D1540974

THE EMC MASTERPIECE SERIES

LITERATURE AND THE LANGUAGE ARTS

Experiencing Literature

EMC/Paradigm Publishing

St. Paul, Minnesota

Staff Credits:

For **EMC/Paradigm Publishing,** St. Paul, Minnesota

Eileen Slater
Editor

Christine Gensmer
Associate Editor

For **Penobscot School Publishing, Inc.,** Danvers, Massachusetts

Robert D. Shepherd
Executive Editor

Kimberly M. Leahy
Managing Editor

Sara Hyry
Christina Kolb
Associate Editors

Camilla Ayers
Sybil Fetter
Sheila Neylon
Copyeditors

Charles Q. Bent
Production Manager

Sara Day
Art Director

Heath P. O'Leary
Compositor

ISBN 0-8219-1266-6

Published by EMC/Paradigm Publishing
300 York Avenue
St. Paul, Minnesota 55101

Printed in the United States of America.
10 9 8 7 6 5 4 3   XXX 01 00 99 98 97 96

Acknowledgments:

Addison-Wesley Publishing Company WHEN I WAS PUERTO RICAN (pp. 3–4), © 1993 by Esmeralda Santiago. Reprinted by permission of Addison-Wesley Publishing Company, Inc. **Toni Cade Bambara** "Geraldine Moore the Poet" is reprinted by permission of the author. © 1972 Toni Cade Bambara. **Robert L. Bell** "Desiderata" from *The Poems of Max Ehrmann.* © 1927 by Max Ehrmann. All rights reserved. Copyright renewed 1954 by Bertha K. Ehrmann. Reprinted by permission Robert L. Bell, Melrose, Mass. 02176. **BOA Editions, Ltd.** LUCILLE CLIFTON. "miss rosie" copyright © 1987, by Lucille Clifton. Reprinted from GOOD WOMAN: POEMS AND A MEMOIR 1969–1980, by Lucille Clifton, with the permission of BOA Editions, Ltd., 92 Park Ave., Brockport NY 14420. **Brandt & Brandt Literary Agents, Inc.** "The Most Dangerous Game" by Richard Connell. Copyright 1924 by Richard Connell. Copyright renewed © 1952 by Louise Fox Connell. Reprinted by permission of Brandt & Brandt Literary Agents, Inc. "Nightmare Number Three" by Stephen Vincent Benet from THE SELECTED WORKS OF STEPHEN VINCENT BENET. Copyright 1935 by Stephen Vincent Benet. Renewed © 1963 by Thomas C. Benet, Stephanie B. Mahin, and Rachel Benet Lewis. Reprinted by permission of Brandt & Brandt Literary Agents, Inc. **Diana Chang** "Saying Yes" is reprinted by permission of the author. © Diana Chang. **Don Congdon Associates, Inc.** Ray Bradbury, "There Will Come Soft Rains." Reprinted by permission of Don Congdon Associates, Inc. Copyright © 1950, renewed 1977 by Ray Bradbury. **Doubleday** "The Bat," copyright 1938 by Theodore Roethke from THE COLLECTED POEMS OF THEODORE ROETHKE by Theodore Roethke. Used by permission of Doubleday, a division of Bantam Doubleday Dell Publishing Group, Inc. O. Henry, "The Gift of the Magi," Doubleday, 1945. "The Lesson of the Moth", from ARCHY AND MEHITABEL by Don Marquis. Copyright 1927 by Doubleday, a division of Bantam, Doubleday, Dell Publishing Group, Inc. Used by permission of Doubleday, a division of Bantam Doubleday Dell Publishing Group, Inc. **Mari Evans** *I Am a Black Woman,* published by Wm. Morrow & Co., 1970, by permission of the author. **The Feminist Press at the City University of New York** "Bury Me in a Free Land," by Frances Ellen Watkins Harper. The Feminist Press at The City University of New York.

(continued on page 975)

LITERATURE AND THE LANGUAGE ARTS

MAPLE LEVEL
THE BRITISH TRADITION

PINE LEVEL
THE AMERICAN TRADITION

WILLOW LEVEL
UNDERSTANDING LITERATURE

BIRCH LEVEL
EXPERIENCING LITERATURE

Consultants and Writers

Edmund J. Farrell, Ph.D.
Emeritus Professor of English
  Education
University of Texas at Austin

Roger Dick
Teacher of English and Humanities
Brooklyn Center High School
Brooklyn Center, Minnesota

David England, Ph.D.
Associate Dean for Teacher
  Education
Louisiana State University

Ellen Gabin
Consultant, Hispanic Literature
Rockport, Massachusetts

Donald Gray, Ph.D.
Professor of English
Indiana University

Susan Gubar, Ph.D.
Professor of English
Indiana University

Dael Angelico-Hart
Director of Language Arts
Danvers Public Schools
Danvers, Massachusetts

Gail Ross Hatcher
English Department Chairperson
T. Wingate Andrews High School
High Point, North Carolina

Jim O'Laughlin
Lecturer
University College
Northwestern University

Jane S. Shoaf, Ph.D.
Instructional Specialist for
  Communication Skills (retired)
North Carolina Department of
  Public Instruction

Kendra Sisserson
Language Arts Curriculum
  Facilitator
Academy for Aerospace Technology
Cocoa, Florida

Donald L. Stephan
English Department Chair
Sidney High School
Sidney, Ohio

James W. Swanson
English Instructor
Robbinsdale Armstrong High School
Plymouth, Minnesota

Jill Triplett
Special Collections Librarian
Wellesley College

Hope Vasholz
Teacher of English
Hammond High School
Columbia, Maryland

Arlette Ingram Willis, Ph.D.
Assistant Professor in the
  Department of Curriculum and
  Instruction
University of Illinois at Urbana-
  Champaign

James Worley, Ph.D.
Teacher of English (retired)
Columbus East High School
Columbus, Indiana

Contents

LANGUAGE ARTS SURVEY

1   ESSENTIAL SKILLS: WRITING

2 ESSENTIAL SKILLS: LANGUAGE

GRAMMAR HANDBOOK

Introduction to Grammar

The Parts of Speech

3 ESSENTIAL SKILLS: SPEAKING AND LISTENING

4 ESSENTIAL SKILLS: STUDY AND RESEARCH

THINKING SKILLS

READING SKILLS

RESEARCH SKILLS

To the Student

Reading Literature

Have you ever become so wrapped up in a movie that when the credits started to roll and the lights came up, you felt a kind of shock? One moment you were in the world on the screen, perhaps identifying with some hero and feeling her joys and sorrows. The next moment you were back in your own world again. The art of the filmmaker transported you to another time and place.

When you read a good story, poem, or play, the same sort of transport should take place. The key to reading literature is to use your imagination to take the journey planned for you by the writer. This willingness to extend yourself imaginatively is the most important characteristic that you can have as a reader. Suppose, for example, that you read the following passage in a story:

> Three lions, a male and two females, lay sunning beside what remained of a kill—an eland, perhaps. We approached in the Range Rover. They ignored us. Chico stopped about fifty meters away, and we both took out binoculars for a closer look. The lions lay heavily, dreamily, sated, self-satisfied. A slight breeze ruffled their fur, yellow-brown like the savannah grass in this season between the rains. It was Chico who noticed that the kill wasn't an eland at all, for attached to part of it was, unmistakably, a large black boot.

It is possible to read that passage and comprehend it, intellectually, without having experienced it. However, reading literature is all about having experiences. To read the passage well, you need to picture three lions, to imagine what it might be like to approach them, to see in your mind's eye the yellow grass, to feel the slight breeze, to notice the boot. If you have done that—if you have imagined the scene vividly—then it will have an impact on you. That impact will be its significance—its meaning for you.

Imagine that you have taken a journey. You have hiked up a mountainside in Peru or have wandered through the Valley of the Kings in Egypt. You have gone shopping in the Ginza district of Tokyo or have bounced in a spacesuit over the surface of the moon. After such an experience, you return home a different person. You think about the experience and what it meant to you.

A work of literature is an opportunity to take just such an exotic journey. Using your imagination, you take the writer's trip. You have an experience. Then you reflect on the experience that you had. You think about what you thought and felt, about what the experience meant to you. That reflection is called **reader response.**

When you sit down to read a literary work, remember that your task, at that moment, is not to prepare for a quiz or to get ready for a class discussion. Your task is to use your imagination to have the experience that the writer has prepared for you. Think of the writer as a tour guide to interesting times and places. In those times and places, you will meet fascinating people and have powerful, moving experiences, ones that will enrich your life immeasurably.

Sharing Your Responses with Others

No two people are exactly alike. Because of this wonderful fact, the experience that you have when reading a particular story, poem, or play will be different from the experience had by the student who sits next to you. That's what makes discussing literature with other students interesting. You can share your experiences with others and learn from them. In this course you will have many opportunities to share responses in class discussion and in collaborative projects.

Educating Your Imagination

You might naturally ask, at the beginning of a course such as this, what you stand to gain from it. Two answers to that question have already been suggested: First, reading literature will provide you with many fascinating imaginative experiences. Second, discussing that literature and doing collaborative projects will provide opportunities for sharing with others. A third answer is implicit in the first two: reading literature and sharing responses with others will educate your imagination. It will train you to think and feel in new ways.

Life is short, opportunities for real-life experience are limited, and events often

happen only once, without your having had the chance to practice, or even think about, how you might react to them. Reading literature is a way around all those difficulties. Through reading, you can find out what it might be like to sail around the globe, to march into battle, to fall in love, to lose a friend, to win a great prize, to live in the rain forest, to be faced with a moral dilemma, to confront your greatest fear, to travel backward in time or forward into the future. Writers write because they want to share interesting, valuable experiences with you—the reader. In the process of reading literary works and thinking about your own and others' responses to them, you will exercise your imaginative faculties and grow in ways that might otherwise have been impossible.

Using This Text

This text is first and foremost a literature anthology. The selections in Units 1–12 have been chosen both for their historical importance and for their current relevance to the interests of students like you. To assist you in understanding the selections, the authors and editors have created activities that appear before and after the selections. These activities will also help you to develop your abilities in many language arts areas. Most of these activities ask you to refer to the section at the back of the book called the Language Arts Survey. Before doing the activity, you will read a section of the Survey, which will introduce you to some key concepts. Then you will apply what you have learned from the Survey when doing the activity.

Part One

UNDERSTANDING LITERATURE

Geese in Flight. *Lelia T. Bauman, 1850 or later. National Gallery of Art, Washington, DC. Gift of Edgar William and Bernice Chrysler Garbisch*

here there is no vision, the people perish.

—Proverbs

"The Story of Echo and Narcissus"
retold by Edith Hamilton

"The Story of Dædalus and Icarus"
from the *Metamorphoses*
by Ovid, trans. by Rolfe Humphries

ABOUT THE AUTHOR

Ovid (43 BC–AD 18), one of the greatest of the Latin poets, lived at the time of the emperor Augustus when the Roman Empire was in its golden age. Popular in his time, he was best known for his love poetry, including *Ars amatoria (The Art of Love)*. Ovid's masterpiece is considered to be the *Metamorphoses,* an epic poem in fifteen books that covers the history of the world and focuses on changes, often on the transformation of beings into different forms. In the *Metamorphoses,* Ovid retold many myths of the ancient world.

Edith Hamilton (1869–1963) spent much of her life teaching, studying, and writing about classical literature. Hamilton, the child of American parents, was born in Dresden, Germany. She was educated first in the United States, receiving degrees in Greek and Latin from Bryn Mawr College, and later in Germany, where she was the first woman to enter the University of Munich. Hamilton is praised for her exceptional ability to explain and translate classical literature.

ABOUT THE SELECTIONS

Background: History. The world of the ancient Greeks and Romans was populated with gods and goddesses. These supernatural beings were more powerful than humans, but they experienced human emotions such as jealousy and passion. The Greeks and the Romans worshiped many of the same gods and goddesses but had different names for them. In the first selection on the following pages, the gods and goddesses are referred to by their Greek names; in the second, by their Roman names. Two of the gods that are referred to in these selections are Zeus, or Jove, the ruler of all living creatures, and Hera, or Juno, his wife. Also important in the first story are naiads. These are lesser goddesses who lived in lakes, rivers, or springs.

Background: Genre. The works of Ovid present Roman myths, many of which were borrowed from the ancient Greeks. Such myths were part of the culture of the ancient world and were carried about by traveling singers and poets before they were written down by poets such as Ovid. They tell the stories of gods and goddesses, as well as of the origins of natural phenomena. **"The Story of Echo and Narcissus"** is of the latter type. **"The Story of Dædalus and Icarus"** is about the brilliant mythical inventor Dædalus and his son who escape from captivity in Crete, a land ruled by King Minos.

"The Story of Echo and Narcissus"

RETOLD BY EDITH HAMILTON

Long ago there lived a beautiful lad, whose name was Narcissus. His beauty was so great, all the girls who saw him longed to be his, but he would have none of them. He would pass the loveliest carelessly by, no matter how much she tried to make him look at her. Heartbroken maidens were nothing to him. Even the sad case of the fairest of the nymphs, Echo, did not move him. She was a favorite of Artemis, the goddess of woods and wild creatures, but she came under the displeasure of a still mightier goddess, Hera herself, who was at her usual occupation of trying to discover what Zeus was about. She suspected that he was in love with one of the nymphs and she went to look them over to try to discover which. However, she was immediately <u>diverted</u> from her investigation by Echo's gay chatter. As she listened amused, the others silently stole away and Hera could come to no conclusion as to where Zeus's wandering <u>fancy</u> had alighted. With her usual injustice she turned against Echo. That nymph became another unhappy girl whom Hera punished. The goddess condemned her never to use her tongue again except to repeat what was said to her. "You will always have the last word," Hera said, "but no power to speak first."

This was very hard, but hardest of all when Echo, too, with all the other lovelorn maidens, loved Narcissus. She could follow him, but she could not speak to him. How then could she make a youth who never looked at a girl pay attention to her? One day, however, it seemed her chance had come. He was calling to his companions. "Is anyone here?" and she called back in rapture, "Here—Here." She was still hidden by the trees so that he

How does Narcissus react to those attracted to him?

Who has punished Echo? What is the punishment?

WORDS FOR EVERYDAY USE:

di • vert • ed (də vʉrt´id) *part.,* distracted
fan • cy (fan´sē) *n.,* fondness

Why does Narcissus become disgusted with Echo? What happens to her?

did not see her, and he shouted, "Come!"—just what she longed to say to him. She answered joyfully "Come!" and stepped forth from the woods with her arms outstretched. But he turned away in angry disgust. "Not so," he said; "I will die before I give you power over me." All she could say was, humbly, entreatingly, "I give you power over me," but he was gone. She hid her blushes and her shame in a lonely cave, and never could be comforted. Still she lives in places like that, and they say she has so wasted away with longing that only her voice now is left to her.

So Narcissus went on his cruel way, a <u>scorner</u> of love. But at last one of those he wounded prayed a prayer and it was answered by the gods: "May he who loves not others love himself." The great goddess Nemesis, which means righteous anger, undertook to bring this about. As Narcissus bent over a clear pool for a drink and saw there his

What happens to Narcissus when he bends over the pool for a drink? Who witnesses the death of Narcissus? What did his spirit do before crossing the river that encircles the world of the dead?

own reflection, on the moment he fell in love with it. "Now I know," he cried, "what others have suffered from me, for I burn with love of my own self—and yet how can I reach that loveliness I see mirrored in the water? But I cannot leave it. Only death can set me free." And so it happened. He <u>pined</u> away, leaning <u>perpetually</u> over the pool, fixed in one long gaze. Echo was near him, but she could do nothing; only when, dying, he called to his image, "Farewell—farewell," she could repeat the words as a last good-by to him.

They say that when his spirit crossed the river that encircles the world of the dead, it leaned over the boat to catch a final glimpse of itself in the water.

The nymphs he had scorned were kind to him in death and sought his body to give it burial, but they could not find it. Where it had lain there was blooming a new and lovely flower, and they called it by his name, Narcissus. ■

WORDS FOR EVERYDAY USE:

scorn • er (skôrnʹər) *n.*, person who treats with contempt

pine (pīn) *vi.*, waste away through grief; yearn

per • pet • u • al • ly (pər pechʹo͞o əl lē) *adv.*, forever

Responding to the Selection

How do you feel toward Narcissus? Do you feel sympathy toward him, or do you think that he deserved his fate? Discuss your ideas with your classmates.

Reviewing the Selection

RECALLING

1. What is unusual about Echo's speech? What caused this peculiarity?

2. How is Narcissus described? What does he look like? What effect does he have on other creatures?

3. How does Narcissus respond to Echo?

4. With whom does Narcissus fall in love? Who intervened in this process?

INTERPRETING

5. How does Echo manage to express herself despite her speech limitation? How well does she succeed?

6. How would you describe Narcissus's character?

7. What happened to Echo? What remained of her?

8. Why did Nemesis punish Narcissus? What does Narcissus learn when he sees himself?

SYNTHESIZING

9. What metamorphoses, or transformations, occur in this story? This story also explains two phenomena in nature. What are these phenomena, and how are they explained?

10. What common human failing does Narcissus represent?

READER'S JOURNAL

It is fun to think of improbable, fantastic things to do. In this story, humans showed their fascination for flying in an age long before modern technology made human flight possible. In your journal, write about an improbable adventure you would like to experience.

"The Story of Dædalus and Icarus"

FROM THE *METAMORPHOSES*

OVID, TRANS. BY ROLFE HUMPHRIES

What is Dædalus's plan for leaving Crete? What does he create?

Homesick for homeland, Dædalus hated Crete
And his long exile there, but the sea held him.
"Though Minos blocks escape by land or water,"
Dædalus said, "surely the sky is open,

5   And that's the way we'll go. Minos' <u>dominion</u>
Does not include the air." He turned his thinking
Toward unknown arts, changing the laws of nature.
He laid out feathers in order, first the smallest,
A little larger next it, and so continued,

10 The way that pan-pipes[1] rise in gradual sequence.
He fastened them with twine and wax, at middle,
At bottom, so, and bent them, gently curving,
So that they looked like wings of birds, most surely.
And Icarus, his son, stood by and watched him,

15 Not knowing he was dealing with his downfall,
Stood by and watched, and raised his shiny face
To let a feather, light as down, fall on it,
Or stuck his thumb into the yellow wax,
Fooling around, the way a boy will, always,

20 Whenever a father tries to get some work done.

---

1. **pan-pipes.** Instruments made of reeds of various lengths

WORDS FOR EVERYDAY USE: do • min • ion (də min′yən) *n.,* governed territory

Still, it was done at last, and the father hovered,
Poised, in the moving air, and taught his son:
"I warn you, Icarus, fly a middle course:
Don't go too low, or water will weigh the wings down;
25 Don't go too high, or the sun's fire will burn them.
Keep to the middle way. And one more thing,
No fancy steering by star or constellation,
Follow my lead!" That was the flying lesson,
And now to fit the wings to the boy's shoulders.
30 Between the work and warning the father found
His cheeks were wet with tears, and his hands trembled.
He kissed his son (*Good-bye,* if he had known it),
Rose on his wings, flew on ahead, as fearful
As any bird launching the little nestlings
35 Out of high nest into thin air. *Keep on,*
Keep on, he signals, *follow me!* He guides him
In flight—O fatal art!—and the wings move
And the father looks back to see the son's wings moving.
Far off, far down, some fisherman is watching
40 As the rod dips and trembles over the water,
Some shepherd rests his weight upon his crook,
Some ploughman on the handles of the ploughshare,
And all look up, in absolute amazement,
At those air-borne above. They must be gods!
45 They were over Samos, Juno's sacred island,
Delos and Paros toward the left, Lebinthus
Visible to the right, and another island,
Calymne, rich in honey. And the boy
Thought *This is wonderful!* and left his father,
50 Soared higher, higher, drawn to the vast heaven,
Nearer the sun, and the wax that held the wings
Melted in that fierce heat, and the bare arms
Beat up and down in air, and lacking oarage[2]
Took hold of nothing. *Father!* he cried, and *Father!*
55 Until the blue sea hushed him, the dark water
Men call the Icarian now. And Dædalus,
Father no more, called "Icarus, where are you!
Where are you, Icarus? Tell me where to find you!"
And saw the wings on the waves, and cursed his talents,
60 Buried the body in a tomb, and the land
Was named for Icarus.
                    During the burial
A noisy partridge, from a muddy ditch,

According to Dædalus, what should Icarus avoid?

Who looks up in amazement as Icarus flies?

What ends the flight of Icarus? Where does Icarus fall?

---

2. **oarage.** Ability to propel

The Fall of Icarus. *Bruegel. Musées royaux des Beaux-Arts, Brussels*

Looked out, drummed with her wings in loud approval.
No other bird, those days, was like the partridge,
65   Newcomer to the ranks of birds; the story
Reflects no credit on Dædalus. His sister,
Ignorant of the fates, had sent her son
To Dædalus as apprentice, only a youngster,
Hardly much more than twelve years old, but clever,
70   With an inventive turn of mind. For instance,
Studying a fish's backbone for a model,
He had notched a row of teeth in a strip of iron,
Thus making the first saw, and he had bound
Two arms of iron together with a joint
75   To keep them both together and apart,

Why had Dædalus's sister sent her son to Dædalus? What sort of mind did the boy have?

One standing still, the other <u>traversing</u>
In a circle, so men came to have the compass.
And Dædalus, in envy, hurled the boy
Headlong from the high temple of Minerva,
80   And lied about it, saying he had fallen
Through accident, but Minerva, kind protectress
Of all inventive wits, stayed him in air,
Clothed him with <u>plumage</u>; he still retained his aptness
In feet and wings, and kept his old name, Perdix,
85   But in the new bird-form, Perdix, the partridge,
Never flies high, nor nests in trees, but flutters
Close to the ground, and the eggs are laid in hedgerows.
The bird, it seems, remembers, and is fearful
Of all high places.   ■

*What did
Dædalus do to
his nephew?
Why?*

*What becomes of
the young boy?*

Responding to the Selection

This is one of the most familiar stories in Western literature. Why do think that people have responded to it over the centuries? What aspects of this story might appeal to people throughout many generations?

WORDS FOR
EVERYDAY USE:

tra • verse   (trə vʉrs´) *vi.,* turn; swivel
plum • age   (plo͞om´ij) *n.,* bird's feathers

Reviewing the Selection

1. What is the problem Dædalus has at the beginning of the story? How does he try to solve it?

2. What advice does Dædalus give Icarus before they try to fly?

3. What happens to Icarus at the end of the story?

4. What inventions does Dædalus's nephew make? What is the fate of Dædalus's nephew?

5. What special gift does Dædalus have?

6. Why doesn't Icarus follow Dædalus's advice about how to fly?

7. What is the reason for Icarus's fate? Should the boy's fate be blamed on Dædalus, who defied the laws of nature, or does the blame lie with Icarus? What do you think the ancients thought? What do you think?

8. What does the episode of Dædalus's nephew tell about Dædalus?

9. Dædalus was considered the greatest inventor in ancient times. What did you learn about Dædalus from Ovid's story? What did you learn about the ancient world?

10. How does the role of the supernatural differ in the stories of Echo and Narcissus and Dædalus and Icarus?

Understanding Literature (Questions for Discussion)

1. **Foreshadowing.** Writers often give hints about what is going to happen later in a story. Can you find two examples of such **foreshadowing** in the first part of "The Story of Dædalus and Icarus"? The episode of Icarus's playing with the wax can also be said to foreshadow or at least explain his later actions. Explain why.

2. **Myth.** Read the section on *myth* in the Handbook of Literary Terms. Discuss how the two selections show the characteristics of myths.

Responding in Writing

1. **Children's Story.** The stories you have just read are written using formal language. How would you retell each story for an audience of six- or seven-year-old children? Rewrite one of the stories so that a child would understand and enjoy it. You might also wish to illustrate your story.

   > **Prewriting Suggestion:** Think about what background information would help a child to understand the story. Write this information to be included at the beginning of your story. Also make a list of the key events that you need to include in the story.

2. **Myth.** Write a myth to tell the origin of something in the world around you. You could tell about the origin of something in nature like a flower or a bird or about the origin of something artificial such as television or computers. You might want to include supernatural elements such as the ability to fly found in "The Story of Dædalus and Icarus" or the intervention of the gods as in "The Story of Echo and Narcissus."

   > **Prewriting Suggestion:** Think about an everyday object that interests you or seems mysterious to you. Think of a fanciful way in which it might have come about. Freewrite about this in your journal.

3. **Description.** Icarus became so caught up in the thrill of flying that he forgot about the danger of flying too close to the sun. Think about a time when you did something thrilling, such as going on an amusement park ride, skateboarding, or rollerblading. Write a description about how you felt during the experience and afterward.

   > **Prewriting Suggestion:** Freewrite about the experience you have chosen. Write down all the impressions you had, all the emotions you experienced, and all the thoughts that went through your mind. Use these details in your story.

PROJECT

Retelling Myths. Work in groups of five to eight. Select gods and goddesses from Greek or Roman mythology. Make a poster that includes the names, descriptions, and, if possible, pictures of traditional representations of the gods and goddesses. Find myths or tales in which each god or goddess has an important role. Each of you should select a myth for a different god or goddess and be prepared to retell it to the class as your group displays its poster.

"The White Snake"
by Jacob and Wilhelm Grimm, trans. by Lucy Crane

ABOUT THE AUTHOR

Jacob Grimm (1785–1863) and his brother **Wilhelm** (1786–1859) were German scholars. Among young people around the globe, they are famous for collecting folk songs and folk tales from the European oral tradition. The brothers transcribed these traditional tales as people related them and are credited with giving folk tales a readable form without changing their essential character. The Grimms' collection became a classic of world literature. The two hundred stories they collected convey the souls and imaginations of generations of people. Jacob was also a highly esteemed scholar of the history of European languages. He demonstrated that sounds change in regular ways and showed how certain languages in Europe and western Asia evolved from other languages.

ABOUT THE SELECTION

Background: Genre. Most fairy tales tell about supernatural occurrences and fanciful creatures, including fairies. The Grimm brothers collected oral stories in their native Germany, including "Rapunzel." In France, Charles Perrault (1628–1703) wrote down other folk stories, including "Cinderella" and "Sleeping Beauty." In Denmark, Hans Christian Andersen (1805–1875) retold such tales as "The Princess and the Pea" and "The Emperor's New Clothes." Similar tales are told in many different countries and cultures. For example, versions of the Cinderella tale have been told for centuries by native peoples of China and North America. **"The White Snake"** contains many common fairy tale elements, or **motifs**, including magical animals, princes and princesses, items that occur in threes, and a series of tests for characters to perform.

READER'S JOURNAL

In this story, a king grants the hero one favor. If a powerful person promised you one favor, what would you choose? Write about this question in your journal.

"The White Snake"

JACOB AND WILHELM GRIMM, TRANS. BY LUCY CRANE

A long time ago there lived a King whose wisdom was noised <u>abroad</u> in all the country. Nothing remained long unknown to him, and it was as if the knowledge of hidden things was brought to him in the air. However, he had one curious custom. Every day at dinner, after the table had been cleared and every one gone away, a trusty servant had to bring in one other dish. But it was covered up, and the servant himself did not know what was in it, and no one else knew, for the King waited until he was quite alone before he uncovered it. This had gone on a long time, but at last there came a day when the servant could restrain his curiosity no longer, but as he was carrying the dish away he took it into his own room. As soon as he had fastened the door securely, he lifted the cover, and there he saw a white snake lying on the dish. After seeing it he could not resist the desire to taste it, and so he cut off a small piece and put it in his mouth. As soon as it touched his tongue he heard outside his window a strange chorus of delicate voices. He went and listened, and found that it was the sparrows talking together, and telling each other all they had seen in the fields and woods. The virtue of the snake had given him power to understand the speech of animals.

Now it happened one day that the Queen lost her most splendid ring, and suspicion fell upon the trusty servant, who had the general <u>superintendence</u>, and he was accused of stealing it. The King summoned him to his presence, and after many reproaches told him that if by the next day he was not able to name the thief he should be considered guilty, and punished. It was in vain that he protested his innocence; he could get no better sentence. In his uneasiness and <u>anxiety</u> he went out into the courtyard, and began to consider

What ability does the servant acquire? What gives him this ability?

How does the servant learn the king's secret? What is the secret?

WORDS FOR EVERYDAY USE:

a • broad (ə brôd´) *adv.,* far and wide

su • per • in • tend • ence (soō´pər in tend´ens) *n.,* supervision; management

anx • i • e • ty (aŋ zī´ə tē) *n.,* worry; apprehension

what he could do in so great a necessity. There sat the ducks by the running water and rested themselves, and plumed themselves with their flat bills, and held a comfortable chat. The servant stayed where he was and listened to them. They told how they had waddled about all yesterday morning and found good food; and then one of them said pitifully,

"Something lies very heavy in my craw,—it is the ring that was lying under the Queen's window; I swallowed it down in too great a hurry."

Then the servant seized her by the neck, took her into the kitchen, and said to the cook,

"Kill this one, she is quite ready for cooking."

"Yes," said the cook, weighing it in her hand; " there will be no trouble of fattening this one—it has been ready ever so long."

She then slit up its neck, and when it was opened the Queen's ring was found in its craw. The servant could now clearly prove his innocence, and in order to make up for the injustice he had suffered the King permitted him to ask some favour for himself, and also promised him the place of greatest honour in the royal household.

But the servant refused it, and only asked for a horse and money for travelling, for he had a fancy to see the world, and look about him a little. So his request was granted, and he set out on his way; and one day he came to a pool of water, by which he saw three fishes who had got entangled in the rushes, and were panting for water. Although fishes are usually considered dumb creatures, he understood very well their lament that they were to perish so miserably; and as he had a compassionate heart he dismounted from his horse, and put the three fishes back again into the water. They quivered all over with joy, stretched out their heads, and called out to him,

"We will remember and reward thee, because thou hast delivered us." He rode on, and after a while he heard a small voice come up from the sand underneath his horse's feet. He listened, and understood how an ant-king was complaining,

"If only these men would keep off, with their great awkward beasts! here comes this stupid horse treading down my people with his hard hoofs!"

The man then turned his horse to the side-path, and the ant-king called out to him,

"We will remember and reward thee!"

The path led him through a wood, and there he saw a father-raven and mother-raven standing by their nest and throwing their young ones out.

"Off with you! young gallows-birds!"[1] cried they; "we cannot stuff you any more; you are big enough to fend for yourselves!" The poor young ravens lay on the ground, fluttering, and beating the air with their pinions, and crying,

"We are poor helpless things, we cannot fend for ourselves, we cannot even fly! we can only die of hunger!"

---

1. **gallows-birds.** Creatures who deserve to be hanged

In what way does the servant's new ability help him?

What does the young man do for the three fishes? for the ants? What do both the fishes and the ants say to him?

WORDS FOR EVERYDAY USE:

plume (plo͞om) *vt.,* preen

craw (krô) *n.,* stomach of an animal

Then the kind young man dismounted, killed his horse with his dagger, and left it to the young ravens for food. They came hopping up, feasted away at it, and cried,

"We will remember and reward thee!"

So now he had to use his own legs, and when he had gone a long way he came to a great town. There was much noise and thronging in the streets, and there came a man on a horse, who proclaimed,

"That the King's daughter seeks a husband, but he who wishes to marry her must perform a difficult task, and if he cannot carry it through successfully, he must lose his life."

Many had already tried, but had lost their lives, in vain. The young man, when he saw the King's daughter, was so dazzled by her great beauty, that he forgot all danger, went to the King and offered himself as a wooer.

Then he was led to the sea-side, and a gold ring was thrown into the water before his eyes. Then the King told him that he must fetch the ring up again from the bottom of the sea, saying,

"If you come back without it, you shall be put under the waves again and again until you are drowned."

Every one pitied the handsome young man, but they went, and left him alone by the sea. As he was standing on the shore and thinking of what he should do, there came three fishes swimming by, none other than those he had set free. The middle one had a mussel in his mouth, and he laid it on the strand at the young man's feet; and when he took it up and opened it there was the gold ring inside! Full of joy he carried it to the King, and expected the promised reward; but the King's daughter, proud of her high birth,[2] despised him, and set him another task to perform. She went out into the garden, and strewed about over the grass ten sacks full of millet seed.[3]

"By the time the sun rises in the morning you must have picked up all these," she said, "and not a grain must be wanting."

The young man sat down in the garden and considered how it was possible to do this task, but he could contrive nothing, and stayed there, feeling very sorrowful, and expecting to be led to death at break of day. But when the first beams of the sun fell on the garden he saw that the ten sacks were all filled, standing one by the other, and not even a grain was missing. The ant-king had arrived in the night with his thousands of ants, and the grateful creatures had picked up all the millet seed, and filled the sacks with great industry. The King's daughter came herself into the garden and saw with astonishment that the young man had performed all that had been given him to do. But she could not let her proud heart melt, but said,

"Although he has completed the two tasks, he shall not be my <u>bridegroom</u> unless he brings me an apple from the tree of life."

---

2. **high birth.** Being born into a noble family
3. **millet seed.** Seed of a grain grown for food

What other animals does the young man help?

What is the reward for completing the difficult task? What danger lies in attempting this task? Why does the young man decide to undertake the task?

What enables the young man to complete the second task?

WORDS FOR EVERYDAY USE: **bride • groom** (brīd´ grōōm´) *n.*, man who is about to be married or who has recently been married

The young man did not know where the tree of life was to be found, but he set out and went on and on, as long as his legs could carry him, but he had no hope of finding it. When he had gone through three kingdoms he came one evening to a wood, and seated himself under a tree to go to sleep; but he heard a rustling in the boughs, and a golden apple fell into his hand. Immediately three ravens flew towards him, perched on his knee, and said,

"We are the three young ravens that you delivered from starving; when we grew big, and heard that you were seeking the golden apple, we flew over the sea to the end of the earth, where the tree of life stands, and we fetched the apple."

Full of joy the young man set off on his way home, and brought the golden apple to the King's beautiful daughter, who was without any further excuse.

So they divided the apple of life, and ate it together; and their hearts were filled with love, and they lived in undisturbed happiness to a great age. ∎

How was the young man able to find the apple from the tree of life?

What kind of ending does this story have? Why might this sort of ending be common in fairy tales?

Responding to the Selection

Do you like fairy tales? Do you remember any that were told to you when you were younger? Which were your favorites? Do a survey of your class. Have each student write down the name of his or her favorite tale. Graph the results. Have volunteers explain the plots and key elements in their favorite tales.

Reviewing the Selection

1. What does the servant do out of curiosity at the beginning of the story? How does his curiosity help him with the problem he has concerning the ring?

2. What does the servant choose when the king grants him a favor?

3. What three groups of animals does the servant meet? How does he help them?

4. Why does the servant choose to perform the tasks set for him? How do the animals he previously met help him?

5. What elements in the first two paragraphs make it clear that this is a fairy tale?

6. Why do you think the servant chose the favor he did?

7. What do the servant's encounters with the animals show about his character?

8. What is the nature of the tasks that the servant has to perform to win the princess's hand? Do you think that these tests of the servant are fair? Why are supernatural helpers necessary for the servant to perform these tasks?

9. How is this fairy tale similar to the myths you just read? How is it different?

10. How is this tale similar to other fairy tales you know? List the similar elements. For example, the tale has a happy ending.

Understanding Literature (Questions for Discussion)

1. **Motif.** A **motif** is any element that recurs in a literary work. Read the entry on *motif* in the Handbook of Literary Terms. One common fairy tale motif found in "The White Snake" is items or events occurring in sets of three. List all the examples of the motif of threes you can find in the story.

2. **Fairy Tale.** A **fairy tale** is a story that deals with mischievous spirits and other supernatural occurrences. What elements occur frequently in fairy tales that you know? List these elements. Here are some ideas to prompt your thinking: tests, curses, good versus evil. Why do you think that fairy tales are traditionally told or read to children?

3. **Character.** A **character** is a person (or sometimes an animal) who figures in the action of a literary work. List the details you know about the servant in this fairy tale. Do you think that character development is a strong element in folk tales?

Responding in Writing

1. **Fantasy.** In this fairy tale, animals speak. What would happen if your pet or another animal you encountered suddenly talked? What do you think the animal would want to tell you? What could the animal tell you that might be particularly interesting or unusual? Write a short story about a talking animal. Be sure to include dialogue in which the animal talks.

> **Prewriting Suggestion:** Think about the characteristics the animal would have. Would it be shy, helpful, hip, or haughty? Write five key adjectives to describe the animal. Make sure that the animal's characteristics come across in the dialogue you write.

2. **Fairy Tale.** Many people have rewritten fairy and folk tales as if they occurred in modern times. Rewrite the fairy tale "The White Snake," but change it to take place in the present. For example, you can change the challenges that the hero faces and how he meets them. You can also include modern machinery to help the hero, but make sure to retain some supernatural elements to make your story fit the fairy tale genre.

> **Prewriting Suggestion:** Make a chart that lists the characters, settings, and events of the fairy tale. Note those elements that you plan to change and how you plan to change them.

PROJECT

Fairy Tales Across Cultures, Times, and Media. Working with other students in a small group, choose a popular fairy tale to research. Gather several versions of the tale from various sources and analyze them to discover differences in their settings, plots, characters, and themes. Present the results of your comparisons to the rest of the class.

"The Prodigal Son"
from the King James Bible

ABOUT THE AUTHOR

The **King James Bible** was published in England in 1611 during the reign of King James I. This work was a translation into English done by forty-seven scholars who used both previous translations and texts in the original ancient languages in which the Bible was written. The poetic King James translation had a profound effect on the English language. Words and quotations from the King James Bible, familiar from Sunday services and from Bible reading, became interwoven in the speech of everyday life.

ABOUT THE SELECTION

Background: Genre. A **parable** is a very brief story told to teach a moral lesson. **"The Prodigal Son"** is one of several parables found in the New Testament of the Bible told by Jesus to answer questions posed to him and to serve as a guide to moral behavior.

Background: Technique. An **allusion** is a reference in a literary work to some other part of a culture with which readers are expected to be familiar. The Bible has had a profound effect on Western culture. The stories and teachings of the Bible are part of the tradition of Western Europe. People are expected to know them, and writers often refer to them and use them in their works. As a result, a knowledge of the Bible is helpful in understanding the classics of Western literature.

If suddenly you had a lot of money to spend, what would you do with it? Think about the way in which you would spend your money and what that says about your personal values. Write about this in your journal.

"The Prodigal¹ Son"

FROM THE KING JAMES BIBLE

Then drew near unto him all the publicans² and sinners for to hear him.

2   And the Pharisees³ and scribes murmured, saying, This man receiveth sinners, and eateth with them.

3   And he spake this parable unto them, saying,

4   What man of you, having an hundred sheep, if he lose one of them, doth not leave the ninety and nine in the wilderness, and go after that which is lost, until he find it?

5   And when he hath found it, he layeth it on his shoulders, rejoicing.

6   And when he cometh home, he calleth together his friends and neighbors, saying unto them, Rejoice with me; for I have found my sheep which was lost.

7   I say unto you, that likewise joy shall be in heaven over one sinner that repenteth,⁴ more than over ninety and nine just persons, which need no repentance.

8   Either what woman having ten pieces of silver, if she lose one piece, doth not light a candle and sweep the house, and seek <u>diligently</u> till she find it?

9   And when she hath found it, she calleth her friends and her neighbors together, saying, Rejoice with me for I have found the piece which I had lost.

10   Likewise, I say unto you, there is joy in the presence of the angels of God over one sinner that repenteth.

11   And he said, A certain man had two sons:

12   And the younger of them said to his father, Father, give me the portion

What would a person do if a sheep or a piece of silver were lost? What would happen when the sheep or the silver was found? What would cause a similar reaction in heaven?

---

1. **Prodigal.** Extravagant; characterized by wasteful expenditure
2. **publicans.** Collectors of revenue in ancient Judea
3. **Pharisees.** Members of an ancient Jewish party or fellowship
4. **repenteth.** Repents, feels sorry for sins

WORDS FOR
EVERYDAY USE:
dil • i • gent • ly (dil´ə jənt lē) *adv.*, carefully and steadily

of goods that falleth to me. And he divided unto them his living.

13 And not many days after the younger son gathered all together, and took his journey into a far country, and there wasted his substance with <u>riotous</u> living.

14 And when he had spent all, there arose a mighty <u>famine</u> in that land; and he began to be in want.

15 And he went and joined himself to a citizen of that country; and he sent him into his fields to feed swine.

16 And he would fain[5] have filled his belly with the husks that the swine did eat: and no man gave unto him.

17 And when he came to himself, he said, How many hired servants of my father's have bread enough and to spare, and I perish with hunger!

18 I will arise and go to my father, and will say unto him, Father, I have sinned against heaven, and before thee,

19 And am no more worthy to be called thy son: make me as one of the hired servants.

20 And he arose, and came to his father. But when he was yet a great way off, his father saw him, and had <u>compassion</u> and ran, and fell on his neck and kissed him.

21 And the son said unto him Father, I have sinned against heaven, and in thy sight and am no more worthy to be called thy son.

22 But the father said to his servants, Bring forth the best robe, and put it on him; and put a ring on his hand, and shoes on his feet:

23 And bring hither the fatted calf, and kill it, and let us eat, and be merry:

24 For this my son was dead, and is alive again; he was lost, and is found. And they began to be merry.

25 Now his elder son was in the field: and as he came and drew nigh to the house, he heard music and dancing.

26 And he called one of the servants, and asked what these things meant.

27 And he said unto him, Thy brother is come; and thy father hath killed the fatted calf, because he hath received him safe and sound.

28 And he was angry, and would not go in: therefore came his father out, and <u>entreated</u> him.

29 And he answering said to his father, Lo, these many years do I serve thee, neither <u>transgressed</u> I at any time thy commandment: and yet thou never gavest me a kid, that I might make merry with my friends:

30 But as soon as this thy son was come, which hath devoured thy living with harlots, thou hast killed for him the fatted calf.

31 And he said unto him, Son, thou art ever with me, and all that I have is thine.

32 It was meet that we should make merry, and be glad: for this thy brother was dead, and is alive again; and was lost, and is found. ∎

What does the younger son do with his money?

How does the older son react?

What explanation does the father give for his actions?

_____

5. **fain.** Gladly

WORDS FOR EVERYDAY USE:

ri • ot • ous (rī´ət əs) *adj.,* without restraint; dissolute

fam • ine (fam´in) *n.,* widespread shortage of food

com • pas • sion (kəm pash´ən) *n.,* sympathy; pity

en • treat (en trēt´) *vt.,* implore; beg

trans • gress (trans gres´) *vt.,* break a commandment; sin

Responding to the Selection

Have you ever forgiven someone for a wrong that he or she committed? What had the other person done? How did forgiving the other person make you feel? Why? Put yourself in the father's place. How would you have reacted when the son returned? Discuss these questions with your classmates.

Reviewing the Selection

RECALLING

1. What does the younger son request at the beginning?

2. How does the younger son spend his money?

3. Why does the younger son decide to return home?

4. How is the younger son greeted when he returns home? What is his father's reaction? What is his brother's reaction?

INTERPRETING

▶▶ 5. Do you consider what the younger son does at the beginning of the parable usual or unusual for a young person to do? Give reasons to support your opinion.

▶▶ 6. Why is "The Prodigal Son" an appropriate name for the parable?

▶▶ 7. Do you think it takes courage for the son to return home?

▶▶ 8. How would you describe each of the three characters—the prodigal son, the father, and the elder son? What is the relationship of the father to each of his sons? What role does the elder son play in the parable?

SYNTHESIZING

9. What lesson does the parable teach?

10. How is this parable different from works in other genres you have studied in this unit?

Understanding Literature (Questions for Discussion)

1. **Symbol.** A **symbol** is a thing that stands for or represents itself and something else. In this parable, the father and the prodigal son are symbols. Use your knowledge of Christian beliefs and the information in the text to tell who the father and son represent. (If you need help, you can look in the King James Bible, in Luke 15, where the context provides an explanation.)

2. **Foil.** A **foil** is a character whose attributes, or characteristics, contrast with and therefore throw into relief the attributes of another character. What are the differences between the younger son and the elder son? How does the inclusion of the elder son affect your reactions to the younger son?

Responding in Writing

Persuasive Writing. Do you think the prodigal son has truly reformed or will he go back to his old ways if he gets a chance? Form an opinion. Then support that opinion in a one- or two-paragraph essay.

> **Prewriting Suggestion:** Make a pro and con chart to gather information on which to base your opinion. List the following statement at the top of your paper: "The prodigal son has truly reformed." Then list facts that support (pro) and that contradict (con) that statement. See the Language Arts Survey, 1.22, "Pro and Con Charts."

PROJECT

Debate. Use your writing from Responding in Writing as the basis for a class debate about the prodigal son.

"The Fox and the Crow"	"The Fox and the Crow"
by Æsop	by James Thurber

ABOUT THE AUTHORS

Æsop may or may not have been a real person. The name has traditionally been associated with a collection of ancient Greek fables, but no reliable historical record of this person exists. Ancient writers invented biographies of this author of fables, some saying he was a slave who was later freed for his storytelling abilities and others saying that he was an advisor to a king. The truth is probably that the fables originated in the oral tradition of ancient Greece.

James Thurber (1894–1961) was a humorist and writer. He attended Ohio State University and later worked as a reporter. Many of his writings appeared in the *New Yorker* magazine, to which he contributed beginning in 1927. Thurber's stories often focused on befuddled characters unable to figure out the modern world. His whimsical biography *My Life and Hard Times* (1931) was popular, and "The Secret Life of Walter Mitty," about a timid, ineffectual man with a vivid fantasy life, was made into a movie. In *Fables for Our Times* (1940), Thurber turned his wry, perceptive eye on human nature, retelling classical fables to apply them to the modern world.

ABOUT THE SELECTIONS

Background: Genre. A **fable** is a brief story with animal characters told to express a moral. Many fables from ancient times featured foxes, crows, mice, and lions. From the European Middle Ages comes a series of fables featuring clever Renart, or Reynard, the fox. In the seventeenth century, the French writer Jean La Fontaine wrote versions of classic fables for his contemporaries. Thurber's fable demonstrates that the process of updating fables continues into the twentieth century.

Background: Technique. A **parody** is a literary work that imitates another work for humorous, often satirical, purposes. Overtly, Thurber's work seems a parody of Æsop. Yet in many ways, the satire seems aimed more at human nature than at Æsop's work. Consider this issue as you read Thurber's modernization of "**The Fox and the Crow.**"

READER'S JOURNAL

How do you respond to flattery? How do you feel when someone says you look nice or have done a good job? Is all praise flattery? Is there a difference between flattery and praise? Explain the difference in your journal.

"The Fox and the Crow"

ÆSOP

A Fox once saw a Crow fly off with a piece of cheese in its beak and settle on a branch of a tree. "That's for me, as I am a Fox," said Master Reynard,[1] and he walked up to the foot of the tree.

"Good day, Mistress Crow," he cried. "How well you are looking today: how glossy your feathers; how bright your eye. I feel sure your voice must <u>surpass</u> that of other birds, just as your figure does; let me hear but one song from you that I may greet you as the Queen of Birds."

The Crow lifted up her head and began to caw her best, but the moment she opened her mouth the piece of cheese fell to the ground, only to be snapped up by Master Fox. "That will do," said he. "That was all I wanted. In exchange for your cheese I will give you a piece of advice for the future—

"Do not trust flatterers." ■

What does the Fox say to the Crow? What does he ask her to do? Why does he make this request?

---

1. **Master Reynard.** Fox in the medieval beast epic *Reynard the Fox*

WORDS FOR EVERYDAY USE: **sur • pass** (sər pas´) *vt.*, go beyond

Responding to the Selection

How do you think the Crow feels about the Fox's flattery? Have you ever offered insincere flattery to somebody? Why did you do it? Discuss these questions with your classmates.

Reviewing the Selection

RECALLING

1. What is the Fox's decision at the start of the story?

2. How does the Fox convince the Crow to open her mouth?

3. Why does the Crow lose the cheese?

INTERPRETING

4. What does the Fox's decision at the start of the story tell about his character?

5. What is humorous about the Fox's flattery of the Crow?

6. Why doesn't the Crow realize that she is going to lose the cheese?

SYNTHESIZING

7. In fables, animals often have particular traits. How would you describe the Fox? How would you describe the Crow?

8. How would you state the lesson of the fable?

Responding in Writing

Children's Story. Many children's stories, like the stories of Æsop, are told to relate moral lessons. Choose such a story and retell it in a few paragraphs.

Prewriting Suggestion: Begin by making a list of the characters and events in your story. Also list its moral. Use these lists to develop your story.

READER'S JOURNAL

When is it inappropriate to praise yourself? What are situations in which it is appropriate for you to say good things about yourself? (Think, for example, of job interviews.) Write about these questions in your journal.

"The Fox and the Crow"

JAMES THURBER

A crow, perched in a tree with a piece of cheese in his beak, attracted the eye and nose of a fox. "If you can sing as prettily as you sit," said the fox, "then you are the prettiest singer within my scent and sight." The fox had read somewhere, and somewhere, and somewhere else, that praising the voice of a crow with a cheese in his beak would make him drop the cheese and sing. But this is not what happened to this particular crow in this particular case.

"They say you are sly and they say you are crazy," said the crow, having carefully removed the cheese from his beak with the claws of one foot, "but you must be <u>nearsighted</u> as well. Warblers wear gay hats and colored jackets and bright vests, and they are a dollar a hundred. I wear black and I am unique." He began nibbling the cheese, dropping not a single crumb.

"I am sure you are," said the fox, who was neither crazy nor nearsighted, but sly. "I recognize you, now that I look more closely, as the most famed and talented of all birds, and I fain would hear you tell about yourself, but I am hungry and must go."

"Tarry[1] awhile," said the crow quickly, "and share my lunch with me." Whereupon he tossed the cunning fox the lion's share of the cheese, and began to tell about himself. "A ship that sails without a crow's nest sails to doom," he said. "Bars may come and bars may go, but crow bars last forever. I am the pioneer of flight, I am the map maker. Last, but never least, my flight is known to scientists and engineers, geometrists and scholars, as the shortest distance between two points. Any two points," he concluded arrogantly.

How does the fox demonstrate his craftiness?

How does the crow in this fable respond to the fox's flattery?

---

1. **Tarry.** Linger; stay

WORDS FOR EVERYDAY USE: **near • sight • ed** (nir´sīt´id) *adj.,* having better vision for near objects than for distant ones

Fox Hunt. Winslow Homer, 1893. The Pennsylvania Academy of the Fine Arts, Philadelphia. Joseph E. Temple Fund

How does the moral of this story differ from Æsop's moral?

"Oh, every two points, I am sure," said the fox. "And thank you for the lion's share of what I know you could not spare." And with this he trotted away into the woods, his appetite appeased, leaving the hungry crow perched <u>forlornly</u> in the tree.

MORAL: *'Twas true in Æsop's time, and La Fontaine's, and now, no one else can praise thee quite so well as thou.* ∎

WORDS FOR EVERYDAY USE: **for • lorn • ly** (fôr lôrn´lē) *adv.,* hopelessly; miserably

Responding to the Selection

Do you feel sympathy for the crow? Do you like it when people praise themselves? Think of ways in which the moral of the fable could apply to your life. Discuss these applications with your classmates.

Reviewing the Selection

RECALLING

1. In this version of the fable, what is the crow's initial reaction to the fox's flattery? Does the fox get the cheese at first?

2. What is the fox's reaction to the crow's statement that a crow is unique?

3. What reasons does the crow give to show that crows are important and unique? On what are the reasons based?

4. What happens at the end of the fable?

INTERPRETING

5. Why does the crow not believe the fox's flattery at first? Is it because he is humble?

6. How does the fox's reaction to the crow's statement show that the fox is clever and quick-witted?

7. Are the crow's arguments for the importance of crows convincing? Why, or why not?

8. Why is the crow forlorn at the end? Is he sorry about losing the cheese?

SYNTHESIZING

9. What makes Thurber's fable humorous? What events and reactions in Thurber's tale do you not expect from having read Æsop's fable?

10. How is the lesson of Thurber's fable different from the lesson of Æsop's fable? How does it go beyond telling people to beware of flatterers? Explain.

Understanding Literature (Questions for Discussion)

Character. A **character** is a person (or sometimes an animal) who figures in the action of a literary work. There is more character development in Thurber's tale than in Æsop's. This means that you know more about the fox and crow in Thurber's fable. One way of developing characters is by describing their actions. What does the fox do and say in Thurber's fable? the crow? What do you learn about these characters from their words and actions? Explain.

Responding in Writing

1. **Fable.** Find a traditional fable. Write your own version of it either by giving it a twist, as Thurber has done, or by adding to it. You could, for example, rewrite the fable of the fox and the crow so that the crow keeps the cheese, perhaps outsmarting the fox and teaching him a lesson, or you could continue the story of the fox to show how he outsmarts another animal, getting food by exploiting the weakness or vanity of another animal. As an alternate assignment, make up your own fable. Start with a moral that you want to teach, such as "Be satisfied with what you have" or "You have to work to succeed." Then think of animals and situations with which to teach the moral.

> **Prewriting Suggestion:** Make a story map for the elements of your story. See the Language Arts Survey, 1.21, "Story Maps."

2. **Advice Letter.** The crow is always being tricked by the fox, so she (or he) writes a letter to an advice columnist, asking how to outfox the fox. Write a letter back to the crow. Help her (or him) decide what to do.

> **Prewriting Suggestion:** Think of situations or settings where the fox and crow might meet. Think of something that the crow could say to the fox to attract his attention or appeal to the fox's vanity.

PROJECT

Contest. Find a book of fables. Choose one that appeals to you and make a copy of it. Write out the moral of the fable on a separate sheet of paper, indicating what you think it can teach you and your classmates. You and your classmates should put the copies of the fables you found on a bulletin board, labeled with numbers, and put the morals scattered underneath, labeled with letters. Then have a contest in which the fables are matched to the morals.

"Paul Bunyan of the North Woods"
by Carl Sandburg

ABOUT THE AUTHOR

Carl Sandburg (1878–1967), who was born in Galesburg, Illinois, wrote in a wide range of genres—poetry, fiction, nonfiction, and history. Much of his writing was based on his own personal experiences traveling around the country and holding a variety of jobs such as barbershop porter, milk truck driver, and wheat harvester. He described these experiences in his autobiography *Always the Young Strangers* (1953). He focused his interests on the history and folkways of the American people. For example, he published two collections of folk songs, *The American Songbag* (1927) and *The New American Songbag* (1950). His poetry often celebrated American people, places, and events, as did his poem "Chicago," which describes the city as "Hog-butcher, Tool-maker, Stacker of Wheat, Player with Railroads, and Freight-handler to the Nation." Sandburg wrote several biographies of Abraham Lincoln and won the Pulitzer Prize in history in 1940.

ABOUT THE SELECTION

Background: Genre. A **tall tale** is a story, often lighthearted or humorous, that contains highly exaggerated, unrealistic elements. Tall tales seem to give a typically American twist to the traditional folk tale, although other cultures do have tales with the exaggeration that distinguishes this type of story. Also important in American folk tales, as in **"Paul Bunyan of the North Woods,"** is struggle with the natural elements, which, of course, was part of the daily experience of pioneers in the American West. Among these pioneers were lumberjacks who lived in isolated logging camps in the wilderness, spending their time cutting down trees. The hero of the following selection is one of these lumberjacks—but a very, very extraordinary one. As you read, note that the tone of a tall tale is lighthearted and humorous.

READER'S JOURNAL

What kinds of heroes appeal to you? What qualities do they have? Why do you find these qualities especially appealing? Answer these questions in your journal.

"Paul Bunyan of the North Woods"

CARL SANDBURG

Who made Paul Bunyan, who gave him birth as a myth, who joked him into life as the Master Lumberjack, who fashioned him forth as an <u>apparition</u> easing the hours of men amid axes and trees, saws and lumber? The people, the bookless people, they made Paul and had him alive long before he got into the books for those who read. He grew up in <u>shanties</u>, around the hot stoves of winter, among socks and mittens drying, in the smell of tobacco smoke and the roar of laughter mocking the outside weather. And some of Paul came overseas in wooden bunks below decks in sailing vessels. And some of Paul is old as the hills, young as the alphabet.

The Pacific Ocean froze over in the winter of the Blue Snow and Paul Bunyan had long teams of oxen hauling regular white snow over from China. This was the winter Paul gave a party to the Seven Axmen. Paul fixed a granite floor sunk two hundred feet deep for them to dance on. Still, it tipped and tilted as the dance went on. And because the Seven Axmen refused to take off their hobnailed boots, the sparks from the nails of their dancing feet lit up the place so that Paul didn't light the kerosene lamps. No women being on the Big Onion river at that time the Seven Axmen had to dance with each other, the one left over in each set taking Paul as a partner. The commotion of the dancing that night brought on an earthquake and the Big Onion river moved over three counties to the east.

One year when it rained from St. Patrick's Day till the Fourth of July, Paul Bunyan got disgusted because his celebration on the Fourth was spoiled.

What is the answer to the narrator's opening question?

WORDS FOR EVERYDAY USE:	**ap • pa • ri • tion** (ap´ə rish´ən) *n.,* strange figure that appears suddenly
	shan • ty (shan´tē) *n.,* shack; hut

He dived into Lake Superior and swam to where a solid pillar of water was coming down. He dived under this pillar, swam up into it and climbed with powerful swimming strokes, was gone about an hour, came splashing down, and as the rain stopped, he explained, "I turned the thing off." This is told in the Big North Woods and on the Great Lakes, with many particulars.

Two mosquitoes lighted on one of Paul Bunyan's oxen, killed it, ate it, cleaned the bones, and sat on a grub shanty picking their teeth as Paul came along. Paul sent to Australia for two special bumblebees to kill these mosquitoes. But the bees and the mosquitoes intermarried; their children had stingers on both ends. And things kept getting worse till Paul brought a big boatload of sorghum[1] up from Louisiana and while all the bee mosquitoes were eating at the sweet sorghum he floated them down to the Gulf of Mexico. They got so fat that it was easy to drown them all between New Orleans and Galveston.

Paul logged on the Little Gimlet in Oregon one winter. The cookstove at that camp covered an acre of ground.

They fastened the side of a hog on each snowshoe and four men used to skate on the griddle while the cook flipped the pancakes. The eating table was three miles long; elevators carried the cakes to the ends of the table where boys on bicycles rode back and forth on a path down the center of the table dropping the cakes where called for.

Benny,[2] the Little Blue Ox of Paul Bunyan, grew two feet every time Paul looked at him, when a youngster. The barn was gone one morning and they found it on Benny's back: he grew out of it in a night. One night he kept pawing and bellowing for more pancakes, till there were two hundred men at the cook-shanty stove trying to keep him fed. About breakfast time Benny broke loose, tore down the cook-shanty, ate all the pancakes piled up for the loggers' breakfast. And after that Benny made his mistake: he ate a red hot stove; and that finished him. This is only one of the hot-stove stories told in the North Woods. ∎

---

1. **sorghum.** Tropical grass grown and harvested to produce grain or syrup
2. **Benny.** In most retellings of the Bunyan story, the blue ox is named Babe. Such variations are common in stories from the oral tradition.

What threatens to spoil Paul's Fourth of July celebration? What does he do to solve the problem?

How does Paul get rid of the bee mosquitoes?

What is one of the red hot stove stories? What might another be?

Responding to the Selection

Did you find this tale entertaining? Why, or why not? What aspects of the tale do you think might have been so appealing that it was retold over many generations in the United States?

Reviewing the Selection

1. What information does the author give in the opening paragraph? What do you learn from that paragraph about the Bunyan stories?

2. How does Paul Bunyan stop the rain that spoiled his Fourth of July?

3. How does Paul Bunyan get rid of the bee mosquitoes?

4. Describe Benny. What happens to him?

5. Why does Sandburg include the introduction? What does he mean by the "bookless people"? What does he mean when he says that "Paul is as old as the hills, young as the alphabet"?

6. Which of Paul Bunyan's qualities are revealed in the episode in which he stops the rain?

7. Which of Paul Bunyan's qualities are revealed in the episode of the bee mosquitoes?

8. A **pun** is a play on words. Explain the play on words in the phrase "hot-stove story" in the last line of the story about Benny. What is the double meaning? (Bear in mind that in frontier America, people often sat around a fire or stove in the evening, spinning yarns.)

9. What do all the episodes in this selection have in common?

10. Why would these tales of Paul Bunyan be appealing to the people that Sandburg describes in the opening paragraph of the selection? What do you learn about the lives and values of pioneer Americans from these tales?

Understanding Literature (Questions for Discussion)

---

1. **Hyperbole.** A **hyperbole** is an exaggeration made for rhetorical effect. In the tale you have just read, there are exaggerations of size and exaggerations of actions. List at least eight examples of hyperbole in the selection. How does the use of hyperbole contribute to the tone of the tall tale?

2. **Genre.** A **genre** is a one of the types or categories into which literary works are divided. "Paul Bunyan of the North Woods" is a tall tale. From the reading you have done in this unit, compare tall tales with myths and fairy tales. How are these genres alike? How are they different?

Responding in Writing

1. **Tall Tale.** Write a tall tale with Paul Bunyan as the main character. Here are two ideas for situations: how Bunyan put out a huge forest fire or how he replanted a forest that was destroyed by a fire. As an alternative, you might write a description related to Paul Bunyan's life similar to the one of the cookstove at Little Gimlet in the story. For example, you might write about what Bunyan's bed looked like. If you are feeling really adventurous, you can invent a character of your own for a tall tale.

   Prewriting Suggestion: Make a list of events for your tall tale. Then, next to each event, describe how it might be exaggerated to achieve a humorous effect.

2. **Oral History.** Paul Bunyan is part of American oral history. What do you know about the history of your family? Interview one or two family members about a particular event in your family history. Use the information that you gather to write a brief account of the event.

   Prewriting Suggestion: Before interviewing, make a list of questions you would like to ask or subjects on which you would like to focus. Make sure that these questions are related to a single interesting event. For additional information on questioning, see the Language Arts Survey, 1.27, "Interviewing."

PROJECT

Comic Strip. Paul Bunyan was a hero of the past, particularly for Americans who were pioneers and struggled with the natural environment as part of their daily living. With your class, invent a hero for contemporary times, perhaps even one that would be a hero in your school setting. Give the hero a name, and list his or her qualities in a chart. Then, with a group, produce a comic strip telling particular adventures of the hero in which his or her strengths or special powers are revealed.

FOLK SONGS/SPIRITUALS

"John Henry"
from *Mules and Men*
by Zora Neale Hurston

ABOUT THE AUTHOR

Zora Neale Hurston (1891–1960) was an African-American writer and novelist. Her best-known novel, *Their Eyes Were Watching God* (1937), tells the story of an African-American woman's discovery of her identity as a woman. Hurston was born in Eatonville, Florida, a town founded by African Americans. She graduated in 1928 from Barnard College, where she studied anthropology. Her interest in folklore led to her publication of Southern folk tales and customs in *Mules and Men,* from which this selection is taken.

ABOUT THE SELECTION

Background: History. John Stephens of Hoboken, New Jersey, built the first steam locomotive in 1825. Over the next fifty years, railroads played a key role in the expansion of settlement across the United States. **"John Henry,"** an African-American folk song, tells the story of a railroad worker, or driver, whose job it was to hammer into rails the large metal stakes that secured those rails to the ground. In the song, a contest is held between John Henry, using a hammer, and a new steam drill. The effort to beat the steam drill kills John Henry, but he is remembered in song and legend as a symbol of the unconquerable spirit of the American worker.

"John Henry"

FROM *MULES AND MEN*

ZORA NEALE HURSTON

John Henry driving[1] on the right hand side,
Steam drill driving on the left,
Says, 'fore I'll let your steam drill beat me down
I'll hammer my fool self to death,
5 Hammer my fool self to death.

John Henry told his Captain,
When you go to town
Please bring me back a nine pound hammer
And I'll drive your steel on down,
10 And I'll drive your steel on down.

John Henry told his Captain,
Man ain't nothing but a man,
And 'fore I'll let that steam drill beat me down
I'll die with this hammer in my hand,
15 Die with this hammer in my hand.

Captain ast John Henry,
What is that storm I hear?
He says Cap'n that ain't no storm,
'Tain't nothing but my hammer in the air,
20 Nothing but my hammer in the air.

What does John Henry decide about the steam drill?

What did John Henry ask his captain to bring? What will John Henry do?

---

1. **driving.** Using a hammer to drive metal stakes into railroad ties

His Hammer in His Hand. Palmer Hayden. From the John Henry Series, Museum of African American Art, Los Angeles, CA. Palmer C. Hayden collection Gift of Miriam A. Hayden

John Henry told his Captain,
Bury me under the sills of the floor,
So when they get to playing good old Georgy skin,[1]
Bet 'em fifty to a dollar more,
25   Fifty to a dollar more.

John Henry had a little woman,
The dress she wore was red,
Says I'm going down the track,
And she never looked back.
30   I'm going where John Henry fell dead,
Going where John Henry fell dead.

Who's going to shoe your pretty lil feet?
And who's going to glove your hand?
Who's going to kiss your dimpled cheek?
35   And who's going to be your man?

Who is the woman in the folk song?

---

1. **Georgy skin.** Gambling game played by railroad workers

Who's going to be your man?

My father's going to shoe my pretty lil feet;
My brother's going to glove my hand;
My sister's going to kiss my dimpled cheek;
40   John Henry's going to be my man,
John Henry's going to be my man.

Where did you get your pretty lil dress?
The shoes you wear so fine?
I got my shoes from a railroad man,
45   My dress from a man in the mine,
My dress from a man in the mine.   ■

Responding to the Selection

The story of John Henry is about a person whose job is being taken by a machine. How do you feel about machines, generally? In what situations do you find them pleasant? In what situations do you find them unpleasant? What can machines do better than you? What can you do better than they can? Discuss these questions with your classmates.

Reviewing the Selection

RECALLING

1. What does John Henry decide in verse 1 of the song?

2. What is John Henry doing in verse 4?

3. What does John Henry's woman decide in verse 6 of the song?

INTERPRETING

▶▶ 4. What tone and mood are set in verse 1? What elements of the verse help to establish this tone and mood?

▶▶ 5. What example of exaggeration is there in verse 4?

▶▶ 6. What do verses 7–9 tell about the role of women in the society in which "John Henry" was written?

SYNTHESIZING

7. What is special about John Henry? Is he a hero?

8. How are John Henry and Paul Bunyan alike? How are they different?

Understanding Literature (Questions for Discussion)

1. **Repetition. Repetition** is the use, again, of a sound, word, phrase, sentence, or other element. It is important in most songs. In folk singing, repetition allows people to join in at regular points. Find examples of repetition in the song "John Henry." If possible, obtain a recording of "John Henry" and sing along with it.

2. **Dialect.** A **dialect** is a version of a language spoken by the people of a particular place, time, or social group. Some of the language of "John Henry" is from a dialect spoken in the past in the rural South. Find some examples of dialect in the song. How does keeping this dialect in modern versions of the song help to make it more realistic and help the listener to imagine the time and place in which the song was composed?

Responding in Writing

Diary Entry/Science Fiction. Imagine a time in the future when all work is done by machines. Write a diary entry that might be written by a person living in such a time.

> **Prewriting Suggestion:** Make a chart in which you write in the left-hand column what a person might actually do in a typical day in our time and write in the right-hand column how various tasks might change if machines did them.

PROJECT

Song Writing. Working with other students in a small group, retell a familiar story as a song. You can choose one of the stories in this unit or another story or tale you know. Either choose a melody you know or compose one of your own. Present the song by singing it to the class, with or without accompaniment by piano, guitar, or another instrument.

"Steal Away"
"Go Down, Moses

Anonymous

ABOUT THE SELECTIONS

Background: Genre. "Steal Away" and "Go Down, Moses" are examples of a kind of music called the **spiritual**, part of the African-American folk tradition. As the name suggests, spirituals deal with religious subjects. "Steal Away" tells of Judgment Day and stealing away from earthly life to an afterlife in heaven. "Go Down, Moses" tells a story from the Bible. According to the book of Exodus in the Bible, Moses was the Hebrew prophet who led his people, the Israelites, out of captivity in Egypt, which was ruled by a king, or Pharaoh.

Most spirituals were composed by anonymous singers during the era of slavery in the United States, and many have a secondary meaning related to escape from slavery into a better life (or into the afterlife). For example, both "Steal Away" and "Go Down, Moses" can be interpreted as expressions of the desire of an enslaved people to gain freedom. Thus the Israelites can be seen as African Americans under slavery, Egypt as slave states, Pharaoh as a typical slave master or plantation owner, and Moses as a potential liberator. (Note that Harriet Tubman, who led many African Americans to freedom in the North during the mid-nineteenth century, is often called "the Moses of Her People.") Songs or poems that can be read as having two different meanings are known as **allegories.**

Although spirituals had long been part of the African-American tradition, it was only in the 1870s that the country at large began to become aware of this rich tradition, when the Fisk Jubilee Singers from Fisk University in Nashville, Tennessee, began to tour the country, singing programs of these songs. Since that time, spirituals have had an important influence on the development of several American musical styles, including gospel, blues, jazz, country, and rock.

"Steal Away"

ANONYMOUS

1

My Lord calls me, He calls me by the thunder;
The trumpet sounds within my soul, I don't have long to stay here.

Chorus

Steal away, steal away, steal away to Jesus.
Steal away, steal away home, I don't have long to stay here.

2

Green trees are bending, poor sinners, they stand trembling,
The trumpet sounds within my soul, I don't have long to stay here.

(Repeat Chorus)

3

My Lord he calls me, He calls me by the lightning,
The trumpet sounds within my soul, I don't have long to stay here.

(Repeat Chorus)

■

Verse

My Lord____ calls me, he calls me by the thun-der; the

trum-pet sounds with-in___ my soul, I don't have long to stay here.

Chorus

Steal a - way, steal a - way, steal a - way to Je - sus.

Steal a - way, steal a - way, home, I don't have long to stay here.

Responding to the Selection

Why might an anonymous African American living under slavery have been moved to write this song? Why might he or she have wanted to "steal away home"? Why would it be necessary for a slave to "steal away" if he or she wanted freedom?

Reviewing the Selection

RECALLING

1. Who is calling to the speaker in this song?

2. To what are green trees compared?

3. What does the speaker say is sounding in his or her soul?

INTERPRETING

▶▶ 4. What message is the speaker receiving? from whom? To what is the voice calling the speaker compared?

▶▶ 5. What similarity might exist between green trees and sinners?

▶▶ 6. What does the sound of the trumpet in this song represent? (See Matthew 24:31.)

SYNTHESIZING

7. Why might this song be interpreted as an expression of the desire of slaves for freedom? What elements of the song support that interpretation? How might singing such songs have kept people's spirits strong during the difficult times of slavery?

Think of the different roles that music plays in people's lives. Think, for example, of lullabies, of songs that people sing while they work, and of music that is played for pep rallies and celebrations. Freewrite in your journal about the many purposes that music serves and give examples.

"Go Down, Moses"

ANONYMOUS

1

When Israel was in Egypt's land,
Let my people go!
Oppressed so hard they could not stand,
Let my people go!

Chorus

"Go down, Moses,
'Way down in Egypt's land,
Tell old Pharaoh
To let my people go!"

2

"Thus spoke the Lord," bold Moses said,
"Let my people go!
If not, I'll smite your firstborn dead,
Let my people go!"

(Repeat Chorus)

3

"No more shall they in bondage toil,
Let my people go!
Let them come out with Egypt's spoil,
Let my people go!"

(Repeat Chorus)

■

Verse

When Is - rael was in E-gypt's land, Let my peo-ple go! Op-

pressed so hard they could not stand, Let my peo-ple go!

Chorus

Go down,_____ Mo- ses,_____ 'Way down in E- gypt's land.

Tell old_____ Pha - raoh To let my peo-ple go!_____

Responding to the Selection

In what way might this song have helped to raise the spirits of people? Discuss with your classmates the power of music. Describe different types of music. Which types do people seem to find most uplifting?

Reviewing the Selection

RECALLING

1. According to the song, who is "in Egypt's land"?

2. In whose name does Moses speak in stanza 2?

INTERPRETING

3. According to stanza 1, what was life like for the Israelites in Egypt?

4. What message does Moses deliver to Pharaoh?

SYNTHESIZING

5. Why might someone living in slavery have found the story of the deliverance of the Israelites from slavery so appealing? Why might Moses have been a hero to such a person?

Understanding Literature (Questions for Discussion)

1. **Allusion.** An **allusion** is a figure of speech in which reference is made to a person, event, object, or work from history or literature. Read the following passages from the Bible: Matthew 24:29–31 and 25:30–46. Then read Exodus 9–11. What allusions to materials from the Bible are made in "Steal Away" and "Go Down, Moses"?

2. **Repetition.** **Repetition** is the use, again, of a sound, word, phrase, sentence, or other element in a literary work. Spirituals often contain repeated lines or phrases. Often a lone singer sings most of the song and several singers join in to sing the repeated parts. What examples of such repetition can you find in "Steal Away" and "Go Down, Moses"?

Responding in Writing

Personal Essay. Spirituals offered consolation and a source of hope to the African Americans who composed and sang them. What role does music play in your life? Does it help you in any way? Do you get any of your self-image or identity from music? What particular music is important to you? What music is important to your friends? to your acquaintances or to members of your family? Why? Write a personal essay about music and what it means to you.

> **Prewriting Suggestion:** Begin by freewriting in your journal about music. Think of times when particular songs or pieces of music have been important to you. Write about those times. Try to come up with some general statement about what music means to you. Then give several examples. Use the general statement in the introduction to your essay and present the examples in the body of the essay. Refer to the Language Arts Survey, 1.41 and 1.42, "Drafting: Compositions."

PROJECT

African-American Music Festival. African Americans have played central roles in creating and developing many of the most interesting and important American musical forms, including spirituals, gospel, blues, jazz, ragtime, rock, rap, and classical. As a class, organize a festival to honor African-American contributions to American music. Divide into groups and assign each group a particular type of music to research. Prepare presentations on various artists, styles, and famous pieces, and find recordings to play. Give each group the responsibility of preparing a presentation on one type of music, including introductory speeches and selections from recorded music.

UNIT REVIEW

The Folk Tradition

VOCABULARY FROM THE SELECTIONS

abroad, 15
anxiety, 15
apparition, 34
bridegroom, 17
compassion, 23
craw, 16
diligently, 22
diverted, 5
dominion, 8

entreat, 23
famine, 23
fancy, 5
forlornly, 30
nearsighted, 29
perpetually, 6
pine, 6
plumage, 11
plume, 16

riotous, 23
scorner, 6
shanty, 34
superintendence, 15
surpass, 27
transgress, 23
traverse, 11

LITERARY TERMS

allegory, 43
allusion, 21, 48
character, 20, 31
dialect, 42
fable, 26
fairy tale, 19

foil, 25
foreshadowing, 12
genre, 36
hyperbole, 36
motif, 14, 19
myth, 12

parable, 21
parody, 26
repetition, 42, 48
spiritual, 43
symbol, 24
tall tale, 33

SYNTHESIS: QUESTIONS FOR WRITING, RESEARCH, OR DISCUSSION

1. What are the differences between myths, fairy tales, fables, and tall tales? Explain, using examples from the unit.

2. The stories, poems, and songs of the folk tradition serve many purpose other than simple entertainment. What are some of the purposes served by myths, parables, fables, and spirituals?

LANGUAGE LAB   THE PARTS OF SPEECH

When speaking with teachers or other students about your writing, it is useful to have a vocabulary for naming different types of words. Grammarians classify words into eight categories known as the parts of speech, as shown on the following chart.

THE EIGHT PARTS OF SPEECH
A **noun** is the name of a person, place, thing, or idea. *Paul Bunyan, Australia, crow, myth, North Woods, patience*
A **pronoun** is a word that stands for or refers to a noun. *she, it, them, anyone, something, which, that, whose*
A **verb** is a word that describes an action or a state of being. *tell, chased, is, are, were, be, appear, grow*
An **adjective** is a word that modifies a noun or pronoun. *white, prodigal, legendary, waltzing, heroic*
An **adverb** is a word that modifies a verb, an adjective, or another adverb. *carefully, very, hopefully, outside, quite, sometimes, too*
A **preposition** is a word that shows a relationship between a noun or a pronoun and some other word in a sentence. *about, among, at, beside, by, down, for, from, in, of, through, out, with*
A **conjunction** is a word that is used to join words, groups of words, or complete sentences. *and, or, nor, for, but, so, yet, because, since, unless, when, but also*
An **interjection** is a word used to express an emotion or to indicate a pause in speech or writing. *wow, yes, aha, yuck, oh, hurrah, well, thanks*

Sentence Model

INT	ADJ	N	ADV	V	CONJ	V	PRO	V	N
"Yikes!	slimy	toads	suddenly	jumped	and	attacked	me!"	screamed	Rita.

EXERCISE A Identifying the Parts of Speech

Identify the part of speech of each italicized word in the following paragraph. Use *n.* for noun, *pro.* for pronoun, *v.* for verb, *adj.* for adjective, *adv.* for adverb, *prep.* for preposition, *conj.* for conjunction, and *int.* for interjection.

EXAMPLE: The *rich* tradition of American folklore *began* thousands of years ago.

How long has the folk tradition existed in America? [1] *Well,* Native Americans have been creating and telling [2] *myths,* legends, and folk stories for thousands of years. Although some Plains and Northwest Coast peoples made pictographs and carvings of their stories, [3] *they* transmitted most of their literature orally. This oral literature [4] *was* shared through ritual dramas [5] *and* ceremonies, as well as [6] *through* storytelling, singing, and public speaking. Native American myths [7] *explain* the creation of the world and the origins of specific peoples through stories [8] *about* animals, gods and heroes. Especially interesting are the Native American stories about tricksters who behave [9] *deceitfully.* Native American myths and legends display a [10] *strong* connection to the natural world.

LANGUAGE ARTS
SURVEY

For additional help, see the Language Arts Survey, 2.3.–2.31.

EXERCISE B Using the Parts of Speech in Writing

Many words in English can be used as more than one part of speech. Identify the part of speech of each italicized word below. Then, write a new sentence using each word as the part of speech given in parentheses.

EXAMPLE: The *drama* class will perform some well-known folk tales. (Use as a noun.)

The audience found the drama very entertaining.

LANGUAGE ARTS
SURVEY

For additional help, see the Language Arts Survey, 2.32–2.35.

1. The operator isn't able to make the telephone call go *through*. (Use as a preposition.)

2. "*Well,* I guess I'll sing the folk song," Tony volunteered reluctantly. (Use as an adverb.)

3. It looks like an either/*or* situation to me. (Use as a conjunction.)

4. Benjamin Franklin originated the aphorism "*Time* is money." (Use as a verb.)

5. Admission to the *storytelling* festival is free. (Use as a noun.)

6. The second baseman made the third *out* to finish the inning. (Use as a preposition.)

7. When Icarus flew too close to the sun, the *wax* fasteners on his wings melted and he fell to the sea. (Use as a verb.)

8. This summer, I will *visit* the north country that gave birth to the Paul Bunyan legend. (Use as a noun.)

9. The crowd grew hushed as the golfer walked onto the *green*. (Use as an adjective.)

10. Many myths tell about the great *beyond*. (Use as a preposition.)

LANGUAGE ARTS WORKSHOP

THE ELEMENTS OF EFFECTIVE SPEAKING

Long before people had written language, they depending upon speaking and listening skills to communicate with one another. The following charts provide guidelines for effective speaking and listening.

LANGUAGE ARTS SURVEY

For additional help, see the Language Arts Survey, 2.61.

GUIDELINES FOR EFFECTIVE SPEAKING

THE VERBAL ELEMENTS OF SPEAKING

- **Volume.** Speak loudly enough to be heard, but not so loudly as to make your audience uncomfortable.
- **Pitch.** When you speak, vary your pitch (the highness or lowness of your voice) to make your speech sound more melodic. Avoid speaking at a single pitch (in a monotone).
- **Enunciation.** Pronounce each word or syllable clearly. Do not drop or clip the ends of words or sentences.
- **Pace.** Do not speak too slowly or too quickly.
- **Stress.** Emphasize important ideas by saying them more forcefully (that is, with more stress).
- **Tone.** Suit the emotion, or tone, of what you say to the message that you wish to communicate.
- **Variety.** Vary your volume, pitch, pace, stress, and tone to suit the parts of your message.

THE NONVERBAL ELEMENTS OF SPEAKING

- **Eye Contact.** Look at your audience as you speak.
- **Facial Expressions.** Make sure that the emotions that you display match the messages that you wish to communicate.
- **Body Language.** Use good posture, and make sure that the positions and movements of your body match your message. Do not slouch or move around a great deal while speaking.
- **Gestures.** Use motions of the hands and arms sparingly to emphasize points that you are making.
- **Proximity.** Stay a comfortable distance from your audience, not too far away or too close.

LANGUAGE ARTS SURVEY

For additional help, see the Language Arts Survey, 2.62.

EXERCISE A

Answer the following questions about the elements of verbal and nonverbal communication.

1. A public speaker wants to get the attention of a large, noisy audience before speaking to them. What elements of verbal and nonverbal communication might the speaker use to call the audience to order?

2. What change in pitch at the end of a sentence indicates that the sentence is a question. (Hint: try saying a couple of questions aloud to see how the pitch changes.)

3. What elements of verbal communication does a speaker have to control carefully in order to speak a tongue twister such as "Peter Piper picked a peck of pickled peppers"?

4. When people become too excited as they are speaking, what problems sometimes happen with regard to volume and pace?

5. Consider the following sentences:

> Are YOU going to the Jim's party?
> ARE you going to Jim's party?
> Are you going to JIM'S party?

   How does the meaning of the question change if you stress, or emphasize, the words in call capital letters?

EXERCISE B

What gestures, facial expressions, and body language could be used to emphasize a point? to communicate sadness? to communicate that something is puzzling or confusing?

EXERCISE C

Choose a short selection from the unit or a paragraph from a long selection. Copy the selection or paragraph onto a piece of paper. Write on every other line. Prepare to read the selection or paragraph aloud by marking it to show the following:

- places where you will increase or decrease your volume;
- places where you will increase or decrease your pace;
- words or phrases that you should emphasize by means of volume, pitch, or stress;
- words or phrases that present enunciation problems and that require special attention; and
- changes in tone or emotion throughout the piece.

EXERCISE D

Rehearse the piece that you chose or Exercise A, above, and present it in class.

The Starry Night. *Vincent van Gogh, 1889. Oil on canvas, 29" x 36^1/$_4$" (73.7 x 92.1 cm). The Museum of Modern Art, NY. Acquired through the Lillie P. Bliss Bequest*

The success of the poem is determined not by how much the poet felt in writing it, but by how much the reader feels in reading it.

—John Ciardi

"The Bells"
by Edgar Allan Poe

ABOUT THE AUTHOR

Edgar Allan Poe (1809–1849), the child of two actors, was born in Boston. A year after his birth, his father deserted the family, and in 1811 Poe's mother died while acting in Richmond, Virginia. Poe was taken in by the Richmond merchant John Allan. He traveled to England with the Allan family and lived with them on good terms until about 1824, when Allan's once kind feelings toward Poe began to change. Poe attended the University of Virginia, where he did well in his studies. After a quarrel with Allan, Poe returned to Boston. There he paid for the printing of *Tamerlane and Other Poems*. He then joined the army and, after his release from the army, was admitted to West Point. When he realized that a successful military career would not make him Allan's heir, Poe got himself expelled.

From the age of twenty-one until his death at forty, Poe divided his time between Baltimore, Richmond, Philadelphia, and New York. During his stay in Baltimore, Poe wrote a number of stories that were published in newspapers and magazines. He married in 1835. That year he returned to Richmond, where he worked as an editor of the *Southern Literary Messenger*. It was during this time that Poe's critical pieces gained acclaim. Fired in 1837, Poe moved again, this time to New York City. Poe managed to get by on some stories and reviews. After New York, he moved to Philadelphia, where he contributed many stories, including "The Fall of the House of Usher," to *Burton's Gentleman's Magazine,* of which he was coeditor. Returning to New York, he wrote "The Raven" and stories such as "The Tell-Tale Heart" and "The Pit and the Pendulum." Poe is known for his musical verse, his gripping psychological horror stories, and his detective fiction (a genre that he invented).

ABOUT THE SELECTION

Background: Technique. A friend of Poe's, Marie Louise Shew, suggested the idea for **"The Bells."** Poe was in poor mental and physical health, and the ringing of the many church bells near Ms. Shew's house disturbed him greatly. When he expressed the need to write a poem for immediate publication, she suggested the topic of the bells. Poe wrote a brief poem that was later expanded into the poem that exists today. Through techniques such as **assonance, alliteration,** and **repetition,** the poem creates an **onomatopoeic** rendering of the sounds of four types of bells and the resulting emotional responses.

READER'S JOURNAL

Freewrite about a sound that doesn't occur in nature, such as the sound of traffic, a siren, an alarm clock, or static from a radio. With what do you associate this sound? Is it a pleasant sound, or an annoying sound, or can it be both?

"The Bells"

EDGAR ALLAN POE

I

Hear the sledges[1] with the bells—
Silver bells!
What a world of merriment their melody foretells!
How they tinkle, tinkle, tinkle,
In the icy air of night!
While the stars that oversprinkle
All the heavens seem to twinkle
With a crystalline delight;
Keeping time, time, time,
In a sort of Runic rhyme,[2]
To the tintinnabulation[3] that so musically wells
From the bells, bells, bells, bells,
Bells, bells, bells—
From the jingling and the tinkling of the bells.

5

10

What kind of bells are described here? What do these bells foretell? What sound do they make?

---

1. **sledges.** Sleds or sleighs
2. **Runic rhyme.** Ancient verse written in an alphabet
known as Runic
3. **tintinnabulation.** Ringing sound

II

15 Hear the mellow wedding bells,
    Golden bells!
What a world of happiness their harmony foretells!
    Through the <u>balmy</u> air of night
    How they ring out their delight!
20   From the molten-golden notes,
     And all in tune,
    What a liquid ditty floats
To the turtle-dove that listens, while she gloats
     On the moon!
25   Oh, from out the sounding cells
What a gush of euphony[4] <u>voluminously</u> wells!
     How it swells!
     How it dwells
    On the Future! how it tells
30   Of the rapture that impels
    To the swinging and the ringing
    Of the bells, bells, bells,
Of the bells, bells, bells, bells,
     Bells, bells, bells—
35 To the rhyming and the chiming of the bells!

III

Hear the loud alarum bells[5]—
    Brazen bells!
What a tale of terror, now, their turbulency[6] tells!
    In the startled ear of night
40   How they scream out their affright![7]
    Too much horrified to speak,
    They can only shriek, shriek,
     Out of tune,
In a clamorous appealing to the mercy of the fire,
45 In a mad expostulation[8] with the deaf and frantic fire,
    Leaping higher, higher, higher,
    With a desperate desire,

What sounds do the wedding bells make? What do they tell?

What message do the alarm bells have? What noise do they use to convey this message?

---

4. **euphony.** Pleasing sound
5. **alarum bells.** Alarm bells (Archaic)
6. **turbulency.** Violent agitation
7. **affright.** Great fright or terror (Archaic)
8. **expostulation.** Objection, disagreement

WORDS FOR
EVERYDAY USE:

balm • y (bäm´ē) *adj.,* soothing; mild; pleasant
vo • lu • mi • nous • ly (və lōō´ mə nəs lē) *adv.,* largely; fully

And a resolute endeavor
Now—now to sit, or never,
50   By the side of the pale-faced moon.
Oh, the bells, bells, bells!
What a tale their terror tells
Of despair!
How they clang, and clash, and roar!
55   What a horror they outpour
On the bosom of the <u>palpitating</u> air!
Yet the ear it fully knows,
By the twanging,
And the clanging,
60   How the danger ebbs and flows;
Yet the ear distinctly tells,
In the jangling,
And the wrangling,
How the danger sinks and swells,
65   By the sinking or the swelling in the anger of the bells—
Of the bells—
Of the bells, bells, bells, bells,
Bells, bells, bells—
In the clamor and the clangor of the bells!

IV
70   Hear the tolling of the bells
Iron bells!
What a world of solemn thought their melody compels!
In the silence of the night,
How we shiver with affright
75   At the <u>melancholy</u> menace of their tone!
For every sound that floats
From the rust within their throats
Is a groan.
And the people—ah, the people—
80   They that dwell up in the steeple,
All alone,
And who tolling, tolling, tolling,
In that muffled monotone,
Feel a glory in so rolling
85   On the human heart a stone—

What does the ear know of danger?

What effect do the iron bells have on us?

They are neither man nor woman—
They are neither brute nor human—
        They are Ghouls:[9]
And their king it is who tolls;
And he rolls, rolls, rolls,
                Rolls
        A pæan[10] from the bells!
And his merry bosom swells
        With the pæan of the bells!
And he dances, and he yells;
Keeping time, time, time,
In a sort of Runic rhyme,
        To the pæan of the bells—
                Of the bells:
Keeping time, time, time,
In a sort of Runic rhyme,
        To the throbbing of the bells—
Of the bells, bells, bells—
        To the sobbing of the bells;
Keeping time, time, time,
        As he <u>knells</u>, knells, knells,
In a happy Runic rhyme,
        To the rolling of the bells—
Of the bells, bells, bells—
                To the tolling of the bells,
Of the bells, bells, bells, bells—
        Bells, bells, bells—
To the moaning and the groaning of the bells. ■

90

95

100

105

110

What does the king of the Ghouls do?

How does this contrast with the bells in the opening stanza?

---

9. **Ghouls.** Evil spirits
10. **pæan.** Song of joy, triumph, or praise

WORDS FOR EVERYDAY USE: **knell** (nel) *vi.*, sound ominously or mournfully

Responding to the Selection

Choose the sound of the bell featured in this poem that you find most pleasant or the one you find least pleasant. Write about the sound, how it makes you feel, and why you think it affects you in this way. Discuss your responses in class.

Reviewing the Selection

RECALLING

1. What does the melody of the sleigh bell foretell?

2. What kind of bell is referred to in stanza 2? What does this type of bell foretell?

3. What is the third kind of bell in the poem? What kind of tale do these bells tell?

4. What kind of bell does the speaker describe in stanza 4? What do these bells make people do?

INTERPRETING

5. What kind of sound do the sleigh bells make? When might a person hear these bells?

6. How do the bells in stanza 2 differ from the bells in stanza 1? In what way are they similar?

7. What kind of sound is produced by the bells in stanza 3? How does that differ from the sounds made by the bells in stanzas 1 and 2? What different feelings do these sounds produce?

8. What description is used for the bells in both stanza 1 and stanza 4? Does the meaning of this line differ for the two types of bells?

SYNTHESIZING

9. What different meanings do bells have for the speaker? Why are bells so expressive?

10. Note the difference in stanza lengths for the different types of bells. Which stanzas are longer? Why do you think this is so?

Understanding Literature (Questions for Discussion)

1. **Onomatopoeia. Onomatopoeia** is the use of words or phrases that sound like the things to which they refer. What onomatopoeic words refer to the sounds of the bells? What phrases throughout the poem sound like the ringing of bells? Which words sound like small, light bells? Which words sound like large, heavy bells?

2. **Repetition. Repetition** is the use, again, of a sound, word, phrase, sentence, or other element. The word *bells* is repeated many times within each stanza. What other words and phrases are repeated? What two-line phrase is repeated twice exactly and a third time, slightly altered, in stanza 4? Where else in the poem is this line repeated?

3. **Alliteration. Alliteration** is the repetition of initial consonant sounds. Examples of alliteration in the poem include the repeated *w* and *m* sounds in "What a world of merriment their melody foretells!" Find five other examples of alliteration in the poem. Try reading the alliterative lines aloud. What effect does the alliteration have?

4. **Assonance. Assonance** is the repetition of vowel sounds in stressed syllables that end with different consonant sounds. An example is the repetition of the long *o* sound in "From the molten-golden notes." Find an example of assonance in each stanza.

Responding in Writing

Sound Poem. Consider the way Poe uses the sounds of words to create the sounds and moods of different bells. Think about another sound that can have different meanings. For example, a dog might make a welcoming bark, a pained yelp, or a menacing growl. Choose a sound and write a poem about it. Try to use some of the techniques of sound that you have studied in this lesson, such as onomatopoeia, assonance, and alliteration. You may also wish to refer to the entries on *cacophony* and *rhyme* in the Handbook of Literary Terms.

> **Prewriting Suggestion:** Make a list of words that you will use in your poem. Choose them carefully for both sound and meaning. You may find it helpful to use a thesaurus to find synonyms with appropriate sounds. For more information refer to the Language Arts Survey, 4.25, "Using Thesauruses."

"Something Told the Wild Geese"
by Rachel Field

ABOUT THE AUTHOR

Rachel Field (1894–1942) was from Massachusetts, but her writing is often set in Maine. She wrote and illustrated children's books, including *The Cross-Stitch Heart and Other One-Act Plays* (1927), *Polly Patchwork* (1928), and *Hitty, Her First Hundred Years* (1929). Her poetry and novels were also popular with adults. Field's collection of poetry, *Points East,* was published in 1930. Her widely successful novels for adults include *Time Out of Mind* (1935), *All This, and Heaven Too* (1938), and *And Now Tomorrow* (1942).

ABOUT THE SELECTION

Background: Theme. In **"Something Told the Wild Geese"** Field writes on a nature theme. In her poem, wild geese know that the seasons are changing and begin to fly south. This would be a common event in the autumn for Field, a native of New England.

"Something Told the Wild Geese"

RACHEL FIELD

*What tells the
wild geese that it
is time to go?*

Something told the wild geese
    It was time to go.
Though the fields lay golden
    Something whispered, "Snow."
5   Leaves were green and stirring,
    Berries, luster-glossed,[1]
But beneath warm feathers
    Something cautioned, "Frost."
All the sagging orchards

*What contrasts
are presented in
the poem?*

10   Steamed with amber spice,
But each wild breast stiffened
    At remembered ice.
Something told the wild geese
    It was time to fly—
15   Summer sun was on their wings,
    Winter in their cry. ∎

---

1. **luster-glossed.** Shiny

Responding to the Selection

Imagine you are the "Something" that tells the wild geese to fly south for the winter. Write what you would tell them when it was time to return in the spring. What clues would there be that it was time to migrate again?

Reviewing the Selection

RECALLING

1. What signs are there that summer still reigns?

2. What warnings do the geese receive?

INTERPRETING

3. Why are the geese warned even though there seems to be no reason to go?

4. How do the geese respond to the warnings?

SYNTHESIZING

5. How do the geese know to go south? What does the departure of the geese symbolize for the speaker?

Understanding Literature (Questions for Discussion)

1. **Image.** An **image** is a word picture—a word or phrase that names something that can be seen, heard, touched, tasted, or smelled. What images does Field use to show the current weather? the coming weather? Which different senses does she use to create these images?

2. **Alliteration. Alliteration** is the repetition of initial consonant sounds as in *Frost on the furrows.* What examples of alliteration can you find in the poem?

Responding in Writing

Science Report. Choose a type of wild animal that changes its habits dramatically depending on the season (such as geese, bears, snakes, or frogs). Do some research on the changes that occur in this animal's life during a given year. Prepare a report on the physiological changes that occur in this animal during the course of a year and on the consequences of those changes for the animal's behavior.

"Sarah Cynthia Sylvia Stout Would Not Take the Garbage Out"
by Shel Silverstein

ABOUT THE AUTHOR

Shel Silverstein (1932–) enjoys traveling and makes his home on a houseboat in California. He was born in Chicago, Illinois, and as a child dreamed of becoming a basketball player or a dancer. Instead, his talents led him to write stories, poems, and songs and to draw cartoons. Many of his books, such as *Where the Sidewalk Ends, A Light in the Attic,* and *The Giving Tree,* are popular with both adults and children.

ABOUT THE SELECTION

Background: Technique. In "Sarah Cynthia Sylvia Stout Would Not Take the Garbage Out" Silverstein relies on exaggeration for humor. He relays an anecdote about a little girl who will not take out the garbage for so long that the situation becomes ridiculous. Note how Silverstein ties together this exaggerated situation (which often takes the form of lists of objects) through the use of a simple, catchy rhyme scheme and alliteration. A **rhyme scheme** is a pattern of rhyming words at the ends of lines in a poem. **Alliteration** is the replication of initial consonant sounds as in **P**eter **P**iper **p**icked a **p**eck of **p**ickled **p**eppers.

READER'S JOURNAL

What is one chore that you absolutely hate to do? Why do you hate it so much? Imagine that you refused to do this chore and nobody else did it either. What would happen? Would the results be humorous? disastrous? dangerous?

"Sarah Cynthia Sylvia Stout Would Not Take the Garbage Out"

SHEL SILVERSTEIN

Sarah Cynthia Sylvia Stout
Would not take the garbage out!
She'd scour the pots and scrape the pans.
Candy the yams[1] and spice the hams.

5   And though her daddy would scream and shout,
She simply would not take the garbage out.
And so it piled up to the ceilings:
Coffee grounds, potato peelings,
Brown bananas, rotten peas,

10   Chunks of sour cottage cheese.
It filled the can, it covered the floor,
It cracked the window and blocked the door
With bacon rinds and chicken bones,
Drippy ends of ice cream cones,

15   Prune pits, peach pits, orange peel,
Gloppy glumps of cold oatmeal,
Pizza crusts and withered greens,
Soggy beans and tangerines,
Crusts of black burned buttered toast,

20   Gristly bits of beefy roasts . . .
The garbage rolled on down the hall,
It raised the roof, it broke the wall . . .

What was Sarah willing to do? What wasn't she willing to do?

What does all this garbage do to the Stout home?

---

1. **yams.** Orange-colored variety of sweet potato

Greasy napkins, cookie crumbs,
Globs of gooey bubblegum,
25 Cellophane from green baloney,
Rubbery blubbery macaroni,
Peanut butter, caked and dry,
Curdled milk and crusts of pie,
Moldy melons, dried up mustard,
30 Eggshells mixed with lemon custard,
Cold french fries and <u>rancid</u> meat,
Yellow lumps of Cream of Wheat.
At last the garbage reached so high
That finally it touched the sky.
35 And all the neighbors moved away,
And none of her friends would come to play.
And finally Sarah Cynthia Stout said,
"OK, I'll take the garbage out!"
But then, of course, it was too late
40 The garbage reached across the state,
From New York to the Golden Gate
And there, in the garbage she did hate,
Poor Sarah met an awful fate,
That I cannot right now relate
45 Because the hour is much too late.
But children, remember Sarah Stout
And always take the garbage out! ∎

What does the garbage finally do? Why does Sarah change her mind?

What is Sarah's fate? Why is the narrator relating this poem?

WORDS FOR EVERYDAY USE: ran • cid (ran′sid) *adj.*, having a bad smell or taste

Responding to the Selection

Imagine you are one of Sarah Cynthia Sylvia Stout's friends. Explain why you will not come to play at her house. Do you encourage her to perform her chore? How would you try to persuade her?

Reviewing the Selection

RECALLING

1. What chores will Sarah Stout do? What is the thing she refuses to do?

2. What are five things that pile up in her house? How far does the garbage pile up?

INTERPRETING

3. What happens as a result of Sarah Stout's refusal to do one chore?

4. What warning does the speaker give at the end of the poem?

SYNTHESIZING

5. Do you think that the warning the speaker issues in this poem is a serious one or not? What makes you come to this conclusion?

Understanding Literature (Questions for Discussion)

1. **Rhyme. Rhyme** is the repetition of sounds at the ends of words. Types of rhyme include *end rhyme* (the use of rhyming words at the ends of lines), *internal rhyme* (the use of rhyming words within lines), *exact rhyme* (in which the rhyming words end with the same sound or sounds), and *slant rhyme* (in which the rhyming sounds are similar but not identical). Find an example of each type of rhyme in this poem.

2. **Alliteration. Alliteration** is the repetition of initial consonant sounds. The most obvious example of alliteration is the name Sarah Cynthia Sylvia Stout in which the *s* sound is repeated. In the list of garbage that piles up, Silverstein uses alliteration several times. Find five examples of alliteration in the list. You might find it helpful to read the poem aloud. Why do you think that Silverstein decided to use alliteration?

3. **Description and Sensory Detail.** A **description**, one of the modes of writing, portrays a character, an object, or a scene. Descriptions make use of **sensory details**—words and phrases that describe how things look, sound, smell, taste, or feel. What sensory details does Silverstein use in his description of the garbage?

"Fog"
by Carl Sandburg

ABOUT THE AUTHOR

Carl Sandburg (1878–1967), a son of Swedish immigrants, grew up in Galesburg, Illinois, and attended school until the age of thirteen. During his youth, he traveled from job to job throughout the Midwest working as a brick maker, a carpenter's helper, a house painter, and a milk wagon driver. Such experiences gave Sandburg a deep appreciation for ordinary working people. He served as a soldier during the Spanish-American War and then attended Lombard College but never received a degree. After college, he worked as an advertising writer and as a journalist and became involved in populist politics. In his poetry, Sandburg often wrote of the nobility of ordinary people and often praised the American experiment in democracy. In keeping with his political beliefs, Sandburg wrote "simple poems for simple people." These poems are collected in such volumes as *Chicago Poems* (1918), *Cornhuskers* (1918), *Smoke and Steel* (1920), and *The People, Yes* (1936). Sandburg traveled throughout the United States, reading his poetry and performing folk songs, which he accompanied on the guitar. He collected many of the best of these folk songs in *The New American Songbag* (1927). Sandburg is also known for his popular biographies *Abraham Lincoln: The Prairie Years* (1926) and *Abraham Lincoln: The War Years* (1939).

ABOUT THE SELECTION

Background: Technique. A **metaphor** is a figure of speech in which something is spoken or written about as though it were something else. In **"Fog,"** Sandburg captures and recreates a scene over time, using a vivid, unusual, perfectly appropriate metaphor. As you read the poem, identify the two things that are being related to one another and ask yourself what these things have in common.

Freewrite about fog. What images come to your mind in relation to fog? What do you see, smell, hear, taste, and feel on a foggy day?

"Fog"

CARL SANDBURG

The fog comes
on little cat feet

It sits looking
over harbor and city
on silent haunches[1]
and then moves on. ■

---

1. **haunches.** Animal's hips and thighs taken together

Responding to the Selection

What feelings do you have on a foggy day? Did this selection arouse those feelings in you? Do you think this is an accurate way to depict fog? How would you describe other types of weather?

Reviewing the Selection

RECALLING

1. On what kind of feet does the fog come?

2. What does the fog do?

INTERPRETING

▶▶ 3. How would you describe the movement of cat feet?

▶▶ 4. How is the action of the fog catlike?

SYNTHESIZING

5. What sounds does this poem suggest?

Understanding Literature (Questions for Discussion)

Metaphor. A **metaphor** is a figure of speech that describes a thing as though it were something else. Metaphorical writing invites the reader to make a comparison between two things. What two things are compared in this poem? In what ways are movements of these two things similar?

Responding in Writing

Lyric Poem. Create your own poem to describe a tornado or hurricane as a destructive animal.

> **Prewriting Suggestion:** Begin by choosing an animal whose actions are similar in some way to the activity of a tornado or hurricane. A falcon or eagle, for example, is powerful and swoops down quickly from the sky. Brainstorm a list of words or phrases that can be used to describe both the animal and the tornado or hurricane.

"Gus: The Theatre Cat"
by T. S. Eliot

ABOUT THE AUTHOR

Thomas Stearns Eliot (1888–1965) was born in St. Louis, Missouri, but he spent many years of his life in England. He studied philosophy and linguistics at Harvard, the Sorbonne, and Oxford. While a student in Paris, Eliot wrote his first major poems, including "The Love Song of J. Alfred Prufrock," which was published in 1917 and contributed to creating a revolution in twentieth-century poetry. An innovative poet, dramatist, literary critic, and editor, Eliot had a profound impact on twentieth-century writing and thought. Eliot dealt with such weighty themes as the sordidness of life and the lack of spirituality in the world. He also published a book of poetry called *Old Possum's Book of Practical Cats* on which the hit musical *Cats* was based.

ABOUT THE SELECTION

Background: Technique. Most of the poems in *Old Possum's Book of Practical Cats* are character sketches of various cats. In **"Gus: The Theatre Cat,"** Gus is an aged actor who enjoys recalling his days of glory on the stage. Eliot creates this character by direct description of his appearance and background. Gus's character is also revealed indirectly through his actions and speech.

READER'S JOURNAL

Think of some older people you know. What kinds of stories do they tell about antics in their younger days? Can you remember any of these stories? If so, relate one of them in your journal. If not, write in your journal about some memory that you would like to have when you are very old.

"Gus: The Theatre Cat"

T. S. ELIOT

Gus is the Cat at the Theatre Door.
His name, as I ought to have told you before,
Is really Asparagus. That's such a fuss
To pronounce, that we usually call him just Gus.

5   His coat's very shabby, he's thin as a rake,
And he suffers from palsy[1] that makes his paw shake.
Yet he was, in his youth, quite the smartest of Cats—
But no longer a terror to mice and to rats.
For he isn't the Cat that he was in his prime;

10   Though his name was quite famous, he says, in its time.
And whenever he joins his friends at their club
(Which takes place at the back of the neighbouring pub)[2]
He loves to regale them, if someone else pays,
With anecdotes drawn from his palmiest days.

15   For he once was a Star of the highest degree—
He has acted with Irving, he's acted with Tree.[3]
And he likes to relate his success on the Halls,
Where the Gallery[4] once gave him seven cat-calls.

In what ways has Gus changed since he has grown older?

What does Gus enjoy doing now? Does he live more in the present, the past, or the future?

---

1. **palsy.** Body tremors, usually of the limbs, hands, or feet
2. **pub.** Tavern/casual family restaurant, typical in Great Britain
3. **Irving . . . Tree.** Sir Henry Irving (1838–1905), an English actor; Sir Herbert Tree (1853–1917), an English actor
4. **Gallery.** Theater balcony; audience sitting in the balcony

WORDS FOR EVERYDAY USE:

re • gale (ri gāl´) *vt.,* entertain; amuse

palm • i • est (päm´ ē est) *adj.,* most prosperous; richest

But his grandest creation, as he loves to tell,
20　Was Firefrorefiddle, the Fiend of the Fell.[5]

'I have played', so he says, 'every possible part,
And I used to know seventy speeches by heart.
I'd <u>extemporize</u> back-chat, I knew how to gag,
And I knew how to let the cat out of the bag.
25　I knew how to act with my back and my tail;
With an hour of rehearsal, I never could fail.
I'd a voice that would soften the hardest of hearts,
Whether I took the lead, or in character parts.[6]
I have sat by the bedside of poor Little Nell;[7]
30　When the Curfew[8] was rung, then I swung on the bell.
In the Pantomime season I never fell flat
And I once <u>understudied</u> Dick Whittington's[9]
But my grandest creation, as history will tell,
Was Firefrorefiddle, the Fiend of the Fell.'

35　Then, if someone will give him a toothful of gin,
He will tell how he once played a part in *East Lynne*.[1]
At a Shakespeare performance he once walked on pat,[1]
When some actor suggested the need for a cat.
He once played a Tiger—could do it again—
40　Which an Indian Colonel[1]　　　[2]　　　pursued
And he thinks that he still can, much better than most,
Produce blood-curdling noises to bring on the Ghost.
And he once crossed the stage on a telegraph wire,
To rescue a child when a house was on fire.
45　And he says: 'Now, these kittens, they do not get trained

---

5. **Fell.** Moor; British word for a field overgrown with brambles and tall bushes, often used as the setting for a frightening story or murder mystery

6. **character parts.** Supporting roles in a play; for example, the gruff-voiced, stern but dull-witted police officer in a detective story

7. **Little Nell.** Character from a melodrama, someone who is a victim and needs to be rescued by a hero

8. **Curfew.** Bell signaling that people should be in their houses for the night

9. **Dick Whittington's.** Richard Whittington (1358?–1423), Lord mayor of London, on whose life numerous legends were based, including one about a remarkable cat called Puss in Boots who saves the day at the king's court

10. **East Lynne.** Speaker may be alluding to a play about a place in Britain, perhaps a lake. (West Lynn is a British lake.)

11. **pat.** Spontaneously, without preparation

12. **Indian Colonel.** Colonel of the East Indian military

Of which role is Gus most proud?

What does Gus believe about his skill as an actor?

Words for Everyday Use:

ex • tem • po • rize (eks tem´pə rīz´) *vi.*, speak or perform without preparation

un • der • stud• y (un´dər stud´ē) *vt.*, learn the part of another actor to serve as a substitute when necessary

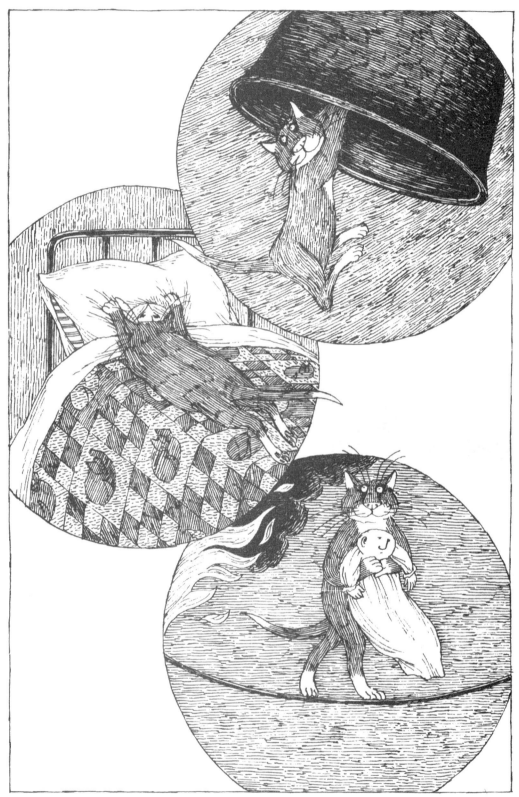

Illustration from **Old Possum's Book of Practical Cats** *by T. S. Eliot, ©1982 by Edward Gorey, reproduced with permission of Harcourt Brace & Company.*

As we did in the days when Victoria[13] reigned.
They never get drilled in a regular troupe,
And they think they are smart, just to jump through a hoop.'
And he'll say, as he scratches himself with his claws,
50   'Well, the Theatre's certainly not what it was.
These modern productions are all very well,
But there's nothing to equal, from what I hear tell,
        That moment of mystery
        When I made history
55   As Firefrorefiddle, the Fiend of the Fell.'

What does Gus think of the next generation of actors?

Does Gus ever tell us what this role is or what it involved?

---

13. **Victoria.** Queen Victoria; Alexandrina Victoria (1819–1901), queen of Great Britain and Ireland from 1837 to 1901

Responding to the Selection

What do you think of Gus the theater cat? Are you impressed by the stories he tells? What do you think he was like in his prime?

Reviewing the Selection

RECALLING

1. What is Gus the cat's full name? Where will you find him?

2. What does Gus look like?

3. With whom has Gus acted? What accolades has he received?

4. What claims does he make about his abilities? What do the younger kittens do? What was Gus's big role?

INTERPRETING

5. What was Gus's role at the theater in the past?

6. The speaker says that Gus is past his prime. What signs show that this is true?

7. Where and under what conditions does Gus tell the stories of his illustrious past?

8. What is Gus's opinion of himself? What does he think of younger actors?

SYNTHESIZING

9. Why is the role of Firefrorefiddle, the Fiend of the Fell, mentioned three times? Why might Gus believe there is no need to explain further who Firefrorefiddle is?

10. In what way is Gus portrayed as a human? What references throughout the poem remind you that he is a cat?

Understanding Literature (Questions for Discussion)

Characterization. Characterization is the use of literary techniques to create a character. Eliot uses direct description and portrayal of behavior to create the character of Gus. What examples of direct description can you find? What examples of portrayal of behavior can you find? What kind of overall picture do you get of Gus?

Responding in Writing

Speech. Imagine that you have been chosen to present Gus with a special theater lifetime achievement award. Write the speech that you would give about Gus, his career, and why he has been chosen to receive this award.

> **Prewriting Suggestion:** Some of the information included in the poem will be useful as you prepare your speech. Other parts of your speech will require more imagination. Brainstorm a list of questions that you have about Gus and his career such as: Why did he once receive seven cat-calls? What was so amazing about his role as Firefrorefiddle, the Fiend of the Fell? What stories do his friends at the pub tell about him? Freewrite to come up with answers to your questions. Use this information to create an interesting speech about Gus and his theater feats.

PROJECT

A Celebration of Cats. With other students in you class, plan a celebration of cats in literature, art, and music. Do some research in the library to identify pieces to share with the rest of the class, beginning with T. S. Eliot's book *Old Possum's Book of Practical Cats* and Andrew Lloyd Webber's musical *Cats*.

"I'm Nobody! Who are you?"

by Emily Dickinson

ABOUT THE AUTHOR

Emily Dickinson (1830–1886) was born and spent most of her life in Amherst, Massachusetts. She did travel to Boston, Cambridge, and Worcester several times to visit relatives and to Philadelphia and Washington with her father, who was a member of Congress. When she was seventeen, she attended Mount Holyoke Female Seminary, but after a year she left and never returned. As time went on, Dickinson became more and more reclusive. In later life she was seldom seen at all. The elusive recluse who dressed all in white was considered quite eccentric, but Dickinson felt seclusion offered her the freedom necessary to write. In her seclusion, Dickinson read widely, exploring the works of such authors as Shakespeare, Milton, Keats, George Eliot, and Elizabeth Barrett Browning. Only eight of her poems were published during her life. The rest of her poems were discovered only after her death.

ABOUT THE SELECTION

Background: Theme. The theme of solitude and privacy is important in Dickinson's work. In **"I'm Nobody! Who are you?"** Dickinson subtly criticizes those who clamor for fame. She finds dignity in quietude and a sort of fellowship in the unadvertised, private life.

READER'S JOURNAL

READER'S JOURNAL

Are you a private person, or do you seek fame and acknowledgment from others? What benefits do you think being an "unknown" has? Freewrite about these questions in your journal.

"I'm Nobody! Who are you?"

EMILY DICKINSON

I'm Nobody! Who are you?
Are you—Nobody—Too?
Then there's a pair of us?
Don't tell! they'd advertise—you know!

5   How dreary—to be—Somebody!
How public—like a Frog—
To tell one's name—the livelong June—
To an admiring <u>Bog</u>! ∎

WORDS FOR EVERYDAY USE: **bog** (bäg, bôg) *n.,* wet, spongy ground; small marsh or swamp

Responding to the Selection

Imagine that reporters have found this "Nobody." How might such a retiring person feel about being discovered?

Reviewing the Selection

RECALLING

1. Who does the speaker say she is?

2. What does the speaker not want the other person to do?

INTERPRETING

3. How does the speaker feel about her identity?

4. Why doesn't the speaker want the other person to tell that there are two of them?

SYNTHESIZING

5. How does the speaker feel about fame? How does she feel about people who admire the famous?

Understanding Literature (Questions for Discussion)

Simile. A **simile** is a comparison using *like* or *as*. What simile does Dickinson use in stanza 2? What two things is she comparing? In what way are they similar? What feelings does she express about fame and publicity by using this simile? Think of a contrasting feeling about fame and publicity. What is a simile that would express that idea?

Responding in Writing

Dialogue. Imagine a discussion between Nobody and Gus the Theatre Cat (see page 74) about fame. Write a short dialogue in which both parties present their opinions.

> **Prewriting Suggestion:** You might have a debate with some of your classmates about the benefits and drawbacks of fame and privacy. To get ideas flowing on each side, you might role play the characters of Nobody and Gus.

PREREADING

"Metaphor"
by Eve Merriam

ABOUT THE AUTHOR

Eve Merriam (1916–   ) is an award-winning poet and playwright who has written more than thirty books. Among her poetry collections are *Family Circle, The Trouble with Love,* and *It Doesn't Have to Rhyme.* Her books *After Nora Slammed the Door* and *Growing Up Female in America: Ten Lives* are about women's rights. Merriam has also written television scripts, advertising copy, song lyrics, and fiction.

ABOUT THE SELECTION

Background: Technique. This poem, titled **"Metaphor,"** is an extended metaphor. A metaphor is a figure of speech in which one thing is spoken or written about as if it were another. This figure of speech invites the reader to make a comparison between the two things.

READER'S JOURNAL

How do you feel at the start of each new day? As a high school student, you do not control everything in your own life. Do you still feel it is within your power to make your days special, exciting, or generally positive? How? Write about this in your journal.

"Metaphor"

EVE MERRIAM

Morning is
a new sheet of paper
for you to write on.

Whatever you want to say,
5   all day,
until night
folds it up
and files it away.

The bright words and the dark words
10   are gone
until dawn
and a new day
to write on. ∎

According to the speaker, what is morning?

What happens at night? What does dawn bring?

Responding to the Selection

What do you want to write on your paper today? What would make you want to crumple up your paper and start all over again? How does Merriam's poem make you feel, in terms of freedom and the ability to control the quality of your own life? Discuss your ideas in class.

Reviewing the Selection

RECALLING

1. What is morning?

2. What does night do?

INTERPRETING

3. What does the new day mean if viewed as it is in this poem?

4. What happens to everything that one does during the day?

SYNTHESIZING

5. Is Merriam's metaphor for morning positive? Do you like the idea of having a blank sheet of paper on which to write a "script" for each day?

Understanding Literature (Questions for Discussion)

Metaphor. A **metaphor** is a figure of speech in which one thing is spoken or written about as if it were another. The poem "Metaphor" is an extended metaphor. This figure of speech invites the reader to make a comparison between the two things. What two things does Merriam invite her reader to compare in the first two lines? How is this metaphor continued throughout the poem?

Responding in Writing

Essay. Part of growing up is learning to make more and more of your own choices. What life decisions do you see yourself making when you are an adult? How will you fill your blank sheet of paper? Write a short essay in which you explore this.

Prewriting Suggestion: Start with a blank sheet of paper, just like the one in Merriam's poem. Make a list of your current goals and values. What steps might you take to pursue your goals? How will you continue to honor your values?

"Boast Not, Proud English"
by Roger Williams

ABOUT THE AUTHOR

Roger Williams (*circa* 1603–1683), colonist, minister, and reformer, developed an interest in church reform while serving as a chaplain to Sir William Masham at Otis in Essex County. He became a Puritan and left England for the American colonies. He soon dissociated himself from the Puritans, however, and moved first to the Separatist Plymouth Colony and then to Salem where he served as a pastor and practiced his democratic views of church government. The Massachusetts General Court sentenced him to exile for his firm opposition to authoritarianism. He fled, seeking refuge in Rhode Island. There he founded the city of Providence and became governor for several years. Williams believed deeply in personal and religious freedom and made Providence Plantations open to all religions. While Williams contributed greatly to establishing religious freedom, he did oppose some groups himself.

Williams's religious ideas were not popular, nor were his relatively liberal ideas about Native Americans. He developed a good relationship with the Native American people of Rhode Island, but in his last years as governor, difficulties developed between the colonists and the indigenous people. One of Williams's most impressive writings is *A Key into the Language of America.* This book became a useful tool for people who wanted to convert Native Americans to Christianity.

ABOUT THE SELECTION

Background: History. Roger Williams recognized that Native Americans were not the uncivilized savages that many of the colonists believed them to be. He criticized people who called them heathens, realizing that no Christian is completely good and free of sin. Williams expresses these beliefs in his poem **"Boast Not, Proud English."**

READER'S JOURNAL

Have you ever held an unpopular belief? Did you ever have to suffer for this belief? What made you persist in your belief despite the difficulties it created for you? Did you ever try to convince somebody else of your belief? What are you willing to risk for your beliefs? Why do you think that some people are willing to hazard all for their beliefs?

"Boast Not, Proud English"

ROGER WILLIAMS

Whom does the speaker address in this poem?

Boast not, proud English, of thy birth and blood:
    Thy brother Indian is by birth as good.
Of one blood God made him, and thee, and all.
    As wise, as fair, as strong, as personal.[1]
By nature, wrath's his portion, thine, no more
    Till Grace his soul and thine in Christ restore.[2]
Make sure thy second birth,[3] or thou shalt see
    Heaven ope[4] to Indians wild, but shut to thee. ∎

In what way, according to the speaker, are the Native Americans and the English connected?

What does the speaker warn that boastful English people might see?

---

1. **as personal.** As much a person (as you)
2. **wrath's his portion, . . . restore.** The Puritans believed that every person deserved no more than God's wrath because of Adam's original sin and that only through God's grace could people be saved, or "restored." Williams is saying that in this respect, as in others, the Native American and the English settler are alike.
3. **second birth.** Religious or spiritual awakening
4. **ope.** Open

Responding to the Selection

How do you feel about Williams's view and the way he expressed it in this poem? How do you think the English people to whom Williams was speaking in this poem might have reacted when they read it? Today Williams is considered one of the visionaries who helped to formulate the ideas of pluralism, democracy, freedom of speech and religion, and equality under the law enshrined in the United States Constitution. Why do you think this might be so?

Reviewing the Selection

RECALLING

1. What does the speaker tell the English not to do?

2. What might the English find if they do not make sure of their "second birth"?

INTERPRETING

3. What reasons does the speaker give for the warning he issues to the English?

4. Why might the possibility suggested by the speaker in the last line surprise the English?

SYNTHESIZING

5. What beliefs about religion and freedom are expressed in this poem?

Understanding Literature (Questions for Discussion)

Aim. A writer's **aim** is the primary purpose that his or her work is meant to achieve. What ideas does Williams express in this poem about equality among different people? How might his views differ from those of many of the people in the communities in which he lived? Why might he have written this poem, or what was his aim? Do you think Williams achieved his purpose?

"The Bat"
by Theodore Roethke

ABOUT THE AUTHOR

Theodore Roethke (1908–1963) grew up in Saginaw, Michigan. Both his father and grandfather kept greenhouses. These greenhouses had a profound effect on Roethke and would figure largely in his future writing. He graduated from Michigan State University, continued his education at Harvard, and went on to teach English at various universities. His first book of poetry, *Open House,* was full of the imagery of plants and growth that would characterize his later work as well.

ABOUT THE SELECTION

Background: Technique. In **"The Bat"** Roethke skillfully creates a picture of a bat by day and by night using vivid imagery. Roethke not only creates a picture of the bat but also evokes the feelings of fear that bats often cause in humans.

What animals are generally loved by human beings? What animals are generally despised by them? Make lists of these animals in your journal. Then study your lists to see if you can identify those characteristics that humans find attractive and unattractive in their fellow creatures.

"The Bat"

THEODORE ROETHKE

By day the bat is cousin to the mouse.
He likes the attic of an aging house.

His fingers make a hat about his head.
His pulse beat is so slow we think him dead.

5   He loops in crazy figures half the night
Among the trees that face the corner light.

But when he brushes up against a screen,
We are afraid of what our eyes have seen:

For something is amiss[1] or out of place
10   When mice with wings can wear a human face. ■

---

1. **amiss.** Wrong; faulty; improper

Responding to the Selection

Did the poem change your feelings about bats? How do you feel about the bat the speaker describes at the beginning of the poem? How do you feel about the bat as described by the speaker at the end of the poem? Discuss with your classmates how people generally feel toward bats and why they feel this way.

Reviewing the Selection

RECALLING

1. What is the bat by day? Where does the bat like to be during the day?

2. What does the bat do at night? What do we see when it brushes up against the screen?

INTERPRETING

3. What feelings does the speaker have toward the bat during the day?

4. What emotions does the bat evoke when it brushes up against the screen? Why does the bat have this effect?

SYNTHESIZING

5. Why are bats mysterious creatures? Why might they arouse fright in humans?

Understanding Literature (Questions for Discussion)

Image. An **image** is a word or phrase that names something that can be seen, heard, touched, tasted, or smelled. What does the bat look like during the day? What specific image of his fingers is created? What image of the bat at night is given in the last line? How does this image contrast with the daytime image of the bat?

Responding in Writing

Point of View. Point of view is the vantage point from which a story is told or something is described. In this poem, a human describes a bat and his or her reaction to the bat. Imagine that you are a bat. Write a paragraph or a poem about a human from a bat's point of view.

> **Prewriting Suggestion:** Imagine you are the bat who "loops in crazy figures half the night" and consider the following questions: How would you see a human? Where do humans spend their time during the day? Where do they spend their time at night? What do they do in these places? What do they look like to you? How do you feel when you see one up close? Use your responses to these questions to help you describe humans and your feelings about them from your "bat's point of view."

"Birches"
by Robert Frost

ABOUT THE AUTHOR

Robert Frost (1874–1963) was born in San Francisco and raised in New Hampshire and Massachusetts. In 1892, he graduated from high school in Lawrence, Massachusetts, as covaledictorian with Elinor White whom he married three years later. He entered Dartmouth College in the fall of 1892, but left before the end of the first semester. Instead he returned to Lawrence where he worked in a textile mill and taught school. Five years later, Frost entered Harvard. There he studied Latin, which he felt helped him to develop word sense. He studied at Harvard for three years before leaving for an experiment in poultry farming. In 1900, Frost moved to a farm in Derry, New Hampshire. He also began teaching at Pinkerton Academy. When he was thirty-eight, he sold his farm and sailed with his wife and four children from Boston to Glasgow, determined to make his reputation as a poet in England. He published his first book of poetry, *A Boy's Will,* in 1913, and his second, *North of Boston,* a year later. Frost returned home in 1915 with the reputation he had been seeking. Frost was a frequent lecturer at many schools, including the Bread Loaf School of English at Middlebury College. Recognition for his poetry included an invitation to read at the inauguration of President John F. Kennedy. Frost received many awards and honors in his lifetime, including Pulitzer Prizes for several of his books and over forty honorary degrees from colleges and universities.

ABOUT THE SELECTION

Background: Setting. The setting is the time and place of a literary work. Frost's **"Birches"** recalls a scene from rural New England in winter. Sometimes, in that part of the country in the winter, rain falls on trees and becomes frozen, so that the branches and twigs appear to be made of crystal. Young birches, carrying that heavy load of ice, are often bent to the ground.

READER'S JOURNAL

Think of some oddity you have noticed and explain how the oddity may have come about. You can make up your own imaginative reason even if you know the factual one. Use your creativity to explain how a certain odd natural condition came to be.

"Birches"

ROBERT FROST

What does the speaker like to think bends the birches? What actually bends the birches?

When I see birches bend to left and right
Across the lines of straighter darker trees,
I like to think some boy's been swinging them.
But swinging doesn't bend them down to stay
5   As ice storms do. Often you must have seen them
Loaded with ice a sunny winter morning
After a rain. They click upon themselves
As the breeze rises, and turn many-colored
As the stir cracks and crazes their enamel.[1]

To what does the speaker compare the broken ice?

10   Soon the sun's warmth makes them shed crystal shells
Shattering and avalanching on the snow crust—
Such heaps of broken glass to sweep away
You'd think the inner dome of heaven had fallen.
They are dragged to the withered <u>bracken</u> by the load,
15   And they seem not to break; though once they are bowed
So low for long, they never right themselves:

To what does the speaker compare the bent birches?

You may see their trunks arching in the woods
Years afterwards, trailing their leaves on the ground
Like girls on hands and knees that throw their hair
20   Before them over their heads to dry in the sun.
But I was going to say when Truth broke in

---

1. **crazes their enamel.** Scratches the shiny white surface of the birch trunks

WORDS FOR EVERYDAY USE:	**brack • en** (brak´ən) *n.,* large, coarse, weedy ferns occurring in meadows and woods

With all her matter of fact about the ice storm,
I should prefer to have some boy bend them
As he went out and in to fetch the cows—
25 Some boy too far from town to learn baseball,
Whose only play was what he found himself,
Summer or winter, and could play alone.
One by one he <u>subdued</u> his father's trees
By riding them down over and over again
30 Until he took the stiffness out of them,
And not one but hung limp, not one was left
For him to conquer. He learned all there was
To learn about not launching out too soon
And so not carrying the tree away
35 Clear to the ground. He always kept his poise
To the top branches, climbing carefully
With the same pains you use to fill a cup
Up to the brim, and even above the brim.
Then he flung outward, feet first, with a swish,
40 Kicking his way down through the air to the ground.
So was I once myself a swinger of birches.
And so I dream of going back to be.
It's when I'm weary of considerations,
And life is too much like a pathless wood
45 Where your face burns and tickles with the cobwebs[2]
Broken across it, and one eye is weeping
From a twig's having <u>lashed</u> across it open.
I'd like to get away from earth awhile
And then come back to it and begin over.
50 May no fate willfully misunderstand me
And half grant what I wish and snatch me away
Not to return. Earth's the right place for love:
I don't know where it's likely to go better.
I'd like to go by climbing a birch tree,
55 And climb black branches up a snow-white trunk
Toward heaven, till the tree could bear no more,
But dipped its top and set me down again.
That would be good both going and coming back.
One could do worse than be a swinger of birches. ∎

What kind of boy does the speaker imagine bending the birches?

What kind of endeavor is bending a birch? To what activity is swinging a birch compared?

When does the speaker dream of becoming a swinger of birches? Why does he wish for this?

Does the speaker wish to leave the Earth forever? Why, or why not?

---

2. **cobwebs.** The speaker refers to the weblike pattern
of lines across the face, perhaps brought on by his grief as
well as his age.

WORDS FOR
EVERYDAY USE:

sub • due (sub do͞o´) *vt.*, overcome; control; reduce

lash (lash) *vt.*, strike hard with great force

Responding to the Selection

Which explanation for the bent birches do you prefer, that they were bent by ice or by the boy? Why do you prefer one explanation over the other?

Reviewing the Selection

RECALLING

1. What does the speaker like to think is the cause when he sees bent birches? What really causes them to bend?

2. What does the speaker say you must have seen on a sunny winter morning? What happens when the sun begins to shed its warmth?

3. What happens to the trees after an ice storm? What makes the narrator talk about ice storms?

4. What does the boy learn about trees? What happens when he gets to the top?

INTERPRETING

5. Why does the speaker prefer to think a swinging boy has caused the trees to bend?

6. What does the shattering of ice look like? What image does this bring to the speaker's mind?

7. What does it say about human frailty and the power of nature if an ice storm and not a boy bent the trees?

8. What does the speaker know about swinging from trees? Why does the speaker want to climb a tree?

SYNTHESIZING

9. How does the speaker's imagination show in both his idea about the ice storm and his story of the boy?

10. In the last line, the narrator says, "One could do worse than be a swinger of birches." What does it mean to be a swinger of birches? Why would being a swinger of birches be a good thing?

Understanding Literature (Questions for Discussion)

1. **Metaphor.** A **metaphor** is a figure of speech in which one thing is spoken or written about as if it were another. This figure of speech invites the reader to make a comparison between the two things. To what does the speaker invite the reader to compare an ice storm in this poem? In what way is the ice storm similar to this thing? To what is broken ice compared? What are some other metaphors in the poem? How do these metaphors illuminate the similarities and differences between nature and humankind?

2. **Simile.** A **simile** is a comparison using *like* or *as.* To what are the arching trunks with trailing leaves compared? How does the use of a simile increase the vividness of the image of the bent tree? Frost also uses a simile for life. To what is life compared? In what way are the two things similar? Do you think that this is an accurate description of life?

3. **Symbol.** A **symbol** is something that represents both itself and something beyond itself; for example, a dove can symbolize peace or a rose, beauty. In this poem, what does the speaker symbolize by describing swinging toward heaven on a birch limb? What does he mean when he says that he would "like to get away from earth for awhile"?

Responding in Writing

Explanation. Write an explanation of a natural event you have seen such as a sunset, a covering of frost on a cold morning, or a violent thunderstorm. You may wish to explain some of the actual reasons for such an occurrence, but you should focus on an imaginative reason of your own.

> **Prewriting Suggestion:** Ask yourself the following questions: How is this natural event accomplished? What if this didn't happen? What effect would it have on the world? Who might be responsible for this event? What does happen as a result of this occurrence? When did this start happening? Where does it (the frost, the color of the sunset, etc.) come from? Why do people feel the way they do about this event (for example, afraid of or exhilarated by a storm)? Answering these questions should get some ideas flowing. Then, to make your piece vivid, choose images that evoke the natural event you are describing.

"The Creation"
by James Weldon Johnson

ABOUT THE AUTHOR

James Weldon Johnson (1871–1938) was born in Jacksonville, Florida, and educated at Atlanta University and Columbia. Johnson's talents ran the gamut from writing poetry and prose to writing songs for Broadway productions, teaching, and practicing law and politics. In a rich and varied career, Johnson worked as a high school principal, a vaudeville comedian, a national secretary to the NAACP, a United States Consul to Venezuela and Nicaragua, and a professor of creative literature at Fisk University in Nashville, Tennessee. He edited several collections of poetry and wrote poetry of his own. Collections of Johnson's poetry include *God's Trombones* (1927) and *Selected Poems* (1935). The anonymously published novel *Autobiography of an Ex-Colored Man* (1912) garnered new attention when Johnson was revealed as its author after its reissue in 1927. Another influential prose work by Johnson was his autobiography, *Along This Way* (1933).

ABOUT THE SELECTION

Background: Theme. "The Creation" was included in Johnson's book *God's Trombones,* a collection of seven sermons and a prayer. The theme of the creation of the world and the beginning of life is a common one in religions around the world. Johnson's poem, with its vivid imagery and magnificent rhetoric reminiscent of southern preaching, is widely considered one of the most beautiful of all retellings of this familiar story.

READER'S JOURNAL
What things fill you with wonder or awe? Freewrite about these things in your journal.

"The Creation"

JAMES WELDON JOHNSON

And God stepped out on space,
And he looked around and said:
I'm lonely—
I'll make me a world.

5   And far as the eye of God could see
Darkness covered everything,
Blacker than a hundred midnights
Down in a cypress swamp.[1]

Then God smiled,
10   And the light broke,
And the darkness rolled up on one side,
And the light stood shining on the other,
And God said: That's good!

Then God reached out and took the light in His hands,
15   And God rolled the light around in His hands
Until He made the sun;
And He set that sun a-blazing in the heavens.
And the light that was left from making the sun
God gathered it up in a shining ball
20   And flung it against the darkness,
Spangling the night with the moon and stars.
Then down between
The darkness and the light

What exists before creation?

How does God create light? What does God say when it is created? What does this passage reveal about God?

To what is the creation of celestial elements (moon, stars, and the world) compared?

---

1. **cypress swamp.** Swamp of evergreen, cone-bearing trees native to North America, Europe, and Asia

He hurled the world;
25   And God said: That's good!

Then God himself stepped down—
And the sun was on His right hand,
And the moon was on His left;
The stars were clustered about His head,
30   And the earth was under His feet.
And God walked, and where He trod
His footsteps hollowed the valleys out
And bulged the mountains up.

Then He stopped and looked and saw
35   That the earth was hot and <u>barren</u>.
So God stepped over to the edge of the world
And He spat out the seven seas—
He batted His eyes, and the lightnings flashed—
He clapped His hands, and the thunders rolled—
40   And the waters above the earth came down,
The cooling waters came down.

Then the green grass sprouted,
And the little red flowers blossomed,
The pine tree pointed his finger to the sky,
45   And the oak spread out his arms,
The lakes cuddled down in the hollows of the ground,
And the rivers ran down to the sea;
And God smiled again,
And the rainbow appeared,
50   And curled itself around His shoulder.

Then God raised His arm and He waved His hand
Over the sea and over the land,
And He said: Bring forth! Bring forth!
And quicker than God could drop His hand,
55   Fishes and fowls
And beasts and birds
Swam the rivers and the seas,
Roamed the forests and the woods,
And split the air with their wings.
60   And God said: That's good!

How does God create the geographical features of the Earth? In what way does the creation of the Earth's features differ from the creation of light?

How does life come to be? To what extent are God and the Earth and sea interacting in creating life? Does the process of creation seem to gain strength as it proceeds?

WORDS FOR EVERYDAY USE: **bar • ren** (bar´ən) *adj.,* empty; not producing crops

The Creation. *Aaron Douglas, 1935. The Howard University Gallery of Art, Washington, DC*

Then God walked around,
And God looked around
On all that He had made.
He looked at His sun,
65   And He looked at His moon,
And He looked at His little stars;
He looked on His world
With all its living things,
And God said: I'm lonely still.

70   Then God sat down—
On the side of a hill where He could think;
By a deep, wide river He sat down;
With His head in His hands,
God thought and thought,
75   Till He thought: I'll make me a man!

Up from the bed of the river
God scooped the clay;
And by the bank of the river
He kneeled Him down;
80   And there the great God Almighty
Who lit the sun and fixed it in the sky,
Who flung the stars to the most far corner of the night,
Who rounded the earth in the middle of His hand;
This Great God,
85   Like a mammy[2] bending over her baby,
Kneeled down in the dust
Toiling over a lump of clay
Till He shaped it in His own image;

Then into it He blew the breath of life,
90   And man became a living soul.
Amen. Amen.

2. **mammy.** Child's term for *mother*

What feelings does God have after surveying His work?

What is special about the creation of the first human? What details signify God's emotional involvement with this creation?

Responding to the Selection

What do you think of the reason God had for creating the world? Do you think it was a good reason? Do you think that the creation of the world and of the life forms on it was the solution to God's problem? How might a creative act relieve loneliness?

Reviewing the Selection

RECALLING

1. What does God see when He looks around? What does God decide to do?

2. How does God create light? How does He make the sun, stars, and moon?

3. What happens when God walks on the land? How does He create the seas?

4. Describe the creation of humans as told in this poem.

INTERPRETING

▶▶ 5. How does God feel at the beginning of the poem? How is this emotion related to the creation of the world?

▶▶ 6. Why is light the first thing that God makes? How does He feel when He has created the sun, the moon, and the stars?

▶▶ 7. How does God feel about what He has made? How do you know? Is He satisfied after creating the "Fishes and fowls/And beasts and birds"?

▶▶ 8. Why does God create humans?

SYNTHESIZING

9. How does the creation of people differ from the creation of other life forms? What is significant about the manner in which God creates humans and the time when He chooses to do so?

10. How is this story similar to other creation stories with which you are familiar? How is it different?

Understanding Literature (Questions for Discussion)

1. **Narrative Poem.** A **narrative poem** is a verse that tells a story. What story does "The Creation" tell? Why do you think the story was written in verse? How might the fact that it was written as a sermon have affected the way that it was written?

2. **Simile.** A **simile** is a comparison using *like* or *as*. What simile is used to describe God creating a person? To what is God compared? How are these two things similar? Johnson says that God "kneeled down in the dust toiling over a lump of clay," so he could have compared God to a sculptor. What kind of relationship would that have established between God and humans? How would that differ from the relationship developed through the simile Johnson does use?

"Casey at the Bat"
by Ernest Lawrence Thayer

ABOUT THE AUTHOR

Ernest Lawrence Thayer (1863–1940) was born in Worcester, Massachusetts. He majored in philosophy at Harvard, where he was editor-in-chief of the student humor magazine, *The Lampoon*. While at Harvard, he befriended William Randolph Hearst, who founded the Hearst chain of newspapers. Thayer left Harvard when Hearst was thrown out because of a practical joke. For several years, Thayer worked with Hearst on the *San Francisco Examiner*. He then left to take over his father's textile business, but he continued to contribute short pieces to the paper. Although Thayer wrote many other works, none achieved the fame of his classic ballad "Casey at the Bat."

ABOUT THE SELECTION

Background: History. "Casey at the Bat" first appeared in the *San Francisco Examiner* on June 3, 1888. A year later, actor DeWolf Hopper read the poem to a baseball crowd, and the crowd responded with a rousing standing ovation. Thayer's spirited, humorous poem about America's "national pastime" has remained popular for over a hundred years.

Background: Technique. "Casey at the Bat" is a **narrative poem,** one that tells a story. Like most stories, this one has a setting; a main character, or **protagonist**; and a struggle, or **conflict**, that the main character faces. As you read, identify these elements of the story that the poem tells.

READER'S JOURNAL

Think about a time when you were part of a crowd that got caught up in excitement over some occurrence. Write about what was happening and how the crowd reacted. What sounds did people make? what movements? What was the overall feeling when the event was over?

"Casey at the Bat"

ERNEST LAWRENCE THAYER

The outlook wasn't brilliant
   for the Mudville nine that day:
The score stood four to two
   with but one inning more to play.

5   And then when Cooney died at first,
   and Barrows did the same,
A sickly silence fell
   upon the patrons of the game.

A straggling few got up
10   to go in deep despair. The rest
Clung to that hope which springs eternal
   in the human breast;
They thought if only Casey[1]
   could but get a whack at that—
15   We'd put up even money now
   with Casey at the bat.

But Flynn preceded Casey,
   as did also Jimmy Blake,
And the former was a lulu[2]
20   and the latter was a cake;[3]

What is the struggle faced by the "Mudville nine"?

What do "the patrons of the game" do when the first two batters strike out?

---

1. **Casey.** Famous baseball player
2. **lulu.** Slang for odd, extraordinary, or peculiar person
3. **cake.** Slang for insubstantial or weak person

So upon that <u>stricken</u> multitude
    grim melancholy sat.
For there seemed to be little chance
    of Casey's getting to the bat.

25   But Flynn let drive a single,
        to the wonderment of all,
And Blake, the much despis-ed,
        tore the cover off the ball;
And when the dust had lifted,
30   and the men saw what had occurred,
There was Jimmy safe at second
        and Flynn a-hugging third.

How do the spectators react when they realize that there is still hope for the team?

Then from 5,000 throats and more
        there rose a lusty yell;
35   It rumbled through the valley,
        it rattled in the <u>dell</u>;
It knocked upon the mountain
        and recoiled upon the flat,
For Casey, mighty Casey,
40   was advancing to the bat.

In what manner is Casey described? How does he react to the crowd?

There was ease in Casey's manner
        as he stepped into his place;
There was pride in Casey's bearing
        and a smile on Casey's face.
45   And when, responding to the cheers,
        he lightly <u>doffed</u> his hat,
No stranger in the crowd could doubt
        'twas Casey at the bat.

Ten thousand eyes were on him
50   as he rubbed his hands with dirt;
Five thousand tongues applauded
        when he wiped them on his shirt.
Then while the <u>writhing</u> pitcher
        ground the ball into his hip,
55   Defiance gleamed in Casey's eye,
        a sneer curled Casey's lip.

WORDS FOR EVERYDAY USE:

strick • en (strik´ən) *adj.,* wounded, afflicted, distressed

dell (del) *n.,* small valley or glen, usually wooded

doff (däf, dôf) *vt.,* take off; remove or lift (one's hat)

writh • ing (rīth´ing) *part.,* twisting or turning in distress

And now the leather-covered sphere
 came hurtling through the air,
And Casey stood a-watching it
60 in <u>haughty</u> grandeur there.
Close by the sturdy batsman
 the ball unheeded sped—
"That ain't my style," said Casey.
 "Strike one," the umpire said.

65 From the benches, black with people,
  there went up a muffled roar,
Like the beating of the storm-waves
 on a stern and distant shore.
"Kill him! Kill the umpire!"
70 shouted someone on the stand;
And it's likely they'd have killed him
 had not Casey raised his hand.

What is Casey's attitude toward the game? How can his demeanor be described?

In what way does the crowd react to the umpire's call?

WORDS FOR
EVERYDAY USE:

haugh • ty (hôt´ē) *adj.*, showing great pride in oneself and scorn for others; arrogant

Is the description of Casey heroic? What makes it so?

With a smile of Christian charity
    great Casey's <u>visage</u> shone;
75 He stilled the rising tumult;
    he bade the game go on;
He signaled to the pitcher,
    and once more the spheroid flew;
But Casey still ignored it,
80   and the umpire said, "Strike two."

"Fraud!" cried the maddened thousands,
    and echo answered fraud;
But one scornful look from Casey
    and the audience was awed.
85 They saw his face grow stern and cold,
    they saw his muscles strain,
And they knew that Casey
    Wouldn't let that ball go by again.

What is Casey's attitude after the umpire's second call?

The sneer is gone from Casey's lip,
90   his teeth are clenched in hate;
He pounds with cruel violence
    his bat upon the plate.
And now the pitcher holds the ball.
    and now he lets it go,
95 And now the air is shattered
    by the force of Casey's blow.

In what way is this other setting, somewhere, described? To what place is it compared?

Oh, somewhere in this favored land
    the sun is shining bright;
The band is playing somewhere,
100   and somewhere hearts are light,
And somewhere men are laughing,
    and somewhere children shout;

But there is no joy in Mudville—
    mighty Casey has struck out.   ■

WORDS FOR EVERYDAY USE: **vis • age** (viz´ ij) *n.,* facial features or expression

Responding to the Selection

How does the crowd in the poem feel about Casey? Have you ever felt this way about an athlete? Do you think that people are more or less interested in sports stars now than they were in the past? Is a live or a televised game more exciting? Have the media changed how we perceive sports and athletes?

Reviewing the Selection

RECALLING

1. At the beginning of the poem, what is the outlook like for the Mudville nine? What is the score? What inning is it?

2. Which two players bat before Casey? What do those two players do?

3. What is Casey's manner and bearing as he steps up to the plate? What does Casey say when the first pitch flies by him?

4. What happens on the third pitch?

INTERPRETING

5. What happens at the beginning of the inning that discourages the fans? How do the fans react?

6. When the dust settles after Blake is up, how do the fans react? Why do they react in this way?

7. What does Casey's comment about the pitch say about him? How does the crowd react to the umpire's call? How does Casey calm the crowd?

8. What is the mood like in Mudville at the end of the poem?

SYNTHESIZING

9. What is Casey's overall manner? What do his actions, facial expressions, and words reveal about him? How do the fans feel about him? What does this tell you about Casey?

10. Trace the feelings of the crowd throughout the poem. How many times does its mood change? What happens to cause each change? What details does Thayer use to create these changes?

Understanding Literature (Questions for Discussion)

1. **Irony. Irony** is a difference between appearance and reality. Irony of situation occurs when an event violates the expectations of the characters, the reader, or the audience. What do the characters expect to happen when Casey gets to bat? How is this expectation developed in the readers? What might you assume based on the line "And now the air is shattered/by the force of Casey's blow"? What is revealed in the last line of the poem? Why is this line ironic?

2. **Hyperbole. Hyperbole** is exaggeration for effect, as when someone says, "I'm so hungry, I could eat a horse." In this poem, Thayer achieves a humorous effect by describing ordinary things and actions using fancy, formal, elevated, "highfalutin" language, such as *spheroid* for *baseball.* What other examples of such grandiose language can you find in the poem? What makes the use of such language funny?

Responding in Writing

Headlines. Write the newspaper headlines for the story about Casey striking out. How would it appear in the Mudville paper? What would the paper in the hometown of the other team say?

> **Prewriting Suggestion:** Make a list of key words related to the story. Choose exciting words that will capture people's attention. Read the Language Arts Survey, 2.32, "Using Precise Nouns," and 2.33, "Using Vivid Verbs." Try to use these types of words in your writing. You may wish to use baseball jargon in your headlines. Remember to keep them brief and exciting!

PROJECT

The Thrill of Victory and the Agony of Defeat. Have you ever been on a team that lost the big game, been the player to score the game-winning point right at the buzzer, or watched as an athlete stumbled and lost his or her dream of glory? At such times, emotions run high among both participants and spectators. With your classmates, prepare a presentation of dramatic moments in sports. Each student can choose a particular event to present. Use pictures or video footage of thrilling or agonizing moments to accompany an oral presentation to the class.

"Paul Revere's Ride"
by Henry Wadsworth Longfellow

ABOUT THE AUTHOR

Henry Wadsworth Longfellow (1807–1882), the most beloved American poet of his time, was born in what is now Portland, Maine, and died in Cambridge, Massachusetts. His father, hoping Longfellow would become a lawyer, sent him to Bowdoin College in Brunswick, Maine. There, Longfellow became so skilled in languages that Bowdoin created for him the then-rare position of professor of modern languages. After three years of additional language study in Europe, Longfellow reported to his teaching position at Bowdoin in 1829. Having concentrated on the Romance languages, Longfellow later became proficient in Germanic languages and became a professor at Harvard in 1836. Later at Harvard, he taught a wide range of European literatures and produced the anthology *The Poets and Poetry of Europe.* Longfellow had married in 1831, but his wife died in 1835. He then fell in love with Fanny Appleton, a Boston heiress, and wrote about their meeting in the prose romance *Hyperion* (1839). They married in 1843 and lived an elegant life. His poem *Hiawatha* was commercially successful, and his other poetry was popular. He continued at Harvard until 1854. Fanny died in 1861, and a grief-stricken Longfellow turned to translating the *Divine Comedy* by the Italian Renaissance poet Dante Alighieri.

ABOUT THE SELECTION

Background: History. In **"Paul Revere's Ride"** (1893) Longfellow immortalized Boston silversmith Paul Revere as an American hero. There is controversy over the historical accuracy of Longfellow's poem, although it is generally agreed that Revere did indeed make at least part of this famous ride. The purpose of the ride to Concord was to warn colonists that the British were moving to destroy military supplies and to capture the patriot leaders John Hancock and Samuel Adams. The ride was successful, for because of the warning the colonists received, they were waiting the following morning on the common in the village of Lexington for the battle that began the Revolutionary War.

READER'S JOURNAL

  Choose some historical event with which you are familiar such as the Boston Tea Party or the Battle of Gettysburg. Imagine that you are a young person living at the time when this event took place. Write a brief journal entry describing the event and your feelings about it. Try to envision what it must be like to be living during a turning point in history.

"Paul Revere's Ride"

HENRY WADSWORTH LONGFELLOW

To whom is the poem addressed?

LISTEN, my children, and you shall hear
Of the midnight ride of Paul Revere,
On the eighteenth of April, in Seventy-five;
Hardly a man is now alive
5   Who remembers that famous day and year.

He said to his friend, "If the British march
By land or sea from the town tonight,
Hang a lantern aloft[1] in the belfry arch[2]

What signals are planned and for what purpose?

Of the North Church[3] tower as a signal light,—
10   One, if by land, and two, if by sea;
And I on the opposite shore will be,
Ready to ride and spread the alarm
Through every Middlesex[4] village and farm,
For the country folk to be up and to arm."

15   Then he said, "Good night!" and with muffled oar
Silently rowed to the Charlestown[5] shore,
Just as the moon rose over the bay,
Where swinging wide at her moorings lay

What mood is created by the description of the ship?

The Somerset, British man-of-war;[6]
20   A phantom ship, with each mast and spar[7]
Across the moon like a prison bar,

---

1. **aloft.** Up high
2. **belfry arch.** Archway in the bell tower
3. **North Church.** Church in Boston's North End where the lantern signal was given in April of 1775
4. **Middlesex.** County in eastern Massachusetts, just west of Boston

5. **Charlestown.** Waterfront town just north of Boston's North End and the main Boston Harbor
6. **man-of-war.** Warship
7. **spar.** Pole or mast supporting a ship's sail

And a huge black hulk, that was magnified
By its own reflection in the tide.
Meanwhile, his friend, through alley and street,
25   Wanders and watches with eager ears,
Till in the silence around him he hears
The muster of men at the barrack door,
The sound of arms, and the tramp of feet,
And the measured tread of the grenadiers,[8]
30   Marching down to their boats on the shore.

Then he climbed the tower of the Old North Church,
By the wooden stairs, with stealthy tread,
To the belfry chamber[9] overhead,
And startled the pigeons from their perch
35   On the sombre rafters, that round him made
Masses and moving shapes of shade,—
By the trembling ladder, steep and tall,
To the highest window in the wall,
Where he paused to listen and look down
40   A moment on the roofs of the town,
And the moonlight flowing over all.

What mood is created by the description of the belfry chamber, the churchyard, the town, and the river?

Beneath, in the churchyard, lay the dead,
In their night-encampment on the hill,
Wrapped in silence so deep and still
45   That he could hear, like a sentinel's tread,
The watchful night-wind, as it went
Creeping along from tent to tent,
And seeming to whisper, "All is well!"
A moment only he feels the spell
50   Of the place and the hour, and the secret dread
Of the lonely belfry and the dead;
For suddenly all his thoughts are bent
On a shadowy something far away,
Where the river widens to meet the bay,—
55   A line of black that bends and floats
On the rising tide, like a bridge of boats.

Meanwhile, impatient to mount and ride,
Booted and spurred, with a heavy stride
On the opposite shore walked Paul Revere.

How does the description of Revere contrast with the descriptions in the preceding two stanzas?

---

8. **grenadiers.** Soldiers employed to throw hand grenades
9. **belfry chamber.** Bell tower room

Midnight Ride of Paul Revere. *Grant Wood, 1931. The Metropolitan Museum of Art, Arthur Hoppock Hearn Fund, 1950. (50.117)*

60   Now he patted his horse's side,
      Now gazed at the landscape far and near,
      Then, <u>impetuous</u>, stamped the earth,
      And turned and tightened his saddle-girth;[10]
      But mostly he watched with eager search
65   The belfry tower of the Old North Church,
      As it rose above the graves on the hill,
      Lonely and <u>spectral</u> and sombre and still.
      And lo! as he looks, on the belfry's height
      A glimmer, and then a gleam of light!

---

10. **saddle-girth.** Leather strap that hangs from the saddle and fastens around the horse's belly to keep the saddle in place

WORDS FOR EVERYDAY USE:

im • pet • u • ous (im pech´ o͞o əs) *adj.*, impulsive; rash
spec • tral (spek´trəl) *adj.*, ghostly

70   He springs to the saddle, the bridle he turns,
        But lingers and gazes, till full on his sight
        A second lamp in the belfry burns!

What do the two lamps signify?

        A hurry of hoofs in a village street,
        A shape in the moonlight, a bulk in the dark,
75   And beneath, from the pebbles, in passing, a spark
        Struck out by a steed[11] flying fearless and fleet:
        That was all! And yet, through the gloom and the light,
        The fate of a nation was riding that night;
        And the spark struck out by that steed, in his flight,
80   Kindled the land into flame with its heat.

What examples of alliteration can you find in these lines?

        He has left the village and mounted the steep,
        And beneath him, tranquil and broad and deep,
        Is the Mystic,[12] meeting the ocean tides;
        And under the alders that skirt its edge,
85   Now soft on the sand, now loud on the ledge,
        Is heard the tramp of his steed as he rides.

In what sense is "the fate of a nation riding" on this night?

        It was twelve by the village clock,
        When he crossed the bridge into Medford[13] town.
        He heard the crowing of the cock,
90   And the barking of the farmer's dog,
        And felt the damp of the river fog,
        That rises after the sun goes down.

        It was one by the village clock,
        When he galloped into Lexington.[14]
95   He saw the gilded weathercock
        Swim in the moonlight as he passed,
        And the meeting-house[15] windows, blank and bare,
        Gaze at him with a spectral glare,
        As if they already stood aghast
100   At the bloody work they would look upon.

To what "bloody work" is Longfellow referring?

        It was two by the village clock,
        When he came to the bridge in Concord[16] town.
        He heard the bleating of the flock,
        And the twitter of birds among the trees,
105   And felt the breath of the morning breeze

---

11. **steed.** Horse
12. **Mystic.** River west of Boston
13. **Medford.** Town just west of Boston
14. **Lexington.** Town some miles northwest of Boston
15. **meeting-house.** Building used for town meetings or worship
16. **Concord.** Town next to Lexington where the Revolutionary colonists stockpiled weapons for war

Blowing over the meadows brown.
And one was safe and asleep in his bed
Who at the bridge would be first to fall,
Who that day would be lying dead,
110 Pierced by a British musket-ball.[17]

What happened as a result of the ride?

You know the rest. In the books you have read,
How the British Regulars fired and fled,—
How the farmers gave them ball for ball,
From behind each fence and farm-yard wall,
115 Chasing the red-coats[18] down the lane,
Then crossing the fields to emerge again
Under the trees at the turn of the road,
And only pausing to fire and load.

So through the night rode Paul Revere;
120 And so through the night went his cry of alarm
To every Middlesex village and farm,—
A cry of defiance and not of fear,
A voice in the darkness, a knock at the door,
And a word that shall echo forevermore!

What will people in the future hear? at what times?

125 For, borne on the night-wind of the Past,
Through all our history, to the last,
In the hour of darkness and peril and need,
The people will waken and listen to hear
The hurrying hoof-beats of that steed,
130 And the midnight message of Paul Revere. ■

---

17. **musket-ball.** Large bullet used in a musket, a rifle with a trumpet-shaped barrel
18. **red-coats.** Refers to British soldiers who wore red coats as part of their uniform

Responding to the Selection

Longfellow's poem made Paul Revere into a national folk hero. Why do you think people in the United States have found this story so moving? What elements of the story are particularly gripping?

Reviewing the Selection

RECALLING

1. What date and time is given for the famous ride? What signal is to be given from the belfry arch?

2. What sound does Revere's friend hear?

3. What town did Revere enter at midnight? at one? at two?

4. What happened when the British showed up? How, according to the speaker, does his audience know about this?

INTERPRETING

5. What is the purpose of the signal?

6. What does Revere's friend do as a result of hearing the sound?

7. How does the poet show the passing of time during the night?

8. What were the immediate consequences of Revere's ride? the long-term consequences?

SYNTHESIZING

9. What elements in this poem work to create suspense? to indicate the importance of the events described?

10. Do you think this poem is an effective way of teaching history? Explain your answer.

Understanding Literature (Questions for Discussion)

1. **Mood. Mood,** or **atmosphere,** is the emotion created in the reader by part or all of a literary work. A writer creates mood through judicious use of concrete details. What mood is created by the following details: "muffled oar," "phantom ship," "mast and spar across the moon like a prison bar," "huge black hulk," and "stealthy tread"? What other details contribute to this mood?

2. **Foreshadowing. Foreshadowing** is the act of presenting materials that hint at events to occur later in a story. Find two parts of the poem that foreshadow the battle that will follow Revere's ride. Why you think Longfellow chose to foreshadow these events in this way? What purpose does foreshadowing serve in the poem? What effect does it have on the reader?

3. **Alliteration. Alliteration** is the repetition of initial consonant sounds, as in "Paul Revere's Ride." What examples of alliteration can you find in this poem?

Responding in Writing

Historical Account. Choose a historical event that you find interesting and write a poem, story, or nonfiction account of it. You may choose to use poetic license with the facts of your story as Longfellow did, or you may try to stick to the facts very closely.

> **Prewriting Suggestion:** Do some research to gather information about the event. Then make a time line that shows what happened and in what order. Think about each item on your time line, making notes about details that you could use to make your account of that part of the event come alive. If you choose to write a literary account such as a poem or story, choose a central character involved in the event, and tell about that character's involvement, as Longfellow did.

PROJECT

History and Legend. Research the early days of the Revolutionary War and try to determine what really happened on the night of Revere's ride. Use a variety of sources to see what different versions of the story exist. Which do you think is the most historically sound? Compare what you feel is the most accurate source with the Longfellow poem to see how they differ. Discuss with your classmates why you think Longfellow made these changes and why you think the version of history Longfellow presented has so captured people's imaginations.

"Desiderata"
by Max Ehrmann

ABOUT THE AUTHOR

Max Ehrmann is the author of a piece commonly believed to be an ancient, anonymous writing. It has been said that "Desiderata" was copied from an inscription dated 1692 and found in Old Saint Paul's Church in Baltimore, but Ehrmann wrote the poem and registered it with the Copyright Office of the Library of Congress in 1927.

ABOUT THE SELECTION

Background: Theme. The ideas presented in "Desiderata" are timeless views on life. This popular philosophy has made its way onto cards and posters as well as into books. The appeal of the poem lies in the hope and peace it offers in the midst of a chaotic, troubled world.

READER'S JOURNAL

Do you ever feel that the world is overrun with problems? What good do you see in the world? How do you keep up your spirits in the face of the chaos and tragedy of the world?

"Desiderata"

Max Ehrmann

Why shouldn't you compare yourself to others? What is another way to assess yourself?

Go placidly amid the noise and the haste, and remember what peace there may be in silence . . . As far as possible, without surrender, be on good terms with all persons. Speak your truth quietly and clearly; and listen to others, even to the dull and the ignorant; they too have their story. Avoid loud and aggressive persons; they are vexatious to the spirit . . . If you compare yourself with others, you may become bitter or vain, for always there will be greater and lesser persons than yourself. Enjoy your achievements as well as your plans. Keep interested in your own career, however humble; it is a real possession in the changing fortunes of time . . . Exercise caution in your business affairs, for the world is full of trickery. But let this not blind you to what virtue there is; many persons strive for high ideals and everywhere life is full of heroism . . . Be yourself. Especially do not feign[1] affection. Neither be cynical about love; for in the face of all aridity[2] and disenchantment it is as perennial as the grass . . . Take kindly the counsel of the years, gracefully surrendering the things of

How should you act in regard to love? Why?

---

1. **feign.** Pretend
2. **aridity.** Dryness; lifelessness

Words for Everyday Use:

pla • cid • ly (plas´id lē) *adv.,* calmly; quietly
vex • a • tious (veks ā´shəs) *adj.,* annoying; troublesome

The Lost Balloon. William Holbrook Beard, 1882. National Museum of American Art Washington, DC/ Art Resource, NY

youth. Nurture strength of spirit to shield you in sudden misfortune. But do not distress yourself with dark imaginings. Many fears are born of fatigue and loneliness . . . Beyond a wholesome discipline, be gentle with yourself. You are a child of the universe no less than the trees and the stars; you have a right to be here. And whether or not it is clear to you, no doubt the universe is unfolding[3] as it should. Therefore be at peace with God, whatever you conceive Him to be . . . And whatever your labors and <u>aspirations,</u> in the noisy confusion of life, keep peace in your soul. With all its sham,[4] drudgery and broken dreams, it is still a beautiful world. Be cheerful. Strive to be happy. ∎

What does the speaker say you are? How should you treat yourself?

What negative aspects of the world are noted? What is true in spite of this? What three things does the speaker urge you to do?

---

3. **unfolding.** Disclosing or explaining
4. **sham.** False or deceptive action

WORDS FOR EVERYDAY USE: **as • pi • ra • tion** (as´pə rā´ shən) *n.,* strong desire or ambition

Responding to the Selection

Which lines in the poem spoke most strongly to you? Write about these lines and why they have special meaning in your life.

Reviewing the Selection

RECALLING

1. What advice does the speaker have about noise and silence?

2. What might happen if you compare yourself to others? Who should you be?

3. What does the speaker say you are? What right do you have?

4. What words does the speaker use to describe the world? What does the speaker instruct the reader to do at the end of the poem?

INTERPRETING

5. What benefit does silence offer? What suggestions does the speaker offer about relationships with other people?

6. Rather than judging yourself in comparison to other people, what guides should you use to assess yourself?

7. What should you do because of who you are? Why shouldn't you worry if things seem to be going wrong?

8. Of what evils in the world does the speaker warn the reader to beware? Against what must the reader guard in face of these evils?

SYNTHESIZING

9. Many people think of "Desiderata" as an ancient piece of writing written by an anonymous author. What about the selection makes this idea conceivable? Why might it appeal to people of many different places and times?

10. According to the advice given by the speaker, describe an appropriate response in the following situations: an angry customer is shouting at you, your younger sister was just made captain of a team of which you are also a member, somebody offers you a sure-fire scheme to make money.

Understanding Literature (Questions for Discussion)

Simile. A **simile** is a comparison that uses *like* or *as.* To what does the speaker in "Desiderata" compare love? In what way are these two things similar? Why does the speaker make this comparison?

Responding in Writing

Guide to Life. In this selection, the speaker makes a number of suggestions about how to live life. Think about your own views on the best way to live and write your own set of guidelines for life.

> **Prewriting Suggestion:** First answer the following questions: What makes you happy? What kind of person do you want to be? What does it mean to be successful? What advice would you put in a book for children called *My Guide to Life?* You may wish to discuss these questions with your classmates. Then speak to some people older than yourself, such as a teacher, your parents, grandparents, or older siblings, and ask them what life lessons they have to share. Perhaps they wish they had followed their dreams when they were younger, or maybe they understand the importance of laughter and wish more people felt the same way. Consider these ideas as well as the ones you have generated and combine the ones you think are the most important in a short essay about how to live.

PROJECT

Guide to Life Book. Work with your classmates to prepare a book of your writings from the Responding in Writing assignment above. Photocopy your book on three-hole paper, create covers, and bind the books together with string or strips of leather.

from *The Odyssey*

by Homer, trans. by Robert Fitzgerald

ABOUT THE AUTHOR

In ancient Greece, before the development of writing, poets created long poems that told stories of heroic adventures. These poems, partly memorized and partly improvised, were written down long after their creation. According to tradition, the greatest of the oral poets, or bards, of ancient Greece was **Homer.** Nothing is known of the historical Homer. However, according to legend, he was blind and came from Ionia, in Asia Minor (site of modern-day Turkey). To Homer is attributed the composition of the two greatest poems of ancient Greece, *The Iliad* and *The Odyssey,* both of which probably date from the seventh century BC.

ABOUT THE SELECTION

Background: Genre. An **epic** is a long, narrative work that relates stories of heroes and gods. One of the oldest and greatest of all epic poems is ***The Odyssey.*** This poem, attributed to Homer, tells the story of the hero Odysseus, king of the Greek city of Ithaca, whose name in ancient Greek means "wanderer" or "voyager." In *The Odyssey,* a Greek people named the Achaeans go to war against the city of Troy to rescue Helen, the wife of the Achaean king Menelaus. For ten long years, the Achaeans attempt unsuccessfully to conquer the walled city. Finally, they are able to do so by means of a famous trick thought up by the crafty Odysseus. They build a large wooden horse and secretly put soldiers inside it. Then they pretend to leave. The Trojans, believing the wooden horse to be a gift left by the defeated Achaeans, wheel the horse into their city. Then, at night, the Greeks steal out of the horse and open the city gates, allowing their soldiers to enter. After the defeat of the Trojans, Odysseus sets sail for Ithaca, which lies across the Mediterranean Sea.

Much of *The Odyssey* tells of Odysseus's ten-year voyage home, during which his son Telemachus and his wife Penelope wait in Ithaca, attempting to maintain their authority in Odysseus's absence. On his journey, Odysseus has many adventures. In the land of the Lotus-Eaters, his shipmates become lazy and unwilling to leave because they have eaten the lotus plant, and only with difficulty does Odysseus rescue them. In the land of the Cyclopes, the giant, one-eyed sons of the sea god Poseidon, Odysseus and his men are captured and escape only by means of another of Odysseus's tricks. Of Odysseus's twelve ships, eleven are destroyed by a cannibal named Laistrygones.

Odysseus then travels to the land of a sorceress, Circe, who turns many of his men into pigs. Odysseus has numerous other adventures, including visiting the land of the dead and navigating in a narrow stretch of water between two monsters, Scylla and Charybdis. He is lured into staying for years on the island of the nymph Calypso but eventually he returns home. Back in Ithaca, he is recognized at first only by his dog and by his now elderly nurse. With Telemachus, he fights against the many suitors who have come in his absence to win Penelope's hand and to become king of Ithaca.

The following pages present two selections from Robert Fitzgerald's magnificent translation of *The Odyssey.* In the first, Odysseus and his sailors meet the mighty Cyclops Polyphemus. In the second, they encounter the Sirens whose singing is so enchanting that sailors are tempted to follow the sound and so steer their ships into death-dealing rocks.

Homer

READER'S JOURNAL

What qualities do you think make a person a hero? Write about what you think a hero is in your journal. Give examples of heroes from real life and from literature.

FROM

The Odyssey

HOMER, TRANS. BY ROBERT FITZGERALD

In the next land we found were Cyclopes,[1]
giants, louts, without a law to bless them.
In ignorance leaving the fruitage of the earth in mystery
to the immortal gods, they neither plow

How do the Cyclopes' lives differ from those of civilized people?

5   nor sow by hand, nor till the ground, though grain—
wild wheat and barley—grows untended, and
wine-grapes, in clusters, ripen in heaven's rain.
Cyclopes have no muster and no meeting,
no consultation or old tribal ways,

10   but each one dwells in his own mountain cave
dealing out rough justice to wife and child,
indifferent to what the others do.

                       Well, then:
across the wide bay from the mainland
there lies a desert island, not far out

15   but still not close inshore. Wild goats in hundreds
breed there; and no human being comes
upon the isle to startle them—no hunter
of all who ever tracked with hounds through forests
or had rough going over mountain trails.

Why haven't the Cyclopes cultivated the land on the island?

20   The isle, unplanted and untilled, a wilderness,
pastures goats alone. And this is why:
good ships like ours with cheekpaint at the bows
are far beyond the Cyclopes. No shipwright

---

1. **Cyclopes.** One-eyed giants

25 toils among them, shaping and building up
symmetrical trim hulls to cross the sea
and visit all the seaboard towns, as men do
who go and come in commerce over water.
This isle—seagoing folk would have <u>annexed</u> it
and built their homesteads on it: all good land,
30 fertile for every crop in season: lush
well-watered meads along the shore, vines in profusion,
prairie, clear for the plow, where grain would grow
chin high by harvest time, and rich sub-soil.
The island cove is landlocked, so you need
35 no hawsers[2] out astern, bow-stones or mooring:
run in and ride there till the day your crews
<u>chafe</u> to be under sail, and a fair wind blows.
You'll find good water flowing from a cavern
through dusky poplars into the upper bay.
40 Here we made harbor. Some god guided us
that night, for we could barely see our bows
in the dense fog around us, and no moonlight
filtered through the overcast. No look-out,
nobody saw the island dead ahead,
45 nor even the great landward rolling billow
that took us in: we found ourselves in shallows,
keels grazing shore: so furled our sails
and disembarked where the low ripples broke.
There on the beach we lay, and slept till morning.

50 When Dawn spread out her finger tips of rose
we turned out marvelling, to tour the isle,
while Zeus's shy nymph daughters flushed wild goats
down from the heights—a breakfast for my men.
We ran to fetch our hunting bows and long-shanked
55 lances from the ships, and in three companies
we took our shots. Heaven gave us game a-plenty:
for every one of twelve ships in my squadron
nine goats fell to be shared; my lot was ten.
So there all day, until the sun went down,
60 we made our feast on meat galore, and wine—
wine from the ship, for our supply held out,

---

2. **hawsers.** Large ropes for mooring or towing a ship

**WORDS FOR
EVERYDAY USE:**

an • nex (ə neks´) *vt.,* add on or attach

chafe (chāf) *vi.,* be impatient or vexed

so many jars were filled at Ismaros
from stores of the Cicones[3] that we <u>plundered</u>.
We gazed, too, at Cyclopes Land, so near;
65 we saw their smoke, heard bleating from their flocks.
But after sundown, in the gathering dusk,
we slept again above the wash of ripples.

When the young Dawn with finger tips of rose
came in the east, I called my men together
and made a speech to them:

70   "Old shipmates, friends,
the rest of you stand by; I'll make the crossing
in my own ship, with my own company,
and find out what the mainland natives are—
for they may be wild savages, and lawless,
75 or hospitable and god fearing men."

At this I went aboard, and gave the word
to cast off by the stern. My oarsmen followed,
filing in to their benches by the rowlocks,
and all in line dipped oars in the gray sea.

80 As we rowed on, and nearer to the mainland,
at one end of the bay, we saw a cavern
yawning above the water, screened with laurel,
and many rams and goats about the place
inside a sheepfold—made from slabs of stone
85 earthfast between tall trunks of pine and rugged
towering oak trees.

A <u>prodigious</u> man
slept in this cave alone, and took his flocks
to graze afield—remote from all companions,
knowing none but savage ways, a brute
90 so huge, he seemed no man at all of those
who eat good wheaten bread; but he seemed rather
a shaggy mountain reared in solitude.

---

3. **Cicones.** Allies of the Trojans and Odysseus's enemies. Odysseus and his men had attacked the Cicones and taken jars of supplies from them.

WORDS FOR EVERYDAY USE:

plun • der (plun´dər) *vt.*, steal or take by trickery or by force

pro • di • gious (prō dij´əs) *adj.*, exceptional; of great size or power

We beached there, and I told the crew
to stand by and keep watch over the ship;
95   as for myself I took my twelve best fighters
and went ahead. I had a goatskin full
of that sweet liquor that Euanthês' son,
Maron, had given me. He kept Apollo's
holy grove at Ismaros; for kindness
100   we showed him there, and showed his wife and child,
he gave me seven shining golden talents[4]
perfectly formed, a solid silver winebowl,
and then this liquor—twelve two-handled jars
of brandy, pure and fiery. Not a slave
105   in Maron's household knew this drink; only
he, his wife and the storeroom mistress knew;
and they would put one cupful—ruby-colored,
honey-smooth—in twenty more of water,
but still the sweet scent hovered like a <u>fume</u>
110   over the winebowl. No man turned away
when cups of this came round.

                            A wineskin full
I brought along, and victuals[5] in a bag,
for in my bones I knew some towering brute
would be upon us soon—all outward power,
115   a wild man, ignorant of <u>civility</u>.

We climbed, then, briskly to the cave. But Cyclops
had gone afield, to pasture his fat sheep,
so we looked round at everything inside:
a drying rack that sagged with cheeses, pens
120   crowded with lambs and kids, each in its class:
firstlings apart from middlings, and the "dewdrops,"
or newborn lambkins, penned apart from both.
And vessels full of whey[6] were brimming there—
bowls of earthenware and pails for milking.
My men came pressing round me, pleading:

125   "Why not
take these cheeses, get them <u>stowed</u>, come back,

What does Odysseus bring along to offer to the Cyclops?

---

4. **talents.** Coins
5. **victuals.** Food
6. **whey.** Milky liquid left over from the making of cheese

WORDS FOR
EVERYDAY USE:

fume (fyo͞om) *n.*, smoke, gas, or vapor

civ • il • i • ty (sə vil´ə tē) *n.*, manners; civilized ways

stow (stō) *v.*, put away, especially aboard a ship

throw open all the pens, and make a run for it?
We'll drive the kids and lambs aboard. We say
put out[7] again on good salt water!"

What mistake does Odysseus make? What is foreshadowed, or hinted at, in these lines?

                                            Ah,

130   how sound that was! Yet I refused. I wished
to see the caveman, what he had to offer—
no pretty sight, it turned out, for my friends.

We lit a fire, burnt an offering,
and took some cheese to eat; then sat in silence
135   around the embers, waiting. When he came
he had a load of dry boughs on his shoulder
to stoke his fire at suppertime. He dumped it
with a great crash into that hollow cave,
and we all scattered fast to the far wall.
140   Then over the broad cavern floor he ushered
the ewes he meant to milk. He left his rams
and he-goats in the yard outside, and swung
high overhead a slab of solid rock
to close the cave. Two dozen four-wheeled wagons,

How strong is the Cyclops? How do you know?

145   with heaving wagon teams, could not have stirred
the tonnage of that rock from where he wedged it
over the doorsill. Next he took his seat
and milked his bleating ewes. A practiced job
he made of it, giving each ewe her suckling;
150   thickened his milk, then, into curds and whey,
sieved out the curds to drip in withy[8] baskets,
and poured the whey to stand in bowls
cooling until he drank it for his supper.
When all these chores were done, he poked the fire,
155   heaping on brushwood. In the glare he saw us.

"Strangers," he said, "who are you? And where from?
What brings you here by sea ways—a fair traffic?[9]
Or are you wandering <u>rogues</u>, who cast your lives
like dice, and ravage other folk by sea?"

---

7. **put out.** Set sail
8. **withy.** Made of willow twigs
9. **fair traffic.** Honest trade

WORDS FOR EVERYDAY USE: **rogue** (rōg) *n.*, wicked or rascally person

160   We felt a pressure on our hearts, in dread
       of that deep rumble and that mighty man.
       But all the same I spoke up in reply:

       "We are from Troy, Achaeans, blown off course
       by shifting gales on the Great South Sea;
165   homeward bound, but taking routes and ways
       uncommon; so the will of Zeus would have it.
       We served under Agamemnon, son of Atreus—
       the whole world knows what city
       he laid waste, what armies he destroyed.
170   It was our luck to come here; here we stand,
       beholden for your help, or any gifts
       you give—as custom is to honor strangers.[10]
       We would entreat you, great Sir, have a care
       for the gods' courtesy; Zeus will <u>avenge</u>
       the unoffending guest."

175   He answered this
       from his brute chest, unmoved:

                            "You are a ninny,
       or else you come from the other end of nowhere,
       telling me, mind the gods! We Cyclopes
       care not a whistle for your thundering Zeus
180   or all the gods in bliss; we have more force by far.
       I would not let you go for fear of Zeus—
       you or your friends—unless I had a whim to.
       Tell me, where was it, now, you left your ship—
       around the point, or down the shore, I wonder?"

185   He thought he'd find out, but I saw through this,
       and answered with a ready lie:

                            "My ship?
       Poseidon Lord,[11] who sets the earth a-tremble,
       broke it up on the rocks at your land's end.

*Why doesn't
Odysseus tell the
Cyclops the
truth?*

---

10. **as custom . . . strangers.** Among the ancient Greeks,
treating visitors well was considered a sacred obligation.
11. **Poseidon Lord.** Greek god of the sea

WORDS FOR
EVERYDAY USE: **a • venge** (ə venjʹ) *vt.*, get revenge for a wrongdoing

How large would you estimate the Cyclops to be?

190 | A wind from seaward served him, drove us there.
We are survivors, these good men and I."

Neither reply nor pity came from him,
but in one stride he clutched at my companions
and caught two in his hands like squirming puppies
to beat their brains out, spattering the floor.

To what is the Cyclops compared?

195 | Then he dismembered them and made his meal,
gaping and crunching like a mountain lion—
everything: innards, flesh, and marrow bones.
We cried aloud, lifting our hands to Zeus,
powerless, looking on at this, appalled;

200 | but Cyclops went on filling up his belly
with manflesh and great gulps of whey,
then lay down like a mast among his sheep.
My heart beat high now at the chance of action,
and drawing the sharp sword from my hip I went

Why can't Odysseus kill the Cyclops?

205 | along his flank to stab him where the midriff
holds the liver. I had touched the spot
when sudden fear stayed me: if I killed him
we perished there as well, for we could never
move his <u>ponderous</u> doorway slab aside.

210 | So we were left to groan and wait for morning.

When the young Dawn with finger tips of rose
lit up the world, the Cyclops built a fire
and milked his handsome ewes, all in due order,
putting the sucklings to the mothers. Then,

215 | his chores being all dispatched, he caught
another brace of men to make his breakfast,
and whisked away his great door slab
to let his sheep go through—but he, behind,
reset the stone as one would cap a quiver.[12]

220 | There was a <u>din</u> of whistling as the Cyclops
rounded his flock to higher ground, then stillness.
And now I pondered how to hurt him worst
if but Athena[13] granted what I prayed for.
Here are the means I thought would serve my turn:

---

12. **cap a quiver.** Put the top on a container for arrows
13. **Athena.** Greek goddess of wisdom to whom Odysseus, known for his intelligence, often turns for guidance

WORDS FOR EVERYDAY USE:

pon • der • ous (pän´dər es) *adj.,* heavy; bulky; massive
din (din) *n.,* noise

225   a club, or staff, lay there along the fold—
an olive tree, felled green and left to season
for Cyclops' hand. And it was like a mast
a lugger of twenty oars, broad in the beam—
a deep-sea-going craft—might carry:
230   so long, so big around, it seemed. Now I
chopped out a six-foot section of this pole
and set it down before my men, who scraped it;
and when they had it smooth, I hewed again
to make a stake with pointed end. I held this
235   in the fire's heart and turned it, toughening it,
then hid it, well back in the cavern, under
one of the dung piles in profusion there.

Now came the time to toss for it: who ventured
along with me? whose hand could bear to thrust
240   and grind that spike in Cyclops' eye, when mild
sleep had mastered him? As luck would have it,
the men I would have chosen won the toss—
four strong men, and I made five as captain.
At evening came the shepherd with his flock,
245   his woolly flock. The rams as well, this time,
entered the cave: by some sheep-herding whim—
or a god's bidding—none were left outside.
He hefted[14] his great boulder into place
and sat him down to milk the bleating ewes
250   in proper order, put the lambs to suck,
and swiftly ran through all his evening chores.
Then he caught two more men and feasted on them.
My moment was at hand, and I went forward
holding an ivy bowl of my dark drink,
looking up, saying:

255   "Cyclops, try some wine.
Here's liquor to wash down your scraps of men.
Taste it, and see the kind of drink we carried
under our planks. I meant it for an offering
if you would help us home. But you are mad,
260   unbearable, a bloody monster! After this,
will any other traveler come to see you?"

He seized and drained the bowl, and it went down
so fiery and smooth he called for more:

---

14. **hefted.** Lifted

How big is the Cyclops's club or staff? What does Odysseus do with it?

What does Odysseus plan to do with the stake?

265 "Give me another, thank you kindly. Tell me,
how are you called? I'll make a gift will please you.
Even Cyclopes know the wine-grapes grow
out of grassland and loam in heaven's rain,
but here's a bit of nectar and ambrosia!"[15]

270 Three bowls I brought him, and he poured them down.
I saw the fuddle and flush come over him,
then I sang out in <u>cordial</u> tones:

                                    "Cyclops,
you ask my honorable name? Remember
the gift you promised me, and I shall tell you.
My name is Nohbdy: mother, father, and friends,
everyone calls me Nohbdy."

275   And he said:

"Nohbdy's my meat, then, after I eat his friends.
Others come first. There's a noble gift, now."
Even as he spoke, he reeled and tumbled backward,
his great head lolling to one side; and sleep
280 took him like any creature. Drunk, hiccuping,
he dribbled streams of liquor and bits of men.

Now, by the gods, I drove my big hand spike
deep in the embers, charring it again,
and cheered my men along with battle talk
285 to keep their courage up: no quitting now.
The pike of olive, green though it had been,
reddened and glowed as if about to catch.
I drew it from the coals and my four fellows
gave me a hand, lugging it near the Cyclops
290 as more than natural force nerved them; straight
forward they sprinted, lifted it, and rammed it
deep in his crater eye, and I leaned on it
turning it as a shipwright turns a drill
in planking, having men below to swing
295 the two-handled strap that spins it in the groove.
So with our brand we bored that great eye socket

What "gift" does the Cyclops offer to Odysseus in exchange for the drink?

What parts of the description of the Cyclops show him to be monstrous and revolting?

What do Odysseus and his companions do to the Cyclops?

---

15. **ambrosia.** Food of the gods

WORDS FOR EVERYDAY USE: cor • dial (kôr´jəl) adj., friendly

while blood ran out around the red hot bar.
Eyelid and lash were seared; the pierced ball
hissed broiling, and the roots popped.

                                    In a smithy
300   one sees a white-hot axehead or an adze[16]
plunged and wrung in a cold tub, screeching steam—
the way they make soft iron hale and hard—:
just so that eyeball hissed around the spike.
The Cyclops bellowed and the rock roared round him,

305   and we fell back in fear. Clawing his face
he tugged the bloody spike out of his eye,
threw it away, and his wild hands went groping;
then he set up a howl for Cyclopes
who lived in caves on windy peaks nearby.
310   Some heard him; and they came by <u>divers</u> ways
to clump around outside and call:

                                    "What ails you,
Polyphemos? Why do you cry so sore
in the starry night? You will not let us sleep.
Sure no man's driving off your flock? No man
has tricked you, ruined you?"

315   Out of the cave
the mammoth Polyphemos roared in answer:

"Nohbdy, Nohbdy's tricked me, Nohbdy's ruined me!"

To this rough shout they made a <u>sage</u> reply:

"Ah well, if nobody has played you foul
320   there in your lonely bed, we are no use in pain
given by great Zeus. Let it be your father,
Poseidon Lord, to whom you pray."

                                    So saying
they trailed away. And I was filled with laughter
to see how like a charm the name deceived them.

---

16. **adze.** Axe-like tool with a curved blade

Why do you think Odysseus told the Cyclops that his name is Nohbdy? What mistake is made by the other Cyclopes when they hear this name?

| WORDS FOR EVERYDAY USE: | **di • vers** (dī′vərz) *adj.*, various, several |
| | **sage** (sāj) *adj.*, wise |

325   Now Cyclops, wheezing as the pain came on him,
    fumbled to wrench away the great doorstone
    and squatted in the breach with arms thrown wide
    for any silly beast or man who bolted—
    hoping somehow I might be such a fool.
330   But I kept thinking how to win the game:
    death sat there huge; how could we slip away?
    I drew on all my wits, and ran through tactics,
    reasoning as a man will for dear life,
    until a trick came—and it pleased me well.
335   The Cyclops' rams were handsome, fat, with heavy
    fleeces, a dark violet.

*What is
Odysseus's plan?*

                                 Three abreast
    I tied them silently together, twining
    cords of willow from the ogre's bed;
    then slung a man under each middle one
340   to ride there safely, shielded left and right.
    So three sheep could convey each man. I took
    the woolliest ram, the choicest of the flock,
    and hung myself under his kinky belly,
    pulled up tight, with fingers twisted deep
345   in sheepskin ringlets for an iron grip.
    So, breathing hard, we waited until morning.

    When Dawn spread out her finger tips of rose
    the rams began to stir, moving for pasture,
    and peals of bleating echoed round the pens
350   where dams[17] with udders full called for a milking.
    Blinded, and sick with pain from his head wound,
    the master stroked each ram, then let it pass,
    but my men riding on the <u>pectoral</u> fleece
    the giant's blind hands blundering never found.
355   Last of them all my ram, the leader, came,
    weighted by wool and me with my meditations.
    The Cyclops patted him, and then he said:

    "Sweet cousin ram, why lag behind the rest
    in the night cave? You never linger so

---

17. **dams.** Female sheep

WORDS FOR
EVERYDAY USE: **pec • tor • al** (pek´tə rəl) *adj.,* located in or on the chest

360 but graze before them all, and go afar
to crop sweet grass, and take your stately way
leading along the streams, until at evening
you run to be the first one in the fold.
Why, now, so far behind? Can you be grieving
365 over your Master's eye? That <u>carrion</u> rogue
and his accurst companions burnt it out
when he had conquered all my wits with wine.
Nohbdy will not get out alive, I swear.
Oh, had you brain and voice to tell
370 where he may be now, dodging all my fury!
Bashed by this hand and bashed on this rock wall
his brains would strew the floor, and I should have
rest from the outrage Nohbdy worked upon me."

He sent us into the open, then. Close by,
375 I dropped and rolled clear of the ram's belly,
going this way and that to untie the men.
With many glances back, we rounded up
his fat, stiff-legged sheep to take aboard,
and drove them down to where the good ship lay.
380 We saw, as we came near, our fellows' faces
shining; then we saw them turn to grief
tallying those who had not fled from death.
I hushed them, jerking head and eyebrows up,
and in a low voice told them: "Load this herd;
385 move fast, and put the ship's head toward the breakers."
They all pitched in at loading, then embarked
and struck their oars into the sea. Far out,
as far off shore as shouted words would carry,
I sent a few back to the adversary:

390 "O Cyclops! Would you feast on my companions?
Puny, am I, in a Caveman's hands?
How do you like the beating that we gave you,
you damned cannibal? Eater of guests
under your roof! Zeus and the gods have paid you!"

395 The blind thing in his doubled fury broke
a hilltop in his hands and heaved it after us.

What do the Greeks do with the Cyclops's sheep?

How has the Cyclops paid for not honoring his guests?

WORDS FOR EVERYDAY USE: **car • ri • on** (kar´ē ən) *adj.*, literally, like a piece of dead meat; figuratively, something disgusting or repulsive

What happens as a result of Odysseus's taunts?

Ahead of our black prow it struck and sank
whelmed in a spuming geyser, a giant wave
that washed the ship stern foremost back to shore.
400   I got the longest boathook out and stood
fending us off, with furious nods to all
to put their backs into a racing stroke—
row, row, or perish. So the long oars bent
kicking the foam sternward,[18] making head
405   until we drew away, and twice as far.
Now when I cupped my hands I heard the crew
in low voices protesting:

                                    "Godsake, Captain!
Why bait the beast again? Let him alone."

"That tidal wave he made on the first throw
all but beached us."

410   "All but stove us in!"
"Give him our bearing with your trumpeting,
he'll get the range and lob a boulder."

                                    "Aye.
He'll smash our timbers and our heads together!"

I would not heed them in my glorying spirit,
but let my anger flare and yelled:

415   "Cyclops,
if ever mortal man inquire
how you were put to shame and blinded, tell him
Odysseus, raider of cities, took your eye:
Laërtês' son, whose home's on Ithaca!"

420   At this he gave a mighty sob and rumbled:

"Now comes the weird[19] upon me, spoken of old.
A wizard, grand and wondrous, lived here—Télemos,
a son of Eurymos; great length of days
he had in wizardry among the Cyclopes,
425   and these things he foretold for time to come:
my great eye lost, and at Odysseus's hands.
Always I had in mind some giant, armed
in giant force, would come against me here.

---

18. **sternward.** Toward the rear of a ship or boat
19. **weird.** Fate or destiny

But this, but you—small, pitiful and twiggy—
430   you put me down with wine, you blinded me.
Come back, Odysseus, and I'll treat you well,
praying the god of earthquake[20] to befriend you—
his son I am, for he by his avowal
fathered me, and, if he will, he may
435   heal me of this black wound—he and no other
of all the happy gods or mortal men."
Few words I shouted in reply to him:

"If I could take your life I would and take
your time away, and hurl you down to hell!
440   The god of earthquake could not heal you there!"

At this he stretched his hands out in his darkness
toward the sky of stars, and prayed Poseidon:
"O hear me, lord, blue girdler of the islands,
if I am thine indeed, and thou art father:
445   grant that Odysseus, raider of cities, never
see his home: Laërtês' son, I mean,
who kept his hall on Ithaca. Should destiny
intend that he shall see his roof again
among his family in his father land,
450   far be that day, and dark the years between.
Let him lose all companions, and return
under strange sail to bitter days at home."

In these words he prayed, and the god heard him.
Now he laid hands upon a bigger stone
455   and wheeled around, <u>titanic</u> for the cast,
to let it fly in the black-prowed vessel's track.
But it fell short, just aft the steering oar,
and whelming seas rose giant above the stone
to bear us onward toward the island.
                                    There
460   as we ran in we saw the squadron waiting,
the trim ships drawn up side by side, and all

Who is Polyphemos's father?

As it turns out, it takes Odysseus ten years to get back home. Why might this be so?

---

20. **the god of earthquake.** Poseidon, god of the seas,
who could cause earthquakes and tidal waves with his
three-pronged spear, or trident

WORDS FOR EVERYDAY USE: ti • tan • ic (tī tan´ik) *adj.*, of great size, strength, or power

our troubled friends who waited, looking seaward.
We beached her, grinding keel[21] in the soft sand,
and waded in, ourselves, on the sandy beach.
465   Then we unloaded all the Cyclops' flock
to make division, share and share alike,
only my fighters voted that my ram,
the prize of all, should go to me. I slew him
by the sea side and burnt his long thighbones
470   to Zeus beyond the stormcloud, Kronos' son,[22]
who rules the world. But Zeus disdained my offering;
destruction for my ships he had in store
and death for those who sailed them, my companions.
Now all day long until the sun went down
475   we made our feast on mutton and sweet wine,
till after sunset in the gathering dark
we went to sleep above the wash of ripples.

When the young Dawn with finger tips of rose
touched the world, I roused the men, gave orders
480   to man the ships, cast off the mooring lines;
and filing in to sit beside the rowlocks
oarsmen in line dipped oars in the gray sea.
So we moved out, sad in the vast offing,[23]
having our precious lives, but not our friends.

BOOK TWELVE

As Circe[24] spoke, Dawn mounted her golden throne,
and on the first rays Circe left me, taking
her way like a great goddess up the island.
I made straight for the ship, roused up the men
5   to get aboard and cast off at the stern;
They scrambled to their places by the rowlocks
and all in line dipped oars in the gray sea.
But soon an off-shore breeze blew to our liking—
a canvas-bellying breeze, a lusty shipmate
10   sent by the singing nymph with sunbright hair.
So we made fast the braces,[25] and we rested,
letting the wind and steersman work the ship.

What offering does Odysseus make to Zeus? Is his offering successful?

Why are Odysseus and his companions sad despite the fact that they have escaped with their lives?

---

21. **keel.** Bottom ridge of a ship
22. **Kronos' son.** Kronos, or Chronos, the god of time, was the father of Zeus, the chief of the Greek gods.
23. **offing.** Leaving
24. **Circe.** Sorceress
25. **made fast the braces.** Tied down the ropes that control the movement of the sails

Ulysses and the Sirens. John Waterhouse, 1849–1917. British. Oil on canvas, 100.0 cm x 201.07 cm. Purchased 1891. Reproduced by permission of the National Gallery of Victoria, Melbourne, Australia

The crew being now silent before me, I
addressed them, sore at heart:

                              "Dear friends,
15   more than one man, or two, should know those things
        Circe foresaw for us and shared with me,
        so let me tell her forecast: then we die
        with our eyes open, if we are going to die,
        or know what death we baffle if we can. Sirens
20   weaving a haunting song over the sea
        we are to shun, she, and their green shore
        all sweet with clover; yet she urged that I
        alone should listen to their song. Therefore
        you are to tie me up, tight as a splint,
25   erect along the mast, lashed to the mast,
        and if I shout and beg to be untied,
        take more turns of the rope to muffle me."

Of what has Circe warned Odysseus?

What does Odysseus ask his men to do? Why doesn't he want to be free to move when he hears the Sirens' song?

I rather dwelt on this part of the forecast,
while our good ship made time, bound outward down
30   the wind for the strange island of Sirens.
Then all at once the wind fell, and a calm
came over all the sea, as though some power
lulled the swell.

                                    The crew were on their feet
briskly, to furl the sail, and stow it; then,
35   each in place, they poised the smooth oar blades
and sent the white foam scudding by. I carved
a massive cake of beeswax into bits
and rolled them in my hands until they softened—
no long task, for a burning heat came down

*Why does
Odysseus stop the
ears of the sailors
with wax?*

40   from Helios,[26] lord of high noon. Going forward
I carried wax along the line, and laid it
thick on their ears. They tied me up, then, plumb
amidships, back to the mast, lashed to the mast,
and took themselves again to rowing. Soon,
45   as we came smartly within hailing distance,
the two Sirens, noting our fast ship
off their point, made ready, and they sang:

        This way, oh turn your bows,
            Achaea's glory,
50   *As all the world allows—*
            Moor and be merry.

        Sweet coupled airs we sing.
            No lonely seafarer
        Holds clear of entering
55   *Our green mirror.*
        Pleased by each <u>purling</u> note
            Like honey twining

---

26. **Helios.** Sun god

**WORDS FOR
EVERYDAY USE:**   **purl • ing** (pʉrlʹŋ) *part.*, swirling; rippling

From her throat and my throat,
    Who lies a-pining?

60   *Sea rovers here take joy*
        Voyaging onward,
    As from our song of Troy
    Graybeard and rower-boy
        Goeth more learnèd.[27]

65   *All feats on that great field*
        In the long warfare,
    Dark days the bright gods willed,
        Wounds you bore there,

    Argos'[28] *old soldiery*
70   *On Troy beach teeming,*
    Charmed out of time we see.
    No life on earth can be
        Hid from our dreaming.

The lovely voices in <u>ardor</u> appealing over the water
75 made me crave to listen, and I tried to say,
"Untie me!" to the crew, jerking my brows;
but they bent steady to the oars. Then Perimêdês
got to his feet, he and Eurýlokhos,
and passed more line about, to hold me still.
80 So all rowed on, until the Sirens
dropped under the sea rim, and their singing
dwindled away.
                    My faithful company
rested on their oars now, peeling off
the wax that I had laid thick on their ears;
85 then set me free.   ■

How does Odysseus try to communicate with his crew? Why do they ignore him?

---

27. **learnèd.** The accent over the e shows that it is to be
pronounced as a separate syllable.
28. **Argos.** Ancient Greek city-state

Responding to the Selection

With your classmates, discuss the following questions about Odysseus: Which qualities do you admire in him? What makes him a good leader? What faults does he have? How well do you think he handled the situations involving the Cyclops and the Sirens?

Reviewing the Selection

RECALLING

1. What do Odysseus's men suggest when they arrive at the land of the Cyclopes? Why do they not follow this plan?

2. What does Odysseus tell the Cyclops his name is? How do Odysseus and his men escape from the Cyclops?

3. What does Odysseus do when he and his sailors have left the island of the Cyclops?

4. What warning does Odysseus share with his men? What preparations are made to meet this next peril?

INTERPRETING

5. What does Odysseus's desire to wait for the inhabitant of the cave tell you about his personality? What happens as a result of Odysseus's decision?

6. Why does Odysseus tell the Cyclops a false name? What aspects of Odysseus's character are revealed by the plan he concocts to free himself and his remaining men from the Cyclops?

7. Why does Odysseus shout to the Cyclops when they are away from the island? What happens as a result of Odysseus's action?

8. Why were the Sirens so tempting? How are Odysseus and his sailors able to avoid this danger? Why does Odysseus choose to face this danger differently than his shipmates? What does Odysseus's desire to hear the Sirens' song tell you about him?

SYNTHESIZING

9. What kind of relationship does Odysseus have with the sailors on his ship? How do they feel about him? Use examples from the text to support your answer.

10. What aspects of Odysseus's character are revealed by the episodes of the Cyclops and the Sirens?

Understanding Literature (Questions for Discussion)

1. **Heroic Epic.** An **epic** is a long story, often told in verse, involving heroes and gods. Grand in length and scope, an epic provides a portrait of an entire culture, of the legends, beliefs, values, laws, arts, and ways of life of a people. A heroic epic's main purpose is telling the life story of a great hero. What references to gods or supernatural powers are made in *The Odyssey*? What do you learn about Odysseus's people? What aspects of Odysseus's character are revealed in these excerpts from *The Odyssey*? What makes him a hero?

2. **Personification. Personification** is a figure of speech in which an idea, animal, or thing is described as if it were a person. Dawn is personified in both the story of the Cyclops and the story of the Sirens. In what way is Dawn repeatedly personified? What variations of the formula that describes Dawn appear in these selections?

Responding in Writing

Adventure. Having read about two of Odysseus's adventures, try your hand at writing another. What danger will he face? How will his courage and wit get him through it? What loss will he face?

> **Prewriting Suggestion:** In a small group, brainstorm a list of adventures that could befall Odysseus. Choose one of these and develop the idea for the story. Begin by having Odysseus and his men reach a new land. Describe the inhabitants of this land and how they will imperil Odysseus. Have Odysseus draw on his courage, strength, or cunning to extricate his men and himself from the dangerous situation.

PROJECT

Illustrating *The Odyssey*. Working with other students in a small group, choose another story from *The Odyssey*, read the story, and create one or more illustrations for it. Share the story and illustration(s) with your classmates.

UNIT REVIEW

Poetry

VOCABULARY FROM THE SELECTIONS

annex, 125	dell, 104	palpitating, 59	stow, 127, 140
ardor, 141	din, 130	pectoral, 134	stricken, 104
aspiration, 119	divers, 133	placidly, 118	subdue, 93
avenge, 129	doff, 104	plunder, 126	titanic, 137
balmy, 58	extemporize, 75	ponderous, 130	ardor, 141
barren, 98	fume, 127	prodigious, 126	understudy, 75
bog, 80	haughty, 105	purling, 140	vexatious, 118
bracken, 92	impetuous, 112	rancid, 68	visage, 106
carrion, 135	knell, 60	regale, 74	voluminously, 58
chafe, 125	lash, 93	rogue, 128, 135	writhing, 104
civility, 127	melancholy, 59, 104	sage, 133	
cordial, 132	palmiest, 74	spectral, 112-113	

LITERARY TERMS

aim, 87	heroic epic, 143	narrative poem, 101,	sensory detail, 69
alliteration, 56, 62,	hyperbole, 108	102	simile, 81, 95, 101,
65, 66, 69, 115	image, 65, 90	onomatopoeia, 61	121
assonance, 56, 62	irony, 108	personification, 143	symbol, 95
characterization, 78	metaphor, 70, 72,	point of view, 90	
description, 69	82, 84, 95	repetition, 56, 62,	
foreshadowing, 115	mood, 115	rhyme, 66, 69	

SYNTHESIS: QUESTIONS FOR WRITING, RESEARCH, OR DISCUSSION

1. What are the defining characteristics of lyric poetry and narrative poetry? Explain using examples from the unit.

2. What examples can you find in the unit of each of the following techniques of sound: alliteration, assonance, onomatopoeia, repetition, and rhyme?

3. What examples can you find in the unit of each of the following techniques of sense: hyperbole, imagery, irony, metaphor, personification, simile, and symbol?

LANGUAGE LAB   THE SENTENCE

A **sentence** contains a subject and a verb and expresses a complete idea. A group of words that does not contain both a subject and a verb and that does not express a complete idea is a **sentence fragment.**

CORRECTING SENTENCE FRAGMENTS	
SENTENCE FRAGMENT:	writing under the pseudonym "Phin" (*does not express a complete idea*)
COMPLETE SENTENCE:	Writing under the pseudonym "Phin," Ernest Lawrence Thayer published "Casey at the Bat" in the *San Francisco Examiner.*
SENTENCE FRAGMENT:	tells of the baseball hero Casey(*does not contain a subject*)
COMPLETE SENTENCE:	The humorous poem tells of the baseball hero Casey.
SENTENCE FRAGMENT:	Casey, the hero of Mudville (*does not contain a verb*)
COMPLETE SENTENCE:	Casey, the hero of Mudville, strikes out and loses the game.

LANGUAGE ARTS SURVEY

For additional help, see the Language Arts Survey, 2.61.

When two sentences are run together without proper punctuation or conjunctions, they are called a **run-on.** The following chart shows ways to correct run-on sentences

CORRECTING RUN-ONS	
RUN-ON:	Emily Dickinson was an extremely gifted and prolific poet, most of her poems were not published until after her death.
CORRECTED USING A COMMA AND A COORDINATING CONJUNCTION:	Emily Dickinson was an extremely gifted and prolific poet, but most of her poems were not published until after her death.
CORRECTED BY TURNING ONE SENTENCE INTO A SUBORDINATE CLAUSE:	Although Emily Dickinson was an extremely gifted and prolific poet, most of her poems were not published until after her death.
CORRECTED BY ADDING A SEMICOLON AND A CONJUNCTIVE ADVERB:	Emily Dickinson was an extremely gifted and prolific poet; however, most of her poems were not published until after her death.

LANGUAGE ARTS SURVEY

For additional help, see the Language Arts Survey, 2.62.

To add variety, interest, and clarity to your writing, combine sentences by adding words, phrases, and clauses. Use the methods described in the following chart.

LANGUAGE ARTS
SURVEY

For additional help,
see the Language
Arts Survey,
2.51–2.53.

METHODS FOR COMBINING SENTENCES

Combine by Adding a Word

ORIGINAL SENTENCES: Longfellow wrote a poem about Paul Revere's ride. Paul Revere's ride was historic.

EXPANDED SENTENCE: Longfellow wrote a poem about Paul Revere's historic ride.

Combine by Adding a Phrase

ORIGINAL SENTENCES: The train sped. It sped across the hills.

EXPANDED SENTENCE: The train sped across the hills.

Combine by Adding a Clause

ORIGINAL SENTENCES: Robert Frost lived in and wrote about New England. He was born in San Francisco.

EXPANDED SENTENCES: Although Robert Frost was born in San Francisco, he lived in and wrote about New England.

Robert Frost was born in San Francisco, but he lived in and wrote about New England.

LANGUAGE ARTS
SURVEY

For additional help,
see the Language
Arts Survey,
2.61–2.62.

EXERCISE A   Correcting Fragments and Run-ons

Rewrite the following paragraph, correcting all sentence fragments and run-ons.

EXAMPLE: Most Americans remember Paul Revere as the famous American Revolutionary hero of Longfellow's poem, Revere made a name for himself many years before his historic ride.

Most Americans remember Paul Revere as the famous American Revolutionary hero of Longfellow's poem, but Revere made a name for himself many years before his historic ride.

From a young age Paul Revere learned about the craft of silversmithing, his father, who was a French silversmith, taught the craft to the young Paul. Like most boys his age who acquired only a very basic education. The young Revere concentrated most of his "educational" efforts on learning a trade. When his father died the nineteen-year-old Revere took over his father's shop, he worked with many kinds of precious metals, including silver and gold. Revere, along with his apprentices and journeymen, created many fine silver pieces. Including bowls, flatware, and utensils, some of these pieces are now displayed in museums. Revere also created engravings. Used to print cartoons, bookplates, and other types of printed matter during the twenty years of his lively and prosperous career. Revere gained a reputation as one of the best silversmiths in the American colonies.

EXERCISE B   Combining Sentences

Revise the following paragraph, combining the numbered sentences.

LANGUAGE ARTS
SURVEY

For additional help,
see the Language
Arts Survey,
2.51–2.53.

[1] Some writers begin their careers when they are quite young. Robert Frost did not publish his first book until he was in his forties. [2] After working in the United States as a teacher and farmer, Frost moved his family. He moved them to England. [3] There he published the book called A Boy's Will. It was a book of poetry. [4] The book brought him fame. The fame was immediate.

LANGUAGE ARTS WORKSHOP

GIVING A SPEECH

Three types of public speech are the impromptu speech, the memorized speech, and the extemporaneous speech. An **impromptu speech** is given "off the cuff," with little or no preparation. A **memorized speech** is written out and then memorized before delivery. An **extemporaneous speech** combines the informality of the impromptu speech with the careful preparation of the memorized speech. To prepare an extemporaneous speech, a person gathers notes on index cards but does not memorize the entire speech. The speaker delivers the speech, referring to the note cards but not reading them word for word.

EXERCISE

Read the Language Arts Survey, 3.7, "Public Speaking." Then prepare and deliver an extemporaneous speech by following these steps:

1. Choose one of the following topics or one of your own (The topics are all related to selections in this unit).

   - Advice to young people about living a happy, productive life ("Desiderata")
   - Lessons to be learned from playing sports ("Casey at the Bat")
   - The greatest American hero ("Paul Revere")
   - The advantages and disadvantages of fame ("I'm Nobody! Who are you?")
   - The importance of preserving the natural environment ("Birches")
   - What makes a person a hero? (selections from *The Odyssey*)

2. Make an outline of your speech. Make sure that the outline shows a beginning, middle, and end. (You may have to do some initial research in the library before outlining your speech.)

3. Gather information and write note cards for your speech. Create at least one note card each for the introduction and conclusion and several note-cards for the body of your speech. Write one major point or idea on each note card.

4. Rehearse your speech using your note cards and a tape recorder, video recorder, a mirror, or a practice audience. Run through the speech several times, revising it as necessary.

5. Deliver your speech, attending to both verbal and nonverbal elements of your delivery.

LANGUAGE ARTS SURVEY

For additional help on preparing speeches, see the Language Arts Survey, 3.7.

LANGUAGE ARTS SURVEY

For additional help on organizing ideas and making outlines, see the Language Arts Survey, 1.32–1.34.

LANGUAGE ARTS SURVEY

For additional help on taking notes and preparing note cards, see the Language Arts Survey, 4.31 and 4.32.

LANGUAGE ARTS SURVEY

For additional help on using the elements of verbal and nonverbal communication, See the Language Arts Survey, 3.2 and 3.3.

The Farm. Joan Miró. National Gallery of Art, Washington, DC. Gift of Mary Hemingway

F iction is truth's elder sister.

—Rudyard Kipling

PREREADING

SETTING AND MOOD

"The Monkey's Paw"
by W. W. Jacobs

ABOUT THE AUTHOR

W. W. Jacobs (1863–1943) was born in London, England. He grew up in a house along the Thames River wharf and later drew upon his childhood memories to write comic tales about the misadventures of sailors. *Many Cargoes,* Jacobs's first collection of stories, was immediately successful. His work is collected in more than twenty volumes, but it is for the horror story "The Monkey's Paw" that Jacobs is best known.

ABOUT THE SELECTION

Background: History. "The Monkey's Paw" was published in 1902. One year later, Louis Napoleon Parker dramatized the story as a one-act play for the stage. It was produced in 1903 at the London Haymarket.

Background: Technique. A classic horror story, "The Monkey's Paw" creates in the reader an overwhelming sense of dread. Jacobs achieves this suspenseful effect by introducing to the ordinary, everyday life of the White family the odd artifact of the monkey's paw. As you read the story, note the details that help to create its suspenseful mood.

"The Monkey's Paw"

W. W. JACOBS

Without, the night was cold and wet, but in the small parlor of Laburnum Villa the blinds were drawn, and the fire burned brightly. Father and son were at chess, the former, who possessed ideas about the game involving radical changes, putting his king into such sharp and unnecessary perils that it even pro-voked comment from the white-haired old lady knitting placidly by the fire.

"Hark at the wind," said Mr. White, who, having seen a fatal mistake after it was too late, was amiably desirous of preventing his son from seeing it.

"I'm listening," said the latter, grimly surveying the board as he stretched out his hand. "Check."

"I should hardly think that he'd come tonight," said his father, with his hand poised over the board.

"Mate,"[1] replied the son.

"That's the worst living so far out," bawled Mr. White, with sudden and unlooked-for violence. "Of all the beastly slushy, out-of-the-way places to live in, this is the worst. Pathway's a bog, and the road's a torrent. I don't know what people are thinking about. I suppose because only two houses in the road are let; they think it doesn't matter."

"Never mind, dear," said his wife soothingly. "Perhaps you'll win the next one."

Mr. White looked up sharply, just in time to intercept a knowing glance between mother and son. The words died away on his lips, and he hid a guilty grin in his thin gray beard.

"There he is," said Herbert White, as the gate banged loudly and heavy footsteps came toward the door.

What words and phrases in this passage create a suspenseful, ominous mood?

---

1. **Mate.** The winning move in chess, capturing your opponent's king, is announced with "Checkmate."

WORDS FOR EVERYDAY USE:

pro • voke (prō vōk´) *vt.*, stir up action or feeling
a • mi • a • bly (ā´mē ə blē) *adv.*, pleasantly
poised (poizd) *part.*, suspended

tor • rent (tôr´ənt) *n.*, swift, violent stream
in • ter • cept (in´tər sept´) *vt.*, seize or stop on the way

The old man rose with hospitable haste, and opening the door, was heard <u>condoling</u> with the new arrival. The new arrival also condoled with himself, so that Mrs. White said, "Tut, tut!" and coughed gently as her husband entered the room, followed by a tall, <u>burly</u> man, beady of eye and rubicund of visage.[2]

"Sergeant-Major Morris," he said, introducing him.

The sergeant-major shook hands, and taking the <u>proffered</u> seat by the fire, watched contentedly while his host got out whisky and tumblers and stood a small copper kettle on the fire.

At the third glass, his eyes got brighter, and he began to talk; the little family circle regarding with eager interest this visitor from distant parts, as he squared his broad shoulders in the chair and spoke of wild scenes and doughty[3] deeds; of wars and plagues and strange peoples.

"Twenty-one years of it," said Mr. White, nodding at his wife and son. "When he went away he was a slip of a youth in the warehouse. Now look at him."

"He don't look to have taken much harm," said Mrs. White politely.

"I'd like to go to India myself," said the old man, "just to look round a bit, you know."

"Better where you are," said the sergeant-major, shaking his head. He put down the empty glass, and sighing softly, shook it again.

"I should like to see those old temples and fakirs[4] and jugglers," said the old man. "What was that you started telling me the other day about a monkey's paw or something, Morris?"

"Nothing," said the soldier hastily. "Leastways, nothing worth hearing."

"Monkey's paw?" said Mrs. White curiously.

"Well, it's just a bit of what you might call magic, perhaps," said the sergeant-major offhandedly.

His three listeners leaned forward eagerly. The visitor absentmindedly put his empty glass to his lips and then set it down again. His host filled it for him.

"To look at," said the sergeant-major, fumbling in his pocket, "it's just an ordinary little paw, dried to a mummy."

He took something out of his pocket and proffered it. Mrs. White drew back with a grimace, but her son, taking it, examined it curiously.

"And what is there special about it?" inquired Mr. White as he took it from his son, and having examined it, placed it upon the table.

"It had a spell put on it by an old fakir," said the sergeant-major, "a very holy man. He wanted to show that fate ruled people's lives, and that those who interfered with it did so to their sorrow. He put a spell on it so that three separate men could each have three wishes from it."

His manner was so impressive that his hearers were conscious that their light laughter jarred somewhat.

---

2. **rubicund of visage.** Pink-faced
3. **doughty.** Brave
4. **fakir.** Person who, for religious purposes, lives a thoughtful life of poverty and self-denial

Do you find the sergeant-major's story believable? Why, or why not?

WORDS FOR EVERYDAY USE:

con • dole (kən dōl´) vi., commiserate

bur • ly (bʉr´lē) adj., big and strong

prof • fered (präf´ərd) part., offered courteously

"Well, why don't you have three, sir?" said Herbert White cleverly.

The soldier regarded him in the way that middle age is wont to regard <u>presumptuous</u> youth. "I have," he said quietly, and his blotchy face whitened.

"And did you really have the three wishes granted?" asked Mrs. White.

"I did," said the sergeant-major, and his glass tapped against his strong teeth.

"And has anybody else wished?" <u>persisted</u> the old lady.

"The first man had his three wishes. Yes," was the reply. "I don't know what the first two were, but the third was for death. That's how I got the paw."

His tones were so grave that a hush fell upon the group.

"If you've had your three wishes, it's no good to you now, then, Morris," said the old man at last. "What do you keep it for?"

The soldier shook his head. "Fancy, I suppose," he said slowly. "I did have some idea of selling it, but I don't think I will. It has caused enough mischief already. Besides, people won't buy. They think it's a fairy tale; some of them, and those who do think anything of it, want to try it first and pay me afterward."

"If you could have another three wishes," said the old man, eyeing him <u>keenly</u>, "would you have them?"

"I don't know," said the other. "I don't know."

He took the paw, and dangling it between his forefinger and thumb, suddenly threw it upon the fire.

White, with a slight cry, stooped down and snatched it off.

"Better let it burn," said the soldier solemnly.

"If you don't want it, Morris," said the other, "give it to me."

"I won't," said his friend doggedly. "I threw it on the fire. If you keep it, don't blame me for what happens. Pitch it on the fire again like a sensible man."

The other shook his head and examined his new possession closely. "How do you do it?" he inquired.

"Hold it up in your right hand and wish aloud," said the sergeant-major, "but I warn you of the consequences."

"Sounds like the *Arabian Nights*," said Mrs. White, as she rose and began to set the supper. "Don't you think you might wish for four pairs of hands for me?"

Her husband drew the talisman[5] from his pocket, and then all three burst into laughter as the sergeant-major, with a look of alarm on his face, caught him by the arm.

"If you must wish," he said gruffly, "wish for something sensible."

Mr. White dropped it back into his pocket, and placing chairs, motioned his friend to the table. In the business of supper, the talisman was partly forgotten, and afterward the three sat listening in an <u>enthralled</u> fashion to a second installment of the soldier's adventures in India.

"If the tale about the monkey's paw is not more truthful than those he has been telling us," said Herbert, as the

Why is the sergeant-major alarmed?

---

5. **talisman.** Magic charm

door closed behind their guest, just in time for him to catch the last train, "we shan't make much out of it."

"Did you give him anything for it, Father?" inquired Mrs. White, regarding her husband closely.

"A trifle," said he, coloring slightly. "He didn't want it, but I made him take it. And he pressed me again to throw it away."

"Likely," said Herbert, with pretended horror. "Why, we're going to be rich, and famous and happy. Wish to be an emperor, Father, to begin with; then you can't be henpecked."

He darted round the table, pursued by the <u>maligned</u> Mrs. White armed with an antimacassar.[6]

Why doesn't Mr. White know what to wish for?

Mr. White took the paw from his pocket and eyed it <u>dubiously</u>. "I don't know what to wish for, and that's a fact," he said slowly. "It seems to me I've got all I want."

"If you only cleared the house, you'd be quite happy, wouldn't you?" said Herbert, with his hand on his shoulder. "Well, wish for two hundred pounds, then; that'll just do it."

His father, smiling shamefacedly at his own <u>credulity</u>, held up the talisman, as his son, with a solemn face, somewhat marred by a wink at his mother, sat down at the piano and struck a few impressive chords.

"I wish for two hundred pounds," said the old man distinctly.

What happens when Mr. White makes his wish?

A fine crash from the piano greeted the words, interrupted by a shuddering cry from the old man. His wife and son ran toward him.

"It moved," he cried, with a glance of disgust at the object as it lay on the floor. "As I wished, it twisted in my hand like a snake."

"Well, I don't see the money," said his son as he picked it up and placed it on the table, "and I bet I never shall."

"It must have been your fancy, Father," said his wife, regarding him anxiously.

He shook his head. "Never mind, though; there's no harm done, but it gave me a shock all the same."

They sat down by the fire again while the two men finished their pipes. Outside, the wind was higher than ever, and the old man started nervously at the sound of a door banging upstairs. A silence unusual and depressing settled upon all three, which lasted until the old couple rose to retire for the night.

"I expect you'll find the cash tied up in a big bag in the middle of your bed," said Herbert, as he bade them good night, "and something horrible squatting up on top of the wardrobe watching you as you pocket your ill-gotten gains."

He sat alone in the darkness, gazing at the dying fire, and seeing faces in it. The last face was so horrible and so <u>simian</u> that he gazed at it in amazement. It got so vivid that, with a little uneasy laugh, he felt on the table for a glass containing a little water to throw over it. His hand grasped the monkey's paw, and with a little shiver, he wiped

6. **antimacassar.** Cover on a chair or sofa, which prevents soiling

WORDS FOR EVERYDAY USE:

ma • ligned (mə lind´) *adj.*, slandered

du • bi • ous • ly (d$\overline{oo}$´bē əs lē) *adv.*, skeptically, doubtfully

cre • du • li • ty (krə d$\overline{oo}$´lə tē) *n.*, tendency to believe too readily

sim • i • an (sim´ē ən) *adj.*, like an ape or a monkey

Photograph courtesy of Digital Stock Corp.

his hand on his coat and went up to bed.

In the brightness of the wintry sun next morning as it streamed over the breakfast table, he laughed at his fears. There was an air of <u>prosaic</u> wholesomeness about the room that it had lacked on the previous night, and the dirty, shrivelled little paw was pitched on the sideboard with a carelessness which betokened[7] no great belief in its virtues.

"I suppose all old soldiers are the same," said Mrs. White. "The idea of our listening to such nonsense! How could wishes be granted in these days? And if they could, how could two hundred pounds hurt you, Father?"

"Might drop on his head from the sky," said the <u>frivolous</u> Herbert.

"Morris said the things happened so naturally," said his father, "that you

---

7. **betokened.** Indicated

WORDS FOR EVERYDAY USE:

pro • sa • ic (prō zā´ik) *adj.*, commonplace, dull

friv • o • lous (friv´ə ləs) *adj.*, not properly serious

might if you so wished <u>attribute</u> it to coincidence."

"Well, don't break into the money before I come back," said Herbert as he rose from the table. "I'm afraid it'll turn you into a mean, <u>avaricious</u> man, and we shall have to disown you."

His mother laughed, and following him to the door, watched him down the road; and returning to the breakfast table, was very happy at the expense of her husband's credulity. All of which did not prevent her from scurrying to the door at the postman's knock, nor prevent her from referring somewhat shortly to retired sergeant-majors of bibulous[8] habits when she found that the post brought a tailor's bill.

"Herbert will have some more of his funny remarks, I expect, when he comes home," she said, as they sat at dinner.

"I dare say," said Mr. White, pouring himself out some beer. "But for all that, the thing moved in my hand; that I'll swear to."

"You thought it did," said the old lady soothingly.

"I say it did," replied the other. "There was no thought about it; I had just—What's the matter?"

His wife made no reply. She was watching the mysterious movements of a man outside, who, peering in an undecided fashion at the house, appeared to be trying to make up his mind to enter. In mental connection with the two hundred pounds, she noticed that the stranger was well dressed, and wore a silk hat of glossy newness. Three times he paused at the gate, and then walked on again. The fourth time he stood with his hands upon it, and then with sudden resolution flung it open and walked up the path. Mrs. White at the same moment placed her hands behind her, and hurriedly unfastening the strings of her apron, put that useful article of apparel beneath the cushion of her chair.

She brought the stranger, who seemed ill at ease, into the room. He gazed at her <u>furtively</u>, and listened in a preoccupied fashion as the old lady apologized for the appearance of the room, and her husband's coat, a garment that he usually reserved for the garden. She then waited, as patiently as her sex would permit, for him to broach his business; but he was at first strangely silent.

"I—was asked to call," he said at last, and stooped and picked a piece of cotton from his trousers. "I come from Maw and Meggins."

The old lady started. "Is anything the matter?" she asked breathlessly. "Has anything happened to Herbert? What is it? What is it?"

Her husband interposed. "There, there, Mother," he said hastily. "Sit down, and don't jump to conclusions. You've not brought bad news, I'm sure, sir;" and he eyed the other wistfully.

"I'm sorry—" began the visitor.

What are the family's feelings about the wish in the morning?

8. **bibulous.** Tending to drink too much

Words for Everyday Use:	at • trib • ute (ə trib´yōōt) *vt.*, think of as resulting from
	av • a • ri • cious (av´ə rish´əs) *adj.*, greedy
	fur • tive • ly (fur´tiv lē) *adv.*, stealthily, not openly

"Is he hurt?" demanded the mother wildly.

The visitor bowed in assent. "Badly hurt," he said quietly, "but he is not in any pain."

"Oh, thank God!" said the old woman, clasping her hands. "Thank God for that! Thank—"

She broke off suddenly as the sinister meaning of the assurance dawned upon her, and she saw the awful confirmation of her fears in the other's <u>averted</u> face. She caught her breath, and turning to her slower-witted husband, laid her trembling old hand upon his. There was a long silence.

"He was caught in the machinery," said the visitor at length in a low voice.

"Caught in the machinery," repeated Mr. White, in a dazed fashion, "yes."

He sat staring blankly out at the window, and taking his wife's hand between his own, pressed it as he had been wont to do in their old courting days nearly forty years before.

"He was the only one left to us," he said, turning gently to the visitor. "It is hard."

The other coughed, and rising, walked slowly to the window. "The firm wished me to convey their sincere sympathy with you in your great loss," he said, without looking round. "I beg that you will understand I am only their servant and merely obeying orders."

There was no reply. The old woman's face was white, her eyes staring, and her breath <u>inaudible</u>. On the husband's face was a look such as his friend the sergeant-major might have carried into his first action.

"I was to say that Maw and Meggins disclaim all responsibility," continued the other. "They admit no <u>liability</u> at all, but in consideration of your son's services, they wish to present you with a certain sum as <u>compensation</u>."

Mr. White dropped his wife's hand, and rising to his feet, gazed with a look of horror at his visitor. His dry lips shaped the words, "How much?"

"Two hundred pounds," was the answer.

Unconscious of his wife's shriek, the old man smiled faintly, put out his hands like a sightless man, and dropped, a senseless heap, to the floor.

In the huge new cemetery, some two miles distant, the old people buried their dead, and came back to a house steeped in shadow and silence. It was all over so quickly that at first they could hardly realize it, and remained in a state of expectation as though of something else to happen—something else that was to lighten this load, too heavy for old hearts to bear.

But the days passed, and expectation gave place to resignation—the hopeless resignation of the old, sometimes miscalled <u>apathy</u>. Sometimes they hardly exchanged a word, for now they had nothing to talk about, and their days were long to weariness.

It was about a week after, that the old man, waking suddenly in the night, stretched out his hand and found him-

How does the first wish come true?

WORDS FOR EVERYDAY USE:

a • vert • ed (ə vʉrt id) *adj.,* turned away
in • au • di • ble (in ôd´ə bəl) *adj.,* that cannot be heard
li • a • bil • i • ty (lī´ə bil´ə tē) *n.,* state of legal obligation
com • pen • sa • tion (käm´ pən sā´shən) *n.,* payment in amends for something
ap • a • thy (ap´ə thē) *n.,* indifference, lack of emotion

self alone. The room was in darkness, and the sound of <u>subdued</u> weeping came from the window. He raised himself in bed and listened.

"Come back," he said tenderly. "You will be cold."

"It is colder for my son," said the old woman, and wept afresh.

The sound of her sobs died away on his ears. The bed was warm, and his eyes heavy with sleep. He dozed fitfully, and then slept, until a sudden wild cry from his wife awoke him with a start.

"*The paw!*" she cried wildly. "The monkey's paw!"

He started up in alarm. "Where? Where is it? What's the matter?"

She came stumbling across the room toward him. "I want it," she said quietly. "You've not destroyed it?"

"It's in the parlor, on the bracket," he replied, marvelling. "Why?"

She cried and laughed together, and bending over, kissed his cheek.

"I only just thought of it," she said hysterically. "Why didn't I think of it before? Why didn't *you* think of it?"

"Think of what?" he questioned.

"The other two wishes," she replied rapidly. "We've only had one."

"Was not that enough?" he demanded fiercely.

"No," she cried triumphantly. "We'll have one more. Go down and get it quickly, and wish our boy alive again."

The man sat up in bed and flung the bedclothes from his quaking limbs. "Good God, you are mad!" he cried, aghast.

Why does Mrs. White want the monkey's paw?

What fear does Mr. White have?

"Get it," she panted. "Get it quickly, and wish—Oh, my boy, my boy!"

Her husband struck a match and lit the candle. "Get back to bed," he said unsteadily. "You don't know what you are saying."

"We had the first wish granted," said the old woman feverishly. "Why not the second?"

"A coincidence," stammered the old man.

"Go and get it and wish," cried his wife, quivering with excitement.

The old man turned and regarded her, and his voice shook. "He has been dead ten days, and besides he—I would not tell you else, but—I could only recognize him by his clothing. If he was too terrible for you to see then, how now?"

"Bring him back," cried the old woman, and dragged him toward the door. "Do you think I fear the child I have nursed?"

He went down in the darkness, and felt his way to the parlor, and then to the mantelpiece. The talisman was in its place, and a horrible fear that the unspoken wish might bring his mutilated son before him ere he could escape from the room seized upon him, and he caught his breath as he found that he had lost the direction of the door. His brow cold with sweat, he felt his way round the table, and groped along the wall until he found himself in the small passage with the unwholesome thing in his hand.

Even his wife's face seemed changed as he entered the room. It was white

WORDS FOR EVERYDAY USE: **sub • dued** (səb do͞od´) *part.,* diminished, lessened in intensity

and expectant, and to his fears, seemed to have an unnatural look upon it. He was afraid of her.

"*Wish!*" she cried, in a strong voice.

"It is foolish and wicked," he faltered.

"*Wish!*" repeated his wife.

He raised his hand. "I wish my son alive again."

The talisman fell to the floor, and he regarded it fearfully. Then he sank trembling into a chair as the old woman, with burning eyes, walked to the window and raised the blind.

He sat until he was chilled with the cold, glancing occasionally at the figure of the old woman peering through the window. The candle-end, which had burned below the rim of the china candlestick, was throwing pulsating shadows on the ceiling and walls, until, with a flicker larger than the rest, it expired. The old man, with an unspeakable sense of relief at the failure of the talisman, crept back to his bed, and a minute or two afterward the old woman came silently and apathetically beside him.

Neither spoke, but lay silently listening to the ticking of the clock. A stair creaked, and a squeaky mouse scurried noisily through the wall. The darkness was <u>oppressive</u>, and after lying for some time screwing up his courage, he took the box of matches, and striking one, went downstairs for a candle.

At the foot of the stairs the match went out, and he paused to strike another; and at the same moment a knock, so quiet and stealthy as to be scarcely audible, sounded on the front door.

The matches fell from his hand and spilled in the passage. He stood motionless, his breath suspended until the knock was repeated. Then he turned and fled swiftly back to his room, and closed the door behind him. A third knock sounded through the house.

"*What's that?*" cried the old woman, starting up.

"A rat," said the old man in shaking tones—"a rat. It passed me on the stairs."

His wife sat up in bed listening. A loud knock resounded through the house.

"It's Herbert!" she screamed. "It's Herbert!"

She ran to the door, but her husband was before her, and catching her by the arm, held her tightly.

"What are you going to do?" he whispered hoarsely.

"It's my boy; it's Herbert!" she cried, struggling mechanically. "I forgot it was two miles away. What are you holding me for? Let go. I must open the door."

"For God's sake, don't let it in," cried the old man, trembling.

"You're afraid of your own son," she cried, struggling. "Let me go. I'm coming, Herbert; I'm coming."

There was another knock, and another. The old woman, with a sudden wrench, broke free and ran from the room. Her husband followed to

Why does the man hesitate before making the wish?

Why is the man afraid?

What was the man's third wish?

the landing, and called after her appealingly as she hurried downstairs. He heard the chain rattle back and the bottom bolt drawn slowly and stiffly from the socket. Then the old woman's voice, strained and panting.

"The bolt," she cried loudly. "Come down. I can't reach it."

But her husband was on his hands and knees, groping wildly on the floor in search of the paw. If he could only find it before the thing outside got in. A perfect fusillade[9] of knocks <u>reverberated</u> through the house, and he heard the scraping of a chair as his wife put it down in the passage against the door. He heard the creaking of the bolt as it came slowly back, and at the same moment he found the monkey's paw, and frantically breathed his third and last wish.

The knocking ceased suddenly, although the echoes of it were still in the house. He heard the chair drawn back, and the door opened. A cold wind rushed up the staircase, and a long, loud wail of disappointment and misery from his wife gave him courage to run down to her side, and then to the gate beyond. The street lamp flickering opposite shone on a quiet and deserted road. ■

---

9. **fusillade.** Simultaneous discharge of many firearms

WORDS FOR EVERYDAY USE: re • ver • ber • ate (ri vʉrˊbə rātˊ) *vi.*, resound, echo

Responding to the Selection

Imagine that you are the father in this selection. Reflect on the night of Sergeant-Major Morris's visit, when he brought the monkey's paw to your home. In your journal, express how your feelings about the monkey's paw changed during that night and on the following day.

Reviewing the Selection

RECALLING

1. What does the sergeant-major pull from his pocket?

2. What spell was put on the paw by a fakir?

3. What is Mr. White's first wish?

4. What is Mr. White's second wish?

INTERPRETING

5. What immediate responses do the members of the White family have to the monkey's paw?

6. What is probably troubling the sergeant-major about the White family's lightheartedness toward the paw?

7. What event reveals the power of the monkey's paw?

8. What is probably Mr. White's third wish?

SYNTHESIZING

9. What human weaknesses are revealed by members of the White family in this story?

10. What relationship between human life and fate is described in this story? How are the fakir's ideas about fate proved true?

Understanding Literature (Questions for Discussion)

1. **Foreshadowing. Foreshadowing** is the act of presenting materials that hint at events to occur later in a story. In the selection, when Sergeant-Major Morris talks about the first man who made three wishes, he says, "I don't know what the first two were, but the third was for death." What later event in the story does this statement foreshadow? Find another example of foreshadowing in the selection.

2. **Description and Effect.** A **description**, one of the modes of writing, portrays a character, an object, or a scene. Descriptions make use of sensory details—words and phrases that describe how things look, sound, feel, taste, and smell. The **effect** of a literary work is the general impression or emotional impact that it achieves. What overall effect is created by the descriptions in this story? What specific descriptions contribute to that effect?

3. **Irony. Irony** is a difference between appearance and reality. In one type of irony, **irony of situation**, an event occurs that violates the expectations of the characters, the reader, or the audience. In the selection, Herbert rather lightheartedly expects the monkey's paw to bring his family wealth, fame, and happiness. How are Herbert's expectations violated?

Responding in Writing

Descriptive Paragraph. Write a descriptive paragraph about an object that creates in the reader an effect of suspense, dread, or horror. Try to use as many sensory details as possible when describing the object.

> **Prewriting Suggestion:** To get started, write the name of the object at the top of a piece of paper. Then write the words *sight, sound, touch, smell,* and *taste* down the left-hand side of the paper. Close your eyes and visualize the object in your mind. Then open your eyes. On your paper, list as many details as you can about the object in each of the sensory detail categories. For more information on using a sensory detail chart, see the Language Arts Survey, 1.18, "Sensory Detail Charts."

PROJECT

Dramatic Skit. Collaborate with two or three other students to write a dramatization of one of the scenes in the selection. Choose a scene that you feel is particularly effective in creating suspense. Write parts for each student in your group. You may want to use music to add to the suspenseful effect of your scene. Rehearse your skit and present it to the class.

"The Most Dangerous Game"
by Richard Connell

ABOUT THE AUTHOR

Richard Connell (1893–1949) was born in Poughkeepsie, New York. At the age of ten, he took on his first writing assignment, covering baseball games for the local newspaper. He attended Georgetown University for one year, then entered and graduated from Harvard University. During World War I, Connell served with the American Expeditionary Force. After the war, he moved to New York City and became a freelance writer. The author of screenplays and hundreds of short stories, Connell also wrote numerous novels, including *Apes and Angels* and *The Mad Lover.* "The Most Dangerous Game" was published in 1924.

ABOUT THE SELECTION

Background: Theme. The **theme** of conflict between opposing forces is an age-old element of fiction. The conflict in this story is an example of person-versus-person conflict. The two opposing forces are Rainsford and General Zaroff. To survive his conflict with Zaroff, Rainsford must escape Zaroff's hunt for three days. Other kinds of conflicts in fiction are person versus nature, person versus society, person versus self, person versus machine, and person versus the supernatural.

Background: Technique. Techniques of **characterization** are used in **"The Most Dangerous Game"** to create the characters of Rainsford and Zaroff. Highly skilled and experienced hunters, the famous Rainsford and cultured Zaroff share an enthusiasm for the sport of big game hunting. Through various techniques of characterization, such as direct description, the different physical traits, actions, and beliefs of each character are created.

READER'S JOURNAL

How would it feel to be trapped on a mysterious island? How would you solve the problems essential to your survival—food, shelter, and warmth? Think about these questions. Then write in your journal about dangers you might face on the island.

"The Most Dangerous Game"

RICHARD CONNELL

What is ominous about the name of the island?

"Off there to the right—somewhere—is a large island," said Whitney. "It's rather a mystery—"

"What island is it?" Rainsford asked.

"The old charts call it 'Ship-Trap Island,' " Whitney replied. "A suggestive name, isn't it? Sailors have a curious dread of the place. I don't know why. Some superstition—"

"Can't see it," remarked Rainsford, trying to peer through the <u>dank</u> tropical night that was <u>palpable</u> as it pressed its thick warm blackness in upon the yacht.

"You've good eyes," said Whitney, with a laugh, "and I've seen you pick off a moose moving in the brown fall bush at four hundred yards, but even you can't see four miles or so through a moonless Caribbean night."

"Nor four yards," admitted Rainsford. "Ugh! It's like moist black velvet."

"It will be light enough in Rio,"[1] promised Whitney. "We should make it in a few days. I hope the jaguar guns have come from Purdey's. We should have some good hunting up the Amazon. Great sport, hunting."

"The best sport in the world," agreed Rainsford.

"For the hunter," amended Whitney. "Not for the jaguar."

"Don't talk rot, Whitney," said Rainsford. "You're a big-game hunter, not a philosopher. Who cares how a jaguar feels?"

"Perhaps the jaguar does," observed Whitney.

"Bah! They've no understanding."

What doesn't Rainsford understand?

"Even so, I rather think they understand one thing—fear. The fear of pain and the fear of death."

"Nonsense," laughed Rainsford. "This hot weather is making you soft, Whitney. Be a <u>realist</u>. The world is

---

1. **Rio.** Rio de Janeiro, the capital of Brazil

WORDS FOR EVERYDAY USE:

dank (daŋk) *adj.,* disagreeably damp

pal • pa • ble (pal´pə bəl) *adj.,* perceptible; noticeable

re • al • ist (rē´ə list) *n.,* person concerned with real things

made up of two classes—the hunters and the huntees. Luckily, you and I are the hunters. Do you think we've passed that island yet?"

"I can't tell in the dark. I hope so."

"Why?" asked Rainsford.

"The place has a reputation—a bad one."

"Cannibals?" suggested Rainsford.

"Hardly. Even cannibals wouldn't live in such a God-forsaken place. But it's gotten into sailor lore, somehow. Didn't you notice that the crew's nerves seemed a bit jumpy today?"

"They were a bit strange, now you mention it. Even Captain Nielsen—"

"Yes, even that tough-minded old Swede, who'd go up to the devil himself and ask him for a light. Those fishy blue eyes held a look I never saw there before. All I could get out of him was: 'This place has an evil name among sea-faring men, sir.' Then he said to me, very gravely: 'Don't you feel anything?'—as if the air about us was actually poisonous. Now, you mustn't laugh when I tell you this—I did feel something like a sudden chill.

"There was no breeze. The sea was as flat as a plate-glass window. We were drawing near the island then. What I felt was a—a mental chill; a sort of sudden dread."

"Pure imagination," said Rainsford. "One superstitious sailor can <u>taint</u> the whole ship's company with his fear."

"Maybe. But sometimes I think sailors have an extra sense that tells them when they are in danger. Sometimes I think evil is a <u>tangible</u> thing—with wave lengths, just as sound and light have. An evil place can, so to speak, broadcast vibrations of evil. Anyhow, I'm glad we're getting out of this zone. Well, I think I'll turn in now, Rainsford."

"I'm not sleepy," said Rainsford. "I'm going to smoke another pipe on the afterdeck."[2]

"Good night, then, Rainsford. See you at breakfast."

"Right. Good night, Whitney."

There was no sound in the night as Rainsford sat there, but the muffled throb of the engine that drove the yacht swiftly through the darkness, and the swish and ripple of the wash of the propeller.

Rainsford, reclining in a steamer chair, <u>indolently</u> puffed on his favorite brier. The sensuous drowsiness of the night was on him. "It's so dark," he thought, "that I could sleep without closing my eyes; the night would be my eyelids—"

An abrupt sound startled him. Off to the right he heard it, and his ears, expert in such matters, could not be mistaken. Again he heard the sound, and again. Somewhere, off in the blackness, someone had fired a gun three times.

Rainsford sprang up and moved quickly to the rail, mystified. He strained his eyes in the direction from which the reports had come, but it was like trying to see through a blanket.

---

2. **afterdeck.** Part of a ship's deck between the middle and the rear

WORDS FOR EVERYDAY USE:	**taint** (tānt) *vt.*, infect
	tan • gi • ble (tan´jə bəl) *adj.*, having actual form
	in • do • lent • ly (in´də lənt lē) *adv.*, idly, lazily

He leaped upon the rail and balanced himself there, to get greater elevation; his pipe, striking a rope, was knocked from his mouth. He lunged for it; a short, hoarse cry came from his lips as he realized he had reached too far and had lost his balance. The cry was pinched off short as the blood-warm waters of the Caribbean Sea[3] closed over his head.

He struggled up to the surface and tried to cry out, but the wash from the speeding yacht slapped him in the face and the salt water in his open mouth made him gag and strangle. Desperately he struck out with strong strokes after the <u>receding</u> lights of the yacht, but he stopped before he had swum fifty feet. A certain cool-headedness had come to him; it was not the first time he had been in a tight place. There was a chance that his cries could be heard by some one aboard the yacht, but that chance was slender, and grew more slender as the yacht raced on. He wrestled himself out of his clothes, and shouted with all his power. The lights of the yacht became faint and ever-vanishing fireflies; then they were blotted out entirely by the night.

Rainsford remembered the shots. They had come from the right, and doggedly he swam in that direction, swimming with slow, deliberate strokes, conserving his strength. For a seemingly endless time he fought the sea. He began to count his strokes; he could do possibly a hundred more and then—

What is unusual about the sound that Rainsford hears?

Why does Rainsford swim in the direction of the shots?

Rainsford heard a sound. It came out of the darkness, a high screaming sound, the sound of an animal in an <u>extremity</u> of anguish and terror.

He did not recognize the animal that made the sound; he did not try to; with fresh vitality he swam toward the sound. He heard it again; then it was cut short by another noise, crisp, staccato.

"Pistol shot," muttered Rainsford, swimming on.

Ten minutes of determined effort brought another sound to his ears— the most welcome he had ever heard— the muttering and growling of the sea breaking on a rocky shore. He was almost on the rocks before he saw them; on a night less calm he would have been shattered against them. With his remaining strength he dragged himself from the swirling waters. Jagged crags appeared to jut into the opaqueness, he forced himself upward, hand over hand. Gasping, his hands raw, he reached a flat place at the top. Dense jungle came down to the very edge of the cliffs. What perils that tangle of trees and underbrush might hold for him did not concern Rainsford just then. All he knew was that he was safe from his enemy, the sea, and that utter weariness was on him. He flung himself down at the jungle edge and tumbled headlong into the deepest sleep of his life.

---

3. **Caribbean Sea.** Tropical and subtropical body of water near the eastern coast of the Americas in the western Atlantic

Words for
Everyday Use:

re • ced • ing (ri sēd´iŋ) *part.*, moving away from, becoming more distant

ex • trem • i • ty (ek strem´ə tē) *n.*, greatest degree

When he opened his eyes he knew from the position of the sun that it was late in the afternoon. Sleep had given him new vigor; a sharp hunger was picking at him. He looked about him, almost cheerfully.

"Where there are pistol shots, there are men. Where there are men, there is food," he thought. But what kind of men, he wondered, in so forbidding a place? An unbroken front of snarled and jagged jungle fringed the shore.

He saw no sign of a trail through the closely knit web of weeds and trees; it was easier to go along the shore, and Rainsford floundered along by the water. Not far from where he had landed, he stopped.

Some wounded thing, by the evidence a large animal, had thrashed about in the underbrush; the jungle weeds were crushed down and the moss was <u>lacerated</u>; one patch of weeds was stained crimson. A small, glittering object not far away caught Rainsford's eye and he picked it up. It was an empty cartridge.

"A twenty-two," he remarked. "That's odd. It must have been a fairly large animal too. The hunter had his nerve with him to tackle it with a light gun. It's clear that the brute put up a fight. I suppose the first three shots I heard was when the hunter flushed his quarry[4] and wounded it. The last shot was when he trailed it here and finished it."

He examined the ground closely and found what he had hoped to find—the print of hunting boots. They pointed along the cliff in the direction he had been going. Eagerly he hurried along, now slipping on a rotten log or a loose stone, but making headway; night was beginning to settle down on the island.

Bleak darkness was blacking out the sea and jungle when Rainsford sighted the lights. He came upon them as he turned a crook in the coast line and his first thought was that he had come upon a village, for there were many lights. But as he <u>forged</u> along he saw to his great astonishment that all the lights were in one enormous building—a lofty structure with pointed towers plunging upward into the gloom. His eyes made out the shadowy outlines of a palatial château; it was set on a high bluff, and on three sides of it cliffs dived down to where the sea licked greedy lips in the shadows.

"Mirage," thought Rainsford. But it was no mirage, he found, when he opened the tall spiked iron gate. The stone steps were real enough; the massive door with a leering gargoyle for a knocker was real enough; yet about it all hung an air of unreality.

He lifted the knocker, and it creaked up stiffly, as if it had never before been used. He let it fall, and it startled him with its booming loudness. He thought he heard steps within; the door remained closed. Again Rainsford lifted the heavy knocker, and let it fall. The door opened then, opened as suddenly as if it were on a spring, and Rainsford stood blinking in the river of <u>glaring</u> gold light that poured out. The first thing Rainsford's eyes discerned was the largest man Rainsford had ever seen—a gigantic creature, solidly made and black-bearded to the waist. In his hand the man held a long-barreled revolver, and he was pointing it straight at Rainsford's heart.

Out of the snarl of beard two small eyes regarded Rainsford.

"Don't be alarmed," said Rainsford, with a smile which he hoped was <u>disarming</u>. "I'm no robber. I fell off a yacht. My name is Sanger Rainsford of New York City."

The menacing look in the eyes did not change. The revolver pointed as rigidly as if the giant were a statue. He gave no sign that he understood Rainsford's words, or that he had even heard them. He was dressed in uniform, a black uniform trimmed with gray astrakhan.[5]

"I'm Sanger Rainsford of New York," Rainsford began again. "I fell off a yacht. I am hungry."

The man's only answer was to raise with his thumb the hammer of his

---

4. **flushed his quarry.** Forced the animal out of its hiding place
5. **astrakhan.** Fur made from the pelt of young lambs

What sign does Rainsford find? Why is he glad to see this sign?

Words for Everyday Use:	forge (fôrg) *vi.*, move forward
	glar • ing (glerˊiŋ) *adj.*, shining too brightly
	dis • arm • ing (dis ärmˊiŋ) *adj.*, removing fear or hostility

revolver. Then Rainsford saw the man's free hand go to his forehead in a military salute, and he saw him click his heels together and stand at attention. Another man was coming down the broad marble steps, an erect, slender man in evening clothes. He advanced to Rainsford and held out his hand.

In a cultivated voice marked by a slight accent that gave it added precision and deliberateness, he said: "It is a very great pleasure and honor to welcome Mr. Sanger Rainsford, the celebrated hunter, to my home."

Automatically Rainsford shook the man's hand.

"I've read your book about hunting snow leopards in Tibet, you see," explained the man. "I am General Zaroff."

Rainsford's first impression was that the man was singularly handsome; his second was that there was an original, almost bizarre quality about the general's face. He was a tall man past middle age, for his hair was a vivid white; but his thick eyebrows and pointed military mustache were as black as the night from which Rainsford had come. His eyes, too, were black and very bright. He had high cheek bones, a sharp-cut nose, a spare, dark face, the face of a man used to giving orders, the face of an aristocrat. Turning to the giant in uniform, the general made a sign. The giant put away his pistol, saluted, withdrew.

"Ivan is an incredibly strong fellow," remarked the general, "but he has the misfortune to be deaf and dumb. A simple fellow, but I'm afraid, like all his race, a bit of a savage."

"Is he Russian?"

"He is a Cossack,"[6] said the general, and his smile showed red lips and pointed teeth. "So am I."

"Come," he said, "we shouldn't be chatting here. We can talk later. Now you want clothes, food, rest. You shall have them. This is a most restful spot."

Ivan had reappeared, and the general spoke to him with lips that moved but gave forth no sound.

"Follow Ivan, if you please, Mr. Rainsford," said the general. "I was about to have my dinner when you came. I'll wait for you. You'll find that my clothes will fit you, I think."

It was to a huge, beam-ceilinged bedroom with a canopied bed big enough for six men that Rainsford followed the silent giant. Ivan laid out an evening suit, and Rainsford, as he put it on, noticed that it came from a London tailor who ordinarily cut and sewed for none below the rank of duke.

The dining room to which Ivan <u>conducted</u> him was in many ways remarkable. There was a <u>medieval</u> magnificence about it; it suggested a baronial hall of feudal times[7] with its oaken panels, its high ceiling, its vast refectory table where twoscore men could sit down to eat. About the hall

For what is Rainsford known?

---

6. **Cossack.** Member of a group of people from southern Russia known for horsemanship and fighting ability

7. **baronial hall of feudal times.** Dining room in mansion during the Middle Ages

---

WORDS FOR EVERYDAY USE:

con • duct (kən dukt´) vt., lead

me • di • e • val (mə dē´vəl) adj., suggestive of the Middle Ages

were the mounted heads of many animals—lions, tigers, elephants, moose, bears; larger or more perfect specimens Rainsford had never seen. At the great table the general was sitting, alone.

"You'll have a cocktail, Mr. Rainsford," he suggested. The cocktail was surpassingly good; and, Rainsford noted, the table appointments were of the finest—the linen, the crystal, the silver, the china.

They were eating *borscht*,[8] the rich, red soup with whipped cream so dear to Russian palates. Half apologetically General Zaroff said: "We do our best to preserve the <u>amenities</u> of civilization here. Please forgive any lapses. We are well off the beaten track, you know. Do you think the champagne has suffered from its long ocean trip?"

"Not in the least," declared Rainsford. He was finding the general a most thoughtful and affable host, a true cosmopolite. But there was one small trait of the general's that made Rainsford uncomfortable. Whenever he looked up from his plate he found the general studying him, <u>appraising</u> him narrowly.

"Perhaps," said General Zaroff, "you were surprised that I recognized your name. You see, I read all books on hunting published in English, French, and Russian. I have but one passion in my life, Mr. Rainsford, and it is the hunt."

"You have some wonderful heads here," said Rainsford as he ate a particularly well cooked filet mignon.

"That Cape buffalo is the largest I ever saw."

"Oh, that fellow. Yes, he was a monster."

"Did he charge you?"

"Hurled me against a tree," said the general. "Fractured my skull. But I got the brute."

"I've always thought," said Rainsford, "that the Cape buffalo is the most dangerous of all big game."

For a moment the general did not reply; he was smiling his curious red-lipped smile. Then he said slowly: "No. You are wrong, sir. The Cape buffalo is not the most dangerous big game." He sipped his wine. "Here in my <u>preserve</u> on this island," he said in the same slow tone, "I hunt more dangerous game."

Rainsford expressed his surprise. "Is there big game on this island?"

The general nodded. "The biggest."

"Really?"

"Oh, it isn't here naturally, of course. I have to stock the island."

"What have you imported, General?" Rainsford asked. "Tigers?"

The general smiled. "No," he said. "Hunting tigers ceased to interest me some years ago. I exhausted their possibilities, you see. No thrill left in tigers, no real danger. I live for danger, Mr. Rainsford."

The general took from his pocket a gold cigarette case and offered his guest a long black cigarette with a silver tip; it was perfumed and gave off a smell like incense.

---

8. **borscht.** Soup made of beets

What about General Zaroff makes Rainsford uncomfortable?

WORDS FOR EVERYDAY USE:	a • men • i • ty (ə men´ə tē) n., desirable feature
	ap • praise (ə prāz´) vt., judge the worth of
	pre • serve (prē zʉrv´) n., place maintained for regulated hunting

"We will have some capital hunting, you and I," said the general. "I shall be most glad to have your society."

"But what game—" began Rainsford.

"I'll tell you," said the general. "You will be amused, I know. I think I may say, in all modesty, that I have done a rare thing. I have invented a new sensation. May I pour you another glass of port, Mr. Rainsford?"

"Thank you, General."

The general filled both glasses and said: "God makes some men poets. Some He makes kings, some beggars. Me He made a hunter. My hand was made for the trigger, my father said. He was a very rich man with a quarter of a million acres in the Crimea,[9] and he was an ardent sportsman. When I was only five years old he gave me a little gun, specially made in Moscow for me, to shoot sparrows with. When I shot some of his prize turkeys with it, he did not punish me; he complimented me on my marksmanship. I killed my first bear in the Caucasus when I was ten. My whole life has been one prolonged hunt. I went into the army—it was expected of noblemen's sons—and for a time commanded a division of Cossack cavalry, but my real interest was always the hunt. I have hunted every kind of game in every land. It would be impossible for me to tell you how many animals I have killed."

The general puffed at his cigarette.

"After the debacle in Russia[10] I left the country, for it was imprudent for an officer of the Czar to stay there.

Many noble Russians lost everything. I, luckily, had invested heavily in American securities, so I shall never have to open a tea room in Monte Carlo or drive a taxi in Paris. Naturally, I continued to hunt—grizzlies in your Rockies, crocodiles in the Ganges,[11] rhinoceroses in East Africa. It was in Africa that the Cape buffalo hit me and laid me up for six months. As soon as I recovered I started for the Amazon to hunt jaguars, for I had heard they were unusually <u>cunning</u>. They weren't." The Cossack sighed. "They were no match at all for a hunter with his wits about him and a high-powered rifle. I was bitterly disappointed. I was lying in my tent with a splitting headache one night when a terrible thought pushed its way into my mind. Hunting was beginning to bore me! And hunting, remember, had been my life. I have heard that in America business men often go to pieces when they give up the business that has been their life."

"Yes, that's so," said Rainsford.

The general smiled. "I had no wish to go to pieces," he said. "I must do something. Now, mine is an <u>analytical</u> mind, Mr. Rainsford. Doubtless that is why I enjoy the problems of the chase."

"No doubt, General Zaroff."

---

9. **Crimea.** Peninsula on the Black Sea in southwestern Russia
10. **debacle in Russia.** Russian Revolution of 1917 during which the czar was overthrown and wealthy landowners lost their property
11. **Ganges.** River in India, viewed by the Hindus as sacred

---

WORDS FOR EVERYDAY USE:

cun • ning (kun´iŋ) *adj.*, crafty, skillful

an • a • lyt • ic •al (an´ə lit´i kəl) *adj.*, skilled in breaking a whole into its parts and examining relationships

"So," continued the general, "I asked myself why the hunt no longer fascinated me. You are much younger than I am, Mr. Rainsford, and have not hunted as much, but you perhaps can guess the answer."

"What was it?"

"Simply this: hunting had ceased to be what you call 'a sporting proposition.' It had become too easy. I always got my quarry. Always. There is no greater bore than perfection."

The general lit a fresh cigarette.

"No animal had a chance with me any more. That is no boast; it is a mathematical certainty. The animal had nothing but his legs and his instinct. Instinct is no match for reason. When I thought of this it was a tragic moment for me, I can tell you."

Rainsford leaned across the table, absorbed in what his host was saying.

"It came to me as an inspiration what I must do," the general went on.

"And that was?"

The general smiled the quiet smile of one who has faced an obstacle and surmounted it with success. "I had to invent a new animal to hunt," he said.

"A new animal? You're joking."

"Not at all," said the general. "I never joke about hunting. I needed a new animal. I found one. So I bought this island, built this house, and here I do my hunting. The island is perfect for my purposes—there are jungles with a maze of trails in them, hills, swamps—"

"But the animal, General Zaroff?"

"Oh," said the general, "it supplies me with the most exciting hunting in the world. No other hunting compares with it for an instant. Every day I hunt, and I never grow bored now, for I have a quarry with which I can match my wits."

Rainsford's bewilderment showed in his face.

"I wanted the ideal animal to hunt," explained the general. "So I said: 'What are the attributes of an ideal quarry?' And the answer was, of course: 'It must have courage, cunning, and, above all, it must be able to reason.' "

"But no animal can reason," objected Rainsford.

"My dear fellow," said the general, "there is one that can."

"But you can't mean—" gasped Rainsford.

"And why not?"

"I can't believe you are serious, General Zaroff. This is a <u>grisly</u> joke."

"Why should I not be serious? I am speaking of hunting."

"Hunting? General Zaroff, what you speak of is murder."

The general laughed with entire good nature. He regarded Rainsford quizzically. "I refuse to believe that so modern and civilized a young man as you seem to be harbors romantic ideas about the value of human life. Surely your experiences in the war—"

"Did not make me <u>condone</u> cold-blooded murder," finished Rainsford stiffly.

Laughter shook the general. "How extraordinarily droll you are!" he said.

Words for Everyday Use:

gris • ly (griz´lē) *adj.,* terrifying, horrifying

con • done (kən dōn´) *vt.,* forgive or overlook an offense

"One does not expect nowadays to find a young man of the educated class, even in America, with such a naive, and, if I may say so, mid-Victorian point of view.[12] It's like finding a snuff-box in a limousine. Ah, well, doubtless you had Puritan ancestors. So many Americans appear to have had. I'll wager you'll forget your notions when you go hunting with me. You've a genuine new thrill in store for you, Mr. Rainsford."

"Thank you, I'm a hunter, not a murderer."

"Dear me," said the general, quite unruffled, "again that unpleasant word. But I think I can show you that your <u>scruples</u> are quite ill founded."

"Yes?"

"Life is for the strong, to be lived by the strong, and, if need be, taken by the strong. The weak of the world were put here to give the strong pleasure. I am strong. Why should I not use my gift? If I wish to hunt, why should I not? I hunt the scum of the earth—a thoroughbred horse or hound is worth more than a score of them."

"But they are men," said Rainsford hotly.

"Precisely," said the general. "That is why I use them. It gives me pleasure. They can reason, after a fashion. So they are dangerous."

"But where do you get them?"

The general's left eyelid fluttered down in a wink. "This island is called Ship-Trap," he answered. "Sometimes an angry god of the high seas sends them to me. Sometimes, when Provi-dence is not so kind, I help Providence a bit. Come to the window with me."

Rainsford went to the window and looked out toward the sea.

"Watch! Out there!" exclaimed the general, pointing into the night. Rainsford's eyes saw only blackness, and then, as the general pressed a button, far out to sea Rainsford saw the flash of lights.

The general chuckled. "They indicate a channel," he said, "where there's none; giant rocks with razor edges crouch like a sea monster with wide-open jaws. They can crush a ship as easily as I crush this nut." He dropped a walnut on the hardwood floor and brought his heel grinding down on it. "Oh, yes," he said casually, as if in answer to a question, "I have electricity. We try to be civilized here."

"Civilized? And you shoot down men?"

A trace of anger was in the general's black eyes; but it was there for but a second, and he said, in his most pleasant manner: "Dear me, what a righteous young man you are! I assure you I do not do the thing you suggest. That would be <u>barbarous</u>. I treat these visitors with every consideration. They get plenty of good food and exercise. They get into splendid physical condition. You shall see for yourself tomorrow."

"What do you mean?"

"We'll visit my training school," smiled the general. "It's in the cellar. I

What indication does General Zaroff give of his civilization?

What justification does General Zaroff give for his hobby?

12. **mid-Victorian point of view.** During the reign of Queen Victoria, in the late nineteenth century, the English had a very strict code of moral behavior.

WORDS FOR EVERYDAY USE:

scru • ple (skrōō´pəl) *n.*, qualm; uneasiness about something one thinks is wrong

bar • ba • rous (bär´bə rəs) *adj.*, cruel, brutal, uncultured

have about a dozen pupils down there now. They're from the Spanish bark San Lucar that had the bad luck to go on the rocks out there. A very inferior lot, I regret to say. Poor specimens and more accustomed to the deck than to the jungle."

He raised his hand, and Ivan, who served as waiter, brought thick Turkish coffee. Rainsford, with an effort, held his tongue in check.

"It's a game, you see," pursued the general blandly. "I suggest to one of them that we go hunting. I give him a supply of food and an excellent hunting knife. I give him three hours' start. I am to follow, armed only with a pistol of the smallest caliber and range. If my quarry eludes me for three whole days, he wins the game. If I find him" —the general smiled—"he loses."

"Suppose he refuses to be hunted?"

"Oh," said the general, "I give him his option, of course. He need not play the game if he doesn't wish to. If he does not wish to hunt, I turn him over to Ivan. Ivan once had the honor of serving as official knouter to the Great White Czar,[13] and he has his own ideas of sport. Invariably, Mr. Rainsford, invariably they choose the hunt."

"And if they win?"

The smile on the general's face widened. "To date I have not lost," he said.

Then he added, hastily: "I don't wish you to think me a braggart, Mr. Rainsford. Many of them afford only the most elementary sort of problem. Occasionally I strike a tartar.[14] One almost did win. I eventually had to use the dogs."

"The dogs?"

"This way, please. I'll show you."

The general steered Rainsford to a window. The lights from the windows sent a flickering illumination that made grotesque patterns on the courtyard below, and Rainsford could see moving about there a dozen or so huge black shapes; as they turned toward him, their eyes glittered greenly.

"A rather good lot, I think," observed the general. "They are let out at seven every night. If anyone should try to get into my house—or out of it—something extremely regrettable would occur to him." He hummed a snatch of song from the Folies Bergére.

"And now," said the general, "I want to show you my new collection of heads. Will you come with me to the library?"

"I hope," said Rainsford, "that you will excuse me tonight, General Zaroff. I'm really not feeling at all well."

"Ah, indeed?" the general inquired solicitously. "Well, I suppose that's only natural, after your long swim. You need a good, restful night's sleep. Tomorrow you'll feel like a new man, I'll wager. Then we'll hunt, eh? I've one rather promising prospect—"

Rainsford was hurrying from the room.

What is the real reason why Rainsford feels ill?

---

13. **Ivan . . . Czar.** During the reign of Alexander III (1881–1894) of Russia, Ivan was the official flogger, who whipped prisoners severely.
14. **strike a tartar.** Meet one who is difficult to control

WORDS FOR EVERYDAY USE: **pros • pect** (prä´spekt´) *n.,* likely candidate

"Sorry you can't go with me tonight," called the general. "I expect rather fair sport—a big, strong sailor. He looks resourceful—Well, good night, Mr. Rainsford; I hope you have a good night's rest."

The bed was good and the pajamas of the softest silk, and he was tired in every fiber of his being, but nevertheless Rainsford could not quiet his brain with the opiate of sleep. He lay, eyes wide open. Once he thought he heard stealthy steps in the corridor outside his room. He sought to throw open the door; it would not open. He went to the window and looked out. His room was high up in one of the towers. The lights of the château were out now, and it was dark and silent; but there was a fragment of sallow moon, and by its <u>wan</u> light he could see, dimly, the courtyard; there, weaving in and out in the pattern of shadow, were black, noiseless forms; the hounds heard him at the window and looked up, expectantly, with their green eyes. Rainsford went back to the bed and lay down. By many methods he tried to put himself to sleep. He had achieved a doze when, just as morning began to come, he heard, far off in the jungle, the faint report of a pistol.

General Zaroff did not appear until luncheon. He was dressed faultlessly in the tweeds of a country squire. He was <u>solicitous</u> about the state of Rainsford's health.

"As for me," sighed the general, "I do not feel so well. I am worried, Mr. Rainsford. Last night I detected traces of my old complaint."

To Rainsford's questioning glance the general said: "Ennui. Boredom."

Then, taking a second helping of crêpes suzette,[15] the general explained: "The hunting was not good last night. The fellow lost his head. He made a straight trail that offered no problems at all. That's the trouble with these sailors. They have dull brains to begin with, and they do not know how to get about in the woods. They do excessively stupid and obvious things. It's becoming most annoying. Will you have another glass of Chablis, Mr. Rainsford?"

"General," said Rainsford firmly, "I wish to leave this island at once."

The general raised his thickets of eyebrows; he seemed hurt. "But, my dear fellow," the general protested, "you've only just come. You've had no hunting—"

"I wish to go today," said Rainsford. He saw the dead black eyes of the general on him, studying him. General Zaroff's face suddenly brightened.

He filled Rainsford's glass with venerable Chablis from a dusty bottle.

"Tonight," said the general, "we will hunt—you and I."

Rainsford shook his head. "No, General," he said, "I will not hunt."

The general shrugged his shoulders and delicately ate a hothouse grape. "As you wish, my friend," he said.

Why can't Rainsford sleep?

---

15. **crêpes suzette.** Thin pancakes eaten as a dessert

WORDS FOR EVERYDAY USE:

wan (wän) *adj.,* pale, faint

so • lic • i • tous (sə lis ´ə təs) *adj.,* showing concern

Whom does Zaroff propose to hunt?

"The choice rests entirely with you. But may I not venture to suggest that you will find my idea of sport more diverting than Ivan's?"

He nodded toward the corner to where the giant stood, scowling, his thick arms crossed on his huge chest.

"You don't mean—" cried Rainsford.

"My dear fellow," said the general, "have I not told you I always mean what I say about hunting? This is really an inspiration. I drink to a foe worthy of me at last."

The general raised his glass, but Rainsford sat staring at him.

"You'll find this game worth playing," the general said enthusiastically. "Your brain against mine. Your woodcraft against mine. Your strength and stamina against mine. Outdoor chess! And the stake is not without value, eh?"

"And if I should win—" began Rainsford huskily.

"I'll cheerfully acknowledge myself defeated if I do not find you by midnight of the third day," said General Zaroff. "My sloop will place you on the mainland near a town."

The general read what Rainsford was thinking.

"Oh, you can trust me," said the Cossack. "I will give you my word as a gentleman and a sportsman. Of course you, in turn, must agree to say nothing of your visit here."

"I'll agree to nothing of the kind," said Rainsford.

"Oh," said the general, "in that case— But why discuss that now? Three days hence we can discuss it over a bottle of Veuve Cliquot, unless—"

The general sipped his wine.

Then a businesslike air animated him. "Ivan," he said to Rainsford, "will supply you with hunting clothes, food, a knife. I suggest you wear moccasins; they leave a poorer trail. I suggest too that you avoid the big swamp in the southeast corner of the island. We call it Death Swamp. There's quicksand there. One foolish fellow tried it. The deplorable part of it was that Lazarus followed him. You can imagine my feelings, Mr. Rainsford. I loved Lazarus; he was the finest hound in my pack. Well, I must beg you to excuse me now. I always take a siesta after lunch. You'll hardly have time for a nap, I fear. You'll want to start, no doubt. I shall not follow till dusk. Hunting at night is so much more exciting than by day, don't you think? *Au revoir,*[16] Mr. Rainsford, *au revoir.*"

General Zaroff, with a deep, courtly bow, strolled from the room.

From another door came Ivan. Under one arm he carried khaki hunting clothes, a haversack of food, a leather sheath containing a long-bladed hunting knife; his right hand rested on a cocked revolver thrust in the crimson sash about his waist. . . .

Rainsford had fought his way through the bush for two hours. "I

---

16. **Au revoir.** Until we meet again (French)

WORDS FOR EVERYDAY USE:	di • vert • ing (də vʉrt´iŋ) *adj.*, amusing	de • plor • a • ble (dē plôr´ə bəl) *adj.*, unfortunate
	ac • knowl • edge (ak näl´ij) *vt.*, admit to be true	
	an • i • mate (an´i māt´) *vt.*, put into motion	

must keep my nerve. I must keep my nerve," he said through tight teeth.

He had not been entirely clear-headed when the château gates snapped shut behind him. His whole idea at first was to put distance between himself and General Zaroff, and, to this end, he had plunged along, spurred on by the sharp rowels of something very like panic. Now he had got a grip on himself, had stopped, and was taking stock of himself and the situation.

He saw that straight flight was <u>futile</u>; inevitably it would bring him face to face with the sea. He was in a picture with a frame of water, and his operations, clearly, must take place within that frame.

"I'll give him a trail to follow," muttered Rainsford, and he struck off from the rude paths he had been following into the trackless wilderness. He executed a series of <u>intricate</u> loops; he doubled on his trail again and again, recalling all the lore of the fox hunt, and all the dodges of the fox. Night found him leg-weary, with hands and face lashed by the branches, on a thickly wooded ridge. He knew it would be insane to blunder on through the dark, even if he had the strength. His need for rest was <u>imperative</u> and he thought: "I have played the fox, now I must play the cat of the fable."[17] A big tree with a thick trunk and outspread branches was nearby, and, taking care to leave not the slightest mark, he climbed up into the crotch, and stretching out on one of the broad limbs, after a fashion, rested. Rest brought him new confidence and almost a feeling of security. Even so zealous a hunter as General Zaroff could not trace him there, he told himself; only the devil himself could follow that complicated trail through the jungle after dark. But, perhaps, the general was a devil—

An apprehensive night crawled slowly by like a wounded snake, and sleep did not visit Rainsford, although the silence of a dead world was on the jungle. Toward morning when a dingy gray was varnishing the sky, the cry of some startled bird focused Rainsford's attention in that direction. Something was coming through the bush, coming slowly, carefully, coming by the same winding way Rainsford had come. He flattened himself down on the limb, and through a screen of leaves almost as thick as tapestry, he watched. The thing that was approaching was a man.

It was General Zaroff. He made his way along with his eyes fixed in utmost concentration on the ground before him. He paused, almost beneath the tree, dropped to his knees and studied the ground. Rainsford's impulse was to hurl himself down like a panther, but he saw the general's right hand held something metallic—a small automatic pistol.

The hunter shook his head several times, as if he were puzzled. Then he straightened up and took from his case

What is Rainsford's plan?

How does Rainsford plan to outwit General Zaroff?

---

17. **I have played . . . fable.** He has used the wiliness of the fox to escape his pursuer; now he must use the guile of a cat to further escape.

one of his black cigarettes; its pungent incense-like smoke floated up to Rainsford's nostrils.

Rainsford held his breath. The general's eyes had left the ground and were traveling inch by inch up the tree. Rainsford froze there, every muscle tensed for a spring. But the sharp eyes of the hunter stopped before they reached the limb where Rainsford lay; a smile spread over his brown face. Very deliberately he blew a smoke ring into the air; then he turned his back on the tree and walked carelessly away, back along the trail he had come. The swish of the underbrush against his hunting boots grew fainter and fainter.

The pent-up air burst hotly from Rainsford's lungs. His first thought made him feel sick and numb. The general could follow a trail through the woods at night; he could follow an extremely difficult trail; he must have <u>uncanny</u> powers; only by the merest chance had the Cossack failed to see his quarry.

Rainsford's second thought was even more terrible. It sent a shudder of cold horror through his whole being. Why had the general smiled? Why had he turned back?

Rainsford did not want to believe what his reason told him was true, but the truth was as evident as the sun that had by now pushed through the morning mists. The general was playing with him! The general was saving him for another day's sport! The Cossack was the cat; he was the mouse. Then it

Why does Zaroff blow the smoke ring? What does he want to communicate?

was that Rainsford knew the full meaning of terror.

"I will not lose my nerve. I will not."

He slid down from the tree, and struck off again into the woods. His face was set and he forced the machinery of his mind to function. Three hundred yards from his hiding place he stopped where a huge dead tree leaned <u>precariously</u> on a smaller, living one. Throwing off his sack of food, Rainsford took his knife from its sheath and began to work with all his energy.

The job was finished at last, and he threw himself down behind a fallen log a hundred feet away. He did not have to wait long. The cat was coming again to play with the mouse.

Following the trail with the sureness of a bloodhound, came General Zaroff. Nothing escaped those searching black eyes, no crushed blade of grass, no bent twig, no mark, no matter how faint, in the moss. So intent was the Cossack on his stalking that he was upon the thing Rainsford had made before he saw it. His foot touched the <u>protruding</u> bough that was the trigger. Even as he touched it, the general sensed his danger and leaped back with the agility of an ape. But he was not quite quick enough; the dead tree, delicately adjusted to rest on the cut living one, crashed down and struck the general a glancing blow on the shoulder as it fell; but for his alertness, he must have been smashed beneath it. He staggered, but he did not fall; nor did he drop his revolver. He stood there, rubbing his

WORDS FOR EVERYDAY USE:	**un • can • ny** (un kan´ē) *adj.,* beyond normal
	pre • car • i • ous • ly (prē ker´ē əs lē) *adv.,* insecurely
	pro • trud • ing (prō trood´iŋ) *adj.,* jutting out

injured shoulder, and Rainsford, with fear again gripping his heart, heard the general's mocking laugh ring through the jungle.

"Rainsford," called the general, "if you are within the sound of my voice, as I suppose you are, let me congratulate you. Not many men know how to make a Malay man-catcher. Luckily, for me, I too have hunted in Malacca.[18] You are proving interesting, Mr. Rainsford. I am going now to have my wound dressed; it's only a slight one. But I shall be back. I shall be back."

When the general, nursing his bruised shoulder, had gone, Rainsford took up his flight again. It was flight now, a desperate, hopeless flight, that carried him on for some hours. Dusk came, then darkness, and still he pressed on. The ground grew softer under his moccasins; the vegetation grew ranker, denser; insects bit him savagely. Then, as he stepped forward, his foot sank into the ooze. He tried to wrench it back, but the muck sucked viciously at his foot as if it were a giant leech. With a violent effort, he tore his foot loose. He knew where he was now. Death Swamp and its quicksand.

His hands were tight closed as if his nerve were something tangible that some one in the darkness was trying to tear from his grip. The softness of the earth had given him an idea. He stepped back from the quicksand a dozen feet or so, and, like some huge prehistoric beaver, he began to dig.

Rainsford had dug himself in in France, when a second's delay meant death. That had been a placid pastime compared to his digging now. The pit grew deeper; when it was above his shoulders, he climbed out and from some hard saplings cut stakes and sharpened them to a fine point. These stakes he planted in the bottom of the pit with the points sticking up. With flying fingers he wove a rough carpet of weeds and branches and with it he covered the mouth of the pit. Then, wet with sweat and aching with tiredness, he crouched behind the stump of a lightning-charred tree.

He knew his pursuer was coming; he heard the padding sound of feet on the soft earth, and the night breeze brought him the perfume of the general's cigarette. It seemed to Rainsford that the general was coming with unusual swiftness; he was not feeling his way along, foot by foot. Rainsford, crouching there, could not see the general, nor could he see the pit. He lived a year in a minute. Then he felt an impulse to cry aloud with joy, for he heard the sharp crackle of the breaking branches as the cover of the pit gave way; he heard the sharp scream of pain as the pointed stakes found their mark. He leaped up from his place of concealment. Then he <u>cowered</u> back. Three feet from the pit a man was standing, with an electric torch[19] in his hand.

---

18. **Malacca.** Region in the southwestern Malay Peninsula in Asia
19. **torch.** Flashlight (British)

"You've done well, Rainsford," the voice of the general called. "Your Burmese tiger pit[20] has claimed one of my best dogs. Again you score. I think, Mr. Rainsford, I'll see what you can do against my whole pack. I'm going home for a rest now. Thank you for a most amusing evening."

At daybreak Rainsford, lying near the swamp, was awakened by a sound that made him know that he had new things to learn about fear. It was a distant sound, faint and wavering, but he knew it. It was the baying of a pack of hounds.

What happens to Ivan? How?

Rainsford knew he could do one of two things. He could stay where he was and wait. That was suicide. He could flee. That was postponing the <u>inevitable</u>. For a moment he stood there, thinking. An idea that held a wild chance came to him, and, tightening his belt, he headed away from the swamp.

The baying of the hounds drew nearer, then still nearer, nearer, ever nearer. On a ridge Rainsford climbed a tree. Down a watercourse, not a quarter of a mile away, he could see the bush moving. Straining his eyes, he saw the lean figure of General Zaroff; just ahead of him Rainsford made out another figure whose wide shoulders surged through the tall jungle weeds; it was the giant Ivan, and he seemed pulled forward by some unseen force; Rainsford knew that Ivan must be holding the pack in leash.

They would be on him any minute now. His mind worked frantically. He thought of a native trick he had learned in Uganda. He slid down the tree. He caught hold of a springy young sapling and to it he fastened his hunting knife, with the blade pointing down the trail; with a bit of wild grapevine he tied back the sapling. Then he ran for his life. The hounds raised their voices as they hit the fresh scent. Rainsford knew now how an animal at bay feels.

He had to stop to get his breath. The baying of the hounds stopped abruptly, and Rainsford's heart stopped too. They must have reached the knife.

He shinned excitedly up a tree and looked back. His pursuers had stopped. But the hope that was in Rainsford's brain when he climbed died; for he saw in the shallow valley that General Zaroff was still on his feet. But Ivan was not. The knife, driven by the <u>recoil</u> of the springing tree, had not wholly failed.

Rainsford had hardly tumbled to the ground when the pack took up the cry again.

"Nerve, nerve, nerve!" he panted, as he dashed along. A blue gap showed between the trees dead ahead. Ever nearer drew the hounds. Rainsford forced himself on toward that gap. He reached it. It was the shore of the sea. Across a cove he could see the gloomy gray stone of the château. Twenty feet below him the sea rumbled and hissed.

---

20. **Burmese tiger pit.** Deep pit used to trap tigers in Burma, a country located in Southeast Asia that is today known as Myanmar

WORDS FOR
EVERYDAY USE:

in • ev • i • ta • ble (in ev´i̇ tə bəl) *n.*, that which cannot be avoided

re • coil (rē´koil´) *n.*, state of flying back when released

Rainsford hesitated. He heard the hounds. Then he leaped far out into the sea. . . .

When the general and his pack reached the place by the sea, the Cossack stopped. For some minutes he stood regarding the blue-green expanse of water. He shrugged his shoulders. Then he sat down, took a drink of brandy from a silver flask, lit a perfumed cigarette, and hummed a bit from *Madame Butterfly*.[21]

General Zaroff had an exceedingly good dinner in his great paneled dining hall that evening. With it he had a bottle of Pol Roger and half a bottle of Chambertin. Two slight annoyances kept him from perfect enjoyment. One was the thought that it would be difficult to replace Ivan; the other was that his quarry had escaped him; of course the American hadn't played the game—so thought the general as he tasted his after-dinner liqueur. In his library he read, to soothe himself, from the works of Marcus Aurelius.[22] At ten he went up to his bedroom. He was deliciously tired, he said to himself, as he locked himself in. There was a little moonlight, so, before turning on his light, he went to the window and looked down at the courtyard. He could see the great hounds, and he called: "Better luck another time," to them. Then he switched on the light.

A man, who had been hiding in the curtains of the bed, was standing there.

"Rainsford!" screamed the general. "How in God's name did you get here?"

"Swam," said Rainsford. "I found it quicker than walking through the jungle."

The general sucked in his breath and smiled. "I congratulate you," he said. "You have won the game."

Rainsford did not smile. "I am still a beast at bay," he said, in a low, hoarse voice. "Get ready, General Zaroff."

The general made one of his deepest bows. "I see," he said. "Splendid! One of us is to furnish a repast for the hounds. The other will sleep in this very excellent bed. On guard, Rainsford. . . ."

He had never slept in a better bed, Rainsford decided. ∎

What two things bother General Zaroff?

---

21. **Madame Butterfly.** Opera by Puccini
22. **Marcus Aurelius.** Roman emperor and philosopher who ruled from AD 160 to 180

Responding to the Selection

Imagine that you are the famous hunter Rainsford in this story. Think about an early comment you made to Whitney, "Who cares how a jaguar feels?" Then write an entry in your journal, responding to that comment in light of your experience on the island.

Reviewing the Selection

1. What kind of reputation does Ship-Trap Island have among sailors?

2. What sport does Rainsford consider to be the best in the world?

3. What reason does General Zaroff give "why the hunt no longer fascinated" him?

4. What is the first trap that Rainsford makes with which to snare Zaroff?

5. What facts in the story show that the island is appropriately named?

6. What statements support Rainsford's allegiance to the hunter, not the hunted, at the beginning of the story?

7. What actions has General Zaroff taken to regain his interest in hunting?

8. What actions on the part of Rainsford show his extraordinary skill as a hunter?

9. What different meanings does the word *game* have in the story? What different meanings might the title of the story have?

10. What changes have taken place in Rainsford because of his experience on the island? How are these changes revealed in the closing scene of the story?

Understanding Literature (Questions for Discussion)

1. **Foreshadowing. Foreshadowing** is the act of presenting materials that hint at events to occur later in a story. While still aboard the yacht, Rainsford hears gunshots: "An abrupt sound startled him. Off to the right he heard it, and his ears, expert in such matters, could not be mistaken. Again he heard the sound, and again. Somewhere, off in the blackness, someone had fired a gun three times." How is this occurrence an example of foreshadowing? Later in the story, the narrator relates that Rainsford "was finding the general a most thoughtful and affable host, a true cosmopolite. But, there was one small trait of the general's that made Rainsford uncomfortable. Whenever he looked up from his plate he found the general studying him, appraising him narrowly." What later situation is foreshadowed by this observation?

2. **Irony. Irony** is a difference between appearance and reality. **Verbal irony** is one type of irony in which a statement is made that implies its opposite. In the story, General Zaroff states, "We do our best to preserve civilization here." Why is that

statement ironic? In another type of irony, **irony of situation,** an event occurs that violates the expectations of the characters, the reader, or the audience. What irony of situation violates the expectations of Rainsford and is central to the story?

3. **Plot/Conflict.** A **plot** is a series of events related to a central **conflict,** or struggle. A typical plot involves the introduction of a conflict, its development, and its eventual resolution. How does the opening dialogue between Whitney and Rainsford establish a major conflict of the story?

Responding in Writing

Folklore Tale. Imagine that many years have passed since Rainsford's experience on Ship-Trap Island. Now his experience has become part of sailor folklore. Write Rainsford's story as it might be told by a sailor on a dark and stormy night at sea.

> **Prewriting Suggestion:** To get started, brainstorm a list of details or events from "The Most Dangerous Game" that create a sense of fear or dread.

PROJECTS

1. **Storyboard.** A **storyboard** is a large board on which the events of a story are sketched in sequence. These sketches often appear with captions and dialogue. As a class, identify the following plot elements in the story: **introduction, inciting incident, rising action, climax, turning point, falling action,** and **resolution.** Then form seven small groups, assigning one plot element to each group. Within each group, create the appropriate portion of a storyboard illustrating the key event for that plot element. Display all seven portions of the storyboard in the class.

2. **Hunting Debate.** After researching the pros and cons of hunting, class members should form teams to debate the issue.

"A Smart Cookie"
from *The House on Mango Street*
by Sandra Cisneros

ABOUT THE AUTHOR

Sandra Cisneros (1954–   ) is a poet and novelist who was born in Chicago and now lives in San Antonio, Texas. Her large Mexican-American family includes her mother, father, and six brothers. She has worked as a teacher, a college recruiter, and an arts administrator. Her books include a collection of short stories, *Woman Hollering Creek;* a volume of poetry; and a series of fictional vignettes, *The House on Mango Street* from which this selection is taken.

ABOUT THE SELECTION

Background: Technique. An **allusion** is a figure of speech in which reference is made to a person, event, object, or work from history or literature. "**A Smart Cookie**" contains an allusion to *Madame Butterfly*, a well-known opera written by the Italian composer Giacomo Puccini in 1906. The opera tells the story of Cho-Cho-San, a Japanese woman who becomes romantically involved with Pinkerton, an American naval lieutenant. The two have conflicting ideas about how committed their relationship is, and Pinkerton marries another woman while Cho-Cho-San waits for him in Japan. Esperanza's mother mentions this story as she talks about friends of hers who have not taken care of themselves as individuals or pursued their own dreams.

"A Smart Cookie"

FROM THE HOUSE ON MANGO STREET

SANDRA CISNEROS

I could've been somebody, you know? my mother says and sighs. She has lived in this city her whole life. She can speak two languages. She can sing an opera. She knows how to fix a T.V. But she doesn't know which subway train to take to get downtown. I hold her hand very tight while we wait for the right train to arrive.

She used to draw when she had time. Now she draws with a needle and thread, little knotted rosebuds, tulips made of silk thread. Someday she would like to go to the ballet. Someday she would like to see a play. She borrows opera records from the public library and sings with velvety lungs powerful as morning glories.[1]

Today while cooking oatmeal she is Madame Butterfly[2] until she sighs and points the wooden spoon at me. I could've been somebody, you know? Esperanza, you go to school. Study hard. That Madame Butterfly was a fool. She stirs the oatmeal. Look at my *comadres*.[3] She means Izaura whose husband left and Yolanda whose husband is dead. Got to take care all your own, she says shaking her head.

Then out of nowhere:

Shame is a bad thing, you know. It keeps you down. You want to know why I quit school? Because I didn't have nice clothes. No clothes, but I had brains.

Yup, she says disgusted, stirring again. I was a smart cookie then. ■

---

1. **morning glories.** Trumpet-shaped flowers
2. **Madame Butterfly.** Main character in the famous opera of the same name
3. *comadres.* Spanish for fellow mothers

What are some of Esperanza's mother's hobbies?

What has happened to Izaura and Yolanda?

What has kept Esperanza's mother down?
What does she tell Esperanza to do?

Responding to the Selection

Does Esperanza think her mother is still "a smart cookie"? Do you?

Reviewing the Selection

RECALLING

1. Where has Esperanza's mother spent her life? What can she do? What does she have difficulty doing?

2. What does Esperanza's mother say about her *comadres,* the women who are her friends? Why did Esperanza's mother quit school?

INTERPRETING

▶▶ 3. How does Esperanza sound in the second paragraph as she describes her mother's hobbies? Does Esperanza have respect for her mother? Explain.

▶▶ 4. Why does Esperanza's mother say, "Got to take care all your own"?

SYNTHESIZING

5. How did shame keep Esperanza's mother down? In what ways can Esperanza "take care all your own" and not have regrets in her own life?

Understanding Literature (Questions for Discussion)

1. **Point of View. Point of view** is the vantage point from which a story is told. This selection is written from a first-person point of view. The narrator of the story is a participant of the action and uses the "I". What are advantages to using this point of view? Why did the author choose to write the story in this way?

2. **Genre.** A **genre** is one of the types or categories into which literary works are divided. *The House on Mango Street* is a **novel,** which is a long work of prose fiction. This book's structure is slightly different than that of many novels in that each chapter is a **vignette,** or a short sketch or description. Each vignette makes a single point or creates a single effect or impression. What point or effect is made by this vignette from *The House on Mango Street?*

3. **Simile.** A **simile** is a comparison using *like* or *as*. Find an example of simile in "A Smart Cookie." What sort of picture does the simile create in your mind?

Responding in Writing

Vignette. Notice how much we learn about Esperanza's mother as she listens to records, stands at the stove, and stirs a pot of oatmeal. Our lives are full of short, everyday activities that may serve as backdrops for brief vignettes. Write your own vignette in the style of "A Smart Cookie."

> **Prewriting Suggestion:** In a notebook, make a list of everyday activities that take place over brief periods of time—for example, brushing your teeth, walking your dog, riding an elevator, or waiting in line at a supermarket. Then freewrite about each activity. What story ideas come to mind? What might you be thinking of during these times?

PROJECT

Skits. Get a copy of *The House on Mango Street* from your school or local library. As a group, read the entire book out loud. Then vote on which chapters are your favorites. Get organized into small groups and adapt each of the favorite chapters into skits. Rehearse your skits and perform them one after the other in your classroom. You may also want to invite other classes to see your performances. If some people haven't read the book, elect one person to give a short introduction.

"The Handsomest Drowned Man in the World"
by Gabriel García Márquez, trans. by Gregory Rabassa

ABOUT THE AUTHOR

Gabriel García Márquez (1928–   ) was born in Aracataca, Colombia. He studied at Bogotá University, then left for Cartagena, where he began his journalism career. Two years later, he went to Europe on assignment as a newspaper reporter. He spent many years away from Colombia. In *Leaf Storm,* his first book, Márquez introduced the imaginary town of Macondo, the setting for many of his later works, including his epic masterpiece *One Hundred Years of Solitude.* Other notable works by Márquez include *No One Writes to the Colonel and Other Stories, Chronicle of a Death Foretold, Love in the Time of Cholera, The General in His Labyrinth,* and *Strange Pilgrims.* In 1982 García Márquez was awarded the Nobel Prize for literature. Now recognized as one of the world's greatest living writers, Márquez resides in Mexico City, Mexico.

ABOUT THE SELECTION

Background: Genre. Every culture on the globe has its legends. In the United States, legendary characters include Pocahantas, Paul Bunyan, Annie Oakley, Davy Crockett, Daniel Boone, and Johnny Appleseed. All of these characters, with the exception of Bunyan, were actual historical figures. However, over time, many fantastic tales were told about them. The folk imagination transformed them from extraordinary actual people into mythical personages. **"The Handsomest Drowned Man in the World"** shows how such transformations of the historical into the mythical take place. It is a story about how myths are born.

Background: Technique. García Márquez is recognized as the master of **Magical Realism.** Magical Realism is writing that includes marvelous, supernatural events but that treats them as though they were ordinary, realistic occurrences. Nothing magical, in a supernatural sense, occurs in Márquez's story; however, the story does show how people's feelings can lead them to magical ideas about actual, ordinary people and things.

"The Handsomest Drowned Man in the World"

GABRIEL GARCÍA MÁRQUEZ, TRANS. BY GREGORY RABASSA

The first children who saw the dark and slinky bulge approaching through the sea let themselves think it was an enemy ship. Then they saw it had no flags or masts and they thought it was a whale. But when it washed up on the beach, they removed the clumps of seaweed, the jellyfish tentacles, and the remains of fish and <u>flotsam</u>, and only then did they see that it was a drowned man.

They had been playing with him all afternoon, burying him in the sand and digging him up again, when someone chanced to see them and spread the alarm in the village. The men who carried him to the nearest house noticed that he weighed more than any dead man they had ever known, almost as much as a horse, and they said to each other that maybe he'd been floating too long and the water had got into his bones. When they laid him on the floor they said he'd been taller than all other men because there was barely enough room for him in the house, but they thought that maybe the ability to keep on growing after death was part of the nature of certain drowned men. He had the smell of the sea about him and only his shape gave one to suppose that it was the corpse of a human being, because the skin was covered with a crust of mud and scales.

They did not even have to clean off his face to know that the dead man was a stranger. The village was made up of only twenty-odd wooden houses that had stone courtyards with no flowers and which were spread about

What do the men notice about the drowned man?

on the end of a desertlike <u>cape</u>. There was so little land that mothers always went about with the fear that the wind would carry off their children and the few dead that the years had caused among them had to be thrown off the cliffs. But the sea was calm and <u>bountiful</u> and all the men fit into seven boats. So when they found the drowned man they simply had to look at one another to see that they were all there. That night they did not go out to work at sea. While the men went to find out if anyone was missing in neighboring villages, the women stayed behind to care for the drowned man. They took the mud off with grass swabs, they removed the underwater stones entangled in his hair, and they scraped the crust off with tools used for scaling fish. As they were doing that they noticed that the vegetation on him came from faraway oceans and deep water and that his clothes were in tatters, as if he had sailed through <u>labyrinths</u> of coral. They noticed too that he bore his death with pride, for he did not have the lonely look of other drowned men who came out of the sea or that haggard, needy look of men who drowned in rivers. But only when they finished cleaning him off did they become aware of the kind of man he was and it left them breathless. Not only was he the tallest, strongest, most virile, and best built man they had ever seen, but even though they were looking at him there was no room for him in their imagination.

They could not find a bed in the village large enough to lay him on nor was there a table solid enough to use for his wake. The tallest men's holiday pants would not fit him, nor the fattest ones' Sunday shirts, nor the shoes of the one with the biggest feet. Fascinated by his huge size and his beauty, the women then decided to make him some pants from a large piece of sail and a shirt from some bridal brabant linen[1] so that he could continue through his death with dignity. As they sewed, sitting in a circle and gazing at the corpse between stitches, it seemed to them that the wind had never been so steady nor the sea so restless as on that night and they supposed that the change had something to do with the dead man. They thought that if that magnificent man had lived in the village, his house would have had the widest doors, the highest ceiling, and the strongest floor, his bedstead would have been made from a midship frame held together by iron bolts, and his wife would have been the happiest woman. They thought that he would have had so much authority that he could have drawn fish out of the sea simply by calling their names and that he would have put so much work into his land that springs would have burst forth from among the rocks so that he would have been able to plant flowers on the cliffs. They secretly compared him to their own men, thinking that for all their lives theirs were incapable

---

1. **brabant linen.** Linen from Brabant, a province on the border between Belgium and the Netherlands

Why do the people know right away that the man is a stranger? What is their village like?

What did the women notice as they cleaned the man?

What did they imagine the drowned man would do if he were a villager?

<u>W</u>ORDS FOR <u>E</u>VERYDAY <u>U</u>SE:

cape (kāp) *n.*, piece of land projecting into a body of water

boun • ti • ful (boun´tə fəl) *adj.*, plentiful; abundant

lab • y • rinth (lab´ ər inth´) *n.*, complicated maze

After the Tornado, Texas. Winslow Homer, American, 1836–1910. Watercolor, 1899, 36.8 x 53.3 cm.
Mr. and Mrs. Martin A. Ryerson Collection, 1933.1235

of doing what he could do in one night, and they ended up dismissing them deep in their hearts as the weakest, meanest, and most useless creatures on earth. They were wandering through that maze of fantasy when the oldest woman, who as the oldest had looked upon the drowned man with more compassion than passion, sighed:

"He has the face of someone called Esteban."

It was true. Most of them had only to take another look at him to see that he could not have any other name. The more stubborn among them, who were the youngest, still lived for a few hours with the <u>illusion</u> that when they put his clothes on and he lay among the flowers in patent leather shoes his name might be Lautaro. But it was a vain illusion. There had not been enough canvas, the poorly cut and worse sewn pants were too tight, and the hidden strength of his heart popped the buttons on his shirt. After midnight the whistling of the wind died down and the sea fell into its Wednesday drowsiness. The silence put an end to any last doubts: he was Esteban. The women who had dressed him, who had combed his hair, had cut his nails and shaved him were unable to hold back a shudder of pity when they had to resign themselves to his being dragged along the ground. It was then that they understood how

WORDS FOR
EVERYDAY USE:

il • lu • sion (i lo͞o´zhən) *n.,* false perception

unhappy he must have been with that huge body since it bothered him even after death. They could see him in life, condemned to going through doors sideways, cracking his head on crossbeams, remaining on his feet during visits, not knowing what to do with his soft, pink, sea lion hands while the lady of the house looked for her most resistant chair and begged him, frightened to death, sit here, Esteban, please, and he, leaning against the wall, smiling, don't bother, ma'am, I'm fine where I am, his heels raw and his back roasted from having done the same thing so many times whenever he paid a visit, don't bother, ma'am, I'm fine where I am, just to avoid the embarrassment of breaking up the chair, and never knowing perhaps that the ones who said don't go, Esteban, at least wait till the coffee's ready, were the ones who later on would whisper the big boob finally left, how nice, the handsome fool has gone. That was what the women were thinking beside the body a little before dawn. Later, when they covered his face with a handkerchief so that the light would not bother him, he looked so forever dead, so defenseless, so much like their men that the first <u>furrows</u> of tears opened in their hearts. It was one of the younger ones who began the weeping. The others, coming to, went from sighs to wails, and the more they sobbed the more they felt like weeping, because the drowned man was becoming all the more Esteban for them, and so they wept so much, for he was the most <u>destitute</u>,

most peaceful, and most obliging man on earth, poor Esteban. So when the men returned with the news that the drowned man was not from the neighboring villages either, the women felt an opening of jubilation in the midst of their tears.

"Praise the Lord," they sighed, "he's ours!"

The men thought the fuss was only womanish <u>frivolity</u>. Fatigued because of the difficult nighttime inquiries, all they wanted was to get rid of the bother of the newcomer once and for all before the sun grew strong on that arid, windless day. They <u>improvised</u> a litter[2] with the remains of foremasts and gaffs, tying it together with rigging so that it would bear the weight of the body until they reached the cliffs. They wanted to tie the anchor from a cargo ship to him so that he would sink easily into the deepest waves, where fish are blind and divers die of nostalgia, and bad currents would not bring him back to shore, as had happened with other bodies. But the more they hurried, the more the women thought of ways to waste time. They walked about like startled hens, pecking with the sea charms on their breasts, some interfering on one side to put a scapular of the good wind[3] on the drowned man, some on the other side to put a wrist compass[4] on him,

---

2. **litter.** Transportable cot used for moving injured or ill people

3. **scapular of the good wind.** Garment with religious significance

4. **wrist compass.** Compass placed on the wrist for the purpose of directing the soul to God

How do the men of the village feel about Esteban? What do they want to do with him? How do the women respond to this?

WORDS FOR EVERYDAY USE:

fur • row (fur´ō) n., narrow groove

des • ti • tute (des´tə tōot) adj., abandoned; forsaken

fri • vol • i • ty (fri väl´ə tē) n., act of being trivial

im • pro • vise (im´prə vīz´) vt., bring about with tools and materials

and after a great deal of *get away from there, woman, stay out of the way, look, you almost made me fall on top of the dead man*, the men began to feel mistrust in their livers and started grumbling about why so many main-altar decorations for a stranger, because no matter how many nails and holy-water jars he had on him, the sharks would chew him all the same, but the women kept piling on their junk relics, running back and forth, stumbling, while they released in sighs what they did not in tears, so that the men finally exploded with *since when has there ever been such a fuss over a drifting corpse, a drowned nobody, a piece of cold Wednesday meat.* One of the women, <u>mortified</u> by so much lack of care, then removed the handkerchief from the dead man's face and the men were left breathless too.

He was Esteban. It was not necessary to repeat it for them to recognize him. If they had been told Sir Walter Raleigh, even they might have been impressed with his gringo accent, the macaw on his shoulder, his cannibal-killing blunderbuss,[5] but there could be only one Esteban in the world and there he was, stretched out like a sperm whale, shoeless, wearing the pants of an undersized child, and with those stony nails that had to be cut with a knife. They only had to take the handkerchief off his face to see that he was ashamed, that it was not his fault that he was so big or so heavy or so handsome, and if he had known that this was going to happen, he would have looked for a more <u>discreet</u> place

to drown in, seriously, I even would have tied the anchor off a galleon around my neck and staggered off a cliff like someone who doesn't like things in order not to be upsetting people now with this Wednesday dead body, as you people say, in order not to be bothering anyone with this filthy piece of cold meat that doesn't have anything to do with me. There was so much truth in his manner that even the most mistrustful men, the ones who felt the bitterness of endless nights at sea fearing that their women would tire of dreaming about them and begin to dream of drowned men, even they and others who were harder still shuddered in the marrow of their bones at Esteban's sincerity.

That was how they came to hold the most splendid funeral they could conceive of for an abandoned drowned man. Some women who had gone to get flowers in the neighboring villages returned with other women who could not believe what they had been told, and those women went back for more flowers when they saw the dead man, and they brought more and more until there were so many flowers and so many people that it was hard to walk about. At the final moment it pained them to return him to the waters as an orphan and they chose a father and mother from among the best people, and aunts and uncles and cousins, so

What makes some of the men shudder?

What do the people do before they return the man to the waters?

5. **Sir Walter Raleigh . . . blunderbuss.** English navigator and statesman (1552–1618). He is portrayed here as having an English accent, a tropical bird on his shoulder, and a blunderbuss, an obsolete gun with a large muzzle, accurate only at short range.

WORDS FOR EVERYDAY USE:

mor • ti • fied (môrʹə fīdʹ) *adj.*, shamed, humiliated

dis • creet (di skrētʹ) *adj.*, careful about what one says or does

that through him all the inhabitants of the village became <u>kinsmen</u>. Some sailors who heard the weeping from a distance went off course and people heard of one who had himself tied to the mainmast, remembering ancient fables about sirens.[6] While they fought for the privilege of carrying him on their shoulders along the steep <u>escarpment</u> by the cliffs, men and women became aware for the first time of the desolation of their streets, the dryness of their courtyards, the narrowness of their dreams as they faced the splendor and beauty of their drowned man. They let him go without an anchor so that he could come back if he wished and whenever he wished, and they all held their breath for the fraction of centuries the body took to fall into the abyss. They did not need to look at one another to realize that they were no longer all present, that they would never be. But they also knew that everything would be different from then on, that their houses would have wider doors, higher ceilings, and stronger floors so that Esteban's memory could go every-

where without bumping into beams and so that no one in the future would dare whisper the big boob finally died, too bad, the handsome fool has finally died, because they were going to paint their house fronts gay colors to make Esteban's memory <u>eternal</u> and they were going to break their backs digging for springs among the stones and planting flowers on the cliffs so that in future years at dawn the passengers on great liners would awaken, suffocated by the smell of gardens on the high seas, and the captain would have to come down from the bridge in his dress uniform, with his astrolabe,[7] his pole star, and his row of war medals and, pointing to the promontory of roses on the horizon, he would say in fourteen languages, look there, where the wind is so peaceful now that it's gone to sleep beneath the beds, over there, where the sun's so bright that the sunflowers don't know which way to turn, yes, over there, that's Esteban's village. ∎

How would Esteban's memory live on in the community?

---

6. **sirens.** Sea nymphs who lured sailors to their deaths
7. **astrolabe.** Ancient marine navigational instrument

WORDS FOR EVERYDAY USE:

kins • man (kinz´ mən) *n.*, relative
es • carp • ment (e skärp´mənt) *n.*, steep slope
e • ter • nal (ē tur´nəl) *adj.*, timeless; everlasting

194 *UNIT THREE / THE SHORT STORY*

Responding to the Selection

Imagine that you are a traveler visiting the village of Esteban. In your journal, write what you have learned from the villagers about how the doors on their houses came to be so wide and the ceilings so tall.

Reviewing the Selection

RECALLING

1. Who finds the drowned man?

2. Who takes care of the drowned man?

3. From what do the village women make a pair of pants for the drowned man?

4. What name do the village women give to the drowned stranger?

INTERPRETING

5. What is probably the reason the drowned man is mistaken for an enemy ship?

6. What details show that he "came from faraway oceans and deep water"?

7. What is probably the reason that the village women begin to think of their husbands as "the weakest, meanest, and most useless creatures on earth"?

8. What is probably the reason that the villagers "became aware for the first time of the desolation of their streets"?

SYNTHESIZING

9. What actions on the part of the villagers ensure that the memory of Esteban will be kept alive?

10. What sort of relationship between the villagers and the drowned stranger is described in this story? What is the significance of Esteban's size and appearance?

Understanding Literature (Questions for Discussion)

1. **Point of View. Point of view** is the vantage point from which a story is told. "The Handsomest Drowned Man in the World" is told from a third-person point of view. In third-person point of view, the narrator generally stands outside the action. Why might the author have chosen to tell this story from a third-person point of view?

2. **Myth.** A **myth** is a story that explains objects or events in the natural world as resulting from the action of some supernatural force or entity, most often a god. Myths often tell about how things came to be as they are. Why are the doors in the village so wide and the ceilings so tall? Why does the village have so many flower gardens? Why do people refer to the village as "Esteban's village"?

3. **Hyperbole.** A **hyperbole** is an exaggeration made for rhetorical effect. For example, in the selection the narrator relates that "Not only was he the tallest, strongest, most virile, and best built man they had ever seen, but even though they were looking at him, there was no room for him in their imagination." What impression of the drowned stranger does the hyperbole create? Find another example of hyperbole in the story. Explain what effect is created by the hyperbole.

Responding in Writing

Myth. Write a myth that explains the existence of a particular manufactured object in the world, such as an automobile, a skateboard, or a billboard.

> **Prewriting Suggestion.** To get started, write the name of the object at the top of a piece of paper. Then, down the left-hand side of the paper, write the words *who, what, where, when, why,* and *how.* For each of the words, brainstorm a few questions you'd like to answer in your myth, such as *Who found the object? What does the object look like? Where was the object first seen?*

PROJECT

Myth History. As a class, do research on the myths of various cultures and civilizations. You may wish to look at Greek, Roman, Incan, Mayan, Native American, African, and Asian myths. Divide into groups. Assign one culture or civilization to each group. Research myths that explain how elements in the natural world came to be. Then present the results of your research in class, combining a brief discussion of each culture with a retelling of three or four myths.

"A Mother in Mannville"
by Marjorie Kinnan Rawlings

ABOUT THE AUTHOR

Marjorie Kinnan Rawlings (1896–1953) was born in Washington, D.C. As a young girl, Rawlings wanted to become a writer and often entertained the neighbors' children with stories. After graduating from the University of Wisconsin, she worked as a journalist for ten years. During this time, Rawlings tried unsuccessfully to sell her stories. In 1928, she moved to Cross Creek, Florida, where she devoted herself to writing fiction. Cross Creek became the setting for most of her work, which she finally succeeded in having published. Rawlings received the Pulitzer Prize in 1939 for her novel *The Yearling*.

ABOUT THE SELECTION

Background: Technique. Rawlings is noted for her descriptions of the land, dialect, and customs of rural Florida. In **"A Mother in Mannville,"** Rawlings uses three techniques of **characterization**—direct description, portrayal of characters' behavior, and representations of characters' internal states—to characterize the narrator and the young boy who befriends her.

"A Mother in Mannville"

MARJORIE KINNAN RAWLINGS

Why was the narrator at the cabin?

The orphanage is high in the Carolina mountains. Sometimes in winter the snowdrifts are so deep that the institution is cut off from the village below, from all the world. Fog hides the mountain peaks, the snow swirls down the valleys, and a wind blows so bitterly that the orphanage boys who take the milk twice daily to the baby cottage reach the door with fingers stiff in an agony of numbness.

"Or when we carry trays from the cookhouse for the ones that are sick," Jerry said, "we get our faces frostbit, because we can't put our hands over them. I have gloves," he added. "Some of the boys don't have any."

He liked the late spring, he said. The rhododendron was in bloom, a carpet of color, across the mountainsides, soft as the May winds that stirred the hemlocks. He called it laurel.

"It's pretty when the laurel blooms," he said. "Some of it's pink and some of it's white."

I was there in the autumn. I wanted quiet, <u>isolation</u>, to do some troublesome writing. I wanted mountain air to blow out the malaria from too long a time in the subtropics. I was homesick, too, for the flaming of maples in October, and for corn shocks and pumpkins and black-walnut trees and the lift of hills. I found them all, living in a cabin that belonged to the orphanage, half a mile beyond the orphanage farm. When I took the cabin, I asked for a boy or man to come and chop wood for the fireplace. The first few days were warm, I found what wood I needed about the cabin, no one came, and I forgot the order.

I looked up from my typewriter one late afternoon, a little startled. A boy stood at the door, and my pointer dog,

---

WORDS FOR EVERYDAY USE:

i • so • la • tion (ī sə lā´shən) *n.,* being set apart from others

my companion, was at his side and had not barked to warn me. The boy was probably twelve years old, but undersized. He wore overalls and a torn shirt, and was barefooted.

He said, "I can chop some wood today."

I said, "But I have a boy coming from the orphanage."

"I'm the boy."

"You? But you're small."

"Size don't matter, chopping wood," he said. "Some of the big boys don't chop good. I've been chopping wood at the orphanage a long time."

I visualized mangled and inadequate branches for my fires. I was well into my work and not <u>inclined</u> to conversation. I was a little blunt.

"Very well. There's the ax. Go ahead and see what you can do."

I went back to work, closing the door. At first the sound of the boy dragging brush annoyed me. Then he began to chop. The blows were rhythmic and steady, and shortly I had forgotten him, the sound no more of an interruption than a <u>consistent</u> rain. I suppose an hour and a half passed, for when I stopped and stretched, and heard the boy's steps on the cabin stoop, the sun was dropping behind the farthest mountain, and the valleys were purple with something deeper than the asters.

The boy said, "I have to go to supper now. I can come again tomorrow evening."

I said, "I'll pay you now for what you've done," thinking I should proba-bly have to insist on an older boy. "Ten cents an hour?"

"Anything is all right."

We went together back of the cabin. An astonishing amount of solid wood had been cut. There were cherry logs and heavy roots of rhododendron, and blocks from the waste pine and oak left from the building of the cabin.

"But you've done as much as a man," I said. "This is a splendid pile."

I looked at him, actually, for the first time. His hair was the color of the corn shocks and his eyes, very direct, were like the mountain sky when rain is pending—gray, with a shadowing of that miraculous blue. As I spoke, a light came over him, as though the setting sun had touched him with the same <u>suffused</u> glory with which it touched the mountains. I gave him a quarter.

"You may come tomorrow," I said, "and thank you very much."

He looked at me, and at the coin, and seemed to want to speak, but could not, and turned away.

"I'll split kindling tomorrow," he said over his thin, ragged shoulder. "You'll need kindling and medium wood and logs and backlogs."

At daylight I was half-wakened by the sound of chopping. Again it was so even in texture that I went back to sleep. When I left my bed in the cool morning, the boy had come and gone, and a stack of kindling was neat against the cabin wall. He came again after school in the afternoon and worked until time to return to the orphanage.

What surprises the narrator?

What does the boy look like? To what does the narrator compare him?

WORDS FOR EVERYDAY USE:	**in • clined** (in klīnd´) *adj.,* willing
	con • sis • tent (kən sis´tənt) *adj.,* steady
	suf • fused (sə fyo͞oz´d) *adj.,* filled, as with color

In what ways does Jerry show integrity?

His name was Jerry; he was twelve years old, and he had been at the orphanage since he was four. I could picture him at four, with the same grave gray-blue eyes and the same—independence? No, the word that comes to me is "integrity."

The word means something very special to me, and the quality for which I use it is a rare one. My father had it—there is another of whom I am almost sure—but almost no man of my acquaintance possesses it with the clarity, the purity, the simplicity of a mountain stream. But the boy Jerry had it. It is bedded on courage, but it is more than brave. It is honest, but it is more than honesty. The ax handle broke one day. Jerry said the wood-shop at the orphanage would repair it. I brought money to pay for the job, and he refused it.

What is granite like? What would it mean for a person to be like granite?

"I'll pay for it," he said. "I broke it. I brought the ax down careless."

"But no one hits accurately every time," I told him. "The fault was in the wood of the handle. I'll see the man from whom I bought it."

It was only then that he would take the money. He was standing back of his own carelessness. He was a free-will agent, and he chose to do careful work; and if he failed, he took the responsibility without subterfuge.

And he did for me the unnecessary thing, the gracious thing, that we find done only by the great of heart. Things no training can teach, for they are done on the instant, with no predicated experience. He found a cubbyhole beside the fireplace that I had not noticed. There, of his own accord, he put kindling and "medium" wood, so that I might always have dry fire material ready in case of sudden wet weather. A stone was loose in the rough walk to the cabin. He dug a deeper hole and steadied it, although he came, himself, by a short cut over the bank. I found that when I tried to return his thoughtfulness with such things as candy and apples, he was wordless. "Thank you" was, perhaps, an expression for which he had had no use, for his courtesy was instinctive. He only looked at the gift and at me, and a curtain lifted, so that I saw deep into the clear well of his eyes, and gratitude was there, and affection, soft over the firm granite of his character.

He made simple excuses to come and sit with me. I could no more have turned him away than if he had been physically hungry. I suggested once that the best time for us to visit was just before supper, when I left off my writing. After that, he waited always until my typewriter had been some time quiet. One day I worked until nearly dark. I went outside the cabin, having forgotten him. I saw him going up over the hill in the twilight toward the orphanage. When I sat down on my stoop, a place was warm from his body where he had been sitting.

He became intimate, of course, with my pointer, Pat. There is a strange communion between a boy and a dog. Perhaps they possess the same single-ness of spirit, the same kind of wisdom.

WORDS FOR EVERYDAY USE:

in • teg • ri • ty (in teg′rə tē) *n.*, quality of honesty and sincerity

clar • i • ty (klar′ə tē) *n.*, state of being clear

sub • ter • fuge (sub′tər fyo͞oj′) *n.*, deceit used to escape a difficult or unpleasant situation

com • mu • nion (kə myo͞on′yən) *n.*, close relationship with deep understanding

Photo courtesy of Digital Stock Corp.

It is difficult to explain, but it exists. When I went across the state for a weekend, I left the dog in Jerry's charge. I gave him the dog whistle and the key to the cabin, and left <u>sufficient</u> food. He was to come two or three times a day and let out the dog, and feed and exercise him. I should return Sunday night, and Jerry would take out the dog for the last time Sunday afternoon and then leave the key under an agreed hiding place.

My return was belated, and fog filled the mountain passes so <u>treacherously</u> that I dared not drive at night. The fog held the next morning, and it was Monday noon before I reached the cabin. The dog had been fed and cared for that morning. Jerry came early in the afternoon, anxious.

"The superintendent said nobody would drive in the fog," he said. "I came just before bedtime last night and you hadn't come. So I brought Pat some of my breakfast this morning. I wouldn't have let anything happen to him."

"I was sure of that. I didn't worry."

"When I heard about the fog, I thought you'd know."

How does Jerry feel when the narrator returns?

What does Jerry tell the narrator?

He was needed for work at the orphanage, and he had to return at once. I gave him a dollar in payment, and he looked at it and went away. But that night he came in the darkness and knocked at the door.

"Come in, Jerry," I said, "if you're allowed to be away this late."

"I told maybe a story," he said. "I told them I thought you would want to see me."

"That's true," I assured him, and I saw his relief. "I want to hear about how you managed with the dog."

He sat by the fire with me, with no other light, and told me of their two days together. The dog lay close to him, and found a comfort there that I did not have for him. And it seemed to me that being with my dog, and caring for him, had brought the boy and me, too, together, so that he felt that he belonged to me as well as to the animal.

How does the narrator feel toward Jerry? Why?

"He stayed right with me," he told me, "except when he ran in the laurel. He likes the laurel. I took him up over the hill and we both ran fast. There was a place where the grass was high and I lay down in it and hid. I could hear Pat hunting for me. He found my trail and he barked. When he found me, he acted crazy, and he ran around and around me, in circles."

We watched the flames.

"That's an apple log," he said. "It burns the prettiest of any wood."

We were very close.

He was suddenly <u>impelled</u> to speak of things he had not spoken of before, nor had I cared to ask him.

"You look a little bit like my mother," he said. "Especially in the dark, by the fire."

"But you were only four, Jerry, when you came here. You have remembered how she looked, all these years?"

"My mother lives in Mannville," he said.

For a moment, finding that he had a mother shocked me as greatly as anything in my life has ever done, and I did not know why it disturbed me. Then I understood my distress. I was filled with a passionate resentment that any woman should go away and leave her son. A fresh anger added itself. A son like this one— The orphanage was a wholesome place, the executives were kind, good people, the food was more than adequate, the boys were healthy, a ragged shirt was no hardship, nor the doing of clean labor. Granted, perhaps, that the boy felt no lack, what blood fed the bowels of a woman who did not yearn over this child's lean body that had come in <u>parturition</u> out of her own? At four he would have looked the same as now. Nothing, I thought, nothing in life could change those eyes. His quality must be apparent to an idiot, a fool. I burned with questions I could not ask. In any case, I was afraid, there would be pain.

"Have you seen her, Jerry—lately?"

"I see her every summer. She sends for me."

I wanted to cry out, "Why are you not with her? How can she let you go away again?"

WORDS FOR EVERYDAY USE:

im • pel (im pel´) *vi.*, force, urge

par • tu • ri • tion (pär´too rish´ən) *n.*, childbirth

He said, "She comes up here from Mannville whenever she can. She doesn't have a job now."

His face shone in the firelight.

"She wanted to give me a puppy, but they can't let any one boy keep a puppy. You remember the suit I had on last Sunday?" He was plainly proud. "She sent me that for Christmas. The Christmas before that"—he drew a long breath, savoring the memory— "she sent me a pair of skates."

"Roller skates?"

My mind was busy, making pictures of her, trying to understand her. She had not, then, entirely deserted or forgotten him. But why, then—I thought, "I must not condemn her without knowing."

"Roller skates. I let the other boys use them. They're always borrowing them. But they're careful of them."

What circumstance other than poverty—

"I'm going to take the dollar you gave me for taking care of Pat," he said, "and buy her a pair of gloves."

I could only say, "That will be nice. Do you know her size?"

"I think it's 8$\frac{1}{2}$," he said.

He looked at my hands.

"Do you wear 8$\frac{1}{2}$?" he asked.

" No. I wear a smaller size, a 6."

"Oh! Then I guess her hands are bigger than yours."

I hated her. Poverty or no, there was other food than bread, and the soul could starve as quickly as the body. He was taking his dollar to buy gloves for her big stupid hands, and she lived away from him, in Mannville, and contented herself with sending him skates.

"She likes white gloves," he said. "Do you think I can get them for a dollar?"

"I think so," I said.

I decided that I should not leave the mountains without seeing her and knowing for myself why she had done this thing.

The human mind scatters its interests as though made of thistledown,[1] and every wind stirs and moves it. I finished my work. It did not please me, and I gave my thoughts to another field. I should need some Mexican material.

I made arrangements to close my Florida place. Mexico immediately, and doing the writing there, if conditions were favorable. Then, Alaska with my brother. After that, heaven knew what or where.

I did not take time to go to Mannville to see Jerry's mother, nor even to talk with the orphanage officials about her. I was a <u>trifle</u> abstracted about the boy, because of my work and plans. And after my first fury at her—we did not speak of her again—his having a mother, any sort at all, not far away, in Mannville, relieved me of the ache I had had about him. He did not question the <u>anomalous</u> relation. He was not lonely. It was none of my concern.

He came every day and cut my wood and did small helpful favors and stayed to talk. The days had become cold,

---

1. **thistledown.** Fine, feathery seedlings from a thistle plant

To what does the narrator compare the human mind? In what way are these two things similar?

What feelings does the narrator have toward Jerry's mother? Why does she feel this way?

WORDS FOR EVERYDAY USE:

tri • fle (trī´fəl) n., small amount

a • nom • a • lous (ə näm´ə ləs) adj., strange, abnormal

and often I let him come inside the cabin. He would lie on the floor in front of the fire, with one arm across the pointer, and they would both doze and wait quietly for me. Other days they ran with a common ecstasy through the laurel, and since the asters were now gone, he brought me back <u>vermilion</u> maple leaves, and chestnut boughs dripping with imperial yellow. I was ready to go.

I said to him, "You have been my good friend, Jerry. I shall often think of you and miss you. Pat will miss you too. I am leaving tomorrow."

He did not answer. When he went away, I remember that a new moon hung over the mountains, and I watched him go in silence up the hill. I expected him the next day, but he did not come. The details of packing my personal belongings, loading my car, arranging the bed over the seat, where the dog would ride, occupied me until late in the day. I closed the cabin and started the car, noticing that the sun was in the west and I should do well to be out of the mountains by nightfall. I stopped by the orphanage and left the cabin key and money for my light bill with Miss Clark.

"And will you call Jerry for me to say goodbye to him?"

"I don't know where he is," she said. "I'm afraid he's not well. He didn't eat his dinner this noon. One of the other boys saw him going over the hill into the laurel. He was supposed to fire the boiler this afternoon. It's not like him; he's unusually reliable."

I was almost relieved, for I knew I should never see him again, and it would be easier not to say goodbye to him.

I said, "I wanted to talk with you about his mother—why he's here—but I'm in more of a hurry than I expected to be. It's out of the question for me to see her now too. But here's some money I'd like to leave with you to buy things for him at Christmas and on his birthday. It will be better than for me to try to send him things. I could so easily duplicate— skates, for instance."

She blinked her eyes.

"There's not much use for skates here," she said.

Her stupidity annoyed me.

"What I mean," I said, "is that I don't want to duplicate things his mother sends him. I might have chosen skates if I didn't know she had already given them to him."

She stared at me.

"I don't understand," she said. "He has no mother. He has no skates." ■

Why do you think Jerry didn't eat or do his work? What might have been troubling him?

Why might Jerry have made up the stories about his mother and his skates?

WORDS FOR EVERYDAY USE: ver • mil • ion (vər mil´yən) adj., bright red

Responding to the Selection

Imagine that you are the narrator in this story. Write a letter to Jerry telling him goodbye. In your letter, express your feelings toward Jerry, explaining to him what his friendship means to you.

Reviewing the Selection

RECALLING

1. What reasons does the narrator give for coming to live near the orphanage?

2. What word comes to the narrator when describing Jerry?

3. What is the narrator's first reaction to learning that Jerry has a mother in Mannville?

4. What does the narrator learn when she gives money to Miss Clark at the orphanage?

INTERPRETING

5. What conclusion does the narrator first draw about Jerry?

6. What actions on the part of Jerry show his integrity?

7. What is probably the reason for the narrator's reaction?

8. What is probably the reason Jerry created the story about having a mother in Mannville?

SYNTHESIZING

9. What kind of person is the narrator? Is she truly concerned about Jerry? How do you know?

10. What sort of relationship between Jerry and the natural setting is described in this story? What does this relationship reveal about Jerry's character?

Understanding Literature (Questions for Discussion)

1. **Setting.** The **setting** of a literary work is the time and place in which it occurs, together with all the details used to create a sense of a particular time and place. In fiction, setting is most often revealed by means of description of such elements as landscape, scenery, buildings, furniture, clothing, the weather, the seasons, and so on. What elements of the season are described at the beginning of the story? What details later in the story show that the time of year has changed?

2. **Characterization. Characterization** is the use of literary techniques to create a character. In the selection, the techniques of direct description and portrayal of a character's behavior are used to create the character of Jerry. Early in the story, when the narrator looked at Jerry "actually, for the first time," the details of Jerry's description are taken from nature: "His hair was the color of the corn shocks, and his eyes, very direct, were like the mountain sky when rain is pending—gray, with a shadowing of that miraculous blue." What does this description reveal about Jerry? What does the narrator's statement, "I looked at him, actually, for the first time," reveal about the narrator?

3. **Mood. Mood** is the emotion created in the reader by part or all of a literary work. A writer creates mood by using concrete details. When the narrator tells Jerry that she is leaving, he goes away without answering. "When he went away, I remember that a new moon hung over the mountains, and I watched him go in silence up the hill." What mood is evoked by the concrete detail of the moon?

Responding in Writing

Lyric Poem. A **lyric poem** is a highly musical verse that expresses the emotions of a speaker. Think about how the loss of a friendship can change everything. Then consider how Jerry may feel at losing the friendship of the narrator. Write a lyric poem from Jerry's point of view about the loss of a friendship. In your poem, use a concrete detail that symbolizes the friendship.

> **Prewriting Suggestion:** Freewrite about friendship. What might symbolize friendship? How would you feel about losing a friend? Use details generated in your freewrite to help your reader experience your emotions about losing a friend.

PROJECT

Photographic History. As a class, research working and living conditions of rural areas in the United States during the 1930s. To begin, check out from the school library books featuring the photographs of Dorothea Lange. As a class, examine the photographs she took from 1935 to 1942 for the Farm Security Administration. Have each person in the class choose one photograph. Write a brief essay about the photograph, expressing what you think it reveals about the working and living conditions of people in rural areas during the Great Depression. Display the photographs on a table in the classroom and read aloud each essay.

"Gwilan's Harp"
by Ursula K. Le Guin

ABOUT THE AUTHOR

Ursula K. Le Guin (1929–   ) was born in Berkeley, California. She received her bachelor's degree from Radcliffe College and her master's degree from Columbia University and went to Paris on a Fulbright scholarship. Returning to the United States to live in Oregon, Le Guin began her prolific writing career, which has included such diverse categories as fantasy, science fiction, and realistic or mainstream fiction. The works for which she is best known include the novels *The Left Hand of Darkness, The Dispossessed,* and *Always Coming Home.* Collections of her short stories include *The Wind's Twelve Quarters, Orsinian Tales,* and *The Compass Rose.*

ABOUT THE SELECTION

Background: Genre. "Gwilan's Harp" is a short story, but it contains many elements of **fables, fairy tales,** and **folk tales.** Like a fable, which is often told to express a moral, this story teaches a lesson. The setting of the story suggests the medieval setting of a fairy tale. Like a folk tale, a story passed from one generation to another in the oral tradition, this story tells of characters in a preliterate culture, one that depends upon oral poets and singers rather than on the written word for the transmission of tales and legends.

Background: Theme. In this story, Le Guin explores the capacity of people to deal with terrible loss and misfortune and to rise above it. "Gwilan's Harp" is a story about the resilience and strength of the human spirit.

"Gwilan's Harp"

URSULA K. LE GUIN

How does Gwilan acquire the harp and her talent for playing the harp?

The harp had come to Gwilan from her mother, and so had her mastery of it, people said. "Ah," they said when Gwilan played," you can tell, that's Diera's touch," just as their parents had said when Diera played, "Ah, that's the true Penlin touch!" Gwilan's mother had had the harp from Penlin, a musician's dying gift to the worthiest of pupils. From a musician's hands Penlin too had received it: never had it been sold or <u>bartered</u> for, nor any value put upon it that can be said in numbers. A princely and most incredible instrument it was for a poor harper to own. The shape of it was perfection, and every part was strong and fine: the wood as hard and smooth as bronze, the fittings of ivory and silver. The grand curves of the frame bore silver mountings chased with long <u>intertwining</u> lines that became waves and the waves became leaves, and the eyes of gods and stags looked out from among the leaves that became waves and the waves became lines again. It was the work of great craftsmen, you could see that at a glance, and the longer you looked the clearer you saw it. But all this beauty was practical, obedient, shaped to the service of sound. The sound of Gwilan's harp was water running and rain and sunlight on the water, waves breaking and the foam on the brown sands, forests, the leaves and branches of the forest and the shining eyes of gods and stags among the leaves when the wind blows in the valleys. It was all that and none of that. When Gwilan played, the harp made music; and what is music but a little wrinkling of the air?

Play she did, wherever they wanted her. Her singing voice was true but had no sweetness, so when it was songs and ballads she accompanied the singers. Weak voices were borne up by her playing, fine voices gained a glory from it; the loudest, proudest singers might keep still a verse to hear her play alone. She played with flute and reed-flute and tambour,[1] and the music made for the harp to play alone, and the music that sprang up of itself when her fingers touched the strings. At weddings and festivals it was, "Gwilan will be here to play," and at music-day competitions, "When will Gwilan play?"

She was young; her hands were iron and her touch was silk; she could play all night and the next day too. She travelled from valley to valley, from town to town, stopping here and staying there and moving on again with other musicians on their wanderings. They walked, or a wagon was sent for them, or they got a lift on a farmer's cart. However they went, Gwilan carried her harp in its silk and leather case at her back or in her hands. When she rode she rode with the harp and when she walked she walked with the harp, and when she slept, no, she didn't sleep with the harp, but it was there where she could reach out and touch it. She was not jealous of it, and would change instruments with another harper gladly; it was a great pleasure to her when at last they gave her back her own, saying with <u>sober</u> envy, "I never played so fine an instrument." She kept it clean, the mountings[2] polished, and strung it with the harpstrings made by old Uliad, which cost as much apiece as a whole set of common harp-

strings. In the heat of summer she carried it in the shade of her body, in the bitter winter it shared her cloak. In a firelit hall she did not sit with it very near the fire, nor yet too far away, for changes of heat and cold would change the voice of it, and perhaps harm the frame. She did not look after herself with half the care. Indeed she saw no need to. She knew there were other harpers, and would be other harpers; most not as good, some better. But the harp was the best. There had not been and there would not be a better. Delight and service were due and fitting to it. She was not its owner but its player. It was her music, her joy, her life, the noble instrument.

She was young; she travelled from town to town; she played *A Fine Long Life* at weddings, and *The Green Leaves* at festivals. There were funerals, with the burial feast, the singing of elegies, and Gwilan to play *The <u>Lament</u> of Orioth*, the music that crashes and cries out like the sea and the seabirds, bringing relief and a burst of tears to the grief-dried heart. There were music-days, with a <u>rivalry</u> of harpers and a shrilling of fiddlers and a mighty outshouting of <u>tenors</u>. She went from town to town in sun and rain, the harp on her back or in her hands. So she was going one day to the yearly music-day at Comin, and the landowner of Torm Vale was giving her a lift, a man who so loved music that he had traded

What does the harp mean to Gwilan?

---

1. **tambour.** Small drum
2. **mountings.** Knobs that hold the harp's strings

a good cow for a bad horse, since the cow would not take him where he could hear music played. It was he and Gwilan in a rickety cart, and the lean-necked <u>roan</u> stepping out down the steep, sunlit road from Torm.

A bear in the forest by the road, or a bear's ghost, or the shadow of a hawk: the horse shied half across the road. Torm had been discussing music deeply with Gwilan, waving his hands to conduct a choir of voices, and the reins went flipping out of those startled hands. The horse jumped like a cat, and ran. At the sharp curve of the road the cart swung round and smashed against the rocky cutting. A wheel leapt free and rolled, rocking like a top, for a few yards. The roan went <u>plunging</u> and sliding down the road with half the wrecked cart dragging behind, and was gone, and the road lay silent in the sunlight between the forest trees.

Torm had been thrown from the cart, and lay stunned for a minute or two.

Gwilan had clutched the harp to her when the horse shied, but had lost hold of it in the smash. The cart had tipped over and dragged on it. It was in its case of leather and embroidered silk, but when, one-handed, she got the case out from under the wheel and opened it, she did not take out a harp, but a piece of wood, and another piece, and a tangle of strings, and a sliver of ivory, and a twisted shell of silver chased with lines and leaves and eyes, held by a silver nail to a fragment of the frame.

It was six months without playing after that, since her arm had broken at the wrist. The wrist healed well enough, but there was no mending the harp; and by then the landowner of Torm had asked her if she would marry him, and she had said yes. Sometimes she wondered why she had said yes, having never thought much of marriage before, but if she looked steadily into her own mind she saw the reason why.

She saw Torm on the road in the sunlight kneeling by the broken harp, his face all blood and dust, and he was weeping. When she looked at that she saw that the time for rambling and roving was over and gone. One day is the day for moving on, and overnight, the next day, there is no more good in moving on, because you have come where you were going to.

Gwilan brought to the marriage a gold piece, which had been the prize last year at Four Valleys music-day; she had sewn it to her bodice as a brooch, because where on earth could you spend a gold piece. She also had two silver pieces, five coppers, and a good winter cloak. Torm contributed house and household, fields and forests, four tenant farmers even poorer than himself, twenty hens, five cows, and forty sheep.

They married in the old way, by themselves, over the spring where the stream began, and came back and told the household. Torm had never suggested a wedding, with singing and harp-playing, never a word of all that.

WORDS FOR EVERYDAY USE:

roan (rōn) *n.*, solid-colored horse with a sprinkling of white hair

plunge (plunj´) *vi.*, move rapidly downward

He was a man you could trust, Torm was.

What began in pain, in tears, was never free from the fear of pain. The two of them were gentle to each other. Not that they lived together thirty years without some quarreling. Two rocks sitting side by side would get sick of each other in thirty years, and who knows what they say now and then when nobody is listening. But if people trust each other they can grumble, and a good bit of grumbling takes the fuel from <u>wrath</u>. Their quarrels went up and burnt out like bits of paper, leaving nothing but a feather of ash, a laugh in bed in the dark. Torm's land never gave more than enough, and there was no money saved. But it was a good house, and the sunlight was sweet on those high stony fields. There were two sons, who grew up into cheerful sensible men. One had a taste for roving, and the other was a farmer born; but neither had any gift of music.

Gwilan never spoke of wanting another harp. But about the time her wrist was healed, old Uliad had a traveling musician bring her one on loan; when he had an offer to buy it at its worth he sent for it back again. At that time Torm would have it that there was money from selling three good heifers[3] to the landowner of Comin High Farm, and the money should buy a harp, which it did. A year or two later an old friend, a flute player still on his travels and rambles, brought her a harp from the south as a present.

The three-heifers harp was a common instrument, plain and heavy; the Southern harp was delicately carved and gilt, but cranky to tune and thin of voice. Gwilan could draw sweetness from the one and strength from the other. When she picked up a harp, or spoke to a child, it obeyed her.

She played at all festivities and funerals in the neighborhood, and with the musician's fees she bought good strings; not Uliad's strings, though, for Uliad was in his grave before her second child was born. If there was a music-day nearby she went to it with Torm. She would not play in the competitions, not for fear of losing but because she was not a harper now, and if they did not know it, she did. So they had her judge the competitions, which she did well and mercilessly. Often in the early years musicians would stop by on their travels, and stay two or three nights at Torm; with them she would play the Hunts of Orioth, the Dances of Cail, the difficult and learned music of the North, and learn from them the new songs. Even in winter evenings there was music in the house of Torm: she played the harp—usually the three-heifers one, sometimes the fretful Southerner—and Torm's good tenor voice, and the boys singing, first a sweet treble, later on in husky unreliable baritone;[4] and one of the farm's men was a lively fiddler; and the shep-

What made it possible for Gwilan to start playing the harp again?

---

3. **heifers.** Young cows
4. **baritone.** Male singing voice lower than a tenor but higher than a bass

herd Keth, when he was there, played on the pipes, though he never could tune them to anyone else's note. "It's our own music-day tonight," Gwilan would say. "Put another log on the fire, Torm, and sing *The Green Leaves* with me, and the boys will take the descant."[5]

Her wrist that had been broken grew a little stiff as the years went on; then the arthritis came into her hands. The work she did in house and farm was not easy work. But then who, looking at a hand, would say it was made to do easy work? You can see from the look of it that it is meant to do difficult things, that it is the noble, willing servant of the heart and mind. But the best servants get clumsy as the years go on. Gwilan could still play the harp, but not as well as she had played, and she did not much like half-measures. So the two harps hung on the wall, though she kept them tuned. About that time the younger son went wandering off to see what things looked like in the north, and the elder married and brought his bride to Torm. Old Keth was found dead up on the mountain in the spring rain, his dog crouched silent by him and the sheep nearby. And the drouth[6] came, and the good year, and the poor year, and there was food to eat and to be cooked and clothes to wear and to be washed, poor year or good year. In the depth of a winter Torm took ill. He went from a cough to a high fever to quietness, and died while Gwilan sat beside him.

Thirty years, how can you say how long that is, and yet no longer than the saying of it: thirty years. How can you say how heavy the weight of thirty years is, and yet you can hold all of them together in your hand lighter than a bit of ash, briefer than a laugh in the dark. The thirty years began in pain; they passed in peace, contentment. But they did not end there. They ended where they began.

Gwilan got up from her chair and went into the hearthroom. The rest of the household were asleep. In the light of her candle she saw the two harps hung against the wall, the three-heifers harp and the gilded Southern harp, the dull music and the false music. She thought, "I'll take them down at last and smash them on the hearthstone, crush them till they're only bits of wood and tangles of wire, like my harp." But she did not. She could not play them at all any more, her hands were far too stiff. It is silly to smash an instrument you cannot even play.

"There is no instrument left that I can play," Gwilan thought, and the thought hung in her mind for a while like a long chord, until she knew the notes that made it. "I thought my harp was myself. But it was not. It was destroyed, I was not. I thought Torm's wife was myself, but she was not. He is dead, I am not. I have nothing left at all now but myself. The wind blows from the valley, and there's a voice on the wind, a bit of a tune. Then the wind falls, or changes. The work has to be done, and we did the work. It's their turn now for that, the children. There's nothing left for me to do but sing. I never could sing. But you play the instrument you have." So she stood by the cold hearth and sang the melody of Orioth's Lament. The people of the household wakened in their

Why does Gwilan have to stop playing again?

What instrument does Gwilan decide to use? What prompts her to use this instrument?

---

5. **descant.** Musical line sung above the main melody to create harmony

6. **drouth.** Archaic spelling of *drought*, a prolonged period of time with no rain

beds and heard her singing, all but Torm; but he knew that tune already. The untuned strings of the harps hung on the wall wakened and answered softly, voice to voice, like eyes that shine among the leaves when the wind is blowing. ∎

Responding to the Selection

Imagine that you are the young Gwilan and have just been given your mother's harp. In your journal, write about the meaning that the harp holds for you. Express your feelings about being part of the long line of musicians to whom the harp has been given.

Reviewing the Selection

RECALLING

1. What do people say about Gwilan's mastery of the harp?

2. What kind of beauty does the harp have?

3. What happens to the harp during Gwilan's journey to Comin?

4. Why does Gwilan hang the two harps on the wall but not play them?

INTERPRETING

5. What gift is passed on with the harp?

6. What details show the harp's beauty?

7. What is probably the reason that Gwilan marries Torm?

8. What events at the end of the story show the passage of time?

SYNTHESIZING

9. How can thirty years be both long and short, heavy and light?

10. For years, Gwilan defined herself as Torm's wife and as a harpist. What does she learn at the end of the story? How does the story demonstrate the capacity of people to rise above suffering and obstacles?

Understanding Literature (Questions for Discussion)

1. **Purpose.** The **purpose** of a piece of writing is the goal that the writer wants his or her work to accomplish. One purpose of "Gwilan's Harp" is to teach a lesson. What lesson does the selection teach?

2. **Metaphor.** A **metaphor** is a figure of speech in which one thing is spoken or written about as if it were another. This figure of speech invites the reader to make a comparison between two things. To what does the narrator of "Gwilan's Harp" compare hands? What characteristics do hands and the other subject of the comparison have in common?

Responding in Writing

Metaphor. Write a metaphor to describe one of the following topics: *music, extreme old age, loneliness,* or *courage.*

> **Prewriting Suggestion:** Begin by looking up *metaphor* in the Handbook of Literary Terms. Then choose your main subject, the **tenor** of your metaphor (example: someone you love). Make a list of its characteristics (example: beauty). Then think of a second, very different thing that has one of these characteristics (example: a rose). This will be the **vehicle** of your metaphor. Finally, write a sentence relating the tenor and the vehicle (example: My love is a red, red rose).

PROJECT

Favorite Music. Bring to class one of your favorite recordings or pieces of music and share it with the class. After you play it, describe in detail why you like it. Try to use musical terms such as tempo, rhythm, and melody in your description.

THEME

"The Gift of the Magi"
by O. Henry

ABOUT THE AUTHOR

O. Henry (1862–1910) was the pseudonym of William Sydney Porter. Born in Greensboro, North Carolina, Henry moved to Texas, where he edited and published a humorous magazine, *The Rolling Stone,* and wrote for a newspaper. The magazine failed, and two years later Henry faced charges for embezzling funds from a bank. He escaped to Central America but later returned and served over three years in an Ohio federal prison. While in prison, Henry began to write short stories. After his release, he moved to New York City, the setting with which most of his work is identified, and published a story a week in *World.* Among the collections of O. Henry stories are *The Four Million, Heart of the West, The Voice of the City, Options,* and *Strictly Business.*

ABOUT THE SELECTION

Background: Technique. O. Henry's stories are famous for their distinctive surprise endings, and **"The Gift of the Magi"** contains, perhaps, the most famous ending of all. In these endings, an ironic event occurs that violates the expectations of the characters, the reader, or the audience.

Background: History. "The Gift of the Magi" was published in the 1906 short story collection *The Four Million.* The twenty-five stories in the collection are set in O. Henry's favorite locale, New York City, and peopled with his favorite characters, lower-middle-class workers, the unemployed, the homeless, and the forgotten. The title of the collection refers to the population of New York City in 1906. O. Henry selected the title in direct rebuttal to an infamous, elitist remark that "there are only about four hundred people in New York society."

"The Gift of the Magi"

O. Henry

How much money does Della have? How did she manage to save it?

One dollar and eighty-seven cents. That was all. And sixty cents of it was in pennies. Pennies saved one and two at a time by bulldozing the grocer and the vegetable man and the butcher until one's cheeks burned with the silent <u>imputation</u> of <u>parsimony</u> that such close dealing implied. Three times Della counted it. One dollar and eighty-seven cents. And the next day would be Christmas.

There was clearly nothing to do but flop down on the shabby little couch and howl. So Della did it. Which instigates the moral reflection that life is made up of sobs, sniffles, and smiles, with sniffles <u>predominating</u>.

While the mistress of the home is gradually <u>subsiding</u> from the first stage to the second, take a look at the home. A furnished flat at $8 per week. It did not exactly beggar description, but it certainly had that word on the lookout for the mendicancy squad.

In the vestibule below was a letter box into which no letter would go, and an electric button from which no mortal finger could coax a ring. Also <u>appertaining</u> thereunto was a card bearing the name "Mr. James Dillingham Young."

The "Dillingham" had been flung to the breeze during a former period of prosperity when its possessor was being paid $30 per week. Now, when the income was shrunk to $20, the letters of "Dillingham" looked blurred, as though they were thinking seriously of contracting to a modest and unassuming D. But whenever Mr. James Dillingham Young came home and reached his flat above he was called "Jim" and greatly hugged by Mrs. James Dillingham Young, already introduced to you as Della. Which is all very good.

Della finished her cry and attended to her cheeks with the powder rag. She

WORDS FOR EVERYDAY USE:

im • pu • ta • tion (im pyo͞o tā´shən) *n.,* charge
par • si • mo • ny (pär´sə mō´nē) *n.,* stinginess
pre • dom • i • nate (prē däm´ə nāt´) *vi.,* prevail

sub • side (səb sīd´) *vi.,* settle, lessen in intensity
ap • per • tain (ap´ər tān´) *vi.,* be a part of

stood by the window and looked out dully at a gray cat walking a gray fence in a gray backyard. Tomorrow would be Christmas Day, and she had only $1.87 with which to buy Jim a present. She had been saving every penny she could for months, with this result. Twenty dollars a week doesn't go far. Expenses had been greater than she had calculated. They always are. Only $1.87 to buy a present for Jim. Her Jim. Many a happy hour she had spent planning for something nice for him. Something fine and rare and sterling—something just a little bit near to being worthy of the honor of being owned by Jim.

There was a pier glass[1] between the windows of the room. Perhaps you have seen a pier glass in an $8 flat. A very thin and very <u>agile</u> person may, by observing his reflection in a rapid sequence of longitudinal strips, obtain a fairly accurate conception of his looks. Della, being slender, had mastered the art.

Suddenly she whirled from the window and stood before the glass. Her eyes were shining brilliantly, but her face had lost its color within twenty seconds. Rapidly she pulled down her hair and let it fall to its full length.

Now, there were two possessions of the James Dillingham Youngs in which they both took a mighty pride. One was Jim's gold watch that had been his father's and his grandfather's. The other was Della's hair. Had the Queen of Sheba[2] lived in the flat across the air shaft, Della would have let her hair hang out the window some day to dry

just to depreciate Her Majesty's jewels and gifts. Had King Solomon[3] been the janitor, with all his treasures piled up in the basement, Jim would have pulled out his watch every time he passed, just to see him pluck at his beard from envy.

So now Della's beautiful hair fell about her rippling and shining like a cascade of brown waters. It reached below her knee and made itself almost a garment for her. And then she did it up again nervously and quickly. Once she <u>faltered</u> for a minute and stood still while a tear or two splashed on the worn red carpet.

On went her old brown jacket; on went her old brown hat. With a whirl of skirts and with the brilliant sparkle still in her eyes, she fluttered out the door and down the stairs to the street.

Where she stopped the sign read: "Mme. Sofronie. Hair Goods of All Kinds." One flight up Della ran, and collected herself, panting. Madame, large, too white, chilly, hardly looked the "Sofronie."

"Will you buy my hair?" asked Della.

"I buy hair," said Madame. "Take yer hat off and let's have a sight at the looks of it."

Down rippled the brown cascade.

"Twenty dollars," said Madame, lifting the mass with a practiced hand.

"Give it to me quick," said Della.

---

1. **pier glass.** Narrow mirror set between two windows
2. **Queen of Sheba.** Biblical queen
3. **King Solomon.** Biblical king

Why does Della need money?

What does Della sell? How much money does she get?

Of what two possessions are the James Dillingham Youngs most proud?

Oh, and the next two hours tripped by on rosy wings. Forget the hashed metaphor. She was ransacking the stores for Jim's present.

She found it at last. It surely had been made for Jim and no one else. There was no other like it in any of the stores, and she had turned all of them inside out. It was a platinum fob chain[4] simple and chaste in design, properly proclaiming its value by substance alone and not by <u>meretricious</u> ornamentation—as all good things should do. It was even worthy of The Watch. As soon as she saw it she knew that it must be Jim's. It was like him. Quietness and value—the description applied to both. Twenty-one dollars they took from her for it, and she hurried home with the eighty-seven cents. With that chain on his watch Jim might be properly anxious about the time in any company. Grand as the watch was, he sometimes looked at it on the sly on account of the old leather strap that he used in place of a chain.

When Della reached home her intoxication gave way a little to <u>prudence</u> and reason. She got out her curling irons and lighted the gas and went to work repairing the ravages made by generosity added to love. Which is always a tremendous task, dear friends— a mammoth task.

Within forty minutes her head was covered with tiny, close-lying curls that made her look wonderfully like a truant schoolboy. She looked at her reflection in the mirror long, carefully, and critically.

"If Jim doesn't kill me," she said to herself, "before he takes a second look at me, he'll say I look like a Coney Island[5] chorus girl. But what could I do—oh! what could I do with a dollar and eighty-seven cents?"

At seven o'clock the coffee was made and the frying pan was on the back of the stove hot and ready to cook the chops.

Jim was never late. Della doubled the fob chain in her hand and sat on the corner of the table near the door that he always entered. Then she heard his step on the stair away down on the first flight, and she turned white for just a moment. She had a habit of saying little silent prayers about the simplest everyday things, and now she whispered: "Please God, make him think I am still pretty."

The door opened and Jim stepped in and closed it. He looked thin and very serious. Poor fellow, he was only twenty-two—and to be burdened with a family! He needed a new overcoat and he was without gloves.

Jim stopped inside the door, as immovable as a setter at the scent of quail. His eyes were fixed upon Della, and there was an expression in them that she could not read, and it terrified her. It was not anger, nor surprise, nor disapproval, nor horror, nor any of the sentiments that she had been prepared

What does Della buy for Jim?

What does Della do when she gets home?

---

4. **fob chain.** Chain for a pocket watch
5. **Coney Island.** Section of Brooklyn, New York, known for its amusement park

WORDS FOR EVERYDAY USE:

mer • e • tri • cious (mer´ə trish´əs) *adj.,* alluring in a false, showy way

pru • dence (prŏŏd´´ns) *n.,* sound judgment

Only a Lock of Hair. *Sir John Everett Millais.*
Manchester City Art Galleries

for. He simply stared at her fixedly with that peculiar expression on his face.

Della wriggled off the table and went for him.

"Jim, darling," she cried, "don't look at me that way. I had my hair cut off and sold it because I couldn't have lived through Christmas without giving you a present. It'll grow out again—you won't mind, will you? I just had to do it. My hair grows awfully fast. Say 'Merry Christmas,' Jim, and let's be happy. You don't know what a nice—what a beautiful, nice gift I've got for you."

"You've cut off your hair?" asked Jim, <u>laboriously</u>, as if he had not arrived at that patent fact yet even after the hardest mental labor.

"Cut it off and sold it," said Della. "Don't you like me just as well, anyhow? I'm me without my hair, ain't I?"

Jim looked about the room curiously.

"You say your hair is gone?" he said, with an air almost of idiocy.

"You needn't look for it," said Della. "It's sold, I tell you—sold and gone, too. It's Christmas Eve, boy. Be good to me, for it went for you. Maybe the hairs of my head were numbered," she went on with a sudden serious sweetness, "but nobody could ever count my love for you. Shall I put the chops on, Jim?"

Out of his trance Jim seemed quickly to wake. He enfolded his Della. For ten seconds let us regard with discreet <u>scrutiny</u> some <u>inconsequential</u> object in the other direction. Eight dollars a

How does Jim react to Della's appearance at first?

week or a million a year—what is the difference? A mathematician or a wit would give you the wrong answer. The magi[6] brought valuable gifts, but that was not among them. This dark assertion will be illuminated later on.

Jim drew a package from his overcoat pocket and threw it upon the table.

"Don't make any mistake, Dell," he said, "about me. I don't think there's anything in the way of a haircut or a shave or a shampoo that could make me like my girl any less. But if you'll unwrap that package you may see why you had me going awhile at first."

White fingers and <u>nimble</u> tore at the string and paper. And then an ecstatic scream of joy; and then, alas! a quick feminine change to hysterical tears and wails, necessitating the immediate employment of all the comforting powers of the lord of the flat.

For there lay The Combs—the set of combs, side and back, that Della had worshipped for long in a Broadway window. Beautiful combs, pure tortoise shell, with jeweled rims just the shade to wear in the beautiful vanished hair. They were expensive combs, she knew, and her heart had simply craved and yearned over them without the least hope of possession. And now, they were hers, but the tresses that should have adorned the coveted <u>adornments</u> were gone.

But she hugged them to her bosom, and at length she was able to look up with dim eyes and a smile and say: "My hair grows so fast, Jim!"

And then Della leaped up like a little singed cat and cried, "Oh, oh!"

Jim had not yet seen his beautiful present. She held it out to him eagerly upon her open palm. The dull precious metal seemed to flash with a reflection of her bright and ardent spirit.

"Isn't it a dandy, Jim? I hunted all over town to find it. You'll have to look at the time a hundred times a day now. Give me your watch. I want to see how it looks on it."

Instead of obeying, Jim tumbled down on the couch and put his hands under the back of his head and smiled.

"Dell," said he, "let's put our Christmas presents away and keep 'em awhile. They're too nice to use just at present. I sold the watch to get the money to buy your combs. And now suppose you put the chops on."

The magi, as you know, were wise men—wonderfully wise men—who brought gifts to the Babe in the manger. They invented the art of giving Christmas presents. Being wise, their gifts were no doubt wise ones, possibly bearing the privilege of exchange in case of <u>duplication</u>. And here I have lamely related to you the uneventful chronicle of two foolish children in a flat who most unwisely sacrificed for each other the greatest treasures of their house. But in a last word to the wise of these days let it be said that of all who give gifts these two were the wisest. Of all who give and receive gifts, such as they are wisest. Everywhere they are wisest. They are the magi. ∎

---

6. **magi.** Wise men from the East who brought gifts to the infant Jesus

Is Jim really upset about the haircut? What has he purchased for Della?

What similarity exists between the magi and the characters in this story? Why does the narrator call Della and Jim not foolish but wise?

WORDS FOR EVERYDAY USE:

nim • ble (nim´bəl) *adj.*, agile

a • dorn • ment (ə dôrn´mənt) *n.*, ornament, decoration

du • pli • ca • tion (dōō´ pli kā´shən) *n.*, copy, double

Responding to the Selection

Imagine that you are either Della or Jim in this story. In your journal, write about what you learned about the art of giving presents.

Reviewing the Selection

RECALLING

1. What amount of money has Della saved for Jim's Christmas present?

2. What information does the narrator provide about Jim and Della's furnished flat?

3. What possession does Della sell for money to buy Jim's gift?

4. What possession does Jim sell for money to buy Della's gift?

INTERPRETING

5. What troubles Della at the beginning of the story?

6. What facts in the story show that Jim and Della enjoyed a "former period of prosperity"?

7. What reaction does Della fear that Jim may have upon seeing her bobbed hair?

8. What action on the part of Jim shows that his love for Della is greater than any gift?

SYNTHESIZING

9. What is probably the reason that the narrator says about Della and Jim, "of all who give gifts these two were the wisest"?

10. What comparison is made between the gifts that Della and Jim exchange and the gifts brought by the magi to the infant Jesus?

Understanding Literature (Questions for Discussion)

1. **Purpose.** The **purpose** of a piece of writing is the goal that the writer wants his or her work to accomplish. One purpose of "The Gift of the Magi" is to teach a lesson. What lesson does the story teach?

2. **Irony.** **Irony** is a difference between appearance and reality. The ending of this story uses a particular type of irony—the **irony of situation.** Irony of situation occurs when an event in the story violates the expectations of the characters, the reader, or the audience. Which of Della's expectations are violated? which of Jim's expectations? which of the reader's expectations?

Responding in Writing

Personal Essay. Write a one-page personal essay in which you tell about a special experience relating to a gift you have either given or received.

> **Prewriting Suggestion:** To brainstorm a list of gift-giving experiences, write the phrase *"special gifts I have given"* on the left-hand side of a piece of paper. On the right-hand side of the paper, write *"special gifts I have received."* Remember that a gift doesn't have to be a thing. Draw a line underneath both headings. Create an idea chart by listing experiences for each heading. Then select the gift-giving experience you wish to write about from your idea chart. On another piece of paper, write the idea you selected and circle it. Then, create a cluster diagram of details that made that experience special. For more information on cluster charts, see the Language Arts Survey, 1.17, "Clustering."

PROJECT

Community Activity. Visit a nursing home or retirement center with several of your classmates and interview some of the residents about their remembrances of special holiday or birthday gifts during economically difficult times. (Make sure to check with the nursing home staff first to make an appointment and to make sure your questions are appropriate.) As a group, write down descriptions of each of the interviews. Then share with the class what you learned about gift giving from the elderly people's experiences.

UNIT REVIEW

The Short Story

VOCABULARY FROM THE SELECTIONS

acknowledge, 176
adornment, 220
agile, 217
amenity, 170
amiably, 151
analytical, 171
animate, 176
anomalous, 203
apathy, 157
appertain, 216
appraise, 170
attribute, 156
avaricious, 156
averted, 157
barbarous, 173
barter, 208
bountiful, 190
burly, 152
cape, 190
clarity, 200

communion, 200
compensation, 157
condole, 152
condone, 172
conduct, 169,
consistent, 199
cower, 179
credulity, 154,
cunning, 171
dank, 164
deplorable, 176
destitute, 192
disarming, 168
discreet, 193
diverting, 176
dubiously, 154
duplication, 220
enthralled, 153
escarpment, 194
eternal, 194

extremity, 166
falter, 217
flotsam, 189
forge, 168
frivolity, 192
frivolous, 155
furrow, 192
furtively, 156
futile, 177
glaring, 168
grisly, 172
illusion, 191
impel, 202
imperative, 177
improvise, 192
imputation, 216
inaudible, 157
inclined, 199
inconsequential, 219
indolently, 165

inevitable, 180
integrity, 200
intercept, 151
intertwining, 208
intricate, 177
isolation, 198
keenly, 153
kinsman, 194
laboriously, 219
labyrinth, 190
lacerated, 167
lament, 209
liability, 157
maligned, 154
medieval, 169
meretricious, 218
mortified, 193
nimble, 220
oppressive, 159
palpable, 164
parsimony, 216

parturition, 202
persist, 153
plunge, 210
poised, 151
precariously, 178
predominate, 216
preserve, 170
presumptuous, 153
proffered, 152
prosaic, 155
prospect, 174
protruding, 178
provoke, 151
prudence, 218
realist, 164
recede, 166
recoil, 180
reverberate, 160
rivalry, 209
roan, 210

scruple, 173
scrutiny, 219
simian, 154
sober, 209
solicitous, 175
subdued, 158
subside, 216
subterfuge, 200
sufficient, 201
suffused, 199
taint, 165
tangible, 165,
tenor, 209,
torrent, 151
treacherously, 201
trifle, 203
uncanny, 178
vermilion, 204
wan, 175
wrath, 211

LITERARY TERMS

allusion, 184
characterization, 163, 197, 206
conflict, 183
description, 162
effect, 162

foreshadowing, 161, 182
genre, 186, 188, 207
hyperbole, 196
irony, 162, 182, 222
irony of situation, 162,

183, 222
lyric poem, 206
magical realism, 188
metaphor, 214
mood, 206
myth, 195, 196

personal essay, 222
plot, 183
point of view, 187, 195–196
purpose, 214, 221
setting, 205

simile, 186
theme, 163, 207
verbal irony, 182
vignette, 187

SYNTHESIS: QUESTIONS FOR WRITING, RESEARCH, OR DISCUSSION

1. What elements make up a plot? Identify the central conflict, inciting incident, climax, and resolution of "The Monkey's Paw" and "The Most Dangerous Game." What are the setting and mood of these stories?

2. For each of the following stories, identify the themes, or main idea: "The Most Dangerous Game," "A Smart Cookie," "Gwilan's Harp," and "The Gift of the Magi."

3. Describe the following characters and what motivates them: Rainsford in "The Most Dangerous Game," Jerry in "A Mother in Manville," and Jim and Della in "The Gift of the Magi."

LANGUAGE LAB EDITING FOR ERRORS IN VERBS

During the editing or proofreading stage of the writing process, check your work to make sure that it is free of errors in verb usage. The following chart describes some common errors.

LANGUAGE ARTS SURVEY

For additional help, see the Language Arts Survey, 2.65.

LANGUAGE ARTS SURVEY

For additional help, see the Language Arts Survey, 2.66–2.67.

LANGUAGE ARTS SURVEY

For additional help, see the Language Arts Survey, 2.68.

LANGUAGE ARTS SURVEY

For additional help, see the Language Arts Survey, 2.70–2.71.

COMMON ERRORS IN VERB USAGE

Improper Shifts in Verb Tense. Throughout a passage, the tenses, or times, of verbs should be consistent.

IMPROPER SHIFT FROM PAST TO PRESENT TENSE:	O. Henry, who publishes many collections of short stories, gained a strong and devoted readership.
CORRECTED SENTENCE:	O. Henry, who published many collections of short stories, gained a strong and devoted readership.

Misuse of Irregular Verb Forms. Many verbs, such as *swim, go, bring, bite, buy, fight,* and *see,* have irregular past tense forms. Make sure to use the proper form in the past tense. If you are unsure about the proper form, check a dictionary.

MISUSE OF IRREGULAR VERB FORM:	In "The Gift of the Magi," the young husband and wife buyed each other Christmas gifts.
CORRECTED SENTENCE:	In "The Gift of the Magi," the young husband and wife bought each other Christmas gifts.

Split Infinitives. An **infinitive** is a verb form made up of the word *to* and the base form of the verb, as in *to play* or *to suggest.* In formal speech and writing, try to avoid placing a modifier between *to* and the verb.

SPLIT INFINITIVE:	It is impossible to definitively say whether the lady or the tiger waits behind the door on the right.
CORRECTED SENTENCE:	It is impossible to say definitively whether the lady or the tiger waits behind the door on the right.

Agreement of Subject and Verb. A verb should agree in number with its subject. If the subject is a compound joined by *and,* the verb should be plural. If the subject is a compound joined by *or, either . . . or,* or *neither . . . nor,* the verb should agree with the nearer subject.

AGREEMENT ERROR:	Ray Bradbury and Ursula K. Le Guin writes science fiction.
CORRECTED SENTENCE:	Ray Bradbury and Ursula K. Le Guin write science fiction.
AGREEMENT ERROR:	Neither "The Gift of the Magi" nor any other O. Henry stories was published under the writer's real name.
CORRECTED SENTENCE:	Neither "The Gift of the Magi" nor any other O. Henry stories were published under the writer's real name.

EXERCISE A   Correcting Errors in Verb Usage

Rewrite the following sentences, correcting the errors in verb usage.

LANGUAGE ARTS SURVEY

For additional help, see the Language Arts Survey, 2.65–2.75.

EXAMPLE: By the time the bus arrived, the students were waiting for half an hour.

By the time the bus arrived, the students had been waiting for half an hour.

1. The monkey's paw brang misery and terror to the White family.

2. What caused the man to suddenly decide to throw the monkey's paw into the fire?

3. O. Henry fans and the uninitiated reader delights in the surprising plot twists in O. Henry's stories.

4. The narrator of "A Smart Cookie" admires her mother and told about her beautiful singing voice.

5. Neither Luisa nor her friends has seen the production of "The Monkey's Paw."

6. When the sun rised on the second day, Rainsford was still alive.

7. Jerry, in "A Mother in Mannville," is honest and worked very hard.

8. Since she is no longer able to play the harp, Gwilan decides to simply sing.

9. Sandra Cisneros and other Mexican-American writers shares their unique cultural perspectives.

10. Could Rainsford have swam away from the island to escape General Zaroff?

EXERCISE B   Revising for Errors in Verb Usage

Rewrite the following paragraph, correcting the errors in verb usage.

LANGUAGE ARTS SURVEY

For additional help, see the Language Arts Survey, 2.65–2.75.

EXAMPLE: "The Monkey's Paw" are one of the most famous of all horror stores.

"The Monkey's Paw" is one of the most famous of all horror stories.

[1] Many people loves to tell stories of horror and the supernatural. [2] When Mary Shelley's *Frankenstein* appears in 1818, it set the standard for horror fiction. [3] In Shelley's classic tale, a young medical student creates a monster from corpses and brang it to life with electricity. [4] Neither the student nor the nearby villagers understands the monster's need for sympathy and acceptance. [5] Shunned by ordinary people, the monster chooses to ultimately punish and destroy its creator.

LANGUAGE ARTS WORKSHOP

SPEAKING AND LISTENING

ORAL INTERPRETATION 3.8

Long before any stories, poems, or songs were written down, people presented stories, poems, and songs orally, as the central character does in Ursula Le Guin's story "Gwilan's Harp." Before the development of writing, oral presentation was the only method available for passing works from generation to generation. In many cultures, entertainers traveled from village to village sharing their own works and their own versions and interpretations of works that they had learned from others. People would come and pay to listen to their retellings. In modern times, people still sometimes go to theaters to hear literary works recited or read aloud. This form of entertainment is less common than it was in the past, but it remains an important part of many jobs. Teachers, librarians, ministers and pastors, lawyers, and television and radio broadcasters, babysitters, and parents, for instance, often present dramatic recitations. The art of presenting a work or group of works orally to an audience is called oral interpretation.

Here are the steps you need to follow to prepare an oral interpretation:

LANGUAGE ARTS SURVEY

For additional help, see the Language Arts Survey, 3.8 and 3.2–3.3.

PREPARING AN ORAL INTERPRETATION
1. **Choose cuttings.** A cutting may be a single piece, a selection from a single piece, or several short, related pieces on a single topic or theme. Most commonly, students choose several short pieces or excerpts on a single theme. Cuttings can be poetry or prose, fiction, nonfiction, or drama. A cutting can be as short as a single line or as long as a page or so.
2. **Write an introduction.** An oral interpretation should begin with a very brief introduction. The introduction should present the overall topic or theme of the interpretation and grab the audience's attention. If you are interpreting a single work, then your introduction should mention the name, the author, and, if appropriate, the translator of each piece. If you are interpreting several short pieces on a single theme, the titles, authors, and translators (if appropriate) should be mentioned in the transitions before each piece.
3. **Write transitions.** Each selection should be introduced by a transition. The transition should mention the title, author, and (if appropriate) the translator of the selection. It should also relate the selection to the overall theme of the interpretation.
4. **Compile the script.** Copy each cutting onto a separate piece of paper. Leave at least one line space between each line of the text. Use this space to make notes on your reading. Make sure to keep the pages of your interpretation in the proper order.

CONTINUED

5. **Develop your interpretation.** Read your script aloud to experiment with variations in volume, pitch, pace, stress, and tone. Try to make your verbal and nonverbal expression mirror what the piece is saying. If there are different voices—for example, if there is a narrator and a character, or if there are two or more characters—distinguish them. As you make decisions about your reading, make notes on your script.

   After your have begun to develop your reading, practice it in front of an audience, a mirror, a video camera, or a tape recorder. Experiment with gestures, facial expressions, stance, and posture to help you communicate your interpretation. However, avoid movement—that's for drama. As you make decisions about your reading, note them on your script.

6. **Revise your script.** As you work on your interpretation, you will develop a better idea of precisely what you want to convey to your audience. Review your introduction and transitions to make sure that they convey your message, and make any necessary revisions. If the revisions are substantial, recopy your script.

7. **Rehearse.** Practice until you have memorized your script.

Outline of an Oral Interpretation, Showing Introduction and Transitions

[Introduction] The city of Philadelphia, the birthplace of the American Constitution, takes its name from Greek words meaning "brotherly love." Learning to love those who are different from us, to recognize them as our brothers and sisters, is a theme that runs throughout American history and literature from the beginning to the present day.

[Transition 1] Long ago, the founder of Rhode Island, Roger Williams, urged his fellow colonists to recognize their similarities with the Native Americans in his poem "Boast Not: Proud English."

[Read Poem.]

[Transition 2] More recently, the Reverend Martin Luther King, Jr., put into immortal words his vision of a future in which people from different backgrounds treat one another as brothers and sisters. These lines come from his famous speech, "I Have a Dream."

[Read Lines from Speech.] Long ago, the founder of Rhode Island, Roger Williams, urged his fellow

---

EXERCISE A   Preparing and Presenting an Oral Interpretation

Choose one of the following themes: friendship, nature, equality, diversity, love. Then choose from two to four cuttings from this text that represent the theme you chose. The cuttings can be either complete selections or excerpts from longer selections. Follow the directions in this lesson to prepare an oral interpretation to present to your class.

Room in Brooklyn. *Edward Hopper. Courtesy, Museum of Fine Arts, Boston*

D rama is life with the dull bits cut out.

—Alfred Hitchcock

The Hitchhiker
by Lucille Fletcher

ABOUT THE AUTHOR

Lucille Fletcher (1912–) wrote radio dramas during the so-called "Golden Age of Radio" in the 1930s and '40s. She has also written short stories, novels, and screenplays for movies and for television. Her most famous works are *Sorry, Wrong Number* and *The Hitchhiker.* The former work has appeared in stage, television, and movie versions.

ABOUT THE SELECTION

Background: Genre and Technique. *The Hitchhiker* is a **radio play.** As such, it depends entirely on sound, for there is no visual component to the audience's experience. Bear this in mind as you read the play. Everything that you read is meant to be heard. In place of the written program that one might receive when going to the theater, the script contains a narrator, who introduces the play. In place of visual presentations of people, objects, and scenes, the script calls for sound effects and descriptions given by the characters. As you read the play, notice how the scenes are carefully painted by the characters, so that a listener can recreate each scene in his or her mind's eye. Many people find that listening to a radio play can be an even more powerful experience than seeing a movie or a television program, because a radio play allows the audience to imagine the action. Often what we imagine is more intense than anything that we might actually see.

The Hitchhiker

LUCILLE FLETCHER

CHARACTERS

ORSON WELLES, *narrator*
RONALD ADAMS
MOTHER
VOICE
MECHANIC
HENRY
WOMAN

GIRL
GALLUP OPERATOR
LONG DISTANCE OPERATOR
ALBUQUERQUE OPERATOR
NEW YORK OPERATOR
MRS. WHITNEY

WELLES. *(narrating)* Good evening, this is Orson Welles. . . .

MUSIC. *In.*

WELLES. Personally I've never met anybody who didn't like a good ghost story, but I know a lot of people who think there are a lot of people who don't like a good ghost story. For the benefit of these, at least, I go on record at the <u>outset</u> of this evening's entertainment with the sober assurance that, although blood may be curdled on the program, none will be spilt. There's no shooting, knifing, throt-tling, axing, or poisoning here. No clanking chains, no cobwebs, no bony and/or hairy hands appearing from secret panels or, better yet, bedroom curtains. If it's any part of that dear old <u>phosphorescent</u> foolishness that people who don't like ghost stories don't like, then again, I promise you we haven't got it. What we do have is a thriller. If it's half as good as we think it is, you can call it a shocker, and we present it proudly and without apologies. After all, a story doesn't have to appeal to the heart—it can also appeal

How will this
ghost story differ
from others?

**WORDS FOR
EVERYDAY USE:**

out • set (out´set´) *n.*, beginning; start

phos • pho • res • cent (fäs´fə re´sənt) *adj.*, luminescent, giving
off light

to the spine. Sometimes you want your heart to be warmed—sometimes you want your spine to tingle. The tingling, it's to be hoped, will be quite audible as you listen tonight to *The Hitchhiker*—That's the name of our story, *The Hitchhiker*—

SOUND.   *Automobile wheels humming over concrete road.*

MUSIC.   *Something weird and shuddery.*

ADAMS. (*narrating*)   I am in an auto camp[1] on Route Sixty-Six just west of Gallup, New Mexico. If I tell it, perhaps it will help me. It will keep me from going mad. But I must tell this quickly. I am not mad now. I feel perfectly well, except that I am running a slight temperature. My name is Ronald Adams. I am thirty-six years of age, unmarried, tall, dark, with a black mustache. I drive a 1940 Ford V-8, license number 6V-7989. I was born in Brooklyn.[2] All this I know. I know that I am, at this moment, perfectly sane. That it is not I, who has gone mad—but something else—something utterly beyond my control. But I must speak quickly . . . very quickly. At any moment the link with life may break. This may be the last thing I ever tell on earth . . . the last night I ever see the stars. . . .

MUSIC.   *In.*

ADAMS. (*narrating*)   Six days ago I left Brooklyn to drive to California. . . .

MOTHER.   Goodbye, son. Good luck to you, my boy. . . .

ADAMS.   Goodbye, mother. Here—give me a kiss, and then I'll go. . . .

MOTHER.   I'll come out with you to the car.

ADAMS.   No. It's raining. Stay here at the door. Hey—what is this? Tears? I thought you promised me you wouldn't cry.

MOTHER.   I know dear. I'm sorry. But I—do hate to see you go.

ADAMS.   I'll be back. I'll only be on the coast three months.

MOTHER.   Oh—it isn't that. It's just—the trip. Ronald—I really wish you weren't driving.

ADAMS.   Oh—mother. There you go again. People do it every day.

MOTHER.   I know. But you'll be careful, won't you. Promise me you'll be extra careful. Don't fall asleep—or drive fast—or pick up any strangers on the road. . . .

ADAMS.   Lord, no. You'd think I was still seventeen to hear you talk—

MOTHER.   And wire me as soon as you get to Hollywood, won't you, son?

ADAMS.   Of course I will. Now don't you worry. There isn't anything going to happen. It's just eight days of perfectly simple driving on smooth, decent, civilized roads, with a hotdog or a hamburger stand every ten miles. . . . (*Fade*)

SOUND.   *Auto hum.*

MUSIC.   *In.*

ADAMS. (*narrating*)   I was in excellent spirits. The drive ahead of me, even the loneliness, seemed like a lark. But I reckoned without *him.*

MUSIC.   *Changes to something weird and empty.*

---

1. **auto camp.** Highway rest area
2. **Brooklyn.** One of the five boroughs of New York City; located south of the island of Manhattan

What does Adams's mother fear?

How does the writer communicate the setting and build suspense and mystery at the beginning of the play?

ADAMS. (*narrating*) Crossing Brooklyn Bridge that morning in the rain, I saw a man leaning against the cables. He seemed to be waiting for a lift. There were spots of fresh rain on his shoulders. He was carrying a cheap overnight bag in one hand. He was thin, <u>nondescript</u>, with a cap pulled down over his eyes. He stepped off the walk right in front of me and, if I hadn't swerved hard, I'd have hit him.

SOUND. *Terrific skidding.*

MUSIC. *In.*

ADAMS. (*narrating*) I would have forgotten him completely, except that just an hour later, while crossing the Pulaski Skyway over the Jersey flats,[3] I saw him again. At least, he looked like the same person. He was standing now, with one thumb pointing west. I couldn't figure out how he'd got there, but I thought probably one of those fast trucks had picked him up, beaten me to the Skyway, and let him off. I didn't stop for him. Then—late that night, I saw him again.

MUSIC. *Changing.*

ADAMS. (*narrating*) It was on the New Pennsylvania Turnpike between Harrisburg and Pittsburgh. It's two hundred and sixty-five miles long, with a very high speed limit. I was just slowing down for one of the tunnels— when I saw him—standing under an arc light by the side of the road. I could see him quite distinctly. The bag, the cap, even the spots of fresh rain spat-

tered over his shoulders. He hailed me this time. . . .

VOICE. (*very spooky and faint*) Hall-ooo. . . . (*It echoes as though coming through the tunnel.*) Hall-ooo. . . !

ADAMS. (*narrating*) I stepped on the gas like a shot. That's lonely country through the Alleghenies, and I had no intention of stopping. Besides, the coincidence, or whatever it was, gave me the willies. I stopped at the next gas station.

SOUND. *Auto tires screeching to stop . . . horn honk.*

MECHANIC. Yes, sir.

ADAMS. Fill her up.

MECHANIC. Certainly, sir. Check your oil, sir?

ADAMS. No, thanks.

SOUND. *Gas being put into car.*

MECHANIC. Nice night, isn't it?

ADAMS. Yes. It—hasn't been raining here recently, has it?

MECHANIC. Not a drop of rain all week.

ADAMS. I suppose that hasn't done your business any harm.

MECHANIC. Oh—people drive through here all kinds of weather. Mostly business, you know. There aren't many pleasure cars out on the Turnpike this season of the year.

---

3. **Pulaski Skyway . . . Jersey flats.** Name of an overpass that crosses a marshy area in northeastern New Jersey

What is unusual about the hitchhiker's voice?

How do the sound effects help to communicate the action?

Why is Adams asking about the rain?

ADAMS. I suppose not. (*casually*) What about hitchhikers?

MECHANIC. (*laughing*) Hitchhikers here?

ADAMS. What's the matter? Don't you ever see any?

MECHANIC. Not much. If we did, it'd be a sight for sore eyes.

ADAMS. Why?

MECHANIC. A guy'd be a fool who started out to hitch rides on this road. Look at it. It's two hundred and sixty-five miles long, there's practically no speed limit, and it's a straightaway. Now what car is going to stop to pick up a guy under those conditions? Would you stop?

ADAMS. No. (*He answers slowly, with puzzled emphasis.*) Then you've never seen anybody?

MECHANIC. Nope. Mebbe they get the lift before the Turnpike starts—I mean, you know—just before the toll house—but then it'd be a mighty long ride. Most cars wouldn't want to pick up a guy for that long a ride. And you know—this is pretty lonesome country here—mountains, and woods . . . You ain't seen anybody like that, have you?

ADAMS. No. (*quickly*) Oh no, not at all. It was—just a—technical question.

MECHANIC. I see. Well—that'll be just a dollar forty-nine—with the tax. . . . (*Fade*)

SOUND. *Auto hum up.*

MUSIC. *Changing.*

How do the mechanic's comments add to the mystery?

ADAMS. (*narrating*) The thing gradually passed from my mind, as sheer coincidence. I had a good night's sleep in Pittsburgh. I did not think about the man all next day—until just outside of Zanesville, Ohio, I saw him again.

MUSIC. *Dark, <u>ominous</u> note.*

ADAMS. (*narrating*) It was a bright sun-shiny afternoon. The peaceful Ohio fields, brown with the autumn stubble, lay dreaming in the golden light. I was driving slowly, drinking it in, when the road suddenly ended in a detour. In front of the barrier, he was standing.

MUSIC. *In.*

ADAMS. (*narrating*) Let me explain about his appearance before I go on. I repeat. There was nothing sinister about him. He was as drab as a mud fence. Nor was his attitude menacing. He merely stood there, waiting, almost drooping a little, the cheap overnight bag in his hand. He looked as though he had been waiting there for hours. Then he looked up. He hailed me. He started to walk forward.

VOICE. (*far off*) Hall-ooo . . . Hall-ooo. . . .

ADAMS. (*narrating*) I had stopped the car, of course, for the detour. And for a few moments, I couldn't seem to find the new road. I knew he must be thinking that I had stopped for him.

VOICE. (*sounding closer now*) Hall-ooo . . . Halll . . . ooo. . . .

SOUND. *Gears jamming . . . sound of motor turning over hard . . . nervous accelerator.*

WORDS FOR EVERYDAY USE: om • i • nous (äm´ə nəs) *adj.*, threatening, sinister

Study for Portrait of Van Gogh III.
Francis Bacon, 1957. Hirshhorn Museum and Sculpture Garden, Smithsonian Institution. Gift of Joseph H. Hirshhorn Foundation, 1966.

VOICE. (*closer*) Hall . . . oooo. . . .

ADAMS. (*with panic in his voice*) No. Not just now. Sorry. . . .

VOICE. (*closer*) Going to California?

SOUND. *Starter starting . . . gears jamming.*

ADAMS. (*as though sweating blood*) No. Not today. The other way. Going to New York. Sorry . . . sorry. . . .

SOUND. *Car starts with squeal of wheels on dirt . . . into auto hum.*

MUSIC. *In.*

ADAMS. (*narrating*) After I got the car back onto the road again, I felt like a fool. Yet the thought of picking him up, of having him sit beside me was somehow unbearable. Yet, at the same time, I felt, more than ever, unspeakably alone.

SOUND. *Auto hum up.*

ADAMS. (*narrating*) Hour after hour went by. The fields, the towns ticked off, one by one. The lights changed. I knew now that I was going to see him again. And though I dreaded the sight, I caught myself searching the side of the road, waiting for him to appear.

SOUND. *Auto hum up . . . car screeches to a halt . . . impatient honk two or three times . . . door being unbolted.*

SLEEPY MAN'S VOICE. Yep? What is it? What do you want?

ADAMS. (*breathless*) You sell sandwiches and pop here, don't you?

VOICE. (*cranky*) Yep. We do. In the daytime. But we're closed up now for the night.

ADAMS. I know. But—I was wondering if you could possibly let me have a cup of coffee—black coffee.

VOICE. Not at this time of night, mister. My wife's the cook and she's in bed. Mebbe further down the road—at the Honeysuckle Rest. . . .

SOUND. *Door squeaking on hinges as though being closed.*

ADAMS. No—no. Don't shut the door. (*shakily*) Listen—just a minute ago, there was a man standing here—right beside this stand—a suspicious looking man. . . .

WOMAN'S VOICE. (*from distance*) Henry? Who is it, Henry?

HENRY. It's nobuddy, mother. Just a feller thinks he wants a cup of coffee. Go back into bed.

ADAMS. I don't mean to disturb you. But you see, I was driving along—when I just happened to look—and there he was. . . .

HENRY. What was he doing?

ADAMS. Nothing. He ran off—when I stopped the car.

HENRY. Then what of it? That's nothing to wake a man in the middle of his sleep about. (*sternly*) Young man, I've got a good mind to turn you over to the local sheriff.

ADAMS. But—I—

HENRY. You've been taking a nip,[4] that's what you've been doing. And you haven't got anything better to do than to wake decent folk out of their hard-earned sleep. Get going. Go on.

Why does Henry react in this way? What is peculiar about the way in which Adams is behaving?

ADAMS. But—he looked as though he were going to rob you.

HENRY. I ain't got nothin' in this stand to lose. Now—on your way before I call out Sheriff Oakes. (*Fade*)

SOUND. *Auto hum up.*

ADAMS. (*narrating*) I got into the car again, and drove on slowly. I was beginning to hate the car. If I could have found a place to stop . . . to rest a little. But I was in the Ozark Mountains of Missouri now. The few resort places there were closed. Only an occasional log cabin, seemingly deserted, broke the monotony of the wild wooded landscape. I had seen him at that roadside stand; I knew I would see him again—perhaps at the next turn of the road. I knew that when I saw him next, I would run him down. . . .

SOUND. *Auto hum up.*

ADAMS. But I did not see him again until late next afternoon . . .

SOUND. *Warning system at train crossing.*

ADAMS. (*narrating*) I had stopped the car at a sleepy little junction just across the border into Oklahoma—to let a train pass by—when he appeared, across the tracks, leaning against a telephone pole.

SOUND. *Distant sound of train chugging . . . bell ringing steadily.*

ADAMS. (*narrating, very tensely*) It was a perfectly airless, dry day. The red clay of Oklahoma was baking under the southwestern sun. Yet there were spots of fresh rain on his shoulders. I couldn't stand that. Without thinking,

---

4. **taking a nip.** Having a drink of something alcoholic

blindly, I started the car across the tracks.

SOUND. *Train chugging closer.*

ADAMS. (*narrating*) He didn't even look up at me. He was staring at the ground. I stepped on the gas hard, veering the wheel sharply toward him. I could hear the train in the distance now, but I didn't care. Then something went wrong with the car. It stalled right on the tracks.

SOUND. *Train chugging closer. Above this, sound of car stalling.*

ADAMS. (*narrating*) The train was coming closer. I could hear its bell ringing, and the cry of its whistle. Still he stood there. And now—I knew that he was beckoning—beckoning me to my death.

SOUND. *Train chugging close. Whistle blows wildly. Then train rushes up and by with pistons going.*

ADAMS. (*narrating*) Well—I frustrated him that time. The starter had worked at last. I managed to back up. But when the train passed, he was gone. I was all alone in the hot dry afternoon.

SOUND. *Train retreating. Crickets begin to sing in background.*

MUSIC. *In.*

ADAMS. (*narrating*) After that, I knew I had to do something. I didn't know who this man was or what he wanted of me. I only knew that from now on, I must not let myself be alone on the road for one single moment.

SOUND. *Auto hum up. Slow down. Stop. Door opening.*

ADAMS. Hello, there. Like a ride?

GIRL. Well what do you think? How far you going?

ADAMS. Amarillo . . . I'll take you all the way to Amarillo.

GIRL. Amarillo Texas?

ADAMS. I'll drive you there.

GIRL. Gee!

SOUND. *Door closes—car starts.*

MUSIC. *In.*

GIRL. Mind if I take off my shoes? My dogs[5] are killing me.

ADAMS. Go right ahead.

GIRL. Gee, what a break this is. A swell car, a decent guy, and driving all the way to Amarillo. All I been getting so far is trucks.

ADAMS. Hitchhike much?

GIRL. Sure. Only it's tough sometimes, in these great open spaces, to get the breaks.

ADAMS. I should think it would be. Though I'll bet if you get a good pickup in a fast car, you can get to places faster than—say, another person, in another car?

GIRL. I don't get you.

ADAMS. Well, take me, for instance. Suppose I'm driving across the country, say, at a nice steady clip of about forty-five miles an hour. Couldn't a girl like you, just standing beside the road, waiting for lifts, beat me to town after town—provided she got picked up every time in a car doing from sixty-five to seventy miles an hour?

GIRL. I dunno. Maybe and maybe not. What difference does it make?

ADAMS. Oh—no difference. It's just a—crazy idea I had sitting here in the car.

---

5. **dogs.** Feet (slang)

GIRL. (*laughing*)   Imagine spending your time in a swell car thinking of things like that!

ADAMS.   What would you do instead?

GIRL. (*admiringly*)   What would I do? If I was a good-looking fellow like yourself? Why—I'd just enjoy myself—every minute of the time. I'd sit back, and relax, and if I saw a good-looking girl along the side of the road . . . (*sharply*) Hey! Look out!

ADAMS. (*breathlessly*)   Did you see him too?

GIRL.   See who?

ADAMS.   That man. Standing beside the barbed wire fence.

GIRL.   I didn't see—anybody. There wasn't nothing but a bunch of steers—and the barbed wire fence. What did you think you was doing? Trying to run into the barbed wire fence?

ADAMS.   There was a man there, I tell you . . . a thin gray man, with an overnight bag in his hand. And I was trying to—run him down.

GIRL.   Run him down? You mean—kill him?

ADAMS.   He's a sort of—phantom. I'm trying to get rid of him—or else prove that he's real. But (*desperately*) you say you didn't see him back there? You're sure?

GIRL. (*queerly*)   I didn't see a soul. And as far as that's concerned, mister . . .

ADAMS.   Watch for him the next time, then. Keep watching. Keep your eyes peeled on the road. He'll turn up again—maybe any minute now. (*excitedly*) There. Look there—

SOUND.   *Auto sharply veering and skidding. Girl screams.*

SOUND.   *Crash of car going into barbed wire fence. Frightened lowing of steer.*

GIRL.   How does this door work? I—I'm gettin' outta here.

ADAMS.   Did you see him that time?

GIRL (*sharply*)   No. I didn't see him that time. And personally, mister, I don't expect never to see him. All I want to do is to go on living—and I don't see how I will very long driving with you—

ADAMS.   I'm sorry. I—I don't know what came over me. (*frightened*) Please—don't go. . . .

GIRL.   So if you'll excuse me, mister—

ADAMS.   You can't go. Listen, how would you like to go to California? I'll drive you to California.

GIRL.   Seeing pink elephants all the way? No thanks.

ADAMS. (*desperately*)   I could get you a job there. You wouldn't have to be a waitress. I have friends there—my name is Ronald Adams—You can check up.

SOUND.   *Door opens.*

GIRL.   Uhn-hunh. Thanks just the same.

ADAMS.   Listen. Please. For just one minute. Maybe you think I am half cracked. But this man. You see, I've been seeing this man all the way across the country. He's been following me. And if you could only help me—stay with me—until I reach the coast—

GIRL.   You know what I think you need, big boy? Not a girl friend. Just a good dose of sleep . . . There, I got it now.

SOUND. *Door opens . . . slams.*

ADAMS. No. You can't go.

GIRL. (*screams*) Leave your hands offa me, do you hear! Leave your—

ADAMS. Come back here, please, come back.

SOUND. *Struggle . . . slap . . . footsteps running away on gravel . . . lowing of steer.*

ADAMS. (*narrating*) She ran from me, as though I were a monster. A few minutes later, I saw a passing truck pick her up. I knew then that I was utterly alone.

SOUND. *Lowing of steer up.*

ADAMS. (*narrating*) I was in the heart of the great Texas prairies. There wasn't a car on the road after the truck went by. I tried to figure out what to do, how to get hold of myself. If I could find a place to rest. Or even, if I could sleep right here in the car for a few hours, along the side of the road . . . I was getting my winter overcoat out of the back seat to use as a blanket, (Hall-ooo), when I saw him coming toward me (Hall-ooo), emerging from the herd of moving steer . . .

VOICE. Hall-ooo . . . Hall-oooo . . .

SOUND. *Auto starting violently . . . up to steady hum.*

MUSIC. *In.*

ADAMS. (*narrating*) I didn't wait for him to come any closer. Perhaps I should have spoken to him then, fought it out then and there. For now he began to be everywhere. Whenever I stopped, even for a moment—for gas, for oil, for a drink of pop, a cup of coffee, a sandwich—he was there.

MUSIC. *Faster.*

ADAMS. (*narrating*) I saw him standing outside the auto camp in Amarillo that night, when I dared to slow down. He was sitting near the drinking fountain in a little camping spot just inside the border of New Mexico.

MUSIC. *Faster.*

ADAMS. (*narrating*) He was waiting for me outside the Navajo Reservation,[6] where I stopped to check my tires. I saw him in Albuquerque where I bought twelve gallons of gas . . . I was afraid now, afraid to stop. I began to drive faster and faster. I was in lunar landscape now—the great arid mesa country of New Mexico. I drove through it with the indifference of a fly crawling over the face of the moon.

MUSIC. *Faster.*

ADAMS. (*narrating*) But now he didn't even wait for me to stop. Unless I drove at eighty-five miles an hour over those endless roads—he waited for me at every other mile. I would see his figure, shadowless, flitting before me, still in its same attitude, over the cold and lifeless ground, flitting over dried-up rivers, over broken stones cast up by old glacial upheavals, flitting in the pure and cloudless air. . . .

MUSIC. *Strikes sinister note of finality.*

ADAMS. (*narrating*) I was beside myself when I finally reached Gallup, New Mexico, this morning. There is an auto camp here—cold, almost deserted at this time of year. I went inside, and asked if there was a telephone. I had the feeling that if only I

Why does the girl run away?

What does this passage confirm about Adams's previous theory that the hitchhiker was getting fast rides and so staying ahead of him?

---

6. **Navajo Reservation.** Land reserved for the Navajo tribe, similar to other reservations for Native American tribes, by the United States government during the period of westward expansion

Why does Adams make the telephone call?

could speak to someone familiar, someone I loved, I could pull myself together.

SOUND. *Nickel put in slot.*

OPERATOR. Number, please?

ADAMS. Long distance.

SOUND. *Return of nickel: buzz.*

LONG DISTANCE. This is long distance.

ADAMS. I'd like to put in a call to my home in Brooklyn, New York. My name is Ronald Adams. The number there is Beechwood 2-0828.

LONG DISTANCE. Thank you. What is your number?

ADAMS. 312.

ALBUQUERQUE OPR. Albuquerque.

LONG DISTANCE. New York for Gallup. (*Pause*)

NEW YORK OPR. New York.

LONG DISTANCE. Gallup, New Mexico, calling Beechwood 2-0828. (*Fade*)

ADAMS. I had read somewhere that love could banish demons. It was the middle of the morning. I knew Mother would be home. I pictured her, tall, white-haired, in her crisp house dress, going about her tasks. It would be enough, I thought, merely to hear the even calmness of her voice. . . .

LONG DISTANCE. Will you please deposit three dollars and eighty-five cents for the first three minutes? When you have deposited a dollar and a half, will you please wait until I have collected the money?

SOUND. *Clunk of six coins.*

LONG DISTANCE. All right, deposit another dollar and a half.

SOUND. *Clunk of six coins.*

LONG DISTANCE. Will you please deposit the remaining twelve cents?

SOUND. *Clunk of four coins.*

LONG DISTANCE. Ready with Brooklyn—go ahead, please.

ADAMS. Hello.

MRS. WHITNEY. Mrs. Adams's residence.

ADAMS. Hello. Hello—Mother?

MRS. WHITNEY. (*very flat and rather proper . . . dumb, too, in a flighty sort of way*) This is Mrs. Adams's residence. Who is it you wished to speak to, please?

ADAMS. Why—who's this?

MRS. WHITNEY. This is Mrs. Whitney.

ADAMS. Whitney? I don't know any Mrs. Whitney. Is this Beechwood 2-0828?

MRS. WHITNEY. Yes.

ADAMS. Where's my mother? Where's Mrs. Adams?

MRS. WHITNEY. Mrs. Adams is not at home. She is still in the hospital.

ADAMS. The hospital!

MRS. WHITNEY. Yes. Who is this calling please? Is it a member of the family?

ADAMS. What's she in the hospital for?

MRS. WHITNEY. She's been prostrated[7] for five days. Nervous breakdown. But who is this calling?

---

7. **prostrated.** The character means *prostrate,* lying flat.

ADAMS. Nervous breakdown? But— my mother was never nervous . . .

MRS. WHITNEY. It's all taken place since the death of her oldest son, Ronald.

ADAMS. The death of her oldest son, Ronald . . . ? Hey—what is this? What number is this?

MRS. WHITNEY. This is Beechwood 2-0828. It's all been very sudden. He was killed just six days ago in an automobile accident on the Brooklyn Bridge.

OPERATOR. (*breaking in*) Your three minutes are up, sir. (*Silence*)

OPERATOR. Your three minutes are up, sir. (*pause*) Your three minutes are up, sir. (*fade*) Sir, your three minutes are up. Your three minutes are up, sir.

ADAMS. (*narrating in a strange voice*) And so, I am sitting here in this deserted auto camp in Gallup, New Mexico. I am trying to think. I am trying to get hold of myself. Otherwise, I shall go mad . . . Outside it is night—the vast, soulless night of New Mexico. A million stars are in the sky. Ahead of me stretch a thousand miles of empty mesa, mountains, prairies—desert. Somewhere among them, he is waiting for me. Somewhere I shall know who he is, and who . . . I . . . am. . . .

MUSIC. *Up.* ■

What inexplicable information does Adams receive from Mrs. Whitney?

Responding to the Selection

Do you agree with the narrator that this is a spine-tingling tale? Why, or why not?

Reviewing the Selection

1. What does Adams tell his mother just before he leaves Brooklyn?

2. What happens as Adams is crossing the Brooklyn Bridge in the rain?

3. Whom does Adams pick up while driving? What does he tell this person? What crazy act does Adams perform?

4. Whom does Adams telephone near the end of the play? What reason does he give for making this call? What does he learn from Mrs. Whitney?

5. What is Adams's mother worried about at the beginning of the play? Given the later events of the play, were her fears justified?

6. What does Adams think happened on the bridge?

7. Why does the person whom Adams picks up run away? Does this person have reason to fear Adams? Why, or why not?

8. What do you think happened to Adams when he swerved on the Brooklyn Bridge?

9. What question does Adams raise at the end of the play? How would you answer this question?

10. What makes the figure beside the road so frightening?

Understanding Literature (Questions for Discussion)

1. **Narrator.** A **narrator** is one who tells a story. In a play, the narrator is the character or person who introduces the work. Not all plays have narrators, but narrators are quite common in radio plays. Who is the narrator of this play? What information does the narrator provide about the play to come? What does the narrator say to capture the attention of the audience and to keep them tuned in?

2. **Foreshadowing. Foreshadowing** is the act of presenting materials that hint at events to occur later in a story. How does the conversation between Adams and his mother at the beginning of the play foreshadow later events?

3. **Suspense. Suspense** is a feeling of expectation, anxiousness, or curiosity created by questions raised in the mind of a reader or viewer. A writer creates suspense by connecting these questions with emotion-producing concrete details. By raising questions, the writer keeps the reader or listener engaged in the action, wondering how the questions will be answered. What about the hitchhiker raises questions in the minds of Adams and the audience for this play? What question does Adams repeat about the hitchhiker at the end of the play? What question does he have about himself at the end of the play? What do you think the answers to these questions might be?

4. **Sound Effects. Sound effects** are sounds used in the production of a play to make the action seem realistic or to signal the presence of something. What are some sound effects used in this play? Why are such effects especially important in a radio play?

Responding in Writing

Ghost Story. The narrator of this play begins by saying that he has "never met anybody who didn't like a good ghost story." Think of a ghost story that you know—perhaps one that you heard when you were a child. Retell the story in your own words. If you can't think of a ghost story that you have heard, create your own.

> **Prewriting Suggestion:** Begin by choosing a central conflict, or struggle, that your story will raise and possibly resolve. On a piece of paper, make a story map describing the other parts of your story: its setting, mood, and main character or characters. Then list the events that will make up your plot. If any of these terms are unfamiliar to you, look them up in the Handbook of Literary Terms. For more information on story maps, read the Language Arts Survey, 1.21, "Story Maps."

PROJECT

Staging a Radio Play. Work with other students to stage all or part of *The Hitchhiker*. Choose a director, actors, and sound effects people. Prepare scripts. Rehearse the play. Then present it to other students. You may wish to tape-record your presentation, listen to the recording, and then do a critique of your performance.

"The Monsters Are Due on Maple Street"
by Rod Serling

ABOUT THE AUTHOR

Rod Serling (1924–1975) grew up in the state of New York and became a major screenwriter for both film and television. Early in his career, Serling wrote realistic dramas. However, he soon switched to writing fantasies to avoid censorship. His television series *The Twilight Zone* became one of the most watched series in the history of the medium. Most *Twilight Zone* teleplays combined science fiction or fantasy elements with biting social criticism and satire. Serling received an Academy Award for Best Screenplay for his feature-length realistic drama *Requiem for a Heavyweight.* He also received a number of Emmy Awards. In addition to *The Twilight Zone,* Serling wrote for and directed the television series *Patterns* and *Night Gallery.*

ABOUT THE SELECTION

Background: Genre and Technique. "The Monsters Are Due on Maple Street" is a **screenplay** for a half-hour television program. Written as an episode for the *Twilight Zone* series, this teleplay is perhaps the best example from the series of Serling's remarkable gift for developing in a few short scenes a believable yet extremely dramatic sequence of events. In typical Serling fashion, these events challenge the characters, causing them to reveal their true selves. As you read the play, you will notice references peculiar to screenwriting, especially notes on camera effects, such as **fading in** (slowly becoming distinct) and **panning** (moving across a field of view).

READER'S JOURNAL

When people join together, they often can accomplish wonderful ends. However, sometimes when people join together, they become a mob. What are the characteristics of a mob? What causes mobs to form? What motivates them? How is mob behavior related to the inability to think and act independently? to rely on one's own values and judgment? Write about these questions in your journal.

"The Monsters Are Due on Maple Street"

ROD SERLING

CHARACTERS

Narrator
Figure One
Figure Two

RESIDENTS OF MAPLE STREET

Steve Brand	**Sally, Tommy's Mother**
Mrs. Brand	**Les Goodman**
Don Martin	**Mrs. Goodman**
Pete Van Horn	**Woman**
Charlie	**Man One**
Charlie's Wife	**Man Two**
Tommy	

ACT I

Fade in on a shot of the night sky. The various nebulae[1] and planet bodies stand out in sharp, sparkling relief, and the camera begins a slow pan across the Heavens.

NARRATOR'S VOICE. There is a fifth dimension[2] beyond that which is known to man. It is a dimension as vast as space, and as timeless as infinity. It is the middle ground between light and shadow—between science and superstition. And it lies between the pit of man's fears and the summit of his knowledge. This is the dimension of imagination. It is an area which we call The Twilight Zone.

What mood is set by the opening of the screenplay?

---
1. **nebulae.** Groups of stars too far away to be seen distinctly; patches of misty light in the night sky
2. **fifth dimension.** Dimension beyond the three spatial dimensions: length, width, and depth—and also beyond the fourth dimension, which is time

The camera has begun to pan down until it passes the horizon and is on a sign which reads "Maple Street." Pan down until we are shooting down at an angle toward the street below. It's a tree-lined, quiet residential American street, very typical of the small town. The houses have front porches on which people sit and swing on gliders, conversing across from house to house. Steve Brand polishes his car parked in front of his house. His neighbor, Don Martin, leans against the fender watching him. A Good Humor man rides a bicycle and is just in the process of stopping to sell some ice cream to a couple of kids. Two women gossip on the front lawn. Another man waters his lawn.

NARRATOR'S VOICE.   Maple Street, U.S.A., late summer. A tree-lined little world of front porch gliders, hop scotch, the laughter of children, and the bell of an ice cream vendor.

There is a pause and the camera moves over to a shot of the Good Humor man and two small boys who are standing alongside, just buying ice cream.

NARRATOR'S VOICE.   At the sound of the roar and the flash of light it will be precisely 6:43 P.M. on Maple Street.

At this moment one of the little boys, Tommy, looks up to listen to a sound of a tremendous screeching roar from overhead. A flash of light plays on both their faces and then it moves down the street past lawns and porches and rooftops and then disappears.

Various people leave their porches and stop what they're doing to stare up at the sky. Steve Brand, the man who's been pol-

ishing his car, now stands there <u>transfixed</u>, staring upwards. He looks at Don Martin, his neighbor from across the street.

STEVE.   What was that? A meteor?

DON. (*Nods*)   That's what it looked like. I didn't hear any crash though, did you?

STEVE. (*Shakes his head*)   Nope. I didn't hear anything except a roar.

MRS BRAND. (*From her porch*)   Steve? What was that?

STEVE. (*Raising his voice and looking toward porch*)   Guess it was a meteor, honey. Came awful close, didn't it?

MRS BRAND.   Too close for my money! Much too close.

The camera pans across the various porches to people who stand there watching and talking in low tones.

NARRATOR'S VOICE.   Maple Street. Six-forty-four P.M. on a late September evening. (*A pause*) Maple Street in the last calm and <u>reflective</u> moment . . . before the monsters came!

The camera slowly pans across the porches again. We see a man screwing a light bulb on a front porch, then getting down off the stool to flick the switch and finding that nothing happens.

Another man is working on an electric power mower. He plugs in the plug, flicks the switch of the power mower, off and on, with nothing happening.

Through the window of a front porch, we see a woman pushing her finger back and forth on the dial hook. Her voice is indistinct and distant, but intelligible and repetitive.

How does the Narrator's last line in the opening contrast with the description that preceded it? What makes this line surprising?

WORDS FOR EVERYDAY USE:

trans • fixed (trans fikst´) *part.*, made motionless
re • flec • tive (ri flek´ tiv) *adj.*, meditative; thoughtful

Photograph courtesy, Digital Stock Corp.

WOMAN. Operator, operator, something's wrong on the phone, operator!

Mrs. Brand comes out on the porch and calls to Steve.

MRS. BRAND. (*Calling*) Steve, the power's off. I had the soup on the stove and the stove just stopped working.

WOMAN. Same thing over here. I can't get anybody on the phone either. The phone seems to be dead.

We look down on the street as we hear the voices creep up from below, small, mildly disturbed voices highlighting these kinds of phrases:

VOICES. Electricity's off.
Phone won't work.
Can't get a thing on the radio.
My power mower won't move, won't work at all.

Radio's gone dead!

Pete Van Horn, a tall, thin man, is seen standing in front of his house.

VAN HORN. I'll cut through the back yard . . . See if the power's still on on Floral Street. I'll be right back!

He walks past the side of his house and disappears into the back yard.

The camera pans down slowly until we're looking at ten or eleven people standing around the street and overflowing to the curb and sidewalk. In the background is Steve Brand's car.

STEVE. Doesn't make sense. Why should the power go off all of a sudden, and the phone line?

DON. Maybe some sort of an electrical storm or something.

Why does Van Horn leave?

CHARLIE. That don't seem likely. Sky's just as blue as anything. Not a cloud. No lightning. No thunder. No nothing. How could it be a storm?

WOMAN. I can't get a thing on the radio. Not even the portable.

The people again murmur softly in wonderment and question.

CHARLIE. Well, why don't you go downtown and check with the police, though they'll probably think we're crazy or something. A little power failure and right away we get all flustered and everything.

STEVE. It isn't just the power failure, Charlie. If it was, we'd still be able to get a broadcast on the portable.

There's a murmur of reaction to this. Steve looks from face to face and then over to his car.

STEVE. I'll run downtown. We'll get this all straightened out.

He walks over to the car, gets in it, turns the key. Looking through the open car door, we see the crowd watching him from the other side. Steve starts the engine. It turns over sluggishly and then just stops dead. He tries it again and this time he can't get it to turn over. Then, very slowly and reflectively, he turns the key back to "off" and slowly gets out of the car.

The people stare at Steve. He stands for a moment by the car, then walks toward the group.

STEVE. I don't understand it. It was working fine before . . .

DON. Out of gas?

STEVE. (*Shakes his head*) I just had it filled up.

WOMAN. What's it mean?

CHARLIE. It's just as if . . . as if every-

Why does Tommy think that Steve shouldn't leave? What is his theory about the strange occurrences on Maple Street?

thing had stopped. (*Then he turns toward Steve.*) We'd better walk downtown. (*Another murmur of assent at this.*)

STEVE. The two of us can go, Charlie. (*He turns to look back at the car.*) It couldn't be the meteor. A meteor couldn't do *this*.

He and Charlie exchange a look, then they start to walk away from the group.

We see Tommy, a serious-faced fourteen-year-old in spectacles who stands a few feet away from the group. He is halfway between them and the two men, who start to walk down the sidewalk.

TOMMY. Mr. Brand . . . you better not!

STEVE. Why not?

TOMMY. They don't want you to.

Steve and Charlie exchange a grin, and Steve looks back toward the boy.

STEVE. *Who* doesn't want us to?

TOMMY. (*Jerks his head in the general direction of the distant horizon*) Them!

STEVE. Them?

CHARLIE. Who are them?

TOMMY. (*Very intently*) Whoever was in that thing that came by overhead.

Steve knits his brows for a moment, cocking his head questioningly. His voice is intense.

STEVE. What?

TOMMY. Whoever was in that thing that came over. I don't think they want us to leave here.

Steve leaves Charlie and walks over to the boy. He kneels down in front of him. He forces his voice to remain gentle. He reaches out and holds the boy.

STEVE. What do you mean? What are you talking about?

TOMMY. They don't want us to leave. That's why they shut everything off.

STEVE. What makes you say that? Whatever gave you that idea?

WOMAN. (*From the crowd*) Now isn't that the craziest thing you ever heard?

TOMMY. (*Persistently but a little <u>intimidated</u> by the crowd*) It's always that way, in every story I ever read about a ship landing from outer space.

WOMAN. (*To the boy's mother, Sally, who stands on the fringe of the crowd*) From outer space, yet! Sally, you better get that boy of yours up to bed. He's been reading too many comic books or seeing too many movies or something.

SALLY. Tommy, come over here and stop that kind of talk.

STEVE. Go ahead, Tommy. We'll be right back. And you'll see. That wasn't any ship or anything like it. That was just a . . . a meteor or something. Likely as not—(*He turns to the group, now trying to weight his words with an optimism he obviously doesn't feel but is desperately trying to <u>instill</u> in himself as well as the others.*) No doubt it did have something to do with all this power failure and the rest of it. Meteors can do some crazy things. Like sunspots.[3]

DON. (*Picking up the cue*) Sure. That's the kind of thing—like sunspots. They raise Cain with[4] radio reception all over the world. And this thing being so close—why, there's no telling the sort of stuff it can do. (*He wets his lips, smiles nervously.*) Go ahead, Charlie. You and Steve go into town

and see if that isn't what's causing it all.

Steve and Charlie again walk away from the group down the sidewalk. The people watch silently.

Tommy stares at them, biting his lips, and finally calling out again.

TOMMY. Mr. Brand!

The two men stop again. Tommy takes a step toward them.

TOMMY. Mr. Brand . . . please don't leave here.

Steve and Charlie stop once again and turn toward the boy. There's a murmur in the crowd, a murmur of irritation and concern as if the boy were bringing up fears that shouldn't be brought up: words which carried with them a strange kind of <u>validity</u> that came without logic but nonetheless registered and had meaning and effect. Again we hear a murmur of reaction from the crowd.

Tommy is partly frightened and partly defiant as well.

TOMMY. You might not even be able to get to town. It was that way in the story. Nobody could leave. Nobody except—

STEVE. Except who?

TOMMY. Except the people they'd sent ahead of them. They looked just like humans. And it wasn't until the ship landed that—

Are Steve and Dan convinced by their own explanations? Why are they trying so desperately to explain what is going on?

---

3. **sunspots.** Temporarily cooler places on the surface of the sun, which appear as dark spots and are sometimes associated with physical disturbances on earth

4. **raise Cain with.** Create commotion with; biblical reference to Cain, the oldest son of Adam and Eve, who murdered his brother Abel

WORDS FOR EVERYDAY USE:

in • tim • i • date (in tim′ə dāt′) *vt.*, make timid or afraid
in • still (in stil′) *vt.*, put in or into little by little
va • lid • i • ty (və lid′ə tē) *n.*, quality of being firmly grounded on facts

The boy suddenly stops again, conscious of the parents staring at them and of the sudden hush of the crowd.

SALLY. (*In a whisper, sensing the antagonism of the crowd*)   Tommy, please son . . . honey, don't talk that way—

MAN ONE.   That kid shouldn't talk that way . . . and we shouldn't stand here listening to him. Why this is the craziest thing I ever heard of. The kid tells us a comic book plot and here we stand listening—

Steve walks toward the camera, stops by the boy.

STEVE.   Go ahead, Tommy. What kind of story was this? What about the people that they sent out ahead?

TOMMY.   That was the way they prepared things for the landing. They sent four people. A mother and a father and two kids who looked just like humans . . . but they weren't.

There's another silence as Steve looks toward the crowd and then toward Tommy. He wears a tight grin.

STEVE.   Well, I guess what we'd better do then is to run a check on the neighborhood and see which ones of us are really human.

There's laughter at this, but it's a laughter that comes from a desperate attempt to lighten the atmosphere. It's a release kind of laugh. The people look at one another in the middle of their laughter.

CHARLIE.   There must be somethin' better to do than stand around makin'

What is unusual about the people's laughter? Why are they laughing in this way?

bum jokes about it. (*Rubs his jaw nervously*) I wonder if Floral Street's got the same deal we got. (*He looks past the houses.*) Where is Pete Van Horn anyway? Didn't he get back yet?

Suddenly there's the sound of a car's engine starting to turn over.

We look across the street toward the driveway of Les Goodman's house. He's at the wheel trying to start the car.

SALLY.   Can you get it started, Les? (*He gets out of the car, shaking his head.*)

GOODMAN.   No dice.

He walks toward the group. He stops suddenly as behind him, <u>inexplicably</u> and with a noise that inserts itself into the silence, the car engine starts up all by itself. Goodman whirls around to stare toward it.

The car idles roughly, smoke coming from the exhaust, the frame shaking gently.

Goodman's eyes go wide, and he runs over to his car.

The people stare toward the car.

MAN ONE.   He got the car started somehow. He got his car started!

The camera pans along the faces of the people as they stare, somehow caught up by this <u>revelation</u> and somehow, illogically, wildly, frightened.

WOMAN.   How come his car just up and started like that?

SALLY.   All by itself. He wasn't anywheres near it. It started all by itself.

Don approaches the group, stops a few feet away to look toward Goodman's car and then back toward the group.

WORDS FOR EVERYDAY USE:

in • ex • pli • ca • bly (in eks´ pli kə blē) *adv.*, without explanation

rev • e • la • tion (rev´ə lā´shən) *n.*, something disclosed

DON. And he never did come out to look at that thing that flew overhead. He wasn't even interested. (*He turns to the faces in the group, his face taut and serious.*) Why? Why didn't he come out with the rest of us to look?

CHARLIE. He always was an oddball. Him and his whole family. Real oddball.

DON. What do you say we ask him?

The group suddenly starts toward the house. In this brief fraction of a moment they take the first step toward performing a <u>metamorphosis</u> that changes people from a group into a mob. They begin to head purposefully across the street toward the house at the end. Steve stands in front of them. For a moment their fear almost turns their walk into a wild stampede, but Steve's voice, loud, <u>incisive</u>, and commanding, makes them stop.

STEVE. Wait a minute . . . wait a minute! Let's not be a mob!

The people stop as a group, seem to pause for a moment, and then much more quietly and slowly start to walk across the street. Goodman stands alone facing the people.

GOODMAN. I just don't understand it. I tried to start it and it wouldn't start. You saw me. All of you saw me.

And now, just as suddenly as the engine started, it stops and there's a long silence that is gradually intruded upon by the frightened murmuring of the people.

GOODMAN. I don't understand. I swear . . . I don't understand. What's happening?

DON. Maybe you better tell us. Nothing's working on this street. Nothing. No lights, no power, no radio. (*And then meaningfully*) Nothing except one car—yours!

The people pick this up and now their murmuring becomes a loud chant filling the air with accusations and demands for action. Two of the men pass Don and head toward Goodman, who backs away, backing into his car and now at bay.

GOODMAN. Wait a minute now. You keep your distance—all of you. So I've got a car that starts by itself—well, that's a freak thing. I admit it. But does that make me some kind of a criminal or something? I don't know why the car works—it just does!

This stops the crowd momentarily and now Goodman, still backing away, goes toward his front porch. He goes up the steps and then stops to stand facing the mob.

We see a long shot of Steve as he comes through the crowd.

STEVE. (*Quietly*) We're all on a monster kick, Les. Seems that the general impression holds that maybe one family isn't what we think they are. Monsters from outer space or something. Different than us. Fifth columnists[5] from the vast beyond. (*He chuckles.*) You know anybody that might fit that description around here on Maple Street?

GOODMAN. What is this, a gag or

About what is Steve worried? What does he want to stop?

What is Steve's attitude toward the neighbors' growing fear of Goodman?

---

5. **Fifth columnists.** Citizens who help the invading enemies of their nation

WORDS FOR EVERYDAY USE:

met • a • mor • pho • sis (met′ə môr′fə sis) *n.,* transformation

in • ci • sive (in sī′siv) *adj.,* penetrating

something? This a practical joke or something?

We see a close-up of the porch light as it suddenly goes out. There's a murmur from the group.

GOODMAN.   Now I suppose that's supposed to <u>incriminate</u> me! The light goes on and off. That really does it, doesn't it?

(*He looks around at the faces of the people.*) I just don't understand this—(*He wets his lips, looking from face to face.*) Look, you all know me. We've lived here five years. Right in this house. We're no different from any of the rest of you! We're no different at all. Really . . . this whole thing is just . . . just weird—

WOMAN.   Well, if that's the case, Les Goodman, explain why—(*She stops suddenly, clamping her mouth shut.*)

GOODMAN. (*Softly*)   Explain what?

STEVE. (*Interjecting*)   Look, let's forget this—

CHARLIE. (*Overlapping him*)   Go ahead, let her talk. What about it? Explain what?

WOMAN. (*A little reluctantly*) Well . . . sometimes I go to bed late at night. A couple of times . . . a couple of times I'd come out on the porch and I'd see Mr. Goodman here in the wee hours of the morning standing out in front of his house . . . looking up at the sky. (*She looks around the circle of faces.*) That's right, looking up at the sky as if . . . as if he were waiting for something. (*A pause*) As if he were looking for something.

What nightmare is beginning on Maple Street?

There's a murmur of reaction from the crowd again.

We cut suddenly to a group shot. As Goodman starts toward them, they back away frightened.

GOODMAN.   You know really . . . this is for laughs. You know what I'm guilty of? (*He laughs.*) I'm guilty of insomnia. Now what's the penalty for insomnia? (*At this point the laugh, the humor, leaves his voice.*) Did you hear what I said? I said it was insomnia. (*A pause as he looks around, then shouts.*) I said it was insomnia! You fools. You scared, frightened rabbits, you. You're sick people, do you know that? You're sick people—all of you! And you don't even know what you're starting because let me tell you . . . let me tell you—this thing you're starting—that should frighten you. As God is my witness . . . you're letting something begin here that's a nightmare!

ACT II

We see a medium shot of the Goodman entry hall at night. On the side table rests an unlit candle. Mrs. Goodman walks into the scene, a glass of milk in hand. She sets the milk down on the table, lights the candle with a match from a box on the table, picks up the glass of milk, and starts out of scene.

Mrs. Goodman comes through her porch door, glass of milk in hand. The entry hall, with table and lit candle, can be seen behind her.

Outside, the camera slowly pans down the sidewalk, taking in little knots of peo-

WORDS FOR EVERYDAY USE: in • crim • i • nate (in krim´i nāt) *vt.*, charge with or show evidence of involvement in a crime *ple who stand around talking in low voices. At the end of each conversation they look toward Les Goodman's house. From the various houses we can see candlelight but no electricity, and there's an <u>all-pervading</u> quiet that blankets the whole area, disturbed only by the almost whispered voices of the people as they stand around. The camera pans over to one group where Charlie stands. He stares across at Goodman's house.*

We see a long shot of the house. Two men stand across the street in almost sentry-like⁶ poses. Then we see a medium shot of a group of people.

SALLY. (*A little timorously*) It just doesn't seem right, though, keeping watch on them. Why . . . he was right when he said he was one of our neighbors. Why, I've known Ethel Goodman ever since they moved in. We've been good friends—

CHARLIE. That don't prove a thing. Any guy who'd spend his time lookin' up at the sky early in the morning—well, there's something wrong with that kind of person. There's something that ain't legitimate. Maybe under normal circumstances we could let it go by, but these aren't normal circumstances. Why, look at this street! Nothin' but candles. Why, it's like goin' back into the Dark Ages or somethin'!

Steve walks down the steps of his porch, walks down the street over to Les Goodman's house, and then stops at the foot of the steps. Goodman stands there, his wife behind him, very frightened.

GOODMAN. Just stay right where you are, Steve. We don't want any trouble, but this time if anybody sets foot on my porch, that's what they're going to get—trouble!

STEVE. Look, Les—

GOODMAN. I've already explained to you people. I don't sleep very well at night sometimes. I get up and I take a walk and I look up at the sky. I look at the stars!

MRS. GOODMAN. That's exactly what he does. Why this whole thing, it's . . . it's some kind of madness or something.

STEVE. (*Nods grimly*) That's exactly what it is—some kind of madness.

CHARLIE'S VOICE. (*Shrill, from across the street*) You best watch who you're seen with, Steve! Until we get this all straightened out, you ain't exactly above suspicion yourself.

STEVE. (*Whirling around toward him*) Or you, Charlie. Or any of us, it seems. From age eight on up!

WOMAN. What I'd like to know is—what are we gonna do? Just stand around here all night?

CHARLIE. There's nothin' else we can do! (*He turns back looking toward Steve and Goodman again.*) One of 'em'll tip their hand. They got to.

STEVE. (*Raising his voice*) There's something you can do, Charlie. You could go home and keep your mouth shut. You could quit strutting around

---

6. **sentry-like.** Like a military guard

What makes Charlie's comment ironic? In what way have the people on Maple Street gone "back into the Dark Ages"? Who has led them there?

WORDS FOR EVERYDAY USE: **all-per • vad • ing** (ôl´ pər vād´iŋ) *adj.*, prevalent throughout

like a self-appointed hanging judge and just climb into bed and forget it.

CHARLIE. You sound real anxious to have that happen, Steve. I think we better keep our eye on you too!

DON. (*As if he were taking the bit from his teeth, takes a hesitant step to the front*) I think everything might as well come out now. (*He turns toward Steve.*) Your wife's done plenty of talking, Steve, about how odd you are!

CHARLIE. (*Picking this up, his eyes widening*) Go ahead, tell us what she's said.

We see a long shot of Steve as he walks toward them from across the street.

STEVE. Go ahead, what's my wife said? Let's get it all out. Let's pick out every <u>idiosyncrasy</u> of every single man, woman, and child on the street. And then we might as well set up some kind of kangaroo court.[7] How about a firing squad at dawn, Charlie, so we can get rid of all the suspects? Narrow them down. Make it easier for you.

DON. There's no need gettin' so upset, Steve. It's just that . . . well . . . Myra's talked about how there's been plenty of nights you spent hours down in your basement workin' on some kind of radio or something. Well, none of us have ever seen that radio—

By this time Steve has reached the group. He stands there <u>defiantly</u> close to them.

CHARLIE. Go ahead, Steve. What kind of "radio set" you workin' on? I never seen it. Neither has anyone else.

How do Don's comments confirm Steve's fears? What is happening to the neighbors' tolerance for differences, or idiosyncrasies?

Who you talk to on that radio set? And who talks to you?

STEVE. I'm surprised at you, Charlie. How come you're so dense all of a sudden? (*A pause*) Who do I talk to? I talk to monsters from outer space. I talk to three-headed green men who fly over here in what look like meteors.

Steve's wife steps down from the porch, bites her lip, calls out.

MRS. BRAND. Steve! Steve, please. (*Then looking around, frightened, she walks toward the group.*) It's just a ham radio set,[8] that's all. I bought him a book on it myself. It's just a ham radio set. A lot of people have them. I can show it to you. It's right down in the basement.

STEVE. (*Whirls around toward her*) Show them nothing! If they want to look inside our house—let them get a search warrant.

CHARLIE. Look, buddy, you can't afford to—

STEVE. (*Interrupting*) Charlie, don't tell me what I can afford! And stop telling me who's dangerous and who isn't and who's safe and who's a menace. (*He turns to the group and shouts.*) And you're with him, too—all of you! You're standing here all set to crucify—all set to find a scapegoat—all desperate to point some kind of a finger at a neighbor! Well now look, friends,

---

7. **kangaroo court.** Unauthorized court that disregards regular legal procedure; named because its enforcement of justice occurs rapidly and unpredictably, in leaps and bounds

8. **ham radio set.** Amateur radio operator's equipment

WORDS FOR EVERYDAY USE:

id • i • o • syn • cra • sy (id´ē ō´sin ´krə sē) *n.,* any personal peculiarity

de • fi • ant • ly (dē fī´ənt lē) *adv.,* openly resisting

the only thing that's gonna happen is that we'll eat each other up alive—

He stops abruptly as Charlie suddenly grabs his arm.

CHARLIE. (*In a hushed voice*) That's not the only thing that can happen to us.

Cut to a long shot looking down the street. A figure has suddenly <u>materialized</u> in the gloom and in the silence we can hear the clickety-clack of slow, measured footsteps on concrete as the figure walks slowly toward them. One of the women lets out a stifled cry. The young mother grabs her boy as do a couple of others.

TOMMY. (*Shouting, frightened*) It's the monster! It's the monster!

Another woman lets out a wail and the people fall back in a group, staring toward the darkness and the approaching figure.

We see a medium group shot of the people as they stand in the shadows watching. Don Martin joins them, carrying a shotgun. He holds it up.

DON. We may need this.

STEVE. A shotgun? (*He pulls it out of Don's hand.*) Good Lord—will anybody think a thought around here? Will you people wise up? What good would a shotgun do against—

Now Charlie pulls the gun from Steve's hand.

CHARLIE. No more talk, Steve. You're going to talk us into a grave! You'd let whatever's out there walk right over us, wouldn't yuh? Well, some of us won't!

He swings the gun around to point it toward the sidewalk.

The dark figure continues to walk toward them.

The group stands there, fearful, apprehensive, mothers clutching children, men standing in front of wives. Charlie slowly raises the gun. As the figure gets closer and closer he suddenly pulls the trigger. The sound of it explodes in the stillness. There is a long angle shot looking down at the figure, who suddenly lets out a small cry, stumbles forward onto his knees and then falls forward on his face. Don, Charlie, and Steve race forward over to him. Steve is there first and turns the man over. Now the crowd gathers around them.

STEVE. (*Slowly looks up*) It's Pete Van Horn.

DON. (*In a hushed voice*) Pete Van Horn! He was just gonna go over to the next block to see if the power was on—

WOMAN. You killed him, Charlie. You shot him dead!

CHARLIE. (*Looks around at the circle of faces, his eyes frightened, his face <u>contorted</u>*) But . . . but I didn't know who he was. I certainly didn't know who he was. He comes walkin' out of the darkness—how am I supposed to know who he was? (*He grabs Steve.*) Steve—you know why I shot! How was I supposed to know he wasn't a monster or something? (*He grabs Don now.*) We're all scared of the same thing. I was just tryin' to . . . tryin' to protect my home, that's all! Look, all of you, that's all I was tryin' to do. (*He looks down wildly*

Again, what is ironic about Charlie's statement? Who actually sends one of his neighbors into a grave?

at the body.) I didn't know it was somebody we knew! I didn't know—

There's a sudden hush and then an intake of breath. We see a medium shot of the living room window of Charlie's house. The window is not lit, but suddenly the house lights come on behind it.

WOMAN. (*In a very hushed voice*) Charlie . . . Charlie . . . the lights just went on in your house. Why did the lights just go on?

DON. What about it, Charlie? How come you're the only one with lights now?

GOODMAN. That's what I'd like to know.

A pause as they all stare toward Charlie.

GOODMAN. You were so quick to kill, Charlie, and you were so quick to tell us who we had to be careful of. Well, maybe you had to kill. Maybe Peter there was trying to tell us something. Maybe he'd found out something and came back to tell us who there was amongst us we should watch out for—

Charlie backs away from the group, his eyes wide with fright.

CHARLIE. No . . . no . . . it's nothing of the sort! I don't know why the lights are on. I swear I don't. Somebody's pulling a gag or something.

He bumps against Steve, who grabs him and whirls him around.

STEVE. A gag? A gag? Charlie, there's a dead man on the sidewalk and you killed him! Does this thing look like a gag to you?

Charlie breaks away and screams as he runs toward his house.

CHARLIE. No! No! Please!

A man breaks away from the crowd to chase Charlie.

We see a long angle shot looking down as the man tackles Charlie and lands on top of him. The other people start to run toward them. Charlie is up on his feet, breaks away from the other man's grasp, lands a couple of desperate punches that push the man aside. Then he forces his way, fighting, through the crowd to once again break free, jumps up on his front porch. A rock thrown from the group smashes a window alongside of him, the broken glass flying past him. A couple of pieces cut him. He stands there perspiring, rumpled, blood running down from a cut on the cheek. His wife breaks away from the group to throw herself into his arms. He buries his face against her. We can see the crowd <u>converging</u> on the porch now.

VOICES. It must have been him.
He's the one.
We got to get Charlie.

Another rock lands on the porch. Now Charlie pushes his wife behind him, facing the group.

CHARLIE. Look, look I swear to you . . . it isn't me . . . but I do know who it is . . . I swear to you, I do know who it is. I know who the monster is here. I know who it is that doesn't belong. I swear to you I know.

GOODMAN. (*Shouting*) What are you waiting for?

WOMAN. (*Shouting*) Come on, Charlie, come on.

MAN ONE. (*Shouting*) Who is it, Charlie, tell us!

DON. (*Pushing his way to the front of the crowd*) All right, Charlie, let's hear it!

Charlie's eyes dart around wildly.

CHARLIE. It's . . . it's . . .

MAN ONE. (*Screaming*) Go ahead, Charlie, tell us.

CHARLIE. It's . . . it's the kid. It's Tommy. He's the one!

There's a gasp from the crowd as we cut to a shot of Sally holding her son Tommy. The boy at first doesn't understand and then, realizing the eyes are all on him, buries his face against his mother.

SALLY. (*Backs away*) That's crazy! That's crazy! He's a little boy.

WOMAN. But he knew! He was the only one who knew! He told us all about it. Well, how did he know? How *could* he have known?

The various people take this up and repeat the question aloud.

VOICES. How could he know?
Who told him?
Make the kid answer.

DON. It was Charlie who killed old man Van Horn.

WOMAN. But it was the kid here who knew what was going to happen all the time. He was the one who knew!

We see a close-up of Steve.

STEVE. Are you all gone crazy? (*Pause as he looks about*) Stop.

A fist crashes at Steve's face, staggering him back out of the frame of the picture.

There are several close camera shots suggesting the coming of violence. A hand fires a rifle. A fist clenches. A hand grabs the hammer from Van Horn's body, etc. Meanwhile, we hear the following lines.

DON. Charlie has to be the one—Where's my rifle—

WOMAN. Les Goodman's the one. His car started! Let's wreck it.

MRS. GOODMAN. What about Steve's radio—He's the one that called them—

MR. GOODMAN. Smash the radio. Get me a hammer. Get me something.

STEVE. Stop—Stop—

CHARLIE. Where's that kid—Let's get him.

MAN ONE. Get Steve—Get Charlie—They're working together.

The crowd starts to converge around the mother, who grabs the child and starts to run with him. The crowd starts to follow, at first walking fast, and then running after him.

We see a full shot of the street as suddenly Charlie's lights go off and the lights in another house go on. They stay on for a moment, then from across the street other lights go on and then off again.

MAN ONE. (*Shouting*) It isn't the kid . . . it's Bob Weaver's house.

WOMAN. It isn't Bob Weaver's house, it's Don Martin's place.

CHARLIE. I tell you it's the kid.

DON. It's Charlie. He's the one.

What are your feelings toward Charlie at this point in the play?

How would you answer Steve's question?

What comment is being made by the aliens about human nature?

We move into a series of close-ups of various people as they shout, accuse, scream, <u>interspersing</u> these shots with shots of houses as the lights go on and off, and then slowly in the middle of this nightmarish <u>morass</u> of sight and sound the camera starts to pull away, until once again we've reached the opening shot looking at the Maple Street sign from high above.

The camera continues to move away until we dissolve to a shot looking toward the metal side of a space craft, which sits shrouded in darkness. An open door throws out a beam of light from the illuminated interior. Two figures silhouetted against the bright lights appear. We get only a vague feeling of form, but nothing more explicit than that.

FIGURE ONE. Understand the procedure now? Just stop a few of their machines and radios and telephones and lawn mowers . . . throw them into darkness for a few hours, and then you just sit back and watch the pattern.

FIGURE TWO. And this pattern is always the same?

Who, according to the aliens, is the most dangerous enemy that people can face? What qualities make this enemy dangerous?

FIGURE ONE. With few variations. They pick the most dangerous enemy they can find . . . and it's themselves. And all we need do is sit back . . . and watch.

FIGURE TWO. Then I take it this place . . . this Maple Street . . . is not unique.

FIGURE ONE. (*Shaking his head*) By no means. Their world is full of Maple Streets. And we'll go from one to the other and let them destroy themselves. One to the other . . . one to the other . . . one to the other—

Now the camera pans up for a shot of the starry sky and over this we hear the Narrator's voice.

NARRATOR'S VOICE. The tools of conquest do not necessarily come with bombs and explosions and fallout.[9] There are weapons that are simply thoughts, attitudes, prejudices—to be found only in the minds of men. For the record, prejudices can kill and suspicion can destroy and a thoughtless frightened search for a scapegoat has a fallout all its own for the children . . . and the children yet unborn. (*A pause*) And the pity of it is . . . that these things cannot be confined to . . . The Twilight Zone! ■

---

9. **fallout.** Radioactive particles falling to earth; for example, after a nuclear explosion

Responding to the Selection

Which character or characters in this selection do you admire? What makes this person or these persons different from the rest of the inhabitants of Maple Street?

WORDS FOR EVERYDAY USE:
in • ter • sperse (in´tər spʉrs´) *vt.*, scatter among other things
mo • rass (mə ras´) *n.*, perplexing state of affairs

Reviewing the Selection

1. What happens at the beginning of the play to all the machines on Maple Street?

2. What explanation does the boy Tommy give of the peculiar events occurring on Maple Street? Where did he get his ideas?

3. Why do the people turn in a mob toward Les Goodman's house? What does Les Goodman do sometimes at night?

4. Where does Pete Van Horn go at the beginning of the play? What happens to him when he returns?

5. How do the people on Maple Street react to what happens to their machines at the beginning of the play? What emotion leads them to react in this way?

6. What are the neighbors' first reactions to Tommy's story? How do their reactions change and why?

7. Why do the neighbors consider Les Goodman's nighttime activity odd? What does their reaction to Goodman's nighttime activity reveal about their level of tolerance for differences?

8. Why does Charlie do what he does to Pete Van Horn? What is the explanation suggested by one of the neighbors?

9. What causes the neighbors on Maple Street to turn into a mob?

10. Who are the real monsters in this play?

Understanding Literature (Questions for Discussion)

1. **Motivation.** A **motivation** is a force that moves a character to think, feel, or behave in a certain way. What motivates the people on Maple Street to turn into a mob? What small differences between people become magnified in their minds? What is this play saying about how people are capable of reacting toward one another in times of stress or crisis?

2. **Analogy.** An **analogy** is a comparison of two things that are alike in some respects but different in others. In the middle of the twentieth century, the countries of

Germany and Italy suffered severe economic hardships. Inflation and unemployment led people to look desperately for solutions and for scapegoats. In both countries, extremely brutal dictators came to power. What similarities are there between the events in Germany and Italy in the mid-1900s and the events described in this play? What political point might the author be making?

3. **Setting.** The **setting** of a literary work is the time and place in which it occurs, together with all the details used to create a sense of a particular time and place. Why is it important that this play be set on an ordinary street, one like thousands of others? What details at the beginning of the teleplay contribute to making the setting seem ordinary and wholesome?

4. **Screenplay.** A **screenplay** is a drama written for television or film. What elements of "The Monsters Are Due on Maple Street" show that it is a screenplay? What special effects might be used in a contemporary production of the play for television or the movies?

Responding in Writing

Ship's Log. Imagine that you are the captain of the alien spaceship in "The Monsters Are Due on Maple Street." Write an entry for your ship's log telling about the experiment that you performed on Maple Street. Explain exactly what you did to bring about the events on Maple Street and why. Also explain the outcome or results of your experiment.

> **Prewriting Suggestion:** Review the play, from beginning to end, making a list of all the strange events that occur. Then decide what the aliens might have done in each case to bring about these events. Finally, think about why the aliens might have done what they did in each case.

PROJECT

Science Fiction Fair. Organize a science fiction fair. Begin by choosing a common theme in science fiction, such as the dangers of technology, visions of the future, or contacts with other intelligences. Then find science fiction stories, plays, and videotapes that deal with this theme. Working with your teacher and with other classmates, organize an event to present selections from these works. You may wish to do readings from stories, to present skits, and to show parts of films. You may also choose to serve refreshments and to come dressed as your favorite science fiction characters.

UNIT REVIEW

Drama

VOCABULARY FROM THE SELECTIONS		
all-pervading, 253	instill, 249	outset, 231
contorted, 255	intersperse, 258	phosphorescent, 231
converge, 256,	intimidate, 249	reflective, 246
defiant, 254	materialize, 255	revelation, 250
idiosyncrasy, 254	metamorphosis, 251	transfixed, 246
incisive, 251	morass, 258	validity, 249
incriminate, 252	nondescript, 233	
inexplicably, 250	ominous, 234	

LITERARY TERMS		
analogy, 259	narrator, 242	setting, 260
foreshadowing, 242	radio play, 230	sound effects, 243
motivation, 259	screenplay, 244, 260	suspense, 243

SYNTHESIS: QUESTIONS FOR WRITING, RESEARCH, OR DISCUSSION

1. What are the major differences between radio and television drama? Explain using examples from *The Hitchhiker* and "The Monsters Are Due on Maple Street."

2. Both *The Hitchhiker* and "The Monsters Are Due on Maple Street" deal with fear of the unknown. What do the characters in these dramas fear? What do they do as a result of their fear? Both dramas have surprise endings. What surprise occurs at the end of each drama?

LANGUAGE LAB EDITING FOR ERRORS IN PRONOUNS

Case is the form that a noun or a pronoun takes to indicate its use in a sentence. The **nominative case** is used for the subject of a verb or for a predicate nominative. The **objective case** is used for a direct object, an indirect object, or the object of a preposition. The **possessive case** is used to show ownership or belonging. The following chart lists common errors in pronoun usage.

COMMON ERRORS IN PRONOUN USAGE

Pronoun as Object of Preposition. Prepositions *always* take an object in the objective case.

EXAMPLES: My mother videotaped *The Twilight Zone* episode for Helen and me.

***Who* and *Whom*.** The pronoun *who* is an interrogative pronoun when it is used to form a question. When it is used to introduce a subordinate clause, it is a relative pronoun. In both situations, the nominative form of the pronoun is *who,* the objective is *whom,* and the possessive is *whose.*

SUBJECT:	The actor who fought with the director is not here.
DIRECT OBJECT:	Whom will the director cast in the lead role?
OBJECT OF PREPOSITION:	To whom should the extras report?

Pronouns in Comparisons. Pronouns in clauses with unexpressed verbs should be the same case as they would have been if the sentence had been completed.

INCORRECT PRONOUN:	I doubt if any of the actors was more nervous than me.
CORRECT PRONOUN:	I doubt if any of the actors was more nervous than I [was].

Agreement of Pronouns and Antecedents. Check the pronouns in your writing to be sure they agree in **number, person,** and **gender** with their **antecedents** (the words to which they refer).

INCORRECT NUMBER:	The stage manager gave each cast member their entrance cues.
CORRECT NUMBER:	The stage manager gave the cast members their entrance cues.

Reference of Pronouns to Antecedents. Avoid weak, ambiguous, indefinite, and general references between pronouns and antecedents.

WEAK REFERENCE:	As the actors entered the stage and the stage lights came on, they squinted.
CLEAR ANTECEDENT:	As the stage lights came on, the actors entering the stage squinted.
AMBIGUOUS REFERENCE:	When the announcer cues the band conductor, he starts the music.
CLEAR REFERENCE:	When the announcer cues him, the band conductor starts the music.
INDEFINITE REFERENCE:	Over the studio door it said, "Taping in progress."
PRONOUN ELIMINATED:	The sign over the studio door read, "Taping in progress."
GENERAL REFERENCE:	Actors sometimes record dialogue to match a scene that has been shot. This is called looping.
SENTENCE REWORDED:	The technique of recording dialogue to match a scene that has been shot is called looping.

EXERCISE A   Avoiding Errors in Pronoun Usage

Rewrite the following sentences, using the correct pronoun from those given in parentheses.

EXAMPLE: My parents took my sister and (I, me) to the premiere of the new play.

My parents took my sister and me to the premiere of the new play.

1. The director heard the rumors that the cast did not like (he, him) but chose to ignore what he had heard.

2. Orson Welles was the actor (who, whom) adapted *War of the Worlds* for the radio.

3. The vain actress complained bitterly when her younger co-star received better reviews than (her, she).

4. Between you and (I, me), I think the character actor stole the show.

5. The movie star, (who, whom) had a reputation of being difficult to work with, could not find a job in Hollywood.

6. The cast gave (us, we) drama critics a private performance.

7. I can't believe that Lyle, who is less experienced than (I, me), was hired as the new producer for the show!

8. Lucille Fletcher is best known for (her, his) dramas *Sorry, Wrong Number* and *The Hitchhiker.*

9. (Who, Whom) did the director cast in the leading role?

10. People in the 1930s and 1940s relied on (our, their) radios for entertainment.

EXERCISE B   Correcting Errors in Pronoun Usage

Rewrite the following sentences, correcting the errors in pronoun usage.

EXAMPLE: When the actors jumped toward the audience, they screamed.

The actors screamed when they jumped toward the audience.

or

The audience screamed when the actors jumped toward them.

1. On some radio programs, one sound-effects person would make all of them.

2. When television competed with radio, it began to decline.

3. In the early days of television, they only broadcast shows in black and white.

4. The stage directions "stage left" and "stage right" are given from the actor's perspective, which might seem backward to someone sitting in the audience.

5. On the play program it announced, "There will be a fifteen-minute intermission between acts."

LANGUAGE ARTS SURVEY

For additional help, see the Language Arts Survey, 2.76–2.82.

LANGUAGE ARTS SURVEY

For additional help, see the Language Arts Survey, 2.83–2.84.

LANGUAGE ARTS WORKSHOP

THINKING SKILLS

LANGUAGE ARTS SURVEY

For additional help, see the Language Arts Survey, 4.1–4.2.

PROBLEM SOLVING

Different problems call for different problem solving strategies. To solve complex problems, you may need to use more than one strategy.

PROBLEM SOLVING STRATEGIES
Rule of Thumb. Think of a strategy that is often used for similar problems and apply it.
Trial and Error. Try various solutions, one after the other.
Represent the Situation. Draw a picture or construct a model.
Divide and Conquer. Divide the problem into parts and then solve the parts one at a time.
Work Backward. Describe in detail the situation that would exist after you solved the problem. Then "work backward" by thinking about what would have to happen for that situation to come about.

EXERCISE A   Selecting Problem Solving Strategies

For each of the following problems, decide which problem solving strategy would be most appropriate and explain your reasoning.

1. Although you're certain that you brought your history textbook home with you, you can't find it when you sit down to study.

2. You've been invited on a ski trip in two months. You want to go, but you will need more money than you have in your savings account.

3. As part of a class project, you and a small group of classmates are creating a bulletin board. The group needs to decide how to organize the display.

DECISION MAKING

LANGUAGE ARTS SURVEY

For additional help, see the Language Arts Survey, 4.3.

You can also use strategies when making decisions.

Pros and Cons. List your options. For each option, list the reasons for choosing it (the pros) and the drawbacks of choosing it (the cons). Then compare the lists.

PROS AND CONS: CHOOSING A SPORT		
	Soccer	Cross Country
Pros	cooperative effort many fans and spectators many teammates	individual achievement more solitude and time for thinking
Cons	can get rough strenuous practices expensive cleats	might get lonely strenuous practices expensive sneakers

Criteria Analysis. List the alternatives across the top of a sheet of paper. List criteria for evaluation along the side of the paper. Assign each alternative and each evaluation criterion a number from one to five. Then add the points for each alternative and choose the one with the highest total.

CRITERIA ANALYSIS: BUYING NEW SHOES				
	Sneakers	Sandals	Brown Loafers	Moccasins
1. Durable	4	2	4	2
2. Attractive	5	5	5	5
3. Affordable	2	3	3	4
4. Versatile	3	2	5	2
5. Comfortable	5	4	4	5
	19	16	21	18

EXERCISE B   Applying Decision Making Strategies

To decide how to spend next summer, you have to choose among working as a counselor at a local day camp, working at the mall, and working on your aunt and uncle's farm 1,200 miles away. Use the pros and cons strategy and then use criteria analysis to evaluate your options. Make charts like those shown in the Language Arts Survey, 4.3, "Decision Making."

Italo-American Celebration, Washington Square. *William James Glackens.*
Courtesy, the Museum of Fine Arts, Boston

f you would not be forgotten as
soon as you are dead, either
write things worth reading or
do things worth writing

—Benjamin Franklin

PREREADING

AUTOBIOGRAPHY

"An Encounter with an Interviewer"
by Mark Twain

ABOUT THE AUTHOR

Samuel Langhorne Clemens (1835–1910) was born in Florida, Missouri. In his late twenties, Clemens adopted his pen name, Mark Twain. The phrase *mark twain,* which means "two fathoms deep," was called from Mississippi riverboats when making depth soundings. When Twain was twelve years old, his father died. Twain was apprenticed to a printer, and soon began writing for his brother's newspaper. Then, from 1857 to 1861, he realized his childhood dream of piloting steamboats on the Mississippi River. At the age of thirty-five, Twain began writing about his early experiences of life on the great river. *The Adventures of Tom Sawyer,* published in 1876, was followed by *Life on the Mississippi* and *The Adventures of Huckleberry Finn.* These are the three books for which Twain will always be remembered. In the 1890s, after Twain suffered a series of financial disasters and the death of his wife and two daughters, the vitality and sly humor of his early work gave way to a dark pessimism. His bitterest works, including *The Mysterious Stranger*, date from this period. Among his numerous other titles are *The Prince and the Pauper, The Tragedy of Pudd'nhead Wilson,* and *A Connecticut Yankee in King Arthur's Court. The Writings of Mark Twain,* published posthumously in 1929, contains thirty-seven volumes.

ABOUT THE SELECTION

Background: Technique. Impostors, frauds, and masters of masquerade crowd the cast of characters in Twain's work. Such characters are central to Twain's humor. In fact, Twain once told an audience that it was a humorist's job to expose all shams. In this selection, the narrator assumes a personality other than his own in order to expose the interviewer's foolishness.

Background: History. In 1894, the same year that he published *The Tragedy of Pudd'nhead Wilson,* the last of his great Mississippi novels, Mark Twain was bankrupt. To pay off his debts, Twain made a worldwide lecture tour. While lecturing, he was interviewed by many journalists. This experience gave him plenty of material to write his satire **"An Encounter with an Interviewer."**

"An Encounter with an Interviewer"

Mark Twain

The nervous dapper, "peart"[1] young man took the chair I offered him, and said he was connected with the "Daily Thunderstorm" and added,—

"Hoping it's no harm, I've come to interview you."

"Come to what?"

"*Interview* you."

"Ah! I see. Yes—yes. Um! Yes—yes. I see."

I was not feeling bright that morning. Indeed, my powers seemed a bit under a cloud. However, I went to the bookcase, and when I had been looking six or seven minutes, I found I was obliged to <u>refer</u> to the young man. I said,—

"How do you spell it?"

"Spell what?"

"Interview."

"Oh my goodness! what do you want to spell it for?"

"I don't want to spell it; I want to see what it means."

"Well, this is astonishing, I must say. I can tell you what it means, if you—if you—"

"Oh, all right! That will answer, and much obliged to you, too."

"In, *in*, ter, *ter*, *in*ter—"

"Then you spell it with an *I?*"

"Why, certainly!"

"Oh, that is what took me so long."

"Why, my *dear* sir, what did *you* <u>propose</u> to spell it with?"

"Well, I—I—hardly know. I had the Unabridged,[2] and I was ciphering

---

1. **peart.** Lively; chipper
2. **Unabridged.** Dictionary that has not been condensed

Why does the narrator search the bookcase? Why does he turn to the interviewer for help? How does the interviewer react to his question?

WORDS FOR EVERYDAY USE:

re • fer (ri fʉr´) *vi.*, direct attention to

pro • pose (prō pōz´) *vt.*, intend

around the back end, hoping I might tree her among the pictures. But it's a very old edition."

"Why, my friend, they wouldn't have a *picture* of it in even the latest e— My dear sir, I beg your pardon, I mean no harm in the world, but you do not look as—as—intelligent as I had expected you would."

"Oh, don't mention it! It has often been said, and by people who would not flatter and who could have no <u>inducement</u> to flatter, that I am quite remarkable in that way. Yes—yes; they always speak of it with <u>rapture</u>."

"I can easily imagine it. But about this interview. You know it is the custom, now to interview any man who has become <u>notorious</u>."

"Indeed, I had not heard of it before. It must be very interesting. What do you do it with?"

"Ah, well—well—well—this is disheartening. It *ought* to be done with a club in some cases; but <u>customarily</u> it consists in the interviewer asking questions and the interviewed answering them. It is all the rage[3] now. Will you let me ask you certain questions calculated to bring out the <u>salient</u> points of your public and private history?"

"Oh, with pleasure,—with pleasure. I have a very bad memory, but I hope you will not mind that. That is to say, it is an irregular memory,—singularly irregular. Sometimes it goes in a gallop, and then again it will be as much as a fortnight[4] passing a given point. This is a great grief to me."

"Oh, it is no matter, so you will try to do the best you can."

"I will. I will put my whole mind on it."

"Thanks. Are you ready to begin?"

"Ready."

Q. How old are you?

A. Nineteen, in June.

Q. Indeed! I would have taken you to be thirty-five or -six. Where were you born?

A. In Missouri.

Q. When did you begin to write?

A. In 1836.

Q. Why, how could that be, if you are only nineteen now?

A. I don't know. It does seem curious, somehow.

Q. It does, indeed. Whom do you consider the most remarkable man you ever met?

A. Aaron Burr.[5]

Q. But you never could have met Aaron Burr, if you are only nineteen years—

A. Now, if you know more about me than I do, what do you ask me for?

Q. Well, it was only a suggestion—nothing more. How did you happen to meet Burr?

A. Well, I happened to be at his funeral one day, and he asked me to make less noise and—

Q. But, good heavens! If you were at his funeral, he must have been dead;

---

3. **all the rage.** Craze; fad
4. **fortnight.** Two weeks
5. **Aaron Burr.** (1756–1836) Vice president of the United States from 1801 to 1805

WORDS FOR EVERYDAY USE:

in • duce • ment (in do͞os´mənt) *n.,* motive; incentive

rap • ture (rap´chər) *n.,* great pleasure

no • to • ri • ous (nō tôr´ē əs) *adj.,* well known

cus • tom • ar • i •ly (kus´tə mer´ə lē) *adv.,* according to what is usually done

sa • lient (sāl´yənt) *adj.,* prominent

and if he was dead, how could he care whether you made a noise or not?

A. I don't know. He was always a particular kind of man that way.

Q. Still, I don't understand it at all! You say he spoke to you, and that he was dead.

A. I didn't say he was dead.

Q. But, wasn't he dead?

A. Well, some said he was, some said he wasn't.

Q. What did you think?

A. Oh, it was none of my business! It wasn't any of my funeral.

Q. Did you—However, we can never get this matter straight. Let me ask about something else. What was the date of your birth?

A. Monday, October 31st, 1693.

Q. What! Impossible! That would make you a hundred and eighty years old. How do you account for that?

A. I don't account for it at all.

Q. But you said at first you were only nineteen, and now you make yourself out to be one hundred and eighty. It is an awful <u>discrepancy</u>.

A. Why, have you noticed that? (Shaking hands.) Many a time it has seemed to me like a discrepancy, but somehow I couldn't make up my mind. How quick you notice a thing!

Q. Thank you for the compliment, as far as it goes.[6] Had you, or have you, any brothers or sisters?

A. Eh! I—I—I think so—yes—but I don't remember.

Q. Well, this is the most extraordinary statement I ever heard!

A. Why, what makes you think that?

Q. How could I think otherwise? Why, look here! Who is this a picture of on the wall? Isn't that a brother of yours?

A. Oh! yes, yes, yes! Now you remind me of it, that *was* a brother of mine. That's William—*Bill* we called him. Poor old Bill!

Q. Why? Is he dead; then?

A. Ah! well, I suppose so. We never could tell. There was a great mystery about it.

Q. That is sad, very sad. He disappeared, then?

A. Well, yes, in a sort of general way. We buried him.

Q. *Buried* him. *Buried* him, without knowing whether he was dead or not?

A. Oh, no! Not that. He was dead enough.

Q. Well, I confess that I can't understand this. If you buried him, and you knew he was dead—

A. No! no! We only thought he was.

Q. Oh, I see! He came to life again?

A. I bet he didn't.

Q. Well, I never heard anything like this. *Somebody* was dead. *Somebody* was buried. Now, where was the mystery?

A. Ah! that's just it! That's it exactly. You see, we were twins,—defunct[7] and I,—we got mixed in the bath-tub

Which two people may or may not have been dead? What doesn't the interviewer realize about the narrator and his story?

What compliment does the narrator give the interviewer? Is he sincere in saying this? Why does he say it?

6. **as far as it goes.** Limited though it is
7. **defunct.** No longer living; dead

WORDS FOR EVERYDAY USE: dis • crep • an • cy (di skrep´ən sē) *n.*, inconsistency

when we were only two weeks old, and one of us was drowned. But we didn't know which. Some think it was Bill. Some think it was me.

Q. Well, that *is* remarkable. What do *you* think?

A. Goodness knows! I would give whole worlds to know. This solemn, this awful mystery has cast a gloom over my whole life. But I will tell you a secret now, which I never have revealed to any creature before. One of us had a peculiar mark—a large mole on the back of his left hand; that was *me. That child was the one that was drowned!*

Q. Very well, then, I don't see that there is any mystery about it, after all.

A. You don't? Well, I do. Anyway, I don't see how they could ever have been such a <u>blundering</u> lot as to go and bury the wrong child. But, 'sh—don't mention it where the family can hear of it. Heaven knows they have heart-breaking troubles enough without adding this.

Q. Well, I believe I have got material enough for the present, and I am very much obliged to you for the pains you have taken. But I was a good deal interested in that account of Aaron Burr's funeral. Would you mind telling me what particular circumstance it was that made you think Burr was such a remarkable man?

A. Oh! it was a mere trifle! Not one man in fifty would have noticed it at all. When the sermon was over, and the procession all ready to start for the cemetery, and the body all arranged nice in the hearse, he said he wanted to take a last look at the scenery, and so he *got up and rode with the driver—*

Then the young man <u>reverently</u> withdrew. He was very pleasant company, and I was sorry to see him go. ■

Responding to the Selection

Imagine that you are the narrator in the selection. In your journal, write about the interviewer who visited you today. Express your feelings toward the interviewer and the experience of being interviewed.

Reviewing the Selection

RECALLING

1. What information does the narrator provide about the interviewer?

2. What word does the narrator attempt to look up in the dictionary?

3. Who does the narrator say is the most remarkable man he ever met?

4. What supposedly happened to the narrator and his twin brother when they were only two weeks old?

INTERPRETING

5. What is probably the reason that the interviewer is "nervous"?

6. What response on the part of the interviewer reveals his gullibility?

7. Why does the narrator's response upset the interviewer?

8. What response on the part of the interviewer shows that the narrator has him completely under control?

SYNTHESIZING

9. What is the narrator trying to do to the interviewer? What early action on the part of the narrator reveals to the reader or listener his intention? Is the narrator successful?

10. What kind of information does the narrator give to the interviewer? Is it possible that the interviewer has "got material enough"? Why, or why not?

Understanding Literature (Questions for Discussion)

1. **Narrator.** A **narrator** is one who tells a story. Writers achieve a wide variety of ends by varying the characteristics of the narrator chosen for a particular work. The narrator in this selection is the person being interviewed. At the beginning of the selection, the narrator describes himself as "not feeling bright that morning. Indeed, my powers seemed a bit under a cloud." Is the narrator's description of himself as a dullard or fool accurate? If not, why do you think he describes himself this way? How would you describe the narrator?

2. **Satire. Satire** is humorous writing or speech intended to point out errors, falsehoods, foibles, or failings. What is being satirized in the selection? What corrective, besides laughter, is implied? How does the writer imply this corrective?

Responding in Writing

Satirical Paragraph. Write a paragraph that satirizes a social convention or custom, such as shaking hands or writing thank-you notes.

> **Prewriting Suggestion:** Write the words *social convention* in the middle of a piece of paper. Then create a cluster diagram on the topic of social conventions. Add whatever words, ideas, or details that come to mind. Review your cluster diagram and choose the social convention and details that would work best for your satirical paragraph.

PROJECT

Dramatic Adaptation. Exchange your satirical paragraph with a partner. Collaborate with your partner to adapt each of your paragraphs into a dramatic scene. In your scene, use a particular event or character to show the errors, falsehoods, foibles, or failings of the social convention you satirized in your paragraph. Write a part for you and for your partner in the scene. Rehearse your adaptation and present it to the rest of the class.

PREREADING

A U T O B I O G R A P H Y

from *I Know Why the Caged Bird Sings*
by Maya Angelou

ABOUT THE AUTHOR

Maya Angelou (1928–) was born Marguerite Johnson in St. Louis, Missouri. Educated in Arkansas and California, Angelou is a poet, playwright, movie and television writer, director, journalist, composer, actor, dancer, and civil rights worker. She has lectured at various American universities and held an administrative position at the University of Ghana. Her collection *Poems,* published in 1986, brings together work from many of her earlier poetry collections. Angelou is most celebrated for her autobiographical work *I Know Why the Caged Bird Sings.* In 1992, Angelou was invited to read a poem at the inauguration of President Clinton.

ABOUT THE SELECTION

Background: History. The following selection is taken from *I Know Why the Caged Bird Sings,* which tells the story of Angelou's life up to the age of sixteen. Angelou continues her life story in the volumes *Gather Together in My Name, Singin' and Swingin' and Gettin' Merry Like Christmas, The Heart of a Woman,* and *All God's Children Need Traveling Shoes.* The selection tells about Marguerite and her brother Bailey first arriving in, and later returning to, Stamps, Arkansas, where they live with their grandmother and uncle in the Wm. Johnson General Merchandise Store.

Background: Technique. In the selection, Angelou's use of concrete words and sensory details creates a portrait of her life in Stamps, Arkansas, that bursts with remembered particulars. Techniques of direct description and portrayal of behavior bring alive the portraits of the inhabitants of Stamps, particularly the portrait of Marguerite's grandmother. However, it is the portrait of Angelou herself that is most striking, as she reveals her thoughts during the twists and turns of her rich and painful life.

READER'S JOURNAL

Have you ever learned a lesson from the way in which someone else lives his or her life? What was the lesson you learned? How did the person's life teach you something of value? Write about these questions in your journal.

FROM

I Know Why the Caged Bird Sings

Maya Angelou

FROM CHAPTER 1

When I was three and Bailey four, we had arrived in the <u>musty</u> little town, wearing tags on our wrists which instructed—"To Whom It May Concern"— that we were Marguerite and Bailey Johnson Jr., from Long Beach, California, en route to Stamps, Arkansas, c/o Mrs. Annie Henderson.

Our parents had decided to put an end to their <u>calamitous</u> marriage, and Father shipped us home to his mother. A porter[1] had been charged with our welfare—he got off the train the next day in Arizona—and our tickets were pinned to my brother's inside coat pocket.

I don't remember much of the trip, but after we reached the segregated southern part of the journey,[2] things must have looked up. Negro passengers, who always traveled with loaded lunch boxes, felt sorry for "the poor little motherless darlings" and <u>plied</u> us with cold fried chicken and potato salad.

Years later I discovered that the United States had been crossed thousands of times by frightened Black children traveling alone to their newly affluent parents in Northern cities, or back to grandmothers in Southern towns when the urban North <u>reneged</u> on its economic promises.

The town reacted to us as its inhabitants had reacted to all things new before our coming. It regarded us a while without curiosity but with caution, and after we were seen to be harmless (and children) it closed in around us, as a real mother embraces a stranger's child. Warmly, but not too familiarly.

Who else has made a journey similar to that of Marguerite and Bailey, and why?

Why are Bailey and Marguerite being sent away? To whom are they being sent?

---

1. **porter.** Carrier; in this case, a railroad employee who carries luggage
2. **segregated . . . journey.** Part of the trip took the children through states in which segregation was still practiced. Segregation is enforced separation of people based on race or ethnic origin.

WORDS FOR EVERYDAY USE:	**mus • ty** (mus´tē) *adj.*, dull; apathetic	**ply** (plī) *vt.*, keep supplying
	ca • lam • i • tous (kə lam´ə təs) *adj.*, deeply troubled or miserable	**re • nege** (ri nig´) *vi.*, back out of an agreement

We lived with our grandmother and uncle in the rear of the Store (it was always spoken of with a capital *s*), which she had owned some twenty-five years.

Early in the century, Momma (we soon stopped calling her Grandmother) sold lunches to the sawmen in the lumberyard (east Stamps) and the seedmen at the cotton gin (west Stamps). Her crisp meat pies and cool lemonade, when joined to her miraculous ability to be in two places at the same time, assured her business success. From being a mobile lunch counter,[3] she set up a stand between the two points of fiscal interest[4] and supplied the workers' needs for a few years. Then she had the Store built in the heart of the Negro area. Over the years it became the lay center[5] of activities in town. On Saturdays, barbers sat their customers in the shade on the porch of the Store, and troubadours[6] on their ceaseless crawlings through the South leaned across its benches and sang their sad songs of The Brazos[7] while they played juice harps and cigar-box guitars.

The formal name of the Store was the Wm. Johnson General Merchandise Store. Customers could find food <u>staples</u>, a good variety of colored thread, mash for hogs, corn for chickens, coal oil for lamps, light bulbs for the wealthy, shoestrings, hair dressing, balloons, and flower seeds. Anything not visible had only to be ordered.

Until we became familiar enough to belong to the Store and it to us, we were locked up in a Fun House of Things where the attendant had gone home for life.

Each year I watched the field across from the Store turn caterpillar green, then gradually frosty white. I knew exactly how long it would be before the big wagons would pull into the front yard and load on the cotton pickers at daybreak to carry them to the remains of slavery's plantations.

During the picking season my grandmother would get out of bed at four o'clock (she never used an alarm clock) and creak down to her knees and chant in a sleep-filled voice, "Our Father, thank you for letting me see this New Day. Thank you that you didn't allow the bed I lay on last night to be my cooling board, nor my blanket my winding sheet.[8] Guide my feet this day along the straight and narrow, and help me to put a bridle on my tongue. Bless this house, and everybody in it. Thank you, in the name of your Son, Jesus Christ, Amen."

Before she had quite arisen, she called our names and issued orders, and pushed her large feet into homemade slippers and across the bare lye-washed[9] wooden floor to light the coal-oil lamp.

How did Momma become an entrepreneur?

For what is Momma grateful?

---

3. **mobile lunch counter.** Lunch stand that could be moved from place to place, for example, in a truck or on a cart

4. **points of . . . interest.** Businesses, here the lumberyard and cotton gin

5. **lay center.** Nonspecialized center for all people to gather and talk

6. **troubadours.** Traveling folk singers and storytellers

7. **The Brazos.** River in southeast and central Texas that flows into the Gulf of Mexico

8. **cooling board . . . winding sheet.** *Cooling board*—place where a corpse lies while being prepared for burial or cremation; *winding sheet*—sheet in which a corpse is wrapped

9. **lye-washed.** Washed with a harsh, strongly alkaline soap

The lamplight in the Store gave a soft make-believe feeling to our world which made me want to whisper and walk about on tiptoe. The odors of onions and oranges and kerosene had been mixing all night and wouldn't be disturbed until the wooden slat was removed from the door and the early morning air forced its way in with the bodies of people who had walked miles to reach the pickup place.

"Sister, I'll have two cans of sardines."

"I'm gonna work so fast today I'm gonna make you look like you standing still."

"Lemme have a hunk uh cheese and some sody crackers."

"Just gimme a coupla them fat peanut paddies." That would be from a picker who was taking his lunch. The greasy brown paper sack was stuck behind the bib of his overalls. He'd use the candy as a snack before the noon sun called the workers to rest.

In those tender mornings the Store was full of laughing, joking, boasting and bragging. One man was going to pick two hundred pounds of cotton, and another three hundred. Even the children were promising to bring home fo' bits and six bits.[10]

The champion picker of the day before was the hero of the dawn. If he prophesied that the cotton in today's field was going to be sparse and stick to the bolls[11] like glue, every listener would grunt a hearty agreement.

The sound of the empty cotton sacks dragging over the floor and the murmurs of waking people were sliced[12] by

Why are the cotton pickers disappointed in the afternoon?

Why is the narrator angered by stereotypes?

the cash register as we rang up the five-cent sales.

If the morning sounds and smells were touched with the supernatural, the late afternoon had all the features of the normal Arkansas life. In the dying sunlight the people dragged, rather than their empty cotton sacks.

Brought back to the Store, the pickers would step out of the backs of trucks and fold down, dirt-disappointed, to the ground. No matter how much they had picked, it wasn't enough. Their wages wouldn't even get them out of debt to my grandmother, not to mention the staggering bill that waited on them at the white commissary[13] downtown.

The sounds of the new morning had been replaced with grumbles about cheating houses, weighted scales, snakes, skimpy cotton and dusty rows. In later years I was to confront the stereotyped picture of gay song-singing cotton pickers with such inordinate rage that I was told even by fellow Blacks that my paranoia was embarrassing. But I had seen the fingers cut by the mean little cotton bolls, and I had witnessed the backs and shoulders and arms and legs resisting any further demands.

Some of the workers would leave their sacks at the Store to be picked up the following morning, but a few had to take them home for repairs. I winced to picture them sewing the coarse material under a coal-oil lamp with fin-

---

10. **fo' bits and six bits.** Fifty cents and seventy-five cents
11. **bolls.** Shell-like top parts of the cotton flower that hold the white seed pod, the cotton
12. **sliced.** Interrupted
13. **commissary.** Store

WORDS FOR EVERYDAY USE:

proph • e • sy (präf´ə sē´) vt., predict
sparse (spärs) adj., meager
ster • e • o • typed (ster´ē ə tīpt) adj., conventional notion, not allowing for individuality

in • or • di • nate (in ôr´də nit) adj., lacking moderation
par • a • noi • a (par´ə noi´ə) n., extreme delusions of persecution

gers stiffening from the day's work. In too few hours they would have to walk back to Sister Henderson's Store, get vittles[14] and load, again, onto the trucks. Then they would face another day of trying to earn enough for the whole year with the heavy knowledge that they were going to end the season as they started it. Without the money or credit necessary to sustain a family for three months. In cotton-picking time the late afternoons revealed the harshness of Black Southern life, which in the early morning had been softened by nature's blessing of grogginess, forgetfulness and the soft lamplight.

FROM CHAPTER 14

The barrenness of Stamps was exactly what I wanted, without will or consciousness. After St. Louis,[15] with its noise and activity, its trucks and buses, and loud family gatherings, I welcomed the obscure lanes and lonely bungalows[16] set back deep in the dirt yards.

The resignation of its inhabitants encouraged me to relax. They showed me a contentment based on the belief that nothing more was coming to them, although a great deal more was due. Their decision to be satisfied with life's inequities was a lesson for me. Entering Stamps, I had the feeling that I was stepping over the border lines of the map and would fall, without fear, right off the end of the world. Nothing more could happen, for in Stamps nothing happened.

Into this cocoon I crept.

For an indeterminate time, nothing was demanded of me or of Bailey. We were, after all, Mrs. Henderson's California grandchildren, and had been away on a glamorous trip way up North to the fabulous St. Louis. Our father had come the year before driving a big, shiny automobile and speaking the King's English[17] with a big city accent, so all we had to do was lie quiet for months and rake in the profits of our adventures.

Farmers and maids, cooks and handymen, carpenters and all the children in town, made regular pilgrimages to the Store. "Just to see the travelers."

They stood around like cutout cardboard figures and asked, "Well, how is it up North?"

"See any of them big buildings?"

"Ever ride in one of them elevators?"

"Was you scared?"

"Whitefolks any different, like they say?"

Bailey took it upon himself to answer every question, and from a corner of his lively imagination wove a tapestry of entertainment for them that I was sure was as foreign to him as it was to me.

He, as usual, spoke precisely. "They have, in the North, buildings so high that for months, in the winter, you can't see the top floors."

"Tell the truth."

Why are the residents of Stamps so interested in city life?

What did the narrator learn from the people of Stamps upon her return?

---

14. **vittles.** Food
15. **St. Louis.** The children had been to St. Louis, Missouri, to visit their mother.
16. **bungalows.** One-story houses
17. **the King's English.** English as spoken by the king of England or well-educated people from England; very proper English

---

WORDS FOR EVERYDAY USE:

ob • scure (əb skyoor´) *adj.*, inconspicuous; hidden
res • ig • na • tion (rez´ig nā shən) *n.*, passive acceptance

in • eq • ui • ty (in ek´wit ē) *n.*, lack of justice
in • de • ter • mi • nate (in´dē tʉr´mi nit) *adj.*, uncertain

Courtesy of Library of Congress Photo Duplication Service

"They've got watermelons twice the size of a cow's head and sweeter than syrup." I distinctly remember his <u>intent</u> face and the fascinated faces of his listeners. "And if you can count the watermelon's seeds, before it's cut open, you can win five zillion dollars and a new car."

Momma, knowing Bailey, warned, "Now Ju, be careful you don't slip up on a not true." (Nice people didn't say "lie.")

"Everybody wears new clothes and have inside toilets. If you fall down in one of them, you get flushed away into the Mississippi River. Some people have iceboxes, only the proper name is Cold Spot or Frigidaire. The snow is so deep you can get buried right out-side your door and people won't find you for a year. We made ice cream out of the snow." That was the only fact that I could have supported. During the winter, we had collected a bowl of snow and poured Pet[18] milk over it, and sprinkled it with sugar and called it ice cream.

Momma beamed and Uncle Willie was proud when Bailey <u>regaled</u> the customers with our <u>exploits</u>. We were drawing cards[19] for the Store and objects of the town's adoration. Our journey to magical places alone was a spot of color on the town's drab can-

Is Momma really angry with Bailey's exaggerations?

---

18. **Pet.** Brand of evaporated milk
19. **drawing cards.** Performers who attract an audience

Words for Everyday Use:

in • tent (in tent´) *adj.*, earnest, fixed
re • gale (ri gāl´) *vt.*, entertain
ex • ploit (eks´ploit) *n.*, daring or bold deed

vas, and our return made us even more the most enviable of people.

High spots in Stamps were usually negative: droughts, floods, lynchings[20] and deaths.

Bailey played on the country folks' need for diversion. Just after our return he had taken to sarcasm, picked it up as one might pick up a stone, and put it snufflike under his lip. The double entendres,[21] the two-pronged sentences, slid over his tongue to dart rapier-like[22] into anything that happened to be in the way. Our customers, though, generally were so straight thinking and speaking that they were never hurt by his attacks. They didn't comprehend them.

"Bailey Junior sound just like Big Bailey. Got a silver tongue. Just like his daddy."

"I hear tell they don't pick cotton up there. How the people live then?"

Bailey said that the cotton up North was so tall, if ordinary people tried to pick it they'd have to get up on ladders, so the cotton farmers had their cotton picked by machines. ■

---

20. **lynchings.** Illegal hangings
21. **double entendres.** Double meanings
22. **rapier-like.** Swordlike

What kinds of things usually caught the interest of the residents of Stamps? What interests them now?

Responding to the Selection

Imagine that you are the narrator in the selection. Write a letter to your grandmother, "Momma." In your letter, express your feelings about living with her in Stamps, Arkansas. Explain what you learned from her and the inhabitants of Stamps.

Reviewing the Selection

RECALLING

1. What reaction do the people of Stamps show toward the newcomers, Marguerite and Bailey?

2. Where do the narrator and her brother, Bailey Jr., live in Stamps?

3. What is the store filled with in the "tender mornings"?

4. What encourages the narrator to relax upon her return to Stamps from St. Louis?

INTERPRETING

5. What does the narrator discover years later that suggests she and Bailey were not the only children traveling alone on a train?

6. What actions on the part of the grandmother show her business talents?

7. What fact about African-American life in the South at the time is revealed to the narrator in the late afternoons in cotton-picking season?

8. What is probably the reason that the inhabitants of Stamps come to the store "just to see the travelers"?

9. What is the difference between the mornings and late afternoons of "Arkansas life"?

10. Upon her return to Stamps, why do you think the narrator refers to Stamps as a cocoon into which she creeps?

Understanding Literature (Questions for Discussion)

1. **Narrator and Point of View.** A **narrator** is one who tells a story. In an autobiography—the story of a person's life written by that person—the narrator is usually the author. This selection is written from a first-person **point of view,** in which the narrator uses words such as *I* and *we.* From this limited point of view, the narrator can reveal her private, internal thoughts. For example, the narrator reveals her pain when imagining cotton-pickers taking home their picking sacks for repairs: "I winced to picture them sewing the coarse material under a coal-oil lamp with fingers stiffening from the day's work. In too few hours they would have to walk back to Sister Henderson's Store, get vittles and load, again, onto the trucks. Then they would face another day of trying to earn enough for the whole year with the heavy knowledge that they were going to end the season as they started it. Without the money or credit necessary to sustain a family for three months." Find another passage in the selection in which the narrator reveals her private, internal thoughts. Explain what emotion the narrator reveals in the passage.

2. **Setting.** The **setting** of a literary work is the time and place in which it occurs, together with all the details used to create a sense of a particular time and place. What details are used to create the setting of the store in the mornings, before "the wooden slat was removed from the door"? Compare the early morning setting in the store with the late afternoon setting.

Responding in Writing

Descriptive Paragraph. Write a paragraph in which you describe a particular person and the place in which he or she lives. Use sensory details to create a clear and vivid picture of the person and place.

> **Prewriting Suggestion:** To get started, write the words *person* and *place* on the top of a piece of paper. Draw a line down the center of the page between the two words. Then, down the left-hand side of the page, write the words *sight, sound, taste, touch,* and *smell.* Fill in the chart with details about your chosen person and place.

from *Blue Highways: A Journey into America*
by William Least Heat-Moon

ABOUT THE AUTHOR

William Least Heat-Moon (1939–) was born in Kansas City, Missouri, of English-Irish-Osage ancestry. He was originally named William Trogdon. He was educated at the University of Missouri and holds a bachelor's degree in photojournalism and a doctorate in English. In 1978, Heat-Moon began a remarkable journey. Taking a leave of absence from teaching, he set out from Missouri in a half-ton truck, named Ghost Dancing, and journeyed throughout America, following thirteen thousand miles of rural roads. From his experiences during this odyssey of self-discovery, Heat-Moon wrote *Blue Highways,* his first published book.

ABOUT THE SELECTION

Background: Technique. Many of the sections in *Blue Highways* consist of a series of conversations, or **dialogues,** between the author and people he met on his travels. Through the dialogues, in which the participants discuss a multitude of topics, each person's life experience and point of view are revealed.

Background: Genre. An autobiographical account of a cross-country journey, *Blue Highways* shares features with *On the Road* by Jack Kerouac and *Travels with Charley* by John Steinbeck. While *Blue Highways* tells the story of Heat-Moon's experience of self-discovery on the road, it also tells the stories of the people he encountered on his journey.

READER'S JOURNAL

Where would you travel if you could make a journey of self-discovery? What method of transportation would you take? What would you take with you? Think about these questions. Then write in your journal about what you would hope to learn about yourself on the journey.

FROM

Blue Highways: A Journey into America

WILLIAM LEAST HEAT-MOON

CHAPTER 14

What was the best name Heat-Moon found in the atlas?

Had it not been raining hard that morning on the Livingston square, I never would have learned of Nameless, Tennessee. Waiting for the rain to ease, I lay on my bunk and read the atlas to pass time rather than to see where I might go. In Kentucky were towns with fine names like Boreing, Bear Wallow, Decoy, Subtle, Mud Lick, Mummie, Neon; Belcher was just down the road from Mouthcard, and Minnie only ten miles from Mousie.

I looked at Tennessee. Turtletown eight miles from Ducktown. And also: Peavine, Wheel, Milky Way, Love Joy, Dull, Weakly, Fly, Spot, Miser Station, Only, McBurg, Peeled Chestnut, Clouds, Topsy, Isoline. And the best of all, Nameless. The logic! I was heading east, and Nameless lay forty-five miles west. I decided to go anyway.

What system does Heat-Moon use to find good food?

The rain stopped, but things looked <u>saturated</u>, even bricks. In Gainesboro, a hill town with a square of businesses around the Jackson County Courthouse, I stopped for directions and breakfast. There is one almost <u>infallible</u> way to find honest food at just prices in blue-highway[1] America: count the wall calendars in a cafe.

No calendar: Same as an interstate pit stop.[2]

---

1. **blue-highway.** Roads that are usually marked in blue on an interstate map; smaller roads rather than major highways
2. **interstate pit stop.** Diner or casual restaurant located at the exit of a major highway

WORDS FOR EVERYDAY USE:

sat • u • rat • ed (sach´ ər rāt´id) *adj.*, soaked through with moisture; wet

in • fal • li • ble (in fal´ə bəl) *adj.*, incapable of error; reliable

One calendar: Preprocessed food assembled in New Jersey.

Two calendars: Only if fish trophies present.

Three calendars: Can't miss on the farm-boy breakfasts.

Four calendars: Try the ho-made pie too.

Five calendars: Keep it under your hat, or they'll franchise.[3]

One time I found a six-calendar cafe in the Ozarks,[4] which served fried chicken, peach pie, and chocolate malts, that left me searching for another ever since. I've never seen a seven-calendar place. But old-time travelers—road men in a day when cars had running boards[5] and lunchroom windows said AIR COOLED in blue letters with icicles dripping from the tops—those travelers have told me the golden legends of seven-calendar cafes.

To the rider of back roads, nothing shows the tone, the voice of a small town more quickly than the breakfast grill or the five-thirty tavern. Much of what the people do and believe and share is <u>evident</u> then. The City Cafe in Gainesboro had three calendars that I could see from the walk. Inside were no interstate <u>refugees</u> with full bladders and empty tanks, no wild-eyed children just released from the glassy cell of a stationwagon backseat, no longhaul truckers talking in CB numbers.[6] There were only townspeople wearing overalls, or catalog-order suits with five-and-dime ties, or uniforms. That is, here were farmers and mill hands, bank clerks, the dry goods merchant,[7] a policeman, and chiropractor's receptionist. Because it was Saturday, there were also mothers and children.

Who was eating in the City Cafe in Gainesboro? What kinds of people were not there? What did this mean to the narrator?

I ordered my standard on-the-road breakfast: two eggs up, hashbrowns, tomato juice. The waitress, whose pale, almost translucent skin shifted <u>hue</u> in the gray light like a thin slice of mother of pearl,[8] brought the food. Next to the eggs was a biscuit with a little yellow Smiley button stuck in it. She said, "You from the North?"

"I guess I am." A Missourian gets used to Southerners thinking him a Yankee, a Northerner considering him a cracker,[9] a Westerner sneering at his <u>effete</u> Easternness, and the Easterner taking him for a cowhand.

What does a Missourian get used to?

"So whata you doin' in the mountains?"

"Talking to people. Taking some pictures. Looking mostly."

"Lookin' for what?"

"A three-calendar cafe that serves Smiley buttons on the biscuits."

---

3. **or they'll franchise.** The speaker means that the restaurant owners will start new restaurants with the same name and quality will suffer.

4. **Ozarks.** Mountain chain (named for the Arkansas Indian tribe) that runs through northwest Arkansas, southwest Missouri, and northeast Oklahoma

5. **running boards.** Footboards, or steps, along the lower edge of the car's side panels

6. **CB numbers.** CB radios were the only way drivers could communicate before car phones became available.

7. **dry goods merchant.** Seller of cloth or clothing products

8. **mother of pearl.** Shiny inner layer of certain marine shells (for example, the pearl oyster or abalone)

9. **cracker.** Insulting term applied to uneducated white persons, especially from the rural south

---

WORDS FOR EVERYDAY USE:

ev • i • dent (ev´ə dənt) *adj.*, easy to see; obvious

ref • u • gee (ref´yoo jē) *n.*, person who flees from home or country to seek safety elsewhere

hue (hyoo) *n.*, particular shade or tint of a given color

ef • fete (e fēt) *adj.*, lacking vigor or force of character

Why does Heat-Moon prefer to travel alone?

"You needed a smile. Tell me really."

"I don't know. Actually, I'm looking for some jam to put on this biscuit now that you've brought one."

She came back with grape jelly. In a land of quince jelly, apple butter, apricot jam, blueberry preserves, pear conserves, and lemon marmalade, you always get grape jelly.

"Whata you lookin' for?"

Like anyone else, I'm embarrassed to eat in front of a watcher, particularly if I'm getting interviewed. "Why don't you have a cup of coffee?"

"Cain't right now. You gonna tell me?"

"I don't know how to describe it to you. Call it harmony."

How did the waitress feel about her life in the beginning? What change occurred in her feelings? What does she suggest to Heat-Moon?

She waited for something more. "Is that it?" Someone called her to the kitchen. I had managed almost to finish by the time she came back. She sat on the edge of the booth. "I started out in life not likin' anything, but then it grew on me. Maybe that'll happen to you." She watched me spread the jelly. "Saw your van." She watched me eat the biscuit. "You sleep in there?" I told her I did. "I'd love to do that, but I'd be scared spitless."

"I don't mind being scared spitless. Sometimes."

"I'd love to take off cross country. I like to look at different license plates. But I'd take a dog. You carry a dog?"

"No dogs, no cats, no budgie birds.[10] It's a one-man campaign to show Americans a person can travel alone without a pet."

"Cain't travel without a dog!"

"I like to do things the hard way."

"Shoot! I'd take me a dog to talk to. And for protection."

What kind of directions does Heat-Moon get to Nameless? What kind of town do you expect Nameless to be?

"It isn't traveling to cross the country and talk to your pug instead of people along the way. Besides, being alone on the road makes you ready to meet someone when you stop. You get sociable traveling alone."

She looked out toward the van again. "Time I get the nerve to take a trip, gas'll cost five dollars a gallon."

"Could be. My rig might go the way of the steamboat." I remembered why I'd come to Gainesboro. You know the way to Nameless?"

"Nameless? I've heard of Nameless. Better ask the amlance driver in the corner booth." She pinned the Smiley on my jacket. "Maybe I'll see you on the road somewhere. His name's Bob, by the way."

"The ambulance driver?"

"The Smiley. I always name my Smileys—otherwise they all look alike. I'd talk to him before you go."

"The Smiley?"

"The amlance driver."

And so I went looking for Nameless, Tennessee, with a Smiley button named Bob.

CHAPTER 15

"I don't know if I got directions for where you're goin'," the ambulance driver said. "I *think* there's a Nameless down the Shepardsville Road."

"When I get to Shepardsville, will I have gone too far?"

"Ain't no Shepardsville."

"How will I know when I'm there?"

"Cain't say for certain."

"What's Nameless look like?"

"Don't recollect."

"Is the road paved?"

"It's possible."

Those were the directions. I was looking for an unnumbered road named after a nonexistent town that

---

10. **budgie birds.** Parakeets

would take me to a place called Nameless that nobody was sure existed.

Clumps of wild garlic lined the county highway that I hoped was the Shepardsville Road. It scrimmaged[11] with the mountain as it tried to stay on top of the ridges; the hillsides were so steep and thick with oak, I felt as if I were following a trail through the misty treetops. Chickens, doing more work with their necks than legs, ran across the road, and, with a battering of wings, half leapt and half flew into the lower branches of oaks. A vicious pair of mixed-breed German shepherds raced along trying to eat the tires. After miles, I decided I'd missed the town—assuming there truly *was* a Nameless, Tennessee. It wouldn't be the first time I'd qualified for the Ponce de Leon[12] Believe Anything Award.

I stopped beside a big man loading tools in a pickup. "I may be lost."

"Where'd you lose the right road?"

"I don't know. Somewhere around nineteen sixty-five."

"Highway fifty-six, you mean?"

"I came down fifty-six. I think I should've turned at the last junction."

"Only thing down that road's stumps and huckleberries, and the berries ain't there in March. Where you tryin' to get to?"

"Nameless. If there is such a place."

"You might not know Thurmond Watts, but he's got him a store down the road. That's Nameless at his store. Still there all right, but I might not vouch you that tomorrow." He came up to the van. "In my Army days, I wrote Nameless, Tennessee, for my place of birth on all the papers, even though I lived on this end of the ridge. All these ridges and hollers[13] got names of their own. That's Steam Mill Holler over yonder. Named after the steam engine in the gristmill. Miller had him just one arm but done a good business."

"What business you in?"

"I've always farmed, but I work in Cookeville now in a heatin' element[14] factory. Bad back made me go to town to work." He pointed to a wooden building not much bigger than his truck. By the slanting porch, a faded Double Cola sign said J M WHEELER STORE. "That used to be my business. That's me—Madison Wheeler. Feller came by one day. From Detroit. He wanted to buy the sign because he carried my name too. But I didn't sell. Want to keep my name up." He gave a cigarette a good slow smoking. "Had a decent business for five years, but too much of it was in credit. Then them supermarkets down in Cookeville opened, and I was buyin' higher than they was sellin'. With these hard roads now, everybody gets out of the hollers to shop or work. Don't stay up in here anymore. This tar road under my shoes done my business in, and it's likely to do Nameless in."

"Do you wish it was still the old way?"

"I got no debts now. I got two boys raised, and they never been in trouble. I got a brick house and some corn and tobacco and a few Hampshire hogs and Herefords. A good bull. Bull's pumpin' better blood than I do. Real generous man in town let me put my cow in with his stud. I couldna paid the fee on that specimen otherwise."[15] He took another

Why did the man from Detroit want to buy the sign? Why didn't the owner sell it?

What has caused the failure of Madison Wheeler's business?

---

11. **scrimmaged.** Wrestled or struggled (as in football)
12. **Ponce de Leon.** Spanish explorer (1460?–1521) who sought the "fountain of youth"; also the first European to discover Florida
13. **hollers.** Hollows or valleys
14. **heatin' element.** Wire coil that becomes glowing hot, as in an electric oven
15. **Bull's . . . otherwise.** Wheeler means that his bull is the offspring of a bull belonging to the generous man.

Gas. Edward Hopper, 1940. Oil on canvas, 26¹/₄" × 40¹/₄" (66.7 × 102.2cm)
The Museum of Modern Art, New York. Mrs. Simon Guggenheim Fund

What doesn't Wheeler like about factory work? Why does he continue to farm?

long, <u>meditative</u> pull on his filtertip. "If you're satisfied, that's all they are to it. I'll tell you, people from all over the nation—Florida, Mississippi—are comin' in here to retire because it's good country. But our young ones don't stay on. Not much way to make a livin' in here anymore. Take me. I been beatin' on these stumps all my life, tryin' to farm these hills. They don't give much up to you. Fightin' rocks and briars all the time. One of the first things I recollect is swingin' a briar blade—filed out of an old saw it was. Now they come in with them crawlers and push out a pasture in a day. Still, it's a grudgin' land—like the gourd. Got to hard cuss[16] gourd seed, they say, to get it up out of the ground."

The whole time, my rig sat in the middle of the right lane while we stood talking next to it and wiped at the mist. No one else came or went. Wheeler said, "Factory work's easier on the back, and I don't mind it, understand, but a man becomes what he does. Got to watch that. That's why I keep at farmin', although the crops haven't ever throve.[17] It's the doin' that's important." He looked up suddenly. "My apologies. I didn't ask what you do that gets you into these hollers."

I told him. I'd been gone only six days, but my account of the trip already had taken on some polish.

16. **hard cuss.** Swear intensely
17. **throve.** Thrived; grown vigorously

WORDS FOR EVERYDAY USE: med • i • ta • tive (med´ə tāt´iv) *adj.,* reflective, thoughtful

He nodded. "Satisfaction is doin' what's important to yourself. A man ought to honor other people, but he's got to honor what he believes in too."

As I started the engine, Wheeler said, "If you get back this way, stop in and see me. Always got beans and taters and a little piece of meat."

Down along the ridge, I wondered why it's always those who live on little who are the ones to ask you to dinner.

CHAPTER 16

Nameless, Tennessee, was a town of maybe ninety people if you pushed it, a dozen houses along the road, a couple of barns, same number of churches, a general merchandise store selling Fire Chief gasoline, and a community center with a lighted volleyball court. Behind the center was an open-roof, rusting metal privy with PAINT ME on the door; in the hollow of a nearby oak lay a full pint of Jack Daniel's Black Label. From the houses, the odor of coal smoke.

Next to a red tobacco barn stood the general merchandise with a poster of Senator Albert Gore, Jr.,[18] smiling from the window. I knocked. The door opened partway. A tall, thin man said, "Closed up. For good," and started to shut the door.

"Don't want to buy anything. Just a question for Mr. Thurmond Watts."

The man peered through the slight opening. He looked me over. "What question would that be?"

"If this is Nameless, Tennessee, could he tell me how it got that name?"

The man turned back into the store and called out, "Miss Ginny! Somebody here wants to know how Nameless come to be Nameless."

Miss Ginny edged to the door and looked me and my truck over. Clearly, she didn't approve. She said, "You know as well as I do, Thurmond. Don't keep him on the stoop in the damp to tell him." Miss Ginny, I found out, was Mrs. Virginia Watts, Thurmond's wife.

I stepped in and they both began telling the story, adding a detail here, the other correcting a fact there, both smiling at the foolishness of it all. It seems the hilltop settlement went for years without a name. Then one day the Post Office Department told the people if they wanted mail up on the mountain they would have to give the place a name you could properly address a letter to. The community met; there were only a handful, but they commenced <u>debating</u>. Some wanted patriotic names, some names from nature, one man recommended in all seriousness his own name. They couldn't agree, and they ran out of names to argue about. Finally, a fellow tired of the talk; he didn't like the mail he received anyway. "Forget the durn Post Office," he said. "This here's a nameless place if I ever seen one, so leave it be." And that's just what they did.

Watts pointed out the window. "We used to have signs on the road, but the

---

18. **Senator Albert Gore, Jr.** Former senator from Tennessee who became vice president of the United States in 1992

How does Wheeler view satisfaction? What should people honor?

How did Nameless get its name?

WORDS FOR EVERYDAY USE: de • bate (dē bāt´) *vi.,* discuss opposing sides of a question

Halloween boys keep tearin' them down."

"You think Nameless is a funny name," Miss Ginny said. "I see it plain in your eyes. Well, you take yourself up north a piece to Difficult or Defeated or Shake Rag. Now them are silly names."

The old store, lighted only by three fifty-watt bulbs, smelled of coal oil and baking bread. In the middle of the rectangular room, where the oak floor sagged a little, stood an iron stove. To the right was a wooden table with an unfinished game of checkers and a stool made from an apple-tree stump. On shelves around the walls sat earthen jugs with corncob stoppers, a few canned goods, and some of the two thousand old clocks and clockworks Thurmond Watts owned. Only one was ticking; the others he just looked at. I asked how long he'd been in the store.

"Thirty-five years, but we closed the first day of the year. We're hopin' to sell it to a churchly couple. Upright people. No athians."[19]

"Did you build this store?"

"I built this one, but it's the third general store on the ground. I fear it'll be the last. I take no pleasure in that. Once you could come in here for a gallon of paint, a pickle, a pair of shoes, and a can of corn."

What did the store provide in the past?

"Or horehound candy," Miss Ginny said. "Or corsets and salves.[20] We had cough syrups and all that for the body. In season, we'd buy and sell blackberries and walnuts and chestnuts, before the <u>blight</u> got them. And outside, Thurmond milled corn and sharpened plows. Even shoed a horse sometimes."

"We could fix up a horse or a man or a baby," Watts said.

"Thurmond, tell him we had a doctor on the ridge in them days."

"We had a doctor on the ridge in them days. As good as any doctor alivin'. He'd cut a crooked toenail or deliver a woman. Dead these last years."

"I got some bad ham meat one day," Miss Ginny said, "and took to vomitin'. All day, all night. Hangin' on the drop edge of yonder. I said to Thurmond, 'Thurmond, unless you want shut of me, call the doctor.' "

"I studied on it,"[21] Watts said.

"You never did. You got him right now. He come over and put three drops of iodeen in half a glass of well water. I drank it down and the vomitin' stopped with the last swallow. Would you think iodeen could do that?"

"He put Miss Ginny on one teaspoon of spirits of ammonia in well water for her nerves. Ain't nothin' works better for her to this day."

"Calms me like the hand of the Lord."

Hilda, the Wattses' daughter, came out of the backroom. "I remember him," she said. "I was just a baby. Y'all

19. **churchly couple. . . . athians.** Religious couple with a strong sense of morality; not atheists
20. **horehound candy . . . corsets and salves.** *Horehound candy*—brown hard candy made with juice from a bitter plant of the mint family; *corsets*—foundation garments used to support the upper torso; *salves*—medicinal creams
21. **I studied on it.** I thought about it.

WORDS FOR
EVERYDAY USE: **blight** (blīt) *n.,* any of several plant diseases that prevent growth

were talkin' to him, and he lifted me up on the counter and gave me a stick of Juicy Fruit and a piece of cheese."

"Knew the old medicines," Watts said. "Only drugstore he needed was a good kitchen cabinet. None of them antee-beeotics that hit you worsen your <u>ailment</u>. Forgotten lore now, the old medicines, because they ain't profit in iodeen."

Miss Ginny started back to the side room where she and her sister Marilyn were taking apart a duck-down mattress to make bolsters. She stopped at the window for another look at Ghost Dancing.[22] "How do you sleep in that thing? Ain't you all cramped and cold?"

"How does the clam sleep in his shell?" Watts said in my defense.

"Thurmond, get the boy a piece of buttermilk pie afore he goes on."

"Hilda, get him some buttermilk pie." He looked at me. "You like good music?" I said I did. He cranked up an old Edison phonograph, the kind with the big morning-glory blossom[23] for a speaker, and put on a wax cylinder. "This will be 'My Mother's Prayer,'" he said.

While I ate buttermilk pie, Watts served as disc jockey of Nameless, Tennessee. "Here's 'Mountain Rose.'" It was one of those moments that you know at the time will stay with you to the grave: the sweet pie, the gaunt man playing the old music, the coals in the stove glowing orange, the scent of kerosene and hot bread. "Here's 'Evening Rhapsody.'" The music was so heavily romantic we both laughed. I thought: It is for this I have come.

Feathered over and giggling, Miss Ginny stepped from the side room. She knew she was a sight. "Thurmond, give him some lunch. Still looks hungry."

Hilda pulled food off the woodstove in the backroom: home-butchered and canned whole-hog sausage, home-canned June apples, turnip greens, cole slaw, potatoes, stuffing, hot cornbread. All delicious.

Watts and Hilda sat and talked while I ate. "Wish you would join me."

"We've ate," Watts said. "Cain't beat a woodstove for flavorful cookin'."

He told me he was raised in a one-hundred-fifty-year-old cabin still standing in one of the hollows. "How many's left," he said, "that grew up in a log cabin? I ain't the last surely, but I must be climbin' on the list."

Hilda cleared the table. "You Watts ladies know how to cook."

"She's in nursin' school at Tennessee Tech. I went over for one of them football games last year there at Coevul." To say *Cookeville*, you let the word collapse in upon itself so that it comes out "Coevul."

"Do you like football?" I asked.

"Don't know. I was so high up in that stadium, I never opened my eyes."

Watts went to the back and returned with a fat spiral notebook that he set

What else has gone the way of Wheeler's and Watts's businesses? How does Watts feel about these losses?

How did Heat-Moon feel about this experience?

---

22. **Ghost Dancing.** The narrator's nickname for his vehicle
23. **morning-glory blossom.** Trumpet-shaped blue flower

| WORDS FOR EVERYDAY USE: | ail • ment (āl´mənt) *n.*, illness; disease |

on the table. His expression had changed. "Miss Ginny's *Deathbook*."

The thing startled me. Was it something I was supposed to sign? He opened it but said nothing. There were scads of names written in a tidy hand over pages <u>incised</u> to crinkliness by a ballpoint. Chronologically, the names had piled up: wives, grandparents, a stillborn infant, relatives, friends close and distant. Names, names. After each, the date of *the* unknown finally known and transcribed. The last entry bore yesterday's date.

What does Miss Ginny record?

"She's wrote out twenty years' worth. Ever day she listens to the hospital report on the radio and puts the names in. Folks come by to check a date. Or they just turn through the books. Read them like a scrapbook."

Hilda said, "Like Saint Peter at the gates inscribin' the names."

Watts took my arm. "Come along." He led me to the fruit cellar under the store. As we went down, he said, "Always take a newborn baby upstairs afore you take him downstairs, otherwise you'll incline him downwards."

What advice does Watts offer as he is taking Heat-Moon to the cellar?

The cellar was dry and full of cobwebs and jar after jar of home-canned food, the bottles organized as a shopkeeper would: sausage, pumpkin, sweet pickles, tomatoes, corn relish, blackberries, peppers, squash, jellies. He held a hand out toward the dusty bottles. "Our tomorrows."

Upstairs again, he said, "Hope to sell the store to the right folk. I see now, though, it'll be somebody offen the ridge.[24] I've studied on it, and maybe it's the end of our place." He stirred the coals. "This store could give a comfortable livin', but not likely get you rich. But just gettin' by is dice rollin' to people nowadays. I never did see my day guaranteed."

When it was time to go, Watts said, "If you find anyone along your way wants a good store—on the road to Cordell Hull Lake—tell them about us."

I said I would. Miss Ginny and Hilda and Marilyn came out to say goodbye. It was cold and drizzling again. "Weather to give a man the weary dismals," Watts grumbled. "Where you headed from here?"

"I don't know."

"Cain't get lost then."

Miss Ginny looked again at my rig. It had worried her from the first as it had my mother. "I hope you don't get yourself kilt in that durn thing gallivantin' around the country."

"Come back when the hills dry off," Watts said. "We'll go lookin' for some of them round rocks all sparkly inside."

I thought a moment. "Geodes?"[25]

"Them's the ones. The country's properly full of them." ∎

---

24. **offen the ridge.** Watts means from beyond his community on the ridge.
25. **Geodes.** The narrator is asking if these are the valuable round stones that contain a cavity lined with crystals.

WORDS FOR EVERYDAY USE: **in • cised** (in sīzd´) *adj.,* engraved or carved

Responding to the Selection

Imagine that you are a member of the Watts family in the selection. Discuss with your classmates the stranger who one day drove into your town—Nameless, Tennessee. Express your feelings about the place where you live, explaining what you do and do not like about it.

Reviewing the Selection

RECALLING

1. What event causes the narrator to learn about Nameless, Tennessee?

2. What information does the narrator provide about "a six-calendar cafe in the Ozarks"?

3. What reason does Madison Wheeler give to explain why people "don't stay up in here anymore"?

4. How did Nameless come to be called "Nameless"?

INTERPRETING

5. What connection does the narrator see between some of the names in the atlas? What "logic" does he see in the name *Nameless*?

6. What is the relationship between the quality of food and the number of calendars in a cafe?

7. What facts emphasize Madison Wheeler's satisfaction with his situation in life?

8. What is probably the reason that "just gettin' by is dice rollin' to people nowadays"?

SYNTHESIZING

9. What circumstances described in this selection cause the reader to feel empathy or understanding for the people with whom the narrator speaks?

10. What sort of relationship between people and place is described in this selection? How is that relationship changing?

Understanding Literature (Questions for Discussion)

1. **Dialogue and Characterization. Dialogue** is conversation involving two or more people or characters. **Characterization** is the use of literary techniques to create a character. One of the three major techniques of characterization is portrayal of a character's behavior. When using portrayal of a character's behavior, the writer presents the actions and speech of the character, allowing readers to draw their own conclusions from what the character says or does. What conclusions can you draw

about the kind of person Madison Wheeler is from his comment, "Factory work's easier on the back, and I don't mind it, understand, but a man becomes what he does. Got to watch that. That's why I keep at farmin', although the crops haven't ever throve. It's the doin' that's important"?

2. **Description. Description**, one of the modes of writing, presents a portrayal of a character, an object, or a scene. Descriptions make use of sensory details—words and phrases that describe how things look, sound, smell, taste, and feel. Consider the following excerpt from the selection: "The old store, lighted only by three fifty-watt bulbs, smelled of coal oil and baking bread. In the middle of the rectangular room, where the oak floor sagged a little, stood an iron stove. To the right was a wooden table with an unfinished game of checkers and a stool made from an apple-tree stump. On shelves around the walls sat earthen jugs with corncob stoppers, a few canned goods, and some of the two thousand old clocks and clockworks Thurmond Watts owned." What particular words and phrases in the excerpt create a vivid picture of the old store?

Responding in Writing

Descriptive Paragraph. Write a descriptive paragraph about a place that you know very well, using concrete words and sensory details to create a vivid picture of that place.

> **Prewriting Suggestion:** Write the words *taste, smell, sound, touch,* and *sight* down the left-hand side of a piece of paper. At the top of the paper, write the name of the place you want to describe. Then, using concrete words, list details in each of the five sensory categories that describe the place.

PROJECT

Community Activity. Form small groups of three or four students. As a group, visit a nursing home and interview some of the residents about the places where they grew up, what kind of work they did, and what town played an important role in their lives and why. (Check with the nursing home staff first to get permission to interview residents and to make sure that your questions are appropriate. If it is not possible or practical to visit a nursing home, interview group members' grandparents.) Have one member of the group write down each person's replies and comments as clearly and accurately as possible. Have another member write a description of the person you are interviewing. As a group, write about each interview, including the dialogue and description of each person. As a class, place the interviews in a notebook for everyone to read.

AUTOBIOGRAPHY

from *An American Childhood*
by Annie Dillard

ABOUT THE AUTHOR

   Annie Dillard (1945–   ) was born in Pennsylvania and grew up in Pittsburgh. She was educated at Hollins College in Virginia. One of the more eloquent contemporary essayists, Dillard has won high praise for *Teaching a Stone to Talk* and for *Pilgrim at Tinker Creek,* which won a Pulitzer Prize. Her other titles include *An American Childhood, Tickets for a Prayer Wheel, Holy the Firm, Living by Fiction, Encounters with Chinese Writers,* and *The Writing Life.*

ABOUT THE SELECTION

Background: Technique. In the selection, Dillard's use of simple sentences, elaboration, and repetition creates a rhythmic, lyrical prose style. The effect of such an eloquent style is to place the reader or listener within the mind of five-year-old Annie Dillard as she learns about the boundaries between herself and the world.

Background: Genre. The selection is taken from Dillard's autobiography, *An American Childhood,* which was published in 1987. In the autobiography, Dillard focuses on her personal experiences, tracing her development from preschool through adolescence.

READER'S JOURNAL

Think of a childhood experience that frightened or puzzled you. Freewrite about that experience in your journal.

FROM

An American Childhood

ANNIE DILLARD

Why didn't Dillard tell anyone of the thing that frightened her?

When I was five, growing up in Pittsburgh in 1950, I would not go to bed willingly because something came into my room. This was a private matter between me and it. If I spoke of it, it would kill me.

Who could breathe as this thing searched for me over the very corners of the room? Who could ever breathe freely again? I lay in the dark.

My sister Amy, two years old, was asleep in the other bed. What did she know? She was innocent of evil. Even at two she <u>composed</u> herself attractively for sleep. She folded the top sheet tidily under her prettily outstretched arm; she laid her perfect head lightly on an unwrinkled pillow, where her thick curls spread evenly in rays like petals. All night long she slept smoothly in a series of pleasant and <u>serene</u>, if artificial-looking, positions, a faint smile on her closed lips, as if she were posing for an ad for sheets.

How does Dillard describe her sleeping sister?

There was no messiness in her, no roughness for things to cling to, only a charming and charmed innocence that seemed then to protect her, an innocence I needed but couldn't <u>muster</u>. Since Amy was asleep, furthermore, and since when I needed someone most I was afraid to stir enough to wake her, she was useless.

I lay alone and was almost asleep when the damned thing entered the room by flattening itself against the open door and sliding in. It was a transparent, <u>luminous</u> oblong. I could see the door whiten at its touch; I could see the blue wall turn pale where it raced over it, and see the maple headboard of Amy's bed glow. It was a swift spirit; it was an awareness. It made noise. It had two joined parts, a head and a tail, like a Chinese dragon.[1]

---

1. **Chinese dragon.** Large costume dragon worn by several people; used especially during Chinese New Year festivities

WORDS FOR EVERYDAY USE:

com • pose (kəm pōz´) *vt.,* put oneself in a state of tranquillity
se • rene (sə rēn´) *adj.,* calm; peaceful; tranquil

mus • ter (mus´ tər) *vt.,* gather together; summon up
lu • mi • nous (loo´mə nəs) *adj.,* filled with light; bright

It found the door, wall, and headboard; and it swiped them, charging them with its luminous glance. After its <u>fleet</u>, searching passage, things looked the same, but weren't.

I dared not blink or breathe; I tried to hush my whooping blood. If it found another awareness, it would destroy it.

Every night before it got to me it gave up. It hit my wall's corner and couldn't get past. It shrank completely into itself and vanished like a cobra down a hole. I heard the rising roar it made when it died or left. I still couldn't breathe. I knew—it was the worst fact I knew, a very hard fact—that it could return again alive that same night.

Sometimes it came back, sometimes it didn't. Most often, restless, it came back. The light stripe slipped in the door, ran searching over Amy's wall, stopped, stretched lunatic at the first corner, raced wailing toward my wall, and vanished into the second corner with a cry. So I wouldn't go to bed.

It was a passing car whose windshield reflected the corner streetlight outside. I figured it out one night.

Figuring it out was as memorable as the oblong itself. Figuring it out was a long and forced <u>ascent</u> to the very rim of being, to the <u>membrane</u> of skin that both separates and connects the inner life and the outer world. I climbed deliberately from the depths like a diver who releases the monster in his arms and hauls himself hand over hand up an anchor chain[2] till he meets the ocean's sparkling membrane and bursts through it; he sights the sunlit, becalmed hull[3] of his boat, which had bulked so <u>ominously</u> from below.

I recognized the noise it made when it left. That is, the noise it made called to mind, at last, my daytime sensations when a car passed—the sight and noise together. A car came roaring down hushed Edgerton Avenue in front of our house, stopped at the corner stop sign, and passed on shrieking as its engine shifted up the gears. What, precisely, came into the bedroom? A reflection from the car's oblong windshield. Why did it travel in two parts? The window sash[4] split the light and cast a shadow.

Night after night I labored up the same long chain of reasoning, as night after night the thing burst into the room where I lay awake and Amy slept prettily and my loud heart thrashed and I froze.

There was a world outside my window and <u>contiguous</u> to it. If I was so all fired bright, as my parents, who had <u>patently</u> no basis for comparison, seemed to think, why did I have to keep learning this same thing over and over? For I had learned it a summer ago, when men with jackhammers broke up Edgerton Avenue. I had watched them from the yard; the street came up in jagged slabs like floes.[5] When I lay to nap, I listened. One restless afternoon I connected the new noise in my bedroom with the jack-

What was the worst thing about "it"?

What did "it" turn out to be?

2. **anchor chain.** Chain attached to a boat's anchor and used to pull up the anchor
3. **becalmed hull.** Body of the boat motionless due to lack of wind
4. **sash.** Frame holding glass panes of a window
5. **floes.** Chunks of ice floating on the water

| WORDS FOR EVERYDAY USE: | fleet (flēt) *adj.*, swift; rapid
as • cent (ə sent´) *n.*, act of rising or climbing
mem • brane (mem´brān) *n.*, thin, soft layer of tissue
om • i • nous • ly (äm´ə nəs lē) *adv.*, in a threat- | ening manner
con • tig • u • ous (kən tig´ yoo əs) *adj.*, near; next; adjacent
pa • tent • ly (pāt´ ´nt lē) *adv.*, clearly; obviously |

Untitled Series #7. Nic Nicosia, 1993

collection of things and people, of items, and I myself was one such item—a child walking up the sidewalk, whom anyone could see or ignore. The things in the world did not necessarily cause my <u>overwhelming</u> feelings; the feelings were inside me, beneath my skin, behind my ribs, within my skull. They were even, to some extent, under my control.

I could be connected to the outer world by reason, if I chose, or I could yield to what amounted to a narrative fiction, to a tale of terror whispered to me by the blood in my ears, a show in light projected on the room's blue walls. As time passed, I learned to amuse myself in bed in the darkened room by entering the fiction deliberately and replacing it by reason deliberately.

When the low roar drew nigh and the oblong slid in the door, I threw my own switches for pleasure. It's coming after me; it's a car outside. It's after me. It's a car. It raced over the wall, lighting it blue wherever it ran; it bumped over Amy's maple headboard in a rush, paused, slithered elongate[6] over the corner, shrank, flew my way, and vanished into itself with a wail. It was a car. ■

How did Dillard amuse herself?

hammer men I had been seeing outside. I understood <u>abruptly</u> that these worlds met, the outside and the inside. I traveled the route in my mind: You walked downstairs from here, and outside from downstairs. "Outside," then, was <u>conceivably</u> just beyond my windows. It was the same world I reached by going out the front or the back door. I forced my imagination yet again over this route.

The world did not have me in mind; it had no mind. It was a <u>coincidental</u>

---

6. **elongate.** Stretched

Responding to the Selection

In small groups, discuss how you interpreted shadows, reflections, and sounds at night when you were a young child. What shapes of shadows do you remember? What sounds frightened or delighted you?

Reviewing the Selection

RECALLING

1. What age is the narrator when she "would not go to bed willingly"?

2. Of what does the narrator believe her younger sister is innocent?

3. What information does the narrator provide about "it"?

4. What does the narrator figure out "it" really is?

INTERPRETING

5. What keeps the narrator awake at night?

6. What details in paragraph 3 emphasize the narrator's characterization of her sister as innocent?

7. What details in paragraph 4 emphasize the narrator's description of "it" as a "swift spirit"?

8. What is the narrator learning to do by "entering the fiction deliberately and replacing it by reason deliberately"?

SYNTHESIZING

9. What sort of relationship between the worlds of "the outside and the inside" is described by the narrator?

10. How does the narrator's point of view allow the reader to know the internal workings of her young mind?

Understanding Literature (Questions for Discussion)

1. **Simile.** A **simile** is a comparison using *like* or *as.* The description invites the reader to compare the two things to see how they are similar. In the selection, the narrator says, "She laid her perfect head lightly on an unwrinkled pillow, where her thick curls spread evenly in rays like petals." What two things are being compared in that sentence? What do these things have in common? In a later paragraph, the narrator says, "It shrank completely into itself and vanished like a cobra down a hole." What two things are being compared in that sentence? What do they have in common? Identify other similes in the selection.

2. **Elaboration.** Elaboration, or **amplification,** is a writing technique in which a subject is introduced and then expanded upon by means of repetition with slight changes, the addition of details, or similar devices. For example, the selection opens with the sentence "When I was five, growing up in Pittsburgh in 1950, I would not go to bed willingly because something came into my room." The narrator then elaborates on that subject, adding the details of her sister sleeping, details of the "transparent, luminous oblong," and closing her five-year-old fictional view of "it" by repeating a slight variation of her opening sentence, "So I wouldn't go to bed." Identify another example of elaboration in the selection and explain what elements are used in the elaboration.

Responding in Writing

Autobiographical Essay. Write an autobiographical essay about a particular event or occurrence that you remember trying to understand when you were a young child. In your essay, describe the event through your young-child eyes. Then describe and explain it through your older eyes.

> **Prewriting Suggestion:** Draw a line vertically down a blank piece of paper. At the top of the left-hand side, write *child eyes.* At the top of the right-hand side, write *older eyes.* Then close your eyes and try to visualize the experience you want to write about in your essay. Try to see the event as you saw it when you were a child. As soon as you have it visualized in your mind, open your eyes and write as many of the details as you can remember in the left-hand column. In the corresponding space in the right-hand column, write an explanation or view of that detail as you understand it or see it now.

PROJECT

Elaboration Circle. Write one or two open-ended sentences (such as, "No one would ever believe that I . . .") on small pieces of paper. Fold the papers in half and place them all in a small box. Sit in a circle and pass the box around. Each person should draw one sentence and keep it until it is his or her turn to start the elaboration. Select someone to start the elaboration, having that person read aloud the open-ended sentence. Then, moving clockwise, have the next person say something to add to the elaboration. Keep moving along the circle, adding details and repetition to the elaboration. Whoever is last in each sequence of elaboration needs to repeat the original sentence, but in a slightly varied form. Begin another elaboration by starting with another open-ended sentence.

"The United States vs. Susan B. Anthony"
by Margaret Truman

ABOUT THE AUTHOR

Margaret Truman (1924–) was born in Independence, Missouri. The only child of Elizabeth (Bess) and President Harry S Truman, she attended a private school in Washington, DC. In 1946, Truman graduated from George Washington University, where she did work in history and international studies. A gifted soprano, Truman has studied voice and performed as a soloist. Truman has written many works of biography and fiction. Her biographies include *Bess Truman, Harry S Truman,* and *Women of Courage,* from which the selection is taken. In her ongoing series of mysteries set in Washington DC, which include *Murder on Capitol Hill* and *Murder at the Pentagon,* Truman writes about the inner circles of Washington politics, arts, business, and bureaucracy.

ABOUT THE SELECTION

Background: Theme. In *Women of Courage,* Margaret Truman describes the lives of twelve courageous women, one of whom is Susan B. Anthony, a pioneering crusader for women's rights. Truman's book explores the meaning of courage and offers a contemporary perspective on "the outstanding women in our past."

Background: Technique. In "The United States vs. Susan B. Anthony," Truman uses a number of writing techniques, such as summarization, quotation, and historical background, to bring alive one particular episode in Susan B. Anthony's life that shows why she was a woman of courage.

READER'S JOURNAL

Have you ever taken a stand on an issue of great importance to you? Did you find the experience of being courageous difficult or easy? Freewrite about courage in your journal. You might write about personal courage or about the courage that someone has demonstrated in your community.

"The United States vs. Susan B. Anthony"

MARGARET TRUMAN

Why wasn't Anthony one of the author's favorite characters?

Susan B. Anthony has never been one of my favorite characters. Stern-eyed and grim-lipped, she seemed utterly <u>devoid</u> of warmth and humor and much too quick to dominate the women she worked with. I always thought her personality could be summed up in one word: battle-ax. On top of that drawback, she was a fanatic. She joined the woman's <u>suffrage</u> movement in 1852, when she was thirty-two years old. From then until her death in 1906, she could think of little else.

The fanatics of one generation have a habit of turning into the heroes and heroines of the next, as Susan B. Anthony proved. And since I've been making a study of heroines, I decided to give Miss Anthony a second look. I have to report that my original <u>assess-</u><u>ment</u> of her character was much too harsh.

Susan B. Anthony came to the woman's movement by a somewhat <u>circuitous</u> route. She was a reformer by inheritance as well as by <u>tempera-</u><u>ment</u>. Her parents were passionate supporters of abolition, temperance,[1] and woman's rights. They numbered among their friends some of the outstanding liberals of the nineteenth century, men like William Lloyd Garrison,[2] Frederick Douglass,[3] and

---

1. **abolition, temperance.** *Abolition*—abolishing, doing away with, as in slavery; *temperance*—moderation or abstinence from drinking alcoholic beverages
2. **William Lloyd Garrison.** (1805–1879) Editor and abolitionist leader
3. **Frederick Douglass.** (1817–1895) Journalist, statesman, African-American leader

---

WORDS FOR EVERYDAY USE:

de • void (di void´) *adj.,* completely without
suf • frage (suf´rij) *n.,* right to vote
as • sess • ment (əs ses´ ment) *n.,* evaluation

cir • cu • i • tous (sər kyōō´ət əs) *adj.,* round-about; indirect
tem • per • a • ment (tem´pər ə mənt) *n.,* customary frame of mind

Prudence Crandall's old ally, the Reverend Samuel J. May.

Daniel Anthony had a <u>succession</u> of homes, a succession of jobs, and a succession of financial ups and downs. He began his career as a farmer in Adams, Massachusetts, but gave up farming to buy a cotton mill near Albany, New York. His business was wrecked by the panic of 1837,[4] and he bought another farm, this one a small plot of land just outside of Rochester, New York.

The collapse of the cotton mill left the Anthony family with a mountain of debts. Susan, by then in her late teens, became a teacher to help pay them off. After ten years in the classroom, she resigned and took over the management of her father's farm so Daniel Anthony could devote his attention to still another business <u>venture</u>—an insurance agency that eventually made him prosperous once more.

As I mentioned earlier, the instinct for <u>reform</u> had been bred into Susan since childhood. She was particularly concerned about temperance, and her work in that movement soon brought her in contact with Amelia Bloomer, who ran a temperance newspaper in Seneca Falls. Mrs. Bloomer introduced her to another temperance advocate, Elizabeth Cady Stanton, who was now pouring most of her energies into a campaign to give women the vote. Mrs. Stanton tried to enlist Susan's support in the suffrage movement, but Susan <u>demurred</u>. She was too busy with temperance activities to have time for anything else.

In 1852, Susan B. Anthony attended a rally in Albany where she was refused permission to speak because of her sex. The incident made her so angry that she withdrew from the regular temperance organization and set up a separate Woman's New York State Temperance Society with Elizabeth Cady Stanton as its president.

Not long after that, Susan went to a convention of the New York State Teachers' Association. More than two-thirds of the members were women, but the men ran the entire meeting, giving the speeches, voting on resolutions,[5] and generally ignoring the women, who sat in an isolated bloc at the back of the room.

When a panel of male speakers began a lengthy debate on the topic: "Why the profession of a teacher is not as much respected as that of lawyer, doctor, or minister," Susan requested permission to state her opinion on the matter. After some discussion, the men agreed to let her be heard.

Susan offered a very simple answer to the question. "Do you not see," she said, "that so long as society says woman is incompetent to be a lawyer, minister, or doctor, but has ample ability to be a teacher, every man of you who chooses this profession <u>tacitly</u> acknowledges that he has no more brains than a woman?"

---

4. **panic of 1837.** Period during which widespread fear of financial disaster resulted in people rushing to sell property for cash

5. **resolutions.** Potential laws or formal opinions presented for approval to a particular group

What angered Anthony? What did she do as a result?

For what cause did Stanton try to enlist Anthony? What was Anthony's response?

WORDS FOR EVERYDAY USE:

suc • ces • sion (sək sesh´ən) *n.,* series

ven • ture (ven´chər) *n.,* enterprise in which there is risk of loss as well as chance for profit

re • form (ri fôrm´) *n.,* improvement by introducing better procedures

de • mur (dē mʉr) *vi.,* hesitate because of one's doubts

tac • it • ly (tas´it lē) *adv.,* silently

How were Anthony's ideas and actions belittled by the press?

She went on to say a few words about the <u>disparity</u> in the salaries of men and women teachers. It would be to the men's advantage to equalize them, she maintained, because their own incomes suffered when they had to compete with the cheap labor of women.

The speech left most of Susan's audience in a state of shock. A few men rushed over to congratulate her; the women remained silent. But she made at least one convert. A woman from Rochester pushed through a resolution <u>affirming</u> the right of women teachers to participate in all of the association's activities, including speaking at meetings, serving on committees, and holding office.

Susan B. Anthony's success with the teachers' association convinced her that discrimination against women should—and could—be overcome. Before long, she had become Elizabeth Cady Stanton's chief lieutenant in the woman's rights movement. Mrs. Stanton had young children at the time and was not free to travel extensively. She concentrated on writing letters and speeches, while Susan did most of the legwork. She proved to be a brilliant organizer and an <u>indefatigable</u> lecturer, a master at circulating petitions,[6] organizing conventions, and browbeating politicians.

What skills made Anthony a good leader for the movement?

All of the women who had the guts to demand the right to vote were cruelly criticized in the press, but Susan was invariably singled out as a special target. The fact that she was unmarried made her particularly vulnerable. This was declared proof positive that her crusade was simply the ranting of an embittered old maid.

The insulting newspaper articles and vicious cartoons must have bothered Susan. But she never let it show. She threw herself into her work. There was always a new speech to write, a new meeting to organize, a new petition to be drawn up and presented to a state legislature.

Susan B. Anthony was a stern and single-minded woman. Like most crusaders for causes—especially unpopular causes—she had little time for fun and games. But I have a sneaky feeling that behind her severe manner and <u>unremitting</u> devotion to duty, she may actually have had a sense of humor. Let me tell you about my favorite episode in Susan B. Anthony's career, and perhaps you'll agree.

It began on Friday morning, November 1, 1872. Susan was reading the morning paper at her home in Rochester. There, at the top of the editorial page of the *Democrat and Chronicle*, was an exhortation[7] to the city's residents:

> Now register! Today and tomorrow are the only remaining opportunities. If you were not permitted to vote, you would fight for the right, undergo all <u>privations</u> for it, face death for it. You have it now at the cost of five minutes' time to be spent in seeking your place of

---

6. **petitions.** Formal requests often signed by people who support the request
7. **exhortation.** Passionate demand, as in a sermon

WORDS FOR EVERYDAY USE:

dis • par • i • ty (di spar´ə tē) *n.,* inequality
af • firm (ə furm´) *vt.,* declare firmly
in • de • fat • i • ga • ble (in´ di fat´ i gə bəl) *adj.,* that cannot be tired out

un • re • mit • ting (uń ri mit´ iŋ) *adj.,* incessant; persistent
pri • va • tion (prī vā´shən) *n.,* lack of the ordinary necessities of life

registration and having your name entered. And yet, on election day, less than a week hence, hundreds of you are likely to lose your votes because you have not thought it worth while to give the five minutes. Today and tomorrow are your only opportunities. Register now!

Susan B. Anthony read the editorial again. Just as she thought, it said nothing about being addressed to men only. With a gleam in her eye, she put down the paper and summoned her sister Guelma, with whom she lived. The two women donned their hats and cloaks and went off to call on two other Anthony sisters who lived nearby. Together, the four women headed for the barber shop on West Street, where voters from the Eighth Ward were being registered.

For some time, Susan B. Anthony had been looking for an opportunity to test the Fourteenth Amendment to the Constitution as a weapon to win the vote for women. Adopted in 1870, the Amendment had been designed to protect the civil rights—especially the voting rights—of recently freed slaves. It stated that:

All persons born or naturalized[8] in the United States, and subject to the jurisdiction thereof, are citizens of the United States and of the State wherein they reside. No State shall make or enforce any law which shall abridge[9] the privileges or immunities of citizens of the United States, nor shall any State deprive any person of life, liberty, or property without due process of law,[10] nor deny to any person within its jurisdiction the equal protection of the laws.

The Amendment did not say that "persons" meant only males, nor did it spell out "the privileges and immunities of citizens." Susan B. Anthony felt perfectly justified in concluding that the right to vote was among the privileges of citizenship and that it extended to women as well as men. I'm sure she must have also seen the humor of outwitting the supposedly superior males who wrote the Amendment.

It was bad enough for a bunch of women to barge into one sacred male precinct—the barber shop—but to insist on being admitted to another holy of holies—the voting booth—was absolutely outrageous. Moustaches twitched, throats were cleared, a whispered conference was held in the corner.

Susan had brought along a copy of the Fourteenth Amendment. She read it aloud, carefully pointing out to the men in charge of registration that the document failed to state that the privilege of voting <u>extended</u> only to males.

Only one man in the barber shop had the nerve to refuse the Anthony sisters the right to register. The rest buckled under Susan's determined <u>oratory</u> and allowed them to sign the huge, leather-

> *What did Anthony notice about the editorial?*

> *What did Anthony read at the voter registration? What point did she make?*

---

8. **naturalized.** Having obtained citizenship in a country not of one's birth
9. **abridge.** Limit
10. **due process of law.** Proper legal process

WORDS FOR EVERYDAY USE:

ju • ris • dic • tion (jo͝or´is dik´ shən) *n.,* authority in general

im • mu • ni • ty (im myo͞on´ i tē) *n.,* freedom from something burdensome

ex • tend (ek stend´) *vt.,* grant

or • a • to • ry (ôr´ ə tôr´ē) *n.,* eloquence in public speaking

bound voter registration book. If the men in the barber shop thought they were getting rid of a little band of crackpots the easy way, they were wrong. Susan urged all her followers in Rochester to register. The next day, a dozen women invaded the Eighth Ward barber shop, and another thirty-five appeared at registration sites elsewhere in the city. The *Democrat and Chronicle*, which had <u>inadvertently</u> prompted the registrations, expressed no editorial opinion on the <u>phenomenon</u>, but its rival, the *Union and Advertiser*, <u>denounced</u> the women. If they were allowed to vote, the paper declared, the poll inspectors[11] "should be prosecuted to the full extent of the law."

The following Tuesday, November 5, was Election Day. Most of the poll inspectors in Rochester had read the editorial in the *Union and Advertiser* and were too intimidated to allow any of the women who had registered to vote. Only in the Eighth Ward did the males weaken. Maybe the inspectors were *Democrat and Chronicle* readers, or perhaps they were more afraid of Susan B. Anthony than they were of the law. Whatever the reason, when Susan and her sisters showed up at the polls shortly after 7 A.M., there was only a minimum of fuss. A couple of inspectors were hesitant about letting the women vote, but when Susan assured them that she would pay all their legal expenses if they were prosecuted, the men relented, and one by one, the women took their ballots and

stepped into the voting booth. There were no insults or sneers, no rude remarks. They marked their ballots, dropped them into the ballot box, and returned to their homes.

Susan B. Anthony's feat quickly became the talk of the country. She was applauded in some circles, <u>vilified</u> in others. But the day of reckoning[12] was not long in arriving. On November 28, Deputy U. S. Marshal E. J. Keeney appeared at her door with a warrant[13] for her arrest. She had violated Section 19 of the Enforcement Act of the Fourteenth Amendment, which held that anyone who voted illegally was to be arrested and tried on criminal charges.

Susan B. Anthony was a great believer in planning ahead. The day after she registered, she decided to get a legal opinion on whether or not she should attempt to vote. A number of lawyers turned her away, but she finally found one who agreed to consider the case. He was Henry R. Selden, a former judge of the Court of Appeals, now a partner in one of Rochester's most prestigious law firms.

On the Monday before Election Day, Henry Selden informed his new client that he agreed with her interpretation of the Fourteenth Amendment and that in his opinion, she had every right to cast her ballot.

Why was Anthony arrested?

---

11. **poll inspectors.** People who supervise voting and registration for an election
12. **day of reckoning.** Day of judgment, as in the Bible
13. **warrant.** Legal document that gives permission to law enforcement personnel to arrest a person or search a piece of property

WORDS FOR EVERYDAY USE:

in • ad • vert • ent • ly (in´ad vʉrt´ ´nt lē) *adv.,* due to oversight; unintentionally

phe • nom • e • non (fə näm´ ə nən´) *n.,* any extremely unusual occurrence

de • nounce (dē nouns´) *vt.,* criticize

vil • i • fy (vil´ə fī´) *vt.,* abuse verbally; slander

The U. S. Commissioner of Elections in Rochester, William C. Storrs, did not <u>concur</u>.

E. J. Keeney, the marshal <u>dispatched</u> to arrest Susan B. Anthony, was not at all happy with his assignment. He nervously twirled his tall felt hat while waiting for her to come to the front door. When she finally appeared, he blushed and stammered, shifted uncomfortably from one foot to the other, and finally blurted out, "The Commissioner wishes to arrest you."

Susan couldn't help being amused at Keeney's embarrassment. "Is this your usual method of serving a warrant?" she asked calmly. With that, the marshal recovered his official dignity, presented her with the warrant, and told her that he had come to escort her to the office of the Commissioner of Elections.

When Susan asked if she could change into a more suitable dress, the marshal saw his opportunity to escape. "Of course," he said, turning to leave. "Just come down to the Commissioner's office whenever you're ready."

"I'll do no such thing," Susan informed him curtly. "You were sent here to arrest me and take me to court. It's your duty to do so."

Keeney had no choice but to wait while his prisoner went upstairs and put on a more appropriate outfit. When she returned, she thrust out her wrists and said, "Don't you want to handcuff me, too?"

"I assure you, madam," Marshal Keeney stuttered, "it isn't at all necessary."

With the U. S. Marshal at her side, Susan was brought before the Federal Commissioner of Elections, William C. Storrs. Her arrest was recorded, and she was ordered to appear the next day for a hearing. It was conducted by U. S. District Attorney Richard Crowley and his assistant, John E. Pound.

Susan answered District Attorney Crowley's questions politely. She said that she thought the Fourteenth Amendment gave her the right to vote. She admitted that she had consulted an attorney on the question but said that she would have voted even if he had not advised her to do so. When Crowley asked if she had voted deliberately to test the law, she said, "Yes, sir. I have been determined for three years to vote the first time I happened to be at home for the required thirty days before an election."

The District Attorney's next step was to <u>convene</u> a grand jury to draw up a bill of indictment.[14] He and his assistant fell to wrangling over a suitable trial date. Susan interrupted them. "I have lecture dates that will take me to central Ohio," she said. "I won't be available until December 10."

"But you're supposed to be in custody until the hearing," Crowley informed her.

"Is that so?" said Susan coolly. "I didn't know that."

The District Attorney backed down without an argument and scheduled the grand jury session for December 23.

How did Keeney feel about arresting Anthony?

What had Anthony been determined to do for three years?

---

14. **bill of indictment.** Formal request to charge an individual with a crime

WORDS FOR EVERYDAY USE:

con • cur (kən kur´) vt., agree

dis • patch (di spach´) vt., send off on an errand

con • vene (kən vēn´) vi., assemble

Sixteen women had voted in Rochester. All sixteen were arrested and taken before the grand jury, but Susan alone was brought to trial. The District Attorney had decided to single her out as a test case. The three poll inspectors who had allowed the women to vote were also arrested. The grand jury indicted them too, set bail at five hundred dollars each, and ordered their trial set for the summer term of the U. S. District Court.

Susan Anthony's case now involved nineteen other men and women. All of them—including Susan—were <u>liable</u> to go to prison if they were found guilty and the judge was in a sentencing mood. Prison in the 1870s was a very unpleasant place. There were no minimum security setups[15] where a <u>benevolent</u> government allowed corrupt politicians, crooked labor leaders, and political <u>agitators</u> to rest and rehabilitate, as we do today. Prison meant a cold cell, wretched food, the company of thieves and murderers.

For a while it looked as if Susan might be behind bars even before her trial. She refused to post a bond for her five-hundred-dollar bail. Henry Selden paid the money for her. "I could not see a lady I respected put in jail," he said.

It must be agonizing to sweat out the weeks before a trial. There is time to look ahead and <u>brood</u> about the possibility of an unfavorable verdict and time to look back, perhaps with regret, at the decision that placed you in the hands of the law. But Susan B. Anthony

had no regrets. Nor did she appear to have any anxieties about her trial. She had already proven her <u>fortitude</u> by devoting twenty years of her life to fighting for the right to vote. If she won her case, the struggle would be over. But even if she lost, Susan was not ready to give up the fight.

Some prospective defendants are too <u>demoralized</u> to do anything but sit around and worry. Not Susan B. Anthony. In the course of the next few months, she attended woman's rights conventions in Ohio, Illinois, and Indiana. She appeared before a session that was meeting in Albany to revise the New York State Constitution and tried to persuade them to include equal suffrage among its <u>provisions</u>. Then she went back to Rochester to cast her

How did Anthony feel about her actions and her upcoming trial?

---

15. **minimum security setups.** Prisons for criminals deemed not dangerous, in which more freedom is given to prisoners than is given to maximum security prisons

---

WORDS FOR
EVERYDAY USE:

li • a • ble (lī´ə bəl) adj., subject to
be • nev • o • lent (bə nev´ə lənt) adj., kind
ag • i • ta • tor (aj´i tāt´ ər) n., person who stirs up people in support of an unfavorable cause
brood (brood) vi., worry

for • ti • tude (fôrt´ ə tood´) n., strength
de • mor • al • ized (dē môr´ə līzd´) adj., weak of spirit and morale
pro • vi • sion (prō vizh´ ən) n., clause or agreement in a legal document

ballot again in the city elections on March 4, 1873.

Deputy Marshal Keeney appeared at the railroad every time she left Rochester. He reminded her that she was not supposed to leave the city while she was out on bail. Susan would smile, nod, and get on the train. Keeney never tried to stop her.

The summer term of the District Court opened in May. In mid-March, Susan launched a new lecture tour. Her topic: Is it a crime for a citizen of the United States to vote? The lecture centered on the U. S. Constitution, particularly the Fourteenth Amendment.

She spoke in every town in New York's Monroe County and drew surprisingly large audiences. When she polled the crowd at the end of each lecture, the majority <u>invariably</u> supported her. Even those who had been <u>skeptics</u> when they entered the hall usually changed their minds when they heard her arguments.

District Attorney Crowley soon decided that Susan was making it difficult for him to find an <u>unprejudiced</u> jury anywhere in the vicinity of Rochester. When he voiced his concern to Susan, she replied by asking him if he honestly believed that a jury could be prejudiced by having the Constitution of the United States read and explained to them.

Crowley became so exasperated that when the District Court opened on May 13, he requested a change of venue[16] from Rochester to Canandaigua in adjacent Ontario County. The change forced a postponement of the

trial until June 17. Susan promptly launched a whirlwind lecture tour of the villages around Canandaigua. She managed to cover twenty-one postal districts on her own, while her good friend and supporter, Matilda Joslyn Gage, covered the remaining sixteen.

The trial of *The United States* vs. *Susan B. Anthony* opened on the afternoon of June 17, 1873, with the tolling of the Canandaigua Courthouse bell. The presiding justice was Ward Hunt, a prim, pale man, who owed his judgeship to the good offices of Senator Roscoe Conkling, the Republican boss of New York State.[17] Conkling was a fierce foe of woman suffrage, and Hunt, who had no wish to offend his powerful <u>patron</u>, had written his decision before the trial started.

District Attorney Crowley opened the arguments for the prosecution.[18] They didn't make much sense at the time and in <u>retrospect</u>, they sound nothing short of ridiculous. The District Attorney mentioned that Susan B. Anthony was a woman and therefore she had no right to vote. His principal witness was an inspector of elections for the Eighth Ward, who swore that on November 5 he had seen Miss Anthony put her ballot in the ballot box. To back up his <u>testimony</u>, the inspector produced the voter registration

What was the subject of Anthony's lecture series? On what did she focus?

What had Hunt done before the trial started? Why did he do this?

---

16. **change of venue.** To hold a trial at a different location
17. **owed his judgeship . . . New York State.** The author means that the judge was given his job as a political favor by the senator.
18. **prosecution.** Legal professionals who attempt to prove the guilt of a defendant in a trial

WORDS FOR EVERYDAY USE:	**in • var • i • a • bly** (in ver´ē ə blē) *adv.*, constantly; uniformly **skep • tic** (skep´tik´) *n.*, doubter **un • prej • u • diced** (un prej´ ə dist) *adj.*, without bias; impartial	**pa • tron** (pā´ trən) *n.*, protector; benefactor **ret • ro • spect** (re´ trə spekt´) *n.*, looking back on **tes • ti • mo • ny** (tes´ tə mō´nē) *n.*, statement made under oath in a court

book with Susan B. Anthony's signature in it.

Henry Selden's reply for the defense was equally simple. He contended that Susan Anthony had registered and voted in good faith, believing that it was her constitutional right to do so. When he attempted to call his client to the stand, however, District Attorney Crowley announced that she was not <u>competent</u> to testify in her own behalf. Judge Hunt agreed, and the only thing Henry Selden could do was read excerpts from the testimony Susan had given at her previous hearings when <u>presumably</u> she was no less incompetent than she was right now.

Henry Selden tried to make up for this gross injustice by making his closing argument a dramatic, three-hour speech on behalf of woman suffrage. District Attorney Crowley replied with a two-hour rehash of the original charge.

By the afternoon of June 18, the case of *The United States* vs. *Susan B. Anthony* was ready to go to the jury. It was impossible to predict what their verdict might be, so Judge Hunt, determined to make it the verdict he and Roscoe Conkling wanted, took matters into his own hands. "Gentlemen of the jury," he said, "I direct that you find the defendant guilty."

Henry Selden leaped to his feet. "I object, your honor," he thundered. "The court has no power to direct the jury in a criminal case."

Judge Hunt ignored him. "Take the verdict, Mr. Clerk," he said.

The clerk of the court must have been another Conkling man.[19] "Gentlemen of the jury," he intoned as if the whole proceeding was perfectly normal, "<u>hearken</u>[20] to the verdict as the court hath recorded it. You say you find the defendant guilty of the offense charged. So say you all."

The twelve jurymen looked stunned. They had not even met to discuss the case, much less agree on a verdict. When Henry Selden asked if the clerk could at least poll the jury, Judge Hunt rapped his gavel sharply and declared, "That cannot be allowed. Gentlemen of the jury, you are <u>discharged</u>."

An enraged Henry Selden lost no time in introducing a <u>motion</u>[21] for a new trial on the grounds that his client had been denied the right to a jury verdict. Judge Hunt denied the motion. He turned to Susan B. Anthony and said, "The prisoner will stand up. Has the prisoner anything to say why sentence shall not be pronounced?"

Thus far in the trial, Susan B. Anthony had remained silent. Now, she rose to her feet and said slowly, "Yes, your honor, I have many things to say."

Without further <u>preliminaries</u>, she launched into a scathing <u>denunciation</u>[22] of Judge Hunt's conduct of her trial. ". . . In your ordered verdict of guilty," she said, "you have trampled underfoot every vital principle of our

---

19. **another Conkling man.** Also appointed, or given his job as a political favor, by Senator Conkling
20. **hearken.** Listen
21. **motion.** Formal request
22. **denunciation.** Harsh criticism

Why wasn't Anthony allowed to testify?

How was the case decided?

WORDS FOR EVERYDAY USE:	com • pe • tent (käm´ pə tənt) *adj.*, capable; fit pre • sum • a • bly (prē zōōm´ ə blē) *adv.*, supposedly; believably	dis • charge (dis chärj´) *vt.*, remove; release pre • lim • i • nar • ies (prē lim´ ə ner´ēz) *n.*, introductory comments

government. My natural rights, my civil rights, my political rights, are all alike ignored. Robbed of the fundamental privilege of citizenship, I am <u>degraded</u> from the status of a citizen to that of a subject;[23] and not only myself individually, but all of my sex, are, by your honor's verdict, doomed to political <u>subjection</u> under this so-called Republican government."

Judge Hunt reached for his gavel, but Susan B. Anthony refused to be silenced.

"May it please your honor," she continued. "Your denial of my citizen's right to vote is the denial of my right to a trial by a jury of my peers as an offender against law, therefore, the denial of my sacred rights to life, liberty, property, and—"

"The court cannot allow the prisoner to go on," Judge Hunt cried out.

Susan ignored him and continued her impassioned <u>tirade</u> against the court. Hunt frantically rapped his gavel and ordered her to sit down and be quiet. But Susan, who must have been taking delight in his <u>consternation</u>, kept on talking. She deplored the fact that she had been denied the right to a fair trial. Even if she had been given such a trial, she insisted, it would not have been by her peers. Jury, judges, and lawyers were not her equals, but her superiors, because they could vote and she could not. Susan was <u>adamant</u> about the fact that she had been denied the justice guaranteed in the Constitution to every citizen of the United States.

Judge Hunt was sufficiently cowed[24] by now to try to defend himself. "The prisoner has been tried according to the established forms of law," he sputtered.

"Yes, your honor," retorted Susan, overlooking his <u>blatant</u> lie, "but by forms of law all made by men, interpreted by men, administered by men, in favor of men, and against women; and hence your honor's ordered verdict of guilty, against a United States citizen for the exercise of that citizen's right to vote, simply because that citizen was a woman and not a man. But yesterday, the same manmade forms of law declared it a crime punishable with a one-thousand-dollar fine and six months imprisonment, for you, or me, or any of us, to give a cup of cold water, a crust of bread, or a night's shelter to a panting fugitive while he was tracking his way to Canada. And every man or woman in whose veins coursed a drop of human sympathy violated that wicked law, reckless of consequences, and was justified in so doing. As, then, the slaves who got their freedom must take it over, or under, or through the unjust forms of law, precisely so now must women, to get their right to a voice in this government, take it, and I have taken mine, and mean to take it at every opportunity."

Judge Hunt flailed his gavel and gave the by now futile order for the prisoner

To what does Anthony compare the laws and legal system that have condemned her?

23. **subject.** Person who submits or surrenders to a monarch or dictator
24. **cowed.** Made afraid

to sit down and be quiet. Susan kept right on talking.

"When I was brought before your honor for trial," she said, "I hoped for a broad and liberal interpretation of the Constitution and its recent Amendments. One that would declare all United States citizens under its protection. But failing to get this justice—failing, even, to get a trial by a jury *not* of my peers—I ask not <u>leniency</u> at your hands—but to take the full rigors of the law."

With that Susan finally obeyed Judge Hunt's orders and sat down. Now he had to reverse himself[25] and order her to stand up so he could <u>impose</u> sentence. As soon as he <u>pronounced</u> the sentence—a fine of one hundred dollars plus the costs of prosecuting the trial—Susan spoke up again. "May it please your honor," she said, "I shall never pay a dollar of your unjust penalty. All the stock in trade[26] I possess is a ten-thousand-dollar debt, incurred by publishing my paper—*The Revolution*—four years ago, the sole object of which was to educate all women to do precisely as I have done, rebel against your manmade, unjust, unconstitutional forms of law, that tax, fine, imprison, and hang women, while they deny them the right of representation in the government; and I shall work on with might and main to pay every dollar of that honest debt, but not a penny shall go to this unjust claim. And I shall earnestly and <u>persistently</u> continue to urge all women to the practical recognition of the old

Revolutionary <u>maxim</u>, that 'Resistance to tyranny is obedience to God.' "

Judge Hunt must have had strict orders not only to see that the defendant was convicted, but to do everything he could to prevent the case from going on to a higher court. He allowed Susan to walk out of the courtroom without imposing a prison sentence in lieu[27] of her unpaid fine. If he had sent her to prison, she could have been released on a writ of habeas corpus[28] and would have had the right to appeal. As it was, the case was closed.

Although she was disappointed that her case would not go to the Supreme Court as she had originally hoped, Susan knew that she had struck an important blow for woman's suffrage. Henry Selden's arguments and her own speech at the end of the trial were widely publicized, and Judge Hunt's conduct of the trial stood as proof that women were treated unjustly before the law.

Susan did not forget the election inspectors who had allowed her to cast her ballot. The men were fined twenty-five dollars each and sent to jail when they refused to pay. In all, they spent about a week behind bars before Susan, through the influence of friends in Washington, obtained presidential

---

25. **reverse himself.** Do the opposite of what was first intended
26. **stock in trade.** Possessions that can be sold for money
27. **in lieu.** Instead
28. **habeas corpus.** Constitutional right that protects against illegal imprisonment

WORDS FOR EVERYDAY USE:

le • ni • en • cy (lē′nē ən sē) *n.,* kindness; flexibility

im • pose (im pōz′) *vt.,* place or set

pro • nounce (prō nouns′) *vt.,* declare officially

per • sist • ent • ly (pər sist ′ənt lē) *adv.,* unre-

lentingly; stubbornly

max • im (maks′ im) *n.,* statement of a general truth

Why didn't Judge Hunt sentence Anthony to prison when she refused to pay her fine?

pardons[29] for each of them. In the meantime, her followers, who included some of the best cooks in Rochester, saw to it that the men were supplied with delicious hot meals and home-baked pies.

True to her promise, Susan paid the legal expenses for the three inspectors. With the help of contributions from sympathetic admirers, she paid the costs of her own trial. But she never paid that one-hundred-dollar fine. Susan B. Anthony was a woman of her word as well as a woman of courage. ■

---

29. **presidential pardons.** Orders by the president of the United States that a convicted prisoner be released from prison and/or further legal penalty

Responding to the Selection

Imagine that you are Susan B. Anthony in this selection. In your journal, write about the right to vote, explaining why you feel it is so important.

Reviewing the Selection

RECALLING

1. What one word sums up Anthony's personality, according to the narrator's original assessment?

2. What temperance advocate does Anthony meet through Amelia Bloomer?

3. What test does Anthony want to give to the Fourteenth Amendment to the Constitution?

4. What does Judge Ward Hunt direct the jury to find?

INTERPRETING

5. What conclusion does the narrator draw about her original assessment of Anthony's personality?

6. What causes Anthony to organize the Woman's New York State Temperance Society?

7. What words in the Fourteenth Amendment reveal the ambiguity of its interpretation?

8. What actions on the part of Judge Hunt show that Anthony was denied a fair trial by jury?

SYNTHESIZING

9. How does the narrator's "favorite episode" in Anthony's career support the narrator's suspicion that "behind her severe manner and unremitting devotion to duty, she may actually have had a sense of humor"?

10. What causes the narrator to conclude that "Susan B. Anthony was a woman of her word as well as a woman of courage"?

Understanding Literature (Questions for Discussion)

1. **Characterization. Characterization** is the use of literary techniques to create a character. Writers use three major techniques to create characters: direct description, portrayal of characters' behavior, and representations of characters' internal states. The following excerpt from the selection is an example of portrayal of characters' behavior: "By the afternoon of June 18, the case of *The United States* vs. *Susan B. Anthony* was ready to go to the jury. It was impossible to predict what their verdict might be, so Judge Hunt, determined to make it the verdict he and Roscoe Conkling wanted, took matters into his own hands. 'Gentlemen of the jury,' he said, 'I direct that you find the defendant guilty.'" What do the actions and speech Judge Ward Hunt reveal about his character?

2. **Narrator.** A **narrator** is one who tells a story. In this selection, the narrator is the writer—Margaret Truman. Of primary importance in a literary work is the narrator's point of view. What qualities does the narrator reveal about herself when she says, "And since I've been making a study of heroines, I decided to give Miss Anthony a second look. I have to report that my original assessment of her character was much too harsh"? Why would, or would not, these be good qualities for a biographer to have?

Responding in Writing

Character Sketch. Write a character sketch about someone you admire. Use a particular moment in the character's life to illustrate the qualities you admire in him or her.

> **Prewriting Suggestion:** Brainstorm a list of questions that you want to answer about the personal characteristics of your subject. To get started on your list, write the following questions on a piece of paper: Where did the person grow up? How did family influence this person? What does the subject do for a living? What kind of person is the subject? What are some of the key moments in this person's life? Now keep adding questions to your list.

PROJECT

People of Courage. As a class, create a display of the courageous people in your neighborhood, town, school, churches, and families—the courageous people in your world. Include a variety of elements in your collective portrait—photographs, poems, essays, posters, and memorabilia. Use whatever materials or literary form that you feel will best illustrate why each person is a hero or heroine to you. Let everyone in the class include a portrait. Set aside a bulletin board or another special place in the classroom specifically for the display.

SPEECHES

Speech to the Convention of the American Equal Rights Association, New York City, 1867

by Sojourner Truth

ABOUT THE AUTHOR

Sojourner Truth (*circa* 1797–1883) was born to slave parents in Ulster County, New York. Named Isabella, Truth served as a slave in New Paltz, New York, for seventeen years, beginning at the age of thirteen. She escaped to freedom in 1827, adopting the name of the Van Wagener family who protected her. One year later, after emancipation became mandatory in New York State, Truth moved to New York City and became involved in social and moral reform. A street-corner preacher, Truth had a wide knowledge of the Bible. In 1843, adopting the name "Sojourner Truth," she became a wandering orator, launching the speaking tours that made her famous. Illiterate, Truth dictated her life story, barely supporting herself by selling the published autobiographical account, *Narrative of Sojourner Truth,* as well as photographs of herself to her audiences. Truth settled in Battle Creek, Michigan, in the mid-1850s, working and traveling from there for the rest of her life.

ABOUT THE SELECTION

Background: History. Influenced by Elizabeth Cady Stanton, a leader in the struggle for women's suffrage, Truth lent her unique oratory skills to the women's suffrage movement. Cady Stanton recorded and printed transcripts of some of Truth's speeches in *The History of Women's Suffrage.*

Background: Technique. The powerful nature of Sojourner Truth's oratory style was born in a combination of elements—a personal magnetism, a strong voice, and the courage to speak directly. Speaking English with a Dutch accent, Truth was legendary for her direct platform style. On one particular occasion, Truth challenged Frederick Douglass's stand on the issue of violence against slavery, exclaiming, "Frederick! Is God dead?"

READER'S JOURNAL

Have you ever spoken aloud your beliefs on a particular issue? Is it more difficult to speak if your views are unpopular? Why, or why not? How would you defend your beliefs if they were challenged? Freewrite about these questions in your journal.

Speech to the Convention of the American Equal Rights Association, New York City, 1867

SOJOURNER TRUTH

My friends, I am rejoiced that you are glad, but I don't know how you will feel when I get through. I come from another field—the country of the slave. They have got their liberty—so much good luck to have slavery partly destroyed; not entirely. I want it root and branch destroyed. Then we will all be free indeed. I feel that if I have to answer for the deeds done in my body just as much as a man, I have a right to have just as much as a man. There is a great stir about colored men getting their rights, but not a word about the colored women; and if colored men get their rights, and not colored women theirs, you see the colored men will be masters over the women, and it will be just as bad as it was before. So I am for keeping the thing going while things are stirring; because if we wait till it is still, it will take a great while to get it

going again. White women are a great deal smarter, and know more than colored women, while colored women do not know scarcely anything. They go out washing, which is about as high as a colored woman gets, and their men go about idle, strutting up and down; and when the women come home, they ask for their money and take it all, and then scold because there is no food. I want you to consider on that, chil'n.[1] I call you chil'n; you are somebody's chil'n, and I am old enough to be mother of all that is here. I want women to have their rights. In the courts women have no rights, no voice; nobody speaks for them. I wish woman to have her voice there among the pettifoggers.[2] If it is not a fit place for women, it is unfit for men to be there.

---

1. **chil'n.** Dialect word meaning "children"
2. **pettifoggers.** Unethical lawyers

> What will happen if African-American men get their rights and African-American women don't? Why should things be stirred up now?

I am above eighty years old; it is about time for me to be going. I have been forty years a slave and forty years free, and would be here forty years more to have equal rights for all. I suppose I am kept here because something remains for me to do; I suppose I am yet to help to break the chain. I have done a great deal of work; as much as a man, but did not get so much pay. I used to work in the field and bind grain, keeping up with the cradler;[3] but men doing no more, got twice as much pay. . . . We do as much, we eat as much, we want as much. I suppose I am about the only colored woman that goes about to speak for the rights of the colored women. I want to keep the thing stirring, now that the ice is cracked. What we want is a little money. You men know that you get as much again as women, when you write, or for what you do. When we get our rights, we shall not have to come to you for money, for then we shall have money enough in our own pockets; and maybe you will ask us for money. But help us now until we get it. It is a good <u>consolation</u> to know that when we have got this battle once fought we shall not be coming to you any more. . . .

I am glad to see that men are getting their rights, but I want women to get theirs, and while the water is stirring I will step into the pool. Now that there is a great stir about colored men's getting their rights is the time for women to step in and have theirs. I am sometimes told that "Women ain't fit to vote. Why, don't you know that a woman had seven devils in her: and do you suppose a woman is fit to rule the nation?" Seven devils ain't no account; a man had a <u>legion</u> in him. The devils didn't know where to go; and so they asked that they might go into the swine. They thought that was as good a place as they came out from. They didn't ask to go into the sheep—no, into the hog; that was the selfish beast; and man is so selfish that he has got women's rights and his own too, and yet he won't give women their rights. He keeps them all to himself. . . . ■

Why should men help women in their struggle for rights?

How does Truth describe men?

---

3. **cradler.** Person who cuts grain with a cradle scythe, a cutting instrument with a frame attached so that grain can be laid out as it is cut

Responding to the Selection

Imagine that you are a member of the audience to whom Sojourner Truth has delivered her speech. In small groups, discuss your response to hearing Sojourner Truth say, ". . . man is so selfish that he has got women's rights and his own too, and yet he won't give women their rights. He keeps them all to himself. . . ."

WORDS FOR EVERYDAY USE:

con • so • la • tion (kän´sə lā´shən) *n.*, comfort; solace

le • gion (lē´jən) *n.*, large number; multitude

Reviewing the Selection

RECALLING

1. At the beginning of her speech, what prediction does Sojourner Truth make about how the audience will feel when she gets through?

2. What does Sojourner Truth want to do "while things are stirring"?

3. For how many years of her life has Sojourner Truth been a slave? For how many years has she been free?

4. For what is Sojourner Truth sometimes told that "women ain't fit"?

INTERPRETING

5. What concerns Sojourner Truth about the "great stir about colored men getting their rights"?

6. What does Sojourner Truth say will prevent African-American women from being slaves to African-American men?

7. What is the conclusion Sojourner Truth draws about why she is still alive?

8. For what reason does Sojourner Truth say that "man is so selfish"?

SYNTHESIZING

9. What sort of relationship between herself and the audience does Sojourner Truth create by calling the audience "chil'n"? What emotional effect does that create in her speech?

10. Are any of the inequalities that Sojourner Truth spoke about still present today? If so, which ones?

Understanding Literature (Questions for Discussion)

1. **Purpose.** The **purpose,** or **aim,** of a speech or piece of writing is the goal that the writer wants his or her work to accomplish. One purpose of Sojourner Truth's speech is to inform her audience of the effect that freedom for African-American men has had on the lives of African-American women. Another purpose of her speech is to persuade her audience. At the beginning of her speech, Truth acknowledges the welcome she has received from her audience, but predicts, "I don't know how you will feel when I get through." Describe the kind of audience to whom you think Truth is speaking. What is she trying to persuade them to do?

2. **Dialect and Style.** A **dialect** is a version of a language spoken by the people of a particular place, time, or social group. A speaker's style or voice is influenced by his or her dialect. **Style** is the manner in which something is said or written. For example, Sojourner Truth says, "I wish woman to have her voice there among the *pettifoggers*." How would the style of that sentence change if she had said, "I wish woman to have her voice there among the *lawyers who practice with petty methods*"? Find another example in the speech of how dialect influences style.

Responding in Writing

Speech. Write a speech that attempts to persuade your audience to act for or against something. You might write about a school or community issue about which you feel strongly.

> **Prewriting Suggestion:** To start thinking about your audience, write the title *Audience Considerations* at the top of a piece of paper. Then write three subheadings underneath, left to right: *Questions about the audience, Evaluation,* and *My speech will need.* Underneath the first subheading, list as many questions as you can think of regarding your audience, starting with the question, "What does the audience already know about this subject?" In the next subheading, write your own evaluation of the situation. For example, you may write "a little" as an evaluation of how much the audience already knows about your subject. Under the third subheading, write what your speech will need, based on your evaluation of each audience consideration.

PROJECT

Oral History. Research the life story of a dynamic person in history, such as Sojourner Truth, Harriet Tubman, Elizabeth Cady Stanton, Susan B. Anthony, Frederick Douglass, or Abraham Lincoln. From detailed notes taken during your research, write an oral history as it might be told by your subject at some specific period in his or her life. Then, rehearse the oral history, playing the part of your subject. Present the oral history to the class.

"I Have a Dream"
by Martin Luther King, Jr.

ABOUT THE AUTHOR

Martin Luther King, Jr., (1929–1968) was born in Atlanta, Georgia, the son and grandson of Baptist ministers. Under a special program for gifted students, King entered Morehouse College in Atlanta at the age of fifteen. In his senior year at Morehouse, King decided to enter the ministry. While studying at Crozer Theological Seminary in Chester, Pennsylvania, King was introduced to and strongly influenced by the nonviolent teachings of Henry David Thoreau and Mohandas Gandhi. He received his Ph.D. from Boston University in 1955.

King founded the Southern Christian Leadership Conference, which gave him a platform from which to speak throughout the United States. As a civil rights leader, minister, and orator, King led protests throughout the South, advocating nonviolent civil disobedience to combat racism and bigotry. King's writings include *Stride Toward Freedom,* an account of the bus system boycott in Alabama, which led to a Supreme Court ruling that segregation of public transportation was unconstitutional. In 1964, the year after his eloquent "I Have a Dream" speech, King was awarded the Nobel Peace Prize. While in Memphis, Tennessee, to show support for striking workers, Martin Luther King, Jr., was assassinated by James Earl Ray.

ABOUT THE SELECTION

Background: History. On August 28, 1963, Martin Luther King, Jr., joined other civil rights leaders in the March on Washington in support of civil rights legislation. To an interracial audience of more than two hundred thousand people, he delivered his speech **"I Have a Dream"** at the foot of the Lincoln Memorial. The Civil Rights Act was enacted in 1964.

Background: Technique. King's dynamic and skillful use of rhetoric can be seen in the selection. An emotional and uplifting effect is created through the repetition of words and phrases, the echoes of biblical language, and the description of his vision of a world in which all people would be sisters and brothers.

READER'S JOURNAL

Have you ever imagined a better world? In what kind of world would you like to live? Freewrite in your journal about the dream you have for a better world.

"I Have a Dream"

MARTIN LUTHER KING, JR.

August 28, 1963
Lincoln Memorial, Washington, D.C.

I'm happy to join with you today in what will go down in history as the greatest demonstration for freedom in the history of our nation.

Fivescore[1] years ago, a great American, in whose symbolic shadow we stand today, signed the Emancipation Proclamation.[2] This momentous decree came as a great beacon light of hope to millions of Negro slaves who had been <u>seared</u> in the flames of withering injustice. It came as a joyous daybreak to end the long night of their captivity.

But one hundred years later, the Negro still is not free; one hundred years later, the life of the Negro is still sadly crippled by the <u>manacles</u> of segregation[3] and the chains of discrimination; one hundred years later, the Negro lives on a lonely island of poverty in the midst of a vast ocean of material prosperity; one hundred years later, the Negro is still <u>languished</u> in the corners of American society and finds himself in exile in his own land. . . .

Nineteen sixty-three is not an end, but a beginning. And those who hope that the Negro needed to blow off steam and will now be content, will have a rude awakening if the nation returns to business as usual. There will be neither rest nor tranquility in America until the Negro is granted his citizenship rights. The whirlwinds of the revolt will continue to shake the foundations of our nation until the bright day of Justice <u>emerges</u>. . . .

According to the speech, why was the African American still not free?

---

1. **Fivescore.** One hundred; one score equals twenty
2. **Emancipation Proclamation.** Document signed by Abraham Lincoln in 1863 that legally set free all people held as slaves in the Confederate states
3. **segregation.** Enforced separation of people based on group characteristics

How did King answer the question, "When will you be satisfied?"

What was the dream King had for his four children?

There are those who are asking the devotees of Civil Rights, "When will you be satisfied?" We can never be satisfied as long as the Negro is the victim of the unspeakable horrors of police <u>brutality</u>; we can never be satisfied as long as our bodies, heavy with the fatigue of travel, cannot gain lodging in the motels of the highways and the hotels of the cities; we cannot be satisfied as long as the Negro's basic <u>mobility</u> is from a smaller ghetto[4] to a larger one; we can never be satisfied as long as our children are stripped of their selfhood and robbed of their dignity by signs stating "For Whites Only"; we cannot be satisfied as long as the Negro in Mississippi cannot vote and a Negro in New York believes he has nothing for which to vote. No! No, we are not satisfied, and we will not be satisfied until "justice rolls down like waters and righteousness like a mighty stream."[5]

I am not unmindful that some of you have come here out of great trials and <u>tribulations</u>. Some of you have come fresh from narrow jail cells. Some of you have come from areas where your quest for freedom left you battered by the storms of persecution and staggered by the winds of police brutality. You have been the veterans of creative suffering. Continue to work with the faith that unearned suffering is <u>redemptive</u>. Go back to Mississippi. Go back to Alabama. Go back to South Carolina. Go back to Georgia. Go back to Louisiana. Go back to the slums and ghettos of our northern cities, knowing that somehow the situation can and will be changed. Let us not wallow in the valley of despair.

I say to you today, my friends, so even though we face the difficulties of today and tomorrow, I still have a dream. It is a dream deeply rooted in the American meaning of its <u>creed</u>, "We hold these truths to be self-evident, that all men are created equal."[6] I have a dream that one day on the red hills of Georgia, sons of former slaves and the sons of former slave owners will be able to sit down together at the table of brotherhood. I have a dream that one day even the state of Mississippi, a state sweltering with the heat of injustice, sweltering with the heat of oppression, will be transformed into an oasis of freedom and justice. I have a dream that my four little children will one day live in a nation where they will not be judged by the color of their skin, but the content of their character.

I have a dream today!

I have a dream that one day down in Alabama—with its vicious racists, with its governor having his lips dripping with the words of interposition and nullification[7]—one day right there in

---

4. **ghetto.** Section of a city in which many members of a minority group live, either by choice or because of economic or social pressure

5. **"justice rolls down . . . stream."** Biblical reference to Amos 5:24

6. **"We hold these truths to be self-evident, that all men are created equal."** First line of the second paragraph of the Declaration of Independence

7. **interposition and nullification.** Dr. King was talking about the Alabama governor's refusal to obey a federal requirement to allow African-American children to attend public schools. Interposition is the disputed theory that a state can reject a federal mandate. Nullification refers to the refusal of a state to enforce any federal law.

WORDS FOR EVERYDAY USE:

bru • tal • i • ty (broo tal´ə tē) *n.*, cruelty
mo • bil • i • ty (mō´ bil´ə tē) *n.*, ability to move from place to place
trib • u • la • tion (trib´yoo lā shən) *n.*, great misery or distress, as from oppression
re • demp • tive (ri demp´tiv) *adj.*, serving to recover or get back
creed (krēd) *n.*, statement of principle or opinion

Alabama, little black boys and black girls will be able to join hands with little white boys and white girls as sisters and brothers.

I have a dream today!

I have a dream that one day "every valley shall be <u>exalted</u> and every hill and mountain shall be made low. The rough places will be made plain and the crooked places will be made straight, and the glory of the Lord shall be revealed, and all flesh shall see it together."[8]

This is our hope. This is the faith that I go back to the South with. With this faith we shall be able to transform the jangling <u>discords</u> of our nation into a beautiful symphony of brotherhood. With this faith we will be able to work together, to pray together, to struggle together, to go to jail together, to stand up for freedom together, knowing that we will be free one day. And this will be the day. This will be the day when all of God's children will be able to sing with new meaning, "My country 'tis of thee, sweet land of liberty, of thee I sing. Land where my fathers died, land of the pilgrim's pride, from every mountainside, let freedom ring."[9] And if America is to be a great nation this must become true . . .

So let freedom ring from the prodigious hilltops of New Hampshire, let freedom ring from the mighty mountains of New York, let freedom ring from the heightening Alleghenies of Pennsylvania; let freedom ring from the snow-capped Rockies of Colorado;

Lincoln Memorial. Washington DC

let freedom ring from the curvaceous slopes of California. But not only that. Let freedom ring from Stone Mountain of Georgia; let freedom ring from Lookout Mountain of Tennessee; let freedom ring from every hill and molehill of Mississippi. From every mountainside, let freedom ring.

And when this happens and when we allow freedom to ring, when we let it ring from every village and every hamlet, from every state and every city, we will be able to speed up that day when all God's children, black men and white men, Jews and gentiles, Protestants and Catholics, will be able to join hands and sing in the words of the old Negro spiritual: "Free at last. Free at last. Thank God Almighty, we are free at last." ■

What did King believe would happen if freedom was allowed to ring?

---

8. **"every valley shall be . . . see it together."** Biblical reference to Isaiah 40:4–9

9. **"My country 'tis of thee, . . . let freedom ring."** Lines from a well-known American anthem

Responding to the Selection

Imagine that you are one of the two hundred thousand people in the audience listening to Dr. Martin Luther King, Jr. In your journal, write your response to his speech, expressing your emotions about his message.

Reviewing the Selection

RECALLING

1. What does King call the demonstration?

2. By what is "the life of the Negro" still crippled?

3. What question is asked of the "devotees of Civil Rights"?

4. In what kind of nation does King dream that his children will live?

INTERPRETING

5. What reference does King make to "a great American, in whose symbolic shadow we stand today"?

6. What is the reason that "those who hope that the Negro . . . will now be content, will have a rude awakening"?

7. What facts emphasize that "we can never be satisfied"?

8. What will happen "when we allow freedom to ring"?

SYNTHESIZING

9. With what kind of faith does King "go back to the South"?

10. Of what kind of relationship between African-American and white human beings does King dream in his speech? Does that kind of relationship exist today? Why, or why not?

Understanding Literature (Questions for Discussion)

1. **Repetition and Style. Repetition** is the use, again, of a sound, word, phrase, sentence, or other element. **Style** is the manner in which something is said or written. King repeats certain phrases in his speech. For example, to emphasize that, one hundred years after the Emancipation Proclamation, "the Negro still is not free," King begins a series of sentences with the phrase, "one hundred years later." What other phrase does King repeat in his speech? What is the effect of the repetition on the style of his speech?

2. **Simile.** A **simile** is a comparison using *like* or *as*. It invites the reader to compare two things to see how they are similar. For example, King says, "This momentous decree came as a great beacon light of hope to millions of Negro slaves who had been seared in the flames of withering injustice." What two things are being compared in that sentence? What do these things have in common? King also says, "It came as a joyous daybreak to end the long night of their captivity." What two things are being compared in these lines? What do they have in common? What emotional effect is created in the reader by these two similes?

Responding in Writing

Speech. Write a speech that informs an audience of your peers about your personal vision for a better world.

> **Prewriting Suggestion:** Brainstorm a list of qualities that your world will have that will make it a better place. Consider the problems that you see in the world as it exists. What changes would need to occur to reach your vision? You may wish to include some changes that have taken place, or that are in the works to give your listeners a sense that change is possible. You may also wish to include actions people can take to help turn your dream into reality.

PROJECT

Persuasion. With a small group of two or three classmates, write a persuasive essay to an imaginary audience of the next generation to convince them to live together as brothers and sisters. To get started you may wish to refer to the better worlds created by group members in their speech (see Responding in Writing, above). In what way do these worlds depend on people working together? Decide if you will try to persuade your audience by showing them the negative aspects of a world in which people do not live as brother and sister, or by showing them the wonderful world it could be if people did live in harmony. You could also try to use a combination of these tactics.

"Thinking Like a Mountain"
by Aldo Leopold

ABOUT THE AUTHOR

Aldo Leopold (1887–1948) was born in Burlington, Iowa. After graduating from Yale Forestry School, he became supervisor of Carson National Forest in New Mexico. In 1933, he began teaching at the University of Wisconsin. Two years later, he helped found the Wilderness Society. Throughout his career as a conservationist, Leopold urged a responsible land ethic, confronting issues of economic and industrial expansion and wasteful land use. *A Sand County Almanac,* which was published the year after Leopold's death, has sold over a million copies.

ABOUT THE SELECTION

Background: Genre. *A Sand County Almanac,* from which **"Thinking Like a Mountain"** is taken, is a collection of essays about nature and ecology. In its criticism of society's exploitation of nature, *A Sand County Almanac* bears a strong likeness to Thoreau's *Walden.*

Background: Theme. In the selection, one of the themes ever present in *A Sand County Almanac* can be seen—that nature was here first, long before human beings arrived on earth; therefore, human beings have a responsibility to nature and to its ecosystems. Behaving responsibly toward nature begins with the recognition that all things in the natural world are interrelated, a point made clear in Leopold's beautiful, provocative essay.

"Thinking Like a Mountain"

ALDO LEOPOLD

A deep chesty bawl echoes from rimrock[1] to rimrock, rolls down the mountain, and fades into the far blackness of the night. It is an outburst of wild <u>defiant</u> sorrow, and of contempt for all the <u>adversities</u> of the world.

Every living thing (and perhaps many a dead one as well) pays heed to that call. To the deer it is a reminder of the way of all flesh, to the pine a forecast of midnight scuffles and of blood upon the snow, to the coyote a promise of gleanings[2] to come, to the cowman a threat of red ink at the bank,[3] to the hunter a challenge of fang against bullet. Yet behind these obvious and immediate hopes and fears there lies a deeper meaning, known only to the mountain itself. Only the mountain has lived long enough to listen <u>objectively</u> to the howl of a wolf.

Those unable to <u>decipher</u> the hidden meaning know nevertheless that it is there, for it is felt in all wolf country, and distinguishes that country from all other land. It tingles in the spine of all who hear wolves by night, or who scan their tracks by day. Even without sight or sound of wolf, it is <u>implicit</u> in a hundred small events: the midnight whinny of a pack horse, the rattle of rolling rocks, the bound of a fleeing deer, the way shadows lie under the spruces. Only the ineducable tyro[4] can fail to sense the presence or absence of wolves, or the fact that mountains have a secret opinion about them.

What different meanings does the howl of the wolf have?

What does Leopold personify, or speak of, as though it had human characteristics? What question is Leopold raising in the mind of the reader?

---

1. **rimrock.** Rock forming on the edge of a cliff
2. **gleanings.** Leftovers; remains
3. **red ink at the bank.** Debt; accountants sometimes use red ink to record debits.
4. **tyro.** Beginner; novice

WORDS FOR EVERYDAY USE:

de • fi • ant (dē fī´ənt) *adj.,* openly resisting
ad • ver • si • ty (ad vɜr´sə tē) *n.,* state of wretchedness and misfortune
ob • jec • tive • ly (əb jək´tiv lē) *adv.,* without bias or prejudice

de • ci • pher (dē sī´fər) *vt.,* make out the meaning of
im • plic • it (im plis´it) *adj.,* understood, though not plainly expressed; implied

Photo courtesy of Digital Stock Corp.

Why did they shoot the wolves?

My own <u>conviction</u> on this score dates from the day I saw a wolf die. We were eating lunch on a high rimrock, at the foot of which a turbulent river elbowed its way. We saw what we thought was a doe <u>fording</u> the torrent, her breast awash in white water. When she climbed the bank toward us and shook out her tail, we realized our error: it was a wolf. A half-dozen others, evidently grown pups, sprang from the willows and all joined in a welcoming <u>mêlée</u> of wagging tails and playful maulings. What was <u>literally</u> a pile of wolves writhed and tumbled in the center of an open flat at the foot of our rimrock.

In those days we had never heard of passing up a chance to kill a wolf. In a second we were pumping lead into the pack, but with more excitement than accuracy: how to aim a steep downhill shot is always confusing. When our rifles were empty, the old wolf was down, and a pup was dragging a leg into impassable slide-rocks.

We reached the old wolf in time to watch a fierce green fire dying in her eyes. I realized then, and have known ever since, that there was something new to me in those eyes—something known only to her and to the mountain. I was young then, and full of trigger-itch; I thought that because

WORDS FOR EVERYDAY USE:	con • vic • tion (kən vik´shən) *n.,* strong belief
	ford (fôrd) *vt.,* cross a stream or river by wading
	mê • lée (mā´lā´) *n.,* confused conflict or mixture
	lit • er • al • ly (lit´ər əl ē) *adv.,* actually; in fact

fewer wolves meant more deer, that no wolves would mean hunters' paradise. But after seeing the green fire die, I sensed that neither the wolf nor the mountain agreed with such a view.

Since then I have lived to see state after state extirpate its wolves. I have watched the face of many a newly wolfless mountain, and seen the south-facing slopes wrinkle with a maze of new deer trails. I have seen every edible bush and seedling browsed, first to anaemic desuetude,[5] and then to death. I have seen every edible tree defoliated to the height of a saddlehorn.[6] Such a mountain looks as if someone had given God a new pruning shears, and forbidden Him all other exercise. In the end the starved bones of the hoped-for deer herd, dead of its own too-much, bleach with the bones of the dead sage, or molder under the high-lined junipers.

I now suspect that just as a deer herd lives in mortal fear of its wolves, so does a mountain live in mortal fear of its deer. And perhaps with better cause, for while a buck pulled down by wolves can be replaced in two or three years, a range pulled down by too many deer may fail of replacement in as many decades.

So also with cows. The cowman who cleans his range of wolves does not realize that he is taking over the wolf's job of trimming the herd to fit the range. He has not learned to think like a mountain. Hence we have dustbowls,[7] and rivers washing the future into the sea.

We all strive for safety, prosperity, comfort, long life, and dullness. The deer strives with his supple legs, the cowman with trap and poison, the statesman with pen, the most of us with machines, votes, and dollars, but it all comes to the same thing: peace in our time. A measure of success in this is all well enough, and perhaps is a requisite to objective thinking, but too much safety seems to yield only danger in the long run. Perhaps this is behind Thoreau's[8] dictum: In wildness is the salvation of the world. Perhaps this is the hidden meaning in the howl of the wolf, long known among mountains, but seldom perceived among men. ■

What idea did the narrator have about killing off all wolves? How did watching the wolf die change this view?

What do mountains know that people sometimes do not? What is the hidden meaning in the howl of the wolf?

Why does a mountain fear deer?

---

5. **anaemic desuetude.** Lifeless disuse
6. **saddlehorn.** Handle at the front of a Western-style saddle
7. **dustbowls.** Dry, dusty lands from which topsoil has been eroded by wind
8. **Thoreau's.** Henry David Thoreau (1817–1862) was a well-known American naturalist and writer.

WORDS FOR EVERYDAY USE:

ex • tir • pate (ek´stər pāt´) vt., destroy or remove completely
de • fo • li • ate (dē fō´lē āt ´ed) vt., strip of leaves
mold • er (mōl´dər) vi., crumble into dust
req • ui • site (rek´wə zit) n., necessity

Responding to the Selection

Imagine that you are the narrator in this essay. In your journal, write an explanation of what it means to think like a mountain.

Reviewing the Selection

1. What echoes "from rimrock to rimrock"?

2. What kind of "opinion" do mountains have about wolves?

3. What has the narrator seen "state after state" do to wolves?

4. Of what does a deer herd live in mortal fear?

5. To what animal does the "outburst of wild defiant sorrow" belong?

6. What kind of "small events" distinguish wolf country "from all other land"?

7. What are the consequences of destroying wolves?

8. What is probably the reason that a mountain lives "in mortal fear of its deer"?

9. Do you think the narrator is still "full of trigger-itch"? Why, or why not?

10. What kind of relationship between animals and nature is described in the essay? How does that relationship change when humans attempt to tame or destroy the "wildness" of nature?

Understanding Literature (Questions for Discussion)

1. **Anecdote.** An **anecdote** is a brief story, usually with a specific point or moral. In the essay, the narrator tells an anecdote about the day he saw a wolf die. What is the narrator's purpose in telling this anecdote? What lesson did the narrator learn from the experience?

2. Personification. Personification is a figure of speech in which an idea, animal, or thing is described as if it were a person. For example, the narrator says, "It is an outburst of wild defiant sorrow, and of contempt for all the adversities of the world." In that sentence, personification is used to describe the wolf and its howl as having the human emotions of sorrow and contempt. Find another example of personification in the selection.

Responding in Writing

Anecdote. Write a brief story that has as its point or moral a lesson learned by a human character's experience in nature. Pretend you are a naturalist who is trying to teach this lesson to others.

> **Prewriting Suggestion:** Draw a line down the center of a piece of paper. At the top of the left-hand column, write the word *before.* At the top of the right-hand column, write the word *after.* Create a character chart by listing details about your character before and after his or her experience in nature. The details listed in the "after" column should reflect some aspect of the lesson that your character has learned from the experience.

PROJECT

Community Project. As a class, research recycling in or near your community. Start by brainstorming a list of questions you want answered about recycling, such as how it is done, what benefits recycling has for the environment, who participates in recycling, and so on. Find out what, if any, recycling centers are nearby. Find out also how your class can become involved in a school or community recycling effort. If a field trip to a local recycling center is possible, create a list of questions specifically for the person who guides your tour.

"In wildness is the salvation of the world."

Henry David Thoreau

from *Silent Spring*
by Rachel Carson

ABOUT THE AUTHOR

Rachel Carson (1907–1964) was born in Springdale, Pennsylvania, where, as a child, she developed a deep interest in wildlife. After receiving her M.A. from Johns Hopkins University, Carson did postgraduate work at the Woods Hole Marine Biological Laboratory. In her long career as a biologist, Carson worked for the U.S. Bureau of Fisheries and the U.S. Fish and Wildlife Service. She won the National Book Award for *The Sea Around Us,* which was published in 1951. Carson's *Silent Spring,* from which this selection is taken, awakened the world to the dangers of environmental pollution. Her other works include *Under the Sea Wind* and *The Edge of the Sea.*

ABOUT THE SELECTION

Background: Theme. The dangers of environmental pollution, particularly the threat to all life brought about by the widespread use of insecticides, is the theme of this selection. In her careful exploration of the theme, Carson asks why we accept such a dangerous threat to the natural world that supports all life, including human life. She also asks how we expect to endure, to survive as a species, if we do not know the facts about the effects of insecticides.

Background: Technique. Carson is well known for her precise observations and clear writing style, both of which are evident in the selection from *Silent Spring.*

READER'S JOURNAL
  If you were given the choice of knowing or not knowing all the facts about environmental pollution and its effects on all forms of life, what choice would you make? Why? Write about these questions in your journal.

FROM

Silent Spring

Rachel Carson

2. THE OBLIGATION TO ENDURE

The history of life on earth has been a history of <u>interaction</u> between living things and their surroundings. To a large extent, the physical form and the habits of the earth's vegetation and its animal life have been molded by the environment. Considering the whole span of earthly time, the opposite effect, in which life actually modifies its surroundings, has been relatively slight. Only within the moment of time represented by the present century has one <u>species</u>—man—acquired significant power to alter the nature of his world.

During the past quarter century this power has not only increased to one of disturbing <u>magnitude</u> but it has changed in character. The most alarming of all man's assaults upon the environment is the contamination of air, earth, rivers, and sea with dangerous and even lethal materials. This pollution is for the most part <u>irrecoverable</u>; the chain of evil it initiates not only in the world that must support life but in living tissues is for the most part irreversible. In this now universal contamination of the environment, chemicals are the sinister and little-recognized partners of radiation in changing the very nature of the world—the very nature of its life. Strontium 90, released through nuclear explosions into the air, comes to earth in rain or drifts down as fallout, lodges in soil, enters into the grass or corn or wheat grown there, and in time takes up its abode in the bones of a human being, there to remain until his death. Similarly, chemicals sprayed on croplands or forests or gardens lie

What is the most alarming change humans have made in the environment? Why is this so disturbing?

WORDS FOR EVERYDAY USE:

in • ter • ac • tion (in´tər ak´shən) *n.,* reciprocal action or effect

spe • cies (spē´ shēz) *n.,* population of highly similar organisms that interbreed only among themselves

mag • ni • tude (mag´nə tood´) *n.,* greatness of importance or influence

ir • re • cov • er • a • ble (ir´ri kuv´ər ə bəl) *adj.,* cannot be corrected or remedied

Why do poisons
have such far-
reaching effects?

long in soil, entering into living organisms, passing from one to another in a chain of poisoning and death. Or they pass mysteriously by underground streams until they emerge and, through the alchemy[1] of air and sunlight, combine into new forms that kill vegetation, sicken cattle, and work unknown harm on those who drink from once pure wells. As Albert Schweitzer[2] has said, "Man can hardly even recognize the devils of his own creation."

It took hundreds of millions of years to produce the life that now inhabits the earth—eons of time in which that developing and evolving and diversifying life reached a state of adjustment and balance with its surroundings. The environment, <u>rigorously</u> shaping and directing the life it supported, contained elements that were hostile as well as supporting. Certain rocks gave out dangerous radiation; even within the light of the sun, from which all life draws its energy, there were short-wave radiations with power to injure. Given time—time not in years but in millennia—life adjusts, and a balance has been reached. For time is the essential ingredient; but in the modern world there is no time.

How do current
changes differ
from natural
changes of
past eons?

The rapidity of change and the speed with which new situations are created follow the <u>impetuous</u> and heedless pace of man rather than the deliberate pace of nature. Radiation is no longer merely the background radiation of rocks, the bombardment of cosmic rays, the ultraviolet of the sun that

have existed before there was any life on earth; radiation is now the unnatural creation of man's tampering with the atom. The chemicals to which life is asked to make its adjustment are no longer merely the calcium and silica and copper and all the rest of the minerals washed out of the rocks and carried in rivers to the sea; they are the synthetic creations of man's inventive mind, brewed in his laboratories, and having no counterparts in nature.

To adjust to these chemicals would require time on the scale that is nature's; it would require not merely the years of a man's life but the life of generations. And even this, were it by some miracle possible, would be futile, for the new chemicals come from our laboratories in an endless stream; almost five hundred annually find their way into actual use in the United States alone. The figure is staggering and its <u>implications</u> are not easily grasped—500 new chemicals to which the bodies of men and animals are required somehow to adapt each year, chemicals totally outside the limits of biologic experience.

Among them are many that are used in man's war against nature. Since the mid-1940's over 200 basic chemicals have been created for use in killing insects, weeds, rodents, and other organisms described in the modern <u>vernacular</u> as "pests"; and they are sold

---

1. **alchemy.** Scientific method of transmutation, changing a thing into something better
2. **Albert Schweitzer.** (1875–1965) Medical missionary to Africa

---

WORDS FOR EVERYDAY USE:

rig • or • ous • ly (rig´ər əs lē) *adv.*, precisely; accurately

im • pet • u • ous (im pech´ o͞o əs) *adj.*, moving with great force or violence

im • pli • ca • tion (im´pli kā´shən) *n.*, something implied; suggestion

ver • nac • u • lar (vər nak´yə lər) *n.*, common, everyday language

Crow with Ribbons. Marsden Hartley, 1941–1942. Hirshhorn Museum and Sculpture Garden, Smithsonian Institution. Gift of Joseph H. Hirshhorn Foundation, 1966

Photograph by Lee Stalsworth

under several thousand different brand names.

These sprays, dusts, and aerosols are now applied almost universally to farms, gardens, forests, and homes—nonselective chemicals[3] that have the power to kill every insect, the "good" and the "bad," to still the song of birds and the leaping of fish in the streams, to coat the leaves with a deadly film, and to linger on in soil—all this though the intended target may be only a few weeds or insects. Can anyone believe it is possible to lay down such a <u>barrage</u> of poisons on the surface of the earth without making it

unfit for all life? They should not be called "insecticides," but "biocides."

The whole process of spraying seems caught up in an endless spiral. Since DDT was released for civilian use, a process of <u>escalation</u> has been going on in which ever more toxic materials must be found. This has happened because insects, in a triumphant <u>vindication</u> of Darwin's principle of the survival of the fittest, have evolved super races immune to the particular insecticide used, hence a deadlier one has always to be developed—and then

What is a major problem with most insecticides?

Why is it necessary to create more and more deadly chemicals?

---

3. **nonselective chemicals.** Substances that contaminate everything they touch

WORDS FOR EVERYDAY USE:

bar • rage (bə räzh´) *n.,* intense attack
es • ca • la • tion (es´kə lā shən) *n.,* step-by-step growth; rapid increase
vin • di • ca • tion (vin´də kā´shən) *n.,* justification

a deadlier one than that. It has happened also because, for reasons to be described later, destructive insects often undergo a "flareback," or <u>resurgence</u>, after spraying, in numbers greater than before. Thus the chemical war is never won, and all life is caught in its violent crossfire.

Along with the possibility of the extinction of mankind by nuclear war, the central problem of our age has therefore become the contamination of man's total environment with such substances of incredible potential for harm—substances that accumulate in the tissues of plants and animals and even penetrate the germ cells to shatter or alter the very material of <u>heredity</u> upon which the shape of the future depends.

Some would-be architects of our future look toward a time when it will be possible to alter the human germ plasm by design. But we may easily be doing so now by <u>inadvertence</u>, for many chemicals, like radiation, bring about gene mutations. It is ironic to think that man might determine his own future by something so seemingly trivial as the choice of an insect spray.

All this has been risked—for what? Future historians may well be amazed by our distorted sense of proportion. How could intelligent beings seek to control a few unwanted species by a method that contaminated the entire environment and brought the threat of disease and death even to their own kind? Yet this is precisely what we have done. We have done it, moreover, for reasons that collapse the moment we examine them. We are told that the enormous and expanding use of pesticides is necessary to maintain farm production. Yet is our real problem not one of *overproduction?* Our farms, despite measures to remove acreages[4] from production and to pay farmers *not* to produce, have yielded such a staggering excess of crops that the American taxpayer in 1962 is paying out more than one billion dollars a year as the total carrying cost of the surplus-food storage program. And is the situation helped when one branch of the Agriculture Department tries to reduce production while another states, as it did in 1958, "It is believed generally that reduction of crop acreages under provisions of the Soil Bank will <u>stimulate</u> interest in use of chemicals to obtain maximum production on the land retained in crops."

All this is not to say there is no insect problem and no need of control. I am saying, rather, that control must be geared to realities, not to mythical situations, and that the methods employed must be such that they do not destroy us along with the insects.

The problem whose attempted solution has brought such a train of disaster in its wake is an <u>accompaniment</u> of our modern way of life. Long before the age of man, insects inhabited the earth—a group of extraordinarily varied and adaptable beings. Over the course of time since man's <u>advent</u>, a small percentage of the more than half

---

4. **acreages.** Large amounts, in acres, of land

WORDS FOR EVERYDAY USE:

re • sur • gence (ri surj´ əns) *n.*, tendency to rise again
he • red • i • ty (hə red´i tē) *n.*, genetic transmission of genes from parent to offspring
in • ad • vert • ence (in´ad vurt´´ns) *n.*, mistake; oversight

stim • u • late (stim´yoo lāt) *vt.*, rouse or excite to increase action
ac • com • pa • ni • ment (ə kum´pə nə mənt) *n.*, something that goes with something else
ad • vent (ad´vent´) *n.*, coming or arrival

a million species of insects have come into conflict with human welfare in two principal ways: as competitors for the food supply and as carriers of human disease.

Disease-carrying insects become important where human beings are crowded together, especially under conditions where sanitation is poor, as in time of natural disaster or war or in situations of extreme poverty and deprivation. Then control of some sort becomes necessary. It is a sobering fact, however, as we shall presently see, that the method of massive chemical control has had only limited success, and also threatens to worsen the very conditions it is intended to curb.

Under primitive agricultural conditions the farmer had few insect problems. These arose with the <u>intensification</u> of agriculture—the devotion of immense acreages to a single crop. Such a system set the stage for explosive increases in specific insect populations. Single-crop farming does not take advantage of the principles by which nature works; it is agriculture as an engineer might <u>conceive</u> it to be. Nature has introduced great variety into the landscape, but man has displayed a passion for simplifying it. Thus he undoes the built-in checks and balances[5] by which nature holds the species within bounds. One important natural check is a limit on the amount of suitable habitat for each species. Obviously then, an insect that lives on wheat can build up its population to much higher levels on a farm

devoted to wheat than on one in which wheat is intermingled with other crops to which the insect is not <u>adapted</u>.

The same thing happens in other situations. A generation or more ago, the towns of large areas of the United States lined their streets with the noble elm tree. Now the beauty they hopefully created is threatened with complete destruction as disease sweeps through the elms, carried by a beetle that would have only limited chance to build up large populations and to spread from tree to tree if the elms were only occasional trees in a richly <u>diversified</u> planting.

Another factor in the modern insect problem is one that must be viewed against a background of geologic[6] and human history: the spreading of thousands of different kinds of organisms from their native homes to invade new territories. This worldwide migration has been studied and <u>graphically</u> described by the British ecologist Charles Elton in his recent[7] book *The Ecology of Invasions.* During the Cretaceous Period,[8] some hundred million years ago, flooding seas cut many land bridges between continents and living things found themselves confined in what Elton calls "colossal separate nature reserves." There, <u>isolated</u> from

What two conflicts are there between humans and insects?

How did new farming techniques create greater insect problems?

---

5. **checks and balances.** Controls and methods of balancing one factor against another

6. **geologic.** Related to the earth, as rocks and minerals

7. **recent.** Carson means recent relative to 1962, the year *Silent Spring* was published.

8. **Cretaceous Period.** Geologic period when, most scientists believe, dinosaurs became extinct and small mammals and plants began to develop on earth

WORDS FOR EVERYDAY USE:	in • ten • si • fi • ca • tion (in ten´ si fi kā´shən) *n.,* increase in magnitude con • ceive (kən sēv´) *vt.,* imagine; think a • dapt (ə dapt) *vi.,* adjust to fit new circumstances	di • ver • si • fied (də vʉr´ sə fīd´) *adj.,* varied graph • i • cal • ly (graf´ik ə lē) *adv.,* vividly i • so • lat • ed (ī´sə lāt ed) *adj.,* set apart from others

others of their kind, they developed many new species. When some of the land masses were joined again, about 15 million years ago, these species began to move out into new territories—a movement that is not only still in progress but is now receiving considerable assistance from man.

The importation of plants is the primary agent in the modern spread of species, for animals have almost invariably gone along with the plants, quarantine being a comparatively recent and not completely effective <u>innovation</u>. The United States Office of Plant Introduction alone has introduced almost 200,000 species and varieties of plants from all over the world. Nearly half of the 180 or so major insect enemies of plants in the United States are accidental imports from abroad, and most of them have come as hitchhikers on plants.

In new territory, out of reach of the restraining hand of the natural enemies that kept down its numbers in its native land, an invading plant or animal is able to become enormously abundant. Thus it is no accident that our most troublesome insects are introduced species.

These invasions, both the naturally occurring and those dependent on human assistance, are likely to continue indefinitely. Quarantine and massive chemical campaigns are only extremely expensive ways of buying time. We are faced, according to Dr. Elton, "with a life-and-death need not just to find new technological means of <u>suppressing</u> this plant or that animal"; instead we need the basic knowledge of animal populations and their relations to their surroundings that will "promote an even balance and damp down the explosive power of outbreaks and new invasions."

Much of the necessary knowledge is now available but we do not use it. We train ecologists in our universities and even employ them in our governmental agencies but we seldom take their advice. We allow the chemical death rain to fall as though there were no alternative, whereas in fact there are many, and our <u>ingenuity</u> could soon discover many more if given opportunity.

Have we fallen into a mesmerized state[9] that makes us accept as <u>inevitable</u> that which is inferior or <u>detrimental</u>, as though having lost the will or the vision to demand that which is good? Such thinking, in the words of the ecologist Paul Shepard, "idealizes life with only its head out of water, inches above the limits of toleration of the corruption of its own environment . . . Why should we tolerate a diet of weak poisons, a home in <u>insipid</u> surroundings, a circle of acquaintances who are not quite our enemies, the noise of motors with just enough relief to prevent insanity? Who would want to live in a world which is just not quite fatal?"

Yet such a world is pressed upon us. The crusade to create a chemically sterile, insect-free world seems to have engendered[10] a fanatic <u>zeal</u> on the part

9. **mesmerized state.** Hypnotized condition
10. **engendered.** Created

| WORDS FOR EVERYDAY USE: | in • no • va • tion (in′ə vā′shən) n., something newly introduced
sup • press (sə pres′) vt., put down by force
in • ge • nu • i • ty (in′jə nōō′ ə tē) n., cleverness; originality | in • ev • i • ta • ble (in ev′i tə bəl) adj., that cannot be avoided or evaded
de • tri • men • tal (de′trə ment′ l) adj., harmful
in • sip • id (in sip′ id) adj., tasteless; dull
zeal (zēl) n., intense enthusiasm |

of many specialists and most of the so-called control agencies. On every hand there is evidence that those engaged in spraying operations exercise a ruthless power. "The regulatory entomologists . . . function as prosecutor, judge and jury,[11] tax assessor and collector and sheriff to enforce their own orders," said Connecticut entomologist Neely Turner. The most flagrant abuses go unchecked in both state and federal agencies.

It is not my <u>contention</u> that chemical insecticides must never be used. I do contend that we have put poisonous and biologically potent chemicals indiscriminately into the hands of persons largely or wholly ignorant of their potentials for harm. We have subjected enormous numbers of people to contact with these poisons, without their consent and often without their knowledge. If the Bill of Rights contains no guarantee that a citizen shall be secure against <u>lethal</u> poisons distributed either by private individuals or by public officials, it is surely only because our forefathers, despite their considerable wisdom and <u>foresight</u>, could conceive of no such problem.

I <u>contend</u>, furthermore, that we have allowed these chemicals to be used with little or no advance investigation of their effect on soil, water, wildlife, and man himself. Future generations are unlikely to condone our lack of <u>prudent</u> concern for the <u>integrity</u> of the natural world that supports all life.

There is still very limited awareness of the nature of the threat. This is an era of specialists, each of whom sees his own problem and is unaware of or intolerant of the larger frame into which it fits. It is also an era dominated by industry, in which the right to make a dollar at whatever cost is seldom challenged. When the public protests, confronted with some obvious evidence of damaging results of pesticide applications, it is fed little tranquilizing pills of half truth. We urgently need an end to these false assurances, to the sugar coating of <u>unpalatable</u> facts. It is the public that is being asked to assume the risks that the insect controllers calculate. The public must decide whether it wishes to continue on the present road, and it can do so only when in full possession of the facts. In the words of Jean Rostand, "The obligation to endure gives us the right to know." ∎

Why is awareness of this threat so limited?

---

11. **regulatory entomologists . . . jury.** Turner means that the entomologists, experts on insects, who work in government agencies have nobody criticizing the laws they create relating to insects.

WORDS FOR EVERYDAY USE:

con • ten • tion (kən ten′ shən) *n.,* argument
le • thal (lē′ thəl) *adj.,* capable of causing death
fore • sight (fôr′ sīt′) *n.,* thoughtful regard for the future
con • tend (kən tend′) *vt.,* hold to be a fact

pru • dent (prōōd′ ′nt) *adj.,* cautious or discreet
in • teg • ri • ty (in teg′rə tē) *n.,* state or condition of perfection
un • pal • at • a • ble (un pal′ə tə bəl) *adj.,* unpleasant

Responding to the Selection

Imagine that you are the narrator of the selection. You are preparing a speech about environmental pollution to present to a group of grade school children. In your journal, write a clear statement about the effects of insecticides on the environment. Express the most important message you hope to convey to the school children.

Reviewing the Selection

RECALLING

1. What "significant power" does humankind have in this century?

2. What two elements are "changing the very nature of the world"?

3. What have human beings been trying to destroy since the 1940s with "over 200 basic chemicals"?

4. What does the narrator say that we "urgently need"?

INTERPRETING

5. What facts emphasize the "disturbing magnitude" of this power?

6. What facts support the prediction that the modern world has "no time" to balance the effects of environmental pollution?

7. What facts support the statement that a more appropriate name for "insecticides" is "biocides"?

8. What is probably the reason that the public is given "false assurances"?

SYNTHESIZING

9. What evidence supports the argument that, in our attempt "to control a few unwanted species," we are bringing destruction to ourselves?

10. What relationship between preservation and knowledge is described in the selection?

Understanding Literature (Questions for Discussion)

1. **Purpose.** The **purpose,** or **aim,** of a piece of writing is the goal that the writer wants his or her work to accomplish. One purpose of the selection from *Silent Spring* is to persuade the reader of the urgent need for "full possession of the facts" about the effects of insecticides. What other purpose does the selection have?

2. **Coherence. Coherence** is the logical arrangement and progression of ideas in a speech or piece of writing. Writers achieve coherence by presenting their ideas in a logical sequence and by using transitions to show how their ideas are connected to one another. For example, in this selection, the writer opens with a perspective of life on earth, establishing a historical context for her ideas and arguments. How is the element of time used to unify and advance the ideas in the selection?

Responding in Writing

Informative Essay. Write an essay informing your peers about an environmental issue, such as the effects of single-crop farming, the public demand for organically grown produce, or the threat of contaminated ground water.

> **Prewriting Suggestion:** To get started, write the words *who, what, where, when, why,* and *how* down the left-hand side of a piece of paper. Next to each word, write questions that you have about the topic that you want to answer or explain in your essay.

PROJECTS

1. **Investigative Report.** As a class, research the topic of acid rain. Investigate what acid rain is, what its effects are on the environment, what its effects are on the food chain, what its effects are on humans, and what solutions to the problem are being attempted. Form five small groups and assign one subtopic to each group. After each group has researched and written a report about its subtopic, present the reports to the entire class.

2. **Amazing Insects.** Insects have long inhabited the earth. These hardy, adaptive creatures have overcome many threats and managed not only to survive but to flourish. Choose an insect and research its natural habitat, life span, and reproductive capacity. Also learn about how this insect affects humans (does it carry disease, destroy crops) and what measures humans have taken to rid themselves of this insect. Does your insect have positive effects on human life? Describe these as well. Present your findings to your class.

Unit Review

Nonfiction

abruptly, 298
accompaniment, 336
adamant, 311
adapted, 337
advent, 336
adversity, 327
affirm, 304
agitator, 308
ailment, 291
ascent, 297
assessment, 302
barrage, 335
benevolent, 308
blatant, 311
blight, 290
blundering, 272
brood, 308
brutality, 322
calamitous, 276
circuitous, 302
coincidental, 298
competent, 310
compose, 296
conceivably, 298
conceive, 337
concur, 307
consolation, 317
consternation, 311
contend, 339
contention, 339
contiguous, 297
convene, 307
conviction, 328
creed, 322
customarily, 270

debate, 289
decipher, 327
defiant, 327
defoliate, 329
degrade, 311
demoralized, 308
demur, 303
denounce, 306
detrimental, 338
devoid, 302
discharge, 310
discord, 323
discrepancy, 271
disparity, 304
dispatch, 307
diversified, 337
effete, 285
emerge, 321
escalation, 335
evident, 285
exalt, 323
exploit, 280
extend, 305
extirpate, 329
fleet, 297
ford, 328
foresight, 339
fortitude, 308
graphically, 337
heredity, 336
hue, 285
immunity, 305
impetuous, 334
implication, 334
implicit, 327
impose, 312

inadvertence, 336
inadvertently, 306
incised, 292
indefatigable, 304
indeterminate, 279
inducement, 270
inequity, 279
inevitable, 338
infallible, 284
ingenuity, 338
innovation, 338
inordinate, 278
insipid, 338
integrity, 339
intensification, 337
intent, 280
interaction, 333
invariably, 309
irrecoverable, 333
isolated, 337
jurisdiction, 305
languish, 321
legion, 317
leniency, 312
lethal, 339
liable, 308
literally, 328
luminous, 296
magnitude, 333
manacle, 321
maxim, 312
meditative, 288
mêlée, 328

membrane, 297
mobility, 322
molder, 329
muster, 296
musty, 276
notorious, 270
objectively, 327
obscure, 279
ominously, 297
oratory, 305
overwhelming, 298
paranoia, 278
patently, 297
patron, 309
persistently, 312
phenomenon, 306
ply, 276
preliminaries, 310
presumably, 310
privation, 304
pronounce, 312
prophesy, 278
propose, 269
provision, 308
prudent, 339
rapture, 270
redemptive, 322
refer, 269
reform, 303
refugee, 285
regale, 280
renege, 276
requisite, 329
resignation, 279

resurgence, 336
retrospect, 309
reverently, 272
rigorously, 334
salient, 270
saturated, 284
sear, 321
serene, 296
skeptic, 309
sparse, 278
species, 333
staple, 277
stereotyped, 278
stimulate, 336
subjection, 311
succession, 303
suffrage, 302
suppress, 338
tacitly, 303
temperament, 302
testimony, 309
tirade, 311
tribulation, 322
unpalatable, 339
unprejudiced, 309
unremitting, 304
venture, 303
vernacular, 334
vilify, 306
vindication, 335
zeal, 338

SYNTHESIS: QUESTIONS FOR WRITING, RESEARCH, OR DISCUSSION

1. One reason for writing a work of nonfiction is to persuade people to believe in a certain way or to take certain actions. Which nonfiction works in this unit are persuasive? Of what does each author want to persuade his or her audience? Other reasons to write include to inform and to entertain. Which pieces in this unit are particularly informative? Which are particularly entertaining? Support your answers with evidence from the selections.

2. What was exceptional about each of the following people whom you have learned about in this unit: Mark Twain, Susan B. Anthony, Martin Luther King, Jr., Aldo Leopold, and Rachel Carson?

LANGUAGE LAB EDITING FOR ERRORS IN MODIFIER USAGE

A **modifier** is a word that modifies—that is, changes or explains—the meaning of another word. The chart below explains common errors in modifier usage. When editing your writing, you should watch carefully for these errors.

LANGUAGE ARTS SURVEY

For additional help, see the Language Arts Survey, 2.85.

LANGUAGE ARTS SURVEY

For additional help, see the Language Arts Survey, 2.86.

LANGUAGE ARTS SURVEY

For additional help, see the Language Arts Survey, 2.87.

COMMON ERRORS IN MODIFIER USAGE

Modifiers with Action and Linking Verbs

To modify the subject of a **linking verb**, use an **adjective**. To modify an **action verb**, use an **adverb**.

LINKING VERB AND ADJECTIVE: The reporter is frustrated by Mark Twain's answers.

ACTION VERB AND ADVERB: Mark Twain answers the reporter's questions humorously.

Comparison of Adjectives and Adverbs

Each modifier has three forms of comparison: **positive, comparative,** and **superlative.** Most one-syllable modifiers and some two-syllable modifiers form the comparative and superlative degrees by adding –er and –est. Other two-syllable modifiers and all modifiers of more than two syllables use more and most to form these degrees. To show a decrease in the quality of any modifier, form the comparative and superlative degrees by using less and least.

EXAMPLES: bright, brighter, brightest
courageous, more courageous, most courageous
certain, less certain, least certain

Illogical and Double Comparisons

An **illogical comparison** occurs when one member of a group is compared with the group of which it is a part. Clarify an illogical comparison by including the word other or else in the sentence. A **double comparison** occurs when two comparative forms or two superlative forms are used to modify the same word. Correct a double comparison by deleting one of the comparative or superlative forms.

ILLOGICAL: Rachel Carson is more concerned about environmental pollution than anything.

LOGICAL: Rachel Carson is more concerned about environmental pollution than anything else.

DOUBLE COMPARISON: Carla felt that Susan B. Anthony's standing up to Judge Hunt was the most bravest act she had ever heard of.

SINGLE COMPARISON: Carla felt that Susan B. Anthony's standing up to Judge Hunt was the bravest act she had ever heard of.

Double Negatives

A **double negative** is a construction in which two negative words are used instead of one. Negative words include no, none, not (and its contraction, –n't), nothing, barely, hardly, and scarcely. Do not use more than one negative word in the same sentence.

DOUBLE NEGATIVE: I couldn't hardly believe there was a town called Nameless.

SINGLE NEGATIVE: I could hardly believe there was a town called Nameless.

Other Problems with Modifiers

Be careful to choose the appropriate modifier from each of the following commonly confused pairs: this and these, that and those, those and them, bad and badly, and good and well.

LANGUAGE ARTS SURVEY

For additional help, see the Language Arts Survey, 2.88.

LANGUAGE ARTS SURVEY

For additional help, see the Language Arts Survey, 2.89.

EXERCISE A   Correcting Errors in Modifier Usage

Rewrite the following sentences, correcting the errors in modifier usage.

EXAMPLE: The problem of violence on television is becoming worser every year.
The problem of violence on television is becoming worse every year.

1. Deer eat more foliage than mountain animals.

2. The early morning lamplight made the Wm. Johnson General Store seem supernaturally.

3. In the nineteenth century, American women didn't have no voting rights.

4. Although she had no formal education, Sojourner Truth spoke good.

5. Five-calendar cafes have the better food in blue-highway America.

6. The 1963 March on Washington was the most large civil rights demonstration ever in the nation's history.

7. My brother watches more television than anyone.

8. Mark Twain moved sly to the bookcase to look up the word *interview*.

9. As a young girl, Annie Dillard couldn't hardly imagine the source of the strange light in her bedroom.

10. The government has banned the use of them insecticides.

EXERCISE B   Avoiding Errors in Modifier Usage

Rewrite the following sentences, using the correct word from those given in parentheses.

EXAMPLE: The mysterious light darted (swift, swiftly) across the bedroom wall.
The mysterious light darted swiftly across the bedroom wall.

1. Although she said her audience might not like what she had to say, Sojourner Truth didn't feel (bad, badly) about the speech she gave at the equal rights convention.

2. Susan B. Anthony was the (most outspoken, most outspokenest) crusader for women's suffrage.

3. Margaret Truman had a (better, more better) opinion of Susan B. Anthony after she reconsidered her.

4. Martin Luther King, Jr., spoke (persuasive, persuasively) for the civil rights cause.

5. With over five hundred new chemicals being produced each year, the earth (can, can't) scarcely adapt to environmental changes.

LANGUAGE ARTS
SURVEY

For additional help,
see the Language
Arts Survey,
2.85–2.89.

LANGUAGE ARTS
SURVEY

For additional help,
see the Language
Arts Survey,
2.85–2.89.

LANGUAGE ARTS WORKSHOP

THINKING SKILLS

AVOIDING FAULTY ARGUMENTS 4.14

A **logical fallacy** is a logical mistake. You commit a fallacy when you make an **invalid** inference, one that is not warranted by the facts at hand.

FAULTY ARGUMENTS

False Analogy. An argument by analogy claims that if two things are alike in one way, then they are also alike in another way.

Circularity. A circular argument is one that assumes the truth of the proposition it is intended to prove. This type of argument is also called **begging the question**.

Fallacies of Affirming the Antecedent and of Denying the Consequent. A **conditional** or "If . . . then . . ." statement says that *if* one thing—the **antecedent**—is true *then* something else—the **consequent**—must be true. However, if the consequent is true, nothing is implied about the antecedent. Likewise, if the antecedent is false, nothing is implied about the consequent.

Non Sequitur. A non sequitur is a conclusion that simply does not follow from the reasons given.

Ad Hominem. An argument that attacks or defends a person instead of addressing the issue at hand is known as an argumentum ad hominem.

Equivocation. An equivocal argument uses words in an ambiguous manner, perhaps using a term to mean one thing at one point in the argument and to mean something else at another point. Equivocation creates a false connection between the premises and the conclusion.

Vague Terms. A faulty argument may use vague terms of approval and disapproval and expect readers or listeners to accept these judgments without the support of logical reasons.

UNDERSTANDING PROPAGANDA TECHNIQUES 4.15

Propaganda refers to messages and materials created with the aim of stirring up support for or opposition to a particular cause. Propaganda messages try to influence people by appealing to their emotions. They may offer faulty arguments or none at all.

PROPAGANDA TECHNIQUES

Bandwagon Appeal. Propaganda that appeals to people's desire to belong to a particular group is using the bandwagon appeal.

False Testimonial. A testimonial is a personal statement endorsing a person, policy, or product. Testimonials by celebrities or other persons who are not true experts are mere propaganda.

Loaded Words. Using words that evoke strong emotions is a way to sway opinion without offering logical arguments.

Character Assassination. This is a form of ad hominem argument that attacks the moral character of one's opponent instead of his or her ideas.

Bias Charges. Another kind of ad hominem argument questions someone's neutrality on an issue.

EXERCISE A Analyzing Faulty Arguments

The following sentences present faulty arguments. Read each statement. Then write the type of faulty argument it uses, and explain your reasoning. Keep in mind that an argument may be faulty in more than one way.

LANGUAGE ARTS SURVEY

For additional help, see the Language Arts Survey, 4.14.

1. Kelly always invites the entire soccer team to parties at her house. Brian has been invited to her parties, so he must be on the soccer team.

2. Yasmin only came to this school last semester. She shouldn't be elected class treasurer.

3. He's an inefficient manager because he does not use his time efficiently.

4. "The Fox and the Crow" is the worst fable ever written because animals can't talk.

5. Kylie, our school's star softball player, has a younger sister who'll be in high school next year. Next year's softball team is going to be amazing!

EXERCISE B Recognizing Propaganda Techniques

The following statements use propaganda techniques. Read each statement. Then write the type of propaganda technique it uses, and explain your reasoning.

LANGUAGE ARTS SURVEY

For additional help, see the Language Arts Survey, 4.15.

1. The Robin Hood Sewage Company has been dumping raw waste into this lake for years. If Lance Marghera didn't own forty percent of Robin Hood, do you think he'd still be telling you that this water is safe to drink?

2. C'mon! Don't go yet. Who cares about what your parents said? Everyone else is going to stay until after midnight.

3. I'm against this new legislation. I think we need to be sensible and stay away from radical proposals such as this.

4. That group is full of ex-cons, flag-burners, and bums. Are you really going to believe what they say?

5. As a wealthy and beautiful model, I can promise you that you'll never drive another car as comfortable and powerful as this Superdog sports sedan.

Part Two
THEMES IN LITERATURE

UNIT 6 DIVERSITY

Photos courtesy, Digital Stock Corp.

have a dream.

—Martin Luther King, Jr.

NONFICTION

from *Black Elk Speaks*
by Black Elk and John G. Neihardt

ABOUT THE AUTHORS

John G. Neihardt (1881–1973) was born in Illinois and grew up in Kansas and Nebraska. The close connections he formed with the indigenous populations of these states influenced his work as a poet and fiction writer. He lived among the Oglala Sioux from 1901 to 1907 and became an adopted member of the group. **Black Elk** (1863–1950), a Sioux medicine man, chose Neihardt as heir to his spiritual powers, the one who would communicate his message to the outside world. Much of Neihardt's work focuses on the time he spent with the Sioux. He has worked as a literary critic and a teacher, has received several awards and honorary degrees, and was chosen poet laureate of the state of Nebraska.

ABOUT THE SELECTION

Background: History. Black Elk was a warrior and medicine man for the Oglala Sioux, a group of Native Americans of the Great Plains. A medicine man is a spiritual advisor as well as a healer. To be a medicine man, one must have a special gift. In this portion of *Black Elk Speaks*, Black Elk tells of his youth, in which he received his first spiritual vision. The vision was a sign that he was indeed gifted and would become a great spiritual leader. The selection also focuses on the difficult time that Black Elk and his people faced as white settlers moved in and claimed ownership of Sioux territory.

READER'S JOURNAL

In your journal, freewrite about respect. What does the word *respect* mean to you? How do you show respect for the beliefs of others? In what ways do people fail to respect one another, on both a large scale and a small scale? How does disrespect feel to you?

FROM

Black Elk Speaks

BLACK ELK AND JOHN G. NEIHARDT

I am a Lakota of the Ogalala[1] band. My father's name was Black Elk, and his father before him bore the name, and the father of his father, so that I am the fourth to bear it. He was a medicine man and so were several of his brothers. Also, he and the great Crazy Horse's father were cousins, having the same grandfather. My mother's name was White Cow Sees; her father was called Refuse-to-go, and her mother, Plenty Eagle Feathers. I can remember my mother's mother and her father. My father's father was killed by the Pawnees when I was too little to know, and his mother, Red Eagle Woman, died soon after.

I was born in the Moon of the Popping Trees (December) on the Little Powder River in the Winter When the Four Crows Were Killed (1863), and I was three years old when my father's right leg was broken in the Battle of the Hundred Slain.[2] From that wound he limped until the day he died, which was about the time when Big Foot's band was butchered on Wounded Knee[3] (1890). He is buried here in these hills.

I can remember that Winter of the Hundred Slain as a man may remember some bad dream he dreamed when he was little, but I can not tell just how much I heard when I was bigger and how much I understood when I was little. It is like some fearful thing in a fog, for it was a time when everything seemed troubled and afraid.

I had never seen a Wasichu[4] then, and did not know what one looked like; but every one was saying that the Wasichus were coming and that they were going to take our country and rub us all out and that we should all have to die fighting. It was the Wasichus who got rubbed out in that

What fear did the Oglala Sioux have about the coming of the settlers?

1. **Ogalala.** Although this spelling is used throughout the text, *Oglala* is now the preferred spelling.

2. **Battle of the Hundred Slain.** Also called the Fetterman Fight, a Sioux victory in which Captain Fetterman and eighty-one men were slain near Peno Creek in December of 1866

3. **Wounded Knee.** Site in South Dakota of a terrible massacre of Native Americans. This massacre symbolized the defeat of the Sioux and the end of the Indian Wars.

4. **Wasichu.** Term used to describe white settlers

battle, and all the people were talking about it for a long while; but a hundred Wasichus was not much if there were others and others without number where those came from.

I remember once that I asked my grandfather about this. I said: "When the scouts come back from seeing the prairie full of <u>bison</u> somewhere, the people say the Wasichus are coming; and when strange men are coming to kill us all, they say the Wasichus are coming. What does it mean?" And he said, "That they are many."

When I was older, I learned what the fighting was about that winter and the next summer. Up on the Madison Fork the Wasichus had found much of the yellow metal that they worship and that makes them crazy, and they wanted to have a road up through our country to the place where the yellow metal was; but my people did not want the road. It would scare the bison and make them go away, and also it would let the other Wasichus come in like a river. They told us that they wanted only to use a little land, as much as a wagon would take between the wheels; but our people knew better. And when you look about you now, you can see what it was they wanted.

Once we were happy in our own country and we were seldom hungry, for then the two-leggeds and the four-leggeds lived together like relatives, and there was plenty for them and for us. But the Wasichus came, and they have made little islands for us and other little islands for the four-leggeds,

and always these islands are becoming smaller, for around them surges the gnawing flood of the Wasichu; and it is dirty with lies and greed.

A long time ago my father told me what his father told him, that there was once a Lakota[5] holy man, called Drinks Water, who dreamed what was to be; and this was long before the coming of the Wasichus. He dreamed that the four-leggeds were going back into the earth and that a strange race had woven a spider's web all around the Lakotas. And he said: "When this happens, you shall live in square gray houses, in a barren land, and beside those square gray houses you shall starve." They say he went back to Mother Earth soon after he saw this vision, and it was sorrow that killed him. You can look about you now and see that he meant these dirt-roofed houses we are living in, and that all the rest was true. Sometimes dreams are wiser than waking.

And so when the soldiers came and built themselves a town of logs there on the Piney Fork of the Powder, my people knew they meant to have their road and take our country and maybe kill us all when they were strong enough. Crazy Horse was only about 19 years old then, and Red Cloud was still our great chief. In the Moon of the Changing Season (October) he called together all the scattered bands of the Lakota for a big council on the Powder River, and when we went on the warpath against the soldiers, a

---

5. **Lakota.** Sioux

What word does Black Elk use to describe the Wasichus' attitude toward the "yellow metal"? What does Black Elk think about that attitude? Do you agree with him?

Who are the "two-leggeds" and the "four-leggeds"? What relationship existed between them before the coming of the Wasichus?

WORDS FOR EVERYDAY USE: bi • son (bī´sən) *n.,* type of mammal having a shaggy mane, short, curved horns, and a humped back; commonly referred to as the American buffalo

horseback could ride through our villages from sunrise until the day was above his head, so far did our camp stretch along the valley of the river; for many of our friends, the Shyela and the Blue Clouds,[6] had come to help us fight.

And it was about when the bitten moon was delayed (last quarter) in the Time of the Popping Trees when the hundred were rubbed out. My friend, Fire Thunder here, who is older than I, was in that fight and he can tell you how it was.

Fire Thunder Speaks:

I was 16 years old when this happened, and after the big council on the Powder we had moved over to the Tongue River where we were camping at the mouth of Peno Creek. There were many of us there. Red Cloud was over all of us, but the chief of our band was Big Road. We started out on horseback just about sunrise, riding up the creek toward the soldiers' town on the Piney, for we were going to attack it. The sun was about half way up when we stopped at the place where the Wasichu's road came down a steep, narrow ridge and crossed the creek. It was a good place to fight, so we sent some men ahead to coax the soldiers out. While they were gone, we divided into two parts and hid in the <u>gullies</u> on both sides of the ridge and waited. After a long while we heard a shot up over the hill, and we knew the soldiers were coming. So we held the noses of our ponies that they might not whinny at the soldiers' horses. Soon we saw our men coming back, and some of them were walking and leading their horses, so that the soldiers would think they were worn out. Then the men we had sent ahead came running down the road between us, and the soldiers on horseback followed, shooting. When they came to the flat at the bottom of the hill, the fighting began all at once. I had a <u>sorrel</u> horse, and just as I was going to get on him, the soldiers turned around and began to fight their way back up the hill. I had a six-shooter that I had traded for, and also a bow and arrows. When the soldiers started back, I held my sorrel with one hand and began killing them with the six-shooter, for they came close to me. There were many bullets, but there were more arrows—so many that it was like a cloud of grasshoppers all above and around the soldiers; and our people, shooting across, hit each other. The soldiers were falling all the while they were fighting back up the hill, and their horses got loose. Many of our people chased the horses, but I was not after horses; I was after Wasichus. When the soldiers got on top, there were not many of them left and they had no place to hide. They were fighting hard. We were told to crawl up on them, and we did. When we were close, someone yelled: "Let us go! This is a good day to die. Think of the helpless ones at home!" Then we all cried, "Hoka hey!" and rushed at them. I was

In what way is an older person like a time machine? What can you learn by listening to the stories that older people tell?

---

6. **Shyela and the Blue Clouds.** Cheyenne and Arapaho, two Native American groups from the Great Plains region

WORDS FOR EVERYDAY USE:

gul • ly (gul´ ē) *n.*, channel or hollow worn by running water

sor • rel (sôr´əl) *adj.*, light reddish-brown

The Last of the Buffalo. *Albert Bierstadt, 1889. In the collection of the Corcoran Gallery of Art. Gift of Albert Bierstadt.*

young then and quick on my feet, and I was one of the first to get in among the soldiers. They got up and fought very hard until not one of them was alive. They had a dog with them, and he started back up the road for the soldiers' town, howling as he ran. He was the only one left. I did not shoot at him because he looked too sweet, but many did shoot, and he died full of arrows. So there was nobody left of the soldiers. Dead men and horses and wounded Indians were scattered all the way up the hill, and their blood was frozen, for a storm had come up and it was very cold and getting colder all the time. We

What was the outcome of the battle?

left all the dead lying there, for the ground was solid, and we picked up our wounded and started back; but we lost most of them before we reached our camp at the mouth of the Peno. There was a big blizzard that night; and some of the wounded who did not die on the way, died after we got home. This was the time when Black Elk's father had his leg broken.

Black Elk Continues:

I am quite sure that I remember the time when my father came home with a broken leg that he got from killing so many Wasichus, and it seems that I can remember all about the battle too, but I think I could not. It must be the fear that I remember most. All this time I was not allowed to play very far away from our tepee, and my mother would say, "If you are not good the Wasichus will get you."

We must have broken camp at the mouth of the Peno soon after the battle, for I can remember my father lying on a pony drag with bison robes all around him, like a baby, and my mother riding the pony. The snow was deep and it was very cold, and I remember sitting in another pony drag beside my father and mother, all wrapped up in fur. We were going away from where the soldiers were, and I do not know where we went, but it was west.

It was a hungry winter, for the deep snow made it hard to find the elk; and also many of the people went snow-blind.[7] We wandered a long time, and some of the bands got lost from each other. Then at last we were camping in the woods beside a creek somewhere, and the hunters came back with meat.

I think it was this same winter when a medicine man, by the name of Creeping, went around among the people curing snowblinds. He would put snow upon their eyes, and after he had sung a certain sacred song that he had heard in a dream, he would blow on the backs of their heads and they would see again, so I have heard. It was about the dragonfly that he sang, for that was where he got his power, they say.

When it was summer again we were camping on the Rosebud, and I did not feel so much afraid, because the Wasichus seemed farther away and there was peace there in the valley and there was plenty of meat. But all the

boys from five or six years up were playing war. The little boys would gather together from the different bands of the tribe and fight each other with mud balls that they threw with willow sticks. And the big boys played the game called Throwing-Them-Off-Their-Horses, which is a battle all but the killing; and sometimes they got hurt. The horsebacks from the different bands would line up and charge upon each other, yelling; and when the ponies came together on the run, they would rear and flounder and scream in a big dust, and the riders would seize each other, wrestling until one side had lost all its men, for those who fell upon the ground were counted dead.

When I was older, I, too, often played this game. We were always naked when we played it, just as warriors are when they go into battle if it is not too cold, because they are swifter without clothes. Once I fell off on my back right in the middle of a bed of prickly pears,[8] and it took my mother a long while to pick all the stickers out of me. I was still too little to play war that summer, but I can remember watching the other boys, and I thought that when we all grew up and were big together, maybe we could kill all the Wasichus or drive them far away from our country.

It was in the Moon When the Cherries Turn Black (August) that all the people were talking again about a battle, and our warriors came back with many wounded. It was The Attacking of the Wagons, and it made me afraid again, for we did not win that battle as we did the other one, and

What hardships did the Sioux experience that winter?

Of what did the young Black Elk dream? What did he want to defend?

---

7. **snowblind.** Blinded temporarily by ultraviolet rays reflected from the snow

8. **prickly pears.** Variety of cactus

there was much mourning for the dead. Fire Thunder was in that fight too, and he can tell you how it was that day.

Fire Thunder Speaks:

It was very bad. There is a wide flat prairie with hills around it, and in the middle of this the Wasichus had put the boxes of their wagons in a circle, so that they could keep their mules there at night. There were not many Wasichus, but they were lying behind the boxes and they shot faster than they ever shot at us before. We thought it was some new medicine of great power that they had, for they shot so fast that it was like tearing a blanket. Afterwards I learned that it was because they had new guns that they loaded from behind, and this was the first time they used these guns. We came on after sunrise. There were many, many of us, and we meant to ride right over them and rub them out. But our ponies were afraid of the ring of fire the guns of the Wasichus made, and would not go over. Our women were watching us from the hills and we could hear them singing and mourning whenever the shooting stopped. We tried hard, but we could not do it, and there were dead warriors and horses piled all around the boxes and scattered over the plain. Then we left our horses in a gulch and charged on foot, but it was like green grass withering in a fire. So we picked up our wounded and went away. I do not know how many of our people were killed, but there were very many. It was bad.

Black Elk Continues:

I do not remember where we camped that winter but it must have been a time of peace and of plenty to eat.

Standing Bear Speaks:

I am four years older than Black Elk, and he and I have been good friends since boyhood. I know it was on the Powder that we camped where there were many cottonwood trees. Ponies like to eat the bark of these trees and it is good for them. That was the winter when High Shirt's mother was killed by a big tree that fell on her tepee. It was a very windy night and there were noises that 'woke me, and then I heard that an old woman had been killed, and it was High Shirt's mother.

Black Elk Continues:

I was four years old then, and I think it must have been the next summer that I first heard the voices. It was a happy summer and nothing was afraid, because in the Moon When the Ponies Shed (May) word came from the Wasichus that there would be peace and that they would not use the road any more and that all the soldiers would go away. The soldiers did go away and their towns were torn down; and in the Moon of Falling Leaves (November), they made a treaty with Red Cloud that said our country would be ours as long as grass should

Why did the Wasichus win this battle?

Why was this a happy summer for the Oglala?

WORDS FOR EVERYDAY USE: **trea • ty** (trēt ´ē) *n.,* formal agreement between two or more nations, resulting in peace

grow and water flow. You can see that it is not the grass and the water that have forgotten.

Maybe it was not this summer when I first heard the voices, but I think it was, because I know it was before I played with bows and arrows or rode a horse, and I was out playing alone when I heard them. It was like somebody calling me, and I thought it was my mother, but there was nobody there. This happened more than once, and always made me afraid, so that I ran home.

It was when I was five years old that my Grandfather made me a bow and some arrows. The grass was young and I was horseback. A thunderstorm was coming from where the sun goes down, and just as I was riding into the woods along a creek, there was a kingbird sitting on a limb. This was not a dream, it happened. And I was going to shoot at the kingbird with the bow my Grandfather made, when the bird spoke and said: "The clouds all over are one-sided." Perhaps it meant that all the clouds were looking at me. And then it said: "Listen! A voice is calling you!" Then I looked up at the clouds, and two men were coming there, headfirst like arrows slanting down; and as they came, they sang a sacred song and the thunder was like drumming. I will sing it for you. The song and the drumming were like this:

> "Behold, a sacred voice is calling you;
> All over the sky a sacred voice is calling."

I sat there gazing at them, and they were coming from the place where the giant lives (north). But when they were very close to me, they wheeled about toward where the sun goes down, and suddenly they were geese. Then they were gone, and the rain came with a big wind and a roaring.

I did not tell this vision to any one. I liked to think about it, but was afraid to tell it. ∎

Based on what Black Elk says, what can you conclude about how well the Wasichus honored the treaty that they made?

Was Black Elk sure that his vision was not a dream? How do you know?

Responding to the Selection

How do you feel about the Oglala? How do you feel about the Wasichus? Imagine that you are holding a meeting during which one person from each side has a chance to voice views, concerns, and plans. What would you say to each person? What view would you express of the conflict between them? Would you try to resolve the conflict? If so, how?

Reviewing the Selection

1. What did the Oglala believe the Wasichus planned to do? What was the "yellow metal" that brought the Wasichus to the area in which Black Elk and his people lived? What did the Wasichus wish to build? Why did the Oglala disagree with their wishes?

2. Was the first battle that Black Elk and Fire Thunder described a success for the Oglala? After the battle, where did the Oglala move and why? What games did the young Oglala play in the summer?

3. What caused the Oglala to lose the second battle that Black Elk and Fire Thunder described? How did events take a turn for the better in the following spring?

4. How old was Black Elk when he had his first vision? What appeared to him in the vision?

5. How did the Wasichus change the lives of the Oglala? How did the Oglala in the selection feel about the Wasichus and the things that they seemed to value?

6. In what ways were the lives of the Oglala difficult? How did real-life events affect the play of the Oglala children?

7. What did the treaty between the Wasichus and Red Cloud say? Why did Black Elk say, "You can see that it is not the grass and the water that have forgotten"? How did the Oglala feel about their country?

8. How did Black Elk feel about his vision? How might you describe the religion of the Oglala Sioux, based on what you have read in this piece?

9. Briefly describe the reason for the conflict in this piece. What lesson might be learned from this selection about respecting the beliefs and dignity of others?

10. How does this selection reflect a respect and appreciation for nature? What specific references are made to the importance of the natural world to the Oglala? How does the way in which the Oglala use language express this importance?

Understanding Literature (Questions for Discussion)

1. **Point of View. Point of view** is the vantage point from which a story is told. This selection is told from the first-person point of view by three different speakers. Who are the three speakers presented in this selection? How do Black Elk's views differ from those of Fire Thunder and Standing Bear? Do you get a better understanding of the events of the selection because three people tell about them? Why, or why not?

2. **Tone.** **Tone** is the emotional attitude toward the reader or toward the subject implied by a literary work. What is the tone of this selection? What specific words, phrases, or scenes create this tone? How does the tone change when Black Elk speaks of his vision at the end of the selection?

Responding in Writing

Calendar. Notice how Black Elk refers to the months of the year. December is "Moon of the Popping Trees," October is "Moon of the Changing Season," November is "Moon of Falling Leaves," May is "Moon When the Ponies Shed," and August is "Moon When the Cherries Turn Black." Each name focuses on something unique about the month to which it refers. Create your own calendar in which you give your own descriptive names to each month of the year. After you name the months, you may want to illustrate the calendar.

> **Prewriting Suggestion:** List all twelve months of the year in a notebook. Then list the special characteristics of each month. Try to concentrate on small details. What do you see and do only in September? How does it feel to walk outside in January or to take a deep breath in May? Black Elk had a strong attachment to nature. Try to see your world as Black Elk saw his when you create your calendar.

PROJECT

Storytelling. Many of the native peoples of North America used storytelling as a way to communicate legends and history. Storytelling is still important in our society; by the time people become teenagers, they are often full of stories. Even if teenagers cannot recall family stories or community legends, they do have personal stories. These stories may come from relationships with others, experiences at school, or interesting articles they have read. As a class, sit in a circle and share stories. These stories should communicate something about yourselves, your history, or how you view the world. When your storytelling session has ended, discuss why this is an effective way of sharing information and getting to know one another.

PREREADING

"The Scarlet Ibis"
by James Hurst

ABOUT THE AUTHOR

James Hurst (1922–   ) was born and raised on a farm in North Carolina and later attended North Carolina State College. He served in the United States Army during World War II, studied singing at the Juilliard School of Music, and traveled to Rome to further pursue his study of music. For thirty-four years, Hurst worked in the international department of a bank in New York. It was during this period of his life that Hurst wrote and published short stories and a play. "The Scarlet Ibis" was first published in *The Atlantic Monthly* in 1960.

ABOUT THE SELECTION

Background: Technique. The **setting** of a literary work is the time and place in which it occurs, together with all the details used to create a sense of a particular time and place. In **"The Scarlet Ibis,"** the setting is particularly important. According to Hurst, it is almost another character. You will notice that Hurst describes colors, weather conditions, plants, and trees in great detail as he creates the world of the two main characters in this story. This world is one with which North Carolina-born Hurst is quite familiar. As you read, notice the important role that the setting plays in the story.

READER'S JOURNAL
What are the different ways in which relationships can be complicated? Have you ever had mixed feelings about a family member or a close friend? Why do you suppose that we might have mixed feelings for the people to whom we are closest?

"The Scarlet Ibis"

JAMES HURST

It was in the clove of seasons,[1] summer was dead but autumn had not yet been born, that the ibis[2] lit in the bleeding tree. The flower garden was stained with rotting brown magnolia petals and ironweeds grew rank amid the purple phlox. The five o'clocks by the chimney still marked time, but the oriole nest in the elm was untenanted and rocked back and forth like an empty cradle. The last graveyard flowers were blooming, and their smell drifted across the cotton field and through every room of our house, speaking softly the names of our dead.

It's strange that all this is still so clear to me, now that that summer has long since fled and time has had its way. A grindstone[3] stands where the bleeding tree stood, just outside the kitchen door, and now if an oriole sings in the elm, its song seems to die up in the leaves, a silvery dust. The flower garden is prim, the house a gleaming white, and the pale fence across the yard stands straight and spruce. But sometimes (like right now), as I sit in the cool, green-draped parlor, the grindstone begins to turn, and time with all its changes is ground away— and I remember Doodle.

Doodle was just about the craziest brother a boy ever had. Of course, he wasn't a crazy crazy like old Miss Leedie, who was in love with President Wilson[4] and wrote him a letter every day, but was a nice crazy, like someone you meet in your dreams. He was born when I was six and was, from the outset, a disappointment. He seemed all head, with a tiny body which was red

Who is Doodle?

What do the graveyard flowers do?

---

1. **clove of seasons.** Time between seasons
2. **ibis.** Large tropical bird
3. **grindstone.** Revolving stone disk for sharpening or polishing tools
4. **President Wilson.** Thomas Woodrow Wilson (1856–1924), twenty-eighth president of the United States

and shriveled like an old man's. Everybody thought he was going to die—everybody except Aunt Nicey, who had delivered him. She said he would live because he was born in a <u>caul</u> and cauls were made from Jesus' nightgown. Daddy had Mr. Heath, the carpenter, build a little mahogany coffin for him. But he didn't die, and when he was three months old Mama and Daddy decided they might as well name him. They named him William Armstrong, which was like tying a big tail on a small kite. Such a name sounds good only on a tombstone.

I thought myself pretty smart at many things, like holding my breath, running, jumping, or climbing the vines in Old Woman Swamp, and I wanted more than anything else someone to race to Horsehead Landing, someone to box with, and someone to perch with in the top fork of the great pine behind the barn, where across the fields and swamps you could see the sea. I wanted a brother. But Mama, crying, told me that even if William Armstrong lived, he would never do these things with me. He might not, she sobbed, even be "all there." He might, as long as he lived, lie on the rubber sheet in the center of the bed in the front bedroom where the white marquisette curtains billowed out in the afternoon sea breeze, rustling like palmetto fronds.[5]

It was bad enough having an invalid brother, but having one who possibly was not all there was unbearable, so I began to make plans to kill him by smothering him with a pillow. However, one afternoon as I watched him, my head poked between the iron posts of the foot of the bed, he looked straight at me and grinned. I skipped through the rooms, down the echoing halls, shouting, "Mama, he smiled. He's all there! He's all there!" and he was.

When he was two, if you laid him on his stomach, he began to try to move himself, straining terribly. The doctor said that with his weak heart this strain would probably kill him, but it didn't. Trembling, he'd push himself up, turning first red, then a soft purple, and finally collapse back onto the bed like an old worn-out doll. I can still see Mama watching him, her hand pressed tight across her mouth, her eyes wide and unblinking. But he learned to crawl (it was his third winter), and we brought him out of the front bedroom, putting him on the rug before the fireplace. For the first time he became one of us.

As long as he lay all the time in bed, we called him William Armstrong, even though it was formal and sounded as if we were referring to one of our ancestors, but with his creeping around on the deerskin rug and beginning to talk, something had to be done about his name. It was I who renamed him. When he crawled, he crawled backwards, as if he were in reverse and couldn't change gears. If you called him, he'd turn around as if he were

---

5. **palmetto fronds.** Fan-shaped leaves of a palm tree

WORDS FOR EVERYDAY USE: **caul** (kôl) *n.*, membrane enclosing a fetus or a newborn baby

Why does the narrator dislike his brother's name?

What does the narrator decide to do to his brother? Why? What causes the narrator to change his mind?

going in the other direction, then he'd back right up to you to be picked up. Crawling backward made him look like a doodlebug, so I began to call him Doodle, and in time even Mama and Daddy thought it was a better name than William Armstrong. Only Aunt Nicey disagreed. She said caul babies should be treated with special respect since they might turn out to be saints. Renaming my brother was perhaps the kindest thing I ever did for him, because nobody expects much from someone called Doodle.

Although Doodle learned to crawl, he showed no signs of walking, but he wasn't idle. He talked so much that we all quit listening to what he said. It was about this time that Daddy built him a go-cart and I had to pull him around. At first I just paraded him up and down the piazza,[6] but then he started crying to be taken out into the yard, and it ended up by my having to lug him wherever I went. If I so much as picked up my cap, he'd start crying to go with me and Mama would call from wherever she was, "Take Doodle with you."

He was a burden in many ways. The doctor had said that he mustn't get too excited, too hot, too cold, or too tired and that he must always be treated gently. A long list of don'ts went with him, all of which I ignored once we got out of the house. To discourage his coming with me, I'd run with him across the ends of the cotton rows and <u>careen</u> him around corners on two wheels. Sometimes I accidentally

turned him over, but he never told Mama. His skin was very sensitive, and he had to wear a big straw hat whenever he went out. When the going got rough and he had to cling to the sides of the go-cart, the hat slipped all the way down over his ears. He was a sight. Finally, I could see I was licked. Doodle was my brother and he was going to cling to me forever, no matter what I did, so I dragged him across the burning cotton field to share with him the only beauty I knew, Old Woman Swamp. I pulled the go-cart through the saw-tooth fern, down into the green dimness where the palmetto fronds whispered by the stream. I lifted him out and set him down in the soft rubber grass beside a tall pine. His eyes were round with wonder as he gazed about him, and his little hands began to stroke the rubber grass. Then he began to cry.

"For heaven's sake, what's the matter?" I asked, annoyed.

"It's so pretty," he said. "So pretty, pretty, pretty."

After that day Doodle and I often went down into Old Woman Swamp. I would gather wildflowers, wild violets, honeysuckle, yellow jasmine, snakeflowers, and water lilies, and with wire grass we'd weave them into necklaces and crowns. We'd bedeck ourselves with our handiwork and loll about thus beautified, beyond the touch of the everyday world. Then when the slanted rays of the sun burned orange

What does Aunt Nicey believe about the narrator's brother?

Why does the narrator stop trying to discourage Doodle's attention?

Why does the narrator find a brother like Doodle to be difficult?

---

6. **piazza.** Large, covered porch

WORDS FOR EVERYDAY USE: **ca • reen** (kə rēn´) *vt.*, lurch from side to side, especially while moving rapidly

in the tops of the pines, we'd drop our jewels into the stream and watch them float away toward the sea.

There is within me (and with sadness I have watched it in others) a knot of cruelty borne by the stream of love, much as our blood sometimes bears the seed of our destruction, and at times I was mean to Doodle. One day I took him up to the barn loft and showed him his casket, telling him how we all had believed he would die. It was covered with a film of Paris green[7] sprinkled to kill the rats, and screech owls had built a nest inside it.

Doodle studied the mahogany box for a long time, then said, "It's not mine."

"It is," I said. "And before I'll help you down from the loft, you're going to have to touch it."

"I won't touch it," he said <u>sullenly</u>.

"Then I'll leave you here by yourself," I threatened, and made as if I were going down.

Doodle was frightened of being left. "Don't go leave me, Brother," he cried, and he leaned toward the coffin. His hand, trembling, reached out, and when he touched the casket he screamed. A screech owl flapped out of the box into our faces, scaring us and covering us with Paris green. Doodle was paralyzed, so I put him on my shoulder and carried him down the ladder, and even when we were outside in the bright sunshine, he clung to me, crying, "Don't leave me. Don't leave me."

When Doodle was five years old, I was embarrassed at having a brother of that age who couldn't walk, so I set out to teach him. We were down in Old Woman Swamp and it was spring and the sick-sweet smell of bay flowers hung everywhere like a mournful song. "I'm going to teach you to walk, Doodle," I said.

He was sitting comfortably on the soft grass, leaning back against the pine. "Why?" he asked.

I hadn't expected such an answer. "So I won't have to haul you around all the time."

"I can't walk, Brother," he said.

"Who says so?" I demanded.

"Mama, the doctor—everybody."

"Oh, you can walk," I said, and I took him by the arms and stood him up. He collapsed onto the grass like a half-empty flour sack. It was as if he had no bones in his little legs.

"Don't hurt me, Brother," he warned.

"Shut up. I'm not going to hurt you. I'm going to teach you to walk." I heaved him up again, and again he collapsed.

This time he did not lift his face up out of the rubber grass. "I just can't do it. Let's make honeysuckle wreaths."

"Oh yes you can, Doodle," I said. "All you got to do is try. Now come on," and I hauled him up once more.

It seemed so hopeless from the beginning that it's a miracle I didn't give up. But all of us must have something or someone to be proud of, and Doodle had become mine. I did not know then that pride is a wonderful,

---

7. **Paris green.** Green powdered insecticide

To what does the narrator compare the cruelty that sometimes accompanies love?

What does the narrator force Doodle to do? What happens when Doodle does it?

WORDS FOR EVERYDAY USE: sul • len • ly (sul´ən lē) *adv.,* gloomily

terrible thing, a seed that bears two vines, life and death. Every day that summer we went to the pine beside the stream of Old Woman Swamp, and I put him on his feet at least a hundred times each afternoon. Occasionally I too became discouraged because it didn't seem as if he was trying, and I would say, "Doodle, don't you *want* to learn to walk?"

He'd nod his head, and I'd say, "Well, if you don't keep trying, you'll never learn. Then I'd paint for him a picture of us as old men, white-haired, him with a long white beard and me still pulling him around in the go-cart. This never failed to make him try again.

Finally one day, after many weeks of practicing, he stood alone for a few seconds. When he fell, I grabbed him in my arms and hugged him, our laughter pealing through the swamp like a ringing bell. Now we knew it could be done. Hope no longer hid in the dark palmetto thicket but perched like a cardinal in the lacy toothbrush tree, brilliantly visible. "Yes, yes," I cried, and he cried it too, and the grass beneath us was soft and the smell of the swamp was sweet.

With success so <u>imminent</u>, we decided not to tell anyone until he could actually walk. Each day, barring rain, we sneaked into Old Woman Swamp, and by cotton-picking time Doodle was ready to show what he could do. He still wasn't able to walk far, but we could wait no longer. Keeping a nice secret is very hard to do, like holding your breath. We chose to reveal all on October eighth, Doodle's sixth birthday, and for weeks ahead we mooned around the house, promising everybody a most spectacular surprise. Aunt Nicey said that, after so much talk, if we produced anything less tremendous than the Resurrection,[8] she was going to be disappointed.

At breakfast on our chosen day, when Mama, Daddy, and Aunt Nicey were in the dining room, I brought Doodle to the door in the go-cart just as usual and had them turn their backs, making them cross their hearts and hope to die if they peeked. I helped Doodle up, and when he was standing alone I let them look. There wasn't a sound as Doodle walked slowly across the room and sat down at his place at the table. Then Mama began to cry and ran over to him, hugging him and kissing him. Daddy hugged him too, so I went to Aunt Nicey, who was thanks praying in the doorway, and began to waltz her around. We danced together quite well until she came down on my big toe with her brogans,[9] hurting me so badly I thought I was crippled for life.

Doodle told them it was I who had taught him to walk, so everyone wanted to hug me, and I began to cry.

"What are you crying for?" asked Daddy, but I couldn't answer. They did not know that I did it for myself; that pride, whose slave I was, spoke to me louder than all their voices, and

---

8. **Resurrection.** Jesus' return to life after the Crucifixion
9. **brogans.** Heavy work shoes

What does the narrator do when Doodle stands on his own? What emotions do the brothers feel when they realize that there is hope for Doodle's success?

What reasons does the narrator have for teaching Doodle to walk?

WORDS FOR EVERYDAY USE: im • mi • nent (im´ə nənt) *adj.,* likely to happen

that Doodle walked only because I was ashamed of having a crippled brother.

Within a few months Doodle had learned to walk well and his go-cart was put up in the barn loft (it's still there) beside his little mahogany coffin. Now, when we roamed off together, resting often, we never turned back until our destination had been reached, and to help pass the time, we took up lying. From the beginning Doodle was a terrible liar and he got me in the habit. Had anyone stopped to listen to us, we would have been sent off to Dix Hill.[10]

My lies were scary, involved, and usually pointless, but Doodle's were twice as crazy. People in his stories all had wings and flew wherever they wanted to go. His favorite lie was about a boy named Peter who had a pet peacock with a ten-foot tail. Peter wore a golden robe that glittered so brightly that when he walked through the sunflowers they turned away from the sun to face him. When Peter was ready to go to sleep, the peacock spread his magnificent tail, enfolding the boy gently like a closing go-to-sleep flower, burying him in the gloriously <u>iridescent</u>, rustling <u>vortex</u>. Yes, I must admit it. Doodle could beat me lying.

Doodle and I spent lots of time thinking about our future. We decided that when we were grown we'd live in Old Woman Swamp and pick dog-tongue for a living. Beside the stream, he planned, we'd build us a house of whispering leaves and the swamp birds would be our chickens. All day long (when we weren't gathering dog-tongue) we'd swing through the cypresses on the rope vines, and if it rained we'd huddle beneath an umbrella tree and play stickfrog. Mama and Daddy could come and live with us if they wanted to. He even came up with the idea that he could marry Mama and I could marry Daddy. Of course, I was old enough to know this wouldn't work out, but the picture he painted was so beautiful and serene that all I could do was whisper Yes, yes.

Once I had succeeded in teaching Doodle to walk, I began to believe in my own <u>infallibility</u> and I prepared a terrific development program for him, unknown to Mama and Daddy, of course. I would teach him to run, to swim, to climb trees, and to fight. He, too, now believed in my infallibility, so we set the deadline for these accomplishments less than a year away, when, it had been decided, Doodle could start to school.

That winter we didn't make much progress, for I was in school and Doodle suffered from one bad cold after another. But when spring came, rich and warm, we raised our sights again. Success lay at the end of summer like a pot of gold, and our campaign got off to a good start. On hot days, Doodle and I went down to Horsehead Landing, and I gave him swimming lessons or showed him how to row a boat. Sometimes we

<hr>

What can Doodle do more skillfully than his brother? What does this skill reveal about Doodle?

10. **Dix Hill.** The location of Dorothea Dix Hospital, a state institution

<hr>

WORDS FOR EVERYDAY USE:

ir • i • des • cent (ir´i des´ənt) *adj.,* having shifting changes in color

vor • tex (vôr´teks´) *n.,* whirlpool or eddy

in • fal • li • bil • i • ty (in fal´ə bil i tē) *n.,* correctness, incapacity for error

descended into the cool greenness of Old Woman Swamp and climbed the rope vines or boxed scientifically beneath the pine where he had learned to walk. Promise hung about us like the leaves, and wherever we looked, ferns unfurled and birds broke into song.

That summer, the summer of 1918, was blighted. In May and June there was no rain and the crops withered, curled up, then died under the thirsty sun. One morning in July a hurricane came out of the east, tipping over the oaks in the yard and splitting the limbs of the elm trees. That afternoon it roared back out of the west, blew the fallen oaks around, snapping their roots and tearing them out of the earth like a hawk at the entrails of a chicken. Cotton bolls were wrenched from the stalks and lay like green walnuts in the valleys between the rows, while the cornfield leaned over uniformly so that the tassels touched the ground. Doodle and I followed Daddy out into the cotton field, where he stood, shoulders sagging, surveying the ruin. When his chin sank down onto his chest, we were frightened, and Doodle slipped his hand into mine. Suddenly Daddy straightened his shoulders, raised a giant knuckly fist, and with a voice that seemed to rumble out of the earth itself began cursing heaven, the weather, hell, and the Republican Party. Doodle and I, prodding each other and giggling, went back to the house, knowing that everything would be all right.

And during that summer, strange names were heard through the house: Château-Thierry, Amiens, Soissons, and in her blessing at the supper table, Mama once said, "And bless the Pearsons, whose boy Joe was lost at Belleau Wood."[11]

So we came to that clove of seasons. School was only a few weeks away, and Doodle was far behind schedule. He could barely clear the ground when climbing up the rope vines and his swimming was certainly not passable. We decided to double our efforts, to make that last drive and reach our pot of gold. I made him swim until he turned blue and row until he couldn't lift an oar. Wherever we went, I purposely walked fast, and although he kept up, his face turned red and his eyes became glazed. Once, he could go no further, so he collapsed on the ground and began to cry.

"Aw, come on, Doodle," I urged. "You can do it. Do you want to be different from everybody else when you start school?"

"Does it make any difference?"

"It certainly does," I said. "Now, come on," and I helped him up.

As we slipped through dog days, Doodle began to look feverish, and Mama felt his forehead, asking him if he felt ill. At night he didn't sleep well, and sometimes he had nightmares, crying out until I touched him and said, "Wake up, Doodle. Wake up."

It was Saturday noon, just a few days before school was to start. I should have already admitted defeat, but my pride wouldn't let me. The excitement of our program had now been gone for weeks, but still we kept on with a tired doggedness. It was too late to turn back, for we had both wandered too far into a net of expectations and had left no crumbs behind.

Daddy, Mama, Doodle, and I were seated at the dining-room table having lunch. It was a hot day, with all the

11. **Château-Thierry . . . Belleau Wood.** World War I battlefields in France

Is Doodle succeeding in learning the new skills the narrator wishes to teach him?

What does the narrator tell Doodle about being different?

The Torn Hat. Thomas Sully. Courtesy, The Museum of Fine Arts, Boston. Gift of Miss Belle Greene and Mr. Henry Copley Greene in memory of their mother Mary Abby Greene (Mrs. J.S. Copley Greene), 1916

What sound signals a coming storm? Has anyone heard such a sound?

windows and doors open in case a breeze should come. In the kitchen Aunt Nicey was humming softly. After a long silence, Daddy spoke. "It's so calm, I wouldn't be surprised if we had a storm this afternoon."

"I haven't heard a rain frog," said Mama, who believed in signs, as she served the bread around the table.

"I did," declared Doodle. "Down in the swamp."

"He didn't," I said contrarily.

"You did, eh?" said Daddy, ignoring my denial.

"I certainly did," Doodle <u>reiterated</u>, scowling at me over the top of his iced-tea glass, and we were quiet again.

Suddenly, from out in the yard, came a strange croaking noise. Doodle stopped eating, with a piece of bread poised ready for his mouth, his eyes popped round like two blue buttons. "What's that?" he whispered.

I jumped up, knocking over my chair, and had reached the door when Mama called, "Pick up the chair, sit down again, and say excuse me."

WORDS FOR EVERYDAY USE: re • it • er • ate (rē it´ə rāt´) *vt.,* repeat

By the time I had done this, Doodle had excused himself and had slipped out into the yard. He was looking up into the bleeding tree. "It's a great big red bird!" he called.

The bird croaked loudly again, and Mama and Daddy came out into the yard. We shaded our eyes with our hands against the hazy glare of the sun and peered up through the still leaves. On the topmost branch a bird the size of a chicken, with scarlet feathers and long legs, was perched precariously. Its wings hung down loosely, and as we watched, a feather dropped away and floated slowly down through the green leaves.

"It's not even frightened of us," Mama said.

"It looks tired," Daddy added. "Or maybe sick."

Doodle's hands were clasped at his throat, and I had never seen him stand still so long. "What is it?" he asked.

Daddy shook his head. "I don't know, maybe it's—"

At that moment the bird began to flutter, but the wings were uncoordinated, and amid much flapping and a spray of flying feathers, it tumbled down, bumping through the limbs of the bleeding tree and landing at our feet with a thud. Its long, graceful neck jerked twice into an S, then straightened out, and the bird was still. A white veil came over the eyes and the long white beak unhinged. Its legs were crossed and its clawlike feet were delicately curved at rest. Even death did not mar its grace, for it lay on the earth like a broken vase of red flowers, and we stood around it, awed by its exotic beauty.

"It's dead," Mama said.

"What is it?" Doodle repeated.

"Go bring me the bird book," said Daddy.

I ran into the house and brought back the bird book. As we watched, Daddy thumbed through its pages. "It's a scarlet ibis," he said, pointing to a picture. "It lives in the tropics— South America to Florida. A storm must have brought it here."

Sadly, we all looked back at the bird. A scarlet ibis! How many miles it had traveled to die like this, in *our* yard, beneath the bleeding tree.

"Let's finish lunch," Mama said, nudging us back toward the dining room.

"I'm not hungry," said Doodle, and he knelt down beside the ibis.

"We've got peach cobbler for dessert," Mama tempted from the doorway.

Doodle remained kneeling. "I'm going to bury him."

"Don't you dare touch him," Mama warned. "There's no telling what disease he might have had."

"All right," said Doodle. "I won't."

Daddy, Mama, and I went back to the dining-room table, but we watched Doodle through the open door. He took out a piece of string from his pocket and, without touching the ibis, looped one end around its neck. Slowly, while singing softly, "Shall We Gather at the River," he carried the bird around to the front yard and dug a hole in the flower garden, next to the petunia bed. Now we were watching him through the front window, but he didn't know it. His awkwardness at digging the hole with a shovel whose handle was twice as long as he was made us laugh, and we covered our mouths with our hands so he wouldn't hear.

What has produced the croaking sound?

How has the bird come to the narrator's yard? What does it do there?

What does Doodle do with the bird?

When Doodle came into the dining room, he found us seriously eating our cobbler. He was pale and lingered just inside the screen door. "Did you get the scarlet ibis buried?" asked Daddy.

Doodle didn't speak but nodded his head.

"Go wash your hands, and then you can have some peach cobbler," said Mama.

"I'm not hungry," he said.

"Dead birds is bad luck," said Aunt Nicey, poking her head from the kitchen door. "Specially *red* dead birds!"

As soon as I had finished eating, Doodle and I hurried off to Horsehead Landing. Time was short, and Doodle still had a long way to go if he was going to keep up with the other boys when he started school. The sun, gilded with the yellow cast of autumn, still burned fiercely, but the dark green woods through which we passed were shady and cool. When we reached the landing, Doodle said he was too tired to swim, so we got into a <u>skiff</u> and floated down the creek with the tide. Far off in the marsh a rail was scolding, and over on the beach locusts were singing in the myrtle trees. Doodle did not speak and kept his head turned away, letting one hand trail limply in the water.

After we had drifted a long way, I put the oars in place and made Doodle row back against the tide. Black clouds began to gather in the southwest, and he kept watching them, trying to pull the oars a little faster. When we reached Horsehead Landing, lightning was playing across half the sky and thunder roared out, hiding even the sound of the sea. The sun disappeared and darkness descended, almost like night. Flocks of marsh crows flew by, heading inland to their roosting trees, and two egrets, squawking, arose from the oyster-rock shallows and careened away.

Doodle was both tired and frightened, and when he stepped from the skiff he collapsed onto the mud, sending an armada of fiddler crabs rustling off into the marsh grass. I helped him up, and as he wiped the mud off his trousers, he smiled at me ashamedly. He had failed and we both knew it, so we started back home, racing the storm. We never spoke (What are the words that can solder cracked pride?), but I knew he was watching me, watching for a sign of mercy. The lightning was near now, and from fear he walked so close behind me he kept stepping on my heels. The faster I walked, the faster he walked, so I began to run. The rain was coming, roaring through the pines, and then like a bursting Roman candle, a gum tree ahead of us was shattered by a bolt of lightning. When the deafening peal of thunder had died, and in the moment before the rain arrived, I heard Doodle, who had fallen behind, cry out, "Brother, Brother, don't leave me! Don't leave me!"

The knowledge that Doodle's and my plans had come to naught was bitter, and that streak of cruelty within

What does Aunt Nicey say about the ibis?

Who has failed? Whose pride has cracked? What has come as Doodle predicted?

WORDS FOR EVERYDAY USE: **skiff** (skif) *n.*, small, open boat

me awakened. I ran as fast as I could, leaving him far behind with a wall of rain dividing us. The drops stung my face like nettles, and the wind flared the wet glistening leaves of the bordering trees. Soon I could hear his voice no more.

I hadn't run too far before I became tired, and the flood of childish spite evanesced as well. I stopped and waited for Doodle. The sound of rain was everywhere, but the wind had died and it fell straight down in parallel paths like ropes hanging from the sky. As I waited, I peered through the downpour, but no one came. Finally I went back and found him huddled beneath a red nightshade bush beside the road. He was sitting on the ground, his face buried in his arms, which were resting on his drawn-up knees. "Let's go, Doodle," I said.

He didn't answer, so I placed my hand on his forehead and lifted his head. Limply, he fell backwards onto the earth. He had been bleeding from the mouth, and his neck and the front of his shirt were stained a brilliant red.

"Doodle! Doodle!" I cried, shaking him, but there was no answer but the ropy rain. He lay very awkwardly, with his head thrown far back, making his vermilion neck appear unusually long and slim. His little legs, bent sharply at the knees, had never before seemed so fragile, so thin.

I began to weep, and the tear-blurred vision in red before me looked very familiar. "Doodle!" I screamed above the pounding storm and threw my body to the earth above his. For a long time, it seemed forever, I lay there crying, sheltering my fallen scarlet ibis from the heresy of rain. ∎

What divides the brothers?

Of what does Doodle remind the narrator? Why?

Responding to the Selection

How did you feel about the narrator and Doodle by the last scene of the story? Which scenes in this story affected you in the strongest way? Why? What is it like to realize that you have lost something important only when it is too late? How do you think you can prevent this from happening?

WORDS FOR EVERYDAY USE:

ev • a • nesce (ev´ən nes´) *vi.,* disappear

her • e • sy (her´i sē) *n.,* rejection of a belief that is part of an established set of beliefs

Reviewing the Selection

1. How is the narrator's younger brother different from other children when he is born? What is the baby's original name? How does the narrator come up with the name "Doodle"?

2. What does the narrator teach Doodle to do? What is the family's reaction to Doodle's accomplishment?

3. What does Doodle do for the scarlet ibis?

4. Where are the boys when the storm first hits?

5. How do the various members of the family respond to the new baby? What does the narrator notice about the baby one afternoon, and how does this observation change how the narrator feels toward him? Why does the narrator feel that renaming his brother is the kindest thing he could do for him?

6. What are the narrator's reasons for taking special interest in his brother and deciding to teach him? What feelings does the narrator display as he spends time with Doodle?

7. How does the scarlet ibis make Doodle feel? To what other scenes in the book might Doodle's feelings be related?

8. What does the narrator do to his brother for the first time as the two make their way through the rain? How might this action affect the narrator for the rest of his life?

9. How would you describe the narrator's relationship with his brother, Doodle? What specific incidents in the story tell the reader about the relationship between these two brothers and how they truly feel about one another?

10. How is the scarlet ibis like Doodle in this story? What do he and the ibis have in common?

Understanding Literature (Questions for Discussion)

1. **Foreshadowing. Foreshadowing** is the act of presenting materials that hint at events to occur later in a story. What images or events in the "The Scarlet Ibis" hint about, or make reference to, the end of the story?

2. **Scene.** A **scene** is a short section of a literary work that presents action that occurs in a single place at a single time. List the important scenes of this story. How do these scenes help you to get to know the characters and the situation? What are your favorite scenes in this piece? Why are they your favorites?

3. **Mood. Mood,** or **atmosphere,** is the emotion created in the reader by all or part of a literary work. How does the author establish mood in the scenes of this story? What bits of dialogue and description make you feel a certain way?

4. **Point of View. Point of view** is the vantage point from which a story is told. How important is point of view in this story? How would the story be different if it were told from the point of view of Doodle, the boys' mother, or Aunt Nicey?

Responding in Writing

Setting and Mood Paragraphs. Write two brief pieces that establish setting and mood in a way that is vivid and clear. One piece should describe a place with which you are quite familiar. The other piece should describe a place to which you have never been but that you can imagine. Try to express the same mood in both pieces.

> **Prewriting Suggestion:** First, decide what mood you would like to convey in your pieces. Then think of appropriate settings. Freewrite about the places you would like to describe, trying to visualize every detail.

PROJECT

Panel Discussion. What is it like to live with expectations—either your expectations of yourself or others' expectations of you? Think about the expectations people had of Doodle and how he proved them wrong. Throughout history, there have always been people who have risen above and beyond what has been expected of them. Many people have had serious illnesses or have been physically challenged in some way, but have surprised and impressed everyone around them by achieving greatness. As a class, brainstorm a list of people who fall into this category. Think about different fields—sports, music, art, literature, politics, and medicine, for example. After you have a list, have each person in the class do some research on one person. Then have a panel discussion that each student in the class attends as his or her "character." The topic for discussion should be expectations and how each member of the panel was able to surpass what was expected of him or her.

from *Mississippi Solo*
by Eddy L. Harris

ABOUT THE AUTHOR

Eddy L. Harris, a 1977 graduate of Stanford University, has lived on the East Coast and in Missouri where he grew up. Harris has worked as a screenwriter and as a journalist and has traveled throughout Europe and Central America. *Mississippi Solo* is his first book.

ABOUT THE SELECTION

Background: Theme. *Mississippi Solo* is a detailed account of a man's trip down the Mississippi River—from Minnesota to Louisiana—in a borrowed canoe. Friends told Harris that paddling the length of the Mississippi River was foolish and dangerous. Harris, however, felt compelled to make this difficult journey. He states in the opening of his book, "But this dream of mine, still suspended on the breeze and delicate as ever, was just as real as those flimsy summer spider webs hanging in the air, and just as clinging. Once the webs attach themselves to you they are hard to get rid of. And so it was with my desire to ride the river." His friend Robinovich, who is mentioned in the selection you are about to read, played a key role in helping Harris to prepare for his journey. She also stayed close to Harris throughout the first day of his journey to make sure he got off to a good start.

Background: History. The Mississippi River flows southeast from Lake Itasca in Minnesota to the Gulf of Mexico. The river stretches some two thousand three hundred fifty miles and, together with the Missouri River, forms a river system surpassed in length only by the Nile in Africa and the Amazon in South America. The Mississippi River was acquired by the United States through the Louisiana Purchase in 1803 and marked the gateway to the western territories. Another American writer fascinated by this impressive river was Mark Twain, who worked as a riverboat pilot.

READER'S JOURNAL

In your journal, make a list of journeys you would like to take, places you would like to visit, or goals you would like to reach. Your list should be a long one; don't leave anything out, even something that seems slightly unrealistic. Then choose one item from your list and try to think of realistic steps you might take toward accomplishing this goal. Write about how you would feel as you pursued your goal and after you accomplished your goal.

FROM

Mississippi Solo

EDDY L. HARRIS

We were up before the sun. The air was soft and fine, but cold. The morning seemed brittle. When the sun finally rose it looked like it would have taken any excuse at all and gone back to bed. The same for me, so it was quickly tea and soup, break camp and head on down to the lake.

Without much <u>ado</u> we unloosed the canoe from its perch atop the car and set it in the water. I tied an extra paddle to one of the cross struts[1] in the canoe, slipped a line through the stern,[2] and I was ready.

Nothing else needed to be stowed in the canoe because Robinovich had agreed to stay on for the day and meet me periodically along this early portion of the river. Just to make sure I got the hang of it and to put both our minds at ease.

I took a long hug and a kiss, <u>donned</u> my yellow life jacket, and I was away.

The lake invites me with its stillness. Any <u>turbulence</u> might have discouraged me, but the water is so calm and pretty and the morning so quiet and finally beginning to take on some color that I shove off easily and paddle straight out to where the water is deep and cold and scariest. I suddenly have no fear of falling in and if not for the river calling me I could easily stay here and paddle up and down this lake all day.

But the river does call. I turn my canoe north and glide toward it.

Right away I discover that canoeing is an art, one which I will eventually have to learn. On the quiet lake my zigzagging poses no problem, but I will need to learn to control this thing or I might find trouble later on. I don't want that.

What is the lake like in the morning? How do the conditions of the lake make Harris feel?

What does Harris learn on the lake? What does he want to avoid?

---

1. **cross struts.** Braces fitted across the framework of a canoe to resist pressure in the direction of its length
2. **stern.** Rear end of a ship or boat

WORDS FOR EVERYDAY USE:

a • do (ə dōō´) *n.*, fuss; trouble; excitement
don (dän) *vt.*, put on (a garment)
tur • bu • lence (tʉr´ byōō ləns) *n.*, violent, irregular motion or swirling agitation of water, air, gas, etc.

I settle in quickly amid the cushioning quiet of this near-wilderness. The lake reflects the dark green trees and the sky striped white and blue. The trail I lay behind me in the water is a soft S-curve of bubbles and swirls. I make so little noise. Only the light swishing of my paddle, the drips of water tapping the lake when I cross the paddle from my left side to my right, a little plop when each time I dig the paddle into the water, and a slight suction sound when I pull it out for the next stroke. And all about me is fine and silent until a handful of ducks skims across the water. Their noise is the flapping of heavy wings and the dragging of duck feet across the lake.

I lengthen my stroking. I'm coming faster and faster across the water now. It's almost effortless, a feeling much like gliding across calm seas in a sail boat. I feel the spirit of this water rising up from the morning's mist and I hear it whispering to me that I have nothing to worry about.

As I carve my path across the water, I see ahead the river falling away as though spilling into a drain. I'm caught in the current. Still paddling, of course; the current isn't *that* strong. It must be a psychological pull that makes me feel I could stop paddling and still not keep from aiming for those rocks and that river.

A father and mother are showing the baby river to their two children. They wave and call to me as I slow to <u>negotiate</u> the rocks that cross the river.

"Where are you headed?"

"New Orleans." I feel like an expert now, an old pro at this. I try to look cool, like I know what I'm doing, but I add, "I hope."

They laugh and wish me luck.

It's a transaction I will undergo a hundred times before I reach the end, each one very much like this one. Some will wish they could go along, others will think I'm a little on the loony side, but each one will encourage me and no one will wish me bad luck or ill. Well, almost no one.

When the river finally falls into the gulf, it will have reached a depth of about two hundred feet, but just beyond these big rocks the Mississippi's bottom lies only inches below the surface. My canoe and its 185- pound paddler have a draft[3] of about six inches and when the creek bed rises to its shallowest point, the canoe touches bottom and I'm stuck. Not ten yards from the beginning and I'm stuck. I hope no one is looking. Is this an <u>omen</u>?

There! I dig my paddle hard into the pebbly bottom and lean against it and just shove until the canoe slides free, dragging bottom at first but finally getting loose and afloat again. This will happen many more times before the river has found a few more inches to <u>accommodate</u> me, but a little strength is all I need. I manage.

Shortly on I come to a little bridge. Lying flat in the canoe I slide under the bridge, scraping bottom again and having to shove my way free while almost lying down. With higher water

---

3. **draft.** Depth to which bottom of boat sinks

What reactions will people that Harris meets have to his trip?

What happens ten yards from the beginning? What might this suggest about the rest of the trip?

WORDS FOR EVERYDAY USE:

ne • go • ti • ate (ni gō′shē āt′) *vt.*, succeed in crossing, surmounting, moving through

o • men (ō′mən) *n.*, thing or event supposed to foretell a future event

ac • com • mo • date (ə käm′ə dāt′) *vt.*, have space for

I could have floated under more easily but my head would have been taken off by the low bridge.

The creek bends left, it bends right. Another footbridge lies across my path and blocks my way. No way can I get under this one, not even if I lie flat and try to slide by again. Easy solution. Get out, set the canoe adrift and let it float under the bridge by itself, then grab it as it comes through the other side. Good idea, but when I get out of the canoe and take the weight of my body with me, the canoe rises in the water and sits too high to squeeze under. The bow[4] of the canoe knocks into the bottom of the bridge. I can stand in the canoe until the front end is under the bridge, climb up onto the bridge myself and then push the canoe through, but the canoe still won't go. It gets stuck in the rafters[5] that support the bridge. I pull it back out and think again.

The bridge is just too low. The embankments are too high to drag the canoe up, but I've no choice. Unless I want to go back and go home. That remains a possible solution to every difficulty I encounter along the way, but I don't take the consideration seriously here. I'm simply forced to get out of the canoe and try to drag this thing up the embankment and across the bridge to the other side.

The canoe is not mine. It's on loan to me from a youth organization in St. Louis, run by a friend of Robinovich's. I hope I don't bend it or break it or put holes in it, but it feels like all of these will happen. In the meantime I'm pulling this boat inch by inch, slipping into the mud and getting my feet wet. At times I go to the back end and lift and shove and finally I get the cursed canoe up and over and back down into the water. No damage to the canoe, only to me and my already weak back.

But soon I'm on my way again along the sparkling waters. I'm in a canyon of trees, two hundred-year-old pines. The river cuts left, it cuts right.

Up ahead another bridge. This time the river has been funneled through what looks like a huge metal sewer pipe and the water builds up there and shoots through to the other side with a rushing noise that sounds like Niagara Falls.[6] I can only go through if I lie down. I do and I'm at the mercy of the river. I hold my breath and go for it. Gathering speed I shoot through the tunnel and out the other side and I feel like I've shot the rapids or done a ride at Disneyland.

For a few minutes I sit in a large, quiet pool at the other end of the tunnel. The river is coming hard and noisily at me. But here it widens and quickly quiets once more and becomes clear and slow again. I move on.

A beaver dam[7] blocks my way. The beavers will create many problems for

How does Harris get by the second bridge? How does this experience make him feel?

What is a possible solution to every difficulty of the trip?

---

4. **bow.** Front part of a ship or boat
5. **rafters.** Boards or planks that slope from the ridge of a roof to the eaves and give support to the roof
6. **Niagara Falls.** Large waterfall on the Niagara River: it is divided by an island into two falls, one on the Canadian border and one on the United States border.
7. **beaver dam.** Barrier that holds back water built from felled trees by rodents with chisel-like teeth. Beavers build these dams to form pools in which they make dome-shaped island dwellings.

WORDS FOR EVERYDAY USE: em • bank • ment (em baŋk´mənt) *n.,* slope of earth; rubble used to keep back water

me before this day is done, and this first dam is the least of them. It stops up the river and a tree has been thrown across half the creek to make getting around it difficult. I wonder if these dams serve a purpose, if beavers really live in them, or if beavers are just great big jokers who like to slow down people in small boats. I'm certainly slowed down. I'm not an expert yet and I struggle to get the canoe going sideways at the right times. Too often I get going backwards. I hit a branch. I'm caught in a snarl of limbs. I get stuck.

What difficulties does Harris face at the beaver dam?

The river here is so gentle. A heron[8] rises up out of nowhere. It squawks: follow me. I do. It drifts downstream to hide, be <u>flushed</u> again, and hide again. It's playing games with me. Eagles in the sky above soar over me and probably laugh at me. Critters scurry through the brush on the banks and never let me see them. The air is crisp and cool but sunny enough and I'm paddling enough to stay warm. Further on I find baby fishes flickering as they dart for cover when I disturb their water. I feel I've got a <u>continuum</u> here, that fish will be with me unlike any other creature all the way to the end and I'll not be so alone. When the river deepens and I encounter the bigger fish <u>loitering</u> in the shade, I know it for certain. But I'm wrong. At the highway bridge just this side of the marsh the river deepens considerably and a school of fish lives here, but they are the last fish I see. The river shallows very quickly again and the fish are gone.

What decision does Harris have to make? What concerns does he have about this decision?

I'm totally alone. This is wilderness.

Now the river really <u>meanders</u>. Soft curves become zigzags and I must cover a lot of ground to gain such a short crow-fly[9] distance. I find myself enmeshed in a maze of meanderings and marsh. The trees stand a long way off now but are still all around, and I'm floating in a plain of rice grass. Tall blades of dense pale yellow, the color of ripened wheat, surround me and the river branches infinitely through. I do not know which branch to take.

Advice from an old man in Wallace, Idaho: When you come to a fork in the road, always take the right road.

The route left looks just as good. The right might be the wrong. Maybe they all come out at the same place. Maybe this way is shorter than that. If I only had a helicopter. Or if I had a motor boat and could just plow through the rice fields. Or a pole instead of a paddle.

The sun is behind me and to my left, high in the sky. I'm okay for time, and the branch to the right seems to go the most north. I take it.

Ducks quack up around me, breaking the quiet. A hawk hovers overhead. The rifle shots of deer hunters echo way off in the distance. Other than that I am so totally alone and the day is so serene and noiseless, I can hear the whooshing of the wind through the tall grass. I feel like singing. Even if I take the wrong way and have to double

---

8. **heron.** Any of various wading birds with a long neck, long legs, and a long, tapered bill that live along marshes and riverbanks

9. **crow-fly.** In a straight line; direct

WORDS FOR EVERYDAY USE:

flush (flush) *vt.*, cause to take wing suddenly

con • tin • u • um (kən tin′yo͞o əm) *n.*, unbroken or connected whole

loi • ter • ing (loit′ər iŋ) *part.*, lingering or spending time in an aimless or idle way

me • an • der (mē an′dər) *vi.*, take a winding course

back, I'm doing fine. The weather is fine, I've got my Nature Valley granola bars to eat, and a canteen filled with tasty spring water. As long as I don't get lost in this maze, I'm okay.

These three miles—by park ranger estimation—take forever. Later in the journey I will expect to do three miles in no time, but these three take so long that by the time I reach Wanagan Landing to stop for lunch, I'm actually considering staying here for the night.

Already my legs are stiff, my hands are sore and my back is tense and tired. I pull the canoe up and lie in the grass. I drink from my canteen.

In a moment, Robinovich arrives. She's been out admiring the area on her own, driving dozens of miles in the time it's taken me to make three. And she's laughing at how tired I am.

We get a small fire going and have a simple lunch. I get warm. Robinovich opens up the treats sent along to me by friends. Trail mix, peanuts, cashews, cookies, and a mountain of granola bars, which I never liked before but which by the time this trip ends will be among my favorite snacks.

Never before could I understand why bicycle racers are surrounded by cars carrying extra bikes, food, and drink. I always thought a racer should be out there doing his job, on his own, and if he has a breakdown he just pulls out. I look at Robinovich, my support team—preparing lunch, encouraging me, prodding me with her presence so I'd be too ashamed to quit—and I understand.

Louisiana Heron. *Rodney Busch. Private collection*

I'm back on my way and we've agreed to meet twelve miles further on at the campsite called Coffee Pot. The Minnesota Parks and Recreation Department has carved into the wilderness along this first sixty-mile stretch of river a series of landings and campsites. They are beautifully done and clean. Some have fire rings and pit toilets and water pumps, others picnic tables. Others are primitive. But they all blend in well with the green surroundings and don't <u>intrude</u> much.

What had Harris thought about bicycle racers? What does he learn from his experience on the river?

Three miles took forever. Twelve more should take four times as long. But no! The next twelve will take much longer. But how can this be? I was rested. The sun was still high. I had just eaten. And the river straightened. On top of that I was gaining experience as a canoeist with every stroke. How could I not make the next twelve miles in a hurry?

I'm feeling really fine. The river deepens and the rice marsh lines only one bank. The other bank is woodsy for now.

Too quickly the marsh and the meanderings are back, but only for a short time. Still, the going is not swift. Soon the sun is slipping down beyond the pines. When the sun goes, the cold comes. And now I'm deeper in the woods where the air is naturally fresher and cooler. I put on my gloves and don a sweatshirt with a hood. Robinovich has my warm jacket. I was thinking she would need it more than I. After all, all this paddling so far has kept me warm. In the sun.

I come to a low wooden dam that threatens to force me out of the canoe. But I'm feeling expert. I can ride this. I do, but the riding is tricky and I get wet. The wet makes me colder. The beaver dams take time. Time takes away my light. There is another obstruction and I'm forced out of my canoe to <u>portage</u> around it. More time. More effort. More cold coming fast into the valley. Whose idea *was* this?

Rapids. They are loud and swift and the rocks are boulders and I'm scared. I may be expert, but I'm not *that* expert. But what choice have I? I've got to shoot them, and shoot them I do. A long series of rapids after rapids—probably because of the shallow water in autumn—and with each one I gain more and more confidence. After each one I shout with triumph and glee. But with each one I get wetter. And as the darkness descends, each one gets more difficult to see and thus trickier to negotiate.

One time the river spins me into a rock and I nearly fly from my seat. The rock spins me around sideways and soon I'm going swiftly downstream backwards. I can't turn around. The river narrows and the canoe won't fit. I'm stuck.

Another time I'm thrown into the side of the river. Low branches force me into the bank and I can't turn around. The water from the side is too fast and strong for me. I have to get out and push the boat around. My shoes get soaked and my feet get cold and my gloves get wet.

To dry the gloves I lay them on the struts. The next set of rapids tosses up the front end of the canoe. Only a keen sense of balance—no canoeing skill—keeps me from falling into the icy water.

I look. My gloves are gone.

The river has become an <u>adversary</u>. I see deer munching leaves on the shore. They know better than to do what I'm doing and they feel safe from me. How can I get at them even if I want to? They watch me and I feel stupid.

WORDS FOR EVERYDAY USE:

por • tage (pôr´ tij) *vi.,* carry boats or supplies overland from one one lake or river to another

ad • ver • sar • y (ad´ vər ser´ē) *n.,* opponent; enemy

Finally it's dark. Then it's night. I'm freezing right through to the bone and my hands and feet are numb. I'm worried about frostbite. I'm worried about being lost. I'm worried about how to find Robinovich out there in the night. I don't know how far I've come or how far I've got to go. I'm scared. So I sing. I worry about running across more rapids, falling in, freezing to death.

That rushing sound, the sound of rapids, terrifies me each time I hear it. The river has begun to meander again and the bank has hidden deep behind the marsh that has popped up again. I can't get out of the river because I can't get out of the canoe. I don't know if I'll find solid ground or if I'll sink to my waist. I'm forced on.

The sound of rapids is the same sound of water falling over those huge beaver dams that threaten my progress. I hate the dams but I fear the rapids even more. The dams I can go around—when I can see them. The ones that completely cross the river I can plow over. The ones that are too thick I can approach and step out on and slide the canoe over. I'm hoping beavers don't bite.

Finally the moon rises and throws down its light. I breathe easier. I can see a bit. But it's still very dark and mostly what I must do is listen. Hearing, smelling: other senses take over when you can't see and right now (despite the moonlight) my eyesight is fairly useless. I rely on a sense I didn't even know I had and it somehow keeps me in the water, upright, away from the marsh and out of too much trouble. I carry on and I sing.

I'm wondering how long before the search party comes looking for me. Off in the distant night sky a signal flare[10] shoots a bright arc and falls. Someone, I'm sure, is looking for me. Pretty soon a helicopter will thump through the air overhead and shine down an intense spotlight on the river. A voice in a loud speaker will ask me if I'm all right and will light my path on the water. I'm sure of it.

But no. I'm still all alone and still miserable. My toes are dead numb and my fingers are swollen. They're locked around the paddle and cannot unbend. Frostbite.

Off in the distance, high on a hill, a light. I aim straight for it and tell myself when I get close, I'll get out and hike. It's a good mile straight up a hill, but at least I know there's a house. I can phone from there or get a ride to Coffee Pot. But dogs are howling up there on the hillside. I keep going.

Beaver dams. Each time I step from the canoe to go over them my feet get wetter. I'm just freezing. In my pocket I do have a box of waterproof matches. If I could find a place to pull out I could at least build a fire and dry off and warm up a little.

Up on a rise, not far from the river, a shed. Old and rickety, but made of wood. I can burn that thing if I need to, burn it to the ground for warmth, and yes I need to. My life or the life of this old shack.

But then I smell smoke. Someone else has built a fire. Hunters maybe, or Robinovich. I keep going.

A big mistake. I find no fire, no hunters, no Robinovich. My spirit is sinking fast. I sing to keep from losing it completely. Between songs I call out to Robinovich. No reply. Just my own voice echoing hollowly back to me from the walls of the night.

10. **flare.** Bright light used as a distress signal

What worries Harris? What does he do to alleviate his fear?

How does Harris compensate for his inability to see in the dark?

What gives Harris hope?

What possible action does Harris consider? What does he actually do?

I can give up, get out right now and just die. It'll be easier.

I find every scrap of energy that's in me and push on. I can't see any better now and I don't need too much speed to make me crash into something or send me into the weeds. I pick my way carefully.

And then I see the light from a fire. I smell smoke. I see the lights from a car. I'm yelling my head off but no sound comes back to me. How far away am I?

Finally I arrive. Coffee Pot. The fire, a big smoky blaze, is ours. Robinovich has built it. She's gone, though, when I pull out from the river, gone to search for me. Not knowing where or how to search she quickly returns. The car lights I saw were hers. ■

Responding to the Selection

Do you admire Harris and his pursuit of his goal? What do you think drives him toward reaching this goal? What do you think, in general, makes some people goal oriented and focused?

Reviewing the Selection

RECALLING

1. At what time of day does Harris begin his journey? Who is assisting him? What is the first major difficulty Harris encounters?

2. At what point in the trip does Harris feel "totally alone"? How does he lose his gloves?

INTERPRETING

3. How does Harris feel on the morning he begins his trip? What clues is the reader given about his state of mind at this time?

4. Does Harris feel positive about being alone in the wilderness? In what way do losing his gloves and being tired and hungry affect his spirit? How do you think he feels when he sees the headlights of Robinovich's car?

SYNTHESIZING

5. What does Harris enjoy about his first day? What does he find frightening? Why does he keep telling himself that "I can give up, get out right now . . ."? Why might this statement make him feel temporarily secure?

Understanding Literature (Questions for Discussion)

1. **Point of View. Point of view** is the vantage point from which a story is told. How does being inside the narrator's head help you appreciate this piece? Would the selection have affected you differently if it had been written in the third person? What might have been lost if the story had been told in the third person?

2. **Image.** An **image** is a word or phrase that names something that can be heard, touched, tasted, or smelled. What are some particularly vivid images in this selection? Try to name images that are unique to the canoe trip.

Responding in Writing

Autobiography. Suppose that you have accomplished the goal that you wrote about in the Reader's Journal activity at the beginning of this selection. Write two pages about something interesting that happened to you as you tried to pursue your goal. Perhaps you encountered a problem that you were not anticipating. Perhaps something especially encouraging happened one day. Try to capture in your piece exactly how you felt at the time. Write using the first-person point of view.

> **Prewriting Suggestion:** Look over the items you listed as steps toward achieving your goal. Choose the step that most captures your imagination, and fill in details that tell who, what, when, where, why, and how. What could have gone wrong with each step? What might unexpectedly have gone right? How did you feel at the time? It might help to freewrite before you try to shape ideas into finished form. Concentrate on vivid details—especially those that only someone who was there would know.

PROJECT

Exploring the Mississippi. Work with a group of your classmates to investigate some aspect of the Mississippi River that you find interesting. For example, you might research major cities along the route and how they use the river, the history of human use of the Mississippi, how the river was formed and has changed over time, or how the river has been treated in literature. Then think of a good way to present this information to others in your class or community.

"I Am a Black Woman"
by Mari Evans

ABOUT THE AUTHOR

Mari Evans credits the writings of author and poet Langston Hughes as a major influence on her decision to become a professional writer. She also credits her father. In fact, when Evans had a story published in her school newspaper when she was in fourth grade, her father was so proud that he named the occasion an important event in the family history. Evans's career did grow from there, and as an adult she became a successful university professor, editor, poet, playwright, children's book writer, and advocate of building pride in the African-American community. Her poetry collections include *Where Is All the Music* (1968), *I Am a Black Woman* (1970), *Nightstar: 1973–1978* (1981), and *A Dark and Splendid Mass* (1992). Evans also wrote, directed, and produced a critically praised television program, "The Black Experience," and edited an important compendium, *Black Women Writers (1950–1980): A Critical Evaluation* (1984). The poem tht follows is considered a classic.

ABOUT THE SELECTION

Background: Technique. An **allusion** is a rhetorical technique in which a reference is made to a person, event, object, or work from history or literature. "**I Am a Black Woman**" is full of allusions to people and events in history. When reading the poem, keep the following historical facts in mind: Nat Turner was a slave who led a slave revolt in the United States in 1831. He was later hanged for organizing this uprising. Anzio, Da Nang, and Pork Chop Hill were battle sites in World War II, the Vietnam War, and the Korean War, respectively. Throughout the history of the United States, African-American soldiers have served valiantly in the country's wars.

"I Am a Black Woman"

MARI EVANS

I am a black woman
the music of my song
some sweet <u>arpeggio</u> of tears
is written in a minor key

Why might the speaker's song be in a minor key?

5 and I
can be heard humming in the night
Can be heard
    humming
in the night

10 I saw my mate leap screaming to the sea[1]
and I/with these hands/cupped the lifebreath
from my issue in the canebrake[2]
I lost Nat's[3] swinging body in a rain of tears
and heard my son scream all the way from Anzio[4]

What do all of the places the speaker mentions have in common?

15 for Peace he never knew. . . . I
learned Da Nang and Pork Chop Hill[5]

---

 1. **screaming to the sea.** The reference here is to an African man jumping from a slave ship.
 2. **canebrake.** Dense growth of sugar cane
 3. **Nat's.** Nat Turner was the valiant leader of a slave uprising in 1831.
 4. **Anzio.** World War II battlefield in Italy
 5. **Da Nang and Pork Chop Hill.** Da Nang, a battlefield of the Vietnam War; Pork Chop Hill, a battlefield of the Korean War

WORDS FOR
EVERYDAY USE:
 ar • peg • gio (är pej´ō) *n.*, playing of the notes of a chord quickly, one after the other, instead of together

What does the speaker seek?

in <u>anguish</u>
Now my nostrils know the gas
and these trigger tire/d fingers
20   seek the softness in my warrior's beard

I
am a black woman
tall as a <u>cypress</u>
strong
25   beyond all definition still
defying place
and time
and circumstance
assailed
30   <u>impervious</u>
                    indestructible
Look
    on me and be
renewed   ∎

How does the speaker describe herself?

Responding to the Selection

How do you feel about the speaker of the poem? In what tone of voice do you think this poem should be read? Is the speaker sad, angry, proud, defiant, or some combination of these? Explain.

WORDS FOR EVERYDAY USE:

an • guish (aŋ´gwish) *n.*, great suffering, as from grief or worry

cy • press (sī´prəs) *n.*, evergreen, native to North America, Europe, and Asia, with dark leaves and a distinctive symmetrical form. The tree is often planted in graveyards and is thus a symbol of mourning.

im • per • vi • ous (im pʉr´vē əs) *adj.*, not affected

Reviewing the Selection

1. How does the speaker describe her song in the first section of the poem?

2. What specific trials or ordeals experienced by African Americans are mentioned in the poem?

3. Is the song the speaker describes upbeat? loud? sad? soft and mellow? How do you know? What kinds of feelings does the speaker have?

4. How have the trials described in this poem affected the speaker?

5. How does the speaker of this poem feel about herself and her ability to survive? How do you know? How do the words "assailed," "impervious," and "indestructible" in the last section relate to what the speaker has described throughout the poem?

Understanding Literature (Questions for Discussion)

1. **Structure. Structure** is the arrangement of elements in a literary work. "I Am a Black Woman" is arranged into three distinct sections. What is the subject of each section of the poem? Restate, or paraphrase, each section of the poem in your own words.

2. **Mood. Mood,** or **atmosphere,** is the emotion created in the reader by all or part of a literary work. What is the mood of this poem? Does the mood change? What specific words and phrases create the mood?

3. **Speaker.** The **speaker** is the character who speaks in, or narrates, a poem—the voice assumed by the writer. Who is the speaker in this poem? What is this speaker like? What has made her that way? What is the speaker saying about how she has been affected by the history of her people?

Responding in Writing

Self Poem. "I Am a Black Woman" is a strong statement of how one person feels about herself and her heritage. Write a short poem about yourself that begins with the statement: I am _____. As you write your poem, experiment with Evans's technique of dividing the work into separate sections, each with one main idea.

> **Prewriting Suggestion:** First read over the notes you made for the Reader's Journal activity at the beginning of the lesson. Then you might want to make three columns, one headed *ideas about myself,* another headed *ideas other people have about me,* and another headed *what I want to be.* List ideas under each heading. These ideas can serve as seeds for your poem. After you have several items listed under each head, underline key words and phrases. Then decide what you want each section of your poem to say.

PROJECTS

1. Time Line of African-American History. Create a class time line of African-American history. Organize trips to the school library to uncover interesting details in books or encyclopedias. You might want to split up the research according to periods in history—four or five people per block of time. This will make the task more manageable and will help ensure that you will include major events and milestones. After facts are collected, you can put together a time line that is as large and as visually complex as the class chooses. For information on creating time lines, see the Language Arts Survey, 1.19, "Time Lines."

2. Heroism Poster. Choose a person from history that you admire and make a poster to honor that person. Include on you poster a picture of the person, a time line of his or her life, and a paragraph explaining why you think that he or she was a hero.

"Saying Yes"
by Diana Chang

ABOUT THE AUTHOR

Diana Chang is a poet, novelist, and painter. Her poems have appeared in many magazines and anthologies and have been collected in three books, *The Horizon Is Definitely Speaking, What Matisse Is After,* and *Earth Water Light.* She has published six novels. Chang has been the recipient of a New York State Council on the Arts award, a Fulbright Scholarship, and a John Hay Whitney Opportunity Fellowship that made it possible for her to complete her first novel, *The Frontiers of Love,* originally published by Random House and reissued in 1994 by the University of Washington Press in Seattle.

ABOUT THE SELECTION

Background: Theme. A **theme** is a central idea in a literary work. **"Saying Yes"** deals with a theme that is important to many people in the United States: the blending of two or more cultures. Look in towns and cities throughout the United States and you will find people who were themselves born in other countries or who have parents, grandparents, or great-grandparents who were born in other countries. The United States has long been a country of immigrants. The only true "natives" of this vast land are those people who lived in the United States before the first European settlers. A serious issue for immigrants in the United States and in countries throughout the world is assimilation, or blending into the new culture. People often ask themselves: "How can I blend into the new culture without losing touch with my heritage?" and "Must I be one or the other, or can I be both?" This idea is addressed in the poem that you are about to read.

READER'S JOURNAL
In your journal, define the word *heritage*. What does it mean to you? List the people, the places, the traditions, and the positive and negative experiences that are part of your heritage.

"Saying Yes"

DIANA CHANG

How does the speaker answer the questions?

"Are you Chinese?"
"Yes."

"American?"
"Yes."

5   "*Really* Chinese?"
"No . . . not quite."

"*Really* American?"
"Well, actually, you see . . ."

But I would rather say
10   yes

Not neither-nor,
not maybe,
but both, and not only

The homes I've had,
15   the ways I am

I'd rather say it
twice,
yes   ■

Responding to the Selection

What is the attitude of the speaker of the poem? How does she feel about herself? What do you imagine about her family life and her daily experiences? Discuss these questions with your classmates.

Reviewing the Selection

RECALLING

1. What four questions are being asked of the speaker?

2. What does the speaker decide to say?

INTERPRETING

3. In what way do the speaker's answers change in lines 5–8? What does she feel the need to explain?

4. What attitude does the speaker have toward the two cultures that are her heritage?

SYNTHESIZING

5. Who might be asking the questions in this poem and why? What does this poem say about pride? about assimilation? Does the speaker believe that one can become part of a new culture without giving up one's old culture? Explain.

Understanding Literature (Questions for Discussion)

1. **Dialogue. Dialogue** is conversation involving two or more people or characters. Why do you think the author chose to use dialogue in this poem? How does the dialogue relate to the theme of the poem? Is the poem more real and interesting to you as a reader because of the dialogue? Why or why not?

2. **Free Verse. Free verse,** or *vers libre,* is poetry that avoids use of regular rhyme, rhythm, meter, or divisions into stanzas. How does "Saying Yes" fit into this category? What do you think are some of the positive aspects of free verse? Do you prefer this type of poetry, or do you prefer regular rhyme and rhythm? Give reasons for your preference.

Responding in Writing

Dialogue Poem. Write a free verse poem that features dialogue. Focus on a short exchange between two people, similar to the one in "Saying Yes." Choose any topic of conversation of interest to you. Maybe you would like to briefly address a serious issue, as Chang does in her poem, or maybe you would like to try writing something light and humorous.

> **Prewriting Suggestion:** To prepare for this assignment, try listening carefully to people and what they say when they are in conversation. Next time you are in the hallway at school, on the bus, or at the supermarket, try to listen for interesting bits of conversation—conversation that reveals something about the people who are talking. Collect these bits of conversation in a journal. Then read through them and decide if anything strikes you as a seed for a poem.

PROJECT

Book of Diversity. As a class, put together a book that shows the diversity within your classroom. Your book might include pages of illustrations, photographs, recipes, stories, poetry, interviews with family members, descriptions of traditions, and personal reflections about heritage and cultures. The book should try to give as many different perspectives as possible. To begin this project, each person in the class might first want to decide what his or her personal contribution to the book could be. Everyone should feel free to include pieces of writing that they have completed for the Reader's Journal and the Responding in Writing sections. Next, create a list of book-production jobs. This list might include assignment editors, researchers, art directors, illustrators, and proofreaders. Each person should be assigned a job according to his or her special interests. Then create a schedule and begin work. When the book is completed, try to distribute it throughout the school and the community. It can be interesting to see how unique each person in your class is.

UNIT REVIEW

Diversity

VOCABULARY FROM THE SELECTIONS

accommodate, 378
ado, 377
adversary, 382
anguish, 388
arpeggio, 387
bison, 354
careen, 365
caul, 364
continuum, 380
cypress, 388
don, 377

embankment, 379
evanesce, 373
flush, 380
gully, 355
heresy, 373
imminent, 367
impervious, 388
infallibility, 368
intrude, 381
iridescent, 368
loitering, 380

meander, 380
negotiate, 378
omen, 378
portage, 382
reiterate, 370
skiff, 372
sorrel, 355
sullenly, 366
treaty, 358
turbulence, 377
vortex, 368

LITERARY TERMS

atmosphere, 375
dialogue, 393
foreshadowing, 374
free verse, 393
image, 385

mood, 375, 389
point of view, 360, 375, 385
scene, 375
setting, 362
speaker, 389

structure, 389
theme, 391
tone, 361

SYNTHESIS: QUESTIONS FOR WRITING, RESEARCH, OR DISCUSSION

1. One message of the selections in this unit is that a person should be proud of his or her unique characteristics and heritage. Choose three speakers or narrators in the unit. Of what is each person particularly proud?

2. Despite superficial differences, people from diverse backgrounds are often quite similar. Choose two characters from different selections in the unit and compare and contrast them. In what ways are these characters similar? In what ways are they different?

LANGUAGE LAB EDITING FOR ERRORS IN USAGE

You can avoid some common writing errors by watching for certain usage problems.

LANGUAGE ARTS SURVEY

For additional help, see the Language Arts Survey, 2.90–2.92.

COMMON USAGE ERRORS

adapt, adopt. *Adapt* means to modify something to fit a specific use or situation. *Adopt* means to make something one's own.

> EXAMPLES: When Neihardt started living with the Oglala Sioux, he had to adapt to a new way of life.
> The Oglala Sioux adopted John G. Neihardt as one of their own people.

affect, effect. If you wish to use a verb meaning "have an effect on," use *affect*. If you wish to use a noun meaning "the result of an action," use *effect*.

> EXAMPLES: Leaving Doodle alone in the storm would affect his brother for the rest of his life.
> What effect would the death of a loved one have on you?

imply, infer. *Imply* means "to express indirectly rather than openly." *Infer* means "to arrive at a conclusion by reasoning from evidence."

> EXAMPLES: Your heavy sigh implies that "The Scarlet Ibis" made you sad.
> Because President Wilson and Belleau Woods were mentioned in "The Scarlet Ibis," Theresa inferred that the story was set during World War I.

like, as, as if. *Like* is a preposition, not a conjunction. Do not use *like* in place of *as* or *as if*.

> EXAMPLE: It seems as if Mari Evans takes great pride in her heritage.

literally. Use *literally* to mean "actually," not to mean "in a manner of speaking" or "in effect."

> EXAMPLE: Black Elk said that a kingbird literally spoke to him before he saw his first vision.

of. The preposition *of* should not be used in place of *have* after verbs such as *could, should, would, might, must,* and *ought*.

> EXAMPLE: Emilio must have liked Mari Evans's poem, because he checked out a book of her poetry from the library.

Avoid *off of*.

> EXAMPLE: Yolanda took *Black Elk Speaks* off the shelf.

than, then. Use *than* as a conjunction in comparisons. Use *then* as an adverb that tells when something occurred.

> EXAMPLE: "I Am a Black Woman" describes historical events, then reveals the speaker's response.
> The speaker feels more strengthened than defeated by her struggles.

EXERCISE A Avoiding Usage Problems

Rewrite the following sentences, using the correct word from those given in parentheses.

> EXAMPLE: "Doodle" was a more suitable name (than, then) "William Armstrong."
> *"Doodle" was a more suitable name than "William Armstrong."*

1. The Wasichus (affected, effected) the Oglalas by taking their land and destroying the buffalo. Perhaps they should not (have, of) done this.

2. Lena (adapted, adopted) "I Am a Black Woman" as her personal anthem.

3. The scarlet ibis had fallen (off, off of) the tree and lay broken on the ground.

4. The names "two-leggeds" and "four-leggeds" (imply, infer) that the Oglala believed humans and animals were connected.

5. Sometimes Doodle's brother acts (as if, like) he doesn't love Doodle, but he only (adapts, adopts) this attitude temporarily.

6. Does Mari Evans's poem have a renewing (affect, effect) on you?

7. Black Elk recounts his memories of the Winter of the Hundred Slain, and (than, then) Fire Thunder, who is much older (than, then) Black Elk, shares his story of the battle.

8. Even though he says his motivation was pride, Doodle's brother must (have, of) had a lot of patience to teach Doodle to walk.

9. What information about African-American history can you (imply, infer) from "I Am a Black Woman"?

10. In Black Elk's vision, two men come down from the clouds, headfirst (as if, like) arrows.

EXERCISE B Proofreading for Usage Errors

Proofread the following paragraph and rewrite it on your own paper, correcting any improperly used words.

John G. Neihardt and Black Elk first met in the summer of 1930. Before the meeting, a Sioux interpreter warned Neihardt that Black Elk might not speak to him. Many writers must of visited the aged medicine man previously, but his silence in their presence inferred that he did not wish to speak about the past. Neihardt might of been discouraged, but, believing he would have better luck then the others, he went to meet the old Sioux man. When Neihardt and the interpreter arrived, Black Elk was standing and waiting for them; the interpreter later remarked that it seemed like he knew Neihardt was coming. Neihardt introduced himself, and than the three men sat down in silence. It seemed like a long time passed before Black Elk finally spoke. He announced that Neihardt had been sent to learn what he knew about the Other World and that he wished to teach him. Neihardt, who was deeply effected by Black Elk's words, agreed to return in the spring to learn from the medicine man. In May 1931, Neihardt and Black Elk began the sessions that Neihardt later adopted into *Black Elk Speaks*. The significance of this book is literally earth-shattering.

LANGUAGE ARTS WORKSHOP

READING ACTIVELY

Reading actively means thinking about what you are reading as you do it. When you read actively, you stay alert and are better able to understand and remember the material you read. Active reading is like having a conversation with the author.

LANGUAGE ARTS SURVEY

For additional help, see the Language Arts Survey, 4.18.

TECHNIQUES FOR ACTIVE READING
Responding to Your Reading. As you are reading, record in your journal any reactions, feelings, comments, or related ideas that occur to you.
Questioning. As you read, ask questions about who, what, where, when, why, and how.
Predicting. Try to guess or develop hypotheses about what is going to happen next.
Summarizing. Pause from reading to state in your own words what you have read.
Identifying Main Ideas. When reading difficult material, you can check your understanding by pausing briefly after each paragraph to restate the main idea in your own words.
Identifying Relationships. Look for words and phrases that reveal how the writing is organized. Pay special attention to passages that describe relationships between people, things, or ideas.
Making Inferences. Use pieces of information from the text to draw conclusions that are not explicitly stated by the author.

READING CHARTS AND GRAPHS

Writers use charts and graphs to present ideas and information visually and compactly. The information necessary for understanding the chart or graph is given in the title, headings, and other labels surrounding the graphic.

LANGUAGE ARTS SURVEY

For additional help, see the Language Arts Survey, 4.19.

READING CHARTS AND GRAPHS
Pie Charts. A pie chart is used to show relative proportions or shares in relation to a whole. It shows how different amounts compare to each other. The whole pie represents all of something, and each piece of the pie represents a portion of that whole.
Bar Graphs. The length of each bar in a bar graph represents an absolute quantity of something. Bar graphs show relative quantities, but unlike pie charts they do not depict relation to a whole.

EXERCISE A Reading Actively

Read "To the Student" on pages *xiv–xv.* As you read, (1) record in your journal two emotional reactions to your reading, (2) write two questions and two predictions about the text, (3) write three or four sentences to summarize the section "Educating Your Imagination," (4) list the main ideas of the section "Reading Literature," and (5) write two inferences that you make from your reading.

EXERCISE B   Reading Pie Charts

Read the pie chart below. Then refer to it to answer the questions that follow.

Favorite Ice Cream Flavors

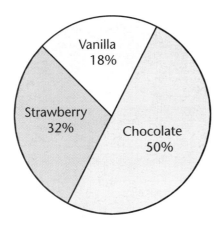

1. What information does the pie chart depict?

2. What is the most popular flavor of ice cream?

3. What percentage of people prefer strawberry?

4. What information does the smallest piece of the pie chart represent?

5. Which flavors are favored equally?

EXERCISE C   Reading Bar Graphs

Read the bar graph below. Then refer to it to answer the questions that follow.

Average Winter Temperatures, Boston, Massachusetts

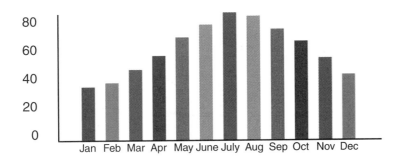

1. What information does the bar graph depict?

2. What does each bar represent?

3. What is the average temperature in February?

4. What is the average temperature in December?

5. On average, which month is coldest?

School's Out. Allan Rohan Crite, 1936. National Museum of American Art, Washington, DC/Art Resource, NY

f a man does not keep pace with his companions,
perhaps it is because he hears a different drummer.

—Henry David Thoreau

"Geraldine Moore the Poet"
by Toni Cade Bambara

ABOUT THE AUTHOR

Toni Cade Bambara (1939–1995) grew up in Harlem and Brooklyn, New York; and Jersey City, New Jersey. After studying theater and English at Queens College and the City College of New York, she worked as a film writer and producer. She also taught college English. During the 1960s and 1970s, she was active in the Civil Rights movement. She has published two collections of stories, *Gorilla, My Love* and *The Sea Birds Are Still Alive.* She has also written a novel, *The Salt Eaters,* as well as scripts for television and film.

ABOUT THE SELECTION

Background: Theme. People are very complex. Everyone has both strengths and weaknesses. Sometimes a person's strengths go unrecognized, even by that person, for a long, long time. What are your strengths? What special abilities do you have? What undiscovered talents might you have that you haven't explored? Think about these questions as you read **"Geraldine Moore the Poet."**

"Geraldine Moore the Poet"

Toni Cade Bambara

Geraldine paused at the corner to pull up her knee socks. The rubber bands she was using to hold them up made her legs itch. She dropped her books on the sidewalk while she gave a good scratch. But when she pulled the socks up again, two fingers poked right through the top of her left one.

"That stupid dog," she <u>muttered</u> to herself, grabbing her books and crossing against traffic. "First he chews up my gym suit and gets me into trouble, and now my socks."

Geraldine shifted her books to the other hand and kept muttering angrily to herself about Mrs. Watson's dog, which she minded two days a week for a dollar. She passed the hot-dog man on the corner and waved. He shrugged as if to say business was very bad.

Must be, she thought to herself. *Three guys before you had to pack up and forget it. Nobody's got hot-dog money around here.*

Geraldine turned down her street, wondering what her sister Anita would have for her lunch. She was glad she didn't have to eat the free lunches in high school any more. She was sick of the funny-looking tomato soup and the dried-out cheese sandwiches and those oranges that were more green than orange.

When Geraldine's mother first took sick and went away, Geraldine had been on her own except when Miss Gladys next door came in on Thursdays and cleaned the apartment and made a meat loaf so Geraldine could have dinner. But in those days Geraldine never quite managed to get breakfast for herself. So she'd sit through social studies class, scraping her feet to cover up the noise of her stomach growling.

WORDS FOR EVERYDAY USE:
mut • ter (mut´ər) *vt.*, utter words in a low tone

Now Anita, Geraldine's older sister, was living at home waiting for her husband to get out of the Army. She usually had something good for lunch—chicken and dumplings if she managed to get up in time, or baked ham from the night before and sweet-potato bread. But even if there was only a hot dog and some baked beans — sometimes just a TV dinner if those soap operas kept Anita glued to the TV set—anything was better than the noisy school lunchroom where <u>monitors</u> kept pushing you into a straight line or rushing you to the tables. Anything was better than that.

Geraldine was almost home when she stopped dead. Right outside her building was a pile of furniture and some boxes. That wasn't anything new. She had seen people get put out in the street before, but this time the ironing board looked familiar. And she recognized the big, ugly sofa standing on its arm, its underbelly showing the hold where Mrs. Watson's dog had gotten to it.

Miss Gladys was sitting on the stoop, and she looked up and took off her glasses. "Well, Gerry," she said slowly, wiping her glasses on the hem of her dress, "looks like you'll be staying with me for a while." She looked at the men carrying out a big box with an old doll sticking up over the edge. "Anita's upstairs. Go on up and get your lunch."

Geraldine stepped past the old woman and almost bumped into the superintendent. He took off his cap to

What was Geraldine feeling when she saw the items outside her building?

What keeps Geraldine from concentrating on her schoolwork?

wipe away the sweat.

"Darn shame," he said to no one in particular. "Poor people sure got a hard row to hoe."

"That's the truth," said Miss Gladys, standing up with her hands on her hips to watch the men set things on the sidewalk.

Upstairs, Geraldine went into the apartment and found Anita in the kitchen.

"I dunno, Gerry," Anita said. "I just don't know what we're going to do. But everything's going to be all right soon as Ma gets well." Anita's voice cracked as she set a bowl of soup before Geraldine.

"What's this?" Geraldine said.

"It's tomato soup, Gerry."

Geraldine was about to say something. But when she looked up at her big sister, she saw how Anita's face was getting all twisted as she began to cry.

That afternoon, Mr. Stern, the geometry teacher, started drawing cubes and cylinders on the board. Geraldine sat at her desk adding up a column of figures in her notebook— the rent, the light and gas bills, a new gym suit, some socks. Maybe they would move somewhere else, and she could have her own room. Geraldine turned the squares and triangles into little houses in the country.

"For your homework," Mr. Stern was saying with his back to the class, "set up your problems this way." He wrote GIVEN: in large letters, and then gave the <u>formula</u> for the first problem. Then he wrote TO FIND: and listed three

WORDS FOR EVERYDAY USE:

mon • i • tor (män´i tər) n., person who keeps order

for • mu • la (fôr´myōō lə) n., rule or fact in mathematics

Endangered Species. Paul T. Goodnight, 1980. National Museum of American Art, Washington, DC/Art Resource, NY

items they were to include in their answers.

Geraldine started to raise her hand to ask what all these squares and angles had to do with solving real problems, like the ones she had. *Better not,* she warned herself, and sat on her hands. *Your big mouth got you in trouble last term.*

In <u>hygiene</u> class, Mrs. Potter kept saying that the body was a wonderful machine. Every time Geraldine looked up from her notebook, she would hear the same thing. "Right now your body is manufacturing all the proteins and <u>tissues</u> and energy you will need to get through tomorrow."

And Geraldine kept wondering, *How? How does my body know what it will need, when I don't even know what I'll need to get through tomorrow?*

As she headed down the hall to her next class, Geraldine remembered that she hadn't done the homework for English. Mrs. Scott had said to write a poem, and Geraldine had meant to do it at lunch-time. After all, there was nothing to it—a flower here, a rain-drop there, moon, June, rose, nose. But the men carrying off the furniture had made her forget.

"And now put away your books," Mrs. Scott was saying as Geraldine tried to scribble a poem quickly.

What does Geraldine think poems are usually like?

"Today we can give King Arthur's[1] knights a rest. Let's talk about poetry."

Mrs. Scott moved up and down the aisles, talking about her favorite poems and <u>reciting</u> a line now and then. She got very excited whenever she passed a desk and could pick up the homework from a student who had remembered to do the assignment.

How does Mrs. Scott define poetry? What has Geraldine felt and seen lately?

"A poem is your own special way of saying what you feel and what you see," Mrs. Scott went on, her lips moist. It was her favorite subject.

"Some poets write about the light that . . . that . . . makes the world sunny," she said, passing Geraldine's desk. "Sometimes an idea takes the form of a picture—an image."

For almost half an hour, Mrs. Scott stood at the front of the room, reading poems and talking about the lives of the great poets. Geraldine drew more houses, and designs for curtains.

"So for those who haven't done their homework, try it now," Mrs. Scott said. "Try <u>expressing</u> what it is like to be . . . to be alive in this . . . this glorious world."

What does Geraldine dream about? What do her dreams tell us about her?

"Oh, brother," Geraldine muttered to herself as Mrs. Scott moved up and down the aisles again, waving her hands and leaning over the students' shoulders and saying, "That's nice," or "Keep trying." Finally she came to Geraldine's desk and stopped, looking down at her.

"I can't write a poem," Geraldine said flatly, before she even realized she was going to speak at all. She said it very loudly, and the whole class looked up.

"And why not?" Mrs. Scott asked, looking hurt.

"I can't write a poem, Mrs. Scott, because nothing lovely's been happening in my life. I haven't seen a flower since Mother's Day, and the sun don't even shine on my side of the street. No robins come sing on my window sill."

Geraldine swallowed hard. She thought about saying that her father doesn't even come to visit any more, but changed her mind. "Just the rain comes," she went on, "and the bills come, and the men to move out our furniture. I'm sorry, but I can't write no pretty poem."

Teddy Johnson leaned over and was about to giggle and crack the whole class up, but Mrs. Scott looked so serious that he changed his mind.

"You have just said the most . . . the most poetic thing, Geraldine Moore," said Mrs. Scott. Her hands flew up to touch the silk scarf around her neck. "'Nothing lovely's been happening in my life.'" She repeated it so quietly that everyone had to lean forward to hear.

"Class," Mrs. Scott said very sadly, clearing her throat, "you have just heard the best poem you will ever hear." She went to the board and stood there for a long time staring at the chalk in her hand.

"I'd like you to copy it down," she said. She wrote it just as Geraldine had said it, bad grammar and all.

---

1. **King Arthur's.** Belonging to the legendary king of Britain and leader of the knights of the Round Table

WORDS FOR EVERYDAY USE:

re • cite (rēs īt) *vt.*, repeat words aloud from memory
ex • press (ek spres´) *vt.*, put into words

Nothing lovely's been happening in my life.
I haven't seen a flower since Mother's Day,
And the sun don't even shine on my side of the street.
No robins come sing on my window sill.
Just the rain comes, and the bills come,
And the men to move out our furniture.
I'm sorry, but I can't write no pretty poem.

Mrs. Scott stopped writing, but she kept her back to the class for a long time—long after Geraldine had closed her notebook.

And even when the bell rang, and everyone came over to smile at Geraldine or to tap her on the shoulder or to kid her about being the school poet, Geraldine waited for Mrs. Scott to put the chalk down and turn around. Finally Geraldine stacked up her books and started to leave. Then she thought she heard a <u>whimper</u>—the way Mrs. Watson's dog whimpered sometimes—and she saw Mrs. Scott's shoulders shake a little. ■

Responding to the Selection

As you read this story, how did you feel toward Geraldine? about her plight? With what details in her story did you identify? Write about these questions in your journal.

Reviewing the Selection

RECALLING

1. What is Geraldine worried about at the very beginning of the story?

2. What does Geraldine see piled up outside her building at lunchtime?

3. What does Geraldine add during math class? What does she draw?

4. What does Mrs. Scott ask her students to write about?

INTERPRETING

5. What greater worries does Geraldine have to contend with later in the story?

6. How does Geraldine feel about what she sees piled up outside her building? How do you know?

7. What do Geraldine's doodles and daydreams during class reveal about her? What does she want?

8. What does Mrs. Scott assume about her students' lives when she frames her writing assignment as she does? Why can't Geraldine write a "pretty poem"?

WORDS FOR EVERYDAY USE: **whim • per** (hwim′pər) *n.*, low, whining cry

9. Think about Mrs. Scott's definition of poetry. What makes Geraldine's poem so good?

10. What do you like or dislike about Geraldine's poem? Do you agree with Mrs. Scott's assessment of it? Why, or why not?

Understanding Literature (Questions for Discussion)

1. **Poetry.** Look back at the Reader's Journal entry that you wrote before reading this story. What words and phrases came to your mind as you thought about poetry? Now think about Geraldine's poem. Do all poems have to be pretty? Do they all have to be filled with beautiful pictures and feelings? Next think about the lyrics of some popular songs that you like. Can any of these lyrics be considered poetry? Why, or why not?

2. **Description and Images. Description,** one of the modes of writing, portrays a character, object, or scene. An **image** is a word or phrase that refers to something that can be seen, heard, touched, tasted, or smelled. Look back at the opening paragraph of this story. What images are used in the description of Geraldine? To what senses do these images appeal? What do you learn about Geraldine from the opening description?

3. **Theme.** The **theme** is the central idea of a literary work. What does Geraldine learn about herself in this story? Why is the story called "Geraldine Moore the Poet"?

Responding in Writing

Character Sketch. Mrs. Scott says, "A poem is your own special way of saying what you feel and what you see." Everyone has his or her own special ways of doing things. Maybe your friend is a good listener. Maybe your teacher has a terrific sense of humor. Maybe your uncle spices up family get-togethers with his delicious chili. Write a one- or two-paragraph description of a character. Write not about a superhero or the president of a nation, but about an ordinary person who in some way is not so ordinary.

> **Prewriting Suggestion:** To get started, make a list of three or four interesting details about your character. Examples: Malcolm loves plants and wants to be a gardener. He tells jokes and he makes good blueberry muffins.

PROJECTS

1. **Improvisation.** Take a few moments to think about the minor characters in "Geraldine Moore the Poet." Try to imagine what they might be thinking and feeling in their scenes with Geraldine. Then get into small groups of four to six students. Take turns dramatizing some of the scenes listed below, with one person playing Geraldine and one person playing the other character. Really try to become your character. (You will have to use your imagination, since you have very little information about some of the characters.)

   • Anita making lunch and talking to Geraldine about how life has been since their mother became ill

   • Geraldine's mother speaking on the phone with Geraldine

   • Mrs. Scott telling Geraldine about when she first discovered poetry

   • Geraldine speaking to the hot-dog man about business

2. **Collaborative Poem.** Get into small groups and work together to write a poem. Pick numbers to see who will write the first line. After the first line is written, pass the paper to the right so that the next person can write a line. After writing, always fold the paper so that only your line is visible to the next poet. Keep passing the paper in a circle until the page is full. After the poem is complete, you may want to share your work with the rest of the class. You will probably find that some of the poems are quite humorous!

POEM

"Nikki-Rosa"
by Nikki Giovanni

ABOUT THE AUTHOR

Nikki Giovanni (1943–   ) is the pen name of Yolande Cornelia Giovanni, a poet, publisher, and educator who gained prominence in the 1960s and 1970s for her poetry and essays on racial issues and the African-American experience. Giovanni was born in Tennessee and grew up in Cincinnati, Ohio. She attended Fisk University, where she received a degree in history, and then went on to study at the University of Pennsylvania and at the Columbia School of Fine Arts. She teaches at Virginia Polytechnic Institute and has received honorary doctorates from many universities. Her books include *Gemini* (1971), a collection of essays on literary, autobiographical, and social topics; poetry collections such as *Black Feeling, Black Talk* (1968), *Re: Creation* (1970), and *Cotton Candy on a Rainy Day* (1978); and two collections of poetry for young people, *Spin a Soft Black Song* (1971) and *Ego Tripping* (1973).

ABOUT THE SELECTION

Background: History. The late 1950s saw the beginnings in the United States of the Civil Rights movement, which was dedicated to achieving equality for all American citizens, regardless of racial or ethnic background. Slowly, over the next two decades, advances were made in many areas. Laws were passed making discrimination in housing, schooling, and public accommodations illegal. Practices that kept African Americans from being able to vote, such as poll taxes, were banned. However, prejudice and economic inequality persisted. In many American cities, persons of African descent lived in poverty. Well-intentioned white social and political commentators wrote many books during that period about the plight of African Americans. However, these books often overlooked strengths in the African-American community. One such oversight is the subject of Giovanni's poem **"Nikki-Rosa."** The title of the poem is Giovanni's childhood nickname.

"Nikki-Rosa"

Nikki Giovanni

childhood remembrances are always a drag
if you're Black
you always remember things like living in Woodlawn[1]
with no inside toilet
5   and if you become famous or something
they never talk about how happy you were to have your mother
all to yourself and
how good the water felt when you got your bath from one of those
big tubs that folk in chicago barbecue in
10   and somehow when you talk about home
it never gets across how much you
understood their feelings
as the whole family attended meetings about Hollydale
and even though you remember
15   your biographers never understand
your father's pain as he sells his stock[2]
and another dream goes
and though you're poor it isn't poverty that
concerns you
20   and though they fought a lot
it isn't your father's drinking that makes any difference
but only that everybody is together and you
and your sister have happy birthdays and very good Christmasses
and I really hope no white person ever has cause to write about me

What positive experiences does the speaker remember from her childhood?

1. **Woodlawn.** Neighborhood in Chicago
2. **stock.** Share of ownership in a business that can be bought, sold, or traded

25 because they never understand Black love is Black wealth and they'll
    probably talk about my hard childhood and never understand that
    all the while I was quite happy   ■

Responding to the Selection

Of what from her childhood is the speaker proud? Do you consider these things to be worth remembering with pride?

Reviewing the Selection

RECALLING

1. With what overstatement does this poem begin? What example does the speaker give of a childhood memory that is "a drag"?

2. What, according to the speaker, do people not say about the childhoods of famous African Americans? What good things do they not talk about because they weren't there to experience them?

INTERPRETING

▶▶ 3. Does the speaker of this poem remember her childhood as being "a drag"? Why, or why not?

▶▶ 4. Why does the speaker hope that "no white person ever has cause to write about" her?

SYNTHESIZING

5. What made the speaker's childhood happy?

Understanding Literature (Questions for Discussion)

Paradox. A **paradox** is a contradictory statement, idea, or event. Often a writer will express a paradox in order to make a point in an arresting or memorable way. What paradox does the speaker of this poem express about poverty? Why, according to the speaker, were the African Americans among whom she grew up not poor, even though they lacked material possessions? What wealth did they have?

Responding in Writing

Autobiographical Essay. Write a brief autobiographical essay describing your own childhood. Fill your account with concrete details that will help your readers to feel what it was like to be you as a child.

> **Prewriting Suggestion:** Begin by making a time line of your life from your earliest memories through the age of six or seven. List on the time line the important events, or milestones, in your early life. Then, think about each of these events and do some focused freewriting to gather details for your essay. For information on time lines and focused freewriting, see the Language Arts Survey, 1.19 and 1.12.

PROJECT

African-American Poetry Recital. The 1960s through the 1980s was a period of great creativity and productivity among African-American poets. Outstanding poets active during this period include Nikki Giovanni, Mari Evans, Gordon Parks, Alice Walker, Gwendolyn Brooks, Imamu Amiri Baraka, and Audre Lorde. Hold a contemporary African-American poetry recital with other students in your class. Assign students to research the poets listed here (and others as well) and to introduce the pieces to be read. Assign other students to memorize poems to be recited. You may wish to add art, music, or dance to your recital and to invite an audience of parents, teachers, and other students to your performance.

"The Secret Life of Walter Mitty"
by James Thurber

ABOUT THE AUTHOR

James Thurber (1894–1961) was born in Columbus, Ohio, and attended Ohio State University. Most of his career was spent as a staff writer and editor for the *New Yorker* magazine, in which much of his work first appeared. At the *New Yorker,* Thurber shared an office with the essayist E. B. White. Both were to become literary legends.

As a child, Thurber suffered an accident that left him blind in one eye and visually impaired in the other. This trauma gave him the sensitivity that is seen in his writing. His essays, fables, cartoons, and stories often deal with underdogs, with people coping comically with the frustrations and disappointments of modern life. Thurber's most famous underdog is Walter Mitty, the subject of this selection.

ABOUT THE SELECTION

Background: History. "The Secret Life of Walter Mitty" was written in 1939, shortly after the beginning of World War II. At the time, Germany, under Adolph Hitler, had invaded Czechoslovakia and Poland and was at war with France and Great Britain. War was very much on the minds of Americans, so it is not surprising that war should figure in the daydreams of Thurber's character Walter Mitty.

In the 1930s, modern mass culture was in the process of developing. Newspapers, radio, and the relatively new medium of cinema were opening the world to a general audience in a way unprecedented in history. Many people were finding escape from their humdrum lives by following the exploits of famous men and women—great military commanders, millionaire industrialists, famous doctors, and the like. All play a role in Walter Mitty's fantasies. Also figuring prominently in Thurber's story are brand names—Kleenex and Squibb—another sign of the emerging modern era.

Background: Genre. A **satire** is a piece of writing that pokes fun at human failings or shortcomings. In "The Secret Life of Walter Mitty," Thurber pokes fun at escapism, the tendency to retreat from unpleasant truths in everyday life into a world of daydreams and fantasy. As you read the story, think about why Mitty feels the need to escape from his life. Also think about the possible sources of Mitty's daydreams.

"The Secret Life of Walter Mitty"

JAMES THURBER

"We're going through!" The Commander's voice was like thin ice breaking. He wore his full-dress uniform, with the heavily braided white cap pulled down rakishly over one cold gray eye. "We can't make it, sir. It's spoiling for a hurricane, if you ask me." "I'm not asking you, Lieutenant Berg," said the Commander. "Throw on the power lights! Rev her up to 8,500! We're going through!" The pounding of the cylinders increased: ta-pocketa-pocketa-pocketa-*pocketa-pocketa*. The Commander stared at the ice forming on the pilot window. He walked over and twisted a row of complicated dials. "Switch on No. 8 <u>auxiliary</u>!" he shouted. "Switch on No. 8 auxiliary!" repeated Lieutenant Berg. "Full strength in No. 3 turret!" shouted the Commander. "Full strength in No. 3 turret!" The crew, bending to their various tasks in the huge, <u>hurtling</u> eight-engined Navy hydroplane,[1] looked at each other and grinned. "The Old Man'll get us through," they said to one another. "The Old Man ain't afraid of Hell!" . . .

"Not so fast! You're driving too fast!" said Mrs. Mitty. "What are you driving so fast for?"

"Hmm?" said Walter Mitty. He looked at his wife, in the seat beside him, with shocked astonishment. She seemed grossly unfamiliar, like a strange woman who had yelled at him in a crowd. "You were up to fifty-five," she said. "You know I don't like to go more than forty. You were up to fifty-five." Walter Mitty drove on toward Waterbury in silence, the roaring of the SN202 through the worst storm in twenty years of Navy flying fading in the remote, intimate airways of his mind. "You're tensed up again," said Mrs. Mitty. "It's one of your days.

How is Mitty's daydream interrupted?

---

1. **hydroplane.** Motorboat built to skim along the top of the water at high speed

---

WORDS FOR EVERYDAY USE:
aux • il • ia • ry (ôg zil´yə rē) *n.*, engine for supplementary power

hur • tling (hʉrt ´liŋ) *adj.*, swift-moving

I wish you'd let Dr. Renshaw look you over."

Walter Mitty stopped the car in front of the building where his wife went to have her hair done. "Remember to get those overshoes while I'm having my hair done," she said. "I don't need overshoes," said Mitty. She put her mirror back into her bag. "We've been all through that," she said, getting out of the car. "You're not a young man any longer." He raced the engine a little. "Why don't you wear your gloves? Have you lost your gloves?" Walter Mitty reached in a pocket and brought out the gloves. He put them on, but after she had turned and gone into the building and he had driven on to a red light, he took them off again. "Pick it up, brother!" snapped a cop as the light changed, and Mitty hastily pulled on his gloves and lurched ahead. He drove around the streets aimlessly for a time, and then he drove past the hospital on his way to the parking lot.

. . . "It's the millionaire banker, Wellington McMillan," said the pretty nurse. "Yes?" said Walter Mitty, removing his gloves slowly. "Who has the case?" "Dr. Renshaw and Dr. Benbow, but there are two specialists here, Dr. Remington from New York and Mr. Pritchard-Mitford from London. He flew over." A door opened down a long, cool corridor and Dr. Renshaw came out. He looked <u>distraught</u> and haggard. "Hello, Mitty," he said. "We're having the devil's own time with McMillan, the millionaire banker and close per-

sonal friend of Roosevelt. Obstreosis of the ductal tract. Tertiary. Wish you'd take a look at him." "Glad to," said Mitty.

In the operating room there were whispered introductions: "Dr. Remington, Dr. Mitty. Mr. Pritchard-Mitford, Dr. Mitty." "I've read your book on streptothricosis," said Pritchard-Mitford, shaking hands. "A brilliant performance, sir." "Thank you," said Walter Mitty. "Didn't know you were in the States, Mitty," grumbled Remington. "Coals to Newcastle, bringing Mitford and me up here for a tertiary." "You are very kind," said Mitty. A huge, complicated machine, connected to the operating table, with many tubes and wires, began at this moment to go pocketa-pocketa-pocketa. "The new anesthetizer is giving way!" shouted an interne. "There is no one in the East who knows how to fix it!" "Quiet, man!" said Mitty, in a low, cool voice. He sprang to the machine, which was now going pocketa-pocketa-queep-pocketa-queep. He began fingering delicately a row of glistening dials: "Give me a fountain pen!" he snapped. Someone handed him a fountain pen. He pulled a faulty piston out of the machine and inserted the pen in its place. "That will hold for ten minutes," he said. "Get on with the operation." A nurse hurried over and whispered to Renshaw, and Mitty saw the man turn pale. "Coreopsis has set in," said Renshaw nervously. "If you would take over, Mitty?" Mitty looked at him and at the <u>craven</u> figure

What detail from real life inspires this fantasy?

WORDS FOR
EVERYDAY USE:

dis • traught (di strôt´) *adj.*, crazed, harassed
cra • ven (krā´vən) *adj.*, cowardly, afraid

of Benbow, who drank, and at the grave, uncertain faces of the two great specialists. "If you wish," he said. They slipped a white gown on him; he adjusted a mask and drew on thin gloves; nurses handed him shining . . .

"Back it up, Mac! Look out for that Buick!" Walter Mitty jammed on the brakes. "Wrong lane, Mac," said the parking-lot attendant, looking at Mitty closely. "Gee. Yeh," muttered Mitty. He began cautiously to back out of the lane marked "Exit Only." "Leave her sit there," said the attendant. "I'll put her away." Mitty got out of the car. "Hey, better leave the key." "Oh," said Mitty, handing the man the ignition key. The attendant <u>vaulted</u> into the car, backed it up with <u>insolent</u> skill, and put it where it belonged.

They're so damn cocky, thought Walter Mitty, walking along Main Street; they think they know everything. Once he had tried to take his chains off, outside New Milford, and he had got them wound around the axles. A man had had to come out in a wrecking car and unwind them, a young, grinning garageman. Since then Mrs. Mitty always made him drive to a garage to have the chains taken off. The next time, he thought, I'll wear my right arm in a sling; they won't grin at me then. I'll have my right arm in a sling and they'll see I couldn't possibly take the chains off myself. He kicked at the slush on the sidewalk. "Overshoes," he said to himself, and he began looking for a shoe store.

When he came out into the street again, with the overshoes in a box under his arm, Walter Mitty began to wonder what the other thing was his wife had told him to get. She had told him, twice, before they set out from their house for Waterbury. In a way he hated these weekly trips to town—he was always getting something wrong. Kleenex, he thought, Squibb's, razor blades? No. Toothpaste, toothbrush, bicarbonate, carborundum, initiative and referendum? He gave it up. But she would remember it. "Where's the what's-its-name?" she would ask. "Don't tell me you forgot the what's-pits-name." A newsboy went by shouting something about the Waterbury trial.

. . . "Perhaps this will refresh your memory." The District Attorney suddenly thrust a heavy automatic at the quiet figure on the witness stand. "Have you ever seen this before?" Walter Mitty took the gun and examined it expertly. "This is my Webley-Vickers 50.80," he said calmly. An excited buzz ran around the courtroom. The Judge rapped for order. "You are a crack shot with any sort of firearms, I believe?" said the District Attorney, <u>insinuatingly</u>. "Objection!" shouted Mitty's attorney. "We have shown that the defendant could not have fired the shot. We have shown that he wore his right arm in a sling on the night of the fourteenth of July." Walter Mitty raised his hand briefly and the bickering attorneys were stilled. "With any known make of gun," he said evenly, "I could have killed

What are Mitty's feelings toward the parking attendant? How is this man like the garageman? Why does Mitty feel this way toward these people?

How does Mitty cope with his own lack of greatness or heroism?

WORDS FOR EVERYDAY USE:

vault (vôlt) *vi.*, jump over

in • so • lent (in´sə lənt) *adj.*, boldly disrespectful

in • sin • u • at • ing • ly (in sin´yoo āt´iŋ lē) *adv.*, suggestively

Gregory Fitzhurst at three hundred feet *with my left hand.*" Pandemonium broke loose in the courtroom. A woman's scream rose above the bedlam and suddenly a lovely, dark-haired girl was in Walter Mitty's arms. The District Attorney struck at her savagely. Without rising from his chair, Mitty let the man have it on the point of the chin. "You miserable cur!" . . .

"Puppy biscuit," said Walter Mitty. He stopped walking and the buildings of Waterbury rose up out of the misty courtroom and surrounded him again. A woman who was passing laughed. "He said 'Puppy biscuit,'" she said to her companion. "That man said 'Puppy biscuit' to himself." Walter Mitty hurried on. He went into an A. & P., not the first one he came to but a smaller one farther up the street. "I want some biscuit for small, young dogs," he said to the clerk. "Any special brand, sir?" The greatest pistol shot in the world thought a moment. "It says 'Puppies Bark for It' on the box," said Walter Mitty.

His wife would be through at the hairdresser's in fifteen minutes, Mitty saw in looking at his watch, unless they had trouble drying it; sometimes they had trouble drying it. She didn't like to get to the hotel first; she would want him to be there waiting for her as usual. He found a big leather chair in the lobby, facing a window, and he put the overshoes and the puppy biscuit on the floor beside it. He picked up an old copy of *Liberty*[2] and sank down into the chair. "Can Germany Conquer the World Through the Air?" Walter Mitty looked at the pictures of bombing planes and of ruined streets.

What detail from Mitty's daydream leads him back to think of the puppy biscuits?

. . . "The cannonading has got the wind up in young Raleigh, sir," said the sergeant. Captain Mitty looked up at him through tousled hair. "Get him to bed," he said wearily. "With the others. I'll fly alone." "But you can't sir," said the sergeant anxiously. "It takes two men to handle that bomber and the Archies are pounding hell out of the air. Von Richtman's circus is between here and Saulier." "Somebody's got to get that ammunition dump," said Mitty. "I'm going over. Spot of brandy?" He poured a drink for the sergeant and one for himself. War thundered and whined around the dugout and battered at the door. There was a rending of wood and splinters flew through the room. "A bit of a near thing," said Captain Mitty carelessly. "The box barrage is closing in," said the sergeant. "We only live once, Sergeant," said Mitty, with his faint, fleeting smile. "Or do we?" He poured another brandy and tossed it off. "I never see a man could hold his brandy like you, sir," said the sergeant. "Begging your pardon, sir." Captain Mitty stood up and strapped on his huge Webley-Vickers automatic. "It's forty kilometers through hell, sir," said the sergeant. Mitty finished one last brandy. "After all," he said softly, "what isn't?" The pounding of the cannon increased; there was the rat-tat-tatting of machine guns, and from somewhere came the menacing pocketa-pocketa-pocketa of the new flame-throwers. Walter Mitty walked to the door of the dugout humming "Auprès de Ma Blonde."[3] He turned and waved to the sergeant. "Cheerio!" he said. . . .

---

2. **Liberty.** Popular magazine of the era
3. **"Auprès de Ma Blonde."** Popular World War II era romantic song

Something struck his shoulder. "I've been looking all over this hotel for you," said Mrs. Mitty. "Why do you have to hide in this old chair? How did you expect me to find you?" "Things close in," said Walter Mitty vaguely. "What?" Mrs. Mitty said. "Did you get the what's-its-name? The puppy biscuit? What's in that box?" "Overshoes," said Mitty. "Couldn't you have put them on in the store?" "I was thinking," said Walter Mitty. "Does it ever occur to you that I am sometimes thinking?" She looked at him. "I'm going to take your temperature when I get you home," she said.

They went out through the revolving doors that made a faintly <u>derisive</u> whistling sound when you pushed them. It was two blocks to the parking lot. At the drugstore on the corner she said, "Wait here for me. I forgot something. I won't be a minute." She was more than a minute. Walter Mitty lighted a cigarette. It began to rain, rain with sleet in it. He stood up against the wall of the drugstore, smoking. . . . He put his shoulders back and his heels together. "To hell with the handkerchief," said Walter Mitty scornfully. He took one last drag on his cigarette and snapped it away. Then, with that faint, fleeting smile playing about his lips, he faced the firing squad; erect and motionless, proud and disdainful, Walter Mitty the Undefeated, <u>inscrutable</u> to the last.   ■

Why might Mitty think that the doors are making a derisive sound? What does this perception reveal about Mitty?

Responding to the Selection

How do you feel toward Walter Mitty after reading this selection? Do you think he is silly or ridiculous? Do you feel sorry for him? Is there anything noble or otherwise attractive about his character? Discuss these questions with your classmates.

WORDS FOR EVERYDAY USE:

de • ri • sive (di rī´siv) *adj.*, ridiculing

in • scru • ta • ble (in skrо̅о̅t´ə bəl) *adj.*, obscure, mysterious

Reviewing the Selection

1. About what is Walter Mitty fantasizing at the beginning of the story? What does he do as a result of his fantasizing? What awakens him from his fantasy?

2. What does Walter Mitty's wife tell him to do while she gets her hair done? How does Mitty react to her instructions?

3. What two events spur Walter Mitty's fantasy about being a famous surgeon? What goes wrong during the operation, and how does surgeon Mitty react?

4. What does the sergeant say to Mitty about the ammunition dump? What is Mitty's response?

5. Why does Mrs. Mitty want Walter to see Dr. Renshaw at the beginning of the story?

6. How does Mitty perceive himself? Why doesn't he like the idea of buying overshoes? Why wouldn't he want to think of himself as the kind of person who is sensitive about such matters as getting his feet wet?

7. What is the surgeon like in Mitty's fantasy? What does Mitty want to be like?

8. In what way is Mitty's response to the sergeant a commentary on his own life? What about Mitty's life is so unpleasant as to merit that description?

9. What drives Mitty to daydream? What aspects of his life are petty and unheroic?

10. What spurs Mitty's final fantasy? Why would he fantasize about being in front of a firing squad? In what sense is Mitty's spirit being killed by events in his everyday life?

Understanding Literature (Questions for Discussion)

1. **Hero and Antihero.** A **hero** is a character who behaves bravely and does great deeds. Heroes are typically strong, resourceful, and self-sacrificing. An **antihero** is a central character who lacks all the qualities traditionally associated with heroes. Often antiheroes are timid, cowardly, and weak, but the reader sympathizes with the struggles that they face. What causes the reader of this story to sympathize with Mitty even though Mitty is the very opposite of a hero? What happens to Mitty's spirit every day? How does life oppress him? What sort of person would Mitty like to be? How do his daydreams reveal this to the reader?

2. **Conflict.** A **conflict** is a struggle between two forces in a literary work. In this story, there is a conflict between the person Walter Mitty fantasizes about being and the person he actually is. How does Mitty cope with the fact that he has no power over his own life? How does he resolve this struggle?

3. **Stereotype.** A **stereotype** is an uncritically accepted or conventional idea, particularly such an idea held about whole groups of people. In what sense are Mitty and his wife stereotypical characters? Bear in mind that in the 1930s, economic and political power lay almost exclusively with men. Given that fact, what makes "The Secret Life of Walter Mitty" unrealistic as a commentary on the actual relations between men and women of the time?

Responding in Writing

Short Story Episode. If Walter Mitty were alive today instead of in the 1930s, how might his daydreams differ? Who might he imagine himself to be? Write an episode, or scene, from a modern update of "The Secret Life of Walter Mitty." Place your episode in the 1990s and have Mitty daydream about being some exceptional contemporary person.

> **Prewriting Suggestion:** Before writing, freewrite in your journal for five to ten minutes about people who are portrayed in contemporary media as idols or heroes. For more information on freewriting, refer to the Language Arts Survey, 1.12, "Freewriting."

PROJECT

Newsreel. In the 1930s, movie houses often showed newsreels before and between feature films. Newsreels contained clips about world and national events. They also contained short news stories about celebrities. The American writer John Dos Passos created a type of writing that he called *Newsreels* in which he attempted to give a picture of daily life at a particular time by gathering together newspaper headlines, bits of popular song, advertisements, quotations, and other materials from popular culture. Create a Dos Passos-style "Newsreel" to describe life in your society today. Gather together bits and pieces of language from the popular media that are typical of life in the latter part of the twentieth century.

Gather materials from as many different sources as you can. Include bits of advertisements, popular songs, newspaper headlines, quotations from famous people alive today, and bits of dialogue from television programs such as talk shows and news shows. Remember that your criterion for inclusion is that the materials you gather be typical of life in the 1990s.

POEM

"the lesson of the moth"
by Don Marquis

ABOUT THE AUTHOR

Don Marquis (1878–1937) was born in Illinois and worked as a newspaper journalist in Atlanta and New York. In addition to his newspaper work, Marquis wrote novels, short stories, plays, and an autobiography. However, he is best known for his humorous poems. Much of his work is satirical. It pokes gentle fun at human failings and foolishness while celebrating our capacity to dream, to love, and to laugh at ourselves.

ABOUT THE SELECTION

Background: Technique. According to Marquis, one morning he came into his office at the *New York Sun* and found he had accidentally left a sheet of paper in his typewriter. To his surprise, a poem had been typed on that paper. The poem was written during the night by a cockroach named Archy. Archy had typed the poem by jumping from key to key. Because Archy couldn't hold down the shift key and type a character at the same time, all the letters in the poem were lowercase. Over the coming years, Marquis made a habit of leaving paper in his typewriter, and Archy wrote many poems about himself and his friends. These friends included Mehitabel the cat, who believed herself to be a reincarnation of Cleopatra. The result was the book *Archy and Mehitabel*, published in 1927. This delightful collection of comic verse features **"the lesson of the moth."**

READER'S JOURNAL
  What do you want most out of life? What are your most cherished dreams? What would you be willing to sacrifice to make those dreams come true? Write about these questions in your journal.

"the lesson of the moth"

DON MARQUIS

i was talking to a moth
the other evening
he was trying to break into
an electric light bulb
5   and fry himself on the wires

why do you fellows
pull this stunt i asked him
because it is the <u>conventional</u>
thing for moths or why
10   if that had been an uncovered
candle instead of an electric
light bulb you would
now be a small unsightly cinder
have you no sense

15   plenty of it he answered
but at times we get tired
of using it
we get bored with the routine
and <u>crave</u> beauty
20   and excitement
fire is beautiful
and we know that if we get

Why does the moth want to "fry himself"?

WORDS FOR EVERYDAY USE:

con • ven • tion • al (kən ven´shə nəl) *adj.*, customary, usual
crave (krāv) *vt.*, long for, desire

too close it will kill us
but what does that matter
25   it is better to be happy
for a moment
and be burned up with beauty
than to live a long time
and be bored all the while
30   so we wad all our life up
into one little roll
and then we shoot the roll
that is what life is for
it is better to be a part of beauty
35   for one instant and then cease to
exist than to exist forever
and never be a part of beauty
our attitude toward life
is come easy go easy
40   we are like human beings
used to be before they became
too civilized to enjoy themselves

and before i could argue him
out of his philosophy
45   he went and <u>immolated</u> himself
on a patent cigar lighter
i do not agree with him
myself i would rather have
half the happiness and twice
50   the <u>longevity</u>

but at the same time i wish
there was something i wanted
as badly as he wanted to fry himself

                      archy   ■

What does the moth want to avoid?

What difference of philosophy do the moth and the speaker of the poem have?

WORDS FOR EVERYDAY USE:

im • mo • late (im´ ə lāt´) *vt.,* kill as a sacrifice

lon • gev • i • ty (län jev´ə tē) *n.,* long life

Responding to the Selection

Which character do you think is saner—the cockroach or the moth? Why does Archy the cockroach admire the moth even though Archy thinks that the moth is crazy? Discuss these questions with your classmates.

Reviewing the Selection

RECALLING

1. What is the moth trying to do at the beginning of the poem?

2. What happens to the moth near the end of the poem?

INTERPRETING

3. How does Archy the cockroach feel about what the moth is trying to do? What does he say to the moth about this?

4. What reason does the moth give for acting as he does? What does the moth want?

SYNTHESIZING

5. What do the last three lines of the poem reveal about Archy? In what way does he wish that he were like the moth? What did the moth have that Archy didn't have?

Understanding Literature (Questions for Discussion)

1. **Personification and Character Trait. Personification** is a figure of speech in which an idea, animal, or thing is described as if it were a person. A **character trait** is a quality or characteristic of a character in a work of literature. What two animals are personified in this selection? What is the moth's major character trait? What sort of creature is the moth? What action on the part of the moth shows that he is not level-headed or sensible? What is the moth's "philosophy"? What does Archy think of that philosophy? What does Archy learn from the moth?

2. **Fable.** A **fable** is a brief story with animal characters told to express a moral. Who are the animal characters in Don Marquis's fable? Think about the title. What is "the lesson of the moth"? In other words, what does Archy learn about himself from thinking about the moth's actions? What is the poem saying about the importance of having dreams? Reread lines 40–42. What is the poem saying about how becoming civilized has affected human beings?

Responding in Writing

Dialogue. Imagine two friends. One is practical and level-headed and plans to go to business school. The other is a dreamer and wants to pursue a career in the arts. Perhaps the second friend wants to make his or her living as a poet, a painter, or a rock musician. Write a dialogue between the two friends in which they debate the pros and cons of the career paths that they want to follow. Then think about the two friends in relation to Don Marquis's poem. Which friend is more like the moth? Which is more like Archy? Which are you more like?

> **Prewriting Suggestion:** For each of the career paths, make a pro and con chart. See the Language Arts Survey, 1.22, "Pro and Con Charts."

PROJECT

Career Fair. With other students in your class, plan a career fair in which you present projects describing various careers. Consult the following sources of information: guidance counselors, adults in the work force, and career-related materials from your school or community library. One excellent source of information is the *Federal Occupational and Career Handbook*, which can be found in many libraries. Each student should choose one career to research and then prepare a poster describing that career. The poster should list the job title, the training or education required, duties, average pay, work conditions, and possibilities for advancement.

NONFICTION

"Prologue: How to Eat a Guava" from *When I Was Puerto Rican*
by Esmeralda Santiago

ABOUT THE AUTHOR

Esmeralda Santiago grew up in Puerto Rico and moved to New York as a young woman. There she accustomed herself to a new language and culture. She attended New York's High School of Performing Arts and went on to graduate with honors from Harvard University. She later received a Master of Fine Arts degree from Sarah Lawrence College in Bronxville, New York. With her husband, she runs a film production company in Boston, Massachusetts. Her writing has appeared in numerous newspapers and magazines.

ABOUT THE SELECTION

Background: Genre. An **autobiography** is the story of a person's life as told by that person. In *When I Was Puerto Rican,* Esmeralda Santiago tells of the difficulties and joys of adapting to life in New York after spending her childhood in Puerto Rico. The introduction to this autobiographical work, **"How to Eat a Guava,"** is written from the point of view of an adult walking through a supermarket and being reminded of her past. A guava is a kind of fruit that grows in rural Puerto Rico.

Background: Technique. An **image** is a word or phrase that describes something that can be seen, touched, tasted, heard, or smelled. Good writers use concrete images to make their descriptions come alive. As you read "How to Eat a Guava," visualize the images that the author presents to you. Imagine how the objects that she describes look, feel, taste, sound, and smell.

READER'S JOURNAL

Imagine that you have moved to some very different place, one where people speak a different language and have very different customs. What would you miss most about your place of origin? Write about this question in your journal.

"*Prologue: How to Eat a Guava*"

FROM *WHEN I WAS PUERTO RICAN*

ESMERALDA SANTIAGO

Barco que no anda, no llega a puerto.

✳

A ship that doesn't sail, never reaches port.

There are guavas at the Shop & Save. I pick one the size of a tennis ball and finger the prickly stem end. It feels familiarly bumpy and firm. The guava is not quite ripe; the skin is still a dark green. I smell it and imagine a pale pink center, the seeds tightly <u>embedded</u> in the flesh.

A ripe guava is yellow, although some varieties have a pink tinge. The skin is thick, firm, and sweet. Its heart is bright pink and almost solid with seeds. The most delicious part of the guava surrounds the tiny seeds. If you don't know how to eat a guava, the seeds end up in the <u>crevices</u> between your teeth.

When you bite into a ripe guava, your teeth must grip the bumpy surface and sink into the thick edible skin without hitting the center. It takes experience to do this, as it's quite tricky to determine how far beyond the skin the seeds begin.

Some years, when the rains have been plentiful and the nights cool, you can bite into a guava and not find many seeds. The guava bushes grow close to the ground, their branches <u>laden</u> with green then yellow fruit that seem to ripen overnight. These guavas are large and juicy, almost seedless, their roundness <u>enticing</u> you to have one more, just one more, because next year the rains may not come.

As children, we didn't always wait for the fruit to ripen. We raided the bushes as soon as the guavas were large enough to bend the branch.

A green guava is sour and hard. You bite into it at its widest point, because it's easier to grasp with your teeth. You

How do the supermarket guavas differ from the ripe guavas the narrator remembers?

Fruit Displayed on a Stand. Gustave Caillebotte. Courtesy, Museum of Fine Arts, Boston. Fanny P. Mason Fund in Memory of Alice Thevin

hear the skin, meat, and seeds crunching inside your head, while the inside of your mouth explodes in little spurts of sour.

You <u>grimace</u>, your eyes water, and your cheeks disappear as your lips purse into a tight O. But you have another and then another, enjoying the crunchy sounds, the acid taste, the gritty texture of the unripe center. At night, your mother makes you drink castor oil,[1] which she says tastes better than a green guava. That's when you know for sure that you're a child and she has stopped being one.

I had my last guava the day we left Puerto Rico.[2] It was large and juicy, almost red in the center, and so fragrant that I didn't want to eat it because I would lose the smell. All the way to the airport I scratched at it with my teeth, making little dents in the skin, chewing small pieces with my front teeth, so that I could feel the texture against my tongue, the tiny pink pellets of sweet.

Today, I stand before a stack of dark green guavas each perfectly round and hard, each $1.59. The one in my hand is tempting. It smells faintly of late summer afternoons and hopscotch under the mango tree. But this is autumn in New York, and I'm no longer a child.

The guava joins its sisters under the harsh fluorescent lights of the exotic fruit display. I push my cart away, toward the apples and pears of my adulthood, their nearly seedless ripeness predictable and bittersweet. ■

Of what does the smell of the guava remind the speaker?

---

1. **castor oil.** Strong-tasting bean oil that is thought to cleanse the digestive system of impurities
2. **Puerto Rico.** Island nation in the West Indies; a commonwealth associated with the United States

Responding to the Selection

How did the writer's descriptions of eating guavas as a child affect you? How do the guavas that she remembers from her childhood compare to the guavas in the supermarket in New York?

Reviewing the Selection

RECALLING

1. What does the narrator pick up in the supermarket at the beginning of the selection? To what does she compare it in paragraph 1? To what does she compare it in paragraph 2?

2. What did the children sometimes eat back in Puerto Rico? What happened as a result of eating these? What did the narrator's mother say to the children at such times?

INTERPRETING

3. Review paragraphs 1 and 2 of the selection. How do the guavas in the supermarket compare to the ripe ones that the narrator remembers from childhood? Review the last two paragraphs. What words does the speaker use to describe the supermarket guavas? the supermarket? What is she saying about supermarkets and about modern urban life in general? How does it compare to the rural life that she left behind?

4. What, according to the narrator, did the mother's comment about the castor oil reveal about her? What did the mother not remember about being a child?

SYNTHESIZING

5. At the end of the selection, the narrator decides to push her cart "toward the apples and pears" of her adulthood. She describes these apples and pears, fruits common in the northern United States, as being "predictable and bittersweet." In what way is her life in the United States bittersweet? Based on the selection, what about her current life is not as good as her childhood? What about it is better?

Understanding Literature (Questions for Discussion)

1. **Image.** An **image** is a word or phrase that describes something that can be seen, touched, tasted, heard, or smelled. What images from this selection are particularly vivid for you? Which ones give you the feeling of actually being there, experiencing what the narrator is describing?

2. **Symbol.** A **symbol** is something that stands for or represents both itself and something beyond itself. For example, a poet who writes about a gift of roses might intend for the roses to stand for love or beauty. What do the hard, green, regularly shaped and priced guavas in the supermarket symbolize for the narrator? What do the ripe, juicy, enticing guavas from her childhood symbolize?

3. **Epigraph.** An **epigraph** is a quotation or motto used at the beginning of the whole or part of a literary work. What is the epigraph at the beginning of this selection? How does that epigraph relate to the narrator's life?

Responding in Writing

Imagist Poem. An **imagist poem** is one that presents a picture in words. Choose a food that you really enjoy and write an imagist poem to describe the experience of eating that food. Your poem should be no more than six lines long and should present a vivid picture in words.

> **Prewriting Suggestion:** Read the Language Arts Survey, 1.18, "Sensory Detail Charts." Then make a sensory detail chart to describe how that food looks, tastes, smells, and feels. In your chart, list vivid nouns and adjectives that you can use to describe the food you've chosen to write about. Next make a list of vivid verbs to use in your poem. For example, instead of listing the vague verb *eat*, you might list vivid verbs such as *crunch, chomp, devour, sip,* and *slurp.*

SHORT STORY

"The Man to Send Rain Clouds"
by Leslie Marmon Silko

ABOUT THE AUTHOR

Leslie Marmon Silko (1948–   ), born in New Mexico, grew up on the Laguna Pueblo Reservation. She attended Bureau of Indian Affairs schools, a Catholic high school, and the University of New Mexico (UNM). Silko left law school in order to work on her writing, and she published her first story in 1969. Among her honors is a prestigious MacArthur Foundation Fellowship. She has taught at several colleges, including the University of New Mexico.

Silko's writings reflect themes from her Native-American heritage, including the relationship between humans and nature and the tensions of living within different cultures. Her first novel, *Ceremony* (1977), tells of the feelings of a World War II veteran of mixed parentage who seeks advice from a Native-American sage.

ABOUT THE SELECTION

Background: History. The Spanish were the first Europeans to explore the American West. They brought with them their Catholic religion and established missions, building beautiful churches out of dried mud, or adobe. Among the native peoples of the West, the Spanish found ancient, established religions that they did not understand. In the Southwest, these religions often involved elaborate ceremonies, including ritual dances such as the dance held for the purpose of bringing rain. Spanish missionaries worked to convert native peoples to the Catholic religion, but many people clung to the older ways, often adding elements of Catholicism to their own rituals and beliefs. **"The Man to Send Rain Clouds"** is a story about the Pueblos who maintain their own identity by adapting the last rites performed by Catholic priests to their own religious purposes. Last rites involve the sprinkling of holy water that has been blessed by a priest.

Background: Technique. The **setting** of a literary work is the time and place of its action. As you read this story, note the details that help to create the setting. These include descriptions of the physical environment and of the customs and ways of life of the people.

READER'S JOURNAL

How do people from various parts of the world differ? What happens when people from very different cultures come into contact with one another? Is it important for people to maintain their own customs and ethnic identity? Why, or why not? Write about these questions in your journal.

"The Man to Send Rain Clouds"

Leslie Marmon Silko

They found him under a big cottonwood tree. His Levi jacket and pants were faded light blue so that he had been easy to find. The big cottonwood tree stood apart from a small grove of winterbare cottonwoods which grew in the wide, sandy arroyo.[1] He had been dead for a day or more, and the sheep had wandered and scattered up and down the arroyo. Leon and his brother-in-law, Ken, gathered the sheep and left them in the pen at the sheep camp before they returned to the cottonwood tree. Leon waited under the tree while Ken drove the truck through the deep sand to the edge of the arroyo. He squinted up at the sun and unzipped his jacket—it sure was hot for this time of year. But high and northwest the blue mountains were still in snow. Ken came sliding down the low, crumbling bank about fifty yards down, and he was bringing the red blanket.

Before they wrapped the old man, Leon took a piece of string out of his pocket and tied a small gray feather in the old man's long white hair. Ken gave him the paint. Across the brown wrinkled forehead he drew a streak of white and along the high cheekbones he drew a strip of blue paint. He paused and watched Ken throw pinches of corn meal and pollen into the wind that fluttered the small gray feather. Then Leon painted with yellow under the old man's broad nose, and finally, when he had painted green across the chin, he smiled.

"Send us rain clouds, Grandfather." They laid the bundle in the back of the pickup and covered it with a heavy tarp before they started back to the pueblo.[2]

They turned off the highway onto the sandy pueblo road. Not long after they passed the store and post office they saw Father Paul's car coming toward them. When he recognized their faces he slowed his car and waved for them to stop. The young priest rolled down the car window.

"Did you find old Teofilo?" he asked loudly.

What does Leon ask of the dead man?

1. **arroyo.** Dry gully
2. **pueblo.** Village

Leon stopped the truck. "Good morning, Father. We were just out to the sheep camp. Everything is O.K. now."

"Thank God for that. Teofilo is a very old man. You really shouldn't allow him to stay at the sheep camp alone."

"No, he won't do that any more now."

"Well, I'm glad you understand. I hope I'll be seeing you at Mass this week—we missed you last Sunday. See if you can get old Teofilo to come with you." The priest smiled and waved at them as they drove away.

Louise and Teresa were waiting. The table was set for lunch, and the coffee was boiling on the black iron stove. Leon looked at Louise and then at Teresa.

"We found him under a cottonwood tree in the big arroyo near sheep camp. I guess he sat down to rest in the shade and never got up again." Leon walked toward the old man's bed. The red plaid shawl had been shaken and spread carefully over the bed, and a new brown flannel shirt and pair of stiff new Levi's were arranged neatly beside the pillow. Louise held the screen door open while Leon and Ken carried in the red blanket. He looked small and <u>shriveled</u>, and after they dressed him in the new shirt and pants he seemed more shrunken.

It was noontime now because the church bells rang the Angelus.[3] They ate the beans with hot bread, and nobody said anything until after Teresa poured the coffee.

Ken stood up and put on his jacket. "I'll see about the gravediggers. Only the top layer of soil is frozen. I think it can be ready before dark."

Leon nodded his head and finished his coffee. After Ken had been gone for a while, the neighbors and clanspeople came quietly to embrace Teofilo's family and to leave food on the table because the gravediggers would come to eat when they were finished.

The sky in the west was full of pale yellow light. Louise stood outside with her hands in the pockets of Leon's green army jacket that was too big for her. The funeral was over, and the old men had taken their candles and medicine bags and were gone. She waited until the body was laid into the pickup before she said anything to Leon. She touched his arm, and he noticed that her hands were still dusty from the corn meal that she had sprinkled around the old man. When she spoke, Leon could not hear her.

"What did you say? I didn't hear you."

"I said that I had been thinking about something."

"About what?"

"About the priest sprinkling holy water for Grandpa. So he won't be thirsty."

Leon stared at the new moccasins that Teofilo had made for the ceremo-

<hr />

3. **Angelus.** Prayer said at morning, noon, and evening to honor the birth of Jesus Christ

WORDS FOR EVERYDAY USE:

shriv • eled (shriv′əld) *adj.*, wrinkled and withered

Sunset Dance–Ceremony to the Evening Sun. John Henry Sharp, 1924. National Museum of American Art, Washington, DC. Gift of Arvin Gottlieb

nial dances in the summer. They were nearly hidden by the red blanket. It was getting colder, and the wind pushed gray dust down the narrow pueblo road. The sun was approaching the long <u>mesa</u> where it disappeared during the winter. Louise stood there shivering and watching his face. Then he zipped up his jacket and opened the truck door. "I'll see if he's there."

Ken stopped the pickup at the church, and Leon got out; and then Ken drove down the hill to the grave-yard where people were waiting. Leon knocked at the old carved door with its symbols of the Lamb.[4] While he waited he looked up at the twin bells from the king of Spain[5] with the last sunlight pouring around them in their tower.

The priest opened the door and smiled when he saw who it was. "Come in! What brings you here this evening?"

---

4. **Lamb.** Symbol of Jesus Christ
5. **twin bells. . . king of Spain.** Spain colonized the Americas in the fifteenth and sixteenth centuries; the Spanish monarchy sent priests and financed the building of churches.

WORDS FOR EVERYDAY USE:

me • sa (māʹsə) *n.,* high, flat tableland

The priest walked toward the kitchen, and Leon stood with his cap in his hand, playing with the earflaps and examining the living room—the brown sofa, the green armchair, and the brass lamp that hung down from the ceiling by links of chain. The priest dragged a chair out of the kitchen and offered it to Leon.

"No thank you, Father. I only came to ask you if you would bring your holy water to the graveyard."

The priest turned away from Leon and looked out the window at the patio full of shadows and the dining-room windows of the nuns' cloister[6] across the patio. The curtains were heavy, and the light from within faintly penetrated; it was impossible to see the nuns inside eating supper. "Why didn't you tell me he was dead? I could have brought the Last Rites[7] anyway."

Leon smiled. "It wasn't necessary, Father."

The priest stared down at his scuffed brown loafers and the worn hem of his cassock. "For a Christian burial it was necessary."

His voice was distant, and Leon thought that his blue eyes looked tired.

"It's O.K. Father, we just want him to have plenty of water."

The priest sank down into the green chair and picked up a glossy missionary magazine. He turned the colored pages full of lepers and pagans[8] without looking at them.

"You know I can't do that, Leon. There should have been the Last Rites and a funeral Mass at the very least."

Leon put on his green cap and pulled the flaps down over his ears. "It's getting late. Father. I've got to go."

When Leon opened the door Father Paul stood up and said, "Wait." He left the room and came back wearing a long brown overcoat. He followed Leon out the door and across the dim churchyard to the adobe steps in front of the church. They both stooped to fit through the low adobe entrance. And when they started down the hill to the graveyard only half of the sun was visible above the mesa.

The priest approached the grave slowly, wondering how they had managed to dig into the frozen ground; and then he remembered that this was New Mexico, and saw the pile of cold loose sand beside the hole. The people stood close to each other with little clouds of steam puffing from their faces. The priest looked at them and saw a pile of jackets, gloves, and scarves in the yellow, dry tumbleweeds that grew in the graveyard. He looked at the red blanket, not sure that Teofilo was so small, wondering if it wasn't some perverse Indian trick—something they did in March to ensure a good harvest—wondering if maybe old Teofilo was actually at sheep camp corraling the sheep for the night. But there he was, facing into a cold dry

---

6. **cloister.** Place of protection and seclusion for people following a religious vocation

7. **Last Rites.** Sacrament performed by a Catholic priest or deacon for someone who is dying

8. **lepers and pagans.** *Lepers* are people afflicted with the disease known as leprosy; *pagan* is a word sometimes used to refer to people who are not Christians

WORDS FOR EVERYDAY USE:	pen • e • trate (pen´i trāt) vi., pass into	a • do • be (ə dō´bē) n., sun-dried brick
	mis • sion • ar • y (mish´ən er´ē) n., person sent to convert others to a religion or to teach religious beliefs	per • verse (pər vurs´) adj., contrary

wind and squinting at the last sunlight, ready to bury a red wool blanket while the faces of his <u>parishioners</u> were in shadow with the last warmth of the sun on their backs.

His fingers were stiff, and it took him a long time to twist the lid off the holy water. Drops of water fell on the red blanket and soaked into dark icy spots. He sprinkled the grave and the water disappeared almost before it touched the dim, cold sand; it reminded him of something—he tried to remember what it was, because he thought if he could remember he might understand this. He sprinkled more water; he shook the container until it was empty, and the water fell through the light from sundown like August rain that fell while the sun was still shining, almost evaporating before it touched the wilted squash flowers.

The wind pulled at the priest's brown Franciscan robe[9] and swirled away the corn meal and pollen that had been sprinkled on the blanket. They lowered the bundle into the ground, and they didn't bother to untie the stiff pieces of new rope that were tied around the ends of the blanket. The sun was gone, and over on the highway the eastbound lane was full of headlights. The priest walked away slowly. Leon watched him climb the hill, and when he had disappeared within the tall, thick walls, Leon turned to look up at the high blue mountains in the deep snow that reflected a faint red light from the west. He felt good because it was finished, and he was happy about the sprinkling of the holy water; now the old man could send them big thunderclouds for sure. ■

Why does Leon feel happy?

---

9. **Franciscan robe.** Robe worn by a member of the Franciscan order, the Order of Saint Francis; hooded brown full-length tunic tied at the waist with a rope

WORDS FOR EVERYDAY USE:

pa • rish • ion • er (pə rish′ə nər) *n.,* member of a church district, or parish

Responding to the Selection

Do the beliefs of the Pueblos in this selection differ from your own? If so, in what ways? How do you feel about these beliefs? How should people react to belief systems that differ from theirs? Discuss these questions with your classmates.

Reviewing the Selection

RECALLING

1. What has happened to the elderly man found by Ken and Leon at the beginning of the story? What word does Leon use to refer to the elderly man?

2. What does Ken put in the elderly man's hair? What does he put on the man's face? What does he ask the elderly man to do?

3. What doesn't Leon tell the priest about Teofilo? Why does Leon decide to go to visit the priest?

4. What does the priest wish that Leon had told him? What would the priest have done if Leon had told him that?

INTERPRETING

5. What purpose might the painting of the elderly man's face serve?

6. Why might the elderly man, according to the beliefs of Ken and Leon, now be in a position to influence the rainfall? What do Ken and Leon probably believe about the afterlife?

7. Why does Louise want the priest to come to the grave?

8. Why didn't Leon consider informing the priest "necessary"?

SYNTHESIZING

9. What is the priest's first reaction to Leon's request? Why does the priest change his mind? What does this tell you about the priest?

10. What non-Christian interpretation do the Pueblos in this story place on the sprinkling of holy water? How does the story illustrate the adaptation of elements from one belief system to another belief system?

Understanding Literature (Questions for Discussion)

1. **Symbol.** A **symbol** is something that stands for or represents both itself and something else. In this story, the dead man is sprinkled with corn meal, pollen, and water. What function does pollen serve in nature? What significance does corn meal have to the Pueblo Indians? Why is rain important to them? Why might they sprinkle the body with corn meal, pollen, and water? What do these things symbolize, or represent?

2. **Theme.** A **theme** is a central idea in a literary work. What does this story tell you about the ways in which traditional peoples attempt to preserve their ethnic identities against changes introduced from the outside?

Responding in Writing

Anthropological Report. Choose a ceremony or ritual that is important in your culture. Possibilities include weddings, birthday parties, bar mitzvahs, high school graduations, first communions, and so on. Write a description of that ceremony to be read by people from a very different culture. In your description, explain what happens at the ceremony. Be sure to explain the symbolic significance of the actions, words, and objects used in the ceremony. For example, each candle on a birthday cake symbolizes one year of life.

> **Prewriting Suggestion:** Make a list of all the objects used in the ceremony and describe the purpose or significance of each object. Then list everything that occurs in the ceremony, from beginning to end. Refer to your lists as you write your draft.

PROJECT

Oral Report. Choose a culture from within your country that is very different from your own. Go to the library and do some research on that culture. Identify some ritual or ceremony that plays an important role in that culture and learn everything you can about it. Then present what you have learned in an oral report to your class.

POEM

"The Road Not Taken"
by Robert Frost

ABOUT THE AUTHOR

Robert Frost (1874–1963), associated by most people with New England, was actually born in San Francisco. At the age of ten, following the death of his father, Frost moved with his mother to New England. He attended Dartmouth and Harvard, worked in a mill, taught school, and farmed. In 1912 he moved to England, where he worked on his poetry. After the publication of his first book at the age of forty, Frost moved back to the United States and bought a farm in New Hampshire. Over the coming years, he became America's most well-known and most beloved poet. In 1961 he was invited to read a poem at President John F. Kennedy's inauguration. Books by Frost include *A Boy's Will, North of Boston,* and *West-Running Brook.*

ABOUT THE SELECTION

Background: Theme. "The Road Not Taken" was published in Frost's 1916 collection *Mountain Interval.* The poem is typical of Frost's work in that it deals with a subject from rural New England, in this case a road that diverges, or forks, in the middle of a forest. The road is a conventional symbol for the path that a person takes through life. As you read the poem, think about what the fork in the road might represent, or symbolize.

Background: Technique. Free verse is poetry that does not follow a regular pattern of rhythm, rhyme, or stanza form. In the early part of this century, many poets were experimenting with free verse, but Frost chose to stick with traditional forms, claiming that writing free verse was like "playing tennis without a net." "The Road Not Taken" is typical of Frost's lyrics in that it uses a regular rhyme scheme, stanza form, and rhythms. Try reading the poem aloud, noting the rhythm, stanza form, and rhyme scheme. Also note the ease and naturalness of the speech. Frost is known for writing poetry in the language of ordinary people. The use of such language is perhaps his greatest contribution to poetry.

READER'S JOURNAL
   Often people make choices in life that have dramatic consequences for the future. In your journal, list some of the most important choices that people make during their lifetimes. Choose one of these choices and write about how you might go about making that choice.

"The Road Not Taken"

ROBERT FROST

Two roads <u>diverged</u> in a yellow wood,
And sorry I could not travel both
And be one traveler, long I stood
And looked down one as far as I could
5   To where it bent in the undergrowth;

Then took the other, as just as fair,
And having perhaps the better claim,
Because it was grassy and wanted wear;
Though as for that, the passing there
10   Had worn them really about the same,

And both that morning equally lay
In leaves no step had <u>trodden</u> black.
Oh, I kept the first for another day!
Yet knowing how way leads on to way,
15   I doubted if I should ever come back.

I shall be telling this with a sigh
Somewhere ages and ages hence:
Two roads diverged in a wood, and I—
I took the one less traveled by,
20   And that has made all the difference. ∎

What decision does the speaker face at the beginning of the poem?

In what ways do the paths differ? How different are they?

WORDS FOR EVERYDAY USE:

di • verge (dī vʉrj´) *vi.,* move in different directions
trod • den (träd´'n) *pp. of tread, vt.,* press or beat with the feet

Responding to the Selection

Describe a situation in life in which someone makes an important decision without enough information about the consequences of that decision. How does that situation parallel the situation described in the poem? Discuss this question with your classmates.

Reviewing the Selection

RECALLING

1. What is the speaker of the poem sorry about in line 2?

2. Where does the speaker look in lines 4 and 5?

3. How does the speaker describe the "other road" in line 6? What slight difference between the two roads is mentioned in lines 7 and 8? What phrase in line 10 shows that the differences between the two roads doesn't seem enormous?

4. Why does the speaker doubt that he would ever come back to take the first road?

INTERPRETING

5. If the road that the speaker is on at the beginning of the poem represents a path through life, what does the fork in the road represent? What does the speaker wish that he could do at the beginning of the poem?

6. What prevents the speaker from seeing clearly what lies ahead on the two roads? What is the speaker saying about people's ability to see into the future and predict the consequences of their decisions?

7. Why does the speaker choose one of the roads over the other? Does the speaker have an overwhelming reason for choosing the one that he takes?

8. What happens as a result of making an important decision? What does one give up by choosing one path over another?

SYNTHESIZING

9. When people sigh, what are they feeling? Why does the speaker say that he will be telling about his decision "with a sigh"? Why might he be wondering about "The Road Not Taken"?

10. What are the speaker's feelings about the choice that he made? What consequences did that choice have? Was the choice made impulsively or for really good reasons? Explain your answer.

Understanding Literature (Questions for Discussion)

1. **Allegory.** An **allegory** is a work in which each element symbolizes, or represents, something else. What do the following parts of this poem stand for?

   the road

   the fork in the road

   the undergrowth

   the grassiness of one of the roads

   the speaker's decision to take one of the roads

2. **Stanza and Rhyme Scheme.** A **stanza** is a recurring pattern of grouped lines in a poem. A **rhyme scheme** is a pattern of rhymes in a poem. Into how many stanzas is this poem divided? What is its rhyme scheme?

Responding in Writing

Personal Essay. Think about something that you would like to do in your life, something very important to you. Then think of an important decision that you will have to make related to that life goal. Write a brief essay in which you describe the goal, tell what important decision you must make related to that goal, and explore the factors, or considerations, that you will have to keep in mind when making that decision.

> **Prewriting Suggestion:** Before writing, read the Language Arts Survey, 4.3, "Strategies For Decision Making." Then, in your journal, write the decision that you want to write about. List under that decision several important factors, or considerations, that will influence the decision that you make.

PROJECT

Interview and Discussion. Interview three adults and ask each to describe to you two important decisions that they have made in their lives. Find out what each decision was, what choices the person had in each case, what factors influenced the person's decision, and what the consequences of that decision were. Then, using the information that you have gathered, join in a class discussion about decision making. Discuss the important decisions that people make in life and their reasons for making the decisions that they do. In your discussion, protect your interviewees' privacy by using different names.

UNIT REVIEW

Identity

VOCABULARY FROM THE SELECTIONS

adobe, 436
auxiliary, 415
conventional, 423
crave, 423
craven, 416
crevice, 428
derisive, 419
distraught, 416
diverge, 441
embed, 428
entice, 428
express, 406

formula, 404
grimace, 429
hurtling, 415
hygiene, 405
immolate, 424
inscrutable, 419
insinuatingly, 417
insolent, 417
laden, 428
longevity, 424
mesa, 435
missionary, 436

monitor, 404
mutter, 403
parishioner, 437
penetrate, 436
perverse, 436
recite, 406
shriveled, 434
tissue, 405
trodden, 441
vault, 417
whimper, 407

LITERARY TERMS

allegory, 443
antihero, 420
autobiography, 427
character trait, 425
conflict, 421
description, 408
epigraph, 431

fable, 425
free verse, 440
hero, 420
image, 408, 427, 431
paradox, 413
personification, 425
poetry, 408

rhyme scheme, 443
satire , 414
setting, 432
stanza, 443
stereotype, 421
symbol, 431,439
theme, 408, 439

SYNTHESIS: QUESTIONS FOR WRITING, RESEARCH, OR DISCUSSION

1. Describe each of the following characters from the unit. In each case, tell what makes the character unique or special: Geraldine Moore, Nikki-Rosa, Walter Mitty, the moth in "the lesson of the moth," and the speaker in "The Road Not Taken."

2. In "The Secret Life of Walter Mitty," "How to Eat a Guava," and "The Man to Send Rain Clouds," the main characters struggle to maintain their identities. Against what does each character struggle? What form does each character's struggle take?

LANGUAGE LAB   PROOFREADING FOR COMMA ERRORS

Commas separate or set off certain elements in a sentence. A comma should be used after a mild exclamation such as *yes, no, oh,* or *well*; after an introductory participial phrase; after two or more introductory prepositional phrases; and after an introductory adverb clause. A comma is also used to set off interrupters such as parenthetical expressions or words used in direct address. Use a comma to separate items in a series unless all items are joined by *and, or,* or *nor.* Two or more adjectives preceding a noun are usually separated by commas. Use commas before *and, but, for, nor, or, so,* and *yet* when they join independent clauses. The comma may be omitted before *and, but, nor,* or *or* if the clauses are very short and the resulting sentence is still clear in meaning. Use commas before and after nonrestrictive phrases and clauses and before and after most appositives and appositive phrases.

LANGUAGE ARTS SURVEY

For additional help, see the Language Arts Survey, 2.94–2.96.

COMMA USAGE

MILD EXCLAMATION:	Well, it appears that Archy the cockroach has written another poem.
PARTICIPIAL PHRASE:	Jumping from key to key, the clever cockroach typed and left many poems for his friend Don Marquis.
TWO PREPOSITIONAL PHRASES:	In his columns for the *New York Sun,* Marquis delighted his readers with stories of Archy and Mehitabel's exploits.
ADVERB CLAUSE:	When Marquis saw Archy's first poem, what did he think?
PARENTHETICAL EXPRESSION:	Archy is, I believe, the only character to whom the stories are attributed.
DIRECT ADDRESS:	Don, what's the topic of this evening's column?
WORDS IN A SERIES:	Marquis, Archy, and Mehitabel became quite famous in New York.
PHRASES IN A SERIES:	The Spanish moved to the Southwest, established missions, and built Catholic churches.
CLAUSES IN A SERIES:	Spanish missionaries believed that the established religions were wrong, that they should convert the native peoples, and that their actions were just.
TWO OR MORE ADJECTIVES:	Many native peoples of the Southwest maintained their ancient, sacred beliefs.
LONG INDEPENDENT CLAUSE:	Leslie Marmon Silko lived in a remote Inuit village in Alaska during the 1970s, and she wrote a short story based on Inuit myth.
SHORT INDEPENDENT CLAUSE:	Silko writes short stories and she also writes poems.
NONRESTRICTIVE PHRASE OR CLAUSE:	Silko, who grew up on the Laguna Pueblo Reservation, is considered one of the most important Native American writers today.
RESTRICTIVE PHRASE OR CLAUSE:	The story that Silko based on Inuit myth is called "Storyteller."
APPOSITIVE OR APPOSITIVE PHRASES:	*Ceremony,* Silko's first novel, tells of Tayo, a World War II veteran.

EXERCISE A   Avoiding Errors in Comma Usage

Rewrite the following sentences, adding commas as necessary.

1. Before she found her voice as a writer Toni Cade Bambara studied acting and mime in Europe.

2. James Thurber a staff writer and editor for the *New Yorker* became a literary legend.

3. Puerto Rico which had been an American colony since 1898 received commonwealth status in 1952.

4. Nikki Giovanni graduated from Fisk University moved on to the University of Pennsylvania and continued her studies at the Columbia School of Fine Arts.

5. Of the two roads in the wood Frost's speaker takes the one less traveled.

6. Giovanni's early poetry is notable for its determined revolutionary view of African-American issues.

7. My that Walter Mitty has quite an imagination!

8. May I if you don't mind borrow your copy of *When I Was Puerto Rican?*

9. When his father died Robert Frost moved from the West Coast to New England.

10. Thurber wrote stories and he drew cartoons.

EXERCISE B   Proofreading for Comma Usage

Rewrite the following paragraph, adding commas as necessary.

[1] At the time of the Spaniards' arrival the peoples of the Southwest lived in an agricultural society that had a long tradition of religious ceremony. [2] These peoples who possessed deep, ancient religious beliefs, were not easily shaken by the appearance of a new religion. [3] True some Pueblo peoples adopted Catholic ritual into their traditional ceremonies. [4] However when they realized that the people would not forsake some of their traditional beliefs some Spanish priests adopted native American traditions into their Roman Catholic ceremonies. [5] Many Native Americans in the Southwest held fast to their traditional beliefs and their religious traditions are alive today.

LANGUAGE ARTS WORKSHOP

USING REFERENCE WORKS

Reference works contain large amounts of information organized for easy access. The following chart lists some common reference works available in most libraries.

LANGUAGE ARTS SURVEY

For additional help, see the Language Arts Survey, 4.23.

REFERENCE WORKS

Almanacs and Yearbooks. An **almanac** contains a wide variety of statistics and lists with an index to help readers locate information. A **yearbook** summarizes major events that occurred in a given year.

Atlases. An **atlas** is basically a collection of maps. Some atlases focus on physical features of the land, political boundaries, roads and highways, or historical developments. A key feature of many atlases is the **gazetteer,** which is an index listing every item located on the maps.

Encyclopedias. An encyclopedia contains knowledge on a broad range of topics. Articles are arranged alphabetically, and all the topics may be listed and cross-referenced in an index.

Indexes. An index is an alphabetical directory to published information and ideas. *The Reader's Guide to Periodic Literature* is a comprehensive index to weekly, monthly, and quarterly publications.

Periodicals. Magazines, daily newspapers, specialized newspapers, trade journals, and professional journals are examples of periodicals, which are published at regular intervals.

Other Reference Works. A library's reference section has collections of quotations, biographies, book reviews, and state and local laws, as well as telephone directories and many other materials.

EXERCISE

For each research need described below, list two reference works that would provide information.

1. Mario is researching the history of the Picts in ancient Britain. He needs to find out when they lived, what areas they occupied, where their battles occurred, and how they interacted with the Romans.

2. Paula needs to find statistics about hazardous waste sites in the Midwest. She also wants to know which sites are currently the focus of controversy.

3. Len is writing a letter to the editor about the impact of a particular political event that occurred last year. He needs to find information that will support his argument.

4. Brenda is writing a paper about Robert Frost. In addition to basic information, such as his place of birth and a list of literary achievements, Brenda wants to find more detailed information about his life and his work that will make her report more comprehensive and interesting.

Snap the Whip. Winslow Homer. The Butler Institute of American Art, Youngstown, Ohio

A friend may well be reckoned the masterpiece of Nature.

—Ralph Waldo Emerson

AUTOBIOGRAPHY

"A Christmas Memory"
by Truman Capote

ABOUT THE AUTHOR

Truman Capote (1924–1984), originally named Truman Streckfus Persons, was born in New Orleans. He took the name Capote after he was adopted by his stepfather. During his early years, he was sent to live with elderly cousins in the small town of Monroeville, Alabama. He had two close friends during this period, Harper Lee, who would later write *To Kill a Mockingbird,* and Sook Faulk, one of his elderly cousins.

After a childhood of feeling neglected and misunderstood, Capote sought acceptance and fame through his writing. His award-winning story "Miriam" caught the attention of a publisher who offered to publish whatever he wished to write. This led to the publication of Capote's first novel, *Other Voices, Other Rooms.* Capote would publish many other works, including *Breakfast at Tiffany's,* which was made into a movie; *In Cold Blood,* a nonfiction novel that Lee helped him to research based on a murder in a small Kansas town; *Music for Chameleons,* a collection of stories and portraits; and *Answered Prayers,* an unfinished work based on the secrets of the large circle of rich and famous friends he had cultivated in his search for fame. Both *In Cold Blood* and *Music for Chameleons* mingle fact and fiction, a technique for which Capote is well known.

ABOUT THE SELECTION

Background: Genre. An **autobiography** is the story of a person's life written by that person. "A Christmas Memory" is based on the time Capote spent with his elderly cousins, and especially on his friendship with Sook Faulk. She was a very shy woman, who possessed a childlike imagination and seldom ventured far from home. Faulk taught Capote to fly a kite, and he helped her gather pecans in the fall. The pecans were for the fruitcakes she made annually to be given to people whom she admired, like the tin peddler and President Franklin Roosevelt. After his parents' divorce, Capote went to live with his mother and later attended military school, where he was in 1938 when he learned about Ms. Faulk's death. Capote later wrote a television script based on this story and used it as part of a trilogy of stories in a film script.

"A Christmas Memory"

TRUMAN CAPOTE

Imagine a morning in late November. A coming of winter morning more than twenty years ago. Consider the kitchen of a spreading old house in a country town. A great black stove is its main feature; but there is also a big round table and a fireplace with two rocking chairs placed in front of it. Just today the fireplace <u>commenced</u> its seasonal roar.

A woman with shorn white hair is standing at the kitchen window. She is wearing tennis shoes and a shapeless gray sweater over a summery calico dress. She is small and <u>sprightly</u>, like a bantam hen; but, due to a long youthful illness, her shoulders are pitifully hunched. Her face is remarkable—not unlike Lincoln's,[1] craggy like that, and tinted by sun and wind; but it is delicate too, finely boned, and her eyes are sherry-colored and timid. "Oh my," she exclaims, her breath smoking the windowpane, "it's fruitcake weather!"

The person to whom she is speaking is myself. I am seven; she is sixty-something. We are cousins, very distant ones, and we have lived together—well, as long as I can remember. Other people inhabit the house, relatives; and though they have power over us, and frequently make us cry, we are not, on the whole, too much aware of them. We are each other's best friend. She calls me Buddy, in memory of a boy who was formerly her best friend. The other Buddy died in the 1880's, when she was still a child. She is still a child.

"I knew it before I got out of bed," she says, turning away from the window with a purposeful excitement in her eyes. "The courthouse bell sounded so cold and clear. And there were no birds singing; they've gone to warmer country, yes indeed. Oh, Buddy, stop stuffing biscuit and fetch our buggy.

How do the other people in the house relate to the speaker and his cousin?

What is the speaker's cousin like? How would you describe her attitude toward life?

---

1. **Lincoln's.** Of Abraham Lincoln (1809–1865), sixteenth president of the United States

WORDS FOR EVERYDAY USE:

com • mence (kə mens´) *vt.*, begin

spright • ly (sprīt lē) *adj.*, full of energy

Help me find my hat. We've thirty cakes to bake."

It's always the same: a morning arrives in November, and my friend, as though officially <u>inaugurating</u> the Christmas time of year that <u>exhilarates</u> her imagination and fuels the blaze of her heart, announces: "It's fruitcake weather! Fetch our buggy. Help me find my hat."

The hat is found, a straw cartwheel corsaged with velvet roses out-of-doors has faded: it once belonged to a more fashionable relative. Together, we guide our buggy, a <u>dilapidated</u> baby carriage, out to the garden and into a grove of pecan trees. The buggy is mine; that is, it was bought for me when I was born. It is made of wicker, rather unraveled, and the wheels wobble like a drunkard's legs. But it is a faithful object; springtimes, we take it to the woods and fill it with flowers, herbs, wild fern for our porch pots; in the summer, we pile it with picnic <u>paraphernalia</u> and sugar-cane fishing poles and roll it down to the edge of a creek; it has its winter uses, too: as a truck for hauling firewood from the yard to the kitchen, as a warm bed for Queenie, our tough little orange and white rat terrier who has survived distemper[2] and two rattlesnake bites. Queenie is trotting beside it now.

Three hours later we are back in the kitchen <u>hulling</u> a heaping buggyload of windfall pecans. Our backs hurt from gathering them: how hard they were to find (the main crop having been shaken off the trees and sold by the orchard's owners, who are not us) among the concealing leaves, the frosted, deceiving grass. Caarackle! A cheery crunch, scraps of miniature thunder sound as the shells collapse and the golden mound of sweet oily ivory meat mounts in the milk-glass bowl. Queenie begs to taste, and now and again my friend sneaks her a mite, though insisting we deprive ourselves. "We mustn't, Buddy. If we start, we won't stop. And there's scarcely enough as there is. For thirty cakes." The kitchen is growing dark. Dusk turns the window into a mirror: our reflections mingle with the rising moon as we work by the fireside in the firelight. At last, when the moon is quite high, we toss the final hull into the fire and, with joined sighs, watch it catch flame. The buggy is empty, the bowl is brimful.

We eat our supper (cold biscuits, bacon, blackberry jam) and discuss tomorrow. Tomorrow the kind of work I like best begins: buying. Cherries and citron, ginger and vanilla and canned Hawaiian pineapple, rinds and raisins and walnuts and whiskey and oh, so much flour, butter, so many eggs, spices, flavorings: why, we'll need a pony to pull the buggy home.

But before these purchases can be made, there is the question of money. Neither of us has any. Except for skin-flint sums persons in the house occasionally provide (a dime is considered very big money); or what we earn

<hr/>

2. **distemper.** Infectious viral disease of young dogs

<table>
<tr><td rowspan="3">WORDS FOR EVERYDAY USE:</td><td>in • au • gu • rate (in ô´gyoo rāt) vt., celebrate the formal beginning of</td><td>broken down and shabby</td></tr>
<tr><td>ex • hil • a • rate (eg zil´ə rāt´) vt., make cheerful and lively</td><td>par • a • pher • na • lia (par´ə fər nāl´yə) n.pl., any collection of articles</td></tr>
<tr><td>di • lap • i • dat • ed (də lap´ə dāt id) adj.,</td><td>hull (hul) vt., take the shell off a seed, fruit, or nut</td></tr>
</table>

What do the speaker and his friend do together throughout the year?

What do the speaker and his friend lack?

ourselves from various activities: holding rummage sales, selling buckets of hand-picked blackberries, jars of homemade jam and apple jelly and peach preserves, rounding up flowers for funerals and weddings. Once we won seventy-ninth prize, five dollars, in a national football contest. Not that we know a fool thing about football. It's just that we enter any contest we hear about: at the moment our hopes are centered on the fifty-thousand-dollar Grand Prize being offered to name a new brand of coffee (we suggested "A.M."; and, after some hesitation, for my friend thought it perhaps <u>sacrilegious</u>, the slogan "A.M.! Amen!"). To tell the truth, our only *really* profitable <u>enterprise</u> was the Fun and Freak Museum we conducted in a back-yard woodshed two summers ago. The Fun was a stereopticon[3] with slide views of Washington and New York lent us by a relative who had been to those places (she was furious when she discovered why we'd borrowed it); the Freak was a three-legged biddy chicken hatched by one of our own hens. Everybody hereabouts wanted to see that biddy: we charged grownups a nickel, kids two cents. And took in a good twenty dollars before the museum shut down due to the decease of the main attraction.

But one way and another we do each year <u>accumulate</u> Christmas savings, a Fruitcake Fund. These moneys we keep hidden in an ancient bead purse under a loose board under the floor under a chamber pot[4] under my friend's bed. The purse is seldom removed from this safe location except to make a deposit, or, as happens every Saturday, a withdrawal; for on Saturdays I am allowed ten cents to go to the picture show. My friend has never been to a picture show, nor does she intend to: "I'd rather hear you tell the story, Buddy. That way I can imagine it more. Besides, a person my age shouldn't <u>squander</u> their eyes. When the Lord comes, let me see Him clear." In addition to never having seen a movie, she has never: eaten in a restaurant, traveled more than five miles from home, received or sent a telegram, read anything except funny papers and the Bible, worn cosmetics, cursed, wished someone harm, told a lie on purpose, let a hungry dog go hungry. Here are a few things she has done, does do: killed with a hoe the biggest rattlesnake ever seen in this county (sixteen rattles), dip snuff[5] (secretly), tame hummingbirds (just try it) till they balance on her finger, tell ghost stories (we both believe in ghosts) so tingling they chill you in July, talk to herself, take walks in the rain, grow the prettiest japonicas[6] in town, know the recipe for every sort of old-time Indian cure, including a magical wart-remover.

Now, with supper finished, we retire to the room in a faraway part of the house where my friend sleeps in a scrap-quilt-covered iron bed painted

What surprises the narrator?

What was their most successful money-making venture?

---

3. **stereopticon.** Slide projector designed to allow one slide to fade out while the next is fading in

4. **chamber pot.** Porcelain bowl kept under the bed, used as a toilet during the night and then emptied in the morning

5. **dip snuff.** Put powdered tobacco between the gums and the lips

6. **japonicas.** Trees, shrubs, or plants that are associated with the Far East

WORDS FOR EVERYDAY USE:

sac • ri • le • gious (sak´rə li´jəs) *adj.*, in violation of something sacred

en • ter • prise (ent´ər prīz´) *n.*, project

ac • cu • mu • late (ə kyo͞om´yo͞o lāt´) *vt.*, gather over time

squan • der (skwän dər´) *vt.*, spend extravagantly; waste

rose pink, her favorite color. Silently, wallowing in the pleasures of <u>conspiracy</u>, we take the bead purse from its secret place and spill its contents on the scrap quilt. Dollar bills, tightly rolled and green as May buds. Somber fifty-cent pieces, heavy enough to weight a dead man's eyes. Lovely dimes, the liveliest coin, the one that really jingles. Nickels and quarters, worn smooth as creek pebbles. But mostly a hateful heap of bitter-odored pennies. Last summer others in the house contracted to pay us a penny for every twenty-five flies we killed. Oh, the <u>carnage</u> of August: the flies that flew to heaven! Yet it was not work in which we took pride. And, as we sit counting pennies, it is as though we were back <u>tabulating</u> dead flies. Neither of us has a head for figures; we count slowly, lose track, start again. According to her calculations, we have $12.73. According to mine, exactly $13. "I do hope you're wrong, Buddy. We can't mess around with thirteen. The cakes will fall. Or put somebody in the cemetery. Why, I wouldn't dream of getting out of bed on the thirteenth." This is true: she always spends thirteenths in bed. So, to be on the safe side, we subtract a penny and toss it out the window.

Of the ingredients that go into our fruitcakes, whiskey is the most expensive, as well as the hardest to obtain: State laws forbid its sale. But everybody knows you can buy a bottle from Mr. Haha Jones. And the next day, having completed our more <u>prosaic</u>

shopping, we set out for Mr. Haha's business address, a "sinful" (to quote public opinion) fish-fry and dancing café down by the river. We've been there before, and on the same errand; but in previous years our dealings have been with Haha's wife, an iodine-dark Indian woman with brassy peroxided hair and a dead-tired <u>disposition</u>. Actually, we've never laid eyes on her husband, though we've heard that he's an Indian too. A giant with razor scars across his cheeks. They call him Haha because he's so gloomy, a man who never laughs. As we approach his café (a large log cabin <u>festooned</u> inside and out with chains of garish-gay naked light bulbs and standing by the river's muddy edge under the shade of river trees where moss drifts through the branches like gray mist) our steps slow down. Even Queenie stops prancing and sticks close by. People have been murdered in Haha's café. Cut to pieces. Hit on the head. There's a case coming up in court next month. Naturally these goings-on happen at night when the colored lights cast crazy patterns and the victrola[7] wails. In the daytime Haha's is shabby and deserted. I knock at the door, Queenie barks, my friend calls: "Mrs. Haha, ma'am? Anyone to home?"

Footsteps. The door opens. Our hearts overturn. It's Mr. Haha Jones himself! And he *is* a giant; he *does* have scars; he *doesn't* smile. No, he <u>glowers</u> at us through Satan-tilted eyes and

---

7. **victrola.** Record player

What bad memory arises from the pennies?

Why are the speaker, his friend, and even the dog afraid of this place?

WORDS FOR EVERYDAY USE:	con • spir • a • cy (kən spir′ə sē) *n.*, a secret plot	dis • po • si • tion (dis′pə zish′ ən) *n.*, one's nature or temperament
	car • nage (kär′nij) *n.*, slaughter	fes • toon (fes tōōn′) *vt.*, adorn with garlands
	tab • u • late (tab′yōō lāt) *vt.*, arrange and count	glow • er (glou′ər) *vt.*, stare with anger
	pro • sa • ic (prō zā′ik) *adj.*, dull and ordinary	

Baby at Play. Thomas Eakins, 1877. John Hay Whitney Collection. ©1995 Board of Trustees, National Gallery of Art, Washington, DC

demands to know: "What you want with Haha?"

For a moment we are too paralyzed to tell. Presently my friend half-finds her voice, a whispery voice at best: "If you please, Mr. Haha, we'd like a quart of your finest whiskey."

His eyes tilt more. Would you believe it? Haha is smiling! Laughing, too. "Which one of you is a drinkin' man?"

"It's for making fruitcakes, Mr. Haha. Cooking."

This sobers him. He frowns. "That's no way to waste good whiskey." Nevertheless, he retreats into the shadowed café and seconds later appears carrying a bottle of daisy-yellow unlabeled liquor. He demonstrates its sparkle in the sunlight and says: "Two dollars."

We pay him with nickels and dimes and pennies. Suddenly, as he jangles the coins in his hand like a fistful of dice, his face softens. "Tell you what," he proposes, pouring the money back into our bead purse, "just send me one of them fruitcakes instead."

"Well," my friend remarks on our way home, "there's a lovely man. We'll put an extra cup of raisins in *his* cake."

The black stove, stoked with coal and firewood, glows like a lighted pumpkin. Eggbeaters whirl, spoons spin round in bowls of butter and

What makes Haha, the gloomy giant, laugh?

What type of person does Haha turn out to be? Why might he be so generous?

sugar, vanilla sweetens the air, ginger spices it; melting, nose-tingling odors <u>saturate</u> the kitchen, <u>suffuse</u> the house, drift out to the world on puffs of chimney smoke. In four days our work is done. Thirty-one cakes, dampened with whiskey, bask on window sills and shelves.

Who are they for?

Friends. Not necessarily neighbor friends: indeed, the larger share is intended for persons we've met maybe once, perhaps not at all. People who've struck our fancy. Like President Roosevelt.[8] Like the Reverend and Mrs. J. C. Lucey, Baptist missionaries to Borneo[9] who lectured here last winter. Or the little knife grinder who comes through town twice a year. Or Abner Packer, the driver of the six o'clock bus from Mobile, who exchanges waves with us every day as he passes in a dust-cloud whoosh. Or the young Wistons, a California couple whose car one afternoon broke down outside the house and who spent a pleasant hour chatting with us on the porch (young Mr. Wiston snapped our picture, the only one we've ever had taken). Is it because my friend is shy with everyone except strangers that these strangers, and merest acquaintances, seem to us our truest friends? I think yes. Also, the scrapbooks we keep of thank-you's on White House stationery, time-to-time communications from California and Borneo, the knife grinder's penny post cards, make us feel connected to eventful worlds beyond the kitchen with its view of a sky that stops.

Now a nude December fig branch grates against the window. The kitchen is empty, the cakes are gone; yesterday we carted the last of them to the post office, where the cost of stamps turned our purse inside out. We're broke. That rather depresses me, but my friend insists on celebrating—with two inches of whiskey left in Haha's bottle. Queenie has a spoonful in a bowl of coffee (she likes her coffee chicory-flavored and strong). The rest we divide between a pair of jelly glasses. We're both quite awed at the prospect of drinking straight whiskey; the taste of it brings screwed-up expressions and sour shudders. But by and by we begin to sing, the two of us singing different songs <u>simultaneously</u>. I don't know the words to mine, just: *Come on along, come on along, to the dark-town strutters' ball.* But I can dance: that's what I mean to be, a tap-dancer in the movies. My dancing shadow rollicks on the walls; our voices rock the chinaware; we giggle: as if unseen hands were tickling us. Queenie rolls on her back, her paws plow the air, something like a grin stretches her black lips. Inside myself, I feel warm and sparky as those crumbling logs, carefree as the wind in the chimney. My friend waltzes round the stove, the

---

8. **President Roosevelt.** Franklin Delano Roosevelt (1882–1945), the thirty-second president of the United States
9. **Baptist missionaries to Borneo.** Members of the Baptist Church who went to Borneo, a large island south of the Philippines, to teach the local people about Jesus

WORDS FOR EVERYDAY USE:

sat • u • rate (sach´ə rāt´) vt. cause to be thoroughly penetrated

suf • fuse (sə fyōōz´) vt., fill

si • mul • ta • ne • ous • ly (sī´məl tā´nē əs lē) adv., occurring at the same time

hem of her poor calico skirt pinched between her fingers as though it were a party dress: *Show me the way to go home*, she sings, her tennis shoes squeaking on the floor. *Show me the way to go home.*

Enter: two relatives. Very angry. <u>Potent</u> with eyes that scold, tongues that scald. Listen to what they have to say, the words tumbling together into a wrathful tune: "A child of seven! whiskey on his breath! are you out of your mind? feeding a child of seven! must be loony! road to ruination! remember Cousin Kate? Uncle Charlie? Uncle Charlie's brother-in-law? shame! scandal! humiliation! kneel, pray, beg the Lord!"

Queenie sneaks under the stove. My friend gazes at her shoes, her chin quivers, she lifts her skirt and blows her nose and runs to her room. Long after the town has gone to sleep and the house is silent except for the chimings of clocks and the sputter of fading fires, she is weeping into a pillow already as wet as a widow's handkerchief.

"Don't cry," I say, sitting at the bottom of her bed and shivering despite my flannel nightgown that smells of last winter's cough syrup, "don't cry," I beg, teasing her toes, tickling her feet, "you're too old for that."

"It's because," she hiccups, "I *am* too old. Old and funny."

"Not funny. Fun. More fun than anybody. Listen. If you don't stop crying you'll be so tired tomorrow we can't go cut a tree."

She straightens up. Queenie jumps on the bed (where Queenie is not allowed) to lick her cheeks. "I know where we'll find real pretty trees, Buddy. And holly, too. With berries big as your eyes. It's way off in the woods. Farther than we've ever been. Papa used to bring us Christmas trees from there: carry them on his shoulder. That's fifty years ago. Well, now: I can't wait for morning."

Morning. Frozen rime[10] lusters the grass; the sun, round as an orange and orange as hot-weather moons, balances on the horizon, <u>burnishes</u> the silvered winter woods. A wild turkey calls. A <u>renegade</u> hog grunts in the undergrowth. Soon, by the edge of knee-deep, rapid-running water, we have to abandon the buggy. Queenie wades the stream first, paddles across barking complaints at the swiftness of the current, the pneumonia-making coldness of it. We follow, holding our shoes and equipment (a hatchet, a burlap sack) above our heads. A mile more: of chastising thorns, burs and briers that catch at our clothes; of rusty pine needles brilliant with gaudy fungus and <u>molted</u> feathers. Here, there, a flash, a flutter, an ecstasy of shrillings remind us that not all the birds have flown south. Always, the path unwinds through lemony sun pools and pitch-black vine tunnels. Another creek to cross: a disturbed armada of speckled trout froths the water round us, and frogs the size of plates practice belly flops; beaver workmen are building a dam. On the

How do their relatives react to their celebration?

What makes the speaker's friend stop crying?

---

10. **rime.** Frost; tiny ice crystals formed on grass and leaves

WORDS FOR EVERYDAY USE:

po • tent (pōt´nt) *adj.,* powerful

bur • nish (bʉr´nish) *vt.,* polish

ren • e • gade (ren´ə gād´) *adj.,* of or like one

who abandons a group to go to the other side

molt • ed (mōlt´id) *part.,* shed

farther shore, Queenie shakes herself and trembles. My friend shivers, too: not with cold but enthusiasm. One of her hat's ragged roses sheds a petal as she lifts her head and inhales the pine-heavy air. "We're almost there; can you smell it, Buddy?" she says, as though we were approaching an ocean.

And, indeed, it is a kind of ocean. Scented acres of holiday trees, prickly-leafed holly. Red berries shiny as Chinese bells: black crows swoop upon them screaming. Having stuffed our burlap sacks with enough greenery and crimson to garland a dozen windows, we set about choosing a tree. "It should be," muses my friend, "twice as tall as a boy. So a boy can't steal the star." The one we pick is twice as tall as me. A brave handsome brute that survives thirty hatchet strokes before it <u>keels</u> with a creaking <u>rending</u> cry. Lugging it like a kill, we commence the long trek out. Every few yards we abandon the struggle, sit down and pant. But we have the strength of triumphant huntsmen; that and the tree's virile, icy perfume revive us, goad us on. Many compliments accompany our sunset return along the red clay road to town; but my friend is sly and <u>noncommittal</u> when passers-by praise the treasure perched in our buggy: what a fine tree and where did it come from? "Yonderways," she murmurs vaguely. Once a car stops and the rich mill owner's lazy wife leans out and whines: "Giveya two-bits cash for that ol tree." Ordinarily my friend is afraid of saying no; but on this occasion she promptly shakes her head: "We wouldn't take a dollar." The mill owner's wife persists. "A dollar, my foot! Fifty cents. That's my last offer. Goodness, woman, you can get another one." In answer, my friend gently reflects: "I doubt it. There's never two of anything."

Home: Queenie slumps by the fire and sleeps till tomorrow, snoring loud as a human.

A trunk in the attic contains: a shoe-box of ermine tails[11] (off the opera cape of a curious lady who once rented a room in the house), coils of frazzled tinsel gone gold with age, one silver star, a brief rope of dilapidated, undoubtedly dangerous candy-like light bulbs. Excellent decorations, as far as they go, which isn't far enough: my friend wants our tree to blaze "like a Baptist window," droop with weighty snows of ornament. But we can't afford the made-in-Japan splendors at the five-and-dime. So we do what we've always done: sit for days at the kitchen table with scissors and crayons and stacks of colored paper. I make sketches and my friend cuts them out: lots of cats, fish too (because they're easy to draw), some apples, some watermelons, a few winged angels devised from saved-up sheets of Hershey-bar tin foil. We use safety pins to attach these creations to the tree; as a final touch, we sprinkle the branches with shredded cotton (picked in August for this purpose). My friend, <u>surveying</u> the

---

11. **ermine tails.** Tails of small weasels native to northern Europe; the animal is brown in summer and white with black tips in winter.

WORDS FOR EVERYDAY USE:

keel (kēl) vt., turn over or upside down
rend • ing (rend´iŋ) adj., showing grief
non • com • mit •tal (nän kə mit ʼl) adj., not committing to one point of view
sur • vey (sər vā´) vt., examine

effect, clasps her hands together. "Now honest, Buddy. Doesn't it look good enough to eat?" Queenie tries to eat an angel.

After weaving and ribboning holly wreaths for all the front windows, our next project is the fashioning of family gifts. Tie-dye scarves for the ladies, for the men a home-brewed lemon and licorice and aspirin syrup to be taken "at the first Symptoms of a Cold and after Hunting." But when it comes time for making each other's gift, my friend and I separate to work secretly. I would like to buy her a pearl-handled knife, a radio, a whole pound of chocolate-covered cherries (we tasted some once, and she always swears: "I could live on them, Buddy, Lord yes I could—and that's not taking His name in vain"). Instead, I am building her a kite. She would like to give me a bicycle (she's said so on several million occasions: "If only I could, Buddy. It's bad enough in life to do without something *you* want; but confound it, what gets my goat is not being able to give somebody something you want *them* to have. Only one of these days I will, Buddy. Locate you a bike. Don't ask how. Steal it, maybe"). Instead, I'm fairly certain that she is building me a kite—the same as last year, and the year before: the year before that we exchanged slingshots. All of which is fine by me. For we are champion kite-fliers who study the wind like sailors; my friend, more accomplished than I, can get a kite aloft when there isn't enough breeze to carry clouds.

Christmas Eve afternoon we scrape together a nickel and go to the butcher's to buy Queenie's traditional gift, a good gnawable beef bone. The bone, wrapped in funny paper, is placed high in the tree near the silver star. Queenie knows it's there. She squats at the foot of the tree staring up in a trance of greed: when bedtime arrives she refuses to budge. Her excitement is equaled by my own. I kick the covers and turn my pillow as though it were a scorching summer's night. Somewhere a rooster crows: falsely, for the sun is still on the other side of the world.

"Buddy, are you awake?" It is my friend, calling from her room, which is next to mine; and an instant later she is sitting on my bed holding a candle. "Well, I can't sleep a hoot," she declares. "My mind's jumping like a jack rabbit. Buddy, do you think Mrs. Roosevelt will serve our cake at dinner?" We huddle in the bed, and she squeezes my hand I-love-you. "Seems like your hand used to be so much smaller. I guess I hate to see you grow up. When you're grown up, will we still be friends?" I say always. "But I feel so bad, Buddy. I wanted so bad to give you a bike. I tried to sell my cameo[12] Papa gave me. Buddy"—she hesitates, as though embarrassed—"I made you another kite." Then I confess that I made her one, too; and we laugh. The candle burns too short to hold. Out it goes, exposing the starlight, the stars spinning at the window like a visible caroling that slowly, slowly daybreak silences. Possibly we doze; but the beginnings of dawn splash us like cold water: we're up, wide-eyed and wandering while we wait for others to waken. Quite deliberately my friend drops a kettle on the kitchen floor. I tap-dance in front of

_____

12. **cameo.** Carved gem or shell, often a head in profile against a background of contrasting color

What is changing in their friendship?

What is worse than doing without something that you want?

closed doors. One by one the household <u>emerges</u>, looking as though they'd like to kill us both; but it's Christmas, so they can't. First, a gorgeous breakfast: just everything you can imagine—from flapjacks and fried squirrel to hominy grits and honey-in-the-comb. Which puts everyone in a good humor except my friend and me. Frankly, we're so impatient to get at the presents we can't eat a mouthful.

Well, I'm disappointed. Who wouldn't be? With socks, a Sunday school shirt, some handkerchiefs, a hand-me-down sweater and a year's subscription to a religious magazine for children. *The Little Shepherd*. It makes me boil. It really does.

My friend has a better haul. A sack of Satsumas,[13] that's her best present. She is proudest, however, of a white wool shawl knitted by her married sister. But she *says* her favorite gift is the kite I built her. And it *is* very beautiful; though not as beautiful as the one she made me, which is blue and scattered with gold and green Good Conduct stars; moreover, my name is painted on it, "Buddy."

"Buddy, the wind is blowing."

The wind is blowing, and nothing will do till we've run to a pasture below the house where Queenie has scooted to bury her bone (and where, a winter hence, Queenie will be buried, too). There, plunging through the healthy waist-high grass, we unreel our kites, feel them twitching at the string like sky fish as they swim into the wind. Satisfied, sun-warmed, we sprawl in the grass and peel Satsumas and watch our kites cavort. Soon I forget the socks and hand-me-down sweater. I'm as happy as if we'd already won the fifty-thousand-dollar Grand Prize in that coffee-naming contest.

"My, how foolish I am!" my friend cries, suddenly alert, like a woman remembering too late she has biscuits in the oven. "You know what I've always thought?" she asks in a tone of discovery, and not smiling at me but a point beyond. "I've always thought a body would have to be sick and dying before they saw the Lord. And I imagined that when He came it would be like looking at the Baptist window: pretty as colored glass with the sun pouring through, such a shine you don't know it's getting dark. And it's been a comfort: to think of that shine taking away all the spooky feeling. But I'll wager it never happens. I'll wager at the very end a body realizes the Lord has already shown Himself. That things as they are"—her hand circles in a gesture that gathers clouds and kites and grass and Queenie pawing earth over her bone—"just what they've always seen, was seeing Him. As for me, I could leave the world with today in my eyes."

This is our last Christmas together.

Life separates us. Those who Know Best decide that I belong in a military school. And so follows a miserable

---

13. **Satsumas.** Small loose-skinned oranges from Florida and Alabama

What does the narrator's friend realize? Why would she be content to die today? What does this passage reveal about the nature of happiness?

WORDS FOR EVERYDAY USE: e • merge (ē mʉrj´) *vi.*, come forth into view

<u>succession</u> of bugle-blowing prisons, grim reveille-ridden[14] summer camps. I have a new home too. But it doesn't count. Home is where my friend is, and there I never go.

And there she remains, puttering around the kitchen. Alone with Queenie. Then alone. ("Buddy dear," she writes in her wild hard-to-read script, "yesterday Jim Macy's horse kicked Queenie bad. Be thankful she didn't feel much. I wrapped her in a Fine Linen sheet and rode her in the buggy down to Simpson's pasture where she can be with all her Bones . . ."). For a few Novembers she continues to bake her fruitcakes single-handed; not as many, but some: and, of course, she always sends me "the best of the batch." Also, in every letter she encloses a dime wadded in toilet paper: "See a picture show and write me the story." But gradually in her letters she tends to confuse me with her other friend, the Buddy who died in the 1880s; more and more thirteenths are not the only days she stays in bed: a morning arrives in November, a leafless birdless coming of winter morning, when she cannot rouse herself to exclaim: "Oh my, it's fruitcake weather!"

And when that happens, I know it. A message saying so merely <u>confirms</u> a piece of news some secret vein had already received, severing from me an irreplaceable part of myself, letting it loose like a kite on a broken string. That is why, walking across a school campus on this particular December morning, I keep searching the sky. As if I expected to see, rather like hearts, a lost pair of kites hurrying toward heaven. ■

Where is home?

What happens to Buddy's friend?

---

14. **reveille-ridden.** The narrator means that "Reveille," a trumpet tune used to awaken soldiers, was played often there.

Responding to the Selection

What do you think of the relationship between Buddy and his friend? Have you ever had a friendship that transcended a difference in ages, cultures, or beliefs? What makes friendship able to cross conventional barriers?

WORDS FOR EVERYDAY USE:

suc • ces • sion (sək sesh´ən) *n.,* number of things coming one after another

con • firm (kən fʉrm´) *vt.,* establish as true

Reviewing the Selection

1. Describe the two characters introduced at the beginning of the story. What type of weather opens the scene? For whom do they make their fruitcakes?

2. How do Buddy and his friend make the money that they need to buy the ingredients for fruitcake? How much money do they have? Why do they get rid of one penny?

3. Why do Buddy and his friend fear Haha's dancing café? How did Haha get his name?

4. What do Buddy and his friend give each other as gifts? How do they wake up the rest of the household on Christmas? What makes this particular Christmas memorable?

5. Describe the relationship between Buddy and his friend. How do they choose the people to whom they give fruitcakes? What does this tell you about their relationships with other people?

6. What characteristics of Buddy and his friend are revealed by the way they make the money for fruitcakes?

7. Does Haha meet Buddy and his friend's expectations? What type of person is Haha? What techniques does Capote use to characterize Haha?

8. How do Buddy and his friend feel about the gifts that they made for each other? How do Buddy and his friend feel as they are flying their kites? What happens to the relationship between Buddy and his friend after their last Christmas together?

9. What is the difference between the words *childish* and *childlike*? Which better describes Buddy's friend? Use examples from the story to explain your answer.

10. Buddy's friend asks him, "When you're grown up will we still be friends?" Buddy answers that they will always be friends. What do you think would have happened if Buddy had not been sent away to school? What is it about their relationship that makes you think this?

Understanding Literature (Questions for Discussion)

Characterization. Characterization is the use of literary techniques to create a character. Examine the description of Buddy's friend in the second paragraph and the list of things that she has done and not done on page 453. What kind of person is revealed by these things? How do you feel about her? Consider how she interacts with Buddy, with Haha, and with the other people in the house. How does this information add to, or alter, your view of her?

Responding in Writing

1. **Friendship Recipe.** When Buddy and his friend make fruitcake, they need certain ingredients, such as flour, butter, sugar, and raisins. What "ingredients" make up a good friend? Write a recipe for friendship. You may choose to write about friendship in general or about a specific friend.

   > **Prewriting Suggestion:** Before you begin writing, freewrite about friendship. What qualities are important in a friend? How do you become friends with someone? What do you do to maintain a friendship? What do you like to do with a friend? If you are thinking about a specific friend, think about some of the memorable moments of your friendship, times when you had a lot of fun, or when you stuck together through a difficult situation.

2. **Autobiographical Sketch.** Choose one episode of your life to write about. You might write about a loss you have experienced, a lesson you have learned, or a challenge you have faced. Why was this event memorable? Describe what happened and how it affected you.

   > **Prewriting Suggestion:** Before you begin writing, think about the chronological events of the episode you wish to relate. Read the Language Arts Survey, 1.34, "Organizing Ideas," for helpful organizational suggestions.

PROJECT

Tradition Record. Think about a specific tradition that you share with family or friends. It may be a personal tradition or one celebrated by your school, town, or city. Create a record of this tradition. Describe who takes part, when it occurs, and what happens. Then explain why this tradition is important to you. Trace the history of the tradition and explain how it started. How has it changed? What is your role in this tradition and how do you feel about it? You may wish to interview others who have participated in this tradition to get another view of it. Using photographs, drawings, or memorabilia from celebrations of this tradition, present your tradition to the class.

PREREADING

from *To Kill a Mockingbird*
by Harper Lee

ABOUT THE AUTHOR

Harper Lee (1926–   ) was born and raised in Monroeville, Alabama. She attended the University of Alabama but left before she finished her law degree to pursue a writing career. While at the university, she wrote for several campus publications, acting on a passion for writing that began when she was seven years old. In the early 1950s she presented two essays and three short stories to a literary agent who suggested that she expand one of the stories. Acting on this suggestion, Lee produced *To Kill a Mockingbird,* her only novel. When she submitted the manuscript for publication, it was criticized for being merely a string of short stories. After extensive rewriting, the novel was published in 1960. The next year the book won the Pulitzer Prize for fiction, and the following year it was made into a movie.

ABOUT THE SELECTION

Background: Theme. *To Kill a Mockingbird* addresses the many facets of persecution and tolerance by describing circumstances surrounding the trial of Tom Robinson, an African-American man falsely accused of attacking a white woman. Atticus, father of the six-year-old narrator Scout, acts as Robinson's attorney. Many people in Maycomb, the town in which the novel is set, disapprove of Atticus's actions, but Atticus has the courage to defend a man he knows to be innocent.

The novel also depicts the persecution of the innocent Arthur (Boo) Radley, a mysterious recluse. Rumors about him abound, and he is feared by both children and adults. He is said to peep through windows in the middle of the night, to eat raw squirrels, and to kill flowers with his breath. This selection shows the beginnings of Scout, Jem, and Dill's fascination with Mr. Radley.

Background: Character. The character of Dill is closely based on Lee's childhood friend Truman Capote, who lived with relatives in Monroeville. Although Lee claims that the novel is not autobiographical, the physical description of Dill matches that of Capote as a boy. Another autobiographical element seems to exist in the description of the activities of Scout and Dill, who enjoyed playing together in a treehouse and acting out scenes from their favorite books and movies, as did Lee and Capote.

READER'S JOURNAL

Have you ever been fascinated by a person or place because it was unfamiliar? Write in your journal about a time when you became interested in something unfamiliar. Why did this person or place intrigue you? How did you satisfy your curiosity? Which is more exciting: the mystery of the unknown or the satisfaction of curiosity?

FROM

To Kill a Mockingbird

HARPER LEE

Maycomb was an old town, but it was a tired old town when I first knew it. In rainy weather the streets turned to red slop; grass grew on the sidewalks, the courthouse sagged in the square. Somehow, it was hotter then: a black dog suffered on a summer's day; bony mules hitched to Hoover carts flicked flies in the sweltering shade of the live oaks on the square. Men's stiff collars wilted by nine in the morning. Ladies bathed before noon, after their three-o'clock naps, and by nightfall were like soft teacakes with frostings of sweat and sweet talcum.

People moved slowly then. They ambled across the square, shuffled in and out of the stores around it, took their time about everything. A day was twenty-four hours long but seemed longer. There was no hurry, for there was nowhere to go, nothing to buy and no money to buy it with, nothing to see outside the boundaries of Maycomb County. But it was a time of vague optimism for some of the people: Maycomb County had recently been told that it had nothing to fear but fear itself.

We lived on the main residential street in town—Atticus, Jem and I, plus Calpurnia our cook. Jem and I found our father satisfactory: he played with us, read to us, and treated us with courteous <u>detachment</u>.

Calpurnia was something else again. She was all angles and bones; she was nearsighted; she squinted; her hand was wide as a bed slat and twice as hard. She was always ordering me out of the kitchen, asking me why I couldn't behave as well as Jem when she knew he was older, and calling me home when I wasn't ready to come. Our battles were <u>epic</u> and one-sided. Calpurnia always won, mainly because

What does Calpurnia look like? How does Scout feel about Calpurnia?

WORDS FOR EVERYDAY USE:	**de • tach • ment** (dē tach´mənt) *n.*, the state of being disinterested
	ep • ic (ep´ik) *adj.*, grand and strong

Who is in the collard patch?

Atticus always took her side. She had been with us ever since Jem was born, and I had felt her tyrannical presence as long as I could remember.

Our mother died when I was two, so I never felt her absence. She was a Graham from Montgomery; Atticus met her when he was first elected to the state legislature. He was middle-aged then, she was fifteen years his junior. Jem was the product of their first year of marriage; four years later I was born, and two years later our mother died from a sudden heart attack. They said it ran in her family. I did not miss her, but I think Jem did. He remembered her clearly, and sometimes in the middle of a game he would sigh at length, then go off and play by himself behind the car-house. When he was like that, I knew better than to bother him.

How did the death of their mother affect Scout and Jem?

When I was almost six and Jem was nearly ten, our summertime boundaries (within calling distance of Calpurnia) were Mrs. Henry Lafayette Dubose's house two doors to the north of us, and the Radley Place three doors to the south. We were never tempted to break them. The Radley Place was inhabited by an unknown <u>entity</u> the mere description of whom was enough to make us behave for days on end; Mrs. Dubose was plain hell.

What do Scout and Jem think about their southern boundary, the Radley Place?

That was the summer Dill came to us.

Early one morning as we were beginning our day's play in the back yard, Jem and I heard something next door in Miss Rachel Haverford's collard patch. We went to the wire fence to see if there was a puppy—Miss Rachel's rat terrier was expecting—instead we found someone sitting looking at us. Sitting down, he wasn't much higher than the collards. We stared at him until he spoke:

"Hey."

"Hey yourself," said Jem pleasantly.

"I'm Charles Baker Harris," he said. "I can read."

"So what?" I said.

"I just thought you'd like to know I can read. You got anything needs readin' I can do it. . . ."

"How old are you," asked Jem, "four-and-a-half?"

"Goin' on seven."

"Shoot no wonder, then," said Jem, jerking his thumb at me. "Scout yonder's been readin' ever since she was born, and she ain't even started to school yet. You look right puny for goin' on seven."

"I'm little but I'm old," he said.

Jem brushed his hair back to get a better look. "Why don't you come over, Charles Baker Harris?" he said. "Lord, what a name."

"'s not any funnier'n yours. Aunt Rachel says your name's Jeremy Atticus Finch."

Jem scowled. "I'm big enough to fit mine," he said. "Your name's longer'n you are. Bet it's a foot longer."

"Folks call me Dill," said Dill, struggling under the fence.

"Do better if you go over it instead of under it," I said. "Where'd you come from?"

WORDS FOR
EVERYDAY USE:

en • ti • ty (en´tə tē) *n.*, being

©1995 Rodney Busch

Dill was from Meridian, Mississippi, was spending the summer with his aunt, Miss Rachel, and would be spending every summer in Maycomb from now on. His family was from Maycomb County originally, his mother worked for a photographer in Meridian, had entered his picture in a Beautiful Child contest and won five dollars. She gave the money to Dill, who went to the picture show twenty times on it.

"Don't have any picture shows here, except Jesus ones in the courthouse sometimes," said Jem. "Ever see anything good?"

Dill had seen *Dracula*,[1] a <u>revelation</u> that moved Jem to eye him with the beginning of respect. "Tell it to us," he said.

Dill was a curiosity. He wore blue linen shorts that buttoned to his shirt, his hair was snow white and stuck to his head like duckfluff; he was a year my senior but I towered over him. As he told us the old tale his blue eyes would lighten and darken; his laugh was sudden and happy; he habitually

---

1. **Dracula.** Film based on a novel written by Bram Stoker about an Eastern European count who becomes a vampire

What is Dill's reaction to the Radley Place?

pulled at a cowlick in the center of his forehead.

When Dill reduced Dracula to dust, and Jem said the show sounded better than the book, I asked Dill where his father was: "You ain't said anything about him."

"I haven't got one."

"Is he dead?"

"No . . ."

"Then if he's not dead you've got one, haven't you?"

Dill blushed and Jem told me to hush, a sure sign that Dill had been studied and found acceptable. Thereafter the summer passed in routine contentment. Routine contentment was: improving our treehouse that rested between giant twin chinaberry trees in the back yard, fussing, running through our list of dramas based on the works of Oliver Optic, Victor Appleton, and Edgar Rice Burroughs.[2] In this matter we were lucky to have Dill. He played the character parts formerly thrust upon me—the ape in *Tarzan*, Mr. Crabtree in *The Rover Boys*, Mr. Damon in *Tom Swift*. Thus we came to know Dill as a pocket Merlin, whose head <u>teemed</u> with eccentric plans, strange longings, and quaint fancies.

Why does Scout enjoy playing with Dill?

But by the end of August our repertoire was <u>vapid</u> from countless reproductions, and it was then that Dill gave us the idea of making Boo Radley come out.

What rumors circulated about the "malevolent phantom"?

The Radley Place fascinated Dill. In spite of our warnings and explanations it drew him as the moon draws water, but drew him no nearer than the light-pole on the corner, a safe distance from the Radley gate. There he would stand, his arm around the fat pole, staring and wondering.

The Radley Place <u>jutted</u> into a sharp curve beyond our house. Walking south, one faced its porch; the sidewalk turned and ran beside the lot. The house was low, was once white with a deep front porch and green shutters, but had long ago darkened to the color of the slate-gray yard around it. Rainrotted shingles drooped over the eaves of the veranda; oak trees kept the sun away. The remains of a picket drunkenly guarded the front yard—a "swept" yard that was never swept—where johnson grass and rabbit-tobacco grew in abundance.

Inside the house lived a <u>malevolent</u> phantom. People said he existed, but Jem and I had never seen him. People said he went out at night when the moon was down, and peeped in windows. When people's azaleas froze in a cold snap, it was because he had breathed on them. Any stealthy small crimes committed in Maycomb were his work. ∎

---

2. **Oliver Optic . . . Burroughs.** Writers of adventure stories; for example, Burroughs wrote *Tarzan*

WORDS FOR EVERYDAY USE:

teem (tēm) *vi.*, be full

vap • id (vap´id) *adj.*, dull, uninteresting

jut (jut) *vi.*, stick out

ma • lev • o • lent (mə lev´ə lənt) *adj.*, wishing evil or harm to others

Responding to the Selection

Write about your summer vacations. Were your activities anything like those of Jem, Scout, and Dill when you were their ages? What do you think is the most interesting thing they did? Would you want to live in a town like Maycomb? Why, or why not?

Reviewing the Selection

RECALLING

1. What kind of town is Maycomb? How does the narrator remember the summers?

2. What do Jem and Scout think of their father? Who else looks after them? What are their summer boundaries?

3. Who is Dill? How old is he? What does he say he can do? How did his mother win money? What did Dill do with the money?

4. How does Scout define "routine contentment"? What new idea does Dill have?

INTERPRETING

5. How does the type of town they live in affect the activities and imaginations of Jem, Scout, and Dill?

6. Why aren't Scout and Jem tempted to break their summer boundaries?

7. What effect does Dill's knowledge of movies have on their play? How does Dill change the summer?

8. Why is Dill fascinated by the Radley house?

SYNTHESIZING

9. Why might Dill be the one who most wants Boo Radley to come out? How is he different from Jem and Scout?

10. Describe Boo Radley as he is perceived by the citizens of Maycomb. Why is Boo Radley blamed for all the "stealthy small crimes" that are committed in Maycomb?

Understanding Literature (Questions for Discussion)

Narrator. In *To Kill a Mockingbird*, the **narrator**, the person who tells the story, is Scout, a six-year-old girl. How does a child's view of the world differ from that of an adult? Why do you think Lee chose to have a child tell the story? How might the story differ if it were told by an adult?

Responding in Writing

1. **Ghost Story.** In Maycomb, Boo Radley is considered a "malevolent phantom" and is a source of fear for many. He was actually a kind but withdrawn person. It was a misunderstanding of his differences that caused him to be viewed as a demon. Think about a situation that frightened you because you didn't know enough about it. How did your imagination take over where your actual knowledge ended? Write a short story about a time when you were frightened and about why you were frightened.

   > **Prewriting Suggestion:** Choose something that has frightened you. Maybe it was a person who looked unusual to you, a shadow in your room at night, or an abandoned house that you believed was haunted. Freewrite about the frightening aspects of this thing, adding and exaggerating details until your subject is quite terrible. Use these details in your story to create a sense of growing fear and dread.

2. **Character Sketch.** Lee based the character of Dill on her childhood friend Truman Capote. Try to turn one of your friends into a character for a story. Imagine that you are meeting this person for the first time. Write about the encounter. Include a physical description of your friend and some realistic dialogue.

   > **Prewriting Suggestion:** Make a chart with the following headings: *appearance, clothes, attitudes, habits, favorite expressions,* and *favorite activities.* Fill in the chart with information about your friend. Then use these bits of information to make a portrait of your character.

PROJECT

Role Play. Think about why Jem, Scout, and Dill were so fascinated by Boo Radley and why they wanted to make him come out. Then, in groups of three, act out the story of Jem, Scout, and Dill trying to make Boo Radley come out. You may wish to discuss reasons for and reasons against getting Boo to come out or plans about how to accomplish this goal. Remember that these characters are ten, six, and seven years old respectively.

NOVELLA

The Snow Goose
by Paul Gallico

ABOUT THE AUTHOR

Paul Gallico (1897–1976) was born in New York City into a musical family. He was not musically inclined, however, and pursued sports and writing instead. He began his career as a sportswriter for a newspaper, manufacturing amusing stories by challenging leading sports figures in their own sports. This method did not win him athletic recognition, but it did earn him a wide readership. In 1936, he turned to fiction. *The Snow Goose,* published in 1940, was a tremendous success. He later turned it into a screenplay. Gallico continued writing for both children and adults. His success with a number of other stories and novels, including *The Poseidon Adventure* (1969), allowed him to travel and live in many countries including England, Mexico, France, and Monaco, where he died in 1976.

ABOUT THE SELECTION

Background: Theme. *The Snow Goose* tells the story of a man whose outward appearance has caused him to be ostracized, or shunned, by others. In this story, a young girl learns to look beyond appearances and to see that beauty lies not on the surface but within.

Background: History. The story is set in England during World War II. After the surrender of the Belgian army in 1940, the Allied American, English, and French troops retreated to Dunkirk, a town on the northern coast of France. With German troops on land and in the English Channel, a massive evacuation of Allied forces was necessary. Many kinds of vessels, including minesweepers, fishing vessels, yachts, and rowboats, carried soldiers from Dunkirk to England. It is in this evacuation that Rhayader, the main character, participates, as told in the second part of *The Snow Goose.*

The Snow Goose

PAUL GALLICO

PART ONE

What mood is created by this description of the setting?

The great marsh lies on the Essex[1] coast between the village of Chelmsbury and the ancient Saxon[2] oyster-fishing hamlet of Wickaeldroth. It is one of the last of the wild places of England, a low, far-reaching expanse of grass and reeds and half-submerged meadowlands ending in the great saltings and mud flats and tidal pools near the restless sea.

Tidal creeks and <u>estuaries</u> and the crooked, meandering arms of many little rivers whose mouths lap at the edge of the ocean cut through the <u>sodden</u> land that seems to rise and fall and breathe with the recurrence of the daily tides. It is desolate, utterly lonely, and made lonelier by the calls and cries of the wildfowl that make their homes in the marshlands and saltings[3]— the wild geese and the gulls, the teal and widgeon, the redshanks and curlews that pick their way through the tidal pools. Of human habitants there are none, and none are seen, with the occasional exception of a wildfowler or native oyster-fishermen, who still ply a trade already ancient when the Normans came to Hastings.[4]

Grays and blues and soft greens are the colors, for when the skies are dark in the long winters, the many waters of the beaches and marshes reflect the cold and somber color. But sometimes,

---

1. **Essex.** County in southeast England
2. **Saxon.** Of the Saxons, Germanic people who conquered and then occupied parts of England around AD 500
3. **saltings.** Grassy land covered by tides
4. **when . . . Hastings.** The narrator means AD 1066, the year the French Normans invaded England and won the Battle of Hastings.

WORDS FOR EVERYDAY USE:
es • tu • ar • y (es´tyoo er ē) *n.,* an inlet of the sea
sod • den (säd´'n) *adj.,* soaked through

Hard by one of the winding arms of the little River Aelder runs the embankment of an old sea wall, smooth and solid, without a break, a <u>bulwark</u> to the land against the encroaching sea. Deep into a salting some three miles from the North Sea[5] it runs, and there turns north. At that corner its face is gouged, broken, and shattered. It has been breached, and at the breach the hungry sea has already entered and taken for its own the land, the wall, and all that stood there.

At low water the blackened and <u>ruptured</u> stones of the ruins of an abandoned lighthouse show above the surface, with here and there, like buoy markers, the top of a sagging fence-post. Once this lighthouse abutted on the sea and was a beacon on the Essex coast. Time shifted land and water, and its usefulness came to an end.

Lately it served again as a human habitation. In it there lived a lonely man. His body was warped, but his heart was filled with love for wild and hunted things. He was ugly to look upon, but he created great beauty. It is about him, and a child who came to know him and see beyond the grotesque form that housed him to what lay within, that this story is told.

It is not a story that falls easily and smoothly into sequence. It has been <u>garnered</u> from many sources and from many people. Some of it comes in the form of fragments from men who looked upon strange and violent scenes. For the sea has claimed its own and spreads its rippled blanket over the site, and the great white bird with the black-tipped <u>pinions</u> that saw it all from the beginning to the end has returned to the dark, frozen silences of the northlands whence it came.

In the late spring of 1930 Philip Rhayader came to the abandoned lighthouse at the mouth of the Aelder. He bought the light and many acres of marshland and salting surrounding it.

He lived and worked there alone the year round. He was a painter of birds and of nature, who, for reasons, had withdrawn from all human society. Some of the reasons were apparent on his fortnightly visits to the little village of Chelmsbury for supplies, where the natives looked askance at his misshapen body and dark visage. For he was a hunchback and his left arm was crippled, thin and bent at the wrist, like the claw of a bird.

They soon became used to his queer figure, small but powerful, the massive, dark, bearded head set just slightly below the mysterious mound on his back, the glowing eyes and the clawed hand, and marked him off as "that queer painter chap that lives down to lighthouse."

Physical deformity often breeds hatred of humanity in men. Rhayader did not hate; he loved very greatly, man, the animal kingdom, and all nature. His heart was filled with pity and understanding. He had mastered

What is the obvious reason that caused Rhayader to withdraw from society?

What type of person is Rhayader?

---

5. **North Sea.** Body of water, part of the Atlantic Ocean, between Great Britain and Scandinavia

---

WORDS FOR EVERYDAY USE:

bul• wark (boŏl´wərk) *n.,* defensive wall, break-water

rup • tured (rup´chərd) *adj.,* broken apart

gar • ner (gär´nər) *vt.,* gather

pin • ion (pin´yən) *n.,* wing

his handicap, but he could not master the <u>rebuffs</u> he suffered due to his appearance. The thing that drove him into seclusion was his failure to find anywhere a return of the warmth that flowed from him. He <u>repelled</u> women. Men would have warmed to him had they got to know him. But the mere fact that an effort was being made hurt Rhayader and drove him to avoid the person making it.

He was twenty-seven when he came to the Great Marsh. He had traveled much and fought valiantly before he made the decision to withdraw from a world in which he could not take part as other men. For all of the artist's sensitivity and woman's tenderness locked in his barrel breast, he was very much a man.

In his retreat he had his birds, his painting, and his boat. He owned a sixteen-footer, which he sailed with wonderful skill. Alone, with no eyes to watch him, he managed well with his deformed hand, and he often used his strong teeth to handle the sheets of his billowing sails in a tricky blow.

He would sail the tidal creeks and estuaries and out to sea and would be gone for days at a time, looking for new species of birds to photograph or sketch, and he became adept at netting them to add to his collection of tamed wildfowl in the pen near his studio that formed the nucleus of a <u>sanctuary</u>.

He never shot over a bird, and wildfowlers were not welcome near his premises. He was a friend to all things wild, and the wild things repaid him with their friendship.

Tamed in his enclosures were the geese that came winging down the coast from Iceland and Spitsbergen[6] each October, in great skeins that darkened the sky and filled the air with the rushing noise of their passage—the brown-bodied pink-feet, white-breasted barnacles with their dark necks and clowns' masks, the wild white fronts with black-barred breasts, and many species of wild ducks—widgeon, mallard, pintails, teal, and shovelers.

Some were pinioned,[7] so that they would remain there as a sign and signal to the wild ones that came down at each winter's beginning that here were food and sanctuary.

Many hundreds came and remained with him all through the cold weather from October to the early spring, when they migrated north again to their breeding grounds below the ice rim.

Rhayader was content in the knowledge that when storms blew, or it was bitter cold and food was scarce, or the big punt guns of the distant bag hunters roared, his birds were safe; that he had gathered to the sanctuary and security of his own arms and heart these many wild and beautiful creatures who knew and trusted him.

They would answer the call of the north in the spring, but in the fall they would come back, barking and

---

6. **Spitsbergen.** Group of Arctic Ocean islands belonging to Norway

7. **pinioned.** Literally, "clipped at the wings" or "bound"

whooping and honking in the autumn sky, to circle the landmark of the old light and drop to earth nearby to be his guests again—birds that he well remembered and recognized from the previous year.

And this made Rhayader happy, because he knew that implanted somewhere in their beings was the germ knowledge of his existence and his safe haven, that this knowledge had become a part of them and, with the coming of the gray skies and the winds from the north, would send them <u>unerringly</u> back to him.

For the rest, his heart and soul went into the painting of the country in which he lived and its creatures. There are not many Rhayaders <u>extant</u>. He hoarded them jealously, piling them up in his lighthouse and storerooms above by the hundreds. He was not satisfied with them, because as an artist he was uncompromising.

But the few that have reached the market are masterpieces, filled with the glow and colors of marsh-reflected light, the feel of flight, the push of birds breasting a morning wind bending the tall flag reeds. He painted the loneliness and the smell of the salt-laden cold, the eternity and age-lessness of marshes, the wild, living creatures, dawn flights, and frightened things taking to the air, and winged shadows at night hiding from the moon.

One November afternoon, three years after Rhayader had come to the Great Marsh, a child approached the lighthouse studio by means of the sea wall. In her arms she carried a burden.

She was no more than twelve, slender, dirty, nervous and timid as a bird, but beneath the grime as <u>eerily</u> beautiful as a marsh faery. She was pure Saxon, large-boned, fair, and a head to which her body was yet to grow, and deep-set, violet-colored eyes.

She was desperately frightened of the ugly man she had come to see, for legend had already begun to gather about Rhayader, and the native wild-fowlers hated him for interfering with their sport.

But greater than her fear was the need of that which she bore. For locked in her child's heart was the knowledge, picked up somewhere in the swampland, that this ogre who lived in the lighthouse had magic that could heal injured things.

She had never seen Rhayader before and was close to fleeing in panic at the dark apparition that appeared at the studio door, drawn by her footsteps—the black head and beard, the sinister hump, and the crooked claw.

She stood there staring, poised like a disturbed marsh bird for instant flight.

But his voice was deep and kind when he spoke to her.

"What is it, child?"

She stood her ground and then edged timidly forward. The thing she carried in her arms was a large white bird, and it was quite still. There were stains of

Why does the girl go to Rhayader despite the horrible legend that surrounds him?

How does Rhayader feel about his art? How does the world at large feel about it? How might the success of his work be related to his own harsh criticism of it?

WORDS FOR EVERYDAY USE:

un • err • ing • ly (un ʉr´iŋ lē) *adv.*, without fail

ex • tant (eks´tənt) *adj.*, still existing

ee • ri • ly (ir´ə lē) *adv.*, mysteriously

blood on its whiteness and on her kirtle[8] where she had held it to her.

The girl placed it in his arms. "I found it, sir. It's hurted. Is it still alive?"

"Yes. Yes, I think so. Come in, child, come in."

Rhayader went inside, bearing the bird, which he placed upon a table, where it moved feebly. Curiosity overcame fear. The girl followed and found herself in a room warmed by a coal fire, shining with many colored pictures that covered the walls, and full of a strange but pleasant smell.

The bird fluttered. With his good hand Rhayader spread one of its immense white pinions. The end was beautifully tipped with black.

Rhayader looked and marveled, and said: "Child, where did you find it?"

"In t' marsh, sir, where fowlers had been. What—what is it, sir?"

"It's a snow goose from Canada. But how in all heaven came it here?"

The name seemed to mean nothing to the little girl. Her deep violet eyes, shining out of the dirt on her thin face, were fixed with concern on the injured bird.

She said: "Can 'ee heal it, sir?"

"Yes, yes," said Rhayader. "We will try. Come, you shall help me."

There were scissors and bandages and splints on a shelf, and he was marvelously deft, even with the crooked claw that managed to hold things.

He said: "Ah, she has been shot, poor thing. Her leg is broken, and the wing tip, but not badly. See, we will clip her primaries, so that we can bandage it, but in the spring the feathers will grow and she will be able to fly again. We'll bandage it close to her body, so that she cannot move it until it has set, and then make a splint for the poor leg."

Her fears forgotten, the child watched, fascinated, as he worked, and all the more so because while he fixed a fine splint to the shattered leg he told her the most wonderful story.

The bird was a young one, no more than a year old. She was born in a northern land far, far across the seas, a land belonging to England. Flying to the south to escape the snow and ice and bitter cold, a great storm had seized her and whirled and <u>buffeted</u> her about. It was a truly terrible storm, stronger than her great wings, stronger than anything. For days and nights it held her in its grip and there was nothing she could do but fly before it. When finally it had blown itself out and her sure instincts took her south again, she was over a different land and surrounded by strange birds that she had never seen before. At last, exhausted by her ordeal, she had sunk to rest in a friendly green marsh, only to be met by the blast from the hunter's gun.

"A bitter reception for a visiting princess," concluded Rhayader. "We will call her 'La Princesse Perdue,' the Lost Princess. And in a few days she will be feeling better. See?" He reached into his pocket and produced a handful of grain. The snow goose

<hr>

8. **kirtle.** Dress or skirt

WORDS FOR EVERYDAY USE:

buf • fet (buf´ it) *vt.,* beat back; thrust

What is different about this bird? Why do you think the author chose to have the girl find a strange bird rather than a common one?

opened its round yellow eyes and nibbled at it.

The child laughed with delight and then suddenly caught her breath with alarm as the full <u>import</u> of where she was pressed in upon her, and without a word she turned and fled out of the door.

"Wait, wait!" cried Rhayader, and went to the entrance, where he stopped so that it framed his dark bulk. The girl was already fleeing down the sea wall, but she paused at his voice and looked back.

"What is your name, child?"

"Frith."

"Eh?" said Rhayader. "Fritha, I suppose. Where do you live?"

"Wi' t' fisherfolk at Wickaeldroth." She gave the name the old Saxon pronunciation.

"Will you come back tomorrow, or the next day, to see how the Princess is getting along?"

She paused, and again Rhayader must have thought of the wild water birds caught motionless in that split second of alarm before they took to flight.

But her thin voice came back to him: "Ay!"

And then she was gone, with her fair hair streaming out behind her.

The snow goose mended rapidly and by midwinter was already limping about the <u>enclosure</u> with the wild pink-footed geese with which it associated, rather than the barnacles, and had learned to come to be fed at Rhayader's call. And the child, Fritha, or Frith, was a frequent visitor. She had overcome her fear of Rhayader. Her imagination was captured by the presence of this strange white princess from a land far over the sea, a land that was all pink, as she knew from the map that Rhayader showed her, and on which they traced the stormy path of the lost bird from its home in Canada to the Great Marsh of Essex.

Then one June morning a group of late pink-feet, fat and well fed from the winter at the lighthouse, answered the stronger call of the breeding grounds and rose lazily, climbing into the sky in ever widening circles. With them, her white body and black-tipped pinions shining in the spring sun, was the snow goose. It so happened that Frith was at the lighthouse. Her cry brought Rhayader running from the studio.

"Look! Look! The Princess! Be she going away?"

Rhayader stared into the sky at the climbing specks. "Ay," he said, unconsciously dropping into her manner of speech. "The Princess is going home. Listen! She is <u>bidding</u> us farewell."

Out of the clear sky came the mournful barking of the pink-feet and above it the higher, clearer note of the snow goose. The specks drifted northward, formed into a tiny *v*, diminished, and vanished.

With the departure of the snow goose ended the visits of Frith to the lighthouse. Rhayader learned all over again the meaning of the word *loneliness*. That summer, out of his memory,

What does the snow goose do after it heals?

Why does Frith stop going to the lighthouse? How does Rhayader feel when she stops visiting?

he painted a picture of a slender grime-covered child, her fair hair blown by a November storm, who bore in her arms a wounded white bird.

In mid-October the miracle occurred. Rhayader was in his enclosure, feeding his birds. A gray northeast wind was blowing and the land was sighing beneath the incoming tide. Above the sea and the wind noises he heard a clear, high note. He turned his eyes upward to the evening sky in time to see first an infinite speck, then a black-and-white-pinioned dream that circled the lighthouse once, and finally a reality that dropped to earth in the pen and came waddling forward importantly to be fed, as though she had never been away. It was the snow goose. There was no mistaking her. Tears of joy came to Rhayader's eyes. Where had she been? Surely not home to Canada. No, she must have summered in Greenland or Spitsbergen with the pink-feet. She had remembered and had returned.

Why is Rhayader overjoyed by the return of the snow goose?

When next Rhayader went into Chelmsbury for supplies, he left a message with the postmistress—one that must have caused her much bewilderment. He said: "Tell Frith, who lives with the fisherfolk at Wickaeldroth, that the Lost Princess has returned."

Three days later, Frith, taller, still <u>tousled</u> and unkempt, came shyly to the lighthouse to visit La Princesse Perdue.

Time passed. On the Great Marsh it was marked by the height of the tides, the slow march of the seasons, the passage of the birds, and, for Rhayader, by the arrival and departure of the snow goose.

How is time marked? What other comings and goings mark time for Rhayader?

The world outside boiled and seethed and rumbled with the eruption that was soon to break forth and come close to marking its destruction. But not yet did it touch upon Rhayader, or, for that matter, Frith. They had fallen into a curious, natural rhythm, even as the child grew older. When the snow goose was at the lighthouse, then she came, too, to visit and learn many things from Rhayader. They sailed together in his speedy boat that he handled so skillfully. They caught wildfowl for the ever increasing colony and built new pens and enclosures for them. From him she learned the lore of every wild bird, from gull to gyrfalcon, that flew the marshes. She cooked for him sometimes and even learned to mix his paints.

But when the snow goose returned to its summer home, it was as though some kind of bar was up between them, and she did not come to the lighthouse. One year the bird did not return, and Rhayader was heartbroken. All things seemed to have ended for him. He painted furiously through the winter and the next summer and never once saw the child. But in the fall the familiar cry once more rang from the sky, and the huge white bird, now at its full growth, dropped from the skies as mysteriously as it had departed. Joyously, Rhayader sailed his boat into Chelmsbury and left his message with the postmistress.

WORDS FOR EVERYDAY USE: **tou • sled** (tou´zeld) *adj.*, rumpled, mussed

Curiously, it was more than a month after he had left the message before Frith reappeared at the lighthouse, and Rhayader, with a shock, realized that she was a child no longer.

After the year in which the bird had remained away, its periods of absence grew shorter and shorter. It had grown so tame that it followed Rhayader about and even came into the studio while he was working.

PART TWO

In the spring of 1940 the birds migrated early from the Great Marsh. The world was on fire. The whine and roar of the bombers and the thudding explosions frightened them. The first day of May, Frith and Rhayader stood shoulder to shoulder on the sea wall and watched the last of the unpinioned pink-feet and barnacle geese rise from their sanctuary; she, tall, slender, free as air, and hauntingly beautiful; he, dark, grotesque, his massive bearded head raised to the sky, his glowing dark eyes watching the geese form their flight tracery.

"Look, Philip," Frith said.

Rhayader followed her eyes. The snow goose had taken flight, her giant wings spread, but she was flying low, and once came quite close to them, so that for a moment the spreading black-tipped white pinions seemed to caress them and they felt the rush of the bird's swift passage. Once, twice, she circled the lighthouse, then dropped to earth again in the enclosure with the pinioned geese and commenced to feed.

"She be'ent going," said Frith, with marvel in her voice. The bird in its close passage seemed to have woven a kind of magic about her. "The Princess be goin' t' stay."

"Ay," said Rhayader, and his voice was shaken too. "She'll stay. She will never go away again. The Lost Princess is lost no more. This is her home now—of her own free will."

The spell the bird had <u>girt</u> about her was broken, and Frith was suddenly conscious of the fact that she was frightened, and the things that frightened her were in Rhayader's eyes—the longing and the loneliness and the deep, welling, unspoken things that lay in and behind them as he turned them upon her.

His last words were repeating themselves in her head as though he had said them again: "This is her home now—of her own free will." The delicate <u>tendrils</u> of her instincts reached to him and carried to her the message of the things he could not speak because of what he felt himself to be, misshapen and grotesque. And where his voice might have soothed her, her fright grew greater and his silence and the power of the unspoken things between them. The woman in her bade her take flight from something that she was not yet capable of understanding.

Frith said: "I—I must go. Goodbye. I be glad the—the Princess will stay. You'll not be so alone now."

What event in the outside world finally affects Rhayader and Frith?

What is Rhayader's hope now that the snow goose is staying?

Words for Everyday Use:

girt (gǝrt) *alt. pp. of gird,* surrounded, encircled

ten • dril (ten´drǝl) *n.,* tender shoot

She turned and walked swiftly away, and his sadly spoken "Goodbye, Frith," was only a half-heard ghost of a sound borne to her ears above the rustling of the marsh grass. She was far away before she dared turn for a backward glance. He was still standing on the sea wall, a dark speck against the sky.

Her fear had stilled now. It had been replaced by something else, a queer sense of loss that made her stand quite still for a moment, so sharp was it. Then, more slowly, she continued on, away from the skyward-pointing finger of the lighthouse and the man beneath it.

It was a little more than three weeks before Frith returned to the light-house. May was at its end, and the day, too, in a long golden twilight that was giving way to the silver of the moon already hanging in the eastern sky.

She told herself, as her steps took her thither, that she must know whether the snow goose had really stayed, as Rhayader said it would. Perhaps it had flown away, after all. But her firm <u>tread</u> on the sea wall was full of eagerness, and sometimes unconsciously she found herself hurrying.

Frith saw the yellow light of Rhayader's lantern down by his little wharf, and she found him there. His sailboat was rocking gently on a flood-ing tide and he was loading supplies into her—water and food and bottles of brandy, gear and a spare sail. When he turned to the sound of her coming, she saw that he was pale, but that his dark eyes, usually so kind and <u>placid</u>, were

glowing with excitement, and he was breathing heavily from his <u>exertions</u>.

Sudden alarm seized Frith. The snow goose was forgotten. "Philip! Ye be goin' away?"

Rhayader paused in his work to greet her, and there was something in his face, a glow and a look, that she had never seen there before.

"Frith! I am glad you came. Yes, I must go away. A little trip. I will come back." His usually kindly voice was hoarse with what was suppressed inside him.

Frith asked: "Where must ye go?"

Words came tumbling from Rhayader now. He must go to Dunkirk.[9] A hun-dred miles across the North Sea. A British army was trapped there on the sands, awaiting destruction at the hands of the advancing Germans. The port was in flames, the position hopeless. He had heard it in the village when he had gone for supplies. Men were putting out from Chelmsbury in answer to the government's call, every tug and fishing boat or power launch that could propel itself was heading across the sea to haul the men off the beaches to the trans-ports and destroyers that could not reach the shallows, to rescue as many as possible from the Germans' fire.

Frith listened and felt her heart dying within her. He was saying that he would cross the sea in his little boat. It could take six men at a time;

---

9. **Dunkirk.** Coastal seaport in northern France where Allied troops had to be evacuated in large numbers during World War II

Where is Rhayader going? What does his action reveal about his character? Has he given up on and set himself apart from the outside world?

What is different about Rhayader? What has caused this change?

Words for Everyday Use:

tread (tred) *n.*, step

plac • id (plas´id) *adj.*, undisturbed, calm

ex • er • tion (eg zʉr´shən) *n.*, effort

in a pinch, seven. He could make many trips from the beaches to the transports.

The girl was young, primitive, <u>inarticulate</u>. She did not understand war, or what had happened in France, or the meaning of the trapped army, but the blood within her told her that here was danger.

"Philip! Must 'ee go? You'll not come back. Why must it be 'ee?"

The fever seemed to have gone from Rhayader's soul with the first rush of words, and he explained it to her in terms that she could understand.

He said, "Men are huddled on the beaches like hunted birds, Frith, like the wounded and hunted birds we used to find and bring to sanctuary. Over them fly the steel peregrines, hawks and gyrfalcons, and they have no shelter from these iron birds of prey. They are lost and storm-driven and <u>harried</u>, like the Princesse Perdue you found and brought to me out of the marshes many years ago, and we healed her. They need help, my dear, as our wild creatures have needed help, and that is why I must go. It is something that I can do. Yes, I can. For once—for once I can be a man and play my part."

Frith stared at Rhayader. He had changed so. For the first time she saw that he was no longer ugly or misshapen or grotesque, but very beautiful. Things were turmoiling in her own soul, crying to be said, and she did not know how to say them.

"I'll come with 'ee, Philip."

Rhayader shook his head. "Your place in the boat would cause a soldier to be left behind, and another and another. I must go alone."

He donned rubber coat and boots and took to his boat. He waved and called back: "Goodbye! Will you look after the birds until I return, Frith?"

Frith's hand came up, but only half, to wave too. "God speed you," she said, but gave it the Saxon turn. "I will take care of t' birds. Godspeed, Philip."

It was night now, bright with moon fragment and stars and northern glow. Frith stood on the sea wall and watched the sail gliding down the swollen estuary. Suddenly from the darkness behind her there came a rush of wings, and something swept past her into the air. In the night light she saw the flash of white wings, black-tipped, and the thrust-forward head of the snow goose.

It rose and cruised over the lighthouse once and then headed down the winding creek where Rhayader's sail was slanting in the gaining breeze and flew above him in slow, wide circles.

White sail and white bird were visible for a long time.

"Watch o'er him. Watch o'er him," Fritha whispered. When they were both out of sight at last, she turned and walked slowly, with bent head, back to the empty lighthouse.

Now the story becomes <u>fragmentary</u>, and one of these fragments is in the words of the men on leave who told it in the public room of the Crown and Arrow, an East Chapel pub.

How does Rhayader help Frith understand his need to go?

What changes Frith's feelings about Rhayader's appearance? What does her change of heart tell you about the nature of beauty? Is beauty something absolute, measurable by agreed-upon standards?

Words for Everyday Use:	in • ar • tic • u • late (in´ăr tik´yo͞o lit) *adj.,* unable to express one's emotions har • ried (har´ēd) *adj.,* tormented, ravaged frag • men • tar • y (frag´mən ter´ē) *adj.,* consisting of disconnected parts

"A goose, a bloomin' goose, so 'elp me," said Private Potton, of His Majesty's London Rifles.

"Garn,"[10] said a bandy-legged artilleryman.

"A goose it was. Jock, 'ere, seed it same as me. It come flyin' down outa the muck an' stink an' smoke of Dunkirk that was over'ead. It was white, wiv black on its wings, an' it circles us like a bloomin' dive bomber. Jock, 'ere, 'e sez: 'We're done for. It's the hangel of death a-come for us.'

" 'Garn,' Hi sez, 'it's a ruddy goose, come over from 'ome wiv a message from Churchill,[11] an' 'ow are we henjoying the bloomin' bathing. It's a omen, that's what it is, a bloody omen. We'll get out of this yet, me lad.'

"We was roostin' on the beach between Dunkirk an' Lapanny,[12] like a lot o' bloomin' pigeons on Victoria Hembankment, waitin' for Jerry to pot us.[13] 'E potted us good too. 'E was be'ind us an' flankin' us an' above us. 'E give us shrapnel and 'e give us H. E., an' 'e peppers us from the bloomin' hatmosphere with Jittersmiths.[14]

"An' offshore is the *Kentish Maid*, a ruddy hexcursion scow[15] wot Hi've taken many a trip on out of Margate in the summer, for two-and-six, waiting to take us off, 'arf a mile out from the bloomin' shallows.

"While we are lyin' there on the beach, done in an' cursin' becos there ain't no way to get out to the boat, a Stuka[16] dives on 'er, an' 'is bombs drop alongside of 'er, throwin' up water like the bloomin' fountains in the palace gardens; a reg'lar display it was.

"Then a destroyer[17] come up an' says: 'No, ye don't,' to the Stuka with ack-acks and pom-poms, but another Jerry dives on the destroyer, an' 'its 'er. Coo, did she go up! She burned before she sunk, an' the smoke an' the stink come driftin' inshore, all yellow an' black, an' out of it comes this bloomin' goose, a-circlin' around us trapped on the beach.

"An' then around a bend 'e comes in a bloody little sailboat, sailing along as cool as you please, like a bloomin' toff[18] out for a pleasure spin on a Sunday hafternoon at 'Enley."[19]

" 'Oo comes?" inquired a civilian.

" 'Im! 'Im that saved a lot of us. 'E sailed clean through a boil of machine gun bullets from a Jerry in a Jittersmith wot was strafin'[20]—Ramsgate motorboat wot 'ad tried to take us off 'ad been sunk there 'arf an hour ago—the water was all frothin' with shell splashes an' bullets, but 'e didn't give it no mind, 'e didn't. 'E didn't 'ave no petrol[21] to burn or hexplode, an' he sailed in between the shells.

"Into the shallows 'e come out of the black smoke of the burnin' destroyer, a little dark man wiv a beard, a bloomin' claw for a 'and, an' a 'ump on 'is back.

" 'E 'ad a rope in 'is teeth that was shinin' white out of 'is black beard, 'is good 'and on the tiller[22] an' the crooked one beckonin' to us to come.

What do the soldiers think of the snow goose?

Why doesn't Rhayader's boat run into the difficulties encountered by the other vessels?

---

10. **Garn.** British slang word meaning "Go on"
11. **Churchill.** Winston Churchill (1874–1965), England's prime minister during World War II
12. **Lapanny.** La Panne, Belgian city on the North Sea near the French border
13. **waitin' . . . us.** Waiting for German soldiers to shoot us
14. **Jittersmiths.** British slang for German combat aircraft
15. **hexcursion scow.** Tourist ferry

16. **Stuka.** German dive bomber
17. **destroyer.** Warship
18. **toff.** Fashionable person
19. **'Enley.** Henley, town in southeastern England, location of an annual rowing race
20. **strafin'.** Strafing; shooting at
21. **petrol.** British word meaning "gasoline"
22. **tiller.** Handle used to turn the rudder of a boat

With Sloping Mast and Dipping Prow. *Albert Pinkham Ryder, before 1906.*
National Museum of American Art, Washington, DC, Gift of John Gellatly/Art Resource, NY

An' over'ead, around and around, flies the ruddy goose.

"Jock, 'ere, says: 'Lawk, it's all over now. It's the bloody devil come for us 'imself. Hi must 'ave been struck an' don't know it.'

What do the soldiers call Rhayader?

" 'Garn,' I sez, 'it's more like the good Lord,'e looks to me, than any bloomin' devil.' 'E did, too, like the pictures from the Sunday-school books, wiv 'is white face and dark eyes an' beard an' all, and 'is bloomin' boat.

" 'Hi can take seven at a time,' 'e sings out when 'e's in close.

"Our horfficer shouts: 'Good, man! . . . You seven nearest, get in.'

"We waded out to where 'e was. Hi was that weary Hi couldn't clumb over the side, but 'e takes me by the collar of me tunic an' pulls, wiv a 'In ye go, lad. Come on. Next man.'

"An' in Hi went. Coo, 'e was strong, 'e was. Then 'e sets 'is sail, part of wot looks like a bloomin' sieve from machine gun bullets, shouts: 'Keep down in the bottom of the boat, boys, in case we meet any of yer friends,' and we're off, 'im sittin' in the stern wiv 'is rope in 'is teeth, another in 'is crooked claw, an' 'is right 'and on the tiller, a-steerin' an' sailin' through the spray of shells thrown by a land battery[23] somewhere back of the coast. An' the bloomin' goose is flyin' around and around, 'onking above the wind and the row Jerry was making', like a bloomin' Morris autermobile on Winchester by-pass.

What does the soldier say about Rhayader? Why might the author have chosen to tell this part of the story from the soldier's point of view?

" 'Hi told you yon goose was a omen,' Hi sez to Jock. 'Look at 'im there, a bloomin' hangel of mercy.'

" 'Im at the tiller just looks up at the goose, wiv the rope in 'is teeth, an' grins at 'er like 'e knows 'er a lifetime.

" 'E brung us out to the *Kentish Maid* and turns around and goes back for another load. 'E made trips all afternoon an' all night, too, because the bloody light of Dunkirk burning was bright enough to see by. Hi don't know 'ow many trips 'e made, but 'im an' a nobby[24] Thames Yacht Club motor-boat an' a big lifeboat from Poole that come along brought off all there was of us on that particular stretch of hell, without the loss of a man.

"We sailed when the last man was off, an' there was more than seven hunder' of us haboard a boat built to take two hunder'. 'E was still there when we left, an' 'e waved us goodbye and sails off toward Dunkirk, and the bird wiv 'im. Blyme, it was queer to see that ruddy big goose flyin' around 'is boat, lit up by the fires like a white hangel against the smoke.

"A Stuka 'ad another go at us, 'arfway across, but 'e'd been stayin' up late nights, an' missed. By mornin' we was safe 'ome.

"Hi never did find out what become of 'im, or 'oo 'e was—'im wiv the 'ump an' 'is little sailboat. A bloody good man 'e was, that chap."

"Coo," said the artilleryman. "A ruddy big goose. Whatcher know?"

In an officers' club on Brook Street, a retired naval officer, sixty-five years old, Commander Keith Brill-Oudener, was telling of his experiences during the evacuation of Dunkirk. Called out of bed at four o'clock in the morning, he had captained a lopsided Lime-

---

23. **land battery.** Emplacement for heavy guns and cannons
24. **nobby.** Stylish

house tug across the Strait of Dover, towing a string of Thames barges, which he brought back four times loaded with soldiers. On his last trip he came in with her funnel shot away and a hole in her side. But he got her back to Dover.

A naval-reserve officer, who had two Brixham trawlers[25] and a Yarmouth drifter[26] blasted out from under him in the last four days of the evacuation, said: "Did you run across that queer sort of legend about a wild goose? It was all up and down the beaches. You know how those things spring up. Some of the men I brought back were talking about it. It was supposed to have appeared at intervals the last days between Dunkirk and La Panne. If you saw it, you were eventually saved. That sort of thing."

"H'm'm'm," said Brill-Oudener, "a wild goose. I saw a tame one. Dashed strange experience. Tragic, in a way, too. And lucky for us. Tell you about it. Third trip back. Toward six o'clock we sighted a <u>derelict</u> small boat. Seemed to be a chap or a body in her. And a bird perched on the rail.

"We changed our course when we got nearer, and went over for a look-see. By Gad, it was a chap. Or had been, poor fellow. Machine gunned, you know. Badly. Face down in the water. Bird was a goose, a tame one.

"We drifted close, but when one of our chaps reached over, the bird hissed at him and struck at him with her wings. Couldn't drive it off. Suddenly young Kettering, who was with me, gave a hail and pointed to starboard. Big mine floating by. One of Jerry's beauties. If we'd kept on our course we'd have piled right into it. Ugh! Head on. We let it get a hundred yards astern[27] of the last barge, and the men blew it up with rifle fire.

"When we turned our attention to the derelict again, she was gone. Sunk. Concussion, you know. Chap with her. He must have been lashed to her. The bird had got up and was circling. Three times, like a plane saluting. Dashed queer feeling. Then she flew off to the west. Lucky thing for us we went over to have a look, eh? Odd that you should mention a goose."

Fritha remained alone at the little lighthouse on the Great Marsh, taking care of the pinioned birds, waiting for she knew not what. The first days she haunted the sea wall, watching, though she knew it was useless. Later she roamed through the storerooms of the lighthouse building with their stacks of canvases on which Rhayader had captured every mood and light of the desolate country and the wondrous graceful, feathered things that inhabited it.

Among them she found the picture that Rhayader had painted of her from memory so many years ago, when she was still a child, and had stood, wind-blown and timid, at his threshold, hugging an injured bird to her.

How does the goose react to the death of Rhayader?

---

25. **trawlers.** Boats used for fishing
26. **drifter.** Particular type of fishing boat
27. **astern.** Behind a ship

WORDS FOR EVERYDAY USE: der • e • lict (der´ ə likt) *adj.,* abandoned

The picture and the things she saw in it stirred her as nothing ever had before, for much of Rhayader's soul had gone into it. Strangely, it was the only time he had painted the snow goose, the lost wild creature, storm-driven from another land, that to each had brought a friend, and which, in the end, returned to her with the message that she would never see him again.

Long before the snow goose had come dropping out of a crimsoned eastern sky to circle the lighthouse in a last farewell, Fritha, from the ancient powers of the blood that was in her, knew that Rhayader would not return.

And so, when one sunset she heard the high-pitched, well-remembered note cried from the heavens, it brought no instant of false hope to her heart. This moment, it seemed, she had lived before many times.

She came running to the sea wall and turned her eyes, not toward the distant sea whence a sail might come, but to the sky from whose flaming arches plummeted the snow goose. Then the sight, the sound, and the solitude surrounding broke the dam within her and released the surging, overwhelming truth of her love, let it well forth in tears.

How is Rhayader's sanctuary destroyed?

Wild spirit called to wild spirit, and she seemed to be flying with the great bird, soaring with it in the evening sky, and hearkening to Rhayader's message.

What message is exchanged by the "wild spirits"?

Sky and earth were trembling with it and filled her beyond the bearing of it. "Frith! Fritha! Frith, my love. Goodbye, my love." The white pinions, black-tipped, were beating it out upon her heart, and her heart was answering; "Philip, I love 'ee."

For a moment Frith thought the snow goose was going to land in the old enclosure, as the pinioned geese set up a welcoming gabble. But it only skimmed low, then soared up again, flew in a wide, graceful spiral once around the old light, and then began to climb.

Watching it, Frith saw no longer the snow goose but the soul of Rhayader taking farewell of her before departing forever.

She was no longer flying with it, but earthbound. She stretched her arms up into the sky and stood on tiptoes, reaching, and cried, "Godspeed! Godspeed, Philip!"

Frith's tears were stilled. She stood watching silently long after the goose had vanished. Then she went into the lighthouse and secured the picture that Rhayader had painted of her. Hugging it to her breast, she wended her way homeward along the old sea wall.

Each night, for many weeks there–after, Frith came to the lighthouse and fed the pinioned birds. Then one early morning a German pilot on a dawn raid mistook the old abandoned light for an active military objective, dived onto it, a screaming steel hawk, and blew it and all it contained into oblivion.

That evening when Fritha came, the sea had moved in through the breached walls and covered it over. Nothing was left to break the utter desolation. No marsh fowl had dared to return. Only the frightless gulls wheeled and soared and mewed their plaint over the place where it had been. ∎

Responding to the Selection

What feelings did you have toward Rhayader at the beginning of the story? Did your feelings change as the story progressed? How and why did they change?

Reviewing the Selection

RECALLING

1. Where does Rhayader live? What does he do there? What does he look like? What do the people in the village call him?

2. Why does Frith go to Rhayader? How does she feel when she sees him? What does he do to put her at ease?

3. What happens when the snow goose leaves? What "miracle" occurs in mid-October? How does the snow goose mark the passage of time? What happens in the spring of 1940?

4. What is Rhayader doing when Frith comes back? Where does he go and what does he do with his boat? What does the snow goose do when Rhayader sails away?

INTERPRETING

5. Why is Rhayader's appearance deceptive? Explain how his home is a sanctuary both for his birds and for himself.

6. What allows Frith to overcome her fear of Rhayader? Why does she leave so suddenly?

7. How does the departure of the snow goose affect Rhayader? What role does the snow goose play in the relationship between Rhayader and Frith? How do things change between them as time passes?

8. Why does Rhayader go to the aid of the soldiers at Dunkirk? Why does Frith suddenly see Rhayader in a new light?

SYNTHESIZING

9. Why might Rhayader's heart have been "filled with love for wild and hunted things"? In what way was he like them?

10. Why is the title of the story appropriate? Explain what the snow goose stands for to Rhayader, to Frith, and to the soldiers.

Understanding Literature (Questions for Discussion)

1. **Simile.** A **simile** is a comparison using *like* or *as*. The following similes are from *The Snow Goose:* "his left arm was crippled, thin and bent at the wrist, like the claw of a bird"; "nervous and timid as a bird"; "she stood there staring, poised like a disturbed marsh bird for instant flight"; "men are huddled on the beaches like hunted birds." What do these comparisons have in common? What types of images do these similes create? Why are these comparisons particularly appropriate for this story?

2. **Foreshadowing. Foreshadowing** is the act of presenting materials that hint at events to occur later in a story. At the end of the first part of this story, the narrator says, "The world outside boiled and seethed and rumbled with the eruption that was soon to break forth and come close to marking its destruction." What events in the second part of the story does this foreshadow? How is Rhayader's death foreshadowed in the first part?

Responding in Writing

1. **Obituary.** Write an obituary for Rhayader to be printed in Chelmsbury's local newspaper. Think about Rhayader's art, what the people of the village thought of him, how Frith got to know him, his love of animals, what he did at the end of the story, and how he was spoken of by the soldiers. Use these ideas as well as other information from the story to write Rhayader's obituary.

> **Prewriting Suggestion:** Before you begin writing, freewrite about what you remember about Rhayader. Then refer back to the story to find other examples of the kind of person he was.

2. **News Story.** Write an imaginary news story about the evacuation of Dunkirk that includes the legend of the snow goose. Describe how the events of the evacuation occurred and how the snow goose figured in these events.

> **Prewriting Suggestion:** Make a list of questions you need answered to write a good story. Think of *who, what, when, where, why,* and *how* questions. You may wish to do some research on the evacuation of Dunkirk to help answer some of your questions. Use the story as another source of information for your report.

PROJECTS

1. **World War II Research.** In small groups, research battles and other aspects of World War II. Possible topics include the Battle of Britain, the attack on Pearl Harbor, D-Day, the role of women in the war, the bombing of Hiroshima, and the birth of the United Nations. Use books as well as newspapers and magazines from the war years. You might also interview a veteran of the war if you know one. Present your findings to the class.

2. **Bird Sanctuary.** Rhayader learned about and cared for the birds that lived in the marsh which surrounded his house. Research some of the birds that live near where you live. What do they eat? Where do they live? Are they endangered or plentiful? Answer these and other questions about the birds that you choose. Visit a bird or wildlife sanctuary and observe the different species of birds. If you can't visit a sanctuary, try to observe birds in the wild. Keep a record of the birds you have observed. Make an indoor "sanctuary" by collecting pictures of the birds you have seen and studied.

UNIT REVIEW

Friendship

VOCABULARY FROM THE SELECTIONS

accumulate, 453
bid, 477
buffet, 476
bulwark, 473
burnish, 457
carnage, 454
commence, 451
confirm, 461
conspiracy, 454
derelict, 485
detachment, 465
dilapidated, 452
disposition, 454
eerily, 475
emerge, 460
enclosure, 477
enterprise, 453

entity, 466
epic, 465
estuary, 472
exertion, 480
exhilarate, 452
extant, 475
festoon, 454
fragmentary, 481
garner, 473
girt, 479
glower, 454
harried, 481
hull, 452
import, 477
inarticulate, 481
inaugurate, 452
jut, 468

keel, 458
malevolent, 468
molted, 457
noncommittal, 458
paraphernalia, 452
pinion, 473
placid, 480
potent, 457
prosaic, 454
rebuff, 474
rending, 458
renegade, 457
repel, 474
revelation, 467
ruptured, 473
sacrilegious, 453
sanctuary, 474

saturate, 456
simultaneously, 456
sodden, 472
sprightly, 451
squander, 453
succession, 461
suffuse, 456
survey, 458
tabulate, 454
teem, 468
tendril, 479
tousled, 478
tread, 480
unerringly, 475
vapid, 468

LITERARY TERMS

autobiography, 450
characterization, 462
foreshadowing, 488

narrator, 469
simile, 488

SYNTHESIS: QUESTIONS FOR WRITING, RESEARCH, OR DISCUSSION

1. Who are the friends in each of the selections in this unit? In what ways are these friends similar to or different from one another? In each case, what binds these friends together?

2. What characteristics make a good friend? Answer the question using examples from the selections in this unit.

LANGUAGE LAB   PROOFREADING FOR OTHER PUNCTUATION ERRORS

When proofreading your writing, check carefully for correct use of semicolons, colons, dashes, hyphens, apostrophes, quotation marks, parentheses, brackets, and ellipses.

LANGUAGE ARTS SURVEY

For additional help, see the Language Arts Survey, 2.97–2.106.

COMMON PUNCTUATION ERRORS

Semicolons. A **semicolon** is used between closely related independent clauses that are not joined by *and, but, for, nor, or, so,* or *yet.* It is also used between items that already contain commas.

EXAMPLES: Buddy helped his friend gather pecans; gathering pecans was a yearly tradition.
Buddy and his friend took along the buggy, which was Buddy's baby carriage; the straw hat, which was decorated with roses; and Queenie, the dog, on their pecan-gathering trip.

Colons. A **colon** introduces a long statement, a long quotation, or a list of items.

EXAMPLE: The typical dinner consisted of the following items: cold biscuits, bacon, and blackberry jam.

Dashes. A **dash** is used to show an abrupt break in thought.

EXAMPLE: The snow goose circled as if to land—but no!

Hyphens. A **hyphen** is used to link words in a compound adjective, adverb, or noun.

EXAMPLES: sherry-colored eyes, six-year-old narrator, Anglo-Saxon, director-producer

Parentheses and Brackets. Parentheses contain additional information not essential to a sentence. **Brackets** enclose comments about quoted material and function as parentheses within parentheses.

EXAMPLES: *The Snow Goose* is set in England during World War II (around 1940).
"Many fishermen set out for Dunkirk in trawlers [fishing boats]."

Apostrophes. An **apostrophe** is used to form the possessive of nouns and some pronouns. See the Language Arts Survey, 2.102, for complete rules about using apostrophes.

Underlining and Italics. Italics are a type of slanted printing used to show emphasis. (When italics are not available, **underlining** is used instead.) Words that receive italics include titles of works of art, books, plays, films, television programs, periodicals, and long musical compositions. Words cited as words, letters used as letters, and foreign language words are also treated with italics.

EXAMPLES: *Tom Swift,* Winslow Homer's *Right and Left,* Beethoven's *Symphony No. 3, mea culpa*

Quotation Marks. Quotation marks are used for a variety of purposes.

DIRECT QUOTATION:	"What are you waiting for?" demanded Renee.
DIRECT WITH PERIOD:	Paul Gallico observes that "physical deformity often breeds hatred of humanity in men."
DIRECT WITH COMMA:	"Without friends no one would choose to live," Aristotle claimed.
TITLE OF SHORT WORK:	"A Christmas Memory"

Ellipses. Ellipsis points are used to indicate where words have been omitted from quoted material or to show a pause in spoken dialogue.

EXAMPLE: "Has anyone seen . . . oh, there she is!"

EXERCISE A   Proofreading Sentences for Punctuation Errors

Proofread the following sentences for correct punctuation.

EXAMPLE: Truman Capotes first novel was Other Voices, Other Rooms.

Truman Capote's first novel was *Other Voices, Other Rooms.*

1. Use the following ingredients to make a fruitcake [flour, butter, eggs, pecans, cherries, citron, ginger, vanilla, pineapple, rinds, raisins, spices; and whiskey.]

2. Buddy and his friend can't afford to buy each other Christmas gifts, instead, they make each other kites.

3. Dill thrilled Jem and Scout with his recounting of the movie "Dracula."

4. The twenty seven year old Rhayader led a lonely, isolated existence on the Great Marsh.

5. "My favorite holiday story is A Christmas Memory," exclaimed Erica.

6. American writer Truman Capote 1924–1984 is known for his technique of blending fact and fiction.

7. Atticus treats his children, Scout and Jem, with 'courteous detachment'.

8. After Rhayaders death, the snow goose probably returned to it's home.

9. Buddy's friend knew what the coming of November meant . . . fruitcake weather.

10. Dill wanted to make Boo Radley come out, Scout and Jem would rather leave the mysterious Boo Radley alone.

EXERCISE B   Proofreading a Paragraph for Correct Punctuation

Proofread the following pararaph for correct punctuation. Rewrite the revised paragraph on your own paper.

EXAMPLE: Harper Lee based Dills character on the young Truman Capote, Lee and Capote had become friends' during their childhood in Alabama.

Harper Lee based Dill's character on the young Truman Capote; Lee and Capote had become friends during their childhood in Alabama.

Dill was very different from any other friend Scout and Jem had known however, they were fascinated and delighted by him. Dill his real name was Charles Baker Harris dressed in linen clothes he had won a childrens' beauty pageant he had seen 'picture shows'. Together the three friends enjoyed typical small town summer activities playing in a treehouse and acting out scenes from movies and books. Some of Dill's, Scout's, and Jem's favorite productions were from the books The Rover Boys and Tom Swift. Before Dills arrival Scout had been stuck with the character roles she was relieved when Dill volunteered to play the ape from Edgar Rice Burroughs's Tarzan. There was one trait that Dill did not share with Scout and Jem a fear of Boo Radley. Dill who didn't have Jem and Scout natural fear of the Radley Place would stare at the slate gray house and wonder about it's 'malevolent phantom.'

LANGUAGE ARTS WORKSHOP

PREPARING A RESEARCH REPORT

A **bibliography** is a list of sources used to write a research paper. See the Language Arts Survey, 4.29, "Bibliographies and Bibliography Cards," to learn about the proper bibliographic forms for books, periodicals, and other types of materials.

> **LANGUAGE ARTS SURVEY**
>
> *For additional help, see the Language Arts Survey, 4.29.*

EXERCISE A

Copy the following bibliography entries onto a separate paper, correcting any errors in bibliographic form. Note the words in parentheses that indicate each type of entry.

1. <u>Jazz</u>. Toni Morrison, Alfred A. Knopf: New York, 1992. *(book; one author)*

2. Perkins, George, Perkins, Barbara and Leininger, Phillip, eds. Benet's Reader's Encyclopedia of American Literature. New York: HarperCollins, 1991 *(book; two or more editors)*

3. United States. U.S. Govt. Printing Office, United States Government Printing Office Style Manual, Washington: GPO, 1984 *(government publication)*

4. James Fallows. "Not Yet Net" in <u>Atlantic Monthly</u> May 1995 (108–112). *(article in a quarterly or monthly magazine)*

Paraphrasing is restating someone else's ideas in your own words. **Summarizing** is reducing a piece of writing to a brief statement of the main points.

EXERCISE B

Follow the instructions for each item below.

1. Read the following quotation and paraphrase it: "Truman Capote (1924–1984), originally named Truman Streckfus Persons, was born in New Orleans. He took the name Capote after he was adopted by his stepfather. During his early years, he was sent to live with elderly cousins in the small town of Monroeville, Alabama."

2. Write a summary of Truman Capote's memoir "A Christmas Memory."

3. Summarize the following quotation: "The character Dill is closely based on Lee's childhood friend Truman Capote, who lived with relatives in Monroeville. Although Lee claims the novel is not autobiographical, the physical description of Dill is certainly true to life. Scout and Dill's playing together in a treehouse and dramatizing scenes from their favorite books and movies, also mirror the real experiences of Lee and Capote."

The City from Greenwich Village. *John Sloan, 1922. ©1995 Board of Trustees, National Gallery of Art, Washington, DC. Gift of Helen Farr Sloan*

 ife is a struggle, but not a warfare.

—John Burroughs

"Through the Tunnel"
by Doris Lessing

ABOUT THE AUTHOR

Doris Lessing (1919–   ) was born in Kermanshah, Persia, and lived for many years in southern Rhodesia, where she was educated. She moved to London in 1949 and one year later published her first novel, *The Grass Is Singing*, which is set in Africa. Throughout her work, Lessing's primary interest is in the subtle and sometimes destructive interactions between women and men. Lessing's experimental novel *The Golden Notebook* has become a classic of feminist literature. She has published numerous novels. Lessing's most highly praised short story collections are *African Stories, The Stories of Doris Lessing,* and *The Habit of Loving,* from which the selection is taken.

ABOUT THE SELECTION

Background: Theme. The passage from childhood to adulthood is the theme of **"Through the Tunnel."** When Jerry first arrives on holiday with his mother, they spend their time together on "the safe beach," but Jerry's thoughts are about "the wild bay." What Jerry experiences and learns about himself in that bay will help him to leave behind the familiar world of childhood and to enter the unfamiliar world of adulthood.

Background: Technique. A **symbol** is something that represents both itself and something beyond itself. For example, a rose is a conventional symbol of beauty and love. In this story, emerging from "the tunnel" may be seen as a symbolic second birth into life as an adult.

"Through the Tunnel"

DORIS LESSING

Going to the shore on the first morning of the vacation, the young English boy stopped at a turning of the path and looked down at a wild and rocky bay, and then over the crowded beach he knew so well from other years. His mother walked on in front of him, carrying a bright striped bag in one hand. Her other arm, swinging loose, was very white in the sun. The boy watched that white, naked arm, and turned his eyes, which had a frown behind them, toward the bay and back again to his mother. When she felt he was not with her, she swung around. "Oh, there you are, Jerry!" she said. She looked impatient, then smiled. "Why, darling, would you rather not come with me? Would you rather—" She frowned, <u>conscientiously</u> worrying over what amusements he might secretly be longing for, which she had been too busy or too careless to imagine. He was very familiar with that anxious, apologetic smile. <u>Contrition</u> sent him running after her. And yet, as he ran, he looked back over his shoulder at the wild bay; and all morning, as he played on the safe beach, he was thinking of it.

Next morning, when it was time for the routine of swimming and sun-bathing, his mother said, "Are you tired of the usual beach, Jerry? Would you like to go somewhere else?"

"Oh, no!" he said quickly, smiling at her out of that unfailing impulse of contrition—a sort of <u>chivalry</u>. Yet, walking down the path with her, he blurted out, "I'd like to go and have a look at those rocks down there."

She gave the idea her attention. It was a wild-looking place, and there was no one there; but she said, "Of course, Jerry. When you've had enough, come to the big beach. Or just go straight back to the villa, if you like." She walked away, that bare arm, now slightly reddened from yesterday's sun, swinging. And he almost ran after her again, feeling it unbearable that she should go by herself, but he did not.

She was thinking, Of course he's old enough to be safe without me. Have I been keeping him too close? He mustn't feel he ought to be with me. I must be careful.

He was an only child, eleven years old. She was a widow. She was determined to be neither possessive nor lacking in devotion. She went worrying off to her beach.

As for Jerry, once he saw that his mother had gained her beach, he began the steep descent to the bay. From where he was, high up among red-brown rocks, it was a scoop of moving bluish green fringed with white. As he went lower, he saw that it spread among small <u>promontories</u> and <u>inlets</u> of rough, sharp rock, and the crisping, lapping surface showed stains of purple and darker blue. Finally, as he ran sliding and scraping down the last few yards, he saw an edge of white surf and the shallow, <u>luminous</u> movement of water over white sand, and, beyond that, a solid, heavy blue.

He ran straight into the water and began swimming. He was a good swimmer. He went out fast over the gleaming sand, over a middle region where rocks lay like discolored monsters under the surface, and then he was in the real sea—a warm sea where irregular cold currents from the deep water shocked his limbs.

When he was so far out that he could look back not only on the little bay but past the promontory that was between it and the big beach, he floated on the <u>buoyant</u> surface and looked for his mother. There she was, a speck of yellow under an umbrella that looked like a slice of orange peel. He swam back to shore, relieved at being sure she was there, but all at once very lonely.

On the edge of a small cape that marked the side of the bay away from the promontory was a loose scatter of rocks. Above them, some boys were stripping off their clothes. They came running, naked, down to the rocks. The English boy swam toward them, but kept his distance at a stone's throw. They were of that coast; all of them were burned smooth dark brown and speaking a language he did not understand. To be with them, of them, was a craving that filled his whole body. He swam a little closer; they turned and watched him with narrowed, alert dark eyes. Then one smiled and waved. It was enough. In a minute, he had swum in and was on the rocks beside them, smiling with a desperate, nervous <u>supplication</u>. They shouted cheerful greetings at him; and then, as he preserved his nervous, uncomprehending smile, they understood that he was a foreigner strayed from his own beach, and they proceeded to forget him. But he was happy. He was with them.

They began diving again and again from a high point into a well of blue sea between rough, pointed rocks.

WORDS FOR EVERYDAY USE:

prom • on • to • ry (präm´ən tô rē) *n.,* peak of high land that juts out into a body of water
in • let (in´let) *n.,* narrow strip of water extending into land
lu • mi • nous (lōō´mə nəs) *adj.,* shining; bright

buoy • ant (boi´ənt) *adj.,* having power to keep something afloat
sup • pli • ca • tion (sup´lə kā shən) *n.,* humble request

After they had dived and come up, they swam around, hauled themselves up, and waited their turn to dive again. They were big boys—men, to Jerry. He dived, and they watched him; and when he swam around to take his place, they made way for him. He felt he was accepted and he dived again, carefully, proud of himself.

Soon the biggest of the boys poised himself, shot down into the water, and did not come up. The others stood about, watching. Jerry, after waiting for the sleek brown head to appear, let out a yell of warning; they looked at him idly and turned their eyes back toward the water. After a long time, the boy came up on the other side of a big dark rock, letting the air out of his lungs in a sputtering gasp and a shout of triumph. Immediately the rest of them dived in. One moment, the morning seemed full of chattering boys; the next, the air and the surface of the water were empty. But through the heavy blue, dark shapes could be seen moving and groping.

Jerry dived, shot past the school of underwater swimmers, saw a black wall of rock looming at him, touched it, and bobbed up at once to the surface, where the wall was a low barrier he could see across. There was no one visible; under him, in the water, the dim shapes of the swimmers had disappeared. Then one, and then another of the boys came up on the far side of the barrier of rock, and he understood that they had swum through some gap or hole in it. He plunged down again. He could see nothing through the stinging salt water but the blank rock. When he came up the boys were all on the diving rock, preparing to attempt the feat again. And now, in a panic of failure, he yelled up, in English, "Look at me! Look!" and he began splashing and kicking in the water like a foolish dog.

They looked down gravely, frowning. He knew the frown. At moments of failure, when he clowned to claim his mother's attention, it was with just this grave, embarrassed inspection that she rewarded him. Through his hot shame, feeling the pleading grin on his face like a scar that he could never remove, he looked up at the group of big brown boys on the rock and shouted, *"Bonjour! Merci! Au revoir! Monsieur, monsieur!"*[1] while he hooked his fingers round his ears and waggled them.

Water <u>surged</u> into his mouth; he choked, sank, came up. The rock, lately weighted with boys, seemed to rear up out of the water as their weight was removed. They were flying down past him, now, into the water; the air was full of falling bodies. Then the rock was empty in the hot sunlight. He counted one, two, three. . . .

At fifty, he was terrified. They must all be drowning beneath him, in the watery caves of the rock! At a hundred, he stared around him at the empty hillside, wondering if he should yell for help. He counted faster, faster, to hurry them up, to bring them to the surface

What is the boy feeling? Why?

---

1. **"Bonjour! . . . monsieur!"** French for "Hello! Thank you! Goodbye! Sir, sir!"

WORDS FOR EVERYDAY USE: **surge** (sʉrj) *vt.*, have a heavy, swelling motion

How long do the boys stay down?

Why is the boy crying?

quickly, to drown them quickly—anything rather than the terror of counting on and on into the blue emptiness of the morning. And then, at a hundred and sixty, the water beyond the rock was full of boys blowing like brown whales. They swam back to the shore without a look at him.

He climbed back to the diving rock and sat down, feeling the hot roughness of it under his thighs. The boys were gathering up their bits of clothing and running off along the shore to another promontory. They were leaving to get away from him. He cried openly, fists in his eyes. There was no one to see him, and he cried himself out.

It seemed to him that a long time had passed, and he swam out to where he could see his mother. Yes, she was still there, a yellow spot under an orange umbrella. He swam back to the big rock, climbed up, and dived into the blue pool among the fanged and angry boulders. Down he went, until he touched the wall of rock again. But the salt was so painful in his eyes that he could not see.

He came to the surface, swam to shore and went back to the villa to wait for his mother. Soon she walked slowly up the path, swinging her striped bag, the flushed, naked arm dangling beside her. "I want some swimming goggles," he panted, defiant and <u>beseeching</u>.

She gave him a patient, inquisitive look as she said casually, "Well, of course, darling."

But now, now, now! He must have them this minute, and no other time.

He nagged and pestered until she went with him to a shop. As soon as she had bought the goggles, he grabbed them from her hand as if she were going to claim them for herself, and was off, running down the steep path to the bay.

Jerry swam out to the big barrier rock, adjusted the goggles, and dived. The impact of the water broke the rubber-enclosed vacuum, and the goggles came loose. He understood that he must swim down to the base of the rock from the surface of the water. He fixed the goggles tight and firm, filled his lungs, and floated, face down, on the water. Now, he could see. It was as if he had eyes of a different kind—fish eyes that showed everything clear and delicate and wavering in the bright water.

Under him, six or seven feet down, was a floor of perfectly clean, shining white sand, rippled firm and hard by the tides. Two grayish shapes steered there, like long, rounded pieces of wood or slate. They were fish. He saw them nose toward each other, poise motionless, make a dart forward, swerve off, and come around again. It was like a water dance. A few inches above them the water sparkled as if sequins were dropping through it. Fish again—<u>myriads</u> of minute fish, the length of his fingernail, were drifting through the water, and in a moment he could feel the innumerable tiny touches of them against his limbs. It was like swimming in flaked silver. The great rock the big boys had swum through rose sheer out of the white

WORDS FOR EVERYDAY USE:

be • seech • ing (bē sēch´iŋ) *adj.,* in an earnest manner

myr • i • ad (mir´ē əd) *n.,* indefinitely large number

sand—black, tufted lightly with greenish weed. He could see no gap in it. He swam down to its base.

Again and again he rose, took a big chestful of air, and went down. Again and again he groped over the surface of the rock, feeling it, almost hugging it in the desperate need to find the entrance. And then, once, while he was clinging to the black wall, his knees came up and he shot his feet out forward and they met no obstacle. He had found the hole.

He gained the surface, clambered about the stones that littered the barrier rock until he found a big one, and, with this in his arms, let himself down over the side of the rock. He dropped, with the weight, straight to the sandy floor. Clinging tight to the anchor of stone, he lay on his side and looked in under the dark shelf at the place where his feet had gone. He could see the hole. It was an irregular, dark gap; but he could not see deep into it. He let go of his anchor, clung with his hands to the edge of the hole, and tried to push himself in.

He got his head in, found his shoulders jammed, moved them in sidewise, and was inside as far as his waist. He could see nothing ahead. Something soft and clammy touched his mouth; he saw a dark <u>frond</u> moving against the grayish rock, and panic filled him. He thought of octopuses, of clinging weed. He pushed himself out backward and caught a glimpse, as he retreated, of a harmless tentacle of seaweed drifting in the mouth of the tunnel. But it was

enough. He reached the sunlight, swam to shore, and lay on the diving rock. He looked down into the blue well of water. He knew he must find his way through that cave, or hole, or tunnel, and out the other side.

First, he thought, he must learn to control his breathing. He let himself down into the water with another big stone in his arms, so that he could lie effortlessly on the bottom of the sea. He counted. One, two, three. He counted steadily. He could hear the movement of blood in his chest. Fifty-one, fifty-two. . . . His chest was hurting. He let go of the rock and went up into the air. He saw that the sun was low. He rushed to the villa and found his mother at her supper. She said only "Did you enjoy yourself?" and he said "Yes."

All night the boy dreamed of the water-filled cave in the rock, and as soon as breakfast was over he went to the bay.

That night, his nose bled badly. For hours he had been under water, learning to hold his breath, and now he felt weak and dizzy. His mother said, "I shouldn't overdo things, darling, if I were you."

That day and the next, Jerry exercised his lungs as if everything, the whole of his life, all that he would become, depended upon it. Again his nose bled at night, and his mother insisted on his coming with her the next day. It was a torment to him to waste a day of his careful self-training, but he stayed with her on that other

What does the boy feel he must do? Why?

How much longer must the boy stay down in order to go through the tunnel?

beach, which now seemed a place for small children, a place where his mother might lie safe in the sun. It was not his beach.

He did not ask for permission, on the following day, to go to his beach. He went, before his mother could consider the complicated rights and wrongs of the matter. A day's rest, he discovered, had improved his count by ten. The big boys had made the passage while he counted a hundred and sixty. He had been counting fast, in his fright. Probably now, if he tried, he could get through the long tunnel, but he was not going to try yet. A curious, most unchildlike <u>persistence</u>, a controlled impatience, made him wait. In the meantime, he lay underwater on the white sand, littered now by stones he had brought down from the upper air, and studied the entrance to the tunnel. He knew every jut and corner of it, as far as it was possible to see. It was as if he already felt its sharpness about his shoulders.

He sat by the clock in the villa, when his mother was not near, and checked his time. He was <u>incredulous</u> and then proud to find he could hold his breath without strain for two minutes. The words "two minutes," authorized by the clock, brought close the adventure that was so necessary to him.

In another four days, his mother said casually one morning, they must go home. On the day before they left, he would do it. He would do it if it killed him, he said defiantly to himself. But two days before they were to leave—a

Why does the boy wait? How has he prepared?

WORDS FOR EVERYDAY USE:

per • sist • ence (pər sist´əns) *n.*, stubborn continuance; tenacity

in • cred • u • lous (in krej´oo ləs) *adj.*, showing disbelief

day of triumph when he increased his count by fifteen—his nose bled so badly that he turned dizzy and had to lie limply over the big rock like a bit of seaweed, watching the thick red blood flow on to the rock and trickle slowly down to the sea. He was frightened. Supposing he turned dizzy in the tunnel? Supposing he died there, trapped? Supposing—his head went around, in the hot sun, and he almost gave up. He thought he would return to the house and lie down, and next summer, perhaps, when he had another year's growth in him—*then* he would go through the hole.

But even after he had made the decision, or thought he had, he found himself sitting up on the rock and looking down into the water; and he knew that now, this moment, when his nose had only just stopped bleeding, when his head was still sore and throbbing—this was the moment when he would try. If he did not do it now, he never would. He was trembling with fear that he would not go; and he was trembling with horror at that long, long tunnel under the rock, under the sea. Even in the open sunlight, the barrier rock seemed very wide and very heavy; tons of rock pressed down on where he would go. If he died there, he would lie until one day—perhaps not before next year—those big boys would swim into it and find it blocked.

He put on his goggles, fitted them tight, tested the vacuum. His hands were shaking. Then he chose the biggest stone he could carry and slipped over the edge of the rock until half of him was in the cool, enclosing water and half in the hot sun. He looked up once at the empty sky, filled his lungs once, twice, and then sank fast to the bottom with the stone. He let it go and began to count. He took the edges of the hole in his hands and drew himself into it, wriggling his shoulders in sidewise as he remembered he must, kicking himself along with his feet.

Soon he was clear inside. He was in a small rockbound hole filled with yellowish-gray water. The water was pushing him up against the roof. The roof was sharp and pained his back. He pulled himself along with his hands—fast, fast—and used his legs as levers. His head knocked against something; a sharp pain dizzied him. Fifty, fifty-one, fifty-two. . . . He was without light, and the water seemed to press upon him with the weight of rock. Seventy-one, seventy-two. . . . There was no strain on his lungs. He felt like an inflated balloon, his lungs were so light and easy, but his head was pulsing.

He was being continually pressed against the sharp roof, which felt slimy as well as sharp. Again he thought of octopuses, and wondered if the tunnel might be filled with weed that could tangle him. He gave himself a panicky, convulsive kick forward, ducked his head, and swam. His feet and hands moved freely, as if in open water. The hole must have widened out. He thought he must be swimming fast, and he was frightened of banging his head if the tunnel narrowed.

A hundred, a hundred and one. . . . The water paled. Victory filled him. His lungs were beginning to hurt. A few more strokes and he would be out. He was counting wildly; he said a hundred and fifteen, and then, a long time later, a hundred and fifteen again. The

What two things make the boy tremble?

How long has the boy been underwater? How does he feel physically and emotionally?

water was a clear jewel-green all around him. Then he saw, above his head, a crack running up through the rock. Sunlight was falling through it, showing the clean, dark rock of the tunnel, a single mussel shell, and darkness ahead.

Why does the boy want, at first, to go through the tunnel? What has changed now that he has actually done it?

He was at the end of what he could do. He looked up at the crack as if it were filled with air and not water, as if he could put his mouth to it to draw in air. A hundred and fifteen, he heard himself say inside his head—but he had said that long ago. He must go on into the blackness ahead, or he would drown. His head was swelling, his lungs cracking. A hundred and fifteen, a hundred and fifteen pounded through his head, and he feebly clutched at rocks in the dark, pulling himself forward, leaving the brief space of sunlit water behind. He felt he was dying. He was no longer quite conscious. He struggled on in the darkness between lapses into unconsciousness. An immense, swelling pain filled his head, and then the darkness cracked with an explosion of green light. His hands, groping forward, met nothing; and his feet, kicking back, propelled him out into the open sea.

He drifted to the surface, his face turned up to the air. He was gasping like a fish. He felt he would sink now and drown; he could not swim the few feet back to the rock. Then he was clutching it and pulling himself up on to it. He lay face down, gasping. He could see nothing but a red-veined, clotted dark. His eyes must have burst, he thought; they were full of blood. He tore off his goggles and a gout of blood went into the sea. His nose was bleeding, and the blood had filled the goggles.

Why is it no longer of importance to go to the bay?

He scooped up handfuls of water from the cool, salty sea, to splash on his face, and did not know whether it was blood or salt water he tasted. After a time, his heart quieted, his eyes cleared, and he sat up. He could see the local boys diving and playing half a mile away. He did not want them. He wanted nothing but to get back home and lie down.

In a short while, Jerry swam to shore and climbed slowly up the path to the villa. He flung himself on his bed and slept, waking at the sound of feet on the path outside. His mother was coming back. He rushed to the bathroom, thinking she must not see his face with bloodstains, or tearstains, on it. He came out of the bathroom and met her as she walked into the villa, smiling, her eyes lighting up.

"Have a nice morning?" she asked, laying her hand on his warm brown shoulder.

"Oh, yes, thank you," he said.

"You look a bit pale." And then, sharp and anxious, "How did you bang your head?"

"Oh, just banged it," he told her.

She looked at him closely. He was strained; his eyes were glazed-looking. She was worried. And then she said to herself, Oh, don't fuss! Nothing can happen. He can swim like a fish.

They sat down to lunch together.

"Mummy," he said, "I can stay under water for two minutes—three minutes, at least." It came bursting out of him.

"Can you, darling?" she said. "Well, I shouldn't overdo it. I don't think you ought to swim any more today."

She was ready for a battle of wills, but he gave in at once. It was no longer of the least importance to go to the bay. ∎

Responding to the Selection

Imagine that you are Jerry in this short story. In your journal, write about your experience swimming through the tunnel. Describe what it felt like to be underwater for that length of time and what emotions you experienced when returning to the water's surface.

Reviewing the Selection

RECALLING

1. What is Jerry's family situation?

2. What information does the narrator provide about the bay where Jerry chooses to swim?

3. What does Jerry do to prepare himself for swimming through the tunnel?

4. What unexpected problems does Jerry encounter as he swims through the tunnel?

INTERPRETING

5. What worries Jerry's mother when Jerry goes to "his own beach"?

6. What is probably the reason Jerry yells "Look at me! Look!" when he realizes that the local boys are able to swim through a hole in the rock and he is not?

7. Why doesn't Jerry tell his mother what he is attempting to do?

8. Why has Jerry no desire to return to the bay and swim again through the tunnel?

SYNTHESIZING

9. What fears does Jerry have about the tunnel and swimming through it? Are his fears understandable? Why, or why not?

10. Of what importance is the sea to the setting of this story? What does Jerry's journey through the underwater tunnel symbolize?

Understanding Literature (Questions for Discussion)

1. **Setting.** The **setting** of a literary work is the time and place in which it occurs, together with all the details used to create a sense of a particular time and place. Consider the following details from the beginning of the story: "rough, sharp rock,

and the crisping, lapping surface showed stains of purple and darker blue." These details suggest the danger of "the wild bay." What details describe the bay after the local boys leave Jerry behind? How does the setting reflect Jerry's feelings during that scene in the story?

2. **Characterization. Characterization** is the use of literary techniques to create a character. The three major techniques used to create characters are direct description, portrayal of characters' behavior, and representations of characters' internal states. When using representations of internal states, a writer reveals directly the character's private thoughts and emotions, often by means of what is known as **internal monologue.** Consider the following internal monologue from the story: "She was thinking, Of course he's old enough to be safe without me. Have I been keeping him too close? He mustn't feel he ought to be with me. I must be careful." What is revealed about Jerry's mother in the monologue?

3. **Conflict.** A **conflict** is a struggle between two forces in a literary work. A struggle that takes place between a character and some outside force is called an **external conflict.** A struggle that takes place within a character is called an **internal conflict.** What is the external conflict in this story? What internal conflict does Jerry experience?

Responding in Writing

Narrative Paragraph. Write a narrative paragraph about an experience you had that challenged you, taught you a lesson, or gave you an opportunity to prove yourself.

> **Prewriting Suggestion:** Begin by writing a sentence that tells what the experience was and what you learned from it. That will become the topic sentence of your paragraph. Then, make a list of the events of the experience in chronological order. Use the list to write the body of your paragraph.

PROJECT

Illustration. Form groups of three or four. As a group, illustrate one emotion, image, or sensation that Jerry experiences while swimming through the tunnel. First, read aloud the passage that describes Jerry's experience underwater. Then choose the one emotion, image, or sensation that you all agree is most visually vivid. For example, you might create a drawing that describes the sharp, slimy roof that Jerry touches with his back, or you might create the image of the crack running up through the rock with the jewel-green water all around Jerry. When each group has completed the assignment, hang the illustrations around the room. Guess what emotion, image, or sensation is portrayed in each illustration.

POEM

"Bury Me in a Free Land"
by Frances Ellen Watkins Harper

ABOUT THE AUTHOR

Frances Ellen Watkins Harper (1825–1911) was born in Maryland. Although Maryland was a slave state at the time of her birth, Harper was born to free African-American parents. She studied at her uncle's school for free African Americans and eventually settled in Pennsylvania. An abolitionist, Harper gave antislavery speeches and worked on the Underground Railroad, a network of safe houses between the slave states of the South and the free states of the North. Escaped or runaway slaves would stay at these houses on their perilous journeys to freedom. Harper's poetry and prose collections include *Eventide,* which appeared under the pseudonym Effie Alton; *Forest Leaves; Poems on Miscellaneous Subjects; Moses: A Story of the Nile;* and *Atlanta Offering: Poems. The Poems of Frances E. W. Harper,* a modern edition of her work, appeared in 1970.

ABOUT THE SELECTION

Background: Theme. Much of Harper's verse focused on social and political issues such as the abolition of slavery and equal rights for women. Harper's most famous poem, **"Bury Me in a Free Land,"** evokes many of the horrors of slavery and presents, in fervent language, her dream to see an end, in her lifetime, to those horrors.

Background: Genre. The **ballad,** a simple narrative poem in four-line stanzas, is a form found in much of Harper's verse, including "Bury Me in a Free Land." The meter of the poem is **iambic tetrameter**, with variations. An iambic tetrameter line has four strong stresses, or beats. The line consists of four iambic feet, each with a weakly stressed syllable followed by a strongly stressed one.

"Bury Me in a Free Land"

FRANCES ELLEN WATKINS HARPER

> The speaker of this poem does not care about having a family grave or monument. What does she care about?

Make me a grave where'er you will,
In a lowly plain or a <u>lofty</u> hill;
Make it among earth's humblest graves,
But not in a land where men are slaves.

5
I could not rest, if around my grave
I heard the steps of a trembling slave;
His shadow above my silent tomb
Would make it a place of fearful gloom.

> What would keep the speaker from resting or sleeping?

I could not sleep, if I heard the tread
10 Of a coffle-gang to the shambles led,[1]
And the mother's shriek of wild despair
Rise, like a curse, on the trembling air.

I could not rest, if I saw the lash
Drinking her blood at each fearful gash;
15 And I saw her babes torn from her breast,
Like trembling doves from their parent nest.

I'd shudder and start, if I heard the bay
Of a bloodhound seizing his human prey;

---

1. **coffle-gang to the shambles led.** Group of slaves chained together, being brought to the place where they would be sold

WORDS FOR
EVERYDAY USE:
lof • ty (lôf´tē) *adj.,* very high, elevated

And I heard the captive plead in vain,
20 As they bound, afresh, his <u>galling</u> chain.

If I saw young girls from their mother's arms
Bartered and sold for their youthful charms,
My eye would flash with a mournful flame,
My death-pale cheek grow red with shame.

25 I would sleep, dear friends, where bloated Might
Can rob no man of his dearest right;
My rest shall be calm in any grave
Where none can call his brother a slave.

I ask no monument, proud and high,
30 To arrest the gaze of the passers by;
All that my yearning spirit craves
Is—*Bury me not in a land of slaves!*

■

What does the speaker want instead of a monument?

WORDS FOR
EVERYDAY USE:

gal • ling (gôl´iŋ) *adj.,* irritating

Responding to the Selection

This ballad describes many of the evils of slavery. To which of these descriptions did you respond most strongly? What do you consider the worst aspect of slavery?

Reviewing the Selection

RECALLING

1. What request does the speaker make in the title of the ballad?

2. What would cause the speaker not to rest, in stanza 4?

3. What would let the speaker sleep, in stanza 7?

4. What kind of grave monument does the speaker request in the last stanza?

INTERPRETING

5. What matters most to the speaker about the location of her grave, in stanza 1?

6. What images in stanza 4 emphasize the horrible realities of slavery?

7. What is the speaker referring to when using the words *sleep* and *rest?*

8. What is probably the reason that the speaker insists "Bury me not in a land of slaves"?

SYNTHESIZING

9. What kind of might is "bloated Might"?

10. What is the "dearest right" that the speaker refers to in this ballad? What emotion is created in the reader when the speaker requests the "dearest right" at the time of death?

Understanding Literature (Questions for Discussion)

1. **Simile.** A **simile** is a comparison using *like* or *as.* A simile contains two parts that are compared because they share some quality. In lines 11–12, the speaker says, "And the mother's shriek of wild despair/Rise, like a curse, on the trembling air." What two things are being compared in these lines? What do these things have in common? What other simile appears in the poem? What two things are being compared in the simile? What do these things have in common?

2. **Image and Objective Correlative.** An **image** is a word or phrase that names something that can be seen, heard, touched, tasted, or smelled. An **objective correlative** is a group of images that together create a particular emotion in the reader. What images are used in lines 17–20 to describe the capturing of a slave? What emotion is created by these images?

Responding in Writing

Ballad. Write a ballad in which an important request is made by the speaker. In the ballad express why this request is so important. Read about iambic tetrameter or iambic pentameter in the entry on *meter* in the Handbook of Literary Terms. Try to use one of these meters in your four-line ballad stanzas.

> **Prewriting Suggestion:** Write a clear and brief statement of your request in the middle of a piece of paper. Underline your request and draw five or six lines outward from the statement. On each line, write one event that will happen if the request is granted.

PROJECT

1. **Research Report.** Frances Ellen Watkins Harper worked on the Underground Railroad, helping to bring African Americans from slave states to free states. With two or three other classmates, prepare a research report on the Underground Railroad. Tell what it was and how it operated.

2. **Monument.** Harper writes in line 30, "I ask no monument, proud and high" because she would rather be buried in a free land. Work in a group to create a monument that recognizes all those who were not "buried in a free land" as well as those who assisted others in getting to a free land. What might be an appropriate design for such a monument? Where should it be erected? What inscription might it bear?

POEM

"Miss Rosie"
by Lucille Clifton

ABOUT THE AUTHOR

Lucille Clifton (1936–   ) was born in DePew, New York. Educated at Howard University and Fredonia State Teachers College, Clifton has taught poetry at many universities. Expressing pride in her heritage and identity, Clifton has said, "I am a Black woman poet, and I sound like one." Her poetry collections include *Good Times, Good News About the Earth, An Ordinary Woman, Two-Headed Woman,* and *Next.* Clifton has also written several children's books, the memoir *Generations,* and *Good Woman: Poems and a Memoir.*

ABOUT THE SELECTION

Background: Theme. The poem **"Miss Rosie"** is from Clifton's first collection, *Good Times,* which was published in 1969. A recurring theme throughout the collection— human resilience and survival in the face of life's hardships—can be seen in this poem.

Background: Technique. Clifton uses **figurative language** and **figures of speech** in the poem "Miss Rosie" to suggest something more than the literal meanings of the poem's words. One particular figure of speech used in the selection, a **simile,** or comparison using *like* or *as,* helps to create a strong, clear portrait of Miss Rosie.

READER'S JOURNAL

Have you ever had to adjust to or recover from a misfortune or difficult change in your life? How did you do it? Freewrite about resilience in your journal. You might write about your own resilience or about the resilience you admire in someone else.

"Miss Rosie"

LUCILLE CLIFTON

When I watch you
wrapped up like garbage
sitting, surrounded by the smell
of too old potato peels
5   or
when I watch you
in your old man's shoes
with the little toe cut out
sitting, waiting for your mind
10   like next week's grocery
I say
when I watch you
you wet brown bag of a woman
who used to be the best looking gal in Georgia
15   used to be called the Georgia Rose
I stand up
through your destruction
I stand up ∎

What startling comparison begins this poem? What does that comparison reveal about Miss Rosie?

Why might the toes be cut out of Miss Rosie's shoes?

How has Miss Rosie changed over the years?

What effect does Miss Rosie have on the speaker?

Responding to the Selection

Imagine that you are Miss Rosie in this poem. In your journal, describe your memory of yourself as Georgia Rose—"the best looking gal in Georgia." Express your feelings about the hardships you have encountered in your life and the effect they have had on how you see yourself now.

Reviewing the Selection

RECALLING

1. What is the speaker doing in the opening line of the poem?

2. What portrait is presented of Miss Rosie in the first four lines?

3. What does the speaker say Miss Rosie is waiting for?

4. What did Miss Rosie "used to be called"?

INTERPRETING

5. What can you infer about where the speaker sees Miss Rosie?

6. What details reinforce the portrait of Miss Rosie?

7. What does Miss Rosie's waiting suggest about her state of mind?

8. What does Miss Rosie's former nickname suggest about her former appearance?

SYNTHESIZING

9. What points in Miss Rosie's life do the "wet brown bag of a woman" and "the Georgia Rose" represent? What can the reader infer about what happened to Miss Rosie during the years between these two points?

10. What different meanings can the phrase "stand up" have? In what sense does the speaker "stand up" through Miss Rosie's destruction?

Understanding Literature (Questions for Discussion)

1. **Speaker.** The **speaker** is the character who speaks, or narrates, in a poem—the voice assumed by the writer. In this poem, the speaker knows and observes Miss Rosie. How does the speaker feel toward Miss Rosie? What emotions are expressed by the way in which the speaker speaks?

2. **Repetition. Repetition** is the use, again, of a sound, word, phrase, sentence, or other element. In the poem, the phrase "when I watch you" is used three times. What other repetitions can you find in the poem? What effect do they create?

3. **Simile.** A **simile** is a comparison using *like* or *as.* A simile contains two parts that are compared because they share some quality. In lines 1–4, the speaker says, "When I watch you/wrapped up like garbage/sitting, surrounded by the smell/of too old potato peels." What two things are being compared in those lines? What do those things have in common? What other simile appears in the poem? What two things are being compared in the simile? What do those things have in common?

Responding in Writing

Poem. Write a poem about human resilience by comparing a current and past portrait of someone's life. In your poem, use similes to show particular characteristics or qualities of the subject. Express the feelings of the speaker through tone and meter.

> **Prewriting Suggestion:** To get started, draw two large intersecting circles to form a Venn diagram on a piece of paper. For more information on Venn diagrams see the Language Arts Survey, 1.24, "Venn Diagrams." Write the name of the person you have chosen to write about at the top of the intersection of the diagram. At the top of the left-hand circle, write the word *then;* at the top of the right-hand circle, write the word *now.* List details in each of the circles that describe the then and now physical and personal traits of your subject. In the center of the diagram, list those details that have remained constant in both periods of your subject's life.

PROJECT

Portraits of Humanity. As a class, brainstorm and list on the chalkboard different qualities that you admire in human beings. Then form small groups and assign one quality to each group. Within your group, plan and create a mixed-media portrait of that quality, using different materials, such as photographs from magazines and quotations. Display the portraits in the classroom.

"The Interlopers"
by Saki

ABOUT THE AUTHOR

Saki (1870–1916) is the pen name of Hector Hugh Munro. He created, in a series of short stories, the characters Reginald and Clovis, two young men who happily take to task the conventional adult world. His collections of short stories include *Reginald, The Chronicles of Clovis, Beasts and Super Beasts,* and *The Square Egg.* Some of Saki's short stories, such as "Sredni Vashtar" and "The Muse on the Hill," are rather somber. He also wrote two novels, three plays, and one history. At the age of forty-four, Saki volunteered for active duty in World War I and was killed in action. Nearly all of his work is included in *The Complete Works of Saki,* which was published in 1976.

ABOUT THE SELECTION

Background: Technique. A **conflict** is a struggle between opposing forces. Common types of conflicts in fiction are person versus nature, person versus society, person versus self, person versus machine, and person versus the supernatural. "**The Interlopers**" presents the first kind of conflict, one between the characters Ulrich von Gradwitz and Georg Znaeym. Their conflict over the border between their lands has been burning between their families for three generations. As you read the story, note how the conflict is described and eventually resolved.

Background: Technique. Through **description**, one of the techniques of characterization, the physical traits, actions, and beliefs of the characters Ulrich von Gradwitz and Georg Znaeym are shown. Through the characterization technique of **portrayal of behavior**, the characters of both men are more fully drawn. While trapped together in the forest, the men reveal in dialogue their thoughts, decisions, and expectations.

READER'S JOURNAL

Have you ever held a grudge against someone? Why? What caused the conflict? Think about these questions. Then write about the relationship between friendship and forgiveness in your journal.

"The Interlopers"[1]

SAKI

In a forest of mixed growth somewhere on the eastern spurs of the Carpathians,[2] a man stood one winter night watching and listening, as though he waited for some beast of the woods to come within the range of his vision, and, later, of his rifle. But the game for whose presence he kept so keen an outlook was none that figured in the sportsman's calendar as lawful and proper for the chase; Ulrich von Gradwitz patrolled the dark forest in quest of a human enemy.

The forest lands of Gradwitz were of wide extent and well stocked with game; the narrow strip of <u>precipitous</u> woodland that lay on its outskirt was not remarkable for the game it harbored or the shooting it afforded, but it was the most jealously guarded of all its owner's territorial possessions. A famous lawsuit, in the days of his grandfather, had wrested it from the illegal possession of a neighboring family of petty landowners;[3] the dispossessed party had never acquiesced in the judgment of the Courts, and a long series of poaching affrays[4] and similar scandals had <u>embittered</u> the relationships between the families for three generations. The neighbor feud had grown into a personal one since Ulrich had come to be head of his family; if there was a man in the world whom he detested and wished ill to it was Georg Znaeym, the inheritor of the quarrel and the tireless game-snatcher and raider of the disputed border-forest. The feud might, perhaps,

With whom has the family of Ulrich von Gradwitz been in dispute? About what?

---

1. **Interlopers.** People who meddle, or intrude, in other people's concerns
2. **eastern spurs . . . Carpathians.** Ridges projecting from a mountain chain; the Carpathian Mountains extend from southern Poland to northeastern Romania
3. **petty landowners.** Owners of small pieces of land
4. **poaching affrays.** Attacks for the purpose of stealing game from someone else's property

WORDS FOR EVERYDAY USE:

pre • cip • i • tous (prë sip′ə təs) *adj.*, steep

em • bit • ter (em bit′ər) *vt.*, make resentful

have died down or been <u>compromised</u> if the personal ill-will of the two men had not stood in the way; as boys they had thirsted for one another's blood, as men each prayed that misfortune might fall on the other, and this wind-scourged winter night Ulrich had banded together his foresters to watch the dark forest, not in quest of four-footed quarry, but to keep a look-out for the prowling thieves whom he suspected of being afoot from across the land boundary. The roebuck,[5] which usually kept in the sheltered hollows during a storm-wind, were running like driven things tonight, and there was movement and unrest among the creatures that were wont to sleep through the dark hours. Assuredly there was a disturbing element in the forest, and Ulrich could guess the quarter from whence it came.

Why does Ulrich watch the forest?

He strayed away by himself from the watchers whom he had placed in ambush on the crest of the hill, and wandered far down the steep slopes amid the wild tangle of undergrowth, peering through the tree-trunks and listening through the whistling and skirling of the wind and the restless beating of the branches for sight or sound of the <u>marauders</u>. If only on this wild night, in this dark, lone spot, he might come across Georg Znaeym, man to man, with none to witness— that was the wish that was uppermost in his thoughts. And as he stepped round the trunk of a huge beech he came face to face with the man he sought.

What happens before either man has a chance to speak or shoot?

The two enemies stood glaring at one another for a long silent moment. Each had a rifle in his hand, each had hate in his heart and murder uppermost in his mind. The chance had come to give full play to the passions of a lifetime. But a man who has been brought up under the code of a <u>restraining</u> civilization cannot easily nerve himself to shoot down his neighbor in cold blood and without word spoken, except for an offense against his hearth and honor.[6] And before the moment of hesitation had given way to action a deed of Nature's own violence overwhelmed them both. A fierce shriek of the storm had been answered by a splitting crash over their heads, and ere they could leap aside a mass of falling beech tree had thundered down on them. Ulrich von Gradwitz found himself stretched on the ground, one arm numb beneath him and the other held almost as helplessly in a tight tangle of forked branches, while both legs were pinned beneath the fallen mass. His heavy shooting-boots had saved his feet from being crushed to pieces, but if his fractures were not as serious as they might have been, at least it was evident that he could not move from his present position till some one came to release him. The descending twigs had slashed the skin of his face, and he had to wink away some drops of blood from his eyelashes before he could take in a general view of the disaster. At his side, so near that under ordinary

---

5. **roebuck.** Male of the roe deer
6. **hearth and honor.** Home and reputation

<small>Words for Everyday Use:</small>

com • pro • mise (käm′prə mīz) *vt.*, settle by having both sides make concessions

ma • raud • er (mə rôd ər) *n.*, one who raids and plunders

re • strain • ing (ri strān′iŋ) *adj.*, controlling or disciplining

circumstances he could almost have touched him, lay Georg Znaeym, alive and struggling, but obviously as helplessly <u>pinioned</u> down as himself. All round them lay a thick-strewn wreckage of splintered branches and broken twigs.

Relief at being alive and exasperation at his captive plight brought a strange medley of pious thank-offerings and sharp curses to Ulrich's lips. Georg, who was nearly blinded with the blood which trickled across his eyes, stopped his struggling for a moment to listen, and then gave a short, snarling laugh.

"So you're not killed, as you ought to be, but you're caught, anyway," he cried; "caught fast. Ho, what a jest, Ulrich von Gradwitz snared in his stolen forest. There's real justice for you!"

And he laughed again, mockingly and savagely.

"I'm caught in my own forest-land," retorted Ulrich. "When my men come to release us you will wish, perhaps, that you were in a better <u>plight</u> than caught poaching on a neighbor's land, shame on you."

Georg was silent for a moment; then he answered quietly:

"Are you sure that your men will find much to release? I have men, too, in the forest tonight, close behind me, and *they* will be here first and do the releasing. When they drag me out from under these damned branches it won't need much clumsiness on their part to roll this mass of trunk right over on the top of you. Your men will find you dead under a fallen beech tree. For form's sake I shall send my condolences to your family."

"It is a useful hint," said Ulrich fiercely. "My men had orders to follow in ten minutes' time, seven of which must have gone by already, and when they get me out—I will remember the hint. Only as you will have met your death poaching on my lands I don't think I can decently send any message of condolence to your family."

"Good," snarled Georg, "good. We fight this quarrel out to the death, you and I and our foresters, with no cursed interlopers to come between us. Death and damnation to you, Ulrich von Gradwitz."

"The same to you, Georg Znaeym, forest-thief, game-snatcher."

Both men spoke with the bitterness of possible defeat before them, for each knew that it might be long before his men would seek him out or find him; it was a bare matter of chance which party would arrive first on the scene.

Both had now given up the useless struggle to free themselves from the mass of wood that held them down; Ulrich limited his <u>endeavours</u> to an effort to bring his one partially free arm near enough to his outer coat-pocket to draw out his wine-flask. Even when he had accomplished that operation it was long before he could manage the unscrewing of the stopper or get any of the liquid down his throat. But what a Heaven-sent draught it seemed! It was an open winter, and little snow had fallen as yet,

Who do the men believe will save them? What do they believe will happen when they are saved?

WORDS FOR EVERYDAY USE:	**pin • ion** (pin´yən) *vt.,* bind
	plight (plīt) *n.,* situation
	en • deav • or or **en • deav • our** (en dev´ər) *n.,* attempt, effort

hence the captives suffered less from the cold than might have been the case at that season of the year; nevertheless, the wine was warming and reviving to the wounded man, and he looked across with something like a throb of pity to where his enemy lay, just keeping the groans of pain and weariness from crossing his lips.

"Could you reach this flask if I threw it over to you?" asked Ulrich suddenly; "there is good wine in it, and one may as well be as comfortable as one can. Let us drink, even if tonight one of us dies."

"No, I can scarcely see anything; there is so much blood caked round my eyes," said Georg, "and in any case I don't drink wine with an enemy."

Ulrich was silent for a few minutes, and lay listening to the weary screeching of the wind. An idea was slowly forming and growing in his brain, an idea that gained strength every time that he looked across at the man who was fighting so grimly against pain and exhaustion. In the pain and <u>languor</u> that Ulrich himself was feeling the old fierce hatred seemed to be dying down.

"Neighbor," he said presently, "do as you please if your men come first. It was a fair compact.[7] But as for me, I've changed my mind. If my men are the first to come you shall be the first to be helped, as though you were my guest. We have quarrelled like devils all our lives over this stupid strip of forest, where the trees can't even stand upright in a breath of wind. Lying here

What does Ulrich begin to think as he looks at Georg? What does he decide?

tonight, thinking, I've come to think we've been rather fools; there are better things in life than getting the better of a boundary dispute. Neighbor, if you will help me to bury the old quarrel I—I will ask you to be my friend."

Georg Znaeym was silent for so long that Ulrich thought, perhaps, he had fainted with the pain of his injuries. Then he spoke slowly and in jerks.

"How the whole region would stare and gabble[8] if we rode into the market-square together. No one living can remember seeing a Znaeym and a von Gradwitz talking to one another in friendship. And what peace there would be among the forester folk if we ended our feud tonight. And if we choose to make peace among our people there is none other to interfere, no interlopers from outside. . . . You would come and keep the Sylvester night[9] beneath my roof, and I would come and feast on some high day at your castle. . . . I would never fire a shot on your land, save when you invited me as a guest; and you should come and shoot with me down in the marshes where the wildfowl are. In all the countryside there are none that could hinder if we willed to make peace. I never thought to have wanted to do other than hate you all my life, but I think I have changed my mind about things too, this last half-hour.

---

7. **compact.** Agreement
8. **gabble.** Chatter; talk
9. **Sylvester night.** New Year's Eve, December 31; named after Saint Sylvester

WORDS FOR EVERYDAY USE: **lan • guor** (laŋ´gər) *n.*, lack of interest, listlessness

And you offered me your wine-flask. . . . Ulrich von Gradwitz, I will be your friend."

For a space both men were silent, turning over in their minds the wonderful changes that this dramatic <u>reconciliation</u> would bring about. In the cold, gloomy forest, with the wind tearing in fitful gusts through the naked branches and whistling round the tree-trunks, they lay and waited for the help that would now bring release and succor to both parties. And each prayed a private prayer that his men might be the first to arrive, so that he might be the first to show honorable attention to the enemy that had become a friend.

Presently, as the wind dropped for a moment, Ulrich broke silence.

"Let's shout for help," he said; "in this lull our voices may carry a little way."

"They won't carry far through the trees and undergrowth," said Georg, "but we can try. Together, then."

The two raised their voices in a prolonged hunting call.

"Together again," said Ulrich a few minutes later, after listening in vain for an answering halloo.

"I heard something that time, I think," said Ulrich.

"I heard nothing but the pestilential[10] wind," said Georg hoarsely.

There was silence again for some minutes, and then Ulrich gave a joyful cry.

"I can see figures coming through the wood. They are following in the way I came down the hillside."

Both men raised their voices in as loud a shout as they could muster.

"They hear us! They've stopped. Now they see us. They're running down the hill towards us," cried Ulrich.

"How many of them are there?" asked Georg.

"I can't see distinctly," said Ulrich; "nine or ten."

"Then they are yours," said Georg; "I had only seven out with me."

"They are making all the speed they can, brave lads," said Ulrich gladly.

"Are they your men?" asked Georg. "Are they your men?" he repeated impatiently as Ulrich did not answer.

"No," said Ulrich with a laugh, the idiotic chattering laugh of a man unstrung with hideous fear.

"Who are they?" asked Georg quickly, straining his eyes to see what the other would gladly not have seen.

"*Wolves.*" ∎

What do the men decide to do?

Whom do the men think they see in the distance? What do they actually see?

---

10. **pestilential.** Of or related to a pestilence, regarded as dangerous or harmful

WORDS FOR EVERYDAY USE: rec • on • cil • i • a • tion (rek´ən sil´ē ā´shən) *n.*, settling of problems or disputes

Responding to the Selection

Imagine that you are one of the men, Ulrich or Georg, trapped underneath the beech tree in the forest. If you could make one more entry in your journal, write your feelings about all of the years you have spent quarreling with your neighbor.

Reviewing the Selection

RECALLING

1. What is Ulrich von Gradwitz pursuing in the forest?

2. What information does the narrator provide about the "famous lawsuit"?

3. What do the two men do when they meet face to face?

4. What does Ulrich offer to Georg as a token of friendship?

INTERPRETING

5. What emotion does Ulrich feel toward Georg Znaeym at the beginning of the story?

6. What information emphasizes that the quarrel between the two families is an impassioned one?

7. What event shows "Nature's own violence" to be stronger than the violence of either man?

8. What thoughts on the part of both men show that even the villagers would find their reconciliation to be dramatic?

SYNTHESIZING

9. What changes take place in both men while they are trapped together underneath the beech tree? Why do you think the changes occur?

10. An ironic situation is one that violates the expectations of the characters, the reader, or the audience. What is ironic about the ending of the story? Who are the "interlopers"?

Understanding Literature (Questions for Discussion)

1. **Plot and Conflict.** A **plot** is a series of events related to a central **conflict**, or struggle. A typical plot involves the introduction of a conflict, its development, and its eventual resolution. Sometimes a **catastrophe**, usually marked by the central character's death, occurs in a plot. How is the conflict in the story resolved? Why is the catastrophe that follows the conflict resolution tragic?

2. **Aim.** A writer's **aim** is the primary purpose that his or her work is meant to achieve. One purpose of "The Interlopers" is to teach a lesson. What lesson does the selection teach?

Responding in Writing

Short Story. Write a short story that revolves around the plot element of conflict between two characters. Use a long-standing grudge or resentment between the characters as the conflict in your story. Resolve the conflict between the two characters, having each character learn something in the process.

> **Prewriting Suggestion:** To get started, write the word *grudge* or *resentment* in the center of a piece of paper. Circle the word and draw a number of lines outward from the circle. On each line, write something about which people hold grudges. Then choose one that you feel would be most interesting in a story. Freewrite about ways that this grudge could incite a dramatic scene between your two characters. Will they end their dispute in this story or will something prevent them from coming to terms with their differences? Experiment with dialogue between your characters to develop the plot and the characters themselves.

PROJECT

Storyboard. As a class, identify the following plot elements in the story: introduction, inciting incident, rising action, climax, turning point, falling action, resolution, and catastrophe. For more information about these plot elements see the entry on *plot* in the Handbook of Literary Terms. Then form eight small groups, assigning one plot element to each group. Within each group, create the appropriate portion of the storyboard, illustrating the key event for that particular plot element. Display in class all eight portions of the storyboard, following the time order used in the story.

Struggle

VOCABULARY FROM THE SELECTIONS

beseeching, 500
buoyant, 498
chivalry, 497
compromise, 518
conscientiously, 497
contrition, 497
embitter, 517

endeavor or
  endeavour, 519
frond, 501
galling 509
incredulous, 502
inlet, 498
languor, 520

lofty, 508
luminous, 498
marauder, 518
myriad, 500
persistence, 502
pinion, 519
plight, 519

precipitous, 517
promontory, 498
reconciliation, 521
restraining, 518
roebuck, 518
supplication, 498
surge, 499

LITERARY TERMS

aim, 523
ballad, 507
catastrophe, 522
characterization, 506
conflict, 506, 516, 522
description, 516
external conflict, 506

figurative language, 512
figure of speech, 512
iambic tetrameter, 507
image, 511
internal conflict, 506
internal monologue, 506
objective correlative, 511

plot, 522
portrayal of behavior, 516
repetition, 515
setting, 505
simile, 510, 512, 515
speaker, 514
symbol, 496

SYNTHESIS: QUESTIONS FOR WRITING, RESEARCH, OR DISCUSSION

1. What is the central struggle, or conflict, in each of the selections in this unit? In which of the selections is the central struggle ended, or resolved? In what ways are these struggles resolved?

2. It is often said that struggle helps people to grow, that it makes them better in some way. What proofs of this statement are offered by selections in this unit?

LANGUAGE LAB PROOFREADING FOR CAPITALIZATION ERRORS

Proper nouns, such as the names of particular people and places, are always capitalized. The following chart shows other cases in which capitalization is required.

CAPITALIZE	EXAMPLES
Awards	Pulitzer Prize, Nobel Prize in literature
Brand and Trade Names	Levi's, Kleenex tissues
Buildings and Structures	Art Institute of Chicago, Stonehenge
Days, Months, and Holidays	Wednesday, April, Thanksgiving
Regions	Badlands, the East
Events and Periods	Great Depression, Roaring Twenties
Family Relationships (without modifiers)	Mother, Aunt Agatha (but: my father)
First Words in Sentences	A penny saved is a penny earned.
Certain Letters	grade of A, high C
Personal Names and Titles	Ms. Clifton, Francis Ellen Watkins Harper
Place Names	Manhattan, New York, United States of America
Pronoun *I*	"Miss Rosie" is the poem I most enjoyed.
Titles of Artworks, Literary Works, and Musical Works	"Bury Me in a Free Land," Gauguin's "The Day of the God"

EXERCISE A   Correcting Capitalization Errors

In each of the following sentences, decide if the underlined words should be capitalized or not. Write each sentence correctly and note any capitalization rules you followed.

1. For most <u>Teenagers</u>, <u>adolescence</u> is an exciting but difficult phase of life.

2. Hector Hugh Munro, who was born in <u>scotland</u>, wrote under the pen name <u>saki</u>.

3. Rhonda procrastinated until late <u>sunday</u> night before reading "<u>through the tunnel</u>."

4. At the time of Frances Ellen Watkins Harper's birth, <u>maryland</u> was still a <u>Slave State</u>.

LANGUAGE ARTS SURVEY

For additional help, see the Language Arts Survey, 2.107– 2.133, on capitalization.

5. <u>at</u> the <u>age of Forty-Four,</u> H. H. Munro was killed in action during <u>world war I</u>.

6. The <u>Underground Railroad</u> was actually a network of safe houses between the slave states of the <u>south</u> and the free states of the <u>north</u>.

7. The first time <u>i</u> read one of Doris Lessing's short stories, <u>i</u> was sitting in the <u>new york city public library</u>.

8. Some of Harper's <u>Poetry</u> appeared under the <u>Pseudonym</u> <u>Effie Alton</u>.

9. Phyllis McGinley, a writer from the <u>northwest</u>, won the <u>pulitzer prize</u> for her volume of poetry, <u>*times three*</u>.

10. <u>Eduardo</u> was pleased with the <u>a</u> he received for his report on the <u>gilded age</u>.

EXERCISE B Proofreading for Capitalization Errors

Copy the following paragraph onto a separate sheet of paper, correcting any errors in capitalization.

LANGUAGE ARTS SURVEY

For additional help, see the Language Arts Survey, 2.107– 2.133, on capitalization.

The theme of Frances Ellen Watkins Harper's poem "Bury Me in a Free Land" is echoed in the writing of many african americans who came before and after Her. famed Abolitionist Frederick Douglass wrote two narratives about his life and experiences. Paul Laurence Dunbar, one of Harper's contemporaries, gained Fame and Critical Acclaim for his poetry, some of which was written in Dialect. The 1920s saw the birth of the harlem renaissance (named for a predominantly african-american Community in new york city). during this period, African-American Art and Culture reached new heights. Poets langston hughes, countee cullen, and Claude McKay came to prominence during these years. in the 1930s Zora Neale Hurston wrote numerous novels. in 1940 Richard Wright published his explosive novel *Native son,* a book that brought African-American literature to the attention of the White Literary establishment. Today, Harper's Poetic Tradition is carried on in the works of contemporary African-American poets, including mari evans, Michael Harper, and Nikki Giovanni.

LANGUAGE ARTS WORKSHOP

TAKING ESSAY TESTS

When taking essay tests, follow the guidelines in the chart below.

ANSWERING AN ESSAY QUESTION
1. Read the entire question carefully before you begin to answer it.
2. Look for key words that tell you what to do. Such words include *analyze, describe, compare, summarize, prove, interpret, define,* and *describe.*
3. Make a rough outline of your answer before you begin. Start with one or more summary statements that answer the essay question in a general way. Then give points that support your general answer. Organize the points in a logical way. If you have time, write a concluding statement that summarizes your answer.
4. Make sure that you answer the question completely. Some essay questions ask you to do two or three different tasks. (Example: Explain the objectives of the Civil Rights movement of the 1950s and 1960s, and describe three landmark events that were part of the movement.)
5. Save time to proofread your answer for errors in spelling, grammar, usage, and mechanics. Be especially careful about the spellings of names.

LANGUAGE ARTS SURVEY

For additional information about rough outlines, see the Language Arts Survey, 1.32.

EXERCISE

Copy the following essay questions onto your own paper. Underline the key words in each question. Then write an answer to each question, following the guidelines outlined above.

LANGUAGE ARTS SURVEY

For additional information about answering essay questions, see the Language Arts Survey, 4.45–4.47.

1. In a brief essay, identify the law that Susan B. Anthony challenged, explain how she challenged it, and tell what consequences she suffered for her actions.

2. In a historic speech given as part of the March on Washington in 1963, Martin Luther King, Jr., presented his vision for the future. Describe that vision and explain whether, in your opinion, that vision has been fulfilled. Support your opinion with examples.

3. Unit 9 presents selections that deal with the theme of struggle. Choose one selection from the unit and analyze it to show what struggle is presented in the piece and what the piece has to say about that struggle.

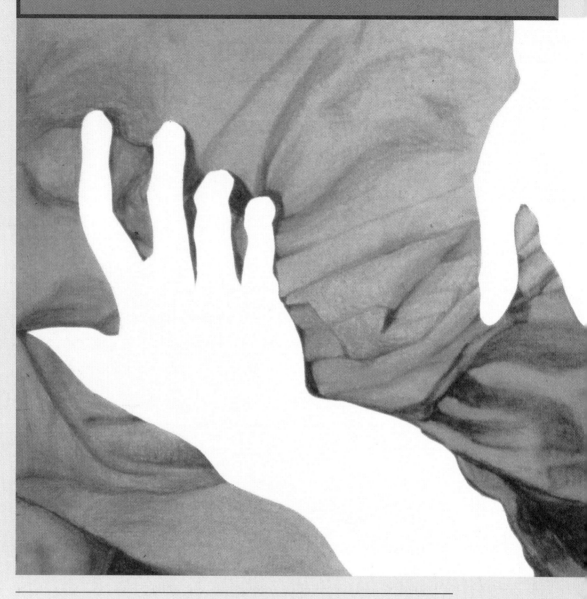

Hot Fuchsia Thermal Blanket. *Jena Busch*

For I dipt into the future, far as human eye could see,
Saw the Vision of the world, and all the wonder that would be.

—Alfred Lord Tennyson

PREREADING

"The Test"
by Theodore L. Thomas

ABOUT THE AUTHOR

Theodore L. Thomas (1920–) has published many stories and articles in anthologies and magazines. After graduating from Massachusetts Institute of Technology, he earned a law degree from Georgetown University. Though employed in fields as diverse as chemical engineering and patent law, Thomas has always found time for his writing.

ABOUT THE SELECTION

Background: History. Theodore L. Thomas originally intended for **"The Test"** to show only what a driver's test of the future might be like. The test was created to judge not only technical driving skills, but moral and emotional fitness as well. The conclusion of the story did not satisfy Thomas, however, and one night before falling asleep he realized the meaning behind the scenes of his story—that human beings never know what is real and what is not real. With this new idea in mind, he was able to write the last two paragraphs of the story.

Background: Genre. **Science fiction** is highly imaginative fiction containing fantastic elements based on scientific principles, discoveries, or laws. The genre allows writers to suspend or alter certain elements of reality in order to create fascinating and sometimes instructive alternatives. As you read the story, consider why Thomas altered the world as he did. What might he be trying to say?

READER'S JOURNAL

Write about a dream you have had that was especially vivid. Have you ever had a dream that seemed so real that when you woke up you were not sure if it had really happened or if it was, indeed, just a dream? What made the dream seem so real? What convinced you that it was not real? Do you ever feel that, as a nursery rhyme says, "life is but a dream"?

"The Test"

THEODORE L. THOMAS

Robert Proctor was a good driver for so young a man. The Turnpike curved gently ahead of him, lightly travelled on this cool morning in May. He felt relaxed and alert. Two hours of driving had not yet produced the twinges of fatigue that appeared first in the muscles in the base of the neck. The sun was bright, but not <u>glaring</u>, and the air smelled fresh and clean. He breathed it deeply, and blew it out noisily. It was a good day for driving.

He glanced quickly at the slim, grey-haired woman sitting in the front seat with him. Her mouth was curved in a quiet smile. She watched the trees and the fields slip by on her side of the pike. Robert Proctor immediately looked back at the road. He said, "Enjoying it, Mom?"

"Yes, Robert." Her voice was as cool as the morning. "It is very pleasant to sit here. I was thinking of the driving I did for you when you were little. I wonder if you enjoyed it as much as I enjoy this."

He smiled, embarrassed. "Sure I did."

She reached over and patted him gently on the arm, and then turned back to the scenery.

He listened to the smooth purr of the engine. Up ahead he saw a great truck, spouting a geyser of smoke as it sped along the Turnpike. Behind it, not passing it, was a long blue convertible, content to drive in the wake of the truck. Robert Proctor noted the arrangement and filed it in the back of his mind. He was slowly <u>overtaking</u> them, but he would not reach them for another minute or two.

He listened to the purr of the engine, and he was pleased with the sound. He had tuned that engine[1] himself over the

---

1. **tuned that engine.** Set the timing and replaced the spark plugs, for example, to improve engine's running condition

How does Robert Proctor feel?

What does Robert notice?

WORDS FOR EVERYDAY USE:

glar • ing (gler´iŋ) *adj.,* shining with a strong light
o • ver • take (ō´vər tāk´) *vt.,* catch up with and go beyond

How does Robert feel about his ability to work with cars?

objections of the mechanic. The engine idled rough now, but it ran smoothly at high speed. You needed a special feel to do good work on engines, and Robert Proctor knew he had it. No one in the world had a feel like his for the tune of an engine.

It was a good morning for driving, and his mind was filled with good thoughts. He pulled nearly abreast of the blue convertible and began to pass it. His speed was a few miles per hour above the Turnpike limit, but his car was under perfect control. The blue convertible suddenly swung out from behind the truck. It swung out without warning and struck his car near the right front fender, knocking his car to the shoulder on the left side of the Turnpike lane.

What happens when Robert starts to pass the convertible?

Robert Proctor was a good driver, too wise to slam on the brakes. He fought the steering wheel to hold the car on a straight path. The left wheels sank into the soft left shoulder, and the car tugged to pull to the left and cross the island and enter the lanes carrying the cars heading in the opposite direction. He held it, then the wheel struck a rock buried in the soft dirt, and the left front tire blew out. The car slewed,[2] and it was then that his mother began to scream.

The car turned sideways and skidded part of the way out into the other lanes. Robert Proctor fought against the steering wheel to straighten the car, but the drag of the blown tire was too much. The scream rang steadily in his ears, and even as he strained at the

What catches the attention of Robert and transfixes him into immobility?

wheel one part of his mind wondered coolly how a scream could so long be <u>sustained</u> without a breath. An oncoming car struck his radiator from the side and spun him viciously, full into the left-hand lanes.

He was flung into his mother's lap, and she was thrown against the right door. It held. With his left hand he reached for the steering wheel and pulled himself erect against the force of the spin. He turned the wheel to the left, and tried to stop the spin and careen out of the lanes of oncoming traffic. His mother was unable to right herself; she lay against the door, her cry rising and falling with the <u>eccentric</u> spin of the car.

The car lost some of its <u>momentum</u>. During one of the spins he twisted the wheel straight, and the car wobblingly stopped spinning and headed down the lane. Before Robert Proctor could turn it off the pike to safety a car loomed ahead of him, bearing down on him. There was a man at the wheel of that other car, sitting rigid, unable to move, eyes wide and staring and filled with fright. Alongside the man was a girl, her head against the back of the seat, soft curls framing a lovely face, her eyes closed in easy sleep. It was not the fear in the man that reached into Robert Proctor; it was the trusting helplessness in the face of the sleeping girl. The two cars sped closer to each other, and Robert Proctor could not change the direction of his car. The

---

2. **slewed.** Turned or pivoted around

WORDS FOR EVERYDAY USE:

sus • tain (sə stān´) vt., keep up or maintain

ec • cen • tric (ək sen´trik) adj., off-center

mo • men • tum (mō men´təm) n., force of an object in motion

Steering Wheel. *David Hockney, October 1982. Photographic Collage, 30 x 36. © David Hockney*

driver of the other car remained frozen at the wheel. At the last moment Robert Proctor sat motionless staring into the face of the <u>onrushing</u>, sleeping girl, his mother's cry still sounding in his ears. He heard no crash when the two cars collided head-on at a high rate of speed. He felt something push into his stomach, and the world began to go grey. Just before he lost consciousness he heard the scream stop, and he knew then that he had been hearing a single, short-lived scream that had only seemed to drag on and on. There came a painless wrench,[3] and then darkness.

Robert Proctor seemed to be at the bottom of a deep black well. There was a spot of faint light in the far distance, and he could hear the rumble of a distant voice. He tried to pull himself toward the light and the sound, but the effort was too great. He lay still and gathered himself and tried again. The light grew brighter and the voice louder. He tried harder, again, and he drew closer. Then

What seems to be happening to Robert Proctor? Is he dying? sleeping? Why might this passage be deliberately ambiguous?

---

3. **wrench.** Jolt; sharp, pulling motion

Words for Everyday Use:

on • rush • ing (än´rush´iŋ) *adj.,* dashing forward

he opened his eyes full and looked at the man sitting in front of him.

"You all right, Son?" asked the man. He wore a blue uniform, and his round, beefy face was familiar.

Robert Proctor <u>tentatively</u> moved his head, and discovered he was seated in a reclining chair, unharmed, and able to move his arms and legs with no trouble. He looked around the room, and he remembered.

The man in the uniform saw the growing intelligence in his eyes and he said, "No harm done, Son. You just took the last part of your driver's test."

Robert Proctor focused his eyes on the man. Though he saw the man clearly, he seemed to see the faint face of the sleeping girl in front of him.

The uniformed man continued to speak. "We put you through an accident under hypnosis—do it to everybody these days before they can get their driver's licenses. Makes better drivers of them, more careful drivers the rest of their lives. Remember it now? Coming in here and all?"

Robert Proctor nodded, thinking of the sleeping girl. She never would have awakened; she would have passed right from a sweet, temporary sleep into the dark heavy sleep of death, nothing in between. His mother would have been bad enough; after all, she was pretty old. The sleeping girl was downright waste.

The uniformed man was still speaking. "So you're all set now. You pay me the ten dollar fee, and sign this application, and we'll have your license in the mail in a day or two." He did not look up.

Robert Proctor placed a ten dollar bill on the table in front of him, glanced over the application and signed it. He looked up to find two white-uniformed men, standing one on each side of him, and he frowned in annoyance. He started to speak, but the uniformed man spoke first. "Sorry, Son. You failed. You're sick; you need treatment."

The two men lifted Robert Proctor to his feet, and he said, "Take your hands off me. What is this?"

The uniformed man said, "Nobody should want to drive a car after going through what you just went through. It should take months before you can even think of driving again, but you're ready right now. Killing people doesn't bother you. We don't let your kind run around loose in society any more. But don't you worry now, Son. They'll take good care of you, and they'll fix you up." He nodded to the two men, and they began to march Robert Proctor out.

At the door he spoke, and his voice was so <u>urgent</u> the two men paused. Robert Proctor said, "You can't really mean this. I'm still dreaming, aren't I? This is still part of the test, isn't it?"

The uniformed man said, *"How do any of us know?"* And they dragged Robert Proctor out the door, knees stiff, feet dragging, his rubber heels sliding along the two grooves worn into the floor. ∎

What does Robert learn about the accident when he wakes up?

How does Robert assess the accident damage?

Is Robert still dreaming?

WORDS FOR EVERYDAY USE:

ten • ta • tive • ly (ten´tə tiv lē) *adv.*, with uncertainty

ur • gent (ʉr´jənt) *adj.*, insistent

Responding to the Selection

What part of the story do you think is real? Was the driving scene real? Was it real when Robert woke up? Was he really being dragged away? Was any of it real, or do you think that Robert woke up to a different "reality"? Discuss these questions with your classmates.

Reviewing the Selection

RECALLING

1. What is Robert Proctor doing when the story begins? Who is with him? What does he notice ahead of him on the road?

2. What happens as he starts to pass the convertible? What sound does he hear throughout the following ordeal? What holds his attention while he is on the collision course with the other car?

3. Who does Robert see when he opens his eyes? What explanation does the man give for what has happened?

4. Who appears after Robert completes his application form? Why do they take him away?

INTERPRETING

5. What kind of mood is Robert in at the beginning of the story? How does he feel about his ability to care for and handle a car?

6. What makes the crash scene seem real to you? Are there things that make it seem unreal?

7. What is Robert's reaction to the crash? How does he feel when he learns it was not real?

8. What do the two grooves on the floor indicate? What does the man mean when he says, "How do any of us know?"

SYNTHESIZING

9. What do you think of the driving test that Robert was given? Do you think it is an accurate way to determine if somebody is fit to drive? Do you think the test serves other purposes? What do you think it says about the people who created it?

10. Do you think Robert had questioned reality before? Do you think he will ever feel that he is in the "real" world again?

Understanding Literature (Questions for Discussion)

1. **Mood. Mood,** or atmosphere, is the emotion created in the reader by part or all of a literary work. What mood is created in the beginning of the story? What details help to create this mood? When does the mood change? What new mood is created?

2. **Theme.** A **theme** is a central idea in a literary work. Do you agree with the uniformed man's suggestion that all of life might be a kind of test? In what ways does life test people every day? In what ways do people pass or fail the tests that life presents to them?

Responding in Writing

Continuation. As this story progresses, twists in the plot continue to distort what is real and what is not. Add another twist of your own. Maybe Robert will be taken to the psychiatric ward. Maybe he'll be taken there and hypnotized again. Maybe he'll wake up somewhere else. Try to think of some other possibilities. With what type of "reality" will your story end?

> **Prewriting Suggestion:** After you decide what will happen to Robert, you will need to use concrete details to make the world he is in seem real. What will Robert see, hear, smell, taste, and feel in his new situation? Read the Language Arts Survey, 1.18, "Sensory Detail Charts," and make a chart based on what Robert experiences. Use these details to create an in-depth picture of this experience.

PROJECT

Choose Your Own Ending. With a group of your classmates, create a choose-your-own-ending book. Use "The Test" as the beginning of your story, and compile the endings that you and your classmates wrote for the preceding assignment. At an appropriate point in the story, insert lines that read something like this: "If you think Robert will escape from the men in white, turn to page 4." Put each new ending on a separate page. Add illustrations and put your story together as a book. Discuss with your classmates which endings you like most.

POEM

"Nightmare Number Three"
by Stephen Vincent Benét

ABOUT THE AUTHOR

Stephen Vincent Benét (1898–1943) was born in Bethlehem, Pennsylvania. His father was a soldier, and the family moved frequently from one army base to the next. His travels and an interest in history greatly affected his writing. Benét began writing at age fifteen and two years later published his first book of poetry. He continued to write poetry while a student at Yale. Later Benét received a Guggenheim Fellowship and went to Paris where he finished a narrative poem about the Civil War, *John Brown's Body* (1928), for which he won a Pulitzer Prize. Later in his career, Benét turned to writing stories and novels. His story "Sobbin Women" (1926) was made into the musical *Seven Brides for Seven Brothers,* and his work *The Devil and Daniel Webster* (1937) was made into an opera and a movie. In 1944, Benét was awarded a second Pulitzer Prize posthumously for his epic poem on the westward migration, *Western Star.*

ABOUT THE SELECTION

Background: Theme. In "Nightmare Number Three" Benét writes on a theme found often in science fiction writing: technology that is out of control. Benét wrote in the early part of the century, when mechanization was in its infancy. Since his time, we have become even more dependent on machines. Benét's poem is humorous, but as you read it, consider this: Does overdependence on machines have a dark side? Might Benét be warning us about our present course?

READER'S JOURNAL

What do you think about the power of machinery? Do you think humans are too dependent on machinery? Do you think machines are used for too many things? What would life be like without machines? Is there a middle ground between accepting conveniences and relinquishing control? Write about these questions in your journal.

"Nightmare Number Three"

STEPHEN VINCENT BENÉT

We had expected everything but <u>revolt</u>
And I kind of wonder myself when they started thinking—
But there's no dice in that[1] now.
                        I've heard fellows say

5   They must have planned it for years and maybe they did.
Looking back, you can find little incidents here and there,
Like the concrete-mixer in Jersey eating the chap[2]
Or the roto press[3] that printed "Fiddle-dee-dee!"
In a three-color process[4] all over Senator Sloop,

10   Just as he was making a speech. The thing about that
Was, how could it walk upstairs? But it *was* upstairs,
Clicking and mumbling in the Senate Chamber.
They had to knock out the wall to take it away
And the wrecking-crew said it grinned.

15   It was only the best
Machines, of course, the <u>superhuman</u> machines,
The ones we'd built to be better than flesh and bone,

What little incidents might have been warnings? What is inexplicable?

---

1. **there's no dice in that.** It doesn't matter
2. **chap.** Man
3. **roto press.** Rotogravure press—printing press used in printing color sections of newspapers

4. **three-color process.** Printing method in which the three primary colors—red, yellow, and blue (cyan)—in a picture, or image, are separated. One color is placed on each of three engraved printing plates; the colors combine as the three plates press on the printing surface.

WORDS FOR
EVERYDAY USE:

re • volt (ri vōlt´) *n.*, rebellion; insurrection
su • per • hu • man (soo´pər hyoo´mən) *adj.*, having power above that of a normal human being

But the cars were in it, of course. . . .

                       and they hunted us

20 Like rabbits through the cramped streets on that Bloody Monday,
The Madison Avenue buses[5] leading the charge.
The buses were pretty bad—but I'll not forget
The smash of glass when the Duesenberg[6] left the show-room
And pinned three <u>brokers</u> to the Racquet Club steps,
25 Or the long howl of the horns when they saw the men run,
When they saw them looking for holes in the solid ground . . .

I guess they were tired of being ridden in,
And stopped and started by pygmies for silly ends,
Of wrapping cheap cigarettes and bad chocolate bars,
30 Collecting nickels and waving[7] platinum hair,
And letting six million people live in a town.
I guess it was that. I guess they got tired of us
And the whole smell of human hands.

                       But it was a shock

35 To climb sixteen flights of stairs to Art Zuckow's office
(Nobody took the elevators twice)
And find him strangled to death in a nest of telephones,
The octopus-tendrils waving over his head,
And a sort of quiet humming filling the air . . .
40 Do they eat? . . . There was red . . . But I did not stop to look.
And it's lonely, here on the roof.

                     For a while I thought

That window-cleaner would make it, and keep me company.
But they got him with his own hoist[8] at the sixteenth floor
45 And dragged him in with a squeal.
You see, they cooperate. Well, we taught them that,
And it's fair enough, I suppose. You see, we built them.
We taught them to think for themselves.
It was bound to come. You can see it was bound to come.

---

5. **Madison Avenue buses.** Buses that run along one
of the main avenues in Manhattan, New York City
6. **Duesenberg.** Elegant automobile produced in the
early part of the twentieth century
7. **waving.** Giving a permanent wave to
8. **hoist.** Mechanical pulley attached to a platform and
used for lifting heavy objects or people

WORDS FOR EVERYDAY USE:	bro • ker (brō´kər) *n.*, person who acts as an agent or intermediary in negotiating contracts, buying, or selling

To what are
humans
compared?

What happened
to Art Zuckow?

In what way are
humans to blame
for the revolt?

To what are
planes
compared?

50 And it won't be so bad, in the country. I hate to think
Of the reapers, running wild in the Kansas fields,
And the transport planes[9] like hawks on a chickenyard,
But the horses might help. We might make a deal with the horses.
At least you've more chance, out there.

What hope do
humans have for
a future?

55   And they need us too.
They're bound to realize that when they once calm down.
They'll need oil and spare parts and adjustments and tuning up.
Slaves? Well, in a way, you know, we were slaves before.
There won't be so much real difference—honest there won't.

60 (I wish I hadn't looked into that beauty-parlor
And seen what was happening there.
But those are female machines and a bit high-strung.)
Oh, we'll settle down. We'll arrange it. We'll <u>compromise</u>.
It wouldn't make sense to wipe out the whole human race.

65 Why, I bet if I went to my old Plymouth now
(Of course, you'd have to do it the tactful way)
And said, "Look here! Who got you the swell French horn?"
He wouldn't turn me over to those police cars.
At least I don't *think* he would.

70   Oh, it's going to be jake.[10]
There won't be so much real difference—honest, there won't—
And I'd go down in a minute and take my chance—
I'm a good American and I always liked them—
Except for one small detail that bothers me

What worries
the speaker?

75 And that's the food proposition. Because you see,
The concrete-mixer may have made a mistake,
And it looks like just high spirits.
But, if it's got so they like the flavor . . . well . . .   ◼

---

9. **transport planes.** Wide-bodied planes, nearly empty
of seating; typically used for carrying freight or soldiers
10. **jake.** Fine (slang)

WORDS FOR
EVERYDAY USE: com • pro • mise (käm´prə mīz´) *vt.*, settle by concessions on
both sides

Responding to the Selection

Imagine that the machines in your home came to life. What kinds of complaints do you think they would have? What might they do to you? Which machine would frighten you the most?

Reviewing the Selection

RECALLING

1. What didn't the speaker expect in the beginning of the poem?

2. The speaker seems to find this bizarre happening explainable for the most part. What is it that cannot be explained? Which machines are involved in the revolt?

3. What reasons does the speaker suggest might have been behind the rebellion?

4. What did humans teach the machines that allowed the revolt to be so successful? What does the speaker think will happen to people?

INTERPRETING

5. What does hindsight allow the speaker to see about the situation?

6. How might the unexplainable be explained? In what way is the machine rebellion like a human rebellion might be?

7. Why is it unreasonable to think that all of the machines in the world got fed up or annoyed with humans?

8. How do the machines work together? Do you think that this is something they would have learned from humans? Do you think humans are slaves to machines? Explain your answers.

SYNTHESIZING

9. Do you think such a revolt could happen? What are machines lacking that would make a revolt of this kind possible?

10. What message do you think the speaker means to communicate about humans and machines?

Understanding Literature (Questions for Discussion)

Simile. A **simile** is a comparison using *like* or *as*. A simile can be analyzed into two parts, the tenor (or subject being described) and the vehicle (or the object used in the description). What simile does Benét use to describe how cars acted in the revolt? What is the tenor of this simile? What is the vehicle? How is the image that is created in this simile continued in line 25? What simile does Benét use to describe planes in line 52? What is the tenor? What is the vehicle? To what are people compared in this line? Why might humans be compared to docile, domesticated animals throughout this poem?

Responding in Writing

Ode. One of the things the machines in this poem seem to feel is that they are not appreciated for the necessary tasks they do. Choose a machine you use frequently, such as a car, a computer, or a CD player. Write an ode to this machine explaining why it is important to you.

> **Prewriting Suggestion:** Make a list of reasons why this machine is helpful in your life. Then freewrite about how your life would be different if this machine did not exist. In your ode, use the reasons that you like your machine and the reasons you would not want to be without it.

PROJECT

Role Play. Imagine a secret meeting of representatives of the various classes of machines. Have each person represent a different group and present their interests. For example, one person might represent small kitchen appliances. Maybe they resent being stuck in the house all the time or feel they are not allowed to live up to their potential. How might these concerns differ from those of a car? In your meeting, debate the issues and make a plan for action that will allow all machines to be free.

"History Lesson"
by Arthur C. Clarke

ABOUT THE AUTHOR

Arthur C. Clarke (1917–) was born in Somerset, England. He studied physics and mathematics at King's College in London and graduated with honors. In the Royal Air Force, he worked with radar. Clarke's fascination with technology led him to write science fiction. Combining his interest in science with a skilled narrative style, he has created many entertaining, instructive stories and novels. Many of his science fiction works focus on exploration and the place of humans in the universe. He has written many nonfiction scientific works as well, including one in which he predicted the use of satellites for communication. Clarke's fictional works include *Childhood's End* (1953), *The City and The Stars* (1956), *The Nine Billion Names of God* (1967), and *2001: A Space Odyssey* (1968), which was later made into a popular movie.

ABOUT THE SELECTION

Background: Theme and Genre. The destruction of the world, exploration of alien civilizations, and the place of humans in the universe—these common themes from science fiction stories are all found in Arthur C. Clarke's amusing and thought-provoking tale, **"History Lesson."** Clarke's story makes us question our society: what values it promotes, how powerful it is, and what weaknesses it possesses. It also offers a unique "history lesson," as well as a unique lesson about history.

READER'S JOURNAL

Do you think that television and movies accurately portray society? In what ways are they accurate? In what ways are they inaccurate? Choose one television show or one movie. If what it depicts were all you knew about life on earth, what would you think? Write about these questions in your journal.

"History Lesson"

ARTHUR C. CLARKE

No one could remember when the tribe had begun its long journey. The land of great rolling plains that had been its first home was now no more than a half-forgotten dream.

For many years, Shann and his people had been fleeing through a country of low hills and sparkling lakes, and now the mountains lay ahead. This summer they must cross them to the southern lands. There was little time to lose. The white terror that had come down from the Poles, grinding continents to dust and freezing the very air before it, was less than a day's march behind.

Shann wondered if the glaciers could climb the mountains ahead, and within his heart he dared to kindle a little flame of hope. This might prove a barrier against which even the <u>remorseless</u> ice would batter in vain. In the southern lands of which the legends spoke his people might find <u>refuge</u> at last.

It took weeks to discover a pass through which the tribe and the animals could travel. When midsummer came, they had camped in a lonely valley where the air was thin and the stars shone with a brilliance no one had ever seen before.

The summer was <u>waning</u> when Shann took his two sons and went ahead to explore the way. For three days they climbed, and for three nights slept as best they could on the freezing rocks, and on the fourth morning there was nothing ahead but a gentle rise to a <u>cairn</u> of gray stones built by other travelers, centuries ago.

Shann felt himself trembling, and not with cold, as they walked toward the little pyramid of stones. His sons had fallen behind. No one spoke, for too much was at stake. In a little while they would know if all their hopes had been betrayed.

Why is Shann leading his people south?

WORDS FOR EVERYDAY USE:	**re • morse • less** (ri môrs´lis) *adj.,* merciless; cruel **ref • uge** (ref´yōōj) *n.,* protection; safety	**wane** (wān´) *vi.,* approach the end **cairn** (kern) *n.,* pile of stones built as a monument or landmark

To east and west, the wall of mountains curved away as if embracing the land beneath. Below lay endless miles of undulating plain, with a great river swinging across it in tremendous loops. It was a fertile land, one in which the tribe could raise crops knowing that there would be no need to flee before the harvest came.

Then Shann lifted his eyes to the south, and saw the doom of all his hopes. For there at the edge of the world glimmered that deadly light he had seen so often to the north—the glint of ice below the horizon.

There was no way forward. Through all the years of flight, the glaciers from the south had been advancing to meet them. Soon they would be crushed beneath the moving walls of ice . . .

Southern glaciers did not reach the mountains until a generation later. In that last summer the sons of Shann carried the sacred treasures of the tribe to the lonely cairn overlooking the plain. The ice that had once gleamed below the horizon was now almost at their feet. By spring it would be splintering against the mountain walls.

No one understood the treasures now. They were from a past too distant for the understanding of any man alive. Their origins were lost in the mists that surrounded the Golden Age,[1] and how they had come at last into the possession of this wandering tribe was a story that now would never be told. For it was the story of a civilization that had passed beyond recall.

Once, all these pitiful relics had been treasured for some good reason, and now they had become sacred though their meaning had long been lost. The print in the old books had faded centuries ago though much of the lettering was still visible—if there had been any to read it. But many generations had passed since anyone had had a use for a set of seven-figure logarithms, an atlas of the world, and the score of Sibelius's[2] Seventh Symphony printed, according to the flyleaf, by H. K. Chu and Sons, at the City of Pekin in the year 2371 AD.

The old books were placed reverently in the little crypt that had been made to receive them. There followed a _motley_ collection of fragments—gold and platinum coins, a broken telephoto lens, a watch, a cold-light lamp, a microphone, the cutter from an electric razor, some midget radio tubes, the _flotsam_ that had been left behind when the great tide of civilization had _ebbed_ forever.

All these treasures were carefully stowed away in their resting place. Then came three more relics, the most sacred of all because the least understood.

The first was a strangely shaped piece of metal, showing the coloration of intense heat. It was, in its way, the most pathetic of all these symbols from the past, for it told of man's greatest achievement and of the future he might have known. The mahogany stand on which it was mounted bore a silver plate with the inscription

---

1. **Golden Age.** Period of great prosperity and cultural achievement
2. **Sibelius's.** By Finnish composer Jean Sibelius (1865–1957)

Where do Shann's sons store their treasures? Why might they do this?

What do these treasures reveal about Shann's people? Why might this revelation be surprising?

Auxiliary Igniter from Starboard Jet
Spaceship "Morning Star"
Earth-Moon, AD 1985

Next followed another miracle of the ancient science—a sphere of transparent plastic with strangely shaped pieces of metal imbedded in it. At its center was a tiny capsule of synthetic radio-element, surrounded by the converting screens that shifted its radiation far down the spectrum. As long as the material remained active, the sphere would be a tiny radio transmitter, broadcasting power in all directions. Only a few of these spheres had ever been made. They had been designed as perpetual beacons to mark the orbits of the asteroids. But man had never reached the asteroids and the beacons had never been used.

Last of all was a flat, circular tin, wide in comparison with its depth. It was heavily sealed, and rattled when shaken. The tribal lore predicted that disaster would follow if it was ever opened, and no one knew that it held one of the great works of art of nearly a thousand years before.

The work was finished. The two men rolled the stones back into place and slowly began to descend the mountainside. Even to the last, man had given some thought to the future and had tried to preserve something for posterity.

That winter the great waves of ice began their first assault on the mountains, attacking from north and south. The foothills were overwhelmed in the first onslaught, and the glaciers ground them into dust. But the mountains stood firm, and when the summer came the ice retreated for a while.

So, winter after winter, the battle continued, and the roar of the avalanches, the grinding of rock and the

explosions of splintering ice filled the air with tumult. No war of man's had been fiercer than this, and even man's battles had not quite engulfed the globe as this had done.

At last the tidal waves of ice began to subside and to creep slowly down the flanks of the mountains they had never quite subdued. The valleys and passes were still firmly in their grip. It was stalemate. The glaciers had met their match, but their defeat was too late to be of any use to man.

So the centuries passed, and presently there happened something that must occur once at least in the history of every world in the universe, no matter how remote and lonely it may be.

The ship from Venus came five thousand years too late, but its crew knew nothing of this. While still many millions of miles away, the telescopes had seen the great shroud of ice that made Earth the most brilliant object in the sky next to the sun itself.

Here and there the dazzling sheet was marred by black specks that revealed the presence of almost buried mountains. That was all. The rolling oceans, the plains and forests, the deserts and lakes—all that had been the world of man was sealed beneath the ice, perhaps forever.

The ship closed in to Earth and established an orbit less than a thousand miles away. For five days it circled the planet, while cameras recorded all that was left to see and a hundred instruments gathered information that would give the Venusian scientists many years of work.

An actual landing was not intended. There seemed little purpose in it. But on the sixth day the picture changed. A panoramic monitor, driven to the limit of its amplification, detected the dying

What is the last sacred object? What do the people know about it? What do they believe?

Why might the Venusian scientists not want to land on Earth?

radiation of the five-thousand-year-old beacon. Through all the centuries, it had been sending out its signals with ever-failing strength as its radioactive heart steadily weakened.

The monitor locked on the beacon frequency. In the control room, a bell clamored for attention. A little later, the Venusian ship broke free from its orbit and slanted down toward Earth, toward a range of mountains that still towered proudly above the ice, and to a cairn of gray stones that the years had scarcely touched. . . .

The great disk of the sun blazed fiercely in a sky no longer veiled with mist, for the clouds that had once hidden Venus had now completely gone. Whatever force had caused the change in the sun's radiation had doomed one civilization, but had given birth to another. Less than five thousand years before, the half-savage people of Venus had seen sun and stars for the first time. Just as the science of Earth had begun with astronomy, so had that of Venus, and on the warm, rich world that man had never seen progress had been incredibly rapid.

Perhaps the Venusians had been lucky. They never knew the Dark Age that held man enchained for a thousand years. They missed the long detour into chemistry and mechanics but came at once to the more fundamental laws of radiation physics. In the time that man had taken to progress from the Pyramids to the rocket-propelled spaceship, the Venusians had passed from the discovery of agriculture to antigravity itself—the ultimate secret that man had never learned.

The warm ocean that still bore most of the young planet's life rolled its breakers <u>languidly</u> against the sandy shore. So new was this continent that the very sands were coarse and gritty. There had not yet been time enough for the sea to wear them smooth.

The scientists lay half in the water, their beautiful reptilian bodies gleaming in the sunlight. The greatest minds of Venus had gathered on this shore from all the islands of the planet. What they were going to hear they did not know, except that it concerned the Third World and the mysterious race that had peopled it before the coming of the ice.

The Historian was standing on the land, for the instruments he wished to use had no love of water. By his side was a large machine which attracted many curious glances from his colleagues. It was clearly concerned with optics, for a lens system projected from it toward a screen of white material a dozen yards away.

The Historian began to speak. Briefly he <u>recapitulated</u> what little had been discovered concerning the Third Planet and its people.

He mentioned the centuries of fruitless research that had failed to interpret a single word of the writings of Earth. The planet had been inhabited by a race of great technical ability. That, at least, was proved by the few pieces of machinery that had been found in the cairn upon the mountain.

Why do the Venusians land on Earth?

What sort of beings are the Venusians?

What caused the Ice Age on Earth? What effect did this have on Venus?

WORDS FOR EVERYDAY USE:

lan • guid • ly (laŋ´gwid lē) adv., sluggishly

re • ca • pit • u • late (rē´kə pich´ə lāt´) vi., summarize

Did humanity necessarily have to be destroyed by the Ice Age?

"We do not know why so advanced a civilization came to an end," he observed. "Almost certainly, it had sufficient knowledge to survive an Ice Age. There must have been some other factor of which we know nothing. Possibly disease or racial <u>degeneration</u> may have been responsible. It has even been suggested that the tribal conflicts <u>endemic</u> to our own species in prehistoric times may have continued on the Third Planet after the coming of technology.

What do the Venusians believe about the effect of technology on war?

"Some philosophers maintain that knowledge of machinery does not necessarily imply a high degree of civilization, and it is theoretically possible to have wars in a society possessing mechanical power, flight, and even radio. Such a conception is alien to our thoughts, but we must admit its possibility. It would certainly account for the downfall of the lost race.

"It has always been assumed that we should never know anything of the physical form of the creatures who lived on Planet Three. For centuries our artists have been depicting scenes from the history of the dead world, peopling it with all manner of fantastic beings. Most of these creations have resembled us more or less closely, though it has often been pointed out that because *we* are reptiles it does not follow that all intelligent life must necessarily be reptilian.

What surprises the Venusians about the life forms from Earth? What did they expect other intelligent life forms would be like?

"We now know the answer to one of the most baffling problems of history. At last, after hundreds of years of research, we have discovered the exact form and nature of the ruling life on the Third Planet."

There was a murmur of astonishment from the assembled scientists. Some were so taken aback that they disappeared for a while into the comfort of the ocean, as all Venusians were apt to do in moments of stress. The Historian waited until his colleagues reemerged into the element they so disliked. He himself was quite comfortable, thanks to the tiny sprays that were continually playing over his body. With their help he could live on land for many hours before having to return to the ocean.

The excitement slowly subsided and the lecturer continued:

"One of the most puzzling of the objects found on Planet Three was a flat metal container holding a great length of transparent plastic material, perforated at the edges and wound tightly into a spool. This transparent tape at first seemed quite featureless, but an examination with the new sub-electronic microscope has shown that this is not the case. Along the surface of the material, invisible to our eyes but perfectly clear under the correct radiation, are literally thousands of tiny pictures. It is believed that they were imprinted on the material by some chemical means, and have faded with the passage of time.

"These pictures apparently form a record of life as it was on the Third Planet at the height of its civilization They are not independent. Consecutive pictures are almost identical, differing only in the detail of movement. The purpose of such a record is obvious. It is only necessary to project

WORDS FOR EVERYDAY USE:

de • gen • er • a • tion (dē jen´ər ā´shən) *n.*, decline; deterioration

en • dem • ic (en dem´ik) *adj.*, present in

the scenes in rapid succession to give an illusion of continuous movement. We have made a machine to do this, and I have here an exact reproduction of the picture sequence.

"The scenes you are now going to witness take us back many thousands of years, to the great days of our sister planet. They show a complex civilization, many of whose activities we can only dimly understand. Life seems to have been very violent and energetic, and much that you will see is quite baffling.

"It is clear that the Third Planet was inhabited by a number of different species, none of them reptilian. That is a blow to our pride, but the conclusion is inescapable. The dominant type of life appears to have been a two-armed <u>biped</u>. It walked upright and covered its body with some flexible material, possibly for protection against the cold, since even before the Ice Age the planet was at a much lower temperature than our own world. But I will not try your patience any further. You will now see the record of which I have been speaking."

A brilliant light flashed from the projector. There was a gentle whirring, and on the screen appeared hundreds of strange beings moving rather jerkily to and fro. The picture expanded to embrace one of the creatures, and the scientists could see that the Historian's description had been correct.

The creature possessed two eyes, set rather close together, but the other facial adornments were a little obscure. There was a large <u>orifice</u> in the lower portion of the head that was continu-

ally opening and closing. Possibly it had something to do with the creature's breathing.

The scientists watched spellbound as the strange being became involved in a series of fantastic adventures. There was an incredibly violent conflict with another, slightly different creature. It seemed certain that they must both be killed, but when it was all over neither seemed any the worse.

Then came a furious drive over miles of country in a four-wheeled mechanical device which was capable of extraordinary feats of locomotion. The ride ended in a city packed with other vehicles moving in all directions at breathtaking speeds. No one was surprised to see two of the machines meet head on with devastating results.

After that, events became even more complicated. It was now quite obvious that it would take many years of research to analyze and understand all that was happening. It was also clear that the record was a work of art, somewhat stylized, rather than an exact reproduction of life as it actually had been on the Third Planet.

Most of the scientists felt themselves completely dazed when the sequence of pictures came to an end. There was a final flurry of motion, in which the creature that had been the center of interest became involved in some tremendous but <u>incomprehensible</u> catastrophe. The picture contracted to a circle, centered on the creature's head.

The last scene of all was an expanded view of its face, obviously expressing

What is surprising about the action in the film?

What do the Venusians recognize about the film?

WORDS FOR EVERYDAY USE:

bi • ped (bī´ped´) *n.,* two-footed animal
or • i • fice (ôr´ə fis) *n.,* opening; mouth
in • com • pre • hen • si • ble (in´käm´prē hen´sə bəl) *adj.,* not understandable

some powerful emotion. But whether it was rage, grief, defiance, resignation or some other feeling could not be guessed. The picture vanished. For a moment some lettering appeared on the screen, then it was all over.

For several minutes there was complete silence, save for the lapping of the waves upon the sand. The scientists were too stunned to speak. The fleeting glimpse of Earth's civilization had had a shattering effect on their minds. Then little groups began to start talking together, first in whispers and then more and more loudly as the implications of what they had seen became clearer. Presently the Historian called for attention and addressed the meeting again.

"We are now planning," he said, "a vast program of research to extract all available knowledge from this record. Thousands of copies are being made for distribution to all workers. You will appreciate the problems involved. The psychologists in particular have an immense task confronting them.

"But I do not doubt that we shall succeed. In another generation, who can say what we may not have learned of this wonderful race? Before we leave, let us look again at our remote cousins, whose wisdom may have sur-

passed our own but of whom so little has survived."

Once more the final picture flashed on the screen, motionless this time, for the projector had been stopped. With something like awe, the scientists gazed at the still figure from the past, while in turn the little biped stared back at them with its characteristic expression of arrogant bad temper.

For the rest of time it would symbolize the human race. The psychologists of Venus would analyze its actions and watch its every movement until they could reconstruct its mind. Thousands of books would be written about it. Intricate philosophies would be contrived to account for its behavior.

But all this labor, all this research, would be utterly in vain. Perhaps the proud and lonely figure on the screen was smiling <u>sardonically</u> at the scientists who were starting on their age-long <u>fruitless</u> quest.

Its secret would be safe as long as the universe endured, for no one now would ever read the lost language of Earth. Millions of times in the ages to come those last few words would flash across the screen, and none could ever guess their meaning.

A Walt Disney Production. ∎

What would symbolize the human race?

What does the Historian expect to learn?

WORDS FOR EVERYDAY USE:

sar • don • i • cal • ly (sär dän´ i kə lē) adv., sarcastically

fruit • less (frōōt´lis) adj., unsuccessful

Responding to the Selection

How do you feel about the Venusian view of humans? What kind of understanding would you wish other intelligent creatures to have of humans? Can you think of something that could be preserved to show humans in the way you would like them to be shown?

Reviewing the Selection

RECALLING

1. What do Shann and his tribe fear in the beginning of the story? What hope do they have for survival?

2. What items do the sons of Shann put into a safe place to save for future generations? Which three items have become the most sacred?

3. Who finds the preserved items? What secret have they learned that humans never learned?

4. What does the Historian show the scientists? What image will come to symbolize the human race?

INTERPRETING

5. What reason is given for the Ice Age? How has this affected the planet Venus?

6. Why do Shann's people place importance on the items the choose to save? Why have the sacred items become so important?

7. How does the progression of Venusian knowledge differ from that of humans? How do the accomplishments of humans compare to those of the Venusians?

8. Why will the Venusians study the film record? What don't they understand about this record?

SYNTHESIZING

9. Reread the passages that describe the cartoon. What misconceptions might the Venusians have about humans based on this film? In what way is it an accurate portrayal of life as we know it on Earth? Imagine that the Venusians had found some footage from the evening news as well. How would the two films compare?

10. What point does this story make about interpreting historical artifacts?

Understanding Literature (Questions for Discussion)

1. **Dramatic Irony. Dramatic irony** is a difference between appearance and reality in which something is known by the reader or audience but unknown to the characters. What does the reader understand about the ending of this story that the characters do not understand? What meaning does the last line have for the reader? What does the reader know at that point about the Venusians' study of human civilization?

2. **Setting.** The **setting** of a literary work is the time and place in which it occurs, together with all the details used to create a sense of a particular time and place. As you began reading, when did you think the story was set? What details created this effect? What details changed your conception of the setting? What purpose was achieved by using such an ambiguous setting?

Responding in Writing

Museum Guide. Review the list of things that Shann's people left in the cairn. Imagine that the Venusians have set up an exhibit about life on the Third Planet. Write a guide to this exhibit that includes a short description of each piece with its name, its material, and its possible function. Try to think about these items from a Venusian point of view.

> **Prewriting Suggestion:** Make a list of the things that were left in the cairn. For each of these things, write what it is made of. Then assign a name and a function to each item. Remember that the Venusians think that humans are the figures they see in a Disney cartoon. How would such beings use these items?

PROJECT

Time Capsule. Shann and his people preserved items that they thought were important within their history and culture. What items would you include in a time capsule? Think about things that have special significance to you. With your classmates, create a list of items you would choose to save. Collect any of these items that you can; for others that are too large or expensive, use pictures of the items. Make a display of the collection. Perhaps you would like to store this away somewhere to be opened at a much later date.

"Southbound on the Freeway"
by May Swenson

ABOUT THE AUTHOR

May Swenson (1919–1989) was born and raised in Logan, Utah. After working as a reporter for a newspaper in Salt Lake City and as an editor in New York City, she published a collection of poems, *Another Animal: Poems* (1954). Her work was well received, and she devoted herself to writing full time. Some of her other works include *Half Sun Half Sleep* (1967), *Iconographs* (1970), and *New and Selected Things Taking Place* (1979). Swenson was a writer in residence at Purdue University and she lectured and gave poetry readings at colleges and universities across the country. Her poems are often noted for their precise, imaginative images and have received both critical acclaim and many awards.

ABOUT THE SELECTION

Background: Technique. The **point of view** of a story or poem is the vantage point from which it is told. In **"Southbound on the Freeway,"** Swenson describes a busy freeway from the point of view of a visitor from another planet. By choosing an unusual point of view, Swenson is able to take a fresh look at a commonplace phenomenon of our culture—the freeway at rush hour.

READER'S JOURNAL

Do you believe there is life on planets other than Earth? What do you think creatures from another planet would look like? Imagine you have just landed on another planet. In your journal, describe the first life forms that you see. How do you know that they are alive? Do they resemble any life forms you know on Earth?

"Southbound on the Freeway"

MAY SWENSON

A tourist came in from Orbitville,[1]
parked in the air, and said:

The creatures of this star[2]
are made of metal and glass.

5   Through the transparent parts
you can see their guts.

Their feet are round and roll
on diagrams—or long

measuring tapes—dark
10   with white lines.

They have four eyes.
The two in the back are red.

Sometimes you can see a five-eyed
one, with a red eye turning

15   on the top of his head.
He must be special—

the others respect him,
and go slow,

*What is the
"special" creature
with the fifth eye?*

---

1. **Orbitville.** Speaker means in orbit, or in outer space
2. **this star.** Speaker means the planet Earth

when he passes, winding
20 among them from behind.

They all hiss as they glide,
like inches, down the marked

tapes. Those soft shapes
shadowy inside

25 the hard bodies—are they
their guts or their brains? ∎

What are the
soft shapes?

Responding to the Selection

How would you describe a crowded freeway? How would it look if you were flying above in a helicopter? What would you see from above? What would you see if
you were in one of the cars? Do you think Swenson's description of a freeway full of
cars is accurate? Is it a flattering picture of life on Earth?

Reviewing the Selection

RECALLING

1. Where is the tourist from? What
materials does the tourist think make
up the creatures of "this star"? How
many eyes do these creatures have?
What makes some of them special?

2. What are the creatures doing? What
does the speaker see inside of the creatures?

INTERPRETING

▶▶ 3. What is the speaker really seeing? Why
doesn't the speaker recognize these
things? Why does the speaker think
that the five-eyed creatures are special?

▶▶ 4. How would you answer the speaker's
last question?

SYNTHESIZING

5. What other situations can you think of that would be confusing for beings from another
planet?

Understanding Literature (Questions for Discussion)

Personification. Personification is a figure of speech in which an idea, animal, or thing is described as if it were a person. What things are personified in this poem? How are the parts of these things described? What relationship between these things is described?

Responding in Writing

Point of View. Write a short description of a place with which you are familiar, such as your bedroom, your school, or a supermarket. Write a detailed description of the place as it appears to you. Then rewrite the description of the place from a completely different point of view; tell, for example, how your dog sees your bedroom, how a five-year-old might see your school, how a visitor from the planet Zephton might see a supermarket. How does a different perspective change things? For example, you might view clothes tossed on the floor as a mess, but your dog might see them as a comfortable bed.

> **Prewriting Suggestion:** To create a detailed description, use details that refer to all the five senses. Make a sensory detail chart. Make five columns with the headings *see, hear, smell, feel,* and *taste*. Make one chart for your point of view and another for some alternate point of view. How would the other person or creature see this place? What would the other person or creature perceive as important? In Swenson's poem, the alien thinks that cars are the creatures that inhabit Earth. What misunderstandings might arise because of the unique point of view of the person or creature about whom you have chosen to write?

PROJECT

Alien Life. What do you think life would be like on another planet? Create your own life forms. Draw a picture or make a model of one or several species. Write a short description of the lifestyle of these beings including habitat, food, means of communication, and any technology they have developed. Display your creations. Are there similarities between your creations and the creations of your classmates?

"There Will Come Soft Rains"
by Ray Bradbury

ABOUT THE AUTHOR

Ray Bradbury (1920–   ) was born in Illinois. He is best known for his science fiction and fantasy stories. He has published more than twenty books, including novels, children's books, and collections of short stories, poetry, and plays. His science fiction stories offer social criticism and warnings against the dangers of uncontrolled technological development. For his work in science fiction and fantasy, he has won the World Fantasy Award for lifetime achievement and the Grand Master Award from the Science Fiction Writers of America.

ABOUT THE SELECTION

Background: Genre. Science fiction is highly imaginative fiction containing fantastic elements based upon scientific principles, discoveries, or laws. "**There Will Come Soft Rains**" is set in the year 2026 in a fully automated house (one in which activities once done by humans are now done by machines). The advanced technology and the futuristic setting make this a science fiction story.

Background: Technique. An **allusion** is a rhetorical technique in which reference is made to a person, event, object, or work from history or literature. The title of this story is an allusion to a poem by Sara Teasdale. This poem is featured in the story. As you read the story and the poem, think about how science fiction writers use stories about the future to warn us about the possible consequences of our present actions. Teasdale's poem, like Bradbury's story, deals with the horrific possibility that people might destroy themselves through war.

"There Will Come Soft Rains"

RAY BRADBURY

To whom is the house speaking? Who is in the house?

In the living room the voice-clock sang, *Tick-tock, seven o'clock, time to get up, time to get up, seven o'clock!* as if it were afraid that nobody would. The morning house lay empty. The clock ticked on, repeating and repeating its sounds into the emptiness. *Seven-nine, breakfast time, seven-nine!*

In the kitchen the breakfast stove gave a hissing sigh and <u>ejected</u> from its warm interior eight pieces of perfectly browned toast, eight eggs sunnyside up, sixteen slices of bacon, two coffees, and two cool glasses of milk.

What is the weather like on August 4, 2026? What does the house recommend?

"Today is August 4, 2026," said a second voice from the kitchen ceiling, "in the City of Allendale, California." It repeated the date three times for memory's sake. "Today is Mr. Featherstone's birthday. Today is the anniversary of Tilita's marriage. Insurance is payable, as are the water, gas, and light bills."

Which conveniences in this passage already exist in today's society?

Somewhere in the walls, relays clicked, memory tapes glided under electric eyes.

Eight-one, tick-tock, eight-one o'clock, off to school, off to work, run, run, eight-one! But no doors slammed, no carpets took the soft <u>tread</u> of rubber heels. It was raining outside. The weather box on the front door sang quietly: "Rain, rain, go away; rubbers, raincoats for today. . . ." And the rain tapped on the empty house, echoing.

Outside, the garage chimed and lifted its door to reveal the waiting car. After a long wait the door swung down again.

At eight-thirty the eggs were shriveled and the toast was like stone. An aluminum wedge scraped them into the sink, where hot water whirled them down a metal throat that digested and flushed them away to the distant sea.

WORDS FOR
EVERYDAY USE:

e • ject (ē jekt´) *vt.,* cast out; emit; discharge

tread (tred) *n.,* step

The dirty dishes were dropped into a hot washer and <u>emerged</u> twinkling dry.

Nine-fifteen, sang the clock, *time to clean.*

Out of warrens[1] in the wall, tiny robot mice darted. The rooms were acrawl with the small cleaning animals, all rubber and metal. They thudded against chairs, whirling their mustached runners, <u>kneading</u> the rug nap, sucking gently at hidden dust. Then, like mysterious invaders, they popped into their burrows. Their pink electric eyes faded. The house was clean.

Ten o'clock. The sun came out from behind the rain. The house stood alone in a city of rubble and ashes. This was the one house left standing. At night the ruined city gave off a radioactive[2] glow which could be seen for miles.

Ten-fifteen. The garden sprinklers whirled up in golden founts, filling the soft morning air with scatterings of brightness. The water pelted windowpanes, running down the charred west side where the house had been burned evenly free of its white paint. The entire west face of the house was black, save for five places. Here the silhouette in paint of a man mowing a lawn. Here, as in a photograph, a woman bent to pick flowers. Still farther over, their images burned on wood in one <u>titanic</u> instant, a small boy, hands flung into the air; higher up, the image of a thrown ball, and opposite him a girl, hands raised to catch a ball which never came down.

The five spots of paint—the man, the woman, the children, the ball—remained. The rest was a thin charcoaled layer.

The gentle sprinkler rain filled the garden with falling light.

Until this day, how well the house had kept its peace. How carefully it had inquired, "Who goes there? What's the password?" and, getting no answer from lonely foxes and whining cats, it had shut up its windows and drawn shades in a <u>preoccupation</u> with self-protection that bordered on a mechanical <u>paranoia</u>.

It quivered at each sound, the house did. If a sparrow brushed a window, the shade snapped up. The bird, startled, flew off! No, not even a bird must touch the house!

The house was an altar with ten thousand attendants, big, small, servicing, attending, in choirs. But the gods had gone away, and the <u>ritual</u> of the religion continued senselessly, uselessly.

Twelve noon.

A dog whined, shivering, on the front porch.

The front door recognized the dog voice and opened. The dog, once huge and fleshy, but now gone to bone and covered with sores, moved in and through the house, tracking mud. Behind it whirred angry mice, angry at

---

1. **warrens.** Tunneled homes produced by small mammals such as mice or rabbits

2. **radioactive.** Capable of producing energy in the form of rays (alpha, beta, and gamma) given off by the disintegration of atomic nuclei, as in uranium and plutonium

What is unusual about the way the house speaks? What is significant about its use of language?

What has happened to the other houses in the city?

What record is left of the family? How was the record created?

WORDS FOR EVERYDAY USE:

e • merge (ē murj´) *vi.*, come forth
knead (nēd) *vt.*, press, rub, or squeeze; massage
ti • tan • ic (tī tan´ik) *adj.*, strong; powerful
pre • oc • cu • pa • tion (prē äk´yoo pā´shən) *n.*, absorption in thought

par • a • noi • a (par´ə noi´ə) *n.*, suspiciousness; delusions of persecution
rit • u • al (rich´oo əl) *n.*, religious or ceremonial act

having to pick up mud, angry at incon-venience.

For not a leaf fragment blew under the door but what the wall panels flipped open and the copper scrap rats flashed swiftly out. The offending dust, hair, or paper, seized in miniature steel jaws, was raced back to the bur-rows. There, down tubes which fed into the cellar, it was dropped into the sighing vent of an incinerator[3] which sat like evil Baal[4] in a dark corner.

What happens to the dog?

The dog ran upstairs, hysterically yelping to each door, at last realizing, as the house realized, that only silence was here.

It sniffed the air and scratched the kitchen door. Behind the door, the stove was making pancakes that filled the house with a rich baked odor and the scent of maple syrup.

The dog frothed at the mouth, lying at the door, sniffing, its eyes turned to fire. It ran wildly in circles, biting at its tail, spun in a frenzy, and died. It lay in the parlor for an hour.

Two o'clock, sang a voice.

Delicately sensing decay at last, the regiments of mice hummed out as softly as blown gray leaves in an elec-trical wind.

Two-fifteen.

The dog was gone.

In the cellar, the incinerator glowed suddenly and a whirl of sparks leaped up the chimney.

Two thirty-five.

---

3. **incinerator.** Furnace designed to burn waste products
4. **Baal.** Pre-Christian god of the Semitic people

Bridge tables[5] sprouted from patio walls. Playing cards fluttered onto pads in a shower of pips.[6] Drinks <u>manifested</u> on an oaken bench with egg-salad sandwiches. Music played.

But the tables were silent and the cards untouched.

At four o'clock the tables folded like great butterflies back through the paneled walls.

Four-thirty.

The nursery walls glowed.

Animals took shape: yellow giraffes, blue lions, pink antelopes, lilac panthers <u>cavorting</u> in crystal substance. The walls were glass. They looked out upon color and fantasy. Hidden films clocked through well-oiled sprockets,[7] and the walls lived. The nursery floor was woven to resemble a crisp, cereal meadow. Over this ran aluminum roaches and iron crickets, and in the hot still air butterflies of delicate red tissue <u>wavered</u> among the sharp aroma of animal spoors![8] There was the sound like a great matted yellow hive of bees within a dark bellows, the lazy bumble of a purring lion. And there was the patter of okapi[9] feet and the murmur of a fresh jungle rain, like other hoofs, falling upon the summer-parched grass. Now the walls <u>dissolved</u> into distances of parched weed, mile on mile, and warm endless sky. The animals drew away into thorn brakes and water holes.

It was the children's hour.

Five o'clock. The bath filled with clear hot water.

Six, seven, eight o'clock. The dinner dishes manipulated like magic tricks, and in the study a *click*. In the metal stand opposite the hearth where a fire now blazed up warmly, a cigar popped out, half an inch of soft gray ash on it, smoking, waiting.

Nine o'clock. The beds warmed their hidden circuits, for nights were cool here.

Nine-five. A voice spoke from the study ceiling:

"Mrs. McClellan, which poem would you like this evening?"

The house was silent.

The voice said at last, "Since you express no preference, I shall select a poem at random." Quiet music rose to back the voice. "Sara Teasdale. As I recall, your favorite . . ."

There will come soft rains and the
*   smell of the ground,*
And swallows circling with their
*   shimmering sound;*
And frogs in the pools singing at
*   night,*
And wild plum trees in <u>tremulous</u>
*   white;*
Robins will wear their feathery fire,
Whistling their whims on a low
*   fence-wire;*

What is ironic about the lifelike images in the nursery?

---

5. **Bridge tables.** Tables where four players can sit to play bridge, a card game involving team strategy

6. **pips.** Suit-indicating figures on playing cards

7. **clocked through well-oiled sprockets.** Moved regularly through holes lined up in a row, as film in a camera

8. **spoors.** Tracks, trails, or droppings of a hunted animal

9. **okapi.** African animal with zebra-like stripes and a giraffe-like neck

And not one will know of the war,
not one
Will care at last when it is done.
Not one would mind, neither bird
nor tree,
If mankind perished utterly;
And Spring herself, when she woke
at dawn
Would scarcely know that we were
gone.

What effect has the death of the family had on the house? What effect do you think the end of humankind has had on the world?

The fire burned on the stone hearth, and the cigar fell away into a mound of quiet ash on its tray. The empty chairs faced each other between the silent walls, and the music played.

At ten o'clock the house began to die.

The wind blew. A falling tree bough crashed through the kitchen window. Cleaning solvent,[10] bottled, shattered over the stove. The room was ablaze in an instant!

"Fire!" screamed a voice. The house lights flashed, water pumps shot water from the ceilings. But the solvent spread on the linoleum, licking, eating, under the kitchen door, while the voices took it up in chorus: "Fire, fire, fire!"

The house tried to save itself. Doors sprang tightly shut, but the windows were broken by the heat and the wind blew and sucked upon the fire.

The house gave ground as the fire in ten billion angry sparks moved with flaming ease from room to room and then up the stairs. While scurrying water rats squeaked from the walls, pistoled their water, and ran for more.

What part of the house does the fire attack? What consequence will this attack have for the house?

And the wall sprays let down showers of mechanical rain.

But too late. Somewhere, sighing, a pump shrugged to a stop. The quenching rain ceased. The reserve water supply which had filled baths and washed dishes for many quiet days was gone.

The fire crackled up the stairs. It fed upon Picassos and Matisses[11] in the upper halls, like delicacies, baking off the oily flesh, tenderly crisping the canvases into black shavings.

Now the fire lay in beds, stood in windows, changed the colors of drapes!

And then, reinforcements.

From attic trapdoors, blind robot faces peered down with faucet mouths gushing green chemical.

The fire backed off, as even an elephant must at the sight of a dead snake. Now there were twenty snakes whipping over the floor, killing the fire with a clear cold venom of green froth.

But the fire was clever. It had sent flame outside the house, up through the attic to the pumps there. An explosion! The attic brain which directed the pumps was shattered into bronze shrapnel[12] on the beams.

The fire rushed back into every closet and felt the clothes hung there.

The house shuddered, oak bone on bone, its bared skeleton cringing from the heat, its wire, its nerves revealed as

---

10. **Cleaning solvent.** Chemical substance that dissolves another substance, such as soil

11. **Picassos and Matisses.** Pieces of art by Spanish artist Pablo Picasso (1881–1973) and French artist Henri Matisse (1869–1964)

12. **shrapnel.** Bits of shattered metal thrown from an explosion

WORDS FOR
EVERYDAY USE:

re • in • force • ment (rē´in fôrs´mənt) *n.*, additional forces

re • veal (ri vēl) *vt.*, show, expose

if a surgeon had torn the skin off to let the red veins and capillaries[13] quiver in the scalded air. Help, help; Fire! Run, run! Heat snapped mirrors like the first brittle winter ice. And the voices wailed Fire, fire, run, run, like a tragic nursery rhyme, a dozen voices, high, low, like children dying in a forest, alone, alone. And the voices fading as the wires popped their sheathings like hot chestnuts. One, two, three, four, five voices died.

In the nursery the jungle burned. Blue lions roared, purple giraffes bounded off. The panthers ran in circles, changing color, and ten million animals, running before the fire, vanished off toward a distant steaming river. . . .

Ten more voices died. In the last instant under the fire avalanche, other choruses, <u>oblivious</u>, could be heard announcing the time, playing music, cutting the lawn by remote-control mower, or setting an umbrella frantically out and in the slamming and opening front door, a thousand things happening, like a clock shop when each clock strikes the hour insanely before or after the other, a scene of maniac confusion, yet unity; singing, screaming, a few last cleaning mice darting bravely out to carry the horrid ashes away! And one voice, with <u>sublime</u> disregard for the situation, read

poetry aloud in the fiery study, until all the film spools burned, until all the wires withered and the circuits cracked.

The fire burst the house and let it slam flat down, puffing out skirts of spark and smoke.

In the kitchen, an instant before the rain of fire and timber, the stove could be seen making breakfasts at a psychopathic rate,[14] ten dozen eggs, six loaves of toast, twenty dozen bacon strips, which, eaten by fire, started the stove working again, hysterically hissing!

The crash. The attic smashing into kitchen and parlor. The parlor into cellar, cellar into subcellar. Deep freeze, armchair, film tapes, circuits, beds, and all like skeletons thrown in a cluttered mound deep under.

Smoke and silence. A great quantity of smoke.

Dawn showed faintly in the east. Among the ruins, one wall stood alone. Within the wall, a last voice said, over and over again and again, even as the sun rose to shine upon the heaped rubble and steam:

"Today is August 5, 2026, today is August 5, 2026, today is . . ." ■

People have often claimed that at death a person's life "flashes before his or her eyes." In what way is the death of the house similar to the death of a person?

---

13. **capillaries.** Small blood vessels that carry blood between the arteries (carrying oxygenated blood away from the heart) and the veins (carrying blood depleted of oxygen back to the heart)
14. **psychopathic rate.** Frantic, insanely rapid rate

Responding to the Selection

Imagine living in an automated house such as this one. What would you like about it? What would you dislike? Might living in an automated house change you in any way? If so, how?

Reviewing the Selection

RECALLING

1. Who is talking in the house on the morning of August 4, 2026? In what ways does the house prepare for people who do not appear?

2. What has happened to the city? What can be seen on the west side of the house? What does the house do when nobody responds to it?

3. What happens just after nine o'clock? Which poem does the house select?

4. What happens at ten o'clock? How does the house react?

INTERPRETING

5. What is ominous about the house in the beginning of the story?

6. What has happened to the people of the house?

7. Why is the action just after nine o'clock somewhat more personal than the others of the day? How does the house choose the poem? Why is it an appropriate poem for the situation?

8. Describe the scene of the destruction of the house. How is the house left in the end? How does the action of the house in the last line compare to its action in the first line?

SYNTHESIZING

9. Why do you think Bradbury waited until paragraph 10 to explain what had happened to the city? Why do you think he waited to show what had happened to the family?

10. What makes the actions of the house senseless? What comment is Bradbury making about the essential stupidity of machines? Why might it be dangerous to put too much of our lives in the hands of machines?

Understanding Literature (Questions for Discussion)

1. **Theme.** A **theme** is a central idea in a literary work. Reread the last four lines of the poem "There Will Come Soft Rains." What do you think the theme of the poem is? Why do you think Bradbury chose to use the name of this poem for the title of his story as well as to incorporate the poem into the story? How are the themes of the poem and the story similar?

2. **Personification. Personification** is a figure of speech in which an idea, animal, or thing is described as if it were a person. In this story the house is personified, and it becomes the main character in the story. Find examples of all the things the house is able to do. What is special about this house that makes it different from other houses? What specific lines, especially in the fire scene, describe the house in human terms?

Responding in Writing

Schedule. In this story the daily schedule is clear because of the frequent chimings of the house. Write a schedule for one day in your life. Write out activities and events in little jingles as the house does to help remind you of things that you have to do.

> **Prewriting Suggestion:** Create a time line or timetable for the day. At the top of a piece of paper, write the date and any special things to remember for the day—a holiday, a birthday, a test you have, a paper that is due. Then, beginning with the hour you get up in the morning, fill in your time line. Some things to include might be the time you leave your house in the morning, the time that school begins, the time you have lunch, and so on.

PROJECT

Machine Show. Have you ever thought, "There has to be a better way to do this"? Well, don your inventor's hat and think of a machine to do your least favorite task. Make a picture or model of your machine and write a description of it. Do you think this machine could really work? Do you think it will ever be made? Why, or why not?

UNIT REVIEW

Visions of the Future

VOCABULARY FROM THE SELECTIONS

biped, 549	flotsam, 545	orifice, 549	sublime, 563
broker, 539	fruitless, 550	overtake, 531	superhuman, 538
cairn, 544	glaring, 531	paranoia, 559	sustain, 532
cavort, 561	incomprehensible,	preoccupation, 559	tentatively, 534
compromise, 540	549	recapitulate, 547	titanic, 559
degeneration, 548	knead, 559	refuge, 544	tread, 558
dissolve, 561	languidly, 547	reinforcement, 562	tremulous, 561
ebb, 545	manifest, 561	remorseless, 544	urgent, 534
eccentric, 532	momentum, 532	reveal, 562	wane, 544
eject, 558	motley, 545	revolt, 538	waver, 561
emerge, 559	oblivious, 563	ritual, 559	
endemic, 548	onrushing, 533	sardonically, 550	

LITERARY TERMS

allusion, 557	personification, 556, 565	setting, 552
dramatic irony, 552	point of view, 556	simile, 542
mood, 536	science fiction, 557	theme, 536, 565

SYNTHESIS: QUESTIONS FOR WRITING, RESEARCH, OR DISCUSSION

1. Works of science fiction often present warnings about the future. Which stories and poems in this unit present warnings? What warnings do they present?

2. Many science fiction works deal with technology. What role is played by technology in each of the selections in this unit?

LANGUAGE LAB   PROOFREADING FOR SPELLING ERRORS

After checking for other errors in your writing, you should read it carefully for errors in spelling. If you come across any words that you are not completely sure about, check them in a dictionary.

LANGUAGE ARTS SURVEY

For additional help, see the Language Arts Survey, 2.134–2.136.

COMMON SPELLING ERRORS

Forming Plurals

Add *es* to nouns ending in *o* preceded by a consonant and to nouns ending in *s, x, z, ch,* or *sh.*
> EXAMPLES: *potatoes, vetoes, tomatoes, tresses, axes, buzzes, scratches, ashes*

Add *s* to most musical terms ending in *o.*
> EXAMPLES: *solos, adagios, pianos*

Add *s* to nouns ending in *y* preceded by a vowel.
> EXAMPLES: *joys, Fridays, lackeys, keys, trays*

In nouns ending in *y* preceded by a consonant, change the *y* to *i* and add *es.*
> EXAMPLES: *candies, quandaries, theories, societies*

Remember irregular plurals of certain words.
> EXAMPLES: *men, feet, geese, teeth*

Form the plural of a compound consisting of a noun and a modifier by making the noun—rather than the last word in the compound—plural.
> EXAMPLES: *justices-of-the-peace, passersby, attorneys general*

Adding Prefixes

A **prefix** is a letter or a group of letters added to the beginning of a word to change its meaning. When a prefix is added to a word, the spelling of the word itself does not change.
> EXAMPLES: dis + like = dislike
> un + natural = unnatural
> over + estimate = overestimate

Adding Suffixes

A **suffix** is a letter or group of letters added to the end of a word to change its meaning. The spelling of most words is not changed when the suffix *–ness* or *–ly* is added.
> EXAMPLES: common + ness = commonness
> common + ly = commonly

If a word has more than one syllable and ends in *y,* change the *y* to *i* before adding *–ly* or *–ness.*
> EXAMPLES: happy + ly = happily
> happy + ness = happiness

In most cases of words ending in a final silent *e,* drop the *e* when adding a suffix beginning with a vowel, and keep the *e* when adding a suffix beginning with a consonant.
> EXAMPLES: strange + ly = strangely
> strange + er = stranger
> excite + ment = excitement
> excite + able = excitable

EXERCISE A   Using Spelling Rules

In the following sentences, make all the underlined words plural, and add prefixes or suffixes to the words in parentheses. Use the spelling rules, and refer to a dictionary if you are unsure of the correct spelling.

1. The <u>echo</u> of the grinding ice sounded (eerie + ly) like the cracking of <u>bone</u>.

2. In the future, <u>person</u> will (probable + ly) develop new <u>theory</u> about the (useful + ness) of technological inventions.

3. Without advances in genetics, growing (seed + less) <u>orange</u> or <u>tomato</u> would be (im + possible).

4. As the Venusian watches the (un + usual) images, he wonders about the (mystery + ous) <u>life</u> of the <u>man</u>, <u>woman</u>, and <u>child</u> from the third planet.

5. The <u>royalty</u> that Ray Bradbury receives for his <u>novel</u> and short <u>story</u> must be (un + believe + able)!

6. Kim wanted to light a few <u>candle</u> to counteract the (heavy + ness) of the stale air, but no one had any <u>match</u>.

EXERCISE B   Proofreading for Spelling Errors

Copy the following paragraph onto a separate sheet of paper, correcting any spelling errors you find. If you are uncertain about any words, refer to a dictionary.

In the 1930s radio programes provided entertainment as well as newes; audiences were glued to their radioes as they listened to readings of popular storys and radio playes. In 1938 a talented young writer and radio personality named Orson Welles adapted the science fiction tale *War of the Worlds* for a radio broadcast. On Halloween night, he broadcast the story of a Martian invasion in a series of news bulletines. Although Welles made several disclaimers during the program, some radio listeners believed the terrifying reports that Martian's had invaded the United States. By 1938 radio audiences had grown accustomed to news interruptiones about the war developing in Europe, and some listeners felt panic when they heard the horrifiing announcments. In some areas of the country, highwaies were jammed with people fleeing their homees after hearing the unbelieveable news.

LANGUAGE ARTS WORKSHOP

TAKING STANDARDIZED TESTS

Standardized tests are almost always multiple choice. Types of questions that appear on standardized tests include analogy; sentence completion; grammar, usage, and mechanics; reading comprehension; and synonym and antonym. See the Language Arts Survey, 4.39–4.44, for information about each of these question types.

EXERCISE

Answer the following questions. Be sure to read instructions carefully.

For questions 1 and 2, choose the pair of words whose relationship is most similar to that of the sample pair.
1.   BANANA : BUNCH ::
(A) key : lock
(B) apple : tree
(C) card : deck
(D) brush : comb
(E) hand : finger

2.   CHILD : ADOLESCENT ::
(A) afternoon : evening
(B) adult : baby
(C) father : daughter
(D) April : January
(E) dinner : breakfast

For questions 3 and 4, select the pair of words that best completes each sentence.
3.   Experts _____ that the powerful hurricane caused _____ damage.
(A) denied . . . seasonable
(B) hesitated . . . noticeable
(C) rejoiced . . . massive
(D) estimated . . . widespread
(E) acknowledged . . . beneficial

4.   Only relief workers who have been _____ may enter the _____ area.
(A) paid . . . disaster
(B) exposed . . . sterile
(C) dismissed . . . volunteer
(D) refused . . . restricted
(E) vaccinated . . . contaminated

Choose the letter that corresponds to any error in the sentence.
5.   <u>Aftershocks</u> from the <u>earthquake</u> <u>was</u> registered <u>for many</u> weeks. <u>No error</u>.
        (A)   (B)   (C)   (D)   (E)

LANGUAGE ARTS SURVEY

For additional help, see the Language Arts Survey, 4.39–4.44.

Part Three

GENRES IN LITERATURE

Kayaker on Eclipse Sound, Northwest Territories, Canada

There's a land where the mountains are nameless
And the rivers all run God knows where;
There are lives that are erring and aimless,
And deaths that just hang by a hair;
There are hardships that nobody reckons;
There are valleys unpeopled and still;
There's a land oh, it beckons and beckons,
And I want to go back and I will.

—Robert W. Service
Spell of the Yukon

NOVEL

The Call of the Wild
by Jack London

ABOUT THE AUTHOR

Jack London (1876–1916) was born in San Francisco, California, to Flora Wellman Chaney. His father had deserted them before he was born. When London was nine months old, his mother married John London, a widower with two daughters. Because of the family's severe poverty, Jack left school at the age of fourteen to work in a cannery and experienced the colorful life of the San Francisco waterfront. By the age of sixteen, London had been both an oyster pirate and a member of the San Francisco Bay Fish Patrol. In 1893, at the age of seventeen, London joined a sealing schooner as an able-bodied seaman and traveled as far as Japan. From this experience, London wrote the essay "Story of a Typhoon off the Coast of Japan," which won a twenty-five-dollar first prize in a San Francisco newspaper contest. After returning to the United States from Japan, London was determined to become a writer; he read voraciously and, at the age of nineteen, continued his education at Oakland High School in California. After one semester at the University of California, London joined countless others in the Klondike gold rush. Ill with scurvy, he returned to Oakland, California, and wrote about his Northland experiences. At the age of twenty-three, London made his literary breakthrough with the story "An Odyssey of the North," which was published by the *Atlantic Monthly* magazine in 1899. London wrote over two hundred short stories in the next twenty years. During that time, he also published twenty novels, more than four hundred nonfiction pieces, and three plays. Despite the extraordinary variety of subjects explored in his work, London's reputation as a writer was established on his works of the Northland, comprising twenty-eight short stories, four novels, one play, and six nonfiction pieces. London's writings about the Northland center on themes of **Naturalism**, a literary movement of the late nineteenth and early twentieth centuries that saw actions and events as arising inevitably from forces in the environment. London's most famous Northland novels are *The Call of the Wild* (1903) and *White Fang* (1906), a companion work to the earlier novel. His novels include *The Sea-Wolf* (1904), *The Game* (1905), *Martin Eden* (1909), *John Barleycorn* (1913), and *Jerry of the Islands* (1917). His several collections of short stories include *Love of Life* (1907), *Lost Face* (1910), and *On the Makaloa Mat* (1919). The work of Jack London greatly influenced many modern writers, including George Orwell and Ernest Hemingway. His work has been translated into over eighty languages.

ABOUT THE SELECTION

The main character in **The Call of the Wild** (1903) is an animal, a Saint Bernard–Scotch shepherd mixed-breed dog named Buck. Buck's adventure begins when he is kidnapped from his civilized life on Judge Miller's farm and placed unprepared in the uncivilized world of the Yukon. During the course of the novel, Buck encounters many different kinds of characters, human and animal, and many types of events, from both of which he learns to adapt, to survive, and, eventually, to return to his wild beginnings.

Background: History. In 1896, when a man by the name of George Washington Carmack struck gold in the Klondike territory of northwest Canada, Jack London was ready for adventure. Hailed as the "Last Frontier," the Klondike captivated London with its promise of gold—certainly an antidote to the miseries of poverty and boredom—and with its rules of survival based not upon a person's bank account, but upon a person's courage, endurance, adaptability, and intelligence. After two years, the rush had exhausted the most easily accessible gold deposits; during those two years, nearly two hundred and fifty thousand prospectors started for the Bonanza River. Of those, only fifty thousand miners reached the Yukon interior. Jack London was one of them.

Background: Theme. Jack London based his personal philosophy on the theory of social Darwinism, the idea—not Darwin's idea, by the way—that human societies are or should be managed according to the principle of "survival of the fittest." This idea seemed to be lived out fully in the wild and harsh Northland, where human laws and law enforcement were virtually nonexistent. In *The Call of the Wild*, London's social Darwinism is combined with the Naturalistic emphasis on natural forces beyond the comprehension and control of the characters subjected to them. When civilizing influences and conditions are absent, the essentially uncivilized and wild nature of Buck expresses itself, and he adapts readily to his new world. The influences of social Darwinism, of the frontier virtues of courage, individuality, endurance, and intelligence, and the experience of surviving a winter eight miles outside Dawson City, Yukon Territory, can be seen in London's *The Call of the Wild.*

READER'S JOURNAL

Have you ever had a dog or another animal as a family pet? Have you had a close friend or relative who did? What are your feelings toward that animal? What role does or did the animal have in your family? In your journal, describe the kind of relationship you have or have had with an animal.

The Call of the Wild

JACK LONDON

CHAPTER I

Into the Primitive

"Old longings nomadic leap,
  Chafing at custom's chain;
Again from its brumal sleep
  Wakens the ferine strain."

Buck did not read the newspapers, or he would have known that trouble was brewing, not alone for himself, but for every tidewater dog, strong of muscle and with warm, long hair, from Puget Sound to San Diego. Because men, groping in the Arctic darkness, had found a yellow metal,[1] and because steamship and transportation companies were booming the find, thousands of men were rushing into the Northland. These men wanted dogs, and the dogs they wanted were heavy dogs, with strong muscles by which to toil, and furry coats to protect them from the frost.

Buck lived at a big house in the sun-kissed Santa Clara Valley. Judge Miller's place, it was called. It stood back from the road, half hidden among the trees, through which glimpses could be caught of the wide cool <u>veranda</u> that ran around its four sides. The house was approached by graveled driveways which wound about through wide-spreading lawns and under the interlacing boughs of tall poplars. At the rear, things were on even a more spacious scale than at the front. There were great stables, where a dozen grooms and boys held forth, rows of vine-clad servants' cottages, an endless and orderly array of outhouses, long grape arbors, green pastures, orchards, and berry patches. Then

Who wants dogs? Why do they want dogs?

---

1. **yellow metal.** Gold

WORDS FOR
EVERYDAY USE: **ve • ran • da** (və ran´də) *n.,* open porch

there was the pumping plant for the artesian well,[2] and the big cement tank where Judge Miller's boys took their morning plunge and kept cool in the hot afternoon.

And over this great <u>demesne</u> Buck ruled. Here he was born, and here he had lived the four years of his life. It was true, there were other dogs. There could not but be other dogs on so vast a place, but they did not count. They came and went, resided in the populous kennels, or lived <u>obscurely</u> in the <u>recesses</u> of the house after the fashion of Toots, the Japanese pug, or Ysabel, the Mexican hairless, strange creatures that rarely put nose out of doors or set foot to ground. On the other hand, there were the fox terriers, a score of them at least, who yelped fearful promises at Toots and Ysabel looking out of the windows at them and protected by a legion of housemaids armed with brooms and mops.

But Buck was neither house-dog nor kennel-dog. The whole realm was his. He plunged into the swimming tank or went hunting with the Judge's sons; he escorted Mollie and Alice, the Judge's daughters, on long twilight or early morning rambles; on wintry nights he lay at the Judge's feet before the roaring library fire; he carried the Judge's grandsons on his back, or rolled them in the grass, and guarded their footsteps through wild adventures down to the fountain in the stable yard, and even beyond, where the <u>paddocks</u> were, and the berry patches. Among the terriers he stalked <u>imperiously</u>, and

Toots and Ysabel he utterly ignored, for he was king,—king over all creeping, crawling, flying things of Judge Miller's place, humans included.

His father, Elmo, a huge St. Bernard, had been the Judge's inseparable companion, and Buck bid fair to follow in the way of his father. He was not so large,—he weighed only one hundred and forty pounds,—for his mother, Shep, had been a Scotch shepherd dog. Nevertheless, one hundred and forty pounds, to which was added the dignity that comes of good living and universal respect, enabled him to carry himself in right royal fashion. During the four years since his puppyhood he had lived the life of a <u>sated</u> aristocrat; he had a fine pride in himself, was even a trifle egotistical, as country gentlemen sometimes become because of their <u>insular</u> situation. But he had saved himself by not becoming a mere pampered house-dog. Hunting and kindred outdoor delights had kept down the fat and hardened his muscles; and to him, as to the cold-tubbing races, the love of water had been a tonic and a health preserver.

And this was the manner of dog Buck was in the fall of 1897, when the Klondike[3] strike dragged men from all the world into the frozen North. But Buck did not read the newspapers, and he did not know that Manuel, one of

What words and details are used to portray Buck's character?

What details show Buck's high status at the Judge's place?

---

2. **artesian well.** Well drilled deep enough to reach water that is draining from higher ground, so that pressure will force a flow upward

3. **Klondike.** Gold was found in 1898 in the Klondike, a river in West Yukon Territory, Canada.

WORDS FOR EVERYDAY USE:

de • mesne (di mān´) *n.*, region; domain
ob • scure • ly (əb skyoor´lē) *adv.*, unnoticed
re • cess (rē´ses) *n.*, secluded place
pad • dock (pad´ək) *n.*, enclosed field

im • per • i • ous • ly (im pir´ē es lē) *adv.*, with an overbearing or imperial manner
sat • ed (sāt´əd) *adj.*, satisfied
in • su • lar (in´sə lər) *adj.*, detached; isolated

the gardener's helpers, was an undesirable acquaintance. Manuel had one <u>besetting</u> sin. He loved to play Chinese lottery. Also, in his gambling, he had one besetting weakness—faith in a system; and this made his damnation certain. For to play a system requires money, while the wages of a gardener's helper do not lap over the needs of a wife and numerous <u>progeny</u>.

The Judge was at a meeting of the Raisin Growers' Association, and the boys were busy organizing an athletic club, on the memorable night of Manuel's treachery. No one saw him and Buck go off through the orchard on what Buck imagined was merely a stroll. And with the exception of a solitary man, no one saw them arrive at the little flag station known as College Park. This man talked with Manuel, and money chinked between them.

"You might wrap up the goods before you deliver 'm," the stranger said gruffly, and Manuel doubled a piece of stout rope around Buck's neck under the collar.

"Twist it, an' you'll choke 'm plentee," said Manuel, and the stranger grunted a ready affirmative.

Buck had accepted the rope with quiet dignity. To be sure, it was an <u>unwonted</u> performance: but he had learned to trust in men he knew, and to give them credit for a wisdom that outreached his own. But when the ends of the rope were placed in the stranger's hands, he growled menacingly. He had merely <u>intimated</u> his displeasure, in his pride believing that

to intimate was to command. But to his surprise the rope tightened around his neck, shutting off his breath. In quick rage he sprang at the man, who met him halfway, grappled him close by the throat, and with a deft twist threw him over on his back. Then the rope tightened mercilessly, while Buck struggled in a fury, his tongue lolling out of his mouth and his great chest panting <u>futilely</u>. Never in all his life had he been so vilely treated, and never in all his life had he been so angry. But his strength ebbed, his eyes glazed, and he knew nothing when the train was flagged and the two men threw him into the baggage car.

The next he knew, he was dimly aware that his tongue was hurting and that he was being jolted along in some kind of a <u>conveyance</u>. The hoarse shriek of a locomotive whistling a crossing told him where he was. He had traveled too often with the Judge not to know the sensation of riding in a baggage car. He opened his eyes, and into them came the unbridled anger of a kidnapped king. The man sprang for his throat, but Buck was too quick for him. His jaws closed on the hand, nor did they relax till his senses were choked out of him once more.

"Yep, has fits," the man said, hiding his mangled hand from the baggageman, who had been attracted by the sounds of struggle. "I'm takin' 'm up for the boss to 'Frisco. A crack dog-doctor there thinks that he can cure 'm."

Concerning that night's ride, the man spoke most eloquently for him-

What does Manuel do to Buck?

What are Buck's first reactions to captivity?

WORDS FOR EVERYDAY USE:	be • set • ting (bē set´ŋ) *part.*, constantly harassing	in • ti • mate (in´tə māt´) *vt.*, hint, imply
	prog • eny (präj´ə nē) *n.*, descendant; offspring	fu • tile • ly (fyoo´til´lē) *adv.*, ineffectively
	un • won • ted (un wän´tid) *adj.*, uncommon	con • vey • ance (kən vā´əns) *n.*, carrying device

self, in a little shed back of a saloon on the San Francisco waterfront.

"All I get is fifty for it," he grumbled; "an' I wouldn't do it over for a thousand, cold cash."

His hand was wrapped in a bloody handkerchief, and the right trouser leg was ripped from knee to ankle.

"How much did the other mug get?" the saloonkeeper demanded.

"A hundred," was the reply. "Wouldn't take a sou[4] less, so help me."

"That makes a hundred and fifty," the saloonkeeper calculated; "and he's worth it, or I'm a squarehead."

The kidnapper undid the bloody wrappings and looked at his <u>lacerated</u> hand. "If I don't get the hydrophoby—"[5]

"It'll be because you was born to hang," laughed the saloonkeeper. "Here, lend me a hand before you pull your freight," he added.

Dazed, suffering intolerable pain from throat and tongue, with the life half throttled out of him, Buck attempted to face his <u>tormentors</u>. But he was thrown down and choked repeatedly, till they succeeded in filing the heavy brass collar from off his neck. Then the rope was removed, and he was flung into a cagelike crate.

There he lay for the remainder of the weary night, nursing his wrath and wounded pride. He could not understand what it all meant. What did they want with him, these strange men? Why were they keeping him pent up in this narrow crate? He did not know why, but he felt oppressed by the vague sense of impending calamity.

Several times during the night he sprang to his feet when the shed door rattled open, expecting to see the Judge, or the boys at least. But each time it was the bulging face of the saloonkeeper that peered in at him by the sickly light of a tallow candle. And each time the joyful bark that trembled in Buck's throat was twisted into a savage growl.

But the saloonkeeper let him alone, and in the morning four men entered and picked up the crate. More tormentors, Buck decided, for they were evil-looking creatures, ragged and unkempt; and he stormed and raged at them through the bars. They only laughed and poked sticks at him, which he promptly assailed with his teeth till he realized that that was what they wanted. Whereupon he lay down <u>sullenly</u> and allowed the crate to be lifted into a wagon. Then he, and the crate in which he was imprisoned, began a passage through many hands. Clerks in the express office took charge of him; he was carted about in another wagon; a truck carried him, with an assortment of boxes and parcels, upon a ferry steamer; he was trucked off the steamer into a great railway depot, and finally he was deposited in an express car.

For two days and nights this express car was dragged along at the tail of shrieking locomotives; and for two days and nights Buck neither ate nor

What hope does Buck still have? How does he feel when that hope is disappointed?

---

4. **sou.** Any of several antique French coins of very small denomination

5. **hydrophoby.** Hydrophobia, or rabies

WORDS FOR EVERYDAY USE:

lac • er • at • ed (las´ər āt´ed) *part.*, cut; wounded

tor • men • tor (tôr ment´ər) *n.*, one who causes great pain or suffering

sul • len • ly (sul´ən lē) *adv.*, showing resentment; gloomily

drank. In his anger he had met the first advances of the express messengers with growls, and they had retaliated by teasing him. When he flung himself against the bars, quivering and frothing, they laughed at him and taunted him. They growled and barked like detestable dogs, mewed, and flapped their arms and crowed. It was all very silly, he knew, but therefore the more outrage to his dignity, and his anger <u>waxed</u> and waxed. He did not mind the hunger so much, but the lack of water caused him severe suffering and fanned his wrath to fever-pitch. For that matter, high-strung and finely sensitive, the ill treatment had flung him into a fever, which was fed by the inflammation of his parched and swollen throat and tongue.

He was glad for one thing: the rope was off his neck. That had given them an unfair advantage; but now that it was off, he would show them. They would never get another rope around his neck. Upon that he was <u>resolved</u>. For two days and nights he neither ate nor drank, and during those two days and nights of torment, he accumulated a fund of wrath that boded ill for whoever first fell foul of him. His eyes turned bloodshot, and he was <u>metamorphosed</u> into a raging fiend. So changed was he that the Judge himself would not have recognized him; and the express messengers breathed with relief when they bundled him off the train at Seattle.

Four men <u>gingerly</u> carried the crate from the wagon into a small, high-walled back yard. A stout man, with a red sweater that sagged generously at the neck, came out and signed the book for the driver. That was the man, Buck divined, the next tormentor, and he hurled himself savagely against the bars. The man smiled grimly, and brought a hatchet and a club.

"You ain't going to take him out now?" the driver asked.

"Sure," the man replied, driving the hatchet into the crate for a pry.

There was an instantaneous scattering of the four men who had carried it in, and from safe perches on top of the wall they prepared to watch the performance.

Buck rushed at the splintering wood, sinking his teeth into it, surging and wrestling with it. Wherever the hatchet fell on the outside, he was there on the inside, snarling and growling, as furiously anxious to get out as the man in the red sweater was calmly intent on getting him out.

"Now, you red-eyed devil," he said, when he had made an opening sufficient for the passage of Buck's body. At the same time he dropped the hatchet and shifted the club to his right hand.

And Buck was truly a red-eyed devil, as he drew himself together for the spring, hair bristling, mouth foaming, a mad glitter in his bloodshot eyes. Straight at the man he launched his one hundred and forty pounds of fury, <u>surcharged</u> with the pent passion of two days and nights. In midair, just as his jaws were about to close on the man, he received a shock that checked his body

How has Buck changed since he was taken from the Judge's?

WORDS FOR EVERYDAY USE:

wax (waks) *vi.*, increase in strength; grow larger
re • solved (ri zälvd´) *adj.*, firm and fixed in purpose; determined
met • a • mor • phose (met´ ə mor´fōz´) *vt.*, change; transform
gin • ger • ly (jin´ jər´lē) *adv.*, very cautiously
sur • charge (sʉr´ chärj´) *vt.*, overload; overburden

and brought his teeth together with an agonizing clip. He whirled over, fetching the ground on his back and side. He had never been struck by a club in his life and did not understand. With a snarl that was part bark and more scream he was again on his feet and launched into the air. And again the shock came and he was brought crushingly to the ground. This time he was aware that it was the club, but his madness knew no caution. A dozen times he charged, and as often the club broke the charge and smashed him down.

After a particularly fierce blow he crawled to his feet, too dazed to rush. He staggered limply about, the blood flowing from nose and mouth and ears, his beautiful coat sprayed and flecked with bloody <u>slaver</u>. Then the man advanced and deliberately dealt him a frightful blow on the nose. All the pain he had endured was as nothing compared with the exquisite agony of this. With a roar that was almost lionlike in its ferocity, he again hurled himself at the man. But the man, shifting the club from right to left, coolly caught him by

What is the man trying to teach Buck?

WORDS FOR EVERYDAY USE:

sla • ver (slav´ər) *n.,* saliva

the under jaw, at the same time wrenching downward and backward. Buck described a complete circle in the air, and half of another, then crashed to the ground on his head and chest.

For the last time he rushed. The man struck the shrewd blow he had purposely withheld for so long, and Buck crumpled up and went down, knocked utterly senseless.

"He's no slouch at dog-breakin', that's wot I say," one of the men on the wall cried enthusiastically.

"Druther break cayuses[6] any day, and twice on Sundays," was the reply of the driver, as he climbed on the wagon and started the horses.

Buck's senses came back to him, but not his strength. He lay where he had fallen, and from there he watched the man in the red sweater.

"Answers to the name of Buck,'" the man soliloquized, quoting from the saloonkeeper's letter which had announced the consignment of the crate and contents. "Well, Buck, my boy," he went on in a genial voice, "we've had our little ruction,[7] and the best thing we can do is to let it go at that. You've learned your place, and I know mine. Be a good dog and all 'll go well and the goose hang high. Be a bad dog, and I'll whale the stuffin' outa you. Understand?"

As he spoke he fearlessly patted the head he had so mercilessly pounded, and though Buck's hair involuntarily bristled at touch of the hand, he endured it without protest. When the man brought him water he drank eagerly, and later bolted a generous meal of raw meat, chunk by chunk, from the man's hand.

He was beaten (he knew that); but he was not broken. He saw, once for all, that he stood no chance against a man with a club. He had learned the lesson, and in all his afterlife he never forgot it. That was a revelation. It was his introduction to the reign of primitive law, and he met the introduction halfway. The facts of life took on a fiercer aspect; and while he faced that aspect uncowed, he faced it with all the latent cunning of his nature aroused. As the days went by, other dogs came, in crates and at the ends of ropes, some docilely, and some raging and roaring as he had come; and, one and all, he watched them pass under the dominion of the man in the red sweater. Again and again, as he looked at each brutal performance, the lesson was driven home to Buck: a man with a club was a lawgiver, a master to be obeyed, though not necessarily conciliated. Of this last Buck was never guilty, though he did see beaten dogs that fawned upon the man, and wagged their tails, and licked his hand. Also he saw one dog, that would neither conciliate nor obey, finally killed in the struggle for mastery.

Now and again men came, strangers, who talked excitedly, wheedlingly, and in all kinds of fashions to the man in the red sweater. And at such times that money passed between them the

---

6. **cayuses.** Small western horses used by cowboys
7. **ruction.** Noisy disturbance or quarrel

WORDS FOR EVERYDAY USE:

so • lil • o • quize (sə lil´ə kwīz´) vi., talk to oneself
con • sign • ment (kən sīn´mənt) n., shipment of goods sent to a dealer for safekeeping
ge • ni • al (jēn´yəl) adj., amiable; cheerful
un • cowed (un koud´) part., unafraid; unintimidated
la • tent (lāt´'nt) adj., hidden
con • cil • i • ate (kən sil´ē āt´) vt., win over

strangers took one or more of the dogs away with them. Buck wondered where they went, for they never came back; but the fear of the future was strong upon him, and he was glad each time when he was not selected.

Yet his time came, in the end, in the form of a little weazened[8] man who spat broken English and many strange and <u>uncouth</u> exclamations which Buck could not understand.

"Sacredam!" he cried, when his eyes lit upon Buck. "Dat one dam bully dog! Eh? How moch?"

"Three hundred, and a present at that," was the prompt reply of the man in the red sweater. "And seein' it's government money, you ain't got no kick coming, eh, Perrault?"

Perrault grinned. Considering that the price of dogs had been boomed skyward by the unwonted demand, it was not an unfair sum for so fine an animal. The Canadian Government would be no loser, nor would its dispatches travel the slower. Perrault knew dogs, and when he looked at Buck he knew that he was one in a thousand—"One in ten t'ousand," he commented mentally.

Buck saw money pass between them, and was not surprised when Curly, a good-natured Newfoundland, and he were led away by the little weazened man. That was the last he saw of the man in the red sweater, and as Curly and he looked at receding Seattle from the deck of the *Narwhal*, it was the last he saw of the warm Southland. Curly and he were taken below by Perrault and turned over to a black-faced giant called François. Perrault was a French-Canadian, and swarthy; François was a French-Canadian, and twice as swarthy. They were a new kind of men to Buck (of which he was destined to see many more), and while he developed no affection for them, he none the less grew honestly to respect them. He speedily learned that Perrault and François were fair men, calm and <u>impartial</u> in administering justice, and too wise in the way of dogs to be fooled by dogs.

In the 'tween-decks of the *Narwhal*, Buck and Curly joined two other dogs. One of them was a big, snow-white fellow from Spitzbergen who had been brought away by a whaling captain, and who had later accompanied a Geological Survey into the Barrens.[9] He was friendly, in a treacherous sort of way, smiling into one's face the while he meditated some underhand trick, as, for instance, when he stole from Buck's food at the first meal. As Buck sprang to punish him, the lash of François's whip sang through the air, reaching the culprit first; and nothing remained to Buck but to recover the bone. That was fair of François, he decided, and the man began his rise in Buck's estimation.

The other dog made no advances, nor received any; also, he did not attempt to steal from the newcomers.

Why does the man curse?

8. **weazened.** Wizened (dried and shrunken, as from aging)
9. **Barrens.** Extremely remote and sparsely populated region of the Northwest Territory, north and west of Hudson Bay

He was a gloomy, <u>morose</u> fellow, and he showed Curly plainly that all he desired was to be left alone, and further, that there would be trouble if he were not left alone. "Dave" he was called, and he ate and slept, or yawned between times, and took interest in nothing, not even when the *Narwhal* crossed Queen Charlotte Sound[10] and rolled and pitched and bucked like a thing possessed. When Buck and Curly grew excited, half wild with fear, he raised his head as though annoyed, favored them with an <u>incurious</u> glance, yawned, and went to sleep again.

Day and night the ship throbbed to the tireless pulse of the propeller, and though one day was very like another, it was apparent to Buck that the weather was steadily growing colder. At last, one morning, the propeller was quiet, and the *Narwhal* was <u>pervaded</u> with an atmosphere of excitement. He felt it, as did the other dogs, and knew that a change was at hand. François leashed them and brought them on deck. At the first step upon the cold surface, Buck's feet sank into a white mushy something very like mud. He sprang back with a snort. More of this white stuff was falling through the air. He shook himself, but more of it fell upon him. He sniffed it curiously, then licked some up on his tongue. It bit like fire, and the next instant was gone. This puzzled him. He tried it again, with the same result. The onlookers laughed uproariously, and he felt ashamed, he knew not why, for it was his first snow.

---

10. **Queen Charlotte Sound.** Body of water off the west coast of British Columbia, Canada

Responding to the Selection

Imagine that you are the dog Buck in this novel. Your place and position in the world have changed drastically and suddenly. Imagine that you can communicate with the Judge back home. Tell him what has happened to you, expressing your feelings about some of the men you've met, such as the man in the red sweater.

WORDS FOR EVERYDAY USE:

mo • rose (mə rōsʹ) *adj.,* gloomy; sullen
in • cu • ri • ous (in kyōōrʹē əs) *adj.,* uninterested
per • vade (pər vādʹ) *vt.,* fill

Reviewing the Selection

RECALLING

1. What kind of dog is Buck? What are some typical events in his life on the Judge's farm?

2. What act of treachery does Manuel commit?

3. What is Buck's "introduction to the reign of primitive law"?

4. Who buys Buck from the man in the red sweater?

INTERPRETING

5. How would you characterize the kind of life that Buck enjoys on the Judge's farm?

6. What causes a demand for strong-muscled, thick-coated dogs?

7. What causes Buck to sense that "the fear of the future was strong upon him"?

8. What does François do that begins "his rise in Buck's estimation"?

SYNTHESIZING

9. What sort of relationship between humans and dogs exists on the Judge's farm? How does that differ from the relationship between the man in the red sweater and the dogs that cross his path?

10. In what kind of life is Buck learning his first lessons? What are those lessons?

Understanding Literature (Questions for Discussion)

1. **Foreshadowing. Foreshadowing** is the act of presenting materials that hint at events to occur later in a story. What events in this chapter foreshadow the kidnapping of Buck?

2. **Conflict/Plot/Inciting Incident.** A **conflict** is a struggle between two forces in a literary work. A **plot** is a series of events related to a central conflict in a literary work. A typical plot involves the following elements: introduction, inciting incident, rising action, climax, turning point, falling action, resolution, and dénouement. The **inciting incident** is the event that introduces the central conflict. What is the inciting incident that occurs in this opening chapter? What conflicts are introduced? Against what forces does Buck struggle?

READER'S JOURNAL

Have you ever moved to a new neighborhood, school, or state? How did you adapt to your new surroundings? Was it difficult or easy to do? Write about adaptability in your journal. You may wish to write about a personal situation in which you needed to adapt to a new environment.

CHAPTER II

The Law of Club and Fang

Buck's first day on the Dyea beach was like a nightmare. Every hour was filled with shock and surprise. He had been suddenly jerked from the heart of civilization and flung into the heart of things <u>primordial</u>. No lazy, sun-kissed life was this, with nothing to do but loaf and be bored. Here was neither peace, nor rest, nor a moment's safety. All was confusion and action, and every moment life and limb were in peril. There was imperative need to be constantly alert; for these dogs and men were not town dogs and men. They were savages, all of them, who knew no law but the law of club and fang.

He had never seen dogs fight as these wolfish creatures fought, and his first experience taught him an unforgettable lesson. It is true, it was a <u>vicarious</u> experience, else he would not have lived to profit by it. Curly was the victim. They were camped near the log store, where she, in her friendly way, made advances to a husky dog the size of a full-grown wolf, though not half so large as she. There was no warning, only a leap in like a flash, a metallic clip of teeth, a leap out equally swift, and Curly's face was ripped open from eye to jaw.

It was the wolf manner of fighting, to strike and leap away; but there was more to it than this. Thirty or forty huskies ran to the spot and surrounded the combatants in an intent and silent circle. Buck did not comprehend that silent intentness, nor the eager way with which they were licking their chops. Curly rushed her <u>antagonist</u>, who struck again and leaped aside. He met her next rush with his chest, in a peculiar fashion that tumbled her off her feet. She never regained them. This was what the onlooking huskies had waited for. They closed in upon her, snarling and yelping, and she was buried, screaming with agony, beneath the bristling mass of bodies.

So sudden was it, and so unexpected, that Buck was taken aback. He saw Spitz run out his scarlet tongue in a way he had of laughing; and he saw François, swinging an axe, spring into the mess of dogs. Three men with clubs were helping him to scatter them.

What happens to Curly? How do the other dogs react? How does Buck react?

It did not take long. Two minutes from the time Curly went down, the last of her assailants were clubbed off. But she lay there limp and lifeless in the bloody, trampled snow, almost literally torn to pieces, the swart fellow standing over her and cursing horribly. The scene often came back to Buck to trouble him in his sleep. So that was the way. No fair play. Once down, that was the end of you. Well, he would see to it that he never went down. Spitz ran out his tongue and laughed again, and from that moment Buck hated him with a bitter and deathless hatred.

Before he had recovered from the shock caused by the tragic passing of Curly, he received another shock. François fastened upon him an arrangement of straps and buckles. It was a harness, such as he had seen the grooms put on the horses at home. And as he had seen horses work, so he was set to work, hauling François on a sled to the forest that fringed the valley, and returning with a load of firewood. Though his dignity was sorely hurt by thus being made a draft animal, he was too wise to rebel. He buckled down with a will and did his best, though it was all new and strange. François was stern, demanding instant obedience, and by virtue of his whip receiving instant obedience; while Dave, who was an experienced wheeler,[1] nipped Buck's hindquarters whenever he was in error. Spitz was the leader, likewise experienced, and while he could not always get at Buck, he growled sharp <u>reproof</u> now and again, or cunningly threw his weight in the traces to jerk Buck into

the way he should go. Buck learned easily, and under the combined tuition of his two mates and François made remarkable progress. Ere they returned to camp he knew enough to stop at "ho," to go ahead at "mush," to swing wide on the bends, and to keep clear of the wheeler when the loaded sled shot downhill at their heels.

"T'ree vair' good dogs," François told Perrault. "Dat Buck, heem pool lak hell. I tich heem queek as anyt'ing."

By afternoon, Perrault, who was in a hurry to be on the trail with his dispatches, returned with two more dogs. "Billee" and "Joe" he called them, two brothers, and true huskies both. Sons of the one mother though they were, they were as different as day and night. Billee's one fault was his excessive good nature, while Joe was the very opposite, sour and <u>introspective</u>, with a <u>perpetual</u> snarl and a <u>malignant</u> eye. Buck received them in comradely fashion, Dave ignored them, while Spitz proceeded to thrash first one and then the other. Billee wagged his tail appeasingly, turned to run when he saw that appeasement was of no avail, and cried (still appeasingly) when Spitz's sharp teeth scored his flank. But no matter how Spitz circled, Joe whirled around on his heels to face him, mane bristling, ears laid back, lips writhing and snarling, jaws clipping together as fast as he could snap, and eyes diabolically gleaming—the <u>incarnation</u> of belligerent fear. So terrible was his appearance that Spitz was forced to

What is Buck made to do? How does he feel about this? How does he respond?

1. **wheeler.** One who urges on animals that pull a cart or sled

WORDS FOR EVERYDAY USE:	re • proof (ri prōōf´) n., rebuke; censure in • tro • spec • tive (in´trō spek´tiv) adj., looking within one's own mind per • pet • u • al (pər pech´ōō əl) adj., constant, permanent	ma • lig • nant (mə lig´nənt) adj., wishing evil; dangerous in • car • na • tion (in´kär nā´shən) n., any person or thing that serves as an embodiment of a quality or concept

forego disciplining him, but to cover his own <u>discomfiture</u> he turned upon the inoffensive and wailing Billee and drove him to the confines of the camp.

By evening Perrault secured another dog, an old husky, long and lean and gaunt, with a battle-scarred face and a single eye, which flashed a warning of <u>prowess</u> that commanded respect. He was called Sol-leks, which means the Angry One. Like Dave, he asked nothing, gave nothing, expected nothing; and when he marched slowly and deliberately into their midst, even Spitz left him alone. He had one peculiarity which Buck was unlucky enough to discover. He did not like to be approached on his blind side. Of this offense Buck was unwittingly guilty, and the first knowledge he had of his indiscretion was when Sol-leks whirled upon him and slashed his shoulder to the bone for three inches up and down. Forever after Buck avoided his blind side, and to the last of their comradeship had no more trouble. His only apparent ambition, like Dave's, was to be left alone; though, as Buck was afterward to learn, each of them possessed one other and even more vital ambition.

That night Buck faced the great problem of sleeping. The tent, illumined by a candle, glowed warmly in the midst of the white plain; and when he, as a matter of course, entered it, both Perrault and François bombarded him with curses and cooking utensils, till he recovered from his <u>consternation</u> and fled <u>ignominiously</u> into the outer cold. A chill wind was blowing that nipped him sharply and bit with especial venom into his wounded shoulder. He lay down on the snow and attempted to sleep, but the frost soon drove him shivering to his feet. Miserable and disconsolate, he wandered about among the many tents, only to find that one place was as cold as another. Here and there savage dogs rushed upon him, but he bristled his neck-hair and snarled (for he was learning fast), and they let him go his way unmolested.

Finally an idea came to him. He would return and see how his own teammates were making out. To his astonishment, they had disappeared. Again he wandered about through the great camp, looking for them, and again he returned. Were they in the tent? No, that could not be, else he would not have been driven out. Then where could they possibly be? With drooping tail and shivering body, very forlorn indeed, he aimlessly circled the tent. Suddenly the snow gave way beneath his forelegs and he sank down. Something wriggled under his feet. He sprang back, bristling and snarling, fearful of the unseen and unknown. But a friendly little yelp reassured him, and he went back to investigate. A whiff of warm air ascended to his nostrils, and there, curled up under the snow in a snug ball, lay Billee. He whined <u>placatingly</u>, squirmed and wriggled to show his good will and intentions, and even ventured, as a bribe for peace, to lick Buck's face with his warm wet tongue.

Another lesson. So that was the way they did it, eh? Buck confidently selected a spot, and with much fuss and wasted

What aspect of Buck's earlier life at the Judge's is contrasted? How has Buck's life changed?

WORDS FOR EVERYDAY USE:

dis • com • fi • ture (dis kum´fi chər) *n.*, feeling of frustration and confusion
prow • ess (prou´is) *n.*, superior ability; skill
con • ster • na • tion (kän´stər nā´shen) *n.*, great fear or shock

ig • no • min • i • ous • ly (ig´nə min´ē əs lē) *adv.*, disgracefully; shamefully
pla • cat • ing • ly (plā´kāt´iŋ lē) *adv.*, pacifyingly; pleasingly

effort proceeded to dig a hole for himself. In a trice[2] the heat from his body filled the confined space and he was asleep. The day had been long and <u>arduous</u>, and he slept soundly and comfortably, though he growled and barked and wrestled with bad dreams.

Nor did he open his eyes till roused by the noises of the waking camp. At first he did not know where he was. It had snowed during the night and he was completely buried. The snow walls pressed him on every side, and a great surge of fear swept through him—the fear of the wild thing for the trap. It was a token that he was harking back through his own life to the lives of his <u>forebears</u>; for he was a civilized dog, an unduly civilized dog, and of his experience knew no trap and so could not of himself fear it. The muscles of his whole body contracted <u>spasmodically</u> and instinctively, the hair on his neck and shoulders stood on end, and with a ferocious snarl he bounded straight up into the blinding day, the snow flying about him in a flashing cloud. Ere he landed on his feet, he saw the white camp spread out before him and knew where he was and remembered all that had passed from the time he went for a stroll with Manuel to the hole he had dug for himself the night before.

A shout from François hailed his appearance. "Wot I say?" the dog-driver cried to Perrault. "Dat Buck for sure learn queek as anyt'ing."

Perrault nodded gravely. As courier for the Canadian Government, bearing important dispatches, he was anxious to secure the best dogs, and he was particularly gladdened by the possession of Buck.

Three more huskies were added to the team inside an hour, making a total of nine, and before another quarter of an hour had passed they were in harness and swinging up the trail toward the Dyea Cañon. Buck was glad to be gone, and though the work was hard he found he did not particularly despise it. He was surprised at the eagerness which animated the whole team and which was communicated to him; but still more surprising was the change wrought in Dave and Sol-leks. They were new dogs, utterly transformed by the harness. All passiveness and unconcern had dropped from them. They were alert and active, anxious that the work should go well, and fiercely irritable with whatever, by delay or confusion, retarded that work. The toil of the traces[3] seemed the supreme expression of their being, and all that they lived for and the only thing in which they took delight.

Dave was wheeler or sled dog, pulling in front of him was Buck, then came Sol-leks; the rest of the team was strung out ahead, single file, to the leader, which position was filled by Spitz.

Buck had been purposely placed between Dave and Sol-leks so that he might receive instruction. Apt scholar that he was, they were equally apt teachers, never allowing him to linger long in error, and enforcing their teaching with

What makes Buck afraid? What is the source of his fear?

How do the dogs feel when harnessed as a team?

---

2. **trice.** Very short time; instant, moment
3. **traces.** Straps, chains, etc., connecting a draft animal's harness to the vehicle drawn

WORDS FOR EVERYDAY USE:	**ar • du • ous** (är´jōō əs) *adj.*, strenuous; hard
	fore • bear (fôr´ ber´) *n.*, ancestor
	spas • mod • i • cal • ly (spaz mäd´ik a lē) *adv.*, suddenly; violently; fitfully

How are Buck's mistakes punished? How is his learning rewarded?

their sharp teeth. Dave was fair and very wise. He never nipped Buck without cause, and he never failed to nip him when he stood in need of it. As François's whip backed him up, Buck found it to be cheaper to mend his ways than to retaliate. Once, during a brief halt, when he got tangled in the traces and delayed the start, both Dave and Sol-leks flew at him and administered a sound trouncing. The resulting tangle was even worse, but Buck took good care to keep the traces clear thereafter; and ere the day was done, so well had he mastered his work, his mates about ceased nagging him. François's whip snapped less frequently, and Perrault even honored Buck by lifting up his feet and carefully examining them.

It was a hard day's run, up the Cañon, through Sheep Camp, past the Scales and the timberline, across glaciers and snowdrifts hundreds of feet deep, and over the great Chilcoot Divide, which stands between the salt water and the fresh and guards forbiddingly the sad and lonely North. They made good time down the chain of lakes which fills the craters of extinct volcanoes, and late that night pulled into the huge camp at the head of Lake Bennett, where thousands of gold-seekers were building boats against the breakup of the ice in the spring. Buck made his hole in the snow and slept the sleep of the exhausted just, but all too early was routed out in the cold darkness and harnessed with his mates to the sled.

That day they made forty miles, the trail being packed; but the next day, and for many days to follow, they broke their own trail, worked harder, and made poorer time. As a rule, Perrault traveled ahead of the team, packing the snow with webbed shoes to make it easier for them. François, guiding the sled at the gee-pole,[4] sometimes exchanged places with him, but not often. Perrault was in a hurry, and he prided himself on his knowledge of ice, which knowledge was indispensable, for the fall ice was very thin, and where there was swift water, there was no ice at all.

Day after day, for days unending, Buck toiled in the traces. Always, they broke camp in the dark, and the first gray of dawn found them hitting the trail with fresh miles reeled off behind them. And always they pitched camp after dark, eating their bit of fish, and crawling to sleep into the snow. Buck was ravenous. The pound and a half of sun-dried salmon, which was his ration for each day, seemed to go nowhere. He never had enough, and suffered from perpetual hunger pangs. Yet the other dogs, because they weighed less and were born to the life, received a pound only of the fish and managed to keep in good condition.

He swiftly lost the <u>fastidiousness</u> which had characterized his old life. A dainty eater, he found that his mates, finishing first, robbed him of his unfinished ration. There was no defending it. While he was fighting off two or three, it was disappearing down the throats of the others. To remedy this, he ate as fast as they; and, so greatly did hunger compel him, he was not above taking what did not belong to him. He

---

4. **gee-pole.** Pole at the front of a dog sled for steering

WORDS FOR EVERYDAY USE: **fas • ti • di • ous • ness** (fas tid´ē əs nes) *n.*, oversensitiveness

watched and learned. When he saw Pike, one of the new dogs, a clever <u>malingerer</u> and thief, slyly steal a slice of bacon when Perrault's back was turned, he duplicated the performance the following day, getting away with the whole chunk. A great uproar was raised, but he was unsuspected; while Dub, an awkward blunderer who was always getting caught, was punished for Buck's misdeed.

This first theft marked Buck as fit to survive in the hostile Northland environment. It marked his adaptability, his capacity to adjust himself to changing conditions, the lack of which would have meant swift and terrible death. It marked, further, the decay or going to pieces of his moral nature, a vain thing and a handicap in the <u>ruthless</u> struggle for existence. It was all well enough in the Southland, under the law of love and fellowship, to respect private property and personal feelings; but in the Northland, under the law of club and fang, whoso took such things into account was a fool, and insofar as he observed them he would fail to prosper.

Not that Buck reasoned it out. He was fit, that was all, and unconsciously he accommodated himself to the new mode of life. All his days, no matter what the odds, he had never run from a fight. But the club of the man in the red sweater had beaten into him a more fundamental and primitive code. Civilized, he could have died for a moral consideration, say the defense of Judge Miller's riding whip, but the completeness of his decivilization was now evidenced by his ability to flee from the defense of a moral consideration and so save his hide. He did not steal for joy of it, but because of the clamor of his stomach. He did not rob openly, but stole secretly and cunningly, out of respect for club and fang. In short, the things he did were done because it was easier to do them than not to do them.

His development (or <u>retrogression</u>) was rapid. His muscles became hard as iron, and he grew callous to all ordinary pain. He achieved an internal as well as external economy. He could eat anything, no matter how loathsome or indigestible, and, once eaten, the juices of his stomach extracted the last least particle of nutriment; and his blood carried it to the farthest reaches of his body, building it into the toughest and stoutest of tissues. Sight and scent became remarkably keen, while his hearing developed such acuteness that in his sleep he heard the faintest sound and knew whether it <u>heralded</u> peace or peril. He learned to bite the ice out with his teeth when it collected between his toes; and when he was thirsty and there was a thick scum of ice over the water hole, he would break it by rearing and striking it with stiff fore legs. His most conspicuous trait was an ability to scent the wind and forecast it a night in advance. No matter how breathless the air when he dug his nest by tree or bank, the wind that later blew inevitably found him to leeward,[5] sheltered and snug.

And not only did he learn by experience, but instincts long dead became

What Northland virtue does Buck prove to possess?

What new rules has Buck come to live by?

---

5. **leeward.** Side or direction away from the wind

Words for Everyday Use:

ma • lin • ger • er (mə liŋ´gər ər) *n.*, someone who avoids duty

ruth • less (rooth´lis) *adj.*, without pity

re • tro • gres • sion (re´trə gresh´ən) *n.*, return to a lower level or stage

her • ald (her´əld) *v.*, announce; introduce

alive again. The domesticated generations fell from him. In vague ways he remembered back to the youth of the breed, to the time the wild dogs ranged in packs through the primeval forest and killed their meat as they ran it down. It was no task for him to learn to fight with cut and slash and the quick wolf snap. In this manner had fought forgotten ancestors. They quickened the old life within him, and the old tricks which they had stamped into the heredity of the breed were his tricks. They came to him without effort or discovery, as though they had been his always. And when, on the still cold nights, he pointed his nose at a star and howled long and wolflike, it was his ancestors, dead and dust, pointing nose at a star and howling down through the centuries and through him. And his cadences were their cadences, the cadences which voiced their woe and what to them was the meaning of the stillness, and the cold, and dark.

Thus, as token of what a puppet thing life is, the ancient song surged through him and he came into his own again; and he came because men had found a yellow metal in the North, and because Manuel was a gardener's helper whose wages did not lap over the needs of his wife and divers small copies of himself.

Why does Buck learn so quickly?

What are the causes of Buck's self-discovery? How much control over these forces did Buck have?

Responding to the Selection

Imagine that you are Perrault. In your journal, write about the dog Buck, describing the changes in him that you are seeing take place.

Reviewing the Selection

RECALLING

1. What was Buck's first day on the Dyea beach like?

2. How do the men react to the fight?

3. Where does Buck try to sleep his first night in camp? Where does he end up sleeping?

4. What action on Buck's part marks him as "fit to survive in the hostile Northland"?

INTERPRETING

5. What event teaches Buck "the law of club and fang"?

6. What is probably the reason that Buck feels toward Spitz "a bitter and deathless hatred"?

7. What action on Buck's part prompts François's exclamation, "Dat Buck for sure learn queek as anyt'ing"?

8. What is probably the reason that adaptability is essential to survival?

WORDS FOR EVERYDAY USE:
ca • dence (kād´ns) *n.*, any rhythmic flow of sound
di • vers (dī´vərz) *adj.*, several

9. What is the law of club and fang?

10. What laws of the Southland are handicaps in the Northland? Why?

Understanding Literature (Questions for Discussion)

1. **Character and Motive.** A **character** is a person or animal who figures in the action of a story. A **motive** is a force that drives a character to act in a certain way. In this novel, the main character is an animal, the dog Buck. In this chapter, Buck develops a new behavior—stealing food. What motivates Buck to act in this way? What motive prevented him in the past from acting this way?

2. **Theme.** A **theme** is a central idea in a literary work. A long work such as a novel may deal with several interrelated themes. One of the themes in *The Call of the Wild* is the decivilization of Buck, a civilized creature who is placed in an uncivilized environment. What moral qualities does Buck shed in this chapter? Why are these qualities superfluous, even dangerous, in an uncivilized environment such as the Northland?

Responding in Writing

Comparison-Contrast Essay. Write an essay in which you compare and contrast the qualities needed to survive in a civilized and an uncivilized environment.

> **Prewriting Suggestion:** First, look up in a dictionary the definitions of the words *civilized* and *uncivilized*. Then draw a line down the middle of a clean sheet of paper. Write the word *civilized* and its definition at the top of the left-hand column; write the word *uncivilized* and its definition at the top of the right-hand column. In each column, brainstorm a list of qualities needed to survive in that particular environment.

READER'S JOURNAL

Are you considered friendly? cautious? skeptical? easygoing? trustworthy? What personal characteristics do you possess? Freewrite in your journal a list of your personal characteristics. Place a checkmark beside those with which you believe you were born. Does anyone else in your family possess some of the same characteristics? If so, write the person's name beside the corresponding characteristic.

CHAPTER III

The Dominant Primordial Beast

The dominant primordial beast was strong in Buck, and under the fierce conditions of trail life it grew and grew. Yet it was a secret growth. His newborn cunning gave him poise and control. He was too busy adjusting himself to the new life to feel at ease, and not only did he not pick fights, but he avoided them whenever possible. A certain deliberateness characterized his attitude. He was not prone to rashness and <u>precipitate</u> action; and in the bitter hatred between him and Spitz he betrayed no impatience, shunned all offensive acts.

On the other hand, possibly because he <u>divined</u> in Buck a dangerous rival, Spitz never lost an opportunity of showing his teeth. He even went out of his way to bully Buck, striving constantly to start the fight which could end only in the death of one or the other. Early in the trip this might have taken place had it not been for an unwonted accident. At the end of this day they made a bleak and miserable camp on the shore of Lake Le Barge. Driving snow, a wind that cut like a white-hot knife, and darkness had forced them to grope for a camping place. They could hardly have fared worse. At their backs rose a perpendicular wall of rock, and Perrault and François were compelled to make their fire and spread their sleeping robes on the ice of the lake itself. The tent they had discarded at Dyea in order to travel light. A few sticks of driftwood furnished them with a fire that thawed down through the ice and left them to eat supper in the dark.

Close in under the sheltering rock Buck made his nest. So snug and warm was it that he was <u>loath</u> to leave it when François distributed the fish which he had first thawed over the fire. But when Buck finished his ration and returned, he found his nest occupied. A warning snarl told him that the trespasser was Spitz. Till now Buck had avoided trouble with his enemy, but this was too much. The beast in him roared. He sprang upon Spitz with a

What extra hardships do the dogs and their masters endure?

What future events might be foreshadowed?

WORDS FOR
EVERYDAY USE:

pre• cip • i • tate (prē sip´ə tit) *adj.*, sudden; impetuous, rash
di • vine (də vīn´) *vt.*, find out by intuition
loath (lōth) *adj.*, hesitant, reluctant

fury which surprised them both, and Spitz particularly, for his whole experience with Buck had gone to teach him that his rival was an unusually timid dog, who managed to hold his own only because of his great weight and size.

François was surprised, too, when they shot out in a tangle from the disrupted nest and he divined the cause of the trouble. "A-a-ah!" he cried to Buck. "Gif it to heem, by Gar! Gif it to heem, the dirty t'eef!"

Spitz was equally willing. He was crying with sheer rage and eagerness as he circled back and forth for a chance to spring in. Buck was no less eager, and no less cautious, as he likewise circled back and forth for the advantage. But it was then that the unexpected happened, the thing which projected their struggle for <u>supremacy</u> far into the future, past many a weary mile of trail and toil.

An oath from Perrault, the resounding impact of a club upon a bony frame, and a shrill yelp of pain, heralded the breaking forth of <u>pandemonium</u>. The camp was suddenly discovered to be alive with <u>skulking</u> furry forms—starving huskies, four or five score of them, who had scented the camp from some Indian village. They had crept in while Buck and Spitz were fighting, and when the two men sprang among them with stout clubs they showed their teeth and fought back. They were crazed by the smell of the food. Perrault found one with head buried in the grub-box.[1]

His club landed heavily on the gaunt ribs, and the grub-box was capsized on the ground. On the instant a score of the famished brutes were scrambling for the bread and bacon. The clubs fell upon them unheeded. They yelped and howled under the rain of blows, but struggled nonetheless madly till the last crumb had been devoured.

In the meantime the astonished team dogs had burst out of their nests only to be set upon by the fierce invaders. Never had Buck seen such dogs. It seemed as though their bones would burst through their skins. They were mere skeletons, draped loosely in <u>draggled</u> hides, with blazing eyes and slavered fangs. But the hunger-madness made them terrifying, irresistible. There was no opposing them. The team dogs were swept back against the cliff at the first onset. Buck was beset by three huskies, and in a trice his head and shoulders were ripped and slashed. The din was frightful. Billee was crying as usual. Dave and Sol-leks, dripping blood from a score of wounds, were fighting bravely side by side. Joe was snapping like a demon. Once, his teeth closed on the foreleg of a husky, and he crunched down through the bone. Pike, the malingerer, leaped upon the crippled animal, breaking its neck with a quick flash of teeth and a jerk. Buck got a frothing adversary by the throat, and was sprayed with blood when his teeth

Who attacks the camp? Why?

---

1. **grub-box.** Feed box

su • prem • a • cy (sə prem′ ə sē) *n.*, authority
pan • de • mo • ni • um (pan′də mō′ nē əm) *n.*, wild noise and disorder

skulk • ing (skulk′ ŋ) *part.*, cravenly or sinisterly lurking about
drag • gled (drag′əld) *part.*, wet and dirty

sank through the jugular.[2] The warm taste of it in his mouth goaded him to greater fierceness. He flung himself upon another, and at the same time felt teeth sink into his own throat. It was Spitz, treacherously attacking from the side.

Perrault and François, having cleaned out their part of the camp, hurried to save their sled dogs. The wild wave of famished beasts rolled back before them, and Buck shook himself free. But it was only for a moment. The two men were compelled to run back to save the grub; upon which the huskies returned to the attack on the team. Billee, terrified into bravery, sprang through the savage circle and fled away over the ice. Pike and Dub followed on his heels, with the rest of the team behind. As Buck drew himself together to spring after them, out of the tail of his eye he saw Spitz rush upon him with the evident intention of overthrowing him. Once off his feet and under that mass of huskies, there was no hope for him. But he braced himself to the shock of Spitz's charge, then joined the flight out on the lake.

Later, the nine team dogs gathered together and sought shelter in the forest. Though unpursued, they were in a sorry plight. There was not one who was not wounded in four or five places, while some were wounded grievously. Dub was badly injured in a hind leg; Dolly, the last husky added to the team at Dyea, had a badly torn throat; Joe had lost an eye; while Billee, the

good-natured, with an ear chewed and <u>rent</u> to ribbons, cried and whimpered throughout the night. At daybreak they limped <u>warily</u> back to camp, to find the <u>marauders</u> gone and the two men in bad tempers. Fully half their grub supply was gone. The huskies had chewed through the sled lashings and canvas coverings. In fact, nothing, no matter how remotely eatable, had escaped them. They had eaten a pair of Perrault's moosehide moccasins, chunks out of the leather traces, and even two feet of lash from the end of François's whip. He broke from a mournful contemplation of it to look over his wounded dogs.

"Ah, my frien's," he said softly, "mebbe it mek you mad dog, dose many bites. Mebbe all mad dog, sacredam! Wot you t'ink, eh, Perrault?"

The courier shook his head <u>dubiously</u>. With four hundred miles of trail still between him and Dawson,[3] he could ill afford to have madness break out among his dogs. Two hours of cursing and <u>exertion</u> got the harnesses into shape, and the wound-stiffened team was under way, struggling painfully over the hardest part of the trail they had yet encountered, and for that matter, the hardest between them and Dawson.

The Thirty Mile River was wide open. Its wild water defied the frost, and it was in the <u>eddies</u> only and in the quiet places that the ice held at all. Six

How does the team escape?

---

2. **jugular.** Large artery that delivers blood to the brain
3. **Dawson.** City in West Yukon, Canada, a base for miners of the gold rush

---

| WORDS FOR EVERYDAY USE: | **rend** (rend) *vt.,* tear
war • i • ly (werʹə lē) *adv.,* cautiously
ma • raud • er (mə rôdʹ ər) *n.,* one who raids, pillages, or plunders | **du • bi • ous • ly** (dooʹ bē əs lē) *adv.,* doubtfully, suspiciously
ex • er • tion (eg zerʹshən) *n.,* effort
ed • dy (edʹē) *n.,* little whirlpool |

days of exhausting toil were required to cover those thirty terrible miles. And terrible they were, for every foot of them was accomplished at the risk of life to dog and man. A dozen times, Perrault, nosing the way, broke through the ice bridges, being saved by the long pole he carried, which he so held that it fell each time across the hole made by his body. But a cold snap was on, the thermometer registering fifty below zero, and each time he broke through he was compelled for very life to build a fire and dry his garments.

Nothing <u>daunted</u> him. It was because nothing daunted him that he had been chosen for government courier. He took all manner of risks, <u>resolutely</u> thrusting his little weazened face into the frost and struggling on from dim dawn to dark. He skirted the frowning shores on rim ice that bent and crackled under foot and upon which they dared not halt. Once, the sled broke through, with Dave and Buck, and they were half-frozen and all but drowned by the time they were dragged out. The usual fire was necessary to save them. They were coated solidly with ice, and the two men kept them on the run around the fire, sweating and thawing, so close that they were singed by the flames.

At another time Spitz went through, dragging the whole team after him up to Buck, who strained backward with all his strength, his forepaws on the slippery edge and the ice quivering and snapping all around. But behind him was Dave, likewise straining backward, and behind the sled was François, pulling till his tendons cracked.

Again, the rim ice broke away before and behind, and there was no escape except up the cliff. Perrault scaled it by a miracle, while François prayed for just that miracle; and with every thong and sled lashing and the last bit of harness rove[4] into a long rope, the dogs were hoisted, one by one, to the cliff crest. François came up last, after the sled and load. Then came the search for a place to descend, which descent was ultimately made by the aid of the rope, and night found them back on the river with a quarter of a mile to the day's credit.

By the time they made the Hootalinqua and good ice, Buck was played out. The rest of the dogs were in like condition; but Perrault, to make up lost time, pushed them late and early. The first day they covered thirty-five miles to the Big Salmon; the next day thirty-five more to the Little Salmon; the third day forty miles, which brought them well up toward the Five Fingers.[5]

Buck's feet were not so compact and hard as the feet of the huskies. His had softened during the many generations since the day his last wild ancestor was tamed by a cave dweller or river man. All day long he limped in agony, and camp once made, lay down like a dead dog. Hungry as he was, he would not move to receive his ration of fish, which François had to bring to him. Also, the dog-driver rubbed Buck's feet for half an hour each night after supper, and sacrificed the tops of his own moccasins to make four moccasins for Buck. This

was a great relief, and Buck caused even the weazened face of Perrault to twist itself into a grin one morning, when François forgot the moccasins and Buck lay on his back, his four feet waving appealingly in the air, and refused to budge without them. Later his feet grew hard to the trail, and the worn-out footgear was thrown away.

At the Pelly one morning, as they were harnessing up, Dolly, who had never been conspicuous for anything, went suddenly mad. She announced her condition by a long, heartbreaking wolf howl that sent every dog bristling with fear, then sprang straight for Buck. He had never seen a dog go mad, nor did he have any reason to fear madness; yet he knew that here was horror, and fled away from it in a panic. Straight away he raced, with Dolly, panting and frothing, one leap behind; nor could she gain on him, so great was his terror, nor could he leave her, so great was her madness. He plunged through the wooded breast of the island, flew down to the lower end, crossed a back channel filled with rough ice to another island, gained a third island, curved back to the main river, and in desperation started to cross it. And all the time, though he did not look, he could hear her snarling just one leap behind. François called to him a quarter of a mile away and he doubled back, still one leap ahead, gasping painfully for air and putting all his faith in that François would save him. The dog-driver held the axe poised in his hand, and as Buck shot past him the axe crashed down upon mad Dolly's head.

Why does Dolly chase Buck? What happens to her?

What disadvantage does Buck have? How does François help Buck?

---

4. **rove.** Woven
5. **Big Salmon . . . Little Salmon . . . Five Fingers.** Three rivers

Buck staggered over against the sled, exhausted, sobbing for breath, helpless. This was Spitz's opportunity. He sprang upon Buck, and twice his teeth sank into his unresisting foe and ripped and tore the flesh to the bone. Then François's lash descended, and Buck had the satisfaction of watching Spitz receive the worst whipping as yet administered to any of the team.

"One devil, dat Spitz," remarked Perrault. "Some dam day heem keel dat Buck."

"Dat Buck two devils," was François's rejoinder. "All de tam I watch dat Buck I know for sure. Lissen: some dam fine day heem get mad lak hell an' den heem chew dat Spitz all up an' spit heem out on de snow. Sure. I know."

From then on it was war between them. Spitz, as lead dog and acknowledged master of the team, felt his supremacy threatened by this strange Southland dog. And strange Buck was to him, for of the many Southland dogs he had known, not one had shown up worthily in camp and on trail. They were all too soft, dying under the toil, the frost, and starvation. Buck was the exception. He alone endured and prospered, matching the husky in strength, savagery, and cunning. Then he was a masterful dog, and what made him dangerous was the fact that the club of the man in the red sweater had knocked all blind pluck and rashness out of his desire for mastery. He was <u>preeminently</u> cunning,

and could bide his time with a patience that was nothing less than primitive.

It was inevitable that the clash for leadership should come. Buck wanted it. He wanted it because it was his nature, because he had been gripped tight by that nameless, incomprehensible pride of the trail and trace—that pride which holds dogs in the toil to the last gasp, which lures them to die joyfully in the harness, and breaks their hearts if they are cut out of the harness. This was the pride of Dave as wheel dog, of Sol-leks as he pulled with all his strength; the pride that laid hold of them at break of camp, transforming them from sour and sullen brutes into straining, eager, ambitious creatures; the pride that spurred them on all day and dropped them at pitch of camp at night, letting them fall back into gloomy unrest and uncontent. This was the pride that bore up Spitz and made him thrash the sled dogs who blundered and <u>shirked</u> in the traces or hid away at harness-up time in the morning. Likewise it was this pride that made him fear Buck as a possible lead dog. And this was Buck's pride, too.

He openly threatened the other's leadership. He came between him and the shirks he should have punished. And he did it deliberately. One night there was a heavy snowfall, and in the morning Pike, the malingerer, did not appear. He was securely hidden in his nest under a foot of snow. François called him and sought him in vain.

How is Buck different from other Southland dogs? How has he become different from the way he was at the Judge's?

WORDS FOR EVERYDAY USE:

pre • em • i • nent • ly (prē em´ə nənt lē) *adv.,* excelling above others

shirk (shʉrk) *vt.,* neglect; evade doing something

Spitz was wild with wrath. He raged through the camp, smelling and digging in every likely place, snarling so frightfully that Pike heard and shivered in his hiding place.

But when he was at last unearthed, and Spitz flew at him to punish him, Buck flew, with equal rage, in between. So unexpected was it, and so shrewdly managed, that Spitz was hurled backward and off his feet. Pike, who had been trembling <u>abjectly</u>, took heart at this open <u>mutiny</u>, and sprang upon his overthrown leader. Buck, to whom fair play was a forgotten code, likewise sprang upon Spitz. But François, chuckling at the incident while unswerving in the administration of justice, brought his lash down upon Buck with all his might. This failed to drive Buck from his <u>prostrate</u> rival, and the butt of the whip was brought into play. Half stunned by the blow, Buck was knocked backward and the lash laid upon him again and again, while Spitz soundly punished the many times offending Pike.

In the days that followed, as Dawson grew closer and closer, Buck still continued to interfere between Spitz and the culprits; but he did it craftily, when François was not around. With the <u>covert</u> mutiny of Buck, a general insubordination sprang up and increased. Dave and Sol-leks were unaffected, but the rest of the team went from bad to worse. Things no longer went right. There was continual bickering and jangling. Trouble was always afoot, and at the bottom of it was Buck. He kept François busy, for the dog-driver was in constant apprehension of the life-and-death struggle between the two which he knew must take place sooner or later; and on more than one night the sounds of quarreling and strife among the other dogs turned him out of his sleeping robe, fearful that Buck and Spitz were at it.

But the opportunity did not present itself, and they pulled into Dawson one dreary afternoon with the great fight still to come. Here were many men, and countless dogs, and Buck found them all at work. It seemed the <u>ordained</u> order of things that dogs should work. All day they swung up and down the main street in long teams, and in the night their jingling bells still went by. They hauled cabin logs and firewood, freighted up to the mines, and did all manner of work that horses did in the Santa Clara Valley. Here and there Buck met Southland dogs, but in the main they were the wild wolf husky breed. Every night, regularly, at nine, at twelve, at three, they lifted a nocturnal song, a weird and eerie chant, in which it was Buck's delight to join.

With the aurora borealis[6] flaming coldly overhead, or the stars leaping in the frost dance, and the land numb and frozen under its <u>pall</u> of snow, this song of the huskies might have been the defiance of life, only it was pitched

---

6. **aurora borealis.** Irregular, luminous phenomena visible at night in a zone surrounding the north magnetic pole; northern lights

---

WORDS FOR EVERYDAY USE:

ab • ject • ly (ab´ jekt lē) *adv.*, miserably, wretchedly

mu • ti • ny (myoot´ 'n ē) *n.*, revolt; rebellion against authority

pros • trate (präs´ trāt´) *adj.*, lying down

cov • ert (kuv´ ərt) *adj.*, concealed, hidden

or • dained (or dānd´) *part.*, commanded

pall (pôl) *n.*, covering

in minor key, with long-drawn wailings and half sobs, and was more the pleading of life, the articulate <u>travail</u> of existence. It was an old song, old as the breed itself—one of the first songs of the younger world in a day when songs were sad. It was invested with the woe of unnumbered generations, this plaint by which Buck was so strangely stirred. When he moaned and sobbed, it was with the pain of living that was of old the pain of his wild fathers, and the fear and mystery of the cold and dark that was to them fear and mystery. And that he should be stirred by it marked the completeness with which he harked back through the ages of fire and roof to the raw beginnings of life in the howling ages.

Seven days from the time they pulled into Dawson, they dropped down the steep bank by the Barracks to the Yukon Trail,[7] and pulled for Dyea and Salt Water. Perrault was carrying dispatches if anything more urgent than those he had brought in; also, the travel pride had gripped him, and he purposed to make the record trip of the year. Several things favored him in this. The week's rest had recuperated the dogs and put them in thorough trim. The trail they had broken into the country was packed hard by later journeyers. And further, the police had arranged in two or three places deposits of grub for dog and man, and he was traveling light.

They made Sixty Mile, which is a fifty-mile run, on the first day; and the second day saw them booming up the Yukon well on their way to Pelly. But such splendid running was achieved not without great trouble and vexation on the part of François. The <u>insidious</u> revolt led by Buck had destroyed the <u>solidarity</u> of the team. It no longer was as one dog leaping in the traces. The encouragement Buck gave the rebels led them into all kinds of petty misdemeanors. No more was Spitz a leader greatly to be feared. The old awe departed, and they grew equal to challenging his authority. Pike robbed him of half a fish one night, and gulped it down under the protection of Buck. Another night Dub and Joe fought Spitz and made him forego the punishment they deserved. And even Billee, the good-natured, was less good-natured, and whined not half so placatingly as in former days. Buck never came near Spitz without snarling and bristling menacingly. In fact, his conduct approached that of a bully, and he was given to swaggering up and down before Spitz's very nose.

The breaking down of discipline likewise affected the dogs in their relations with one another. They quarreled and bickered more than ever among themselves, till at times the camp was a howling bedlam. Dave and Sol-leks alone were unaltered, though they were made irritable by the unending squabbling. François swore strange barbarous oaths, and stamped the snow in futile rage, and tore his hair. His lash was always singing among the

Why do the dogs howl? What does their howling express?

---

7. **Yukon Trail.** Trail running through Yukon Territory of Northwest Canada

WORDS FOR EVERYDAY USE:

trav • ail (trə vāl´) *n.*, intense pain

in • sid • i • ous (in sid´ē əs) *adj.*, sly or treacherous

sol • i • dar • i • ty (säl´ə dar´ə tē) *n.*, unity or agreement on an opinion or purpose

dogs, but it was of small avail. Directly his back was turned they were at it again. He backed up Spitz with his whip, while Buck backed up the remainder of the team. François knew he was behind all the trouble, and Buck knew he knew; but Buck was too clever ever again to be caught red-handed. He worked faithfully in the harness, for the toil had become a delight to him; yet it was a greater delight slyly to <u>precipitate</u> a fight amongst his mates and tangle the traces.

At the mouth of the Tahkeena, one night after supper, Dub turned up a snowshoe rabbit, blundered it, and missed. In a second the whole team was in full cry. A hundred yards away was a camp of the Northwest Police, with fifty dogs, huskies all, who joined the chase. The rabbit sped down the river, turned off into a small creek, up the frozen bed of which it held steadily. It ran lightly on the surface of the snow, while the dogs ploughed through by main strength. Buck led the pack, sixty strong, around bend after bend, but he could not gain. He lay down low to the race, whining eagerly, his splendid body flashing forward, leap by leap, in the wan white moonlight. And leap by leap, like some pale frost <u>wraith</u>, the snowshoe rabbit flashed on ahead.

All that stirring of old instincts which at stated periods drives men out from the sounding cities to forest and plain to kill things by chemically propelled leaden pellets, the blood lust, the joy to kill—all this was Buck's, only it was infinitely more intimate. He was ranging at the head of the pack, running the wild thing down, the living meat, to kill with his own teeth and wash his muzzle to the eyes in warm blood.

There is an ecstasy that marks the summit of life, and beyond which life cannot rise. And such is the paradox of living, this ecstasy comes when one is most alive, and it comes as a complete forgetfulness that one is alive. This ecstasy, this forgetfulness of living, comes to the artist, caught up and out of himself in a sheet of flame; it comes to the soldier, war-mad on a stricken field and refusing quarter; and it came to Buck, leading the pack, sounding the old wolf cry, straining after the food that was alive and that fled swiftly before him through the moonlight. He was sounding the deeps of his nature, and of the parts of his nature that were deeper than he, going back into the womb of Time. He was mastered by the sheer surging of life, the tidal wave of being, the perfect joy of each separate muscle, joint, and sinew in that it was everything that was not death, that it was aglow and <u>rampant</u>, expressing itself in movement, flying <u>exultantly</u> under the stars and over the face of dead matter that did not move.

But Spitz, cold and calculating even in his supreme moods, left the pack and cut across a narrow neck of land where the creek made a long bend around. Buck did not know of this, and as he rounded the bend, the frost

What does Buck enjoy?

WORDS FOR EVERYDAY USE:

pre • cip •i • tate (prē sip′ ə tāt′) v., cause; start

wraith (rāth) n., ghost or specter

ram • pant (ram′pənt) adj., flourishing

ex • ult • ant • ly (eg zult′′nt lē) adv., triumphantly; rejoicing

wraith of a rabbit still flitting before him, he saw another and larger frost wraith leap from the overhanging bank into the immediate path of the rabbit. It was Spitz. The rabbit could not turn, and as the white teeth broke its back in midair it shrieked as loudly as a stricken man may shriek. At the sound of this, the cry of Life plunging down from Life's <u>apex</u> in the grip of Death, the full pack at Buck's heels raised a hell's chorus of delight.

Buck did not cry out. He did not check himself, but drove in upon Spitz, shoulder to shoulder, so hard that he missed the throat. They rolled over and over in the powdery snow. Spitz gained his feet almost as though he had not been overthrown, slashing Buck down the shoulder and leaping clear. Twice his teeth clipped together, like the steel jaws of a trap, as he backed away for better footing, with lean and lifting lips that writhed and snarled.

In a flash Buck knew it. The time had come. It was to the death. As they circled about, snarling, ears laid back, keenly watchful for the advantage, the scene came to Buck with a sense of familiarity. He seemed to remember it all,—the white woods, and earth, and moonlight, and the thrill of battle. Over the whiteness and silence brooded a ghostly calm. There was not the faintest whisper of air—nothing moved, not a leaf quivered, the visible breaths of the dogs rising slowly and lingering in the frosty air. They had made short work of the snowshoe rab-

bit, these dogs that were ill-tamed wolves; and they were now drawn up in an expectant circle. They, too, were silent, their eyes only gleaming and their breaths drifting slowly upward. To Buck it was nothing new or strange, this scene of old time. It was as though it had always been, the wonted way of things.

Spitz was a practiced fighter. From Spitzbergen through the Arctic, and across Canada and the Barrens, he had held his own with all manner of dogs and achieved to mastery over them. Bitter rage was his, but never blind rage. In passion to rend and destroy, he never forgot that his enemy was in like passion to rend and destroy. He never rushed till he was prepared to receive a rush; never attacked till he had first defended that attack.

In vain Buck strove to sink his teeth in the neck of the big white dog. Wherever his fangs struck for the softer flesh, they were countered by the fangs of Spitz. Fang clashed fang, and lips were cut and bleeding, but Buck could not penetrate his enemy's guard. Then he warmed up and enveloped Spitz in a whirlwind of rushes. Time and time again he tried for the snow-white throat, where life bubbled near to the surface, and each time and every time Spitz slashed him and got away. Then Buck took to rushing, as though for the throat, when, suddenly drawing back his head and curving in from the side, he would drive his shoulder at the shoulder of Spitz, as a ram by which to overthrow

What sense does Buck have about the fight?

What had Spitz learned about fighting? Why does this make Buck's goal different?

him. But instead, Buck's shoulder was slashed down each time as Spitz leaped lightly away.

Spitz was untouched, while Buck was streaming with blood and panting hard. The fight was growing desperate. And all the while the silent and wolfish circle waited to finish off whichever dog went down. As Buck grew winded, Spitz took to rushing, and he kept him staggering for footing. Once Buck went over, and the whole circle of sixty dogs started up; but he recovered himself, almost in midair, and the circle sank down again and waited.

But Buck possessed a quality that made for greatness—imagination. He fought by instinct, but he could fight by head as well. He rushed, as though attempting the old shoulder trick, but at the last instant swept low to the snow and in. His teeth closed on Spitz's left foreleg. There was a crunch of breaking bone, and the white dog faced him on three legs. Thrice he tried to knock him over, then repeated the trick and broke the right fore leg. Despite the pain and helplessness, Spitz struggled madly to keep up. He saw the silent circle, with gleaming eyes, lolling tongues, and silvery breaths drifting upward, closing in upon him as he had seen similar circles close in upon beaten antagonists in the past. Only this time he was the one who was beaten.

There was no hope for him. Buck was <u>inexorable</u>. Mercy was a thing reserved for gentler climes. He maneuvered for the final rush. The circle had tightened till he could feel the breaths of the huskies on his flanks. He could see them, beyond Spitz and to either side, half crouching for the spring, their eyes fixed upon him. A pause seemed to fall. Every animal was motionless as though turned to stone. Only Spitz quivered and bristled as he staggered back and forth, snarling with horrible menace, as though to frighten off <u>impending</u> death. Then Buck sprang in and out; but while he was in, shoulder had at last squarely met shoulder. The dark circle became a dot on the moon-flooded snow as Spitz disappeared from view. Buck stood and looked on, the successful champion, the dominant primordial beast who had made his kill and found it good.

What earlier event is recalled?

Responding to the Selection

In this chapter, Buck sheds the constraints of civilization and becomes a "primordial beast." What does it mean to be civilized? Why was Buck compelled to shed the constraints of civilization? Describe the characteristics of Buck, the "primordial beast."

WORDS FOR EVERYDAY USE:

in • ex • o • ra • ble (in eks´ ə rə bəl) *adj.*, that which cannot be moved or influenced; unrelenting

im • pend • ing (im pend´iŋ) *part.*, about to happen; threatening

Reviewing the Selection

RECALLING

1. What primitive nature grows in Buck "under the fierce conditions of trail life"?

2. What kind of dogs invade the camp?

3. What does Buck do when he hears the "nocturnal song" of the huskies in Dawson?

4. What causes the breakdown of the solidarity of the sled team?

INTERPRETING

▶▶ 5. What action on the part of Spitz causes "the beast" in Buck to roar?

▶▶ 6. What facts emphasize the "hunger madness" of these dogs?

▶▶ 7. What qualities of the "nocturnal song" emphasize its connection to the ancient, "raw beginnings of life"?

▶▶ 8. What quality does Buck possess that ensures Spitz's fall from leadership?

SYNTHESIZING

9. What instincts and characteristics does Buck, as a "dominant primordial beast," now possess?

10. What actions of the several dogs, including Buck, are described as hereditary? What sort of relationship between heredity and survival is described in this chapter? How does Buck's fight with Spitz emphasize or exemplify that relationship?

Understanding Literature (Questions for Discussion)

1. **Protagonist and Antagonist.** A **protagonist**, or main character, is the central figure in a story. An **antagonist** is a character who is pitted against a protagonist. Which term describes the character Buck? Which describes Spitz? These characters are created primarily through the characterization techniques of direct description and portrayal of behavior. Compare and contrast the characteristics of Buck and Spitz. How are those characteristics displayed in the battles that eventually lead to the final fight to the death between Spitz and Buck?

2. **Setting and Mood.** The **setting** of a literary work is the time and place in which a story occurs, together with all the details used to create a sense of a particular time and place. The **mood** is the emotion created in the reader by descriptions of the setting, of characters, and of events. In the second paragraph of this chapter, what do the descriptions of the landscape and the weather tell about the conditions of the camp? What kind of mood is created by the description of the camp setting? How does this compare with the mood created by the description of daily life in Dawson?

READER'S JOURNAL

Do you have a particular skill or talent that you wish to master one day? What value do you place on mastering that talent? What personal qualities will you need in order to reach your desired level of mastery? Write about these questions in your journal.

CHAPTER IV

Who Has Won to Mastership

"Eh? Wot I say? I spik true w'en I say dat Buck two devils."

This was François's speech next morning when he discovered Spitz missing and Buck covered with wounds. He drew him to the fire and by its light pointed them out.

"Dat Spitz fight lak hell," said Perrault, as he surveyed the gaping rips and cuts.

"An' dat Buck fight lak two hells," was François's answer. "An' now we make good time. No more Spitz, no more trouble, sure."

While Perrault packed the camp outfit and loaded the sled, the dog-driver proceeded to harness the dogs. Buck trotted up to the place Spitz would have occupied as leader; but François, not noticing him, brought Sol-leks to the coveted position. In his judgment, Sol-leks was the best lead dog left. Buck sprang upon Sol-leks in a fury, driving him back and standing in his place.

"Eh? eh?" François cried, slapping his thighs gleefully. "Look at dat Buck. Heem keel dat Spitz, heem t'ink to take de job."

"Go 'way, Chook!" he cried, but Buck refused to budge.

He took Buck by the scruff of the neck, and though the dog growled threateningly, dragged him to one side and replaced Sol-leks. The old dog did not like it, and showed plainly that he was afraid of Buck. François was <u>obdurate</u>, but when he turned his back Buck again displaced Sol-leks, who was not at all unwilling to go.

François was angry. "Now, by Gar, I feex you!" he cried, coming back with a heavy club in his hand.

Buck remembered the man in the red sweater, and retreated slowly; nor did he attempt to charge in when Sol-leks was once more brought forward. But he circled just beyond the range of the club, snarling with bitterness and rage; and while he circled he watched the club so as to dodge it if thrown by François, for he was become wise in the way of clubs.

The driver went about his work, and he called to Buck when he was

How does Sol-leks respond to Buck's threat?

What does Buck do to Sol-leks? Why?

WORDS FOR EVERYDAY USE:
ob • du • rate (äb´ door it) *adj.*, not easily moved; stubborn

ready to put him in his old place in front of Dave. Buck retreated two or three steps. François followed him up, whereupon he again retreated. After some time of this, François threw down the club, thinking that Buck feared a thrashing. But Buck was in open revolt. He wanted, not to escape a clubbing, but to have the leadership. It was his by right. He had earned it, and he would not be content with less.

Perrault took a hand. Between them they ran him about for the better part of an hour. They threw clubs at him. He dodged. They cursed him, and his fathers and mothers before him, and all his seed to come after him down to the remotest generation, and every hair on his body and drop of blood in his veins; and he answered curse with snarl and kept out of their reach. He did not try to run away, but retreated around and around the camp, advertising plainly that when his desire was met, he would come in and be good.

François sat down and scratched his head. Perrault looked at his watch and swore. Time was flying, and they should have been on the trail an hour gone. François scratched his head again. He shook it and grinned sheepishly at the courier, who shrugged his shoulders in sign that they were beaten. Then François went up to where Sol-leks stood and called to Buck. Buck laughed, as dogs laugh, yet kept his distance. François unfastened Sol-leks's traces and put him back in his old place. The team stood harnessed to the sled in an unbroken line, ready for the trail. There was no place for Buck save at the front. Once more François called, and once more Buck laughed and kept away.

"T'row down de club," Perrault commanded.

François complied, whereupon Buck trotted in, laughing triumphantly, and swung around into position at the head of the team. His traces were fastened, the sled broken out, and with both men running they dashed out on to the river trail.

Highly as the dog-driver had forevalued Buck, with his two devils, he found, while the day was yet young, that he had undervalued. At a bound Buck took up the duties of leadership; and where judgment was required, and quick thinking and quick acting, he showed himself the superior even of Spitz, of whom François had never seen an equal.

But it was in giving the law and making his mates live up to it that Buck excelled. Dave and Sol-leks did not mind the change in leadership. It was none of their business. Their business was to toil, and toil mightily, in the traces. So long as that were not interfered with, they did not care what happened. Billee, the good-natured, could lead for all they cared, so long as he kept order. The rest of the team, however, had grown unruly during the last days of Spitz, and their surprise was great now that Buck proceeded to lick them into shape.

Pike, who pulled at Buck's heels, and who never put an ounce more of his weight against the breast-band than he was compelled to do, was swiftly and repeatedly shaken for loafing; and ere the first day was done he was pulling more than ever before in his life. The first night in camp, Joe, the sour one, was punished roundly[1]—a thing that

Why does Buck rebel?

How does Buck act as lead dog? What qualities does he display?

---

1. **roundly.** Severely; fully

Spitz had never succeeded in doing. Buck simply smothered him by virtue of superior weight, and cut him up till he ceased snapping and began to whine for mercy.

The general tone of the team picked up immediately. It recovered its old-time solidarity, and once more the dogs leaped as one dog in the traces. At the Rink Rapids two native huskies, Teek and Koona, were added; and the <u>celerity</u> with which Buck broke them in took away François's breath.

"Nevaire such a dog as dat Buck!" he cried. "No, nevaire! Heem worth one t'ousan' dollair, by Gar! Eh? Wot you say, Perrault?"

And Perrault nodded. He was ahead of the record then, and gaining day by day. The trail was in excellent condition, well packed and hard, and there was no new-fallen snow with which to contend. It was not too cold. The temperature dropped to fifty below zero and remained there the whole trip. The men rode and ran by turn, and the dogs were kept on the jump, with but infrequent stoppages.

The Thirty Mile River was comparatively coated with ice, and they covered in one day going out what had taken them ten days coming in. In one run they made a sixty-mile dash from the foot of Lake Le Barge to the White Horse Rapids. Across Marsh, Tagish, and Bennett (seventy miles of lakes), they flew so fast that the man whose turn it was to run towed behind the sled at the end of a rope. And on the last night of the second week they topped White Pass and dropped down the sea slope with the lights of Skaguay[2] and of the shipping at their feet.

It was a record run. Each day for fourteen days they had averaged forty miles. For three days Perrault and François threw chests up and down the main street of Skaguay and were <u>del-uged</u> with invitations to drink, while the team was the constant center of a worshipful crowd of dog-busters and mushers.[3] Then three or four western bad men <u>aspired</u> to clean out the town, were riddled like pepperboxes for their pains, and public interest turned to other idols. Next came official orders. François called Buck to him, threw his arms around him, wept over him. And that was the last of François and Perrault. Like other men, they passed out of Buck's life for good.

A Scot took charge of him and his mates, and in company with a dozen other dog teams he started back over the weary trail to Dawson. It was no light running now, nor record time, but heavy toil each day, with a heavy load behind; for this was the mail train, carrying word from the world to the men who sought gold under the shadow of the Pole.

Buck did not like it, but he bore up well to the work, taking pride in it after the manner of Dave and Sol-leks, and seeing that his mates, whether

2. **Skaguay.** City in what is now Alaska that served as the entry point to the Yukon gold fields
3. **dog-busters and mushers.** People who urge sled dogs to go faster

What success does the team led by Buck have? How are Perrault and François received in the city?

How is the team's new work different from its prior work?

WORDS FOR EVERYDAY USE:

ce • ler • i • ty (sə ler´i tē) *n.,* swiftness
del • uge (del´ yōōj) *vi.,* overwhelm as with a flood
as • pire (əs pīr´) *vi.,* try, attempt; desire, aim

they prided in it or not, did their fair share. It was a <u>monotonous</u> life, operating with machine-like regularity. One day was very like another. At a certain time each morning the cooks turned out, fires were built, and breakfast was eaten. Then, while some broke camp, others harnessed the dogs, and they were under way an hour or so before the darkness fell which gave warning of dawn. At night, camp was made. Some pitched the flies, others cut firewood and pine boughs for the beds, and still others carried water or ice for the cooks. Also, the dogs were fed. To them, this was the one feature of the day, though it was good to loaf around, after the fish was eaten, for an hour or so with the other dogs, of which there were five score and odd. There were fierce fighters among them, but three battles with the fiercest brought Buck to mastery, so that when he bristled and showed his teeth they got out of his way.

Best of all, perhaps, he loved to lie near the fire, hind legs crouched under him, forelegs stretched out in front, head raised, and eyes blinking dreamily at the flames. Sometimes he thought of Judge Miller's big house in the sun-kissed Santa Clara Valley, and of the cement swimming-tank, and Ysabel, the Mexican hairless, and Toots, the Japanese pug; but oftener he remembered the man in the red sweater, the death of Curly, the great fight with Spitz, and the good things he had eaten or would like to eat. He was not homesick. The Sunland was very dim and distant, and such memories had no power over him. Far more <u>potent</u> were the memories of his <u>heredity</u> that gave things he had never seen before a seeming familiarity; the instincts (which were but the memories of his ancestors become habits) which had lapsed in later days, and still later, in him, quickened and became alive again.

Sometimes as he crouched there, blinking dreamily at the flames, it seemed that the flames were of another fire, and that as he crouched by this other fire he saw another and different man from the cook before him. This other man was shorter of leg and longer of arm, with muscles that were stringy and knotty rather than rounded and swelling. The hair of this man was long and matted, and his head slanted back under it from the eyes. He uttered strange sounds, and seemed very much afraid of the darkness, into which he peered continually, clutching in his hand, which hung midway between knee and foot, a stick with a heavy stone made fast to the end. He was all but naked, a ragged and fire-scorched skin hanging partway down his back, but on his body there was much hair. In some places, across the chest and shoulders and down the outside of the arms and thighs, it was matted into almost a thick fur. He did not stand erect, but with trunk inclined forward from the hips, on legs that bent at the knees. About his body there was a <u>peculiar</u> springiness, or <u>resiliency</u>, almost catlike,

Who does Buck remember? From where do these memories come?

What is important to Buck?

WORDS FOR EVERYDAY USE:

mo • not • o • nous (mə nät´n əs) *adj.,* unvarying; tiresome because unvarying

po • tent (pōt´ 'nt) *adj.,* strong, powerful

he • red • i • ty (hə red´i tē) *n.,* inherited characteristics

pe • cu • liar (pə kyōol´yər) *adj.,* unique, strange

re • sil • ien • cy (ri zil´ yens ē) *n.,* ability to bounce or spring back to shape; ability to rebound

and a quick alertness as of one who lived in perpetual fear of things seen and unseen.

At other times this hairy man squatted by the fire with head between his legs and slept. On such occasions his elbows were on his knees, his hands clasped above his head as though to shed rain by the hairy arms. And beyond that fire, in the circling darkness, Buck could see many gleaming coals, two by two, always two by two, which he knew to be the eyes of great beasts of prey. And he could hear the crashing of their bodies through the undergrowth, and the noises they made in the night. And dreaming there by the Yukon bank, with lazy eyes blinking at the fire, these sounds and sights of another world would make the hair to rise along his back and stand on end across his shoulders and up his neck, till he whimpered low and <u>suppressedly</u>, or growled softly, and the cook shouted at him, "Hey, you Buck, wake up!" Whereupon the other world would vanish and the real world come into his eyes, and he would get up and yawn and stretch as though he had been asleep.

It was a hard trip, with the mail behind them, and the heavy work wore them down. They were short of weight and in poor condition when they made Dawson, and should have had a ten days' or a week's rest at least. But in two days' time they dropped down the Yukon bank from the Barracks, loaded with letters for the outside. The dogs were tired, the dri-

vers grumbling, and to make matters worse, it snowed every day. This meant a soft trail, greater friction on the runners, and heavier pulling for the dogs; yet the drivers were fair through it all, and did their best for the animals.

Each night the dogs were attended to first. They ate before the drivers ate, and no man sought his sleeping robe till he had seen to the feet of the dogs he drove. Still, their strength went down. Since the beginning of the winter they had traveled eighteen hundred miles, dragging sleds the whole weary distance; and eighteen hundred miles will tell upon life of the toughest. Buck stood it, keeping his mates up to their work and maintaining discipline, though he too was very tired. Billee cried and whimpered regularly in his sleep each night. Joe was sourer than ever, and Sol-leks was unapproachable, blind side or other side.

But it was Dave who suffered most of all. Something had gone wrong with him. He became more morose and irritable, and when camp was pitched at once made his nest, where his driver fed him. Once out of the harness and down, he did not get on his feet again till harness-up time in the morning. Sometimes, in the traces, when jerked by a sudden stoppage of the sled, or by straining to start it, he would cry out with pain. The driver examined him, but could find nothing. All the drivers became interested in his case. They talked it over at mealtime, and over their last pipes before going to bed,

What shows that something is wrong with Dave?

WORDS FOR EVERYDAY USE: sup • pres • sed • ly (sə preś ed lē) *adv.,* with restraint

and one night they held a <u>consultation</u>. He was brought from his nest to the fire and was pressed and prodded till he cried out many times. Something was wrong inside, but they could locate no broken bones, could not make it out.

By the time Cassiar Bar was reached, he was so weak that he was falling repeatedly in the traces. The Scot called a halt and took him out of the team, making the next dog, Sol-leks, fast to the sled. His intention was to rest Dave, letting him run free behind the sled. Sick as he was, Dave resented being taken out, grunting and growling while the traces were unfastened, and whimpering broken-heartedly when he saw Sol-leks in the position he had held and served so long. For the pride of trace and trail was his, and, sick unto death, he could not bear that another dog should do his work.

When the sled started, he <u>floundered</u> in the soft snow alongside the beaten trail, attacking Sol-leks with his teeth, rushing against him and trying to thrust him off into the soft snow on the other side, striving to leap inside his traces and get between him and the sled, and all the while whining and yelping and crying with grief and pain. The musher tried to drive him away with the whip; but he paid no heed to the stinging lash, and the man had not the heart to strike harder. Dave refused to run quietly on the trail behind the sled, where the going was easy, but continued to flounder along-side in the soft snow, where the going was most difficult, till exhausted. Then he fell, and lay where he fell, howling <u>lugubriously</u> as the long train of sleds churned by.

With the last remnant of his strength he managed to stagger along behind till the train made another stop, when he floundered past the sleds to his own, where he stood alongside Sol-leks. His driver lingered a moment to get a light for his pipe from the man behind. Then he returned and started his dogs. They swung out on the trail with remarkable lack of exertion, turned their heads uneasily, and stopped in surprise. The driver was surprised, too; the sled had not moved. He called his comrades to witness the sight. Dave had bitten through both of Sol-leks's traces, and was standing directly in front of the sled in his proper place.

He pleaded with his eyes to remain there. The driver was perplexed. His comrades talked of how a dog could break its heart through being denied the work that killed it, and recalled instances they had known where dogs, too old for the toil, or injured, had died because they were cut out of the traces. Also, they held it a mercy, since Dave was to die anyway, that he should die in the traces, heart-easy and content. So he was harnessed in again, and proudly he pulled as of old, though more than once he cried out involuntarily from the bite of his inward hurt. Several times he fell down and was dragged in the traces, and once the

How does the Scot try to help Dave? How does Dave respond? Why does he respond in this way?

What does Dave want?

WORDS FOR EVERYDAY USE:

con • sul • ta • tion (kän´səl tā´shən) *n.*, meeting to decide or plan
floun • der (floun´dər) *vi.*, struggle awkwardly; stumble
lu • gu • bri • ous • ly (lə gōō´ brē əs lē) *adv.*, sadly, mournfully, often in an exaggerated manner

sled ran upon him so that he limped thereafter in one of his hind legs.

But he held out till camp was reached, when his driver made a place for him by the fire. Morning found him too weak to travel. At harness-up time he tried to crawl to his driver. By convulsive efforts he got on his feet, staggered, and fell. Then he wormed his way forward slowly toward where the harnesses were being put on his mates. He would advance his forelegs and drag up his body with a sort of hitching movement, when he would advance his forelegs and hitch ahead again for a few more inches. His strength left him, and the last his mates saw of him he lay gasping in the snow and yearning toward them. But they could hear him mournfully howling till they passed out of sight behind a belt of river timber.

Here the train was halted. The Scot slowly retraced his steps to the camp they had left. The men ceased talking. A revolver shot rang out. The man came back hurriedly. The whips snapped, the bells tinkled merrily, the sleds churned along the trail; but Buck knew, and every dog knew, what had taken place behind the belt of river trees.

Responding to the Selection

Imagine that you are François. Before heading out on your next official order, you have time to write a brief entry in your journal about the record run into Skaguay. Explain how you managed to average forty miles every day for fourteen days, expressing your feelings about having Buck as the lead dog.

WORDS FOR EVERYDAY USE: **con • vul • sive** (kən vul´ siv) *adj.*, occurring in violent fits; spasmodic

Reviewing the Selection

1. What position on the team does Buck think is his?

2. At what does Buck excel?

3. What memories no longer hold any power over Buck?

4. Which dog suffers most of all from the eighteen hundred miles traveled?

5. What actions on the part of Buck show his ability to outsmart François and Perrault?

6. What actions show Buck's "mastership" over the other dogs?

7. What is probably the reason that "memories of his heredity" are becoming "far more potent" to Buck?

8. What actions on the part of Dave show his perseverance? What else do these actions show about Dave?

9. Who is the other, "different" man in Buck's dream? How is this man described? What purpose is served by this description?

10. How do the dogs feel about pulling the sleds? What sort of relationship between a dog and his work is described in this chapter?

Understanding Literature (Questions for Discussion)

Character and Characterization. Characterization is the use of literary techniques to create a character. When using the characterization technique of portrayal of behavior, the writer presents the actions and speech of the character, allowing the reader to draw his or her own conclusions about the character from what the character says or does. The dog Dave is a **minor character**, a character who plays a lesser role in the action of the story. In this chapter, the character of Dave is described primarily through the portrayal of his behavior. What is revealed about Dave through his behavior? What qualities does he possess? For what qualities is he admired by the men and the rest of the dogs?

Have you ever tried to give advice to somebody who just wouldn't listen? What happened when he or she acted without heeding your advice? How did you feel about the results of those actions?

CHAPTER V

The Toil of Trace and Trail

Thirty days from the time it left Dawson, the Salt Water Mail, with Buck and his mates at the fore, arrived at Skaguay. They were in a wretched state, worn out and worn down. Buck's one hundred and forty pounds had dwindled to one hundred and fifteen. The rest of his mates, though lighter dogs, had relatively lost more weight than he. Pike, the malingerer, who, in his lifetime of deceit, had often successfully feigned a hurt leg, was now limping in earnest. Sol-leks was limping, and Dub was suffering from a wrenched shoulder-blade.

They were all terribly footsore. No spring or rebound was left in them. Their feet fell heavily on the trail, jarring their bodies and doubling the fatigue of a day's travel. There was nothing the matter with them except that they were dead tired. It was not the dead-tiredness that comes through brief and excessive effort, from which recovery is a matter of hours; but it was the dead-tiredness that comes through the slow and prolonged strength drainage of months of toil. There was no power of recuperation left, no reserve strength to call upon. It had been all used, the last least bit of it. Every muscle, every fiber, every cell, was tired, dead tired. And there was reason for it. In less than five months they had traveled twenty-five hundred miles, during the last eighteen hundred of which they had had but five days' rest. When they arrived at Skaguay they were apparently on their last legs. They could barely keep the traces taut, and on the down grades just managed to keep out of the way of the sled.

"Mush on, poor sore feets," the driver encouraged them as they tottered down the main street of Skaguay. "Dis is de las'. Den we get one long res'. Eh? For sure. One bully long res'."

The drivers confidently expected a long stopover. Themselves, they had covered twelve hundred miles with two days' rest, and in the nature of reason and common justice they deserved an interval of loafing. But so many were the men who had rushed into the Klondike, and so many were the sweethearts, wives, and kin that had not rushed in, that the congested mail was taking on Alpine[1] proportions; also, there were official orders. Fresh batches of Hudson Bay dogs

What do the drivers expect? What thwarts their plans?

---

1. **Alpine.** Having the mountainous quality of the Alps, the highest mountains in Europe

were to take the places of those worthless for the trail. The worthless ones were to be got rid of, and, since dogs count for little against dollars, they were to be sold.

Three days passed, by which time Buck and his mates found how really tired and weak they were. Then, on the morning of the fourth day, two men from the States came along and bought them, harness and all, for a song. The men addressed each other as "Hal" and "Charles." Charles was a middle-aged, lightish-colored man, with weak and watery eyes and a mustache that twisted fiercely and vigorously up, giving the lie to the limply drooping lip it concealed. Hal was a youngster of nineteen or twenty, with a big Colt's revolver and a hunting knife strapped about him on a belt that fairly bristled with cartridges. This belt was the most <u>salient</u> thing about him. It advertised his <u>callowness</u>— a callowness sheer and unutterable. Both men were <u>manifestly</u> out of place, and why such as they should adventure the North is part of the mystery of things that passes understanding.

Buck heard the chaffering,[2] saw the money pass between the man and the Government agent, and knew that the Scot and the mail-train drivers were passing out of his life on the heels of Perrault and François and the others who had gone before. When driven with his mates to the new owners' camp, Buck saw a slipshod and <u>slovenly</u> affair, tent half-stretched, dishes unwashed, everything in disorder; also, he saw a woman. "Mercedes"

the men called her. She was Charles's wife and Hal's sister—a nice family party.

Buck watched them apprehensively as they proceeded to take down the tent and load the sled. There was a great deal of effort about their manner, but no businesslike method. The tent was rolled into an awkward bundle three times as large as it should have been. The tin dishes were packed away unwashed. Mercedes continually fluttered in the way of her men and kept up an unbroken chattering of <u>remonstrance</u> and advice. When they put a clothes sack on the front of the sled, she suggested it should go on the back; and when they had it put on the back, and covered it over with a couple of other bundles, she discovered overlooked articles which could abide nowhere else but in that very sack, and they unloaded again.

Three men from a neighboring tent came out and looked on, grinning and winking at one another.

"You've got a right smart load as it is," said one of them; "and it's not me should tell you your business, but I wouldn't tote that tent along if I was you."

"Undreamed of!" cried Mercedes, throwing up her hands in dainty dismay. "However in the world could I manage without a tent?"

"It's springtime, and you won't get any more cold weather," the man replied.

Why is Buck apprehensive?

What does Hal's belt say about him?

---

2. **chaffering.** Bargaining, haggling over price

WORDS FOR EVERYDAY USE:

sa • lient (sāl´yənt) *adj.*, noticeable; prominent
cal • low • ness (kal´ō nes) *n.*, youth; immaturity; state of being inexperienced
man • i • fest • ly (man´ə fest´ lē) *adv.*, clearly; obviously

slov • en • ly (sluv´ən lē) *adj.*, careless; untidy; slipshod
re • mon • strance (ri män´ strəns) *n.*, act of complaining, protesting

She shook her head decidedly, and Charles and Hal put the last odds and ends on top of the mountainous load.

"Think it'll ride?" one of the men asked.

"Why shouldn't it?" Charles demanded rather shortly.

"Oh, that's all right, that's all right," the man hastened meekly to say. "I was just a-wonderin', that is all. It seemed a mite top-heavy."

Charles turned his back and drew the lashings down as well as he could, which was not in the least well.

"An' of course the dogs can hike along all day with that contraption behind them," affirmed a second of the men.

"Certainly," said Hal, with freezing politeness, taking hold of the gee-pole with one hand and swinging his whip from the other. "Mush!" he shouted. "Mush on there!"

The dogs sprang against the breast-bands, strained hard for a few moments, then relaxed. They were unable to move the sled.

"The lazy brutes, I'll show them," he cried, preparing to lash out at them with the whip.

But, Mercedes interfered, crying, "Oh, Hal, you mustn't," as she caught hold of the whip and wrenched it from him. "The poor dears! Now you must promise you won't be harsh with them for the rest of the trip, or I won't go a step."

"Precious lot you know about dogs," her brother sneered; "and I wish you'd leave me alone. They're lazy, I tell you, and you've got to whip them to get any-thing out of them. That's their way. You ask any one. Ask one of those men."

Mercedes looked at them imploringly, untold <u>repugnance</u> at sight of pain written in her pretty face.

"They're weak as water, if you want to know," came the reply from one of the men. "Plum tuckered out, that's what's the matter. They need a rest."

"Rest be blanked," said Hal, with his beardless lips; and Mercedes said, "Oh!" in pain and sorrow at the oath.

But she was a clannish creature, and rushed at once to the defense of her brother. "Never mind that man," she said pointedly. "You're driving our dogs, and you do what you think best with them."

Again Hal's whip fell upon the dogs. They threw themselves against the breast-bands, dug their feet into the packed snow, got down low to it, and put forth all their strength. The sled held as though it were an anchor. After two efforts, they stood still, panting. The whip was whistling savagely, when once more Mercedes interfered. She dropped on her knees before Buck, with tears in her eyes, and put her arms around his neck.

"You poor, poor dears," she cried sympathetically, "why don't you pull hard? Then you wouldn't be whipped." Buck did not like her, but he was feeling too miserable to resist her, taking it as part of the day's miserable work.

One of the onlookers, who had been clenching his teeth to suppress hot speech, now spoke up:—

WORDS FOR EVERYDAY USE: **re • pug • nance** (ri pug´nəns) *n.*, extreme dislike or distaste

"It's not that I care a whoop what becomes of you, but for the dogs' sakes I just want to tell you, you can help them a mighty lot by breaking out that sled. The runners are froze fast. Throw your weight against the gee-pole, right and left, and break it out."

A third time the attempt was made, but this time, following the advice, Hal broke out the runners which had been frozen to the snow. The overloaded and unwieldy sled forged ahead, Buck and his mates struggling frantically under the rain of blows. A hundred yards ahead the path turned and sloped steeply into the main street. It would have required an experienced man to keep the top-heavy sled upright, and Hal was not such a man. As they swung on the turn the sled went over, spilling half its load through the loose lashings. The dogs never stopped. The lightened sled bounded on its side behind them. They were angry because of the ill treatment they had received and the unjust load. Buck was raging. He broke into a run, the team following his lead. Hal cried "Whoa! whoa!" but they gave no heed. He tripped and was pulled off his feet. The capsized sled ground over him, and the dogs dashed on up the street, adding to the gayety of Skaguay as they scattered the remainder of the outfit along its chief thoroughfare.

Kindhearted citizens caught the dogs and gathered up the scattered belongings. Also, they gave advice. Half the load and twice the dogs if they ever expected to reach Dawson, was what was said. Hal and his sister and brother-in-law listened unwillingly, pitched tent, and overhauled the outfit. Canned goods were turned out that made men laugh, for canned goods on the Long Trail is a thing to dream about. "Blankets for a hotel," quoth one of the men who laughed and helped. "Half as many is too much; get rid of them. Throw away that tent, and all those dishes,—who's going to wash them, anyway? Good Lord, do you think you're traveling on a Pullman?"[3]

And so it went, the inexorable elimination of the <u>superfluous</u>. Mercedes cried when her clothes bags were dumped on the ground and article after article was thrown out. She cried in general, and she cried in particular over each discarded thing. She clasped hands about knees, rocking back and forth broken-heartedly. She <u>averred</u> she would not go an inch, not for a dozen Charleses. She appealed to everybody and to everything, finally wiping her eyes and proceeding to cast out even articles of apparel that were imperative necessaries. And in her zeal, when she had finished with her own, she attacked the belongings of her men and went through them like a tornado.

This accomplished, the outfit, though cut in half, was still a <u>formidable</u> bulk. Charles and Hal went out in the evening and bought six Outside

---

What kinds of things did the inexperienced sledders pack? What factors did they consider when packing?

Why does the sled overturn? Why does the load spill? What predictions can you make about the rest of the trip based on this information?

---

3. **Pullman.** Railroad passenger car with convertible berths for sleeping

---

WORDS FOR EVERYDAY USE:

su • per • flu • ous (sə pʉr´floō əs) *adj.,* being more than is needed, excessive

a • ver (ə vʉr´) *vt.,* declare to be true, affirm

for • mi • da • ble (fôr´mə də bəl) *adj.,* large; hard to handle

Why had Hal and Charles never seen a sled with fourteen dogs?

dogs. These, added to the six of the original team, and Teek and Koona, the huskies obtained at the Rink Rapids on the record trip, brought the team up to fourteen. But the Outside dogs, though practically broken in since their landing, did not amount to much. Three were short-haired pointers, one was a Newfoundland, and the other two were mongrels of indeterminate breed. They did not seem to know anything, these newcomers. Buck and his comrades looked upon them with disgust, and though he speedily taught them their places and what not to do, he could not teach them what to do. They did not take kindly to trace and trail. With the exception of the two mongrels, they were bewildered and spirit-broken by the strange savage environment in which they found themselves and by the ill treatment they had received. The two mongrels were without spirit at all; bones were the only things breakable about them.

How are the dogs feeling as they set out? Why is Buck's feeling justified?

With the newcomers hopeless and forlorn, and the old team worn out by twenty-five hundred miles of continuous trail, the outlook was anything but bright. The two men, however, were quite cheerful. And they were proud, too. They were doing the thing in style, with fourteen dogs. They had seen other sleds depart over the Pass for Dawson, or come in from Dawson, but never had they seen a sled with so many as fourteen dogs. In the nature of Arctic travel there was a reason why fourteen dogs should not drag one sled, and that was that one sled could not carry the food for fourteen dogs. But Charles and Hal did not know this. They had worked the trip out with a pencil, so much to a dog, so many dogs, so many days, Q.E.D.[4] Mercedes looked over their shoulders and nodded comprehensively, it was all so very simple.

Late next morning Buck led the long team up the street. There was nothing lively about it, no snap or go in him and his fellows. They were starting dead weary. Four times he had covered the distance between Salt Water and Dawson, and the knowledge that, jaded and tired, he was facing the same trail once more, made him bitter. His heart was not in the work, nor was the heart of any dog. The Outsides were timid and frightened, the Insides without confidence in their masters.

Buck felt vaguely that there was no depending upon these two men and the woman. They did not know how to do anything, and as the days went by it became apparent that they could not learn. They were slack in all things, without order or discipline. It took them half the night to pitch a slovenly camp, and half the morning to break that camp and get the sled loaded in fashion so slovenly that for the rest of the day they were occupied in stopping and rearranging the load. Some days they did not make ten miles. On other days they were unable

---

4. **Q.E.D.** Latin, *quod erat demonstrandum;* which was to be demonstrated or proved

---

WORDS FOR EVERYDAY USE: jad • ed (jād´id) *adj.,* worn out; dulled

to get started at all. And on no day did they succeed in making more than half the distance used by the men as a basis in their dog food computation.

It was inevitable that they should go short on dog food. But they hastened it by overfeeding, bringing the day nearer when underfeeding would commence. The Outside dogs, whose digestions had not been trained by chronic famine to make the most of little, had <u>voracious</u> appetites. And when, in addition to this, the worn-out huskies pulled weakly, Hal decided that the <u>orthodox</u> ration was too small. He doubled it. And to cap it all, when Mercedes, with tears in her pretty eyes and a quaver in her throat, could not cajole him into giving the dogs still more, she stole from the fish sacks and fed them slyly. But it was not food that Buck and the huskies needed, but rest. And though they were making poor time, the heavy load they dragged sapped their strength severely.

Then came the underfeeding. Hal awoke one day to the fact that his dog food was half gone and the distance only quarter covered; further, that for love or money no additional dog food was to be obtained. So he cut down even the orthodox ration and tried to increase the day's travel. His sister and brother-in-law seconded him; but they were frustrated by their heavy outfit and their own incompetence. It was a simple matter to give the dogs less food; but it was impossible to make the dogs travel faster, while their own inability to get under way earlier in the morning prevented them from traveling longer hours. Not only did they not know how to work dogs, but they did not know how to work themselves.

The first to go was Dub. Poor blundering thief that he was, always getting caught and punished, he had nonetheless been a faithful worker. His wrenched shoulder blade, untreated and unrested, went from bad to worse, till finally Hal shot him with the big Colt's revolver. It is a saying of the country that an Outside dog starves to death on the ration of the husky, so the six Outside dogs under Buck could do no less than die on half the ration of the husky. The Newfoundland went first, followed by the three short-haired pointers, the two mongrels hanging more grittily on to life, but going in the end.

By this time all the <u>amenities</u> and gentlenesses of the Southland had fallen away from the three people. Shorn of its glamour and romance, Arctic travel became to them a reality too harsh for their manhood and womanhood. Mercedes ceased weeping over the dogs, being too occupied with weeping over herself and with quarreling with her husband and brother. To quarrel was the one thing they were never too weary to do. Their irritability arose out of their misery, increased with it, doubled upon it, outdistanced it. The wonderful patience of the trail

What did the people do to cause food supply problems?

How does Hal try to remedy the problem? Why doesn't this solution work?

WORDS FOR EVERYDAY USE:

vo • ra • cious (vô rā´shəs) *adj.*, greedy; ravenous

or • tho • dox (ôr ´thō däks´) *adj.*, usual; established (as in beliefs)

a • men • i • ty (ə men´ə tē) *n.*, comfort or convenience

How do Charles, Hal, and Mercedes react to life on the trail?

which comes to men who toil hard and suffer sore, and remain sweet of speech and kindly, did not come to these two men and the woman. They had no inkling of such a patience. They were stiff and in pain; their muscles ached, their bones ached, their very hearts ached; and because of this they became sharp of speech, and hard words were first on their lips in the morning and last at night.

Charles and Hal <u>wrangled</u> whenever Mercedes gave them a chance. It was the cherished belief of each that he did more than his share of the work, and neither forbore to speak this belief at every opportunity. Sometimes Mercedes sided with her husband, sometimes with her brother. The result was a beautiful and unending family quarrel. Starting from a dispute as to which should chop a few sticks for the fire (a dispute which concerned only Charles and Hal), presently would be lugged in the rest of the family, fathers, mothers, uncles, cousins, people thousands of miles away, and some of them dead. That Hal's views on art, or the sort of society plays his mother's brother wrote, should have anything to do with the chopping of a few sticks of firewood, passes comprehension; nevertheless the quarrel was as likely to tend in that direction as in the direction of Charles's political prejudices. And that Charles's sister's tale-bearing tongue should be relevant to the building of a Yukon fire was apparent only to Mercedes, who disburdened herself of <u>copious</u> opinions upon that topic, and incidentally upon a few other traits unpleasantly peculiar to her husband's family. In the meantime the fire remained unbuilt, the camp half pitched, and the dogs unfed.

Mercedes nursed a special grievance—the grievance of sex. She was pretty and soft, and had been chivalrously treated all her days. But the present treatment by her husband and brother was everything save chivalrous. It was her custom to be helpless. They complained. Upon which <u>impeachment</u> of what to her was her most essential sex-prerogative, she made their lives unendurable. She no longer considered the dogs, and because she was sore and tired, she persisted in riding on the sled. She was pretty and soft, but she weighed one hundred and twenty pounds—a lusty last straw to the load dragged by the weak and starving animals. She rode for days, till they fell in the traces and the sled stood still. Charles and Hal begged her to get off and walk, pleaded with her, entreated, the while she wept and <u>importuned</u> Heaven with a recital of their brutality.

On one occasion they took her off the sled by main strength. They never did it again. She let her legs go limp like a spoiled child, and sat down on the trail. They went on their way, but she did not move. After they had traveled three miles they unloaded the sled, came back for her, and by main strength put her on the sled again.

WORDS FOR EVERYDAY USE:

wran • gle (raŋ´gəl) *vi.,* quarrel angrily and noisily
co • pi • ous (kō´pē əs) *adj.,* full of information, wordy
im • peach • ment (im pēch´ment) *n.,* discredit
im • por • tune (im´pôr tōōn´) *vt.,* demand, ask for urgently

In the excess of their own misery they were <u>callous</u> to the suffering of their animals. Hal's theory, which he practiced on others, was that one must get hardened. He had started out preaching it to his sister and brother-in-law. Failing there, he hammered it into the dogs with a club. At the Five Fingers the dog food gave out, and a toothless old squaw offered to trade them a few pounds of frozen horsehide for the Colt's revolver that kept the big hunting knife company at Hal's hip. A poor substitute for food was this hide, just as it had been stripped from the starved horses of the cattlemen six months back. In its frozen state it was more like strips of galvanized iron, and when a dog wrestled it into his stomach it thawed into thin and innutritious leathery strings and into a mass of short hair, irritating and indigestible.

And through it all Buck staggered along at the head of the team as in a nightmare. He pulled when he could; when he could no longer pull, he fell down and remained down till blows from whip or club drove him to his feet again. All the stiffness and gloss had gone out of his beautiful furry

What is Hal's theory? To whom is he unable to teach this lesson? To whom does he teach it instead?

WORDS FOR EVERYDAY USE:
cal • lous (kalʹəs) *adj.,* unfeeling

coat. The hair hung down, limp and draggled, or matted with dried blood where Hal's club had bruised him. His muscles had wasted away to knotty strings, and the flesh pads had disappeared, so that each rib and every bone in his frame were outlined cleanly through the loose hide that was wrinkled in folds of emptiness. It was heartbreaking, only Buck's heart was unbreakable. The man in the red sweater had proved that.

As it was with Buck, so was it with his mates. They were <u>perambulating</u> skeletons. There were seven all together, including him. In their very great misery they had become insensible to the bite of the lash or the bruise of the club. The pain of the beating was dull and distant, just as the things their eyes saw and their ears heard seemed dull and distant. They were not half living, or quarter living. They were simply so many bags of bones in which sparks of life fluttered faintly. When a halt was made, they dropped down in the traces like dead dogs, and the spark dimmed and paled and seemed to go out. And when the club or whip fell upon them, the spark fluttered feebly up, and they tottered to their feet and staggered on.

There came a day when Billee, the good-natured, fell and could not rise. Hal had traded off his revolver, so he took the axe and knocked Billee on the head as he lay in the traces, then cut the carcass out of the harness and dragged it to one side. Buck saw, and his mates saw, and they knew that this

thing was very close to them. On the next day Koona went, and but five of them remained: Joe, too far gone to be malignant; Pike, crippled and limping, only half conscious and not conscious enough longer to malinger; Sol-leks, the one-eyed, still faithful to the toil of trace and trail, and mournful in that he had so little strength with which to pull; Teek, who had not traveled so far that winter and who was now beaten more than the others because he was fresher; and Buck, still at the head of the team, but no longer enforcing discipline or striving to enforce it, blind with weakness half the time and keeping the trail by the loom of it and by the dim feel of his feet.

It was beautiful spring weather, but neither dogs nor humans were aware of it. Each day the sun rose earlier and set later. It was dawn by three in the morning, and twilight lingered till nine at night. The whole long day was a blaze of sunshine. The ghostly winter silence had given way to the great spring murmur of awakening life. This murmur arose from all the land, <u>fraught</u> with the joy of living. It came from the things that lived and moved again, things which had been as dead and which had not moved during the long months of frost. The sap was rising in the pines. The willows and aspens were bursting out in young buds. Shrubs and vines were putting on fresh garbs of green. Crickets sang in the nights, and in the days all manner of creeping, crawling things rustled forth into the sun. Partridges and woodpeckers were

What has happened to the dogs since this journey began?

How does this picture of the spring landscape contrast with the portrait of the travelers?

WORDS FOR EVERYDAY USE:

per • am • bu • lat • ing (pər am´byōō lāt´iŋ) *part.*, walking around

fraught (frôt) *adj.*, filled; charged; loaded

booming and knocking in the forest. Squirrels were chattering, birds singing, and overhead honked the wild fowl driving up from the south in cunning wedges that split the air.

From every hill slope came the trickle of running water, the music of unseen fountains. All things were thawing, bending, snapping. The Yukon was straining to break loose the ice that bound it down. It ate away from beneath; the sun ate from above. Air holes formed, fissures sprang and spread apart, while thin sections of ice fell through bodily into the river. And amid all this bursting, rending, throbbing of awakening life, under the blazing sun and through the soft-sighing breezes, like wayfarers to death, staggered the two men, the woman, and the huskies.

With the dogs falling, Mercedes weeping and riding, Hal swearing <u>innocuously</u>, and Charles's eyes wistfully watering, they staggered into John Thornton's camp at the mouth of White River. When they halted, the dogs dropped down as though they had all been struck dead. Mercedes dried her eyes and looked at John Thornton. Charles sat down on a log to rest. He sat down very slowly and painstakingly what of his great stiffness. Hal did the talking. John Thornton was whittling the last touches on an axe-handle he had made from a stick of birch. He whittled and listened, gave monosyllabic replies, and, when it was asked, <u>terse</u> advice. He knew the breed, and he gave his advice in the certainty that it would not be followed.

"They told us up above that the bottom was dropping out of the trail and that the best thing for us to do was to lay over," Hal said in response to Thornton's warning to take no more chances on the rotten ice. "They told us we couldn't make White River, and here we are." This last with a sneering ring of triumph in it.

"And they told you true," John Thornton answered. "The bottom's likely to drop out at any moment. Only fools, with the blind luck of fools, could have made it. I tell you straight, I wouldn't risk my carcass on that ice for all the gold in Alaska."

"That's because you're not a fool, I suppose," said Hal. "All the same, we'll go on to Dawson." He uncoiled his whip. "Get up there, Buck! Hi! Get up there! Mush on!"

Thornton went on whittling. It was idle, he knew, to get between a fool and his folly, while two or three fools more or less would not alter the scheme of things.

But the team did not get up at the command. It had long since passed into the stage where blows were required to rouse it. The whip flashed out, here and there, on its merciless errands. John Thornton compressed his lips. Sol-leks was the first to crawl to his feet. Teek followed. Joe came next, yelping with pain. Pike made painful efforts. Twice he fell over, when half up, and on the third attempt managed to rise. Buck made no effort.

What does John Thornton recognize about the characters of these people?

What answer does Thornton give to Hal's triumphant sneer? What advice does Thornton give?

<u>W</u>ords for
Everyday Use:

in • no • cu • ous • ly (in năk´yoo əs lē) *adv.*, harmlessly; dully

terse (tʉrs) *adj.*, short; concise

He lay quietly where he had fallen. The lash bit into him again and again, but he neither whined nor struggled. Several times Thornton started, as though to speak, but changed his mind. A moisture came into his eyes, and, as the whipping continued, he arose and walked <u>irresolutely</u> up and down.

This was the first time Buck had failed, in itself a sufficient reason to drive Hal into a rage. He exchanged the whip for the customary club. Buck refused to move under the rain of heavier blows which now fell upon him. Like his mates, he was barely able to get up, but, unlike them, he had made up his mind not to get up. He had a vague feeling of impending doom. This had been strong upon him when he pulled in to the bank, and it had not departed from him. What of the thin and rotten ice he had felt under his feet all day, it seemed that he sensed disaster close at hand, out there ahead on the ice where his master was trying to drive him. He refused to stir. So greatly had he suffered, and so far gone was he, that the blows did not hurt much. And as they continued to fall upon him, the spark of life within flickered and went down. It was nearly out. He felt strangely numb. As though from a great distance, he was aware that he was being beaten. The last sensations of pain left him. He no longer felt anything, though very faintly he could hear the impact of the club upon his body. But it was no longer his body, it seemed so far away.

And then, suddenly, without warning, uttering a cry that was <u>inarticulate</u> and more like the cry of an animal, John Thornton sprang upon the man who wielded the club. Hal was hurled backward, as though struck by a falling tree. Mercedes screamed. Charles looked on wistfully, wiped his watery eyes, but did not get up because of his stiffness.

John Thornton stood over Buck, struggling to control himself, too convulsed with rage to speak.

"If you strike that dog again, I'll kill you," he at last managed to say in a choking voice.

"It's my dog," Hal replied, wiping the blood from his mouth as he came back. "Get out of my way, or I'll fix you. I'm going to Dawson."

Thornton stood between him and Buck, and <u>evinced</u> no intention of getting out of the way. Hal drew his long hunting-knife. Mercedes screamed, cried, laughed, and manifested the chaotic abandonment of hysteria. Thornton rapped Hal's knuckles with the axe-handle, knocking the knife to the ground. He rapped his knuckles again as he tried to pick it up. Then he stooped, picked it up himself, and with two strokes cut Buck's traces.

Hal had no fight left in him. Besides, his hands were full with his sister, or his arms, rather; while Buck was too near dead to be of further use in hauling the sled. A few minutes later they pulled out from the bank and down the river. Buck heard them go and raised his head to see. Pike was leading, Sol-leks was at

What does Buck do for the first time? Why is he different from his mates?

What three reasons does Hal have for giving up Buck?

WORDS FOR EVERYDAY USE:

ir • re • so • lute • ly (ir rez´ ə lo͞ot´lē) adv., indecisively

in • ar • tic • u • late (in´är tik´yo͞o lit) adj., not able to speak understandably

e • vince (ē vins´) vt., show plainly; indicate

the wheel, and between were Joe and Teek. They were limping and staggering. Mercedes was riding the loaded sled. Hal guided at the gee-pole, and Charles stumbled along in the rear.

As Buck watched them, Thornton knelt beside him and with rough, kindly hands searched for broken bones. By the time his search had disclosed nothing more than many bruises and a state of terrible starvation, the sled was a quarter of a mile away. Dog and man watched it crawling along over the ice. Suddenly, they saw its back end drop down, as into a rut, and the gee-pole, with Hal clinging to it, jerk into the air. Mercedes's scream came to their ears. They saw Charles turn and make one step to run back, and then a whole section of ice give way and dogs and humans disappear. A yawning hole was all that was to be seen. The bottom had dropped out of the trail.

John Thornton and Buck looked at each other.

"You poor devil," said John Thornton, and Buck licked his hand.

What happens to the sled? Are you sympathetic toward Charles, Mercedes, and Hal when this happens? Why, or why not?

Responding to the Selection

Imagine that you are John Thornton. In your journal, write about Buck, explaining why you saved his life. Express your feelings about Hal in your journal entry.

Reviewing the Selection

RECALLING

1. In what condition are the dogs when they reach Skaguay?

2. What does Hal claim is the reason the dogs are unable to move the sled?

3. What is the reason that fourteen dogs should not drag one sled?

4. What warning does John Thornton give to Hal about the ice?

INTERPRETING

5. What facts emphasize the grueling effects of the trail upon the dogs' physical condition?

6. What is probably the reason that Buck wildly runs the sled down the street of Skaguay?

7. What actions on the part of Charles and Hal justify the lack of confidence Buck feels toward them?

8. What actions on the part of John Thornton show his courage and compassion?

9. What causes inexperienced people like Charles, Hal, and Mercedes to "adventure the North"? What sort of image do they have of the North? How is that image different from the reality?

10. What kind of people does Thornton recognize Charles, Hal, and Mercedes to be? Does Thornton have respect for them? Why, or why not?

Understanding Literature (Questions for Discussion)

1. **Conflict.** A **conflict** is a struggle between two forces in a literary work. A character may struggle against another character, against the forces of nature, against society or social norms, against fate, or against some element within himself or herself. A struggle that takes place between a character and some outside force is called an **external conflict.** A struggle that takes place within a character is called an **internal conflict.** At the end of this chapter, the character John Thornton experiences both kinds of conflict—external and internal. What external conflict does Thornton struggle against? What internal conflict causes Thornton to hesitate before defending Buck against Hal?

2. **Character.** A **character** is a person (or sometimes an animal) who figures in the action of a literary work. Two types of characters include a **one-dimensional character** and a **three-dimensional character.** Hal, Charles, and Mercedes are examples of one-dimensional characters—characters who exhibit a single dominant quality, or character trait. What dominant quality or trait does each of these characters exhibit? John Thornton is an example of a three-dimensional character—a character who exhibits the complexity of traits associated with actual human beings. What human traits does Thornton exhibit at the end of this chapter?

READER'S JOURNAL

Have you ever pushed yourself to achieve a goal because you wanted to make someone proud of you? Have you ever taken risks to protect somebody you love? What compels you to act in these ways? Write about these questions in your journal.

CHAPTER VI

For the Love of a Man

When John Thornton froze his feet in the previous December, his partners had made him comfortable and left him to get well, going on themselves up the river to get out a raft of saw-logs for Dawson. He was still limping slightly at the time he rescued Buck, but with the continued warm weather even the slight limp left him. And here, lying by the river bank through the long spring days, watching the running water, listening lazily to the songs of birds and the hum of nature, Buck slowly won back his strength.

A rest comes very good after one has traveled three thousand miles, and it must be confessed that Buck waxed lazy as his wounds healed, his muscles swelled out, and the flesh came back to cover his bones. For that matter, they were all loafing,—Buck, John Thornton, and Skeet and Nig,—waiting for the raft to come that was to carry them down to Dawson. Skeet was a little Irish setter who early made friends with Buck, who, in a dying condition, was unable to resent her first advances. She had the doctor trait which some dogs possess; and as a mother cat washes her kittens, so she washed and cleansed Buck's wounds. Regularly, each morning after he had finished his breakfast, she performed her self-appointed task, till he came to look for her <u>ministrations</u> as much as he did for Thornton's. Nig, equally friendly, though less demonstrative, was a huge black dog, half-bloodhound and half-deerhound, with eyes that laughed and a boundless good nature.

To Buck's surprise these dogs manifested no jealousy toward him. They seemed to share the kindliness and largeness of John Thornton. As Buck grew stronger they enticed him into all sorts of ridiculous games, in which Thornton himself could not forebear to join; and in this fashion Buck romped through his convalescence and into a new existence. Love, genuine passionate love, was his for the first time. This he had never experienced at Judge Miller's down in the sun-kissed Santa Clara Valley. With the Judge's

Why is Skeet able to become friends with Buck?

What surprises Buck about these dogs? What past experience causes this surprise?

WORDS FOR EVERYDAY USE: min • is • tra • tion (min´is trā´shən) *n.*, act of giving care, help, or service

sons, hunting and tramping, it had been a working partnership; with the Judge's grandsons, a sort of pompous guardianship; and with the Judge himself, a stately and dignified friendship. But love that was feverish and burning, that was adoration, that was madness, it had taken John Thornton to arouse.

This man had saved his life, which was something; but, further, he was the ideal master. Other men saw to the welfare of their dogs from a sense of duty and business expediency; he saw to the welfare of his as if they were his own children, because he could not help it. And he saw further. He never forgot a kindly greeting or a cheering word, and to sit down for a long talk with them ("gas" he called it) was as much his delight as theirs. He had a way of taking Buck's head roughly between his hands, and resting his own head upon Buck's, of shaking him back and forth, the while calling him ill names that to Buck were love names. Buck knew no greater joy than that rough embrace and the sound of murmured oaths, and at each jerk back and forth it seemed that his heart would be shaken out of his body so great was its ecstasy. And when, released, he sprang to his feet, his mouth laughing, his eyes eloquent, his throat vibrant with unuttered sound, and in that fashion remained without movement, John Thornton would reverently exclaim, "God! you can all but speak!"

Buck had a trick of love expression that was akin to hurt. He would often seize Thornton's hand in his mouth and close so fiercely that the flesh bore the impress of his teeth for some time afterward. And as Buck understood the oaths to be love words, so the man understood this feigned bite for a caress.

For the most part, however, Buck's love was expressed in adoration. While he went wild with happiness when Thornton touched him or spoke to him, he did not seek these tokens. Unlike Skeet, who was wont to shove her nose under Thornton's hand and nudge and nudge till petted, or Nig, who would stalk up and rest his great head on Thornton's knee, Buck was content to adore at a distance. He would lie by the hour, eager, alert, at Thornton's feet, looking up into his face, dwelling upon it, studying it, following with keenest interest each fleeting expression, every movement or change of feature. Or, as chance might have it, he would lie farther away, to the side or rear, watching the outlines of the man and the occasional movements of his body. And often, such was the communion in which they lived, the strength of Buck's gaze would draw John Thornton's head around, and he would return the gaze, without speech, his heart shining out of his eyes as Buck's heart shone out.

For a long time after his rescue, Buck did not like Thornton to get out of his sight. From the moment he left the tent to when he entered it again, Buck would follow at his heels. His <u>transient</u> masters since he had come into the Northland had bred in him a fear that

WORDS FOR EVERYDAY USE: **tran • sient** (tran´shənt) *adj.*, staying only for a short time

no master could be permanent. He was afraid that Thornton would pass out of his life as Perrault and François and the Scot had passed out. Even in the night, in his dreams, he was haunted by this fear. At such times he would shake off sleep and creep through the chill to the flap of the tent, where he would stand and listen to the sound of his master's breathing.

But in spite of this great love he bore John Thornton, which seemed to bespeak the soft civilizing influence, the strain of the primitive, which the Northland had aroused in him, remained alive and active. Faithfulness and devotion, things born of fire and roof, were his; yet he retained his wildness and wiliness. He was a thing of the wild, come in from the wild to sit by John Thornton's fire, rather than a dog of the soft Southland stamped with the marks of generations of civilization. Because of his very great love, he could not steal from this man, but from any other man, in any other camp, he did not hesitate an instant; while the cunning with which he stole enabled him to escape detection.

His face and body were scored by the teeth of many dogs, and he fought as fiercely as ever and more shrewdly. Skeet and Nig were too good-natured for quarreling,—besides, they belonged to John Thornton; but the strange dog, no matter what the breed or valor, swiftly acknowledged Buck's supremacy or found himself struggling for life with a terrible antagonist. And Buck was merciless. He had learned well the law of club and fang, and he never forewent an advantage or drew back from a foe he had started on the way to death. He had lessoned from Spitz, and from the chief fighting dogs of the police and mail, and knew there was no middle course. He must master or be mastered; while to show mercy was a weakness. Mercy did not exist in the primordial life. It was misunderstood for fear, and such misunderstandings made for death. Kill or be killed, eat or be eaten, was the law; and this mandate, down out of the depths of Time, he obeyed.

What two forces are active in Buck? Which is stronger?

He was older than the days he had seen and the breaths he had drawn. He linked the past with the present, and the eternity behind him throbbed through him in a mighty rhythm to which he swayed as the tides and seasons swayed. He sat by John Thornton's fire, a broad-breasted dog, white-fanged and long-furred; but behind him were the shades of all manner of dogs, half-wolves and wild wolves, urgent and prompting, tasting the savor of the meat he ate, thirsting for the water he drank, scenting the wind with him, listening with him and telling him the sounds made by the wildlife in the forest, dictating his moods, directing his actions, lying down to sleep with him when he lay down, and dreaming with him and beyond him and becoming themselves the stuff of his dreams.

In what way is Buck affected by links to the past?

So <u>peremptorily</u> did these shades beckon him, that each day mankind and the claims of mankind slipped farther from him. Deep in the forest a call

What compels
Buck to plunge
into the forest?
What compels
him to come
back?

was sounding, and as often as he heard this call mysteriously thrilling and luring, he felt compelled to turn his back upon the fire and the beaten earth around it, and to plunge into the forest, and on and on, he knew not where or why; nor did he wonder where or why, the call sounding imperiously, deep in the forest. But as often as he gained the soft unbroken earth and the green shade, the love for John Thornton drew him back to the fire again.

Thornton alone held him. The rest of mankind was as nothing. Chance travelers might praise or pet him; but he was cold under it all, and from a too demonstrative man he would get up and walk away. When Thornton's partners, Hans and Pete, arrived on the long-expected raft, Buck refused to notice them till he learned they were close to Thornton; after that he tolerated them in a passive sort of way,

accepting favors from them as though he favored them by accepting. They were of the same large type as Thornton, living close to the earth, thinking simply and seeing clearly; and ere they swung the raft into the big eddy by the sawmill at Dawson, they understood Buck and his ways, and did not insist upon an intimacy such as obtained with Skeet and Nig.

For Thornton, however, his love seemed to grow and grow. He, alone among men, could put a pack upon Buck's back in the summer traveling. Nothing was too great for Buck to do, when Thornton commanded. One day (they had grubstaked themselves from the proceeds of the raft and left Dawson for the headwaters of the Tanana) the men and dogs were sitting on the crest of a cliff which fell away, straight down, to naked bedrock three hundred feet below. John Thornton was sitting near the edge, Buck at his shoulder. A thoughtless whim seized Thornton, and he drew the attention of Hans and Pete to the experiment he had in mind. "Jump, Buck!" he commanded, sweeping his arm out and over the chasm. The next instant he was grappling with Buck on the extreme edge, while Hans and Pete were dragging them back into safety.

"It's uncanny," Pete said, after it was over and they had caught their speech.

Thornton shook his head. "No, it is splendid, and it is terrible, too. Do you know, it sometimes makes me afraid."

"I'm not hankering to be the man that lays hands on you while he's around," Pete announced conclusively, nodding his head toward Buck.

"Py Jingo!" was Hans's contribution. "Not mineself either."

It was at Circle City, ere the year was out, that Pete's apprehensions were realized. "Black" Burton, a man evil-tempered and <u>malicious</u>, had been picking a quarrel with a tenderfoot at the bar, when Thornton stepped good-naturedly between. Buck, as was his custom, was lying in a corner, head on paws, watching his master's every action. Burton struck out, without warning, straight from the shoulder. Thornton was sent spinning, and saved himself from falling only by clutching the rail of the bar.

Those who were looking on heard what was neither bark nor yelp, but a something which is best described as a roar, and they saw Buck's body rise up in the air as he left the floor for Bur-

ton's throat. The man saved his life by instinctively throwing out his arm, but was hurled backward to the floor with Buck on top of him. Buck loosed his teeth from the flesh of the arm and drove in again for the throat. This time the man succeeded only in partly blocking, and his throat was torn open. Then the crowd was upon Buck, and he was driven off; but while a surgeon checked the bleeding, he prowled up and down, growling furiously, attempting to rush in, and being forced back by an array of hostile clubs. A "miners' meeting," called on the spot, decided that the dog had sufficient <u>provocation</u>, and Buck was discharged. But his reputation was made, and from that day his name spread through every camp in Alaska.

Later on, in the fall of the year, he saved John Thornton's life in quite another fashion. The three partners were lining a long and narrow poling-boat down a bad stretch of rapids on the Forty-Mile Creek. Hans and Pete moved along the bank, snubbing with a thin Manila rope[1] from tree to tree, while Thornton remained in the boat, helping its descent by means of a pole, and shouting directions to the shore. Buck, on the bank, worried and anxious, kept abreast of the boat, his eyes never off his master.

At a particularly bad spot, where a ledge of barely submerged rocks jutted out into the river, Hans cast off the rope, and, while Thornton poled the

1. **Manila rope.** Strong rope made of hemp from Manila, capital of the Philippines

What experiment does Thornton try on a whim? What does it prove?

What reputation does Buck gain?

WORDS FOR EVERYDAY USE:

ma • li • cious (mə lish´əs) *adj.,* intentionally spiteful; harmful

prov • o • ca • tion (präv´ə kā´shən) *n.,* something that stirs up feelings or action, especially a cause of resentment or irritation

boat out into the stream, ran down the bank with the end in his hand to snub the boat when it had cleared the ledge. This it did, and was flying downstream in a current as swift as a millrace, when Hans checked it with the rope and checked too suddenly. The boat flirted over and snubbed in to the bank bottom up, while Thornton, flung sheer out of it, was carried downstream toward the worst part of the rapids, a stretch of wild water in which no swimmer could live.

Buck had sprung in on the instant; and at the end of three hundred yards, amid a mad swirl of water, he overhauled Thornton. When he felt him grasp his tail, Buck headed for the bank, swimming with all his splendid strength. But the progress shoreward was slow, the progress downstream amazingly rapid. From below came the fatal roaring where the wild current went wilder and was rent in shreds and spray by the rocks which thrust through like the teeth of an enormous comb. The suck of the water as it took the beginning of the last steep pitch was frightful, and Thornton knew that the shore was impossible. He scraped furiously over a rock, bruised across a second, and struck a third with crushing force. He clutched its slippery top with both hands, releasing Buck, and above the roar of the churning water shouted: "Go, Buck! Go!"

Buck could not hold his own, and swept on downstream, struggling desperately, but unable to win back. When he heard Thornton's command repeated, he partly reared out of the water, throwing his head high, as though for a last look, then turned obediently toward the bank. He swam powerfully and was dragged ashore by Pete and Hans at the very point where swimming ceased to be possible and destruction began.

They knew that the time a man could cling to a slippery rock in the face of that driving current was a matter of minutes, and they ran as fast as they could up the bank to a point far above where Thornton was hanging on. They attached the line with which they had been snubbing the boat to Buck's neck and shoulders, being careful that it should neither strangle him nor impede his swimming, and launched him into the stream. He struck out boldly, but not straight enough into the stream. He discovered the mistake too late, when Thornton was abreast of him and a bare half-dozen strokes away while he was being carried helplessly past.

Hans promptly snubbed with the rope, as though Buck were a boat. The rope thus tightening on him in the sweep of the current, he was jerked under the surface, and under the surface he remained till his body struck against the bank and he was hauled out. He was half drowned, and Hans and Pete threw themselves upon him, pounding the breath into him and the water out of him. He staggered to his feet and fell down. The faint sound of Thornton's voice came to them, and though they could not make out the words of it, they knew that he was in his extremity. His master's voice acted on Buck like an electric shock. He sprang to his feet and ran up the bank ahead of the men to the point of his previous departure.

Again the rope was attached and he was launched, and again he struck out, but this time straight into the stream. He had miscalculated once, but he

What does Buck do to save Thornton's life? What makes progress difficult? What danger lies ahead?

What spurs Buck on to further action?

would not be guilty of it a second time. Hans paid out the rope, permitting no slack, while Pete kept it clear of coils. Buck held on till he was on a line straight above Thornton; then he turned, and with the speed of an express train headed down upon him. Thornton saw him coming, and, as Buck struck him like a battering ram, with the whole force of the current behind him, he reached up and closed with both arms around the shaggy neck. Hans snubbed the rope around the tree, and Buck and Thornton were jerked under the water. Strangling, suffocating, sometimes one uppermost and sometimes the other, dragging over the jagged bottom, smashing against rocks and snags, they veered in to the bank.

Thornton came to, belly downward and being violently propelled back and forth across a drift log by Hans and Pete. His first glance was for Buck, over whose limp and apparently lifeless body Nig was setting up a howl, while Skeet was licking the wet face and closed eyes. Thornton was himself bruised and battered, and he went carefully over Buck's body, when he had been brought around, finding three broken ribs.

"That settles it," he announced. "We camp right here." And camp they did, till Buck's ribs knitted and he was able to travel.

That winter, at Dawson, Buck performed another exploit, not so heroic, perhaps, but one that put his name many notches higher on the totem-pole[2]

of Alaskan fame. This exploit was particularly gratifying to the three men; for they stood in need of the outfit which it furnished, and were enabled to make a long-desired trip into the virgin East, where miners had not yet appeared. It was brought about by a conversation in the Eldorado Saloon, in which men waxed boastful of their favorite dogs. Buck, because of his record, was the target for these men, and Thornton was driven stoutly to defend him. At the end of half an hour one man stated that his dog could start a sled with five hundred pounds and walk off with it; a second bragged six hundred for his dog; and a third, seven hundred.

"Pooh! pooh!" said John Thornton; "Buck can start a thousand pounds."

"And break it out? and walk off with it for a hundred yards?" demanded Matthewson, a Bonanza King, he of the seven-hundred <u>vaunt</u>.

"And break it out, and walk off with it for a hundred yards," John Thornton said coolly.

"Well," Matthewson said, slowly and deliberately, so that all could hear, "I've got a thousand dollars that says he can't. And there it is." So saying, he slammed a sack of gold dust of the size of a bologna sausage down upon the bar.

Nobody spoke. Thornton's bluff, if bluff it was, had been called. He could

---

2. **totem-pole.** Pole or post carved and painted with totems, or images of animals or natural objects believed to be related to a family's heritage, often erected in front of their dwellings by Native Americans from the northwest coast of North America

What boast does Thornton make? What happens as a result of this boast?

What effect does Buck's next act have for him? for Thornton and his friends?

WORDS FOR EVERYDAY USE: **vaunt** (vônt) *n.*, boast or brag

feel a flush of warm blood creeping up his face. His tongue had tricked him. He did not know whether Buck could start a thousand pounds. Half a ton! The enormousness of it appalled him. He had great faith in Buck's strength and had often thought him capable of starting such a load; but never, as now, had he faced the possibility of it, the eyes of a dozen men fixed upon him, silent and waiting. Further, he had no thousand dollars; nor had Hans or Pete.

"I've got a sled standing outside now, with twenty fifty-pound sacks of flour on it," Matthewson went on with brutal directness; "so don't let that hinder you."

Thornton did not reply. He did not know what to say. He glanced from face to face in the absent way of a man who has lost the power of thought and is seeking somewhere to find the thing that will start it going again. The face of Jim O'Brien, a Mastodon King and old-time comrade, caught his eyes. It was as a cue to him, seeming to rouse him to do what he would never have dreamed of doing.

"Can you lend me a thousand?" he asked, almost in a whisper.

"Sure," answered O'Brien, thumping down a <u>plethoric</u> sack by the side of Matthewson's. "Though it's little faith I'm having, John, that the beast can do the trick."

The Eldorado emptied its occupants into the street to see the test. The tables were deserted, and the dealers and gamekeepers came forth to see the outcome of the wager and to lay odds. Several hundred men, furred and mittened, banked around the sled within easy distance. Matthewson's sled, loaded with a thousand pounds of flour, had been standing for a couple of hours, and in the intense cold (it was sixty below zero) the runners had frozen fast to the hard-packed snow. Men offered odds of two to one that Buck could not budge the sled. A quibble arose concerning the phrase "break out." O'Brien contended it was Thornton's privilege to knock the runners loose, leaving Buck to "break it out" from a dead standstill. Matthewson insisted that the phrase included breaking the runners from the frozen grip of the snow. A majority of the men who had witnessed the making of the bet decided in his favor, whereat the odds went up to three to one against Buck.

There were no takers. Not a man believed him capable of the feat. Thornton had been hurried into the wager, heavy with doubt; and now that he looked at the sled itself, the concrete fact, with the regular team of ten dogs curled up in the snow before it, the more impossible the task appeared. Matthewson waxed jubilant.

"Three to one!" he proclaimed. "I'll lay you another thousand at that figure, Thornton. What d'ye say?"

Thornton's doubt was strong in his face, but his fighting spirit was aroused—the fighting spirit that soars above odds, fails to recognize the impossible, and is deaf to all save the

Does Thornton believe Buck can start a thousand pounds? Does he regret his statement?

What rouses Thornton to action? What does he ask O'Brien? Does O'Brien believe Buck can do it?

Words for Everyday Use:

ple • thor • ic (plə thôr′ik) *adj.*, characterized by excess or profusion

clamor for battle. He called Hans and Pete to him. Their sacks were slim, and with his own the three partners could rake together only two hundred dollars. In the ebb of their fortunes, this sum was their total capital; yet they laid it unhesitatingly against Matthewson's six hundred.

The team of ten dogs was unhitched, and Buck, with his own harness, was put into the sled. He had caught the contagion of the excitement, and he felt that in some way he must do a great thing for John Thornton. Murmurs of admiration at his splendid appearance went up. He was in perfect condition, without an ounce of superfluous flesh, and the one hundred and fifty pounds that he weighed were so many pounds of grit and <u>virility</u>. His furry coat shone with the sheen of silk. Down the neck and across the shoulders, his mane, in repose as it was, half bristled and seemed to lift with every movement, as though excess of vigor made each particular hair alive and active. The great breast and heavy forelegs were no more than in proportion with the rest of the body, where the muscles showed in tight rolls underneath the skin. Men felt these muscles and proclaimed them hard as iron, and the odds went down to two to one.

"Gad, sir! Gad, sir!" stuttered a member of the latest dynasty, a king of the Skookum Benches. "I offer you eight hundred for him, sir, before the test, sir; eight hundred just as he stands."

Thornton shook his head and stepped to Buck's side.

"You must stand off from him," Matthewson protested. "Free play and plenty of room."

The crowd fell silent; only could be heard the voices of the gamblers vainly offering two to one. Everybody acknowledged Buck a magnificent animal, but twenty fifty-pound sacks of flour bulked too large in their eyes for them to loosen their pouch-strings.

Thornton knelt down by Buck's side. He took his head in his two hands and rested cheek on cheek. He did not playfully shake him, as was his wont, or murmur soft love curses; but he whispered in his ear. "As you love me, Buck. As you love me," was what he whispered. Buck whined with suppressed eagerness.

The crowd was watching curiously. The affair was growing mysterious. It seemed like a conjuration. As Thornton got to his feet, Buck seized his mittened hand between his jaws, pressing in with his teeth and releasing slowly, half-reluctantly. It was the answer, in terms, not of speech, but of love. Thornton stepped well back.

"Now, Buck," he said.

Buck tightened the traces, then slacked them for a matter of several inches. It was the way he had learned.

"Gee!" Thornton's voice rang out, sharp in the tense silence.

Buck swung to the right, ending the movement in a plunge that took up the slack and with a sudden jerk arrested his one hundred and fifty pounds. The load quivered, and from under the runners arose a crisp crackling.

What does Buck sense?

What does Thornton whisper to Buck?

"Haw!" Thornton commanded.

Buck duplicated the maneuver, this time to the left. The crackling turned into a snapping, the sled pivoting and the runners slipping and grating several inches to the side. The sled was broken out. Men were holding their breaths, intensely unconscious of the fact.

"Now, MUSH!"

Thornton's command cracked out like a pistol shot. Buck threw himself forward, tightening the traces with a jarring lunge. His whole body was gathered compactly together in the tremendous effort, the muscles writhing and knotting like live things under the silky fur. His great chest was low to the ground, his head forward and down, while his feet were flying like mad, the claws scarring the hard-packed snow in parallel grooves. The sled swayed and trembled, half-started forward. One of his feet slipped, and one man groaned aloud. Then the sled lurched ahead in what appeared a rapid succession of jerks, though it never really came to a dead stop again . . . half an inch . . . an inch . . . two inches . . . The jerks perceptibly diminished; as the sled gained momentum, he caught them up, till it was moving steadily along.

Men gasped and began to breathe again, unaware that for a moment they had ceased to breathe. Thornton was running behind, encouraging Buck with short, cheery words. The distance had been measured off, and as he neared the pile of firewood which marked the end of the hundred yards, a cheer began to grow and grow, which burst into a roar as he passed the firewood and halted at command. Every man was tearing himself loose, even Matthewson. Hats and mittens were flying in the air. Men were shaking hands, it did not matter with whom, and bubbling over in a general incoherent babel.

But Thornton fell on his knees beside Buck. Head was against head, and he was shaking him back and forth. Those who hurried up heard him cursing Buck, and he cursed him long and fervently, and softly and lovingly.

"Gad, sir! Gad, sir!" spluttered the Skookum Bench King. "I'll give you a thousand for him, sir, a thousand, sir—twelve hundred, sir."

Thornton rose to his feet. His eyes were wet. The tears were streaming frankly down his cheeks. "Sir," he said to the Skookum Bench King, "no, sir. You can go to hell, sir. It's the best I can do for you, sir."

Buck seized Thornton's hand in his teeth. Thornton shook him back and forth. As though animated by a common impulse, the onlookers drew back to a respectful distance; nor were they again indiscreet enough to interrupt.

How does the crowd react to Buck's success?

What shows that the growing tension has been released?

Responding to the Selection

Which of Buck's actions for Thornton do you find most admirable? Which escapade is most exciting? Discuss your opinions and why you feel this way with two or three of your classmates.

Reviewing the Selection

RECALLING

1. What kind of master is John Thornton to Buck?

2. What command does Thornton give to Buck on the crest of the cliff?

3. What heroic feat does Buck perform on the rapids of Forty-Mile Creek?

4. What feat does Matthewson bet Thornton that Buck cannot do?

INTERPRETING

5. What actions on the part of John Thornton show his particular affection for Buck?

6. What is probably the reason that Thornton gives the command?

7. What value does Thornton show that he places on Buck when saying, "That settles it. We camp right here"?

8. What action on the part of Buck secures his place "on the totem-pole of Alaskan fame"?

SYNTHESIZING

9. What is the difference between the feelings that Buck has toward John Thornton and his feelings toward other men, such as Judge Miller and François and Perrault?

10. What qualities does John Thornton possess that allow him to be the only hold humankind has on Buck?

Understanding Literature (Questions for Discussion)

Characterization. Characterization is the use of literary techniques to create a character. Two of these techniques, direct description and portrayal of a character's behavior, are used in the following passage from this chapter: "He sat by John Thornton's fire, a broad-breasted dog, white-fanged and long-furred; but behind him were the shades of all manner of dogs, half-wolves and wild wolves, urgent and prompting, tasting the savor of the meat he ate, thirsting for the water he drank, scenting the wind with him, listening with him and telling him the sounds made by the wildlife in the forest, dictating his moods, directing his actions, lying down to sleep with him when he lay down, and dreaming with him and beyond him and becoming themselves the stuff of his dreams." What aspects of Buck's character are revealed by the description of the dog sitting by the fire? How does this contrast with the characterization of "the shades of all manner of dogs"? Who are they? What kind of influence or power do they have upon the character of Buck?

READER'S JOURNAL

What kind of call pulls at you? Do you dream about sailing at sea? climbing to the highest mountain peak? plumbing the depths of the deepest cave? In your journal, freewrite about an impulse that secretly calls to you.

CHAPTER VII

The Sounding of the Call

When Buck earned sixteen hundred dollars in five minutes for John Thornton, he made it possible for his master to pay off certain debts and to journey with his partners into the East after a fabled lost mine, the history of which was as old as the history of the country. Many men had sought it; few had found it; and more than a few there were who had never returned from the quest. This lost mine was steeped in tragedy and shrouded in mystery. No one knew of the first man. The oldest tradition stopped before it got back to him. From the beginning there had been an ancient and ramshackle cabin. Dying men had sworn to it, and to the mine the site of which it marked, clinching their testimony with nuggets that were unlike any known grade of gold in the Northland.

But no living man had looted this treasure house, and the dead were dead; wherefore John Thornton and Pete and Hans, with Buck and half a dozen other dogs, faced into the East on an unknown trail to achieve where men and dogs as good as themselves had failed. They sledded seventy miles up the Yukon, swung to the left into the Stewart River, passed the Mayo and the McQuestion, and held on until the Stewart itself became a streamlet, threading the upstanding peaks, which marked the backbone of the continent.

John Thornton asked little of man or nature. He was unafraid of the wild. With a handful of salt and a rifle he could plunge into the wilderness and fare wherever he pleased and as long as he pleased. Being in no haste, Indian fashion, he hunted his dinner in the course of the day's travel; and if he failed to find it, like the Indian, he kept on traveling, secure in the knowledge that sooner or later he would come to it. So, on this great journey into the East, straight meat was the bill of fare, ammunition and tools principally made up the load on the sled, and the timecard was drawn upon the limitless future.

To Buck it was boundless delight, this hunting, fishing, and indefinite wandering through strange places. For weeks at a time they would hold on steadily, day after day; and for weeks upon end they would camp, here and there, the dogs loafing and the men burning holes through frozen muck and gravel and washing countless pans of dirt by the heat of the fire. Sometimes they went hungry, sometimes they feasted riotously, all according to the abundance of game and the fortune of hunting. Summer arrived, and dogs and men packed on their backs, rafted across blue mountain lakes, and descended or ascended unknown rivers in slender boats whipsawed[1] from the standing forest.

The months came and went, and back and forth they twisted through the uncharted vastness, where no men were and yet where men had been if the Lost Cabin were true. They went across divides in summer blizzards, shivered under the midnight sun on naked mountains between the timber line and the eternal snows, dropped into summer valleys amid swarming gnats and flies, and in the shadows of glaciers picked strawberries and flowers as ripe and fair as any the Southland could boast. In the fall of the year they penetrated a weird lake country, sad and silent, where wildfowl had been, but where then there was no life nor sign of life—only the blowing of chill winds, the forming of ice in sheltered places, and the melancholy rippling of waves on lonely beaches.

And through another winter they wandered on the <u>obliterated</u> trails of men who had gone before. Once, they came upon a path blazed through the forest, an ancient path, and the Lost Cabin seemed very near. But the path began nowhere and ended nowhere, and it remained mystery, as the man who made it and the reason he made it remained mystery. Another time they chanced upon the time-graven wreckage of a hunting lodge, and amid the shreds of rotted blankets John Thornton found a long-barreled flintlock.[2] He knew it for a Hudson Bay Company gun of the young days in the Northwest, when such a gun was worth its height in beaver skins packed flat. And that was all—no hint as to the man who in an early day had reared the lodge and left the gun among the blankets.

Spring came on once more, and at the end of all their wandering they found, not the Lost Cabin, but a shallow placer[3] in a broad valley where the gold showed like yellow butter across the bottom of the washingpan. They sought no farther. Each day they worked earned them thousands of dollars in clean dust and nuggets, and they worked every day. The gold was sacked in moosehide bags, fifty pounds to the bag, and piled like so much firewood outside the spruce-bough lodge. Like giants they toiled, days flashing on the heels of days like dreams as they heaped the treasure up.

There was nothing for the dogs to do, save the hauling in of meat now and again that Thornton killed, and Buck spent long hours musing by the fire. The vision of the short-legged hairy man came to him more frequently, now that there was little work to be done; and often, blinking by the fire, Buck wandered with him in that other world which he remembered.

---

1. **whipsawed.** Cut with a whipsaw, a two-handled crosscut saw, five and a half to seven feet long
2. **flintlock.** Gun with a lock in which a flint in the hammer strikes a metal plate to produce a spark that ignites the powder
3. **placer.** Gravel or sand containing ore

WORDS FOR EVERYDAY USE: ob • lit • er • at • ed (ō blit´ər āt əd) *part.*, erased; destroyed

What does the
hairy man feel
most often?

The salient thing of this other world seemed fear. When he watched the hairy man sleeping by the fire, head between his knees and hands clasped above, Buck saw that he slept restlessly, with many starts and awakenings, at which times he would peer fearfully into the darkness and fling more wood upon the fire. Did they walk by the beach of a sea, where the hairy man gathered shellfish and ate them as he gathered, it was with eyes that roved everywhere for hidden danger and with legs prepared to run like the wind at its first appearance. Through the forest they crept noiselessly, Buck at the hairy man's heels; and they were alert and vigilant, the pair of them, ears twitching and moving and nostrils quivering, for the man heard and smelled as keenly as Buck. The hairy man could spring up into the trees and travel ahead as fast as on the ground, swinging by the arms from limb to limb, sometimes a dozen feet apart, letting go and catching, never falling, never missing his grip. In fact, he seemed as much at home among the trees as on the ground; and Buck had memories of nights of <u>vigil</u> spent beneath trees wherein the hairy man roosted, holding on tightly as he slept.

And closely akin to the visions of the hairy man was the call still sounding in the depths of the forest. It filled him with a great unrest and strange desires. It caused him to feel a vague, sweet gladness, and he was aware of wild yearnings and stirrings for he knew not what. Sometimes he pursued the call into the forest, looking for it as though it were a <u>tangible</u> thing, barking softly or defiantly, as the mood might dictate. He would thrust his nose into the cool wood moss, or into the black soil where long grasses grew, and snort with joy at the fat earth smells; or he would crouch for hours, as if in concealment, behind fungus-covered trunks of fallen trees, wide-eyed and wide-eared to all that moved and sounded about him. It might be, lying thus, that he hoped to surprise this call he could not understand. But he did not know why he did these various things. He was impelled to do them, and did not reason about them at all.

Irresistible impulses seized him. He would be lying in camp, dozing lazily in the heat of the day, when suddenly his head would lift and his ears cock up, intent and listening, and he would spring to his feet and dash away, and on and on, for hours, through the forest aisles and across the open spaces. He loved to run down dry watercourses, and to creep and spy upon the bird life in the woods. For a day at a time he would lie in the underbrush where he could watch the partridges drumming and strutting up and down. But especially he loved to run in the dim twilight of the summer midnights, listening to the subdued and sleepy murmurs of the forest, reading signs and sounds as man may read a book, and seeking for the mysterious something that called—called, waking or sleeping, at all times, for him to come.

WORDS FOR
EVERYDAY USE:

vig • il (vij´əl) *n.,* staying awake on watch
tan • gi • ble (tan´jə bəl) *adj.,* touchable

One night he sprang from sleep with a start, eager-eyed, nostrils quivering and scenting, his mane bristling in <u>recurrent</u> waves. From the forest came the call (or one note of it, for the call was many noted), distinct and definite as never before—a long-drawn howl, like, yet unlike, any noise made by a husky dog. And he knew it, in the old familiar way, as a sound heard before. He sprang through the sleeping camp and in swift silence dashed through the woods. As he drew closer to the cry he went more slowly, with caution in every movement, till he came to an open place among the trees, and looking out saw, erect on haunches, with nose pointed to the sky, a long, lean, timber wolf.

He had made no noise, yet it ceased from its howling and tried to sense his presence. Buck stalked into the open, half crouching, body gathered compactly together, tail straight and stiff, feet falling with unwonted care. Every movement advertised <u>commingled</u> threatening and overture of friendliness. It was the menacing truce that marks the meeting of wild beasts that prey. But the wolf fled at sight of him. He followed, with wild leapings, in a frenzy to overtake. He ran him into a blind channel, in the bed of the creek, where a timber jam barred the way. The wolf whirled about, pivoting on his hind legs after the fashion of Joe and of all cornered husky dogs, snarling and bristling, clipping his teeth together in a continuous and rapid succession of snaps.

Buck did not attack, but circled him about and hedged him in with friendly advances. The wolf was suspicious and afraid; for Buck made three of him in weight, while his head barely reached Buck's shoulder. Watching his chance he darted away, and the chase was resumed. Time and again he was cornered, and the thing repeated, though he was in poor condition or Buck could not so easily have overtaken him. He would run till Buck's head was even with his flank, when he would whirl around at bay, only to dash away again at the first opportunity.

But in the end Buck's <u>pertinacity</u> was rewarded; for the wolf, finding that no harm was intended, finally sniffed noses with him. Then they became friendly, and played about in the nervous, half-coy way with which fierce beasts <u>belie</u> their fierceness. After some time of this the wolf started off at an easy <u>lope</u> in a manner that plainly showed he was going somewhere. He made it clear to Buck that he was to come, and they ran side by side through the <u>somber</u> twilight, straight up the creek bed, into the gorge from which it issued, and across the bleak divide where it took its rise.

On the opposite slope of the watershed they came down into a level country where were great stretches of forest and many streams, and through these great stretches they ran steadily, hour after hour, the sun rising higher and the day growing warmer. Buck was wildly glad. He knew he was at last answering the call, running by the side

What wakes up Buck? Why is he attracted to it?

WORDS FOR EVERYDAY USE:	**re • cur • rent** (ri kʉr´ənt) *adj.*, occurring or appearing again or regularly **com • min • gle** (kəm miŋ´ gəl) *vi.*, intermix **per • ti • nac • i • ty** (pʉr´tə nās´ ə tē) *n.*, stubborn persistance, obstinacy **be • lie** (bē lī) *vt.*, disguise, misrepresent **lope** (lōp) *n.*, long, easy stride **som • ber** (säm´bər) *adj.*, dark, dull

of his wood brother toward the place from where the call surely came. Old memories were coming upon him fast, and he was stirring to them as of old he stirred to the realities of which they were the shadows. He had done this thing before, somewhere in that other and dimly remembered world, and he was doing it again, now, running free in the open, the unpacked earth underfoot, the wide sky overhead.

They stopped by a running stream to drink, and, stopping, Buck remembered John Thornton. He sat down. The wolf started on toward the place from where the call surely came, then returned to him, sniffing noses and making actions as though to encourage him. But Buck turned about and started slowly on the back track. For the better part of an hour the wild brother ran by his side, whining softly. Then he sat down, pointed his nose

Why does Buck leave the wolf?

What two desires call Buck in different directions?

upward, and howled. It was a mournful howl, and as Buck held steadily on his way he heard it grow faint and fainter until it was lost in the distance.

John Thornton was eating dinner when Buck dashed into camp and sprang upon him in a frenzy of affection, overturning him, scrambling upon him, licking his face, biting his hand—"playing the general tomfool," as John Thornton characterized it, the while he shook Buck back and forth and cursed him lovingly.

For two days and nights Buck never left camp, never let Thornton out of his sight. He followed him about at his work, watched him while he ate, saw him into his blankets at night and out of them in the morning. But after two days the call in the forest began to sound more imperiously than ever. Buck's restlessness came back on him, and he was haunted by recollections of the wild brother, and of the smiling land beyond the divide and the run side by side through the wide forest stretches. Once again he took to wandering in the woods, but the wild brother came no more; and though he listened through long vigils, the mournful howl was never raised.

He began to sleep out at night, staying away from camp for days at a time; and once he crossed the divide at the head of the creek and went down into the land of timber and streams. There he wandered for a week, seeking vainly for fresh sign of the wild brother, killing his meat as he traveled and traveling with the long, easy lope that seems never to tire. He fished for salmon in a broad stream that emptied somewhere into the sea, and by this stream he killed a large black bear, blinded by the mosquitoes while likewise fishing, and raging through the forest helpless and terrible. Even so, it was a hard fight, and it aroused the last latent remnants of Buck's ferocity. And two days later, when he returned to his kill and found a dozen wolverines quarreling over the spoil, he scattered them like chaff; and those that fled left two behind who would quarrel no more.

The blood-longing became stronger than ever before. He was a killer, a thing that preyed, living on the things that lived, unaided, alone, by virtue of his own strength and prowess, surviving triumphantly in a hostile environment where only the strong survived. Because of all this he became possessed of a great pride in himself, which communicated itself like a contagion to his physical being. It advertised itself in all his movements, was apparent in the play of every muscle, spoke plainly as speech in the way he carried himself, and made his glorious furry coat if anything more glorious. But for the stray brown on his muzzle and above his eyes, and for the splash of white hair that ran midmost down his chest, he might well have been mistaken for a gigantic wolf, larger than the largest of the breed. From his St. Bernard father he had inherited size and weight, but it was his shepherd mother who had given shape to that size and weight. His muzzle was the long wolf muzzle, save that it was larger than the muzzle of any wolf; and his head, somewhat broader, was the wolf head on a massive scale.

His cunning was wolf cunning, and wild cunning; his intelligence, shepherd intelligence and St. Bernard intelligence; and all this, plus an experience gained in the fiercest of schools, made him as formidable a creature as any that roamed the wild. A carnivorous animal, living on a straight meat diet, he was in full flower, at the high tide of his life, overspilling with vigor and virility. When Thornton passed a caressing hand along his back, a snapping and crackling followed the hand, each hair discharging its pent magnetism at the contact. Every part, brain and body, nerve tissue and fiber, was keyed to the most exquisite pitch; and between all the parts there was a perfect <u>equilibrium</u> or adjustment. To

Of what is Buck proud?

sights and sounds and events which required action, he responded with lightning-like rapidity. Quickly as a husky dog could leap to defend from attack or to attack, he could leap twice as quickly. He saw the movement, or heard sound, and responded in less time than another dog required to compass the mere seeing or hearing. He perceived and determined and responded in the same instant. In point of fact the three actions of perceiving, determining, and responding were sequential; but so infinitesimal were the intervals of time between them that they appeared simultaneous. His muscles were surcharged with vitality, and snapped into play sharply, like steel springs. Life streamed through him in splendid flood, glad and rampant, until it seemed that it would burst him asunder in sheer ecstasy and pour forth generously over the world.

"Never was there such a dog," said John Thornton one day, as the partners watched Buck marching out of camp.

"When he was made, the mold was broke," said Pete.

"Py jingo! I t'ink so mineself," Hans affirmed.

They saw him marching out of camp, but they did not see the instant and terrible transformation which took place as soon as he was within the secrecy of the forest. He no longer marched. At once he became a thing of the wild, stealing along softly, cat-footed, a passing shadow that appeared and disappeared among the shadows. He knew how to take advantage of every cover, to crawl on his belly like a snake, and like a snake to leap and strike. He could take a ptarmigan[4] from its nest, kill a rabbit as it slept, and snap in midair the little chipmunks fleeing a second too late for the trees. Fish, in open pools, were not too quick for him; nor were beaver, mending their dams, too wary. He killed to eat, not from wantonness; but he preferred to eat what he killed himself. So a lurking humor ran through his deeds, and it was his delight to steal upon the squirrels, and, when he all but had them, to let them go, chattering in mortal fear to the treetops

As the fall of the year came on, the moose appeared in greater abundance, moving slowly down to meet the winter in the lower and less rigorous valleys. Buck had already dragged down a stray part-grown calf; but he wished strongly for larger and more formidable quarry, and he came upon it one day on the divide at the head of the creek. A band of twenty moose had crossed over from the land of streams and timber, and chief among them was a great bull. He was in a savage temper, and, standing over six feet from the ground, was as formidable an antagonist as ever Buck could desire. Back and forth the bull tossed his great palmated[5] antlers, branching to fourteen points and embracing seven feet

---

4. **ptarmigan.** Bird; type of grouse often hunted for food
5. **palmated.** Shaped like a hand, with spread fingers

How does Buck change upon entering the forest?

within the tips. His small eyes burned with a vicious and bitter light, while he roared with fury at sight of Buck.

From the bull's side, just forward of the flank, protruded a feathered arrow-end, which accounted for his savageness. Guided by that instinct which came from the old hunting days of the primordial world, Buck proceeded to cut the bull out from the herd. It was no slight task. He would bark and dance about in front of the bull, just out of reach of the great antlers and of the terrible <u>splay</u> hoofs, which could have stamped his life out with a single blow. Unable to turn his back on the fanged danger and go on, the bull would be driven into <u>paroxysms</u> of rage. At such moments he charged Buck, who retreated craftily, luring him on by a simulated inability to escape. But when he was thus separated from his fellows, two or three of the younger bulls would charge back upon Buck and enable the wounded bull to rejoin the herd.

There is a patience of the wild—dogged, tireless, persistent as life itself—that holds motionless for endless hours the spider in its web, the snake in its coils, the panther in its ambuscade;[6] this patience belongs peculiarly to life when it hunts its living food; and it belonged to Buck as he clung to the flank of the herd, retarding its march, irritating the young bulls, worrying the cows with their half-grown calves, and driving the wounded bull mad with helpless rage. For half a day this continued.

Buck multiplied himself, attacking from all sides, enveloping the herd in a whirlwind of menace, cutting out his victim as fast as it could rejoin its mates, wearing out the patience of creatures preyed upon, which is a lesser patience than that of creatures preying.

As the day wore along and the sun dropped to its bed in the northwest (the darkness had come back and the fall nights were six hours long), the young bulls retraced their steps more and more reluctantly to the aid of their beset leader. The down-coming winter was <u>harrying</u> them on to the lower levels, and it seemed they could never shake off this tireless creature that held them back. Besides, it was not the life of the herd, or of the young bulls, that was threatened. The life of only one member was demanded, which was a remoter interest than their lives, and in the end they were content to pay the toll.

As twilight fell the old bull stood with lowered head, watching his mates—the cows he had known, the calves he had fathered, the bulls he had mastered—as they <u>shambled</u> on at a rapid pace through the fading light. He could not follow, for before his nose leaped the merciless fanged terror that would not let him go. Three hundredweight more than half a ton he weighed; he had lived a long, strong life, full of fight and struggle, and at the end he faced death at the teeth of a creature whose head did not reach beyond his great knuckled knees.

Why do the younger moose eventually leave?

---

6. **ambuscade.** Ambush

| WORDS FOR EVERYDAY USE: | splay (splā) *adj.*, turning outward; spreading
par • ox • ysm (par´əks iz´əm) *n.*, sudden attack or spasm | har • ry (har´ē) *vt.*, force or push along
sham • ble (sham´bəl´) *vi.*, walk lazily |

How does Buck gain an advantage over his prey? What qualities does he display?

Where does Buck head after eating his kill? Why?

From then on, night and day, Buck never left his prey, never gave it a moment's rest, never permitted it to browse the leaves of trees or the shoots of young birch and willow. Nor did he give the wounded bull opportunity to slake his burning thirst in the slender trickling streams they crossed. Often, in desperation, he burst into long stretches of flight. At such times Buck did not attempt to stay him, but loped easily at his heels, satisfied with the way the game was played, lying down when the moose stood still, attacking him fiercely when he strove to eat or drink.

The great head drooped more and more under its tree of horns, and the shambling trot grew weaker and weaker. He took to standing for long periods, with nose to the ground and dejected ears dropped limply; and Buck found more time in which to get water for himself and in which to rest. At such moments, panting with red lolling tongue and with eyes fixed upon the big bull, it appeared to Buck that a change was coming over the face of things. He could feel a new stir in the land. As the moose were coming into the land, other kinds of life were coming in. Forest and stream and air seemed <u>palpitant</u> with their presence. The news of it was borne in upon him, not by sight, or sound, or smell, but by some other and subtler sense. He heard nothing, saw nothing, yet knew that the land was somehow different; that through it strange things were afoot and ranging; and he resolved to investigate after he had finished the business in hand.

At last, at the end of the fourth day, he pulled the great moose down. For a day and a night he remained by the kill, eating and sleeping, turn and turn about. Then, rested, refreshed, and strong, he turned his face toward camp and John Thornton. He broke into the long easy lope, and went on, hour after hour, never at loss for the tangled way, heading straight home through strange country with a certitude of direction that put man and his magnetic needle to shame.

As he held on he became more and more conscious of the new stir in the land. There was life abroad in it different from the life which had been there throughout the summer. No longer was this fact borne in upon him in some subtle, mysterious way. The birds talked of it, the squirrels chattered about it, the very breeze whispered of it. Several times he stopped and drew in the fresh morning air in great sniffs, reading a message which made him leap on with greater speed. He was oppressed with a sense of calamity happening, if it were not calamity already happened; and as he crossed the last watershed and dropped down into the valley toward camp, he proceeded with greater caution.

Three miles away he came upon a fresh trail that sent his neck hair rippling and bristling. It led straight toward camp and John Thornton. Buck hurried on, swiftly and stealthily, every nerve straining and tense, alert to the

---

Words for Everyday Use:

pal • pi • tant (pal´pə tənt) *adj.,* throbbing, quivering, trembling

multitudinous details which told a story—all but the end. His nose gave him a varying description of the passage of the life on the heels of which he was traveling. He remarked the pregnant silence of the forest. The bird life had flitted. The squirrels were in hiding. One only he saw,—a sleek gray fellow, flattened against a gray dead limb so that he seemed a part of it, a woody excrescence upon the wood itself.

As Buck slid along with the obscureness of a gliding shadow, his nose was jerked suddenly to the side as though a positive force had gripped and pulled it. He followed the new scent into a thicket and found Nig. He was lying on his side, dead where he had dragged himself, an arrow protruding, head and feathers, from either side of his body.

A hundred yards farther on, Buck came upon one of the sled-dogs Thornton had bought in Dawson. This dog was thrashing about in a death-struggle, directly on the trail, and Buck passed around him without stopping. From the camp came the faint sound of many voices, rising and falling in a singsong chant. Bellying forward to the edge of the clearing, he found Hans, lying on his face, feathered with arrows like a porcupine. At the same instant Buck peered out where the spruce-bough lodge had been and saw what made his hair leap straight up on his neck and shoulders. A gust of overpowering rage swept over him. He did not know that he growled, but he growled aloud with a terrible ferocity. For the last time in his life he allowed passion to <u>usurp</u> cunning and reason, and it was because of his great love for John Thornton that he lost his head.

The Yeehats were dancing about the wreckage of the spruce-bough lodge when they heard a fearful roaring and saw rushing upon them an animal the like of which they had never seen before. It was Buck, a live hurricane of fury, hurling himself upon them in a frenzy to destroy. He sprang at the foremost man (it was the chief of the Yeehats), ripping the throat wide open till the rent jugular spouted a fountain of blood. He did not pause to worry the victim, but ripped in passing, with the next bound tearing wide the throat of a second man. There was no withstanding him. He plunged about in their very midst, tearing, rending, destroying, in constant and terrific motion which defied the arrows they discharged at him. In fact, so inconceivably rapid were his movements, and so closely were the Indians tangled together, that they shot one another with the arrows; and one young hunter, hurling a spear at Buck in midair, drove it through the chest of another hunter with such force that the point broke through the skin of the back and stood out beyond. Then a panic seized the Yeehats, and they fled in terror to the woods, proclaiming as they fled the <u>advent</u> of the Evil Spirit.

And truly Buck was the Fiend incarnate, raging at their heels and dragging them down like deer as they raced

WORDS FOR EVERYDAY USE:

u • surp (yōō surp) *vt.*, take over, assume power by force or without right

ad • vent (ad´vent´) *n.*, coming or arrival

through the trees. It was a fateful day for the Yeehats. They scattered far and wide over the country, and it was not till a week later that the last of the survivors gathered together in a lower valley and counted their losses. As for Buck, wearying of the pursuit, he returned to the desolated camp. He found Pete where he had been killed in his blankets in the first moment of surprise. Thornton's desperate struggle was fresh written on the earth, and Buck scented every detail of it down to the edge of a deep pool. By the edge, head and forefeet in the water, lay Skeet, faithful to the last. The pool itself, muddy and discolored from the sluice boxes, effectually hid what it contained, and it contained John Thornton; for Buck followed his trace into the water, from which no trace led away.

All day Buck <u>brooded</u> by the pool or roamed restlessly about the camp. Death, as a cessation of movement, as a passing out and away from the lives of the living, he knew, and he knew John Thornton was dead. It left a great void in him, somewhat akin to hunger, but a void which ached and ached, and which food could not fill. At times, when he paused to contemplate the carcasses of the Yeehats, he forgot the pain of it; and at such times he was aware of a great pride in himself,—a pride greater than any he had yet experienced. He had killed man, the noblest game of all, and he had killed in the face of the law of club and fang. He sniffed the bodies curiously.

They had died so easily. It was harder to kill a husky dog than them. They were no match at all, were it not for their arrows and spears and clubs. Thenceforward he would be unafraid of them except when they bore in their hands their arrows, spears, and clubs.

Night came on, and a full moon rose high over the trees into the sky, lighting the land till it lay bathed in ghostly day. And with the coming of the night, brooding and mourning by the pool, Buck became alive to a stirring of the new life in the forest other than that which the Yeehats had made. He stood up, listening and scenting. From far away drifted a faint, sharp yelp, followed by a chorus of similar sharp yelps. As the moments passed the yelps grew closer and louder. Again Buck knew them as things heard in that other world which persisted in his memory. He walked to the center of the open space and listened. It was the call, the many-noted call, sounding more luringly and compelling than ever before. And as never before, he was ready to obey. John Thornton was dead. The last tie was broken. Man and the claims of man no longer bound him.

Hunting their living meat, as the Yeehats were hunting it, on the flanks of the migrating moose, the wolf pack had at last crossed over from the land of streams and timber and invaded Buck's valley. Into the clearing where the moonlight streamed, they poured in a silvery flood; and in the center of the clearing stood Buck, motionless as a statue, waiting their coming. They

How does Buck feel about Thornton's death? What thoughts help him feel better?

WORDS FOR EVERYDAY USE:　　brood (brōōd) *vi.*, worry

were awed, so still and large he stood, and a moment's pause fell, till the boldest one leaped straight for him. Like a flash Buck struck, breaking the neck. Then he stood, without movement, as before, the stricken wolf rolling in agony behind him. Three others tried it in sharp succession; and one after the other they drew back, streaming blood from slashed throats or shoulders.

This was sufficient to fling the whole pack forward, pell-mell, crowded together, blocked and confused by its eagerness to pull down the prey. Buck's marvelous quickness and agility stood him in good stead. Pivoting on his hind legs, and snapping and gashing, he was everywhere at once, presenting a front which was apparently unbroken so swiftly did he whirl and guard from side to side. But to prevent them from getting behind him, he was forced back, down past the pool and into the creek bed, till he brought up against a high gravel bank. He worked along to a right angle in the bank which the men had made in the course of mining, and in this angle he came to bay, protected on three sides and with nothing to do but face the front.

And so well did he face it, that at the end of half an hour the wolves drew back discomfited. The tongues of all were out and lolling, the white fangs showing cruelly white in the moonlight. Some were lying down with heads raised and ears pricked forward; others stood on their feet, watching him; and still others were lapping water from the pool. One wolf, long and lean and gray, advanced cautiously, in a friendly manner, and Buck recognized the wild brother with whom he had run for a night and a day. He was whining softly, and, as Buck whined, they touched noses.

Then an old wolf, gaunt and battle-scarred, came forward. Buck writhed his lips into the preliminary of a snarl, but sniffed noses with him. Whereupon the old wolf sat down, pointed nose at the moon, and broke out the long wolf howl. The others sat down and howled. And now the call came to Buck in unmistakable accents. He too sat down and howled. This over, he came out of his angle and the pack crowded around him, sniffing in half-friendly, half-savage manner. The leaders lifted the yelp[7] of the pack and sprang away into the woods. The wolves swung in behind, yelping in chorus. And Buck ran with them, side by side with the wild brother, yelping as he ran.

And here may well end the story of Buck. The years were not many when the Yeehats noted a change in the breed of timber wolves, for some were seen with splashes of brown on head and muzzle, and with a rift of white centering down the chest. But more remarkable than this, the Yeehats tell of a Ghost Dog that runs at the head of the pack. They are afraid of this Ghost Dog, for it has cunning greater than they, stealing from their camps in fierce winters, robbing their traps, slaying their dogs, and defying their bravest hunters.

Nay, the tale grows worse. Hunters there are who fail to return to the camp, and hunters there have been whom their tribesmen found with throats slashed cruelly open and with wolf prints about them in the snow greater than the prints of any wolf. Each fall, when the Yeehats follow the

---

7. **lifted the yelp.** Yelped even louder than the rest of the pack

How do the wolves react to Buck? How does he respond?

How is Buck's encounter with the wolves finally resolved?

Whom does Buck meet again?

movement of the moose, there is a certain valley which they never enter. And women there are who become sad when the word goes over the fire of how the Evil Spirit came to select that valley for an abiding-place.

In the summers there is one visitor, however, to that valley, of which the Yeehats do not know. It is a great, gloriously coated wolf, like, and yet unlike, all other wolves. He crosses alone from the smiling timberland and comes down into an open space among the trees. Here a yellow stream flows from rotted moose-hide sacks and sinks into the ground, with long grasses growing through it and vegetable mold overrunning it and hiding its yellow from the sun; and here he muses for a time, howling once, long and mournfully, ere he departs.

But he is not always alone. When the long winter nights come on and the wolves follow their meat into the lower valleys, he may be seen running at the head of the pack through the pale moonlight or glimmering borealis,[8] leaping gigantic above his fellows, his great throat a-bellow as he sings a song of the younger world, which is the song of the pack. ∎

---

8. **borealis.** Northern lights

Responding to the Selection

Imagine that you are a young member of the Yeehat people. Discuss the myth of the Ghost Dog that you have been told by your ancestors. Describe the event that the myth explains.

Reviewing the Selection

RECALLING

1. What does John Thornton set out to find in the East?

2. What vision comes more frequently to Buck, especially when he gazes into the fire?

3. What kind of void does John Thornton's death leave in Buck's heart?

4. With whom is Buck reunited after Thornton's death?

INTERPRETING

5. What qualities does Thornton possess that make him "unafraid of the wild"?

6. What actions on the part of the "hairy man" in Buck's dream show his fear of the world?

7. What causes Buck to forget the pain of Thornton's death?

8. What is probably the reason that Buck "sat down and howled" with the wolves?

9. To what call does John Thornton, in his journey and search, respond? To what call does Buck respond?

10. Why has Buck been able to endure, survive, and master?

Understanding Literature (Questions for Discussion)

1. **Naturalism. Naturalism** was a literary movement of the late nineteenth and early twentieth centuries that saw actions and events as resulting inevitably from forces in the environment. Often these forces were beyond the comprehension or control of the characters subjected to them. Identify a passage in this chapter that conveys through Buck's actions the philosophy of Naturalism. Identify the natural force that is at work. How does Buck respond to this force? Is his response effective? What point might the author be trying to make about how one should respond to over-whelming natural forces?

2. **Plot and Dénouement.** A **plot** is a series of events related to a central conflict, or struggle. A typical plot involves the introduction of a conflict, its development, and its eventual resolution. Following the resolution of a conflict is an element of plot called **dénouement.** The dénouement includes any material that ties up loose ends in the story. *The Call of the Wild* closes with a four-paragraph dénouement that begins, "And here may well end the story of Buck." What loose ends are resolved in this dénouement? What purpose is served by telling the Yeehat stories of the Ghost Dog?

Responding in Writing

Essay. Write an essay that explains how Buck and John Thornton are emblematic of frontier values, such as courage, endurance, self-sufficiency, and individuality.

> **Prewriting Suggestion:** Create three columns on a sheet of paper by drawing two vertical lines. At the top of the first column, write the word *Value.* At the top of the second column, write the word *Buck.* At the top of the third column, write the word *Thornton.* Under the heading *Value,* list at least five frontier values that are emphasized in the novel. Then identify and paraphrase examples of behavior for Buck and for Thornton that exemplify each of the values listed.

PROJECT

Storyboard. As a class, discuss and identify the following plot elements in the novel: introduction, inciting incident, rising action, climax, turning point, falling action, resolution, and dénouement. Then form seven small groups, assigning one plot element to each group, with one group responsible for the last two elements—resolution and dénouement. Within each group, create a portion of a storyboard that illustrates the key event for the group's assigned plot element. Some elements of plot, such as rising action and falling action, may have more than one key event. Underneath each illustration, write a passage from the novel that is especially relevant to that element of plot. When all portions of the storyboard are complete, arrange them in the formation of the diagram known as "Freytag's Pyramid." Display the diagram in the classroom.

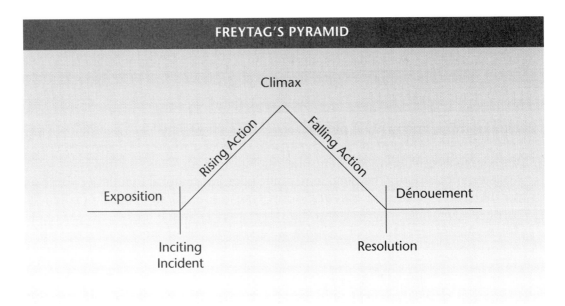

UNIT REVIEW

Adventure

abjectly, 600
advent, 647
amenity, 619
antagonist, 586
apex, 603
arduous, 589
aspire, 608
aver, 617
belie, 641
besetting, 578
brood, 648
cadence, 592
callous, 621
callowness, 615
celerity, 608
commingle, 641
compass, 644
conciliate, 582
consignment, 582
consternation, 588
consultation, 611
conveyance, 578
convulsive, 612
copious, 620
covert, 600
daunt, 597
deluge, 608

demesne, 577
discomfiture, 588
divers, 592
divine, 594
draggled, 595
dubiously, 596
eddy, 596
equilibrium, 643
evince, 624
exertion, 596
exultantly, 602
fastidiousness, 590
flounder, 611
forebear, 589
formidable, 617
fraught, 622
futilely, 578
genial, 582
gingerly, 580
harry, 645
herald, 591
heredity, 609
ignominiously, 588
impartial, 583
impeachment, 620

impending, 604
imperiously, 577
importune, 620
inarticulate, 624
incarnation, 587
incurious, 584
inexorable, 604
infinitesimal, 644
innocuously, 623
insidious, 601
insular, 577
intimate, 578
introspective, 587
irresolutely, 624
jaded, 618
lacerated, 579
latent, 582
loath, 594
lope, 641
lugubriously, 611
malicious, 631
malignant, 587
malingerer, 591
manifestly , 615
marauder, 596
metamorphose, 580
ministration, 627

monotonous, 609
morose, 584
mutiny, 600
obdurate, 606
obliterated, 639
obscurely, 577
ordained, 600
orthodox, 619
paddock, 577
pall, 600
palpitant, 646
pandemonium, 595
paroxysm, 645
peculiar, 609
perambulating, 622
peremptorily, 629
perpetual, 587
pertinacity, 641
pervade, 584
placatingly, 588
plethoric, 634
potent, 609
precipitate, 594, 602
preeminently, 599
primordial, 586

progeny, 578
prostrate, 600
provocation, 631
prowess, 588
quarry, 644
rampant, 602
recess, 577
recurrent, 641
remonstrance, 615
rend, 596
reproof, 587
repugnance, 616
resiliency, 609
resolutely, 597
resolved, 580
retrogression, 591
ruthless, 591
salient, 615
sated, 577
sequential, 644
shamble, 645
shirk, 599
skulking, 595
slaver, 581
slovenly, 615
solidarity, 601
soliloquize, 582

somber, 641
spasmodically, 589
splay, 645
sullenly, 579
superfluous, 617
suppressedly, 610
supremacy, 595
surcharge, 580
tangible, 640
terse, 623
tormentor, 579
transient, 628
travail, 601
uncouth, 583
uncowed, 582
unwonted, 578
usurp, 647
vaunt, 633
veranda, 576
vicarious, 586
vigil, 640
virility, 635
voracious, 619
warily, 596
wax, 580
wraith, 602
wrangle, 620

antagonist, 605
character, 593, 613, 626
characterization, 613, 637

conflict, 585, 626
dénouement, 651
external conflict, 626
foreshadowing, 585
inciting incident, 585

internal conflict, 626
minor character, 613
mood, 605
motive, 593
Naturalism, 574, 651

one-dimensional character, 626
plot, 585, 651
protagonist, 605
setting, 605

theme, 593
three-dimensional character, 626

SYNTHESIS: QUESTIONS FOR WRITING, RESEARCH, OR DISCUSSION

1. How does Buck change from the beginning to the end of this novel? What events cause him to change as he does?

2. What view of nature is presented in *The Call of the Wild?* How does the natural world in this novel differ from the civilized world?

LANGUAGE LAB   VOCABULARY DEVELOPMENT

Most times when you encounter a new word, you can check the meaning in a dictionary. When a dictionary is not available, you can use context clues in the text to deduce the meaning of an unfamiliar word. The chart below lists several types of context clues.

LANGUAGE ARTS SURVEY

For additional help, see the Language Arts Survey, 2.61.

USING CONTEXT CLUES
Restatement. Writers sometimes present an idea and then restate it using different words. A **restatement** can help a reader figure out the meaning of an unfamiliar word. EXAMPLE: The Yukon trapper had lived for years as a **recluse**. When the gold rush hit, his **solitary existence** was abruptly invaded. **Apposition.** A word or phrase that clarifies an unknown word may appear directly before or after it in a sentence, separated by a comma or commas. This technique is called **apposition.** EXAMPLE: Medieval scientists dreamed of creating unimaginable wealth through **alchemy,** or **the process of changing base metals into gold.** **Examples.** Sometimes **examples** are included within the sentence to reveal a word's meaning. EXAMPLE: Besides the **Klondike Gold Rush,** other famous **bonanzas** included the **California Gold Rush of 1849** and the **1876 gold rush** in the Black Hills of the Dakotas. **Comparison and Contrast.** A reader can sometimes deduce a word's meaning by comparing or contrasting it with familiar words that have similar or opposite meanings. EXAMPLES: Gold rush fever created a rash of **miserly** behavior. Most prospectors **jealously guarded their treasures.** Many **refused to loan money** to anyone. While **experienced** prospectors had started the gold rush, most of the people who crowded the boom town were **greenhorns.**

LANGUAGE ARTS SURVEY

For additional help, see the Language Arts Survey, 2.62.

Prefixes and Base Words. Some words are formed by adding a **prefix** to the beginning of a **base word.** If the word is unfamiliar, you can deduce its meaning by looking at the meaning of these parts. The following are some common prefixes and their meanings.

PREFIX	MEANING
pseudo-	"false"
ultra-	"extremely"
semi-	"half, partly"
dis-	"not"

Suffixes. Suffixes are meaning units added to the ends of words. The following are some common suffixes and their meanings.

SUFFIX	MEANING
-able	"capable of"
-ful	"full of"; "amount capable of filling"
-less	"not having"
-logy	"science of"

EXERCISE A   Using Context Clues

Write the meaning of the italicized word in each sentence below. Then write the type of context clue you used to deduce the meaning.

1. Jack London, a *prolific* writer, produced over two hundred short stories, four hundred nonfiction pieces, twenty novels, and three full-length plays.

2. Some *speculators,* or people who assumed business risks in hopes of getting rich, made enormous fortunes in the Klondike Gold Rush.

3. When he was eighteen, London spent a year as a *hobo*. He recorded the experiences of his penniless existence and aimless journey across the Midwest and the East Coast in *The Road* (1907).

4. Eventually, the gold was *depleted*. No longer could prospectors reach a hand into the stream and pull out a handful of gold.

EXERCISE B   Using Prefixes and Suffixes

Identify the prefixes and suffixes in the italicized words. Then write a definition for each word. If necessary, use a dictionary to check the meaning of a particular prefix or suffix.

1. London wrote of his *transcontinental* experiences.

2. To most prospectors, the lure of gold was *undeniable.*

3. People who believed the *pseudoscientific* claims lost their life savings.

4. The miner erected a *semilivable* tent at the river's edge.

5. The sled dog's *mournful* howl echoed across the tundra.

6. *Heedless* of danger, prospectors rushed into the forbidding Yukon territory.

LANGUAGE ARTS WORKSHOP

LETTERS AND FORMS

THE FORM OF A BUSINESS LETTER 5.3

A business letter includes:

- a **return address,** including the writer's address and the date the letter was composed;
- an **inside address,** including the name and title of the person to whom you are writing (or a department name, if you're not writing to a specific individual), the name of the company or organization, and its address;
- a respectful and formal **salutation,** or greeting, followed by a colon (such as *Dear Ms. Watkins:* or *Dear Sir or Madam:*);
- the **body,** or text of the letter;
- a respectful and formal **closing,** followed by a comma, and with only the first word of the closing capitalized (such as *Sincerely,* or *Respectfully yours,*);
- a **signature** (with your full name typed below it); and
- an optional **postscript.**

A business letter should maintain a courteous, formal tone; use standard English; and contain correct grammar, punctuation, capitalization, and spelling.

LANGUAGE ARTS SURVEY

For additional help, see the Language Arts Survey, 5.3.

EXERCISE

Choose one of the following examples and write a letter that would be appropriate to the situation.

A. Imagine that you have checked several video rental stores, local libraries, and retail stores and have not been able to locate a videotape of a certain foreign-language film. Write a business letter to a videocassette warehouse. Ask if the film is available on videocassette, and if so, where it can be purchased. You might wish to order the video directly from the warehouse, in which case you will need to inquire about costs, shipping and handling, and so on. Address your letter to Clear View Pictures, 2000 Scenic Drive, Sun City, Arizona 85351.

B. Imagine that you are interested in learning about forestry and would like to find out about the requirements for becoming a forest ranger. Write a business letter to a forest ranger inquiring whether he would be willing to share information about forestry and his experiences as a forest ranger. Address your letter to Mr. Alejandro Vasquez, Greentree National Park, Three Rivers, California 90009.

127 Wild Wolf Way RETURN ADDRESS
Yellow Metal, AK 99998
June 14, 1999

Ms. Golda Buck INSIDE ADDRESS
Customer Service
Sled Dog Delivery
2 Gold Rush Road
Musherville, AK 99999

Dear Ms. Buck: SALUTATION

BODY

I recently ordered several items from Sled Dog Delivery. Unfortunately, I had several problems upon receiving my order. Two of the items, a Snow Dog Pup Tent and a hand knit red sweater, were damaged, and several were not shipped although they appear on the order slip. The missing items are two bags of Yukon Trail Mix, a case of Snowshoe dog biscuits, and one pair of moccasins, size eight. The only salvageable item in the package was a set of trail maps.

I am returning the tent and the sweater, and I would like replacements for both. I would also like to have the other items shipped to the address above if they can arrive before June 30, otherwise please cancel my order on all items.

As an avid adventurer who often leads expeditions out on the trail, I have recommended Sled Dog products to others for years. I have also placed substantial orders of my own with you in the past and would like to continue to do so. For this reason I hope that the appalling service I have received will not be repeated. If it does I will take my business elsewhere. Thank you for your timely attention to this matter.

Sincerely, CLOSING

Lupe U. Kon SIGNATURE

Lupe U. Kon

Photograph ©1995 Michael Romanos

or never was a story of more woe

Than this of Juliet and her Romeo.

—Shakespeare

The Tragedy of Romeo and Juliet
by William Shakespeare

ABOUT THE AUTHOR

William Shakespeare (1564–1616) is often called the greatest playwright who ever lived. Even now, almost four hundred years after his death, people flock to see his magnificent plays. Shakespeare was born to Mary Arden and John Shakespeare in Stratford-upon-Avon, a small English village on the banks of the river Avon. His father was a glove maker and local political figure. His mother was descended from a prosperous family who owned large amounts of land. He attended Stratford grammar school where he studied Latin, as was common for schoolchildren of his day. Little is known of his early life, but he is believed to have loved the countryside.

Stratford-upon-Avon was a rural town, and the plays that Shakespeare would grow up to write have many references to plants and animals of the woods and fields. As a young man, Shakespeare may have been a school teacher. He married Anne Hathaway, also of Stratford-upon-Avon, and had three children, Susanna, Hamnet, and Judith. By 1592, he was living and working in London, the largest city in England. There he became a successful actor, playwright, and theater owner. He also wrote magnificent poetry. His theater company, the Lord Chamberlain's Men (so called because the group's sponsor, or patron, was Lord Chamberlain, an official of the royal court), became the most popular troupe of actors in London. They performed at the Globe Theater and in a smaller indoor theater called Blackfriars. In 1594, Shakespeare's company performed two plays before Queen Elizabeth I. In 1603, the troupe became servants of King James I and changed their name to the King's Men. In 1597, Shakespeare bought a large house in Stratford called New Place, and it is believed that he divided his time thereafter between Stratford-upon-Avon and London. Increasingly, he devoted himself to writing rather than to acting. Altogether, he wrote at least thirty-six plays, including *Hamlet, Macbeth, Julius Cæsar, King Lear, A Midsummer Night's Dream, The Tempest,* and *The Tragedy of Romeo and Juliet.* In 1613, during a performance of *Henry VIII,* a cannon fired as a sound effect accidentally burned down the Globe Theater. Following that incident, Shakespeare retired to Stratford-upon-Avon. He died at the age of fifty-two, but his plays have lived on to delight audiences through the ages and around the world.

ABOUT THE SELECTION

Background: Genre. *Romeo and Juliet* is a form of drama known as **tragedy.** A tragedy presents a sad tale of the fall of a noble character or characters. In this play, there are two characters who suffer a downfall—the two young people whose names appear in the title. In most tragedies, the downfall of the central character is brought about by a personal failing called a **tragic flaw.** As you read *Romeo and Juliet,* think about what actions on the part of the central characters lead them into trouble. Doing so will help you to identify their tragic flaws.

Background: History. *Romeo and Juliet* is set in "fair Verona," a city in northern Italy. The time is the Renaissance. The central characters in the play are a young man and woman from two noble families, the Montagues and the Capulets, who are feuding with one another. A feud is a fight carried out over a long time between rival groups. In the first scene of the play, servants from these two families are seen dueling with swords. Their duel is typical of the "civil strife," or public quarrelings, that result from the Montague and Capulet feud.

Background: Technique. When Romeo, a Montague, and Juliet, a Capulet, fall in love, they know that their union will not be blessed by their warring families. This creates a **conflict,** or struggle, for the two young people that can only lead to disaster.

This play, like others written during the time of Queen Elizabeth I, is divided into five **acts.** An act is a major section of a play. Each act is divided into several **scenes,** short parts that begin and end with characters entering or exiting the stage.

Act I begins with a **prologue** spoken by a character called Chorus. A prologue is an introduction. It provides information about the work to come. The prologue in this play takes the form of a **sonnet.** A sonnet is a fourteen-line rhymed poem. Try reading the prologue aloud in class. Read the first four lines. Then stop to paraphrase them, or repeat what they are saying in your own words. Then do the same with the next four lines, with the four lines after that, and with the two lines that end the sonnet.

Background: Theme. The word *disaster* comes from Greek words meaning "bad star." In the past, people believed that the stars ruled people's fortunes, or fates. In the opening lines of the play, the character called Chorus speaks of Romeo and Juliet as "star-cross'd lovers." This means that the stars, or fate, are against them because they were born into families that are enemies. One **theme**, or main idea, of the play is that feuding leads inevitably to disaster. The play teaches that people should end their grudges and hatreds, for they stand in the way of love and lead to death and ruination.

Background: Shakespeare's Theater. *Romeo and Juliet* was performed in the Globe Theater, which was partly owned by Shakespeare. This theater, which Shakespeare described in one of his plays as a "wooden O," had eight sides and was open in the middle. The stage jutted into the center. Some members of the audience, who paid one penny for admittance, stood around the stage on three sides and were known as "groundlings." Other audience members stood or sat in the three tiers of seats inside the walls of the theater. The stage was partly covered by a canopy that was supported by two pillars. On either side of the stage were doors for entrances and exits. The floor of the stage contained trap doors through which actors could appear or disappear. In the center of the back part of the stage was an area known as the "tiring house," in which actors could change. Sometimes this area was opened for interior scenes such as throne rooms or bedrooms. Above the tiring house was a second-story balcony, which was used in the famous balcony scene in *Romeo and Juliet.* Above the balcony was a third level that housed musicians and sound-effects technicians.

In Shakespeare's day, very little scenery was used to stage dramas. The audience had to imagine the setting based on characters' descriptions, costumes, and set **properties.** Properties are small objects, such as swords or scepters, that can be carried on and off stage easily. The actors in Shakespeare's time were all men or boys, as it was considered improper for women to act in plays.

On Reading Shakespeare. If you could travel back in time to see a Shakespearean play performed at the Globe Theater, you would find that these plays were enormously popular. People from all walks of life came to see them, from kings and queens to poor peasants who could not read or write. Shakespeare wrote in the language of ordinary men and women of his time. However, over time, language changes. As a result, students reading Shakespeare today often find his language difficult. To help you to understand Shakespeare's language, the editors of this textbook have included footnotes explaining the meanings of words and phrases peculiar to Shakespeare's Elizabethan English (the version of English spoken during the reign of Queen Elizabeth I).

The best way to approach reading this play is to read a scene through quickly, without worrying about figuring out the entire meaning. By doing so, you can get an overall sense of what the scene is about. Then read the scene through a second time, carefully referring to the footnotes. In addition to reading the play, you may want to listen to a recording of it or watch a film or videotape production. All drama comes alive when it is performed by actors and is best experienced that way.

Do you believe in love at first sight? What might lead someone to fall in love with someone whom he or she doesn't really know but has only seen? What dangers might come of falling in love impulsively? Write about these questions in your journal.

The Tragedy of Romeo and Juliet

WILLIAM SHAKESPEARE

CHARACTERS IN THE PLAY

CHORUS

ESCALUS, *Prince of Verona*
PARIS, *a young nobleman, kinsman to the Prince*
MONTAGUE ⎤ *heads of two houses at*
CAPULET ⎦ *variance with each other*
An OLD MAN, *of the Capulet family*
ROMEO, *son to Montague*
MERCUTIO, *kinsman to the Prince, and friend to Romeo*
BENVOLIO, *nephew to Montague, and friend to Romeo*
TYBALT, *nephew to Lady Capulet*
PETRUCHIO, *a (mute) follower of Tybalt*
FRIAR LAWRENCE ⎤ *Franciscans*
FRIAR JOHN ⎦
BALTHASAR, *servant to Romeo*

ABRAM, *servant to Montague*
SAMPSON ⎤
GREGORY ⎥ *servants to Capulet*
CLOWN ⎦
PETER, *servant to Juliet's nurse*
PAGE, *to Paris*
APOTHECARY
Three MUSICIANS

LADY MONTAGUE, *wife to Montague*
LADY CAPULET, *wife to Capulet*
JULIET, *daughter to Capulet*
NURSE, *to Juliet*
CITIZENS *of Verona; several* GENTLEMEN *and* GENTLEWOMEN *of both houses;* MASKERS, TORCH-BEARERS, PAGES, GUARDS, WATCHMEN, SERVANTS, *and* ATTENDANTS

SCENE: *Verona; Mantua*

THE PROLOGUE

Enter CHORUS.

Two households, both alike in dignity,[1]
In fair Verona, where we lay our scene,
From ancient grudge break to new <u>mutiny</u>,
Where civil blood makes civil hands[2] unclean.
5　From forth the fatal loins of these two foes
A pair of star-cross'd[3] lovers take their life;
Whose misadventur'd piteous overthrows
Doth with their death bury their parents' strife.
The fearful passage of their death-mark'd love,
10　And the continuance of their parents' rage,
Which, but their children's end, nought could remove,
Is now the two hours' traffic[4] of our stage;
The which if you with patient ears attend,
What here shall miss, our toil shall strive to mend.[5]

Exit.

What ends the long feud between the two families?

ACT I
SCENE i: a public place in Verona

Enter SAMPSON *and* GREGORY, *with swords and bucklers, of the house of Capulet.*

SAMPSON.　Gregory, on my word, we'll not carry coals.[6]

GREGORY.　No, for then we should be colliers.[7]

SAMPSON.　I mean, and we be in choler,[8] we'll draw.

GREGORY.　Ay, while you live, draw your neck out of collar.[9]

5　**SAMPSON.**　I strike quickly, being mov'd.

GREGORY.　But thou art not quickly mov'd to strike.

SAMPSON.　A dog of the house of Montague moves me.

GREGORY.　To move is to stir, and to be valiant is to stand; therefore, if thou art mov'd, thou run'st away.

PROLOGUE/ACT I, SCENE i

1. **alike in dignity.** Of the same rank (both noble)
2. **civil blood . . . civil hands.** Civil strife on citizens' hands
3. **star-cross'd.** Opposed by the stars, which were believed to control fate
4. **traffic.** Business; action
5. **What here . . . to mend.** What we do not do well in tonight's performance, we shall correct in the future, based on your reactions.
6. **carry coals.** Perform menial work; figuratively, put up with insults
7. **colliers.** Coal miners
8. **be in choler.** Be angry
9. **draw your neck . . . collar.** Keep from being hanged

WORDS FOR EVERYDAY USE:　**mu • ti • ny** (myo͞ot´´n ē) *n.,* revolt against constituted authority

10 SAMPSON. A dog of that house shall move me to stand! I will take the wall[10] of any man or maid of Montague's.

GREGORY. That shows thee a weak slave, for the weakest goes to the wall.[11]

SAMPSON. 'Tis true, and therefore women, being the weaker vessels, are ever thrust to the wall; therefore I will push Montague's men from the wall,
15 and thrust his maids to the wall.

GREGORY. The quarrel is between our masters, and us their men.

SAMPSON. 'Tis all one; I will show myself a tyrant: when I have fought with the men, I will be civil with the maids; I will cut off their heads.

GREGORY. The heads of the maids?

20 SAMPSON. Ay, the heads of the maids, or their maidenheads, take it in what sense thou wilt.

GREGORY. They must take it in sense that feel it.

SAMPSON. Me they shall feel while I am able to stand, and 'tis known I am a pretty piece of flesh.

25 GREGORY. 'Tis well thou art not fish; if thou hadst, thou hadst been poor-John.[12] Draw thy tool, here comes two of the house of Montagues.

Enter two other servingmen ABRAM *and* BALTHASAR.

SAMPSON. My naked weapon is out. Quarrel, I will back thee.[13]

GREGORY. How, turn thy back and run?

SAMPSON. Fear me not.

30 GREGORY. No, marry, I fear thee!

SAMPSON. Let us take the law of our sides,[14] let them begin.

GREGORY. I will frown as I pass by, and let them take it as they list.[15]

SAMPSON. Nay, as they dare. I will bite my thumb[16] at them, which is disgrace to them if they bear it.

35 ABRAM. Do you bite your thumb at us, sir?

SAMPSON. I do bite my thumb, sir.

ABRAM. Do you bite your thumb at us, sir?

SAMPSON. [*Aside to* GREGORY.] Is the law of our side if I say ay?

GREGORY. [*Aside to* SAMPSON.] No.

40 SAMPSON. No, sir, I do not bite my thumb at you, sir, but I bite my thumb, sir.

---

10. **take the wall.** The inner part of a sidewalk, near the wall, was cleaner, so people allowed their superiors to walk there as a matter of courtesy.
11. **weakest . . . wall.** The weakest gives way.
12. **poor-John.** Inexpensive fish

13. **back thee.** Assist you
14. **take the law of our sides.** Have the law on our side
15. **list.** Wish
16. **bite my thumb.** Gesture of contempt or insult

GREGORY. Do you quarrel, sir?

ABRAM. Quarrel, sir? No, sir.

SAMPSON. But if you do, sir, I am for you. I serve as good a man as you.

45 **ABRAM.** No better?

SAMPSON. Well, sir.

Enter BENVOLIO.

GREGORY. Say "better," here comes one of my master's kinsmen.

SAMPSON. Yes, better, sir.

ABRAM. You lie.

50 **SAMPSON.** Draw, if you be men. Gregory, remember thy washing[17] blow.

They fight.

Who tries to stop the fighting?

BENVOLIO. Part, fools!
Put up your swords, you know not what you do.   *Beats down their swords.*

Enter TYBALT.

TYBALT. What, art thou drawn among these heartless hinds?[18]
Turn thee, Benvolio, look upon thy death.

55 **BENVOLIO.** I do but keep the peace. Put up thy sword,
Or manage it to part these men with me.

What does Tybalt feel about peace?

TYBALT. What, drawn and talk of peace? I hate the word
As I hate hell, all Montagues, and thee.
Have at thee, coward!   *They fight.*

Enter three or four CITIZENS *with clubs or partisans.*[19]

60 **CITIZENS.** Clubs, bills,[20] and partisans! Strike! Beat them down!
Down with the Capulets! Down with the Montagues!

Enter old CAPULET *in his gown, and his wife* LADY CAPULET.

CAPULET. What noise is this? Give me my long sword ho!

LADY CAPULET. A crutch, a crutch! why call you for a sword?

CAPULET. My sword, I say! Old Montague is come,
65 And <u>flourishes</u> his blade in spite of me.

---

17. **washing.** Slashing
18. **heartless hinds.** Cowardly creatures
19. **partisans.** Broad-bladed spears
20. **bills.** Hooked blades attached to long shafts

WORDS FOR
EVERYDAY USE:

flour • ish (flur´ish) *vi.,* wave in the air

Enter old MONTAGUE *and his wife* LADY MONTAGUE.

MONTAGUE.   Thou villain Capulet!—Hold me not, let me go.

LADY MONTAGUE.   Thou shalt not stir one foot to seek a foe.

Enter PRINCE ESCALUS *with his* TRAIN.

PRINCE.   Rebellious subjects, enemies to peace,
Profaners of this neighbor-stained steel[21]—
70   Will they not hear?—What ho, you men, you beasts!
That quench the fire of your <u>pernicious</u> rage
With purple fountains issuing from your veins—
On pain of torture, from those bloody hands
Throw your mistempered[22] weapons to the ground,
75   And hear the sentence of your moved prince.
Three civil brawls, bred of an airy word,
By thee, old Capulet, and Montague,
Have thrice[23] disturb'd the quiet of our streets,
And made Verona's ancient citizens
80   Cast by their grave beseeming ornaments[24]
To wield old partisans, in hands as old,
Cank'red[25] with peace, to part your cank'red hate;
If ever you disturb our streets again
Your lives shall pay the <u>forfeit</u> of the peace.
85   For this time all the rest depart away.
You, Capulet, shall go along with me,
And, Montague, come you this afternoon,
To know our farther pleasure in this case,
To old Free-town, our common judgment-place.
90   Once more, on pain of death, all men depart.

Exeunt all but MONTAGUE, LADY MONTAGUE, *and* BENVOLIO.

MONTAGUE.   Who set this ancient quarrel new abroach?[26]
Speak, nephew, were you by when it began?

BENVOLIO.   Here were the servants of your <u>adversary</u>,
And yours, close fighting ere[27] I did approach.

What are "purple fountains"? What fires do they put out?

Why does the fighting between Capulets and Montagues disturb Prince Escalus? What punishment will they face if they do not stop fighting?

---

21. **Profaners . . . steel.** People who profane, or make contemptible, their weapons by staining them with their neighbors' blood
22. **mistempered.** Hardened for an improper use
23. **thrice.** Three times
24. **Cast . . . ornaments.** Throw aside those objects, like canes, appropriate for old age
25. **cank'red.** Malignant
26. **abroach.** Open and flowing freely
27. **ere.** Before

WORDS FOR EVERYDAY USE:
per • ni • cious (pər nish´ əs) *adj.,* fatal; deadly
for • feit (fôr´fit) *n.,* penalty or fine one pays because of a crime
ad • ver • sar • y (ad´ vər ser´ē) *n.,* opponent; enemy

95　I drew to part them. In the instant came
　　The fiery Tybalt, with his sword prepar'd,
　　Which, as he breath'd defiance to my ears,
　　He swung about his head and cut the winds,
　　Who, nothing hurt withal,[28] hiss'd him in scorn.
100　While we were interchanging thrusts and blows,
　　Came more and more, and fought on part and part,
　　Till the Prince came, who parted either part.

Does Benvolio give an honest report of the fight?

LADY MONTAGUE.　O, where is Romeo? Saw you him today?
　　Right glad I am he was not at this <u>fray</u>.

105　**BENVOLIO.**　Madam, an hour before the worshipp'd sun
　　Peer'd forth the golden window of the east,
　　A troubled mind drive[29] me to walk abroad,
　　Where, underneath the grove of sycamore
　　That westward rooteth from this city side,
110　So early walking did I see your son.
　　Towards him I made, but he was ware[30] of me,
　　And stole into the covert[31] of the wood.
　　I, measuring his affections by my own,
　　Which then most sought where most might not be found,
115　Being one too many by my weary self,
　　Pursued my humor not pursuing his,[32]
　　And gladly shunn'd who gladly fled from me.

MONTAGUE.　Many a morning hath he there been seen,
　　With tears <u>augmenting</u> the fresh morning's dew,
120　Adding to clouds more clouds with his deep sighs,
　　But all so soon as the all-cheering sun
　　Should in the farthest east begin to draw
　　The shady curtains from Aurora's[33] bed,
　　Away from light steals home my heavy son,
125　And private in his chamber pens himself,
　　Shuts up his windows, locks fair daylight out,
　　And makes himself an artificial night.
　　Black and portendous[34] must this humor[35] prove,
　　Unless good counsel may the cause remove.

According to his father, how does Romeo spend his nights and days?

---

28. **nothing hurt withal.** Not harmed as a result
29. **drive.** Drove
30. **ware.** Wary
31. **covert.** Cover; hiding place
32. **Pursued . . . his.** Followed my own mood by not
following him
33. **Aurora's.** Of the Roman goddess of dawn
34. **portendous.** Ominous; portentous
35. **humor.** Moody behavior

WORDS FOR EVERYDAY USE:

fray (frā) *n.*, noisy quarrel or fight

aug • ment (ôg ment´) *vt.*, make greater in size, strength, or quantity

130   **BENVOLIO.**   My noble uncle, do you know the cause?

       MONTAGUE.   I neither know it, nor can learn of him.

       BENVOLIO.   Have you importun'd[36] him by any means?

       MONTAGUE.   Both by myself and many other friends,
       But he, his own affections' counsellor,
135   Is to himself (I will not say how true)
       But to himself so secret and so close,
       So far from sounding[37] and discovery,
       As is the bud bit with an envious[38] worm,
       Ere he can spread his sweet leaves to the air
140   Or dedicate his beauty to the sun.
       Could we but learn from whence[39] his sorrows grow,
       We would as willingly give cure as know.

       Enter ROMEO.

       BENVOLIO.   See where he comes. So please you step aside,
       I'll know his <u>grievance</u>, or be much denied.

145   **MONTAGUE.**   I would thou wert[40] so happy by thy stay
       To hear true shrift.[41] Come, madam, let's away.

                            Exeunt MONTAGUE *and* LADY.

       BENVOLIO.   Good morrow, cousin.

       ROMEO.   Is the day so young?

       BENVOLIO.   But new strook[42] nine.

       ROMEO.   Ay me, sad hours seem long.
       Was that my father that went hence[43] so fast?

150   **BENVOLIO.**   It was. What sadness lengthens Romeo's hours?

       ROMEO.   Not having that which, having, makes them short.

       BENVOLIO.   In love?

       ROMEO.   Out—

       BENVOLIO.   Of love?

155   **ROMEO.**   Out of her favor where I am in love.

       BENVOLIO.   Alas that love, so gentle in his view,

What does Benvolio hope to learn?

---

36. **importun'd.** Questioned
37. **sounding.** Being understood
38. **envious.** Vicious
39. **whence.** What place
40. **wert.** Were
41. **shrift.** Confession
42. **strook.** Struck
43. **hence.** From here

WORDS FOR EVERYDAY USE: **griev • ance** (grēv´əns) *n.*, complaint or resentment

Should be so tyrannous and rough in proof!

ROMEO. Alas that love, whose view is muffled still,[44]
Should, without eyes, see pathways to his will!
160 Where shall we dine? O me! what fray was here?
Yet tell me not, for I have heard it all:
Here's much to do with hate, but more with love.
Why then, O brawling love! O loving hate!
O any thing, of nothing first create![45]
165 O heavy lightness, serious vanity,
Misshapen chaos of well-seeming forms,
Feather of lead, bright smoke, cold fire, sick health,
Still-waking sleep, that is not what it is!
This love feel I, that feel no love in this.[46]
Dost thou not laugh?

170 **BENVOLIO.**   No, coz,[47] I rather weep.

ROMEO. Good heart, at what?

BENVOLIO.   At thy good heart's oppression.

ROMEO. Why, such is love's <u>transgression</u>.
Griefs of mine own lie heavy in my breast,
Which thou wilt <u>propagate</u> to have it press'd
175 With more of thine.[48] This love that thou hast shown
Doth add more grief to too much of mine own.
Love is a smoke made with the fume of sighs,
Being <u>purg'd</u>, a fire sparkling in lovers' eyes,
Being <u>vex'd</u>, a sea nourish'd with loving tears.
180 What is it else? a madness most discreet,
A choking gall, and a preserving sweet.
Farewell, my coz.

BENVOLIO.   Soft,[49] I will go along;
And if you leave me so, you do me wrong.

ROMEO. Tut, I have lost myself, I am not here:
185 This is not Romeo, he's some other where.

---

44. **whose view . . . still.** Love is conventionally pictured
as blind.
45. **O any thing . . . create!** All things created (by God)
out of nothing
46. **O brawling love . . . no love in this.** Romeo's string
of contradictions show the confused state he is in. He feels
good because he is in love and also feels bad because his
love is not returned.
47. **coz.** Cousin (said of any relative)
48. **Griefs of mine own . . . of thine.** The grief in my
heart will multiply if it feels the further weight of your
grief.
49. **Soft.** One moment; used as an interjection

WORDS FOR
EVERYDAY USE:

trans • gres • sion (trans gresh´ən) *n.*, act of
going over a limit

prop • a • gate (präp´ə gāt) *vt.*, reproduce;
multiply

purge (pʉrj) *vt.*, cleanse of impurities

vex (veks) *vt.*, disturb; annoy; irritate

BENVOLIO.   Tell me in sadness,[50] who is that you love?

ROMEO.   What, shall I groan and tell thee?

BENVOLIO.   Groan? why, no;
But sadly tell me, who?

ROMEO.   Bid a sick man in sadness make his will—
190   A word ill urg'd to one that is so ill!
In sadness, cousin, I do love a woman.

BENVOLIO.   I aim'd so near when I suppos'd you lov'd.

ROMEO.   A right good mark-man![51] And she's fair I love.

BENVOLIO.   A right fair mark,[52] fair coz, is soonest hit.

195   **ROMEO.**   Well, in that hit you miss: she'll not be hit
With Cupid's arrow, she hath Dian's wit;[53]
And in strong proof[54] of chastity well arm'd,
From Love's weak childish bow she lives uncharm'd.[55]
She will not stay[56] the <u>siege</u> of loving terms,
200   Nor bide th' encounter of assailing eyes,
Nor ope her lap to saint-seducing gold.[57]
O, she is rich in beauty, only poor
That, when she dies, with beauty dies her store.[58]

BENVOLIO.   Then she hath sworn that she will still[59] live chaste?

205   **ROMEO.**   She hath, and in that sparing[60] makes huge waste;
For beauty starv'd with her severity
Cuts beauty off from all <u>posterity</u>.
She is too fair, too wise, wisely too fair,
To merit bliss by making me despair.
210   She hath forsworn to love, and in that vow
Do I live dead that live to tell it now.

BENVOLIO.   Be rul'd by me, forget to think of her.

ROMEO.   O, teach me how I should forget to think.

BENVOLIO.   By giving liberty unto thine eyes:

---

50. **in sadness.** With gravity or seriousness
51. **mark-man.** Marksman, one who shoots well
52. **mark.** Target
53. **Dian's wit.** Ideas or beliefs of Diana, the Roman goddess of chastity and of the hunt
54. **proof.** Armor
55. **uncharm'd.** Not under the spell of
56. **stay.** Abide

57. **Nor ope . . . gold.** The reference is to Danaë, in Roman mythology, whom Jupiter visited in the form of a shower of gold.
58. **dies her store.** Her beauty will die with her, for she left no children.
59. **still.** Always
60. **sparing.** Thriftiness

WORDS FOR EVERYDAY USE:

siege (sēj) *n.,* persistent attempt to gain control

pos • ter • i • ty (päs ter´ə tē) *n.,* all succeeding generations

215   Examine other beauties.

ROMEO.   'Tis the way
To call hers, exquisite, in question more.[61]
These happy masks that kiss fair ladies' brows,
Being black, puts us in mind they hide the fair.
220   He that is strooken[62] blind cannot forget
The precious treasure of his eyesight lost.
Show me a mistress that is passing[63] fair,
What doth her beauty serve but as a note
Where I may read who pass'd that passing fair?
225   Farewell, thou canst not teach me to forget.

BENVOLIO.   I'll pay that doctrine, or else die in debt.[64]

Exeunt.

SCENE ii: a street in Verona

Enter CAPULET, COUNTY PARIS, *and the Clown, Capulet's* SERVANT.

CAPULET.   But Montague is bound as well as I,
In penalty alike, and 'tis not hard, I think,
For men so old as we to keep the peace.

PARIS.   Of honorable reckoning[1] are you both,
5   And pity 'tis you liv'd at odds so long.
But now, my lord, what say you to my suit?[2]

CAPULET.   But saying o'er what I have said before:
My child is yet a stranger in the world,
She hath not seen the change of fourteen years;
10   Let two more summers wither in their pride,
Ere we may think her ripe to be a bride.

PARIS.   Younger than she are happy mothers made.

CAPULET.   And too soon marr'd are those so early made.
Earth hath swallowed all my hopes but she;
15   She's the hopeful lady of my earth.[3]
But woo her, gentle Paris, get her heart,
My will to her consent is but a part;
And she agreed, within her scope of choice
Lies my consent and fair according voice.
20   This night I hold an old accustom'd feast,
Whereto I have invited many a guest,
Such as I love, and you, among the store

What advice does Benvolio give to Romeo who loves someone who does not love him?

How old is Juliet? What age does her father think appropriate for her marriage?

Who wishes to marry Juliet?

---

61. **'Tis the way . . . more.** That's the way to make her great beauty even more evident.
62. **strooken.** Struck
63. **passing.** Extremely; surpassing others
64. **pay that . . . debt.** Teach you that lesson or die still under obligation to you

ACT I, SCENE ii
1. **Of honorable reckoning.** With a favorable reputation
2. **suit.** Pleading
3. **hopeful . . . earth.** The one who will inherit my land, and the one who makes my world seem hopeful

One more, most welcome, makes my number more.
At my poor house look to behold this night
25 Earth-treading stars that make dark heaven light.
Such comfort as do lusty young men feel
When well-apparell'd April on the heel
Of limping winter treads, even such delight
Among fresh fennel[4] buds shall you this night
30 Inherit[5] at my house; hear all, all see;
And like her most whose merit most shall be;
Which on more view of many, mine, being one,
May stand in number, though in reck'ning none.[6]
Come go with me. [*To* SERVANT.] Go, sirrah,[7] trudge about
35 Through fair Verona, find those persons out
Whose names are written there, and to them say,
My house and welcome on their pleasure stay.[8]   *Exit with* PARIS.

SERVANT.   Find them out whose names are written here! It is written that
the shoemaker should meddle with his yard and the tailor with his last, the
40 fisher with his pencil and the painter with his nets; but I am sent to find
those persons whose names are here writ, and can never find what names
the writing person hath here writ. I must to the learned. In good time!

Enter BENVOLIO *and* ROMEO.

BENVOLIO.   Tut, man, one fire burns out another's burning,
One pain is less'ned by another's anguish;
45 Turn giddy, and be holp[9] by backward turning;
One desperate grief cures with another's <u>languish</u>:
Take thou some new infection to thy eye,
And the rank poison of the old will die.

ROMEO.   Your plantan leaf[10] is excellent for that.

50 BENVOLIO.   For what, I pray thee?

ROMEO.   For your broken shin.

BENVOLIO.   Why, Romeo, art thou mad?

ROMEO.   Not mad, but bound more than a madman is;

What advice does Capulet give Paris? Who gave similar advice to Romeo?

What is the servant's problem?

4. **fennel.** Plant with yellow flowers and a sweet aroma
5. **inherit.** Experience
6. **May stand . . . none.** She may be one of a number of women, but when you reckon, or make calculations, about which is the best, you will find that none compares to her.
7. **sirrah.** Form of address used by a person of higher rank when speaking to a person of a lesser social rank
8. **on their pleasure stay.** Wait to see what will be their pleasure
9. **holp.** Helped; cured
10. **plantan leaf.** Leaf of the plantain, applied to soothe minor wounds

WORDS FOR EVERYDAY USE: lan • guish (laŋ´gwish) *vi.*, suffer with longing

Shut up in prison, kept without my food,
Whipt and tormented and—God-den,[11] good fellow.

55 **SERVANT.** God gi' god-den. I pray, sir, can you read?

ROMEO. Ay, mine own fortune in my misery.

SERVANT. Perhaps you have learn'd it without book.
But I pray, can you read any thing you see?

ROMEO. Ay, if I know the letters and the language.

60 **SERVANT.** Ye say honestly, rest you merry!

ROMEO. Stay, fellow, I can read.
(*He reads the letter.*) "Signior Martino and his wife and daughters; County
Anselme and his beauteous sisters; the lady widow of Vitruvio; Signior
Placentio and his lovely nieces; Mercutio and his brother Valentine; mine
65 uncle Capulet, his wife, and daughters; my fair niece Rosaline, and Livia;
Signior Valentio and his cousin Tybalt; Lucio and the lively Helena." A
fair assembly. Whither should they come?

SERVANT. Up.

ROMEO. Whither? to supper?

70 **SERVANT.** To our house.

ROMEO. Whose house?

SERVANT. My master's.

ROMEO. Indeed I should have ask'd thee that before.

SERVANT. Now I'll tell you without asking. My master is the great rich
75 Capulet, and if you be not of the house of Montagues, I pray come and
crush[12] a cup of wine. Rest you merry! *Exit.*

Whom does Romeo love?

BENVOLIO. At this same ancient feast of Capulet's
Sups the fair Rosaline whom thou so loves,
With all the admired beauties of Verona.
80 Go thither,[13] and with unattainted[14] eye
Compare her face with some that I shall show,
And I will make thee think thy swan a crow.

ROMEO. When the <u>devout</u> religion of mine eye
Maintains such falsehood, then turn tears to fires;

---

11. **God-den.** Good evening
12. **crush.** Drink
13. **thither.** There
14. **unattainted.** Untainted; not with preconceived ideas

WORDS FOR   de • vout (di vout´) *adj.*, religious; pious
EVERYDAY USE:

85 And these,[15] who, often drown'd, could never die,
Transparent heretics, be burnt for liars!
One fairer than my love! The all-seeing sun
Ne'er saw her match since first the world begun.

   BENVOLIO.   Tut, you saw her fair, none else being by,
90 Herself pois'd with herself in either eye;
But in that crystal scales let there be weigh'd
Your lady's love against some other maid
That I will show you shining at this feast,
And she shall scant show well that now seems best.

95 **ROMEO.**   I'll go along no such sight to be shown,
But to rejoice in splendor of mine own.   *Exeunt.*

SCENE iii: Capulet's house

Enter CAPULET'S WIFE, *and* NURSE.

LADY CAPULET.   Nurse, where's my daughter? Call her forth to me.

NURSE.   Now by my maidenhead at twelve year old,
I bade her come. What, lamb! What, ladybird!
God forbid! Where's this girl? What, Juliet!

Enter JULIET.

JULIET.   How now, who calls?

NURSE.   Your mother.

5 **JULIET.**   Madam, I am here,
What is your will?

LADY CAPULET.   This is the matter. Nurse, give leave[1] a while,
We must talk in secret. Nurse, come back again,
I have rememb'red me, thou s'[2] hear our counsel.
10 Thou knowest my daughter's of a pretty age.

NURSE.   Faith, I can tell her age unto an hour.

LADY CAPULET.   She's not fourteen.

NURSE.   I'll lay fourteen of my teeth—
And yet, to my teen[3] be it spoken, I have but four—
She's not fourteen. How long is it now
To Lammas-tide?[4]

15 **LADY CAPULET.**   A fortnight[5] and odd days.

NURSE.   Even or odd, of all days in the year,

---

15. **these.** These eyes

ACT I, SCENE iii

1. **give leave.** Leave us

2. **thou s'.** You shall or you should

3. **teen.** Sorrow
4. **Lammas-tide.** First of August
5. **fortnight.** Fourteen nights

Come Lammas-eve at night shall she be fourteen,
Susan and she—God rest all Christian souls!—
Were of an age. Well, Susan is with God,
20   She was too good for me. But as I said,
On Lammas-eve at night shall she be fourteen,
That shall she, marry, I remember it well.
'Tis since the earthquake now aleven[6] years,
And[7] she was wean'd—I never shall forget it—
25   Of all the days of the year, upon that day;
For I had then laid wormwood to my dug,[8]
Sitting in the sun under the dove-house wall.
My lord and you were then at Mantua—
Nay, I do bear a brain—but as I said,
30   When it did taste the wormwood on the nipple
Of my dug and felt it bitter, pretty fool,
To see it teachy[9] and fall out wi' th' dug!
Shake, quoth the dove-house;[10] 'twas no need, I trow,[11]
To bid me trudge.
35   And since that time it is aleven years,
For then she could stand high-lone;[12] nay, by th' rood,[13]
She could have run and waddled all about;
For even the day before, she broke her <u>brow</u>,
And then my husband—God be with his soul!
40   'A[14] was a merry man—took up the child.
"Yea," quoth he, "dost thou fall upon thy face?
Thou wilt fall backward when thou hast more wit,
Wilt thou not, Jule?" and by my holidam,[15]
The pretty wretch left crying and said, "Ay."[16]
45   To see now how a jest shall come about![17]
I warrant,[18] and I should live a thousand years,
I never should forget it: "Wilt thou not, Jule?" quoth he;
And, pretty fool, it stinted[19] and said, "Ay."

LADY CAPULET.   Enough of this, I pray thee hold thy peace.

---

6. **aleven.** Eleven
7. **And.** Since
8. **laid wormwood to my dug.** Applied the bitter herb called wormwood to her breast to wean the child
9. **teachy.** Touchy
10. **Shake . . . dove-house.** The dove house shook because of the earthquake.
11. **trow.** Believe
12. **stand high-lone.** Stand upright

13. **rood.** Cross
14. **'A.** He
15. **holidam.** Holiness, sometimes referring to the Virgin Mary
16. **Ay.** Aye, or yes
17. **To see . . . about!** The nurse is expressing pleasure at seeing her husband's joke come true.
18. **warrant.** Swear or guarantee
19. **stinted.** Stopped (crying)

WORDS FOR
EVERYDAY USE: **brow** (brou) *n.*, forehead

50   **NURSE.**   Yes, madam, yet I cannot choose but laugh
          To think it should leave crying and say, "Ay."
          And yet I warrant it had upon it[20] brow
          A bump as big as a young cock'rel's stone—[21]
          A perilous knock—and it cried bitterly.
55   "Yea," quoth my husband, "fall'st upon thy face?
          Thou wilt fall backward when thou comest to age,
          Wilt thou not, Jule?" It stinted and said, "Ay."

          JULIET.   And stint thou too, I pray thee, nurse, say I.

          NURSE.   Peace, I have done. God mark thee to his grace![22]
60   Thou wast the prettiest babe that e'er I nurs'd.
          And I might live to see thee married once,
          I have my wish.

          LADY CAPULET.   Marry, that "marry" is the very theme
          I came to talk of. Tell me, daughter Juliet,
65   How stands your dispositions to be married?

          JULIET.   It is an honor that I dream not of.

          NURSE.   An honor! were not I thine only nurse,
          I would say thou hadst suck'd wisdom from thy teat.

          LADY CAPULET.   Well, think of marriage now; younger than you,
70   Here in Verona, ladies of esteem,
          Are made already mothers. By my count,
          I was your mother much upon these years
          That you are now a maid. Thus then in brief:
          The valiant Paris seeks you for his love.

75   **NURSE.**   A man, young lady! Lady, such a man
          As all the world—why, he's a man of wax.[23]

          LADY CAPULET.   Verona's summer hath not such a flower.

          NURSE.   Nay, he's a flower, in faith, a very flower.

          LADY CAPULET.   What say you? can you love the gentleman?
80   This night you shall behold him at our feast;
          Read o'er the volume of young Paris' face,
          And find delight writ there with beauty's pen;
          Examine every married[24] <u>lineament</u>,

What do Lady Capulet and the Nurse think of Paris and his wish to marry Juliet?

---

20. **it.** Its
21. **cock'rel's stone.** Part of a young male chicken
22. **God mark . . . grace!** God grant grace to you!
23. **he's a man of wax.** He is as handsome as a wax figure of a man. The nurse means this as a compliment, but a wax figure is less than a real person, so the compliment is unintentionally an insult.
24. **married.** Well-matched or put together; also a pun on the usual sense of the word

WORDS FOR EVERYDAY USE: lin • e • a • ment (lin´ē ə mənt) *n.*, any of the features of the body

And see how one another lends content;
85 And what obscur'd in this fair volume lies
Find written in the margent[25] of his eyes.
This precious book of love, this unbound[26] lover,
To beautify him, only lacks a cover.
The fish lives in the sea, and 'tis much pride
90 For fair without the fair within to hide.[27]
That book in many's eyes doth share the glory,
That in gold clasps locks in the golden story;
So shall you share all that he doth possess,
By having him, making yourself no less.

95 **NURSE.** No less! nay, bigger: women grow by men.

LADY CAPULET. Speak briefly, can you like of Paris' love?[28]

JULIET. I'll look to like, if looking liking move;
But no more deep will I endart[29] mine eye
Than your consent gives strength to make it fly.

Enter SERVINGMAN.

What does Juliet say is important about her choice of a husband?

100 **SERVINGMAN.** Madam, the guests are come, supper serv'd up, you call'd, my young lady ask'd for, the nurse curs'd in the pantry,[30] and every thing in extremity. I must hence to wait; I beseech you follow straight. *Exit.*

LADY CAPULET. We follow thee. Juliet, the County stays.[31]

NURSE. Go, girl, seek happy nights to happy days. *Exeunt.*

SCENE iv: in front of Capulet's house

Enter ROMEO, MERCUTIO, BENVOLIO, *with five or six other* MASKERS;[1] TORCH-BEARERS.

ROMEO. What, shall this speech be spoke for our excuse?
Or shall we on without apology?

BENVOLIO. The date is out of such prolixity:[2]
We'll have no Cupid hoodwink'd with a scarf,[3]
5 Bearing a Tartar's painted bow of lath,[4]
Scaring the ladies like a crow-keeper,[5]
Nor no without-book prologue,[6] faintly spoke

---

25. **margent.** Margin, as in a book
26. **unbound.** Like a book unbound, he is unbound by marriage.
27. **The fish . . . hide.** It is as appropriate for a good man to be handsome as it is for a fish to live in the sea.
28. **like of Paris' love.** Love someone like Paris
29. **endart.** Shoot like a dart
30. **the nurse . . . pantry.** The kitchen help are cursing because the nurse is not there to help.
31. **the County stays.** The Count (Paris) waits.

ACT I, SCENE iv
1. **Maskers.** People wearing masks, dressed in costumes for the party
2. **The date . . . prolixity.** Such a speech, given by maskers arriving at a party, is out of fashion.
3. **Cupid hoodwink'd with a scarf.** Cupid was the Roman god of love, said to pierce lovers with his arrows. To be hoodwinked meant, literally, to be blindfolded with a scarf tied around the head.
4. **Bearing . . . lath.** Carrying, like Cupid or like a Tartar, a small bow of painted strips of wood
5. **crow-keeper.** Scarecrow
6. **without-book prologue.** Memorized introduction

After the prompter,[7] for our entrance;
But let them measure us by what they will,
10 We'll measure them a measure[8] and be gone.

    ROMEO. Give me a torch, I am not for this ambling;[9]
Being but heavy, I will bear the light.

    MERCUTIO. Nay, gentle Romeo, we must have you dance.

    ROMEO. Not I, believe me. You have dancing shoes
15 With nimble soles, I have a soul of lead
So stakes me to the ground I cannot move.

    MERCUTIO. You are a lover, borrow Cupid's wings,
And soar with them above a common bound.[10]

    ROMEO. I am too sore enpiercèd with his shaft
20 To soar with his light feathers, and so bound
I cannot bound a pitch above dull woe;
Under love's heavy burthen[11] do I sink.

    MERCUTIO. And, to sink in it, should you burthen love—
Too great oppression for a tender thing.

25   **ROMEO.** Is love a tender thing? It is too rough,
Too rude, too boist'rous, and it pricks like thorn.

    MERCUTIO. If love be rough with you, be rough with love;
Prick love for pricking, and you beat love down.
Give me a case to put my <u>visage</u> in, [*Puts on a mask.*]
30 A visor for a visor![12] what care I
What curious eye doth cote[13] deformities?
Here are the beetle brows[14] shall blush for me.

    BENVOLIO. Come knock and enter, and no sooner in,
But every man betake him to his legs.[15]

35   **ROMEO.** A torch for me. Let wantons light of heart
Tickle the senseless rushes[16] with their heels.
For I am proverb'd with a grandsire phrase,[17]

What is Mercutio's attitude about Romeo's heavy heart?

---

7. **After the prompter.** Repeating lines given by a prompter, a person whose job it is to help an actor who has forgotten the lines

8. **measure them a measure.** Give them a dance

9. **Give me . . . ambling.** Romeo wishes to carry a torch because he wants to avoid ambling, or dancing, being too heavy-hearted for such frivolity.

10. **a common bound.** Ordinary leap as might be made by an ordinary, untalented dancer

11. **burthen.** Burden

12. **visor for a visor!** A visor is a mask. Mercutio is suggesting that his face is also a mask, because he is a jester, one who hides his feelings behind his wit.

13. **cote.** See; notice

14. **beetle brows.** Bushy eyebrows

15. **betake him to his legs.** Begin dancing

16. **rushes.** Plants used as a floor covering

17. **grandsire phrase.** Proverb, or phrase known to our grandfathers

WORDS FOR EVERYDAY USE: vis • age (viz´ij) *n.*, face

I'll be a candle-holder and look on:[18]
The game was ne'er so fair, and I am done.

40   MERCUTIO.   Tut, dun's the mouse, the constable's own word.[19]
If thou art Dun, we'll draw thee from the mire
Of this sir-reverence love, wherein thou stickest
Up to the ears. Come, we burn daylight,[20] ho!

ROMEO.   Nay, that's not so.

MERCUTIO.   I mean, sir, in delay
45   We waste our lights in vain, like lights by day!
Take our good meaning, for our judgment sits
Five times in that ere once in our five wits.

ROMEO.   And we mean well in going to this mask,
But 'tis no wit to go.

MERCUTIO.   Why, may one ask?

ROMEO.   I dreamt a dream tonight.

50   MERCUTIO.   And so did I.

ROMEO.   Well, what was yours?

MERCUTIO.   That dreamers often lie.[21]

ROMEO.   In bed asleep, while they do dream things true.

MERCUTIO.   O then I see Queen Mab[22] hath been with you.
She is the fairies' midwife, and she comes
55   In shape no bigger than an agot-stone[23]
On the forefinger of an alderman,
Drawn with a team of little atomi[24]
Over men's noses as they lie asleep.
Her chariot is an empty hazel-nut,
60   Made by the joiner squirrel or old grub,
Time out a' mind the fairies' coachmakers.
Her waggon-spokes made of long spinners' legs,
The cover of the wings of grasshoppers,
Her traces of the smallest spider web,
65   Her collars of the moonshine's wat'ry beams,
Her whip of cricket's bone, the lash of film,
Her waggoner a small grey-coated gnat,
Not half so big as a round little worm
Prick'd from the lazy finger of a maid.[25]

Who is Queen Mab?

---

18. **I'll be . . . look on.** Romeo recalls the proverb, "A good candle-holder or spectator makes a good gamester."
19. **dun's . . . word.** A mouse is dun—a dull, grayish brown. Romeo has just suggested that he will be an onlooker, which makes Mercutio think of a hidden, quiet mouse. A constable, or police officer, might describe a stealthy criminal in that way.
20. **burn daylight.** Waste time

21. **lie.** Mercutio puns on the word *lie*, implying both "rest" and "tell falsehoods."
22. **Queen Mab.** Fairy creature
23. **agot-stone.** Agate used as a stone in a ring
24. **atomi.** Tiny beings
25. **Not half . . . maid.** According to a folk belief, worms grew in the fingers of lazy girls.

70   And in this state she gallops night by night
    Through lovers' brains, and then they dream of love;
    O'er <u>courtiers</u>' knees, that dream on cur'sies[26] straight;
    O'er lawyers' fingers, who straight dream on fees;
    O'er ladies' lips, who straight on kisses dream,

75   Which oft the angry Mab with blisters plagues,
    Because their breath with sweetmeats tainted are.
    Sometime she gallops o'er a courtier's nose,
    And then dreams he of smelling out a suit;[27]
    And sometime comes she with a tithe-pig's[28] tail

80   Tickling a parson's nose as 'a lies asleep,
    Then he dreams of another benefice.[29]
    Sometime she driveth o'er a soldier's neck,
    And then dreams he of cutting foreign throats,
    Of breaches, ambuscadoes,[30] Spanish blades,

85   Of healths five fadom deep;[31] and then anon[32]
    Drums in his ear, at which he starts and wakes,
    And being thus frighted, swears a prayer or two,
    And sleeps again. This is that very Mab
    That plats the manes of horses in the night,

90   And bakes the elf-locks in foul sluttish hairs,
    Which, once untangled, much misfortune bodes.[33]
    This is the hag, when maids lie on their backs,
    That presses them and learns them first to bear,
    Making them women of good carriage.[34]
    This is she—

95   **ROMEO.**   Peace, peace, Mercutio, peace!
    Thou talk'st of nothing.

  MERCUTIO.   True, I talk of dreams,
    Which are the children of an idle brain,
    Begot of nothing but vain fantasy,
    Which is as thin of substance as the air,

---

26. **on cur'sies.** Of curtsies, or bows
27. **smelling out a suit.** Thinking of something to request for oneself of a high-born or noble person
28. **tithe-pig.** Pig given as payment of tithes, dues owed to a parish
29. **benefice.** Church office that provides a living for its holder
30. **breaches, ambuscadoes.** Breaching, or breaking through fortifications; ambushes

31. **healths five fadom deep.** Drinks five fathoms deep. A fathom is a unit of measure of water equal to six feet in depth.
32. **anon.** At once
33. **bakes . . . bodes.** A folk belief was that elves matted the hair of lazy or slovenly people and that to unmat this hair was to bring bad luck.
34. **good carriage.** Pun, one sense of which is "women who are carrying (babies)"

100 And more inconstant than the wind, who woos
Even now the frozen bosom of the north,
And, being anger'd, puffs away from thence,
Turning his side to the dew-dropping south.

BENVOLIO. This wind you talk of blows us from ourselves:
105 Supper is done, and we shall come too late.

What does Romeo fear?

ROMEO. I fear, too early, for my mind misgives
Some consequence yet hanging in the stars
Shall bitterly begin his fearful date
With this night's revels, and expire the term
110 Of a despised life clos'd in my breast
By some vile forfeit of untimely death.
But He that hath the steerage of my course
Direct my sail! On, lusty gentlemen!

BENVOLIO. Strike, drum.

They march about the stage and stand to one side.

SCENE V: a hall in Capulet's house

And SERVINGMEN *come forth with napkins.*

1. SERVINGMAN. Where's Potpan, that he helps not to take away? He shift a trencher?[1] he scrape a trencher?

2. SERVINGMAN. When good manners shall lie all in one or two men's hands, and they unwash'd too, 'tis a foul thing.

5 **1. SERVINGMAN.** Away with the join-stools,[2] remove the court-cupboard, look to the plate. Good thou, save me a piece of marchpane,[3] and, as thou loves me, let the porter let in Susan Grindstone and Nell. [*Exit Second Servant.*] Anthony and Potpan!

Enter ANTHONY *and* POTPAN.

ANTHONY. Ay, boy, ready.

10 **1. SERVINGMAN.** You are look'd for and call'd for, ask'd for and sought for, in the great chamber.

POTPAN. We cannot be here and there too. Cheerly, boys, be brisk a while, and the longer liver take all.

Exeunt.

Enter CAPULET, LADY CAPULET, JULIET, TYBALT, NURSE, SERVINGMEN, *and all the* GUESTS *and* GENTLEWOMEN *to the Maskers.*

ACT I, SCENE V
1. **trencher.** Platter
2. **join-stools.** Wooden stools, made by carpenters called joiners
3. **marchpane.** Marzipan, a type of candy

CAPULET.   Welcome, gentlemen! Ladies that have their toes
15   Unplagu'd with corns will walk a bout with you.
Ah, my mistresses, which of you all
Will now deny to dance? She that makes dainty,[4]
She I'll swear hath corns. Am I come near ye now?
Welcome, gentlemen! I have seen the day
20   That I have worn a visor and could tell
A whispering tale in a fair lady's ear,
Such as would please; 'tis gone, 'tis gone, 'tis gone.
You are welcome, gentlemen! Come, musicians, play.

Music plays, and they dance.

A hall, a hall! give room! and foot it, girls.
25   More light, you knaves, and turn the tables up;
And quench the fire, the room is grown too hot.
Ah, sirrah, this unlook'd-for sport comes well.
Nay, sit, nay, sit, good cousin Capulet,
For you and I are past our dancing days.
30   How long is't now since last yourself and I
Were in a mask?

2. CAPULET.   By'r lady, thirty years.

CAPULET.   What, man? 'tis not so much, 'tis not so much:
'Tis since the <u>nuptial</u> of Lucentio,
Come Pentecost as quickly as it will,
35   Some five and twenty years, and then we mask'd.

2. CAPULET.   'Tis more, 'tis more. His son is elder,[5] sir;
His son is thirty.

CAPULET.   Will you tell me that?
His son was but a ward two years ago.

ROMEO.   [*To a Servingman.*] What lady's that which doth enrich the hand
40   Of yonder knight?

SERVINGMAN.   I know not, sir.

ROMEO.   O, she doth teach the torches to burn bright!
It seems she hangs upon the cheek of night
As a rich jewel in an Ethiop's[6] ear—

---

4. **makes dainty.** Behaves shyly by refusing to dance
5. **elder.** Older
6. **Ethiop's.** Of a person from Ethiopia, a country in
Africa

WORDS FOR
EVERYDAY USE: nup • tial (nup´shəl) *n.,* wedding; marriage

45 Beauty too rich for use, for earth too dear!
So shows a snowy dove trooping with crows,
As yonder lady o'er her fellows shows.
The measure done, I'll watch her place of stand,
And touching hers, make blessed my rude hand.
50 Did my heart love till now? Forswear it, sight!
For I ne'er saw true beauty till this night.

Is Romeo speaking of Rosaline?

TYBALT.   This, by his voice, should be a Montague.
Fetch me my rapier, boy. What dares the slave
Come hither, cover'd with an antic face,
55 To fleer[7] and scorn at our solemnity?
Now, by the stock and honor of my kin,
To strike him dead I hold it not a sin.

CAPULET.   Why, how now, kinsman, wherefore storm you so?

TYBALT.   Uncle, this is a Montague, our foe;
60 A villain that is hither come in spite
To scorn at our solemnity this night.

CAPULET.   Young Romeo is it?

TYBALT.   'Tis he, that villain Romeo.

CAPULET.   Content thee, gentle coz, let him alone,
'A bears him like a portly gentleman;[8]
65 And to say truth, Verona brags of him
To be a virtuous and well-govern'd youth.
I would not for the wealth of all this town
Here in my house do him disparagement;
Therefore be patient, take no note of him;
70 It is my will, the which if thou respect,
Show a fair presence and put off these frowns,
An ill-beseeming semblance for a feast.

How does Capulet feel about Romeo's presence at the feast?

TYBALT.   It fits when such a villain is a guest.
I'll not endure him.

CAPULET.   He shall be endured.
75 What, goodman boy?[9] I say he shall, go to!
Am I the master here, or you? go to!
You'll not endure him! God shall mend my soul,
You'll make a mutiny among my guests!
You will set cock-a-hoop![10] you'll be the man!

80 **TYBALT.**   Why, uncle, 'tis a shame.

---

7. **fleer.** Mock
8. **portly gentleman.** Well-mannered nobleman
9. **goodman boy.** The term *goodman* was used to address non-nobles. *Goodman boy* is an insult because Tybalt is being called both common and a boy.
10. **set cock-a-hoop.** Act wildly

CAPULET. Go to, go to,
You are a saucy boy. Is't so indeed?
This trick may chance to scath you,[11] I know what.
You must contrary me![12] Marry, 'tis time.—
Well said, my hearts!—You are a princox,[13] go,
85 Be quiet, or—More light, more light!—For shame,
I'll make you quiet, what!—Cheerly, my hearts!

TYBALT. Patience perforce with willful choler meeting
Makes my flesh tremble in their different greeting.
I will withdraw, but this intrusion shall,
90 Now seeming sweet, convert to bitt'rest gall. *Exit.*

What does Tybalt plan?

ROMEO. [*To Juliet.*] If I profane with my unworthiest hand
This holy shrine, the gentle sin[14] is this,
My lips, two blushing pilgrims, ready stand
To smooth that rough touch with a tender kiss.

95 **JULIET.** Good pilgrim, you do wrong your hand too much,
Which mannerly devotion shows in this:
For saints have hands that pilgrims' hands do touch,
And palm to palm is holy palmers'[15] kiss.

ROMEO. Have not saints lips, and holy palmers too?

100 **JULIET.** Ay, pilgrim, lips that they must use in pray'r.

ROMEO. O then, dear saint, let lips do what hands do,
They pray—grant thou, lest faith turn to despair.

JULIET. Saints do not move, though grant for prayers' sake.

ROMEO. Then move not while my prayer's effect I take.
105 Thus from my lips, by thine, my sin is purg'd. *Kissing her.*

JULIET. Then have my lips the sin that they have took.

ROMEO. Sin from my lips? O trespass sweetly urg'd!
Give me my sin again. *Kissing her again.*

JULIET. You kiss by th' book.

NURSE. Madam, your mother craves a word with you.

ROMEO. What is her mother?

110 **NURSE.** Marry, bachelor,
Her mother is the lady of the house,
And a good lady, and a wise and virtuous.
I nurs'd her daughter that you talk'd withal;[16]

---

11. **trick . . . you.** Behavior will hurt you
12. **contrary me.** Go contrary to me, or contradict me
13. **princox.** Sassy boy
14. **sin.** Fine or penalty
15. **palmers'.** Of pilgrims
16. **withal.** With

I tell you, he that can lay hold of her
Shall have the chinks.[17]

What does Romeo think when he learns Juliet's identity?

115 **ROMEO.**   Is she a Capulet?
O dear account! my life is my foe's debt.[18]

BENVOLIO.   Away, be gone, the sport is at the best.[19]

ROMEO.   Ay, so I fear, the more is my unrest.

CAPULET.   Nay, gentlemen, prepare not to be gone,
120 We have a trifling foolish banquet towards.[20]   *They whisper in his ear.*
Is it e'en so? Why then I thank you all.
I thank you, honest gentlemen, good night.
More torches here! Come on, then let's to bed.
[*To Second Capulet.*] Ah, sirrah, by my fay,[21] it waxes late,
125 I'll to my rest.   *Exeunt all but* JULIET *and* NURSE.

JULIET.   Come hither, nurse. What is yond gentleman?

NURSE.   The son and heir of old Tiberio.

JULIET.   What's he that now is going out of door?

NURSE.   Marry, that, I think, be young Petruchio.

How does Juliet learn Romeo's identity without letting the Nurse know of her interest?

130 **JULIET.**   What's he that follows here, that would not dance?

NURSE.   I know not.

JULIET.   Go ask his name.—If he be married,
My grave is like to be my wedding-bed.

NURSE.   His name is Romeo, and a Montague,
135 The only son of your great enemy.

JULIET.   My only love sprung from my only hate!
Too early seen unknown, and known too late!
Prodigious[22] birth of love it is to me
That I must love a loathed enemy.

NURSE.   What's tis? what's tis!

140 **JULIET.**   A rhyme I learnt even now
Of one I danc'd withal.   *One calls within,* "Juliet!"

NURSE.   Anon, anon!
Come let's away, the strangers all are gone.   *Exeunt.*

---

17. **chinks.** Money
18. **my foe's debt.** Owed to my enemy; in that enemy's power
19. **sport . . . best.** Benvolio cautions Romeo to quit

while he is ahead.
20. **towards.** Coming
21. **fay.** Faith
22. **Prodigious.** Ominous

Responding to the Selection

How do you feel about the feud between the Montagues and the Capulets? Does the feud make sense? What are Romeo and Juliet feeling at the end of act I? Given the situation between their families, what do you think might happen in the rest of the play? Discuss these questions with your classmates.

Reviewing the Selection

RECALLING

1. When Escalus, the prince of Verona, arrives on the scene at the beginning of the play, what does he break up? What does the prince say will happen if the peace of his city is again disturbed in this way?

2. With whom is Romeo in love at the beginning of the play? Why does he go to the Capulet feast?

3. Who do Capulet and Lady Capulet want Juliet to marry?

4. About whom does Mercutio speak in scene iv? Who, according to Mercutio, is the cause of lovers' dreams?

INTERPRETING

5. What is the "ancient grudge" referred to in line 3 of the prologue? In other words, who has a grudge against whom? What have been the consequences of this grudge, or feud, for the city of Verona? Why is the prince so upset in scene i?

6. What happens to Romeo at the Capulet feast? What becomes of the love that he felt at the beginning of the play? What does this tell you about Romeo?

7. How does Juliet react when her mother first speaks of a possible marriage? What does Juliet's reaction reveal about her? Is she a dutiful daughter? In what way was marriage different in the time of this play than it usually is today?

8. What attitude does Mercutio have toward lovers and their dreams? How does he differ, in this respect, from Romeo?

SYNTHESIZING

9. What argument does Tybalt have with Capulet in scene v? Why does Tybalt hate Romeo? What do you think might be the consequences if Tybalt learns that Romeo has fallen in love with Juliet?

10. What does Romeo say on first seeing Juliet? How does Juliet react on first meeting Romeo? How do they feel about one another at the end of the act? What mixed feelings do they both have? What are the causes of these mixed feelings?

Understanding Literature (Questions for Discussion)

1. **Plot, Central Conflict, and Inciting Incident.** A **plot** is the series of events related to a **central conflict**, or **struggle**. The scene that introduces the central conflict is called the **inciting incident**. What struggle is introduced at the end of act I? What conflict is felt by both Romeo and Juliet? In other words, what is the inciting incident in this play?

2. **Foreshadowing. Foreshadowing** is the act of presenting materials that hint at events to occur later in a story. What does Romeo fear in lines 106–111 of scene iv? What future events might be foreshadowed by Romeo's words?

3. **Motif.** A **motif** is an element that recurs in one or more works of literature or art. What is the significance of the motif of stars in the prologue and in scene iv? What is the playwright suggesting about the role of fate in people's lives? Do you agree that fate plays an important role in life? It is often said that "character is destiny." In other words, people's fates are a result of the sorts of people that they are. What sort of people are Romeo and Juliet? In what way do they act impulsively? What fate might result from their impulsiveness?

Responding in Writing

Personal Letter. Imagine that you are Romeo or Juliet at the end of act I of this play. Write a letter to the other person expressing your feelings about having met at the feast. Be sure to express both your feelings about the other person and your fears for the future. Share your letter with classmates in a small group. Then discuss the problem that these characters will face in the rest of the play.

> **Prewriting Suggestion:** Before writing, reread the end of scene v. If you have chosen to write from the point of view of Romeo, copy onto a piece of paper some lines from the scene that reveal what he is feeling. If you have chosen to write from the point of view of Juliet, copy some lines that show what she is feeling.

PROJECT

Artwork. Reread Mercutio's Queen Mab speech from scene iv. Based on Mercutio's description, do a drawing, painting, clay model, cartoon, or woodcut of Queen Mab, the fairies' midwife, who helps give birth to unquiet dreams. If you do not feel comfortable doing a piece of artwork, write a description of Queen Mab in your own words. Describe both how she looks and what she does.

Act II of *Romeo and Juliet* contains a very famous scene in which Romeo climbs over a wall into Juliet's garden, and Juliet speaks to him from a balcony. In this scene you will find some of the most beautiful and famous love poetry in the English language. In your journal, freewrite for five to ten minutes on the subject of romantic love. Answer the following questions: What role does love play in human life? What causes people to fall in love? What risks do people run when they fall in love? What do they stand to gain? What reasons might people have for being cautious and careful about falling in love? Keep your own ideas about love in mind as you read the balcony scene.

ACT II

Enter CHORUS.

Now old desire doth in his death-bed lie,
And young affection gapes[1] to be his heir;
That fair[2] for which love groan'd for and would die,
With tender Juliet match'd[3] is now not fair.

5   Now Romeo is belov'd and loves again,[4]
Alike[5] bewitched by the charm of looks;
But to his foe suppos'd he must complain,[6]
And she steal love's sweet bait from fearful[7] hooks.
Being held a foe, he may not have access

10   To breathe such vows as lovers use to[8] swear,
And she as much in love, her means much less
To meet her new-beloved any where.
But passion lends them power, time means, to meet,
Temp'ring[9] extremities[10] with extreme sweet.   *Exit.*

SCENE i: Capulet's orchard

Enter ROMEO *alone.*

ROMEO.   Can I go forward when my heart is here?
Turn back, dull earth,[11] and find thy center[12] out.

Enter BENVOLIO *with* MERCUTIO. ROMEO *withdraws.*

BENVOLIO.   Romeo! my cousin Romeo! Romeo!

MERCUTIO.   He is wise,
And, on my life, hath stol'n him home to bed.

PROLOGUE/ACT II, SCENE i
1. **gapes.** Desires
2. **fair.** Beauty
3. **match'd.** Compared
4. **loves again.** Loves back
5. **Alike.** Both
6. **complain.** Speak (of his love)
7. **fearful.** Dangerous

8. **use to.** Usually
9. **Temp'ring.** Lessening or making bearable
10. **extremities.** Difficulties
11. **dull earth.** The body, made of earth
12. **center.** Romeo is saying that Juliet is the center of his life. He turns back to her as things on Earth fall toward its center.

5   **BENVOLIO.**   He ran this way and leapt this orchard[13] wall.
Call, good Mercutio.

        MERCUTIO.   Nay, I'll conjure[14] too.
Romeo! humors! madman! passion! lover!
Appear thou in the likeness of a sigh!
Speak but one rhyme, and I am satisfied;
10   Cry but "Ay me!", pronounce but "love" and "dove,"
Speak to my gossip[15] Venus one fair word,
One nickname for her purblind[16] son and heir,
Young Abraham[17] Cupid he that shot so trim,[18]
When King Cophetua lov'd the beggar-maid![19]
15   He heareth not, he stirreth not, he moveth not,
The ape is dead, and I must conjure him.
I conjure thee by Rosaline's bright eyes,
By her high forehead and her scarlet lip,
By her fine foot, straight leg, and quivering thigh,
20   And the demesnes[20] that there <u>adjacent</u> lie,
That in thy likeness thou appear to us!

        BENVOLIO.   And if[21] he hear thee, thou wilt anger him.

        MERCUTIO.   This cannot anger him; 'twould anger him
To raise a spirit in his mistress' circle,[22]
25   Of some strange nature, letting it there stand
Till she had laid it and conjur'd it down.
That were some spite.[23] My <u>invocation</u>
Is fair and honest; in his mistress' name
I conjure only but to raise up him.

30   **BENVOLIO.**   Come, he hath hid himself among these trees
To be <u>consorted</u> with the humorous[24] night.
Blind is his love and best befits the dark.

        MERCUTIO.   If love be blind, love cannot hit the mark.
Now will he sit under a medlar[25] tree,
35   And wish his mistress were that kind of fruit
As maids call medlars, when they laugh alone.

How is Mercutio behind the times?

---

13. **orchard.** Garden
14. **conjure.** Cause a spirit to appear
15. **gossip.** Busybody or crone
16. **purblind.** Weak-sighted
17. **Abraham.** Beggar
18. **trim.** Precisely; accurately
19. **King . . . maid.** Love story from a popular ballad

20. **demesnes.** Regions
21. **And if.** If
22. **To raise . . . circle.** To call up a spirit as in a seance
23. **spite.** Vexation
24. **humorous.** Wet; mood-provoking
25. **medlar.** Fruit

WORDS FOR EVERYDAY USE:

ad • ja • cent (ə jā′sənt) *adj.*, near or close to something

in • vo • ca • tion (in′və kā′ shən) *n.*, the act of calling on a god for blessing or inspiration

con • sort (kän′sôrt) *vi.*, be in harmony or agreement

O, Romeo, that she were, O that she were
An open-arse,[26] thou a pop'rin pear![27]
Romeo, good night, I'll to my truckle-bed,[28]
40   This field-bed is too cold for me to sleep.
Come, shall we go?

BENVOLIO.   Go then, for 'tis in vain
To seek him here that means not to be found.   *Exit with* MERCUTIO.

SCENE ii: Capulet's orchard

ROMEO *advances.*

ROMEO.   He jests at scars that never felt a wound.

Enter JULIET *above at her window.*

ROMEO.   But soft, what light through yonder window breaks?
It is the east, and Juliet is the sun.
Arise, fair sun, and kill the envious moon,
5   Who is already sick and pale with grief
That thou, her maid, art far more fair than she.
Be not her maid,[1] since she is envious;
Her vestal livery[2] is but sick and green,
And none but fools do wear it; cast it off.
10   It is my lady, O, it is my love!
O that she knew she were!
She speaks, yet she says nothing; what of that?
Her eye <u>discourses</u>, I will answer it.
I am too bold, 'tis not to me she speaks.
15   Two of the fairest stars in all the heaven,
Having some business, do entreat her eyes
To twinkle in their spheres[3] till they return.
What if her eyes were there, they in her head?
The brightness of her cheek would shame those stars,
20   As daylight doth a lamp; her eyes in heaven
Would through the airy region stream[4] so bright
That birds would sing and think it were not night.

What request does Romeo think two stars might make of Juliet?

---

26. **open-arse.** Another name for the medlar fruit
27. **pop'rin pear.** Kind of fruit
28. **truckle-bed.** Small bed that fits under a larger bed

ACT II, SCENE ii
1. **maid.** Servant

2. **vestal livery.** Uniform belonging to a servant of Vestia, the virgin Roman goddess
3. **spheres.** Places in the heavens
4. **stream.** Shine

WORDS FOR
EVERYDAY USE: **dis • course** (dis kôrs´) *vi.,* express oneself

See how she leans her cheek upon her hand!
O that I were a glove upon that hand,
That I might touch that cheek!

JULIET.   Ay me!

25 **ROMEO.**   She speaks!
O, speak again, bright angel, for thou art
As glorious to this night, being o'er my head,
As is a winged messenger of heaven
Unto the white-upturned[5] wond'ring eyes
30 Of mortals that fall back to gaze on him,
When he bestrides the lazy puffing clouds,
And sails upon the bosom of the air.

JULIET.   O Romeo, Romeo, wherefore art thou Romeo?
Deny thy father and refuse thy name;
35 Or, if thou wilt not, be but sworn my love,
And I'll no longer be a Capulet.

ROMEO.   [*Aside.*] Shall I hear more, or shall I speak at this?

JULIET.   'Tis but thy name that is my enemy;
Thou art thyself, though not a Montague.[6]
40 What's Montague? It is nor hand nor foot,
Nor arm nor face, nor any other part
Belonging to a man. O, be some other name!
What's in a name? That which we call a rose
By any other word would smell as sweet;
45 So Romeo would, were he not Romeo call'd,
Retain that dear perfection which he owes[7]
Without that title. Romeo, doff thy name,
And for[8] thy name, which is no part of thee,
Take all myself.

ROMEO.   I take thee at thy word.
50 Call me but love, and I'll be new baptiz'd;
Henceforth I never will be Romeo.

JULIET.   What man art thou that thus bescreen'd in night
So stumblest on my counsel?[9]

ROMEO.   By a name
I know not how to tell thee who I am.
55 My name, dear saint, is hateful to myself,
Because it is an enemy to thee;
Had I it written, I would tear the word.

What does
"wherefore"
mean here? What
is Juliet's
dilemma? Does
she know she is
not alone?

---

5. **white-upturned.** When the eyes look up, more of
the whites of them show.

6. **Thou . . . Montague.** If you were to change your
name, it would not change who you are.

7. **owes.** Owns; has
8. **for.** In payment for
9. **counsel.** Meditations; private musings

JULIET. My ears have yet not drunk a hundred words
Of thy tongue's uttering, yet I know the sound.
60   Art thou not Romeo, and a Montague?

ROMEO. Neither, fair maid, if either thee dislike.

JULIET. How camest thou hither, tell me, and wherefore?
The orchard walls are high and hard to climb,
And the place death, considering who thou art,
65   If any of my kinsmen find thee here.

ROMEO. With love's light wings did I o'erperch[10] these walls,
For stony limits cannot hold love out,
And what love can do, that dares love attempt;
Therefore thy kinsmen are no stop to me.

70   **JULIET.** If they do see thee, they will murther[11] thee.

ROMEO. Alack, there lies more peril in thine eye
Than twenty of their swords! Look thou but sweet,
And I am proof[12] against their <u>enmity</u>.

JULIET. I would not for the world they saw thee here.

75   **ROMEO.** I have night's cloak to hide me from their eyes,
And but thou love me,[13] let them find me here;
My life were better ended by their hate,
Than death prorogued,[14] wanting of[15] thy love.

JULIET. By whose direction foundst thou out this place?[16]

80   **ROMEO.** By love, that first did prompt me to inquire;
He lent me counsel, and I lent him eyes.
I am no pilot, yet, wert thou as far
As that vast shore wash'd with the farthest sea,
I should adventure for such merchandise.[17]

85   **JULIET.** Thou knowest the mask of night is on my face,
Else would a maiden blush bepaint my cheek
For that which thou hast heard me speak tonight.
Fain[18] would I dwell on form,[19] fain deny

---

10. **o'erperch.** Fly over
11. **murther.** Murder
12. **proof.** Protected
13. **And but thou love me.** If you do not love me
14. **prorogued.** Postponed
15. **wanting of.** Lacking
16. **By whose . . . place?** Who gave you directions to

this place?
17. **I am . . . merchandise.** Romeo compares his willingness to work for her love to the willingness of sailors to risk dangerous voyages.
18. **Fain.** By my wish
19. **dwell on form.** Act formally

WORDS FOR
EVERYDAY USE:
    en • mi • ty (en´mə tē) *n.*, hostility; antagonism

What I have spoke, but farewell compliment![20]
90 Dost thou love me? I know thou wilt say, "Ay,"
And I will take thy word; yet, if thou swear'st,
Thou mayest prove false: at lovers' perjuries
They say Jove laughs. O gentle Romeo,
If thou dost love, pronounce it faithfully,
95 Or if thou thinkest I am too quickly won,
I'll frown and be perverse, and say thee nay,
So thou wilt[21] woo, but else not for the world.
In truth, fair Montague, I am too fond,[22]
And therefore thou mayest think my behavior light,
100 But trust me, gentleman, I'll prove more true
Than those that have more coying[23] to be strange.
I should have been more strange,[24] I must confess,
But that thou overheardst, ere I was ware,
My true-love passion; therefore pardon me,
105 And not <u>impute</u> this yielding to light love,
Which the dark night hath so discovered.[25]

ROMEO.   Lady, by yonder blessed moon I vow,
That tips with silver all these fruit-tree tops—

JULIET.   O, swear not by the moon, th' <u>inconstant</u> moon,
110 That monthly changes in her circled orb,[26]
Lest that thy love prove likewise variable.[27]

ROMEO.   What shall I swear by?

JULIET.   Do not swear at all;
Or if thou wilt, swear by thy gracious self,
Which is the god of my <u>idolatry</u>,
And I'll believe thee.

115 **ROMEO.**   If my heart's dear love—

JULIET.   Well, do not swear. Although I joy in thee,
I have no joy of this contract tonight,
It is too rash, too unadvis'd, too sudden,
Too like the lightning, which doth cease to be
120 Ere one can say it lightens. Sweet, good night!

What makes Juliet worry?

---

20. **compliment.** Etiquette, social graces
21. **So thou wilt.** So that you will
22. **fond.** Silly
23. **coying.** Coyness
24. **strange.** Distant

25. **discovered.** Shown
26. **circled orb.** Orbit
27. **Lest . . . variable.** Because of its changes, the moon is a traditional symbol of inconsistency, or fickleness.

WORDS FOR EVERYDAY USE:

im • pute (im pyo͞ot´) *vt.,* attribute

in • con • stant (in kän´stənt) *adj.,* not remaining firm in mind or purpose

i • dol • a • try (ī däl´ə trē) *n.,* excessive devotion or reverence

This bud of love, by summer's ripening breath,
May prove a beauteous flow'r when next we meet.
Good night, good night! as sweet <u>repose</u> and rest
Come to thy heart as that within my breast!

125 **ROMEO.**   O, wilt thou leave me so unsatisfied?

JULIET.   What satisfaction canst thou have tonight?

ROMEO.   Th' exchange of thy love's faithful vow for mine.

JULIET.   I gave thee mine before thou didst request it;
And yet I would it were to give again.

130 **ROMEO.**   Wouldst thou withdraw it? for what purpose, love?

JULIET.   But to be frank[28] and give it thee again,
And yet I wish but for the thing I have.
My <u>bounty</u> is as boundless as the sea,
My love as deep; the more I give to thee,

135 The more I have, for both are infinite.   NURSE *calls within.*
I hear some noise within; dear love, adieu!
Anon,[29] good nurse! Sweet Montague, be true.
Stay but a little, I will come again.   *Exit above.*

ROMEO.   O blessed, blessed night! I am afeard,

140 Being in night, all this is but a dream,
Too flattering-sweet to be <u>substantial</u>.

Enter JULIET *above.*

JULIET.   Three words, dear Romeo, and good night indeed.
If that thy bent of love[30] be honorable,
Thy purpose marriage, send me word tomorrow,

What message
does Juliet want
Romeo to send
her?

145 By one that I'll <u>procure</u> to come to thee,
Where and what time thou wilt perform the rite,
And all my fortunes at thy foot I'll lay,
And follow thee my lord throughout the world.

NURSE.   [*Within.*] Madam!

150 **JULIET.**   I come, anon.—But if thou meanest not well,
I do beseech thee—

NURSE.   [*Within.*] Madam!

---

28. **frank.** Generous
29. **Anon.** Now, at once
30. **thy . . . love.** The purpose or inclination of your love

**WORDS FOR
EVERYDAY USE:**

re • pose (ri pōz´) *n.*, rest; sleep

boun • ty (boun´tē) *n.*, something given freely;
generous gift

sub • stan • tial (səb stan´shəl) *adj.*, real;
actual; true

pro • cure (prō kyoor´) *vt.*, get or bring about
by some effort

JULIET.   By and by,[31] I come—
To cease thy strife,[32] and leave me to my grief.
Tomorrow will I send.

ROMEO.   So thrive my soul—

JULIET.   A thousand times good night!   *Exit above.*

155   **ROMEO.**   A thousand times the worse, to want thy light.
Love goes toward love as schoolboys from their books,
But love from love, toward school with heavy looks.   *Retiring.*

Enter JULIET *again above.*

JULIET.   Hist,[33] Romeo, hist! O, for a falc'ner's voice,
To lure this tassel-gentle[34] back again!
160   Bondage is hoarse, and may not speak aloud,
Else would I tear the cave where Echo lies,
And make her airy tongue more hoarse than mine,
With repetition of my Romeo's name. Romeo!

ROMEO.   It is my soul that calls upon my name.
165   How silver-sweet sound lovers' tongues by night,
Like softest music to attending ears!

JULIET.   Romeo!

ROMEO.   My niesse?[35]

JULIET.   What a' clock tomorrow
Shall I send to thee?

ROMEO.   By the hour of nine.

JULIET.   I will not fail, 'tis twenty year till then.
170   I have forgot why I did call thee back.

ROMEO.   Let me stand here till thou remember it.

JULIET.   I shall forget, to have thee still[36] stand there,
Rememb'ring how I love thy company.

ROMEO.   And I'll still stay, to have thee still forget,
175   Forgetting any other home but this.

JULIET.   'Tis almost morning, I would have thee gone—
And yet no farther than a wanton's bird,
That lets it hop a little from his hand,
Like a poor prisoner in his twisted gyves,[37]
180   And with a silken thread plucks it back again,
So loving-jealous of his liberty.

---

31. **By and by.** Now, at this moment
32. **Strife.** Striving
33. **Hist.** Falconer's call
34. **tassel-gentle.** Male falcon of a type

reserved to princes
35. **niesse.** Nestling hawk
36. **still.** Always
37. **gyves.** Chains around ankles

ROMEO.   I would I were thy bird.

JULIET.   Sweet, so would I,
Yet I should kill thee with much cherishing.
Good night, good night! Parting is such sweet sorrow
185   That I shall say good night till it be morrow.   *Exit above.*

ROMEO.   Sleep dwell upon thine eyes, peace in thy breast!
Would I were sleep and peace, so sweet to rest!
Hence will I to my ghostly sire's close cell,[38]
His help to crave, and my dear hap[39] to tell.   *Exit.*

SCENE iii: Friar Lawrence's cell

Enter FRIAR LAWRENCE *alone, with a basket.*

FRIAR LAWRENCE.   The grey-ey'd morn smiles on the frowning night,
Check'ring the eastern clouds with streaks of light,
And fleckled[1] darkness like a drunkard reels
From forth day's path and Titan's fiery wheels.[2]
5   Now ere the sun advance his burning eye,
The day to cheer and night's dank dew to dry,
I must up-fill this osier cage[3] of ours
With <u>baleful</u> weeds and precious-juiced flowers.
The earth that's nature's mother is her tomb;
10   What is her burying grave, that is her womb;
And from her womb children of divers kind
We sucking on her natural bosom find:
Many for many virtues excellent,
None but for some,[4] and yet all different.
15   O, mickle[5] is the powerful grace that lies
In plants, herbs, stones, and their true qualities;
For nought so vile that on the earth doth live
But to the earth some special good doth give;
Nor aught so good but, strain'd from that fair use,
20   Revolts from true birth,[6] stumbling on abuse.

What does Friar Lawrence say about good and evil?

---

38. **ghostly sire's close cell.** Priest's (or confessor's)
secluded room
39. **hap.** Fortune

ACT II, SCENE iii
 1. **fleckled.** Flecked, spotted with color
 2. **Titan's fiery wheels.** Wheels of the chariot belong-

ing to the sun god, Helios, one of the Titans
 3. **osier cage.** Willow basket
 4. **None . . . some.** None without some valuable property
 5. **mickle.** Great
 6. **true birth.** Its nature

WORDS FOR   **bale • ful** (bāl´fəl) *adj.,* sorrowful; wretched
EVERYDAY USE:

Virtue itself turns[7] vice, being misapplied
And vice sometime by action dignified.[8]

Enter ROMEO.

Within the infant rind of this weak flower
Poison hath <u>residence</u> and medicine power;
25   For this, being smelt, with that part cheers each part,
Being tasted, stays all senses with the heart.[9]
Two such opposed kings encamp them still
In man as well as herbs, grace and rude will;
And where the worser is <u>predominant</u>,
30   Full soon the canker[10] death eats up that plant.

ROMEO.   Good morrow, father.

FRIAR LAWRENCE.   *Benedicite!*[11]
What early tongue so sweet saluteth me?
Young son, it argues a distempered[12] head
So soon to bid good morrow to thy bed.
35   Care keeps his watch in every old man's eye,
And where care lodges, sleep will never lie;
But where unbruised youth with unstuff'd brain
Doth couch his limbs, there golden sleep doth reign.
Therefore thy earliness doth me assure
40   Thou art up-rous'd with some distemp'rature;
Or if not so, then here I hit it right—
Our Romeo hath not been in bed tonight.

ROMEO.   That last is true—the sweeter rest was mine.

FRIAR LAWRENCE.   God pardon sin! Wast thou with Rosaline?

45   **ROMEO.**   With Rosaline? my ghostly father, no;
I have forgot that name, and that name's woe.

FRIAR LAWRENCE.   That's my good son, but where hast thou been then?

ROMEO.   I'll tell thee ere thou ask it me again.
I have been feasting with mine enemy,
50   Where on a sudden one hath wounded me
That's by me wounded; both our remedies

Why does Friar Lawrence appear relieved Romeo was not with Rosaline?

---

7. **turns.** Becomes
8. **vice . . . dignified.** Vice may sometimes be made worthy by particular circumstances.
9. **For this . . . heart.** Being smelled, it improves

health; being tasted, it kills.
10. **canker.** Worm in the bud of a plant
11. **Benedicite.** Bless you
12. **distempered.** Disordered, disturbed

WORDS FOR EVERYDAY USE:

res • i • dence (rez´i dəns) *n.,* the place in which a person or thing resides or lives

pre • dom • i • nant (prē däm´ə nənt) *adj.,* having dominating influence over others; superior

Within thy help and holy physic[13] lies.
I bear no hatred, blessed man, for lo
My intercession[14] likewise steads[15] my foe.

55   **FRIAR LAWRENCE.**   Be plain, good son, and homely in thy drift,[16]
Riddling <u>confession</u> finds but riddling shrift.[17]

ROMEO.   Then plainly know my heart's dear love is set
On the fair daughter of rich Capulet.
As mine on hers, so hers is set on mine,
60   And all combin'd, save what thou must combine
By holy marriage. When and where and how
We met, we woo'd, and made exchange of vow,
I'll tell thee as we pass, but this I pray,
That thou consent to marry us today.

65   **FRIAR LAWRENCE.**   Holy Saint Francis, what a change is here!
Is Rosaline, that thou didst love so dear,
So soon forsaken? Young men's love then lies
Not truly in their hearts, but in their eyes.
Jesu Maria, what a deal of brine[18]
70   Hath wash'd thy sallow[19] cheeks for Rosaline!
How much salt water thrown away in waste,
To season love, that of it doth not taste!
The sun not yet thy sighs from heaven clears,
Thy old groans yet ringing in mine ancient ears;
75   Lo here upon thy cheek the stain doth sit
Of an old tear that is not wash'd off yet.
If e'er thou wast[20] thyself and these woes thine,
Thou and these woes were all for Rosaline.
And art thou chang'd? Pronounce this sentence then:
80   Women may fall, when there's no strength in men.

ROMEO.   Thou <u>chidst</u> me oft for loving Rosaline.

FRIAR LAWRENCE.   For <u>doting</u>, not for loving, pupil mine.

ROMEO.   And badst me[21] bury love.

FRIAR LAWRENCE.   Not in a grave,
To lay one in, another out to have.

What does Romeo want Friar Lawrence to do?

For what does Friar Lawrence scold Romeo?

---

13. **physic.** Healing power
14. **intercession.** Petition, request
15. **steads.** Helps
16. **homely . . . drift.** Plain in your speech
17. **shrift.** Forgiveness, absolution of sin

18. **brine.** Salt water; tears
19. **sallow.** Of a sickly, pale yellow color
20. **wast.** Was
21. **badst me.** Bade me, told me to

WORDS FOR
EVERYDAY USE:

con • fes • sion (kən fesh´ən) n., admission of guilt
chide (chīd) vt., scold
dote (dōt) vi., be foolishly or excessively fond

85   **ROMEO.**   I pray thee chide me not. Her I love now
Doth grace for grace and love for love allow;
The other did not so.

   FRIAR LAWRENCE.   O, she knew well
Thy love did read by rote that could not spell.[22]
But come, young waverer, come go with me,
90   In one respect I'll thy assistant be;
For this alliance may so happy prove
To turn your households' <u>rancor</u> to pure love.

   ROMEO.   O, let us hence, I stand on[23] sudden haste.

   FRIAR LAWRENCE.   Wisely and slow, they stumble that run fast.

Exeunt.

What is the hope Friar Lawrence finds in the love between a Montague and a Capulet?

SCENE iv: a street in Verona

Enter BENVOLIO *and* MERCUTIO.

   MERCUTIO.   Where the dev'l should this Romeo be?
Came he not home tonight?

   BENVOLIO.   Not to his father's, I spoke with his man.

   MERCUTIO.   Why, that same pale hard-hearted wench, that Rosaline,
5   Torments him so, that he will sure run mad.

   BENVOLIO.   Tybalt, the kinsman to old Capulet,
Hath sent a letter to his father's house.

   MERCUTIO.   A challenge, on my life.

   BENVOLIO.   Romeo will answer it.

10   **MERCUTIO.**   Any man that can write may answer a letter.

   BENVOLIO.   Nay, he will answer the letter's master, how he dares, being
dar'd.

What does Tybalt send to the Montague house? What does Benvolio think Romeo will do?

   MERCUTIO.   Alas, poor Romeo, he is already dead, stabb'd with a white
wench's black eye, run through the ear with a love-song, the very pin[1] of
15   his heart cleft with the blind bow-boy's butt-shaft;[2] is he a man to
encounter Tybalt?

   BENVOLIO.   Why, what is Tybalt?

---

22. **Thy love . . . spell.** Your love was recited from
memory, not really understood or felt.
23. **stand on.** Require. Haste will prove to be Romeo's
tragic flaw.

ACT II, SCENE iv
  1. **pin.** Bull's eye
  2. **butt-shaft.** Blunt, nonbarbed arrow used for practice
by the love god Cupid

WORDS FOR EVERYDAY USE: **ran • cor** (raŋˊkər) *n.*, bitter hate or ill will

Mercutio describes what skill of Tybalt's?

MERCUTIO. More than Prince of Cats.[3] O, he's the courageous captain of compliments.[4] He fights as you sing prick-song,[5] keeps time, distance, and proportion; he rests his minim rests, one, two, and the third in your bosom: the very butcher of a silk button,[6] a duellist, a duellist; a gentleman of the very first house, of the first and second cause. Ah, the immortal *passado*, the *punto reverso*, the *hay!*[7]

BENVOLIO. The what?

MERCUTIO. The pox of such antic, lisping, affecting phantasimes, these new tuners of accent![8] "By Jesu, a very good blade! a very tall[9] man! a very good whore!" Why, is not this a lamentable thing, grandsire, that we should be thus afflicted with these strange flies, these fashion-mongers, these pardon-me's,[10] who stand so much on the new form,[11] that they cannot sit at ease on the old bench? O, their bones, their bones!

Enter ROMEO.

BENVOLIO. Here comes Romeo, here comes Romeo.

MERCUTIO. Without his roe,[12] like a dried herring: O flesh flesh, how art thou fishified! Now is he for the numbers[13] that Petrarch flow'd in. Laura to his lady was a kitchen wench (marry, she had a better love to berhyme her), Dido a dowdy, Cleopatra a gipsy, Helen and Hero hildings[14] and harlots, Thisby[15] a gray eye or so, but not to the purpose. Signior Romeo, *bon jour!* there's a French salutation to your French slop.[16] You gave us the counterfeit fairly last night.

ROMEO. Good morrow to you both. What counterfeit did I give you?

MERCUTIO. The slip,[17] sir, the slip, can you not conceive?[18]

ROMEO. Pardon, good Mercutio, my business was great, and in such a case as mine a man may strain courtesy.

MERCUTIO. That's as much as to say, such a case as yours constrains a man to bow in the hams.

ROMEO. Meaning to cur'sy.

MERCUTIO. Thou hast most kindly hit it.

ROMEO. A most courteous exposition.

---

3. **Prince of Cats.** Tybalt is the name of the Prince of Cats in a series of medieval tales about Reynard the Fox.
4. **captain of compliments.** Dueling master
5. **prick-song.** Printed music
6. **butcher . . . button.** Swordsman good enough to pierce a particular button on an opponent's clothing
7. **a gentleman . . . hay.** Superb swordsman, knowledgeable about the rules and techniques of swordplay
8. **The pox . . . accent.** The sickness of smart, young people with their modern speech

9. **tall.** Large; intimidating
10. **pardon-me's.** Overly polite, affected people
11. **form.** Contemporary fashions or fads
12. **Without his roe.** Thin from not eating
13. **numbers.** Verses of poetry
14. **hildings.** Good-for-nothings
15. **Laura . . . Thisby.** Famous women in love stories
16. **French slop.** Pants
17. **The slip.** Counterfeit coins were called *slips.*
18. **conceive.** Understand

MERCUTIO. Nay, I am the very pink[19] of courtesy.

50 **ROMEO.** Pink for flower.

MERCUTIO. Right.

ROMEO. Why then is my pump[20] well flower'd.[21]

MERCUTIO. Sure wit! Follow me this jest now, till thou hast worn out thy pump, that when the single[22] sole of it is worn, the jest may remain,
55 after the wearing, soly singular.

ROMEO. O single-sol'd jest, soly <u>singular</u> for the singleness![23]

MERCUTIO. Come between us, good Benvolio, my wits faints.

ROMEO. Swits and spurs,[24] swits and spurs, or I'll cry a match.[25]

MERCUTIO. Nay, if our wits run the wild-goose chase, I am done; for thou
60 hast more of the wild goose in one of thy wits than, I am sure, I have in my whole five. Was I with you there for the goose?

ROMEO. Thou wast never with me for any thing when thou wast not there for the goose.

MERCUTIO. I will bite thee by the ear for that jest.

65 **ROMEO.** Nay, good goose, bite not.

MERCUTIO. Thy wit is a very bitter sweeting,[26] it is a most sharp sauce.

ROMEO. And is it not then well serv'd in to a sweet goose?

MERCUTIO. O, here's a wit of cheverel,[27] that stretches from an inch narrow to an ell[28] broad!

70 **ROMEO.** I stretch it out for that word "broad," which, added to the goose, proves thee far and wide a broad[29] goose.

MERCUTIO. Why, is not this better now than groaning for love? Now art thou sociable, now art thou Romeo; now art thou what thou art, by art as well as by nature, for this <u>drivelling</u> love is like a great natural[30] that
75 runs lolling up and down to hide his bable[31] in a hole.

BENVOLIO. Stop there, stop there.

---

19. **pink.** Flower
20. **pump.** Shoe
21. **flower'd.** Decorated by pinking, or punching with holes
22. **single.** Thin
23. **O single-sol'd . . . singleness.** Feeble jest, unequaled in its silliness
24. **Swits and spurs.** Switches and spurs

25. **cry a match.** Claim victory
26. **sweeting.** Kind of apple
27. **cheverel.** Easily stretched kind of leather
28. **ell.** Measure equal to forty-five inches
29. **broad.** Large or obvious
30. **natural.** Fool, jester
31. **bable.** Bauble, stick carried by a court jester

WORDS FOR EVERYDAY USE:
sin • gu • lar (siŋ´ gyə lər) *adj.*, being the only one of its kind
driv • el • ling (driv´əl iŋ) *part.*, childish

MERCUTIO. Thou desirest me to stop in my tale against the hair.[32]

BENVOLIO. Thou wouldst else have made thy tale large.

80 **MERCUTIO.** O, thou art deceiv'd; I would have made it short, for I was come to the whole depth of my tale, and meant indeed to occupy the argument no longer.

ROMEO. Here's goodly gear!

Enter NURSE *and her man* PETER.

A sail, a sail!

MERCUTIO. Two, two: a shirt and a smock.[33]

85 **NURSE.** Peter!

PETER. Anon!

NURSE. My fan, Peter.

MERCUTIO. Good Peter, to hide her face, for her fan's the fairer face.

NURSE. God ye good morrow, gentlemen.

90 **MERCUTIO.** God ye good den,[34] fair gentlewoman.

NURSE. Is it good den?

MERCUTIO. 'Tis no less, I tell ye, for the bawdy hand of the dial is now upon the prick[35] of noon.

NURSE. Out upon you, what a man[36] are you?

95 **ROMEO.** One, gentlewoman, that God hath made, himself to mar.

NURSE. By my troth,[37] it is well said; "for himself to mar," quoth 'a![38] Gentlemen, can any of you tell me where I may find the young Romeo?

ROMEO. I can tell you, but young Romeo will be older when you have found him than he was when you sought him. I am the youngest of that
100 name, for fault of a worse.

NURSE. You say well.

MERCUTIO. Yea, is the worst well? Very well took, i' faith, wisely, wisely.

NURSE. If you be he, sir, I desire some confidence with you.

BENVOLIO. She will indite[39] him to some supper.

105 **MERCUTIO.** A bawd, a bawd, a bawd! So ho![40]

ROMEO. What hast thou found?

---

32. **against the hair.** Against my wish
33. **shirt . . . smock.** Man and a woman
34. **good den.** Good afternoon
35. **prick.** Mark on a sundial or clock
36. **what a man.** What sort of person

37. **troth.** Faith
38. **quoth 'a.** Says he
39. **indite.** Invite
40. **So ho.** Hunter's cry

MERCUTIO. No hare, sir, unless a hare, sir, in a lenten pie,[41] that is something stale and hoar[42] ere it be spent.[43]

He walks by them and sings.

An old hare hoar,
And an old hare hoar,
Is very good meat in Lent;
But a hare that is hoar
Is too much for a score,[44]
When it hoars ere it be spent.

110

115 Romeo, will you come to your father's? We'll to dinner thither.

ROMEO. I will follow you.

MERCUTIO. Farewell, ancient lady, farewell, *singing* "lady, lady, lady."

Exeunt MERCUTIO *and* BENVOLIO.

NURSE. I pray you, sir, what saucy merchant[45] was this, that was so full of his ropery?[46]

120 **ROMEO.** A gentleman, nurse, that loves to hear himself talk, and will speak more in a minute than he will stand to in a month.

NURSE. And 'a speak any thing against me, I'll take him down, and 'a were lustier than he is, and twenty such Jacks; and if I cannot, I'll find those that shall. Scurvy knave, I am none of his flirt-gills,[47] I am none of 125 his skains-mates.[48] [*She turns to* PETER, *her man.*] And thou must stand by too and suffer every knave to use me at his pleasure!

PETER. I saw no man use you at his pleasure; if I had, my weapon should quickly have been out. I warrant you, I dare draw as soon as another man, if I see occasion in a good quarrel, and the law on my side.

130 **NURSE.** Now, afore God, I am so vex'd that every part about me quivers. Scurvy knave! Pray you, sir, a word: and as I told you, my young lady bid me inquire you out; what she bid me say, I will keep to myself. But first let me tell ye, if ye should lead her in a fool's paradise, as they say, it were a very gross kind of behavior, as they say; for the gentlewoman is young; and 135 therefore, if you should deal double[49] with her, truly it were an ill thing to be off'red to any gentlewoman, and very weak[50] dealing.

ROMEO. Nurse, commend me to thy lady and mistress. I protest unto thee—

NURSE. Good heart, and, i' faith, I will tell her as much.[51] Lord, Lord,

---

41. **lenten pie.** Meatless pie prepared during Lent, into which, Mercutio suggests, one might place an old rabbit left over from before the Lenten season
42. **hoar.** Moldy
43. **spent.** Eaten
44. **Is . . . score.** Costs too much
45. **saucy merchant.** Jesting, vulgar man
46. **ropery.** Vulgar jokes

47. **flirt-gills.** Flirtatious, loose women
48. **skains-mates.** Outlaw women
49. **deal double.** Speak untruly or equivocatingly
50. **weak.** Poor; mean
51. **I will . . . much.** The nurse has not allowed Romeo to say anything.

140   she will be a joyful woman.

ROMEO. What wilt thou tell her, nurse? Thou dost not mark[52] me.

NURSE. I will tell her, sir, that you do protest, which, as I take it, is a gentleman-like offer.

ROMEO. Bid her devise

145 Some means to come to shrift this afternoon,
And there she shall at Friar Lawrence' cell
Be shriv'd and married. Here is for thy pains.

NURSE. No, truly, sir, not a penny.

ROMEO. Go to, I say you shall.

150 **NURSE.** This afternoon, sir? Well, she shall be there.

ROMEO. And stay, good nurse—behind the abbey wall
Within this hour my man shall be with thee,
And bring thee cords made like a tackled stair,[53]
Which to the high top-gallant[54] of my joy

155 Must be my convoy[55] in the secret night.
Farewell, be trusty, and I'll quit[56] thy pains.
Farewell, commend me to thy mistress.

NURSE. Now God in heaven bless thee! Hark you, sir.

ROMEO. What say'st thou, my dear nurse?

160 **NURSE.** Is your man secret?[57] Did you ne'er hear say,
"Two may keep counsel,[58] putting one away"?[59]

ROMEO. 'Warrant thee, my man's as true as steel.

NURSE. Well, sir, my mistress is the sweetest lady—Lord, Lord! when 'twas a little prating thing—O, there is a nobleman in town, one Paris,
165 that would fain lay knife aboard;[60] but she, good soul, had as lieve[61] see a toad, a very toad, as see him. I anger her sometimes and tell her that Paris is the properer[62] man, but I'll warrant you, when I say so, she looks as pale as any clout[63] in the versal[64] world. Doth not rosemary and Romeo begin both with a letter?[65]

170 **ROMEO.** Ay, nurse, what of that? Both with an *R*.

NURSE. Ah, mocker, that's the dog's name.[66] *R* is for the—no, I know it begins with some other letter—and she hath the prettiest sententious[67] of it, of you and rosemary, that it would do you good to hear it.

What plan does Romeo want the Nurse to disclose to Juliet?

---

52. **mark.** Listen to
53. **tackled stair.** Rope ladder
54. **top-gallant.** Highest mast of a ship
55. **convoy.** Means of passage
56. **quit.** Reward
57. **secret.** Discreet
58. **keep counsel.** Keep a secret
59. **putting one away.** If one of them is away
60. **lay knife aboard.** Lay seige, or claim

61. **lieve.** Willingly
62. **properer.** Handsomer
63. **clout.** Cloth
64. **versal.** Universal; whole
65. **a letter.** The same letter
66. **the dog's name.** Because an *r* sounds like the growl of a dog
67. **sententious.** Sayings (The nurse is misusing a big word.)

ROMEO.   Commend me to thy lady.

175 NURSE.   Ay, a thousand times. [*Exit* ROMEO.] Peter!

PETER.   Anon!

NURSE.   [*Handing him her fan.*] Before, and apace.

Exit after PETER.

SCENE v: Capulet's orchard

Enter JULIET.

JULIET.   The clock strook nine when I did send the nurse;
In half an hour she promised to return.
Perchance she cannot meet him—that's not so.
O, she is lame! Love's heralds should be thoughts,
5   Which ten times faster glides than the sun's beams,
Driving back shadows over low'ring hills;
Therefore do nimble-pinion'd doves draw Love,[1]
And therefore hath the wind-swift Cupid wings.
Now is the sun upon the highmost hill
10   Of this day's journey, and from nine till twelve
Is three long hours, yet she is not come.
Had she affections and warm youthful blood,
She would be as swift in motion as a ball;
My words would bandy[2] her to my sweet love,
15   And his to me.
But old folks—many feign as they were dead,
Unwieldy, slow, heavy, and pale as lead.

Enter NURSE *and* PETER.

O God, she comes! O honey nurse, what news?
Hast thou met with him? Send thy man away.

20 NURSE.   Peter, stay at the gate.   *Exit* PETER.

JULIET.   Now, good sweet nurse—O Lord, why lookest thou sad?
Though news be sad, yet tell them merrily;
If good, thou shamest the music of sweet news
By playing it to me with so sour a face.

25 NURSE.   I am a-weary, give me leave a while.
Fie, how my bones ache! What a jaunce[3] have I!

JULIET.   I would thou hadst my bones, and I thy news.
Nay, come, I pray thee speak, good, good nurse, speak.

ACT II, SCENE v
 1. **draw Love.** Pull the chariot of Venus
 2. **bandy.** Toss
 3. **jaunce.** Bounce; difficult journey

NURSE. Jesu, what haste! Can you not stay[4] a while?

30 Do you not see that I am out of breath?

JULIET. How art thou out of breath, when thou hast breath
To say to me that thou art out of breath?
The excuse that thou dost make in this delay
Is longer than the tale thou dost excuse.

35 Is thy news good or bad? Answer to that.
Say either, and I'll stay the circumstance.[5]
Let me be satisfied, is't good or bad?

NURSE. Well, you have made a simple[6] choice, you know not how to choose a man. Romeo! no, not he. Though his face be better than any

40 man's, yet his leg excels all men's, and for a hand and a foot and a body, though they be not to be talk'd on,[7] yet they are past compare. He is not the flower of courtesy, but I'll warrant him, as gentle as a lamb. Go thy ways, wench, serve God. What, have you din'd at home?

JULIET. No, no! But all this did I know before.

45 What says he of our marriage? what of that?

NURSE. Lord, how my head aches! What a head have I!
It beats as it would fall in twenty pieces.
My back a' t'[8] other side—ah, my back, my back!
Beshrew your heart[9] for sending me about

50 To catch my death with jaunticing up and down!

JULIET. I' faith, I am sorry that thou art not well.
Sweet, sweet, sweet nurse, tell me, what says my love?

NURSE. Your love says, like an honest gentleman,
An' a courteous, and a kind, and a handsome,

55 And, I warrant, a virtuous—Where is your mother?

JULIET. Where is my mother! why, she is within,
Where should she be? How oddly thou repliest!
"Your love says, like an honest gentleman,
'Where is your mother?'"

NURSE. O God's lady dear!

60 Are you so hot?[10] Marry,[11] come up,[12] I trow;
Is this the poultice for my aching bones?
Henceforward do your messages yourself.

JULIET. Here's such a coil![13] Come, what says Romeo?

NURSE. Have you got leave to go to shrift to-day?

65 **JULIET.** I have.

What does Juliet do to get the message from the Nurse?

---

4. **stay.** Wait
5. **stay the circumstance.** Wait for details
6. **simple.** Foolish
7. **be not . . . on.** Aren't worth talking about
8. **a' t'.** On the

9. **Beshrew your heart.** (Mild oath)
10. **hot.** Impatient
11. **Marry.** (Interjection)
12. **come up.** Stop now
13. **coil.** Fuss

NURSE. Then hie[14] you hence to Friar Lawrence' cell,
There stays a husband to make you a wife.
Now comes the wanton[15] blood up in your cheeks,
They'll be in scarlet straight at any news.[16]
70   Hie you to church, I must another way,
To fetch a ladder, by the which your love
Must climb a bird's nest soon when it is dark.
I am the drudge, and toil in your delight;
But you shall bear the burthen soon at night.
75   Go, I'll to dinner, hie you to the cell.

JULIET. Hie to high fortune! Honest nurse, farewell.   *Exeunt.*

SCENE vi: Friar Lawrence's cell

Enter FRIAR LAWRENCE *and* ROMEO.

FRIAR LAWRENCE. So smile the heavens upon this holy act,
That after-hours with sorrow chide us not!

ROMEO. Amen, amen! but come what sorrow can,
It cannot countervail[1] the exchange of joy
5   That one short minute gives me in her sight.
Do thou but close our hands with holy words,
Then love-devouring death do what he dare,
It is enough I may but call her mine.

FRIAR LAWRENCE. These violent delights have violent ends,
10   And in their triumph die, like fire and powder,
Which as they kiss consume. The sweetest honey
Is loathsome in his own deliciousness,
And in the taste confounds[2] the appetite.
Therefore love moderately: long love doth so;
15   Too swift arrives as tardy as too slow.

Enter JULIET.

Here comes the lady. O, so light a foot
Will ne'er wear out the everlasting flint;
A lover may bestride the gossamers[3]
That idles in the wanton[4] summer air,
20   And yet not fall; so light is vanity.[5]

JULIET. Good even to my ghostly confessor.

FRIAR LAWRENCE. Romeo shall thank thee, daughter, for us both.

What concerns Friar Lawrence?

---

14. **hie.** Hurry
15. **wanton.** Unrestrained
16. **They'll . . . news.** Any little thing makes you blush.

ACT II, SCENE vi
 1. **countervail.** Match, equal

2. **confounds.** Destroys
3. **gossamers.** Delicate threads like those spun by spiders
4. **wanton.** Sportive
5. **vanity.** Temporary joy of life

JULIET. As much[6] to him, else is his thanks too much.

ROMEO. Ah, Juliet, if the measure of thy joy
25   Be heap'd like mine, and that[7] thy skill be more
To blazon[8] it, then sweeten with thy breath
This neighbor air, and let rich music's tongue
Unfold the imagin'd happiness[9] that both
Receive in either by this dear encounter.

30   **JULIET.** Conceit,[10] more rich in matter than in words,
Brags of[11] his substance, not of ornament;
They are but beggars that can count their worth,
But my true love is grown to such excess
I cannot sum up sum[12] of half my wealth.

35   **FRIAR LAWRENCE.** Come, come with me, and we will make short work,
For by your leaves, you shall not stay alone
Till Holy Church incorporate two in one.   *Exeunt.*

---

6. **As much.** A return of Romeo's greeting and kiss
7. **that.** If
8. **blazon.** Proclaim
9. **imagin'd happiness.** Unexpressed emotion
10. **Conceit.** Understanding
11. **Brags of.** Prides himself on
12. **sum up sum.** Determine the total

Responding to the Selection

Why does Friar Lawrence chide Romeo when the boy first comes to see him? What bothers the monk about Romeo's feelings toward Juliet? Do you share Friar Lawrence's opinion? Do you think that Romeo is making a mistake? Discuss these questions with your classmates.

Reviewing the Selection

1. To what does Romeo compare Juliet's eyes in the opening to scene ii? What does Romeo swear by in line 107 of this scene? What is Juliet's response?

2. What does Juliet say about the name *Montague* in the balcony scene? How does Romeo respond?

3. Why does Romeo go to see Friar Lawrence? What does Romeo hope to do? For what purpose do Romeo and Juliet meet with Friar Lawrence at the end of act II?

4. Who has sent a letter to Romeo's house? What is the purpose of the letter?

▶▶ 5. How do Romeo and Juliet feel about one another, as revealed in the balcony scene? For what does each one hope? What does each one fear?

▶▶ 6. What problem lies in the path of the two lovers? What is Romeo ready to renounce in exchange for Juliet's love?

▶▶ 7. Why does Friar Lawrence want to marry the two young people to one another? What does he hope to accomplish by doing this?

▶▶ 8. How does Tybalt feel toward Romeo? Why does he feel this way? What do you think might happen as a result of Tybalt's feelings toward Romeo? How might that situation affect the relationship between Romeo and Juliet?

9. In what time of year and of day does the balcony scene take place? What do the two lovers both know at the end of the scene? How does what happens between the two young people differ from thinking something over carefully in the cold light of day?

10. In your opinion, is Friar Lawrence doing the right thing? Do you think that Friar Lawrence is correct in believing that his actions will bring the families together? What evidence in the play so far supports your view? Explain.

Understanding Literature (Questions for Discussion)

1. **Plot and Complication.** A **plot** is the series of events related to a central conflict, or struggle. The **complication** is a part of the plot in which events occur that develop the central conflict. In this play, the central conflict is between Romeo and Juliet's love for one another and their families' opposition to this love. The central conflict is introduced in act I. What happens in act II to develop this conflict even further?

2. **Metaphor.** A **metaphor** is a figure of speech in which one thing is spoken or written about as if it were another. The description invites the reader to make a comparison

between the two things. In the opening line of scene ii, Romeo says of Mercutio, "He jests at scars that never felt a wound." To what is Romeo comparing love in this line? What do love and wounds have in common? In what way is Romeo "scarred"? Why, according to Romeo, doesn't Mercutio understand how Romeo feels?

3. **Character and Motivation.** A **character** is a person who figures in the action of a literary work. **Motivation** is a force that moves a character to think, feel, or behave in a certain way. Why does Romeo's presence in the garden make Juliet afraid? What does this part of scene ii reveal about the character of Romeo? What motivates him? How strong is this motivation?

Responding in Writing

Lyric Poem. In the balcony scene, Juliet asks Romeo not to swear by the "inconstant moon" that changes from night to night. Imagine that you are Rosaline, the young woman whom Romeo first loved, and that you have heard of Romeo's feelings toward Juliet. Write a poem, addressed to Romeo, in which you tell how you feel about Romeo's change of heart. In your poem, use the changeableness of the moon as a metaphor or simile to describe Romeo.

> **Prewriting Suggestion:** Begin by writing notes, in prose, about what you think Rosaline might be thinking about Romeo. Include in your notes a sentence or two comparing Romeo to the moon, which is sometimes full, sometimes partially full, and sometimes completely dark. Then study your notes and make a list of rhymes that you might use in your poem, such as *moon* and *soon, Romeo* and *below.*

PROJECT

THE PARTS OF A STAGE		
Up Right	Up Center	Up Left
Right Center	Center	Left Center
Down Right	Down Center	Down Left

Costume and Set Design. Imagine that you are going to stage the balcony scene from act II in a contemporary theater. Working with other students, make plans for the costumes and set design for the scene. What will Romeo wear? What will Juliet wear? Do some research in the library to find out about Elizabethan dress and costumes. Based on this research, create written descriptions and drawings of the costumes. Then turn your attention to the set. Create a written description of the stage set telling what structures should appear there, what painted backdrops might be used, what objects might be placed on the stage, and what lighting effects the scene requires. Do a drawing of the stage that shows the parts of your set design.

What should a person do when someone else picks a fight? Why is it important for people in a civilized society to avoid fighting? What actions can people take to avoid fights? What can they do when other people insist on being spiteful or belligerent? Write about these questions in your journal.

ACT III

SCENE i: a public place in Verona

Enter MERCUTIO, BENVOLIO, PAGE, *and* MEN.

What threatening people and emotions does Benvolio wish to avoid?

BENVOLIO.   I pray thee, good Mercutio, let's retire.
The day is hot, the Capels are abroad,
And if we meet we shall not scape a brawl,
For now, these hot days, is the mad blood stirring.

5   **MERCUTIO.**   Thou art like one of these fellows that, when he enters the confines of a tavern, claps me[1] his sword upon the table, and says, "God send me no need of thee!" and by the operation of the second cup draws him on the drawer,[2] when indeed there is no need.

BENVOLIO.   Am I like such a fellow?

10   **MERCUTIO.**   Come, come, thou art as hot a Jack in thy mood as any in Italy, and as soon mov'd to be moody, and as soon moody[3] to be mov'd.

BENVOLIO.   And what to?

MERCUTIO.   Nay, and there were two[4] such, we should have none shortly, for one would kill the other. Thou? why, thou wilt quarrel with a man that
15   hath a hair more or a hair less in his beard than thou hast. Thou wilt quarrel with a man for cracking nuts, having no other reason but because thou hast hazel eyes. What eye but such an eye would spy out such a quarrel? Thy head is as full of quarrels as an egg is full of meat,[5] and yet thy head hath been beaten as addle[6] as an egg for quarrelling. Thou hast
20   quarrell'd with a man for coughing in the street, because he hath waken'd thy dog that hath lain asleep in the sun. Didst thou not fall out with a tailor for wearing his new doublet[7] before Easter? with another for tying his new shoes with old riband?[8] and yet thou wilt tutor me from[9] quarrelling!

BENVOLIO.   And I were so apt to quarrel as thou art, any man should buy
25   the fee-simple of my life for an hour and a quarter.

ACT III, SCENE i
 1. **claps me.** Throws down
 2. **draws . . . drawer.** Prepares to sword fight with the bartender
 3. **moody.** Irritable

 4. **two.** Retort to Benvolio's *to*
 5. **meat.** Matter that can be eaten
 6. **addle.** Confused, rotten (with reference to eggs)
 7. **doublet.** Close-fitting jacket, with or without sleeves
 8. **riband.** Shoelace
 9. **tutor me from.** Instruct me not to

MERCUTIO.   The fee-simple![10] O simple!

Enter TYBALT, PETRUCHIO, *and others.*

BENVOLIO.   By my head, here comes the Capulets.

MERCUTIO.   By my heel, I care not.

30   **TYBALT.**   Follow me close, for I will speak to them.
Gentlemen, good den, a word with one of you.

MERCUTIO.   And but one word with one of us?
Couple it with something, make it a word and a blow.

TYBALT.   You shall find me apt enough to that, sir, and you will give me
occasion.

35   **MERCUTIO.**   Could you not take some occasion without giving?

TYBALT.   Mercutio, thou consortest with Romeo—

MERCUTIO.   Consort![11] what, dost thou make us <u>minstrels</u>? And thou
make minstrels of us, look to hear nothing but discords. Here's my fiddlestick,[12] here's that shall make you dance. 'Zounds,[13] consort!

40   **BENVOLIO.**   We talk here in the public haunt of men.
Either withdraw unto some private place;
Or reason coldly of[14] your grievances,
Or else depart;[15] here all eyes gaze on us.

MERCUTIO.   Men's eyes were made to look, and let them gaze;
45   I will not budge for no man's pleasure, I.

Enter ROMEO.

TYBALT.   Well, peace be with you, sir, here comes my man.

MERCUTIO.   But I'll be hang'd, sir, if he wear your livery.[16]
Marry, go before to field,[17] he'll be your follower;
Your worship in that sense may call him man.[18]

50   **TYBALT.**   Romeo, the love I bear thee can afford
No better term than this: thou art a villain.

ROMEO.   Tybalt, the reason that I have to love thee
Doth much excuse the appertaining rage[19]

How does Tybalt try to insult Romeo?

---

10. **fee-simple.** Complete ownership
11. **Consort.** Mercutio means to "play music with."
Consort refers to a group of musicians.
12. **fiddlestick.** Rapier, a type of sword
13. **'Zounds.** By God's (Christ's) wounds
14. **reason coldly of.** Speak about dispassionately

15. **depart.** Separate
16. **livery.** Mercutio responds as if Tybalt used *my man* to
mean "my servant."
17. **field.** Setting for a duel
18. **man.** One deserving to be described as a man
19. **excuse . . . rage.** Lessen the appropriate anger

**WORDS FOR
EVERYDAY USE:**   min • strel (min'strəl) *n.,* medieval entertainer who traveled from
place to place

What does Romeo know that Tybalt does not?

To such a greeting. Villain am I none;
55   Therefore farewell, I see thou knowest me not.

TYBALT.   Boy, this shall not excuse the injuries
That thou hast done me, therefore turn and draw.

ROMEO.   I do protest[20] I never injuried[21] thee,
But love thee better than thou canst devise,[22]
60   Till thou shalt know the reason of my love,
And so, good Capulet—which name I tender[23]
As dearly as mine own—be satisfied.

MERCUTIO.   O calm, dishonorable, vile <u>submission</u>!
Alla stoccato[24] carries it away.   *Draws.*
65   Tybalt, you rat-catcher,[25] will you walk?[26]

TYBALT.   What wouldst thou have with me?

MERCUTIO.   Good King of Cats, nothing but one of your nine lives; that
I mean to make bold withal, and as you shall use me hereafter,[27] dry-beat[28]
the rest of the eight. Will you pluck your sword out of his pilcher[29] by the
70   ears?[30] Make haste, lest mine be about your ears ere it be out.

TYBALT.   I am for you.   *Drawing.*

ROMEO.   Gentle Mercutio, put thy rapier up.

MERCUTIO.   Come, sir, your *passado*.[31]   *They fight.*

ROMEO.   Draw, Benvolio, beat down their weapons.
75   Gentlemen, for shame, forbear this outrage!
Tybalt, Mercutio, the Prince expressly hath
Forbid this bandying[32] in Verona streets.

What does Romeo attempt to do?

ROMEO *steps between them.*

Hold, Tybalt! Good Mercutio!

TYBALT *under* ROMEO'S *arm thrusts* MERCUTIO *in.*
Away TYBALT *with his followers.*

MERCUTIO.   I am hurt.

---

20. **protest.** Assert
21. **injuried.** Harmed
22. **devise.** Imagine
23. **tender.** Cherish
24. **Alla stoccato.** Literally, at the thrust (fencing term).
Mercutio suggests that Tybalt's attack has unarmed
Romeo.
25. **rat-catcher.** Reference to his name
26. **walk.** Leave the premises

27. **as . . . hereafter.** Depending on how you treat me in
the future
28. **dry-beat.** Beat up (without drawing blood)
29. **his pilcher.** Its sheath
30. **by the ears.** Implying that the sword resists being
unsheathed
31. **passado.** Thrust
32. **bandying.** Fighting

WORDS FOR EVERYDAY USE: sub • mis • sion (sub mish´ ən) *n.,* yielding or surrendering

A plague a' both houses! I am sped.[33]
Is he gone and hath nothing?

80 **BENVOLIO.**   What, art thou hurt?

MERCUTIO.   Ay, ay, a scratch,[34] a scratch, marry, 'tis enough.
Where is my page? Go, villain,[35] fetch a surgeon.   *Exit* PAGE.

ROMEO.   Courage, man, the hurt cannot be much.

MERCUTIO.   No, 'tis not so deep as a well, nor so wide as a church-door,
85 but 'tis enough, 'twill serve. Ask for me tomorrow, and you shall find me
a grave man. I am pepper'd, I warrant, for this world. A <u>plague</u> a' both
your houses! 'Zounds, a dog, a rat, a mouse, a cat, to scratch a man to death!
a braggart, a rogue, a villain, that fights by the book of arithmetic! Why the
dev'l came you between us? I was hurt under your arm.

90 **ROMEO.**   I thought all for the best.

MERCUTIO.   Help me into some house, Benvolio,
Or I shall faint. A plague a' both your houses!
They have made worms' meat of me. I have it,
And soundly too. Your houses!
                    Exeunt MERCUTIO *and* BENVOLIO.

95 **ROMEO.**   This gentleman, the Prince's near ally,[36]
My very[37] friend, hath got this mortal hurt
In my behalf; my reputation stain'd
With Tybalt's slander—Tybalt, that an hour
Hath been my cousin! O sweet Juliet,
100 Thy beauty hath made me effeminate,
And in my temper[38] soft'ned <u>valor</u>'s steel!

Enter BENVOLIO.

BENVOLIO.   O Romeo, Romeo, brave Mercutio is dead!
That gallant spirit hath aspir'd[39] the clouds,
Which too untimely here did scorn the earth.

105 **ROMEO.**   This day's black fate on moe days doth depend,[40]
This but begins the woe others must end.

Enter TYBALT.

BENVOLIO.   Here comes the furious Tybalt back again.

*What news does
Benvolio bring of
Mercutio?*

---

33. **sped.** Spent, finished
34. **a scratch.** Another reference to Tybalt's name
35. **villain.** Person of lower class; boy
36. **ally.** Relative

37. **very.** Absolute
38. **temper.** Nature
39. **aspir'd.** Ascended to
40. **on . . . depend.** Affects days in the future

WORDS FOR
EVERYDAY USE:

plague (plāg) *n.,* anything that afflicts or troubles

val • or (val´ər) *n.,* marked courage or bravery

ROMEO.   He gone in triumph, and Mercutio slain!
Away to heaven, respective[41] lenity,
110   And fire-ey'd fury be my conduct[42] now!
Now, Tybalt, take the "villain" back again
That late thou gavest me, for Mercutio's soul
Is but a little way above our heads,
Staying for thine to keep him company.
115   Either thou or I, or both, must go with him.

TYBALT.   Thou wretched boy, that didst consort him here,
Shalt with him hence.

ROMEO.   This shall determine that.

They fight; TYBALT *falls.*

BENVOLIO.   Romeo, away, be gone!
The citizens are up,[43] and Tybalt slain.
120   Stand not amazed,[44] the Prince will doom thee death
If thou art taken. Hence be gone, away!

ROMEO.   O, I am fortune's fool!

BENVOLIO.   Why dost thou stay?   *Exit* ROMEO.

Enter CITIZENS.

1. CITIZEN.   Which way ran he that kill'd Mercutio?
Tybalt, that murtherer, which way ran he?

BENVOLIO.   There lies that Tybalt.

125   **1. CITIZEN.**   Up, sir, go with me;
I charge thee in the Prince's name, obey.

Enter PRINCE, *old* MONTAGUE, CAPULET, *their* WIVES, *and all.*

PRINCE.   Where are the vile beginners of this fray?

BENVOLIO.   O noble Prince, I can discover[45] all
The unlucky manage[46] of this fatal brawl:
130   There lies the man, slain by young Romeo,
That slew thy kinsman brave Mercutio.

LADY CAPULET.   Tybalt, my cousin! O my brother's child!
O Prince! O husband! O, the blood is spill'd
Of my dear kinsman! Prince, as thou art true,
135   For blood of ours, shed blood of Montague.
O cousin, cousin!

PRINCE.   Benvolio, who began this bloody fray?

---

41. **respective.** Thoughtful
42. **conduct.** Guide
43. **up.** Have taken arms
44. **amazed.** Bewildered, astounded
45. **discover.** Uncover, divulge
46. **manage.** Process

Why does Romeo challenge Tybalt?

Why must Romeo escape?

What does Lady Capulet demand?

BENVOLIO. Tybalt, here slain, whom Romeo's hand did slay!
Romeo that spoke him fair, bid him bethink
How nice[47] the quarrel was, and urg'd withal
Your high displeasure; all this, uttered
With gentle breath, calm look, knees humbly bowed,
Could not take truce with the unruly spleen
Of Tybalt deaf to peace, but that he tilts
With piercing steel at bold Mercutio's breast,
Who, all as hot, turns deadly point to point,
And, with a martial scorn, with one hand beats
Cold death aside, and with the other sends
It back to Tybalt, whose <u>dexterity</u>
Retorts it. Romeo he cries aloud,
"Hold, friends! friends, part!" and swifter than his tongue,
His <u>agile</u> arm beats down their fatal points,
And 'twixt them rushes; underneath whose arm
An envious[48] thrust from Tybalt hit the life
Of stout[49] Mercutio, and then Tybalt fled;
But by and by comes back to Romeo,
Who had but newly entertain'd[50] revenge,
And to't they go like lightning, for, ere I
Could draw to part them, was stout Tybalt slain;
And as he fell, did Romeo turn and fly.
This is the truth, or let Benvolio die.

LADY CAPULET. He is a kinsman to the Montague,
Affection makes him false, he speaks not true.
Some twenty of them fought in this black strife,
And all those twenty could but kill one life.
I beg for justice, which thou, Prince, must give:
Romeo slew Tybalt, Romeo must not live.

PRINCE. Romeo slew him, he slew Mercutio;
Who now the price of his dear blood doth owe?

MONTAGUE. Not Romeo, Prince, he was Mercutio's friend;
His fault concludes but what the law should end,
The life of Tybalt.

PRINCE. And for that offense

---

47. **nice.** Slight
48. **envious.** Spiteful
49. **stout.** Brave
50. **entertain'd.** Considered

WORDS FOR EVERYDAY USE:

dex • ter • i • ty (deks ter´ə tē) *n.*, skill in using one's hands or body

ag • ile (aj´əl) *adj.*, quick and easy of movement

What is Romeo's
punishment?
What could it
have been?

Immediately we do exile him hence.
I have an interest[51] in your heart's proceeding;
175   My blood[52] for your rude brawls doth lie a-bleeding;
But I'll amerce[53] you with so strong a fine
That you shall all repent the loss of mine.
I will be deaf to pleading and excuses,
Nor tears nor prayers shall purchase out[54] abuses;
180   Therefore use none. Let Romeo hence in haste,
Else, when he is found, that hour is his last.
Bear hence this body and attend our will;[55]
Mercy but murders,[56] pardoning those that kill.   *Exeunt.*

SCENE ii: Capulet's house

Enter JULIET *alone.*

JULIET.   Gallop apace, you fiery-footed steeds,[1]
Towards Phoebus' lodging;[2] such a waggoner
As Phaëton[3] would whip you to the west,
And bring in cloudy night immediately.
5   Spread thy close[4] curtain, love-performing night,
That th' runaway's[5] eyes may wink,[6] and Romeo
Leap to these arms untalk'd of and unseen!
Lovers can see to do their amorous rites
By their own beauties, or, if love be blind,
10   It best agrees with night. Come, civil[7] night,
Thou sober-suited matron all in black,
And learn me how to lose a winning match,
Play'd for a pair of stainless maidenhoods.
Hood[8] my unmann'd blood, bating[9] in my cheeks,
15   With thy black mantle; till strange[10] love grow[11] bold,
Think true love acted simple modesty.[12]
Come, night, come, Romeo, come, thou day in night,

---

51. **interest.** Concern
52. **My blood.** Mercutio and the prince are related
53. **amerce.** Inflict a fine
54. **purchase out.** Make amends for
55. **attend our will.** Listen to my judgment
56. **murders.** Encourages future murders

ACT III, SCENE ii
1. **steeds.** Horses that pull the chariot of the sun-god
2. **Phoebus' lodging.** Beyond the western horizon
3. **Phaëton.** Phaëthon, son of the sun-god, who lost

control of the sun-chariot and was killed by Zeus
4. **close.** Protective
5. **runaway's.** Meaning unclear, possibly corrupt
6. **wink.** Close and so not see
7. **civil.** Solemn
8. **Hood.** Hide
9. **bating.** Beating
10. **strange.** Restrained
11. **grow.** Becomes
12. **modesty.** Virtuousness

WORDS FOR
EVERYDAY USE:

am • o • rous (am´ə res) *adj.,* relating to love
ma • tron (mā´ trən) *n.,* married woman or widow

For thou wilt lie upon the wings of night,
Whiter than new snow upon a raven's back.
20 Come, gentle night, come, loving, black-brow'd night,
Give me my Romeo, and, when I shall die,
Take him and cut him out in little stars,
And he will make the face of heaven so fine
That all the world will be in love with night,
25 And pay no worship to the garish sun.
O, I have bought the mansion of a love,
But not possess'd it, and though I am sold,
Not yet enjoy'd. So tedious is this day
As is the night before some festival
30 To an impatient child that hath new robes
And may not wear them. O, here comes my nurse,

Enter NURSE *wringing her hands, with the ladder of cords in her lap.*

And she brings news; and every tongue that speaks
But Romeo's name speaks heavenly <u>eloquence</u>.
Now, nurse, what news? What hast thou there? the cords
That Romeo bid thee fetch?

35 **NURSE.**   Ay, ay, the cords.   *Throws them down.*

JULIET.   Ay me, what news? Why dost thou wring thy hands?

NURSE.   Ah, weraday,[13] he's dead, he's dead, he's dead!
We are undone, lady, we are undone!
Alack the day, he's gone, he's kill'd, he's dead!

JULIET.   Can heaven be so envious?[14]

40 **NURSE.**   Romeo can,
Though heaven cannot. O Romeo, Romeo!
Who ever would have thought it? Romeo!

JULIET.   What devil art thou that dost torment me thus?
This torture should be roar'd in dismal hell.
45 Hath Romeo slain himself? Say thou but ay,
And that bare vowel *I* shall poison more
Than the death-darting eye of cockatrice.[15]
I am not I, if there be such an ay,

What misunderstanding occurs with the Nurse's words?

---

13. **weraday.** Pity
14. **envious.** Spiteful
15. **cockatrice.** Basilisk, mythical serpent that could kill
with a glance

WORDS FOR   **el • o • quence** (el′ə kwəns) *n.,* speech or writing that is vivid,
EVERYDAY USE: forceful, and persuasive

Or those eyes shut,[16] that makes thee answer ay.
50 If he be slain, say ay, or if not, no.
Brief sounds determine my weal or woe.[17]

NURSE. I saw the wound, I saw it with mine eyes—
God save the mark![18]—here on his manly breast.
A <u>piteous</u> corse,[19] a bloody piteous corse,
55 Pale, pale as ashes, all bedaub'd in blood,
All in gore blood; I sounded[20] at the sight.

JULIET. O, break, my heart, poor bankrout,[21] break at once!
To prison, eyes, ne'er look on liberty!
Vile earth,[22] to earth resign,[23] end motion here,
60 And thou and Romeo press one heavy <u>bier</u>!

NURSE. O Tybalt, Tybalt, the best friend I had!
O courteous Tybalt, honest gentleman,
That ever I should live to see thee dead!

JULIET. What storm is this that blows so contrary?
65 Is Romeo slaught'red? and is Tybalt dead?
My dearest cousin, and my dearer lord?
Then, dreadful trumpet,[24] sound the general doom,
For who is living, if those two are gone?

NURSE. Tybalt is gone, and Romeo banished,
70 Romeo that kill'd him, he is banished.

JULIET. O God, did Romeo's hand shed Tybalt's blood?

NURSE. It did, it did, alas the day, it did!

JULIET. O serpent heart, hid with a flow'ring[25] face!
Did ever dragon keep[26] so fair a cave?
75 Beautiful tyrant! fiend angelical!
Dove-feather'd raven! wolvish ravening lamb!
Despised substance[27] of divinest show![28]
Just opposite to what thou justly seem'st,[29]
A damned saint, an honorable villain!

---

16. **Or . . . shut.** If Romeo dies
17. **determine . . . woe.** Decide whether I am happy or sad
18. **God . . . mark.** Expression used to ward off bad omens
19. **corse.** Dead body
20. **sounded.** Fainted
21. **bankrout.** Emptiness
22. **Vile earth.** Body
23. **resign.** Relinquish yourself

24. **trumpet.** Signal of Judgment Day
25. **flow'ring.** Young, attractive
26. **keep.** Reside in
27. **substance.** Contemptible being
28. **show.** Appearance
29. **Just . . . seem'st.** Exactly the opposite of what you appear to be

WORDS FOR EVERYDAY USE:

pit • e • ous (pit´ē əs) *adj.,* arousing or deserving pity or compassion

bier (bir) *n.,* coffin and its supporting platform

80 O nature, what hadst thou to do in hell
When thou didst bower[30] the spirit of a fiend
In mortal paradise of such sweet flesh?
Was ever book containing such vile matter
So fairly bound? O that deceit should dwell
In such a gorgeous palace!

85 **NURSE.**   There's no trust,
No faith, no honesty in men, all perjur'd,
All forsworn, all naught,[31] all <u>dissemblers.</u>
Ah, where's my man? Give me some aqua-vitae;[32]
These griefs, these woes, these sorrows make me old.
Shame come to Romeo!

90 **JULIET.**   Blister'd be thy tongue
For such a wish! he was not born to shame:
Upon his brow shame is asham'd to sit;
For 'tis a throne where honor may be crown'd
Sole <u>monarch</u> of the universal earth.

95 O, what a beast was I to chide at him!

NURSE.   Will you speak well of him that kill'd your cousin?

JULIET.   Shall I speak ill of him that is my husband?
Ah, poor my lord, what tongue shall smooth thy name,
When I, thy three-hours wife, have mangled it?

100 But wherefore, villain, didst thou kill my cousin?
That villain cousin would have kill'd my husband.
Back, foolish tears, back to your native spring,
Your tributary drops belong to woe,[33]
Which you, mistaking, offer up to joy.[34]

105 My husband lives that Tybalt would have slain,
And Tybalt's dead that would have slain my husband.
All this is comfort, wherefore weep I then?
Some word there was, worser than Tybalt's death,
That murd'red me; I would forget it fain,

110 But O, it presses to my memory
Like damned guilty deeds to sinners' minds:
"Tybalt is dead, and Romeo banished."

*What does Juliet
do when the
Nurse wishes
harm to Romeo?*

---

30. **bower.** Enclose
31. **naught.** Evil
32. **aqua-vitae.** Strong liquor
33. **belong to woe.** Indicate sadness
34. **joy.** Romeo's survival

WORDS FOR
EVERYDAY USE:

dis • sem • bler (di sem´bəlir) *n.*, pretender

mon • arch (män´ərk) *n.*, ruler

That "banished," that one word "banished,"
Hath slain ten thousand Tybalts. Tybalt's death

115 Was woe enough if it had ended there;
Or if sour woe delights in fellowship,
And needly[35] will be rank'd[36] with other griefs,
Why followed not, when she said, "Tybalt's dead,"
Thy father or thy mother, nay, or both,

120 Which modern[37] lamentation might have moved?
But with a rearward[38] following Tybalt's death,
"Romeo is banished," to speak that word,
Is father, mother, Tybalt, Romeo, Juliet,
All slain, all dead: "Romeo is banished"!

125 There is no end, no limit, measure, bound,
In that word's death, no words can that woe sound.[39]
Where is my father and my mother, nurse?

NURSE.   Weeping and wailing over Tybalt's corse.
Will you go to them? I will bring you thither.

130 **JULIET.**   Wash they his wounds with tears? Mine shall be spent,
When theirs are dry, for Romeo's banishment.
Take up those cords. Poor ropes, you are beguil'd,[40]
Both you and I, for Romeo is exil'd.
He made you for a highway to my bed,

135 But I, a maid, die maiden-widowed.
Come, cords, come, nurse, I'll to my wedding-bed,
And death, not Romeo, take my maidenhead!

NURSE.   Hie to your chamber. I'll find Romeo
To comfort you, I wot[41] well where he is.

140 Hark ye, your Romeo will be here at night.
I'll to him, he is hid at Lawrence' cell.

JULIET.   O, find him! Give this ring to my true knight,
And bid him come to take his last farewell.   *Exeunt.*

Why does the Nurse promise to find Romeo?

---

35. **needly.** Inevitably
36. **rank'd.** Grouped
37. **modern.** Customary
38. **rearward.** Rear guard
39. **sound.** Define; measure
40. **beguil'd.** Deceived
41. **wot.** Know

WORDS FOR
EVERYDAY USE:

lam • en • ta • tion (lam´ən tā´shən) *n.,* outward expression of grief

cham • ber (chām´bər) *n.,* room in a house

SCENE iii: Friar Lawrence's cell

Enter FRIAR LAWRENCE.

FRIAR LAWRENCE.   Romeo, come forth, come forth, thou fearful[1] man:
Affliction is enamor'd of thy parts,[2]
And thou art wedded to <u>calamity</u>.

Enter ROMEO.

ROMEO.   Father, what news? What is the Prince's doom?[3]
5   What sorrow craves acquaintance at my hand,
That I yet know not?

FRIAR LAWRENCE.   Too familiar
Is my dear son with such sour company!
I bring thee tidings of the Prince's doom.

ROMEO.   What less than dooms-day[4] is the Prince's doom?

10   **FRIAR LAWRENCE.**   A gentler judgment vanish'd[5] from his lips—
Not body's death, but body's banishment.

ROMEO.   Ha, banishment? Be merciful, say "death";
For exile hath more terror in his look,
Much more than death. Do not say "banishment"!

15   **FRIAR LAWRENCE.**   Here from Verona art thou banished.
Be patient,[6] for the world is broad and wide.

ROMEO.   There is no world without[7] Verona walls,
But purgatory, torture, hell itself.
Hence "banished" is banish'd from the world,
20   And world's exile[8] is death; then "banished"
Is death misterm'd. Calling death "banished,"
Thou cut'st my head off with a golden axe,
And smilest upon the stroke that murders me.

FRIAR LAWRENCE.   O deadly sin! O rude unthankfulness!
25   Thy fault our law calls death,[9] but the kind Prince,
Taking thy part, hath rush'd[10] aside the law,
And turn'd that black word "death" to "banishment."
This is dear[11] mercy, and thou seest it not.

What does Friar Lawrence think of the prince's sentence?

ACT III, SCENE iii
1. **fearful.** Frightened
2. **parts.** Traits
3. **doom.** Fate, outcome
4. **dooms-day.** Death
5. **vanish'd.** Uttered without possibility of recall
6. **Be patient.** Calm yourself
7. **without.** Beyond
8. **world's exile.** Banishment from the world
9. **death.** Capital offense
10. **rush'd.** Pushed
11. **dear.** Unusual

WORDS FOR
EVERYDAY USE: ca • lam • i • ty (kə lam´ə tē) *n.*, disaster, misery

Why does Romeo think banishment is worse than death?

ROMEO.   'Tis torture, and not mercy. Heaven is here

30   Where Juliet lives, and every cat and dog
And little mouse, every unworthy thing,
Live here in heaven and may look on her,
But Romeo may not. More validity,[12]
More honorable state, more courtship[13] lives

35   In carrion flies than Romeo; they may seize
On the white wonder of dear Juliet's hand,
And steal immortal blessing from her lips,
Who, even in pure and vestal modesty
Still blush, as thinking their own kisses sin;

40   But Romeo may not, he is banished.
Flies may do this, but I from this must fly;
They are free men, but I am banished:
And sayest thou yet that exile is not death?
Hadst thou no poison mix'd, no sharp-ground knife,

45   No sudden mean of death, though ne'er so mean,[14]
But "banished" to kill me? "Banished"?
O friar, the damned use that word in hell;
Howling attends it. How hast thou the heart,
Being a divine, a ghostly confessor,

50   A sin-absolver, and my friend profess'd,
To mangle me with that word "banished"?

FRIAR LAWRENCE.   Thou fond[15] mad man, hear me a little speak.

ROMEO.   O, thou wilt speak again of banishment.

FRIAR LAWRENCE.   I'll give thee armor to keep off that word:

55   Adversity's sweet milk, philosophy,
To comfort thee though thou art banished.

ROMEO.   Yet "banished"? Hang up philosophy!
Unless philosophy can make a Juliet,
Displant[16] a town, reverse a prince's doom,

60   It helps not, it prevails not.[17] Talk no more.

FRIAR LAWRENCE.   O then I see that madmen have no ears.

ROMEO.   How should they when that wise men have no eyes?

FRIAR LAWRENCE.   Let me dispute[18] with thee of thy estate.[19]

---

12. **validity.** Honor, worth
13. **courtship.** Courtliness
14. **mean . . . mean.** Means . . . ignoble
15. **fond.** Naïve

16. **Displant.** Relocate
17. **prevails not.** Has no effect
18. **dispute.** Talk
19. **estate.** Situation

WORDS FOR
EVERYDAY USE:

car • ri • on (kar´ē ən) *n.*, decaying flesh of a dead body when regarded as food for scavenging animals

ad • ver • si • ty (ad vʉr´sə tē) *n.*, wretchedness or misfortune

ROMEO.   Thou canst not speak of that thou dost not feel.

65 Wert thou as young as I, Juliet thy love,
An hour but married, Tybalt murdered,
Doting like me, and like me banished,
Then mightst thou speak, then mightst thou tear thy hair,
And fall upon the ground, as I do now,
70 Taking the measure of an unmade grave.

Enter NURSE *within and knock.*

FRIAR LAWRENCE.   Arise, one knocks. Good Romeo, hide thyself.

ROMEO.   Not I, unless the breath of heart-sick groans
Mist-like infold me from the search of eyes.   *Knock.*

FRIAR LAWRENCE.   Hark how they knock!—Who's there?—
75 Romeo, arise,
Thou wilt be taken.—Stay a while![20]—Stand up;   *Loud knock.*
Run to my study.—By and by!—God's will,
What simpleness[21] is this?—I come, I come!   *Knock.*
Who knocks so hard? Whence come you? What's your will?

80 **NURSE.**   [*Within.*] Let me come in, and you shall know my errant.[22]
I come from Lady Juliet.

FRIAR LAWRENCE.   Welcome then.   *Unlocks the door.*

Enter NURSE.

NURSE.   O holy friar, O, tell me, holy friar,
Where's my lady's lord? where's Romeo?

FRIAR LAWRENCE.   There on the ground, with his own tears made drunk.

85 **NURSE.**   O, he is even in my mistress' case,
Just in her case. O woeful sympathy![23]
Piteous predicament! Even so lies she,
Blubb'ring and weeping, weeping and blubb'ring.
Stand up, stand up, stand, and you be a man.
90 For Juliet's sake, for her sake, rise and stand;
Why should you fall into so deep an O?[24]

ROMEO.   Nurse!   *He rises.*

NURSE.   Ah sir, ah sir, death's the end of all.

ROMEO.   Spakest thou of Juliet? How is it with her?
95 Doth not she think me an old[25] murtherer,
Now I have stain'd the childhood of our joy
With blood removed but little from her own?
Where is she? and how doth she? and what says
My conceal'd lady[26] to our cancell'd love?

How do the Nurse and Friar Lawrence compare the actions of Romeo and Juliet?

---

20. **Stay a while.** Wait
21. **simpleness.** Absurdity
22. **errant.** Purpose
23. **sympathy.** Piteous suffering

24. **O.** State of despair
25. **old.** Experienced
26. **conceal'd lady.** Secret wife

NURSE. 100   O, she says nothing, sir, but weeps and weeps,
And now falls on her bed, and then starts up,
And Tybalt calls, and then on Romeo cries,
And then down falls again.

ROMEO.   As if that name,
Shot from the deadly level[27] of a gun,
105   Did murther her, as that name's cursed hand
Murder'd her kinsman. O, tell me, friar, tell me,
In what vile part of this anatomy
Doth my name lodge? Tell me, that I may sack
The hateful mansion.

He offers to stab himself, and the NURSE *snatches the dagger away.*

FRIAR LAWRENCE.   Hold thy desperate hand!

What frightens Friar Lawrence?

110   Art thou a man? Thy form cries out thou art;
Thy tears are womanish, thy wild acts <u>denote</u>
The unreasonable[28] fury of a beast.
Unseemly woman[29] in a seeming man,
And ill-beseeming beast in seeming both,
115   Thou hast amaz'd me! By my holy order,
I thought thy <u>disposition</u> better temper'd.[30]
Hast thou slain Tybalt? Wilt thou slay thyself,
And slay thy lady that in thy life lives,
By doing damned hate upon thyself?
120   Why railest thou on thy birth? the heaven and earth?[31]
Since birth, and heaven, and earth, all three do meet
In thee at once, which thou at once wouldst lose.
Fie, fie, thou shamest thy shape, thy love, thy wit,[32]
Which[33] like a usurer[34] abound'st in all,
125   And usest none in that true use indeed
Which should bedeck thy shape, thy love, thy wit.
Thy noble shape is but a form of wax,[35]
Digressing from the valor of a man;
Thy dear love sworn but hollow perjury,
130   Killing that love which thou hast vow'd to cherish;
Thy wit, that ornament to shape and love,

---

27. **level.** Aim
28. **unreasonable.** Irrational
29. **Unseemly woman.** Romeo's behavior is like that of a woman who offends good taste.
30. **temper'd.** Composed; controlled

31. **heaven and earth.** Soul and body
32. **wit.** Mind
33. **Which.** Who
34. **usurer.** One who misuses possessions
35. **form of wax.** Lifeless figure

WORDS FOR EVERYDAY USE:

de • note (dē nōt´) *vt.,* indicate
dis • po • si • tion (dis´pə zish´ən) *n.,* one's customary frame of mind

Misshapen[36] in the conduct[37] of them both,
Like powder in a skilless soldier's flask,[38]
Is set afire by thine own ignorance,
135   And thou dismemb'red with thine own defense.
What, rouse thee, man! thy Juliet is alive,
For whose dear sake thou wast but lately dead:
There art thou happy.[39] Tybalt would kill thee,
But thou slewest Tybalt: there art thou happy.
140   The law that threat'ned death becomes thy friend,
And turns it to exile: there art thou happy.
A pack of blessings light upon thy back,
Happiness courts thee in her best array,
But like a mishaved[40] and sullen wench,
145   Thou pouts upon thy fortune and thy love.
Take heed, take heed, for such die miserable.
Go get thee to thy love as was decreed,[41]
Ascend her chamber, hence and comfort her.
But look thou stay not till the watch be set,[42]
150   For then thou canst not pass to Mantua,
Where thou shalt live till we can find a time
To blaze[43] your marriage, reconcile your friends,[44]
Beg pardon of the Prince, and call thee back
With twenty hundred thousand times more joy
155   Than thou went'st forth in lamentation.
Go before, nurse; commend me to thy lady,
And bid her hasten all the house to bed,
Which heavy sorrow makes them apt unto.
Romeo is coming.

160   **NURSE.**   O Lord, I could have stay'd here all the night
To hear good counsel. O, what learning is!
My lord, I'll tell my lady you will come.

ROMEO.   Do so, and bid my sweet prepare to chide.

NURSE *offers to go in, and turns again.*

NURSE.   Here, sir, a ring she bid me give you, sir.
165   Hie you, make haste, for it grows very late.

For what should
Romeo be
grateful?

---

36. **Misshapen.** Badly trained
37. **conduct.** Use
38. **flask.** Powder horn
39. **happy.** Lucky
40. **mishaved.** Misbehaved

41. **decreed.** Ordered
42. **watch be set.** Guard is posted
43. **blaze.** Announce
44. **friends.** Family

WORDS FOR
EVERYDAY USE: **as • cend** (ə send´) *vt.,* move upward along; mount; climb; rise

ROMEO.   How well my comfort is reviv'd by this!

Exit NURSE.

FRIAR LAWRENCE.   Go hence, good night; and here stands all your state:[45]
Either be gone before the watch be set,
Or by the break of day disguis'd from hence.
170 Sojourn in Mantua. I'll find out your man,
And he shall signify from time to time
Every good hap to you that chances here.
Give me thy hand. 'Tis late; farewell, good night.

ROMEO.   But that a joy past joy calls out on me,
175 It were a grief, so brief[46] to part with thee.
Farewell.

Exeunt.

SCENE iv: Capulet's house

Enter old CAPULET, *his* WIFE, *and* PARIS.

CAPULET.   Things have fall'n out, sir, so unluckily
That we have had no time to move our daughter.
Look you, she lov'd her kinsman Tybalt dearly,
And so did I. Well, we were born to die.
5 'Tis very late, she'll not come down to-night.
I promise you, but for your company,
I would have been a-bed an hour ago.

PARIS.   These times of woe afford no times to woo.
Madam, good night, commend me to your daughter.

10 **LADY CAPULET.**   I will, and know her mind early tomorrow;
To-night she's mewed up to[1] her heaviness.[2]

PARIS *offers to go in, and* CAPULET *calls him again.*

CAPULET.   Sir Paris, I will make a desperate tender[3]
Of my child's love. I think she will be rul'd
In all respects by me; nay more, I doubt it not.
15 Wife, go you to her ere you go to bed,
Acquaint her here of my son Paris' love,
And bid her—mark you me?—on We'n'sday next—
But soft, what day is this?

PARIS.   Monday, my lord.

CAPULET.   Monday! ha, ha![4] Well, We'n'sday is too soon,
20 A'[5] Thursday let it be—a' Thursday, tell her,

---

45. **here . . . state.** Your situation is this
46. **brief.** Quickly
ACT III, SCENE iv
  1. **mewed up to.** Shut up with (falconry term)

2. **heaviness.** Sadness
3. **desperate tender.** Daring offer
4. **ha, ha.** Sound he mutters as he thinks
5. **A'.** On

She shall be married to this noble earl.
Will you be ready? do you like this haste?
We'll keep no great ado—a friend or two,
For hark you, Tybalt being slain so late,
25 It may be thought we held him carelessly,
Being our kinsman, if we revel much:
Therefore we'll have some half a dozen friends,
And there an end. But what say you to Thursday?

PARIS.   My lord, I would that Thursday were tomorrow.

30 **CAPULET.**   Well, get you gone, a' Thursday be it then.—
Go you to Juliet ere you go to bed,
Prepare her, wife, against[6] this wedding-day.
Farewell, my lord. Light to my chamber ho!
Afore me,[7] it is so very late that we
35 May call it early by and by. Good night.

What does Capulet tell Paris?

Exeunt.

SCENE v: Capulet's orchard

Enter ROMEO *and* JULIET *aloft at the window.*

JULIET.   Wilt thou be gone? it is not yet near day.
It was the <u>nightingale</u>, and not the lark,
That pierc'd the fearful hollow of thine ear;
Nightly she sings on yond <u>pomegranate</u> tree.
5 Believe me, love, it was the nightingale.

ROMEO.   It was the lark, the herald of the morn,
No nightingale. Look, love, what envious streaks
Do lace the severing clouds in yonder east.
Night's candles are burnt out, and jocund day
10 Stands tiptoe on the misty mountain tops.
I must be gone and live, or stay and die.

JULIET.   Yond light is not day-light, I know it, I;
It is some meteor that the sun exhal'd[1]
To be to thee this night a torch-bearer
15 And light thee on thy way to Mantua.
Therefore stay yet, thou need'st not to be gone.

---

6. **against.** For
7. **Afore me.** I say

ACT III, SCENE v
1. **exhal'd.** Meteors were believed to be vapors from earth that were ignited by the sun's heat.

WORDS FOR EVERYDAY USE:

night • in • gale (nīt´'n gāl) *n.,* reddish-brown songbird noted for the sweet song of the male

pome • gran • ate (päm´gran´it) *n.,* round fruit with a red, leathery rind and many seeds covered with red, juicy, edible flesh

ROMEO. Let me be ta'en, let me be put to death,
I am content, so thou wilt have it so.
I'll say yon grey is not the morning's eye,
20 'Tis but the pale reflex[2] of Cynthia's[3] brow;
Nor that is not the lark whose notes do beat
The vaulty heaven so high above our heads.
I have more care[4] to stay than will to go.
Come, death, and welcome! Juliet wills it so.
25 How is't, my soul? Let's talk, it is not day.

JULIET. It is, it is! Hie hence, be gone, away!
It is the lark that sings so out of tune,
Straining harsh <u>discords</u> and unpleasing sharps.[5]
Some say the lark makes sweet division;[6]
30 This doth not so, for she divideth us.
Some say the lark and loathed toad change[7] eyes;
O now I would they had chang'd voices too,
Since arm from arm[8] that voice doth us affray,[9]
Hunting thee hence with hunt's-up[10] to the day.
35 O now be gone, more light and light it grows.

ROMEO. More light and light, more dark and dark our woes!

Enter NURSE *hastily.*

NURSE. Madam!

JULIET. Nurse?

NURSE. Your lady mother is coming to your chamber.
40 The day is broke, be wary, look about.   *Exit.*

JULIET. Then, window, let day in, and let life out.

ROMEO. Farewell, farewell! One kiss, and I'll descend.   *He goeth down.*

JULIET. Art thou gone so, love, lord, ay, husband, friend![11]
I must hear from thee every day in the hour,
45 For in a minute there are many days.
O, by this count I shall be much in years[12]
Ere I again behold my Romeo!

---

2. **reflex.** Reflection
3. **Cynthia's.** The moon's
4. **care.** Wish
5. **sharps.** High-pitched sounds
6. **division.** Melodic variations
7. **change.** Exchange

8. **arm from arm.** From each other's arms
9. **affray.** Startle, scare
10. **hunt's-up.** Song to waken hunters
11. **friend.** Dear one, sweetheart
12. **much in years.** Old

WORDS FOR
EVERYDAY USE: **dis • cord** (dis´kôrds) *n.,* lack of harmony in tones sounded
together

ROMEO.   [*From below.*] Farewell!
I will omit no opportunity
50   That may convey my greetings, love, to thee.

JULIET.   O, think'st thou we shall ever meet again?

ROMEO.   I doubt it not, and all these woes shall serve
For sweet discourses in our times to come.

JULIET.   O God, I have an ill-divining[13] soul!
55   Methinks I see thee now, thou art so low,
As one dead in the bottom of a tomb.
Either my eyesight fails, or thou lookest pale.

ROMEO.   And trust me, love, in my eye so do you;
Dry sorrow drinks our blood.[14] Adieu, adieu!   *Exit.*

60   **JULIET.**   O Fortune, Fortune, all men call thee fickle;
If thou art fickle, what dost thou[15] with him
That is renown'd for faith? Be fickle, Fortune:
For then I hope thou wilt not keep him long,
But send him back.

LADY CAPULET.   [*Within.*] Ho, daughter, are you up?

65   **JULIET.**   Who is't that calls? It is my lady mother.
Is she not down[16] so late, or up so early?
What unaccustom'd cause procures her hither?
                                 She goeth down from the window.[17]

Enter Mother LADY CAPULET.

LADY CAPULET.   Why, how now, Juliet?

JULIET.   Madam, I am not well.

LADY CAPULET.   Evermore weeping for your cousin's death?
70   What, wilt thou wash him from his grave with tears?
And if thou couldst, thou couldst not make him live;
Therefore have done. Some grief shows much of love,
But much of grief shows still some want of wit.

JULIET.   Yet let me weep for such a feeling[18] loss.

75   **LADY CAPULET.**   So shall you feel the loss, but not the friend
Which you weep for.

JULIET.   Feeling so the loss,
I cannot choose but ever weep the friend.

LADY CAPULET.   Well, girl, thou weep'st not so much for his death,
As that the villain lives which slaughter'd him.

What does Lady Capulet believe is causing Juliet's sorrow?

---

13. **ill-divining.** Sensing evil
14. **Dry . . . blood.** Sorrow was thought to deplete the blood.
15. **what dost thou.** What do you have to do
16. **not down.** Still awake

17. **She . . . window.** Apparently she descends and re-enters the main stage, which is no longer the garden but a room in the house.
18. **feeling.** Deep

JULIET.   What villain, madam?

80   LADY CAPULET.   That same villain Romeo.

JULIET.   [*Aside.*] Villain and he be many miles <u>asunder</u>.—
God pardon him! I do with all my heart;
And yet no man like[19] he doth grieve my heart.

LADY CAPULET.   That is because the traitor murderer lives.

85   JULIET.   Ay, madam, from the reach of these my hands.
Would none but I might venge my cousin's death!

LADY CAPULET.   We will have vengeance for it, fear thou not.
Then weep no more. I'll send to one in Mantua,
Where that same banish'd runagate[20] doth live,
90   Shall give him such an unaccustom'd dram
That he shall soon keep Tybalt company;
And then I hope thou wilt be satisfied.

JULIET.   Indeed I never shall be satisfied
With Romeo, till I behold him—dead—
95   Is my poor heart, so for a kinsman vex'd.
Madam, if you could find out but a man
To bear a poison, I would temper[21] it,
That Romeo should, upon receipt thereof,
Soon sleep in quiet. O how my heart <u>abhors</u>
100   To hear him nam'd, and cannot come to him
To wreak the love I bore my cousin
Upon his body that[22] hath slaughter'd him!

LADY CAPULET.   Find thou the means, and I'll find such a man.
But now I'll tell thee joyful tidings, girl.

105   JULIET.   And joy comes well in such a needy time.
What are they, beseech your ladyship?

LADY CAPULET.   Well, well, thou hast a careful[23] father, child,
One who, to put thee from thy heaviness,
Hath sorted out a sudden[24] day of joy,
110   That thou expects not, nor I look'd not for.

JULIET.   Madam, in happy time, what day is that?

LADY CAPULET.   Marry, my child, early next Thursday morn,

What does Lady Capulet plan for Romeo? Why?

What does Juliet mean? What does her mother think she means?

Why does Juliet's father plan joy for her?

---

19. **like.** So much as
20. **runagate.** Renegade
21. **temper.** Prepare

22. **his body that.** Body of the person who
23. **careful.** Caring
24. **sudden.** Fast-approaching

The gallant, young, and noble gentleman,
The County Paris, at Saint Peter's Church,
115 Shall happily make thee there a joyful bride.

    JULIET.   Now, by Saint Peter's Church and Peter too,
He shall not make me there a joyful bride.
I wonder at this haste, that I must wed
Ere he that should be husband comes to woo.
120 I pray you tell my lord and father, madam,
I will not marry yet, and when I do, I swear
It shall be Romeo, whom you know I hate,
Rather than Paris. These are news indeed!

    LADY CAPULET.   Here comes your father, tell him so yourself;
125 And see how he will take it at your hands.

    Enter CAPULET *and* NURSE.

    CAPULET.   When the sun sets, the earth doth drizzle dew,
But for the sunset of my brother's son
It rains downright.
How now, a conduit,[25] girl? What, still in tears?
130 Evermore show'ring? In one little body
Thou counterfeits a bark, a sea, a wind:
For still thy eyes, which I may call the sea,
Do ebb and flow with tears; the bark thy body is,
Sailing in this salt flood; the winds, thy sighs,
135 Who, raging with thy tears, and they with them,
Without a sudden calm,[26] will overset
Thy tempest-tossed body. How now, wife?
Have you delivered to her our decree?

    LADY CAPULET.   Ay, sir, but she will none, she gives you thanks.[27]
140 I would the fool were married to her grave!

    CAPULET.   Soft, take me with you, take me with you,[28] wife.
How, will she none? Doth she not give us thanks?
Is she not proud?[29] Doth she not count her blest,
Unworthy as she is, that we have wrought[30]
145 So worthy a gentleman to be her bride?[31]

    JULIET.   Not proud you have, but thankful[32] that you have.
Proud can I never be of what I hate,
But thankful even for hate that is meant love.

    CAPULET.   How how, how how, chopp'd logic![33] What is this?
150 "Proud," and "I thank you," and "I thank you not,"

What response does Lady Capulet give to Juliet's refusal to wed Paris?

---

25. **conduit.** Fountain
26. **Without . . . calm.** Unless they stop soon
27. **but . . . thanks.** She declines with thanks.
28. **take . . . you.** Tell me what you mean
29. **proud.** Happy

30. **wrought.** Obtained
31. **bride.** Bridegroom
32. **thankful.** Politely grateful
33. **chopp'd logic.** Misleading but clever argument

And yet "not proud," mistress minion[34] you?
Thank me no thankings, nor proud me no prouds,
But fettle[35] your fine joints 'gainst Thursday next,
To go with Paris to Saint Peter's Church,
155   Or I will drag thee on a hurdle[36] thither.
Out,[37] you green-sickness[38] carrion! Out, you baggage![39]
You tallow-face!

LADY CAPULET.   Fie, fie, what, are you mad?

JULIET.   Good father, I beseech you on my knees,
Hear me with patience but to speak a word.   *She kneels down.*

160   **CAPULET.**   Hang thee, young baggage! disobedient wretch!
I tell thee what: get thee to church a' Thursday,
Or never after look me in the face.
Speak not, reply not, do not answer me!
My fingers itch. Wife, we scarce thought us blest
165   That God had lent us but this only child,
But now I see this one is one too much,
And that we have a curse in having her.
Out on her, hilding!

NURSE.   God in heaven bless her!
You are to blame, my lord, to rate[40] her so.

170   **CAPULET.**   And why, my Lady Wisdom? Hold your tongue,
Good Prudence, smatter[41] with your gossips, go.

NURSE.   I speak no treason.

CAPULET.   O, God-i-goden![42]

NURSE.   May not one speak?

CAPULET.   Peace, you mumbling fool!
Utter your <u>gravity</u> o'er a gossip's bowl,
For here we need it not.

175   **LADY CAPULET.**   You are too hot.

CAPULET.   God's bread, it makes me mad! Day, night, work, play,
Alone, in company, still my care hath been
To have her match'd; and having now provided

What does Capulet think of Juliet's refusal?

---

34. **minion.** Spoiled child
35. **fettle.** Ready (a stable term)
36. **hurdle.** Sled on which prisoners were taken
37. **Out.** Rebuke
38. **green-sickness.** Pale

39. **baggage.** Worthless being
40. **rate.** Scold
41. **smatter.** Talk constantly
42. **God-i-goden.** Exclamation of impatience meaning "for God's sake"

WORDS FOR EVERYDAY USE:
grav • i • ty (grav´i tē) *n.*, danger or threat

A gentleman of noble parentage,
180 Of fair demesnes,[43] youthful and nobly lien'd,[44]
Stuff'd, as they say, with honorable parts,
Proportion'd as one's thought would wish a man,
And then to have a wretched puling fool,
A whining mammet,[45] in her fortune's tender,[46]
185 To answer, "I'll not wed, I cannot love;
I am too young, I pray you pardon me."
But and you will not wed, I'll pardon you.
Graze where you will, you shall not house with me.
Look to't, think on't, I do not use[47] to jest.
190 Thursday is near, lay hand on heart, advise.[48]
And you be mine, I'll give you to my friend;
And you be not, hang, beg, starve, die in the streets,
For, by my soul, I'll ne'er acknowledge thee,
Nor what is mine shall never do thee good.
195 Trust to't, bethink you, I'll not be forsworn.   *Exit.*

JULIET.   Is there no pity sitting in the clouds,
That sees into the bottom of my grief?
O sweet my mother, cast me not away!
Delay this marriage for a month, a week,
200 Or if you do not, make the bridal bed
In that dim monument where Tybalt lies.

LADY CAPULET.   Talk not to me, for I'll not speak a word.
Do as thou wilt, for I have done with thee.   *Exit.*

JULIET.   O God!—O nurse, how shall this be prevented?
205 My husband is on earth, my faith in heaven;[49]
How shall that faith return again to earth,
Unless that husband send it me from heaven
By leaving earth?[50] Comfort me, counsel me!
Alack, alack, that heaven should practice[51] stratagems
210 Upon so soft a subject as myself!
What say'st thou? Hast thou not a word of joy?
Some comfort, nurse.

NURSE.   Faith, here it is.

---

43. **demesnes.** Domain
44. **nobly lien'd.** Of good standing
45. **mammet.** Doll
46. **in . . . tender.** When good fortune comes
47. **do not use.** Don't usually

48. **advise.** Think carefully
49. **my . . . heaven.** I swore my marriage vow before God.
50. **How . . . earth?** How can I remarry unless Romeo dies?
51. **practice.** Invent, contrive

WORDS FOR EVERYDAY USE: strat • a • gem (strat´ə jəm) *n.,* trick

What does the
Nurse advise
Juliet to do?

Romeo is banished, and all the world to nothing[52]
That he dares ne'er come back to challenge[53] you;
215   Or if he do, it needs must be by stealth.
Then, since the case so stands as now it doth,
I think it best you married with the County.
O he's a lovely gentleman!
Romeo's a dishclout to[54] him. An eagle, madam,
220   Hath not so green, so quick, so fair an eye
As Paris hath. Beshrow[55] my very heart,
I think you are happy in this second match,
For it excels your first; or if it did not,
Your first is dead, or 'twere as good he were
225   As living here[56] and you no use of him.

JULIET.   Speak'st thou from thy heart?

NURSE.   And from my soul too, else beshrew them both.

JULIET.   Amen![57]

NURSE.   What?

230   **JULIET.**   Well, thou hast comforted me marvellous much.
Go in, and tell my lady I am gone,
Having displeas'd my father, to Lawrence' cell,
To make confession and to be absolv'd.

NURSE.   Marry, I will, and this is wisely done.   *Exit.*

235   **JULIET.**   [*She looks after* NURSE.] Ancient damnation![58] O most wicked
fiend!
Is it more sin to wish me thus forsworn,
Or to dispraise my lord with that same tongue
Which she hath prais'd him with above compare
So many thousand times? Go, counsellor,
240   Thou and my bosom[59] henceforth shall be twain.[60]
I'll to the friar to know his remedy;
If all else fail, myself have power to die.   *Exit.*

Whom does Juliet
turn to?

---

52. **all . . . nothing.** It is a safe bet, the odds are
53. **challenge.** Claim
54. **to.** Compared to
55. **Beshrow.** Beshrew, curse
56. **here.** On earth

57. **Amen.** So be it.
58. **Ancient damnation.** Damned old woman
59. **bosom.** Inner thoughts
60. **twain.** Separate

Responding to the Selection

How do you feel at this point in the play toward Tybalt, Romeo, Benvolio, Mercutio, and Juliet's parents? Which characters do you admire? Which do you not admire? Why do you feel as you do toward these characters? Discuss these questions with your classmates.

Reviewing the Selection

RECALLING

1. Why does Benvolio want to go inside at the beginning of scene i? What does he fear?

2. What name does Tybalt call Romeo? How does Romeo respond? What happens to Mercutio? What is Romeo trying to do when this happens? What happens to Tybalt and why?

3. What order does the prince give as a result of the killing of Tybalt? What mistaken impression does Juliet get from the nurse at the beginning of scene ii? What information does Juliet finally get from the nurse?

4. What is Friar Lawrence's plan for solving Romeo and Juliet's problems? Why are Juliet's parents angry with her at the end of the act? What does the audience know about Juliet that her parents do not know? What advice does the nurse give Juliet at the end of the act?

INTERPRETING

5. What sort of man is Benvolio? What sort of man is Mercutio? How do they differ in personality?

6. What do Romeo's actions during the duel reveal about him? What makes Romeo a sympathetic character?

7. Do you agree with the prince's decision with regard to Romeo? Why, or why not?

8. Why has Juliet withheld important information from her parents? What does she fear might happen if they knew the truth? Do you agree with the nurse's advice to Juliet? Why, or why not?

SYNTHESIZING

9. How might the problems that Romeo and Juliet are facing have been avoided? What tragic mistakes have been made and by whom so far in the play?

10. What do you think will happen in the rest of the play? Discuss possibilities with your classmates.

Understanding Literature (Questions for Discussion)

Plot and Crisis. A **plot** is a series of events related to a central conflict, or struggle. The **crisis** is a part of the plot where something decisive happens to determine the future course of events and the eventual working out of the conflict. In a tragedy, the main character's fortunes improve until the crisis. After the crisis, the main character's fortunes decline, or get worse. What crisis does Romeo face in act III of this play? What event occurs that has negative consequences for him? Was Romeo at fault in this crisis? Do you sympathize with his predicament? Why, or why not?

Responding in Writing

Petition. Imagine that you are Benvolio, Romeo's friend. Write a petition to the prince on Romeo's behalf. In the petition, argue Romeo's case. Explain to the prince everything that has happened and why you feel that Romeo should be pardoned.

> **Prewriting Suggestion:** Before writing, make a list of the major events so far in the play. Then reread act III, scene i, carefully, paying close attention to everything that Romeo says and does. Finally, write your petition. Make sure to address the prince appropriately.

PROJECT

Newspaper. Newspapers did not yet exist in Renaissance Italy or in Elizabethan England. For this project, however, imagine that you live in Romeo and Juliet's Verona and have invented the first newspaper. Create a name for your newspaper and some articles about recent events. Possibilities include a news story about the deaths of Mercutio and Tybalt and the banishment of Romeo, a society column about the Capulets' feast, an announcement of the wedding of Juliet and Paris, a schedule of times for confessions to be heard by Friar Lawrence, a gossip column with information about various people in the play, and an interview with the prince about violence in Verona's streets. Working with other students, choose a managing editor, reporters, copy editors, designers, typesetters, and layout people. Assign articles to be written. Have other students edit the stories. Have some students prepare drawings for the newspaper and others type or word process the articles. When typing the articles, use a fairly narrow column width, like that in a real newspaper. Then paste up the articles and pictures in column format on newspaper-sized pages.

READER'S JOURNAL

If you were Juliet at the end of act III, what would you do? Would you follow your nurse's advice and marry Paris? Would you make a plan to be with Romeo? If so, how would you accomplish that goal? Read the Language Arts Survey, 4.1 and 4.2, "Strategies for Problem Solving I and II." Then write about these questions in your journal.

ACT IV

SCENE i: Friar Lawrence's cell

Enter FRIAR LAWRENCE *and* COUNTY PARIS.

FRIAR LAWRENCE.   On Thursday, sir? The time is very short.

PARIS.   My father Capulet will have it so,
And I am nothing slow to slack his haste.[1]

FRIAR LAWRENCE.   You say you do not know the lady's mind?
5   Uneven is the course, I like it not.

PARIS.   Immoderately she weeps for Tybalt's death,
And therefore have I little talk'd of love,
For Venus smiles not in a house of tears.
Now, sir, her father counts it dangerous
10   That she do give her sorrow so much sway;
And in his wisdom hastes our marriage,
To stop the <u>inundation</u> of her tears,
Which, too much minded by herself alone,
May be put from her by society.[2]
15   Now do you know the reason of this haste.

FRIAR LAWRENCE.   [*Aside.*] I would[3] I knew not why it should be
slowed.—
Look, sir, here comes the lady toward my cell.

Enter JULIET.

ACT IV, SCENE i
  1. **I am . . . haste.** I have no desire to cause him to act less hastily.
  2. **too much . . . society.** Paris suggests that Juliet's sorrow is worse because she is alone and that she would feel better in the company of others.
  3. **would.** Wish

WORDS FOR EVERYDAY USE: in • un • da • tion (in´ən dā´shən) *n.,* flood; deluge

PARIS. Happily met, my lady and my wife!

JULIET. That may be, sir, when I may be a wife.

20 **PARIS.** That may be must be, love, on Thursday next.

JULIET. What must be shall be.

FRIAR LAWRENCE. That's a certain text.

PARIS. Come you to make confession to this father?

JULIET. To answer that, I should confess to you.

PARIS. Do not deny to him that you love me.

25 **JULIET.** I will confess to you that I love him.

PARIS. So will ye, I am sure, that you love me.

JULIET. If I do so, it will be of more price,
Being spoke behind your back, than to your face.

PARIS. Poor soul, thy face is much abus'd with tears.

30 **JULIET.** The tears have got small victory by that,
For it was bad enough before their spite.

PARIS. Thou wrong'st it more than tears with that report.

JULIET. That is no <u>slander</u>, sir, which is a truth,
And what I spake, I spake it to my face.[4]

35 **PARIS.** Thy face is mine, and thou hast sland'red it.

JULIET. It may be so, for it is not mine own.
Are you at leisure, holy father, now,
Or shall I come to you at evening mass?

FRIAR LAWRENCE. My leisure serves me, pensive[5] daughter, now.
40 My lord, we must entreat the time alone.

PARIS. God shield[6] I should disturb devotion!
Juliet, on Thursday early will I rouse ye;
Till then adieu, and keep this holy kiss.   *Exit.*

JULIET. O, shut the door, and when thou hast done so,
45 Come weep with me, past hope, past cure, past help!

FRIAR LAWRENCE. O Juliet, I already know thy grief,
It strains[7] me past the compass[8] of my wits.

What "strain" does Friar Lawrence feel?

---

4. **to my face.** About my own face
5. **pensive.** Sad and thoughtful
6. **shield.** Forbid
7. **strains.** Forces
8. **compass.** Boundaries or borders

WORDS FOR EVERYDAY USE:
slan • der (slan´dər) *n.,* false statement damaging another person's character or reputation

I hear thou must, and nothing may prorogue[9] it,
On Thursday next be married to this County.

50   **JULIET.**   Tell me not, friar, that thou hearest of this,
Unless thou tell me how I may prevent it.
If in thy wisdom thou canst give no help,
Do thou but call my <u>resolution</u> wise,
And with this knife I'll help it presently.[10]
55   God join'd my heart and Romeo's, thou our hands,
And ere this hand, by thee to Romeo's seal'd,
Shall be the label[11] to another deed,
Or my true heart with treacherous revolt
Turn to another, this shall slay them both.
60   Therefore, out of thy long-experienc'd time,
Give me some present counsel, or, behold,
'Twixt my extremes and me this bloody knife
Shall play the umpeer,[12] arbitrating[13] that
Which the commission[14] of thy years and art[15]
65   Could to no issue of true honor bring.
Be not so long to speak, I long to die,
If what thou speak'st speak not of remedy.

     FRIAR LAWRENCE.   Hold, daughter! I do spy a kind of hope,
Which craves as desperate an execution
70   As that is desperate which we would prevent.
If rather than to marry County Paris,
Thou hast the strength of will to slay thyself,
Then is it likely thou wilt undertake
A thing like death to chide away this shame,
75   That cop'st with Death himself to scape from it;[16]
And if thou darest, I'll give thee remedy.

     JULIET.   O, bid me leap, rather than marry Paris,
From off the battlements of any tower,
Or walk in thievish ways, or bid me lurk
80   Where serpents are; chain me with roaring bears,
Or hide me nightly in a charnel-house,[17]

---

9. **prorogue.** Argue against or prevent
10. **presently.** At this moment
11. **label.** Seal
12. **umpeer.** Umpire
13. **arbitrating.** Deciding
14. **commission.** Authority

15. **art.** Ability
16. **That cop'st . . . from it.** You who would have dealings with death in order to escape the death of a marriage to one whom you do not love
17. **charnel-house.** House where corpses are kept

WORDS FOR
EVERYDAY USE:

res • o • lu • tion (rez´ə lōō´ shən) *n.*, resolving or determining

O'ercover'd quite with dead men's rattling bones,
With reeky[18] shanks and yellow chapless[19] skulls;
Or bid me go into a new-made grave,
85 And hide me with a dead man in his <u>shroud</u>—
Things that, to hear them told, have made me tremble—
And I will do it without fear or doubt,
To live an unstain'd wife to my sweet love.

FRIAR LAWRENCE.   Hold then. Go home, be merry, give consent
90 To marry Paris. We'n'sday is to-morrow;
To-morrow night look that thou lie alone,
Let not the nurse lie with thee in thy chamber.
Take thou this vial, being then in bed,
And this distilling liquor drink thou off,
95 When presently through all thy veins shall run
A cold and drowsy humor;[20] for no pulse
Shall keep his native progress,[21] but surcease;[22]
No warmth, no breath shall testify thou livest;
The roses in thy lips and cheeks shall fade
100 To wanny[23] ashes, thy eyes' windows[24] fall,
Like death when he shuts up the day of life;
Each part, depriv'd of supple government,[25]
Shall, stiff and stark and cold, appear like death,
And in this borrowed likeness of shrunk death
105 Thou shalt continue two and forty hours,
And then awake as from a pleasant sleep.
Now when the bridegroom in the morning comes
To rouse thee from thy bed, there art thou dead.
Then, as the manner of our country is,
110 In thy best robes, uncovered on the bier,
Thou shall be borne to that same ancient vault
Where all the kindred of the Capulets lie.
In the mean time, against[26] thou shalt awake,
Shall Romeo by my letters know our drift,[27]
115 And hither shall he come, an' he and I
Will watch thy waking, and that very night

What plan does Friar Lawrence devise so Juliet will not have to marry Paris?

---

18. **reeky.** Reeking, smelly
19. **chapless.** Jawless
20. **humor.** Fluid
21. **keep . . . progress.** Occur as usual
22. **surcease.** Cease

23. **wanny.** Pale
24. **windows.** Lids
25. **supple goverment.** Control over movements
26. **against.** To prepare for the moment when
27. **drift.** Intentions

Shall Romeo bear thee hence to Mantua.
And this shall free thee from this present shame,
If no inconstant toy,[28] nor womanish fear,
120   Abate thy valor in the acting it.

JULIET.   Give me, give me! O, tell not me of fear!

FRIAR LAWRENCE.   Hold, get you gone. Be strong and prosperous
In this resolve. I'll send a friar with speed
To Mantua, with my letters to thy lord.

125   **JULIET.**   Love give me strength! and strength shall help afford.
Farewell, dear father!   *Exeunt.*

SCENE ii: Capulet's house

Enter FATHER CAPULET, *Mother* LADY CAPULET, NURSE, *and*
SERVINGMEN, *two or three.*

CAPULET.   So many guests invite as here are writ.

                           Exit FIRST SERVANT.

Sirrah, go hire me twenty cunning cooks.

2. SERVANT.   You shall have none ill, sir, for I'll try if they can lick
their fingers.

5   **CAPULET.**   How canst thou try them so?[1]

2. SERVANT.   Marry, sir, 'tis an ill cook that cannot lick his own
fingers; therefore he that cannot lick his fingers[2] goes not with me.

CAPULET.   Go, be gone.   *Exit* SECOND SERVANT.
We shall be much unfurnish'd[3] for this time.
10   What, is my daughter gone to Friar Lawrence?

NURSE.   Ay forsooth.

CAPULET.   Well, he may chance to do some good on her.
A peevish self-will'd harlotry it is.

Enter JULIET.

NURSE.   See where she comes from shrift with merry look.

15   **CAPULET.**   How now, my headstrong, where have you been gadding?[4]

---

28. **inconstant toy.** Change of mind

ACT IV, SCENE ii

1. **try them so.** By that means tell whether they can cook
2. **lick . . . fingers.** The servant is suggesting that a

good cook will be willing to taste his own cooking by licking his fingers.
3. **unfurnish'd.** Unprepared
4. **gadding.** Going in a capricious manner

WORDS FOR   **pee • vish** (pēv′ish) *adj.*, hard to please; irritable
EVERYDAY USE:

JULIET.   Where I have learnt me to repent the sin
Of disobedient opposition
To you and your behests, and am enjoin'd
By holy Lawrence to fall <u>prostrate</u> here
20 To beg your pardon. [*She kneels down.*] Pardon, I beseech you!
Henceforward I am ever rul'd by you.

CAPULET.   Send for the County, go tell him of this.
I'll have this knot knit up tomorrow morning.

JULIET.   I met the youthful lord at Lawrence' cell,
25 And gave him what becomed[5] love I might,
Not stepping o'er the bounds of modesty.

CAPULET.   Why, I am glad on't, this is well, stand up.
This is as't should be. Let me see the County;
Ay, marry, go, I say, and fetch him hither.
30 Now, afore God, this reverend holy friar,
All our whole city is much bound to him.

JULIET.   Nurse, will you go with me into my closet[6]
To help me sort such needful ornaments
As you think fit to furnish me tomorrow?

35 **LADY CAPULET.**   No, not till Thursday, there is time enough.

CAPULET.   Go, nurse, go with her, we'll to church tomorrow.

Exeunt JULIET *and* NURSE.

LADY CAPULET.   We shall be short in our provision,
'Tis now near night.

CAPULET.   Tush, I will stir about,
And all things shall be well, I warrant thee, wife;
40 Go thou to Juliet, help to deck up her.
I'll not to bed tonight; let me alone,
I'll play the huswife[7] for this once. What ho!
They are all forth. Well, I will walk myself
To County Paris, to prepare up him
45 Against to-morrow. My heart is wondrous light,
Since this same wayward girl is so reclaim'd.

Exeunt.

Why does Capulet rejoice?

---

5. **becomed.** Fitting
6. **closet.** Room
7. **huswife.** Housewife

WORDS FOR EVERYDAY USE: **pros • trate** (präs´trāt) *adj.,* lying with the face downward in demonstration of great humility

SCENE iii: Capulet's house

Enter JULIET *and* NURSE.

JULIET.   Ay, those attires are best, but, gentle nurse,
I pray thee leave me to myself tonight,
For I have need of many orisons[1]
To move the heavens to smile upon my state,

5   Which, well thou knowest, is cross and full of sin.

Enter Mother LADY CAPULET.

LADY CAPULET.   What, are you busy, ho? Need you my help?

JULIET.   No, madam, we have cull'd such necessaries
As are behoofeful[2] for our state[3] tomorrow.
So please you, let me now be left alone,

10   And let the nurse this night sit up with you,
For I am sure you have your hands full all,
In this so sudden business.

LADY CAPULET.   Good night.
Get thee to bed and rest, for thou hast need.

Exeunt LADY CAPULET *and* NURSE.

JULIET.   Farewell! God knows when we shall meet again.

15   I have a faint cold fear thrills through my veins,
That almost freezes up the heat of life.
I'll call them back again to comfort me.
Nurse!—What should she do here?
My dismal scene I needs must act alone.

20   Come, vial.
What if this mixture do not work at all?
Shall I be married then tomorrow morning?
No, no, this shall forbid it. Lie thou there.

Laying down her dagger.

What if it be a poison which the friar

25   Subtilly hath minist'red to have me dead,
Lest in this marriage he should be dishonor'd
Because he married me before to Romeo?
I fear it is, and yet methinks it should not,
For he hath still[4] been tried[5] a holy man.

30   How if, when I am laid into the tomb,
I wake before the time that Romeo
Come to redeem me? there's a fearful point!
Shall I not then be stifled in the vault,
To whose foul mouth no healthsome air breathes in,

Why does Juliet send the Nurse away?

Why might Friar Lawrence want to poison Juliet?

ACT IV, SCENE iii
 1. **orisons.** Prayers
 2. **behoofeful.** Needed

3. **state.** Ceremony
4. **still.** Always
5. **been tried.** Been shown to be

35   And there die strangled ere my Romeo comes?
     Or if I live, is it not very like
     The horrible conceit[6] of death and night,
     Together with the terror of the place—
     As in a vault, an ancient <u>receptacle</u>,
40   Where for this many hundred years the bones
     Of all my buried ancestors are pack'd,
     Where bloody Tybalt, yet but green in earth,[7]
     Lies fest'ring in his shroud, where, as they say,
     At some hours in the night spirits resort—
45   Alack, alack, is it not like that I,
     So early waking—what with <u>loathsome</u> smells,
     And shrikes like mandrakes'[8] torn out of the earth,
     That living mortals, hearing them, run mad—
     O, if I [wake], shall I not be distraught,
50   Environed with all these hideous fears,
     And madly play with my forefathers' joints,
     And pluck the mangled Tybalt from his shroud,
     And in this rage, with some great kinsman's bone,
     As with a club, dash out my desp'rate brains?
55   O, look! methinks I see my cousin's ghost
     Seeking out Romeo, that did spit his body
     Upon a rapier's point. Stay, Tybalt, stay!
     Romeo, Romeo, Romeo! Here's drink—I drink to thee.

                    She falls upon her bed, within the curtains.

Where will Juliet be taken?

SCENE iv: continues in Capulet's house

Enter lady of the house LADY CAPULET *and* NURSE *with herbs.*

LADY CAPULET.   Hold, take these keys and fetch more spices, nurse.

NURSE.   They call for dates and quinces in the pastry.[1]

Enter old CAPULET.

CAPULET.   Come, stir, stir, stir! the second cock hath crowed,
The curfew-bell hath rung, 'tis three a' clock.

---

6. **conceit.** Idea
7. **green in earth.** Newly buried
8. **shrikes like mandrakes'.** Shrieks like those made by mandrakes. The mandrake root, used in magic because of its supposed resemblance to a human being, was believed to shriek when pulled out of the ground.

ACT IV, SCENE iv
1. **pastry.** Pastry-room

WORDS FOR EVERYDAY USE:

re • cep • ta • cle (ri sep´tə kəl) *n.,* anything used to contain or hold something else

loath • some (lōth´səm) *adj.,* disgusting; detestable

5   Look to the bak'd meats, good Angelica,[2]
       Spare not for cost.

       NURSE.   Go, you cot-quean,[3] go,
       Get you to bed. Faith, you'll be sick tomorrow
       For this night's watching.[4]

       CAPULET.   No, not a whit. What, I have watch'd ere now
10   All night for lesser cause, and ne'er been sick.

       LADY CAPULET.   Ay, you have been a mouse-hunt[5] in your time,
       But I will watch you from such watching now.

                              Exeunt LADY CAPULET *and* NURSE.

       CAPULET.   A jealous hood,[6] a jealous hood!

       Enter three or four SERVINGMEN *with spits and logs and baskets*

       Now, fellow, what is there?

15   **1. SERVANT.**   Things for the cook, sir, but I know not what.

       CAPULET.   Make haste, make haste. Sirrah, fetch drier logs.

                                          Exit FIRST SERVANT.

       Call Peter, he will show thee where they are.

       2. SERVANT.   I have a head, sir, that will find out logs,
       And never trouble Peter for the matter.

20   **CAPULET.**   Mass, and well said, a merry whoreson, ha!
       Thou shalt be logger-head.[7] Good faith, 'tis day.   *Exit* SECOND SERVANT.
       The County will be here with music straight,
       For so he said he would. [*Play music within.*] I hear him near.
       Nurse! Wife! What ho! What, nurse, I say!

       Enter NURSE.

25   Go waken Juliet, go and trim her up,
       I'll go and chat with Paris. Hie, make haste,
       Make haste, the bridegroom he is come already,
       Make haste, I say.   *Exit.*

                 SCENE V: continues in Capulet's house

       NURSE.   Mistress! what, mistress! Juliet!—Fast,[1] I warrant her, she.—
       Why, lamb! why, lady! fie, you slug-a-bed!
       Why, love, I say! madam! sweet heart! why, bride!
       What, not a word? You take your pennyworths[2] now;
5   Sleep for a week, for the next night, I warrant,

---

2. **Angelica.** The Nurse
3. **cot-quean.** Male housekeeper
4. **watching.** Wakefulness
5. **mouse-hunt.** Mouse-hunter, one who is up all night, like a cat

6. **jealous hood.** Jealous person
7. **logger-head.** Blockhead
ACT IV, SCENE V
1. **Fast.** Fast asleep
2. **pennyworths.** Small amounts (of sleep)

The County Paris hath set up his rest
That you shall rest but little. God forgive me!
Marry and amen! How sound is she asleep!
I needs must wake her. Madam, madam, madam!
10 Ay, let the County take you in your bed,
He'll fright you up, i' faith. Will it not be?   *Draws back the curtains.*
What, dress'd, and in your clothes, and down again?
I must needs wake you. Lady, lady, lady!
Alas, alas! Help, help! my lady's dead!
15 O, weraday, that ever I was born!
Some aqua-vitae ho! My lord! my lady!

*What does the
Nurse find?*

Enter Mother, LADY CAPULET.

LADY CAPULET.   What noise is here?

NURSE.   O <u>lamentable</u> day!

LADY CAPULET.   What is the matter?

NURSE.   Look, look! O heavy day!

LADY CAPULET.   O me, O me, my child, my only life!
20 Revive, look up, or I will die with thee!
Help, help! Call help.

Enter Father CAPULET.

CAPULET.   For shame, bring Juliet forth, her lord is come.

NURSE.   She's dead, deceas'd, she's dead, alack the day!

LADY CAPULET.   Alack the day, she's dead, she's dead, she's dead!

25 **CAPULET.**   Hah, let me see her. Out alas, she's cold,
Her blood is settled, and her joints are stiff;
Life and these lips have long been separated.
Death lies on her like an untimely frost
Upon the sweetest flower of all the field.

NURSE. O lamentable day!

30 **LADY CAPULET.**   O woeful time!

CAPULET.   Death, that hath ta'en her hence to make me wail,
Ties up my tongue and will not let me speak.

Enter FRIAR LAWRENCE *and the* COUNTY PARIS *with the* MUSICIANS.

FRIAR LAWRENCE.   Come, is the bride ready to go to church?

CAPULET.   Ready to go, but never to return.—

**WORDS FOR
EVERYDAY USE:**   **lam • en • ta • ble** (lam´ən tə bəl) *adj.,* grievous; deplorable; distressing

35   O son, the night before thy wedding-day
Hath Death lain with thy wife. There she lies,
Flower as she was, deflowered by him.
Death is my son-in-law, Death is my heir,
My daughter he hath wedded. I will die,
40   And leave him all; life, living, all is Death's.

PARIS.   Have I thought long to see this morning's face,
And doth it give me such a sight as this?

LADY CAPULET.   Accurs'd, unhappy, wretched, hateful day!
Most miserable hour that e'er time saw
45   In lasting labor of his <u>pilgrimage</u>![3]
But one, poor one, one poor and loving child,
But one thing to rejoice and solace in,
And cruel Death hath catch'd[4] it from my sight!

NURSE. O woe! O woeful, woeful, woeful day!
50   Most lamentable day, most woeful day
That ever, ever, I did yet behold!
O day, O day, O day, O hateful day!
Never was seen so black a day as this.
O woeful day, O woeful day!

55   **PARIS.**   Beguil'd, divorced, wronged, spited, slain!
Most detestable Death, by thee beguil'd,
By cruel cruel thee quite overthrown!
O love, O life! not life, but love in death!

CAPULET.   Despis'd, distressed, hated, martyr'd, kill'd!
60   Uncomfortable time, why cam'st thou now
To murther, murther our solemnity?[5]
O child, O child! my soul, and not my child!
Dead art thou! Alack, my child is dead,
And with my child my joys are buried.

65   **FRIAR LAWRENCE.**   Peace ho, for shame! Confusion's cure lives not
In these confusions. Heaven and yourself
Had part in this fair maid, now heaven hath all,
And all the better is it for the maid.
Your part in her you could not keep from death,

---

3. **Most miserable . . . pilgrimage.** The worst hour
since the beginning of time
4. **catch'd.** Stolen, taken
5. **solemnity.** Festivity, ceremony

WORDS FOR   **pil • grim • age** (pil´grim ij) *n.,* long journey
EVERYDAY USE:

70 But heaven keeps his part in eternal life.
    The most you sought was her promotion,
    For 'twas your heaven she should be advanc'd,
    And weep ye now, seeing she is advanc'd
    Above the clouds, as high as heaven itself?
75 O, in this love, you love your child so ill
    That you run mad, seeing that she is well.
    She's not well married that lives married long,
    But she's best married that dies married young.
    Dry up your tears, and stick your rosemary[6]
80 On this fair corse, and as the custom is,
    And in her best array, bear her to church;
    For though fond nature bids us all <u>lament</u>,
    Yet nature's tears are reason's merriment.[7]

    CAPULET.   All things that we ordained festival,
85 Turn from their office[8] to black funeral:
    Our instruments to melancholy bells,
    Our wedding cheer to a sad burial feast;
    Our solemn hymns to sullen dirges change;
    Our bridal flowers serve for a buried corse;[9]
90 And all things change them to the contrary.

    FRIAR LAWRENCE.   Sir, go you in, and, madam, go with him;
    And go, Sir Paris. Every one prepare
    To follow this fair corse unto her grave.
    The heavens do low'r upon you for some ill;
95 Move them no more by crossing[10] their high will.

    They all, but the NURSE *and the* MUSICIANS, *go forth, casting rosemary on her, and shutting the curtains.*

    1. MUSICIAN.   Faith, we may put up our pipes and be gone.

    NURSE. Honest good fellows, ah, put up, put up,
    For well you know this is a pitiful case.   *Exit.*

    1. MUSICIAN.   Ay, by my troth, the case may be amended.[11]

    Enter PETER.

What does the planned wedding become?

---

6. **rosemary.** Herb associated with remembrance
7. **nature's . . . merriment.** Human nature weeps at things that reason considers joyful.
8. **office.** Purpose or function

9. **corse.** Corpse, dead body
10. **crossing.** Going against, challenging
11. **amended.** Mended, fixed, repaired

WORDS FOR EVERYDAY USE: la • ment (lə ment´) *vi.,* feel deep sorrow

100   **PETER.**   Musicians, O musicians, "Heart's ease," "Heart's ease"![12] O, and you will have me live, play "Heart's ease."

    1. MUSICIAN.   Why "Heart's ease"?

    PETER.   O musicians, because my heart itself plays "My heart is full." O, play me some merry dump[13] to comfort me.

105   **1. MUSICIAN.**   Not a dump we, 'tis no time to play now.

    PETER.   You will not then?

    1. MUSICIAN.   No.

    PETER.   I will then give it you soundly.

    1. MUSICIAN.   What will you give us?

110   **PETER.**   No money, on my faith, but the gleek;[14] I will give you the minstrel.[15]

    1. MUSICIAN.   Then will I give you the serving-creature.

    PETER.   Then will I lay the serving-creature's dagger on your pate.[16] I will carry no crotchets,[17] I'll *re* you, I'll *fa* you.[18] Do you note[19] me?

115   **1. MUSICIAN.**   And[20] you *re* us and *fa* us, you note us.[21]

    2. MUSICIAN.   Pray you put up your dagger, and put out[22] your wit.

    PETER.   Then have at you with my wit! I will drybeat you with an iron wit,[29] and put up my iron dagger. Answer me like men:
      "When griping griefs the heart doth wound,
120   And doleful dumps the mind oppress,
      Then music with her silver sound"—
why "silver sound"? Why "music with her silver sound"? What say you, Simon Catling?

    1. MUSICIAN.   Marry, sir, because silver hath a sweet sound.

125   **PETER.**   Pretty! What say you, Hugh Rebeck?

    2. MUSICIAN.   I say, "silver sound," because musicians sound for silver.

    PETER.   Pretty too! What say you, James Soundpost?

    3. MUSICIAN.   Faith, I know not what to say.

---

12. **"Heart's ease."** Title of a popular ballad
13. **dump.** Song
14. **gleek.** Jest, insult
15. **give . . . minstrel.** Call you names
16. **pate.** Head
17. **carry no crotchets.** Pun meaning both "sing no quarternotes" and "endure no gibes"

18. **I'll re . . . you.** Pun meaning both "I'll sing the notes *re* and *fa* to you" and "I'll mess you up and clean you up," from *ray*, "to befoul," and *fay*, "to clean up"
19. **note.** Hear, listen to
20. **And.** If
21. **note us.** Set us to music
22. **put out.** Bring out

130 **PETER.** O, I cry you mercy,[23] you are the singer; I will say for you; it is "music with her silver sound," because musicians have no gold for sounding:

> "Then music with her silver sound
> With speedy help doth lend redress." *Exit.*

135 **1. MUSICIAN.** What a pestilent knave is this same!

2. MUSICIAN. Hang him, Jack! Come, we'll in here, tarry for the mourners, and stay[24] dinner. *Exeunt.*

---

23. **cry you mercy.** Ask for mercy from you
24. **stay.** Wait for

Responding to the Selection

How do you feel about Friar Lawrence's plan at this point in the story? Do you think that Juliet has done the right thing? Why, or why not? Discuss these questions with your classmates.

Reviewing the Selection

RECALLING

1. Whom does Juliet meet when she goes to see Friar Lawrence? What is going to happen on Thursday?

2. What is Friar Lawrence's new plan? How does it differ from the old one?

3. What does Juliet fear as she gets ready to drink the potion given to her by Friar Lawrence?

4. What does the Nurse discover when she goes to wake Juliet on her wedding day?

INTERPRETING

5. How does Juliet feel about the prospect of marrying Paris? How do you know? What does her refusal to marry Paris reveal about her?

6. Why was it necessary for Friar Lawrence to change his plan?

7. What contradictory feelings does Juliet have about the killing of Tybalt? How do you know?

8. What consequences have Juliet's actions had for her relationship with her parents? Do her parents share any of the blame for this unfortunate outcome? Why, or why not?

9. How do you feel about Friar Lawrence at this point in the play? Has he always acted kindly? wisely? Explain.

10. What do you think will happen in the rest of the play? Discuss possibilities with your classmates.

Understanding Literature (Questions for Discussion)

1. **Plot and Climax.** A **plot** is the series of events related to a central conflict, or struggle. The **climax** is the point in a plot where something decisive happens to determine the future course of events and the eventual working out of the conflict. Many people would agree that the climax of this play comes when Juliet drinks the Friar's potion. This is a highly emotional, intense scene. What suspense does the reader feel at the end of the scene? What is the reader wondering about at the end of the act? What character echoes some of the reader's worries about the possible outcome of Friar Lawrence's plan?

2. **Motif and Foreshadowing.** A **motif** is any element that recurs in one or more works of literature or art. **Foreshadowing** is the act of presenting materials that hint at events to occur later in a story. When Juliet first sees Romeo in act I, she says to her nurse, "Go ask his name.—If he be married,/My grave is like to be my wedding-bed." What lines from Capulet in act IV echo or repeat Juliet's line from act I? In what way has Juliet's statement turned out to be prophetic, an example of foreshadowing?

3. **Simile.** A **simile** is a comparison using *like* or *as.* Capulet says of Juliet that "Death lies on her like an untimely frost/Upon the sweetest flower of all the field." What is being compared to a flower in this simile? What is being compared to frost? What do the things in those two comparisons have in common?

Responding in Writing

Plot Summary. Brainstorm with a friend about a possible outcome for this play. Then write a summary of the plot of act V as you would write it.

> **Prewriting Suggestion:** Before writing, read the entry on *plot* in the Handbook of Literary Terms. Pay particular attention to the part of the entry that explains the resolution of the plot. Make sure that your plot for act V provides a proper resolution, or end, for the central conflict in the play.

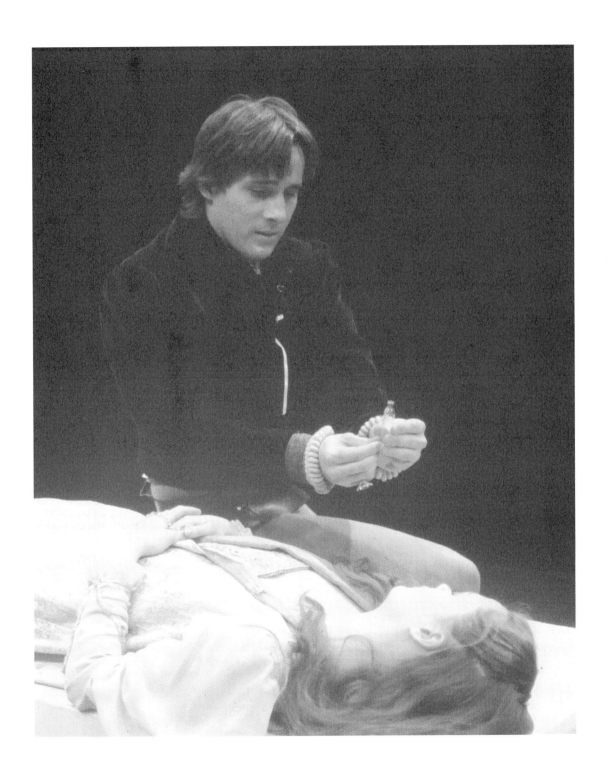

How do you think the play will end? What will become of Romeo and Juliet? Make notes in your journal about how you would end the play if you were Shakespeare. Then, as you read act V, compare your notes to the actual events in the act.

ACT V

SCENE i: a street in Mantua

Enter ROMEO.

ROMEO.   If I may trust the flattering[1] truth of sleep,
My dreams presage some joyful news at hand.
My bosom's lord[2] sits lightly in his throne,[3]
And all this day an unaccustom'd spirit

5   Lifts me above the ground with cheerful thoughts.
I dreamt my lady came and found me dead—
Strange dream, that gives a dead man leave to think!—
And breath'd such life with kisses in my lips
That I reviv'd and was an emperor.

10   Ah me, how sweet is love itself possess'd,
When but love's shadows are so rich in joy!

Enter Romeo's man BALTHASAR, *booted.*

News from Verona! How now, Balthasar?
Dost thou not bring me letters from the friar?
How doth my lady? Is my father well?

15   How doth my Juliet? That I ask again,
For nothing can be ill if she be well.

What was supposed to have reached Romeo before the news?

BALTHASAR.   Then she is well and nothing can be ill:
Her body sleeps in Capel's monument,
And her immortal part with angels lives.

20   I saw her laid low in her kindred's vault,
And presently[4] took post[5] to tell it you.
O, pardon me for bringing these ill news,
Since you did leave it for my office,[6] sir.

ROMEO.   Is it e'en so? Then I defy you, stars!

25   Thou knowest my lodging, get me ink and paper,
And hire post-horses; I will hence tonight.

ACT V, SCENE i
1. **flattering.** Favorable
2. **My bosom's lord.** Love
3. **his throne.** Romeo's heart

4. **presently.** Immediately
5. **took post.** Traveled by horse
6. **office.** Duty

BALTHASAR.   I do beseech you, sir, have patience.
Your looks are pale and wild, and do import
Some <u>misadventure</u>.

ROMEO.   Tush, thou art deceiv'd.
30   Leave me, and do the thing I bid thee do.
Hast thou no letters to me from the friar?

BALTHASAR.   No, my good lord.

ROMEO.   No matter, get thee gone,
And hire those horses; I'll be with thee straight.   *Exit* BALTHASAR.
Well, Juliet, I will lie with thee tonight.
35   Let's see for means.[7] O mischief, thou art swift
To enter in the thoughts of desperate men!
I do remember an apothecary—
And hereabouts 'a dwells—which late I noted
In tatt'red weeds,[8] with overwhelming[9] brows,
40   Culling of simples;[10] meagre were his looks,
Sharp misery had worn him to the bones;
And in his needy shop a tortoise hung,
An alligator stuff'd and other skins
Of ill-shap'd fishes, and about his shelves
45   A beggarly account[11] of empty boxes,
Green earthen pots, bladders, and musty seeds,
Remnants of packthread, and old cakes of roses[12]
Were thinly scattered, to make up a show.
Noting this penury, to myself I said,
50   "An' if[13] a man did need a poison now,
Whose sale is present death[14] in Mantua,
Here lives a caitiff wretch would sell it him."
O, this same thought did but forerun my need,
And this same needy man must sell it me.
55   As I remember, this should be the house.
Being holiday, the beggar's shop is shut.
What ho, apothecary!

Enter APOTHECARY.

APOTHECARY.   Who calls so loud?

What does the apothecary need? What does Romeo need?

---

7. **see for means.** See how
8. **weeds.** Clothes
9. **overwhelming.** Overhanging; large
10. **simples.** Medicines
11. **beggarly account.** Small number

12. **cakes of roses.** Rose petals made into cakes for their scent
13. **An' if.** If
14. **present death.** Capital offense

ROMEO.   Come hither, man. I see that thou art poor.
Hold, there is forty ducats;[15] let me have
60   A dram of poison, such soon-speeding gear[16]
As will disperse itself through all the veins
That the life-weary taker may fall dead,
And that the trunk may be discharg'd of breath
As violently as hasty powder fir'd
65   Doth hurry from the fatal cannon's womb.

APOTHECARY.   Such mortal drugs I have, but Mantua's law
Is death to any he[17] that utters[18] them.

ROMEO.   Art thou so bare and full of wretchedness,
And fearest to die? Famine is in thy cheeks,
70   Need and oppression starveth in thy eyes,
Contempt and beggary hangs upon thy back;
The world is not thy friend, nor the world's law,
The world affords no law to make thee rich;
Then be not poor, but break it, and take this.

75   **APOTHECARY.**   My poverty, but not my will, consents.

ROMEO.   I pay thy poverty, and not thy will.

APOTHECARY.   Put this in any liquid thing you will
And drink it off, and if you had the strength
Of twenty man, it would dispatch[19] you straight.

80   **ROMEO.**   There is thy gold, worse poison to men's souls,
Doing more murther in this loathsome world,
Than these poor compounds that thou mayest not sell.
I sell thee poison, thou hast sold me none.
Farewell! Buy food, and get thyself in flesh.[20]

Exit APOTHECARY.

85   Come, cordial[21] and not poison, go with me
To Juliet's grave, for there must I use thee.   *Exit.*

SCENE ii: Friar Lawrence's cell

Enter FRIAR JOHN.

FRIAR JOHN.   Holy Franciscan friar! brother, ho!

Enter FRIAR LAWRENCE.

FRIAR LAWRENCE.   This same should be the voice of Friar John.
Welcome from Mantua! What says Romeo?
Or, if his mind be writ, give me his letter.

---

15. **ducats.** Gold coins
16. **soon-speeding gear.** Fast-acting stuff
17. **any he.** Anyone
18. **utters.** Dispenses

19. **dispatch.** Kill
20. **get . . . flesh.** Become fat (i.e., prosper)
21. **cordial.** Medicine

5   **FRIAR JOHN.**   Going to find a barefoot brother out,
One of our order, to associate[1] me,
Here in this city visiting the sick,
And finding him, the searchers[2] of the town,
Suspecting that we both were in a house
10   Where the infectious pestilence did reign,
Seal'd up the doors and would not let us forth,
So that my speed to Mantua there was stay'd.

FRIAR LAWRENCE.   Who bare my letter then to Romeo?

FRIAR JOHN.   I could not send it—here it is again—
15   Nor get a messenger to bring it thee,
So fearful were they of infection.

FRIAR LAWRENCE.   Unhappy fortune! By my brotherhood,
The letter was not nice[3] but full of charge,[4]
Of dear[5] import, and the neglecting it
20   May do much danger. Friar John, go hence,
Get me an iron crow,[6] and bring it straight
Unto my cell.

FRIAR JOHN.   Brother, I'll go and bring it thee.   *Exit.*

FRIAR LAWRENCE.   Now must I to the monument alone,
25   Within this three hours will fair Juliet wake.
She will beshrew[7] me much that Romeo
Hath had no notice of these accidents;[8]
But I will write again to Mantua,
And keep her at my cell till Romeo come—
30   Poor living corse, clos'd in a dead man's tomb!   *Exit.*

Why couldn't Friar John get to Mantua?

What does Friar John return?

Friar Lawrence thinks of only one problem with the plan. What is it?

SCENE iii: the churchyard wherein lies the Capulet family tomb

Enter PARIS *and his* PAGE *with flowers and sweet[1] water and a torch.*

PARIS.   Give me thy torch, boy. Hence, and stand aloof.[2]
Yet put it out, for I would not be seen.
Under yond yew trees lay thee all along,[3]
Holding thy ear close to the hollow ground,
5   So shall no foot upon the churchyard tread,
Being[4] loose, unfirm, with digging up of graves,
But thou shalt hear it. Whistle then to me
As signal that thou hearest something approach.
Give me those flowers. Do as I bid thee, go.

ACT V, SCENE ii
1. **associate.** Accompany
2. **searchers.** Health officials
3. **nice.** About small matters
4. **full of charge.** Important, emotion-provoking
5. **dear.** Extreme, great
6. **crow.** Crowbar

7. **beshrew.** Censure
8. **accidents.** Events

ACT V, SCENE iii
1. **sweet.** Perfumed
2. **aloof.** Away from here, distant
3. **all along.** Flat against the ground
4. **Being.** Because the ground is

10   **PAGE.**   [*Aside.*] I am almost afraid to stand[5] alone
Here in the churchyard, yet I will adventure.[6]

Retires. PARIS *strews the tomb with flowers.*

PARIS.   Sweet flower, with flowers thy bridal bed I strew—
O woe, thy canopy is dust and stones!—
Which with sweet water nightly I will dew,
15   Or wanting that, with tears distill'd by moans.
The obsequies[7] that I for thee will keep
Nightly shall be to strew thy grave and weep.

Whistle Boy.

The boy gives warning, something doth approach.
What cursed foot wanders this way tonight,
20   To cross[8] my obsequies and true love's rite?
What, with a torch? Muffle me, night, a while.   *Retires.*

Enter ROMEO *and* BALTHASAR *with a torch, a mattock, and a crow of iron.*

ROMEO.   Give me that mattock and the wrenching iron.
Hold, take this letter; early in the morning
See thou deliver it to my lord and father.
25   Give me the light. Upon thy life I charge thee,
What e'er thou hearest or seest, stand all aloof,
And do not interrupt me in my course.
Why I descend into this bed of death
Is partly to behold my lady's face,
30   But chiefly to take thence from her dead finger
A precious ring—a ring that I must use
In dear employment—therefore hence be gone.
But if thou, jealous, dost return to pry
In what I farther shall intend to do,
35   By heaven, I will tear thee joint by joint,
And strew this hungry churchyard with thy limbs.
The time and my intents are savage-wild,
More fierce and more inexorable far
Than empty tigers or the roaring sea.

40   **BALTHASAR.**   I will be gone, sir, and not trouble ye.

ROMEO.   So shalt thou show me friendship. Take thou that;
Live and be prosperous, and farewell, good fellow.

BALTHASAR.   [*Aside.*] For all this same, I'll hide me hereabout,
His looks I fear, and his intents I doubt.   *Retires.*

---

5. **stand.** Stay
6. **adventure.** Try
7. **obsequies.** Prayers or rites for dead persons
8. **cross.** Interrupt, go against

45   **ROMEO.**   Thou detestable maw,[9] thou womb of death,
      Gorg'd with the dearest morsel of the earth,
      Thus I enforce thy rotten jaws to open,
      And in despite I'll cram thee with more food.

                              ROMEO *begins to open the tomb.*

      PARIS.   This is that banish'd <u>haughty</u> Montague,
50   That murd'red my love's cousin, with which grief
      It is supposed the fair creature died,
      And here is come to do some villainous shame
      To the dead bodies. I will apprehend him.   *Steps forth.*
      Stop thy <u>unhallowed</u> toil, vile Montague!
55   Can vengeance be pursued further than death?
      Condemned villain, I do apprehend thee.
      Obey and go with me, for thou must die.

What does Paris suspect Romeo is doing at Juliet's tomb?

      ROMEO.   I must indeed, and therefore came I hither.
      Good gentle youth, tempt not a desp'rate man.
60   Fly hence and leave me, think upon these gone,
      Let them affright thee. I beseech thee, youth,
      Put not another sin upon my head,
      By urging me to fury: O, be gone!
      By heaven, I love thee better than myself,
65   For I come hither arm'd against myself.
      Stay not, be gone; live, and hereafter say
      A madman's mercy bid thee run away.

      PARIS.   I do defy thy conjuration,
      And apprehend thee for a felon here.

70   **ROMEO.**   Wilt thou provoke me? Then have at thee, boy!   *They fight.*

      PAGE.   O Lord, they fight! I will go call the watch.   *Exit.*

      PARIS.   O, I am slain! [*Falls.*] If thou be merciful,
      Open the tomb, lay me with Juliet.   *Dies.*

What happens to Paris?

      ROMEO.   In faith, I will. Let me peruse this face.
75   Mercutio's kinsman, noble County Paris!
      What said my man, when my betossed soul
      Did not attend him as we rode? I think
      He told me Paris should have married Juliet.
      Said he not so? or did I dream it so?
80   Or am I mad, hearing him talk of Juliet,

---

9. **maw.** Mouth

WORDS FOR EVERYDAY USE:

haugh • ty (hôt´ē) *adj.,* proud; arrogant
un • hal • lowed (un´hal´ōd) *adj.,* unholy; wicked

To think it was so? O, give me thy hand,
One writ with me in sour misfortune's book!
I'll bury thee in a triumphant grave.
A grave? O no, a lanthorn,[10] slaught'red youth;
For here lies Juliet, and her beauty makes
This vault a feasting presence[11] full of light.
Death, lie thou there, by a dead man interr'd.

Laying PARIS *in the tomb.*

How oft when men are at the point of death
Have they been merry, which their keepers call
A lightning before death! O how may I
Call this a lightning? O my love, my wife,
Death, that hath suck'd the honey of thy breath,
Hath had no power yet upon thy beauty:
Thou art not conquer'd, beauty's ensign yet
Is crimson in thy lips and in thy cheeks,
And death's pale flag is not advanced[12] there.
Tybalt, liest thou there in thy bloody sheet?
O, what more favor can I do to thee,
Than with that hand that cut thy youth in twain
To sunder[13] his that was thine enemy?
Forgive me, cousin! Ah, dear Juliet,
Why art thou yet so fair? Shall I believe
That unsubstantial Death is amorous,
And that the lean abhorred monster keeps
Thee here in dark to be his <u>paramour</u>?
For fear of that, I still will stay with thee,
And never from this palace of dim night
Depart again. Here, here will I remain
With worms that are thy chambermaids; O, here
Will I set up my everlasting rest,
And shake the yoke of <u>inauspicious</u> stars
From this world-wearied flesh. Eyes, look your last!
Arms, take your last embrace! and, lips, O you
The doors of breath, seal with a righteous kiss
A dateless bargain to engrossing death!

How does Juliet appear? What does Romeo think?

Line numbers: 85, 90, 95, 100, 105, 110, 115

---

10. **lanthorn.** Lantern (a tower room with glass on all sides)
11. **feasting presence.** Appear like a place decorated for a feast
12. **advanced.** Raised
13. **sunder.** Cut

WORDS FOR EVERYDAY USE:

par • a • mour (par´ə mo͞or) *n.,* sweetheart
in • aus • pi • cious (in´ô spish´əs) *adj.,* unfavorable; unlucky

Come, bitter conduct,[14] come, unsavory guide!
Thou desperate pilot, now at once run on
The dashing rocks thy sea-sick weary bark!
Here's to my love! [*Drinks.*] O true apothecary!
120   Thy drugs are quick. Thus with a kiss I die.   *Dies.*

Enter FRIAR LAWRENCE *with lanthorn, crow, and spade.*

FRIAR LAWRENCE.   Saint Francis be my speed! how oft tonight
Have my old feet stumbled at graves! Who's there?

BALTHASAR.   Here's one, a friend, and one that knows you well.

FRIAR LAWRENCE.   Bliss be upon you! Tell me, good my friend,
125   What torch is yond, that vainly lends his light
To grubs and eyeless skulls? As I <u>discern</u>,
It burneth in the Capels' monument.

BALTHASAR.   It doth so, holy sir, and there's my master,
One that you love.

FRIAR LAWRENCE.   Who is it?

BALTHASAR.   Romeo.

FRIAR LAWRENCE.   How long hath he been there?

130   **BALTHASAR.**   Full half an hour.

FRIAR LAWRENCE.   Go with me to the vault.

BALTHASAR.   I dare not, sir.
My master knows not but I am gone hence,
And fearfully did menace me with death
If I did stay to look on his intents.

135   **FRIAR LAWRENCE.**   Stay then, I'll go alone. Fear comes upon me.
O, much I fear some ill unthrifty[15] thing.

BALTHASAR.   As I did sleep under this yew tree here,
I dreamt my master and another fought,
And that my master slew him.

FRIAR LAWRENCE.   Romeo!
                   FRIAR *stoops and looks on the blood and weapons.*
140   Alack, alack, what blood is this, which stains
The stony entrance of this <u>sepulchre</u>?
What mean these masterless and gory swords

---

14. **conduct.** Guide
15. **unthrifty.** Unlucky

WORDS FOR EVERYDAY USE:

dis • cern (di zʉrn´) *vt.*, recognize; make out clearly

sep • ul • chre or **sep • ul • cher** (sep´əlk ər) *n.*, vault for burial; grave; tomb

What happens to Romeo?

To lie discolor'd by this place of peace? *Enters the tomb.*
Romeo, O, pale! Who else? What, Paris too?
145 And steep'd in blood? Ah, what an unkind[16] hour
Is guilty of this lamentable chance!
The lady stirs. *JULIET rises.*

JULIET. O comfortable friar! where is my lord?
I do remember well where I should be,
150 And there I am. Where is my Romeo? *Noise within.*

FRIAR LAWRENCE. I hear some noise, lady. Come from that nest
Of death, contagion, and unnatural sleep.
A greater power than we can contradict
Hath thwarted our intents. Come, come away.
155 Thy husband in thy bosom there lies dead;
And Paris too. Come, I'll dispose of thee
Among a sisterhood of holy nuns.
Stay not to question, for the watch is coming.
Come go, good Juliet [*noise again*], I dare no longer stay. *Exit.*

160 **JULIET.** Go get thee hence, for I will not away.
What's here? A cup clos'd in my true love's hand?
Poison, I see, hath been his timeless[17] end.
O churl,[18] drunk all, and left no friendly drop
To help me after?[19] I will kiss thy lips,
165 Haply some poison yet doth hang on them,
To make me die with a restorative.[20]
Thy lips are warm.

1. WATCH. [*Within.*] Lead, boy, which way?

JULIET. Yea, noise? Then I'll be brief. O happy dagger,
Taking Romeo's dagger.
170 This is thy sheath [*stabs herself*]; there rust, and let me die.
Falls on Romeo's body and dies.

Enter Paris's BOY and WATCH.

PAGE. This is the place, there where the torch doth burn.

1. WATCH. The ground is bloody, search about the churchyard.
Go, some of you, whoe'er you find attach.[21] *Exeunt some.*
Pitiful sight! here lies the County slain,
175 And Juliet bleeding, warm, and newly dead,
Who here hath lain this two days buried.
Go tell the Prince, run to the Capulets,
Raise up the Montagues; some others search. *Exeunt others.*

---

16. **unkind.** Unnatural, cruel
17. **timeless.** Untimely, premature
18. **churl.** Low person
19. **help me after.** Help me to come after or follow you
20. **restorative.** Juliet feels such pain that she imagines that death will restore her.
21. **attach.** Stop, detain

We see the ground whereon these woes do lie,
180 But the true ground of all these piteous woes
We cannot without circumstance descry.

Enter some of the WATCH *with Romeo's man* BALTHASAR.

2. WATCH. Here's Romeo's man, we found him in the churchyard.

1. WATCH. Hold him in safety till the Prince come hither.

Enter FRIAR LAWRENCE *and another* WATCHMAN.

3. WATCH. Here is a friar, that trembles, sighs, and weeps.
185 We took this mattock and this spade from him,
As he was coming from this churchyard's side.

1. WATCH. A great suspicion. Stay the friar too.

Enter the PRINCE *and* ATTENDANTS.

PRINCE. What misadventure is so early up,
That calls our person from our morning rest?

Enter Capels CAPULET, LADY CAPULET, *and others.*

190 **CAPULET.** What should it be that is so shrik'd abroad?

LADY CAPULET. O, the people in the street cry "Romeo,"
Some "Juliet," and some "Paris," and all run
With open outcry toward our monument.

PRINCE. What fear is this which startles in your ears?

195 **1. WATCH.** Sovereign, here lies the County Paris slain,
And Romeo dead, and Juliet, dead before,
Warm and new kill'd.

PRINCE. Search, seek, and know how this foul murder comes.

1. WATCH. Here is a friar, and slaughter'd Romeo's man,
200 With instruments upon them, fit to open
These dead men's tombs.

CAPULET. O heavens! O wife, look how our daughter bleeds!
This dagger hath mista'en, for lo his house
Is empty on the back of Montague,
205 And it mis-sheathed in my daughter's bosom!

LADY CAPULET. O me, this sight of death is as a bell
That warns my old age to a sepulchre.

Enter MONTAGUE *and others.*

PRINCE. Come, Montague, for thou art early up
To see thy son and heir now early down.

210 **MONTAGUE.** Alas, my liege,[22] my wife is dead tonight;
Grief of my son's exile hath stopp'd her breath.

What other death does Montague report?

---

22. **liege.** Lord or master

What further woe conspires against mine age?

PRINCE.   Look and thou shalt see.

MONTAGUE.   O thou untaught! what manners is in this,
215   To press before thy father to a grave?

PRINCE.   Seal up the mouth of outrage[23] for a while,
Till we can clear these _ambiguities_,
And know their spring, their head,[24] their true descent,
And then will I be general[25] of your woes,
220   And lead you even to death.[26] Mean time forbear,
And let mischance be slave to patience.
Bring forth the parties of suspicion.[27]

FRIAR LAWRENCE.   I am the greatest, able to do least,
Yet most suspected, as the time and place
225   Doth make against me, of this direful murther;
And here I stand both to impeach and purge
Myself condemned and myself excus'd.

PRINCE.   Then say at once what thou dost know in this.

FRIAR LAWRENCE.   I will be brief, for my short date of breath[28]
230   Is not so long as is a tedious tale.
Romeo, there dead, was husband to that Juliet,
And she, there dead, that Romeo's faithful wife.
I married them, and their stol'n marriage-day
Was Tybalt's dooms-day, whose untimely death
235   Banish'd the new-made bridegroom from this city,
For whom, and not for Tybalt, Juliet pin'd.
You, to remove that siege of grief from her,
Betroth'd and would have married her perforce
To County Paris. Then comes she to me,
240   And with wild looks bid me _devise_ some mean
To rid her from this second marriage,
Or in my cell there would she kill herself.
Then gave I her (so tutor'd by my art)
A sleeping potion, which so took effect
245   As I intended, for it wrought on her
The form of death. Mean time I writ to Romeo,

---

23. **outrage.** Impassioned grief
24. **their spring, their head.** Their source
25. **be general.** Learn about

26. **death.** The execution of guilty persons
27. **parties of suspicion.** Suspects
28. **my . . . breath.** The little time left to me in this life

WORDS FOR
EVERYDAY USE:

am • bi • gu • i • ty (am´bə gyo͞o´ ə tē) *n.*, word or statement
that is uncertain or unclear

de • vise (di vīz´) *vt.*, work out or create; plan

That he should hither come as[29] this dire night
To help to take her from her borrowed grave,
Being the time the potion's force should cease.
250 But he which bore my letter, Friar John,
Was stayed by accident, and yesternight
Return'd my letter back. Then all alone,
At the prefixed hour of her waking,
Came I to take her from her kindred's vault,
255 Meaning to keep her closely at my cell,
Till I conveniently could send to Romeo.
But when I came, some minute ere the time
Of her awakening, here untimely lay
The noble Paris and true Romeo dead.
260 She wakes, and I entreated her come forth
And bear this work of heaven with patience.
But then a noise did scare me from the tomb,
And she, too desperate, would not go with me,
But as it seems, did violence on herself.
265 All this I know, and to the marriage
Her nurse is privy; and if aught in this
Miscarried by my fault, let my old life
Be sacrific'd some hour before his time,
Unto the rigor of severest law.

270 **PRINCE.**   We still[30] have known thee for a holy man.
Where's Romeo's man? what can he say to this?

BALTHASAR.   I brought my master news of Juliet's death,
And then in post he came from Mantua
To this same place, to this same monument.
275 This letter he early bid me give his father,
And threat'ned me with death, going in the vault,
If I departed not and left him there.

PRINCE.   Give me the letter, I will look on it.
Where is the County's page that rais'd the watch?
280 Sirrah, what made[31] your master in this place?

PAGE.   He came with flowers to strew his lady's grave,
And bid me stand aloof, and so I did.
Anon comes one with light to ope the tomb,
And by and by my master drew on him,
285 And then I ran away to call the watch.[32]

PRINCE.   This letter doth make good the friar's words,
Their course of love, the tidings of her death;

---

29. **as.** On
30. **still.** Always
31. **made.** Wanted, did
32. **watch.** Watchman

And here he writes that he did buy a poison
Of a poor 'pothecary, and therewithal
290 Came to this vault, to die and lie with Juliet.
Where be these enemies? Capulet! Montague!
See what a scourge is laid upon your hate,
That heaven finds means to kill your joys with love.
And I for winking at your discords too
295 Have lost a brace[33] of kinsmen. All are punish'd.

What finally happens, after all the deaths?

CAPULET. O brother Montague, give me thy hand.
This is my daughter's jointure,[34] for no more
Can I demand.

MONTAGUE. But I can give thee more,
For I will raise her statue in pure gold,
300 That whiles Verona by that name is known,
There shall no figure at such rate be set
As that of true and faithful Juliet.

CAPULET. As rich shall Romeo's by his lady's lie,
Poor sacrifices of our enmity!

305 **PRINCE.** A glooming[35] peace this morning with it brings,
The sun, for sorrow, will not show his head.
Go hence to have more talk of these sad things;
Some shall be pardon'd, and some punished:
For never was a story of more woe
310 Than this of Juliet and her Romeo.   *Exeunt omnes.*[36] ∎

---

33. **a brace.** Two
34. **jointure.** Dowry
35. **glooming.** Gloomy
36. **Exeunt omnes.** Exit all.

Responding to the Selection

Who do you feel is to blame for the tragic fate of Romeo and Juliet? Should several people share the blame?

Reviewing the Selection

RECALLING

1. What news does Romeo receive from Balthasar in scene i?

2. What does Romeo purchase from the apothecary, or druggist?

3. To whom did Friar Lawrence give the letter addressed to Romeo?

4. Whom does Romeo meet in Juliet's tomb? What does Romeo do to this person? What does he then do to himself? What does Juliet do when she wakes and discovers Romeo's death?

INTERPRETING

5. What does the scene between Balthasar and Romeo teach us about secondhand reports? Why is it important to verify information for ourselves when we can?

6. In what way does Romeo act hastily, without considering matters carefully? Is this haste, or impulsiveness, typical of him? Why, or why not?

7. Why wasn't the letter to Romeo delivered? What did the letter say?

8. Why is Paris angry with Romeo? What does Romeo tell Paris to do? What does Paris do instead? Why does Romeo take the poison? Why does Juliet use the dagger?

SYNTHESIZING

9. At the end of the play, the Prince commands that the vault be sealed "Till we can clear these ambiguities,/And know their spring, their head, their true descent." What are the causes of Romeo and Juliet's tragedy? In what ways are they themselves to blame? In what way is their family to blame? In what way is Friar Lawrence to blame?

10. What happens between the Montagues and the Capulets as a result of the deaths of their children? How is order restored at the end of the play? at what cost?

Understanding Literature (Questions for Discussion)

1. **Plot and Resolution.** A **plot** is the series of events related to a central conflict, or struggle. The **resolution** is the point at which the central conflict is ended, or resolved. What is the central conflict, or struggle, in this play? How is that conflict resolved, or ended, in act V? What about this resolution makes the play into a tragedy?

2. **Summary.** A **summary** is a brief account of the main idea or arguments presented in a work. What does Friar Lawrence summarize at the end of the play? Why does he provide this summary?

3. **Moral.** A **moral** is a lesson that a story teaches. According to Prince Escalus, what moral can be drawn from the deaths of Romeo and Juliet? What do Capulet and Montague agree to do at the end of the play? Why? What have they learned?

4. **Couplet.** A **couplet** is a pair of rhyming lines that expresses a complete thought. With what couplet does this play end? What, in your own words, does that couplet say?

5. **Tragic Flaw.** A **tragic flaw** is a personal weakness that brings about the fall of a character in a tragedy. From what tragic flaw do both Romeo and Juliet suffer? Give examples to support your answer. Why do you think they do so? What does this play teach about the dangers of impulsive young love?

6. **Theme.** A **theme** is a central idea in a literary work. Working with other students, name at least three central themes of this play. Support your ideas by citing, or noting, particular lines that illustrate these themes.

Responding in Writing

Advice Column. Imagine that you write an advice column for a newspaper. You have received the following letter from one of your readers. Answer the letter for your paper. In your answer, refer to *Romeo and Juliet* as an example.

Dear Mr. Lonelihearts:

  I am fourteen years old. Recently I met a girl whom I like very much. She sits beside me in English class, and we often talk together about our writing and other work. I think that she likes me as much as I like her. However, our families are at odds. My father and her father used to be great friends, but years ago they had a quarrel. To this day they do not speak to one another. Recently my father told me not to have anything to do with "that family." Should I tell him about Marissa, the girl in my class? Is it OK for me to ask Marissa to a dance? What should I do?

Confused in Columbus

> **Prewriting Suggestion:** Before writing, think about how the lessons of the play *Romeo and Juliet* might be applied to this situation. Also think about the possible consequences for the boy if he acts in various ways. Remember that as a newspaper columnist, you have a responsibility to offer sound, sensible advice.

UNIT REVIEW

Romance

▷ SYNTHESIS: QUESTIONS FOR WRITING, RESEARCH, OR DISCUSSION

1. In what ways do Romeo and Juliet act impulsively? How does their impulsiveness contribute to their tragic end?

2. What message does this play teach about feuding and grudges between rival groups? How might this message be applied to society today?

LANGUAGE LAB   VARIETIES OF ENGLISH

Formal English is used in writing papers, some magazine articles and nonfiction books, and some literary works. It is spoken at public ceremonies and in official speeches. Check your writing to be sure it is free of informal English, jargon, gobbledygook, clichés, euphemisms, and connotations that might make your writing unclear or inappropriate. The following chart describes these varieties of English.

VARIETIES OF ENGLISH

Informal English. This style of English allows nonstandard grammatical constructions that would be unacceptable in a formal context. Informal English includes **colloquialisms**, which are words and phrases that people use naturally in spoken conversation. It is also peppered with **slang**, a form of speech consisting of coined words, words whose meanings have been changed for no known reason, and words used facetiously or ironically.

NONSTANDARD:	**How come** you look so sad?
COLLOQUIALISM:	It looks like your date **stood you up!**
SLANG:	That wasn't a very **cool** move.

Jargon and Gobbledygook. Jargon is specialized vocabulary used by members of a profession. **Gobbledygook** is unclear, wordy jargon used by bureaucrats or government officials.

JARGON:	After the play's final performance, the stage crew **strikes the set.**
GOBBLEDYGOOK:	The government agency announced plans to **downsize** its staff.

Clichés and Euphemisms. A **cliché** is a figurative expression that has been used so often it has become colorless and uninteresting. A **euphemism** is a "nice" or inoffensive term that substitutes for one that may sound too blunt or offensive to a certain audience.

CLICHÉ:	Juliet's eyes **twinkled like stars.**
EUPHEMISM:	Juliet believed that Romeo had **passed away.**

Denotations and Connotations. The **denotation** of a word is its dictionary definition. A word's **connotations** are all the associations it has in addition to its literal meaning. For example, the denotation of *immature* is "not fully developed," but its connotations can suggest silly behavior.

EXERCISE A Recognizing Varieties of English

Rewrite the following sentences, eliminating any instances of informal English, jargon, gobbledygook, clichés, euphemisms, or inappropriate connotations.

EXAMPLE: Cyrano de Bergerac had a large honker.

Cyrano de Bergerac had a large nose.

1. William Shakespeare sure had a way with words.
2. When Juliet believed that Romeo had died, she freaked out.
3. Cyrano thought Roxanne was drop-dead gorgeous.
4. The teacher accused the student of borrowing ideas for the term paper.
5. If you don't step on it, we won't catch the opening of *Romeo and Juliet!*
6. The characters in Shakespeare's dramas speak a ridiculous form of English.
7. Because the boom was out of position, the sound crew didn't get the actors' voices on tape.
8. The Capulets and the Montagues hated each other's guts.
9. Every summer, the city's theater company stages cheap productions of Shakespearean plays.
10. Although the actor hoped to get the gig, the director cast someone else.

LANGUAGE ARTS SURVEY

For additional help, see the Language Arts Survey, 2.147 and 2.151–2.153.

EXERCISE B Using Formal English

Rewrite the following paragraph, eliminating any instances of informal English, jargon, gobbledygook, clichés, euphemisms, or inappropriate connotations.

So, the other day I went to the theater to catch this new production of *Romeo and Juliet.* These guys knocked my socks off! Don't be put off by the fact that everyone in the play has a stuck-up way of speaking. At first, I was afraid I'd have trouble understanding what was going on; but once I caught on, I was totally into it. Basically, it goes like this: There's this hunk, Romeo, who digs this chick, Juliet. The problem is, they aren't supposed to fall in love because their families don't get along and no one thinks it's a good idea. But Romeo and Juliet fight against all odds because they know they were made for each other. I don't want to blow the ending, but let me just say you won't believe your eyes! I totally give this one a thumbs up.

LANGUAGE ARTS SURVEY

For additional help, see the Language Arts Survey, 2.147 and 2.151–1.153.

LANGUAGE ARTS WORKSHOP

WRITING ON THE JOB

TECHNICAL WRITING 5.7

Follow these guidelines for documenting technical procedures:

- First, make sure you are very familiar with the procedure you will be documenting.
- Break the task into a series of short, simple steps.
- Warn the reader of any potentially hazardous steps or materials.
- List any tools or equipment needed to complete the process.
- List each step in the proper sequence.
- Use the second person imperative. Write "Press the enter key," not "The user should press the enter key."
- Keep your vocabulary simple, avoiding unexplained technical jargon.
- If appropriate, incorporate pictures and diagrams.
- Do not leave out any steps or include unnecessary steps.
- Proofread your instructions to make sure they are easy to follow and unambiguous.
- Ask someone who is not familiar with the operation to follow the directions you have written. If necessary, adjust your instructions based on his or her experience.

EXERCISE A

Imagine that you are writing documentation for an audio cassette recorder. Write the steps for recording sound with a microphone. Use the following information about the tape recorder to write your instructions:

- The tape recorder has the following buttons: play, record, rewind, fast forward, stop, eject.
- The microphone plugs into an outlet labeled "MIC" on the side of the recorder.
- A cassette tape must be placed in the cassette holder before recording can begin.
- The side of the cassette to be recorded must face outward when placed in the cassette holder.
- Recording begins when the "record" button is pressed down.
- Recording ends when the "stop" button is pressed down.
- The microphone should face the noise source for the best quality recording.
- The microphone can be held in the hand or propped up by placing it on its stand.

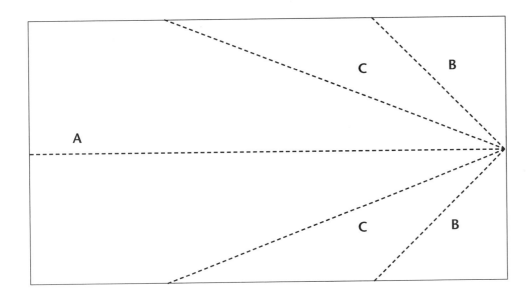

EXERCISE B

The diagram above shows where to fold a piece of paper to make a simple paper air-plane. Look at the diagram carefully. Then read the instructions below, which are incomplete and out of order. Rewrite the instructions, putting the steps in the proper order and adding steps as needed. You can create another kind of diagram if you think the one above is unclear or incomplete.

• Fold along lines C.

• Fold the paper in half lengthwise and then unfold it again. The fold now shows where the middle of the paper is.

• Fold the paper in half again.

• Fold the top right and top left corners down (B) so that the corners touch the middle fold.

• Use sturdy paper (not tissue paper, for example), but nothing too heavy or stiff.

• Make the wings by folding down again.

LANGUAGE ARTS
SURVEY

ESSENTIAL SKILLS:
Writing

INTRODUCTION TO WRITING

Students sometimes assume that writing is a specialized skill, like surfing or opera singing, that only a few people have. The truth is, writing is something every person can learn. Like any other skill it takes practice. You learn to write by writing—as much as you can and as often as you can—and by reading. If you give yourself plenty of writing experiences, in time you'll find yourself not only writing well but writing with confidence and pleasure.

1.1 THE PROCESS OF WRITING

Writing is a process. Although each person's writing process is somewhat unique, almost all writers go through a getting-ready stage, a writing stage, and a refining stage. For the purpose of instruction the writing process is often divided into six stages:

SIX STAGES IN THE PROCESS OF WRITING	
1. **Prewriting**	Choose a topic, audience, purpose, and form. Then gather ideas and organize these in a reasonable way.
2. **Drafting**	Get your ideas down on paper in rough form without worrying about perfecting spelling, grammar, usage, and mechanics.
3. **Peer and Self-Evaluation**	Study your draft by yourself or with one or more of your peers to find ways to improve it.
4. **Revising**	Revise your draft to improve its content, organization, and style.
5. **Proofreading**	Check your revised draft for errors in spelling, grammar, usage, and mechanics (including punctuation and capitalization). Then prepare a final copy in an appropriate manuscript form and proofread again.
6. **Publishing and Presenting**	Share your work with an audience.

▶ ▶ ▶ A C T I V I T Y **1.1**

Think about your past experiences as a writer. Answer the following questions on a sheet of paper or in your journal.

1. Do you find writing difficult or easy? Do you enjoy writing? What do you think are your strengths and weaknesses as a writer?

2. Is there a particular kind of writing that you enjoy doing the most? (Consult the list of Forms of Writing on pages 000–000.) What do you like about this kind of writing? What kind of writing would you like to learn more about?

3. Writers often have favorite tools for writing. What sort of writing materials do you prefer? Do you use a pencil or a pen? Is it a certain color? Do you like to write on ruled pages in a notebook? on blank pages in a record book? on a computer or typewriter?

4. Do you tend to devote a lot of time to prewriting? In the past, what sorts of prewriting activities did you do? Which activities were the most helpful?

5. As a writer, do you like to get everything down on paper quickly in rough form and then rework it, or do you prefer to work more slowly, refining your ideas and expression as you go?

6. What stage of the writing process tends to give you the most trouble?

7. How do you feel about sharing your writing with others? What kinds of responses to your writing have helped you in the past?

1.2 KEEPING A WRITER'S JOURNAL

A **writer's journal** is a place to store ideas you can use in your writing. You can keep your journal in a spiral notebook, a loose-leaf binder, a composition book, a bound record book of the kind sold in stationery stores, or on a computer. To get the most out of your journal, keep it in a separate notebook and write in it every day. The following ideas can help you to start:

IDEAS FOR JOURNAL ENTRIES	
The Journal as Diary	Record observations and experiences from your daily life. Explore your feelings about people and events.
The Journal as Commonplace Book	Record interesting phrases or ideas that you hear from others or that you encounter in your reading.
The Journal as Writer's Lab	Record your ideas for pieces of writing to do in the future. Do freewriting on subjects of interest to you. Try out different kinds of writing, such as monologues, dialogues, song lyrics, concrete poetry, and riddles.

CONTINUED

The Journal as Planner	Write about what you want to do over the next week, month, year, or ten years. Explore your goals and dreams. Think on paper about how to meet your goals. Make lists of activities to help yourself grow.
The Journal as Reader Response Forum	Record your reactions to works that you read for class and on your own. Talk back to the authors, take issue with them, expand on what they say, and explore their ideas.

► ► ► ACTIVITY 1.2

Begin a journal. For one week, write at least one journal entry of each kind discussed in the preceding chart. Date each entry. Be sure to write your name and address somewhere on your journal so that it can be returned to you if it gets lost.

1.3 KEEPING A WRITER'S PORTFOLIO

A **writer's portfolio** is a folder in which you store your drafts and finished pieces of writing. Your teacher may ask you to keep a portfolio so the two of you can assess your progress over time.

You may be asked to keep all the writing that you do for the class, along with evaluation forms for that writing, in a **comprehensive portfolio.** Alternatively, you may be asked to keep a **selected portfolio**, which contains the pieces of writing that you think are your best. The pieces that you choose for a selected portfolio should reflect the various skills you have developed and the various types of writing you have done.

If you keep a selected portfolio, you should still save the pieces of writing that you do not include. Put them in a safe place in case you or your teacher wants to refer to these pieces later.

For each piece of writing that you place in your portfolio, be sure to attach any earlier notes or drafts. Your teacher can use these to see how each piece of writing developed. Also, include any completed evaluation forms requested by your teacher.

If you keep a portfolio, your teacher will ask you to evaluate it from time to time. After the two of you evaluate the portfolio separately, you will probably have a meeting, or **student-teacher conference,** to discuss your work and to set goals for further development.

► ► ► ACTIVITY 1.3

Following your teacher's instructions, begin a writer's portfolio. You might put in this portfolio pieces of writing you have done in the past that you think are especially successful. You could also include your answers to the questions in Activity 1.1.

1.4 Using Computers for Writing

A computer is not an essential tool for writing. Mark Twain did just fine with a typewriter that had only capital letters! Using a personal computer, however, can simplify many parts of the writing process.

Computer Hardware

Hardware refers to the machinery of a computer. The core of this machinery is the **central processing unit,** or **CPU.** It carries out the instructions given by the computer user. Connected to the CPU, or sometimes in the same case with it, are various **peripherals,** devices for storing, inputting, and outputting information, or **data.**

COMMON COMPUTER PERIPHERALS	
Storage Devices	• **Floppy diskettes,** or **floppies,** are small, flat media used to store and to transport limited amounts of data, such as individual computer files and programs. • **Hard drives** store large amounts of data on revolving disks. A hard drive can be **internal** (located inside the case with the CPU) or **external** (housed in a separate case and connected to the CPU by a cable). • **Removable media,** like hard drives, store large amounts of data. However, unlike hard drives, they can be inserted and ejected, like floppy disks. Common removable media include CD/ROMs, optical disks, and DAT tapes.
Input Devices	• **Keyboards,** the most common of all input devices, allow you to type numbers, alphabetic characters, and special computer commands. • **Mice** and **trackballs** are devices that are used to point to and select items on a computer monitor. • **Digitizing tablets** allow you to write in longhand and to draw directly onto the computer screen. • **Scanners** allow you to turn pictures or words into computer files that can then be edited or otherwise manipulated. • **Voice recognition devices** allow you to speak commands to the computer. Some will even transcribe, or write, your speech into a computer file that can then be edited.
Output Devices	• **Monitors** are the most common output devices. A monitor is a screen, similar to the ones on televisions, that shows you the work that you are doing on the computer. • **Printers** are machines that create **hard copies,** or printed paper, of the work that you have done on the computer. • **Modems** are devices for communicating, over telephone lines, with other computers.

Computer Software

Software is the set of instructions for making a computer do particular tasks. A particular piece of software is called a **program.** The following chart describes types of programs commonly used by writers.

SOFTWARE FOR WRITERS	
Operating System	An **operating system,** or **OS,** is a program that tells the computer how to do general tasks—how to create, save, and store files; what to do when specific commands are given; how to print files; and so on.
Application Software	An **application program** enables the user to accomplish a particular kind of task. Common application programs include the following: • **Word-processing programs** allow you to key in words. Most such programs also allow you to revise your writing, to check its spelling, to add special formatting such as boldface or italic letters, and to save and print your work. Many of these programs also allow you to consult a built-in dictionary and/or thesaurus and to check your grammar, usage, capitalization, and punctuation. • **Page-layout programs** allow you to put your writing into columns and boxes and to add graphic elements such as lines, borders, photographs, and illustrations. Such programs are used to produce newsletters, posters, flyers, newspapers, magazines, and books. • **Graphics programs** allow you to create illustrations and to edit photographs. • **Telecommunications programs** allow you to use a **modem** to connect over telephone lines to other computers, to **on-line information services,** or to **computer networks** such as the **Internet.** Other types of programs often used by writers include ones for creating outlines, graphs, charts, indexes, and bibliographies.

Applications of Computers to Writing

Like a typewriter, a computer is a useful tool for getting words onto a page. However, computers can do more. They allow you to

• revise, or edit, your writing easily, simply by moving around words, sentences, or paragraphs;
• format your writing in special ways—by specifying bold or italic type, by specifying a particular style of lettering, by automating functions such as paragraph, page, and line breaks, and so on;
• look up definitions, synonyms, and antonyms and automatically check spelling, grammar, usage, and mechanics;
• print multiple copies of your work;
• add photographs and illustrations to your work;
• use computer-accessed information sources such as on-line information services and encyclopedias on CD/ROM.

Although the computer offers advantages, many writers prefer to work in longhand or to use a typewriter. The choice of writing instrument is a personal one. Of course, it also depends on the availability of machines and instruction on how to use them. Many schools have **writing labs** where computers are available to students. Computers may also sometimes be available in school or public libraries.

> ► ► ► **A C T I V I T Y 1.4 a**
>
> Interview two writers, one who uses a computer regularly and one who prefers not to use a computer. Ask the writers what they like and dislike about using a computer as a writing tool. Make notes of their responses and share them with another student.

PREWRITING: DEVELOPING A PLAN FOR WRITING

Imagine that you have been given a week to explore the scenic lakes of northern Minnesota by canoe. Would you just show up with paddle in hand, or would you come up with some plans beforehand? Most likely, you would do some planning, because a plan can help ensure the success of the trip. The same is true of writing. Good writing can sometimes occur spontaneously. If you make a plan ahead of time, however, the writing is likely to go more smoothly and to be more fun. The following elements are part of a good writing plan:

ELEMENTS OF A WRITING PLAN	
Topic	The specific subject that you will be writing about
Purpose	The aim, or goal, that you want the piece of writing to accomplish: to express yourself, to create a literary work, to inform, or to persuade
Audience	The person or persons who will read or hear your work
Form	The specific type of writing that you will be doing (for example, a press release or a short story)
Mode	The method of presentation of the ideas in a piece of writing. Common modes, often combined in actual pieces of writing, include narration, dialogue, description, and various kinds of exposition, such as analysis or comparison and contrast.

> ► ► ► **A C T I V I T Y 1.4b**
>
> In your journal, sketch a plan for a piece of writing that you could do at a future time. List the form, topic, purpose, audience, and mode of the piece. Refer to the Language Arts Survey, 1.5–1.8, to help you complete this activity.

1.5 CHOOSING AND FOCUSING A TOPIC

Choosing a Topic

When trying to think of a topic to write about, many students draw a blank. If you find yourself in this situation, don't despair. Most writers find it difficult to come up with good ideas for writing. The following list of tips will help you find a topic that engages you:

TIPS FOR DISCOVERING WRITING TOPICS	
Read Your Journal	Make a habit of jotting down ideas for writing in your journal. Pretty soon, you will have a store of good ideas to draw from.
Draw on Your Experience	Think about experiences that you have had in the past, from early childhood on. People, places, and events from personal experience make excellent topics for writing. Making a time line of your life might help to jog your memory.
Consult Reference Works and Other Media	Browsing through reference works, looking through the shelves in a library, paging through magazines or newspapers, exploring the contents of informational CD/ROMs—all can help you to find topics worth writing about.
Do Some Freewriting	One interesting way to come up with a writing idea is simply to put your pen to paper and start writing about whatever pops into your mind, without stopping to think about spelling, grammar, usage, and mechanics. Don't force yourself to stick to one subject. Freewriting is one situation in which it's actually good to let your mind wander. Write for five to ten minutes. Then look over your freewriting for topic ideas.
Talk to People	Other people can be excellent resources for writing ideas. Draw on the experiences of the people around you. Ask them about subjects of interest to you and to them.

> ► ► ► A C T I V I T Y 1.5a
>
> Select a place in your journal to list possible topics for writing. Using the techniques discussed above, come up with at least ten topics for future pieces of writing. Add to your list whenever other ideas for topics occur to you. Be sure to keep the list in a separate part of your journal so you can find it easily when you have a writing assignment.

Focusing a Topic

A good way to select a topic is to start with a general topic and then to focus on some part of that general topic. Here is an example:

General topic: Shakespeare's writings

Focused topic 1: moral lessons in Shakespeare's historical plays

Focused topic 2: minor characters in Shakespeare's *Romeo and Juliet*

Writers may choose general topics or focused topics. Generally, the shorter the piece of writing you plan to do, the more focused the topic should be. For example, in a two-page composition on a general topic such as Shakespeare's writings, you would not be able to include much detail. If you wrote a piece of the same length about minor characters in Shakespeare's *Romeo and Juliet*, a narrower topic, you could go into more depth.

TECHNIQUES FOR FOCUSING TOPICS	
Analyze the Topic	Break the topic down into its parts. Then think about how the parts relate to one another.
Do a Tree Diagram	Write the topic at the top of a page. Then break it into parts, and break those parts into parts.
Ask Questions	Write questions about the topic beginning with the words *who, what, where, when, why,* and *how.* Decide which answers to these questions are most important for your piece.

Other techniques for focusing topics include freewriting and clustering (see the Language Arts Survey, 1.12, "Freewriting," and 1.17, "Clustering").

► ► ► A C T I V I T Y **1.5b**

Choose one of the general topics below or choose a topic from the list in your journal. List three narrower topics that are related to the general topic:

General topics:	museums	math	cities
	the past	popular music	sports

1.6 CHOOSING A PURPOSE OR AIM

Writing is one way of communicating with others. **Communication** is the act of sending and receiving **messages.** Four elements are involved in every communication: the **sender** of the message; the **receiver,** or **recipient,** of the message; the **subject** of the message; and the **code** (the signs or symbols) used to communicate the message. These elements of communication are often pictured as a **communication triangle.**

The Communication Triangle

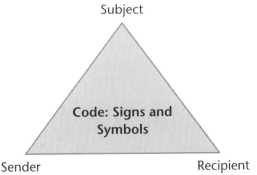

Subject

Code: Signs and Symbols

Sender   Recipient

The **purpose,** or **aim,** of a piece of writing is the goal that the writer wants to achieve. The study of purpose in writing and speaking is called **rhetoric.** Teachers of rhetoric since the time of the ancient Greeks have worked out various systems for classifying types of writing and speech. One useful classification scheme has the four classes described below. Each class of writing in this scheme emphasizes one part of the communication triangle. Each class also has a different primary purpose.

THE CLASSIFICATION OF WRITING AND SPEECH BY PURPOSE OR AIM			
Type	Focus is on . . .	Purpose is to . . .	Examples
Expressive Writing	the sender (the writer or speaker)	express the feelings of the writer or speaker	journal entry, credo
Informative Writing	the subject	provide information about the subject	accident reports, book report
Persuasive Writing	the recipient (the reader or listener)	move the reader or listener to adopt a point of view or to act in a particular way	campaign speech, public service ad
Literary Writing	the signs or symbols used to communicate the message	create a work of art	lyric poem, short story

Limitations of Classification Systems

A classification scheme like the one above is useful for thinking about and discussing writing and speech. However, an actual piece of writing rarely falls neatly into a single category. Most pieces of writing have more than one purpose. Take, for example, Henry Wadsworth Longfellow's poem, "Paul Revere's Ride," on page 000. The writer obviously had in mind the purpose of creating a literary work of art. The poem, however, also *informs* the reader about a historical event and attempts to *persuade* the reader about the importance of that event.

Purpose and the Writing Process

Thinking about purpose can be useful to you as a writer. For example, if you have decided that your main purpose is to inform, then your main task during prewriting will be to gather information. If your primary purpose is to persuade, then you will focus on finding persuasive arguments. Thinking about purpose also can help you during revision. A good question to ask before you start to revise is, "Have I accomplished my purpose?" Your answer will guide you in changing the piece of writing so that it better accomplishes your purpose.

> ▶ ▶ ▶ A C T I V I T I E S **1.6**
>
> **A.** Draw and label a communication triangle for each communications situation below. Identify the sender, the recipient, the subject, and the code.
>
> 1. A coach gives a speech to her team, praising the team's performance in a recent game.
>
> *CONTINUED*

2. A teenager uses sign language to tell a friend about a new movie.

3. A child writes a letter to his parents about his experiences at summer camp.

4. A hula dancer at a public festival performs a story about her Hawaiian ancestors.

B. Identify the primary purpose of each of type of writing below.

1. a poem

2. an entry in a journal

3. a magazine interview with a rock musician

4. a newspaper editorial supporting a political candidate

1.7 CHOOSING AND ANALYZING AN AUDIENCE

You may not always know exactly who will be reading or hearing your writing, but it's still a good idea to have a specific audience in mind as you write. Thinking about a specific audience will help you to

- select details, examples, or arguments that will be interesting or persuasive to your reader;
- determine what information to include or to leave out;
- decide how formal or informal and how complex or simple your language should be.

QUESTIONS TO ASK ABOUT YOUR AUDIENCE

How much does my audience already know about the subject? How much background information do I have to provide to make my writing understandable to this audience? Does the audience know enough about the subject to make it possible for me to write technically or to use jargon?

What interests, wishes, or goals does my audience have? How can I relate what I am writing to those interests, wishes, and goals?

How old and how well educated is my audience? How complex or sophisticated should my writing be?

Which would be more effective and appropriate for my audience, formal or informal language?

► ► ► A C T I V I T Y 1.7

Rewrite each of the following passages for the audience indicated in parentheses. Explain to a classmate what changes you made to make the passage appropriate for its new audience.

1. From a short story: The fire-engine red Toyota pickup was parked in front of the Rose Bowl. (Rewrite for a person who is new to the United States and has a very limited English vocabulary.)

CONTINUED

2. From an advertisement: This exciting eighteen-minute video lets you experience in the privacy of your home the thrills and luxuries of a sailboat cruise through the sparkling Caribbean. (Rewrite as a description for a friend.)

3. From the Pledge of Allegiance: "I pledge allegiance to the flag of the United States of America and to the republic for which it stands." (Rewrite as an explanation for adult citizens of a former dictatorship that has just become a democracy.)

4. From an instruction manual: WARNING: Not submersible. Danger of electrical shock. (Rewrite as directions for a young child.)

1.8 Choosing a Form

What form will your writing take? This is one of the most important decisions that a writer makes. The following chart lists forms that you might consider using in writing you do for class and on your own.

FORMS OF WRITING

Abstract	Bylaws	Dialogue
Acceptance speech	Campaign speech	Diary
Ad copy	Captions	Diatribe
Address to a jury	Cartoon	Dictionary entry
Adventure	Cause-and-effect essay	Directions
Advice column	Chant	Docudrama
Afterword	Character sketch	Dramatic narrative
Agenda	Charter	Dream analysis
Allegory	Cheer	Dream report
Annals	Children's story	Editorial
Annotation	Cinquain	Elegy
Annual report	Classified ad	Encyclopedia article
Apology	Comeback speech	Epic
Appeal	Comedy	Epic poem
Autobiography	Comic strip	Epilogue
Ballad	Community calendar	Epistolary fiction
Ballet	Concrete poem	Epitaph
Bibliography	Constitution	Essay
Billboard	Constructive speech	Eulogy
Biography	Consumer report	Experiment
Birth announcement	Contract	Explication
Blank verse	Court decision	Exposé
Book review	Credo	Fable
Brief	Critical analysis	Fabliaux
Brochure	Curriculum	Family history
Bulletin board	Daydream	Fantasy
Business letter	Debate	Filmstrip
Business proposal	Detective story	Flyer

CONTINUED

Foreword	Nature guide	Riddle
Fortune cookie insert	News story	Roast
Found poem	Nomination speech	Romance
Free verse	Nonsense rhyme	Sales letter
Gothic tale	Novel	Schedule
Graduation speech	Novella	Science fiction
Graffiti	Nursery rhyme	Screenplay
Grant application	Obituary	Sermon
Greeting card	One-act play	Short short story
Haiku	Oracle	Short story
Headline	Ottava rima	Sign
History	Packaging copy	Situation comedy
Horoscope	Parable	Slide show
Human interest story	Paragraph	Slogan
Informative essay	Paraphrase	Song lyric
Instructions	Parody	Sonnet (Petrarchan,
Insult	Party platform	Elizabethan, or
Interview questions	Pastoral	Spenserian)
Introduction	Persuasive essay	Specifications
Invitation	Petition	Spell
Itinerary	Play	Sports story
Jingle	Police/Accident	Storyboard
Joke	report	Stream-of-consciousness
Journal entry	Political advertisement	fiction
Keynote address	Prediction	Summary
Lament	Preface	Summation
Law (statute)	Press release	Survey
Learning log	Proclamation	Sutra
Letter of complaint	Profile	Tall tale
Letter to the editor	Prologue	Tanka
Libretto	Proposal	Technical writing
Limerick	Prose poem	Terza rima
Love letter	Protocol	Test
Lyric poem	Public service announcement	Thank-you note
Magazine article	Quatrain	Theater review
Manifesto	Radio play	Toast
Manual	Radio spot	Tour guide
Memorandum	Rap	Tragedy
Memorial plaque	Reader's theater production	Translation
Menu	Rebuttal	Treaty
Minutes	Recipe	TV spot
Monologue	Recommendation	Villanelle
Monument inscription	Referendum question	Vows
Movie review	Research report	Want ad
Mystery	Resignation	Wanted poster
Myth	Restaurant review	Warrant
Narrative poem	Résumé	Wish list

A good way to get acquainted with the possibilities and limitations of forms of writing is to try to convert one form into a different form. Refer to the Handbook of Literary Terms if you need more information about the forms of writing given below.

1. Rewrite a fable or folk tale as a poem or song lyric.

2. Find a biography or biographical sketch in a history textbook. Choose a portion of the material to rewrite as an interview with the subject.

1.9 Modes of Writing

Writing can be classified by **mode** as well as by form. A mode is a way of presenting ideas, information, and details in a piece of writing. Although most pieces of writing combine several different modes, in any particular piece one type usually dominates. The following chart lists the most common modes:

COMMON MODES OF WRITING		
Mode	**Explanation**	**Forms in Which This Mode Dominates**
Narration	Presents events, usually in chronological order	Short story News report Process/How-to writing
Dialogue	Presents the speech of characters	Drama Dramatic poem Docudrama
Description	Uses images to present a portrait in words	Imagist poem Tour guide
Exposition	Presents information	(See below)

Exposition can take many different forms. The most common are analysis, comparison and contrast, classification, and cause-and-effect analysis.

An **analysis** divides a subject into its parts and then shows how the parts are related to each other and to the whole. For example, an analysis of a daily diet might break it down into carbohydrates, proteins, and fats. An analysis of a short story might break it down into setting, characters, plot, and theme.

Exposition based on **comparison and contrast** shows similarities and differences between one or more subjects. For example, a writer might compare a road to the path a person takes through life.

Classification divides a group into smaller groups, or classes, of things that are similar in some way. A writer discussing popular music might divide the subject into country music, rock music, rap music, and so on.

A **cause-and-effect** analysis describes a sequence of events in which one or more events cause, or bring about, one or more other events. For instance, a writer explaining why a basketball team lost a critical game (the effect) might discuss several causes, such as the team's stamina, rebounding, defense, and strategy.

Sometimes a writer will use a single mode almost exclusively. For example, a radio play is almost entirely dialogue. Most pieces of writing combine two or more modes. Thus, a short story will typically contain narration to present events in sequence, description to flesh out the characters and setting, dialogue to show characters interacting, and exposition to comment on what is happening in the story.

► ► ► A C T I V I T Y **1.9**

Choose one of the following topics. Write four short pieces about that topic, using a different one of the four major modes—narration, description, dialogue, and exposition—in each piece.

computers   summer
school facilities a cultural celebration

PREWRITING: EXPLORING IDEAS ON YOUR OWN

Have you ever thought of yourself as a rich person? Most of us are richer than we know—rich in personal experiences and in knowledge and understanding that increase day by day. This section of the Language Arts Survey will give you some suggestions on how to mine those riches for ideas and details you can use in your writing.

1.10 RECALLING

Experienced writers often advise young people to "write about what you already know." You probably know more than you are aware of. You may know what it's like to live in a large family or to live with a single parent. You may know a lot about computer games or street basketball or butterflies. You may have had an important emotional experience that changed the way you look at the world or yourself. The key to turning such experiences into good writing is **recalling,** or remembering, them vividly. Here are some hints for recalling past experiences that might serve as writing topics:

USING RECALL TO GATHER WRITING IDEAS

1. Choose some time in your life that you want to think about. It might be early childhood, for example, when you were first learning about the world around you. It might be the time when you started going to a new school or working at a new part-time job.

2. Make a time line of events that occurred during that period. (See the Language Arts Survey, 1.19, for more information on making time lines.)

3. Make a list of questions, problems, opinions, wishes, dreams, or goals that you had during that time.

CONTINUED

---

4. List important things that you learned during that time. How did you grow or change? What brought about this growth or change?

5. Make a list of the important people in your life at that time. What was interesting, engaging, or unusual about each of these people? How did they look, dress, talk, and behave? What ideas, opinions, attitudes, and habits did they have? What did you learn from them? How did they act toward you and you toward them? Why?

6. Make a list of specific places that you associate with that time. Close your eyes and try to imagine one of these places. Think about what it looked like. What sights, sounds, smells, or tastes come to mind when you think of this place? How did the place make you feel?

7. If you wish to do a piece of imaginative writing, think of past experiences as raw material to be reshaped and transformed. Choose aspects of your past experience and ask yourself questions about them. Begin your questions with the words *what if.*

What if my family had lived in the country instead of in the city?

What if I had chosen to pursue football instead of soccer?

What if my mother, a fourth-grade teacher, had turned out to be *my* teacher?

Once you have selected a particular person, place, thing, or event from your past to write about, try to recall as many details about it as you can. Use a graphic device such as a cluster diagram, sensory detail chart, or time line to generate specific details to use in your writing. For information about these devices, see the Language Arts Survey, 1.18–1.24.

> ▶ ▶ ▶ **A C T I V I T I E S   1.10**

A. In your journal, make a time line of your life. On the time line, list specific places that you associate with a certain year or a certain period of your life.

B. Choose one place from your time line and do a sensory detail chart about this place (see the Language Arts Survey, 1.18).

C. Using your sensory detail chart to vivify your memories, freewrite about this place (see the Language Arts Survey, 1.12).

1.11 OBSERVING

In many ways, it's the details that make life interesting, from your classmate's dirty fingernails to the last rose of summer. Good writers know this and develop their powers of observation. They also develop the habit of noticing interesting sights, sounds, statements, and events wherever they go and recording these in their journals. Of special interest to writers is the **telling detail**—one that implies a great deal. For example, in a description of the coming of winter, one small detail—a last autumn leaf clinging to a bare vine—could suggest the bleakness of the season.

As a writer, you may also call upon your powers of observation to write about present events. For example, you might want to review a school play or report on a controversial issue. In such situations, ask yourself the questions that reporters typically ask when gathering information for a news story: *who? what? where? when? why?* and *how?* As you view the event, jot down answers to these questions in brief form and record details of sight, sound, touch, taste, and smell.

► ► ► **A** CTIVITIES **1.11**

A. The next time you are riding on a bus or in a car, make observations about what you see in the passing scenes outside the window. Record interesting, unusual, and telling details.

B. Choose a busy scene, such as a restaurant, playground, or market. Observe the scene carefully and record what you see, hear, feel, taste, and smell.

C. Describe a particular tree, flower, or other plant in minute detail. Use a full range of sensory details.

1.12 FREEWRITING

Many students find that they can come up with writing ideas and interesting details about a topic by **freewriting.** Freewriting is simply putting pen or pencil to paper and then writing whatever comes into your mind, without pausing to judge or revise or correct your work. You should try to write for several minutes without stopping. If you get stuck, simply repeat the last few words you wrote until something new pops into your mind. Here's a sample of what one student wrote during a freewriting session:

> I never know where to start. I don't like looking at a blank page. At least it's not blank now. blank blank blank—a field of snow, a blank look, a blank wall. Walls. Like the Berlin Wall, the Great Wall. hey, there's a climbing wall at the new backpacking store at the mall. It looks like a vertical rock face. And there are tiny ledges and hollows to put your feet and hands. They have free climbing clinics sometimes. I'd love to try it. I wonder if my folks would let me. Now that would be something interesting to write about! but freewriting's not over yet, over yet, over yet. I used to climb trees a lot, when I was little, especially this one old oak tree. It was my special private spot when I was nine.

Another approach to freewriting is **focused freewriting.** In a focused freewrite you still write nonstop for a short period, but you begin with one topic and keep bringing yourself back to it whenever your mind wanders to something else. Focused freewriting is a good way to explore what you already know about a topic.

► ► ► **A** CTIVITIES **1.12**

A. Reread the freewrite above. List four possible topics for writing based on this freewrite.

B. Choose a topic from the list of topics in your journal and freewrite about it for five minutes.

CONTINUED

C. Do a focused freewrite about one of the following topics:

clouds	forgetfulness	music videos
dogs	going to the dentist	people I admire
friendship	maps	teaching

1.13 QUESTIONING

Another excellent technique for gathering ideas and focusing a writing topic is to ask questions. Try asking the well-known **reporting questions:** *who? what? where? when? why?* and *how?* This approach is especially useful when you are gathering information about an event or planning a narrative such as a news report or short story.

If you are doing literary or expressive writing, try asking questions that begin with the words *what if.* "What if" questions can spark your imagination and lead you down unexpected and interesting paths. Here are some examples:

EXAMPLES   *What if* animals could speak? What would a pet cat say? What would cows and other livestock say? What would dolphins say?

What if young people weren't required to go to school? What would they do instead? How would they learn? How would their lives be affected? How would society be affected?

What if intelligent life were discovered on a planet in another galaxy?

What if someone were to become lost in the frozen Arctic? What would that person think and feel? How would the person survive?

> ► ► ► A C T I V I T I E S   1.13

A. Choose one of the following topics. In your journal, write questions about the topic beginning with *who, what, where, when, why,* and *how.*

bicycling	commercials	flight	junk food
Canada	counseling	horses	Native Americans
college	deserts	jokes	twins

B. Choose three topics from the list above and write "what if" questions about them.

1.14 ANALYZING

Analyzing is a way to gather and sort information about a topic. To analyze something, you break it down into its parts and then think about how the parts are related. An **analysis chart** can help you list the parts, describe each one, and explain how each is related to the whole.

ANALYSIS OF "THE ROAD NOT TAKEN" (PAGE 441)

Part	Description	Relationship of Part to Whole
Stanza 1 (lines 1–5)	The speaker describes a decision he must make—choose one of two roads.	Introduces basic situation—the need to make a choice
Stanza 2 (lines 6–10)	The speaker compares the two roads and tells which road he took (the one less traveled) and why.	Presents the speaker's response to the situation described in stanza 1
Stanza 3 (lines 11–15)	The speaker compares the roads further (they now seem more similar) and realizes that he probably will never have the chance to take the other road.	Presents the speaker's reflection on the choice made in stanza 2
Stanza 4 (lines 16–20)	The speaker restates the choice he made and reflects ("with a sigh") on the consequences of his choice (it "has made all the difference").	Summarizes the speaker's choice and his feelings and thoughts about it

►►► ACTIVITIES 1.14

A. Select a poem from Unit 2 that is divided into stanzas. Do an analysis chart for the poem, following the model given above.

B. Choose a process or activity that you know well: for example, washing a dog, patching a pair of jeans, or flying a kite. Create an analysis chart to describe that process.

C. Choose a group or organization with which you are very familiar, perhaps your school, a club or sports team, or a workplace. Create an analysis chart to describe that group's structure.

1.15 IMAGINING

When you think of things not as they actually are but as they might be, you are **imagining.** Writers use their ability to imagine to create new settings, characters, plots, and themes. While the actual processes of creativity remain mysterious, there are some simple techniques, known as **heuristics,** that you can use to spark and drive your imagination and to develop creative ideas for writing.

1. Ask questions beginning with the words *what if.* (Example: What if you could be as small as a flea? What if medical doctors did not have to be licensed? What if the United States ran out of electricity?)

2. Combine previously existing things in a new way. (Example: Use your grandmother's accounts of coming to America as a young girl to create a character in a short story about a family of immigrants.)

3. Magnify something, making it bigger or more significant than it is now. (Example: Write a poem about a winter snowstorm that lasts for thirty days.)

4. Simplify something to make it more manageable to write about. (Example: Create a minor character for a story based on your younger brother, who has the amusing habit of speaking in short rhymes. Let this particular trait be the defining quality of the character.)

5. Make a drawing, sketch, or diagram of something you want to write about. (Example: Draw a picture of the unusual restaurant that will be the main setting for your story.)

6. Start with something as it is and change it systematically. (Example: Create a story about a family that is like your family in the Midwest except that the family members live in Australia, raise sheep instead of beans, have Australian accents instead of Midwest accents, and so on.)

7. Project a trend into the future. (Example: Write about a time when cities occupy every square mile of your state.)

8. Work against type. (Example: Write a poem about a president who is shy.)

▶ ▶ ▶ A C T I V I T Y **1.15**

Choose one heuristic from the chart above and use it to come up with an idea for a piece of imaginative writing.

1.16 ROLE PLAYING

When you use **role playing** to generate ideas for writing, you work with others to enact an imagined situation. Each person adopts a certain character or role in the situation. Role playing can be especially helpful when you are developing characters or exploring a controversial issue for a piece of persuasive writing. When you use role playing, you may want to record the session on audio- or videotape for closer study later on. Alternatively, you could ask someone to watch the role play and take notes on it.

▶ ▶ ▶ A C T I V I T I E S **1.16**

A. Role play one of the following situations with a partner:
  • Two neighbors discussing the city's plan to build a freeway through their neighborhood

CONTINUED

- An argument between an older sister (or brother) and a younger sister (or brother) about privacy
- Two citizens with opposite opinions discussing whether prayer should be allowed in public schools
- A conversation between two friends, one of whom has just been forsaken by a former best friend

B. Using the role play above as source material, write a scene for a play.

1.17 CLUSTERING

Sample Cluster Chart

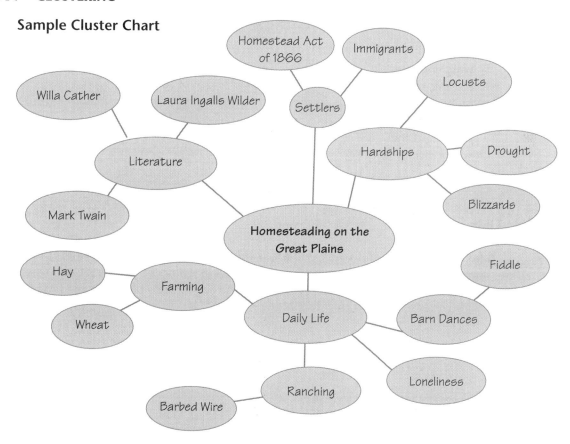

▶ ▶ ▶ **A C T I V I T Y 1.17**

Draw a cluster chart for one of the topics in Activity 1.13.

1.18 SENSORY DETAIL CHARTS

A **sensory detail chart** is a useful tool when you are preparing to do a piece of descriptive writing. Begin by listing your subject at the top of a page. Beneath the subject, list the five senses: *sight, hearing, touch, taste,* and *smell.* Then, under each heading, list details about your subject.

CAMPFIRE AT MCGEE LAKE				
Sight	Hearing	Touch	Taste	Smell
yellow flames glowing faces dancing shadows	snap and pop of fire owl hooting in distance	log seats hot face, cold back	burnt marsh- mallows burnt corn burnt fish	smoke pine trees

► ► ► **A C T I V I T Y 1.18**

A. Create a sensory detail chart for one of the following situations. Include as many details as you can.

watching a movie
a picnic on the beach
building a snowman
mowing a lawn
washing dishes
scuba diving

1.19 TIME LINES

A **time line** can be useful when you are planning a piece of narrative writing. To make a time line, draw a line on a piece of paper and divide it into a number of equal segments. Label each segment, and then add key events at the appropriate places on the time line.

Sample Time Line: My Family History

❶ Grandma Henrietta born (Santa Clara: 1915)
❷ Grandpa Joz joins Army, sent to California (1919)
❸ Grandma and Grandpa married (San Francisco: 1935)
❹ Mom born (Honolulu: 6/15/52)
❺ Dad born (San Francisco: 3/26/55)
❻ Mom arrives San Francisco (1975)
❼ Mom and Dad meet (1/1/77)
❽ Mom and Dad married (11/11/81)
❾ Brother Sam born (7/12/83)
❿ My birth (7/4/85)

1.20 FLOW CHARTS

A **flow chart** is a good way to organize ideas and information when you are planning to write about a process or sequence of events, as you might in an expository piece. A flow chart shows what happens and in what order. In this type of chart, a rectangle around a step means "perform an action and continue to the next step," a diamond means "make a decision," and a triangle means "stop."

Using an On-line Card Catalog

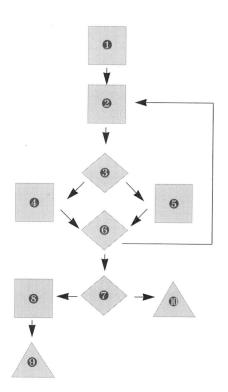

❶ Select type of search (author, title, subject)

❷ Type search request

❸ Is book available?

❹ If yes, note call number

❺ If no, complete book request slip

❻ Any more books to search for?
   If yes, return to step 2

❼ If no, any books to retrieve from shelves?

❽ If yes, retrieve books from shelves

❾ Stop

❿ If no, stop

1.21 STORY MAPS

A **story map** is a chart that shows the elements of a short story. Most story maps include the following elements: setting, mood, conflict, plot, major characters, and theme.

Setting and Mood	Conflict _____ internal __✓__ external
Time _____1830s_____	Eliza must find her way safely to freedom in the North.
Place _the Ohio River_	**Plot**
Mood _suspenseful_	Inciting incident _Eliza flees from a Kentucky plantation and is pursued by slave hunters._
Major characters	Climax _Eliza comes to the Ohio River, full of dangerous ice floes._
Eliza Harris (runaway slave)	Resolution _Eliza leaps from floe to floe to cross the river to freedom and is helped by Reverend Rankin to travel on to Canada._
Reverend John Rankin (guide on Underground Railroad)	Themes _courage; determination; personal integrity_

Story maps can take many forms. They may describe elements of the setting, traits of the characters, and specific events in the plot.

► ► ► **A C T I V I T Y 1.21**

Create a story map for a story that you have read.

1.22 PRO AND CON CHARTS

A **pro and con chart** can be helpful when planning a piece of persuasive writing or when making a decision. At the top of the chart, write a proposition. This could be a statement of fact, of a policy, or of a personal value. Create two columns under the proposition. Label one *Pro* and the other *Con.* In these columns, list arguments or evidence in support of (pro) and against (con) the proposition.

Proposition: All students should be required to take a foreign language.	
Pro	**Con**
—gain familiarity with another culture	—may never be used
—gain deeper understanding of language	—time better spent on other courses
—may be useful in future	

► ► ► **A C T I V I T Y 1.22**

Make a pro and con chart for a decision you will soon face.

1.23 ANALYSIS CHARTS

An **analysis chart** divides a thing into its parts and then shows how these parts are related to the whole. (See the sample analysis chart in the Language Arts Survey, 1.14.)

Create an analysis chart to show the elements of a forest.

1.24 VENN DIAGRAMS

A **Venn diagram** is commonly used to show the similarities and differences between two things. This graphic device can help you plan a piece of writing based on comparison and contrast. To create a Venn diagram, draw two intersecting circles. Label each with the name of one of your subjects. In the area where the circles overlap, list properties shared by the two subjects. In the areas that do not overlap, write properties that are unique to the two subjects, respectively.

Rhymed Verse **Free Verse**

imagery

—rhyme at end of lines   rhythmic effects   —usually lacks end rhymes

—regular meter   figures of speech   —irregular meter

► ► ► A C T I V I T Y **1.24**

Choose one of the graphic devices described in the previous sections (1.17–1.24). Use it to develop an idea for a piece of writing.

PREWRITING: USING OUTSIDE SOURCES

1.25 BRAINSTORMING

Brainstorming is a process in which you try to think of as many different ideas as you can, as quickly as possible, without stopping to evaluate or comment on the ideas. You can brainstorm in a small group or by yourself. The most important point to remember is that no idea should be rejected during this activity. The more ideas, the better.

► ► ► A C T I V I T Y **1.25**

With a small group, choose a subject about which you can brainstorm for ten minutes. For example, you might brainstorm about ideas for a story set on a tropical island. Designate one person to record the ideas on the board or on a flip chart. Give everyone a chance to speak, and keep the atmosphere spontaneous.

1.26 Discussion

Discussion is an idea-generating technique that involves other people. A discussion is a conversation focused on a specific topic. Discussion members sometimes assume particular roles. The **group leader** presents the topic, asks questions, draws out responses, and generally keeps the discussion on track. The **participants** in the discussion offer their thoughts, listen attentively to others, and respond to others' comments. All discussion members should speak calmly and politely. Sometimes the group appoints a **secretary** to record the ideas discussed.

> ► ► ► **A C T I V I T Y   1.26**
>
> Hold a discussion with four other students about publicizing a school concert. Choose names out of a hat to designate a group leader and a secretary.

1.27 Interviewing

Sometimes you will want to gather ideas for writing by **interviewing** a person who has some experience or understanding of your subject. Newspaper articles, for example, frequently contain information taken from interviews. When you interview, remember these tips:

- Get permission from the interviewee to print his or her statements.
- Ask questions that start with the words *who, what, when, where, why,* and *how.*
- Write down the interviewee's most important statements word for word so you can quote some of them in your piece.
- Get the correct spelling of the interviewee's name so you can cite accurately the source of your information.

> ► ► ► **A C T I V I T Y   1.27**
>
> Choose a topic that interests you and about which someone you know is an expert. For example, if you are curious about sailing and you know someone who has learned to sail, you could interview that person. Use a notepad and, if available, a tape recorder to record your interview. Then write a brief article that includes a quotation from your expert.

1.28 Using Print Sources

No matter what your subject, there probably are print sources that contain information about it. Books, magazines, newspapers, brochures, and reference works are the most common print sources. To locate books, use your library's card catalog or on-line catalog. For magazines, consult the *Readers' Guide to Periodical Literature.* To find newspaper articles, use the print, microfilm, or microfiche indexes to newspapers.

> ► ► ► **A C T I V I T Y   1.28**
>
> Choose a subject that interests you, such as folk art, Catherine de Medici, or three-toed sloths. Find three different print sources of information on that subject. Briefly identify each source by title, author, date, and publication name (if appropriate).

1.29 USING NONPRINT SOURCES

The number and kind of nonprint sources of information have grown terrifically in recent years. These sources can also be useful to you when gathering information and ideas for writing. Nonprint sources include television and radio programs, films, videos, slides, photographic prints, filmstrips, audiocassette tapes, and CD/ROMs, as well as various kinds of on-line computer services. You can find many of these materials in libraries. For specific information about accessing information via computer, talk to a resource person at your school or library.

> ▶ ▶ ▶ A C T I V I T Y 1.29
>
> Find at least three nonprint sources offering information on one of the following subjects. Then write a brief description of each source.
>
> | | | |
> |---|---|---|
> | nursing | soccer | careers |
> | tornadoes | gourmet cooking | workplace safety |

PREWRITING: ORGANIZING YOUR IDEAS

1.30 REVISING YOUR WRITING PLAN

After you have gathered information for a piece of writing, you should review your writing plan. Think about the topic, purpose, audience, form, and mode of writing you have chosen. The information you have gathered may prompt you to change parts of your plan. For example, while researching the Harlem Renaissance, you may have found especially interesting information about Langston Hughes. You might now decide to narrow your topic to this particular poet. This decision, in turn, might lead you to change other parts of your plan, such as the form or mode of writing.

> ▶ ▶ ▶ A C T I V I T Y 1.30
>
> Choose a general subject and a narrower subject related to it. Make a writing plan for each subject, listing a topic, purpose, audience, form, and primary mode.

1.31 IDENTIFYING MAIN IDEAS AND SUPPORTING DETAILS

Once you have gathered information for a piece of writing, read through your notes to identify the main ideas that you want to present. Next, look for details that support these main ideas. For a short piece of writing such as a paragraph, you will want to identify a single main idea and several supporting details. For a longer piece of writing, you could begin by creating a **thesis statement** that expresses the major idea you want to communicate and then look for several main ideas related to your thesis and for details to support each main idea.

> ▶ ▶ ▶ A C T I V I T Y 1.31
>
> Choose one of the following subjects for a descriptive paragraph:
>
> - Your first day of school as a freshman
> - The view from a particular window
>
> CONTINUED

- A place where you feel comfortable
- Approaching the finish line in a running race

Write a topic sentence to express a main idea about the subject. Then write at least three supporting details to support your main idea.

1.32 Making a Rough Outline

A **rough outline**, also called an **informal outline**, can help you organize ideas for writing. When you create a rough outline, you list main ideas in some logical order. Under each main idea you list supporting details preceded by dashes or bullets. Here is a rough outline for a paper about primitive camping.

Primitive Camping

What it is
—Living in the wild for a short time
—Walking is only transportation
—Camping gear is carried on back
—No water or toilet facilities

Why people like it
—Get away from busy life
—Natural surroundings
—Quiet

How to do it
—Necessary gear
—Places to go
—Take a buddy for safety

► ► ► A C T I V I T Y 1.32

Choose a topic related to the outdoors. Make a rough outline for a composition on your topic.

1.33 Making a Formal Outline

In a **formal outline**, Roman numerals, letters, and numbers identify headings and subheadings. The entries at each level should be parallel in grammatical structure and should begin with capital letters. There are two types of formal outline. A **topic outline** has entries that are words, phrases, or clauses. A **sentence outline** has complete sentences for entries. The following sample is from a topic outline:

Interesting birds of coastal Florida

I. Diving birds

   A Cormorants

   B. Anhingas

II. Wading birds

A. Herons

   1. Green herons

   2. Yellow-crowned night herons

B. Roseate spoonbills

C. White ibises

▶ ▶ ▶ **A C T I V I T Y 1.33**

Create a formal topic outline or sentence outline for a paper on a subject of your own choosing.

1.34 ORGANIZING IDEAS

Writers use outlines to put their ideas into some logical order. The chart that follows shows some common ways in which writers organize ideas.

METHODS FOR ORGANIZING IDEAS	
Chronological Order	Events are organized in order of their occurrence, often from first to last. Ideas are connected by transitional words and phrases that indicate time or sequence, such as *first, second, finally, next, then, afterward,* and *before.*
Spatial Order	Subjects are organized according to their positions or locations, often from top to bottom, left to right, front to back, clockwise, or the reverse of any of these. Ideas are connected by transitional words and phrases that indicate position or location, such as *beside, in the middle, next, to the right, on top,* and *in front.*
Degree Order	Ideas are presented in order of degree from most to least or vice versa. For example, they might be presented from most important to least important. Ideas are connected by transitional words and phrases that indicate degree, such as *more, less, most, least, most important,* and *least promising.*
Comparison and Contrast Order	Details about two subjects are presented in one of two ways. In the first method, the characteristics of one subject are presented, followed by the characteristics of a second subject. In the second method, both subjects are compared and contrasted with regard to one characteristic, then with regard to a second characteristic, and so on. Ideas are connected by transitional words and phrases that indicate similarities or differences, such as *likewise, similarly, in contrast, a different kind,* and *another difference.* *CONTINUED*

METHODS FOR ORGANIZING IDEAS	
Cause-and-Effect Order	One or more causes are presented followed by one or more effects, or one or more effects are presented followed by one or more causes. Ideas are connected by transitional words and phrases that indicate cause and effect, such as *one cause, another effect, as a result, consequently,* and *therefore.*
Classification Order	Subjects are divided into groups, or classes. These groups are then presented, one by one, in some reasonable order. Ideas are connected by transitional words and phrases that indicate class membership or the method by which the writer has organized the classes, such as *another group, the first type, one kind,* and *other sorts.*
Part-by-Part Order	Ideas are presented according to no *overall* organizational pattern. However, each idea is connected logically to the one that precedes it and/or to the one that follows it. After chronological order, this is the most common method for organizing ideas in writing. Ideas are connected by any transitional word or phrase that indicates the relationship or connection between the ideas.

► ► ► A C T I V I T Y **1.34**

Choose an appropriate method of organizing ideas for each piece of writing below. Then briefly explain your choice.

1. a composition about different types of guitar music
2. a description of the Grand Canyon
3. a report on the causes of the Depression
4. an account of a football game
5. an article on the pros and cons of owning your own home

DRAFTING: APPROACHES TO WRITING A DRAFT

1.35 WRITING A DISCOVERY DRAFT

When you have completed your prewriting and are ready to begin your first draft, there are several approaches you can take. You might write a **discovery draft.** In a discovery draft, you work to get all of your ideas down on paper quickly, without giving much thought to organization, style, grammar, spelling, mechanics, and so on. This type of draft is extremely rough. It gives the writer raw material that is later refined, through one or more extensive revisions, into the final piece of writing.

> > > **A C T I V I T Y 1.35**

Choose one of the following topics. Then write a discovery draft of a paragraph about the topic. Write quickly, simply putting all of your ideas down on paper.

> a good friend
> a rainy day
> a store that you like
> frustration

1.36 WRITING A CAREFUL DRAFT

Another approach to drafting is to write a **careful draft.** This type of draft works best if it is based on a thorough outline. Writers who prefer to write careful drafts work slowly and carefully, revising and polishing the initial draft as they go. For example, a writer might draft a topic sentence first and then revise it until it seems just right before going on to the next sentence. Other writers prefer to do several drafts, each more polished than the one before. Both approaches can produce great writing.

> > > **A C T I V I T Y 1.36**

Choose a topic from the following list. Make an outline of your topic by listing the main idea and three supporting details. Then write a careful draft of a paragraph based on your outline. Revise each sentence as you go.

> a favorite item to wear
> a favorite song
> a pet you might like to own
> what you might do after high school

1.37 THE PREWRITING, DRAFTING, AND REVISING CYCLE

Writing does sometimes occur in neatly separated parts—prewriting, drafting, and revising. More often, however, writers move back and forth between the stages. For example, you might discover during drafting that you need more information about some aspect of your topic, so you would do some more prewriting. You might also draft a particular paragraph and then revise a weak topic sentence in that paragraph before drafting the next paragraph. The order of stages of the writing process is as flexible as you need it to be.

DRAFTING: PARAGRAPHS

1.38 PARAGRAPHS WITH TOPIC SENTENCES

A paragraph often includes a **topic sentence** that presents its main idea. The topic sentence can be placed at the beginning, middle, or end of the paragraph. Most paragraphs also contain two or more sentences related to the topic sentence. These sentences may illustrate or elaborate on the topic sentence. Often, these **supporting sentences** begin with transitions that relate them to the other sentences or to the topic sentence. The paragraph may also end with a **clincher sentence**, which sums up what has been said in the paragraph. Read the following paragraph to identify its parts.

Topic Sentence	The solitary stone house at the edge of the darkening moor was a welcome sight. The travelers had been walking over the
Supporting Sentences	rough, soggy ground all day. Their feet were cold and wet, their bodies tired. Hours ago, they had eaten the last of their provisions—a few stale biscuits and a small bit of cheese. As they
Clincher Sentence	spotted a warm light glowing from one of the tiny windows in the house, their pace quickened and their spirits rose.

▶ ▶ ▶ A C T I V I T Y **1.38**

Write a paragraph about one of the following topics or a topic of your own choosing. Begin the paragraph with a topic sentence. Then write three sentences that elaborate on the topic sentence. End with a clincher sentence that wraps up the paragraph.

a description of a food associated with a particular celebration
your opinion on when teenagers should begin dating
your favorite musician

1.39 PARAGRAPHS WITHOUT TOPIC SENTENCES

Most paragraphs do not have topic sentences. In such paragraphs, the topic sentence is often implied rather than stated directly. For example, narrative paragraphs often simply state a series of events, and no sentence in the paragraph sums up the events, as in this example:

To get to the sixteenth-century fort, we started from the north end of the village. Then we walked uphill along Via San Marco until we reached a small, white church that looks out over the countryside. About two hundred feet beyond the church, the dark-gray fortress loomed above everything else.

Other paragraphs may serve simply as transitions between other paragraphs or as parts of a dialogue.

▶ ▶ ▶ A C T I V I T Y **1.39**

Write a narrative paragraph about what happens as you travel from home to school on a typical school day. Organize your paragraph in chronological order, and do not include a topic sentence.

1.40 Elaboration: Types of Supporting Details

If a paragraph has a topic sentence, the rest of the paragraph will elaborate on the main idea presented in the topic sentence. There are many types of supporting details. **Sensory details** are facts about things seen, smelled, touched, heard, and tasted. **Anecdotes** are brief stories from everyday life intended to demonstrate a point. **Facts and statistics, illustrations and examples,** and **quotations** are other types of supporting details. In the sample paragraph in the Language Arts Survey, 1.38, notice that the main idea is elaborated using sensory details.

> ► ► ► A C T I V I T Y **1.40**
>
> Some topic sentences are listed below. For each sentence, write at least two supporting sentences containing details of the type specified.
>
> 1. The desert heat was beginning to take its toll on the travelers. (illustrations)
> 2. The king's guests were delighted by the magnificent banquet spread out before them. (sensory details)
> 3. One must often make sacrifices in order to achieve one's goals. (anecdote)

DRAFTING: COMPOSITIONS

1.41 Writing a Thesis Statement and Topic Sentences

A **thesis statement** expresses the main idea of a composition. Writers usually state the thesis in the first paragraph. The remainder of the paragraph introduces the thesis statement and the composition as a whole. A thesis statement should be direct and concise. It should also show clearly whether the composition is primarily expressive, informative, or persuasive.

An excellent way to draft a composition is to write a thesis statement first and then write the **topic sentences** for the body paragraphs of the composition. These sentences should lay out the major ideas that support your thesis. Once you have this basic skeleton, you can flesh out the thesis statement and topic sentences with the rest of your introduction, supporting sentences for the body paragraphs, and your conclusion.

> ► ► ► A C T I V I T Y **1.41**
>
> Write a focused thesis statement for an informative or persuasive composition on one of the following topics. Then write three supporting topic sentences for the body paragraphs.
>
> volunteering on community projects   ways to earn money
>
> getting along with brothers and sisters   a current school controversy

1.42 ORGANIZING A COMPOSITION

Every composition should have three parts: an introduction, a body, and a conclusion.

Introduction. The purpose of the introduction is to capture the reader's attention and express the main idea of the composition. You might use one or more of the following elements in your introduction:

- Describe a scene
- Offer a fascinating fact
- Pose a question

- Present a quotation
- Give a summary
- Provide an anecdote

Body. The body of the composition consists of several paragraphs that support the thesis statement. Generally, each paragraph has a topic sentence that expresses a supporting main idea. Other sentences in each paragraph elaborate on its main idea.

Conclusion. The conclusion of the composition should round out the composition and give the reader a sense of completeness. Here are some common techniques used in writing conclusions:

- Restate the main idea
- Make a generalization
- Pose a question

- Make a prediction
- Imagine the future
- Present the last event

▶ ▶ ▶ **A C T I V I T I E S 1.42**

A. Search for some essays in magazines. Find one that has an opening that you really like. Read the opening out loud in a small group of students. Be prepared to explain what technique the writer used to attract the reader's attention and what the essay is about.

B. Repeat the previous activity with conclusions instead of openings. Before reading the conclusion that you choose, give your listeners some background about the essay so they can place the conclusion in context. Be prepared to explain what technique the writer used to create a sense of completeness.

REVISING: APPROACHES TO REVISION

1.43 SELF-EVALUATION

When your draft is finished, you will want to reread it to **evaluate,** or judge, its effectiveness. Many writers recommend waiting a day or two before doing a **self-evaluation.** By waiting, you will be able to experience the piece more as a first-time reader would.

A good self-evaluation practice is to read the composition through three times. On the first reading, check the content and unity. The second time, check organization and coherence. On the third reading, check voice and style. Use the following checklists to guide you in adding, deleting, replacing, or moving material. When you have made your revisions, read the piece aloud to spot and adjust any awkward passages.

REVISION CHECKLIST: CONTENT AND UNITY

1. Does the writing achieve its purpose?
2. Are the main ideas related to the thesis statement?
3. Are the main ideas clearly stated and supported by details?

REVISION CHECKLIST: ORGANIZATION AND COHERENCE

1. Are the ideas arranged in a logical order?
2. Do transitions connect ideas to one another both within and between paragraphs?

REVISION CHECKLIST: VOICE AND STYLE

1. Is the voice—the tone, word choice, and perspective of the writing—authentic? Is it consistent?
2. Is the level of language appropriate to the audience and purpose?
3. Is the mood appropriate to the purpose and form of the writing?

► ► ► A C T I V I T Y **1.43**

Select a piece of writing that you have done previously. Read it through three times to make revisions using the three checklists given above.

1.44 PEER EVALUATION

Peer evaluation is a form of evaluation in which a fellow writer gives you feedback on the effectiveness of a piece of writing. To maximize the benefits of peer evaluation, follow these guidelines.

For the Writer

- Tell your evaluator what aspect of the composition you are concerned about. Here are some examples:

   —**Content.** I'm not sure the topic is narrow enough.

   —**Organization.** I'm wondering if the reader can easily follow the sequence of events.

   —**Style.** Do you think the mood comes across clearly in the opening paragraph?

- Thank the evaluator and accept the comments politely. If you do not understand or if you disagree with a particular comment, ask the evaluator to clarify it. Avoid taking criticisms of your writing personally.

For the Evaluator

- Be focused. You should evaluate content, organization, and style. Ignore proofreading matters, such as spelling, punctuation, and mechanics, which will be dealt with later.

- Be positive. Let the writer know what he or she has done right. Discuss weak spots by pointing out what the writer would gain by making a certain change.

- Be specific. Give the writer concrete ideas for improving the piece. For example, if you think that organizing the piece using spatial order makes more sense than using degree order, suggest how the writer could rearrange the content of the piece to fit this pattern.

- Be tactful. Use constructive language and a pleasant tone of voice. Word your comments so the writer knows you are critiquing the writing, not the person behind the writing.

> ► ► ► **A C T I V I T Y 1.44**
>
> Choose a "work in progress" that you think is ready to be evaluated by a peer. Ask a classmate to read your writing and comment on strong points and weak points in the composition.

1.45 FOUR TYPES OF REVISION

During revision, writers use four basic processes to change what they have written: **adding, deleting, replacing,** and **moving.** They use these processes to manipulate words, sentences and parts of sentences, and even entire paragraphs. For example, as you revise a paragraph, you might add transitions between the sentences. You might delete, or cut out, a detail that does not support the main idea. You might replace a dull description with a vivid one. And you might move a sentence that is out of order to its correct place.

> ► ► ► **A C T I V I T Y 1.45**
>
> Revise the following paragraph. Add, delete, replace, or move material as necessary to produce a well-written final draft.
>
> Have you ever thought to get rich by giving up junk food? With that money you could buy yourself something worth a lot more pleasure than junk food. How many junk food lunches do you eat a week and what does each lunch cost? Just answer these simple questions. Say you eat out twice a week and spend $3 for each meal. In a typical school year, you would be spending $192 on nothing but hamburgers, fries, tacos, etc. Well, maybe not become rich, but you could save an extremely high amount of money. That's sufficient to buy a CD-player, some great clothes, or a used computer. My advice is to think twice the next time you expend a few bucks at the burger joint. Get rich instead.

1.46 MARKING A MANUSCRIPT

When you mark revisions on your writing, use the standard proofreading symbols. After just a little practice you'll find them very easy and convenient.

SYMBOL AND EXAMPLE	MEANING OF SYMBOL
The very first time	Delete this material.
french toast	Capitalize this letter.
the vice-President	Lowercase this letter.
cat' cradle	Insert something that is missing. Write the missing letter(s) or punctuation above the line.
Geor̩ze	Replace this letter or word.
housŝe	Take out this letter and close up space.
book keeper	Close up space.
gebril	Change the order of these letters.
All the horses (king's)	Move this word to where the arrow points.
end. "Watch out," she yelled.	Begin a new paragraph.
Love conquers all.	Put a period here.
Welcome friends.	Put a comma here.
Getthe stopwatch	Put a space here.
Dear Madam	Put a colon here.
She walked he rode.	Put a semicolon here.
name-brand products	Put a hyphen here.
cats meow	Put an apostrophe here.
cat's cradle (stet)	Let it stand. (Leave it be.)

PROOFREADING AND PUBLISHING

1.47 PROOFREADING CHECKLIST

After you have revised your draft, make a clean copy and proofread it for errors in spelling, grammar, usage, and mechanics. Use the following proofreading checklist.

PROOFREADING CHECKLIST	
Spelling	• Are all words, including names, spelled correctly?
Grammar	• Does each verb agree in number with its subject? • Are verb tenses consistent and correct? • Are irregular verbs formed correctly? • Is the referent of each pronoun clear? • Does every pronoun agree with its antecedent? • Are subject and object forms of pronouns used correctly? • Are there any sentence fragments or run-ons? • Have double negatives been avoided?

CONTINUED

PROOFREADING CHECKLIST	
Usage	• Have frequently confused words, such as *affect* and *effect*, been used correctly?
Mechanics	• Does every sentence end with an end mark? • Are commas, semicolons, hyphens, and dashes used correctly? • Do all proper nouns and proper adjectives begin with capital letters? • Has proper manuscript form been used?

► ► ► A C T I V I T Y **1.47**

Using the proofreading checklist, correct the following paragraph for spelling, grammar, usage, and mechanics errors.

In the summertime, whenever Im not doing 101 chores, playing soft ball, or hanging out with friends: you can find me in an apple tree. The old tree in back of our house has too branches exactly the right distance a part for a hammock. I read there. I doze there I birdwatch there. sometimes I just gaze up into the branches, when they is covered with apple blossoms or loaded down with ripening apples, and think. My "hang-out" is a great place to daydream. It's also a place I like go to cool out or to reflect on something that's ben bothering me. My tree place is a nest, a study a beauty spot, a thinking spot

1.48 PREPARING YOUR MANUSCRIPT

Once you have proofread your draft, you are ready to prepare the final manuscript. Follow the guidelines given by your teacher. Your teacher may prefer that you use the guidelines below, which are common.

Guidelines for preparing your manuscript:

1. Type, word process, or write neatly in blue or black ink.
2. Double-space your paper. In other words, leave one blank line between every line of type.
3. Use one side of the paper.
4. Leave one-inch margins on all sides of the text.
5. Indent the first line of each paragraph.
6. In the upper right-hand corner, put your name, class, and date. On every page after the first, include the page number in this heading as follows:

> Gloria Ramirez
> English 12
> May 6, 1999
> p. 2

7. Make a cover sheet containing the title of the work, your name, the date, and the class.

After preparing a final manuscript based on these guidelines, proofread it one last time for errors introduced in the typing, word processing, or handwriting.

1.49 PUBLISHING OR PRESENTING YOUR WORK

Some writing is done just for one's self. Journal writing usually falls into that category. However, most writing is meant to be shared with others. There are many, many ways in which to share your work. Here are several ways in which you can publish your writing or present it to others:

- Find a local publication that will accept such work (a school literary magazine, a school newspaper, or a community newspaper are possibilities).

- Submit the work to a regional or national publication. Check a reference work such as *Writer's Market* to find information on types of manuscripts accepted, manuscript form, methods and amounts of payment, and so on.

- Enter the work in a contest. Your teacher may be able to tell you about writing contests for students. You can also find out about such contests by looking for announcements in writer's magazines and literary magazines.

- Read your work aloud to classmates, friends, or family members.

- Obtain permission to read your work aloud over the school's public address system.

- Work with other students to prepare a publication—a brochure, literary magazine, anthology, or newspaper.

- Prepare a poster or bulletin board, perhaps in collaboration with other students, to display your writing.

- Make your own book by typing or word processing the pages and binding them together in some way. Another possibility is to copy your work into a blank book.

- Hold a recital of student writing as a class or school-wide project.

- Share your writing with other students in a small writer's group that meets periodically to discuss one or two students' recent work. (Members of the group should receive the work to be discussed beforehand so they can read it and make notes on it.)

- If the work is dramatic in nature, work with other students to present a performance of it, either as straight drama or as reader's theater. If the work is poetry, fiction, or nonfiction, work with others to present it as an oral interpretation. (One possibility is to pair with another student, exchange pieces, and then coach one another in oral interpretations of the pieces.)

ESSENTIAL SKILLS:
Language

GRAMMAR HANDBOOK

INTRODUCTION TO GRAMMAR

2.1 THE GRAMMAR YOU ALREADY KNOW

Grammar is something you know, even if you have never studied it. Inside the head of every person is a sophisticated device that works, all by itself, to learn how to put words and phrases together grammatically. Even if you don't know an adverb from an aardvark, you know, if you are a speaker of English, that

the big blue sky

is grammatical and that

the sky big blue

is not. You can tell that one string of words is grammatical and the other isn't because you have learned, unconsciously, many thousands of rules governing how words can be put together and how they can't.

When you study a grammar textbook, therefore, what you are really learning is not the grammar of the language—for the most part, that's something you already know. What you are learning is terminology for describing what you know so that you can use that terminology when discussing language. Incidentally, as you study textbook grammar, you will also learn a few rules that you never quite learned unconsciously. Remember, however, that most of the grammar is already inside your head. Learning to describe that grammar can therefore be viewed as learning more about yourself and your amazing unconscious abilities.

2.2 THE USES OF GRAMMAR

Why study grammar? After all, no amount of grammar study can match the value of hands-on reading and writing. Grammar is useful, however. It gives you a way to speak about and understand your own writing and that of others. Contrast the following examples:

After her return to the prison, Hester Prynne was found to be in a state of nervous excitement that demanded constant watchfulness, lest she should perpetuate violence on herself, or do some half-frenzied mischief to the poor babe. As night approached, it proving impossible to quell her insubordination by rebuke or threats of punishment, Master Brackett, the jailer, thought fit to introduce a physician.

—Nathaniel Hawthorne, *The Scarlet Letter*

The folks have all gone away. They thought that they left me alone, and contrived things to amuse me should they stay long, and *I* be lonely. Lonely indeed. They didn't look, and they couldn't have seen if they had, who should bear me company. *Three* here instead of *one*—wouldn't it scare them?

—Emily Dickinson, Letter to Abiah Root

If you had to describe the difference between these two passages, you would find it useful to have precise grammatical terms. The first sentence in Hawthorne's passage begins with two prepositional phrases, which are followed by an independent clause expressed in the passive voice and modified by an adverbial clause. Dickinson's letter, in contrast, begins with a short simple sentence. Although the following longer sentence is made more complicated than the first by a compound predicate and infinitive phrase, it is still simpler than Hawthorne's. Dickinson follows this sentence with a sentence fragment, which makes her writing more casual. You may sense the differences in these two styles of writing, but grammar gives you a way to *understand* and *communicate* those differences.

THE PARTS OF SPEECH

2.3 COMMON AND PROPER NOUNS

A **noun** is a word used to refer to a person, place, thing, or idea.

NOUNS   Carrie Nation, Rhode Island, statue, freedom

A **common noun** is a name that belongs to (is *common* to) all the persons, places, or things in a group. A **proper noun** refers to a *particular* person, place, or thing and begins with a capital letter.

COMMON NOUNS	man, city, war
PROPER NOUNS	Paul Revere, Boston, War of Independence

2.4 CONCRETE AND ABSTRACT NOUNS

A **concrete noun** refers to an object that you can perceive by hearing, seeing, smelling, tasting, or touching. An **abstract noun** names a quality, characteristic, or idea.

CONCRETE NOUNS	cry, child, perfume, candy, clothing
ABSTRACT NOUNS	fear, beauty, truth

2.5 COMPOUND AND COLLECTIVE NOUNS

A **compound noun** is made up of two or more words used together as a single noun. A **collective noun** refers to a group of similar things.

COMPOUND NOUNS   book review, boogie-woogie, boondoggle
COLLECTIVE NOUNS   dozen, gang, club, jury, family, Congress, Dodgers

2.6 PERSONAL PRONOUNS

A **pronoun** is a word used as a substitute for a noun. The word a pronoun stands for is called an **antecedent** or **referent**. In the following example, *door* is the antecedent of the pronoun *it*.

ANTECEDENT AND PRONOUN   As the **door** swung open, **it** creaked.

A **personal pronoun** is a pronoun that substitutes for a person's name. The personal pronouns are *I, me, my, mine, we, us, our, ours, you, your, yours, he, him, his, she, her, hers, it, its, they, them, their,* and *theirs.*

PERSONAL PRONOUNS   **She** watches the stars and marks the time.
It's **your** work that will be famous.

2.7 REFLEXIVE AND INTENSIVE PRONOUNS

A **reflexive pronoun** is a pronoun used to show that an action is done to or reflects upon someone or something. An **intensive pronoun** is a pronoun used to emphasize a noun or pronoun already given. The reflexive and intensive pronouns are *myself, ourselves, yourself, yourselves, himself, herself, itself,* and *themselves.*

REFLEXIVE PRONOUN   I wrote **myself** a letter but didn't mail it.
INTENSIVE PRONOUN   The Grimms **themselves** wouldn't have told such a tale.

2.8 DEMONSTRATIVE PRONOUNS

A **demonstrative pronoun** is a pronoun used to point out a particular person, place, or thing. The demonstrative pronouns are *this, that, these,* and *those.*

DEMONSTRATIVE PRONOUNS   Look here! **These** are the books to read.
What is **this**?

2.9 INDEFINITE PRONOUNS

An **indefinite** pronoun is a pronoun that points out a person, place, or thing, but not a particular one. Some of the most common indefinite pronouns are *some, someone, somebody, something, any, anyone, anybody, anything, everyone, everybody, everything, other, another, either, neither, all, many, few, each, both, one, none, nobody,* and *nothing.*

INDEFINITE PRONOUNS Not **anyone** could have played the part.
Nothing should stand between you and your goal.

2.10 INTERROGATIVE PRONOUNS

An **interrogative pronoun** is a pronoun used in asking a question. The interrogative pronouns are *who, whose, what, whom,* and *which.*

INTERROGATIVE PRONOUNS **What** is the meaning of this?
Who will have the last word?

2.11 RELATIVE PRONOUNS

A **relative pronoun** is a pronoun that connects a group of words with an antecedent. The relative pronouns are *that, which, who, whom,* and *whose.*

RELATIVE PRONOUNS Cummings is a poet **who** didn't use capital letters.
Have you heard the news **that** the game will be played on Saturday?

2.12 ACTION VERBS

A **verb** is a word that expresses action or a state of being. An **action verb** expresses physical or mental activity.

ACTION VERBS play, believe, run, laugh, quit, shrug

2.13 LINKING VERBS

A **linking verb** connects a noun with another noun, pronoun, or adjective that describes it or identifies it. Most linking verbs are forms of the verb *to be.* They include *am, are, is, was,* and *been.* Other words that can be used as linking verbs include *seem, sound, look, stay, feel, remain,* and *become.*

LINKING VERBS The butler **is** the main suspect.
He **looks** guilty.

2.14 Auxiliary Verbs

An **auxiliary verb** is a verb that helps to make some form of another verb. Common auxiliary verbs are *can, could, may, might, must, shall, should, will, would,* and forms of the verbs *to be, to have,* and *to do.*

<table>
<tr><td>AUXILIARY VERBS</td><td>has played, should pay, will be coming, must be going
We had finally completed our work.</td></tr>
</table>

2.15 Transitive and Intransitive Verbs

The **direct object** of a verb is a noun or pronoun that names the person or thing upon which the verb acts. Verbs that must have direct objects are **transitive verbs**. Verbs that do not need direct objects are **intransitive verbs**. Some verbs are both transitive and intransitive.

<table>
<tr><td>TRANSITIVE VERB</td><td>Penelope wove a tapestry.</td></tr>
<tr><td>INTRANSITIVE VERB</td><td>While she worked, she waited.</td></tr>
</table>

2.16 Verbals: Participles

A **participle** is a form of a verb that can be used as an adjective. (See the Language Arts Survey, 2.19, for the definition of an adjective.)

<table>
<tr><td>PARTICIPLES</td><td>A sleeping poet seldom produces.
Having no money, I couldn't go.
He tipped his hat to a passing motorist.</td></tr>
</table>

2.17 Verbals: Gerunds

A **gerund** is a form of a verb ending in *–ing* that is used as a noun. Be careful not to confuse gerunds with participles, verbal adjectives that end in *–ing.*

<table>
<tr><td>GERUNDS</td><td>Flipping the pages isn't reading.
Her singing was sadly off key.
I thought you'd given up waiting for us.</td></tr>
</table>

2.18 Verbals: Infinitives

An **infinitive** is a form of a verb that can be used as a noun, an adjective, or an adverb. Most infinitives begin with *to.* (See the Language Arts Survey, 2.19 and 2.22, for more information about adjectives and adverbs.)

INFINITIVES   **To read** is to live many lives.
"I like **to see** it lap the miles" is both a title and a first line.
Help me **write** my own poem.

2.19 ADJECTIVES AND ARTICLES

An **adjective** is a word used to modify a noun or pronoun. *To modify* means to change the meaning of something. Adjectives change the meaning of nouns or pronouns by answering the questions *What kind? Which one?* or *How many?*

ADJECTIVES   **small** town, **second** try, **ten** players

The adjectives *a, an,* and *the* are called **articles.** *A* and *an* are **indefinite articles** because they refer indefinitely to any one of a group. *The* is the **definite article** because it refers to a definite person, place, thing, or idea.

ARTICLES   **a** hobby, **an** expert, **the** force

2.20 PROPER ADJECTIVES

A **proper adjective** is an adjective formed from a proper noun.

PROPER ADJECTIVES   **Greek** myths, **Biblical** passages, **Shakespearean** drama

2.21 PREDICATE ADJECTIVES

Every sentence is made up of two parts, a **subject** and a **predicate.** The subject is what or whom the sentence is about. The predicate tells something about the subject's actions or condition.

SUBJECT   **Susan B. Anthony** did much for women.
PREDICATE   The tiger **was behind the door**.

A **predicate adjective** is an adjective that follows a linking verb and modifies the subject of a verb.

PREDICATE ADJECTIVES   This book is **dull**.
His speech was **longer** than we expected.

2.22 ADVERBS

An **adverb** is a word used to modify a verb, an adjective, or another adverb.

ADVERBS   She **always** arrives **early** and stays **late**.
They are **unusually** good students.
Everyone behaved **very** well.

2.23 Adjective or Adverb?

If you know a word is either an adjective or adverb but are not sure which it is, look at the word it modifies. Adjectives modify nouns and pronouns. Adverbs modify verbs, adjectives, and adverbs.

ADJECTIVES   **blue** eyes, **large** city, **strong** wind
ADVERBS   **Quietly**, the fog crept **forward**.

Many, but not all words with –ly endings are adverbs. Generally speaking, if you take the –ly ending off a word and are left with a noun, the –ly word is an adjective. If you are left with an adjective, the –ly word is an adverb.

ADJECTIVES   timely, scholarly, kingly, friendly
ADVERBS   kindly, happily, heartily, steadily

2.24 Prepositions

A **preposition** is used to show how a noun or a pronoun, its **object,** is related to some other word in the sentence. Common prepositions are *after, among, at, behind, beside, off, through, until, upon,* and *with.* A preposition introduces a **prepositional phrase**. The following examples show prepositional phrases in sentences.

PREPOSITIONAL PHRASES   I finished the book **before lunch**.
Among her papers was the one I wanted.

2.25 Coordinating Conjunctions

A **conjunction** is a word used to join words or groups of words. A **coordinating conjunction** connects words or groups of words that are used in the same way—nouns with nouns, verbs with verbs, and so on. Thus a coordinating conjunction *coordinates*, or orders the relationship between, two words or groups of words. The main coordinating conjunctions are *and, but, for, nor, or, so,* and *yet.*

COORDINATING CONJUNCTIONS   She read aloud to you **and** me.
Eleanor Roosevelt was a politician **but** not a president.
We attended, **yet** we did not listen.

2.26 CORRELATIVE CONJUNCTIONS

Correlative conjunctions are two conjunctions that join words or groups of words that are used in the same way. Some common correlative conjunctions are *both . . . and; either . . . or; neither . . . nor; not only . . . but also;* and *whether . . . or.*

CORRELATIVE CONJUNCTIONS   **Either** stay here **or** come with us.
We read **both** the plays **and** the sonnets of Shakespeare.

2.27 SUBORDINATING CONJUNCTIONS

A **clause** is a group of words with its own subject and verb.

CLAUSES   **A thing of beauty is a joy forever.**
Great writing must express great thoughts.
The library, **which was seldom open**, contained ten computers.

A **subordinate clause** is a clause that cannot stand by itself as a complete sentence. It depends on another clause and adds information about that clause. A **subordinating conjunction** connects a subordinate clause to another clause. Some common subordinating conjunctions are *after, as, as well as, because, if, in order that, provided, since, so that, than, that, though, unless, when,* and *why.*

SUBORDINATING CONJUNCTIONS   **When** you see Sammy, say hello.
I will, **provided** that I recognize him.

2.28 CONJUNCTIVE ADVERBS

A **conjunctive adverb** is a conjunction that both introduces and modifies a clause. Some conjunctive adverbs are *accordingly, furthermore,* and *moreover.*

CONJUNCTIVE ADVERBS   I think; **therefore,** I am.
She studied every day; **moreover,** she did extra work.

2.29 INTERJECTIONS

An **interjection** is a word used to express emotion. It stands apart from the rest of a sentence. Common interjections are *ah, oh, say, well,* and *wow.*

INTERJECTIONS   **Oh,** what a tangled web we have woven.
Say, have you seen my best friend?

2.30 Words as Other Parts of Speech I

Words often serve as more than one part of speech. A noun, for instance, can become an adjective when it is used to modify another noun.

NOUNS AS ADJECTIVES   **police** officer, **fiction** writer, **opera** singer

Sometimes pronouns can be used as adjectives. Such pronouns show who possesses something and are called **possessive pronouns.**

PRONOUNS AS ADJECTIVES   **my** work, **her** strength, **their** courage

2.31 Words as Other Parts of Speech II

A word that is commonly used as a preposition may also be used as an adverb. In such cases, you can tell that such a word is being used as an adverb because it will not have a **prepositional object.** A prepositional object is the noun or pronoun that ends the prepositional phrase.

PREPOSITION   We walked **around** the block.
ADVERB   We walked **around**.

Not only can other parts of speech serve as adjectives and adverbs, but nearly any word can serve as a noun or verb if necessary.

INTERJECTION AS NOUN   The "**alas**" that he sighed could be heard by all.
INTERJECTION AS VERB   He **wowed** them with his smile.

USING THE PARTS OF SPEECH IN WRITING

2.32 Using Precise Nouns

When you are writing, choose nouns that tell your reader precisely what you mean. If you use precise nouns, rather than nouns with a vague or general meaning, your writing will be more effective. Avoid using an adjective and a noun, as in *expensive house,* when using a single precise noun, such as *mansion,* will do.

VAGUE   The **house** was covered with **plants**.
PRECISE   The **cottage** was covered with **vines**.

Note the precise nouns in this passage from *A Sylph's Song*, by Edith Sitwell.

PRECISE NOUNS   Amid this hot green glowing **gloom**
A word falls with a raindrop's **boom**.

2.33 USING VIVID VERBS

Like precise nouns, vivid verbs create a picture in the reader's mind. Instead of using a vague, general verb like *walk,* a writer can produce a concrete picture by using a vivid verb such as *hobble, stroll, meander, saunter, march, tramp, pace, stride, trudge, trek, hoof,* or *hike.* Instead of using an adverb and a verb, as in *ran quickly,* a writer can use a single precise verb such as *sprinted.*

DULL   Maya **liked** being on her own.
VIVID   Maya **relished** being on her own.

Note the vivid verb Oscar Wilde chose instead of "moves" in the following lines:

An omnibus across the bridge
Crawls like a yellow butterfly

2.34 REPLACING LINKING VERBS WITH ACTION VERBS

To give color to your writing, avoid using linking verbs, especially forms of the verb *to be* (*am, are, is, was,* and so on). Instead, use action verbs. Using action verbs will force you to restructure your sentences for greater impact.

LINKING   *The Odyssey* **is** a timeless story.
ACTION   *The Odyssey* **speaks** to us from the distant past.

Note how, in the following passage, May Sarton has used action verbs to describe self-reflection:

ACTION VERB   We think of all the women **hunting** for themselves

2.35 USING COLORFUL MODIFIERS

A **modifier** is a word that modifies—that is, changes or explains—the meaning of another word. Adjectives and adverbs are modifiers. Rather than use trite or vague modifiers in your writing, search out adjectives and adverbs that add freshness and meaning. Consider the modifiers Thomas Gray chose in these lines from his poem "Elegy Written in a Country Churchyard."

COLORFUL MODIFIERS   Beneath those **rugged** elms, that yew-tree's shade,
　　　　　　　　　　　　Where heaves the turf in many a **mould'ring** heap,
　　　　　　　　　　Each in his **narrow** cell for ever laid,
　　　　　　　　　　　　The **rude** forefathers of the hamlet sleep.

By using precise nouns, vivid action verbs, and colorful modifiers, you can turn bland prose into dynamic reading.

DULL   Robert Frost was famous as a writer about the outdoors.
COLORFUL   Robert Frost found fame as a poet of the natural world.

BUILDING SENTENCES

2.36 THE FUNCTIONS OF SENTENCES

Sentences are classified according to their functions. They may be **declarative, imperative, interrogative,** or **exclamatory.** A **declarative sentence** makes a statement and is followed by a period.

DECLARATIVE SENTENCES   Poems should be memorized.
　　　　　　　　　　　　T. S. Eliot seldom recited his poems.

An **interrogative sentence** asks a question. It ends with a question mark.

INTERROGATIVE SENTENCES   Why are grammatical terms important?
　　　　　　　　　　　　　Must I learn all of them?

An **imperative sentence** gives a command or makes a request. It usually ends with a period but may end with an exclamation point.

IMPERATIVE SENTENCES   Learn the grammatical terms, students!
　　　　　　　　　　　Don't give up until you known them all.

An **exclamatory sentence** expresses a strong feeling about something. It ends with an exclamation point.

EXCLAMATORY SENTENCES   Oh, no! I confused my nouns and verbs!
　　　　　　　　　　　　You lost your prepositions!

2.37 SUBSTANTIVES

A **substantive** is a noun or any other word or group of words that is used as a noun. If a word is used as a subject, direct object, indirect object, object of a preposition, predicate nominative, or objective complement, then it is a substantive. The following are some examples of substantives used as **subjects,** words that name the thing that does the action of the verb.

	SUBSTANTIVES
NOUN	**Anonymous** has written much.
PRONOUN	**I** write every day.
INFINITIVES	**To write** well is **to think** well.
GERUND	Good **writing** requires practice.
CLAUSE	**That you write** to me is all that matters.

2.38 SIMPLE SENTENCES: SUB + V

The most basic sentence is one that combines a **substantive** and a verb in the form SUB + V. A substantive is anything used as a noun—a noun, pronoun, gerund, infinitive, or noun clause.

NOUN	The **sun** rose.
PRONOUN	**Everyone** rejoiced.
GERUND	**Reading** is essential.
INFINITIVE	**To stop** would be a loss.
NOUN CLAUSE	**That you keep reading** is most important.

2.39 SIMPLE SENTENCES: SUB + AV + SUB

You can build the next kind of basic sentence by adding another substantive as the direct object of an action verb, producing a sentence with the form SUB + AV + SUB. In the following examples, the direct object is boldfaced.

EXAMPLES	Great literature stirs the **mind.**
	It challenges **you.**
	Reading makes you a better **person.**

2.40 SIMPLE SENTENCES: SUB + LV + SUB OR ADJ

Imagine you had a linking verb in your simple sentence instead of an action verb. Your sentence would then follow the pattern SUB + LV + SUB. The second substantive would be a **predicate nominative**, which is a word or group of words that follows a linking verb and refers to the same person or thing as the subject of the verb. In the following examples, the predicate nominative is boldfaced.

Monday was a **day** to forget.
It's **music**.
His life is **swimming**.

Now imagine you made the element after the verb a predicate adjective. (See the Language Arts Survey, 2.21, for the definition of a predicate adjective.) Then the sentence pattern would be SUB + LV + ADJ. In the following examples, the predicate adjective is boldfaced.

EXAMPLES   Dorothy Parker was **famous**.
Her dogs seemed **friendly**.
That's **important**.
They all felt **loved**.

2.41 SIMPLE SENTENCES: SUB + AV + SUB + SUB

Another type of simple sentence can be formed by following the pattern substantive + action verb + substantive + substantive (SUB + AV + SUB + SUB). One of the substantives after the action verb will be a direct object. The other may be an **indirect object**. An indirect object is a noun or pronoun that comes between an action verb and a direct object. It shows *to whom, to what, for whom,* or *for what* the action of the verb is done. In the following examples, the indirect object is boldfaced.

EXAMPLES   He gave **everyone at the party** his permission.
She promised **him** she'd use it well.
Working made **her** a stronger person.
To succeed gives **a person** pleasure.

Instead of an indirect object, however, one of the elements may be an **objective complement**. An objective complement is a word or group of words that helps complete the meaning of an action verb by identifying or modifying the direct object. The words *to be* may be inferred as appearing before the objective complement. In the following examples, the objective complement is boldfaced.

EXAMPLES   You made me **the leader**.
Ms. Helen named him **chief aide**.
We all considered her **the boss**.

2.42 INDEPENDENT CLAUSES

An **independent clause** expresses a complete thought and can stand by itself as a sentence. All the examples in the Language Arts Survey, 2.38–2.41, are also examples of independent clauses.

2.43 COMPOUND SENTENCES

You can expand on a sentence that has only one independent clause by adding another independent clause. You will then have a **compound sentence**—one formed of two or more independent clauses but no subordinate clauses. (See the Language Arts Survey, 2.27, for the definition of a subordinate clause.) Related independent clauses can be joined by a semi-colon; by a coordinating conjunction such as *and, or, for, nor, but, so,* or *yet* and a comma; or by a semicolon followed by a conjunctive adverb such as *however* or *therefore* and a comma.

COMPOUND SENTENCES The books lie unread; the library is closed.
The library has opened, **and** the books are off the shelves.
The books have been removed; **therefore**, they will be read.

2.44 COMPLEX SENTENCES

You can also expand a sentence that has only one independent clause by adding a subordinate clause. You will then have a **complex sentence**—one formed of an independent clause and at least one subordinate clause. In the following examples, the subordinate clauses are boldfaced.

COMPLEX SENTENCES Great books, **which challenge the reader**, are the best.
I met an author **who showed me his new book**.
Because he had written it, I took a second look.

2.45 COMPOUND-COMPLEX SENTENCES

If you combine a compound sentence and a complex sentence, you will have a **compound-complex** sentence. This kind of sentence must have two or more independent clauses and at least one subordinate clause. In the following examples, the subordinate clauses are boldfaced.

COMPOUND-COMPLEX SENTENCES **Although writing expands the mind**, walking exercises the body, and praying feeds the soul.
Nothing could be done **until the water receded**, yet the people waited patiently.

EXPANDING SENTENCES

2.46 ADDING MODIFIERS

Simple, compound, complex, and compound-complex sentences can be expanded by adding modifiers such as adjectives and adverbs.

BASIC SENTENCE The boy ran.
SENTENCE WITH ADDED MODIFIERS The **young** boy ran **away terrified**.
BASIC SENTENCE I met an author.
SENTENCE WITH ADDED MODIFIERS I **eagerly** met a **rich** and **famous** author.
BASIC SENTENCE Dancing made her a star.
SENTENCE WITH ADDED MODIFIERS Dancing **gracefully** made her a **beautifully shining** star.

2.47 Adding Prepositional Phrases

Adding a prepositional phrase is another way to expand sentences. The prepositional phrase you add can be an **adjectival phrase** or an **adverbial phrase.** An adjectival phrase modifies a noun or pronoun. An adverbial phrase modifies a verb, an adjective, or an adverb. The following examples are from the Language Arts Survey, 2.46, with added prepositional phrases.

WITH ADDED PREPOSITIONAL PHRASES The young boy ran away terrified **through the fog.**
I eagerly met a rich and famous author **with her own publishing company.**
Dancing gracefully **in full view of the judges** made her a shining star **in their eyes for a moment.**

Note that expanding sentences can cause problems instead of adding interest and variety. The third sentence, above, is bloated and should be trimmed down.

2.48 Adding Appositives and Appositive Phrases

Still another way to expand sentences is to add an **appositive** or an **appositive phrase.** An appositive is a noun or pronoun placed beside another noun or pronoun to identify or explain it. An appositive phrase is the appositive and its modifiers. The modifiers can be adjectives or adverbs.

BASIC SENTENCE Your friend is in trouble.
WITH APPOSITIVES Your friend **Bill** is in trouble.
WITH APPOSITIVE PHRASES Your friend Bill, **the spooky one with the criminal record,** is in trouble.

2.49 Adding Predicates

A **predicate** is a main verb and any auxiliary verbs, together with any words, phrases, or clauses that modify or complement the verb. You can expand sentences by adding predicates.

BASIC SENTENCE Homer told stories.
WITH ADDED VERB PHRASE Homer told stories and **preserved them for future students.**

2.50 Adding Subordinate Clauses

Subordinate clauses may also be used to expand the meaning of a sentence.

BASIC SENTENCE More students are taking advanced courses.
WITH SUBORDINATE CLAUSES More students **who want to go to college** are taking advanced courses, **which help them do well on admissions tests.**

COMBINING SENTENCES

2.51 COMBINING SENTENCES USING SINGLE WORDS

Often you can combine two sentences that deal with the same topic to make your writing briefer and more effective. Rather than repeat information, you take the vital information from one sentence and insert it in the other, either in its original form or slightly altered.

GIVEN SENTENCES   The game ended. It was early.
COMBINED SENTENCE   The game ended **early**.

GIVEN SENTENCES   The meat loaf tasted terrible. It was green.
COMBINED SENTENCE   The **green** meat loaf tasted terrible.

2.52 COMBINING SENTENCES USING PHRASES

A second way to combine two sentences that deal with the same topic is to take a prepositional phrase or a participial phrase from one sentence and move it into the other.

GIVEN SENTENCES   We ordered pizza. We ordered it with pepperoni.
COMBINED SENTENCE   We ordered pizza **with pepperoni**.

GIVEN SENTENCES   We were standing there asking for more. We could hear our stomachs rumble.
COMBINED SENTENCE   **Standing there asking for more**, we could hear our stomachs rumble.

Sometimes you may need to change a part of the sentence into a prepositional phrase or change a verb into a participle before you can insert the idea into another sentence.

GIVEN SENTENCES   I ate too quickly. I upset my stomach.
COMBINED SENTENCE   I ate too quickly, **upsetting my stomach**.

GIVEN SENTENCES   He skimmed the newspaper. He read only news of his friends.
COMBINED SENTENCE   **Skimming the newspaper**, he read only news of his friends.
He skimmed the newspaper, **reading only news of his friends**.

2.53 COMBINING SENTENCES USING CLAUSES

A third way to combine two sentences that have the same topic is to make one the independent clause and the other the subordinate clause in a combined sentence.

GIVEN SENTENCES	I grew cold. I decided to go inside.
COMBINED SENTENCE	**Because I grew cold**, I decided to go inside.
GIVEN SENTENCES	You must finish the symphony. I can write the program notes.
COMBINED SENTENCE	You must finish the symphony **before I can write the program notes.**

EDITING SENTENCES

2.54 Varying Sentence Openings

Many of the examples in this handbook begin with a subject for the sake of simplicity. When you are writing, however, you will find that *always* beginning with a subject makes for a dull style. You can make your writing more varied and interesting by beginning sentences with adjectives, adverbs, participles—just about any part of speech—as well as with phrases and clauses. You may have to reword your sentences slightly as you vary the sentence openings.

GIVEN SENTENCE	I gained more energy by jogging every day.
EDITED SENTENCE	**By jogging every day**, I gained more energy.
GIVEN SENTENCE	He mixed the chemicals carefully.
EDITED SENTENCE	**Carefully**, he mixed the chemicals.
GIVEN SENTENCE	The television was often blaring in the afternoon.
EDITED SENTENCE	**Often** the television was blaring in the afternoon.

2.55 Varying Sentence Length and Structure

Repeated sentences of the same length and structure soon become monotonous. Use a variety of simple, compound, complex, and compound-complex sentences in your writing.

PASSAGE WITH SIMPLE SENTENCES

My mother told stories. She had to warn us about life. They ran like this one. This was a story to grow up on. She tested our strength to establish realities. Some were in the emigrant generations. If they could not reassert brute survival, they died young and far from home. Some of us are in the first American generations. The emigrants built an invisible world around our childhoods. We have had to figure out how to fit in solid America.

PASSAGE WITH VARIED SENTENCE LENGTH AND STRUCTURE

Whenever she had to warn us about life, my mother told stories that ran like this one, a story to grow up on. She tested our strength to establish realities. Those in the emigrant generations who could not reassert brute survival died young and far from home. Those of us in the first American generations have had to figure out how the invisible world the emigrants built around our childhoods fits in solid America.

—Maxine Hong Kingston, *The Woman Warrior*

2.56 USING THE ACTIVE VOICE

A verb is in the **active voice** when the subject of the verb performs the action. It is in the **passive voice** when the subject of the verb receives the action.

ACTIVE   Lightning **struck** the barn.
PASSIVE   The barn **was struck** by lightning.

A common characteristic of poor writing is overuse of the passive voice. Keep your verbs in the active voice unless you have a good reason for using the passive voice. In the examples that follow, note how the active verbs make the writing more natural, interesting, and concise.

WITH PASSIVE VERBS   Pink blossoms **were plucked** by me from my apple tree
                And **were worn** by me all that evening in my hair:
                Then in due season when I went to see
                No apples **were found** by me there.

WITH ACTIVE VERBS   I **plucked** pink blossoms from mine apple tree
                And **wore** them all that evening in my hair:
                Then in due season when I went to see
                I **found** no apples there.

                —Christina Rossetti, "An Apple-Gathering"

2.57 ACHIEVING PARALLELISM

A sentence has **parallelism** when it uses the same grammatical forms to express ideas of equal, or parallel, importance. When you edit your sentences during revision, check to be sure that your parallelism is not faulty.

FAULTY   After the camping trip, I was tired, irritable, and wanted to eat.
PARALLEL After the camping trip, I was tired, irritable, and hungry.

FAULTY   He spends his free time reading and listening to music, and he works in the
          garden.
PARALLEL He spends his free time reading, listening to music, and gardening.

FAULTY   With her pale skin and her eyes that were green, she appeared ghostly.
PARALLEL With her pale skin and green eyes, she appeared ghostly.

FAULTY   Her pale skin made her appear ghostly, and she seemed cat-like because of her
          green eyes.
PARALLEL Her pale skin made her appear ghostly, and her green eyes made her seem
          cat-like.

2.58 Deleting Repeated or Unnecessary Ideas

When you edit your writing, check carefully for repeated or unnecessary ideas.

SENTENCE WITH REPETITION On January 1, **the first of the year**, we had a **New Year's Day** brunch.

CORRECTED SENTENCE On January 1 we had a brunch.

SENTENCE WITH UNNECESSARY IDEA We wrote the letter together, but **then** we mailed **our copies of it** separately.

CORRECTED SENTENCE We wrote the letter together but mailed our copies separately.

2.59 Reducing Wordiness

When you write, use only as many words as you need to express your meaning. While editing, remove words that do not contribute to your meaning and replace complicated or unclear words with ones that are simple and clear.

WORDY At this point in time, I believe I shall depart from this place and from all of you.

DIRECT I'm going now.

WORDY Way back in the past, when my grandmother was a young girl, many people didn't have the advantages provided by electricity and running water.

DIRECT When my grandmother was young, many people lacked electricity and running water.

Look for ways to reduce the length of your sentences by replacing a clause with a phrase that conveys the same meaning. In some cases, you can even replace a lengthy phrase with a single word.

WORDY Edgar Allan Poe, **who was a poet**, wrote about the dark side of humanity.

DIRECT The **poet** Edgar Allan Poe wrote about the dark side of humanity.

WORDY I am amazed at **the rudeness that so many people demonstrate**.

DIRECT I am amazed at **people's** rudeness.

2.60 Correcting Sentence Strings

Sentence strings are formed of several sentences strung together with conjunctions. Edit sentence strings by breaking them up into separate sentences and subordinate clauses. In the examples that follow, the first passage is a sentence string; the second is a passage broken up into separate sentences and clauses.

| STRINGY | The story begins with a family that came over to America from Europe years ago, and most family members went west on a wagon train, but they had trouble with their wagon, so they told their friends to go ahead, and then they caught up with their friends. |
| REVISED | The story begins with a European family that came to America and joined a westward wagon train. Having wagon trouble, they told their friends to go ahead. Later, they caught up with their friends again. |

2.61 CORRECTING SENTENCE FRAGMENTS

A **sentence** should express a complete thought and contain both a subject and a verb. A **sentence fragment** is a phrase or clause that does not express a complete thought but has been punctuated as though it did. You can correct a sentence fragment by changing its punctuation or structure so that it expresses a complete thought.

FRAGMENTED	He promised us a shorter school day. Because class was canceled.
CORRECTED	He promised us a shorter school day because class was canceled.
FRAGMENTED	She spent the day discouraged. Trying to find a job.
CORRECTED	She spent the day discouraged, trying to find a job.

In sentences in which the subject will be understood by the reader, the subject can be left unexpressed. Such sentences are not sentence fragments.

SENTENCE WITH IMPLIED, UNEXPRESSED SUBJECT   [You] Promise me you'll be there.

2.62 CORRECTING RUN-ONS

A **run-on** is formed of two or more sentences that have been run together as if they were one complete thought. Edit a run-on by making it into two sentences, by adding a comma and a coordinating conjunction, or by adding a semicolon.

RUN-ON	He was not a success at his job his mouth moved faster than his hands.
TWO SENTENCES	He was not a success at his job. His mouth moved faster than his hands.
COORDINATED CLAUSES	He was not a success at his job, because his mouth moved faster than his hands.

2.63 CORRECTING DANGLING OR MISPLACED MODIFIERS

A **dangling modifier** is a phrase or clause that seems to modify a word it is not intended to modify. Sometimes this error occurs because the modifier is too far from the word it is supposed to modify. It is then called a **misplaced modifier**. You can edit dangling and misplaced modifiers by adding a word for the phrase or clause to modify or by rewording the sentence.

DANGLING	Luke fell out of bed while in the shower.
WORDS ADDED	Luke fell out of bed while his sister was in the shower.
DANGLING	Working in the yard, a dog attacked me.
REWORDED	Working in the yard, I was attacked by a dog.
MISPLACED	Tickets for next week's game in the lounge have gone on sale.
REWORDED	Tickets for next week's game have gone on sale in the lounge.

2.64 INVERTING SENTENCES FOR EMPHASIS

When editing your writing, look for opportunities to add emphasis and clarify your meaning. One way to add emphasis is to **invert** a sentence—to change the usual order of its parts.

REGULAR ORDER	She would travel across the world to help her friend.
INVERTED ORDER	To help her friend she would travel across the world.
REGULAR ORDER	"God created the heaven and the earth in the beginning."
INVERTED ORDER	"In the beginning, God created the heaven and the earth."

—King James Bible

EDITING FOR ERRORS IN VERB TENSE

2.65 IMPROPER SHIFTS IN VERB TENSE

When the verbs in a sentence or group of sentences shift from past to present or from present to past without reason, the reader may not be able to follow the intended meaning. Correct the shift by using consistent tenses for all verbs.

WITH TENSE SHIFT	The president **makes** a speech but **refused** to answer questions.
CORRECTED	The president **made** a speech but **refused** to answer questions.

2.66 IRREGULAR VERBS I

Every verb has four **principle parts**: the **base form**, the **present participle**, the **past**, and the **past participle**. All the other verb forms can be made from these parts. As you can see from the table below, the present participle is formed by adding –ing to the base form (sometimes dropping an e), and the past and past participle are formed by adding –d or –ed (or sometimes –t) to the base form.

BASE FORM	PRESENT PARTICIPLE	PAST	PAST PARTICIPLE
call	[is] calling	called	[have] called
delight	[is] delighting	delighted	[have] delighted
judge	[is] judging	judged	[have] judged
mean	[is] meaning	meant	[have] meant

Some verbs, however, form the past and past participle in some other way than by adding –d or –ed (or sometimes –t) to the base form. These verbs are called *irregular verbs*. English has dozens of them. The table below shows just a few examples. If you are in doubt about whether a verb is irregular, look it up in the dictionary; if it is irregular, you will find its principal parts listed.

BASE FORM	PRESENT PARTICIPLE	PAST	PAST PARTICIPLE
beat	[is] beating	beat	[have] beaten
fall	[is] falling	fell	[have] fallen
fly	[is] flying	flew	[have] flown
ring	[is] ringing	rang	[have] rung
speak	[is] speaking	spoke	[have] spoken

2.67 IRREGULAR VERBS II

When using irregular verbs in the so-called perfect tenses (with *has* or *have*), make sure you do not use the past form instead of the past participle.

NONSTANDARD PARTICIPLE	I **have spoke** my piece.
STANDARD PARTICIPLE	I **have spoken** my piece.

Another error to watch for is using the past participle form without a helping verb or mistaking the past participle for the past.

NONSTANDARD	My friends **seen** me do it.
STANDARD	My friends **have seen** me do it.
NONSTANDARD	Yesterday, we **run** up the hill.
STANDARD	Yesterday, we **ran** up the hill.

Finally, do not add *–d* or *–ed* or *–t* to the past form of an irregular verb.

NONSTANDARD	The man **bited** the dog.
STANDARD	The man **bit** the dog.

2.68 Split Infinitives

In English, the infinitive often takes the form of two words, *to* and the base. In their discussion of this form, the first English grammarians—influenced by their knowledge of Latin, in which the infinitive is a single word—decreed that the infinitive should never be "split" in English. Under this rule, adverbs and other sentence components should not stand between *to* and the base form.

NONSTANDARD	She decided **to comfortably recline** on the sofa.
STANDARD	She decided **to recline comfortably** on the sofa.

However, the normal sentence rhythms of English, and the demands of sense, often call for an infinitive to be split. In using the infinitive, keep *to* and the base form together where possible, but do not hesitate to separate them where the rhythm or sense of the sentence requires it. (Note that a phrase such as *to be proudly aware* is not a split infinitive; it is an infinitive of the verb *to be* followed by a predicate nominative modified by an adverb.)

STRAINED WORD ORDER	He wanted **to remember happily** these days.
NATURAL WORD ORDER	He wanted **to happily remember** these days.

Although the rule that infinitives should not be split was based on Latin rather than English, it has been widely accepted. You should be aware that some people may find fault with the use of a split infinitive even in cases where such a use is required by sound and sense. (For more information on the use of split infinitives, see the entry on split infinitives in Fowler's *Modern English Usage*.)

2.69 Voice and Mood

Shifts in **voice** from active to passive can be as confusing as shifts in tense. Check your sentences to be sure voice is consistent. Rewrite and change subjects as necessary.

WITH VOICE SHIFT	We **made the trip**, but **no hardship was endured**.
CORRECTED	We made the trip but endured no hardship.

In addition to watching for voice shifts, check to be sure your verbs are in the appropriate **mood.** Mood is a characteristic that shows the way in which a verb is used. Each verb has three moods: **indicative**, **imperative**, and **subjunctive.**

Use a verb in the *indicative mood* to express a fact, an opinion, or a question.

INDICATIVE MOOD	Delilah **found** the scissors before I did.
	My mother **believed** that everyone was entitled to learn ballroom dancing.
	Wasn't he **going** to read it?

Use the *imperative mood* to express a direct command or request.

IMPERATIVE MOOD	**Don't** delay!
	Please **finish** on time.

Use the *subjunctive mood* in the present to express a suggestion or a necessity.

SUBJUNCTIVE MOOD	I suggested that he **be** admitted to the club.
	It is important that we first **know** who he is.

Use the *past subjunctive* to express a wish or a condition that is not true (contrary to fact).

PAST SUBJUNCTIVE	If I **were** rich, I wouldn't be here.
	If all **were** well, you wouldn't either.

Notice that the singular of most verbs in the subjunctive looks like a plural of a verb in the indicative.

INDICATIVE PLURAL	We **were** all wishing for more.
SUBJUNCTIVE SINGULAR	I was wishing I **were** somewhere else.

EDITING FOR ERRORS IN SUBJECT/VERB AGREEMENT

2.70 AGREEMENT OF SUBJECT AND VERB

A word that refers to one person or thing is said to be **singular in number.** A word that refers to more than one person or thing is said to be **plural in number.** Most nouns that end in *s* are plural, but most verbs that refer to the present and end in *s* are singular.

SINGULAR NOUNS	cat, song, writing
PLURAL NOUNS	cats, songs, writings
SINGULAR VERBS	crashes, drags, gives
PLURAL VERBS	crash, drag, give

Each verb in a sentence should be singular if its subject is singular and plural if its subject is plural. In other words, a verb must **agree in number** with its subject.

EXAMPLES   The **roots** of the tree **are** shallow.
A **cup** of coffee **is** not a breakfast.

The pronouns *I* and *you,* though singular, almost always take forms that look plural. The only exceptions are the forms *I am* and *I was.*

EXAMPLES   **I write** almost every day.
You read everything I write.

2.71 AGREEMENT WITH COMPOUND SUBJECTS

A **compound subject** is formed of two or more nouns or pronouns that are joined by a conjunction and have the same verb. A compound subject joined by the conjunction *and* usually takes a plural verb.

EXAMPLE   **Frost and Eliot are** poets.

A compound subject in which the subjects are joined by the conjunction *and* takes a singular verb if the compound subject really names only one person or thing.

EXAMPLE   My **friend and teammate** is not here.

A compound subject formed of two singular subjects joined by the conjunctions *or* or *nor* takes a singular verb.

EXAMPLES   Either a **cat** or a **dog** is enough to make her happy.
Neither a **bird** nor a **mouse** could do the job.

A compound subject formed of a singular subject and a plural subject joined by the conjunctions *or* or *nor* takes a verb that agrees in number with the subject nearer the verb.

EXAMPLES   Either the **coach** or the **players were** at fault.
Neither my **brothers** nor **I am** going.

2.72 Agreement with Indefinite Pronouns

These indefinite pronouns are singular and take a singular verb: *anybody, anyone, anything, each, either, everybody, everyone, everything, neither, nobody, no one, nothing, one, somebody, someone,* and *something.*

EXAMPLES   **Everyone likes** my new hat.
              None of them **is** interested.

These indefinite pronouns are plural and take a plural verb: *both, few, many,* and *several.*

EXAMPLES   **Few** bargains **are** available at Fran's.
              Several have been taken already.

The following indefinite pronouns can be singular or plural: *all, any, most, none,* and *some.*

EXAMPLES   You've finished your work. That **is all** you need to do. (*All* refers to *work.*)
              The students are arriving. **All will be** counted. (*All* refers to *students.*)

2.73 Agreement in Inverted Sentences

When you invert sentences for emphasis, make sure you maintain agreement in number between subject and verb.

EXAMPLES   Rather quiet **he is**, eh?
              There **go I**, but for my trust fund.

2.74 Agreement with *Doesn't* and *Don't*

The contraction *doesn't* (from *does not*) is singular and should be used only with a singular subject. The contraction *don't* (from *do not*) is plural and should be used only with a plural subject.

EXAMPLES   **She doesn't like** the theater.
              They don't want to take her anyway.

2.75 Other Problems in Subject/Verb Agreement

When a sentence begins with *here, there, when,* or *where,* often the subject follows the verb. These are called **inverted sentences.** In editing your writing, use extra care to check that the subject and verb of such sentences agree in number. Remember that the contractions *here's, there's, when's,* and *where's* contain a singular verb (*is*) and should only be used with a singular subject.

EXAMPLES   Here's the best way.
                 There are seven days in a week.
                 When is your assignment due?
                 When's the first day of class?
                 Where are the table and chairs?

Also check to be sure a verb in a **sentence with a predicate nominative** agrees in number with the subject and not with the predicate nominative.

EXAMPLES   **Cats are** a curious species.
                 The most curious **species is** cats.

A **collective noun** takes a singular verb when the noun refers to the group as a unit, and it takes a plural verb when it refers to the members of the group as individuals.

AS SINGULAR   The crew **is** growing larger than planned.
AS PLURAL   The crew **are** demanding their wages.

While editing your work, check for **singular nouns with plural forms**. They should take singular verbs.

EXAMPLES   news, ethics, mumps, gallows

Titles and groups of words used as a unit take a singular verb.

EXAMPLES   "The Fox and the Crow" **is** a folk tale.
                 The expression *p's and q's* **is** not as commonly heard as it once was.

Words of amount are singular and take a singular verb when the amount is considered as one unit. They are plural and take a plural verb when the amount is considered as something with many parts.

AS SINGULAR   **Five sandwiches** is too much to eat.
AS PLURAL   **Five sandwiches** are lying on the desk.

Fractions and percentages are singular when they refer to a singular word and plural when they refer to a plural word.

AS SINGULAR   **Nine-tenths** of the **student body is passing**.
AS PLURAL   **Nine-tenths** of the **students are passing**.

Expressions of measurement, such as area, length, volume, and weight, are usually singular.

EXAMPLE   **Twenty pounds doesn't feel** so heavy.

EDITING FOR ERRORS IN PRONOUN USAGE

2.76 PRONOUN CASE I

Case is the form that a noun or a pronoun takes to indicate its use in a sentence. English nouns and pronouns have three cases: **nominative, objective,** and **possessive.** The nominative case is used for the subject of a verb or for a predicate nominative. The objective case is used for a direct object, an indirect object, or the object of a preposition. The possessive case is used to show possession. The form of the nominative and objective cases of nouns is the same, and most nouns form possessives by adding an apostrophe and an *s* to the singular and an apostrophe only to the plural. Many pronouns have different forms to show nominative, objective, and possessive cases.

PERSONAL PRONOUNS		
SINGULAR		
Nominative Case (for subjects or predicate nominatives)	**Objective Case** (for direct objects, indirect objects, and objects of prepositions)	**Possessive Case** (to show possession)
I	me	my, mine
you	you	your, yours
he, she, it	him, her, it	his, her, hers, its
PLURAL		
we	us	our, ours
you	you	your, yours
they	them	their, theirs

To determine which form of the pronoun to use when writing a sentence, first decide whether the pronoun is used as a subject, predicate nominative, as some kind of object, or as a possessive. Doing so will tell you what case the pronoun should be.

SUBJECT	**He** knows more than she does.
PREDICATE NOMINATIVE	It was **they** who let the cat out of the bag.
DIRECT OBJECT	I love **you** a lot.
INDIRECT OBJECT	The letter carrier gave **him** the address.
OBJECT OF PREPOSITION	Between **us,** we should manage.

Remember that in standard English, prepositions *always* take an object in the objective case. The phrase *between you and I* is nonstandard English.

2.77 PRONOUN CASE II

Use the possessive pronouns *mine, yours, his, hers, its, ours,* and *theirs* just as you use the pronouns in the nominative and objective cases.

AS SUBJECT	**Mine** is the first chair.
AS PREDICATE NOMINATIVE	The last chair is **hers**.
DIRECT OBJECT	I read my essay, and then I read **his**.
INDIRECT OBJECT	Her column gave **ours** a bad review.
OBJECT OF PREPOSITION	That dog barked at **yours**!

Use the possessive pronouns *my, your, his, her, its, our,* and *their* as adjectives before nouns.

EXAMPLES	**Her** project won first prize.
	Only **their** disappointment was evident.

As you edit your writing, check the case of nouns and pronouns before a gerund. They should always be in the possessive case.

WITH GERUND	**His writings** made sense only to him.

Do not confuse the gerund and the present participle (see the Language Arts Survey, 2.17). Compare the example above with the following example, in which no possessive is required before the participle:

WITH PARTICIPLE	I saw **him writing** the book.

2.78 *WHO* AND *WHOM*

The pronoun *who* is referred to as an **interrogative pronoun** when it is used to form a question. When it is used to introduce a **subordinate clause**, it is referred to as a **relative pronoun**. In both cases, the nominative is *who,* the objective is *whom,* and the possessive is *whose.* As you edit your writing, check these pronouns to see if the form of the pronoun you have used is appropriate for its use in the sentence or subordinate clause in which it appears.

SUBJECT	**Who** is it?
SUBJECT	The small boy **who** entered seemed hungry.
DIRECT OBJECT	**Whom** did we see last night?
DIRECT OBJECT	The ghost **whom** we saw did not speak.
OBJECT OF PREPOSITION	Of **whom** are you thinking?
OBJECT OF PREPOSITION	I don't know to **whom** the letter was sent.

In spoken English, *whom* is gradually being replaced by *who.* In some formal speech, however, and in all writing of standard English except dialogue, the form *whom* should still be used where grammatically correct.

2.79 PRONOUNS WITH APPOSITIVES

When a pronoun is used with an appositive, its form matches its use in the sentence.

SUBJECT	**She**, the president, is conducting our meeting.
PREDICATE NOMINATIVE	The hungriest people are **we campers** who hiked all day.
INDIRECT OBJECT	Give **us newcomers** an extra week.
OBJECT OF PREPOSITION	The day belongs to **us early birds**.

2.80 PRONOUNS AS APPOSITIVES

When a pronoun is itself used as an appositive, it should be in the same case as the word to which it refers.

PRONOUN IN APPOSITION TO SUBJECT	The greatest athletes, **you** and **he**, will be honored.
PRONOUN IN APPOSITION TO THE OBJECT OF A PREPOSITION	Awards will be given to the co-captains, **you** and **him**.

2.81 PRONOUNS IN COMPARISONS

The ends of sentences that compare people or things are often left unexpressed. Pronouns in such sentences should be in the same case as they would have been if the sentence had been completed.

EXAMPLES	I know you better than **he** [does].
	I know you better than [I know] **him**.

2.82 AGREEMENT OF PRONOUNS AND ANTECEDENTS

Check the pronouns in your writing to be sure they agree in **number, person,** and **gender** with their antecedents. (For a discussion of number, see the Language Arts Survey, 2.70.) Person is the form a word takes to indicate the person speaking (the *first person,* corresponding to *I* or *we*), the person spoken to (the *second person,* corresponding to *you*), or the person spoken of or about (the *third person,* corresponding to *he, she, it,* or *they*). Gender is the form a word takes to indicate whether it is *masculine, feminine,* or *neuter* (neither masculine nor feminine).

INCORRECT NUMBER	If **anyone** calls, tell **them** I'll be back.
CORRECT NUMBER	If **people** call, tell **them** I'll be back.
	If **anyone** calls, tell **him or her** I'll be back.

CONTINUED

INCORRECT GENDER	Mary Ann Evans (pen name **George Eliot**) wrote novels that made **him** famous.
CORRECT GENDER	Mary Ann Evans (pen name **George Eliot**) wrote novels that made **her** famous.

2.83 REFERENCE OF PRONOUNS TO ANTECEDENTS I

As you edit, check each pronoun to be sure that it refers clearly to its antecedent.

CLEAR REFERENCE	Each **language** has idioms of **its** own.
CLEAR REFERENCES	Listening to the **teacher** explain the <u>problem</u>, the students believed that **he** understood <u>it</u>.

Weak reference occurs when a pronoun refers to an antecedent that has not been expressed. If you find a weak reference while editing your writing, either change the pronoun into a noun or give the pronoun a clear antecedent.

WEAK REFERENCE	My brother is an auto mechanic, but I'm not interested in it.
PRONOUN CHANGED TO NOUN	My brother is a mechanic, but I'm not interested in **auto repair**.
WEAK REFERENCE	We buy vegetables at that store because **they** charge so little.
PRONOUN GIVEN CLEAR ANTECEDENT	We buy vegetables at that store because **the owners** charge so little.

Ambiguous reference occurs when a pronoun can refer to either of two antecedents. Clarify ambiguous references by rewording the sentence or by replacing the pronouns with a noun.

AMBIGUOUS	Tom told Bill that **he** had learned to cook.
CLEAR	Tom told Bill that Bill had learned to cook.
CLEAR	Tom told Bill that Tom had learned to cook.

2.84 REFERENCE OF PRONOUNS TO ANTECEDENTS II

An **indefinite reference** occurs when the pronouns *you, it,* or *they* have no reference to a specific person or thing. Edit out an indefinite reference by rewording the sentence to explain to whom or what the pronoun refers or by eliminating the pronoun altogether.

INDEFINITE REFERENCE	I like city living because **you** always have something to do.
PRONOUN ELIMINATED	I like city living because **there is** always something to do.

CONTINUED

INDEFINITE REFERENCE	On the billboard **it** read, "Place your ad here."
PRONOUN ELIMINATED	The **billboard** read, "Place your ad here."
INDEFINITE REFERENCE	In the future, **they** might send explorers into space for years at a time.
PRONOUN REPLACED	In the future, **scientists** might send explorers into space for years at a time.

A **general reference** occurs when a pronoun refers to a general idea implied in the previous clause, rather than to a specific antecedent. Edit general references by replacing the pronoun with a noun or by rewording the sentence.

GENERAL REFERENCE	The teacher's explanation was careful and slow, **which** made me feel better.
SENTENCE REWORDED	The teacher's explanation, **which made me feel better**, was careful and slow.
GENERAL REFERENCE	We hiked over mountains and forded streams. **This** made us stronger.
PRONOUN REPLACED AND SENTENCES REWORDED	**Hiking over mountains and fording streams** made us stronger.

EDITING FOR ERRORS IN MODIFIER USAGE

2.85 MODIFIERS WITH ACTION AND LINKING VERBS

When you wish to modify the subject of a linking verb, use an adjective. When you wish to modify an action verb, use an adverb.

LINKING VERB AND ADJECTIVES	She **is quiet** and **sullen**.
ACTION VERB AND ADVERBS	She **sat quietly** and **sullenly**.

Check whether your use of an adjective or adverb is correct by temporarily replacing the verb you have written with the verb *seem.* If the sentence still makes some kind of sense, the original verb is a linking verb and should take an adjective. If the substitution of *seem* produces nonsense, the original verb is an action verb and should take an adverb. You can see how this works by substituting *seem* in each of the examples given above.

SUBSTITUTION MAKES SENSE	She **seems quiet** and **sullen**.
SUBSTITUTION MAKES NO SENSE	She **seemed quietly** and **sullenly**.

2.86 COMPARISON OF ADJECTIVES AND ADVERBS

Comparison refers to the change in the form of a modifier to show an increase or a decrease in the quality expressed by the modifier. Each modifier has three forms of comparison: **positive**, **comparative**, and **superlative**. Most one-syllable modifiers and some two-syllable modifiers form the comparative and superlative degrees by adding *-er* and *-est*. Other two-syllable modifiers, and all modifiers of more than two syllables, use *more* and *most* to form these degrees.

	POSITIVE	COMPARATIVE	SUPERLATIVE
ADJECTIVES	big	bigger	biggest
	pretty	prettier	prettiest
	hopeful	more hopeful	most hopeful
	difficult	more difficult	most difficult
ADVERBS	fast	faster	fastest
	early	earlier	earliest
	easily	more easily	most easily
	quickly	more quickly	most quickly

To show a decrease in the quality of any modifier, form the comparative and superlative degrees by using *less* and *least*.

EXAMPLES   bright, less bright, least bright
steadily, less steadily, least steadily

Some modifiers form their comparative and superlative degrees irregularly. Check the dictionary if you are unsure about the comparison of a modifier.

EXAMPLES   good, better, best   well, better, best   bad, worse, worst

Use the comparative degree when comparing two things. Use the superlative degree when comparing more than two things.

COMPARATIVE   Of my sister and I, she is the **better** singer.
SUPERLATIVE   I am the **worst** singer in our family of eight.

2.87 ILLOGICAL AND DOUBLE COMPARISONS

As you edit your writing, check sentences for **illogical comparison.** Such comparison occurs when one member of a group is compared with the group of which it is a part. Clarify illogical comparison by including the word *other* or *else* in the sentence.

ILLOGICAL   He has better teeth than anyone in his grade.
LOGICAL   He has better teeth than anyone **else** in his grade.

Another problem to check for is **double comparison.** This occurs when two comparative forms or two superlative forms are used to modify the same word. Correct double comparison by editing out one of the comparative or superlative forms.

DOUBLE COMPARISON   This sentence is **more clearer** than the one you erased.
SINGLE COMPARISON   This sentence is **clearer** than the one you erased.

2.88 DOUBLE NEGATIVES

In English a **double negative** is a nonstandard construction in which two negative words are used instead of one. Check your writing to be sure you have not used a negative word such as *no, none, not* (and its contraction, *–n't*), *nothing, barely, hardly,* or *scarcely* with any other negative word. If you find a double negative, change it by deleting one of the negative words.

DOUBLE NEGATIVE   There **wasn't hardly** enough food.
SINGLE NEGATIVE   There **was hardly** enough food.
SINGLE NEGATIVE   There **wasn't** enough food.

DOUBLE NEGATIVE   He **didn't** give me **none.**
SINGLE NEGATIVE   He **didn't** give me **any.**
SINGLE NEGATIVE   He gave me **none.**

2.89 OTHER PROBLEMS WITH MODIFIERS

The demonstrative pronouns *this* and *these* are used to refer to things near the speaker. The pronouns *that* and *those* refer to objects at some distance. Thus you might say, "This apple in my hand is poisonous" if you were referring to an apple you were actually holding, but if you were pointing at an apple in a picture of yourself, you might say, "That apple in my hand is poisonous." The two pairs of pronouns are often used to distinguish between objects or sets of objects.

EXAMPLE   I'll check out **these** books; **those** books can be put back on the shelves.

Check your writing to see that your use of *this* and *these,* and *that* and *those* makes sense.

NONSENSICAL   **Those** are my fingers, and **these** are yours.
SENSIBLE   **These** are my fingers, and **those** are yours.

The pronoun *them* is a personal pronoun in standard English and should not be substituted for the demonstrative pronoun *those.*

NONSTANDARD   **Them** friends of yours are loud and raucous.
STANDARD   **Those** friends of yours are loud and raucous.

Modifiers that often give writers trouble are *bad* and *badly*. Check instances of these words in your writing to make sure you have used *bad* as an adjective and *badly* as an adverb. Only the adjective should follow a linking verb such as *feel, hear, see, smell,* or *taste.*

NONSTANDARD   Near the factory the air smelled **badly**.
STANDARD   Near the factory the air smelled **bad**.

Similarly distinguish between *good* and *well. Good* is an adjective and should not be used to modify an action verb. *Well,* however, can be used either as an adverb meaning "capably" or "in a satisfactory way," or as an adjective meaning "healthy" or "of a satisfactory condition."

NONSTANDARD   Socrates taught **good**.
STANDARD   Socrates taught **good** classes.
STANDARD   Socrates taught **well**.
STANDARD   Socrates was a **good** teacher.
STANDARD   Socrates was **well** until he drank the poison.

USAGE HANDBOOK

2.90 USAGE PROBLEMS I

Sections 2.90–2.92 explain some common problems to watch for as you edit your writing.

adapt, adopt. *Adapt* means "to make [something] fit a specific use or situation by modifying"; *adopt* means to "take something and make it in some sense one's own."

EXAMPLES   The twins were **adopted** by different families.
The twins **adapted** to survive in their new environments.

affect, effect. If you wish to use a verb meaning "have an effect on," use *affect.* If you wish to use a noun meaning "the result of an action," use *effect.*

VERB   How did the victory **affect** the team?
NOUN   Was the **effect** long-lasting?

As a verb, *effect* means to bring something about despite obstacles.

EXAMPLE   She **effected** a change in plan.
The change **affected** our plans.

2.91 Usage Problems II

imply, infer. Most writers accept the following meanings for these words: *imply* means "to express indirectly rather than openly"; *infer* means "to arrive at a conclusion by reasoning from evidence." Although this distinction between *imply* and *infer* has not always been observed, it is a useful one.

EXAMPLES   When you spoke, you **implied** that he was your friend.
I **inferred** from your explanation that he was your friend.

like, as, as if. Although *like* is frequently used to introduce subordinate clauses in informal English, it is considered a preposition, not a conjunction. Do not use it in place of *as* or *as if* in your writing.

INFORMAL   It looks **like** we're going.
FORMAL   It looks **as if** we're going.
FORMAL   The map looks **like** a checkerboard.

literally. Most writers limit their use of *literally* to the sense "actually" and avoid using it in the sense "not actually, but in effect, or for all practical purposes." This distinction, though sometimes ignored, is worth observing.

CLEAR   I **literally** awoke at noon to start the day.
CONFUSING   I **literally** turned myself inside out to finish on time.

2.92 Usage Problems III

of. The preposition *of* should not be used in place of *have* after verbs such as *could, should, would, might, must,* and *ought.*

NONSTANDARD   I **should of** taken a taxi.
STANDARD   I **should've** taken a taxi.
STANDARD   I **should have** taken a taxi.

Avoid *off of.*

NONSTANDARD   I fell **off of** my bike the first time I tried to ride.
STANDARD   I fell **off** my bike the first time I tried to ride.

then, than. Use *than* as a conjunction in comparisons. Use *then* as an adverb that tells when something occurred.

EXAMPLES   You are a faster writer **than** I.
First I outline; **then** I write.

PROOFREADING FOR ERRORS IN END MARKS AND COMMAS

2.93 END MARKS

An **end mark** signals the end of a sentence. It also shows the purpose of the sentence. A declarative sentence ends with a **period.** If a declarative sentence already has a period at the end because an abbreviation occurs there, no other end mark is needed. If a declarative sentence ends with a quotation, place the period inside the quotation marks.

DECLARATIVE	Summer vacation begins soon.
WITH ABBREVIATION AT END	The meeting starts at 7:30 P.M.
WITH QUOTATION AT END	I said, "Summer vacation begins soon."

A question ends with a **question mark.** Indirect questions, however, do not require a question mark. If a question ends with an abbreviation, add a question mark after the final period. If a question is quoted, the question mark appears inside the closing quotation marks; if a question contains a quotation, the question mark appears outside the closing quotation marks. Polite questions often end with a period instead of a question mark.

DIRECT QUESTION	Where's the library?
ENDING IN ABBREVIATION	Are you sure it's at the end of Creaky Rd.?
INDIRECT QUESTION	She asked where the library was.
QUOTED QUESTION	She asked, "Where's the library?"
QUESTION INCLUDING QUOTATION	Did she really say, "I've never been to the library"?
POLITE QUESTION	Will you please wait for me in the library.

An exclamation ends with an **exclamation point.** If an exclamation is quoted, the exclamation point appears inside the closing quotation marks; if an exclamation contains a quotation, the exclamation point appears outside the closing quotation marks. An imperative sentence may end with a period instead of an exclamation point.

MILD EXCLAMATION	**Yes**, I'm quite sure.
EXCLAMATION	What a beautiful book!
QUOTED EXCLAMATION	The student complained, "I can't finish reading this in one night!"
EXCLAMATION CONTAINING QUOTE	I can't believe she said, "I can't finish"!
IMPERATIVE SENTENCE	Do try to finish.

2.94 COMMAS I

As you proofread your writing, check to see that you have used commas after certain introductory elements. Such elements include mild exclamations such as *yes, no, oh,* and *well;* participial phrases; two or more prepositional phrases; and adverb clauses.

MILD EXCLAMATION	**Oh,** I thought you were asleep.
PARTICIPIAL PHRASE	**Having finished the book,** you are probably ready to sleep.
TWO PREPOSITIONAL PHRASES	**With my book on my face,** I took a nap.
ADVERB CLAUSE	**When I awoke,** I was sure I remembered everything I'd read.

A comma is also used to set off an element that interrupts a sentence, such as a parenthetical expression or a word used in direct address.

PARENTHETICAL EXPRESSION	I thought, **however,** that I should read it again.
DIRECT ADDRESS	**My friend,** do you agree?

2.95 COMMAS II

A **serial comma** is a comma used to separate items in a series, whether the items are words, phrases, or clauses. Some writers omit the last comma when *and, or,* or *nor* joins the last two items in a series, but this construction sometimes makes a sentence unclear.

WORDS	The pins in the map marked London, Paris, and Rome.
PHRASES	During the summer, the crew had installed a new gym floor, a new stage in the theater, and a new heating system.
CLAUSES	We had to push the car whenever it rained, whenever the engine stalled, and whenever it ran out of gas.

Some paired words may be considered a single item.

PAIRED WORDS	We brought paper, **pen and ink,** and a picnic lunch.

If all the items in a series are joined by *and, or,* or *nor,* do not separate them with commas.

EXAMPLE	The weather forecast predicted either rain or sleet or snow.

Two or more adjectives preceding a noun are separated by commas.

EXAMPLE	We sat through a long, dull, dry performance.

Use a comma before *and, but, for, nor, or, so,* and *yet* when they join two independent clauses. The comma may be omitted before *and, but, nor,* and *or* if the clauses are very short and the resulting sentence is still clear in meaning.

LONG CLAUSE	Yesterday's meeting was harmonious, for no one raised any objections.
SHORT CLAUSE	The rain fell and the wind blew.

Do not use a comma between two parts of a compound verb or compound predicate.

EXAMPLE   Doreen repaired the old bicycle and sold it at a tag sale.

2.96 COMMAS III

A **nonrestrictive** participial phrase or clause is one that does not restrict or limit the meaning of the substantive to which it refers. You can test a phrase or clause when proofreading your writing by seeing if the main meaning of the sentence is lost if you omit the phrase or clause. If the phrase or clause is indeed nonrestrictive, make sure it is set off by commas.

RESTRICTIVE	People **who live in glass houses** shouldn't throw stones.
NONRESTRICTIVE	Sacramento, **which is the capital of California,** escaped the earthquake.

Appositives and appositive phrases can be either restrictive or nonrestrictive.

RESTRICTIVE	That book **that you loaned me** is lost.
NONRESTRICTIVE	That book, **the one you loaned me,** is lost.

PROOFREADING FOR OTHER PUNCTUATION ERRORS

2.97 SEMICOLONS

A **semicolon** is used as punctuation between clauses in several situations. Use a semicolon between closely related independent clauses that are not joined by *and, but, for, nor, or, so,* or *yet.*

EXAMPLE   Holiday traffic always threatens safety; this year should be no different.

Use a semicolon between independent clauses joined by a conjunctive adverb or transitional expression that is followed by a comma.

EXAMPLE   At the first meeting, excellent refreshments were served; consequently, everyone stayed until the end.

Use a semicolon between linked independent clauses or items in a list if the clauses or items already contain commas.

INDEPENDENT CLAUSES	Tranh is the new president, elected unanimously; Barb is the new vice president; and Cesar is the new treasurer.
LIST OF ITEMS WITH COMMAS	The committee showed that its members could work together; that they could work efficiently, fairly, and quickly; and that everyone could arrive on time.

2.98 COLONS

A **colon** introduces a long statement or quotation or a list of items.

QUOTATION	She made this astute observation: "To err is human."
LIST	You will be expected to know these rules: punctuation, spelling, capitalization, and usage.

2.99 DASHES

A **dash** is used to show an abrupt break in thought.

EXAMPLE	He could—and might yet—pass the test.

Sometimes the dash serves in place of an expression such as *in other words, that is,* or *namely.*

EXAMPLE	The referees had the power—they could have stopped the game.

2.100 HYPHENS

A **hyphen** is used to link words in a compound adjective, adverb, or noun.

EXAMPLES	all-around athlete, twentieth-century literature, middle-class voter, self-styled poet, best-loved teacher, little-known writer, five-mile hike, eighth-grade student, twenty-odd students, long-suffering patient

If you have questions about whether you should hyphenate a particular compound word, look it up in the dictionary. If the dictionary offers no information, consider whether the hyphen is needed to make the meaning of the sentence clear.

UNCLEAR	We too eagerly agreed.
CLEAR	We too-eagerly agreed.

2.101 PARENTHESES AND BRACKETS

Parentheses are used to enclose an aside or information that is less important than the main information offered in a sentence.

ASIDE	She asked **(without any tact)** whether he'd been fired.
LESS IMPORTANT	The results are on display in the lobby **(the exhibit ends a week from Friday)**.

Brackets are used to enclose a writer's corrections or comments in someone else's quoted material and as parentheses within parentheses.

QUOTED MATERIAL	"I am honored by it **[the appointment]** and will strive to be an effective minister."
PARENTHESES WITHIN	The court of appeals upheld the lower court's decision (the details of the hearing are given in Alberta Smythe's *Trial Lawyer!* **[1894]**).

2.102 APOSTROPHES

An **apostrophe** is used to form the possessive of nouns and some—but not all—pronouns. To form the possessive of a singular noun, add an apostrophe and an *s*. If the noun already ends in an *s* sound, has two or more syllables, and would be hard to pronounce with an additional *s,* add only an apostrophe. These rules apply also to hyphenated words, names of organizations, and indefinite pronouns.

WITH ADDED *S*	citizen's right, dog's collar, girl's dress, man's neckties, princess's ball, Gus's hat, day's pay
WITHOUT ADDED *S*	Jesus' name, series' topic, conscience' sake

To form the possessive of a plural noun, add only an apostrophe if the plural form ends in *s*. If the plural form ends in some other letter, add an apostrophe and an *s*.

ENDING WITH *S*	boys' gym, writers' block, cats' meow
ENDING WITHOUT *S*	children's hour, women's room, data's source, people's choice

While proofreading, check to see that you have not used an apostrophe to form the plural of a noun. Note also that the possessive pronouns, including *yours, ours, hers,* and *its,* do not have an apostrophe.

INCORRECT PLURAL	The **student's** disagree.
CORRECT PLURAL	The **students** disagree.
INCORRECT POSSESSIVE	The ship made **it's** way to port.
CORRECT POSSESSIVE	The ship made **its** way to port.

To show joint possession by all people in a group, add 's (or an apostrophe only) to the last word. To show individual possession of similar items by each member of a group, add 's (or an apostrophe only) to each noun in the group.

JOINT POSSESSION The prize was the **husband and wife's**.
INDIVIDUAL POSSESSION The chairs at the head table were the **husband's** and **wife's**.

Use an apostrophe to form the possessive of words that refer to time or that indicate amounts in dollars or cents.

EXAMPLES today's bread, an hour's drive, a dime's worth

2.103 UNDERLINING AND ITALICS

Italics are a type of slanted printing used to show emphasis. (**Underlining** is used instead of italics in handwritten documents or in forms of printing in which italics are not available.) The following examples show the categories of words that should receive italics (underlining) for emphasis.

WORKS OF ART *Blue Boy, The Thinker, Humoresque*
BOOKS, PLAYS *Mississippi Solo, The Miracle Worker, The Monsters Are Due on Maple Street*
FILMS, TELEVISION PROGRAMS, PERIODICALS *The Wizard of Oz, Meet the Press, The Globe, Mademoiselle*
AIRCRAFT, SHIPS, SPACECRAFT, TRAINS *Concorde, Mayflower, Challenger, Empire Builder*

Italicize the titles of long musical compositions unless they are merely the names of musical forms such as *fantasy, symphony, concerto, sonata,* and *nocturne.* The titles of short pieces such as songs should be placed in quotation marks.

SHORT MUSICAL COMPOSITION "Ave Maria," "Nocturne"
LONG MUSICAL COMPOSITION *New World Symphony*, Mozart's Symphony no. 40

As you proofread your writing, check for words used as words, letters used as letters, and words from foreign languages. These should all be in italics (or underlined).

EXAMPLES Use of the word *got* is sometimes scorned.
Macintosh left an *s* in the sand.
Look up the meaning of *caveat emptor.*

2.104 Quotation Marks I

Quotation marks are used to enclose a **direct quotation,** or a person's exact words. They are not used to enclose an **indirect quotation,** which is a reworded version of a person's words. Commas and periods that follow a quotation should be placed inside closing quotation marks; colons and semicolons should be placed outside. Do not, however, use a period to separate a direct quotation from the rest of a sentence.

DIRECT	"May I have the car?" my sister asked.
DIRECT WITH PERIOD	Mother promised, "You may have the car this afternoon."
DIRECT WITH COMMA	"I'll be back for dinner," my sister shouted back.
DIRECT WITH SEMICOLON	My mother responded, "I won't wait for you"; she had waited too many times.
INDIRECT	I promised my sister that I'd wait anyway.

When writing **dialogue,** a conversation between speakers, begin a new paragraph each time the speaker changes and enclose each speaker's words in quotation marks. When an indication of the speaker, such as *she said,* divides a sentence into two parts, the second part begins with a small letter.

EXAMPLES   Then suddenly Wilhelm rose and said,
"That's enough of this. Tamkin, let's go
back to the market."
"I haven't finished my melon."
"Never mind that. You've had enough
to eat. I want to go back."

—Saul Bellow, *Seize the Day,* ch. 6

2.105 Quotation Marks II

Quotation marks are also used to enclose titles of short works.

PARTS OF BOOKS	"Grammar Handbook"
SONGS	"I Could Have Danced All Night"
SHORT POEMS	"Gus: the Theatre Cat"
STORIES	"The Gift of the Magi"
ESSAYS, ARTICLES	"Thinking Like a Mountain"

Single quotation marks are used to enclose a quotation within a quotation.

EXAMPLE   Martin Luther King, Jr. explained, "I still strive for the goals I sought the day I said, 'I have a dream.'"

2.106 ELLIPSIS

Ellipsis points are used to indicate an omission in quoted material. Use three ellipsis points (with a space before the first point) if the quoted material that precedes the omission is not a complete sentence; if it is a complete sentence, keep the end mark and add the ellipsis points.

INCOMPLETE SENTENCE BEFORE OMISSION   "The result is . . . that he had altered his treatment. It worked."

COMPLETE SENTENCE BEFORE OMISSION   "The result is this. . . . It worked."

Ellipsis points are also used in much the same way to show a pause in a written passage.

EXAMPLE   Yes, but . . . I cannot possibly learn my lines.

PROOFREADING FOR ERRORS IN CAPITALIZATION

2.107 ASTRONOMICAL TERMS

Capitalize the names of astronomical bodies.

PLANETS   Mars, Venus, Saturn
STARS   North Star, Alpha Centauri, Betelgeuse
CONSTELLATIONS   Milky Way, Ursa Major, Little Dipper

2.108 AWARDS

Capitalize the names of awards and prizes. Some words that go with prize names are not capitalized, however.

EXAMPLES   Medal of Honor, Nobel Peace Prize, Nobel Prize in literature, Emmy Award, National Merit scholarship

2.109 BRAND AND TRADE NAMES

Capitalize the brand names and trademarks of products made by businesses. The dictionary may indicate if a name is trademarked. Do not capitalize the noun following a trade name that indicates what type of product it is.

EXAMPLES   Kleenex, Vaseline, Xerox copy

2.110 BUILDINGS AND STRUCTURES

Capitalize the names of important or widely recognized buildings and other structures or monuments. Capitalize the noun following a building, structure, or monument name that indicates its type.

EXAMPLES   White House, Lincoln Memorial, Statue of Liberty, the Pyramids, Leaning Tower of Pisa, Times Square, Brooklyn Bridge

Contrast the absence of capitalization in the following example of a building that is not widely known:

EXAMPLE   The **gray tower** stands in the middle of town.

2.111 DAYS, MONTHS, YEARS, AND HOLIDAYS

Capitalize the names of days, months, and holidays.

DAYS OF THE WEEK   Monday, Saturday
MONTHS   January, March
HOLIDAYS   Fourth of July, Labor Day

Do not capitalize references to decades or centuries.

EXAMPLES   the sixties, the twentieth century

2.112 DIRECTIONS AND REGIONS

Capitalize the names of commonly recognized geographical regions.

EXAMPLES   the Arctic, the Nile Delta, Great Barrier Reef, Black Forest, Texas Panhandle

Do not capitalize words such as *east, west, north,* and *south* when they are used only to indicate direction.

EXAMPLES   Go **west**, young man!
I went out **West**, but I've returned to the **East**.

The adjectives *eastern, western, northern,* and *southern* are not capitalized when they are used as temporary designations.

TEMPORARY   **n**orthern Atlantic, **s**outhern United States
STANDARD   Western Hemisphere, Middle Eastern journey, Southern California, the South

2.113 EVENTS AND PERIODS

Capitalize historical events, special events, and recognized periods of time.

HISTORICAL EVENTS	Fall of Rome, War on Poverty
HISTORICAL PERIODS	Enlightenment, Ice Age, Middle Ages
SPECIAL EVENTS	World Series, Olympics

2.114 FAMILY RELATIONSHIPS

Capitalize the names of family relationships used as titles unless they are preceded by a modifier.

MODIFIED	my mother, your dad, Sam's sister
NOT MODIFIED	Why, Father, must I stay home tonight?

If the name of a family relationship precedes a proper name, capitalize it even if it is modified.

EXAMPLES Grandpa Hann, good old Aunt Clara

2.115 FIRST WORDS

Capitalize the first word in a sentence.

EXAMPLES Do not confuse *capital* and *capitol*.
The doctor said, "This may hurt a little."

2.116 INTERJECTIONS

Do not capitalize the interjection *oh* unless it begins a sentence or stands alone. Do, however, capitalize the word *O*, which is technically not an interjection but a **vocative**—a word used to call someone.

EXAMPLES Ouch, it did hurt!
Oh my, don't do it again.
This time, I'll scream, and oh will you be sorry.
Tell me, O Silent One.

2.117 LETTERS

Capitalize letters used as grades, as musical tones, or as a designation for a person, thing, or location.

EXAMPLES Gone are the days of the gentleman's C.
Beethoven wrote his first symphony in the key of C.

CONTINUED

If **A** equals **B**, **A** also equals **C**.
The shortest distance between point **A** and point **B** is a straight line.

2.118 ORGANIZATIONS AND INSTITUTIONS

Capitalize the names of organizations and institutions, whether they are public, private, athletic, business, or government bodies.

PUBLIC	Democratic Party, University of North Dakota, National Guard
PRIVATE	Boy Scouts of America, New York Stock Exchange
ATHLETIC	Boston Celtics, Los Angeles Dodgers
BUSINESS	Texaco, MCI Communications
GOVERNMENT	Congress, Department of Labor

2.119 OUTLINES

Capitalize the first word of each entry in an outline. Most of the index letters that identify parts of the outline are also capitalized. The following example is the first part of an outline for a report on teaching; observe that lowercase letters are used as index letters after the Arabic numeral level.

Title: You Should Teach

Thesis statement: Everyone should try teaching.

I. Varieties of teaching
   A. Professional
      1. School
      2. College
      3. Industry
      4. Educational media
         a. Films
         b. Books
   B. Volunteer
      1. Peer tutoring
      2. Literacy volunteers

II. Benefits of teaching others
   A. Personal

2.120 PERSONAL NAMES

Capitalize the names of persons and titles of address such as *Mr., Mrs., Ms., Miss, Madame,* or *Monsieur* when used in addressing a person or before a name.

EXAMPLES   Eleanor Roosevelt, Ursula K. Le Guin, O. Henry, Ray Bradbury, Madame Curie

Check a reference book if you are unsure about the capitalization of *de la, du, van, von,* and other parts of names. Sometimes the part of a name that follows *Mc–* or *Mac–* is capitalized and sometimes it is not.

EXAMPLES   Daphne du Maurier, Lee De Forest, Martin Van Buren, Harold Macmillan,
            Alister McAllister

2.121 PLACE NAMES

Capitalize the names of places, including terms such as *lake, mountain, river,* or *valley,* if it is used as part of a name.

BODIES OF WATER	Mississippi River, Lake Placid
CITIES AND TOWNS	San Francisco, Cairo
COUNTIES	Dade County, Western County
COUNTRIES	France, South Africa, India
ISLANDS	Georges Island, Honshu
MOUNTAINS	Mount Rushmore, Grand Tetons
STATES	Idaho, Alabama, Texas
STREETS AND HIGHWAYS	Main Street, Route 66

Do not capitalize generic terms for places without specific modifiers.

EXAMPLES   The **square** in the center of town was decorated with medals.
            Mom and Dad took us camping on an **island** in a little **lake**.

2.122 POETRY

The first word in each line of a poem was capitalized in English until recent times.

EXAMPLE   Often I think of the beautiful town
               That is seated by the sea

                                    —Henry Wadsworth Longfellow

Most writers in this century, however, have broken with this tradition.

EXAMPLE   love is not Love is not LOVE
           love is, LOVE is not

                                    —Anonymous

2.123 PROPER NOUNS AND ADJECTIVES

Capitalize proper nouns and adjectives.

EXAMPLES   Achilles, Achilles' heel
French, French fries

2.124 QUOTATIONS

Capitalize the first word of a sentence in a direct quotation even if it begins within the sentence where it is quoted.

EXAMPLE   Robert Frost wrote, "Good fences make good neighbors."

Do not capitalize a quoted fragment that completes the sense of part of the sentence outside the quotation marks.

EXAMPLE   Henry explained that he "prefers surprise endings."

2.125 SACRED BEINGS AND WRITINGS

Capitalize references to sacred beings or persons, including God, gods, prophets, apostles, and saints. Some adjectives traditionally linked to such beings and persons are sometimes capitalized as well.

EXAMPLES   Allah, Jehovah, the Holy One, Buddha, Messiah

Capitalize the names of sacred writings and parts of such writings.

EXAMPLES   the Bible, Exodus, Quran, Sutra, Torah

2.126 SCHOOL SUBJECTS, COURSES, GRADES, AND YEARS

Capitalize a school subject when it is also the name of a language or when it is followed by a number indicating that it is the name of a specific course.

EXAMPLES   English, social studies, science, math, Algebra I

Expressions such as *tenth grade, twelfth grade, sophomore, junior,* or expressions such as *freshman year, junior year,* are not capitalized unless they are part of the title of an official program.

EXAMPLES   ninth-grade science, Science Fair Scholars

2.127 THE PRONOUN *I*

Capitalize the pronoun *I* wherever it appears, except in quoted material where the pronoun is lowercased in the original.

EXAMPLES   I am what I am.
somewhere i have never travelled, gladly beyond
any experience . . .

—E. E. Cummings

2.128 TITLES OF ARTWORKS

Apply **title capitalization** to titles of works of art. In title capitalization, the following are capitalized: the first word, the last word, all nouns, pronouns, adjectives, verbs, adverbs, and subordinating conjunctions. Articles *(a, an, the)* are written lowercase unless they are the first or last word. Some writers also capitalize any preposition over five letters long.

EXAMPLES   Wood's *American Gothic,* Rodin's *Balzac,* El Greco's *View of Toledo*

2.129 TITLES OF LITERARY WORKS

Apply title capitalization to titles of literary works.

EXAMPLES   Sandburg's "Fog," Twain's "Encounter with an Interviewer," Shakespeare's *Merchant of Venice*

2.130 TITLES OF MUSICAL WORKS

Apply title capitalization to titles of musical works.

EXAMPLES   "Waltzing Matilda," *Hungarian Rhapsody, Adagio for Strings*

2.131 TITLES OF PERSONS AND OCCUPATIONS

Capitalize official titles of persons when they immediately precede a person's name or when they are used instead of a name in direct address.

EXAMPLES   President Abraham Lincoln, Lady Thatcher, Pope John, General Douglas MacArthur
Mr. President, I beg you to reconsider!

Do not capitalize references to occupations.

EXAMPLES   the **p**resident, the **g**eneral, the **p**rince, the **p**ope, the **l**ords and **l**adies

2.132 UNITS OF TIME

Do not capitalize units of time such as the words *second, minute, hour, day, year, decade, century,* or the names of the seasons.

EXAMPLES   A decade from now, we'll be in the twenty-first century.
If winter's here, can spring be far behind?

2.133 VEHICLES

Capitalize the names of vehicles only if they are trade names.

EXAMPLES   **C**hevrolet, **H**onda **A**ccord, station wagon, train, automobile, spacecraft

SPELLING HANDBOOK

2.134 PROOFREADING FOR SPELLING ERRORS

After you have checked your writing for other problems, read it through for spelling errors. Even if you have confidence in your spelling, you may make a mistake in keyboarding your work or writing it out by hand. Of course, the difficulty in detecting errors is that you will tend to see the words as you meant to write them, rather than as they really stand on the page. Professional proofreaders have a helpful technique: they read the text backward word by word. If you come across a word that causes the slightest doubt, check it in the dictionary.

2.135 USING SPELLING RULES I

Many spelling problems arise from a common operation: forming plurals. Form the plurals of most nouns by simply adding *s*.

EXAMPLES   book**s**, computer**s**, compact disc**s**

Some nouns ending in *o* preceded by a consonant have plurals ending in *es*, as do nouns ending in *s, x, z, ch,* or *sh*.

EXAMPLES   Mosquit**oes** swarmed around the potat**oes**.
her**oes**, dress**es**, box**es**, buzz**es**, bir**ches**, bu**shes**

Form the plurals of most musical terms ending in *o* by adding *s.*

EXAMPLES   The alt**os** sang sol**os** like virtuos**os**.

Form the plurals of nouns ending in *y* preceded by a vowel by adding *s.* (The **vowels** are the letters *a, e, i, o, u.* Sometimes the letter *y* also represents a vowel sound.)

EXAMPLES   On Mond**ays**, the b**oys** visit the monk**eys** and donk**eys**.

Form the plurals of nouns ending in *y* preceded by a consonant by changing the *y* to *i* and adding *es.* (The **consonants** are all the letters that are not vowels.)

EXAMPLES   The lady was beset by a fly.
The lad**ies** were surrounded by fl**ies**.

The plurals of some nouns are irregular.

EXAMPLES   The **goose** amused the **child** by pecking at her **foot**.
The **geese** amused the **children** by pecking at their **feet**.

Form the plural of a compound noun consisting of a noun and a modifier by making the main noun component plural.

EXAMPLES   The treasonous brother**s**-in-law faced court**s** martial.

2.136 USING SPELLING RULES II

Another operation that causes spelling errors is adding **prefixes** or **suffixes** to a word. A prefix is a letter or a group of letters added to the beginning of a word to change its meaning. When adding a prefix to a word, do not change the word itself.

EXAMPLES   mis + spell = **mis**spell
il + legal = **il**legal
over + turned = **over**turned

A **suffix** is a letter or group of letters added to the end of a word to change its meaning. The spelling of most words is not changed when the suffix *–ness* or *–ly* is added.

EXAMPLES   mean + ness = mean**ness**
final + ly = final**ly**

In the case of many words of more than one syllable ending in *y*, however, change the *y* to *i* before adding *–ly* or *ness*.

EXAMPLES   ready + ly = read**ily**
happy + ness = happ**iness**

In most cases of words ending in a final silent *e*, drop the *e* when adding a suffix beginning with a vowel, and keep the *e* when adding a suffix beginning with a consonant.

EXAMPLES   care + ing = car**ing**
use + able = us**able**
name + less = name**less**
nine + ty = nine**ty**

VOCABULARY DEVELOPMENT

2.137 MAKING A PLAN FOR VOCABULARY DEVELOPMENT

You can increase your **vocabulary**—the words you have at your command that empower you in communicating with others—by taking a few simple steps. When you encounter a new word, whether in reading, in speaking with others, in class, or outside school altogether, write it down in a list in your journal. Check the meaning in a dictionary and jot that down, too. Then review your vocabulary list from time to time. This procedure will vastly increase the chances that you will recall the new words you encounter.

2.138 USING CONTEXT CLUES I

Although a dictionary is the best resource to check when you encounter a new word, sometimes a dictionary is not at hand. Even if a dictionary is available, you may prefer not to break the stream of your thought by consulting it. At times like these, you can often deduce the meaning of a word from context clues.

One type of context clue to look for is **restatement**. The author may tell you the meaning of a word you do not know by using different words to express the same idea in another sentence. Consider the following example.

EXAMPLE   The defendant claims that the crime was not **premeditated**. The man was found, however, with a large bag of burglar's tools, showing that **he intended to rob the house**.

An alert reader will guess from the restatement (printed here in boldface) that *premeditated* means "planned in advance."

A second and related type of context clue is **apposition.** Look for a word or phrase that is specifically intended to clarify or modify the word you do not know.

EXAMPLE Your assignment is to write a **précis,** or **summary**.

A third related type of context clue is the use of **examples.**

EXAMPLE **Illative** expressions include *therefore, thus, in conclusion, ergo,* **and** *it follows that.*

The examples suggest that *illative* means "introducing an inference or conclusion."

2.139 Using Context Clues II

Another context clue is the use of **comparison.** Imagine a reader does not know the meaning of the word *sexagenarian.* The comparison in the following passage will allow him or her to deduce the meaning from the context.

EXAMPLE Today there are advantages for **sexagenarians**. Many businesses give substantial discounts to **persons over sixty**. Improvements in health care have made **the later years of life** much more comfortable and vigorous. And since **most people retire at this time of life**, they can enjoy their newfound leisure time.

Comparison indicates that a sexagenarian is a person over the age of sixty (specifically between the ages of sixty and seventy).

Contrast is a similar type of context clue.

EXAMPLE Although the medical team quickly administered the **antidote**, the patient died from the poison.

Contrast suggests that an antidote is something that counteracts poison.

2.140 Base Words and Prefixes

Building vocabulary is easier if you know the building blocks of words. Many words are formed by adding **prefixes** to a **base.** For example, imagine you come across the word *counterrevolution* and are unfamiliar with it. You do, however, recognize the **base word,** *revolution.* And you know from words such as *counterclockwise* and *countermeasure* that the prefix *counter–* means "against" or "contrary to." You can then quickly deduce that a counterrevolution is a movement in opposition to a revolution. The following table gives further examples.

PREFIX	MEANING	EXAMPLE	MEANING
bi–	"two," "twice"	bivalve	having two valves
pre–	"before"	prejudge	to judge before
hemi–	"half"	hemisphere	half a sphere
a–	"not," "without"	amoral	without morality
im–	"against," "not"	immoral	against morality

2.141 SUFFIXES

Like prefixes, **suffixes** can provide valuable clues to words you do not know. The following table lists a few examples.

SUFFIX	MEANING	EXAMPLE	MEANING
–ar	"one who"	scholar	one who studies
–ling	"small being"	duckling	small duck
–ic	"like"	angelic	like an angel
–ish	"like"	boyish	like a boy
–ous	"full of"	famous	full of fame

2.142 GREEK AND LATIN ROOTS

Although English is primarily a Germanic language, its vocabulary is in large part based on ancient Greek and Latin. Some Greek and Latin words came to English by way of other languages such as French; others were borrowed directly from Greek and Latin sources by scientists, researchers, and writers, who have always looked to Greek and Latin for components to build new words. The word *telephone,* for instance, comes from the Greek root *tele–*, meaning "far away," and *phone,* meaning "voice."

The following table shows some words with **Greek and Latin roots.**

FROM GREEK	FROM LATIN	MEANING OF GREEK AND LATIN ROOTS
dys-function	mal-function	"bad-operating"
hypo-dermals	sub-dermal	"under-skin"
peri-phery	circum-ference	"around-boundary"
sym-pathy	com-passion	"with-feeling"
dia-ry	trans-cript	"across-writing"
mono-cycle	uni-cycle	"one-wheel"
poly-morph	multi-form	"many-form"

2.143 WORD ORIGINS I

Knowing how speakers of English form words can help you recognize new words when you see them. **Names of people and places** are a common source of new words. The following table gives several examples.

WORD	ORIGIN
cashmere	From Cashmere, or Kashmir, a region in the Himalayas, where mountain goats produce a downy wool known as "cashmere."
quisling	From the name of a Norwegian traitor, Vidkum Quisling, who served the Germans when Germany occupied Norway during World War II. The word now means "traitor."
braille	From the name of the French musician and inventor Louis Braille, who was blind from childhood. Braille developed a system of writing and reading for the blind that carries his name.

Another source of new words are **acronyms**, or words formed from the first letter or letters of each of the major parts of a compound term.

EXAMPLES   laser, from "**l**ight **a**mplification-**s**timulated **e**mission **r**adiation"; scuba, from "**s**elf-**c**ontained **u**nderwater **b**reathing **a**pparatus"

Many words are simply **borrowed** from other languages.

EXAMPLES   **calico** (Hindi), **blitz** (German), **samba** (Portuguese), **sushi** (Japanese), **collage** (French), **concerto** (Italian), **raccoon** (Algonquin), **caboose** (Dutch), **gung ho** (Chinese)

2.144 WORD ORIGINS II

New words are also formed by shortening longer words. The word *phone,* short for *telephone,* is one such **clipped form.**

EXAMPLES   **ad** (from *advertisement*), **exam** (from *examination*), **gym** (from *gymnasium*), **lab** (from *laboratory*), **math** (from *mathematics*), **photo** (from *photograph*), **typo** (from *typographical error*)

New words are often **coined,** or deliberately created to fill a need.

EXAMPLES   **e-mail,** from *electronic mail.* The term refers to written communication transferred between people by means of computers.

CONTINUED

ESSENTIAL SKILLS: LANGUAGE

Brand names are often taken into the language, even though their owners may struggle to protect their exclusive status.

EXAMPLES   Ping-Pong, Teflon, Jell-O

2.145 WORDS FROM OTHER CURRICULAR AREAS I

As you study other subjects besides English, be alert for colorful words that have extended meanings that might be of use in your writing. Keep a list of these words in your journal. The table below gives a few examples of words of this type, as well as sample sentences showing how these words might be used in the study of English.

SUBJECT	WORDS
Arts and Humanities	You guys are real **characters**. Few would say that *The Iliad* is but a **prelude** to *The Odyssey*. The short story seemed so familiar; it **struck a chord** deep within me.
Mathematics	You cannot make an **equation** between fiction and nonfiction. The **common denominator** of all mythology is an explanation of the human experience. Plays differ from short stories and poems because a theatrical performance involves more **variables**.

2.146 WORDS FROM OTHER CURRICULAR AREAS II

More examples of words from other curricular areas are shown in the table below.

SUBJECT	WORDS
Social Studies	What would it **cost** you to be a little more polite? Few politicians are prepared to tackle the **sacred cow** of Social Security.
Science	A short story can become the **germ** of a novel that further develops the plot and character. The **evolution** of the English novel began in the early eighteenth century. Dryden was the center of literary England, and other poets **orbited** about him.
Technical Preparatory	Capote's prose was **honed** as sharp as anyone's. King **hammered** home his point by deft use of repetition. I thought that Dave was supposed to pick me up here at 6:00; I guess our **wires got crossed**.

VARIETIES OF ENGLISH

2.147 FORMAL AND INFORMAL ENGLISH

Formal English is the kind of English used in writing papers, some magazine articles and nonfiction books, and some literary works. It is spoken at public ceremonies and in official speeches. **Informal English** is the kind of English used in personal notes and letters, in most newspaper and magazine articles, in some nonfiction and fiction books, and in some short stories and plays. It is spoken in everyday conversation.

How do you decide whether to use formal or informal English? You will naturally tend to use informal English, so all you need to bear in mind are those situations (just described) in which formal English may be expected instead.

How do you distinguish formal from informal English? First, informal English allows grammatical constructions that would not be acceptable in formal English. Second, informal English is enlivened by **colloquialisms.** These are the words and phrases that speakers of a language use naturally in conversation.

EXAMPLES It was hard **to get going** this morning.
I waited a bit, but then I **wanted out**.

Third, informal English is often salted with **slang,** a form of speech made up of coined words, words whose meaning has been changed for no known reason, and words used facetiously.

EXAMPLES I hear you **whipped right through** [finished quickly] the multiple-choice questions.
My sister was really **bent out of shape** [very upset] after losing the contest.

Informal grammatical constructions, colloquialisms, and slang sometimes have a place even in writing that is otherwise formal. Literary works, for example, may rely on these devices to make dialogue colorful and realistic.

2.148 REGISTER

To understand the concept of **register,** imagine that all the different kinds of usage in a language—both formal and informal—form one large set. A register is a subset of language usage that is used in a particular relationship between people. In talking to a friend, for example, you speak in a register that is casual, warm, and open. In speaking to a little child, you speak in a register that is nonthreatening and simple to understand. In speaking to an official such as a police officer or a government clerk, you speak in a register that is polite but firm—the same register they should use with you. The words you choose, the grammar you employ to say those words, and your tone of voice will change depending on the register in which you are speaking.

Another way to understand register is to think of the meaning of the musical term. In music, *register* means the range of notes a singer or instrument is capable of producing. Your speaking and writing, however, are not limited to one range of usage. You can use any part of a broad scale of usage from a grunt to a complex and formal declaration of your thought.

One hallmark of people who adapt to society is their ability to choose and use the appropriate register for whatever situation they are in. They do not offend strangers by being too familiar or puzzle their friends by being too formal. The same is true of written language. When you write, use language that is appropriate for the context and for your intended reader. Your personal journal will be in a different register from a term paper, and a story you write for a child will be in a different register from a short story you write for your English class.

2.149 TONE AND VOICE

Tone is the quality of a work that shows the attitude of the person writing or supposedly writing it. The whimsical tone of "Sarah Cynthia Sylvia Stout Would Not Take the Garbage Out," "Gus: The Theatre Cat," or "Casey at the Bat" is in contrast to the reverent tone in James Weldon Johnson's "The Creation" or Max Ehrmann's "Desiderata."

In any writing you do, you can adopt a tone appropriate for the message you wish to convey. Your **diction,** or choice of words, determines much of your tone. For instance, when writing a letter to a government official protesting a new regulation, do you want to say, "Your new regulation is utterly unacceptable to the honest citizens of this state," or "The new regulation is unpopular among many of your constituents"? The tone you convey will depend upon your choice.

Voice is the quality of a work that tells you that one person in particular wrote it—not several, and not just anyone. Voice is one feature that makes a work unique. The voice of a work can be difficult to define; it may have to do with the way a writer views people, events, objects, ideas, the passage of time, even life itself. If this treatment of the subject is consistent throughout, despite variations in tone, register, point of view, and so forth, then the writer has **established a voice,** a sense of individuality, in the work.

Voice is difficult to illustrate in a small space. Consider, however, the following passages:

> Arcadio waited for her that night trembling with fever in his hammock. He waited without sleeping, listening to the aroused crickets in the endless hours of early morning and the implacable telling of time by the curlews, more and more convinced that he had been deceived. Suddenly, when anxiety had broken down into rage, the door opened. A few months later, facing the firing squad, Arcadio would relive the wandering steps in the classroom, the stumbling against benches, and finally the bulk of a body in the shadows of the room and the breathing of air that was pumped by a heart that was not his.
> —Gabriel García Márquez, *One Hundred Years of Solitude*, ch. 6

> This man, this night, did not look as though he wished to amuse her with imitations of Laurence Olivier. He looked preoccupied. In fact, the more she watched him, the more she realized that he was almost grotesquely preoccupied. He was restless; he could not sit still: he kept picking up one book from his pile, then another, then turning over the pages of his *New Statesman*, then staring out into the corridor and onto the dark platform.
> —Margaret Drabble, "A Voyage to Cythera"

Each of these passages describes a man waiting, but the two differ greatly in the kind of person they describe, in what they say about that person, and in the types of words and sentences they use. Consider Márquez's main subjects and verbs—"Arcadio waited . . . ," "He waited . . . ," " . . . the door opened," " . . . Arcadio would relive. . . ." Márquez uses phrases (prepositional and participial) that make the passage flow and undulate; he describes repetitive nighttime background noises that lull the reader into a trance; he describes the future as if it affected what happens in the present. Reading the passage is like watching a dream. Compare Drabble's subjects and verbs: "This man . . . did not look . . . ," "He looked . . . ," " . . . she looked . . . she realized . . . ," "He was . . . ; he could not . . . : he kept picking up . . . turning . . . staring. . . ." Drabble's short clauses with action verbs make the reader feel the man's intensity and anxiety. Even the linking verb "looked" expresses action. The reader jumps after her here, then there. Her descriptions are always from the observer's point of view, giving the reader an idea of how stressful it is to watch someone who is "grotesquely" nervous.

2.150 DIALECTS OF ENGLISH

Dialects are varieties of a language. Dialects fall into one of two main classes: dialects based on **social differences** (for example, upper class, middle class, and lower class) and dialects based on **regional differences** (in the United States, the major regional dialects are northern, southern, midland, and western).

All dialects are equally capable of expressing thought, which is what language is for. Therefore, no dialect is *better* than any other dialect. Some dialects are accepted by social classes that hold power; their dialect is generally considered the **standard** form of a language, and other dialects are considered **nonstandard**. But *standard* does not mean "correct" or "better than others." Knowledge of the standard dialect is useful because it is widely understood and because, in many situations, speaking or writing in the standard dialect will ensure that people focus on *what* you say rather than *how* you say it. They will understand your meaning, without being distracted by your use of an unfamiliar dialect.

Knowledge of nonstandard dialects is also useful to writers. Consider Thomas Hardy's poem "The Man He Killed," which is made more lively and authentic through Hardy's use of dialect words such as *nipperkin,* meaning a half-pint container, and the form *'list,* for the standard *enlist.*

> They's something kindo' harty°-like about the atmusfere   *hearty*
>   When the heat of summer's over and the coolin' fall is here—
> Of course we miss the flowers, and the blossums° on the trees,   *blossoms*
> And the mumble of the hummin'-birds and the buzzin' of the bees;
> But the air's so appetizin'; and the landscape through the haze
> Of a crisp and sunny morning of the airly° autumn days   *early*
>   Is a pictur' that no painter has the colorin' to mock
>   When the frost is on the punkin and the fodder's in the shock
>
>   —James Whitcomb Riley,
>   "When the Frost is on the Punkin"

2.151 Jargon and Gobbledygook

Jargon is the specialized vocabulary used by members of a profession. It tends to be incomprehensible to people outside the profession. A plumber may speak of a "hubless fitting" or a "street elbow" (kinds of pipe). A computer programmer may talk of "RAM cache" (part of computer memory) or a "shell" (a type of operating software for computers).

Jargon is useful to writers who want to lend authenticity to their description of situations in which jargon would naturally be used. For instance, a novel about fighter pilots on an aircraft carrier would probably be full of aviation jargon. A scriptwriter developing a science fiction film would be sure to work in futuristic jargon about warps in space, energy shields, and tractor beams.

Gobbledygook is unclear, wordy jargon used by bureaucrats or government officials. For instance, instead of saying, "raise taxes," a bureaucrat might say "proactively maximize voluntary revenue income." In requesting six billion dollars for a kind of paper handkerchief for the armed services, a military planner might call the product a "disposable fiber wipeage utensil."

The most famous literary examples of gobbledygook occur in the novel *Nineteen Eighty-four,* by the English writer George Orwell. Gobbledygook is there raised to a standard of its own; called *doublespeak,* it is the officially approved form of communication between the government and the people.

2.152 Clichés and Euphemisms

A **cliché** is an expression that has been used so often it has become colorless and uninteresting.

The use of clichés makes writing dull.

EXAMPLES break the ice
drop in the bucket
last but not least
at a loss for words

A **euphemism** (from the Greek verb meaning "to speak with good words") is an inoffensive term that substitutes for one considered offensive.

EXAMPLES the necessary, rest room, little boys'/girls' room (for "toilet")
pass away, leave this world, go to a/the better place (for "die")

2.153 CONNOTATION AND DENOTATION

A **denotation** of a word is its dictionary definition. A **connotation** of a word is all the associations that it has in addition to its literal meaning. For example, the denotations of *mud* and *muck* are identical; but *muck* carries a connotation of moral filthiness that makes it a much stronger word than *mud*. Contrast the denotations and connotations of the following examples.

Writers should be aware of the connotations as well as the denotations of the words they use. You would be remiss to say, "The honcho jabbered for eons about his pet proposition," when what you meant was, "The president spoke for a long time about the proposal he favored."

EXAMPLES   speak, talk, prattle, gab, pontificate, jabber
child, tot, kid, youngster, brat, squirt, tyke

ESSENTIAL SKILLS:
Speaking and Listening

3.1 A COMMUNICATION MODEL

An actor gives a speech and the audience applauds. A traffic cop holds up a red sign and a driver stops. You order a taco and the server says, "That'll be $1.49." These all are examples of communication. In each case, there is a **sender** and a **receiver** of a **message.** The sender encodes the message using symbols. The English language is one set of symbols; traffic signs are another. The message is sent by a channel, or medium. The channel for spoken English is sound; the channel for traffic signs is sight. A receiver decodes the message and provides a response, or feedback. The following chart describes this communication model.

COMMUNICATION MODEL	
Sender	You
Message	"I'd like a taco with extra onions."
Symbols Used	Words in the English language
Channel	Sound
Recipient	Restaurant clerk
Feedback	"That'll be $1.49."

Communication is successful only when all six elements are working together: the sender must use the same symbols as the receiver and encode the message correctly, the channel must be clear so the receiver can get the message, and the receiver must decode the message correctly. If communication is not successful, one or more of these elements must be changed. For example, if the restaurant were noisy and the server couldn't hear you, you might repeat your order in a louder voice, or you might "change channels" (from sound to sight) and point to the item on the menu.

> ► ► ► A C T I V I T Y 3.1

A. Name the sender, the message, the receiver, and the feedback in each communication situation described below.

1. A parent waves to a child on the school bus, and the child waves back.

CONTINUED

2. A friend keeps looking over your shoulder as he is talking to you. You ask, "Are you waiting for someone?"

3. A driver spots a traffic light turning yellow and begins to slow down.

B. What are two channels you could use to send each of the following messages?

1. I like you.

2. Come on, let's go.

3. My stomach hurts.

C. Explain how communication might break down in each of the following situations.

1. A student is reading a poem in front of the class.

2. Hikers are looking for blue paint marks on trees that mark the trail through a forest.

3.2 ELEMENTS OF VERBAL COMMUNICATION

Communication can be verbal or nonverbal. **Verbal communication** uses spoken words and other sounds uttered by speakers. **Nonverbal communication** uses symbols other than spoken words or sounds. The most important elements of verbal, or oral, communication are described in the following chart:

ELEMENTS OF VERBAL COMMUNICATION		
ELEMENT	**DESCRIPTION**	**GUIDELINES FOR SPEAKERS**
Volume	The loudness or softness of the voice	Speak loudly enough to be heard, but not so loudly as to make your audience uncomfortable.
Pitch, or Intonation	The highness or lowness of the voice	Vary your pitch to give your expressions a musical quality and to communicate meaning (for example, a rising pitch at the end of a sentence indicates a question). Avoid using a single pitch, or **monotone**.
Enunciation	The clearness with which syllables are spoken	Slightly exaggerate the clearness of your syllables to ensure that you are understood. Do not drop or clip the ends of words or sentences.
Pace	The speed with which something is said	Do not speak too slowly or too quickly.
Stress	The emphasis given to syllables, words, or phrases	Use stress to emphasize important ideas. Vary stress along with pitch to avoid monotony.

CONTINUED

ELEMENTS OF VERBAL COMMUNICATION

ELEMENT	DESCRIPTION	GUIDELINES FOR SPEAKERS
Tone	The emotional quality of the speech	Suit the tone to the message. Vary the tone appropriately throughout the communication.

Being aware of these elements of verbal communication is especially important for public speaking. When speaking in front of a group, follow these guidelines:

USING ELEMENTS OF VERBAL COMMUNICATION IN PUBLIC SPEAKING

1. Make sure that you can be heard and understood by using an appropriate volume and pace.
2. Suit your volume, pitch, pace, stress, and tone to your message.
3. Vary all the verbal elements of your speech to make the presentation more lively, colorful, and interesting.
4. Slightly heighten or exaggerate each of the verbal elements of your speech over the level that you would use in ordinary conversation.

► ► ► A C T I V I T Y 3.2

Choose a poem from this textbook to read aloud to your classmates. Make a copy of the poem and mark it to show the following:

1. places where you will increase or decrease your volume
2. places where you will increase or decrease your pace
3. words or phrases that you should emphasize by means of volume, pitch, or stress
4. words or phrases that you might have trouble pronouncing, or enunciating (You will want to give special attention to these when practicing.)
5. changes in tone or emotion throughout the piece

Practice reading the selection aloud following the notes that you have made.

3.3 ELEMENTS OF NONVERBAL COMMUNICATION

Much of everyday communication is nonverbal. Many nonverbal messages are communicated unconsciously or unintentionally. Speakers addressing an audience, however, deliberately use nonverbal communication to make their verbal messages stronger and clearer. The following chart offers some guidelines for using nonverbal communication.

ELEMENTS OF NONVERBAL COMMUNICATION

ELEMENT	DESCRIPTION	GUIDELINES FOR SPEAKERS
Eye contact	Looking your audience in the eye	Maintain eye contact to keep your audience engaged in what you are saying.
Facial expressions	Displays of emotion using the face (e.g., smiles, scowls, frowns, etc.)	Match your facial expressions to your message.
Body language	Positions of the body that have meaning to an audience	Match your body language to your message. Maintain good posture.
Gestures	Meaningful motions of the hands and arms	Use gestures sparingly to emphasize points. Match gestures to your message.
Proximity	Distance from the audience	Maintain a comfortable distance, not too close for comfort, but not so far away as to hamper communication.

▶ ▶ ▶ A C T I V I T Y 3.3

Mark the same poem that you chose in Activity 3.2 to show how you will use appropriate facial expressions, gestures, and body language. Practice reading the poem aloud using the nonverbal communication techniques you have noted.

3.4 ACTIVE LISTENING

Listening, like speaking, is an active process. You've probably heard the expression "in one ear and out the other." This expression suggests that when someone is speaking with or to you, you must listen actively, with your mind as well as your ears. Here are some ways you can listen actively:

- **Mentally process what you hear.** As you listen, try to summarize and ask yourself questions about what you hear. Try to organize the information by identifying main ideas and supporting details.

- **Take notes.** Jot down especially interesting ideas or details. If you are listening to a lecture, you may want to take notes in outline form.

- **Ask questions and give other feedback.** Use both nonverbal feedback—eye contact, gestures, facial expressions, and body language—and verbal feedback. In conversation, you might show that you have understood the speaker by saying "uh-huh" or "I see." If you are confused by something the speaker said, pause and rephrase it; ask "Are you saying that . . . ?" to check your understanding. Wait until the speaker has finished a whole thought before asking questions.

► ► ► A C T I V I T Y   3.4

Role play a listening session with a classmate. Choose one of the following topics and write some notes or make an outline for what you will say. Then take turns actively listening to each other. Practice using the preceding techniques.

- explaining how to repair something
- telling about a disagreement you had with an adult
- describing your street or neighborhood

3.5 INTERPERSONAL COMMUNICATION

Communication between individuals is called **interpersonal communication.** Individuals use interpersonal communication to

- transmit information;
- establish relationships;
- maintain relationships;
- confirm their identity;
- form personal bonds.

You can use verbal and nonverbal techniques to improve your interpersonal communication:

- Make eye contact.
- Stand in a relaxed way.
- Provide feedback by asking questions or reflecting back what the speaker said. For example:

  SPEAKER   "I can't believe Nell didn't invite me to her party."
  LISTENER   "You sound disappointed. Were you expecting an invitation?"

- Think before you speak. Consider how your listener might interpret what you are saying.
- Keep strong emotions under control. If you begin to feel angry, for example, tell your listener how you feel and why you feel that way.

► ► ► A C T I V I T Y   3.5

Choose a partner and role play a conversation about a personal disappointment. (For this exercise, the disappointment selected should be an imaginary one.) Take turns being speaker and listener. As you speak or listen, apply the techniques for improving interpersonal communication given above.

3.6 DISCUSSION

Discussion is a way of sharing ideas or information with several people at one time. Discussions may range from very formal, as in a congressional committee meeting, to very informal, as in a lunchtime conversation among friends. Your teacher probably will want you to have semiformal discussions, in which group members have assigned roles, and the discussion is focused and structured in some way. The following chart describes the basic elements of a semiformal discussion.

DISCUSSION	
Roles	• **Group leader or chairperson.** Keeps the discussion on track when people begin to digress or veer away from the subject, asks questions when the discussion starts to lag, makes sure everyone participates • **Secretary.** Takes notes or records what is said and later prepares a description (**minutes**) of the discussion • **Participants.** Take part in the discussion, listen attentively to others, provide feedback
Process	• **Discussion question.** States the goal or main idea of the discussion and is usually put forward by the group leader. In a formal discussion, the discussion question is called a **proposition.** • **Agenda.** A step-by-step plan for the discussion, usually written and distributed at the beginning of the discussion by the group leader or secretary

► ► ► A C T I V I T Y   3.6

Imagine that you and a group of classmates are planning an oral interpretation program. Participants will read poems, perform excerpts from plays, tell folk tales, and so on. Think about what decisions must be made and what jobs need to be assigned. Then write an agenda for a meeting at which you will plan the program.

3.7 PUBLIC SPEAKING

If you feel afraid of or anxious about speaking before a group, you are in the majority. Most people, even some famous stage actors and politicians, admit to feeling anxious when they must face a crowd. If you feel nervous about speaking in front of others, you should know that some preparation and a basic understanding of good public speaking techniques can make you feel much more at ease and can even enable you to turn your anxiety into an advantage.

Types of speeches. There are three main types of speeches. A speech given on the spur of the moment, with no preparation, is called an **impromptu speech.** An example would be a thank-you speech made immediately after receiving a surprise award. A **memorized speech** is written out entirely and then committed to memory word for word and recited to the audience. Impromptu speeches can be spontaneous and intimate, but they can be very ineffective because there is little thought behind them; on the other hand, memorized speeches do have preparation and thought behind them, but when delivered, they tend to sound stilted and dull. An **extemporaneous speech** combines the informality of an impromptu speech with the careful preparation of a memorized speech. In an extemporaneous speech the speaker gathers concise and organized notes on index cards but does not memorize the entire speech, leaving room for spontaneity and improvisation.

Writing a speech. Like other forms of writing, a written speech should have a beginning, a middle, and an end. The **beginning,** or **introduction,** should capture the audience's attention and present your main idea. The **middle,** or **body,** should expand on the main idea, adding details or presenting reasons and evidence. The **end, or conclusion,** should be memorable and give the audience a sense that the message of your speech is complete. For more information on writing introductions and conclusions, see the Language Arts Survey, 1.42, "Organizing a Composition."

Preparing an extemporaneous speech. To prepare an extemporaneous speech, follow the steps described in the chart below.

STEPS IN PREPARING AN EXTEMPORANEOUS SPEECH
1. Do prewriting.
2. Do research.
3. Prepare note cards.
4. Make a plan for using verbal and nonverbal elements of communication in your speech.
5. Rehearse with your note cards, using a tape recorder, a video recorder, a mirror, or a practice audience.
6. Deliver your speech, attending to both verbal and nonverbal elements of the delivery.

▶ ▶ ▶ A C T I V I T Y 3.7

Choose an audience and a topic for an extemporaneous speech. Your audience might be a group of classmates, children, or parents. Prepare an extemporaneous speech for that audience by completing steps 1 through 5 in the chart above.

3.8 ORAL INTERPRETATION

Oral interpretation is the process of presenting a dramatic reading of a literary work or group of works. The goal is to give the audience your individual sense, or interpretation, of the work. Oral interpretation is an ancient form of literature. Before they were ever written down, epic poems such as Homer's *The Odyssey*, ballads such as "Robin Hood," and many other poems, songs, and tales were recited orally for generations.

To prepare an oral interpretation, follow these steps:

1. **Choose a cutting.** The cutting may be a single piece, a selection from a single piece, or several short, related pieces on a single topic.

2. **Write the introduction.** In the introduction, you should present the overall topic or theme of the presentation and identify the author and title of each selection.

3. **Write any needed transitions.** The transitions should introduce and connect the different parts or cuttings that you will be interpreting.

4. **Rehearse.** Experiment using volume (loud/soft), pitch (high/low), pace (slow/fast), stress (strong/weak), and tone (formal/informal/elegant/serious/exaggerated/etc.) to help you convey what you think the piece is saying. If there is more than one speaker or character, use different voices to distinguish them. Also practice gestures, facial expressions, and overall body language; however, avoid moving around the stage—that's for a drama.

► ► ► A C T I V I T Y   **3.8**

Choose three short pieces or portions of pieces in this text for an oral interpretation. All the cuttings should relate to a single theme or topic, such as animals in the wild or growing up in the city. Copy your cuttings onto notebook paper, skipping lines to leave room for your notes. On separate pieces of paper, write your introduction and transitions. In the introduction, present your topic or theme in an interesting way and state the title and author of each selection. In your transitions, make brief statements to connect each piece to the overall topic or theme. Then combine the introduction, the cuttings, and the transitions to make a script. Practice reading your script. As you make decisions about how you will interpret the cuttings, mark the script to show variations in volume, pitch, pace, stress, tone, gestures, facial expressions, and body language. Rehearse the final version until you have memorized it. Then present your oral interpretation to a group.

ESSENTIAL SKILLS:
Study and Research

THINKING SKILLS

Every day you use a great number of thinking skills to make decisions, to solve problems, and to understand new ideas and information. Probably without realizing it, you already use many of the thinking strategies presented in this section. Becoming aware of your thinking processes and practicing a few strategies can help you be more efficient and effective in using your thinking skills.

4.1 STRATEGIES FOR PROBLEM SOLVING I

All problem solving involves four steps.

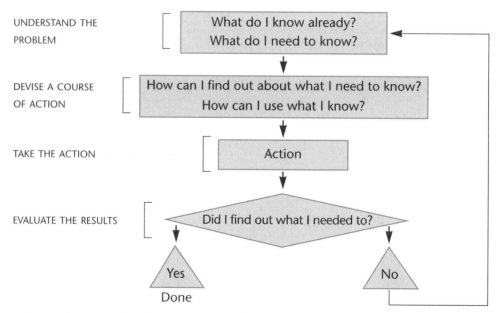

The problem-solving framework described by the diagram is general. For any problem that you face, there are many particular strategies you can use to decide what actions to take. Keep your mind flexible: even a good strategy does not guarantee that you will solve a given problem. For a complex problem you will probably need to use more than one strategy.

Trial and error. When you guess at a solution and see if it works, you are using trial and error. This is the simplest of all problem-solving strategies. Trial and error is useful when only a few possible solutions seem likely. You might also use this strategy when there are a great many possibilities and you need to get familiar with the problem in order to find a more systematic strategy. As a rule, though, the trial-and-error method is usually not very effective.

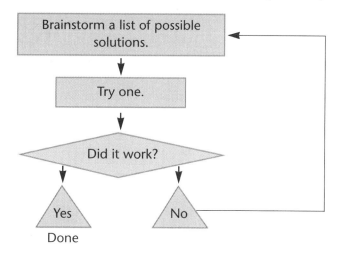

Represent the situation. When a problem is complex or confusing, making a visual or physical **representation** of the problem can be very useful. A representation could be a picture, a diagram, or a model. This technique often helps you to see more clearly how different parts of a problem are related.

4.2 STRATEGIES FOR PROBLEM SOLVING II

Divide and conquer. One strategy that is often helpful is to divide the problem into parts and then solve each part one at a time in a logical sequence. If a particular part is still difficult to solve, you can divide it into smaller parts and tackle each part step by step.

PROBLEM   You have decided to write a short story about someone your age who has an adventure on a bicycle. How can you build a story around these elements?

SOLUTION   1. Break the goal into parts: (1) main character; (2) adventure, or plot; and
STRATEGY   (3) setting. Then solve each part separately: (1a) What traits does the character have? (1b) Does the character ride a bike for pleasure or for practical reasons? (2a) When the story begins, why is the character riding? (2b) What might go wrong on the ride? (2c) What will the character do to solve the problem? (2d) Whom will the character encounter? (3a) To where is the character riding? in what part of the world? (3b) What time of year is it? what time of day? (3c) What is the weather?

Work backward. Describe in detail the situation that would exist after you solved the problem. Then think about what would have to happen for that situation to come about. Continue working backward until you get to a situation that you know how to bring about.

PROBLEM	How can I budget my time to enable me to finish my English project by Friday?
SOLUTION STRATEGY	If I'm going to turn in the project Friday morning, I have to have it done by 11:00 Thursday night. It will take two hours to type, so I must begin typing by 9:00 Thursday night. Before I can type it I have to finish writing it. I have gymnastics practice Thursday until 8:00, and math homework due Friday, which I can do Thursday after school, so I have to finish the writing by 11:00 Wednesday night. It will take me six hours to write after I have my note cards in order, so I have to have my note cards ready by 5:00; except that I have to eat dinner and do chores, so let's say I must have my cards ready by 3:00 Wednesday afternoon. . . .

4.3 STRATEGIES FOR DECISION MAKING

Pros and cons. Make a list of your options. For each option, list the reasons for choosing it (the *pros*) and the drawbacks of choosing it (the *cons*). Then compare the lists.

PROS AND CONS: POSSIBLE PETS			
	Cat	**Dog**	**Iguana**
Pros	cuddly will catch mice independent	companionship will catch disk at park loyal	appearance will catch insects quiet
Cons	house training might kill birds at feeder	house training daily walks be home for feeding every evening	house training not friendly hard to find good vet care?

Criteria analysis. Criteria (plural; singular = *criterion*) are the standards or yardsticks you use in an evaluation. For instance, your criteria for a new pair of shoes might be that they are durable, that they're comfortable, that they cost less than $40, and that they don't clash with your new jacket. When you use the strategy of criteria analysis, you compare each of your options with each of the standards you have set for your decision.

CRITERIA ANALYSIS: CHOOSING A JOURNAL			
	Hardcover "Book"	**Spiral-bound Notebook**	**Three-ring Binder**
1. Durable	5	3	4
2. Portable	4	4	4
3. Attractive	5	2	3
4. Affordable	2	5	4
	16	14	15

You can make a chart for criteria analysis. List the results you want to achieve, your criteria, on the left side of a sheet of paper. List your options across the top of the page. Then, assign each option from 1 to 5 points based on how well it will meet each criterion you have listed. Add up the points under each option, and choose the option with the highest total. If one criterion is more important than the others you can assign it points from 1 to 10.

4.4 MEMORIZING

Memory is an essential part of learning. There are two parts to remembering: storing the information securely in your mind and retrieving the information when you need it. Retrieving will be easier if, when storing information, you spend a little time thinking about how you might use the information and what it means to you. For example, you are studying plants and are introduced to the formula for photosynthesis: carbon dioxide + water + sunlight = sugar + oxygen. You will remember this formula more easily if you put it in a larger context and think about the relationships between plants and animals and different parts of the environment (for instance, that animals inhale the oxygen produced by plants, or that plants use the sugar to grow).

Sometimes you will have particular bits of information that you will want to be able to recall quickly. For example, you will find it convenient to be able to remember how to spell the word *separate* instead of having to look it up in a dictionary every time you use it.

Mnemonics. A **mnemonic** is an association that helps you remember. To use a mnemonic, you put together information that you need to remember with information you already know or can remember very easily. For example, you probably learned the alphabet by associating it with an easy-to-remember tune. Mnemonics also can be based on images and on words; for instance, you may have learned that "there is *a rat* in *separate.*"

MNEMONICS			
Name of Strategy	**Strategy**	**Information to be Learned**	**Information Easy to Remember**
Embellished Letter	Form an acronym using the first letters of the information to be remembered.	Items in a series, e.g. the colors of the spectrum (<u>r</u>ed, <u>o</u>range, <u>y</u>ellow, <u>g</u>reen, <u>b</u>lue, <u>i</u>ndigo, <u>v</u>iolet)	Roy G. Biv
Method of Loci	Imagine a place you know well (a baseball diamond, etc.). Form an image of each object to be recalled in a particular spot or room in that place.	Items in a series, e.g., the first ten presidents (Washington, Adams, Jefferson, Adams, Madison, Monroe, Jackson, Van Buren, Harrison, Tyler)	Washington is pitcher, Adams is catcher, Jefferson at first base, etc.
Key Word	Form an image of the items doing something to or with each other.	Associations, e.g., a server at a restaurant must remember that the man in the blue shirt ordered chicken with baked potato.	Bizarre images, e.g., a man is terrified (chicken) of a potato.

Repetition. In general, simply repeating information over and over is not a good way to remember it. If you want to remember something for more than a few minutes or a few days, you need to get to know it in a variety of ways. For example, to remember the formula for photosynthesis, you might perform an experiment with plants, write out the formula in your notebook, and read about how photosynthesis by rain forest plants affects the climate of the earth.

Repetition, however, does play a *part* in remembering. For example, you probably know your best friend's phone number by heart, but you probably cannot recite the phone number of a new movie theater that you have called only once. If you need to memorize by repetition, first divide the information into parts. Repeat each part separately until you have memorized them all. Then repeat two of the parts together, and once you have memorized that chunk, continue to add on parts one at a time until you can repeat all the information.

4.5   REMEMBERING AND VISUALIZING

Think of a place where you feel extremely comfortable. Can you see the place in your mind? Take a moment and try. . . .

Visualizing a place, person, or object can be helpful when you want to describe it accurately and vividly. When you are trying to visualize and remember something, using thinking skills such as classifying and analyzing can help you recall interesting and significant details. For example, while visualizing the scene you chose, you might think first about what you see, then about what sounds you hear, then about what you can feel, and so on.

4.6   OBSERVING

Imagine that five people are observing Niagara Falls: a tourist, a geologist, a boat captain, a painter, and a stuntperson. Would all of these people make the same observations about the falls? Probably not. Each of these persons probably has different interests in the falls, and a person tends to notice what he or she is interested in.

OBSERVATIONS OF COUGARS VS. PUMAS GAME

	Cougars	Pumas
Leading Scorers		
Leading Rebounders		
Assists		
Steals		
Type of Offense		
Type of Defense		
Turnovers		

Whenever you observe a situation, decide ahead of time what you want to know about the situation; knowing what you want to observe will help you focus your observations. For example, suppose you are gathering material for an essay about how basketball coaches interact with players. With this objective, you would probably go to a game, sit near the bench, and focus your observations on what goes on between the coach and the players. On the other hand, if you wanted information for an article about the team's conditioning, you might focus your observations on players as they come out of the game for a rest.

When you gather evidence, you want to avoid interpreting people's words and actions and to avoid making judgments. Write down only what you actually observe and not what you think or feel about it.

A chart can help you record your observations. More importantly, it can remind you of your purposes and thus help you to focus your observations and to gather the information that you need.

4.7 CLASSIFYING

To **classify** is to put into classes or categories. Items in the same category share one or more characteristics. For example, "The Fox and the Crow" and "The Lion and the Mouse" are classified as fables because each has the basic features of a fable (they are short narratives, they have animal characters with human traits, and they make a point about how people should behave).

The key step in classifying is choosing categories that fit your purpose. For example, if you wanted to compare how Æsop's "The Fox and the Crow" and Diane Ackerman's "Whales" present animals, you might classify the two works according to literary form—the first work is fiction, the second is nonfiction—and then explain how the different depictions of the animals reflect the differences between fiction and nonfiction. This example also shows how classifying can provide a natural and sensible way to organize a piece of writing.

When you classify, be sure to base your decisions on the traits that define the class. If the things that you are classifying fit into more than one of your categories, this often is because the categories are imprecisely defined. Make sure that your categories are clearly defined before you use them.

4.8 COMPARING AND CONTRASTING

Comparing and contrasting are closely related processes that involve observing and analyzing two (or more) things at the same time. When you **compare** one thing **to** another, you describe similarities between the two things. (Notice that in English, to **compare** a thing **with** another means to examine the two to find similarities *and* differences.) When **contrasting,** you describe differences between the two things.

Most often, a writer both compares and contrasts the things he or she is writing about. In your literature class, you can expect to be asked to compare and contrast authors, works, techniques, and various aspects of works. Remember to discuss both points of similarity and points of difference. (See the Language Arts Survey, 1.18, "Sensory Detail Charts," and 1.34, "Organizing Ideas," for tips on organizing a "compare and contrast" essay.)

When you are asked to compare and contrast, begin by listing the noteworthy features of each subject. At first, list every feature you can think of. Then go down both lists point by point, checking whether each feature is shared or not. When you have a list of points of comparison and contrast (similarities and differences), eliminate the obvious and trivial points and select the few most interesting points to discuss.

4.9 Estimating and Quantifying

To support your points in a persuasive essay or speech, you need to provide facts. Often the facts you need are numbers or **quantities.** For example, if you claim that too many people in the United States are illiterate, you ought to **quantify** your claim by stating **how many.** The number you need may be available in reference works (see the Language Arts Survey, 4.23, "Using Reference Works"). If you cannot find the number you need, you may be able to **estimate,** or find the approximate quantity. Sometimes you will have only enough knowledge to estimate a **range** within which the actual number probably falls.

UNQUANTIFIED	The number of single-parent families has greatly increased over the last twenty-five years.
QUANTIFIED	In 1993, almost 30 percent of all family groups had one parent, compared to 12 percent in 1970. (Source: *World Almanac,* 1995)
ESTIMATED	The number of single-parent families today is almost three times greater than it was twenty-five years ago. (This estimate is based on the data in the quantified statement; it assumes that the trend has been continuing since 1993.)

4.10 Analyzing

To **analyze** a thing is to break it down mentally into logical parts and then study the parts and how they are related. There is almost no limit on the number of ways you can analyze a particular thing. Suppose, for instance, that you are analyzing a dinner in a restaurant. You might analyze it in terms of nutritional categories, such as carbohydrates, proteins, and fats; you might analyze the individual courses, such as appetizer, salad, soup, entree, and dessert; or you might analyze its effect on the diner, in terms of flavor, texture, and color. Just as in classifying, your purpose will guide your decision about what parts to use. In the example, if you are writing about eating and health, you might use the nutritional analysis; if you are writing a restaurant review, you might use the course analysis; if you are writing a poem, you might use the sensory effects analysis.

When analyzing a work of literature, you also have many choices. You might divide a speech into introduction, body, and closing. You might analyze a poem according to the types of figurative language it uses, such as metaphors, similes, and personification. You might analyze a novel by examining each main character, or perhaps by examining each major event in the plot. You might analyze a persuasive essay by examining its several arguments. (For other ideas on analyzing written works, see the Language Arts Survey, 1.14, "Analyzing," and 1.34, "Organizing Ideas.")

4.11 Generalizing

To **generalize** is to make a general or universal claim based on particular observations. Generalizations that are based on a limited number of observations are often unjustified. For example, if Seth has looked for falcons in the city where he lives and has never seen one, he might generalize, "Falcons do not live in cities." In fact, falcons frequently make their homes on the ledges of tall city buildings (just as they do on tall cliffs in the wild). Seth, however, has not been able to observe this. A generalization is on flimsy ground if it is based only on what you can observe.

Generalizations may be based on reasoning as well as on observation. Seth knows that if he provides water and sunlight to a potted geranium plant, it will grow and flower. He can know this even though he has never grown a geranium plant before. He has observed other plants growing when given water and light, but he knows more than what he has observed. He knows the principle that plants require light and water in order to grow. Generalizing about a particular situation based on a general rule is called **induction**.

4.12 DEDUCING

Deducing, or **inferring**, is coming to a logical conclusion from certain facts, called **premises.**

PREMISES   (1) A myth is an ancient story about a supernatural hero.

                 (2) "The Story of Daedalus and Icarus" is an ancient Greek story about a hero with supernatural powers.

CONCLUSION   "The Story of Daedalus and Icarus" is a myth.

A deduction is **valid** if the conclusion follows from, or is forced by, the premises. Otherwise, the conclusion is **invalid.** The above conclusion is valid. If, from the same premises, you had concluded, "'The Story of Daedalus and Icarus is exciting," that conclusion would be invalid.

Notice that validity and truth are separate elements in any deduction. The conclusion in the previous paragraph is invalid, because it does not follow from the premises, but it may nonetheless be true.

A deduction is often based on a **conditional**, or "If . . ., then . . ." statement. A conditional says that *if* something is true, *then* something else must be true: if a story is ancient and has a supernatural hero, then it is a myth. In a conditional, the part of the statement following *if* is called the **antecedent,** and the part following *then* is called the **consequent.**

INFERENCE RULE 1. If the antecedent in a conditional is true, you can infer that the consequent is true.

EXAMPLE   If the library is closed, then I can't get a library book.

       The library is closed. (antecedent true)

       Therefore, I can't get a library book. (consequent also true)

INFERENCE RULE 2. If the consequent in a conditional is false, you can infer that the antecedent is also false.

EXAMPLE   If the library is closed, then I can't get a library book.

       I got a library book. (consequent false)

       Therefore, the library is not closed. (antecedent also false)

INFERENCE RULE 3. You cannot make a valid inference from a conditional when the antecedent is false or when the consequent is true (see the Language Arts Survey, 4.14, "Avoiding Faulty Arguments").

4.13 MAKING HYPOTHESES

A **hypothesis** (singular; plural = *hypotheses*) is an educated guess about a cause. Suppose that your cactus plant died. You might guess that the plant received too much water. When you observe something and then suggest a possible explanation, your explanation is a hypothesis. A prediction based on a theory is also a hypothesis. Hypotheses always need to be tested against experience. You can test hypotheses by conducting actual experiments, by examining many relevant examples, or by conducting a **thought experiment,** asking "What if" questions (see the Language Arts Survey, 1.13, "Questioning: 'What if' Questions").

A hypothesis cannot be proven merely by gathering examples (see the Language Arts Survey, 4.11, "Generalizing"). For example, if you overwatered fifty cactus plants and they all died, you would have strong evidence to support your hypothesis, but you would not have ruled out other possible explanations, such as cold temperatures or atmospheric pollution. A single counterexample, however, is enough to disprove a hypothesis.

4.14 AVOIDING FAULTY ARGUMENTS

A **logical fallacy** is a mistake in reasoning. You commit a fallacy when you make an **invalid** inference, one that is not justified by the facts at hand.

A conclusion that is not justified may be false, but it also may be true. To say that an argument or inference is fallacious is only to say that the conclusion has not been *proven*.

Not every mistake in reasoning involves a logical fallacy. Errors might also be due to incorrect information, lack of information, carelessness, and so on. Often it is hard to tell if a mistake in thinking is the result of faulty logic or some other factor.

A list of some common types of fallacy, or logical mistakes, follows.

EXAMPLE   "My ten-year-old brother loves this book. Your ten-year-old brother will love it too."

ANALYSIS   People have different tastes and interests. Just because two people are alike in age does not mean they will be alike in what books they like.

False analogy. An argument by analogy claims that if two things are alike in some way, then they are alike in another way.

An interesting analogy (say, comparing the human mind to a computer) can offer much food for thought. An argument by analogy, however, does not *prove* what it states, and is thus invalid.

Circularity. A circular argument is one that assumes the truth of what it is trying to prove. This type of argument is also called **question-begging.** A common type of circular argument merely restates an assumption in different words.

EXAMPLE   "I like this book because it really appealed to me."

ANALYSIS   The "reason" the speaker gives for liking the book is just a different way of saying that the speaker liked the book.

Post hoc (ergo) propter hoc. If one event is caused by another, the effect always follows the cause. A speaker who commits **post hoc** fallacy assumes that because one event follows another, then the first event must have *caused* the second one.

EXAMPLE	"Every morning, just before dawn, the rooster crows. The rooster did not crow early this morning. Will the sun still rise?"
ANALYSIS	This simple example clearly shows that sequence and consequence are not the same thing. The sun rises *after* the rooster crows, but the sun does not rise *because* the rooster crows.

Fallacies of affirming the antecedent and of denying the consequent. A **conditional** states that *if* something (the antecedent) is true, *then* something else (the consequent) must be true. You can draw a valid conclusion from a conditional when the antecedent is true or when the consequent is false (see the Language Arts Survey, 4.12, "Deducing"). If the consequent is true, however, nothing is implied about the antecedent.

EXAMPLE	"The more you practice writing, the more confident you will feel about writing." What can you conclude about someone who does not feel confident about writing?
ANALYSIS	Not much. To infer that the person does not practice writing would be fallacious. Perhaps the person has high standards or has experienced harsh criticism. Not practicing is not the only cause of lack of confidence about writing.

In addition, if the antecedent is false, nothing is implied about the consequent.

EXAMPLE	"The more you practice writing, the more confident you will feel about writing." What can you conclude about the feelings of someone who doesn't practice writing?
ANALYSIS	Again, not much. You cannot conclude that the person does not feel confident about writing. The person might feel confident because he or she has received a writing award or good grades on essay tests, or perhaps the person is naturally confident about everything he or she does.

Non sequitur. A **non sequitur** is a conclusion that simply does not follow from the reasons given, and may have nothing to do with them.

Ad hominem. An argument that attacks or defends a person instead of a point under discussion is an **ad hominem** argument. Whether a person is a good student or a poor student, a Democrat or a Republican, a gang member or a Boy Scout, does not determine the truth of what the person says.

EXAMPLE	"That ad was published by tree-hugging environmentalists. You can't believe anything it says."
ANALYSIS	This statement does not address the information in the ad. It simply attacks the people who created the ad.

Equivocation. To equivocate is to shift the meaning of an ambiguous term in the middle of an argument. Equivocation creates the appearance of a logical connection between the reasons and the conclusion where there is no logical connection.

EXAMPLE   "The Declaration of Independence states that 'all men are created equal.' Therefore, the Founders intended for men but not women to vote."

ANALYSIS   The word *men,* as used by the Founders, means "human beings." However, the term is ambiguous, and in the second part of the argument, the speaker shifts the meaning to "adult male human beings."

Vague terms. In everyday speaking, people use words very casually. They rarely clarify exactly what they mean by terms such as *good, large, harmful,* or *wrong.* Imprecise language often gets in the way of clear communication and can lead to misunderstanding. Before you agree to an assertion, think about whether the statement is clear and precise. Before you argue with someone about an assertion, ask the person to explain any vague terms.

EXAMPLE   "The students in this class are very intelligent."

ANALYSIS   *Intelligent* is a vague term. Is the speaker saying that the students in the class get good grades? that they have high IQs? that they are knowledgeable about many subjects? that they can use their powers of reasoning effectively? To be clear, the speaker should be more specific.

4.15 UNDERSTANDING PROPAGANDA TECHNIQUES

Propaganda refers to messages and materials created with the aim of stirring up support for (or opposition to) a particular cause. Propaganda messages try to influence people by appealing to their emotions instead of by reasoning logically. To avoid being manipulated by propaganda appeals, keep an eye out for these fallacies.

Bandwagon. Sometimes it's hard to resist a trend, to set yourself apart from everyone else. People like to feel included. Propaganda that tries to make people worry about being unique or that appeals to the desire to be part of a crowd is using the **bandwagon appeal.**

EXAMPLE   "These neon bookbags are selling like hotcakes! It's the 'in' thing for the new school year. So hurry down to Beeman's back-to-school sale and get yours now!"

ANALYSIS   This message is designed to make listeners feel anxious about being left out: you won't be part of the "in" crowd if you don't have a neon bookbag. Ask yourself, if you don't own a neon bookbag, will you lose friends? If you wanted to have more friends, would you want people to like you because of something you own or because of who you are?

Transfer. The propaganda technique of **transfer** makes a positive (or negative) association between two unrelated things. A television commercial shows a famous athlete eating a certain brand of corn flakes. A newspaper photograph shows a political candidate laughing with a movie star. In each example, the sender of the message hopes that the positive qualities of one thing (the athlete, the movie star) will "rub off," or transfer, to another thing (the corn flakes, the politician). Neither message appeals to your powers of reasoning.

False testimonial. A testimonial is a statement endorsing a person, object, or idea. When experts offer testimonials without being paid for them, it is wise to listen. When an expert is paid to endorse a product, as in many commercials, or when celebrities are asked to promote a cause, as in a political campaign, you should be on guard.

Loaded words. Different words can refer to the same thing but carry radically different connotations (see the Language Arts Survey, 2.153, "Connotation and Denotation"). A word may have a strongly positive, strongly negative, or relatively neutral connotation. Using words with strong connotations can be a way to sway opinion without offering reasons.

Character assassination. This is a form of ad hominem argument that tries to persuade by attacking the character of one's opponent.

EXAMPLE	"Senator Grinch is a corrupt, back-stabbing, power-hungry politician. Don't believe him when he says we need welfare reform."
ANALYSIS	There may or may not be a need for welfare reform. You should decide whether you think there is such a need based on the facts about the welfare system. You should not base your decision on Senator Grinch's personal character.

Bias charges. Another form of ad hominem argument attacks a speaker's neutrality on an issue. A person who has a personal stake in the outcome of an issue may not be able to judge both sides of the issue impartially, or may even go so far as to intentionally deceive. If a person has a bias, you should examine carefully that person's arguments to make sure they are logical, and you should examine carefully his or her facts to make sure they are complete.

EXAMPLE	"Some electric companies are against this environmental regulation because it would reduce their profits. Don't listen to their arguments."
ANALYSIS	The power companies may have sound arguments to present against the regulation, even if they have a bias. The possibility of bias is not reason enough to reject a particular point of view. However, you should be alert for distorted facts that a biased party might introduce.

READING SKILLS

4.16 READING RATES

The purpose you have for reading something affects how, and how quickly, you read it. Slow and careful reading is required in some situations, scanning and skimming in others.

READING RATES		
Technique	**Purpose**	**Tips**
Scanning	Finding specific information quickly	Look for key words; look at chapter and part headings.
Skimming	Getting a general idea of the content of a piece	Ask questions; look at introductions; look at chapter and part headings.
Slow and careful reading	Learning and enjoyment	Read actively.

Scanning

Scanning is very quickly looking through written material to locate some particular information that you want. For example, in the Sunday paper you might scan the classified ads for portable tape players that are for sale. You would look down the columns of the classified ads section quickly until you spotted an appropriate heading such as "Audiovisual Equipment." Then you would scan the listings beneath it for ads that mention portable tape players, ignoring all the other ads.

Scanning is a useful technique for using reference works and other materials when you are doing research for a writing assignment or project. You can also use scanning to find answers for written exercises or to find quotations or other support for your opinions.

When you scan, pick out a few key words to look for. Then glance quickly down each page, one at a time, looking for those key words. When you find a key word, stop scanning and begin reading carefully to gather the information you need.

Skimming

Skimming is glancing quickly through a piece of writing to get the general idea. This reading technique is useful when you do research. For example, say you have located eight magazine articles about AIDS and you want to select the three that will be most useful to you. By skimming, you could find out quickly that one article emphasizes scientific research, another contains interesting profiles of people with AIDS, and another provides statistics about AIDS worldwide. Skimming is also useful as a way to preview your reading (see the Language Arts Survey, 4.17, "Previewing Your Reading") or to review your reading before taking a test or planning an essay.

When you skim, keep the following questions in mind:

QUESTIONS FOR SKIMMING
• What is this piece of writing about?
• What does the author say about the subject?
• What evidence or support is given?

To answer the first question, read the title and any headings within the piece. Then read the opening paragraphs to find a general answer to the second question. Also glance at any material that is set off from the main text, such as captions or boxed paragraphs. Spot-read a few paragraphs from the middle of the piece as well as the last few paragraphs to get an answer to the third question.

Slow and Careful Reading

When you are reading for pleasure or for instruction, you will read more slowly and thoroughly than when you are scanning or skimming for some particular bit of information. If you are reading a novel, you will read every word from the first to the last. You may try to imagine what it would be like to be one of the characters or what will happen next. If you are reading a textbook or nonfiction book, you will reread any passages that you found confusing the first time through. You also may think about the causes and consequences of the events. If you are reading a persuasive essay, you may think about the author's reasons and the quality of his or her evidence. Another important part of slow and careful reading is looking up in a dictionary any words you do not know. In all of these ways, you become an active, comprehending reader. Specific techniques for active reading are described in the Language Arts Survey, 4.18, "Reading Actively."

4.17 PREVIEWING YOUR READING

A movie preview gets an audience thinking about and interested in a movie. With reading, you can create your own preview that will get you thinking about what you are about to read. To **preview** your reading, try the sequence of activities below:

PREVIEWING ACTIVITIES	
1. **Read** the title.	**Ask:** What is the piece about? What is the author's attitude toward the subject?
2. **Skim** the first paragraph(s).	**Ask:** What is the main point of the piece?
3. **Skim** the last paragraph(s) (but not if the piece to be read is a work of literature).	**Ask:** What is the author's conclusion?
4. **Read** the headings.	**Ask:** What are the main points?
5. **Summarize** and **Plan** your reading.	**Ask:** Do all the parts seem to fit together? Do I have any unresolved questions?

4.18 READING ACTIVELY

When you think about what you are reading as you read, you are reading actively. Active reading is something like having a conversation with the author.

Responding to Your Reading

Keep your journal close by as you read so you can record reactions to what you are reading (see the Language Arts Survey, 1.2, "Keeping a Writer's Journal"). You might pause after a section or paragraph to ask yourself questions:

- "Do I agree with the author's point?"
- "If I were in the same situation as this character, would I feel the same way?"

Sometimes you'll want to wait until after you've finished reading to describe or analyze your thoughts and feelings.

Questioning

Asking yourself questions as you read keeps your mind more alert and helps you digest what you are reading. You might ask questions based on *who? what? where? when? why?* and *how?* When you are reading this book, you can use the Guided Reading questions and the Reviewing the Selection questions in addition to your own questions.

TYPES OF READER RESPONSE QUESTIONS	
Who?	• Questions about characters or persons in the text • Questions about the author
What?	• Questions about objects and events
Where?	• Questions about location
When?	• Questions about sequence • Questions about time period
Why?	• Questions about motivation • Questions about reasoning and evidence
How?	• Questions about possibilities • Questions about actions

Predicting

Have you ever read a book that was a real "page-turner"? When you turn a page eagerly, it's often because your mind is trying to predict what will happen next. Predicting is a natural part of reading. Trying to guess what will happen next, and why, is a good way to become more actively involved in your reading.

Summarizing

Summarizing is simplifying a piece of writing, such as an essay or paragraph, into a briefer statement of main points. Summarizing can help you understand what you have read by forcing you to select the points that are most important to remember. Whenever you summarize ideas in your own words, you are more likely to remember and understand them.

Identifying Main Ideas

The main idea of a piece of nonfiction writing is often expressed in the introduction, in a thesis statement. The main idea of a single paragraph is often stated in a topic sentence. In other cases, the main idea is strongly implied by all the sentences in the paragraph but is not directly stated. When you are reading difficult material, a good way to check your understanding is to pause briefly after each paragraph to restate the main idea in your own words.

Identifying Relationships

Keeping an eye out for words and phrases that reveal the writer's plan of order can help you better understand what you are reading. For example, phrases such as *on the other hand* and *in contrast* may indicate comparison-and-contrast order. Some other phrases that indicate relationships include *for example, thus, however, in general, as well,* and *in conclusion.* In general, pay special attention to passages that describe relationships between people, things, or ideas. For example, a writer might say that two sisters were as opposite as day and night.

Making Inferences

When **making an inference** you put together pieces of information to draw a conclusion that is not explicitly stated. In nonfiction works, an author may provide certain information but leave it up to the reader to infer the author's meaning or intention. Sometimes you make an inference by putting together new facts and facts you already know. For example, when you evaluate an author's argument, you might spot a piece of information or an inference that the author overlooked.

4.19 READING CHARTS AND GRAPHS

Writers use charts and graphs to present ideas and information in a compact, visual form. The information readers need to understand the chart or graph is given in the title, headings, and labels on the graph.

Pie charts. A **pie chart** is a circle divided into pie-shaped sections that represent portions of some whole thing. It shows how different amounts compare to each other and to the whole.

EXAMPLE   The whole pie below represents all of the games played by a softball team (16 games). The pie is divided into two pieces, one representing wins (11 games) and the other losses (5 games). The size of each piece is proportional to the number of games that were won (69%) or lost (31%). From the chart you can quickly see that the team had about twice as many wins as losses.

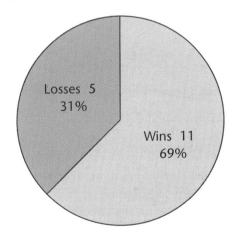

Bar graphs. A **bar graph** compares absolute amounts of something by representing the amounts as parallel bars of different lengths.

EXAMPLE   The bar graph below shows the yearly earnings for women and men based on the level of education completed. The earnings of women and men are grouped together, and each bar represents the earnings of those with a particular level of education. You can see right away how women's earnings compared to men's and how education level affected earnings in 1992.

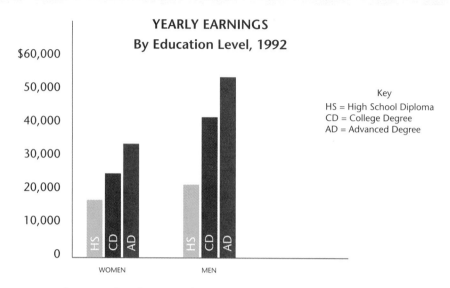

You may come across bar graphs that are drawn in unusual ways to make them visually appealing. The "bars" in such graphs may be distorted and give a misleading impression. Read the graph labels and related text carefully before drawing a conclusion.

Line graphs. A **line graph,** like a bar graph, shows how one thing changes in relation to some other thing. Line graphs are useful for showing a continuous process, a pattern, or a trend over time.

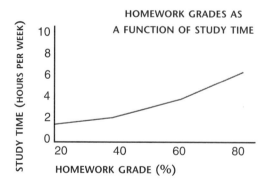

Researching is looking for ideas and information. The process of researching is a bit like detective work. You have a problem to solve or an overall goal. You start with the most promising "leads," or sources of information that might lead you to what you want to know. These sources, in turn, lead you to other sources of information, until you have fully answered your question.

Libraries offer a number of research paths, each of which has its own logic. The suggestions in the following sections will help you navigate these paths efficiently.

4.20 THE CLASSIFICATION OF LIBRARY MATERIALS

Each book in a library has a unique number, called a **call number,** printed on the **spine,** or edge, of the book. This number is used to classify the book. It also helps the library keep track of the books.

There are two common systems for classifying library books. The **Dewey Decimal System** is used in most school and public libraries. The **Library of Congress Classification System** (known as the LC system) is used in most college libraries.

The first part of the call number categorizes the book by its general subject. Then, each part of the call number narrows down its subject. For example, in the Dewey Decimal System the book *Introduction to Buddhism* by Peter Harvey might have the call number [294.344 / Ha]. This book is in the 200s; thus its general subject is religion. Within that class, books in the 290s are about non-Christian religions, and books numbered 294 are about non-Christian religions of Indic origin. The addition of the numbers after the decimal narrow the topic further to Buddhism.

THE DEWEY DECIMAL SYSTEM

Call Numbers	Subjects[1]
000–099	Reference and General Works
100–199	Philosophy, Psychology
200–299	Religion
300–399	Social Studies
400–499	Language
500–599	Science, Mathematics
600–699	Technology
700–799	Arts
800–899	Literature
900–999	History, Geography, Biography[2]

1. The Dewey Decimal System does not number fiction. Works of fiction are arranged alphabetically by author.
2. Biographies (920s) are arranged alphabetically by subject.

In the LC system, the initial letters in a call number identify the general subject area, and the numbers after the letters identify the precise topic within that area. The book above might have the call number BQ4131. BQ shows that the subject is Buddhism; the number 4131 shows that the more specific topic is the history of Buddhism.

THE LIBRARY OF CONGRESS SYSTEM

Call Letters	Subjects
A	Reference and General Works
B–BJ	Philosophy, Psychology
BK–BX	Religion
C–F	History
G	Geography, Autobiography, Recreation
H	Social Sciences
J	Political Science
K	Law
L	Education
M	Music
N	Fine Arts
P	Language, Literature
Q	Science, Mathematics
R	Medicine
S	Agriculture
T	Technology
U	Military Science
V	Naval Science
Z	Bibliography, Library Science

The second part of the call number distinguishes individual books on the same subject. In the Dewey Decimal System, the first one to three letters of the author's last name may be added on a second line; notice the [Ha] in the Dewey number. In the LC system, the second part of the number usually includes a letter (the author's last initial) and a number that uniquely identify the author. This second element falls after a decimal point, as in the LC number BQ4131 / .H37 / 1990. An LC call number may also include a date of publication.

Locating Materials in the Library. You can find many other types of publications besides books in a library, such as magazines, newspapers, audio and video recordings, and government documents. Typically, each type of material is stored in a distinct place in the library and has its own classification system. For example, back issues of magazines stored on microfilm have their own index and numbering system, and the microfilm materials and equipment may be located in the periodicals department.

Books are stored on shelves, or **stacks,** that are labeled by the range of call numbers they contain. If you know the call number or the subject classification number you want, use the signs at the ends of the rows to locate the right stack. Then find the particular shelf that contains call numbers close to yours. Large libraries may provide maps or signs showing where different call number areas are located. These signs may be posted near elevators, room entrances, or assistance desks.

4.21 USING SEARCHING TOOLS

To find out the call numbers of books that will help you with your research, use the library's **catalog.** If your library has a computerized catalog, you will need to learn how to use your library's particular system. At most libraries, a sign or flier explains how to use the system, and the computer keys are labeled to assist you. There is also usually a "help" button.

In most computerized systems, you have a choice of searching by author, title, subject, or key words. The chart on page 908 gives you some tips for doing each type of search.

When you search by subject on computer, it is important to use a subject heading that the computer will recognize. For example, if you look up "how to paint" and do not find any books on this subject, it is probably because the library uses a different wording for this subject, such as "painting—handbooks." Sometimes the system will give **cross-references,** which direct you to related subject headings. If you search under "blimps," the system may respond with a cross-reference such as "Blimps. *See* Dirigibles." Before you look for books on a subject, it's best to check the library's list of subjects to see what wording your library uses.

Author	Conway, Jill K., 1934–
Title	The Road From Coorain
Publication info.	Knopf, 1993
No. of pages/size	238 p. :24 cm.
ISBN	ISBN 0-394-57456-7
Subjects	Conway, Jill K., 1934–
	Women scholars—Australia—Biography
	Country life—Australia
Dewey call number	305.4 Ke

When you type your entry, capitalization does not matter. You should double-check your spelling, however, since the computer cannot compensate for spelling errors.

You can use the results of your initial search to zoom in more closely on your topic. Once you locate a title related to your subject, you can usually call up a screen with more information about that particular book, such as subject headings or number of pages. Use this information to evaluate the book further. If you spot a book that seems to be just what you are looking for, jot down its subjects or key words and use those in new searches. For each book you want, write down the call number and then head for the stacks (see the Language Arts Survey, 4.20, "The Classification of Library Materials).

COMPUTERIZED CATALOG SEARCHES

Search by . . .	Example	Hints
author	gould, stephen j	Type last name first. Type as much of the name as you know.
title	mismeasure of man	Omit articles such as *a, an,* or *the* at the beginning of titles.
subject	intelligence tests; ability—testing	Use the list of subjects provided by the library.
key words	darwin; intelligence; craniology	Use related topics if you can't find anything in your subject.

Interlibrary loan. In many libraries, the computerized catalog spans the collections of several libraries that are members of the same network. In these cases, you usually can obtain books and articles from those other libraries through an **interlibrary loan.** The catalog will tell you which library holds the book you want. If the book is in a different library, you will need to request the book, either through the system or by giving a request slip to a librarian. The book is then shipped to your library. If the book you want is not checked out, the wait is often only a few days.

4.22 USING THE CARD CATALOG

The library's catalog contains basic information about each book in the library. If the library uses a **card catalog,** the information is typed on paper cards. The cards are arranged alphabetically in drawers. For each book, there is a **title card,** one **author card** for each author, and at least one **subject card.** All of these cards give the book's title, author, and call number. Thus, you can find a book in several different ways: by author, title, or subject (see the Language Arts Survey, 4.21, "Using Searching Tools," for tips on how to search).

AN AUTHOR CARD

author

call number   305.4   Conway, Jill Ker, 1934-

The road from Coorain.—New York:
    Knopf, 1993

length   348 p. :24 cm.   page size

Subject
identifiers   1. Conway, Jill K., 1934-.2. Women
        scholars—Australia—Biography.

    2. Country life—Australia. I.
        Title.

ISBN   ISBN 0-394-57456-7

A TITLE CARD

```
305.4    The road from Coorain.
Ke

         Conway, Jill Ker, 1934-
           The road from Coorain.

         1. Conway, Jill K., 1934-.2. Women
            scholars—Australia—Biography.

         2. Country life—Australia. I.
            Title.
```

A SUBJECT CARD

```
305.4    Country life—Australia
Ke

         Conway, Jill Ker, 1934-
           The road from Coorain.

         1. Conway, Jill K., 1934-.2. Women
            scholars—Australia—Biography.

         2. Country life—Australia. I.
            Title.

         ISBN 0-394-57456-7
```

Once you have located the books you want, copy the call number of each book and then go to the shelves (see the Language Arts Survey, 4.20, "The Classification of Library Materials). If you are looking for a particular book and cannot find it in the card catalog, ask the librarian if your library can get books from other libraries through an interlibrary loan.

4.23 USING REFERENCE WORKS

Most libraries have an assortment of **reference works,** works in which knowledge is compiled and organized for easy access. Some reference works, such as the library catalog and **indexes,** are designed to help you find works that contain the ideas and information you want. Other reference works contain the ideas and information themselves. Generally, current reference works cannot be checked out of the library.

Almanacs and yearbooks. An **almanac** provides statistics and lists of all sorts. You could use an almanac to find basic facts about the fifty states, names of Nobel Prize winners, lists of national parks, crime and education statistics, population figures, and brief summaries of the world's major religions. To find information in an almanac, use the index.

Most almanacs also include a summary of major events that occurred in the past year. A more detailed overview of the events of the year can be found in a **yearbook,** which is published separately. Some yearbooks are published by encyclopedia publishers and are shelved with the encyclopedias.

Atlases. An **atlas** is primarily a collection of maps, but each atlas has a particular focus and offers additional information. Some atlases show natural features, such as mountains and rivers, or other geographic information, such as climate or population; others show political features, such as countries and cities. A **historical atlas** contains maps of places as they used to be, and is useful for tracing historical events. If you need to locate a particular feature on a map in an atlas, refer to the **gazetteer,** an index that lists every item shown on the maps—countries, cities, counties, continents, roads, lakes, rivers, bays, canals, mountains, mountain ranges, deserts, parks, and many others.

Encyclopedias. Encyclopedias provide a survey of knowledge. **General encyclopedias,** such as *World Book, Compton's,* or *Britannica,* contain information on almost any topic. **Specialized encyclopedias,** such as *The Encyclopedia of Adolescence,* contain information on one particular area of knowledge. The different topics in an encyclopedia are treated in **articles,** which are arranged in alphabetical order.

If you look up a topic in an encyclopedia and do not find it, check the index. Most likely, the topic is covered somewhere, but a different word or phrase has been used to identify the subject. Another reason for using the index is that ideas and information related to your topic may be treated in more than one article. The index of a multivolume encyclopedia is found in one or two separate volumes.

Encyclopedias are useful for getting an overview and outline of a particular topic. For more detailed information, however, you are likely to need other sources of information such as books and magazine articles. You might start with the list of additional sources of information at the end of the encyclopedia article.

Indexes. An **index** is an alphabetical directory of published articles or other works, arranged alphabetically by subject. Each index covers a specific group of publications. For example, *The Readers' Guide to Periodic Literature* is a comprehensive index to nearly all the popular weekly, monthly, and quarterly publications. Some other indexes list only newspapers, or only periodicals that deal with a particular subject. Some periodicals, such as *National Geographic* and the *New York Times,* publish their own indexes, covering articles in past issues of that periodical only. A number of indexes are available on microfilm or computer.

Periodicals. A **periodical** is a publication issued at regular intervals, such as once a week, once a month, or four times a year. Magazines, daily newspapers, specialized newspapers, and professional journals are all periodicals. Because they are published frequently and quickly, periodicals are an excellent source for the latest news and information. Information in periodicals, however, is less likely to have been evaluated carefully by experts.

Current issues of periodicals are usually available in a reading room in the library. Recent issues may be stored beneath or behind the current issues. If the library retains older issues, these are either bound and stored in the stacks, or copied onto microfilm or microfiche.

Other reference works. Are you looking for a review of a particular book? a biography of a living author? a quotation by a famous American? Other reference works at your library can help you with these kinds of research. Most libraries have a range of basic reference works such as *Book Review Digest, Contemporary Authors,* and *Bartlett's Familiar Quotations,* in addition to those mentioned above. Your library may also have specialized dictionaries, business directories, guidebooks and manuals, and many other materials. Check with a reference librarian to find out about particular reference works that might help you with your research.

4.24 USING DICTIONARIES

The entries in a dictionary provide much more information about words than just their spellings and definitions.

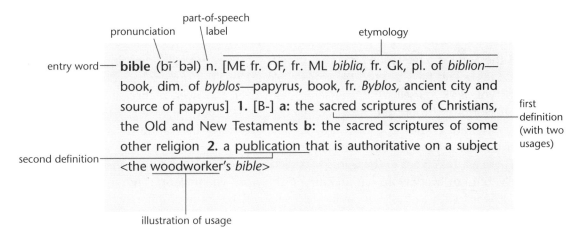

The **pronunciation** is given immediately after the entry word, usually in parentheses. You can find a complete key to pronunciation symbols by looking in the Table of Contents. In some dictionaries, a simplified key is provided at the bottom of each page.

An abbreviation of the **part of speech** usually follows the pronunciation. This label tells the ways in which a word can be used (see the Language Arts Survey, 2.3–2.31, "The Parts of Speech"). In the example, the letter *n.* shows that the word is used as a noun. If a word can be used in more than one way, definitions in the entry are grouped by part of speech.

An **etymology** is the history of a word. In the example, the word *bible* traces back—through Middle English (ME), Old French (OF), and Medieval Latin (ML)—to the Greek (Gk) word for papyrus, *byblos,* which comes from the name of a city in the ancient country of Phoenicia.

Each **definition** in the entry gives a different meaning the word can take. When a word has more than one meaning, the different definitions are numbered. The first definition in an entry is the most common meaning of the word. Sometimes one meaning of a word has two or more submeanings; these are identified with lowercase letters. For example, the first definition of *bible* (sacred writings) can be used in two different senses: it can mean (a) scripture of the Christian religion (most commonly) or (b) the scripture of another religion. The "[B–]" before the definition shows that when the word is used in this meaning, it is spelled with a capital B.

Sometimes you will see more than one entry for a word. Words are listed as separate entries when they have different meanings and etymologies, even if they are spelled the same. Such words are called **homographs.** A superscript number before each entry word shows that the word is a homograph. Notice the three different origins in the entries for *yak* on the next page.

¹**yak** ('yak) n. [Tibetan *gyak*] a long-haired ox of Tibet

²**yak** ('yak) n. [imitative] *slang:* laugh

³**yak** ('yak) vi. [origin unknown] talk persistently

Usage notes, such as "slang" or "colloquial," describe any nonstandard usages. In the example above, the second word *yak* is slang. Sometimes the entry gives an illustration of how the word is used. In the second definition of *bible,* the **usage illustration** is given in angle brackets after the meaning.

4.25 USING THESAURUSES

A thesaurus is a reference book that groups words with similar meanings. Suppose you are writing and have a word that means almost but not quite what you want. Or perhaps you find yourself using the same word over and over. A thesaurus can give you fresh words and more precise words to use. In fact, you might enjoy reading through several entire entries in a thesaurus to get a sense of the subtle differences between words that have some shared meaning.

There are two types of thesauruses. A dictionary-type thesaurus is organized alphabetically, but not every word has an entry. If the word you look up is not listed, try looking up a word with a similar meaning. If the word has several different senses, the synonyms will be grouped by meaning. Antonyms are listed at the end of the entry. The entry may also include cross-references to entries for related words.

Roget's Thesaurus is organized by idea rather than alphabetically. Each numbered section in the front part of the book covers an idea. To use *Roget's Thesaurus,* look up your word in the index at the back of the book. Beneath the word you'll find a number of related words followed by a number. Choose the related word whose meaning is closest to what you want. Then look in the front part of the book to find the numbered section or subsection. Although *Roget's Thesaurus* takes a little time to master, it is a very interesting and useful tool.

4.26 COMPUTER-ASSISTED RESEARCH

On-line Research

Using a computer, you can connect to various sources of information that are available electronically. If you, your school, or your library subscribes to an on-line service, you may have access to current news, on-line encyclopedias, homework assistance, and research services. You may also be able to use the service to connect to the Internet, which links you to universities, libraries, businesses, government agencies, and individuals around the world. Your school may also be connected to a special education network, such as TENET (Texas Education Network). Find out from your school or public librarian if you can use these services.

CD/ROM and Other Computer Media

A CD/ROM database works just like an on-line database. The difference is that you retrieve the information directly from a CD instead of working through a network. Your library may have a collection of CDs that you can insert into the computer, or the CDs may be changed only by the librarians.

4.27 OTHER SOURCES OF INFORMATION

Vertical files. Libraries collect many sources of information besides books and periodicals. Among these sources are brochures, pamphlets, maps, clippings, photographs, and posters. These items are not cataloged. They are stored in folders in filing cabinets. When doing research, you might look through the files to see if there is anything on your topic.

Organizations and associations. Many businesses and business associations; religious, political, and human services organizations; and professional societies are eager to provide information on topics of concern to them. Sometimes these groups are the best source of information on a topic. Sometimes, though, a group strongly supports a particular point of view; you should scrutinize materials from organizations and associations for possible bias.

Community institutions such as historical societies, colleges, museums, art galleries, orchestras, dance troupes, and other performing arts groups can be good sources of ideas and information on certain topics.

Information about many of these groups is available in the *Encyclopedia of Associations.* You can find names and addresses of local groups in your local telephone book.

Experts. As you gather information for your research, don't overlook individuals who have a great deal of knowledge on your topic. An expert is anyone who has learned a great deal about a certain thing through experience, whether through work or recreation. Some experts, such as lawyers or engineers, are working professionals. Others, such as college professors, have made a study of their specialty for many years. Many of these people are glad to share their knowledge and experience with students and others.

To find someone who knows about your topic, ask your teachers, parents, friends, and relatives for ideas. Ask your contact if he or she can arrange an interview, or arrange an interview yourself by calling the person directly (see the Language Arts Survey, 1.27, "Interviewing").

Before you contact an expert for assistance, remember that you are requesting a favor. Be courteous, and be specific about what you are seeking from the person. Also, be prepared for your interview, so you can accomplish your goal without wasting the expert's time; you can gather a great deal of information in fifteen minutes.

4.28 EVALUATING SOURCES

In conducting any research project, you'll find that it is impossible to read everything that has been written on your topic. You'll also find that you can't believe everything you read. To do your research efficiently, you need to evaluate your sources and rank them. Ideally, a source will be

- **unbiased.** All authors take a personal interest in their subject. When an author has something to gain from what people think about a subject, however, that author may distort or leave out certain facts. Ask yourself: Is the author associated with a particular group? Does the author use loaded words or overlook obvious counterarguments? If the answer is yes, the author may be biased.

- **authoritative.** An authoritative source is one that is reliable and trustworthy. An author's reputation, especially her or his reputation among others in the same field, is a sign of authoritativeness. In addition, certain publications have a reputation for being responsible and precise, while others are known for "playing loose" with the truth.

- **timely.** In some subject areas, knowledge is expanding and changing very rapidly. For example, a book about personal computers can go out of date very fast. In other subjects, such as gardening, a book that is ten years old may be perfectly adequate. If your topic is historical, you might seek out older works deliberately, but most often you will want current information. Consult with your teacher or a librarian to decide how current your sources should be.

- **available.** Sometimes you will have to wait for materials to be mailed to you or for a book that is checked out by another person. Once you have selected materials, make sure that they are available or will be available in time to be useful.

- **at the appropriate level.** In order to be useful, a source must not only contain the right information but present it in a way that you can understand. Materials written for experts may presume knowledge that you do not have. On the other hand, you may be able to mine for the information you need if you allow yourself extra time.

4.29 BIBLIOGRAPHIES AND BIBLIOGRAPHY CARDS

Bibliographies. A **bibliography** is a list of sources on a particular topic. If you are writing a research paper, your teacher will ask you to include one of the following types of bibliography:

TYPES OF BIBLIOGRAPHY	
Complete Bibliography	A comprehensive list of works on your topic
Works Cited *or* **References**	A list of all the works referred to or quoted in your paper
Works Consulted	A list of every work you learned from in your research, even if you did not directly use or cite these works in your paper

The chart on pages 915–918 provides examples of proper bibliographic form for many different types of materials.

To prepare your bibliography, first arrange your bibliography cards (see page 919) in alphabetical order. Type or copy the information from each card onto your paper. Follow the correct form for each type of entry, as shown in the chart. Set up your pages and type the bibliography as described in the chart on page 919.

ABBREVIATIONS FOR BIBLIOGRAPHIES	
ed., eds.	editor *or* edition, editors *or* editions
et al.	and others
nd.	no date
prod.	producer *or* produced by
trans.	translator *or* translated by
vol., vols.	volume, volumes
writ.	written by

FORMS FOR BIBLIOGRAPHY ENTRIES

A. A book with one author

Turkel, Studs. <u>Hard Times: An Oral History of the Depression</u>. New York: Avon, 1970.

B. A book with two authors

Note that only the first author's name is inverted.

Collins, Marie, and Virginia Davis. <u>A Medieval Book of Seasons</u>. New York, HarperCollins, 1992.

C. A book with three authors

Note that only the first author's name is inverted.

Kinzer, Charles, Robert Sherwood, and John Bransford. <u>Computer Strategies for Education</u>. Columbus, OH: Merrill, 1986.

D. A book with four or more authors

The abbreviation *et al.* means "and others." Use *et al.* instead of listing all the authors.

Bellah, Robert N., et al. <u>Habits of the Heart: Individualism and Commitment in American Life</u>. New York: Harper and Row, 1985.

E. A book with no author given

<u>Calculator Activities and Games to Play at Home</u>. Washington, DC: National Council of Teachers of Mathematics, 1981.

F. A book with an editor, but no single author

Fairchild, Jill, ed. <u>Trees: A Celebration</u>. New York: Weidenfield and Nicolson, 1989.

G. A book with two or three editors

Kowalchik, Claire, and William H. Hylton, eds. <u>Rodale's Illustrated Encyclopedia of Herbs</u>. Emmaus, PA: Rodale, 1987.

H. A book with four or more editors

The abbreviation *et al.* means "and others." Use *et al.* instead of listing all the authors.

Metzger, Lindsay, et al. <u>Black Writers: A Selection of Sketches from Contemporary Authors</u>. Detroit, MI: Gale Research, 1989.

I. A book with an author and a translator

Saint-Exupery, Antoine de. <u>Night Flights</u>. Trans. Stuart Gilbert. New York: New American Library, 1961.

J. A second or later edition of a book

Chaet, Bernard. <u>The Art of Drawing</u>. 3rd ed. Orlando, FL: Harcourt, 1983.

K. A book or monograph that is part of a series

Chan, Sucheng. <u>Asian Americans: An Interpretive History</u>. Twayne's Immigrant Heritage of America Series. Boston: Twayne, 1991.

CONTINUED

L. A multivolume work

If you use only one volume of a multivolume work, cite only that volume; otherwise cite only the entire work.

Foote, Shelby. <u>The Civil War: A Narrative</u>. Vol. 1. New York: Random, 1958.

Foote, Shelby. <u>The Civil War: A Narrative</u>. 3 vols. New York: Random, 1958-1974.

M. A titled volume with its own title that is part of a multivolume work with a different title

Hakim, Joy. <u>Reconstruction and Reform</u>. Vol. 7. <u>A History of Us</u>. New York: Oxford UP, 1994.

N. A republished book or literary work available in several editions

Give the original publication date after the title. Then give complete information for the edition that you have used.

Stephen, Leslie, Sir. <u>Hours in a Library</u>. 1892. New York: Johnson Reprint Corp., 1968.

O. A government publication

United States. Department of Health and Human Services. <u>The Health Consequences of Smoking: Nicotine Addiction: A Report to the Surgeon General</u>. Washington, DC: GPO, 1988.

Parts of Books

A. A poem, short story, essay, or chapter in a collection of works by one author

Anderson, Sherwood. "The Corn Planting." <u>Sherwood Anderson: Short Stories</u>. Ed. and with an introd. by Maxwell Geismar. New York: Hill and Wang, 1962. 199-202.

B. A poem, short story, essay, or chapter in a collection of works by several authors

Lopez, Barry. "The Stone Horse." <u>On Nature: Nature, Landscape, and Natural History</u>. Ed. Daniel Halpern. San Francisco, North Point Press, 1987. 220-229.

C. A novel or play in a collection under one cover

Waugh, Evelyn. <u>A Handful of Dust</u>. <u>A Handful of Dust and Decline and Fall</u>. New York: Dell, 1956.

D. An introduction, preface, foreword, or afterword written by the author(s) of a work

Keillor, Garrison. Preface. <u>Lake Wobegon Days</u>. New York: Viking, 1985.

E. An introduction, preface, foreword, or afterword written by someone other than the author(s) of a work

Myrdal, Jan. Introduction. <u>Report from a Swedish Village</u>. By Sture Källberg. Trans. Angela Gibbs. New York: Penguin, 1969.

CONTINUED

F. A reprint of a previously published article or essay
Give complete information for the original publication, followed by "Rpt. in" and complete information for the collection.

```
Hawthorne, Manning. "Nathaniel Hawthorne at Bowdoin College."
    New England Quarterly 13 (1940): 246-249. Rpt. in Nathaniel
    Hawthorne at Bowdoin College. Orono, ME: University P, 1940.
```

Magazines, Encyclopedias, Reports, Newspapers, and Newsletters

A. An article in a quarterly or monthly magazine or journal
Give the volume number, the year, and the page number(s) after the title of the magazine or journal. For periodicals that begin page numbering with each issue:

```
Mitchell, W. J. "When Is Seeing Believing?" Scientific American
    Feb. 1994: 68-73.
```

For periodicals that number pages consecutively throughout a volume:

```
Mitchell, W. J. "When Is Seeing Believing?" Scientific American
    270 (Feb. 1994): 68-73.
```

B. An article in a weekly magazine

```
Layden, Tim. "The Long Road Back." Sports Illustrated
    23 May 1995: 44-50.
```

C. A magazine article with no author given

```
"On the Northern Border." National Parks Jan./Feb. 1994: 54-55.
```

D. An article in a daily newspaper

```
Biskupic, Joan. "Federal Labeling Law Struck Down." Washington
    Post 20 April 1995: B12.
```

E. An editorial in a newspaper

```
"Community of Interests." Editorial. Wall Street Journal
    24 April 1995: A14.
```

F. An article in an encyclopedia, dictionary, or other alphabetically organized reference work
Give the title of the article, the title of the work, and the year.

```
"Emancipation Proclamation." Encyclopedia of African-American
    Civil Rights. Ed. Charles Lowery and John Marszalek. New York:
    Greenwood, 1992.
```

G. A review

```
Rich, Frank. "'The Twentieth Century Should Have Been the
    Best.'" Rev. of From Time to Time. By Jack Finney. New York:
    Simon, 1995. New York Times Book Review 19 Feb. 1995: 10.
```

H A report for a pamphlet
Same as for a book.

Media and Other Sources

A. An interview that you have conducted

```
Yolen, Jane. Personal interview. 4 May 1995.
```

CONTINUED

B. A letter or fax that you have received

Kennedy, Edward. Letter to the author. 17 December 1994.

C. A thesis or dissertation

Fine, Richard. "Hollywood and the Profession of Authorship, 1928–1940." Diss., U of Pennsylvania, 1979.

D. A film

Dead Poets Society. With Robin Williams. Dir. Peter Weir. Writ. Tom Schulman. 128 min. Touchstone Pictures in assoc. with Silver Screen Partners IV, 1989.

E. A work of visual art

Brueghel, Pieter. Harvest. 1565. Metropolitan Museum, New York.

F. A television or radio program

Give the episode name; the names of the episode's writer, director, producer, or actors; the series or program title; and any information that you wish to include about the series' writer, director, or producer. Then give the network, station call letters, city, and date.

"And Justice for All." Prod. Kathleen Hughes. Dir. Joseph Camp. Listening to America with Bill Moyers. PBS. WOSU-TV, Columbus, OH. 14 April 1992.

G. A musical composition

Handel, George Frideric. Messiah.

H. An audio recording (LP, compact disc, audiocassette tape)

Angelou, Maya. Maya Angelou (audiocassette). Washington, DC: Tapes for Readers, nd.

I. A lecture, speech, or address

Give the name of the speaker and the name of the speech. If there is no title, give the kind of speech—e.g., lecture, introduction, address. Then give the event, place, and date.

Carus, Marianne. "Writing for Magazines." 22nd Annual Writer's Conference in Children's Literature. Marina Del Rey, CA, 7 Aug. 1993.

MANUSCRIPT FORM FOR BIBLIOGRAPHIES

1. Begin on a new page.

2. Indent one inch from both side margins, one and one-half inches on the left side and one inch on the right side if the report is to be bound.

3. Place your last name and the page number, flush right, a half inch from the top of the paper.

4. Drop down another half inch and insert the title "Works Consulted" or "Works Cited." Use uppercase and lowercase letters, and do not underscore.

5. Begin each entry at the left margin. Single space within each entry. Indent run-over lines five spaces from the left margin.

6. Double-space between the title and the first entry and between each entry.

Bibliography cards. For each possible source that you find, prepare a 3" x 5" card listing complete bibliographical information. You will use this information to document your sources as you write (see the Language Arts Survey, 4.33, "Documenting Sources in a Report") and to prepare your bibliography. The cards can also help you find the book again at a later time. Include all of the information listed in the chart below when preparing your cards. A sample bibliography card is shown below the chart.

INFORMATION TO INCLUDE ON A BIBLIOGRAPHY CARD	
Author(s)	Write the complete name(s) of all author(s), editor(s), and translator(s).
Title	Write the complete title, including any subtitle and any series title. If the piece is an article or chapter in a periodical or book, write • the title of the particular piece; • the beginning and ending page numbers; and • the title of the larger work.
Edition	Note "2nd edition," "revised edition," etc.
Publisher	Write exactly as it appears on the title page.
Place and date of publication	For periodicals, write the date as well as the issue and volume numbers. For republished works, write both the original publication date and the date of your edition.
Location and call number	Note where you found the book. If it is in a library collection, write the call number.
Card number	Give each bibliography card that you prepare a number. Write that number in the top right-hand corner of the card and circle it. When you take notes from the source, include this number on each note card so that you will be able to identify the source of the note later on.

SAMPLE BIBLIOGRAPHY CARD

①

Campbell, Joseph. <u>The Power of Myth: Joseph Campbell, with Bill Moyers</u>. Ed. Betty Sue Flowers. New York: Anchor Books, 1988.

Springfield Public Library
BL304 / C36 / 1988

4.30 PARAPHRASING AND SUMMARIZING

Quoting. When you need to prove that someone made a specific statement about something, you will want to quote your source directly. **Quoted** words are those borrowed exactly from someone else. Place quotation marks before and after the words to show that they are not your own (see the Language Arts Survey, 2.104 and 2.105, on punctuation with quotations, and 2.124, on capitalization with quotations). When you add a quotation to your writing, be sure to check its accuracy word for word and to provide proper documentation (see the Language Arts Survey, 4.33, "Documenting Sources in a Report").

Paraphrasing. Paraphrasing is restating someone else's ideas in your own words. When taking notes from a source, your note-taking will be more accurate if you quote directly rather than paraphrase. However, when you draft your piece, you are likely to paraphrase many of your notes. Having the exact quote to look at will help you avoid quoting a source without realizing it.

Paraphrasing is still a form of borrowing. So when you paraphrase someone else's ideas, you have a responsibility to give credit to the source of those ideas (see the Language Arts Survey, 4.33, "Documenting Sources in a Report").

Summarizing. To summarize a piece of writing is to simplify it in a brief statement of the main points, leaving out most details. When you summarize, you condense someone else's words into fewer words that are all your own. The purpose of your summary will help you determine how much supporting detail to include. For example, think about how a summary of a movie in a video guide might compare to a summary printed on the case of the actual video.

A summary should tell what the author said. Be sure you don't inadvertently inject your own opinions or ideas into the summary.

Outlining. An excellent way to summarize a piece of nonfiction is to outline it (see the Language Arts Survey, 1.32 and 1.33, on outlining). You can paraphrase the title and headings (if any) in the piece you are summarizing and use these as the title and headings in your own outline. After each heading, note the main points made in the section.

4.31 INFORMAL NOTE-TAKING

Informal note-taking is a way of gathering information for personal use only, such as when you take notes in a class or at a live event or performance. In informal note-taking, you are not concerned with quoting and documenting sources.

Informal note-taking is much like outlining (see the Language Arts Survey, 1.32, "Making a Rough Outline"). You make each important idea a heading and write related details below each heading. For efficiency, use phrases and abbreviations. However, if you use a special shorthand or way of abbreviating, it's a good idea to look back over your notes as soon as you can and write out any notes that might be confusing at a later time.

SOURCE MATERIAL "Desktop publishing is the production of printed matter by means of a desktop computer having a layout program that integrates text and graphics."

NOTES Desktop publishing
—produces printed materials
—uses d.t. computer
—uses layout program (text + graphics)

If you are taking notes at a performance, be sure to record information to identify the event such as the date, time, place, speaker or performer, and so on.

4.32 FORMAL NOTE-TAKING

Use **formal note-taking** when you may need to quote or document your sources. In formal note-taking, you write each quotation, paraphrase, or summary on a separate 4" x 6" index card. The chart below can help you decide when each type of note is appropriate.

FORMAL NOTE-TAKING		
Type of Note	**When to Use**	**What to Watch for**
Quotation	When the exact wording of a primary source is important to your topic; or When you are providing a definition; or When the wording of a secondary source is particularly elegant, pithy, concise, amusing, etc.	Be sure you exactly copy spelling, capitalization, punctuation, and numbers. Place quotation marks around all direct quotations. Record, when appropriate, explanatory background information about the speaker or the context of a quotation.
Paraphrase	Most of the time	Bear in mind your main purpose, and note only points that are related to your topic. Place quotation marks around any quoted words or phrases.
Summary	When the point in which you are interested does not require the detail of a paraphrase	Reread the source after writing your summary to be sure that you have not altered the meaning.

Formal note-taking is appropriate for a research paper, debate, or other school-related project. Follow the guidelines in the chart when preparing individual note cards. A sample note card is shown on the following page.

PREPARING NOTE CARDS

1. Identify the source at the top right corner of the card. (Use the source numbers from your bibliography cards.)

2. Identify the subject or topic of the note on the top line of the card. (This will make it easier to organize the cards later.)

3. Use a separate card for each fact or quotation. (This will make it easier to organize the cards later.)

4. Write the page number or numbers after the note.

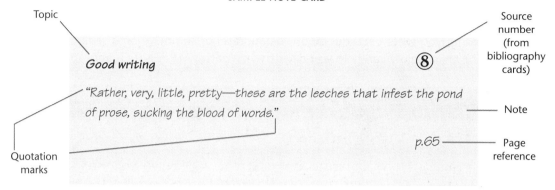

Topic

Source number (from bibliography cards)

Good writing

⑧

"*Rather, very, little, pretty—these are the leeches that infest the pond of prose, sucking the blood of words.*"

Note

p.65

Page reference

Quotation marks

4.33 DOCUMENTING SOURCES IN A REPORT

Documentation. In your writing, you need to make it clear to your readers when you are presenting or using the words or ideas of others. You do this by **documenting** your sources. A note that tells the source of an idea or statement is called a **citation** or a **reference.**

Presenting someone else's words or ideas as if they were your own is called **plagiarism.** Plagiarism is a form of stealing. Unlike other forms of stealing, "I didn't mean to" is not an excuse. A writer who borrows words or ideas without giving credit is guilty of plagiarism whether or not it was intentional. In most schools, committing plagiarism brings a severe penalty, such as a failing grade for a project or course. Outside of school, plagiarism is a violation of copyright law and can result in being sued.

There are other important reasons for documenting your sources. Your readers will find your writing more credible if you tell them exactly where you obtained your facts. Documentation is also a courtesy to your readers, in case they want to follow up on some point you discuss. Finally, documentation is a sign of honesty; it shows that you recognize and appreciate the contributions to human knowledge made by others.

Parenthetical documentation. Currently, parenthetical documentation is the most widely used method for citing sources. To use this method, you place a brief note identifying the source in parentheses immediately after the borrowed material. This type of note is called a **parenthetical citation,** and the act of placing such a note is called **citing a source.**

A parenthetical citation has two parts. The first part refers the reader to an entry in your list of "Works Cited" or "Works Consulted." The second part refers the reader to a specific page number or place in the source. If the source is clearly identified in the text, omit the source and give only the page number.

ABBREVIATIONS FOR CITATIONS	
pt.	part
bk.	book
ch.	chapter
sec.	section
sc.	scene
par.	paragraph

A. For works listed by author or editor, use the author's or editor's last name.

Sample bibliographic entry

"Fable." <u>Encyclopedia Americana</u>, 1995 ed.

Sample citation

Humans' anthropomorphizing of animals goes back to prehistoric times ("Fable," 824).

B. For works listed by title, use an abbreviated title.

Sample bibliographic entry

Bettmann, Otto L. <u>The Delights of Reading: Quotes, Notes and Anecdotes</u>. Boston: Godine, 1987.

Sample citation

"Books remind us that we are not alone" (Bettmann xii).

C. When the listed name or title is stated in the text, cite only the page number.

Sample citation

Bettmann's <u>Delights of Reading</u> contains several quotations about public libraries (36-40).

D. For works of multiple volumes, use a colon after the volume number.

Sample bibliographic entry

Foner, Philip, ed. <u>The Life and Writings of Frederick Douglass</u>. 4 vols. New York: International, 1950.

Sample citation

. . . , as he said in his farewell speech to the British people in March 1847 (Foner 1: 103).

E. For works quoted in secondary sources, use the abbreviation "qtd. in."

Sample citation

Paul Valery once noted, "A poem is never finished—only abandoned." (qtd. in Bettmann 69)

F. For classic works that are available in various editions, give the page number from the edition you are using, followed by a semicolon; then identify the section of the work to help people with other editions find the reference.

Sample bibliographic entry

Dickens, Charles. <u>Bleak House</u>. Boston: Houghton, 1956.

Sample citation

. . . in the scene where Lady Dedlock meets Mr. Jarndyce for the first time (194-196; ch. 18), . . .

G. For classic works of poetry or drama you may omit the page reference completely and cite the section and line numbers.

Sample citation

Orsino speaks of falling in love with Olivia at first sight (<u>Twelfth Night</u>, act 1, sc. 1, 17-22)

4.34 Footnotes and Endnotes

The alternatives to parenthetical documentation are footnoting and endnoting. These two forms of documentation are less widely used and occur mainly in scholarly works.

Footnotes. A **footnote** is a citation placed at the bottom, or "foot," of the page. With this system, a number or symbol is placed in the text at the end of the passage to be documented. At the bottom of the page, a matching number or symbol identifies the note. In addition to identifying sources, footnotes may supply information that is useful to the reader but not important enough to be placed in the text. For example, in this book, numbered footnotes in the literature selections define obscure words and provide background information.

Endnotes. Many readers find footnotes distracting, especially if they are numerous, and typists and typesetters find them difficult to place on the page. For these reasons, many books and periodicals use **endnotes** instead of footnotes. Endnotes are exactly like footnotes except that they are gathered at the end of a book, chapter, or article.

TEST-TAKING SKILLS

OBJECTIVE TESTS

4.35 Strategies for Taking Objective Tests

Tests are a fact of life (both in school and beyond), yet they needn't be a cause for great distress. The tips in the chart below and in the following sections can help you to do your best and to feel more at ease when taking tests.

STRATEGIES FOR TAKING OBJECTIVE TESTS
Before the Test
• Get ample sleep the night before the test.
• Eat a nutritious breakfast.
• Study over as long a period of time as possible.
• Review frequently.
• Try to predict questions that may be on the test, and make sure you can answer them.
• Bring extra pencils, erasers, and any other required materials.
During the Test
• Determine how much time is allowed for each question. If a question takes too long, guess and/or come back to it if you have time.
• *Read each question carefully.*
• Work quickly but do not rush.
• Write legibly.
• Review all your work before submitting it.

Whenever you are taking a test, if a question seems too difficult, skip it and go on to the next one. Make a note to come back to it if you have extra time at the end of the test period.

4.36 TRUE/FALSE QUESTIONS

A true/false question gives you a statement and asks you to decide whether the statement is true or false. If you think you do not know the answer, try to guess. There are only two possible answers, so you have a 50/50 chance of guessing correctly. If you are given a true/false test, be alert for these traps:

Negatives and double negatives. The word *not* completely changes the meaning of a sentence. To evaluate a sentence with a negative, see if its opposite makes sense or is plausible. If so, the original must be false.

Quantifiers and qualifiers. Look for words such as *all, sometimes, never,* and so on. Few statements are true without exception.

Excess information. The more information a sentence in a true/false test contains, the more likely it is to be false. Remember, if any one part of the statement is false, then the statement is false.

4.37 MULTIPLE-CHOICE QUESTIONS

Multiple-choice tests are very common. A multiple-choice test item asks a question and then lists several possible answers from which to choose. If you know the answer from reading the question, look for it in the choices. Otherwise, read through each answer to rule out incorrect choices. Remember that sometimes you must choose the *best* answer, even if none appears exactly correct to you.

EXAMPLE What is the best word to describe the character of Alice in *Alice in Wonderland*?
1. naughty   4. young
2. curious   5. circumspect
3. educated

4.38 SHORT-ANSWER QUESTIONS

On quizzes and in class discussions you will frequently be given short-answer questions. These are answered with a word, a phrase, or a sentence. Many teachers require that responses to short-answer questions be complete sentences.

EXAMPLE Was Sojourner Truth an abolitionist or a feminist?
She was both.

STANDARDIZED TESTS

4.39 STRATEGIES FOR TAKING STANDARDIZED TESTS

You are likely to encounter standardized tests at several points in your school career. States and school districts use standardized tests to assess achievement, and colleges use them to evaluate students for admission and scholarships.

SOME STANDARDIZED TESTS	
Common Abbreviation	**Test**
PSAT/NMSQT	Pre-Scholastic Aptitude Test/National Merit Scholarship Qualifying Test
ACT	American College Testing Program
MAT	Miller Analogies Test
SAT	Scholastic Aptitude Test
ACH	College Board Achievement Tests

These tests are all multiple-choice tests. You mark your answer by filling in a bubble on a special sheet that can be read and graded by a computer. When taking one of these tests, use the type of pencil or pen specified by the test monitor. Be sure to fill in bubbles *completely* and *neatly.*

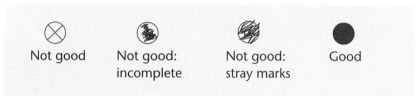

Not good   Not good: incomplete   Not good: stray marks   Good

When selecting an answer on a standardized test, remember these points. If you do not know the answer, try to rule out some choices and then guess from those remaining. If a question seems too difficult, skip it and go on to the next one. If you have extra time later, you can come back to it. If you forgot to make a note of which question you skipped, look for a blank space on your answer sheet. Be aware, however, that most tests do not allow you to return to a previous section; you can go back to questions only within a section. Always follow the instructions of the test monitor.

4.40 ANALOGY QUESTIONS

Analogy questions ask you to find the relationship between a given pair of words and then recognize a similar relationship between another pair of words.

EXAMPLE   CHIRP : CRICKET
(A) whisper : sound   (C) shout : pain   (E) song : voice
(B) thunder : storm   (D) buzz : bee

To answer an analogy question you must examine *all* of the answers. If more than one answer seems correct, choose the *best* answer. Do not be misled by irrelevant relationships between individual words in the example and words in the choices. Focus on the *relationship* between the two words in the example.

4.41 SENTENCE-COMPLETION QUESTIONS

Sentence-completion questions present a sentence in which one or two words are missing. You must recognize the relationship among the parts of the sentence, and then choose the word or words that best complete the sentence.

EXAMPLE   The play was so _____ that I couldn't stop _____.
   (A) beneficial . . . wondering   (D) lengthy . . . watching
   (B) amusing . . . laughing   (E) amended . . . yawning
   (C) tragic . . . smiling

You can answer a sentence-completion question only by trying all the choices to see which answer works best in the sentence. You can often eliminate one or two answers right away because they do not make sense or fit the structure of the sentence.

4.42 GRAMMAR, USAGE, AND MECHANICS QUESTIONS

Grammar, usage, and mechanics questions are designed to test your knowledge of correct English. Often these questions present a sentence or paragraph containing underlined and labeled words or passages for you to evaluate.

Error-identification questions ask you to identify the passage that contains an error. You do not have to tell the type of error. **Error-correction questions** ask you to correct the error by choosing a word or passage to replace it.

Error-identification question

EB White, the much-loved author of *Charlotte's Web*, was a
A   B   C
writer for the *New Yorker* for many years. No error.
             D   E

(A) (B) (C) (D) (E)

Error-correction question

Select the letter of the word or words that should replace the underlined word.

White is wellknown for his insightful essays.
              1
1. (A) No change   (C) well-known   (E) well-knowed
   (B) well known   (D) known-well

ANSWERING ERROR-IDENTIFICATION AND ERROR-CORRECTION QUESTIONS

1. Ignore the underlining and proofread the sentence or paragraph carefully.
   • Proofread for errors in grammar, usage, and mechanics.
   • Look especially for agreement—in tense, person, number, and mood.
2. If you do not find the error, look specifically at the underlined passages.
3. Read the whole sentence through before settling on your answer.

You can practice for all grammar, usage, and mechanics questions by working on the activities in 2.1–2.153 of the Language Arts Survey and completing your reading and writing assignments conscientiously.

4.43 READING COMPREHENSION QUESTIONS

Reading comprehension questions give you a short piece of writing and then ask you several questions about it. Often the questions ask you to make an inference or interpretation from the text. To select the correct answer, you will need to try all the choices. Be sure that your answers are based only on the passage and not on "outside" information or opinions you have.

STEPS IN ANSWERING READING COMPREHENSION QUESTIONS

1. Read all the questions quickly.
2. Read the passage.
3. Reread the first question carefully.
4. Reread the passage while bearing in mind the first question.
5. Answer the first question.
6. Continue with each subsequent question in the same manner.

4.44 SYNONYM AND ANTONYM QUESTIONS

Synonym and antonym questions give you a word and ask you to select the word that has the same meaning (for a synonym) or the opposite meaning (for an antonym). You must select the *best* answer, even if none is exactly correct.

For this type of question, you should try all the choices to see which one works best. You will usually find both synonyms and antonyms among the answers, so make sure you know what the question is asking for. Don't select an answer just because it reminds you of the given word or because it is a long or unfamiliar word.

EXAMPLE   Write the letter of the word that is most nearly the *same* in meaning to the word in capital letters.
1. PREJUDICE
(A) bias   (B) justice   (C) predicate   (D) fairness   (E) belief

STRATEGIES FOR TAKING ESSAY TESTS

4.45 ANALYZING AN ESSAY QUESTION

One of the keys to writing a good answer to an essay question is to take a few moments to analyze the question. Once you understand clearly what tasks are being requested, you will be able to organize and write a more effective essay in the time available.

After reading the *entire* question carefully, look for key words in the question that tell you what is expected. Underline these words or write them on your own note paper. Many questions ask for more than one type of response; make sure you answer *all* parts of the question.

UNDERSTANDING AN ESSAY QUESTION	
Type of Essay Question	**Tasks of Essay**
analyze (1.14, 1.33, 4.11)	break into parts and describe the parts and their relationships
compare; compare and contrast (1.33, 4.8)	identify and describe similarities and differences
describe; explain (1.33, 4.6)	tell the steps in a process; identify causes and effects
define; describe; identify (4.7)	classify and tell the features of
interpret (4.13)	tell the meaning and significance of
summarize (4.30)	retell very briefly, stating only the main points
argue; prove; show (4.12)	tell and evaluate reasons for believing a statement

4.46 ORGANIZING AN ANSWER TO AN ESSAY QUESTION

Because in most testing situations your time is limited, deciding how you will spend that time is an important part of planning your essay. Allow time for planning, drafting, and reviewing. If you have a plan and pace yourself, you will not have any trouble writing a complete essay in the time available.

Before you begin writing, make a brief outline of the main points you will make. Then add notes about key details, such as examples and quotations, that will support those points. Later, if you do find yourself running out of time, attempt to complete the essay by at least stating your remaining main points and adding a conclusion. Even if you cannot fully execute your plan, revealing your plan allows you to show your understanding.

Do write a clear introduction. This will help keep you on track as you write each paragraph. Your introduction should state your main point or points and lead logically into the body of your essay.

4.47 REVIEWING AN ANSWER TO AN ESSAY QUESTION

Before you submit your completed essay, you should take time to review and polish it. The guidelines in the chart below will help you.

QUESTIONS FOR REVIEWING AN ANSWER TO AN ESSAY QUESTION
• Does the essay answer all parts of the question?
• Does the introduction state clearly the main point of the essay?
• Is the conclusion consistent with the main point?
• Does the essay cover all the points in your outline?
• Are there any points that could be made more strongly or clearly?
• Is every word in the essay easily legible?
• Is the essay free of errors in grammar, usage, and mechanics?

ESSENTIAL SKILLS:
Applied English/Tech Prep

LETTERS AND FORMS

Suppose you want to comfort a friend who is far away, apply for a summer job, strike up an acquaintance with an e-mail pen pal, or tell your community how you feel about an issue that affects teens. You can accomplish all of these things with letters. Letters can be expressive, informative, or persuasive. They can involve description and exposition. They may be addressed to close friends or to individuals you've never met but want to impress in some way. Thus, all of your writing skills come into play when you write a letter.

5.1 FILLING OUT FORMS AND APPLICATIONS

Sometimes your first opportunity to make a good impression on others through your writing comes when you must fill out a form or application. Forms are efficient tools for collecting information, and you will encounter them frequently, such as when entering contests, applying for work, or going to a new dentist. Generally, when you complete a form or application, your basic task is to provide clearly and accurately the information requested; but most often, your main aim should be to make a positive impression.

Guidelines for completing forms:

- If possible, obtain an extra copy of the form or application.
- Gather any information you will need to complete the form.
- Read all the directions before you begin to enter your data.
- Be neat. Type or print your responses legibly, in pencil or ink, as directed. Avoid smudges or cross-outs.
- Write "N.A." or "not applicable," rather than leave a space blank, if a section of the form or application does not apply to you.
- Proofread. When you've completed the form, check your spelling, grammar, and punctuation, and review the information you've provided.
- If the form is messy or inaccurate, discard it and complete the extra form or application if you have one.
- When you've completed the form to your satisfaction, submit it to the appropriate person, or mail it to the correct address.

SAMPLE APPLICATION FORM

Application for Youth Employment
Florida State Fair

Position Desired: __Information Booth Attendant__

Personal Data

Applicant's Name: __Alvarez__   __Alicia__   __M.__
                  Last name   *First Name*   *Middle Initial*

Address: __255 Hudson__   __Springfield__   __FL__   __00823__
         Street   *City*   *State*   *Zip*

Phone: __(586) 555-7056__   Date of Birth: __7/16/82__

Previous Work Experience

(List last two positions held, beginning with the most recent.)

Employer: __Adam Johnson__   __105 E. Miami St., Springfield, FL   00823__
          Name   *Address*

Phone: __(586) 555-2122__

Employment Period: __9/95–present__

Job Title: __Babysitter__

Hours Worked: __Flexible, 5–10 hrs./wk.__

Salary: __$5.00/hr.__

Description: __Supervise 2 children aged 5 and 11__

Reason for Leaving: __N.A.__

Employer: __Central School__   __2 Main St., Springfield, FL   00823__
          Name   *Address*

Phone: __(586) 555-0455__

Employment Period: __9/95–5/96__

Job Title: __Hall Monitor__

Hours Worked: __8:00–9:30, Monday–Friday__

Salary: __N. A.__

Description: __Check students for passes, give directions to new students and visitors__

Reason for Leaving: __End of school year__

CONTINUED

Education

(List last school attended.)

Springfield High School	Springfield, FL	9/96–	Business	
School Name	Address	Dates Attended	Field of Study	Date Graduated

References

Name: Sally and Lincoln Garfield

Relationship to
Job Applicant: Friends of family   Years Acquainted: 12

Address: 29 A Mars Court, Oslo, FL   00825   Phone: (586) 555-4725

Name: Dr. Lonnie Carson

Relationship to
Job Applicant: Teacher   Years Acquainted: 2

Address: Central School, Springfield, FL 00823   Phone: (586) 555-0455

Signature: *Alicia M. Alvarez*   Date: 6/14/96

5.2 THE FORM OF A PERSONAL LETTER

In an age of mobile telephones and e-mail, personal letters are much less common than they once were; however, personal letters remain an important way to correspond with friends and relatives, to say "thank you" for a gift or kindness, to offer congratulations and condolences, and to extend invitations. Personal letters offer some advantages over speaking by telephone. They tend to carry more weight than spontaneous comments. When you write a letter, you can say what you have to say without interruption and play with language in ways that express your personality. Furthermore, written communications can be saved and savored time and again.

A personal letter may be quite informal or semiformal, depending on the writer's relationship with the person who will receive the letter. It will typically include the following parts:

1. a **return address,** including the writer's address and the date the letter was composed;
2. a **salutation,** or greeting, followed by a comma;
3. the **body,** or text, of the letter;
4. an appropriate **closing,** followed by a comma;
5. a **signature;** and
6. an optional **postscript,** preceded by the abbreviation "P.S."

SAMPLE THANK-YOU LETTER

❶ 236 Van Buren Avenue
Nicely, NM 99290
July 7, 1996

❷ Dear Grandmother,

❸   I love the book on masks that you sent. It's really the perfect gift. I've seen it so many times at the Bookworm, and it has been on my birthday wish list for months. I can't wait to get started on the papier-mâché dragon mask.
    Did I tell you that our class is putting an art display in the main hall at school? I am going to try to finish my dragon mask in time for the display.
    Thanks again for your thoughtfulness.

❹ Love,

❺ *Fred*

5.3 THE FORM OF A BUSINESS LETTER

You can express your emotions and thoughts freely in a personal letter, and even use slang or pet expressions, because you know these will be acceptable and of interest to the recipient. A business letter, however, is typically addressed to someone who does not know you personally. When writing this type of letter, it makes sense to use a more formal tone.

You also should follow the widely accepted format for a business letter. This will help to ensure that your letter makes a positive impression. Like a typical personal letter, a business letter includes a **heading, salutation, body, closing**, and **signature**. In addition, it includes an **inside address.** The inside address is located below the heading and above the salutation. It includes the name and title of the person to whom you are writing and the name and address of that person's company or organization. If you do not know the name of a person at an organization, you can use a department name instead, or you can phone the organization and ask to whom you should address your letter.

The salutation and closing of a business letter should be respectful and formal. The salutation typically begins with the word "Dear" followed by the courtesy or professional title used in the inside address, such as "Ms.," "Mr.," "Dr.," "Miss," or "Mrs.," and a colon. If you are not writing to a specific person, you can use "Dear Sir or Madam" or "Ladies and Gentlemen."

To end a business letter, it's best to stick with one of the standard closings, such as "Sincerely," "Yours truly," or "Respectfully yours." Capitalize only the first word of the closing. Skip down three lines to leave room for your signature, and type your full name. Finally, sign your name, in either blue or black ink, below the closing.

Arrange the parts of your business letter in either block form or modified block form. When you use **block form** you begin each part of the letter at the left margin and do not indent paragraphs. A sample letter in block form is on page 934. To use **modified block form,** begin the heading and the closing just to the right of the center of the page. Make sure they align with each other. Indent each body paragraph five spaces from the left margin. A sample letter in modified block form is on page 936.

Remember that one of your basic goals is to give your reader a positive impression. Your letter should get to the point quickly, be easy to read, and be as brief as possible. Outline your main points before you begin to compose, so that your letter will be well organized. In the body of your letter, be courteous and formal. Use standard English and avoid slang expressions. Before you seal the envelope, carefully recheck your grammar, punctuation, and spelling.

Guidelines for writing a business letter:

- Outline your letter's main points before you begin the writing process.
- Type your letter, if at all possible, and use clean 8½" × 11" white or off-white paper. Type on one side of the paper only.
- Select a standard business-letter format, either block form or modified block form.
- Use single-spacing, leaving a blank line between paragraphs.
- Select a standard salutation and closing.
- Stick to the subject, keeping the letter brief and informative.
- Be neat. A sloppy appearance may make your letter less effective.
- Check your grammar, usage, punctuation, capitalization, and spelling.
- Reread your letter. Have you conveyed your main points clearly and effectively? Don't make your reader guess at your intentions.

5.4 TYPES OF BUSINESS LETTERS I

Follow the form and guidelines for business letters even when you are not writing to an actual business. For example, you would write a business letter to request information from a chamber of commerce, to complain to the mayor about poor lighting on your street, or to thank the local Kiwanis for an award they gave you.

In any of these cases, you might use a phone call for the same purpose, but people often pay more attention to written communications, and they appreciate the extra effort that goes into writing a letter. In addition, when you write a letter, you can save a copy of it. Having a record of your correspondence can be very useful. For example, if you were to receive a reply to a letter of complaint that you wrote, you would want to refer to your original letter to see which of your points were answered.

SAMPLE LETTER OF REQUEST

442 Grandview Avenue
Springs, ND 78799
May 22, 1996

High Mountain Adventures
P.O. Box 81212
Seattle, WA 99134

Dear Director:

In a recent issue of the *Cincinnati Enquirer,* I read about your mountain-biking camp in the Rocky Mountains. I would like to receive more information about the camp, including the dates, costs, and daily schedule.

CONTINUED

Also, would it be possible for me to contact a former camper in my area? I'm hoping you might be able to give me the name and address of a satisfied customer, with that person's permission of course. I look forward to hearing from you.

Sincerely,

Zenobia Mafouz

5.5 Types of Business Letters II

Of all the letters you write in your lifetime, some of the most important might be those you send to potential employers. As a high school student, you can also use your skills in writing business letters when you apply for special academic or extracurricular programs or seek summer jobs and internships.

When applying for a position, it is common to submit both a **résumé** and a letter of application, also called a **cover letter.** The purpose of these two documents is to tell the most important facts about your education, skills, and work experience. The information in your résumé and cover letter must be honest and accurate, but you should present your experience in a positive light.

Cover letters. In your letter you can explain how your background is especially suited to the particular job or educational opportunity at hand, and suggest how your unique mix of skills and abilities could help the organization you hope to join.

Guidelines for composing a cover letter:

- Limit your cover letter to a single page.
- State your interest in obtaining a position within the organization, indicating the type of position (or specific job opening) for which you'd like to be considered.
- If you are applying for a specific position, describe how you learned of the job's availability.
- Briefly describe your qualifications.
- Refer to your résumé, enclosed with your letter.
- Mention your interest in scheduling an interview and where and when you may be reached (typically by telephone) to make arrangements.
- Thank the reader for considering your application.

SAMPLE COVER LETTER

2482 Ocean Avenue
Pacifica, NE 69890
May 21, 1996

Mr. Harry Yang
Texon Company
9929 Red Bank Road
Vespucci, NE 69804

Dear Mr. Yang:

While attending a science day at the University of Nebraska recently, I met Ms. Beverly Myers, a member of your Research and Development department, at your company booth. When Ms. Myers told me about the Texon Summer Institute for Young Scientists, I knew immediately that I wanted to apply.

My special interest is physics. One of my earliest accomplishments in this area was winning second prize in the citywide science fair for a project on the random movement of molecules. I am an avid reader of books and magazine articles about physics. At Anthony High, where I am now a freshman, I am a member of the science club, tutor younger students in science, and continue to create science projects on physics topics.

I hope someday to have a career in science. The summer institute, I believe, would help me reach that goal. If you need any additional information or have any questions, please call me at (471) 555-6645.

Sincerely,

Consuelo Alvarez

Consuelo Alvarez

Résumés. The information in your résumé may be organized in many different ways. Your guidance counselor or librarian may have a file of sample résumés for you to review. Select a style that looks neat and businesslike. Most résumés list the applicant's **objective**, or career goal, **work experience; education; extracurricular activities; skills;** and **references.** Be sure to list any special accomplishments or awards you have had in school or in a job.

Limit your résumé to a single page. It should be typed and printed on high-quality paper; you can use the same paper stock used for your cover letter. Check the quality of the print to make sure it's easy to read.

SAMPLE RÉSUMÉ

Consuelo Alvarez
2482 Ocean Avenue
Pacifica, NE 69890
(471) 555-6645

Objective:
An educational or work opportunity that will help me prepare for a career in science

Work Experience:

9/95–Present   Science tutor, Jones Middle School, Pacifica, NE

Helped sixth-grade science students understand basic science concepts and develop lab and study skills.

Summer 1994   Crew member, City Parks Clean-up Program, Pacifica, NE
Assisted with trash pickup and landscape improvement at four city parks (12 hours per week).

Education:
Susan B. Anthony High School, Class of '99, Business program
Grade point average: 2.9
Awards: Second Prize, Central County Schoolwide Science Fair, 1992
(Topic: Random Motion of Molecules)
Honorable Mention, Anthony High School Science Fair, 1995
(Topic: Lift and Wing Design)

Extracurricular Activities:
Vice President, Science Club
Intramural volleyball

References:

Mr. Tyrone Griffith	Mr. Sam Liebowitz
Teacher, Anthony High School	Maintenance Director
Pacifica, NE	Pacifica Parks System
(471) 555–8221	(471) 555-1993

WRITING ON THE JOB

For some working people, such as journalists and technical writers, writing is the primary task of their jobs. For others, writing is still a necessary part of most jobs. As important as writing is, employers today often complain that many employees cannot write well enough to communicate with each other or with clients and customers. If you learn to organize and express your thoughts on paper, you'll be ahead of the crowd by the time you take your first job.

5.6 WRITING MEMORANDA

Workers usually send **memoranda**, or **memos**, to communicate with other workers in the organization. Memos can be used to communicate information and ideas on a wide variety of topics. You might write a memo to call a meeting, to explain changes in a procedure, to introduce a new employee, or to give a work assignment.

SAMPLE MEMO

MEMORANDUM

TO: Janetta Davidson
FROM: Bernice Dean, Personnel Department
DATE: July 17, 1997
SUBJECT: Dental insurance

I just want to let you know that as a new employee you are eligible for the optional dental coverage as part of your health benefits. The cost is $12 per month for an individual. I have a booklet that describes the coverage in the personnel office. You can pick it up any time. I'd be happy to answer any questions you might have.

5.7 TECHNICAL WRITING

Nearly every worker in every profession will be called on some day to explain a procedure or complex process in writing. For example, you might be asked to document, or describe in detail, a procedure you have mastered so that others can learn it. This type of practical, skill-related writing is called **technical writing.**

Guidelines for documenting technical procedures:

- First, make sure you are very familiar with the procedure you'll be documenting.
- Break the task into a series of short, simple steps.
- Warn the reader of any potentially hazardous steps or materials.
- List any tools or equipment needed to complete the process.
- List each step in the proper sequence.
- Use the second person imperative. Write "Press the enter key," not "The user should press the enter key."
- Keep your vocabulary simple, avoiding unexplained technical jargon.
- If appropriate, incorporate pictures and diagrams.
- Don't leave out any steps or include unnecessary steps.
- Proofread your instructions to make sure they are easy to follow and unambiguous.
- Ask someone who isn't familiar with the operation to follow the directions you have written. If necessary, adjust your instructions based on his or her experience.

5.8 WRITING PROMOTIONAL AND PUBLIC RELATIONS COPY

Promotional writing is writing intended to capture a reader's attention and persuade the reader to purchase a product or accept a particular viewpoint. Promotional materials include press releases; ads for radio, television, and newspapers; news and feature articles; scripts for films and slide shows; letters to magazine editors; and annual reports. Although the aim of promotional copy is to persuade, its content must be based on fact. A press release should include the name and telephone number of the person to contact for details or verification, the date the information can be released,the location of the event, and the word *end* surrounded by dashes at the bottom of the release.

SAMPLE PRESS RELEASE

For immediate release:

January 6, 1997

Contact:

Kwami Fields
(397) 555-7211

Bloomsbury:

Wickliffe's Book Store, the leading used bookstore in the tricounty area, will sponsor the 12th Annual Book and Print Collectors' Bookfair at the Convention Center, March 12–13, from 10 A.M. to 9 P.M. each day.

More than 100 dealers from twelve states will offer more than 50,000 used books of all types on all subjects. Old and rare prints will also be offered for sale.

Visitors on Saturday will have the opportunity to enter a raffle for a signed first edition of Toni Morrison's *The Bluest Eye.* Door prizes are available on both days.

Discount tickets may be purchased at Wickliffe's Book Store, 246 North High Street, open 10–5.

— *END* —

HANDBOOK OF
Literary Terms

abstract **1.** *n.* An **abstract,** *précis,* or **summary** is a brief account of the main ideas or arguments presented in a work. Writing an abstract is an excellent way to remember the ideas of an essay or a chapter in a textbook. See *paraphrase.* **2.** *adj.* An **abstract** word or phrase is one that refers to something that cannot be directly perceived by the senses. *Freedom, justice,* and *loyalty* are examples of abstract terms. The opposite of *abstract* in this sense is *concrete.* See *concrete.*

accent See *stress.*

acronym An **acronym** is a word created from the first, or initial, letters of a series of words. The word *scuba* is an acronym. It is created from the words *self-contained underwater breathing apparatus.*

acrostic An **acrostic** is a poem organized so that the first or last letters of each line form a word, a phrase, or a regular sequence of letters of the alphabet.

act An **act** is a major division of a drama. The plays of Shakespeare are generally divided into five acts. In modern times, plays are often divided into three acts. Short one-act plays are quite common. Lucille Fletcher's *The Hitchhiker* is a one-act play.

action The **action** is the sequence of events that actually occur in a literary work, as opposed to those that occur off-scene or that precede or follow the events in the work itself. Some works begin in the middle of the action, or *in medias res.* In this situation, background details are filled in through flashbacks. See *flashback.*

actor An **actor** is one who performs the role of a character in a play. The term is now used for both male and female performers.

adage See *aphorism.*

adaptation An **adaptation** is a rewriting of a literary work in another form. Novels, musicals, and plays are often adapted for film. Italian director Franco Zeffirelli directed an award-winning screen version of *Romeo and Juliet.* The hit Broadway musical *Cats* was adapted from T. S. Eliot's *Old Possum's Book of Practical Cats.* "Gus: The Theatre Cat" is both a selection in Eliot's book and a number in the musical.

afterword An **afterword** is a statement made at the end of a work, often an analysis, a summary, or a celebration of the preceding work. See *epilogue.*

aim A writer's **aim** is the primary purpose that his or her work is meant to achieve. James Kinneavey describes four major aims in his book *A Theory of Discourse.* These aims are to express oneself (expressive writing), to persuade (persuasive writing), to inform (informative writing), and to create a work of literary art (literary writing).

allegory An **allegory** is a work in which each element *symbolizes,* or represents, something else. The spiritual "Go Down, Moses" is an allegory that tells a story from the Bible. This story of the Hebrew prophet Moses leading the Israelites out of captivity in Egypt can be read as a story about slavery in the United States. The Israelites can be seen as African Americans under slavery.

alliteration **Alliteration** is the repetition of initial consonant sounds. Some writers also use the term to describe repeated initial vowel sounds. Shel Silverstein's poem "Sarah Cynthia Sylvia Stout Would Not Take the Garbage Out" contains several examples of alliteration, including the repetition of the *s* sound in *Sarah, Cynthia, Sylvia,* and *Stout.* In the following passage from this poem, notice the repetition of the *p* sound in *prune, pits, peach,* and *peel;* the repetition of the *g* sound in *gloppy* and *glumps;* and the repetition of the *b* sound in *black, burned, buttered, bits,* and *beefy.*

> **P**rune **p**its, **p**each **p**its, orange **p**eel,
> **G**loppy **g**lumps of cold oatmeal,
> Pizza crusts and withered greens
> Soggy beans and tangerines,
> Crusts of **b**lack **b**urned **b**uttered toast,
> Gristly **b**its of **b**eefy roasts . . .

allusion   An **allusion** is a rhetorical technique in which reference is made to a person, event, object, or work from history or literature. In "I Am a Black Woman," Mari Evans makes historical allusions to World War II, the Vietnam War, and the Korean War. The selection "A Smart Cookie" by Sandra Cisneros features an allusion to the opera *Madame Butterfly.*

ambiguity   An **ambiguity** is a statement that has a double meaning or a meaning that cannot be clearly resolved. Many literary *figures of speech,* including *metaphors, similes, personifications,* and *symbols,* are examples of intentional ambiguity.

analogy   An **analogy** is a comparison of two things that are alike in some respects but different in others. A *simile* is a type of analogy. See *simile.*

anapest   An **anapest** is a poetic foot containing two weakly stressed syllables followed by one strongly stressed syllable, as in the words *unimpressed* and *correlate.* A line of poetry made up of anapests is said to be *anapestic.*

anecdote   An **anecdote** is a brief story, usually with a specific point or moral.

antagonist   See *character.*

antihero   An **antihero** is a central character who lacks all the qualities traditionally associated with heroes. An antihero may be lacking in beauty, courage, grace, intelligence, or moral scruples. Antiheroes are common figures in modern fiction and drama. Walter Mitty, from "The Secret Life of Walter Mitty," is a well-known antihero.

aphorism   An **aphorism** is a short saying or pointed statement. "Do not trust flatterers " is an aphorism that appears at the end of Æsop's "The Fox and the Crow." An aphorism that is passed from generation to generation, such as "A stitch in time saves nine," is called a *proverb* or *adage.*

apostrophe   **Apostrophe** is a rhetorical technique in which someone or something is directly addressed. "Boast Not, Proud English" by Roger Williams is an example of apostrophe. In the poem the speaker addresses the English colonists.

apposition   An **apposition** is a grammatical form in which a thing is renamed, in different words, in a word, phrase, or clause. The following example of apposition appears in Edgar Allan Poe's "The Bells":

> Hear the mellow wedding bells,
> Golden bells!

archaic language   **Archaic language** consists of old or obsolete words or phrases such as the following words from William Shakespeare's *The Tragedy of Romeo and Juliet*: *fortnight* for *fourteen nights,* and *strooken* for *struck.*

argument   In nonfiction writing, an **argument** is the case for accepting or rejecting a proposition or course of action.

argumentation   **Argumentation,** one of the modes of writing, presents reasons or arguments for accepting a position or for adopting a course of action. See *mode.*

article   An **article** is a brief work of nonfiction on a specific topic. The term *article* is typically used for encyclopedia entries and short nonfiction works that appear in newspapers and popular magazines. The term is sometimes used as a synonym of *essay,* though the latter term often connotes a more serious, important, or lasting work. See *essay.*

assonance   **Assonance** is the repetition of vowel sounds in stressed syllables that end with different consonant sounds. An example is the repetition of the long *o* sound in the following line from Edgar Allan Poe's "The Bells":

> From the molten-golden notes

atmosphere   See *mood.*

autobiography   An **autobiography** is the story of a person's life, written by that person. Examples of autobiography include Maya Angelou's *I Know Why the Caged Bird Sings* and William Least Heat-Moon's *Blue Highways: A Journey into America.*

background information   See *flashback, plot,* and *setting.*

ballad   A **ballad** is a simple narrative poem in four-line stanzas, usually meant to be sung and usually rhyming *abcb.* One popular ballad tells the story of John Henry.

> When John Henry was a little baby
> Sitting on his daddy's knee,

He picked up a hammer and a little piece of
    steel
Said, "This hammer's gonna be the death of
    me."

For a different version of the John Henry tale, see
page 39.

bibliography   A **bibliography** is a list of works
on a given subject or of works consulted by an
author. See *List of Works Cited.*

biography   A **biography** is the story of a person's life, told by someone other than that
person. Margaret Truman's "The United States vs.
Susan B. Anthony" is an example of biography.

blank verse   **Blank verse** is unrhymed poetry
written in iambic pentameter. An *iambic
pentameter* line consists of five *feet,* each containing two syllables, the first weakly stressed and the
second strongly stressed. Shakespeare adopted it
as the standard medium for his dramatic works.
The following lines from *Romeo and Juliet* are
examples of blank verse:

But soft, what light through yonder window
    breaks?
It is the east, and Juliet is the sun.
Arise, fair sun, and kill the envious moon,
Who is already sick and pale with grief
That thou, her maid, art far more fair than she.

blend   A **blend**, or **portmanteau**, is a word
created by joining together two previously existing words, such as *smoke* and *fog* for *smog* and
chuckle and *snort* for *chortle.*

broadside   A **broadside** is a form of short,
printed work common in England after the introduction of printing. Broadsides were printed in
columns and on one side only. Many early ballads and short political and religious tracts
survive in the form of broadsides.

cæsura   A **cæsura** is a major pause in a line of
poetry, represented in scansion by the symbol ||,
as in the following line from "Something Told the
Wild Geese" by Rachel Field:

Something told the wild geese || It was
    time to go.

See *scansion* and *meter.*

caricature   In literature, a **caricature** is a piece
of writing that exaggerates certain qualities of a
character in order to satirize or ridicule that character or type. See *satire.*

catastrophe   A **catastrophe** is the conclusion
of a play, particularly of a tragedy, marked by the
fall of the central character. In a catastrophe, the
central conflict of the play is ended, or resolved.
See *plot.*

central conflict   A **central conflict** is the primary
struggle dealt with in the plot of a story or
drama. See *conflict* and *plot.*

character   A **character** is a person (or some-
times an animal) who figures in the action of a
literary work. A *protagonist,* or *main character,* is
the central figure in a literary work. Examples of
protaganists include Rainsford in "The Most
Dangerous Game" by Richard Connell, and Walter
Mitty in "The Secret Life of Walter Mitty" by James
Thurber. An *antagonist* is a character who is pitted
against a protagonist. Antagonists include General
Zaroff in "The Most Dangerous Game" and
Walter Mitty's wife in "The Secret Life of Walter
Mitty." *Major characters* are ones who play significant roles in a work. *Minor characters* are ones
who play lesser roles. A *one-dimensional character,*
flat character, or *caricature* is one who exhibits a
single dominant quality, or *character trait.* A *three-
dimensional, full,* or *rounded character* is one who
exhibits the complexity of traits associated with
actual human beings. A *static character* is one who
does not change during the course of the action.
A *dynamic character* is one who does change. A
stock character is one found again and again in
different literary works.

characterization   **Characterization** is the use of
literary techniques to create a character. Writers use
three major techniques to create characters: direct
description, portrayal of characters' behavior, and
representations of characters' internal states. When
using direct description, the writer, through a
speaker, a narrator, or another character, simply
comments on the character, telling the reader
about such matters as the character's appearance,
habits, dress, background, personality, motivations,
and so on. When using portrayal of a character's
behavior, the writer presents the actions and
speech of the character, allowing the reader to
draw his or her own conclusions from what the
character says or does. When using representations
of internal states, the writer reveals directly the
character's private thoughts and emotions, often
by means of what is known as the *internal monologue.* See *character* and *internal monologue.*

chronological order   **Chronological order** is
the arrangement of details in order of their
occurrence. It is the primary method of organization used in narrative writing. It is also common
in nonfiction writing that describes processes,
events, and cause-and-effect relationships.

classic A **classic** is a work of literature that is widely held to be one of the greatest creations within a given literary tradition. The question of just what works may be considered classics is a much-debated one.

cliché A **cliché** is a tired or hackneyed expression such as *slow as molasses* or *cold as ice.* Most clichés originate as vivid, colorful expressions but soon lose their interest because of overuse. Careful writers and speakers avoid clichés, which are dull and signify lack of originality.

climax The **climax** is the point of highest interest and suspense in a literary work. The term also is sometimes used to describe the *turning point* of the action in a story or play, the point at which the rising action ends and the falling action begins. See *crisis* and *plot.*

closed couplet A **closed couplet** is a pair of rhyming lines that presents a complete statement.

> For never was a story of more woe
> Than this of Juliet and her Romeo.
>
> —Shakespeare, *Romeo and Juliet*

coherence **Coherence** is the logical arrangement and progression of ideas in a speech or piece of writing. Writers achieve coherence by presenting their ideas in a logical sequence and by using transitions to show how their ideas are connected to one another. See *transition.*

coined words **Coined words** are ones that are intentionally created, often from the raw materials provided by already existing words and word parts. Examples of recently coined words include *E-mail, yuppie,* and *flextime.*

colloquialism **Colloquialism** is the use of informal language. The following passage, which appears in *To Kill a Mockingbird* by Harper Lee, contains colloquialisms.

> "How old are you," asked Jem, "four-and-a-half?"
> "**Goin'** on seven."
> "**Shoot** no wonder, then," said Jem, jerking his thumb at me. "**Scout yonder's been readin'** ever since she was born, and she **ain't** even started to school yet. You look **right puny for goin'** on seven."

comedy Originally a literary work with a happy ending, a **comedy** is any lighthearted or humorous work, especially one prepared for the stage or the screen. Comedies typically present less-than-exalted characters who display all-too-human limitations, foibles, faults, and misunderstandings.

The typical progression of the action in a comedy is from initial order to a humorous misunderstanding or confusion and back to order again. Stock elements of comedy include mistaken identities, word play, satire, and exaggerated characters and events. See *tragedy.*

comic relief Writers sometimes insert into a serious work of fiction or drama a humorous scene that is said to provide **comic relief** because it relieves the seriousness or emotional intensity felt by the audience. Paradoxically, a scene introduced for comic relief can sometimes, because of the contrast it provides, increase the perceived intensity or seriousness of the action around it.

complication The **complication** is the part of a plot in which the conflict is developed or built to its high point of intensity. See *plot.*

concrete A **concrete** word or phrase is one that names or describes something that can be directly perceived by one or more of the five senses. *Sunset, rainbow, snake, street,* and *beach* are examples of concrete terms. See *abstract* and *concrete universal.*

concrete poem A **concrete poem** is one printed or written in a shape that suggests its subject matter. This type of poem tries to suggest its theme visually. Below is an example of a one-word concrete poem.

$$j \overset{o}{} y$$

concrete universal A **concrete universal** is a particular object, person, action, or event that provides an instance or example of a general type. For example, in Thurber's "The Secret Life of Walter Mitty," Mitty can be seen as a concrete example of a man living in a fantasy world. Buck in Jack London's *The Call of the Wild* can be seen as a concrete example of the struggle between civilization and nature.

conflict A **conflict** is a struggle between two forces in a literary work. A *plot* involves the introduction, development, and eventual resolution of a conflict. One side of the *central conflict* in a story or drama is usually taken by the *main character.* That character may struggle against another character, against the forces of nature, against society or social norms, against fate, or against some element within himself or herself. A struggle that takes place between a character and some outside force is called an *external conflict.* A struggle that takes place within a character is called an *internal conflict.* Geraldine in Toni Cade Bambara's "Geraldine Moore the Poet" experiences both external conflict and internal conflict. She experiences external conflicts with her mother's illness and her family's financial troubles. Her internal conflict centers around feelings of pessimism and her lack of self-confidence.

connotation   A **connotation** is an emotional association or implication attached to an expression. For example, the word *unique* has positive emotional associations, whereas the word *strange* has negative ones, even though the two words both *denote*, or refer to, something highly unusual or extraordinary. Good writers choose their words carefully in order to express appropriate connotations. See *denotation*.

consonance   **Consonance** is the repetition of a consonant sound preceded by a different vowel sound, as in

The garbage rolled down the ha**ll**

from Silverstein's "Sarah Sylvia Cynthia Stout Would Not Take the Garbage Out."

convention   A **convention** is an unrealistic element in a literary work that is accepted by readers or viewers because the element is traditional. One of the conventions of fiction, for example, is that it uses the past tense to describe current or present action. Rhyme schemes and organization into stanzas are among the many commonly employed conventions of poetry. Violation of accepted conventions is one of the hallmarks of *avant garde* or *Modernist* literature. See *dramatic convention*.

conventional symbol   See *symbol*.

couplet   A **couplet** is a pair of rhyming lines that expresses a complete thought. These lines from Shakespeare's *Romeo and Juliet* provide an example:

But passion lends them power, time means,
   to meet,
Temp'ring extremities with extreme sweet.

A pair of rhyming iambic pentameter lines is called a *heroic couplet*.

crisis   In the plot of a story or a drama, the **crisis** is that point in the development of the conflict at which a decisive event occurs that causes the main character's situation to become better or worse. See *plot*.

critic   A literary **critic** is a person who evaluates or interprets a work of literature. See *criticism*.

critical essay   A **critical essay** is a type of informative or persuasive writing that presents an argument in support of a particular interpretation or evaluation of a work of literature. A well-constructed critical essay presents a clear *thesis*, or main idea, supported by ample evidence from the work or works being considered.

criticism   **Criticism** is the act of evaluating or interpreting a work of art or the act of developing general guidelines or principles for such evaluation or interpretation. Over the centuries, many schools, or philosophies, of criticism have been developed. However, most readers and teachers are eclectic critics, drawing consciously or unconsciously upon various schools of critical thought.

dactyl   A **dactyl** is a poetic foot made up of a strongly stressed syllable followed by two weakly stressed syllables, as in the word *feverish*. A line of poetry made up of dactyls is said to be *dactylic*.

dead metaphor   A **dead metaphor** is one that is so familiar that its original metaphorical meaning is rarely thought of when the expression is used. An example would be the word *nightfall*, which describes the coming of darkness as a falling object.

definition   A **definition** is an explanation of the meaning of a word or phrase. A dictionary definition typically consists of two parts: the *genus*, or class to which the thing belongs, and the *differentia*, or differences between the thing and other things of its class.

denotation   The **denotation** is the basic meaning or reference of an expression, excluding its emotional associations, or *connotations*. See *connotation*.

dénouement   See *plot*.

description   A **description**, one of the modes of writing, portrays a character, an object, or a scene. Descriptions make use of *sensory details*—words and phrases that describe how things look, sound, touch, taste, or feel. See *mode*.

dialect   A **dialect** is a version of a language spoken by the people of a particular place, time, or social group. Writers often use dialect, as in London's *The Call of the Wild* or Lee's *To Kill a Mockingbird*, to give their works a realistic flavor. A *regional dialect* is one spoken in a particular place. A *social dialect* is one spoken by members of a particular social group or class.

dialogue   **Dialogue** is conversation involving two or more people or characters. Plays are made up of dialogue and stage directions. Fictional works are made up of dialogue, narration, and description.

diary   A **diary** is a day-to-day record of a person's activities, experiences, thoughts, and feelings. See *journal.*

diction   **Diction,** when applied to writing, refers to word choice. Much of a writer's *style* is determined by his or her diction, the types of words that he or she chooses. Diction can be formal or informal, simple or complex, contemporary or archaic, ordinary or unusual, foreign or native, standard or dialectical, euphemistic or blunt. See *style.*

dimeter   See *meter.*

dominant impression   See *effect.*

drama   A **drama** is a story told through characters played by actors. The script of a drama typically consists of characters' names, *dialogue* spoken by the characters, and *stage directions.* Because it is meant to be performed before an audience, drama can be distinguished from other, nonperformance-based forms of literary works by the central role played in it by the *spectacle*—the sensory presentation to the audience, which includes such elements as lighting, costumes, makeup, properties, set pieces, music, sound effects, and the movements and expressions of actors. Another important distinguishing feature of drama is that it is *collaborative.* The interpretation of the work depends not only upon the author and his or her audience but also upon the director, the actors, and others involved in mounting a production.

dramatic convention   A **dramatic convention** is an unreal element in a drama that is accepted as realistic by the audience because it is traditional. Such conventions include the impersonation of characters by actors, the use of a curtain to open or close an act or a scene, the revelation of a character's thoughts through *asides* and *soliloquies,* and the removal of the so-called *fourth wall* at the front of the stage that allows the audience to see action taking place in an imagined interior. See *convention* and *suspension of disbelief.*

dramatic irony   See *irony.*

dream record   A **dream record** is a *diary* or *journal* in which a writer records his or her dreams. See *diary* and *journal.*

editorial   An **editorial** is a short persuasive piece that appears in a newspaper, magazine, or other periodical.

effect   The **effect** of a literary work is the general impression or emotional impact that it

achieves. Some writers and critics, notably Edgar Allan Poe, have insisted that a successful short story or poem is one in which each detail contributes to the overall effect, or *dominant impression,* produced by the piece.

elaboration   **Elaboration,** or **amplification,** is a writing technique in which a subject is introduced and then expanded upon by means of repetition with slight changes, the addition of details, or similar devices.

emphasis   **Emphasis** is importance placed on an element in a literary work. Writers achieve emphasis by various means, including repetition, elaboration, stress, restate- ment in other words, and placement in a strategic position at the beginning or end of a line or a sentence.

end rhyme   **End rhyme** is rhyme that occurs at the ends of lines of verse, as in Theodore Roethke's "The Bat."

> By day the bat is cousin to the **mouse.**
> He likes the attic of an aging **house.**

See *rhyme.*

epic   An **epic** is a long story, often told in verse, involving heroes and gods. Grand in length and scope, an epic provides a portrait of an entire culture, of the legends, beliefs, values, laws, arts, and ways of life of a people. Famous epic poems include Homer's *The Odyssey.*

epigram   An **epigram** is a short, often witty, saying. Alexander Pope's "To err is human, to forgive divine" is an example.

epigraph   An **epigraph** is a quotation or motto used at the beginning of the whole or part of a literary work to help establish the work's theme. An epigraph can be found before Esmeralda Santiago's "Prologue: How to Eat a Guava," from *When I Was Puerto Rican.*

epilogue   An **epilogue** is a concluding section or statement, often one that comments on or draws conclusions from the work as a whole.

episode   An **episode** is a complete action within a literary work.

epithet   An **epithet** is a word or phrase used to describe a characteristic of a person, place, or thing. In Homer's *The Odyssey,* the description of dawn as "rosy-fingered" is an epithet.

eponym   An **eponym** is a person or character from whose name a word or title is derived, or a name that has become synonymous with some general characteristic or idea. The mythological character Narcissus is the eponym of the word *narcissism*, which means extreme preoccupation with one's own appearance and importance.

essay An **essay** is a brief work of prose nonfiction. The original meaning of *essay* was "a trial or attempt," and the word retains some of this original force. An essay need not be a complete or exhaustive treatment of a subject but rather a tentative exploration of it. A good essay develops a single idea and is characterized by *unity* and *coherence*. See *coherence* and *unity*.

euphemism A **euphemism** is an indirect word or phrase used in place of a direct statement that might be considered offensive. The phrase *pass away*, used instead of *die*, and the phrase *waste managment*, used in place of *garbage collection*, are euphemisms.

euphony **Euphony** is pleasing sound. Writers achieve euphony by various means, including repetitions of vowel and consonant sounds, rhyme, and parallelism.

exposition **1. Exposition**, one of the modes of writing, presents factual information. See *mode*. **2.** In a plot, the **exposition** is that part of a narrative that provides background information, often about the characters, setting, or conflict. See *plot*.

extended metaphor An **extended metaphor** is a point-by-point presentation of one thing as though it were another. The description is meant as an implied comparison, inviting the reader to associate the thing being described with something that is quite different from it. Eve Merriam's poem "Metaphor" is an example of extended metaphor. In this poem, morning is described as being a blank sheet of paper. Each day's activities, thoughts, and feelings are words on the paper.

external conflict See *conflict*.

eye rhyme See *sight rhyme*.

fable A **fable** is a brief story with animal characters told to express a moral. The fables of Æsop, including "The Fox and the Crow," are famous examples.

fairy tale A **fairy tale** is a story that deals with mischievous spirits and other supernatural occurrences, often in medieval settings. The name is generally applied to stories of the kinds collected by Charles Perrault in France and the Brothers Grimm in Germany or told by Hans Christian Andersen of Denmark. "Cinderella," "The White Snake," and "The Ugly Duckling" are famous fairy tales.

falling action See *plot*.

fantasy A **fantasy** is a literary work that contains highly unrealistic elements. Ursula Le Guin's "Gwilan's Harp" and Stephen Vincent Benét's "Nightmare Number Three" both contain elements of fantasy. Fantasy is often contrasted with *science fiction*, in which the unreal elements are given a scientific or pseudoscientific basis. See *science fiction*.

fiction **Fiction** is prose writing about imagined events or characters. The primary forms of fiction are the *novel* and the *short story*.

figurative language **Figurative language** is language that suggests something more than the literal meanings of the words might be taken to suggest. See *figures of speech*.

figures of speech **Figures of speech**, or **tropes**, are expressions that have more than a literal meaning. Hyperbole, metaphor, personification, simile, and understatement are all figures of speech. See *hyperbole, metaphor, personification, simile,* and *understatement*.

first-person point of view See *point of view*.

flashback A **flashback** is a section of a literary work that presents an event or series of events that occurred earlier than the current time in the work. Writers use flashbacks for many purposes, but most notably to provide *background information*, or exposition. In popular melodramatic works, including modern romance fiction and detective stories, flashbacks are often used to end suspense by revealing key elements of the plot such as a character's true identity or the actual perpetrator of a crime. One common technique is to begin a work with a final event and then to tell the rest of the story as a flashback that explains how that event came about. Another common technique is to begin a story *in medias res* (in the middle of the action) and then to use a flashback to fill in the events that occurred before the opening of the story.

flash fiction See *short short*.

flat character See *character*.

foil A **foil** is a character whose attributes, or characteristics, contrast with and therefore throw into relief the attributes of another character. Walter Mitty and his wife are foils for one another in Thurber's "The Secret Life of Walter Mitty." The loud, overbearing personality of the wife is meant to be in contrast with Walter's meek personality.

folk ballad   See *ballad.*

folklore   **Folklore** is a body of orally transmitted beliefs, customs, rituals, traditions, songs, verses, or stories. Folk tales, fables, fairy tales, tall tales, nursery rhymes, proverbs, legends, myths, parables, riddles, charms, spells, and ballads are all common kinds of folklore, though each of these can be found, as well, in literary forms made in imitation of works from the *oral tradition.*

folk song   A **folk song** is an anonymous song that is transmitted orally. Examples include the ballad "John Henry," the sea chantey "Blow the Man Down," the children's song "Row, Row, Row Your Boat," the spiritual "Go Down, Moses," the railroad song "Casey Jones," and the cowboy song "The Streets of Laredo." The term *folk song* is sometimes used for works composed in imitation of true folk songs. Modern composers of songs in the folk tradition include Bob Dylan; Livingston Taylor; Peter, Paul, and Mary; and the Indigo Girls. See *ballad.*

folk tale   A **folk tale** is a brief story passed by word-of-mouth from generation to generation. Writers often make use of materials from folk tales. Famous collections of folk tales include the German *Märchen,* or fairy tales, collected by the Brothers Grimm; and Zora Neale Hurston's collections of African-American folk tales and other folklore materials, *Mules and Men* and *Tell My Horse.* See *fairy tale, folklore,* and *oral tradition.*

foot   In a poem, a **foot** is a unit of rhythm consisting of strongly and weakly stressed syllables. See *meter* and *scansion.* Also see the specific types of feet: *anapest, dactyl, iamb, spondee,* and *trochee.*

foreshadowing   **Foreshadowing** is the act of presenting materials that hint at events to occur later in a story.

foreword   See *preface.*

free verse   **Free verse,** or *vers libre,* is poetry that avoids use of regular rhyme, rhythm, meter, or division into stanzas. Much of the English and American poetry written in the twentieth century is in free verse.

full character   See *character.*

genre   A **genre** (zhän´rə) is one of the types or categories into which literary works are divided. Some terms used to name literary genres include *autobiography, biography, comedy, drama, epic, essay, lyric, narrative, novel, poetry, short story,* and *tragedy.* Literary works are sometimes classified into genres based on subject matter. Such a classification might describe *detective stories, mysteries, adventure stories, romances, westerns,* and *science fiction* as different genres of fiction.

haiku   A **haiku** is a traditional Japanese three-line poem containing five syllables in the first line, seven in the second, and five again in the third. A haiku presents a picture, or image, in order to arouse in the reader a specific emotional and/or spiritual state.

half rhyme   See *slant rhyme.*

heptameter   See *meter.*

heroic couplet   See *couplet.*

heroic epic   A **heroic epic** is an epic that has a main purpose of telling the life story of a great hero. Examples of the heroic epic include Homer's *The Iliad* and *The Odyssey.* See *epic.*

hexameter   See *meter.*

high style   See *style.*

hymn   A **hymn** is a song or verse of praise, often religious.

hyperbole   A **hyperbole** (hī pʉr´bə lē) is an exaggeration made for rhetorical effect. Ernest Lawrence Thayer uses hyperbole in "Casey at the Bat" when he writes

> Then from 5,000 throats or more
>   there rose a lusty yell;
>
> It rumbled through the valley,
>   it rattled in the dell;
>
> It knocked upon the mountain
>   and recoiled upon the flat.

iamb   An **iamb** is a poetic foot containing one weakly stressed syllable followed by one strongly stressed syllable, as in the words *afraid* and *release.* A line of poetry made up of iambs is said to be *iambic.*

iambic   See *iamb.*

image   An **image** is a word or phrase that names something that can be seen, heard, touched, tasted, or smelled. The images in a literary work are referred to, collectively, as the work's *imagery.*

imagery   See *image.*

inciting incident   See *plot.*

in medias res   See *action* and *flashback.*

internal conflict   See *conflict.*

internal monologue   An **internal monologue** presents the private sensations, thoughts, and emotions of a character. The reader is allowed to step inside the character's mind and overhear what is going on in there. Which characters' internal states can be revealed in a work of fiction depends on the point of view from which the work is told. See *point of view.*

introduction   See *preface.*

inversion   An **inversion** is a poetic technique in which the normal order of words in an utterance is altered. Robert Frost's "Whose woods these are, I think I know" is an inversion of the usual order of expression: "I think I know whose woods these are." See *syntax.*

irony   **Irony** is a difference between appearance and reality. Types of irony include the following: *dramatic irony,* in which something is known by the reader or audience but unknown to the characters; *verbal irony,* in which a statement is made that implies its opposite; and *irony of situation,* in which an event occurs that violates the expectations of the characters, the reader, or the audience. O. Henry's "The Gift of the Magi" is a classic example of irony of situation. See *paradox.*

irony of situation   See *irony.*

journal   A **journal,** like a *diary,* is a day-to-day record of a person's activities, experiences, thoughts, and feelings. In contrast to *diary,* the word *journal* connotes an outward rather than an inward focus. However, the two terms are often used interchangeably. See *diary.*

limited point of view   See *narrator* and *point of view.*

List of Works Cited   A **List of Works Cited** is a type of bibliography that lists works used or referred to by an author. A standard feature of a research paper, the List of Works Cited appears at the end of the paper and is arranged in alphabetical order.

low style   See *style.*

lyric poem   A **lyric poem** is a highly musical verse that expresses the emotions of a speaker. Edgar Allen Poe's "The Bells" and Emily Dickinson's "I'm Nobody! Who are you?" are examples of lyric poetry. Lyric poems are often contrasted with narrative poems, which have telling a story as their main purpose.

Magical Realism   **Magical Realism** is a kind of fiction that is for the most part realistic but that contains elements of fantasy. W. W. Jacobs's "The Monkey's Paw" is an example of Magical Realism.

main character   See *character.*

major character   See *character.*

metaphor   A **metaphor** is a figure of speech in which one thing is spoken or written about as if it were another. This figure of speech invites the reader to make a comparison between the two things. The two "things" involved are the writer's actual subject, the *tenor* of the metaphor, and another thing to which the subject is likened, the *vehicle* of the metaphor.

Personifications and similes are types of metaphor. See *dead metaphor, mixed metaphor, personification,* and *simile.*

meter   The **meter** of a poem is its rhythmical pattern. English verse is generally described as being made up of rhythmical units called *feet,* as follows:

TYPE OF FOOT	STRESS PATTERN	EXAMPLE
iambic	⌣ /	insist
trochaic	/ ⌣	freedom
anapestic	⌣ ⌣ /	unimpressed
dactylic	/ ⌣ ⌣	feverish
spondaic	/ /	baseball

Terms used to describe the number of feet in a line include the following:

monometer for a one-foot line

dimeter for a two-foot line

trimeter for a three-foot line

tetrameter for a four-foot line

pentameter for a five-foot line

hexameter, or *Alexandrine,* for a six-foot line

heptameter for a seven-foot line

octameter for an eight-foot line

A seven-foot line of iambic feet is called a *fourteener.*

A complete description of the meter of a line includes both the term for the type of foot that predominates in the line and the term for the number of feet in the line. The most common English meters are iambic tetrameter and iambic pentameter. The following are examples of each:

IAMBIC TETRAMETER:

⌣ / ⌣ / ⌣ / ⌣ /
O slow | ly, slow | ly rose | she up

IAMBIC PENTAMETER:

⏑ / ⏑ / ⏑ / ⏑ /
The cur | few tolls | the knell | of part |

⏑ /
ing day,

middle style   See *style*.

minor character   See *character*.

mixed metaphor   A **mixed metaphor** is an expression or passage that conflates, or garbles together, two or more metaphors. An example of mixed metaphor would be the sentence "The chariot of the sun screamed across the sky," in which the sun is described, inconsistently, as both a chariot and as something that screams. See *metaphor*.

mode   A **mode** is a form of writing. One common classification system, based on content, divides types of writing into four modes: argumentation, description, exposition, and narration. See *argumentation, description, exposition,* and *narration*.

monometer   See *meter*.

mood   **Mood**, or **atmosphere**, is the emotion created in the reader by part or all of a literary work. A writer creates a mood through judicious use of concrete details.

motif   A **motif** is any element that recurs in one or more works of literature or art. Examples of common folk tale motifs found in oral traditions throughout the world include grateful animals or the grateful dead, three wishes, the trial or quest, and the magical metamorphosis, or transformation of one thing into another. "Cinderella," "The Ugly Duckling," and the Arthurian "Sword in the Stone" are examples of the transformation motif of the person or creature of humble station who is revealed to be exceptional. Much can be revealed about a literary work by studying the motifs within it.

motivation   A **motivation** is a force that moves a character to think, feel, or behave in a certain way.

Muse   In ancient Greek and Roman myth, the **Muses**—the nine daughters of Zeus and Mnemosyne, or Memory—were believed to provide the inspiration for the arts and sciences. Calliope was the Muse of epic poetry; Clio, the Muse of history; Erato, the Muse of lyrical poetry; Euterpe, the Muse of music; Melpomene, the Muse of tragedy; Polyhymnia, the Muse of sacred choral poetry; Terpischore, the Muse of choral dance and song; Thalia, the Muse of comedy; and Urania, the Muse of astronomy.

The idea of the Muse has often been used by later writers to explain the vagaries and mysteries of literary inspiration. The connection of the Muses with entertainments and the arts survives in our English words *amusing* and *amusement*.

myth   A **myth** is a story that explains objects or events in the natural world as resulting from the action of some supernatural force or entity, most often a god. Every early culture around the globe has produced its own myths. A typical example is the Greek myth of the origin of the Narcissus flower. Narcissus was a vain boy who liked to look at his own reflection in pools of water. The punishment for his vanity was to be turned into a flower that grows near water. There he can look at his own reflection for as long as the world lasts. Literature in English often alludes to or makes use of materials from Greek, Roman, Germanic, and Celtic myths.

narration   **Narration**, one of the modes of writing, tells a story. The story is made up of occurrences, or events. See *mode*.

narrative poem   A **narrative poem** is a verse that tells a story. Henry Wadsworth Longfellow's "Paul Revere's Ride" is an example of a narrative poem. See *ballad* and *epic*.

narrator   A **narrator** is one who tells a story. In a drama, the narrator may be a character who introduces, concludes, or comments upon the action of the play. However, dramas typically do not have narrators. Works of fiction, on the other hand, always do, unless they consist entirely of dialogue without *tag lines,* in which case they become no longer fictions but *closet dramas,* ones meant to be read but not performed. The narrator in a work of fiction may be a central or minor character or simply someone who witnessed or heard about the events being related. Writers achieve a wide variety of ends by varying the characteristics of the narrator chosen for a particular work. Of primary importance is the choice of the narrator's *point of view*. Will the narrator be *omniscient,* knowing all things, including the internal workings of the minds of the characters in the story, or will the narrator be *limited* in his or her knowledge? Will the narrator participate in the action of the story or stand outside that action and comment on it? Will the narrator be reliable or unreliable? That is, will the reader be able to trust the narrator's statements? These are all questions that a writer must answer when developing a narrator. See *point of view* and *speaker*.

Naturalism **Naturalism** was a literary movement of the late nineteenth and early twentieth centuries that saw actions and events as resulting inevitably from biological or natural forces or from forces in the environment. Often these forces were beyond the comprehension or control of the characters subjected to them. Taken to its extreme, Naturalism views all events as mechanically determined by external forces, including decisions made by people. Much of modern fiction, with its emphasis on social conditions leading to particular consequences is Naturalistic in this sense. Jack London was one of many authors informed by the philosophy of Naturalism.

near rhyme See *slant rhyme.*

nonfiction Nonfiction is writing about real events. Essays, autobiographies, biographies, and news stories are all types of nonfiction. See *prose.*

nonsense verse A **nonsense verse** is a kind of light verse that contains elements that are silly, absurd, or meaningless.

> And there in a wood a Piggy-wig stood,
> With a ring at the end of his nose,
>> His nose,
>> His nose,
> With a ring at the end of his nose.
>
> —Edward Lear, from "The Owl and the Pussy-Cat"

novel A **novel** is a long work of prose fiction. Often novels have involved plots; many characters, both major and minor; and numerous settings. Examples of novels include *The Call of the Wild, To Kill a Mockingbird,* and *A House on Mango Street.*

novella A **novella** is a short novel. *The Snow Goose* is a novella. See *novel.*

nursery rhyme A **nursery rhyme** is a children's verse. Famous English writers of nursery rhymes include Rudyard Kipling and Edward Lear.

objective correlative An **objective correlative** is a group of images that together create a particular emotion in the reader. The term was coined by T. S. Eliot. See *image.*

occasional verse An **occasional verse** is one written to celebrate or commemorate some particular event. "Paul Revere's Ride" is an occasional verse.

octameter See *meter.*

octave An **octave** is an eight-line stanza. A Petrarchan sonnet begins with an octave. See *meter* and *sonnet.*

off rhyme See *slant rhyme.*

omniscient point of view See *narrator* and *point of view.*

one-act See *act.*

one-dimensional character See *character.*

onomatopoeia **Onomatopoeia** is the use of words or phrases that sound like the things to which they refer. Examples of onomatopoeia include words such as *buzz, click,* and *pop.* Poe's poem "The Bells" contains onomatopoetic words.

oral tradition An **oral tradition** is a work, a motif, an idea, or a custom that is passed by word-of-mouth from generation to generation. Materials transmitted orally may be simplified in the retelling. They also may be sensationalized because of the tendency of retellers to add to or elaborate upon the materials that come down to them. Often, works in an oral tradition contain miraculous or magical elements. Common works found in the oral traditions of peoples around the world include *folk tales, fables, fairy tales, tall tales, nursery rhymes, proverbs, legends, myths, parables, riddles, charms, spells,* and *ballads.* See *folklore.*

oxymoron An **oxymoron** is a statement that contradicts itself. Words like *bittersweet, tragicomedy,* and *pianoforte* (literally, "soft-loud") are oxymorons that develop a complex meaning from two seemingly contradictory elements.

palindrome A **palindrome** is a word, a phrase, or a sentence that reads the same backward as forward. Examples include the word *radar* and the sentence *Able was I ere I saw Elba,* which describes Napoleon's condition prior to his exile to the island of Elba.

parable A **parable** is a very brief story told to teach a moral lesson. The most famous parables are those such as "The Parable of the Prodigal Son" told by Jesus in the Bible.

paradox A **paradox** is a seemingly contradictory statement, idea, or event. All forms of *irony* involve paradox. An *oxymoron* is a paradoxical statement. See *irony* and *oxymoron.*

parallelism **Parallelism** is a rhetorical technique in which a writer emphasizes the equal value or weight of two or more ideas by expressing them in the same grammatical form. James Weldon

Johnson uses parallelism in these lines from "The Creation":

> Who lit the sun and fixed it in the sky,
> Who flung the stars to the most far corner
>   of the night,
> Who rounded the earth in the middle of his
>   hand.

paraphrase   A **paraphrase** is a rewriting of a passage in different words. A paraphrase is often distinguished from an *abstract* or *summary* as follows: a summary is shorter than the original, whereas a paraphrase may be as long as or longer than the original. One of the central ideas of the so-called New Criticism was that it is impossible to paraphrase a literary work precisely. Much of the content or meaning of a literary work lies in how it is expressed. Changing the expression therefore inevitably changes the meaning. See *abstract.*

parody   A **parody** is a literary work that imitates another work for humorous, often satirical, purposes.

pentameter   See *meter.*

periodical   A **periodical** is a newspaper, magazine, journal, newsletter, or other publication that is produced on a regular basis.

personal essay   A **personal essay** is a short work of nonfictional prose on a single topic related to the life or interests of the writer. Personal essays are characterized by an intimate and informal style and tone. They often, but not always, are written in the first person. See *essay.*

personal symbol   See *symbol.*

personification   **Personification** is a figure of speech in which an idea, animal, or thing is described as if it were a person.

plagiarism   **Plagiarism** is the act of using material gathered from another person or work without crediting the source of the material.

plot   A **plot** is a series of events related to a central *conflict,* or struggle. A typical plot involves the introduction of a conflict, its development, and its eventual resolution. Terms used to describe elements of plot include the following:

- The **exposition,** or **introduction,** sets the tone or mood, introduces the characters and the setting, and provides necessary background information.

- The **inciting incident** is the event that introduces the central conflict.

- The **rising action,** or **complication,** develops the conflict to a high point of intensity.

- The **climax** is the high point of interest or suspense in the plot.

- The **crisis,** or **turning point,** often the same event as the climax, is the point in the plot where something decisive happens to determine the future course of events and the eventual working out of the conflict.

- The **falling action** is all of the events that follow the climax.

- The **resolution** is the point at which the central conflict is ended, or resolved.

- The **dénouement** is any material that follows the resolution and that ties up loose ends.

- The **catastrophe,** in tragedy, is the event that marks the ultimate tragic fall of the central character. Often this event is the character's death.

Plots rarely contain all these elements in precisely this order. Elements of exposition may be introduced at any time in the course of a work. A work may begin with a catastrophe and then use flashback to explain it. The exposition or dénouement or even the resolution may be missing. The inciting incident may occur before the beginning of the action actually described in the work. These are but a few of the many possible variations that plots can exhibit. See *conflict.*

poetic license   **Poetic license** is the right claimed by writers to change elements of reality to suit the purposes of particular works that they create. In Don Marquis's "the lesson of the moth" the speaking moth and cockroach are examples of poetic license. Such things do not happen in reality, but they are accepted by readers willing to suspend disbelief in order to have imaginary experiences. See *suspension of disbelief.*

point of view   **Point of view** is the vantage point from which a story is told. Stories are typically written from a *first-person point of view,* in which the narrator uses words such as *I* and *we,* or from a *third-person point of view,* in which the narrator uses words such as *he, she, it,* and *they* and avoids the use of *I* and *we.* In stories written from a first-person point of view, the narrator may be a participant or witness of the action. In stories told from a third-person point of view, the narrator generally stands outside the action. In some stories, the narrator's point of view is *limited.* In such stories, the narrator can reveal the private, internal thoughts of himself or herself or of a single character. In other stories, the narrator's point of view is *omniscient,* or all-encompassing. In such stories the narrator can reveal the private, internal thoughts of any character.

portmanteau   See *blend.*

précis   See *abstract.*

preface   A **preface** is a statement made at the beginning of a literary work, often by way of introduction. The terms *foreword*, *preface*, and *introduction* are often used interchangeably.

proscenium stage   See *stage.*

prose   **Prose** is the broad term used to describe all writing that is not drama or poetry, including fiction and nonfiction. Types of prose writing include novels, short stories, essays, and news stories. Most biographies, autobiographies, and letters are written in prose. See *fiction* and *nonfiction.*

prose poem   A **prose poem** is a work of prose, usually a short work, that makes such extensive use of poetic language, such as figures of speech and words that echo their sense, that the line between prose and poetry, never a clear one, becomes blurred. An example of a prose poem is Max Ehrmann's "Desiderata."

protagonist   See *character.*

proverb   See *aphorism.*

pseudonym   A **pseudonym** is a name assumed by a writer. Mark Twain is the pseudonym of Samuel Langhorne Clemens.

psychological fiction   **Psychological fiction** is fiction that emphasizes the interior, subjective experiences of its characters, and especially fiction that deals with emotional or mental disturbance or anguish.

pun   A **pun** is a play on words, one that wittily exploits a double meaning. In act III of Shakespeare's *Romeo and Juliet,* Mercutio's line, "Ask for me tomorrow, and you shall find me a grave man" is a pun. The word *grave*, in this context, means "having serious thoughts." However, he is also hinting that he might be dead and in a *grave* tomorrow.

purpose   See *aim.*

pyrrhic   See *meter.*

quatrain   A **quatrain** is a stanza containing four lines.

quintain   A **quintain**, or **quintet**, is a stanza containing five lines.

quintet   See *quintain.*

rap   A **rap** is an improvised rhymed verse that is chanted or sung, often to a musical accompaniment.

Realism   **Realism** is the attempt to render in art an accurate portrayal of reality. The theory that the purpose of art is to imitate life is at least as old as Aristotle. The eighteenth-century development of the novel, with its attention to details of character, setting, and social life, can be thought of as a step toward increased Realism in writing. However, the term *Realism* is generally applied to literature of the late nineteenth century written in reaction to Romanticism and emphasizing details of ordinary life.

redundancy   **Redundancy** is needless repetition. The phrase *firmly determined* is redundant because the word *determined* already implies firmness.

refrain   A **refrain** is a line or group of lines repeated in a poem or song. Many ballads contain refrains.

regional dialect   See *dialect.*

repetition   **Repetition** is the use, again, of a sound, word, phrase, sentence, or other element. In his "I Have a Dream" speech Martin Luther King, Jr., repeats the phrase "I have a dream."

resolution   See *plot.*

reversal   A **reversal** is a dramatic change in the direction of events in a drama or narrative, especially a change in the fortunes of the protagonist. See *plot.*

review   A **review** is a written evaluation of a work of art, a performance, or a literary work, especially one that appears in a periodical or on a broadcast news program. Common subjects of reviews include books, films, art exhibitions, restaurants, and performances of all kinds, from rock concerts to ballets.

rhetoric   **Rhetoric** is the study of ways in which speech and writing affect or influence audiences.

rhetorical question   A **rhetorical question** is one asked for effect but not meant to be answered because the answer is clear from context, as in Dickinson's lines, "I'm Nobody! Who are you?/Are you—Nobody—too?"

rhetorical technique   A **rhetorical technique** is an extraordinary but literal use of language to achieve a particular effect on an audience.

Common rhetorical techniques include *apostrophe, parallelism, repetition,* and the *rhetorical question.*

rhyme   **Rhyme** is the repetition of sounds at the ends of words. Types of rhyme include *end rhyme* (the use of rhyming words at the ends of lines), *internal rhyme* (the use of rhyming words within lines), *exact rhyme* (in which the rhyming words end with the same sound or sounds), and *slant rhyme* (in which the rhyming sounds are similar but not identical). An example of exact rhyme is the word pair *moon/June.* Examples of slant rhyme are the word pairs *rave/rove* and *rot/rock.* See *slant rhyme.*

rhythm   **Rhythm** is the pattern of beats or stresses in a line of verse or prose. See *meter.*

riddle   A **riddle** is a word game in which something is described in an unusual way and the reader or listener must figure out what that something is. Riddles are common in folklore and myth throughout the world.

rising action   See *plot.*

romance   **Romance** is a term used to refer to four types of literature: **1.** medieval stories about the adventures and loves of knights; **2.** novels and other fictions involving exotic locales and extraordinary or mysterious events and characters; **3.** nonrealistic fictions in general; and **4.** in popular modern usage, love stories of all kinds.

rounded character   See *character.*

run-on line   A **run-on line** is a line of verse in which the sense or the grammatical structure does not end with the end of the line but rather is continued on one or more subsequent lines. The following lines from Robert Frost's "Birches" form a single sentence:

> Soon the sun's warmth makes them shed crystal shells
> Shattering and avalanching on the snow crust—
> Such heaps of broken glass to sweep away
> You'd think the inner dome of heaven had fallen.

The act of continuing a statement beyond the end of a line is called *enjambment.*

satire   **Satire** is humorous writing or speech intended to point out errors, falsehoods, foibles, or failings. It is written for the purpose of reforming human behavior or human institutions. Mark Twain's "An Encounter with an Interviewer" is an example of satire.

scansion   **Scansion** is the art of analyzing poetry to determine its meter. See *meter.*

scene   A **scene** is a short section of a literary work that presents action that occurs in a single place or at a single time. Long divisions of dramas are often divided into scenes.

science fiction   **Science fiction** is highly imaginative fiction containing fantastic elements based on scientific principles, dis- coveries, or laws. It is similar to *fantasy* in that it deals with imaginary worlds but differs from fantasy in having a scientific basis. Arthur C. Clarke's short story "History Lesson," which is set on Venus, is an example of science fiction. Often science fiction deals with the future, the distant past, or with worlds other than our own such as distant planets, parallel universes, and worlds under the ground or the sea. The genre allows writers to suspend or alter certain elements of reality in order to create fascinating and sometimes instructive alternatives. Important writers of science fiction include H. G. Wells, Jules Verne, Ray Bradbury, Arthur C. Clarke, Isaac Asimov, Ursula K. Le Guin, Robert Heinlein, and Kurt Vonnegut, Jr. See *fantasy.*

sensory detail   See *description.*

sentimentality   **Sentimentality** is an excessive expression of emotion. Much popular literature of the nineteenth and twentieth centuries is characterized by sentimentality.

septet   A **septet** is a stanza with seven lines.

sestet   A **sestet** is a stanza with six lines, such as the second part of a Petrarchan sonnet. See *meter* and *sonnet.*

set   A **set** is a collection of objects on a stage arranged in such a way as to create a scene.

setting   The **setting** of a literary work is the time and place in which it occurs, together with all the details used to create a sense of a particular time and place. Writers create setting by various means. In drama, the setting is often revealed by the stage *set* and the costumes, though it may be revealed through what the characters say about their surroundings. In fiction, setting is most often revealed by means of description of such elements as landscape, scenery, buildings, furniture, clothing, the weather, and the season. It can also be revealed by how characters talk and behave. In its widest sense, setting includes the general social, political, moral, and psychological conditions in which characters find themselves. See *set.*

shape poem   See *concrete poem.*

short short   A **short short,** or **flash fiction,** is an extremely brief short story. This recently recognized genre of the short story is currently enjoying considerable popularity among readers of literary magazines and short story collections published in the United States. Short shorts sometimes take the form of *anecdotes,* or retellings of single incidents. Alternatively, they may attempt to develop an entire plot within the compass of a few paragraphs. Many short shorts are highly poetic and may be considered prose poems.

sight rhyme   A **sight rhyme,** or **eye rhyme,** is a pair of words, generally at the ends of lines of verse, that are spelled similarly but pronounced differently. These lines from Shakespeare's *Romeo and Juliet* provide an example:

> The fearful passage of their death-mark'd **love,**
> And the continuance of their parent's rage,
> Which, but their children's end, nought could **remove,**

simile   A **simile** is a comparison using *like* or *as.*

> A phantom ship, with each mast and spar
> Across the moon **like** a prison bar,
> —Henry Wadsworth Longfellow, "Paul Revere's Ride"

> His coat's very shabby, he's thin **as** a rake,
> —T. S. Eliot, "Gus: The Theatre Cat"

A simile is a type of *metaphor,* and like any other metaphor, can be analyzed into two parts, the *tenor* (or subject being described), and the *vehicle* (or object being used in the description). In the simile "your smile is like the sun," the tenor is *smile* and the vehicle is *sun.* They can be compared because they share some quality, in this case, warmth and brightness. See *metaphor.*

slang   **Slang** is extremely colloquial speech not suitable for formal occasions and usually associated with a particular group of people. Among young people in the United States, the verb *dis* and the participle *dissing* are sometimes used as slang terms meaning "disrespect," and "disrespecting," as in "Don't *dis* the teacher," or "They are *dissing* the rules." In the 1940s the slang term "cut a rug" was used to mean "to dance," as in "Lets put on some music and cut a rug." Writers sometimes use slang in an attempt to render characters and setting vividly.

slant rhyme   A **slant rhyme, half rhyme, near rhyme,** or **off rhyme** is substitution of assonance or consonance for true rhyme. The pairs *talk/sulk* and *run/ride* are examples. See *assonance, consonance,* and *rhyme.*

social dialect   See *dialect.*

soliloquy   A **soliloquy** is a speech delivered by a lone character that reveals the speaker's thoughts and feelings. In Shakespeare's *Romeo and Juliet,* Juliet's speech, "Farewell! God knows when we shall meet again" (act IV, scene iii), is an example of a soliloquy.

sonnet   A **sonnet** is a fourteen-line poem that follows one of a number of different rhyme schemes. The *English, Elizabethan,* or *Shakespearean sonnet* is divided into four parts: three *quatrains* and a final *couplet.* The rhyme scheme of such a sonnet is *abab cdcd efef gg.* The sonnets that open act I and act II of Shakespeare's *Romeo and Juliet* are examples. The *Italian* or *Petrarchan sonnet* is divided into two parts: an *octave* and a *sestet.* The rhyme scheme of the octave is *abbaabba.* The rhyme scheme of the sestet can be *cdecde, cdcdcd,* or *cdedce.*

source   A **source** is a work, person, or experience from which an author takes his or her materials. For example, the source for John G. Neihardt's book *Black Elk Speaks* is the life of Black Elk, a warrior and medicine man for the Oglala Sioux, Native American people from the Great Plains.

speaker   The **speaker** is the character who speaks in, or narrates, a poem—the voice assumed by the writer. The speaker and the writer of a poem are not necessarily the same person.

spectacle   In drama, the **spectacle** is all the elements that are presented to the senses of the audience, including the lights, setting, costumes, makeup, music, sound effects, and movements of the actors.

spondee   A **spondee** is a poetic foot containing two strongly stressed syllables, as in the words *compound* and *roughhouse.* Such a foot is said to be *spondaic.*

stage   A **stage** is any arena on which the action of a drama is performed. In the Middle Ages, stages often consisted of the beds of wagons, which were wheeled from place to place for performances. From the use of such wagons in innyards, the *thrust stage* developed. This was a platform that extended out into the audience and that was closed at the back. In front of the platform in the first English theaters, such as Shakespeare's Globe Theater, was an open area, the pit, where common people stood. Around the pit were balconies in imitation of the balconies of inns. The modern *proscenium stage* typically is closed on three sides and open at the front, as though the fourth wall had been removed. Sometimes contemporary plays are performed as *theater in the round,* with the audience seated on all sides of the playing area.

stage directions   **Stage directions** are notes included in a play in addition to the dialogue for the purpose of describing how something should be performed on stage. Stage directions describe setting, lighting, music, sound effects, entrances and exits, properties, and the movements of characters. They are usually printed in italics and enclosed in brackets or parentheses.

stanza   A **stanza** is a recurring pattern of grouped lines in a poem. The following are some types of stanza:

two-line stanza	couplet
three-line stanza	tercet or triplet
four-line stanza	quatrain
five-line stanza	quintain
six-line stanza	sestet
seven-line stanza	heptastich
eight-line stanza	octave

static character   See *character.*

stereotype   A **stereotype** is an uncritically accepted fixed or conventional idea, particularly such an idea held about whole groups of people. A *stereotypical,* or *stock,* character is one who does not deviate from conventional expectations of such a character. Examples of stereotypical characters include the merciless villain, the mad scientist, and the hard-boiled private eye. See *character.*

stock character   See *character* and *stereotype.*

story   A **story,** or **narrative,** is writing or speech that relates a series of events. When these events are causally connected and related to a conflict, they make up a *plot.* See *plot.*

stress   **Stress,** or **accent,** is the level of emphasis given to a syllable. In English *metrics,* the art of rhythm in written and spoken expression, syllables are generally described as being *strongly* or *weakly stressed,* in other words, *accented* or *unaccented.* A strongly stressed or accented syllable receives a strong emphasis. A weakly stressed or unaccented syllable receives a weak one. In the following line from Longfellow's "Paul Revere's Ride," the strongly stressed or accented syllables are marked with a slash mark (/).

/   /   /   /
Listen my children, and you shall hear

/   /   /   /
Of the midnight ride of Paul Revere

style   **Style** is the manner in which something is said or written. Traditionally, critics and scholars have referred to three levels of style: *high style,* for formal occasions or lofty subjects; *middle style,* for ordinary occasions or subjects; and *low style,* for extremely informal occasions or subjects. A writer's style depends upon many things, including his or her *diction* (the words that the writer chooses), selection of grammatical structures (simple versus complex sentences, for example), and preference for abstract or concrete words. Any recurring feature that distinguishes one writer's work from another can be said to be part of that writer's style. See *diction.*

subplot   A **subplot** is a subordinate story told in addition to the major story in a work of fiction. Often a subplot mirrors or provides a foil for the primary plot. See *plot* and *story.*

summary   See *abstract.*

suspense   **Suspense** is a feeling of expectation, anxiousness, or curiosity created by questions raised in the mind of a reader or viewer.

suspension of disbelief   **Suspension of disbelief** is the act by which the reader willingly sets aside his or her skepticism in order to participate imaginatively in the work being read. Readers may not believe that animals can talk, but they are willing to suspend that disbelief when reading fairy tales such as "The White Snake" or fables like "The Fox and the Crow." The willingness to suspend disbelief, to participate imaginatively in a story being read, is the most important attribute, beyond literacy, that a person can bring to the act of reading.

symbol   A **symbol** is a thing that stands for or represents both itself and something else. Writers use two types of symbols—conventional and personal, or idiosyncratic. A *conventional symbol* is one with traditional, widely recognized associations. Such symbols include doves for peace; laurel wreaths for heroism or poetic excellence; the color green for jealousy; the color purple for royalty; the color red for anger; morning or spring for youth; winter, evening, or night for old age; wind for change or inspiration; rainbows for hope; roses for beauty; the moon for fickleness or inconstancy; roads or paths for the journey through life; woods or darkness for moral or spiritual confusion; thorns for troubles or pain; stars for unchangeableness or constancy; mirrors for vanity or introspection; snakes for evil or duplicity; and owls for wisdom. A *personal* or *idiosyncratic symbol* is one that assumes its secondary meaning because of the special use to which it is put by a writer. For example, in James Hurst's story "The Scarlet Ibis," the scarlet ibis becomes a symbol of the uniqueness and fragility of the character Doodle.

syntax   **Syntax** is the pattern of arrangement of words in a statement. Poets often vary the syntax of ordinary speech or experiment with unusual syntactic arrangements. See *inversion*.

tag line   A **tag line** is an expression in a work of fiction that indicates who is speaking and sometimes indicates the manner of speaking. Examples include the familiar *he said* as well as more elaborate expressions such as *Gabriella whispered quietly.*

tall tale   A **tall tale** is a story, often light-hearted or humorous, that contains highly exaggerated, unrealistic elements. Stories about Paul Bunyan and John Henry are well-known tall tales.

tenor   See *metaphor.*

tercet   See *triplet.*

tetrameter   See *meter.*

theater (playing area)   See *stage.*

theater in the round   See *stage.*

theme   A **theme** is a central idea in a literary work. The theme of Dickinson's "I'm Nobody! Who are you?" is solitude and privacy.

thesis   A **thesis** is a main idea that is supported in a work of nonfictional prose.

third-person point of view   See *point of view.*

three-dimensional character   See *character.*

thrust stage   See *stage.*

tone   **Tone** is the emotional attitude toward the reader or toward the subject implied by a literary work. Examples of the different tones that a work may have include familiar, ironic, playful, sarcastic, serious, and sincere.

tragedy   A **tragedy** is a drama (or by extension any work of literature) that tells the story of the fall of a person of high status. Tragedy tends to be serious. It celebrates the courage and dignity of a tragic hero in the face of inevitable doom.

Sometimes that doom is made inevitable by a *tragic flaw* in the hero. In the twentieth century, writers have extended the definition of *tragedy* to cover works that deal with the fall of any sympathetic character, despite his or her status.

tragic flaw   A **tragic flaw** is a personal weakness that brings about the fall of a character in a tragedy. In Shakespeare's *Romeo and Juliet,* for example, both Romeo and Juliet suffer from the tragic flaw of impulsiveness. They follow their hearts rather than their heads, and this leads to the play's tragic ending.

transition   A **transition** is a word, phrase, sentence, or paragraph used to connect ideas and to show relationships between them. *However, therefore, in addition,* and *in contrast* are common transitions. Repeated nouns, synonyms, and pronouns can also serve as transitions. For more information on transitions, see the Language Arts Survey, 1.34, "Organizing Ideas"; 1.38, "Paragraphs with Topic Sentences"; and 1.39, "Paragraphs without Topic Sentences." See *coherence.*

translation   **Translation** is the art of rendering speech or writing into another language.

trimeter   See *meter.*

triplet   A **triplet**, or **tercet**, is a stanza of three lines.

trochee   A **trochee** is a poetic foot consisting of a strongly stressed syllable followed by a weakly stressed syllable, as in the word *winter.* A line of poetry made up of trochees is said to be *trochaic.*

turning point   See *plot.*

understatement   An **understatement** is an ironic expression in which something of importance is emphasized by being spoken of as though it were not important, as in the statement "I would say the sailors were slightly nervous during the monsoon."

unity   A work has **unity** when its various parts all contribute to creating an integrated whole. An essay with unity, for example, is one in which all the parts help to support the thesis statement, or main idea. See *essay.*

unreliable narrator   An **unreliable narrator** is one whom the reader cannot trust. See *narrator.*

vehicle   See *metaphor.*

verbal irony   See *irony.*

vers libre   See *free verse.*

Glossary

OF WORDS FOR EVERYDAY USE

PRONUNCIATION KEY

VOWEL SOUNDS

a	hat	i	sit	o͞o	blue, stew	ə	extra
ā	play	ī	my	oi	boy		under
ä	star			ou	wow		civil
		ō	go				honor
e	then	ô	paw, born	u	up		bogus
ē	me	o͝o	book, put	ʉ	burn		

CONSONANT SOUNDS

b	but	j	jump	p	pop	th	the
ch	watch	k	brick	r	rod	v	valley
d	do	l	lip	s	see	w	work
f	fudge	m	money	sh	she	y	yell
g	go	n	on	t	sit	z	pleasure
h	hot	ŋ	song, sink	th	with		

A

ab • hor (ab hôr´) *vt.,* hate; detest

ab • ject • ly (ab jekt´ lē) *adv.,* miserably, wretchedly

a • broad (ə brôd´) *adv.,* far and wide

a • brupt • ly (ə brupt´lē) *adv.,* in a sudden manner

ac • com • mo • date (ə käm´ ə dāt´) *vt.,* have space for

ac • com • pa • ni • ment (ə kum´pə nə mənt) *n.,* something that goes with something else

ac • cu • mu • late (ə kyo͞om´ yo͞o lāt´) *vt.,* gather over time

ac • knowl • edge (ak näl´ij) *vt.,* admit to be true

ad • a • mant (ad´ə mənt) *adj.,* inflexible

a • dapt (ə dapt´) *vi.,* adjust to fit new circumstances

ad • ja • cent (ə jā´sənt) *adj.,* near or close to something

a • do (ə do͞o´) *n.,* fuss; trouble; excitement

a • do • be (ə dō´bē) *n.,* sun-dried brick

a • dorn • ment (ə dôrn´mənt) *n.,* ornament, decoration

ad • vent (ad´ vent´) *n.,* coming or arrival

ad • ver • sar • y (ad´ vər ser´ē) *n.,* opponent; enemy

ad • ver • si • ty (ad vʉr´sə tē) *n.,* wretchedness or misfortune

af • firm (ə furm´) *vt.,* declare firmly

ag • ile (aj´əl) *adj.,* able to move quickly and easily

ag • i • ta • tor (aj´i tāt´ ər) *n.,* person who stirs up people in support of an unfavorable cause

ail • ment (āl´mənt) *n.,* illness; disease

all-per • vad • ing (ôl´ pər vād´iŋ) *adj.,* prevalent throughout

am • bi • gu • i • ty (am´bə gyo͞o´ ə tē) *n.,* word or statement that is uncertain or unclear

a • men • i • ty (ə men´ə tē) *n.,* comfort or convenience; desireable feature

a • mi • a • bly (ā´mē ə blē) *adv.,* pleasantly

am • o • rous (am´ə res) *adj.,* relating to love

an • a • lyt • ic • al (an´ə lit´i kəl) *adj.,* skilled in breaking a whole into its parts and examining relationships

an • guish (aŋ´gwish) *n.,* great suffering, as from grief or worry

an • i • mate (an´i māt´) *vt.,* put into motion

an • nex (ə neks´) *vt.,* add on or attach

a • nom • a • lous (ə näm´ə ləs) *adj.,* strange, abnormal

an • tag • o • nist (an tag´ə nist) *n.,* opponent; enemy

anx • i • e • ty (aŋ zī´ə tē) *n.,* worry; apprehension

ap • a • thy (ap´ə thē) *n.,* indifference, lack of emotion

a • pex (ā´peks´) *n.,* highest point

ap • pa • ri • tion (ap´ə rish´ən) *n.,* strange figure that appears suddenly

ap • per • tain (ap´ər tān´) *vi.,* be a part of

ap • praise (ə prāz´) *vt.,* judge the worth of

ar • dor (är´dər) *n.,* eagerness; passion; enthusiasm

ar • du • ous (är´jo͞o əs) *adj.,* strenuous; hard

ar • peg • gio (är pej´ō) *n.,* playing of the notes of a chord quickly, one after the other, instead of together

as • cend (ə send´) *vt.,* move upward along; mount; climb; rise

as • cent (ə sent´) *n.,* act of rising or climbing

as • pi • ra • tion (as´pə rā´ shən) *n.,* strong desire or ambition

as • pire (əs pīr´) *vi.,* try, attempt; desire, aim

as • sess • ment (ə ses´ ment) *n.,* evaluation

a • sun • der (ə sun´ dər) *adv.,* apart or separate in direction

at • trib • ute (ə trib´yо̄ot) *vt.,* think of as resulting from

aug • ment (ôg ment´) *vt.,* make greater in size, strength, or quantity

aux • il • ia • ry (ôg zil´yə rē) *n.,* engine for supplementary power

av • a • ri • cious (av´ə rish´əs) *adj.,* greedy

a • venge (ə venj´) *vt.,* get revenge for a wrongdoing

a • ver (ə vʉr´) *vt.,* declare to be true, affirm

a • vert • ed (ə vʉrt´id) *adj.,* turned away

B

bale • ful (bāl´fəl) *adj.,* sorrowful; wretched

balm • y (bäm´ē) *adj.,* soothing; mild; pleasant

bar • ba • rous (bär´bə rəs) *adj.,* cruel, brutal, uncultured

bar • rage (bə räzh´) *n.,* intense attack

bar • ren (bar´ən) *adj.,* empty; not producing crops

bar • ter (bärt´ər) *vt.,* trade for goods or services

be • lie (bē lī´) *vt.,* disguise, misrepresent

be • nev • o • lent (bə nev´ə lənt) *adj.,* kind

be • seech • ing (bē sēch´iŋ) *adj.,* in an earnest manner

be • set • ting (bē set´iŋ) *part.,* constantly harassing

bid (bid) *vt.,* express in leave-taking

bier (bir) *n.,* coffin and its supporting platform

bi • ped (bī´ped´) *n.,* two-footed animal

bi • son (bī´sən) *n.,* type of mammal having a shaggy mane, short, curved horns, and a humped back; commonly referred to as the American buffalo

bla • tant (blāt´ 'nt) *adj.,* glaringly conspicuous

blight (blīt) *n.,* any of several plant diseases that prevent growth

blun • der • ing (blun´dər iŋ) *adj.,* clumsy; careless; foolish

bog (bäg, bôg) *n.,* wet, spongy ground; small marsh or swamp

boun • ti • ful (boun´tə fəl) *adj.,* plentiful; abundant

boun • ty (boun´tē) *n.,* something given freely; generous gift

brack • en (brak´ən) *n.,* large, coarse, weedy ferns occurring in meadows and woods

bride • groom (brīd´gro̅o̅m´) *n.,* man who is about to be married or who has recently been married

bro • ker (brō´kər) *n.,* person who acts as an agent or intermediary in negotiating contracts, buying, or selling

brood (bro̅o̅d) *vi.,* worry

brow (brou) *n.,* forehead

bru • tal • i • ty (bro̅o̅ tal´ə tē) *n.,* cruelty

buf • fet (buf´it) *vt.,* beat back; thrust

bul • wark (bo̅o̅l´wərk) *n.,* defensive wall, breakwater

buoy • ant (boi´ənt) *adj.,* having power to keep something afloat

bur • ly (bʉr´lē) *adj.,* big and strong

bur • nish (bʉr´nish) *vt.,* polish

C

ca • dence (kād´ 'ns) *n.,* any rhythmic flow of sound

cairn (kern) *n.,* pile of stones built as a monument or landmark

ca • lam • i • tous (kə lam´ə təs) *adj.,* deeply troubled or miserable

ca • lam • i • ty (kə lam´ə tē) *n.,* disaster, misery

cal • lous (kal´əs) *adj.,* unfeeling

cal • low • ness (kal´ō nes) *n.,* youth; immaturity; state of being inexperienced

cape (kāp) *n.,* piece of land projecting into a body of water

ca • reen (kə rēn´) *vt.,* lurch from side to side, especially while moving rapidly

car • nage (kär´nij) *n.,* slaughter

car • ri • on (kar´ē ən) *n.,* decaying flesh of a dead body when regarded as food for scavenging animals—*adj.,* literally, like a piece of dead meat; figuratively, something disgusting or repulsive

caul (kôl) *n.,* membrane enclosing a fetus or a newborn baby

ca • vort (kə vôrt´) *vi.,* leap about; romp

ce • ler • i • ty (sə ler´i tē) *n.,* swiftness

chafe (chāf) *vi.,* be impatient or vexed

cham • ber (chām´bər) *n.,* room in a house

chide (chīd) *vt.,* scold

chiv • al • ry (shiv´əl rē) *n.,* sense of courage and honor

cir • cu • i • tous (sər kyo̅o̅´ət əs) *adj.,* roundabout; indirect

civ • il • i • ty (sə vil´ə tē) *n.,* manners; civilized ways

clar • i • ty (klar´ə tē) *n.,* state of being clear

co • in • ci • den • tal (kō in´sə dent´ 'l) *adj.,* characterized by an accidental occurrence of events

com • mence (kə məns´) *vt.,* begin

com • min • gle (kəm miŋ´gəl) *vi.,* intermix

com • mu • nion (kə myo̅o̅n´yən) *n.,* close relationship with deep understanding

com • pass (kum´pəs) *vt.,* accomplish

com • pas • sion (kəm pash´ən) *n.,* sympathy; pity

com • pen • sa • tion (käm´pən sā´shən) *n.,* payment in amends for something

com • pe • tent (käm´pə tənt) *adj.,* capable; fit

com • pose (kəm pōz´) *vt.,* put oneself in a state of tranquillity

com • pro • mise (käm´prə mīz´) *vt.,* settle by concessions on both sides

con • ceiv • a • bly (kən sēv´ə blē) *adv.,* that can be understood, imagined, or believed

con • ceive (kən sēv´) *vt.,* imagine; think

con • cil • i • ate (kən sil´ē āt´) *vt.,* win over

con • cur (kən kʉr´) *vi.,* agree

con • dole (kən dōl´) *vi.,* commiserate

con • done (kən dōn´) *vt.,* forgive or overlook an offense

con • duct (kən dukt´) *vt.,* lead

con • fes • sion (kən fesh´ən) *n.,* admission of guilt

con • firm (ken fʉrm´) *vt.,* establish as true

con • sci • en • tious • ly (kän shē en´shəs lē) *adv.,* in a manner governed by doing what one knows is right

con • sign • ment (kən sīn´mənt) *n.,* shipment of goods sent to a dealer for safekeeping

con • sis • tent (kən sis´tənt) *adj.,* steady

con • so • la • tion (kän´sə lā´shən) *n.,* comfort; solace

con • sort (kən sôrt´) *vi.,* be in harmony or agreement

con • spir • a • cy (kən spir´ə sē) *n.,* secret plot

con • ster • na • tion (kän´stər nā´shen) *n.,* great fear or shock

con • sul • ta • tion (kän´səl tā´shən) *n.,* meeting to decide or plan

con • tend (kən tend´) *vt.,* hold to be a fact

con • ten • tion (kən ten´shən) *n.,* argument

con • tig • u • ous (kən tig´yo̅o̅ əs) *adj.,* near; next; adjacent

con • tin • u • um (kən tin´yo̅o̅ əm) *n.,* unbroken or connected whole

con • tort • ed (kən tôrt´ əd) *part.*, twisted out of its usual form

con • tri • tion (kən trish´ən) *n.*, remorse

con • vene (kən vēn´) *vi.*, assemble

con • ven • tion • al (kən ven´shə nəl) *adj.*, customary, usual

con • verge (kən vʉrj´) *vi.*, come together

con • vey • ance (kən vā´əns) *n.*, carrying device

con • vic • tion (kən vik´shən) *n.*, strong belief

con • vul • sive (kən vul´ siv) *adj.*, occurring in violent fits; spasmodic

co • pi • ous (kō´pē əs) *adj.*, full of information, wordy

cor • dial (kôr´jəl) *adj.*, friendly

cour • ti • er (kôrt´ē ər) *n.*, attendant at a royal court

cov • ert (kuv´ərt) *adj.*, concealed, hidden

cow • er (kau´ər) *vi.*, crouch in fear

crave (krāv) *vt.*, long for, desire

cra • ven (krā´vən) *adj.*, cowardly, afraid

craw (krô) *n.*, stomach of an animal

cre • du • li • ty (krə dōō´lə tē) *n.*, tendency to believe too readily

creed (krēd) *n.*, statement of principle or opinion

crev • ice (krev´is) *n.*, narrow opening, crack

cun • ning (kun´iŋ) *adj.*, crafty, skillful

cus • tom • ar • i • ly (kus´tə mer´ə lē) *adv.*, according to what is usually done

cy • press (sī´prəs) *n.*, evergreen, native to North America, Europe, and Asia, with dark leaves and a distinctive symmetrical form. The tree is often planted in graveyards and is thus a symbol of mourning.

D

dank (daŋk) *adj.*, disagreeably damp

daunt (dônt) *vt.*, make afraid, intimidate

de • bate (dē bāt´) *vi.*, discuss opposing sides of a question

de • ci • pher (dē sī´fər) *vt.*, make out the meaning of

de • fi • ant (dē fī´ənt) *adj.*, openly resisting

de • fi • ant • ly (dē fī´ənt lē) *adv.*, openly resisting

de • fo • li • ate (dē fō´lē āt´) *vt.*, strip of leaves

de • gen • er • a • tion (dē jen´ər ā´shən) *n.*, decline; deterioration

de • grade (dē grād´) *vt.*, lower in moral character

dell (del) *n.*, small valley or glen, usually wooded

del • uge (del´ yōōj) *vi.*, overwhelm as with a flood

de • mesne (di mān´) *n.*, region; domain

de • mor • al • ized (dē môr´ə līzd´) *adj.*, weak of spirit and morale

de • mur (dē mʉr´) *vi.*, hesitate because of one's doubts

de • note (dē nōt´) *vt.*, indicate

de • nounce (dē nouns´) *vt.*, criticize

de • plor • a • ble (dē plôr´ə bəl) *adj.*, unfortunate

der • e • lict (der´ə likt´) *adj.*, abandoned

de • ri • sive (di rī´siv) *adj.*, ridiculing

des • ti • tute (des´tə tōōt´) *adj.*, abandoned; forsaken

de • tach • ment (dē tach´mənt) *n.*, state of being disinterested

de • tri • men • tal (de´trə ment´′l) *adj.*, harmful

de • vise (di vīz) *vt.*, work out or create; plan

de • void (di void´) *adj.*, completely without

de • vout (di vout´) *adj.*, religious; pious

dex • ter • i • ty (deks ter´ə tē) *n.*, skill in using one's hands or body

di • lap • i • dat • ed (də lap´ə dāt id) *adj.*, broken down and shabby

dil • i • gent • ly (dil´ə jənt lē) *adv.*, carefully and steadily

din (din) *n.*, noise

dis • arm • ing (dis ärm´iŋ) *adj.*, removing fear or hostility

dis • cern (di zʉrn´) *vt.*, recognize; make out clearly

dis • charge (dis chärj´) *vt.*, remove; release

dis • com • fi • ture (dis kum´fi chər) *n.*, feeling of frustration and confusion

dis • cord (dis´kôrd) *n.*, 1. conflict; 2. lack of harmony in tones sounded together

dis • course (dis kôrs´) *vi.*, express oneself

dis • creet (di skrēt´) *adj.*, careful about what one says or does

dis • crep • an • cy (di skrep´ən sē) *n.*, inconsistency

dis • par • i • ty (di spar´ə tē) *n.*, inequality

dis • patch (di spach´) *vt.*, send off on an errand

dis • po • si • tion (dis´pə zish´ən) *n.*, one's customary frame of mind; one's nature or temperament

dis • sem • bler (di sem´blir) *n.*, pretender

dis • solve (di zälv´) *vi.*, decompose or disintegrate

dis • traught (di strôt´) *adj.*, crazed; harassed

di • verge (dī vʉrj´) *vi.*, move in different directions

di • vers (dī´vərz) *adj.*, various, several

di • ver • si • fied (də vʉr´sə fīd´) *adj.*, varied

di • vert • ed (də vʉrt´id) *part.*, distracted

di • vert • ing (də vʉrt´iŋ) *adj.*, amusing

di • vine (də vīn´) *vt.*, find out by intuition

doff (däf, dôf) *vt.*, take off; remove or lift (one's hat)

do • min • ion (də min´yən) *n.*, governed territory

don (dän) *vt.*, put on (a garment)

dote (dōt) *vi.*, be foolishly or excessively fond

drag • gled (drag´əld) *part.*, wet and dirty

driv • el • ling (driv´əl iŋ) *part.*, childish

du • bi • ous • ly (dōō´ bē əs lē) *adv.*, doubtfully, suspiciously

du • pli • ca • tion (dōō´ pli kā´shən) *n.*, copy, double

E

ebb (eb) *vi.*, recede; decline

ec • cen • tric (ək sen´trik) *adj.*, off-center

ed • dy (ed´ē) *n.*, little whirlpool

ee • ri • ly (ir´ə lē) *adv.*, mysteriously

ef • fete (e fēt´) *adj.*, lacking vigor or force of character

e • ject (ē jekt´) *vt.*, cast out; emit; discharge

el • o • quence (el´ə kwəns) *n.*, speech or writing that is vivid, forceful, and persuasive

em • bank • ment (em baŋk´mənt) *n.*, slope of earth; rubble used to keep back water

em • bed (em bed´) *vt.*, set in a surrounding mass

em • bit • ter (em bit´ər) *vt.*, make resentful

e • merge (ē mʉrj´) *vi.*, become apparent or known; come forth into view

en • clo • sure (en klō´zher) *n.*, fenced-in area

en • deav • or or **en • deav • our** (en dev´ər) *n.*, attempt, effort

en • dem • ic (en dem´ik) *adj.,* present in
en • mi • ty (en´mə tē) *n.,* hostility; antagonism
en • ter • prise (ent´ər prīz´) *n.,* project
en • thralled (en thrôld´) *adj.,* captivated
en • tice (en tīs´) *vt.,* tempt
en • ti • ty (en´tə tē) *n.,* being
en • treat (en trēt´) *vt.,* implore; beg
ep • ic (ep´ik) *adj.,* grand and strong
e • qui • lib • ri • um (ē´kwi lib´rē um) *n.,* state of balance
es • ca • la • tion (es´kə lā´shən) *n.,* step-by-step growth; rapid increase
es • carp • ment (e skärp´mənt) *n.,* steep slope
es • tu • ar • y (es´tyoo er ē) *n.,* inlet of the sea
e • ter • nal (ē tʉr´nəl) *adj.,* timeless; everlasting
ev • a • nesce (ev´ən nes´) *vi.,* disappear
ev • i • dent (ev´ə dənt) *adj.,* easy to see; obvious
e • vince (ē vins´) *vt.,* show plainly; indicate
ex • alt (eg zôlt´) *vt.,* raise in status
ex • er • tion (eg zer´shən) *n.,* effort
ex • hil • a • rate (eg zil´ə rāt´) *vt.,* make cheerful and lively
ex • ploit (eks´ploit) *n.,* daring or bold deed
ex • press (ek spres´) *vt.,* put into words
ex • tant (eks´tənt) *adj.,* still existing
ex • tem • po • rize (eks tem´pə rīz´) *vi.,* speak or perform without preparation
ex • tend (ek stend´) *vt.,* grant
ex • tir • pate (ek´stər pāt´) *vt.,* destroy or remove completely
ex • trem • i • ty (ek strem´ə tē) *n.,* greatest degree
ex • ult • ant • ly (eg zult´'nt lē) *adv.,* triumphantly; rejoicingly

F

fal • ter (fôl´tər) *vi.,* hesitate
fam • ine (fam´in) *n.,* widespread shortage of food
fan • cy (fan´sē) *n.,* fondness
fas • ti • di • ous • ness (fas tid´ē əs nes) *n.,* oversensitiveness
fes • toon (fes toon´) *vt.,* adorn with garlands
fleet (flēt) *adj.,* swift; rapid
flot • sam (flät´səm) *n.,* debris floating on the sea; odds and ends
floun • der (floun´dər) *vi.,* struggle awkwardly; stumble
flour • ish (flʉr´ish) *vi.,* wave in the air
flush (flush) *vt.,* cause to take wing suddenly
ford (fôrd) *vt.,* cross a stream or river by wading
fore • bear (fôr´ber´) *n.,* ancestor
fore • sight (fôr´sīt´) *n.,* thoughtful regard for the future
for • feit (fôr´fit) *n.,* penalty or fine one pays because of a crime
forge (fôrg) *vi.,* move forward
for • lorn • ly (fôr lôrn´lē) *adv.,* hopelessly; miserably
for • mi • da • ble (fôr´mə də bəl) *adj.,* large; hard to handle
for • mu • la (fôr´myoo lə) *n.,* rule or fact in mathematics
for • ti • tude (fôrt´ə tood´) *n.,* strength
frag • men • tar • y (frag´mən ter´ē) *adj.,* consisting of disconnected parts
fraught (frôt) *adj.,* filled; charged; loaded
fray (frā) *n.,* noisy quarrel or fight
fri • vol • i • ty (fri väl´ə tē) *n.,* act of being trivial

friv • o • lous (friv´ə ləs) *adj.,* not properly serious
frond (fränd) *n.,* leaflike part of seaweed
fruit • less (froot´lis) *adj.,* unsuccessful
fume (fyoom) *n.,* smoke, gas, or vapor
fur • row (fʉr´ō) *n.,* narrow groove
fur • tive • ly (fʉr´tiv lē) *adv.,* stealthily, not openly
fu • tile (fyoot´'l) *adj.,* hopeless
fu • tile • ly (fyoo´til lē) *adv.,* ineffectively

G

gal • ling (gôl´iŋ) *adj.,* irritating
gar • ner (gär´nər) *vt.,* gather
ge • ni • al (jēn´yəl) *adj.,* amiable; cheerful
gin • ger • ly (jin´jər lē) *adv.,* very cautiously
girt (gʉrt) *alt. pp. of gird,* surrounded, encircled
glar • ing (gler´iŋ) *adj.,* shining too brightly
glow • er (glou´ər) *vt.,* stare with anger
graph • i • cal • ly (graf´ik ə lē) *adv.,* vividly
grav • i • ty (grav´i tē) *n.,* danger or threat
griev • ance (grēv´əns) *n.,* complaint or resentment
gri • mace (grim´is) *vi.,* twist one's face in distaste, disgust, or pain
gris • ly (griz´lē) *adj.,* terrifying, horrifying
gul • ly (gul´ē) *n.,* channel or hollow worn by running water

H

har • ried (har´ēd) *adj.,* tormented, ravaged
har • ry (har´ē) *vt.,* force or push along
haugh • ty (hôt´ē) *adj.,* proud; arrogant; showing great pride in oneself and scorn for others
her • ald (her´əld) *vt.,* announce; introduce
he • red • i • ty (hə red´i tē) *n.,* transmission of genes from parent to offspring; inherited characteristics
her • e • sy (her´i sē) *n.,* rejection of a belief that is part of an established set of beliefs
hue (hyoo) *n.,* particular shade or tint of a given color
hull (hul) *vt.,* take the shell off a seed, fruit, or nut
hur • tling (hʉrt´liŋ) *adj.,* swift-moving
hy • giene (hī´jēn) *n.,* health and cleanliness

I

id • i • o • syn • cra • sy (id´ē ō´sin´krə sē) *n.,* any personal peculiarity
i • dol • a • try (ī däl´ə trē) *n.,* excessive devotion or reverence
ig • no • min • i • ous • ly (ig´nə min´ē əs lē) *adv.,* disgracefully; shamefully
il • lu • sion (i loo´zhən) *n.,* false perception
im • mi • nent (im´ə nənt) *adj.,* likely to happen
im • mo • late (im´ə lāt´) *vt.,* kill as a sacrifice
im • mu • ni • ty (im myoon´i tē) *n.,* freedom from something burdensome
im • par • tial (im pär´shəl) *adj.,* without prejudice or bias
im • peach • ment (im pēch´mənt) *n.,* discredit
im • pel (im pel´) *vi.,* force, urge
im • pend • ing (im pend´iŋ) *part.,* about to happen; threatening

im • per • a • tive (im per´ə tiv) *adj.,* necessary

im • per • i • ous • ly (im pir´ē es lē) *adv.,* with an overbearing or imperial manner

im • per • vi • ous (im pʉr´vē əs) *adj.,* not affected

im • pet • u • ous (im pech´o͞o əs) *adj.,* moving with great force or violence; impulsive; rash

im • pli • ca • tion (im´pli kā´shən) *n.,* something implied; suggestion

im • plic • it (im plis´it) *adj.,* understood, though not plainly expressed; implied

im • port (im´pôrt´) *n.,* significance

im • por • tune (im´pôr to͞on´) *vt.,* demand, ask for urgently

im • pose (im pōz´) *vt.,* place or set

im • pro • vise (im´prə vīz´) *vt.,* bring about with tools and materials on hand

im • pu • ta • tion (im pyo͞o tā´shən) *n.,* charge

im • pute (im pyo͞ot´) *vt.,* attribute

in • ad • vert • ence (in´ad vʉrt´´ns) *n.,* mistake; oversight

in • ad • vert • ent • ly (in´ad vʉrt´´nt lē) *adv.,* due to oversight; unintentionally

in • ar • tic • u • late (in´är tik´yo͞o lit) *adj.,* not able to speak understandably; unable to express one's emotions

in • au • di • ble (in ôd´ə bəl) *adj.,* that cannot be heard

in • au • gu • rate (in ô´gyo͞o rāt) *vt.,* celebrate the formal beginning of

in • aus • pi • cious (in´ô spish´əs) *adj.,* unfavorable; unlucky

in • car • na • tion (in´kär nā´shən) *n.,* any person or thing that serves as an embodiment of a quality or concept

in • cised (in sīzd´) *adj.,* engraved or carved

in • ci • sive (in sī´siv) *adj.,* penetrating

in • clined (in klīnd´) *adj.,* willing

in • com • pre • hen • si • ble (in´käm´prē hen´sə bəl) *adj.,* not understandable

in • con • se • quen • tial (in kän´si kwen´shəl) *adj.,* unimportant

in • con • stant (in kän´stənt) *adj.,* not remaining firm in mind or purpose

in • cred • u • lous (in krej´o͞o ləs) *adj.,* showing disbelief

in • crim • i • nate (in krim´i nāt´) *vt.,* charge with or show evidence of involvement in a crime

in • cu • ri • ous (in kyo͞or´ē əs) *adj.,* uninterested

in • de • fat • i • ga • ble (in´di fat´i gə bəl) *adj.,* that cannot be tired out

in • de • ter • mi • nate (in´dē tʉr´mi nit) *adj.,* uncertain

in • do • lent • ly (in´də lənt lē) *adv.,* idly, lazily

in • duce • ment (in do͞os´mənt) *n.,* motive; incentive

in • eq • ui • ty (in ek´wit ē) *n.,* lack of justice

in • ev • i • ta • ble (in ev´i tə bəl) *adj.,* that cannot be avoided or evaded

in • ex • o • ra • ble (in eks´ə rə bəl) *adj.,* that which cannot be moved or influenced; unrelenting

in • ex • pli • ca • bly (in eks´pli kə blē) *adv.,* without explanation

in • fal • li • bil • i • ty (in fal´ə bil´i tē) *n.,* correctness, incapacity for error

in • fal • li • ble (in fal´ə bəl) *adj.,* incapable of error; reliable

in • fin • i • tes • i • mal (in´fin i tes´i məl) *adj.,* too small to be measured

in • ge • nu • i • ty (in´jə no͞o´ə tē) *n.,* cleverness; originality

in • let (in´let) *n.,* narrow strip of water extending into land

in • no • cu • ous • ly (in näk´yo͞o əs lē) *adv.,* harmlessly; dully

in • no • va • tion (in´ə vā´shən) *n.,* something newly introduced

in • or • di • nate (in ôr´də nit) *adj.,* lacking moderation

in • scru • ta • ble (in skro͞ot´ə bəl) *adj.,* obscure, mysterious

in • sid • i • ous (in sid´ē əs) *adj.,* sly or treacherous

in • sin • u • at • ing • ly (in sin´yo͞o āt´iŋ lē) *adv.,* suggestively

in • sip • id (in sip´id) *adj.,* tasteless; dull

in • so • lent (in´sə lənt) *adj.,* boldly disrespectful

in • still (in stil´) *vt.,* put in or into little by little

in • su • lar (in´sə lər) *adj.,* detached; isolated

in • teg • ri • ty (in teg´rə tē) *n.,* quality of honesty and sincerity; state of perfection

in • ten • si • fi • ca • tion (in ten´si fi kā´shən) *n.,* increase in magnitude

in • tent (in tent´) *adj.,* earnest, fixed

in • ter • ac • tion (in´tər ak´shən) *n.,* reciprocal action or effect

in • ter • cept (in´tər sept´) *vt.,* seize or stop on the way

in • ter • sperse (in´tər spʉrs´) *vt.,* scatter among other things

in • ter • twin • ing (in´tər twīn´iŋ) *adj.,* twisted together

in • ti • mate (in´tə māt´) *vt.,* hint, imply

in • tim • i • date (in tim´ə dāt´) *vt.,* make timid or afraid

in • tri • cate (in´tri kit) *adj.,* complex

in • tro • spec • tive (in´trō spek´tiv) *adj.,* looking within one's own mind

in • trude (in tro͞od´) *vi.,* force upon others without being asked or welcomed

in • un • da • tion (in´ən dā´shən) *n.,* flood; deluge

in • var • i • a • bly (in ver´ē ə blē) *adv.,* constantly; uniformly

in • vo • ca • tion (in´və kā´shən) *n.,* act of calling on a god for blessing or inspiration

ir • i • des • cent (ir´i des´ənt) *adj.,* having shifting changes in color

ir • re • cov • er • a • ble (ir´ri kuv´ər ə bəl) *adj.,* cannot be corrected or remedied

ir • re • so • lute • ly (ir rez´ə lo͞ot´lē) *adv.,* indecisively

i • so • lat • ed (ī´sə lāt ed) *adj.,* set apart from others

i • so • la • tion (ī sə lā´shən) *n.,* being set apart from others

J

jad • ed (jād´id) *adj.,* worn out; dulled

ju • ris • dic • tion (jo͞or´is dik´shən) *n.,* authority in general

jut (jut) *vi.,* stick out

K

keel (kēl) *vt.,* turn over or upside down

keen • ly (kēn´lē) *adv.,* sharply

kins • man (kinz´mən) *n.,* relative

knead (nēd) *vt.,* press, rub, or squeeze; massage

knell (nel) *vi.,* sound ominously or mournfully

L

la • bo • ri • ous • ly (lə bôr´ē əs lē) *adv.,* with difficulty

lab • y • rinth (lab´ər inth´) *n.,* complicated maze

lac • er • at • ed (las´ər āt´ed) *part.,* cut; wounded

lad • en (lād´´n) *adj.,* loaded

la • ment (lə ment´) *n.,* song of mourning—*vi.,* feel deep sorrow

lam • en • ta • ble (lam´ən tə bəl) *adj.,* grievous; deplorable; distressing

lam • en • ta • tion (lam´ən tā´shən) *n.,* outward expression of grief

la • tent (lāt´´nt) *adj.,* hidden

lan • guid • ly (laŋ´gwid lē) *adv.,* sluggishly

lan • guish (lan´gwish) *vi.,* lose vigor or vitality; suffer with longing

lan • guor (laŋ´gər) *n.,* lack of interest, listlessness

lash (lash) *vt.,* strike hard with great force

le • gion (lē´jən) *n.,* large number; multitude

le • ni • en • cy (lē´nē ən sē) *n.,* kindness; flexibility

le • thal (lē´ thəl) *adj.,* capable of causing death

li • a • bil • i • ty (lī´ə bil´ə tē) *n.,* state of legal obligation

li • a • ble (lī´ə bəl) *adj.,* subject to

lin • e • a • ment (lin´ē ə mənt) *n.,* any of the features of the body

lit • er • al • ly (lit´ər əl ē) *adv.,* actually; in fact

loath (lōth) *adj.,* hesitant, reluctant

loath • some (lōth´səm) *adj.,* disgusting; detestable

lof • ty (lôf´tē) *adj.,* very high, elevated

loi • ter • ing (loit´ər iŋ) *part.,* lingering or spending time in an aimless or idle way

lon • gev • i • ty (län jev´ə tē) *n.,* long life

lope (lōp) *n.,* long, easy stride

lu • gu • bri • ous • ly (lə gōō´ brē əs lē) *adv.,* sadly, mournfully, often in an exaggerated manner

lu • mi • nous (lōō´mə nəs) *adj.,* filled with light; bright; shinning

M

mag • ni • tude (mag´nə tōōd´) *n.,* greatness of importance or influence

ma • lev • o • lent (mə lev´ə lənt) *adj.,* wishing evil or harm to others

ma • li • cious (mə lish´əs) *adj.,* intentionally spiteful; harmful

ma • lig • nant (mə lig´nənt) *adj.,* wishing evil; dangerous

ma • ligned (mə lind´) *adj.,* slandered

ma • lin • ger • er (mə liŋ´gər ər) *n.,* someone who avoids duty

man • a • cle (man´ə kəl) *n.,* handcuff, shackle, or any restraint

man • i • fest (man´ə fest) *vi.,* appear

man • i • fest • ly (man´ə fest´lē) *adv.,* clearly; obviously

ma • raud • er (mə rôd´ər) *n.,* one who raids and plunders

ma • te • ri • al • ize (mə tir´ē əl īz) *vt.,* appear in bodily form

ma • tron (mā´trən) *n.,* married woman or widow

max • im (maks´im) *n.,* statement of a general truth

me • an • der (mē an´dər) *vi.,* take a winding course

me • di • e • val (mə dē´vəl) *adj.,* suggestive of the Middle Ages

med • i • ta • tive (med´ə tāt´iv) *adj.,* reflective, thoughtful

mel • an • chol • y (mel´ən käl´ē) *adj.,* sad; gloomy; depressed

mê • lée (mā´lā´) *n.,* confused conflict or mixture

mem • brane (mem´brān) *n.,* thin, soft layer of tissue

mer • e • tri • cious (mer´ə trish´əs) *adj.,* alluring in a false, showy way

me • sa (mā´sə) *n.,* high, flat tableland

met • a • mor • phose (met´ə mor´fōz´) *vt.,* change; transform

met • a • mor • pho • sis (met´ə môr´fə sis) *n.,* transformation

min • is • tra • tion (min´is trā´shən) *n.,* act of giving care, help, or service

min • strel (min´strəl) *n.,* medieval entertainer who traveled from place to place

mis • ad • ven • ture (mis´əd ven´chər) *n.,* unlucky accident; mishap

mis • sion • ar • y (mish´ən er´ē) *n.,* person sent to convert others to a religion or to teach religious beliefs

mo • bil • i • ty (mō´bil´ə tē) *n.,* ability to move from place to place

mold • er (mōl´dər) *vi.,* crumble into dust

molt • ed (mōlt´id) *part.,* shed

mo • men • tum (mō men´təm) *n.,* force of an object in motion

mon • arch (män´ərk) *n.,* ruler

mon • i • tor (män´i tər) *n.,* person who keeps order

mo • not • o • nous (mə nät´´n əs) *adj.,* unvarying; tiresome because unvarying

mo • rass (mə ras´) *n.,* perplexing state of affairs

mo • rose (mə rōs´) *adj.,* gloomy; sullen

mor • ti • fied (môrt´ə fīd´) *adj.,* shamed, humiliated

mot • ley (mät´lē) *adj.,* made of many different elements

mus • ter (mus´tər) *vt.,* gather together; summon up

mus • ty (mus´tē) *adj.,* dull; apathetic

mu • ti • ny (myōōt´´n ē) *n.,* revolt against constituted authority

mut • ter (mut´ər) *vt.,* utter words in a low tone

myr • i • ad (mir´ē əd) *n.,* indefinitely large number

N

near • sight • ed (nir´sīt´id) *adj.,* having better vision for near objects than for distant ones

ne • go • ti • ate (ni gō´shē āt´) *vt.,* succeed in crossing, surmounting, moving through

night • in • gale (nīt´´n gāl) *n.,* reddish-brown songbird noted for the sweet song of the male

nim • ble (nim´bəl) *adj.,* agile

non • com • mit •tal (nän´kə mit´´l) *adj.,* not committing to one point of view

non • de • script (nän´di skript´) *adj.,* lacking in recognizable characteristics or qualities

no • to • ri • ous (nō tôr´ē əs) *adj.,* well known

nup • tial (nup´shəl) *n.,* wedding; marriage

O

ob • du • rate (äb´door it) *adj.,* not easily moved; stubborn

ob • jec • tive • ly (əb jək´tiv lē) *adv.,* without bias or prejudice

ob • lit • er • at • ed (ō blit´ər āt əd) *part.,* erased; destroyed

ob • liv • i • ous (ə bliv´ē əs) *adj.,* forgetful or unmindful

ob • scure (əb skyōōr´) *adj.,* inconspicuous; hidden

ob • scure • ly (əb skyōōr´lē) *adv.,* unnoticed

o • men (ō´mən) *n.,* thing or event supposed to foretell a future event

om • i • nous (äm´ə nəs) *adj.,* threatening, sinister

om • i • nous • ly (äm´ə nəs lē) *adv.,* in a threatening manner

on • rush • ing (än´rush´iŋ) *adj.,* dashing forward

op • pres • sive (ə pres´iv) *adj.*, hard to put up with

or • a • to • ry (ôr´ə tôr´ē) *n.*, eloquence in public speaking

or • dained (or dānd´) *part.*, commanded

or • i • fice (ôr´ə fis) *n.*, opening; mouth

o • paque • ness (ō pāk´nis) *n.*, darkness

or • tho • dox (ôr´thō däks´) *adj.*, usual; established (as in beliefs)

out • set (out´set´) *n.*, beginning; start

o • ver • take (ō´vər tāk´) *vt.*, catch up with and go beyond

o • ver • whelm • ing (ō´vər hwelm´iŋ) *adj.*, overpowering

P

pad • dock (pad´ək) *n.*, enclosed field

pall (pôl) *n.*, covering

palm • i • est (päm´ē est) *adj.*, most prosperous; richest

pal • pa • ble (pal´pə bəl) *adj.*, perceptible; noticeable

pal • pi • tant (pal´pə tənt) *adj.*, throbbing, quivering, trembling

pal • pi • tat • ing (pal´pə tāt´ing) *part.*, beating rapidly; fluttering

pan • de • mo • ni • um (pan´də mō´nē əm) *n.*, wild noise and disorder

par • a • mour (par´ə mōōr) *n.*, sweetheart

par • a • noi • a (par´ə noi´ə) *n.*, extreme delusions of persecution; suspiciousness

par • a • pher • na • lia (par´ə fər nāl´yə) *n.pl.*, any collection of articles

pa • rish • ion • er (pə rish´ə nər) *n.*, member of a church district, or parish

par • ox • ysm (par´əks iz´əm) *n.*, sudden attack or spasm

par • si • mo • ny (pär´sə mō´nē) *n.*, stinginess

par • tu • ri • tion (pär´tōō rish´ən) *n.*, childbirth

pa • tent • ly (pāt´´nt lē) *adv.*, clearly; obviously

pa • tron (pā´trən) *n.*, protector; benefactor

pec • tor • al (pek´tə rəl) *adj.*, located in or on the chest

pe • cu • liar (pə kyōōl´yər) *adj.*, unique, strange

pee • vish (pēv´ish) *adj.*, hard to please; irritable

pen • e • trate (pen´i trāt) *vi.*, pass into

per • am • bu • lat • ing (pər am´byōō lāt´iŋ) *part.*, walking around

per • emp • to • ri • ly (pər emp´tə rē lē) *adv.*, finally; absolutely

per • ni • cious (pər nish´əs) *adj.*, fatal; deadly

per • pet • u • al (pər pech´ōō əl) *adj.*, constant, permanent

per • pet • u • al • ly (pər pech´ōō əl lē) *adv.*, forever

per • sist (pər sist´) *vi.*, continue insistently

per • sist • ence (pər sist´əns) *n.*, stubborn continuance; tenacity

per • sist • ent • ly (pər sist´ənt lē) *adv.*, unrelentingly; stubbornly

per • ti • nac • i • ty (pʉr´tə nās´ə tē) *n.*, stubborn persistance, obstinacy

per • vade (pər vād´) *vt.*, fill

per • verse (pər vʉrs´) *adj.*, contrary

phe • nom • e • non (fə näm´ə nən´) *n.*, any extremely unusual occurrence

phos • pho • res • cent (fäs´fə re´sənt) *adj.*, luminescent, giving off light

pil • grim • age (pil´grim ij) *n.*, long journey

pine (pīn) *vi.*, waste away through grief; yearn

pin • ion (pin´yən) *n.*, wing—*vt.*, bind

pit • e • ous (pit´ē əs) *adj.*, arousing or deserving pity or compassion

pla • cat • ing • ly (plā´kāt´iŋ lē) *adv.*, pacifyingly; pleasingly

plac • id (plas´id) *adj.*, undisturbed, calm

plac • id • ly (plas´id lē) *adv.*, calmly; quietly

plague (plāg) *n.*, anything that afflicts or troubles

ple • thor • ic (plə thôr´ik) *adj.*, characterized by excess or profusion

plight (plīt) *n.*, situation

plum • age (plōōm´ij) *n.*, bird's feathers

plume (plōōm) *vt.*, preen

plun • der (plun´dər) *vt.*, steal or take by trickery or by force

plunge (plunj) *vi.*, move rapidly downward

ply (plī) *vt.*, keep supplying

poised (poizd) *part.*, suspended

pome • gran • ate (päm´gran´it) *n.*, round fruit with a red, leathery rind and many seeds covered with red, juicy, edible flesh

pon • der • ous (pän´dər əs) *adj.*, heavy; bulky; massive

por • tage (pôr´tij) *vi.*, carry boats or supplies overland from one one lake or river to another

pos • ter • i • ty (päs ter´ə tē) *n.*, all succeeding generations

po • tent (pōt´´nt) *adj.*, strong, powerful

pre • car • i • ous • ly (prē ker´ē əs lē) *adv.*, insecurely

pre • cip • i • tate (prē sip´ə tāt´) *vt.*, cause; start—(prē sip´ə tit) *adj.*, sudden; impetuous; rash

pre • cip • i • tous (prē sip´ə təs) *adj.*, steep

pre • dom • i • nant (prē däm´ə nənt) *adj.*, having dominating influence over others; superior

pre • dom • i • nate (prē däm´ə nāt´) *vi.*, prevail

pre • em • i • nent • ly (prē em´ə nənt lē) *adv.*, excelling above others

pre • lim • i • nar • ies (prē lim´ə ner´ēz) *n.*, introductory comments

pre • oc • cu • pa • tion (prē äk´yōō pā´shən) *n.*, absorption in thought

pre • serve (prē zʉrv´) *n.*, place maintained for regulated hunting

pre • sum • a • bly (prē zōōm´ə blē) *adv.*, supposedly; believably

pre • sump • tu • ous (prē zump´chōō əs) *adj.*, arrogant

pri • mor • dial (prī môr´dē əl) *adj.*, existing from the beginning of time; primitive

pri • va • tion (prī vā´shən) *n.*, lack of the ordinary necessities of life

pro • cure (prō kyōōr´) *vt.*, get or bring about by some effort

pro • di • gious (prō dij´əs) *adj.*, exceptional; of great size or power

prof • fered (präf´ərd) *part.*, offered courteously

prog • eny (präj´ə nē) *n.*, descendant; offspring

prom • on • to • ry (präm´ən tô rē) *n.*, peak of high land that juts out into a body of water

pro • nounce (prō nouns´) *vt.*, declare officially

prop • a • gate (präp´ə gāt) *vt.*, reproduce; multiply

proph • e • sy (präf´ə sē´) *vt.*, predict

pro • pose (prō pōz´) *vt.*, intend

pro • sa • ic (prō zā´ik) *adj.*, commonplace, dull

pros • pect (prä´spekt´) *n.*, likely candidate

pros • trate (präs´trāt) *adj.*, lying with the face downward in demonstration of great humility

pro • trud • ing (prō trōōd´iŋ) *adj.*, jutting out

pro • vi • sion (prō vizh´ ən) *n.*, clause or agreement in a legal document

prov • o • ca • tion (präv´ə kā´shən) *n.*, something that stirs up feelings or action, especially a cause of resentment or irritation

pro • voke (prō vōk´) *vt.*, stir up action or feeling

prow • ess (prou´is) *n.*, superior ability; skill

pru • dence (prōōd´´ns) *n.*, sound judgment

pru • dent (prōōd´´nt) *adj.*, cautious or discreet

purge (pʉrj) *vt.*, cleanse of impurities

purl • ing (pʉrl´iŋ) *part.*, swirling; rippling

Q

quar • ry (kwôr´ē) *n.*, anything being hunted or pursued

R

ram • pant (ram´pənt) *adj.*, flourishing

ran • cid (ran´sid) *adj.*, having a bad smell or taste

ran • cor (raŋ´kər) *n.*, bitter hate or ill will

rap • ture (rap´chər) *n.*, great pleasure

re • al • ist (rē´ə list) *n.*, person concerned with real things

re • buff (ri buf´) *n.*, abrupt refusal

re • ca • pit • u • late (rē´kə pich´ə lāt´) *vi.*, summarize

re • ced • ing (ri sēd´iŋ) *part.*, moving away from, becoming more distant

re • cep • ta • cle (ri sep´tə kəl) *n.*, anything used to contain or hold something else

re • cess (rē´ses) *n.*, secluded place

re • cite (ri sīt´) *vt.*, repeat words aloud from memory

re • coil (rē´koil´) *n.*, state of flying back when released

rec • on • cil • i • a • tion (rek´ən sil´ē ā´shən) *n.*, settling of problems or disputes

re • cur • rent (ri kʉr´ənt) *adj.*, occurring or appearing again or regularly

re • demp • tive (ri demp´tiv) *adj.*, serving to recover or get back

re • fer (ri fʉr´) *vi.*, direct attention to

re • flec • tive (ri flek´tiv) *adj.*, meditative; thoughtful

re • form (ri fôrm´) *n.*, improvement by introducing better procedures

ref • uge (ref´yōōj) *n.*, protection; safety

ref • u • gee (ref´yōō jē) *n.*, person who flees from home or country to seek safety elsewhere

re • gale (ri gāl´) *vt.*, entertain; amuse

re • in • force • ment (rē´in fôrs´mənt) *n.*, additional forces

re • it • er • ate (rē it´ə rāt´) *vt.*, repeat

re • mon • strance (ri män´strəns) *n.*, act of complaining, protesting

re • morse • less (ri môrs´lis) *adj.*, merciless; cruel

rend (rend) *vt.*, tear

rend • ing (rend´iŋ) *adj.*, showing grief

ren • e • gade (ren´ə gād´) *adj.*, of or like one who abandons a group to go to the other side

re • nege (ri nig´) *vi.*, back out of an agreement

re • pel (ri pel´) *vt.*, cause distaste or disgust

re • pose (ri pōz´) *n.*, rest; sleep

re • proof (ri prōōf´) *n.*, rebuke; censure

re • pug • nance (ri pug´nəns) *n.*, extreme dislike or distaste

req • ui • site (rek´wə zit) *n.*, necessity

res • i • dence (rez´i dəns) *n.*, place in which a person or thing resides or lives

res • ig • na • tion (rez´ig nā´shən) *n.*, passive acceptance

re • sil • ien • cy (ri zil´yens ē) *n.*, ability to bounce or spring back to shape; ability to rebound

res • o • lute • ly (rez´ə lōōt´lē) *adv.*, with determination or fixed purpose

res • o • lu • tion (rez´ə lōō´shən) *n.*, resolving or determining

re • solved (ri zälvd´) *adj.*, firm and fixed in purpose; determined

re • strain • ing (ri strān´iŋ) *adj.*, controlling or disciplining

re • sur • gence (ri sʉrj´əns) *n.*, tendency to rise again

re • tro • gres • sion (re´trə gresh´ən) *n.*, return to a lower level or stage

ret • ro • spect (re´trə spekt´) *n.*, looking back on

re • veal (ri vēl´) *vt.*, show, expose

rev • e • la • tion (rev´ə lā´shən) *n.*, something disclosed; striking announcement

re • ver • ber • ate (ri vʉr´bə rāt´) *vi.*, resound, echo

rev • er • ent • ly (rev´ər ənt lē) *adv.*, showing great respect

re • volt (ri vōlt´) *n.*, rebellion; insurrection

rig • or • ous • ly (rig´ər əs lē) *adv.*, precisely; accurately

ri • ot • ous (rī´ət əs) *adj.*, without restraint; dissolute

rit • u • al (rich´ōō əl) *n.*, religious or ceremonial act

ri • val • ry (rī´vəl rē) *n.*, competition

roan (rōn) *n.*, solid-colored horse with a sprinkling of white hair

rogue (rōg) *n.*, wicked or rascally person

rup • tured (rup´chərd) *adj.*, broken apart

ruth • less (rōōth´lis) *adj.*, without pity

S

sac • ri • le • gious (sak´rə li´jəs) *adj.*, in violation of something sacred

sage (sāj) *adj.*, wise

sa • lient (sāl´yənt) *adj.*, prominent; noticeable

sanc • tu • ar • y (saŋk´chōō er´ē) *n.*, place of refuge or protection

sar • don • i • cal • ly (sär dän´i kə lē) *adv.*, sarcastically

sat • ed (sāt´əd) *adj.*, satisfied

sat • u • rate (sach´ə rāt´) *vt.* cause to be thoroughly penetrated

sat • u • rat • ed (sach´ər rāt´id) *adj.*, soaked through with moisture; wet

scorn • er (skôrn´ər) *n.*, person who treats with contempt

scru • ple (skrōo´pəl) *n.*, qualm; uneasiness about something one thinks is wrong

scru • ti • ny (skrōot´'n ē) *n.*, careful, searching look

sear (sir) *vt.*, burn; wither

sep • ul • chre or **sep • ul • cher** (sep´əlk ər) *n.*, vault for burial; grave; tomb

se • quen • tial (si kwen´shəl) *adj.*, in a regular series or order

se • rene (sə rēn´) *adj.*, calm; peaceful; tranquil

sham • ble (sham´bəl) *vi.*, walk lazily

shan • ty (shan´tē) *n.*, shack; hut

shirk (shʉrk) *vt.*, neglect; evade doing something

shriv • eled (shriv´əld) *adj.*, wrinkled and withered

shroud (shroud) *n.*, cloth used to wrap a corpse for burial

siege (sēj) *n.*, persistent attempt to gain control

sim • i • an (sim´ē ən) *adj.*, like an ape or a monkey

si • mul • ta • ne • ous • ly (sī´məl tā´nē əs lē) *adv.*, occurring at the same time

sin • gu • lar (siŋ´ gyə lər) *adj.*, being the only one of its kind

skep • tic (skep´tik) *n.*, doubter

skiff (skif) *n.*, small, open boat

skulk • ing (skulk´ iŋ) *part.*, lurking about in a craven or sinister manner

slan • der (slan´dər) *n.*, false statement damaging another person's character or reputation

sla • ver (slav´ər) *n.*, saliva

slov • en • ly (sluv´ən lē) *adj.*, careless; untidy; slipshod

so • ber (sō´bər) *adj.*, serious, solemn

sod • den (säd´'n) *adj.*, soaked through

so • lic • i • tous (sə lis´ə təs) *adj.*, showing concern

sol • i • dar • i • ty (säl´ə dar´ə tē) *n.*, unity or agreement on an opinion or purpose

so • lil • o • quize (sə lil´ə kwīz´) *vi.*, talk to oneself

som • ber (säm´bər) *adj.*, dark, dull

sor • rel (sôr´əl) *adj.*, light reddish-brown

sparse (spärs) *adj.*, meager

spas • mod • i • cal • ly (spaz mäd´ik ə lē) *adv.*, suddenly; violently; fitfully

spe • cies (spē´ shēz) *n.*, population of highly similar organisms that interbreed only among themselves

spec • tral (spek´trəl) *adj.*, ghostly

splay (splā) *adj.*, turning outward; spreading

spright • ly (sprīt´lē) *adj.*, full of energy

squan • der (skwän´dər) *vt.*, spend extravagantly; waste

sta • ple (stā´pəl) *n.*, item of trade, regularly stocked and in constant demand

ster • e • o • typed (ster´ē ə tīpt) *adj.*, conventional notion, not allowing for individuality

stim • u • late (stim´yōo lāt) *vt.*, rouse or excite to increase action

stow (stō) *v.*, put away, especially aboard a ship

strat • a • gem (strat´ə jəm) *n.*, trick

strick • en (strik´ən) *adj.*, wounded, afflicted, distressed

sub • due (sub dōo´) *vt.*, overcome; control; reduce

sub • dued (səb dōod´) *part.*, diminished, lessened in intensity

sub • jec • tion (sub jek´ shən) *n.*, state of being under another's control

sub • lime (sə blīm´) *adj.*, outstanding

sub • mis • sion (sub mish´ ən) *n.*, yielding or surrendering

sub • side (səb sīd´) *vi.*, settle, lessen in intensity

sub • stan • tial (səb stan´shəl) *adj.*, real; actual; true

sub • ter • fuge (sub´tər fyōoj´) *n.*, deceit used to escape a difficult or unpleasant situation

suc • ces • sion (sək sesh´ən) *n.*, number of things coming one after another; series

suf • fi • cient (sə fish´ənt) *adj.*, as much as is needed

suf • frage (suf´rij) *n.*, right to vote

suf • fuse (sə fyōoz´) *vt.*, fill

suf • fused (sə fyōozd´) *adj.*, filled, as with color

sul • len • ly (sul´ən lē) *adv.*, showing resentment; gloomily

su • per • flu • ous (sə pʉr´flōo əs) *adj.*, being more than is needed, excessive

su • per • hu • man (sōo´pər hyōo´mən) *adj.*, having power above that of a normal human being

su • per • in • tend • ence (sōo´pər in tend´ens) *n.*, supervision; management

sup • pli • ca • tion (sup´lə kā´shən) *n.*, humble request

sup • press (sə pres´) *vt.*, put down by force

sup • pres • sed • ly (sə pres´ed lē) *adv.*, with restraint

su • prem • a • cy (sə prem´ə sē) *n.*, authority

sur • charge (sʉr´chärj´) *vt.*, overload; overburden

surge (sʉrj) *vi.*, have a heavy, swelling motion

sur • pass (sər pas´) *vt.*, go beyond

sur • vey (sər vā´) *vt.*, examine

sus • tain (sə stān´) *vt.*, keep up or maintain

T

tab • u • late (tab´yōo lāt) *vt.*, arrange and count

tac • it • ly (tas´it lē) *adv.*, silently

taint (tānt) *vt.*, infect

tan • gi • ble (tan´jə bəl) *adj.*, having actual form; touchable

teem (tēm) *vi.*, be full

tem • per • a • ment (tem´pər ə mənt) *n.*, customary frame of mind

ten • dril (ten´drəl) *n.*, tender shoot

ten • or (ten´ər) *n.*, singer with voice range one octave above and one octave below middle C

ten • ta • tive • ly (ten´tə tiv lē) *adv.*, with uncertainty

terse (tʉrs) *adj.*, short; concise

tes • ti • mo • ny (tes´tə mō´nē) *n.*, statement made under oath in a court

ti • rade (tī´rād´) *n.*, vehement speech

tis • sue (tish´ōo) *n.*, group of cells that work together in the body

ti • tan • ic (tī tan´ik) *adj.,* of great size, strength, or power

tor • men • tor (tôr ment´ər) *n.,* one who causes great pain or suffering

tor • rent (tôr´ənt) *n.,* swift, violent stream

tou • sled (tou´zəld) *adj.,* rumpled, mussed

trans • fixed (trans fikst´) *part.,* made motionless

trans • gress (trans gres´) *vt.,* break a commandment; sin

trans • gres • sion (trans gresh´ən) *n.,* act of going over a limit

tran • sient (tran´shənt) *adj.,* staying only for a short time

trav • ail (trə vāl´) *n.,* intense pain

tra • verse (trə vʉrs´) *vi.,* turn; swivel

treach • er • ous • ly (trech´ər əs lē) *adv.,* dangerously

tread (tred) *n.,* step

trea • ty (trēt´ē) *n.,* formal agreement between two or more nations, resulting in peace

trem • u • lous (trem´yoo ləs) *adj.,* trembling, quivering

tri • fle (trī´fəl) *n.,* small amount

trib • u • la • tion (trib´yoo lā shən) *n.,* great misery or distress, as from oppression

trod • den (träd´'n) *pp. of tread, vt.,* pressed or beaten with the feet

tur • bu • lence (tʉr´byoo ləns) *n.,* violent, irregular motion or swirling agitation of water, air, gas, etc.

U

un • can • ny (un kan´ē) *adj.,* beyond normal

un • couth (un kooth´) *adj.,* uncultured; crude; strange

un • cowed (un koud´) *part.,* unafraid; unintimidated

un • der • stud • y (un´dər stud´ē) *vt.,* learn the part of another actor to serve as a substitute when necessary

un • err • ing • ly (un ʉr´iŋ lē) *adv.,* without fail

un • hal • lowed (un´hal´ōd) *adj.,* unholy; wicked

un • pal • at • a • ble (un pal´ə tə bəl) *adj.,* unpleasant

un • prej • u • diced (un prej´ ə dist) *adj.,* without bias; impartial

un • re • mit • ting (un´ri mit´ iŋ) *adj.,* incessant; persistent

un • won • ted (un wän´tid) *adj.,* uncommon

ur • gent (ʉr´jənt) *adj.,* insistent

u • surp (yoo sʉrp´) *vt.,* take over, assume power by force or without right

V

va • lid • i • ty (və lid´ə tē) *n.,* quality of being firmly grounded on facts

val • or (val´ər) *n.,* marked courage or bravery

vap • id (vap´id) *adj.,* dull, uninteresting

vault (vôlt) *vi.,* jump over

vaunt (vônt) *n.,* boast or brag

ven • ture (ven´chər) *n.,* enterprise in which there is risk of loss as well as chance for profit

ve • ran • da (və ran´də) *n.,* open porch

ver • mil • ion (vər mil´yən) *adj.,* bright red

ver • nac • u • lar (vər nak´yə lər) *n.,* common, everyday language

vex (veks) *vt.,* disturb; annoy; irritate

vex • a • tious (veks ā´shəs) *adj.,* annoying; troublesome

vi • car • i • ous (vī ker´ē əs) *adj.,* experienced by imagined participation in another's experience

vig • il (vij´əl) *n.,* staying awake on watch

vil • i • fy (vil´ə fī´) *vt.,* abuse verbally; slander

vin • di • ca • tion (vin´də kā´shən) *n.,* justification

vi • ril • i • ty (və ril´ə tē) *n.,* state of having strength or vigor

vis • age (viz´ ij) *n.,* face; facial features or expression

vo • lu • mi • nous • ly (və loo´ mə nəs lē) *adv.,* largely; fully

vo • ra • cious (vô rā´shəs) *adj.,* greedy; ravenous

vor • tex (vôr´teks´) *n.,* whirlpool or eddy

W

wan (wän) *adj.,* pale, faint

wane (wān´) *vi.,* approach the end

war • i • ly (wer´ə lē) *adv.,* cautiously

wa • ver (wā´vər) *vi.,* swing or sway; flutter

wax (waks) *vi.,* increase in strength; grow larger

whim • per (hwim´pər) *n.,* low, whining cry

wraith (rāth) *n.,* ghost or specter

wran • gle (raŋ´gəl) *vi.,* quarrel angrily and noisily

wrath (rath) *n.,* anger

writh • ing (rī th´iŋ) *part.,* twisting or turning in distress

Z

zeal (zēl) *n.,* intense enthusiasm

Index of Titles and Authors

Index of Skills

Reading and Literature

mixed metaphor, 949
mode, 949
mood, 115, 206, 375, 393, 536, 605, 949
moral, 772
motif, 14, 19, 756, 949
motivation, 259, 712, 949
motive, 593
Muse, 949
myth, 12, 195, 949
narration, 949
narrative poem, 101, 102, 949
narrator, 242, 314, 469, 949
Naturalism, 574, 651, 950
nonfiction, 950
nonsense verse, 950
novel, 950
novella, 950
nursery rhyme, 950
objective correlative, 511, 950
occasional verse, 950
octave, 950
one-dimensional character, 626, 950
onomatopoeia, 61, 950
oral tradition, 950
oxymoron, 950
palindrome, 950
parable, 21, 950
paradox, 413, 950
parallelism, 950
paraphrase, 951
parody, 26, 951
periodical, 951
personal essay, 222, 951
personification, 143, 331, 425, 556, 565, 951
plagiarism, 951
plot, 183, 522, 585, 651, 711, 740, 756, 771, 951
poetic license, 951
point of view, 90, 187, 195–196, 282, 360, 375, 385, 556, 951
portrayal of behavior, 516
preface, 952
prose poem, 952
protagonist, 605, 952
proverb, 952
pseudonym, 952
psychological fiction, 952
pun, 952

purpose, 214, 221, 318, 340, 952
quatrain, 952
quintain, 952
radio play, 230
rap, 952
Realism, 952
redundancy, 952
refrain, 952
repetition, 42, 48, 56, 62, 324, 515, 952
resolution, 771, 952
reversal, 952
review, 952
rhetoric, 952
rhetorical question, 952
rhetorical technique, 952
rhyme, 66, 69, 953
rhyme scheme, 443
rhythm, 953
riddle, 953
romance, 953
run-on line, 953
satire , 274, 414, 953
scansion, 953
scene, 375, 953
science fiction, 557, 953
screenplay, 244, 260
sensory detail, 69, 953
sentimentality, 953
septet, 953
sestet, 953
set, 953
setting, 205, 260, 282, 362, 432, 505, 552, 605, 953
short short, 954
sight rhyme, 954
simile, 81, 95, 101, 121, 187, 299, 325, 488, 510, 512, 515, 542, 756, 954
slang, 954
slant rhyme, 954
soliloquy, 954
sonnet, 954
source, 954
sound effects, 243
speaker, 393, 514, 954
spectacle, 954
spiritual, 43
spondee, 954
stage, 954

stage directions, 955
stanza, 443, 955
stereotype, 421, 955
story, 955
stress, 955
structure, 393
style, 319, 324, 955
subplot, 955
summary, 771, 955
suspense, 243, 955
suspension of disbelief, 955
symbol, 24, 95, 431, 439, 496, 955
syntax, 956
tag line, 956
tall tale, 33, 956
theme, 163, 207, 391, 408, 439, 536, 565, 593, 772, 956
three-dimensional character, 626, 956
tone, 361, 956
tragedy, 956
tragic flaw, 772, 956
transition, 956
translation, 956
triplet, 956
trochee, 956
understatement, 956
unity, 956
unreliable narrator, 956
verbal irony, 182, 956
vignette, 187

Writing

adventure, 143
advice column, 772
advice letter, 32
analysis charts, 802
analyzing, 796
anecdotes, 331, 811
anthropological report, 439
audience, 785, 789
autobiographical essay, 300, 413
autobiographical sketch, 463
autobiography, 385
ballad, 511
brainstorming, 803
calendar, 361
careful draft, 809
character sketch, 314, 408, 470

Language

Study and Research

Speaking and Listening

Applied English/Tech Prep

Index of Fine Art

Art Acknowledgments

Greywhisker's Daughter. Ross Stefan, Rosequist Gallery Tucson, Arizona, **cover;** Geese in Flight. Lelia T. Bauman, 1850 or later. National Gallery of Art, Washington, DC. Gift of Edgar William and Bernice Chrysler Garbisch, **2;** Rodney Busch, **6;** The Fall of Icarus. Bruegel. Musées royaux des Beaux-Arts, Brussels, **10;** Jacob and Wilhelm Grimm. Library of Congress Photoduplication Service, **14;** Fox. Rodney Busch, **27;** Fox Hunt. Winslow Homer, 1893. The Pennsylvania Academy of the Fine Arts, Philadelphia. Joseph E. Temple Fund, **30;** Carl Sandburg. Library of Congress Photoduplication Service, **33;** His Hammer in His Hand. Palmer Hayden. From the John Henry Series, Museum of African American Art, Los Angeles, CA. Palmer C. Hayden collection. Gift of Miriam A. Hayden, **40;** The Starry Night. Vincent van Gogh, 1889. Oil on canvas, 29" x 36¹/₄" (73.7 x 92.1 cm). The Museum of Modern Art, NY. Acquired through the Lillie P. Bliss Bequest, **54;** Edgar Allan Poe. Library of Congress Photoduplication Service, **56;** Bells. Jena Busch, **57;** Carl Sandburg. Library of Congress Photoduplication Service, **70;** Illustration from Old Possum's Book of Practical Cats by T. S. Eliot, ©1982 by Edward Gorey, reproduced with permission of Harcourt Brace & Company, **76**; Roger Williams. Library of Congress Photoduplication Service, **85**; Robert Frost. Library of Congress Photoduplication Service, **91**; The Creation. Aaron Douglas, 1935. The Howard University Gallery of Art, Washington, DC, **99**; Casey at the Bat. Ed Parker, **105**; Henry Wadsworth Longfellow. Library of Congress Photoduplication Service **109**; Midnight Ride of Paul Revere. Grant Wood, 1931. The Metropolitan Museum of Art, Arthur Hoppock Hearn Fund, 1950. (50.117), **112**; The Lost Balloon. William Holbrook Beard, 1882. National Museum of American Art Washington, DC/Art Resource, NY, **119**; Homer. Library of Congress Photoduplication Service, **123**; Ulysses and the Sirens. John Waterhouse, 1849–1917. British. Oil on canvas, 100.0 cm × 201.07 cm. Purchased 1891. Reproduced by permission of the National Gallery of Victoria, Melbourne, Australia, **139**; The Farm. Joan Miró. National Gallery of Art, Washington, DC. Gift of Mary Hemingway, **148**; W. W. Jacobs. Library of Congress Photoduplication Service, **150**; Photo courtesy of Natalie and Quincy Bent, **167**; After the Tornado, Texas. Winslow Homer, American, 1836–1910. Watercolor, 1899, 36.8 × 53.3 cm. Mr. and Mrs. Martin A. Ryerson Collection, 1933.1235, **191**; Only a Lock of Hair. Sir John Everett Millais. Manchester City Art Galleries, **219**; Room in Brooklyn. Edward Hopper. Courtesy, Museum of Fine Arts, Boston, **228**; Study for Portrait of Van Gogh III. Francis Bacon, 1957. Hirshhorn Museum and Sculpture Garden, Smithsonian Institution. Gift of Joseph H. Hirshhorn Foundation, 1966. Photograph by Lee Stalsworth, **235**; Rod Serling. Library of Congress Photoduplication Service, **244**; Italo-American Celebration, Washington Square. William James Glackens. Courtesy, the Museum of Fine Arts, Boston, **266**; Courtesy of Library of Congress Photo Duplication Service, **280**; Gas. Edward Hopper, 1940. Oil on canvas, 26¼" × 40¼" (66.7 × 102.2cm) The Museum of Modern Art, New York. Mrs. Simon Guggenheim Fund, **288**; Untitled Series #7. Nic Nicosia, 1993, **298**; Martin Luther King Jr. Library of Congress Photoduplication Service, **320**; Crow with Ribbons. Marsden Hartley, 1941–1942. Hirshhorn Museum and Sculpture Garden, Smithsonian Institution. Gift of Joseph H. Hirshhorn Foundation, 1966. Photograph by Lee Stalsworth, **335**; The Last of the Buffalo. Albert Bierstadt, 1889. In the collection of the Corcoran Gallery of Art. Gift of Albert Bierstadt, **356**; The Torn Hat. Thomas Sully. Courtesy, The Museum of Fine Arts, Boston. Gift of Miss Belle Greene and Mr. Henry Copley Greene in memory of their mother Mary Abby Greene (Mrs. J.S. Copley Greene), 1916, **370**; Louisiana Heron. Rodney Busch. Private collection, **381**; School's Out. Allan Rohan Crite, 1936. National Museum of American Art, Washington, DC/Art Resource, NY, **400**; Endangered Species. Paul T. Goodnight, 1980. National Museum of American Art, Washington, DC/Art Resource, NY, **405**; Illustration by George Herriman, from ARCHY and MEHITABEL by Don Marquis. Copyright 1927 by Doubleday, a division of Bantom, Doubleday Dell Publishing Group, Inc. Used by permission of Doubleday Dell Publishing Group Inc., **426**; Fruit Displayed on a Stand. Gustave Caillebotte. Courtesy, Museum of Fine Arts, Boston. Fanny P. Mason Fund in Memory of Alice Thevin, **429**; Sunset Dance–Ceremony to the Evening Sun. John Henry Sharp, 1924. National Museum of American Art, Washington, DC. Gift of Arvin Gottlieb, **435**; Snap the Whip. Winslow Homer. The Butler Institute of American Art, Youngstown, Ohio, **448**; Truman Capote. Library of Congress Photoduplication Service, **450**; Baby at Play. Thomas Eakins, 1877. John Hay Whitney Collection. ©1995 Board of Trustees, National Gallery of Art, Washington, DC, **455**; Rodney Busch, **467**; With Sloping Mast and Dipping Prow. Albert Pinkham Ryder, before 1906. National Museum of American Art, Washington, DC, Gift of John Gellatly/Art Resource, NY, **483**; The City from Greenwich Village. John Sloan, 1922. ©1995 Board of Trustees, National Gallery of Art, Washington, DC. Gift of Helen Farr Sloan, **494**; Illustration from abolitionist literature. Library of Congress Photoduplication Service, **509**; Paper Bag. Jena Busch, **513**; Hot Fuchsia Thermal Blanket. Jena Busch, **528**; Steering Wheel. David Hockney, October 1982. Photographic Collage, 30 × 36. © David Hockney, **533**; '73 Malibu. Robert Bechtle. Courtesy OK Harris, **538**; Ray Bradbury. Library of Congress Photoduplication Service, **557**; Jack London. Library of Congress Photoduplication Service, **574**; Engraving of Shakespeare from the First Folio. Wellesley College Library, Special Collections, **660**.

Additional Photo and Illustration Credits

Rodney Busch: 64, 467, 489; **Courtesy Digital Stock Corp.:** 34, 92, 155, 201, 247, 328, 348–349, 350, 363, 392, 517, 560, 570, 571, 778, 780, 818, 879, 880, 888, 930, 940; **Courtesy Corel Professional Photos:** 18, 25, 46, 68, 71, 80, 83, 86, 89, 185, 208, 231, 269, 274, 284, 302, 316, 321, 323, 387, 409, 411, 415, 428, 441, 497, 502, 508, 544, 554, 572, 576, 581, 586, 594, 597, 606, 621, 626, 630, 642, 652; ©**1995 Michael Romanos:** 658, 663, 689, 690, 713, 714, 741, 742, 757, 758.

Literary Acknowledgments (continued from copyright page)

Harcourt Brace & Company "Fog" from CHICAGO POEMS by Carl Sandburg, copyright 1916 by Holt, Rinehart and Winston, Inc. and renewed 1944 by Carl Sandburg, reprinted by permission of Harcourt Brace & Company. "Paul Bunyan of the North Woods" from THE PEOPLE, YES by Carl Sandburg, copyright 1936 by Harcourt Brace & Company and renewed 1964 by Carl Sandburg, reprinted by permission of the publisher. "Gus: The Theatre Cat" from OLD POSSUM'S BOOK OF PRACTICAL CATS, copyright 1939 by T. S. Eliot and renewed 1967 by Esme Valerie Eliot, reprinted by permission of Harcourt Brace & Company.
HarperCollins Publishers SELECTED EXCERPTS FROM PAGES 20–23 from AN AMERICAN CHILDHOOD by ANNIE DILLARD. Copyright © 1987 by Annie Dillard. Reprinted by permission of

HarperCollins Publishers, Inc. Pages 197–201 from "THE HANDSOMEST DROWNED MAN IN THE WORLD" FROM LEAF STORM AND OTHER STORIES by GABRIEL GARCIA MARQUEZ. Copyright © 1971 by Gabriel Garcia Marquez. Reprinted by permission of HarperCollins Publishers, Inc. "JOHN HENRY" from MULES AND MEN by ZORA NEALE HURSTON. Copyright 1935 by Zora Neale Hurston. Copyright renewed 1963 by John C. Hurston and Joel Hurston. Reprinted by permission of HarperCollins Publishers, Inc. Unabridged Text of "SARAH CYNTHIA SYLVIA STOUT WOULD NOT TAKE THE GARBAGE OUT" from WHERE THE SIDEWALK ENDS by Shel Silverstein COPYRIGHT © 1974 by EVIL EYE MUSIC, INC. SELECTION REPRINTED BY PERMISSION OF HarperCollins Publishers. ALL PAGES from "THROUGH THE TUNNEL" FROM THE

HABIT OF LOVING by DORIS LESSING. Copyright © 1955 by Doris Lessing. Originally appeared in The New Yorker. Copyright renewed. Reprinted by permission of HarperCollins Publishers, Inc. 4 PAGES from TO KILL A MOCKINGBIRD by HARPER LEE. Copyright © 1960 by Harper Lee. Copyright Renewed © 1988 by Harper Lee. Reprinted by permission of HarperCollins Publishers, Inc. **Henry Holt and Company, Inc.** "Birches" and "The Road Not Taken" from *The Poetry of Robert Frost.* Edited by Edward Connery Lathem. Holt, Rinehart and Winston, Inc., 1969. **Houghton Mifflin Company** "The Obligation to Endure", from SILENT SPRING. Copyright © 1962 by Rachel L. Carson. Copyright © renewed 1990 by Roger Christie. Reprinted by permission of Houghton Mifflin Co. All rights reserved. **James Hurst** "The Scarlet Ibis" from *The Atlantic Monthly* July 1960. By permission of the author. **Indiana University Press** "The Story of Dædalus and Icarus" by Ovid. From *Metamorphoses,* translated by Rolfe Humphries. Copyright, 1955, Indiana University Press. **James Thurber Literary Properties** "The Fox and the Crow," by James Thurber. Copyright © 1956 James Thurber. Copyright © 1984 Rosemary A. Thurber. From *Further Fables for Our Time,* published by Simon & Schuster. "The Secret Life of Walter Mitty," by James Thurber. Copyright © 1942 James Thurber. Copyright © 1970 Rosemary A. Thurber. From *My World - And Welcome To It,* published by Harcourt Brace Company. **Joan Daves Agency** Martin Luther King, Jr., "I Have a Dream." Reprinted by arrangement with The Heirs to the Estate of Martin Luther King, Jr., c/o Joan Daves Agency as agent for the proprietor. Copyright 1963 by Martin Luther King, Jr., copyright renewed 1991 by Coretta Scott King. **Virginia Kidd** Ursula K. Le Guin, "Gwilan's Harp" Copyright © 1977 by Ursula K. Le Guin; first appeared in *Redbook;* reprinted by permission of the author and the author's agent, Virginia Kidd. **Little, Brown and Company** From BLUE HIGHWAYS: A JOURNEY INTO AMERICA by William Least Heat Moon. Copyright © 1982 by William Least Heat Moon. By permission Little, Brown and Company. From MYTHOLOGY by Edith Hamilton. Copyright 1942 by Edith Hamilton; © renewed 1969 by Dorian Fielding Reid and Doris Fielding Reid. By permission of Little, Brown and Company. "I'm Nobody! Who are you?" by Emily Dickinson. From THE COMPLETE POEMS OF EMILY DICKINSON edited by Thomas H. Johnson. Copyright 1929 by Martha Dickinson Bianchi; Copyright © renewed 1957 by Mary L. Hampson. By permission Little, Brown and Company. **Lyons & Burford, Publishers** Reprinted with permission from *Mississippi Solo: A River Quest,* by Eddy Harris. copyright 1988, Lyons & Burford, Publishers. **The Magazine of Fantasy and Science Fiction** "Test" by Theodore L. Thomas. © 1962 by MERCURY PRESS, INC. Reprinted from THE MAGAZINE OF FANTASY AND SCIENCE FICTION. © renewed 1990. **Oxford University Press** "Thinking Like a Mountain," by Aldo Leopold. From *A Sand County Almanac,* with other essays on conservation from *Round River* by Aldo Leopold. Copyright © 1949, 1953, 1966 renewed 1977, 1981 by Oxford University Press, Inc. Reprinted by permission. **Penguin USA** "The Interlopers," by Saki. 1976. "The Creation," from GOD'S TROMBONES by James Weldon Johnson. Copyright © 1927 The Viking Press, Inc., renewed © 1955 by Grace Nail Johnson. Used by permission of Viking Penguin, a division of Penguin Books USA Inc. **Random House, Inc.** From I KNOW WHY THE CAGED BIRD SINGS by Maya Angelou Copyright © 1969 by Maya Angelou. Reprinted by permission of Random House, Inc. From A CHRISTMAS MEMORY by Truman Capote. Copyright © 1956 by Truman Capote. Reprinted by permission of Random House, Inc. From THE SNOW GOOSE by Paul Gallico. Copyright 1940 by the Curtis Publishing Company and renewed 1968 by Paul Gallico. Reprinted by permission of Alfred A Knopf Inc. Sandra Cisneros, "A Smart Cookie" from *A House on Mango Street.* Random House, 1989. **Marian Reiner** "Metaphor" From A SKY FULL OF POEMS by Eve Merriam. Copyright © 1964, 1970, 1973 by Eve Merriam. Reprinted by permission of Marian Reiner. **Scovil Chichak Galen Literary Agency, Inc.** "History Lesson," by Arthur C. Clarke. Reprinted by permission of the author and the author's agents, Scovil Chichak Galen Literary Agency, Inc., New York. **Seaver Books** "The Man to Send Rain Clouds," by Leslie Marmon Silko. Copyright © 1981 by Leslie Marmon Silko. Reprinted from *Storyteller* by Leslie Marmon Silko, published by Seaver Books, New York, New York. **Rod Serling.** "The Monsters Are Due on Maple Street" Reprinted by permission of The Rod Serling Trust. All rights reserved. © 1960 Rod Serling; © 1988 by Carolyn Serling, Jodi Serling and Anne Serling. **Simon & Schuster, Inc.** "A Mother in Mannville." Reprinted with the permission of Scribner, an imprint of Simon & Schuster, Inc. from WHEN THE WHIPPOORWILL by Marjorie Kinnan Rawlings. Copyright 1936, 1940 Marjorie Kinnan Rawlings; copyright renewed © 1964, 1968 Norton Baskin. "Something Told the Wild Geese." Reprinted with permission of Atheneum Books for Young Readers, an imprint of Simon & Schuster Children's Publishing Division, from POEMS by Rachel Field. Copyright 1934 by Macmillan Publishing Company, renewed 1962 by Arthur S. Pederson. "Southbound on the Freeway." Reprinted with permission of Simon & Schuster Books for Young Readers, an imprint of Simon & Schuster Children's Publishing Division, from THE COMPLETE POEMS TO SOLVE by May Swenson. Copyright © 1953 by May Swenson. Copyright renewed © 1991. Originally appeared in *The New Yorker.* "There Will Come Soft Rains." Reprinted with permission of Simon & Schuster, Inc. from COLLECTED POEMS OF SARA TEASDALE. Copyright 1920 by Macmillan Publishing Company, renewed 1948 by Marnie T. Wheless. As it appears in Ray Bradbury's short story, "There Will Come Soft Rains." **The Society of Authors** "The Monkey's Paw," by W. W. Jacobs. By permission of The Society of Authors as the literary representative of the Estate of W. W. Jacobs. **University of Nebraska Press** Reprinted from *Black Elk Speaks,* by Black Elk and John G. Neihardt, by permission of the University of Nebraska Press. Copyright 1932, 1959, 1972, by John G. Neihardt. Copyright © 1961 by the John G. Neihardt Trust. **Vintage Books** from *The Odyssey* of Homer, trans. by Robert Fitzgerald, © 1961, 1963 by Robert Fitzgerald, © renewed 1989, 1991 by Benedict R. C. Fitzgerald on behalf of the Fitzgerald children. Reprinted by permission of Vintage Books. **William Morris Agency, Inc.** *The Hitchhiker* by Lucille Fletcher. Reprinted by permission of the William Morris Agency, Inc. on behalf of the Author. Copyright © 1947 by Lucille Fletcher. **William Morrow & Company, Inc.** Text of "Nikki-Rosa" from BLACK FEELING, BLACK TALK, BLACK JUDGMENT by Nikki Giovanni. Text: Copyright © 1968, 1970 by Nikki Giovanni. By permission of William Morrow and Company, Inc. Text excerpt "The United States vs. Susan B. Anthony" pgs. 145–161 from WOMEN OF COURAGE by Margaret Truman. Text: Copyright © 1976 by Margaret Truman Daniel. By permission of William Morrow and Company, Inc.

Every effort has been made to trace the ownership of all copyrighted selections found in this book. Omissions brought to our attention will be corrected in subsequent editions.